P9-DMG-400

The LIBRARY

A Guide to the LDS Family History Library

The LIBRARY

A Guide to the LDS Family History Library

Edited by Johni Cerny & Wendy Elliott

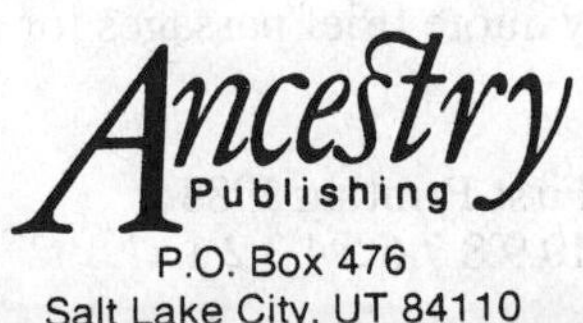

P.O. Box 476
Salt Lake City, UT 84110

Library of Congress
Catalog Card Number 87-70109

ISBN Number 0-916489-21-3

First Printing 1988
10 9 8 7 6 5 4 3 2 1

Printed in the United States of America.

Dedication

To our parents:
Vivian Elaine West and the late John Steve Cerny
Alva Thomas Bebout and Rena Leon Hill

Foreword

I was an officer in British Intelligence from 1940 to 1957, and on marrying an American lady had hoped to be employed in intelligence here. Alas, I was an alien and no longer *persona grata.* Therefore, I decided to return to my former career, librarianship, first in rare books at the Cambridge University Library and then as director of the University Science Library in the years preceding World War II.

Without a library science degree in America it was going to be tough, but by good fortune a vacancy at the Peabody Institute Library (now George Peabody Library of The Johns Hopkins University), was available. The library had 300,000 books, mostly historical, and also a fantastic collection of British genealogy and general heraldry. The Depression hit the Peabody very badly, and almost all book buying ceased. Nevertheless, it was and still is one of the best collections in America.

At the time I came to the Peabody, genealogists were intensely disliked, partly because most were sure that they descended "straight from Edward III" or certainly an earl or duke. They proudly bore coats of arms belonging to German princes or British nobility because they had the same name as the holders! This snobbery undoubtedly contributed to the librarians' scorn, and, too, there were many "little old ladies in tennis shoes" intent upon recounting to a bored librarian the family tree for five generations.

My real problem was that I was not a genealogist and did not know the first thing about its literature. But, I had a certain sympathy for family researchers and realized that not only did librarians have no wish to help, but they, too, knew little about the subject. Therefore, I decided to join the genealogists. *American & British Genealogy & Heraldry: A Bibliography* was the result, and, since about 1,000 definitive publications are published annually, this bibliography has increased from 1,800 to 13,000 titles. I am told that it has served readers and librarians equally well.

The foregoing covers my first decade in an American library. I became Director of the Maryland Historical Society and instantly changed the atmosphere by welcoming genealogists. In general, a change was coming about in libraries. Genealogy was becoming legitimate, and I credit the Church of Jesus Christ of Latter-day Saints for much of the change. Latter-day Saints were not concerned with nobility; they simply wanted to find their ancestors–no matter whether they were convicts, indentured servants or humble steerage pasasengers with just a sack over their shoulders. To do this the Latter-day Saints gathered together a vast number of books and microfilms copied from many collections throughout the world. This was a costly undertaking, and it is to their credit that the Family History Library in Salt Lake City is open free to anyone who wishes to use it.

It is possible to visit the library without making an appointment, and it is not difficult to work on your own genealogy. I first went to the library in the early 1960s when it and its microfilm readers were in a former store. There my wife and I met the famous Hill sisters, who administered the library. We were invited to witness the opening of the main reading room and were astonished at the mad rush for seats. The technical aspects of the library have changed somewhat since then and, as far as possible, the authorities are keeping abreast of the influx of readers.

Many users are flying into Salt Lake City and staying in hotels, therefore, every minute is costly. In sympathy with this problem, Ancestry, Incorporated decided to compile a book which would be useful both to visitors and genealogists in general. The Family History Library is by far the largest genealogical library in the world, and, thus, *The Library: A Guide to the LDS Family History Library* is timely.

This is not a review of the work so ably edited by Johni Cerny and Wendy Elliott, but from the point of view of a user I can state what is to my liking. Firstly, the compilers of each chapter are experts and, obviously, work or have worked in the area they have written about. The arrangement is excellent and uniform for all countries. Secondly, as a bibliographer, I am delighted to find several titles omitted from my own Bibliography. I pounced upon what I thought was an error in the title but found the error to be mine. In such a work as this, which must have taken considerable time to complete, the bibliography will become, as all bibliographies do, slightly out of date; but for each county, it is beyond reproach. The illustrations are most helpful and, occasionally, show the difficulty of transcription. I found only one ommission, which the editors and compilers could hardly mention.

In this book we are told how to use the library and its contents, and what we should expect to find; and these things are tangible. But, the researcher will also find an abundance of staff members who, time permitting, are eager to help with any question–even to the extent of translating a foreign passage to the reader. I suppose I speak so personally because certain members of the staff continually alert me to the presence of yet another list of passengers in periodicals which cross their desks. In short, this is a *compleat* library and *The Library* makes all this knowledge so much more accessible.

Although I do not act as a genealogist but rather as one who compiles works for genealogists, I can confidently claim that this guide is quite the best I have ever seen.

P. William Filby, F.S.G., F.M.S.
Former Director of the Maryland Historical Society

Foreword

Preface

The Family History Library of the Church of Jesus Christ of Latter-day Saints is a mecca to genealogists who travel great distances to use the largest collection of genealogical sources in existence today with its equivalent of more than 5 million volumes in print and in microform. *The Library: A Guide to the LDS Family History Library* is designed to assist the genealogical community in using the library's major collections and its branches.

The major collections include books, microfilms, and microfiche of original records and secondary sources from the United States and Canada, the British Isles, Scandinavia, Central Europe, Mexico and Central America, and South America. There are noteworthy collections for Australia and the South Pacific, South Africa, and the Caribbean – countries that became home to untold numbers of British emigrants. This volume discusses the Family History Library's collection for each of the countries within these geographic areas. It also covers the outstanding collection of sources for Latter-day Saints.

The Family History Library's holdings include something for nearly every country in the world. However, the collections for those countries not discussed in *The Library* primarily consist of gazetteers, histories, guides to archival and library materials in the country itself, and some family histories and genealogies. As these collections include microfilmed original records and materials of greater genealogical content, they will be treated in future editions. Thus, the library's major collections are also the most-often used sources.

Our goal throughout has been to make the Family History Library's collection more accessible to its patrons – first-time users and professionals alike. Admittedly, these chapters are representative in their discussion of subjects and titles. The bulk of the library's holdings were created at the local level, such as the town, parish, and county level, and to offer a comprehensive guide to the library's collection would have meant reproducing the Family History Library Catalog (FHLC). The charts following most chapters on a particular geographical area list each local jurisdiction for which the library has some holdings, a list of subjects, and a dot telling you that there are titles in the library's collection about that subject. For example: If you wanted to know if the library had Culpeper County, Virginia, probate records, you would look down the list of Virginia counties to find Culpeper County and then follow the Probate Records column down to the Culpeper entry. If there is a dot in the appropriate square, you then check the FHLC under **Virginia/Culpeper/Probate Records** for a complete list of holdings and call numbers.

New England, Germany, and several other areas did not lend themselves well to tabulating local jurisdiction holdings. Records in the library's collection are maintained respectively on the town and parish level in those areas. Listing the holdings for each town or parish would require several independent volumes. Thus, you will have to consult the FHLC to determine what is available. For example, if you want to know what records the library has for Fairfield, Connecticut, look under **Connecticut/Fairfield/Fairfield.** If you want to find records for Schwaigern, Germany, look under FHLC heading **Wuerttemberg/Schwaigern.**

Due to inconsistencies in cataloging, topic headings in each chapter vary depending upon the area being discussed. For example, atlases, gazetteers, and maps may be listed in the FHLC under **Atlases and Gazetteers,** or **Maps, Atlases, and Gazetteers,** or **Gazetteers,** or **Maps.** Rather than confuse the reader by changing the headings for standardization, all headings in this book are listed as in the FHLC.

The Library is not designed to teach you how to do research. However, rich insights into record-keeping systems, geographic jurisdictions, pitfalls that may be encountered in using some records, and other helpful hints are offered by genealogists who use the library's collection almost daily. Richard Dougherty's discussion of the U.S. General Collection is an introduction not only to the collection, but to genealogical research in the United States. Insights into using the library's vast New England collection come as a result of Clifford Stott's years of tracking down every possible source to solve tough research problems as a professional genealogist. Much of the information in William Arbuckle's discussions of the Canada and Scotland collections is made available for the first time.

Gordon Remington's introduction to "The Old South" will help you through the difficult process of understanding the library's collection of Southern records, thus easing the burden of research there. Some of the U.S. chapters discuss states whose collections are still being developed. Hopefully, future editions of this publication will find those chapters greatly expanded.

The Library represents the combined efforts of many genealogists, all of whom went far beyond what was expected of them to meet the goals of comprehensiveness, thoroughness, and accuracy. Many of them expressed appreciation throughout the project for the helpfulness and cordiality of the reference, acquisitions, and cataloging staffs at the Family History Library of the Church of Jesus Christ of Latter-day Saints.

We, as authors and readers, owe specific thanks to the General Authorities of The Church of Jesus Christ of Latter-day Saints for their commitment to family history and genealogical research as seen in the aggressive acquisition of valuable research source materials, both original and secondary, the excellent facilities provided to LDS Church members and the general public without charge, and the patron services and programs that are continually upgraded and expanded to meet changing needs.

In addition, we express special thanks to Glade I. Nelson, Manager, Family History Centers Support at the Family History Library, for conceptualizing this project; Robert J. Welsh who coordinated the project for the publisher; Robb Barr, also of the production team; Lavina Fielding Anderson and her staff at Editing, Inc.; the staff at Extras, Inc., and Cindy Radford, word-processors; Dennis McCafferty and Kyle Betit of Lineages, Inc., who did the tabular charts for England; Steve Newman and Bob Passey of Newman Passey Design (Salt Lake City); our staff at Lineages, Inc., who carried the everyday load; and our families who coped through another project.

Johni Cerny
Wendy Elliott
Salt Lake City, Utah

Contents

Chapter 1

Introduction to the Family History Library

Glade I. Nelson

The Main Family History Library

It is difficult to describe the main Family History Library of the Church of Jesus Christ of Latter-day Saints without using superlatives, as it contains the largest single collection of genealogical information in the world. The library, located at 35 North West Temple in Salt Lake City, Utah (84150), is in the center of downtown Salt Lake City, immediately west of Temple Square. Even though the Family History Library is a private library, it may be used free of charge for interested researchers of any denomination or nationality.

The library is closed on Sundays. It opens at 7:30 a.m. Monday through Saturday. It closes at 6:00 p.m. on Monday, at 10:00 p.m. from Tuesday through Friday, and at 5:00 p.m. on Saturday. The holidays for which the library closes are New Year's Day, Memorial Day, Independence Day, Pioneer Day (July 24, a Utah state holiday), Labor Day, Thanksgiving Day, and Christmas Day.

The library is located in a new building which opened in October 1985. It contains five floors, two underground and three above ground. The top floor is for administrative offices and staff; the other four are public areas.

Location of Collections

The genealogical collection is organized so that each public floor of the library contains records from specific geographical areas. Each floor contains the book records, microfilm records, microfilm and microfiche reading machines, tables, and study areas for its collection. Each public floor contains an information center, a copy center, and rest rooms. Classrooms are located on most floors. The Family Registry, Family History Library Catalog (FHLC), and appropriate portions of the International Genealogical Index (IGI) are also found on each public floor.

The by-floor arrangement of the collections is as follows:

Basement 2. British Isles, plus some British Commonwealth areas such as Australia, New Zealand, and South Africa. The original forms of the Family Group Records Collection: Archive Section are also located here.

Basement 1. International Area. The collections from continental Europe, Scandinavia, Latin America, Asia, Oceania, Africa, and the Middle East are located on this floor.

Main Floor. General Information and LDS Records. An orientation room and two small theaters are located near the main entrance. The collections include U.S. and Canada family history books, the original forms of the Family Group Records Collection, the Patron Section, General Reference books, and Special Collections. A small patron snack room with vending machines and a few tables is located on this floor. This is the only public area where food is allowed.

Second Floor. United States and Canada. This collection is the most heavily used in the library. As indicated, the U.S. and Canada family history books are located on the main floor.

Third Floor. This floor is reserved for administrative and staff offices and work areas, such as cataloging, the book bindery, acquisitions, and secretarial support. Access to this floor is restricted after 5:00 p.m. and on Saturdays when the staff is not there.

Size of Collections

The library has a collection of over 165,000 books which do not circulate or go out on interlibrary loan.

The heart of the collection, however, is not its printed materials but its massive microfilm and microfiche records. On the average, each of the library's more than

1.4 million reels of microfilms is the equivalent of three printed books of over 300 pages each, or the equivalent of over 5 million printed volumes of genealogical material.

Nearly 450,000 reels–over 31 percent–deal with United States records. Six states–New York, North Carolina, Massachusetts, Pennsylvania, Tennessee, and Ohio–comprise 35 percent of the U.S. collection.

The international countries with the largest number of microfilm are, in order, Mexico, France, Germany, Great Britain, the Netherlands, and Denmark, each with more than 75,000 reels. Other countries with significant collections (more than 10,000 reels) include Sweden, Belgium, Austria, Canada, Italy, Brazil, Poland, Finland, Chile, Spain, Japan, and the Philippines.

"Little-Used" Microfilms

All of the microfilms from countries or areas with heavily used collections, such as the United States, Canada, British Isles, Germany, Scandinavia, Poland, Belgium, the Netherlands, Luxembourg, Austria, and Switzerland are located in the main Family History Library at all times.

However, the main Family History Library has limited space to accommodate resources and patrons. If a country's records are designated as "little-used" by the rate of past use, only selected records such as indexes are kept in the library.

Countries or areas so classified have included Latin America, Asia, Africa, France, Spain, Portugal, Italy, and some eastern European countries. However, with the expanded facilities and broader patron use, more microfilms will be kept in the main library.

Microfilms from these countries can be ordered from the Granite Mountain Records Vault and sent to the main library, a process which usually requires at least three days when handled on a "rush" basis.

If you are planning to visit the main library, you should consult the Family History Library Catalog (FHLC) in the nearest family history center. (For a list of family history centers in your geographical area, write to the Family History Library, 35 North West Temple, Salt Lake City, UT 84150.) Note the catalog call numbers for the microfilms you wish to consult. If you have any question about whether the microfilm is housed in the main Family History Library, please write to the Family History Library, at the address above at least four weeks in advance, indicating the microfilms you wish to use (cite catalog call number and country) and the dates you expect to be in Salt Lake City.

Special Services

The Family History Library also provides the following services:

Library Orientation. A fifteen-minute narration with slides, presented in the theaters near the main entrance, is helpful to first-time visitors in explaining the organization of the library and how to begin research using the library's facilities. The program begins approximately every ten minutes or on request. A booklet containing the same information is available at the copy centers on each floor.

Information Counters. Near the entrance to each floor is an information counter staffed by employees and volunteers who will help answer questions regarding research and records in that floor's collection. The library staff will not do your research, but they will help direct you to the records you need to use. It is helpful to show them a pedigree chart, family group record form, and other records to explain what information you are interested in obtaining.

Copy Centers. Materials in the library may be copied within copyright rules. Each copy center contains self-service equipment to copy material from books, microfilm, or microfiche. A small fee is charged per page copied. Genealogical supplies, such as pedigree charts, family group record forms, and research aids, are also available in each copy center.

Library Classes. Throughout the year, experts offer one-hour classes on various aspects of genealogical research. Basic classes are offered regularly. In addition, each month several in-depth one-hour classes on a specific theme, such as British Isles research, or Latin American research, are presented. Class schedules are available at the information centers throughout the library. Each month's schedule may be requested by mail approximately two weeks before the beginning of the month.

Gifts to the Library. Gifts of compiled family histories and genealogies, as well as original records are welcomed. For further information, contact the Gifts Librarian on the third floor of the library.

Special Rules. The Family History Library is a private library, open to the public on condition of compliance with established rules and procedures. First-time visitors should read these rules in "Library Services," (Library Publication, Series GEN LIB, No. 1), available by mail or at the main library. Smoking is not permitted in the building or on the grounds.

Family History Centers and Microfilm Ordering Centers

Local Centers

Basic church policy allows for genealogical facilities to be placed in LDS Church meetinghouses worldwide in four phases or categories:

Family History Center (Phase IV). A complete family history center is established where church members are prepared to do advanced research. If located in the United States and Canada, they receive microfilm circulation from Salt Lake City. In international areas, a family history center receives its microfilms from a Microfilm Ordering Center (MOC). A family history center will generally contain, as a minimum, three or four microfilm readers, one or two microfiche readers, a few microfilms permanently housed in the library, a few basic reference books, a complete set of the Family History Library Catalog (FHLC), the International Genealogical Index (IGI), and selected reference material on microfiche.

You may order microfilms from the main collection in Salt Lake City for a small fee. Currently microfilm may be ordered for three weeks, six months, or for an indefinite period, with fees scaled to the length of the loan. For a list of family history center addresses in your geographic area, write to the Family History Library, 35 North West Temple, Salt Lake City, UT 84150.

In areas with high concentrations of LDS Church members, several LDS stakes (ecclesiastical groupings of several congregations), may join together to operate considerably larger facilities with expanded microfilm reader, microfiche reader, and book collection resources.

Family History Center (Phase III). Sometimes referred to as an auxiliary family history center, this facility differs from a Phase IV center only in scale. All genealogical research possible in one is also possible in the other. A Phase III center can be expected to have fewer microfilm and microfiche readers and smaller facilities, but it will still have a complete set of the FHLC, IGI, and selected reference material on microfiche.

Phase III centers may also borrow microfilms from Salt Lake City. A Phase III facility will be found only in an LDS Church stake which will also have, somewhere in its boundaries, a Phase IV center.

As of 1987, more than 1,000 Phase IV and Phase III facilities were in operation – more than 250 of them outside the United States and Canada.

Family History Center (Phase II). A family history center may be found where LDS Church members are ready to begin basic genealogical research and where there is no convenient access to a Phase III or a Phase IV center. These may be found in the United States and Canada, as well as in international areas.

A Phase II facility normally will contain only one or two microfiche readers and a few basic reference books. A Phase II facility may not order microfilm from Salt Lake City; however, it may obtain all of the microfiche holdings, including the FHLC and the IGI, that are available from the main collection in Salt Lake City.

Family History Center (Phase I). These facilities are established in areas where church members are just beginning to learn genealogical concepts and gather genealogical records, usually only in developing countries, and not in the United States or Canada.

The equipment in this ceter would be only a filing cabinet to store genealogical records and forms, a table and chairs. A Phase I facility may not order microfilms or microfiche resources.

All family history center facilities receive guidelines from the Family History Department in Salt Lake City. However, daily operations, within those guidelines, are determined by local ecclesiastical leaders. There is, thus, considerable flexibility in determining such items as hours of operation, collection development, physical facilities, equipment, and furnishings.

In all cases, personnel in the family history centers are volunteers. Some have extensive experience; others may be novices. These facilities have been established by the LDS Church for the use of its members. Others are welcome insofar as local resources, space, and equipment can effectively accommodate them.

Microfilm Ordering Centers

To better serve overseas family history centers, seventeen (as of 1987) Microfilm Ordering Centers (MOC), or regional film distribution facilities, serve family history centers in more than forty countries.

As an example, a patron in the family history center in Perth, Australia, fills out a microfilm order request form and sends it to the MOC in Sydney, Australia. If that reel is in the Sydney MOC collection, it is sent to Perth by return mail. If the roll of microfilm is not in the Sydney collection, a copy is ordered from Salt Lake City. The copy is then sent to Perth, via Sydney. When the loan period expires, the Perth center will return the film to Sydney where it will become part of the Sydney MOC circulating collection.

Several MOCs are developing a core collection of the major available genealogical records microfilmed by the LDS Church for their country. For example, all of the microfilmed records from Mexico are available in the Mexico City MOC. No copies need be ordered from Salt Lake City. Moreover, the Mexico City MOC may order films from other countries, such as Spain, for its patrons.

The Genealogical Society of Utah and the Worldwide Records Gathering Program

The Genealogical Society of Utah was incorporated in 1894 as the entity dealing with genealogical activity in The Church of Jesus Christ of Latter-day Saints (LDS). When the church began acquiring genealogical records and particularly when it began its microfilming program, it acted through this corporate body. Since 1894, there have been structural and name changes in the LDS organizations responsible for genealogy, but the name of the Genealogical Society of Utah has been maintained for negotiations, acquisitions, and microfilming of records.

LDS doctrines teach that its members should participate in the sacred temple ordinances of endowment and celestial marriage for themselves, then submit identifying data on their ancestors so that the same temple ordinances plus baptisms, confirmations, and ordination to the priesthood (for men) can be performed by proxy.

The Church's General Authorities have assigned the Family History Department of the LDS Church the task of helping church members identify their ancestors. This is the basic reason why the LDS Church acquires records of genealogical value and makes them available.

For more than forty years, the Genealogical Society of Utah has been microfilming records throughout the world. Because of obvious storage and retrieval characteristics, microfilm has been an excellent medium for acquiring and maintaining a genealogical record collection.

The original microfilm is preserved in the specially designed Granite Mountain Records Vault located in a mountain canyon just east of Salt Lake City. Copies are placed in the main library in Salt Lake City and distributed through the family history center system for genealogical research as needed by church members.

Categories of Genealogical Records

There are many different categories of genealogical records. Some provide only minimal identifying information. Other records are detailed and definitive. Some records cover a large segment of the population of a given area, while others are limited to a small percentage of individuals in a given time and place. A key criterion for acquisition has been the desire to reduce duplication of temple ordinances. Therefore, unique identification based upon a single source is considered desirable.

Three evaluation questions influence acquisition decisions: (1) How complete is the genealogical information in this single source? (2) What is the cost of filming related to the genealogical value of the record? and (3) What percentage of the population is covered in this record? Four categories of records, in descending order, are established by using these criteria. Examples of the types of records, by category, are:

Category 1 Records: are primary records – church and vital records which provide names, dates, and family relationships, and some census records. From this category come the extracted records which make up the bulk of the International Genealogical Index (IGI).

Category 2 Records: immigration/emigration, probate, and military records.

Category 3 Records: tax lists, school, and pension records.

Category 4 Records: criminal court records, business records, and hospital records.

Area Profiles

The Family History Department prepares, for internal use only, Area Profiles for each geographical area of the world, including areas where little or no microfilming is currently taking place. Area Profiles generally cover only one country, but in a few cases a group of similar countries.

Area Profiles identify and define each specific record of genealogical value known to be in existence for that country and designate the relative genealogical research value of each record type. They identify the extent of the department's current holdings. The result is a description of what the Family History Department should acquire. Area Profiles do not specify when records will be acquired, nor do they presuppose a priority of one area over any other area.

The objective of the Area Profiles is to describe which records, collectively, provide information to sufficiently identify individuals and link families for at least 80 percent of the recorded population in that area. In some areas and for some time periods, this ideal can never be achieved because such records do not exist. Furthermore, acquiring specific records, no matter how desirable to the department, depends upon the cooperation of the local record custodian.

Country Levels

Current department policy categorizes countries which will receive greatest acquisition attention in three ways:

Level 1 Countries: countries where many LDS Church members have ancestors.

Level 2 Countries: countries with substantial current LDS Church member growth.

Level 3 Countries: countries of probable future LDS Church member growth.

Every modern country has been assigned to one of the three levels. The level designation could change as the LDS Church grows in a given country. Countries that are now designated as church member growth (level 2) may become countries of church member ancestry (level 1). Countries of future church member growth (level 3) might migrate into the category of church member growth (level 2). In theory, this process could continue until all countries became areas of church member ancestry.

The lists are reviewed, modified as needed, and approved annually by department management.

Placement of Microfilm Cameras

With the tools of the area profiles and the country level assignments, the Family History Department is then in a position to allocate effectively its records acquisition resources. Currently about 70 percent of the microfilm cameras operate in Level 1 countries, 25 percent in Level 2 countries, and 5 percent in Level 3 countries.

The department assigns a filming crew for periods ranging from a few days to many months, depending on the amount of material to be microfilmed, but tries to gather all of the approved records from all four levels completely and methodically so that reentry and refilming will not be necessary.

Why Latter-day Saints Do Genealogical Research

When individuals find out that the largest collection of genealogical material in the world has been accumulated by the Church of Jesus Christ of Latter-day Saints, they often ask why a church would be interested in such an undertaking. Why does this church expend so many resources in gathering and making available records of genealogical value? And why do its members spend so much time doing genealogical research?

Central to the reasons why Latter-day Saints are interested in genealogy are the following LDS Church beliefs:

1. Every person's identity is eternal. It did not begin at birth and will not end at death.
2. As part of earth life, individuals obtain a mortal

body and join a family. Family relationships have the potential to continue forever.

3. Christ's teachings apply to everyone. Each person must believe in the Savior and receive baptism from someone with proper authority. A way has been provided for those who, because of when or where they lived, did not have the opportunity to be baptized.

Latter-day Saints believe that baptisms, marriages, and the "sealing" of parents and children may be done by proxy in its temples, located in many countries of the world. Only faithful members may enter these temples to perform such ordinances, first for themselves and then for the dead. Thus, it is possible to continue each family unit back through as many generations as individual identification is possible. To identify each ancestor and perform these sacred ordinances requires genealogical research.

Latter-day Saints believe that an ordinance performed on behalf of a deceased ancestor does not limit his or her free agency. The belief is that no one in the spirit world is bound to accept the gospel or the family sealing ordinances. Each person may accept or reject these ordinances. But if this vicarious work is not done in their behalf, they have no choice.

Why, then do Latter-day Saints undertake genealogical research? They do it to identify accurately their ancestors so that the ordinances can be performed for them and for all the children of God. The Church of Jesus Christ of Latter-day Saints gathers records of genealogical value from the four corners of the earth to help its members fulfill this objective.

Chapter 2

Tools, Resources, and Previous Research

Gary J. Zimmerman

The Family History Library Catalog (FHLC)

Until 1969 all the holdings of the Family History Library were listed in a standard card catalog. With the introduction of the computer system that year, all new materials were cataloged on computer, while all previously cataloged holdings were converted from the cards to the new system over a period of eighteen years. The conversion was completed in 1987. Oriental and Asiatic collections are still largely intact in the card file, which should be consulted along with the computer listings.

The computer listing of holdings, called the Family History Library Catalog (FHLC), is a set of microfiche computer print-outs under five arrangements: Locality, Author-Title, Surname, Subject, and Foreign-Language-Locality. Each of these arrangements is different in format and content, and each requires a different approach to be searched effectively.

Locality: The locality portion of the catalog is probably the most heavily used, since many of the records of genealogical value are records kept by different levels of government or are the records of specific towns and villages. In the catalog, the world is broken down into geographic units, most corresponding to modern countries and their governmental districts. For the sake of simplicity, some countries are cataloged according to their pre-World War I boundaries. A numbered sequence of fiche exists for each country of the world, and within each country localities are further broken down under other geographical divisions, from largest to smallest. These divisions have different names in different countries but correspond roughly to similar divisions used in the United States (state, county, township). Examples of the variously named divisions in some countries follow:

United States: STATE/COUNTY/TOWN
Britain: COUNTY/PARISH/TOWN
Germany: STATE/PROVINCE/PARISH
(German: LAND/PROVINZ/ORT)
France: STATE/TOWN
(French: DEPARTMENT, COMMUNE)
Mexico: STATE/TOWN
(Spanish: ESTADO/MUNICIPIO)

These types of divisions are standard in the catalog, most countries having no more than three subdivisions. The arrangement is alphabetical under each country. To find records for Reamstown, Pennsylvania, for example, begin with the largest division and then keep sub-dividing: **United States/Pennsylvania/Lancaster/Reamstown.** (Reamstown is in Lancaster County.) At the beginning of each set of fiche is an alphabetical index fiche of towns and villages (the smallest divisions), with a key about how they are arranged in the catalog. Figure 2:1 is a page from the Locality FHLC.

Under each of the several catalog divisions, differing types of records will be listed. Listings are determined by the geographical area covered by the records themselves. Thus, records created by the federal government which relate to the United States as a whole (such as U.S. Army enlistments, federal land grants, military pensions, etc.) will simply be listed under **United States**, and then under a specified record category. In the same way, records created on a state basis (such as census records, state vital records, militia rolls, etc.) are listed under the state and category.

Counties are then listed, with records created by, or pertaining to that particular county (such as deeds, probates, cemeteries, taxes, etc.). Within each county, the individual villages and townships are listed, where one finds the most specific of records: church records, town histories, city maps, and port records.

Most of the world is cataloged according to modern boundaries with the exception of most of central Europe, which is cataloged under older boundaries. Germany is divided according to its boundaries of 1871, encompassing areas now in Poland and the USSR. Listings are found under both the old German divisions and names of places, as well as under their corresponding modern names and boundaries. Thus, it is possible to find the same set of records under two countries.

Poland is likewise cataloged in several ways. The old division of Poland appears (Germany, Austria, and Russian-Poland, when Poland was not a country), as well as corresponding modern boundaries. This multiple entry system of places has the distinct advantage of allowing searches under either the old or the new names of places, and the index fiche as a guide greatly facilitates finding the corresponding old or new divisions. (The index fiche for Poland gives the corresponding Polish-language divisions, whereas the index fiche for Germany provides the German names and political divisions.)

No matter how the headings are broken down, the content of the catalog entry is always the same. These entries are in the native language of the country with notations in English. Some of the German entries are written, not just in German, but also in Polish. Similarly, areas now in Czechoslovakia once belonging to Hungary are also cataloged under their Hungarian names, with the catalog text in Hungarian.

U.S. church records are frequently cataloged under the name of the village where the church itself is located, rather than under the township where the village is located. This causes no small difficulty in determining how many churches existed in a particular township. You must first find the names of all the villages within that township, and then search under the names of those villages.

In most cases, types of records fit easily under their assigned headings by locality, but occasionally a particular group of records is so unusual that it becomes harder to classify appropriately. Here are the headings used in the Locality FHLC:

Archives & Libraries
Bible Records
Bibliography
Biography
Business & Commerce
Cemeteries
Census
Centennials
Chronology
Church Directories
Church Records
Church Histories
Civil Registration
Collected Works
Colonization
Correctional Institutions
Court Records
Description & Travel
Dictionaries
Directories
Dwellings
Emigration & Immigration
Encyclopedias
Manors
Maps
Medical Records
Merchant Marine
Migration (Internal)
Military History
Military Records
Minorities
Names-Geographic
Names-Personal
Native Races
Naturalization
Newspapers
Nobility
Notarial Records
Obituaries
Occupations
Officials & Employees
Orphans
Pensions
Periodicals
Politics & Government
Poor Houses
Ethnology
Folklore
Gazetteers
Genealogy
Guardian & Ward Records
Guide Books
Handbooks & Manuals
Handwriting
Heraldry
Historical Geography
History
Indexes
Inventories & Registers
Jewish History
Jewish Records
Land & Property
Languages
Law & Legislation
Population
Portraits
Postal Guides
Probate Records
Public Records
Religion
Schools
Slavery & Bondage
Social Life & Customs
Societies
Statistics
Taxation
Town Records
Visitations-Heraldic
Vital Records
Voting Registers
Yearbooks

If you are looking for deeds in a particular county, you would find them under **[State]/[County]/Land Records.** Wills are listed under **/Probate Records.** New editions of all parts of the catalog are distributed every six months. Pending new editions, you can search for new records on computer access terminals located at the Information Desk on each floor in the main library.

Sometimes you must be creative in finding how records are cataloged. New Mexico's majority population was Mexican by nationality and it still has a large Mexican population base; however, the IGI lists all records pertaining to Mexicans in New Mexico under the heading **New Mexico/Minorities.**

Changes in cataloging procedures have caused inconsistencies and incompleteness in bibliographic citations and the descriptive information included with each entry.

Some titles are cataloged in the Author-Title FHLC without separate entries in the Locality FHLC. Thus, it is important to check both sections for a complete list of titles.

Finally, a significant portion of the titles listed in the United States Locality section of the 1986 edition of the FHLC do not appear in the 11 March 1987 edition. Either consult the older edition, use the computer access terminals at the main library, or check the Author-Title section of the FHLC to identify the library's complete holdings.

Here are explanations of the five different sections of the catalog:

Author-Title: Look for particular books or authors in this part of the catalog, which is organized strictly alphabetically. All books (in any language) are cataloged here under both their titles and authors. Descriptions of books written in foreign languages are in the foreign language with brief notes in English. Since most of the library's film collection consists of parish and vital records without exact titles, those records are included under an Author-Title listing for the organization creating the records. The entire collection of Danish parish registers can thus be found under the name of the church (Den Danske Folkekirke), with the parishes following in alphabetical order.

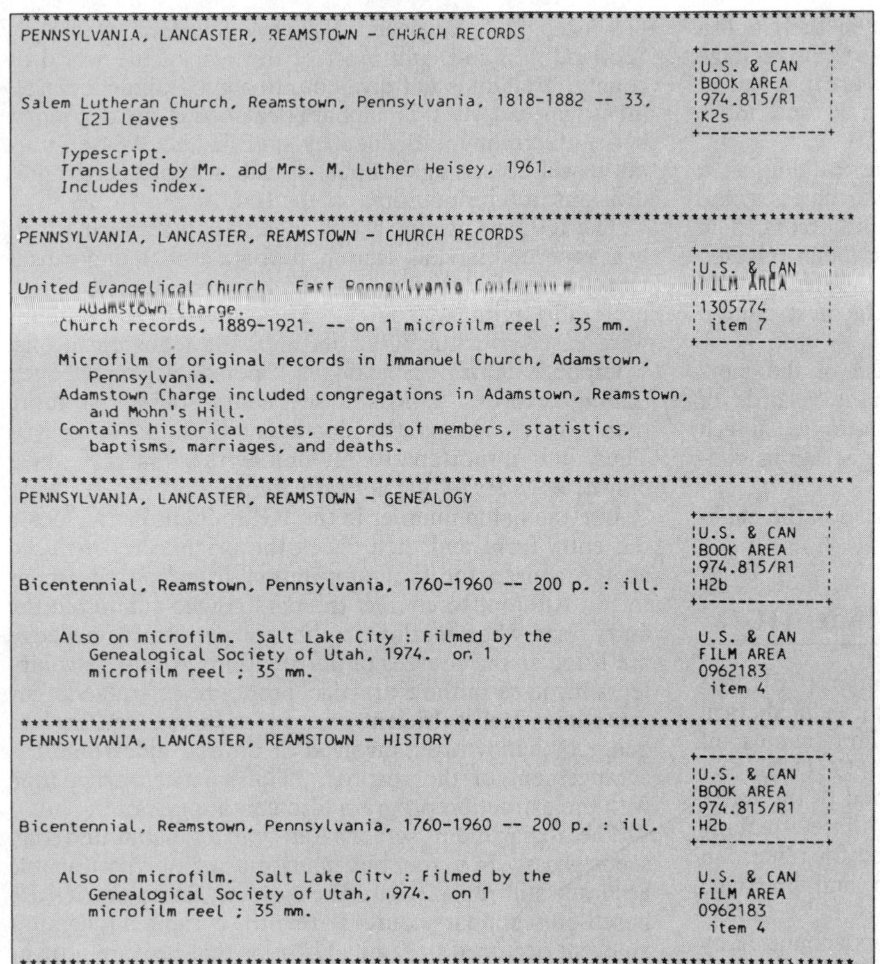

```
PENNSYLVANIA, LANCASTER, REAMSTOWN - CHURCH RECORDS
                                                                  U.S. & CAN
                                                                  BOOK AREA
Salem Lutheran Church, Reamstown, Pennsylvania, 1818-1882 -- 33,  974.815/R1
    [2] leaves                                                    K2s

    Typescript.
    Translated by Mr. and Mrs. M. Luther Heisey, 1961.
    Includes index.

PENNSYLVANIA, LANCASTER, REAMSTOWN - CHURCH RECORDS
                                                                  U.S. & CAN
United Evangelical Church  East Pennsylvania Conference          FILM AREA
      Adamstown Charge.                                           1305774
    Church records, 1889-1921. -- on 1 microfilm reel ; 35 mm.    item 7

    Microfilm of original records in Immanuel Church, Adamstown,
       Pennsylvania.
    Adamstown Charge included congregations in Adamstown, Reamstown,
       and Mohn's Hill.
    Contains historical notes, records of members, statistics,
       baptisms, marriages, and deaths.

PENNSYLVANIA, LANCASTER, REAMSTOWN - GENEALOGY
                                                                  U.S. & CAN
                                                                  BOOK AREA
                                                                  974.815/R1
Bicentennial, Reamstown, Pennsylvania, 1760-1960 -- 200 p. : ill. H2b

    Also on microfilm.  Salt Lake City : Filmed by the            U.S. & CAN
       Genealogical Society of Utah, 1974.  on 1                  FILM AREA
       microfilm reel ; 35 mm.                                    0962183
                                                                  item 4

PENNSYLVANIA, LANCASTER, REAMSTOWN - HISTORY
                                                                  U.S. & CAN
                                                                  BOOK AREA
                                                                  974.815/R1
Bicentennial, Reamstown, Pennsylvania, 1760-1960 -- 200 p. : ill. H2b

    Also on microfilm.  Salt Lake City : Filmed by the            U.S. & CAN
       Genealogical Society of Utah, 1974.  on 1                  FILM AREA
       microfilm reel ; 35 mm.                                    0962183
                                                                  item 4
```

Figure 2:1 Locality Section of the Family History Library microfiche catalog.

The text of an entry never changes, no matter in which portion of the catalog it is found; only the catalog headings change. Within the text of the entry are numbered references to alternate filing headings for that same entry.

Surname: The surname catalog is used largely for locating compiled family histories and genealogies. Sources are listed alphabetically by surname. Listed under that surname are all entries where that surname is in the title of a book or manuscript, or included in its description. Several entries may be found under a certain surname; the entries under that name are filed alphabetically by the name of the author. A brief description of the work is also included. Since there are many families named Clark, for example, you would scan all the entries under the Clark name, looking for descriptive references to particular places or years to identify the family of interest. By using the catalog this way, you would not waste time finding the history of a Clark family in Massachusetts, when the family being researched lived in Georgia.

Some of the histories listed under a particular surname are not chiefly about that family, even though the book's description contains that name. In these cases, the descriptive entry lists the included surnames, even though they may be only briefly mentioned in the work.

After general works on a surname, the catalog then begins a new list of books about a specific individual of that surname, or the descendants of a certain individual of that name. Thus, a book about the descendants of John Smith, born 1612, will be listed first under the collection of Smith histories, and then again under "Smith, John born 1612." If a particular surname is not listed in the surname file, it does not mean that something about that family is not already in print. Books of descendants of a common ancestor have a multiplicity of surnames included, particularly if the descendants of the daughters are traced. Only those surnames appearing in the descriptions are entered in the surname file. Collections of research on certain families are also found in the surname file. A collection of inscriptions from a family cemetery, where the cemetery bears the name of the family, would also be included, as are other types of research papers and files–so long as the surname is reflected in the title or description thereof.

Subject: This section of the catalog is probably the least used. The generalities represented by a subject listing are not particularly helpful because in doing genealogical research very specific types of records are used. Certain topics can nevertheless be located more quickly in the subject catalog than in the locality file, since some books of general interest would be difficult to pin down to a particular locality.

A book containing a list of the recipients of the Presidential Medal of Honor, for example, might be difficult to find under the "United States" locality heading. Similarly, books concerning laws of divorce in various states or countries are listed here under the heading "Divorce."

Foreign-Language Locality: The foreign-language locality file is an exact duplicate of the regular locality file, except that the geographic headings and categories are in the native languages of those countries. Germany is broken down in exactly the same manner, except that it is called Deutschland.

This arrangement is intended to help native language speakers, who might otherwise have difficulty locating places under their English equivalents. Besides the names of the countries, the category listings are also in local languages: what in the English listing appears as **/Directories** would in German be listed as **/Adressbucher.** But again, only the headings vary. The text of the catalog entry is still identical to that in the English edition. Often it is beneficial to use the foreign-language edition, since it and the English edition are put out at different times, making the foreign edition at times more up-to-date.

The alphabetical arrangement of the catalog as a whole greatly enhances its usability. Nevertheless, some records have been misfiled because of input errors. The town of Czarnikau, Posen, Germany, has been misfiled as "Carnikau," because the typist accidentally dropped the "z." Such errors are corrected in the next edition when they are found.

Other cataloging errors occur because of the inexperience of the cataloger. A great many records of German-Poland were cataloged under **/Catholic Church Records,** when they were actually civil registrations containing all religions.

Other FHLC idiosyncracies are discussed in the chapters dealing with each geographic locality.

The International Genealogical Index (IGI)

Formerly called the Computer File Index (CFI), the International Genealogical Index is an alphabetical microfiche print-out of over 80 million names of deceased persons in alphabetical order (1984 edition). Approximately 10 million names are added to the index each year; new editions are released at three- to four-year intervals. A new edition is scheduled for release in 1988 with nearly 40 million new birth and marriage entries.

The IGI consists of entries from names submitted by professional and amateur genealogists from information taken from family and original records or by trained extractors who enter information from birth and marriage records, church registers, probate records, and census enumerations worldwide. Until 1987, names were submitted on Individual Entry or Marriage Entry forms. A newly released 8 1/2 x 11 family group record form has replaced them. (See Figure 2:2.)

The IGI lists the name of the person, names of parents or spouse, sex, date and place of event, LDS ordinance dates, and input source reference number. The names are in alphabetical sequence with cross-references for marriages. (Spelling variants are indexed together.) The input reference number is coded to show the type of record used and whether it was submitted by an individual or as part of the name-extraction program. See Figure 2:3 for an annotated example.

The source number (more commonly called the batch number) is used to identify the individual or marriage entry form from which the data was taken. Each entry form is given a batch number and microfilmed. Learning to identify batch numbers and locate the microfilmed individual and marriage entry forms is important because entry forms usually contain more information than that listed in the IGI, along with the name and address of the person who submitted the form.

The IGI is arranged differently by country with the United States being subdivided by state; Canada by province; and England, Norway, Sweden, Denmark, Scotland, Finland, and most of the rest of the world by county. Ireland is not divided into a geographic arrangement, instead it is in alphabetical order on a country basis. Germany is divided by state in the 1984 edition, but it will be arranged alphabetically without geographic divisions in future editions of the IGI.

The IGI was originally designed to contain facts exactly as recorded in vital, church, probate (wills), and census records. Each entry was to be supported by a *single*, preferably primary, source. Those initial requirements were eased over the IGI's lifetime, and many entries list "compiled family genealogy," "personal knowledge," "family records," a printed secondary source, or more than one source as the documentation for the entry. Thus, it is important to remember that *the IGI serves only as an index to original entry forms.*

Use the batch number in the IGI to identify and locate the entry form and then check the original record used as the source for the information listed on the entry form. Attempt to contact the person who submitted the entry form when family members or personal knowledge are listed as the sources of information. Although volunteers involved in the extraction program are trained, they sometimes lack sufficient experience in reading the language or handwriting involved or do not understand the arrangement of the records. Thus, entries originating with the extraction program also contain errors.

The department screens out entries submitted that seem grossly in error, but many entries of questionable accuracy still make it into the system. Some entries are based on secondary sources – records compiled long after an event occurred or family histories that provide little or no citation of research evidence. Such entries frequently contain errors.

Extraction records also are less complete than the original source document. In some countries, for example, it is customary to give a child several personal names; however, the IGI will list only the first two names. Thus, a child christened John Henry Albert who used Albert during his lifetime might be overlooked in the IGI where he would be listed as John Henry.

Royal and noble family members may also be difficult to locate because they didn't retain fixed surnames, and are indexed by either the place they ruled or by their places of birth or marriage. For example, King George II of England is listed under Prussia as "England-R/N" (meaning "England-Royalty/Nobility") because he was born in Prussia.

In cases of illegitimate or adopted children, the IGI lists the parents to whom the child is sealed. (Sealings are an LDS religious ordinance involving couples and their children. See Chapter 1.) No reference is made to an adoption, although the original input source may include it. If the illegitimate child's mother married later, the child may be listed under the surname of the step-father. In many instances, the child is listed under a double entry, the biological father's surname and the step-father's surname.

Besides the massive IGI index by surname, special indexes have been prepared by given name for areas where

Family Group Record

Page ____ of ____

LDS ORDINANCE DATA
B = Baptized E = Endowed
S = Sealed to spouse P = Sealed to parents

Husband's name

			Date	Temple
Born	Place	B		
Chr.	Place	E		
Mar.	Place	S		
Died	Place	P		
Bur.	Place			

Father ____ Mother ____

Husband's other wives

Wife's name

			Date	Temple
Born	Place	B		
Chr.	Place	E		
Died	Place	P		
Bur.	Place			

Father ____ Mother ____

Wife's other husbands

Children List each child (whether living or dead) in order of birth

				Date	Temple
1 Sex	Name	Spouse			
	Born	Place	B		
	Chr.	Place	E		
	Mar.	Place	S		
	Died	Place	P		
2 Sex	Name	Spouse			
	Born	Place	B		
	Chr.	Place	E		
	Mar.	Place	S		
	Died	Place	P		
3 Sex	Name	Spouse			
	Born	Place	B		
	Chr.	Place	E		
	Mar.	Place	S		
	Died	Place	P		
4 Sex	Name	Spouse			
	Born	Place	B		
	Chr.	Place	E		
	Mar.	Place	S		
	Died	Place	P		

☐ Check here if additional children are listed on reverse side.

Additional Information

Record on the back:
- **Sources of information**
- **Other marriages, sealings, and explanations**

Check the box for one of the following options (applies to all names submitted on this form):

☐ **OPTION 1— FAMILY FILE** Send all names to my family file at the ____ Temple. I will provide proxies for: ☐ Baptism ☐ Endowment ☐ Sealing
I understand that ordinances not checked will have proxies assigned by the temple.

☐ **OPTION 2 — TEMPLE FILE** Send all names to any temple and assign proxies for all approved ordinances.

☐ **OPTION 3 — ANCESTRAL FILE** Send all names to the Ancestral File. (You must include a pedigree chart or required form.) No ordinances will be done.

Name and address of person submitting form

Phone ( ) Date prepared

Stake/Mission Stake/Mission unit no.

Relationship of above to:
Husband____ Wife____

Figure 2:2 Family Group Record form used for submitting names for inclusion in the International Genealogical Index. (1987 version)

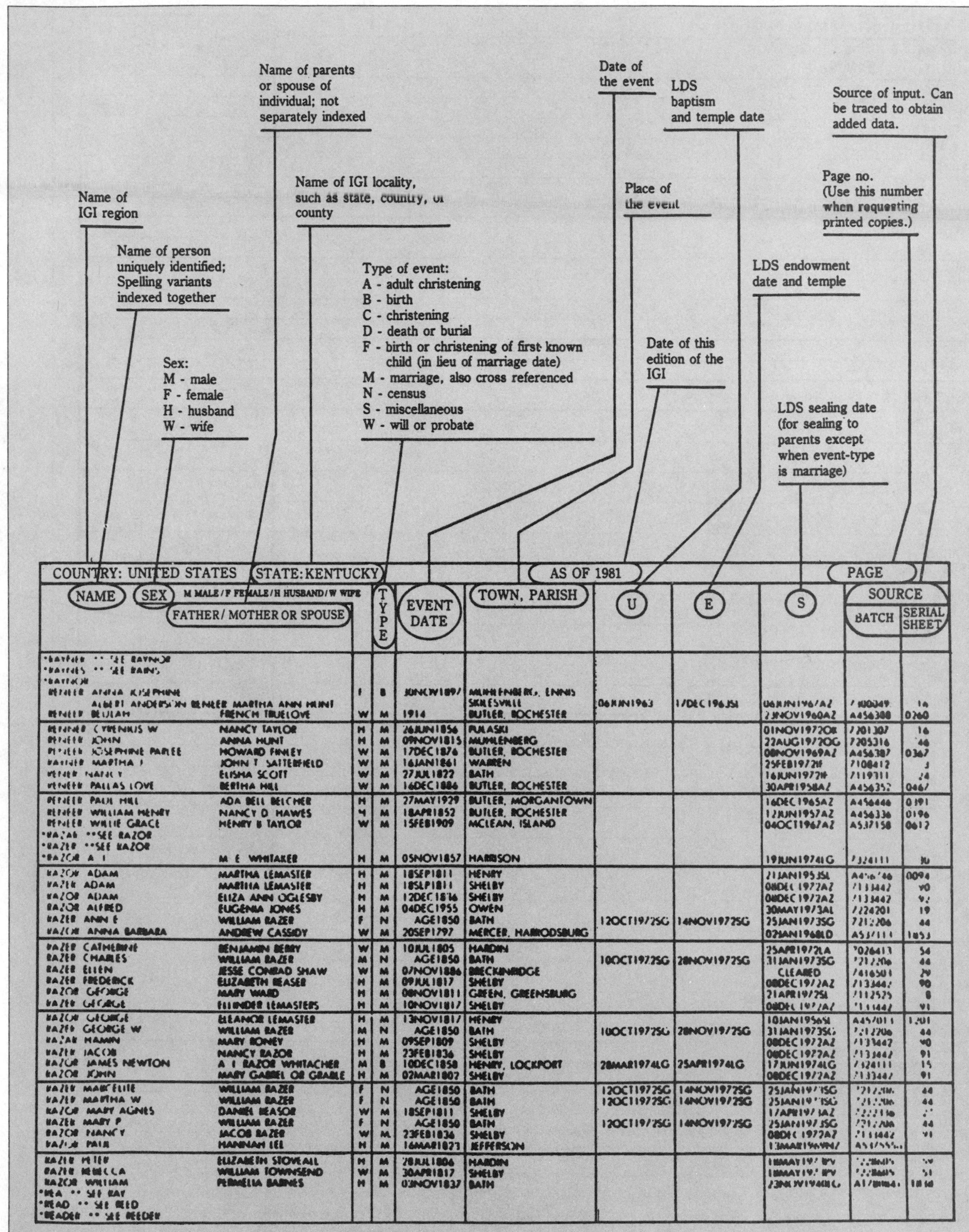

Figure 2:3 The International Genealogical Index.

the patronymic naming system was in effect. All Scandinavian countries have them, as well as Wales and Monmouthshire, England. Other places using patronymics, such as the Netherlands and East Frisia, and Prussia, do not have given name indexes.

Another supplemental index to the IGI is the *Index to Old Parochial Registers of Scotland*, consisting of entries extracted from Scottish parish registers from their earliest dated entry to 1855. Separate sections exist for births and marriages in which entries are listed by actual surname spellings rather than standard spellings. This index is used primarily as a finding tool, so the dates of LDS ordinances are not included, but can be obtained from the IGI.

In the early years of the extraction program, names taken from a particular parish were printed out in alphabetical order and then filmed or bound for use in the library. The *Parish and Vital Records Listing*, included as front matter with each copy of the IGI, contains the microfilm or book call numbers for these print-outs. This process was eliminated during the 1970s and now extracted names go directly into the IGI.

The IGI is available on every floor of the Family History Library, at each of its centers, and at selected public and private libraries throughout the United States. Most of the batch/input sources are available on microfilm through the family history centers.

For further information on the IGI and its use, refer to the following publications:

1. *Genealogical Research Paper Series F, No. 6, 1983* (stock no. PRGS2020), $2.50, Genealogical Society of Utah, 35 North West Temple, Salt Lake City, UT 84150 or from the General Church Distribution Center, 1999 West 1700 South, Salt Lake City, UT 84104.

2. "IGI Instructions and Regions," on microfiche, available wherever copies of the IGI are found, dated September 1983 or later.

3. Elizabeth L. Nichols, "The International Genealogical Index," *New England Historical Genealogical Register* 87 (July 1983): 193-217.

4. Lance J. Jacob, "The International Genealogical Index: A Tool to Be Used with Understanding," *Genealogical Magazine* 21 (June 1983): 60-63; (Sept. 1983): 165-70. A British perspective on using the IGI.

The IGI is an index and should be used as such, not a replacement for original source material. Its size makes the IGI one of the finest genealogical finding aids in existence. Experienced IGI users would forewarn the beginner of some of the less obvious pitfalls of searching the IGI. For instance, foreign names are not always listed as they were spelled after a family immigrated to the United States. They often appear in Latin or in abbreviated form. Someone named George in America may appear in the German segment of the IGI as Georg, Georgius, Geo (no period) or Geo. (with period).

The entries in the IGI are arranged by columns, each with a heading. Since the list is alphabetical, the individual's name appears first. For birth entries, the names of the parents are then listed. On marriage entries, the name of spouse is listed. The sex of the person, event type (birth, marriage, or death), date, and place are also provided. Columns are also devoted to dates of LDS Temple Ordinances, and source references. Here is an explanation of the information in each column:

Name: Names in the IGI were, for several years, indexed under standardized spellings. Some of these standardizations make good sense, because the different spellings are just varying forms of the same name (like "Smith" and "Smythe"). Other names, less likely variants of the same, were also alphabetized together (like "Schmidt" and "Schmidtke"). Cross references are included in the IGI to each of these standard spellings.

Many names are also entered exactly as they appeared in the original source. Records written using abbreviations and foreign name forms (as in Catholic Church records written in Latin) may make locating an entry more difficult. The computer indexes abbreviations with and without periods under separate listings.

The IGI serves only as an index to original sources–entries for marriages including only the names of the bride and groom. Much more information may have been given in the original document, however. For example, in many cases the names of the parents of the bride and groom are also given. For that reason, you should always check the original source, using the references provided.

Sex: The sex of the individual is always listed. On birth entries, M or F (male or female) and on marriages, H or W (husband or wife) are standard indications. Entries where the original source did not include sex or where the sex cannot be determined from the name have largely been listed as males.

Event Type: Information in the IGI is derived from many sources. Some of these sources do not allow for clearly establishing dates of birth or marriage. The "Event Type" letter codes what type of document was used to establish minimum identification. Some of these codes are:

A–Adult christening
B–Birth
C–Child christening
D–Death (infants for whom no christening is found)
F–Birth of first known child (in lieu of marriage date)
M–Marriage
N–Census
S–Miscellaneous
W–Will or probate record

When information is derived from census or probate records, the date under which the listing is indexed is not the calculated/approximated date of birth or marriage, but the date of the census or probate record. Thus, a fifteen-year-old entered from the 1850 U.S. census would not be found under a calculated birth of 1835 but under the year 1850, with the notation "age 15." Similarly, that person may be listed in the census living in Illinois, but born in Arkansas. Since the 1850 census was in Illinois, the person is listed in Illinois, rather than the state of birth.

Date: Event dates listed in the IGI are not necessarily dates of birth or marriage. When the information is obtained from church records, the date of christening is used, even if the record contains the exact birth date. In most instances, a christening date is very close to the date of birth, in some cases the same. But in areas where it was customary to christen a child later (often several months after birth), the christening date could be misleading. Calculated or approximated years of birth have recently been introduced into the system. Such entries are marked with an "F" before the source batch number.

Place: Specific places of birth or marriage are required for submission of entries. In the U.S., at least a county must be provided; in most other countries, the name of a city or parish is required. Where parish registers provide the name of a village of birth which differs from the name of the parish, the parish name is nevertheless used as the locality. In this sense, the IGI represents the locality of the record, rather than the locality of the event. When records come from localities with more than one parish (as in a city) or parishes of different denominations, the event place column will often include specific reference to the parish or denomination. The words "Vital" or "Civil" might also appear if the record was from Civil Registers.

B,E,S: The next three columns refer to dates of LDS baptism, endowment, and sealing, all of them religious ordinances performed by proxy in LDS temples. (See Chapter 1.) These dates are a clue to how recently the entry was filed since the ordinances are usually performed the same year the information is submitted. The more recently an entry was filed, the greater the possibility of locating the individual who submitted it at the address listed on the submission form. Ordinance dates prior to 1969 are usually conversions from the older (TIB) indexing system. Sealing dates on birth entries refer to sealing to parent, on marriage entries, sealing to spouse. Besides the ordinance dates, the name of the temple where they were performed is also provided, using standard abbreviations, in case the temple records should ever need to be consulted.

The word "infant" appears in the baptism and endowment columns for children who died under eight years of age; the word "cleared" for entries still in process. The abbreviation "BIC" may appear in the sealing column (Born in Covenant), if the individual was born after his or her parents had been sealed in the temple. Finally, the words "Do not seal" may be found in cases of illegitimacy.

Source: Batch and serial sheet numbers appearing in these columns are your references to track the original source. An entry can be input into the system in a variety of ways. If the batch number is composed solely of digits, then the entry was submitted by an LDS Church member acting as an individual. The original submission form can be viewed on microfilm by locating that same batch number on the microfiche "Batch Number Index," which provides the number of the microfilm for that batch. The "Batch Number Index" is included as front matter with each copy of the IGI and is found on the same microfiche holder with the IGI. The serial sheet number is actually the page number for the sheet on which the entry appears.

If the batch number is preceded by a letter, then the Family History Department itself entered that information as part of its names extraction program from the microfilms already held in its collection. Entries preceded by a "C" or "M" are christenings and marriages derived in that manner. A list of localities and film numbers for records extracted by the department, called the "Parish and Vital Records Listing" is used to keep track of the original sources for these entries.

Other letters preceding batch numbers do not necessarily refer to original sources but rather to the conversion of earlier entries from earlier entry systems. The computerization process began in 1969. "A" refers to the Family Group Archives, a collection of family group sheets used for records processing from 1941 to 1969. This whole set of sheets (600,000) are slowly being converted to the computer system. "E" refers to an "Early Marriage Extraction," a program of isolating obscure marriage records from a variety of sources. Batch numbers preceded by an "E" can be traced using the batch number index for a corresponding number with the "M" prefix, which then lists an input film number. Batch numbers beginning with a "T" are conversions from the Temple Index Bureau (TIB), a 30 million-name file-card index to the Family Group Archives. A photocopy of the original TIB index card can be obtained from the copy center; the information should be identical, however, with that entered on a sheet in the Family Group Archives, if the ordinance dates are after 1941. Prior to that date, the TIB indexed only the temple records.

More unusual are batch numbers preceded by J, K, or P. These are similar to those with a "C." Entries with "F" are records processed under the Family Entry Program, which provided for submitting records where dates were calculated or approximated. This batch number can be consulted in normal alpha-numeric order on the batch number index for a source film number.

New batch numbers (and accompanying prefixes) are always being created. The LDS counter at the Family History Library maintains a current listing of numbers and prefixes and what they signify.

Family Group Records Collection

One of the largest collections of genealogical information in existence, the Family Group Records Collection (FGRC) or Family Group Records Archives contains over 600,000 family group sheets. These sheets were submitted by members of the Church of Jesus Christ of Latter-day Saints for processing between 1941 and 1969. The collection is organized alphabetically in binders, arranged by father's surname, then given name, then year of birth. Figure 2:4 is an archive record from the FGRC. Note the asterisk after several names indicating that the

HUSBAND WILLHEIT OR WILLET, Michael

Born 1645 Place Schwaigern, Neckar, Wrtt
Chr. Place
Marr. 3 Nov 1668 Place Schwaigern, Neckar, Wrtt
Died 23 Sep 1711 Place " " "
Bur. Place
HUSBAND'S FATHER WILLHEIT, Georg — HUSBAND'S MOTHER LUTZ, Barbara
HUSBAND'S OTHER WIVES (2) 18 Nov 1690 NELLINGER, Anna Barbara *

WIFE (1) RIFLIN , Anna Marie * T

Born abt 1647 Place Schwaigern, Neckar, Wrtt
Chr. Place
Died 27 Dec 1689 Place Schwaigern, Neckar, Wrtt
Bur. Place
WIFE'S FATHER RIFLIN OR RIEFLE, Martin * — WIFE'S MOTHER [illegible]
WIFE'S OTHER HUSBANDS

Husband WILLHEIT, Michael 1645
Wife RIFLIN, Anna Marie

NAME & ADDRESS OF PERSON SUBMITTING RECORD — J. S.
Mrs. Paula Shomaker
Manti, Utah 84642

FAMILY REPRESENTATIVE
SHOMAKER, (Mrs) Paula A. Schwender
RELATION OF F.R. TO HUSBAND 6 gg dau — RELATION OF F.R. TO WIFE 6 gg dau

TEMPLE ORDINANCE DATA

	BAPTIZED (DATE)	ENDOWED (DATE)	SEALED (Date & Temple) WIFE TO HUSBAND
HUSBAND	7 FEB 1967	27 FEB 1967	10 JAN '68 MT
WIFE	6 FEB 1967	24 FEB 1967	//////////

ARCHIVE RECORD

	SEX M F	CHILDREN (List Each Child (Whether Living or Dead) in Order of Birth) SURNAME (CAPITALIZED) GIVEN NAMES	WHEN BORN (DAY MONTH YEAR)	WHERE BORN: TOWN	COUNTY	STATE OR COUNTRY	DATE OF FIRST MARRIAGE / TO WHOM	WHEN DIED (DAY MONTH YEAR)	BAPTIZED (DATE)	ENDOWED (DATE)	SEALED (Date & Temple) CHILDREN TO PARENTS
1	F	WILLHEIT, Anna Marie	9 Aug 1669	Schwaigern	Neckar	Wrtt			6 FEB 1967	24 FEB 1967	10 JAN '68 MT
2	M	WILLHEIT, Matthias (twin)	25 Jan 1671	"	"	"		8 Feb 1671	child	child	10 JAN '68 MT
3	M	WILLHEIT Johann Michael (twin)	25 Jan 1671	"	"	"	29 Jan 1696 MUELLER, Anna Dorothea		7 FEB 1967	27 FEB 1967	10 JAN '68 MT
4	F	WILLHEIT, Barbara	29 July1674	"	"	"	6 Sep 1698 BERINGER, Hans Paul		6 FEB 1967	27 FEB 1967	10 JAN '68 MT
5	F	WILLHEIT, Elisabethe	18 Nov 1677	"	"	"		10 Nov 1677	child	child	10 JAN '68 MT
6	F	WILLHEIT, Catharine	31 Aug 1679	"	"	"	23 Jan 1700 BAUMGARTNER, Hans Jacob		6 FEB 1967	27 FEB 1967	10 JAN '68 MT
7	M	WILLHEIT, Johann Georg	21 Mar 1682	"	"	"		22 June1710	7 FEB 1967	27 FEB 1967	10 JAN '68 MT
8	x F	WILLHEIT, Susanna	11 Apr 1684	"	"	"	4 May 1706 BOGER, Hans Jerg	14 Sep 1731	6 FEB 1967	27 FEB 1967	10 JAN '68 MT
9	F	WILLHEIT, Anna Marie	27 Dec 1689	"	"	"			6 FEB 1967	27 FEB 1967	10 JAN '68 MT
10											
11											

SOURCES OF INFORMATION Parish rec. of Schwaigern 1963-1964-1965 by researcher Josef Schurr, Heilbronn, Neckar, Wrtt. now 2327 So. 250 West, Bountiful, Utah

NECESSARY EXPLANATIONS: Husband was also called WILLETT. Wife was also known as RIEFLE, RIFFEL OR RUEFFLIN. Wife's father was also known as RIFFEL OR RUEFFLIN.

Figure 2:4 Archive Record from the Family Group Records Collection (FGRC).

individual appears on a separate group record as a husband or wife.

The bulk of the collection consists of the ancestors of LDS families; and since many of the early members of the church were from the eastern seaboard and England, the collection is particularly strong in those areas. Many colonial New England families have their whole lineages outlined in this collection. It also contains research efforts submitted for processing, in an era of genealogical research known as the "name gathering," where researchers were encouraged to collect all instances of a surname they were researching, whether or not a direct connection to the ancestral family could be established.

Such a massive collection is not without drawbacks. Since information was submitted by individual members of the church and processed with practically no evaluation, many of the sheets have errors – some slight, others gross, even to the point of connecting unrelated families.

All sheets obtained from the archives should be closely scrutinized. The sources listed are good indications of the reliability of the information. Generally, the more complete a source citation, the more accurate a sheet will be. When original records are cited, such as wills and vital records, the information on the sheet is most likely correct. When secondary sources are cited, such as family histories or "family records," you should probably verify the information in original records. The term "family records" has been so loosely used that it is nearly impossible to tell what type of records it was intended to mean. In some cases, it could refer to a family Bible, a very good source; in other cases, it could refer to someone's memories or family tradition.

Furthermore, the closer the specified relationship of the submitter to the ancestors listed on the sheet, the more likely it is that the submitter had access to accurate data from a reliable source.

This collection is available for use in the library on original paper as well as on microfilm. Many times, a particular sheet, if damaged or worn, will be removed from the collection. The filming was made fairly early and thus better represents the whole of the original collection. Asterisks marked by the names of the husband or wife's parents's names indicate that there is a sheet in the collection for those persons too. Sometimes there is no asterisk, but you may still find a sheet for the earlier generation.

Besides the main FGRC, the library has a few smaller family group collections, more limited in scope. The first is the Patron's Section, and it has also been microfilmed. Between 1962 and 1974, members of the church were encouraged to submit sheets for four generations on their family lines, beginning with themselves. As a result, most of the information comes from the late nineteenth and twentieth centuries. The collection also deals almost exclusively with early LDS families.

Since the sheets were provided by individuals, with no cross-referencing of sheets, there are duplicates of many sheets, submitted by different persons. Sometimes the

C INDEX CARD TO End. House TEMPLE RECORDS
No. **M** No. 2167 Book F Page 194
Name in full Jarvis- George Frederick
When born 16 June 1847
Where born London, Middlesex, England
When died 1 Jan [illegible] lvg.
Father George Jarvis [illegible]
Mother Ann Prior
When Married 21 Oct 1872 to [illegible]
Children
Heir Self Rel.
When baptized 1855 When endowed 21 Sept. 1867
When sealed Husband Wife 21 Oct 1872 EH To Parents
Baptized 2 6 MAY 1964 Proxy Olof K. Olsen
All prev. Church bless- ings reconfirmed in the
confirmation ordinances. Dan K. Hansen, R co...

Figure 2:5 Temple Index Bureau Card.

data on all the sheets matches; but more often than not, there are discrepancies. The source of information listed should also be closely scrutinized.

Older groups of sheets have been filmed. A collection of family groups submitted about 1924 to 1950, called the "Oldest Patron's Section" was filmed in 1953. In 1965 the same collection was again filmed, including sheets submitted 1953-62. This second filming is called the "Old Patron's Section."

A collection of family groups prepared from the work of Swiss genealogist Julius Billeter is also on film, as is a collection of Italian (Waldensian) sheets called the Piedmont Project.

Despite their limitations, these family group sheet collections are of tremendous benefit, enabling you to track what has previously been researched and determine the sources used in that research.

Temple Index Bureau

The Temple Index Bureau (TIB) is a 30 million-name index to the records listed on the archives sheets. Since all the archive sheets are filed by father's name, it is first necessary to know the name of the father of the sought-for ancestor, or scan all the sheets of a particular surname looking for an ancestor listed as a child. This card index is alphabetical by surname, providing a faster way of identifying a name in the collection than examining each sheet. Listed on the TIB card is the person's name, birth date and place, parents, spouse, etc. Also entered on the card is a small P or C in the upper left corner, signifying that the individual appears either as a parent or as a child on an archive sheet. Dates of LDS ordinances and temple references are also included. Figure 2:5 is a sample TIB card.

Besides indexing the names appearing on archives sheets, the TIB indexes all LDS temple endowments beginning with the Nauvoo Temple in 1844 and coming up to the work of modern temples in 1969. These include both endowments for the living and proxy work for the dead. If research culminating in LDS ordinances was conducted prior to 1941, searching the TIB may be the only way to uncover it.

Direct access to the TIB and its microfilm copies is limited to LDS patrons. Requests for searches and copies can be made by anyone, however, and the department itself conducts them.

The TIB and accompanying temple records provide the name of the individual who supplied the name but no reference to source material. Thus, any name processed prior to 1941, when the archives was established, cannot be traced back to its source of origin. Since the TIB indexes both documents for the living and the dead, TIB cards for living endowments can be considered rather accurate, because an individual provided that information about himself or herself.

Other information indexed in the TIB or obtained from temple records without source identification should be verified in original documents, when possible.

Family Registry

The Family Registry is a research coordination program, established by the Family History Library. Individuals can enter the name and vital dates of a particular ancestor being researched, so others working on the same person or line can contact them. In this way, several individuals can pool their research efforts, saving time and duplication. This is an on-going program, with periodic microfiched updates.

Registration forms contain information about the individual being researched, and the researcher's name and address. The forms are arranged by the date they are received, then numbered for cross-reference. Space is also provided for the name and address of a second individual to contact, in case the person submitting the form moves and inquiries are not forwarded.

The Family Registry Index contains an alphabetical listing of the ancestors, abbreviated vital data for identification, and the names, addresses, and registration form numbers for persons researching that ancestor. Using the form number, you can view the original registration form. This step is not absolutely necessary, since the index itself contains most of the sought-for particulars.

The value of the Family Registry is in its networking. Names submitted to the International Genealogical Index (IGI) are entered only once. All subsequent submissions of the same name are refused. Thus, the names and addresses of others working on that individual are discarded. This can sometimes be quite disadvantageous, since the first person submitting a name is not necessarily always the one with the best information. It also limits research scope – researchers are encouraged to enter only the names of ancestors that are currently being sought – channeling research, then, to the "problem" ancestors. Figures 2:6 and 2:7 are the forms used to submit information to the Family Registry.

Personal Ancestral File (PAF)

The Personal Ancestral File (PAF) is a computer software program designed by the Family History Department for individual home use on a personal computer (PC). It is available in versions suited to MS-DOS (IBM compatibles), Apple (II+, IIe, IIc), and CP/M (Kaypro). It does not currently access any files of the Family History Department but simply provides an organizing system for a researcher's own data.

The program comes in three parts: a family records program, for entering data and printing out forms; a research data filer to document information sources; and a Genealogical Data Communications (GEDCOM) program, for transmitting or receiving data. The GEDCOM program can only be used with MS-DOS, however.

The family records program is a menu-driven program, containing menus for data entry, data modification, data deletion, pedigree searches, note-taking, form printing, and utility (formatting and address labeling). Data is not entered onto family group sheets, but each individual has his or her own record and computer-generated identification number (RIN). Using the RIN numbers, the computer can assemble family group sheets.

Where no RIN number is known, the program directs you on a name-search until you find a RIN number. Since the RIN numbers are generated by the system, they do not follow the "Ahnentafel" numbering system where the number of a person's father is always twice his or her own. The system allows you to input self-generated identification numbers but does not access records using them.

You can search for a pedigree using a RIN, and the display provides the individual, his or her spouse and children, and abbreviated data on the parents (with RINs). Thus, three generations are displayed on the screen at once. Further search options include scrolling upwards or downwards on the pedigree or the spouse's pedigree and viewing children born to the individual's other spouses.

Note-taking provides for an unlimited number of pages of text identified by RIN. These notes can be source references, biographies, etc. If requested, these notes will be printed at the bottom of a family group sheet. If a note is preceded by an exclamation point "!," that line and all other lines so preceded will print while the unmarked lines are suppressed. In that way, only selected notes will be printed on the family group (like sources), and other notes will simply be stored (like biography). The same command can be given without the exclamation point. The computer will print notes at the bottom of the group sheet until it hits a line break code. Thus, if a line break is included between the source notes and the biographical ones, only the source notes will print.

The print program will print seven different forms and lists: (1) a standard five-generation pedigree chart (dimensions variable 8 1/2 x 11, 8 1/2 x 14), (2) standard family group sheets (with or without LDS ordinance data), (3) individual and marriage entry forms for LDS ordinances, (4) an individual summary sheet (one person, no family), (5) a descendant's chart (all individuals on record descended from a certain RIN), and (6) lists sorted alphabetically, by RIN or MRIN (marriage record number), by self-generated identification number, or an individual record with notes.

The entry-form printing does not use the Family History Department's former "One-Source" policy, but all information known about an individual is entered in the record. The source of information comes up blank on the terminal, however, and must be filled in by the user.

The utilities menu contains only three options – formatting a disk, including a name and address for reports printing, and changing the specified titles on the various reports.

Besides the family records program, a research data filer stores original research notes by RIN as well as event (birth, marriage, death, military, etc.). You can make searches and sort on any of these fields. The program (MS-DOS only) can also tell you the relationship between two persons on file (by their RINs). The Data Filer organizes research notes, making analysis easier. It does not, however, contain any research instructions or strategies.

The GEDCOM portion of the program is simply a data-transmission system. It will convert specified data into a format for telephone modem transfer and allow it to be transmitted to another individual with a GEDCOM system. You do not necessarily have to have the PAF program in order to transfer data back and forth. GEDCOM alone is sufficient. GEDCOM also provides a retrieval system for information you receive and will convert that data into a family records format for entry into your file. GEDCOM can also be used to copy a portion of a data disk onto another one.

Two versions of PAF have already been released. Data entered using the first release for the IBM computer and compatible systems can be converted for use with the second version. The software package includes the program and a three-ring binder user manual. It can be obtained from the Church Distribution Center 1999 West 1700 South, Salt Lake City, Utah 84104 for $35.

Other commercial software programs include interfaces with the PAF, including Roots II and Family Roots.

THE CHURCH OF JESUS CHRIST OF LATTER-DAY SAINTS

Research Coordination Registration

Family Registry, Genealogical Department
50 East North Temple Street
Salt Lake City, Utah 84150

FR

By registering, you indicate your willingness to coordinate your research efforts with others. Your name and address and some of the genealogical information on this form will be computerized to produce the Family Registry Index. TYPE or PRINT with black or blue-black ink. This form will be microfilmed.

Registrant Information

Your name	Alternate person to contact in case of returned mail	
Your street address	Alternate's street address	
City, state, zip code	City, state, zip code	
Telephone (optional) ( )	Telephone (optional) ( )	Today's date

Information About Deceased Individual Being Researched Please register only one individual per form

Name of individual (given, surname) ☐ Male ☐ Female

Birth/Christening date (day, month, year)

Place (parish/town, county, state/country)

Death/Burial date (day, month, year)

Place (parish/town, county, state/country)

Father:

b.
m.
d.

Mother:

b.
d.

Marriage Information About Individual

Name of first spouse (given, surname)

Marriage date (day, month, year) | Place (parish/town, county, state/country)

Name of second spouse (given, surname)

Marriage date (day, month, year) | Place (parish/town, county, state/country)

Name of third spouse (given, surname)

Marriage date (day, month, year) | Place (parish/town, county, state/country)

Additional spouses
☐ Yes ☐ No

Variant surname spellings

Additional information

PFGS2501 1/84 Printed in USA

Figure 2:6 Research Coordination Registration form used to submit information to the Family Registry.

THE CHURCH OF JESUS CHRIST OF LATTER-DAY SAINTS

Family Organization Registration

Family Registry, Genealogical Department
50 East North Temple Street
Salt Lake City, Utah 84150

FR

The registrant's name and address and some of the genealogical information on this form will be computerized to produce the Family Registry Index.
If you wish to register specific names you are actively researching, use the Research Coordination form.
TYPE or PRINT with black or blue black ink. This form will be microfilmed.

Family Organization Information Please register only one organization per form.

Name of organization | Year organized | ☐ Not yet organized

Check type of organization
☐ Ancestral Family Organization—Fill out Section A
☐ Surname Family Organization—Fill out Section B

Today's date

Name of registrant (person to contact) | Alternate contact

Street address | Street address

City, state, zip code | City, state, zip code

Telephone (optional) ( ) | Telephone (optional) ( )

A. Ancestral Family Organization This section is for organizations formed around a deceased ancestor.

Name of common ancestor (given, surname) ☐ Male ☐ Female

Birth/Christening date (day, month, year) | Place of birth/christening (parish/town, county, state/country)

Death/Burial date (day, month, year) | Place of death/burial (parish/town, county, state/country)

Father's name (given, surname) | Mother's name (given, maiden surname)

Name of first spouse (given, surname)

Marriage date (day, month, year) | Place of marriage (parish/town, county, state/country)

Name of second spouse (given, surname)

Date of marriage (day, month, year) | Place of marriage (parish/town, county, state/country)

Name of third spouse (given, surname)

Date of marriage (day, month, year) | Place of marriage (parish/town, county, state/country)

Additional spouses
☐ Yes ☐ No

Additional information

B. Surname Organization DO NOT complete this section if you have filled out Section A. This section is for organizations centered around researching a surname in a particular location and time period.

Surname | Year or year range of records you are researching ________ to ________

Locality

Variant surname spellings

Additional information

PFGS2512 1/84 Printed in USA

Figure 2:7 Family Organization Registration form used to submit family organization for inclusion in the Family Registry

Family Histories

The Family History Collection of the Family History Library, with well over 30,000 titles of printed family histories, manuscript genealogies, and family history periodicals, is among the largest in the world.

The key to searching the collection successfully is, of course, the catalog. Since most of the collection is family histories based on surname (that is, books of descendants of a certain ancestor), the titles and call numbers of these books are found under that surname in the Surname FHLC.

The actual books themselves are shelved alphabetically by surname. A large part of the collection consists of family histories which have been filmed, after which the original book is discarded. *Thus, only the catalog, not a shelf search, will tell you what is available.* Many of the more recently published works cannot be microfilmed, and are thus in book form only. As a result, they cannot circulate to the family history centers; but it is possible that they can be obtained through other interlibrary loan systems.

Although a well-researched and carefully documented family history is invaluable, one that has been compiled from family traditions, hearsay, or second-hand research cannot be relied upon with any confidence. The documentation included in a particular work is the chief determination of its reliability. The more often original sources are cited and quoted, the more likely the history is accurate.

The collection is very strong in pre-turn-of-the-century New England/New York genealogies. For this reason, if you have a research problem family in those areas with a particularly New England-sounding name, you should check the histories under that surname. Persons searching a Booth ancestor in New York, for example, should check the Booth family history, for many descendants of the immigrant Richard Booth of Connecticut went to New York and are included in the history, despite its title.

Other family histories are not about a certain family, but contain research notes about various groups of the same surname. This pattern is particularly true with families in the South. The book *Wilhoits of Virginia,* then, may not contain the descendants of just one Wilhoit, but information on several immigrant branches of Wilhoits, all of whom lived in Virginia.

The collection also contains the periodicals and newsletters of certain surname societies.

Any work which contains a surname as part of its title is cataloged in the Surname FHLC.

Special Registers

Available only at the main library are printed sets of call-number microfilm registers, which greatly assist finding call numbers for heavily used items. These Special Registers are extremely helpful, not just because they help find numbers faster, but also because some of the collections they represent may be more difficult to find in the catalog. The Danish Census of Schleswig-Holstein, for example, is almost impossible to locate in the catalog, but the numbers are easily found in the Danish Census Register.

These volumes are found on register tables and credenzas in the reference area specified. Here are the registers available:

USA/Canada Reference Area
Passenger Lists (United States)
Passenger Lists (New York)
State Vital Records (Where to Write)
State Census Records
Federal Census Records
United States Maps
Register of Gazetteers
County Census Indexes
City Ward Maps
Mortality Schedules
American Indian Census
1890 Veterans' Census
Cook County, Illinois, Records
1915 Census New York City, Street Index
United States Military Records
United States City Directories
Canadian Census
Supplementary Index to Canadian Records

LDS Reference Area
LDS Temple Register
Archives Collection Film Numbers
Salt Lake City Street Guide
Register of LDS Records
1850 Utah Census
1852 Bishop's Report Utah
Research Department Files
LDS Periodicals Index
Journal History Call Numbers
Form Two Family Group Sheets Numbers

British Reference Area
England Probate Districts
Marriage Bonds and Allegations
Boyd's Marriage Index Register
Phillimore's Marriage Index Register
BTs, Worcester, York, Suffolk
England/Wales Census Register
Census Street Indexes
Apprenticeships
India Office Records
Sherwood Collection
Civil Registration Indexes England/Wales
Merchant Vessels
Militia and Army Records
Chancery Proceedings
Welsh Non-Parochial Registers
Welsh Probates
Welsh National Library Manuscripts
Welsh Bishops' Transcripts (BT's)
Scottish Parish Registers
Scotland Censuses

Scotland Civil Registration
Scottish Testaments
Scottish Sasines
Scottish Service of Heirs
Ireland 1901 Census
Ireland Civil Registration
Ireland Catholic Parish Registers
Ireland Probates
Ireland Census Substitutes
Irish Deeds
Ireland Tithes and Griffiths
New Zealand Election Rolls
Australian Census Records
Australian Civil Registration

Continental Europe
German Hamburg Passenger Lists
Various Emigration Sources
Germans in Russia
Netherland Handschriften
Amsterdam Civil Registers
Amsterdam Parish Registers
Drenthe Civil Registers
Rotterdam Civil Registers
Den Haag Civil Registers
Groningen Civil Registers
Dutch Military Records
Limburg pre-1812 Parish Registers
Friesland Parish Registers
Zuid Holland Parish Register Indexes
Amsterdam Census
Brabant, Belgium Civil Registers
Liege, Belgium Census Records

Scandanavia
Danish Census Register
Danish Military Records
Danish Probate Records
Various Probate Extracts for Denmark
Copenhagen Passenger Lists
Norway Census Records
Norway Clerical Maps
Norway Farm Histories (Bygdeboker)
Sweden Parish Registers
Sweden post-1861 Parish Extracts
Swedish Probates
Swedish Tax Lists

It should be mentioned that many of these registers contain old call numbers, and registers in some areas are in the process of being eliminated or updated. Regardless of these limitations, using the registers for these heavily used items is still the fastest way of obtaining the call numbers.

Accelerated Indexing Systems (AIS) Index

Accelerated Indexing Systems (AIS) Index is a microfiche master-index of U.S. census records, some tax rolls, and other miscellaneous records which were originally published in book form on a state-by-state basis. The Family History Library has purchased the first edition of *AIS Index* and the rights to distribute it and future editions among the family history centers.

Although primarily an index to U.S. census records, a complete listing of what is included in the database is found in *Records Indexed by AIS,* a guide prepared by the Family History Library staff, which accompanies each set of microfiche. It contains abbreviations for places and sources indexed, explains how to locate an individual in the index, tells you what to do if the person being sought is not listed in the index, and where to go for further help.

The collection is divided into nine groups, called searches. Each search covers a different time period and/or area as follows:

1. Whole United States 1607-1819
2. Whole United States 1820-29
3. Whole United States 1830-39
4. Whole United States 1840-50
5. United States South 1850-60
6. United States North/Northeast 1850
7. United States West/Midwest 1850-1906

7a. Combination of Searches 5, 6, & 7 1850-1906

8. United States Mortality Schedules 1850-1885

Column arrangement for searches 1 through 7a is identical: six columns with the headings: Name, County, State, Page Number, Additional Information, and Year. Search 8 lists: Name, County, State, Age, Sex, Month [of death], Birthplace, Cause of Death, and Occupation.

Like all indexes, the *AIS Index* has both strengths and weaknesses. It can save an incredible amount of time because so much information is indexed together. The large geographical area covered and the large units of time are also extremely useful. So is the fact that other sources have been included besides the federal census records.

Americans always have been on the move and in the absence of early vital records, locating people in the census has been the only way to document those belonging to a particular family. Since the *AIS Index* is a nation-wide index, it is extremely valuable in pinpointing migration patterns and helps identify variant surname spellings. Without census indexes, genealogical research in the United States would be painstakingly slow; however, the *AIS Index* is not without its problems.

Since the *AIS Index* is a compilation of the widely used printed census indexes published by Accelerated Indexing Systems, the microfiche nation-wide index contains the same errors as the printed volumes. A study conducted at Brigham Young University estimates that a 20 percent error rate exists in the *AIS Index* with names misspelled, people listed in the census were left out of the index, typographical errors, and incorrect page numbers to mention a few of the problems. Most of the errors are attributable to the the fact that the indexing was not done by persons trained in early American paleography. Furthermore, data entry was accomplished by entering data directly from the film into the computer, without verification or editing.

Typographical errors made in the data entry process show up in the index. One would never expect to find an entry for "Smith" under a transposition "MSITH," but this frequently occurs. Brown is found transposed as "Bronw." Transcription errors also occur where a "u" is read as an "n" etc. All these problems must be kept in mind when you cannot find an entry.

Some counties have been entered under the wrong census year – as a hypothetical example, Montgomery County, New York, Census of 1820 is titled 1830 in the index. The abbreviations used for counties within a state also can be confusing. In Pennsylvania it is difficult to tell whether an individual is residing in Northumberland or Northampton County, since both counties are abbreviated "North." The same occurs in New York with Chanango and Chemung Counties abbreviated "Che."

Since the *AIS Index* contains errors and ommissions, it cannot be the final word on whether a person or family lived in a particular place during a census year. If evidence suggests that a person or family lived in a specific county and they do not appear in the index, *always search the original census entry.*

Despite these problems, the *AIS Index* is one of the best finding tools available to genealogists and it can reduce research time by hundreds of hours.

Center Microfiche Core Collection

The reference staffs in each of the library's units have compiled a list of titles of reference works frequently used by library patrons. Included in this list of 100 titles (divided by geographical area) are the most frequently used reference books, gazetteers, and indexes. The titles have all been microfiched (about 1,200 fiche).

The core collection is excellent in most areas, since the titles were chosen by specialists with research experience. It represents as many of the basic/general research tools as possible, but it is not always complete. Some of the best reference works cannot yet be fiched, due to copyright restrictions, so titles of similar scope and value have sometimes been substituted. For example, under France one finds listed the "Code Postal," a zip-code directory, but the best gazetteer and atlas "Bottin" is not listed, since it cannot be legally copied. Other titles had to be deleted because of the limitations of the project.

Each family history center can either purchase a complete set or selected titles on fiche or, if it prefers, locate book copies of those volumes still in print.

About half of the collection is gazetteers, domestic and foreign. These are particularly noteworthy, since some of them are old and out of print, and likely the only place where a certain locality is mentioned. For Germany, the *Meyers Orts-und Verkegrs Lexikon des Deutschen Reiches.* 2 vols. (Leipzig: Bibliographisches Institut, 1912-13) (FHL# 6000001-6000029) is not available in book form since it is long out of print. However, it is the only gazetteer listing places formerly in Germany but ceded to Poland and Russia since World War II. Having this gazetteer available on fiche to family history center users was imperative.

Other works on the list are general indexes to different types of records: street indexes to large cities of England for use with the census; an index to wills of South Carolina; a roster of Iowa soldiers in the Civil War, etc. See Appendix A for the list.

Computer Resource Files (OPR, AF, GIS)

Besides the International Genealogical Index (IGI), the Family History Department has several other computer-generated resources. The Old Parish Registers (OPR) for Scotland have previously been discussed under the IGI heading. The Ancestral File (AF) and Genealogical Information System (GIS) still need clarification.

Prior to the development of the GIS, names processed on computer were entered in a system called GIANT, the printout of which was the IGI. As the sophistication of the system progressed, the GIANT system became inadequate, so an umbrella system was developed. It included GIANT but allowed for increased expansion and development. This umbrella system is the GIS. As an umbrella system, the GIS uses the IGI, the pre-1970 computer file (Temple Records Conversion) and the Ancestral File as resource files within the system. In this way, all computer files generated by the department fall into a logical system.

At present, you cannot use files under the GIS system except in the form of the microfiche printouts made by the department (the IGI and OPR being some of those). Currently the department is working out a method for users to search the GIS files using a communications modem software, such as, but not limited to, GEDCOM.

The Ancestral File (AF) is one of the resource files under the GIS umbrella. Originally, it was a four-generation program of the departments, consisting of a five-generation pedigree chart beginning with the individual submitting the form and eight family group sheets, submitted on paper to the department. Since then, the forms submitted have been computerized. The AF information is on a main-frame program, not currently accessible to users.

Permanent on-line access terminals are scheduled to be installed in the library sometime during 1987. While not initially available for access by a PC user through a telephone modem, eventually it will be using generic modem software. Presently, AF information is being prepared for down-loading (user-reading, not writing) in the GEDCOM format, but the exact nature of the files has not yet been determined.

With this in mind, the Ancestral File will eventually also be open to up-loading (writing to the system), so the AF will contain on-going updates of information. With many decisions yet to be made about the system and its format (tab and column formats also being considered), it may be some time before the system is open to PC users.

Chapter 3

Services of the Family History Library

Glade I. Nelson

Ordering Microfilm and Microfiche

If you are using the services of a branch of the Family History Library, then one of your most useful tools is the Family History Library Catalog (FHLC) and one of the library's most useful services is its microfilm/fiche ordering capacity. (See Chapter 2 for detailed information on the FHLC.) Each branch library has a microfiche copy of the main library catalog. Thus, you can easily determine what records are available on microfilm and microfiche.

Microfilm

Ordering Microfilm. If the FHLC indicates that a record you would like to view is available on microfilm, you can probably order it at your family history center with the exception of restricted items. Some records cannot be circulated to family history centers because the original custodian specified this restriction as a condition for microfilming. In some cases a record may not be circulated back to the country where it was microfilmed, but it may be circulated to family history centers elsewhere. If a record is restricted from circulating, the FHLC entry will so indicate.

Loan Periods. Films loan out for three weeks at a time to be used in the family history center. This is the time the film is available to be used in the family history center. Time required for processing the order and returning the film is not charged against the patron's use time.

If you think three weeks will not be long enough, you should request it for six months, the next longest loan period. An indefinite loan can be requested if a significant number of patrons at the center will use it extensively. If only a few patrons need the record, an indefinite loan may be periodically evaluated by the center staff and returned to Salt Lake City if its storage space is needed for another roll of microfilm.

In all cases, films are the property of the Family History Department, which reserves the right to recall any film at any time.

If you receive a film on a three-week loan and then discover that you need more time, you may request that the loan terms be changed to either six months or indefinite status.

This loan schedule operates in the United States and Canada. International areas served by microfilm ordering centers may have slight variations in the loan periods.

Loan Fees. When you order the microfilm, you will pay the center staff a fee based on the type of loan you are requesting. Changing loan status will also cost a fee. These fees are set by the Family History Department, which also pays the postage to send the film to the family history center. You will pay the postage to return a three-week or six-month loan.

Sometimes, you may find a record so valuable that you want to have your own copy of the microfilm. In general, the Family History Department does not encourage private purchase of its microfilms because they were acquired for public, not private use. You must obtain written permission from the original record owner before the department will duplicate a roll of microfilm for you. For further information, contact the Administrative Services Section, Family History Department, 50 East North Temple Street, Salt Lake City, UT 84150.

Photocopying Restrictions. You should be aware that a few records cannot be photocopied because of restrictions placed by the original record owner. These records will circulate but are on red microfilm reels to distinguish them from others.

In some cases (some Australian records, for instance), you may make photocopies if you sign a statement that you will not use the information on the record to embarrass or harm any living person.

Microfiche. If the FHLC indicates that a record you would like to view is available on microfiche, you may order it at your branch center library. Microfiche call numbers are always seven-digit numbers beginning with 6, for example, 6876543.

Because microfiche are easier to store than microfilm and less expensive to produce, they are simply sent to a family history center and remain there permanently unless they need to be replaced. A nominal fee of ten cents is charged per fiche; however, that fee is subject to change without notice. The Family History Department pays postage.

You may purchase many of the microfiche in the Family History Library collection for a nominal fee. An example is the International Genealogical Index (IGI) or portions of it. For further information contact the Administrative Services Section, Family History Department, 50 East North Temple Street, Salt Lake City, UT 84150.

The Accreditation Program

Background

The Family History Library discontinued its paid research services in 1966; but to meet the needs of many individuals who are either unable to do their own research or who have research problems requiring particular expertise, it accredits professional genealogical researchers who are not employed by the library but who are experts in using its facilities and resources.

Applicants for accreditation must demonstrate an acceptable level of knowledge, expertise, and skill in solving genealogical problems and compiling genealogies through a series of written and oral examinations.

Applicants must have a good working knowledge of the records of the area or subject to be tested. The tests for non-English-speaking countries include records in the principal language of that country.

Each geographical area or subject area of specialization has its own test for accreditation. Here is a list of the geographic areas for which accreditation is currently offered. Those with an asterisk require a working knowledge of the primary language(s) of that area. Other accreditation tests may be developed in response to need.

United States

1. New England States: Connecticut, Maine, Massachusetts, New Hampshire, Rhode Island, and Vermont.
2. Eastern States: Delaware, New Jersey, New York, and Pennsylvania.
3. Southern States: Alabama, Arkansas, Florida, Georgia, Kentucky, Louisiana, Maryland, Mississippi, North Carolina, Oklahoma, South Carolina, Tennessee, Texas, Virginia, and West Virginia.
4. Midwestern States: Illinois, Indiana, Iowa, Michigan, Minnesota, Missouri, Ohio, and Wisconsin.

British Isles

1. England
2. Ireland
3. Isle of Man
4. Scotland
5. Wales

Canada

1. British Canada
2. French Canada and Acadia*

Scandinavia

1. Denmark*
2. Finland*
3. Norway*
4. Sweden*

Pacific Area

1. Australia
2. New Zealand
3. Polynesia* (non-English-speaking)

Asia

1. China, Taiwan, and Hong Kong*

Latin America

1. Central America*
2. Mexico*

Africa

1. South Africa*

Continental Europe

1. Austria*
2. Belgium*
3. Czechoslovakia*
4. France*
5. Germany*
6. Italy*
7. Netherlands*
8. Poland*
9. Spain*
10. Switzerland*

Accreditation tests are also offered in the research specialties of American Indians and LDS Church Records.

Geographic specialties in order of numbers of accredited researchers are: England, Southern United States, Midwestern States, Denmark, New England States, Germany, Eastern States, and Sweden. Some categories show more than ten accredited genealogists on current lists; others currently have none.

Prerequisites and Application

Any person who feels qualified may apply to take the examination. Membership in the LDS Church is not a prerequisite. However, the examinations are given only in Salt Lake City and only to persons who have access to either the main family history in Salt Lake City or one of the branch family history centers.

For application forms, contact the Accreditation Committee, Family History Library, 35 North West Temple Street, Salt Lake City, UT 84150.

The application requires general information, specific notice of experience in the requested area of accreditation, attestation that the applicant has completed at least 1,000 hours of research in the area of desired accreditation, and submission of a pedigree which the applicant has extended for at least four generations prior to 1875.

This pedigree should be presented in report form and include well-documented family group record forms for each family shown on the pedigree. The report should also indicate each research step taken and explain why it was taken. At least three weeks should be allowed to schedule the written examination after submission of the application and accompanying papers.

Each applicant must also sign an agreement that he or she is willing to maintain high ethical and research standards; reply promptly to all letters received as a result of accreditation; clearly inform his or her clients of fees charged, the use of other agents, and methods of reporting research progress; make regular research reports indicating procedures used, records searched, results found, and recommendations for future research; maintain an adequate accounting system to protect fully any funds deposited by the patron; and abide by "The Genealogist's Code" prepared by the Board for Certification of Genealogists, Washington, D.C. This code outlines the obligations the genealogist has to the public, to his or her client, and to the profession.

Testing Procedures and Contents

The examinations are free and are given individually and only at the Family History Library in Salt Lake City. After an application is accepted, the Accreditation Committee will schedule an appointment. The written portion of the examination is open book and requires using book and microfilm records in the main library's public collection. It takes approximately eight hours to complete and consists of the following items:

Handwriting. Tests ability to read genealogical documents of the area and time period.

Document Recognition. Tests ability to identify important types of documents and reference sources for the area of accreditation.

Brief Pedigree Evaluation. Tests knowledge of sources necessary to extend a pedigree and types of information to be found in them.

General Questions and Answers. Tests knowledge of pertinent history and records (such as types of records, time period covered, content, and availability) of the area of accreditation.

LDS Church Records. Tests knowledge of the content and usefulness to researchers of LDS records relating to the area of accreditation. Although a knowledge of LDS Church records may have little bearing on a person's ability to use records of a given geographic area, this requirement recognizes that many requests for assistance come from LDS Church members.

Pedigree Problem. The examination includes an actual pedigree problem for which the applicant carries out research in the main library, writes a research report detailing the results of the search, and makes recommendations for future action.

Applicants must successfully complete a written examination before the oral portion is scheduled. The oral examination takes approximately one and one-half hours and is conducted by a committee of two to four individuals well-versed in the area of accreditation. The examination consists of a review of the written examination and a defense of the pedigree case study submitted with the application.

Successful applicants may use "A.G." following their names and are listed with the library's other accredited genealogists.

Limits of Family History Department Responsibility

The Family History Department assumes no responsibility for providing the accredited genealogist with clients. It provides a list of accredited genealogists, by area and subject, to any person who requests it. The department will not recommend any specific accredited genealogist over another one nor are department employees authorized to make such a recommendation.

Some accredited genealogists earn their livelihood solely from fees for genealogical research. From this standpoint they can be considered "professional." The majority of accredited genealogists, however, do research for a fee for less than forty hours per week. Nevertheless, all accredited genealogists must be "professional" in their scholarship and businesslike in their dealings with clients.

The Family History Department further assumes no responsibility for work performed by any accredited genealogist. All contractual arrangements are between the accredited genealogist and the client. Only when complaints are lodged against an accredited genealogist that, upon investigation, are reasonable and justified, will the department intervene, first to insure an equitable arrangement between the genealogist and the client, and possibly to rescind accreditation status. Persons having any complaints regarding the work or conduct of an accredited genealogist may write to Manager of Public Relations, Family History Library, 35 North West Temple Street, Salt Lake City, UT 84150.

Photoduplication Services

If you do not have access to either the main library or one of the branch center libraries with photoduplication equipment, the Family History Library will generally make copies of materials in its collection for a fee. However, a few records may not be photocopied because of restrictions placed by the original record owner. These records are on red microfilm reels to distinguish them from others. See *Photocopy Restrictions* above.

Many of the published materials in the main library are covered by copyright and are protected by U.S. copyright law. This law provides that copies may be made as long as they will not be "used for any purpose other than private study, scholarship, or research." If you ask the Family History Library to supply you with photocopies of copyright material, you assume legal responsibility for how those copies are used.

Photoduplication order forms are available at branch genealogical libraries. It is wise, if the record is on microfilm, to order it sent to the branch library so that you can review it and be sure it contains the information you want. If your library does not have copying facilities, then you can complete a copy request form and send it to the main library. Be sure that you identify the record completely, correctly, and exactly. If, for example, you request the 1843 tax record for Hancock County but omit the pages on which it occurs in the microfilm, you will be charged a substantially higher fee because it will require staff time in Salt Lake City to identify the information.

Here are examples of the types of records which can be copied:

1. Microfiche, such as the International Genealogical Index (IGI) and the Family History Library Catalog (FHLC).
2. United States census records.
3. Books in the main library collection.
4. Most original documents on microfilm, such as parish registers, civil registration, land records, and probate records.

International Genealogical Index (IGI) Sources

Photoduplication Services probably receives more requests to copy International Genealogical Index (IGI) sources than any other. You need to understand what you will receive if you make this request. As explained in Part 1, Chapter 2, the IGI consists of information from two sources: extraction submissions and patron submissions.

IGI extraction-submission entries come from controlled extraction projects conducted by trained volunteers who extract all of the genealogical information on a given record. The IGI entry thus usually includes all of the genealogical information available in the original record. Chances for any additional information from an English parish register or most New England entries would be extremely small, but some notable exceptions are French civil registration marriage records and some Mexican parish register entries.

Patron submissions are records submitted by LDS Church members in order to have temple ordinances performed. Generally, if you ask for a patron submission, it is with the intention of corresponding with a researcher working on the same genealogical lines. However, you should be aware that some of the addresses date as far back as 1970 and may no longer be current. No updating of these addresses is provided.

Patron submissions numbers in the IGI are all seven digits long, for example, 7612603. The first two numbers, "76" in this example, indicate that the submission was received in 1976.

Services Offered by Correspondence

To help individuals identify their ancestors, the Family History Library provides a correspondence service which will answer questions not requiring extensive research and/or explain how you can find the needed information. However, it will not undertake research projects for you. See "The Accreditation Program," in this chapter for information on trained experts who do genealogical research for a fee.

Individuals in the Family History Library's correspondence unit are skilled researchers and experts on records and research methodology for specific localities. They receive and answer requests in most major languages of Western Europe.

The Correspondence Unit will:

1. Explain library services.
2. Answer questions about research procedures in a given geographical area.
3. Attempt to identify specific localities, especially in some European areas where boundary changes and language differences make identification difficult.
4. Fill orders for Genealogical Library publications.
5. Provide information on accommodations and tourist sites for people planning to visit Salt Lake City.

Correspondence service will not do pedigree research, translate documents in foreign languages, or make reservations for Salt Lake City accommodations or activities.

Since many research questions deal with the same subject, a patron asking a common question, such as the library services available, may receive a prepared handout or a letter that includes a standard word-processed paragraph of information along with a customized section answering a unique or unusual question.

Most inquiries are answered within three weeks from the time received in Salt Lake City, although this time may vary depending on the seasonal highs and lows of correspondence received, the volume of requests for a given geographical area, and the vacation schedule of correspondence specialists.

When requesting information from the Family History Library, include sufficient information to identify the problem clearly. It is sometimes helpful to include a pedigree chart or a family group record form.

Do not make more than one or two major requests per letter. Do not ask questions about two different geographical areas in the same letter, because they will be answered by different correspondence specialists.

No permanent file is kept on incoming and outgoing correspondence, so a correspondence specialist cannot refer to any previous correspondence.

Genealogical Supplies

Genealogical Forms

The Family History Department has developed several genealogical forms to make it easier for LDS Church members to record their genealogical information and temple ordinance data. (See in Chapter 1, "Why Latter-day Saints Do Genealogy.") Aside from columns for these unique ordinances, the forms look very much like pedigree charts and family group record forms available from other outlets.

Certain Family History Department forms are also used to submit names of individuals for temple ordinance processing. The main library and center libraries supply free Marriage Entry Forms, Individual Entry Forms, and Family Group Record Forms in limited amounts when you plan to submit names for temple ordinances.

Pedigree charts, IGI Extraction Sheets, and many additional genealogical forms are available at the copy centers on each floor of the Family History Library in Salt Lake City. Each center library may also, at its discretion, carry such genealogical forms. Contact the Family History Library, 35 North West Temple, Salt Lake City, UT 84150 for a current list of prices, and forms available.

Genealogical Research Publications

Staff experts at the Family History Library with expertise in specialized research sources and methods have prepared many publications to aid researchers. The three basic types of publications are:

Research Guides. This series provides relatively detailed genealogical research sources and methods for specific areas or collections. Examples are "Basic Genealogy Research Guide for Ireland," and "The International Genealogical Index."

Research Outlines. This series contains basic "how-to" information on subjects like "France: Genealogical Research by Mail" and "Jewish Genealogical Research Outline." Eventually this series will outline research guidelines for each state in the United States and each province in Canada.

Patron and Staff Aids. This series consists of patron and staff training manuals for the main and center libraries, registers of special collections, and other material designed to provide more efficient and effective service. Examples are "Genealogical Library Catalog: Instructional Materials," and "Spanish: Genealogical Word List."

For a price list of the research guides, write to the Family History Library, 35 North West Temple Street, Salt Lake City, UT 84150.

Selected research outlines and patron aids designed to meet a specific need are generally free. It is planned that many of the major research guides and all of the United States/Canada research outlines will be duplicated and distributed to selected centers in the United States and Canada.

World Conference on Records Publications

In 1980, the Family History Library hosted a World Conference on Records entitled "Preserving Our Heritage," whose speakers included internationally renowned genealogists and family historians from many nations.

The proceedings of that conference are available as 269 papers and 22 cassette tapes. The tapes of general assemblies and lectures of broad appeal include "Backyard History" by David L. Weitzman, "American Jewish Family History" by Rabbi Malcolm H. Stern, "Genealogical Records as Family History Sources in Scotland" by Donald J. Steel, "The Archives of Northwestern Mexico" by Rudecinda Lo Buglio, and "The Search for My Japanese Roots" by Kin-itsu Hirata.

Individual lecture papers and cassettes are available as well as volumes dealing with a specific geographic area or topic. Papers and cassette tapes are limited to the supply on hand. For an order form, contact the Family History Library, 35 North West Temple, Salt Lake City, UT 84150.

Pamphlets

The Family History Department has produced several pamphlets intended to describe its functions and services. They are available in the main library and some may be available in center libraries. There is a minimal charge of up to fifty cents (as of spring 1987) for these pamphlets:

"Why Genealogy"

"Introducing the Genealogical Library"

"A Guide to Research: Using the LDS Library in Salt Lake City"

"A Guide to Research: Using an LDS Branch Library"

"The Family Registry" (no charge)

Computer Software and Supplies

The Personal Ancestral File, a genealogical management system for home computers, has been developed by the Family History Department and is currently available for MS-DOS, Apple II, and CP/M computers. It enables users to organize genealogical data and print it out in many useful formats. A descriptive brochure is available at no charge; for it, or additional information concerning computer system requirements, write to the Ancestral File Operation Unit, Family History Department, 50 East North Temple Street, Salt Lake City, UT 84150.

You may purchase this program for $35.00 at the main library and at the Church Distribution Center, 1999 West 1700 South, Salt Lake City, UT 84104.

Ordering Information

You may order some genealogical forms, some research publications, pamphlets, and the Personal Ancestral File from the Salt Lake Distribution Center, 1999 West 1700 South, Salt Lake City, UT 84104. Money must accompany orders so you should consult a current price list available at a branch center or from the Family History Library, 35 North West Temple, Salt Lake City, UT 84150.

Chapter 4

Introduction to the United States Collection

Richard W. Dougherty

The precise relationship of genealogy to history has provoked a great deal of discussion and debate over the decades. One author, Archibald F. Bennett, (*A Guide for Genealogical Research*. Salt Lake City: Church of Jesus Christ of Latter-day Saints, 1951, p. 151) described history as the "twin sister of genealogy." A more generally adopted definition would be that genealogy is that branch of history which concerns itself with establishing family relationships.

Regardless of how you define the relationship, few experienced genealogists will quarrel with Derek Harland's advice (*Genealogical Research Standards*. Salt Lake City: Bookcraft, 1963, p. 138) that "No genealogist, professional or beginner, should even attempt the solving of a pedigree problem without first equipping himself with a map of that locality and an understanding of those historical facts likely to have affected persons living in that locality." Harland's dictum is just as valid for an early twentieth-century problem in a large metropolitan city as it is for a rural area of Pennsylvania or Massachusetts c. 1750.

Church records offer an excellent illustration of this point. Prior to the establishment of vital records, they provided the most precise genealogical data of any major record type. But determining which church an ancestral family attended may require extensive research using county histories, city directories, and detailed maps.

Hence, a knowledge of local history may be necessary to achieve even the most basic genealogical goal of filling out a pedigree chart. But if one's goal is not merely the compilation of names and dates, but the reconstruction of a family's history, then an intimate knowledge of the local geography and history of an ancestral home becomes mandatory. For only then can you acquire the empathy necessary to recreate mentally the actual experiences of your ancestors, to understand the driving forces in their lives.

Realizing the value of local history, the Family History Library constantly strives to acquire new and old works of local history for its collection. Indeed, in areas such as the Plains States where little or no microfilming of court records and other primary source material has yet occurred, local histories may comprise the only material the library currently possesses on the area other than United States or state census returns. These histories are cataloged according to locality–that is, by state, county, and town. In the case of a county history, it will appear under the heading of the county, for example, **South Dakota/Clark/History.**

Two useful guides are P. William Filby, *A Bibliography of American County Histories* (Baltimore: Genealogical Publishing Co., 1985) (FHL# US REF/973/H23bi) and Marion J. Kaminkow, *United States Local Histories in the Library of Congress,* 5 vols. (Baltimore: Magna Charta Book Co., 1975-76) (FHL# US REF/973/ A3ka).

Migration and Settlement

A vivid way to experience the importance of migration and settlement patterns in America is to travel north from Louisville, Kentucky, through the state of Indiana to Chicago. In southern Indiana, the local accent is strikingly similar to that heard across the Ohio River in Kentucky. Somewhere in central Indiana, roughly where Interstate 70 bisects the state, the accent changes. By the time you reach Hammond, the gas station attendant sounds like those you hear in Wisconsin or Michigan. Thus, the myth of a standard midwestern accent dissolves in one auto trip across the length of a single state.

What accounts for these varying patterns of speech? Most authorities attribute it to migration patterns of the early nineteenth century. Southern Indiana was primarily settled by people from Kentucky and Virginia. The family of Abraham Lincoln is the best known example. But a glance at the 1850 census returns of a southern Indiana county confirms that the Lincoln family was not an isolated case.

On the other hand, northern Indiana was largely settled by people moving west from New York and Pennsylvania. In later decades, immigrants poured in from central Europe. But the English their children learned in school was taught by school teachers who considered their own accent as the standard American.

The implications of this and other migration patterns should be obvious to the genealogist. If one's ancestors settled in southern Indiana, one would be more likely to extend the line by searching in Kentucky or Virginia rather than Maine or New Hampshire.

Indiana offers a particularly vivid example of the long-term effect migration patterns have on speech, local attitudes, and regional history. But the lessons it offers can be applied elsewhere. For instance, the formidable geographical barrier of the Pre-Cambrian Shield in central Canada diverted many residents of Ontario seeking cheap land and better opportunity from western Canada into the American upper Midwest. Residents of eastern Canada did not enjoy direct access to the prairie provinces until the construction of the Canadian Pacific Railway to Winnipeg in 1881. Hence, many descendants of midwestern settlers must explore Canadian records if they wish to extend their ancestral lines to Europe.

Nor does the importance of migration patterns end at the water's edge. Many Americans recall from high school history classes that large scale immigration to the United States after 1880 came primarily from southern and eastern Europe. This signaled a significant shift from previous patterns, which saw millions of people leaving northwestern Europe and the British Isles for opportunities in the new land.

Novice genealogists do not always realize that emigrants tended to migrate in groups. A rural township often was settled by individuals from the same village or local region in Europe. The same pattern often held true in larger cities, where a given neighborhood block might consist of immigrants from the same area in Europe. Thus, a knowledge of local history combined with a knowledge of migration patterns can yield rich dividends in the genealogical quest.

The American collection in the Family History Library has a substantial number of general reference books which can aid the researcher in his or her genealogical searches. Many of these books are shelved on low credenza-style bookcases directly in front of the American Reference Desk. Hence, they are sometimes called the "Reference Credenza Collection." The following bibliography includes some, though by no means all, of the "Credenza" collection. In addition, other key books of general interest are listed.

Atlases, Maps, and Gazetteers

As the opening remarks indicated, maps play a key role in most genealogical searches. Of all the atlases and gazetteers in the Family History Library, the single most useful to me has been the John L. Androit, comp. and ed. *Township Atlas of the United States* (McLean, Va.: Andriot Associates, 1977), (FHL# 973/E7an). This book is extraordinarily useful when conducting searches of unindexed census returns. Often, a family source may state an ancestor's birthplace as a village, when in fact, the ancestor was born on a farm near that village. If you know the county and state, a quick check of the *Township Atlas* may show in which township the village is situated. With this information, you can search the township returns for the appropriate census and sometimes locate the ancestral family in a few minutes.

Of course, not all census searches are that easy. The family may not know the county in which the ancestor was born. If the village or town is known, and still exists, it can be located in the current *Rand McNally Commercial Atlas and Marketing Guide* (Chicago, New York, San Francisco, 1987) (FHL# 973/E7rc).

A more complete work is *Bullinger's Postal and Shippers Guide for the United States and Canada* (Westwood, N.J.: Bullinger Guides, 1987) (FHL# 970/E8b, 1987). However, it does not include maps.

In some cases, you can't find the name of the place in any of these sources. It has long since disappeared from standard road atlases and gazetteers and exists only in the memories of older residents of the area and in older reference works. One of the more useful of these works is L. De Colange, *The National Gazetteer* subtitled *A Geographical Dictionary of the United States* (London: Hamilton, Adams and Co., 1884) (FHL# US REF 973/E5c/1884 or microfilm 0845264).

The Credenza Collection houses other nineteenth-century and late eighteenth-century gazetteers including one published in 1795.

But none of these books deal with the vexing problem of changing county boundaries. Fortunately, the collection now includes the five-volume *Historical Atlas and Chronology of County Boundaries 1788-1980,* John H. Long, ed. (Boston: G. K. Hall, 1984) (FHL# US/CAN REF 973/E7hl/ Vols.1-5). Unfortunately, it only covers fourteen states.

More comprehensive in the geographical area it covers is the *Map Guide to the U.S. Federal Censuses, 1790-1920* by William Thorndale and William Dollarhide (Baltimore, Md.: Genealogical Publishing Co., 1987). (FHL# US/CAN REF 973/X2th).

Two standard works included in the collection are *Atlas of American History* by Kenneth A. Jackson, 2nd Rev. Ed. (New York: Scribners, 1984) (FHL# US/CAN REF 973/E7at) and *Atlas of the Historical Geography of the United States* (New York: Carnegie Institution of Washington and the American Geographical Society of New York, 1932) (FHL# US/CAN REF Q 973/E3p). A more recent and somewhat more accessible work is Hilde Heun Kagan, ed., *Pictorial Atlas of United States History* (New York, American Heritage, 1966) (FHL# US/CAN REF 973/E3am).

A beautifully written companion to these works is Ray Allen Billington and Martin Ridge, *Westward Expansion,* 5th Ed. (New York: Macmillan, 1982) (FHL# 973/H2bw/1982). While neither an atlas nor a gazetteer, it contains excellent maps showing the principal migration routes and discusses the settlement of various areas in some depth. Rounding out its virtues is an excellent bibliography.

Naturally, no single volume is likely to contain every place-name or local map that ever existed concerning the United States. For these, the researcher must turn to the collections cataloged under states and localities.

A useful guide to the Family History Library's United States map collection is G. Eileen Buckway, comp., *United States Map Register,* (Salt Lake City: Genealogical Library of the Church of Jesus Christ of Latter-day Saints, 1985). No catalog number is available; however, it is located at the U.S. Reference Register Credenza. This compilation categorizes maps by county and city as well as by state.

A companion volume to the *Map Register* is Cherry Sale Brown, comp., *Gazetteers and Place-Name References in States and Territories of the United States* (Salt Lake City: Genealogical Library of the Church of Jesus Christ of Latter-day Saints, 1985). No catalog number is available, but it is located at the U.S. Reference Area. Current plans are to make these two works available in the center system, but it is difficult to say when these plans will be carried out.

A standard book available in the center collection is E. K. Kirkham, *A Genealogical and Historical Atlas of the U.S.A.* (Salt Lake City: E. K. Kirkham, 1976) (FHL# 973/Esd or microfiche 6010066-6010069). This book features capsule histories of the states and territories illustrated with contemporary maps.

Another book by E. K. Kirkham is *A Handy Guide to Record Searching in the Larger Cities of the United States* (Logan, Utah: Everton Publishers, 1974) (FHL# US/CAN REF 973/D27kc). As the title indicates, the book contains contemporary maps of the larger cities in the United States indicating ward boundaries coupled with street indexes by wards at various points in time, e.g., 1860, 1900, etc. Other data listed include names of early newspapers of the city in question as well as useful addresses such as local libraries and vital records offices.

Cemetery Records

While church records are extremely important sources of genealogical information, they can be very difficult to locate if they still exist. With luck, one may discover the journal of a circuit riding preacher who noted baptisms and marriages tucked away in a denominational archive. But for many frontier churches, the only records that still exist are written on stone tablets in the churchyard.

I refer, of course, to tombstone inscriptions. In many areas of the country, but especially in the South, cemeteries may be the only source of information regarding birth, death, and even marriage dates. In later decades of the nineteenth century, one may find other genealogically useful data such as military and lodge affiliations. In Canada, an immigrant's tombstone often listed his county of birth in the British Isles, sometimes even the exact parish; occasionally this sort of information appears in American immigrant cemeteries.

In a sense, it may be a bit misleading to connect cemeteries too closely with churchyards. For in many American frontier communities, family cemeteries were far more typical. In part, this simply reflected the fact that families had preceded the organizing of churches, sometimes by a decade or two. But it also reflected the more individualistic religious attitude of American Protestants, especially after the Great Awakening of the eighteenth century. In some areas of the Midwest, churchyard cemeteries only became common after Lutheran and Catholic immigrants from Europe settled in the mid-nineteenth century.

Exploring the rural byways for long defunct family cemeteries can be one of the most pleasant aspects of the genealogical quest. Instead of thumbing through dusty records in county courthouses or falling asleep over microfilm readers in a library, the genealogist may become a pathfinder in the literal sense of the term. But this can lead to frustration if you cannot find the cemetery. Hence, it is usually advisable to contact local genealogical and historical societies for precise instructions for locating obscure family plots or relocated cemeteries.

Fortunately, an increasing number of local societies are compiling guides to cemeteries. The best of these include maps showing the location of virtually every cemetery in a given county. The Family History Library attempts to obtain these compilations as they appear. They are cataloged according to locality.

Space does not permit the listing of all the cemetery records available at the Family History Library. However, a book which attempted to do just that and more is John D. and E. Diane Stemmons, comps., *The Cemetery Record Compendium* (Logan, Utah: Everton Publishers, 1979) (FHL# US/CAN REF 973/V34s). Records available in the Family History Library at that time are listed alphabetically by state, county, and locality followed by the name of the cemetery and the microfilm number. In addition, the compilers list cemetery records which have been compiled and published in various genealogical and historical journals as well as many housed in the DAR Library in Washington, D.C. As useful as this book is, it must be supplemented by other works. Also, the Family History Library has acquired many cemetery records since the book was published.

One such supplementary work would be *Directory of United States Cemeteries* Vol. I, 1974 (San Jose, Calif.: Cemetery Research Inc., 1974). (FHL# US/CAN REF 973/V34c). Most of the cemeteries listed are still active, and many of them do not appear in the Stemmons compilation.

A second general directory is the *International Cemetery Directory* (Columbus, Ohio: American Cemetery Association, 1974) (FHL# US/CAN REF 973/B2ca/Vol.38). Again, most of the cemeteries listed are active.

This leads to another type of cemetery record, namely sextons' records. While most modern cemetery managers no longer call themselves sextons, the value of their records has not changed. Sexton's records are invaluable for information on individuals buried in a given cemetery for whom there are no headstones. In addition, they may contain information as to place of birth of the deceased, place of death, which may be far distant from the place of burial, name of undertaker, etc.

This leads to still another type of record, notably undertakers records. The term undertaker has gone out of style. But their records have not and can often provide valuable genealogical information. The standard directory is *The American Blue Book of Funeral Directors* (New York: Kates-Boylston, 1978-79) (FHL# US/CAN/REF 973/U24a). Actually, this directory has been published every even-numbered year since 1932. Again, the Family History Library has acquired microfilms of the records of many funeral homes, which are cataloged according to locality.

Census Records

The decennial federal census returns have been called the "backbone" of American genealogical research for good reason. Given the highly migratory nature of American society, the task of tracing ancestors from one state to another would be extremely difficult, at times impossible, without the census records.

As the term "decennial" implies, the federal census is taken every ten years, beginning in 1790. Its original purpose was to provide information for apportioning the House of Representatives. Hence, the returns for the early censuses (1790-1840) list only the head of the household. Others in the household are arranged by age and gender groupings, for example, males over the age of 45, females aged 5-10, etc. Other information listed included the number of slaves in the household, an important clue to wealth in the Old South, number of individuals not naturalized, etc.

Beginning with the 1850 census, the names of all the members of the household are listed together with age, gender, birthplace (country or state), and occupation. In addition, the value of an individual's real and personal property was listed. In 1880, the census returns began listing the birthplaces of each person's parents and the relationship between the various members of the household.

Almost all of the 1890 census returns were destroyed by fire. Apart from a few scattered fragments, the only portion to survive were the Civil War Veterans schedules for those states in the last half of the alphabet beginning with Kentucky.

The 1900 census listed month and year of birth, number of years a couple had been married, the number of children a woman had borne, the number still living, the year of immigration, and citizenship status. The 1910 census contains similar information, although it does not list the month of birth. It also lists the native language, a valuable clue for tracing European immigrants. Indexes exist for all of the surviving census returns for 1790 to 1850 and for many of those 1860-70. Complete indexes exist for a few states in 1880 and for most of the veterans' schedules which have survived.

Most of these indexes have been published in book form, although a few–for example, Wisconsin for 1860 and 1870–exist only on microfilm. For some states, several versions of a given census index have been published. It is generally wise to check all available versions. Census returns can be very difficult to read, and errors and omissions almost invariably occur.

In addition to its printed indexes, Accelerated Indexing Systems has compiled a series of indexes combining the returns for several states for a given census, for example, 1850. These indexes have been published in microfiche format and are available at the Family History Library and its centers.

Soundex indexes for the federal censuses beginning in 1880 are available. The term *Soundex* refers to the fact that names are grouped together according to the way they sounded rather than in pure alphabetical order. A partial Soundex for families with children ten and under exists for the 1880 census for all states and territories. The 1900 Soundex covers all households in all states and territories. For the 1910 census, Soundex or the similar Miracode indexes are available.

For those states which were not indexed in 1910, one must rely on city directories, county landowners' atlases, and other such guides. A particularly useful tool for cities in states not indexed was originally produced by the Census Bureau, *1910 Street Index for 39 Cities,* National Archives Publication N1283 (Washington, D.C.: National Archives, n.d.) (FHL# microfiche 6331480-6331489).

In addition to the published statewide indexes and the federal Soundex and Miracode indexes, many county historical societies or individuals have prepared county indexes for a given census year, for example, 1860. These indexes are often of very high quality as the compilers are acquainted with the variant spellings of the local surnames. Check the locality catalog of the Family History Library Catalog under the individual county census.

In addition, the Family History Library staff has prepared a guide to county indexes labeled *County Indexes to Federal Census Returns* (Salt Lake City: Genealogical Library, n.d.) (no catalog number). It is shelved adjacent to the special schedules discussed below.

In addition to the standard population schedules, the federal government created a number of special schedules which contain invaluable genealogical information. One of these has already been mentioned, the Veterans' Schedules of 1890. Although some were destroyed by fire in 1921, the schedules for thirty-four states, plus Washington, D.C. and about one-half of Kentucky have survived and are available.

Another veterans schedule was made in 1840, which listed the names of Revolutionary War pensioners on the second page of the 1840 population schedule. The names were published the following year in *A Census of Pensioners for Revolutionary or Military Services* (1841; reprint ed. Baltimore, Md.: Genealogical Publishing Co., 1967) (FHL# 973/X2pc/1967). The Genealogical Society of Utah prepared an index to this volume *Index to Pensioners Listed in the 1840 Census* (Baltimore, Md.: Genealogical Publishing Co., 1965) (FHL# 973/X2pc/-1965 index).

While many states made off-year or interdecennial censuses, that taken in 1885 was unique in that the federal government offered partial reimbursement for the costs. Three states, Colorado, Florida, and Nebraska, and two territories, Dakota and New Mexico, which included Arizona, took advantage of the offer and returned schedules to the Secretary of the Interior. the Family History Library has microfilm copies or transcriptions of all these 1885 returns which have survived. Unfortunately, those for a number of counties are missing. Statewide indexes for some of these have been compiled, for example, Nebraska – and some have been published, for example, South Dakota. Consult the locality catalog of the Family History Library Catalog or check the published indexes shelved adjacent to the credenza shelves for those available in the Family History Library.

Mortality Schedules

A forerunner of the vital records later kept by states are the mortality schedules. These were taken in conjunction with the federal census beginning in 1850. Those for 1850, 1860, 1870, 1880, and the special 1885 federal censuses still exist. They list deaths for twelve months prior to the census, e.g., 1 June 1849 through 31 May 1850. The Family History Library has some, but not all, of these schedules. Those available are listed in the Family History Library Catalog under **[State]/Census** or **[State]/Vital Records.**

Slave Schedules

Slaves were enumerated separately in the 1850 and 1860 censuses. The names of the owners are recorded, followed by the number of the slave, age, sex, and color. On rare occasions individual names of the slaves appear. These records when used in conjunction with other records, such as probate inventories, can be useful in the extremely difficult task of tracing black ancestry before the Civil War.

The federal census returns and those special schedules in the Family History Library's collection are listed in the locality catalog of the Family History Library Catalog under **[State]/Census.** In addition, the Family History Library has prepared four bound volumes found in the credenza shelf area. One volume contains the film numbers of the first eight censuses, including the slave schedules, arranged by census year, state, and county. Separate volumes exist for the 1880, 1900, and 1910 census returns. The Sondex or Miracode film numbers for each year are bound together with the film numbers of the actual returns.

Colonial, Territorial, and State Censuses

In addition to the federal censuses, many state, territorial, and colonial governments made census enumerations. Censuses prior to 1790 may exist only for some towns or counties. Some of these compilations are actually census substitutes reconstructed from tax lists or land records.

Most of the state censuses were taken in the off-years between federal censuses – that is, 1895, 1905, etc. Often they contain information equal in value to the federal records. For instance, the Iowa State Census of 1885 recorded whether the individual listed was a Civil War Veteran, and if so, the name of his unit. Thus, this census serves as a substitute for the Iowa 1890 federal veterans' schedule which was burned.

The Family History Library has state census returns for some states from about 1800 to 1925. A special set of registers listing all the state censuses available in the Family History Library's collection is shelved near the guides to the federal census returns in the credenza shelf area. However, it is always wise to check the locality catalog for local censuses or census substitutes.

Church Records

Church records rank among the best genealogical sources available. They provide names, dates, and places in various types of records, such as baptismal, confirmation, marriage and burial registers, membership lists, minutes of council meetings, and published histories of the congregation or parish.

Identifying which church an ancestor belonged to can be very difficult, particularly if the congregation no longer exists. Once the church has been identified and its records have been located, you may face a problem of gaining access to the records. Roman Catholic and some Protestant churches may have a policy limiting access to the pastor and/or the parish secretary.

The Family History Library makes a concerted effort to microfilm all vailable church records by purchasing published transcriptions of church records, microfilms of records in church archives made by the church itself or by some other agency. These records are cataloged according to the locality where the original record was made.

Once the Family History Library has these older church records in its possession, it extracts the names from the christening and marriage registers and enters them into the International Genealogical Index. Hence, a check of the IGI for the state in question should be a routine step in the quest for church records. The IGI will list the name and location of the church in which the event originally took place.

Since the vast majority of American church records have not yet been microfilmed by the Family History Library, the directories issued by the major denominations and unions are extremely important tools in locating church records. The following are available in the Family History Library:

Jacquet, Constant H. ed. *Yearbook of American and Canadian Churches.* Nashville, Tenn.: Abingdon Press, annual. (FHL# US/CAN/REF 970/K2wh). Lists all the major current denominations in the United States and Canada and the names and addresses of current officers. It contains a capsule history of each denomination, its distinctive doctrinal position, main depositories of church historical material, and church-related colleges and universities in the United States and Canada.

The Official Catholic Directory. Wilmette, Ill.: P. J. Kenedy, annual. (FHL# GEN REF 282.025/Of2). A very complete directory listing the name, address, and pastor of every active parish in the United States, arranged according to diocese. It also lists other officials in a given diocese, including the archivist, and ethnic affiliations of parishes. Invaluable for tracing Catholic church records.

Directory of Southern Baptist Churches. Nashville, Tenn.: Sunday School Board of the Southern Baptist Convention, annual. (FHL# 973/K24n) Lists churches alphabetically by state followed by the post office, specific mailing address, and telephone. Since the mailing address may be the pastor's residence, it does not necessarily reveal the precise location of the church.

Lutheran Church Directory for the United States. New York: Lutheran Council of the United States of America, 1976. (FHL# 973/K24L/1976). Lists all United States congregations of the major Lutheran synods, arranged alphabetically by state, city, county, name of congregation, synodical affiliation, and exact location. This may or may not be the post office or mailing address.

Yearbook United Church of Christ. New York: United Church of Christ, annual. (FHL# 973/K25yb/1973). Lists churches arranged by conferences (administrative districts within the church) rather than by state. Some coincide with state boundaries, but others do not. Within multi-state conferences, the member churches are alphabetically arranged according to the city or town, and by church name within a given city. The church's mailing address is listed, as is the name of the current pastor and the total number of members, plus other statistical data.

The works of a more general nature which are valuable guides to church records are:

Kirkham, E. Kay. *A Survey of American Church Records.* 4th ed. Logan, Utah: Everton Publishers, 1978. (FHL# 973/K2K/1978). While by no means complete, this volume contains a substantial list of church records arranged by state and county. Information listed includes denomination, name of church, location (town or city), kind of records and years covered, and present location of records.

Suelflow, August R. *A Preliminary Guide to Church Records Repositories.* St. Louis: Church Archives Committee, Society of American Archivists, 1969. (FHL# 973/A5s). Describes the holdings of many church archives, arranged alphabetically by denomination, plus access of the records and the services available at the archive.

Mead, Frank. *Handbook of American Denominations in the United States.* 5th ed. Nashville, Tenn.: Abingdon Press, 1970. (FHL# 973/K2mf). Useful guide to the maze of denominational history in the United States.

The Family History Library has microfilmed many archival collections of church records, for instance, the collection of Pennsylvania church records housed in the Fackenthal Library at Franklin and Marshall College, Lancaster, Pennsylvania. Other major collections available on microfilm include the holdings of the Presbyterian Historical Society in Philadelphia and the registers of the parishes in the Roman Catholic Archdiocese of San Antonio. These records are cataloged according to the original locality of the church, for example, **Pennsylvania/Berks/Albany Township.**

In addition to these collections on microfilm, the Family History Library also has published collections of church records such as the multi-volume series of Louisiana Catholic records translated and described by the Reverend Donald J. Hebert, for example, *Southwest Louisiana Records* (Eunice, La.: Hebert Publications, 1974-pres.) (FHL# 976.35/V2h/Vols. 1-28).

Court Records

Court records rank just behind census and church records in genealogical value. They may include marriage, death, probate, naturalization, divorce, debt, and adoption records. Thus, they can be crucial in determining family relationships, especially in pre-1850 America where census data was minimal and church records scarce or non-existent. For this reason, the Family History Library has microfilmed thousands of rolls of court records, primarily from the county level.

A great deal of American court terminology dates back to medieval England. Furthermore, even in a relatively young country such as the United States, local usage has created special terms for certain types of courts. For instance, in Pennsylvania, guardianship and certain other probate matters are handled by the orphans' court. In certain states, the circuit court may cover several counties, reflecting its origins as a court where the presiding judge traveled around a circuit. On the other hand, it may be confined to one county because of the press of business in modern society.

Regardless of local terminology, certain basic types of court records can be identified. Probate and naturalization records are discussed elsewhere in this chapter. Other court records include:

Civil Court Records:

These concern civil actions, stemming from disputes between individuals of corporations such as debts or suits.

Criminal Court Records:

Criminal actions involve the protection of society. They include serious crimes classified as felonies (e.g., murder, robbery, burglary, or rape) and lesser offenses called misdemeanors (petty theft, vagrancy, drunkenness, or prostitution).

Equity and Chancery Court Records:

These generally concern questions of property. Probate, divorce, and adoption also come under this category. However, probate records are so important genealogically speaking that they are treated separately.

Each state has its own system of courts. A useful guide for determining the specific responsibilities and recording systems of each court are the county record inventories, published by the Historical Records Survey of the Works Progress Administration. They are listed in the locality catalog of the Family History Library Catalog under **[State]/[County]/Archives and Libraries.**

Directories (Personal Names)

Directories can be of great assistance in locating a person in place. Two basic types of directories exist. One categorizes people according to residence, while the other categorizes them by attribute, for example, occupation or profession.

City directories can be extraordinarily useful for gaining access to unindexed census returns. They can also be used to determine an approximate date of death.

The Family History Library has a large collection of city directories, some in book form, but mostly on microform, including a comprehensive collection dating from the late 1700s to 1901. It is described in *City Directories of the United States.* (Woodbridge, Conn.: Research Publications, 1983). (FHL# US/CAN REF 973/E43c).

E. Kay Kirkham's *A Handy Guide to Record Searching in the Larger Cities of the United States* (Logan, Utah: Everton Publishers, 1974) (FHL# 973/D27kc or microfiche 6010054-6010060) with its printed city maps is a useful supplement to the city directory collection. However, it is by no means complete.

Telephone directories, now kept on microfiche forms in the Family History Library, can be classified as a special type of city directory. While only of marginal use in locating ancestors, they can be valuable in determining whether a given church or funeral home still exists.

Other types of city directories include county and regional business directories and various professional directories. Religious directories in the Family History Library are discussed under church records earlier in this chapter.

Genealogical Collections

Determining whether a published history exists on a given family should be one of the first steps in any genealogical investigation. Although many of these are rife with errors, they can still save the researcher a vast amount of time.

The Family History Library has gathered a large collection of compiled genealogies. Family histories and newsletters are listed alphabetically in the surname section of the Family History Library Catalog (FHLC). Other collections are listed in the Locality FHLC under **United States/** or **[State]/Genealogy**. For example, the important collection of Pennsylvania German family material gathered by the late Adolf H. Gerberich is cataloged under **Pennsylvania/Genealogy**.

Compiled lineages and applications for lineage societies such as the Sons of the American Revolution may appear in various sections of the United States general catalog. Compiled lineages and applications for the SAR are cataloged under **United States/Genealogy** and **United States/Societies.** However, compiled lineages and applications for the Daughters of the American Revolution are cataloged under **United States/Genealogy** and **United States/Societies,** but not under **United States/Genealogy/Societies.** So it is best to check all three categories when using the FHLC.

A useful guide to the Family History Library's holdings of lineage societies is J. Roberts, comp. *U.S. Lineage Societies Register* (Salt Lake City: Genealogical Library, 1982.) (FHL# REF 973/C43r).

Beyond that, a great deal of material collected or compiled by the DAR such as local cemetery records or Bible records are cataloged according to the locality of origin. Unfortunately, much of this data is rather haphazardly organized and thus time consuming to use.

The Genealogical Library's collection contains several important indexes to published family histories. The most comprehensive of these is Fremont Rider, ed., *The American Genealogical-Biographical Index (AGBI)*, Series 2, (Middletown, Conn.: Godfrey Memorial Library, 1952-Present) (FHL# 973/D22ag).

Another important index is the *Genealogical Index of the Newberry Library,* 4 vols. (Boston: G. K. Hall and Co., 1960) (FHL# REF 929/N24g). This index does not cover books published after 1917. Technically a catalog, but in effect a valuable index is Marion J. Kaminkow, *Genealogies in the Library of Congress: A Bibiography,* two volumes and supplements (Baltimore, Md.: Magna Charta Book Co., 1971, 1977, 1981) (FHL# REF 016.9291/K128g).

An extremely important catalog which lists numerous family papers and unpublished manuscript collections is the *National Union Catalog of Manuscript Collections,* multi-volumed, (Washington D.C.: Library of Congress, 1959) (FHL# REF/016.091/ N21).

Immigration

Virtually all Americans except those of native American stock are descendants of immigrants. Hence, emigration and immigration records comprise an important and ever-expanding portion of the Family History Library collection.

Many, but not all of these are listed under the FHLC under **United States/Emigration and Immigration.** This section contains a fairly complete list of United States sources such as passenger arrival lists and indexes. It also lists some, although by no means all, foreign sources such as the Hamburg passenger lists and articles published in periodicals listing emigrants from a specific locality. For a list of the latter, check the locality FHLC for the country in question, e.g., **Germany/Prussia/Westfalen/Emigration.**

For immigrants arriving in the United States prior to 1820, you must consult published lists. Fortunately, an outstanding index to published passenger and immigration lists is P. William Filby and Mary K. Meyer, eds., *Passenger and Immigration Lists Index,* (Detroit: Gale Research Co., 1981 and annual supplements) (FHL# REF/973/W32p). This index also includes names of emigrants published in foreign-language articles, especially in Germany.

The Filby-Meyer index, while an impressive piece of work, lists only a fraction of the 50 million immigrants who have come to America. For the vast majority, you must check the passenger arrival lists required by the United States government after 1820. Originally these were filed with the customs officer, but later with the Immigration and Naturalization Service.

Microfilms of the passenger arrival lists and indexes for the following ports of entry are available at the Genealogical Library:

New York City

Indexes: 1820-46, 1897-1943
Lists: 1820-1919

Boston

Indexes: 1848-91, 1902-20
Lists: 1820-74, 1883-1935

Baltimore

Indexes: 1820-1952, 1833-66
Lists: 1820-1909

Philadelphia

Indexes: 1800-1906, 1883-1948
Lists: 1800-1916

New Orleans

Indexes: 1820-50, 1853-99
Lists: 1820-1903

The Family History Library has combined indexes for major ports 1820-74, minor ports 1820-73, and 1890-1924. Other ports for which passenger lists are available include Galveston, San Francisco, and Seattle. For a complete list, consult the **United States/Emigration and Immigration** in the FHLC. It is important to note that the ports are not listed in alphabetical order. Hence, it is necessary to read through the entire **/Emigration/Immigration** listings to discover whether a given port's lists are available or not.

At the main library in Salt Lake City, the staff has prepared two three-ring looseleaf binders–one devoted solely to New York City passenger arrivals and the other covering the smaller ports. This is much quicker and easier to use than the microfiche catalog. It is located at the U.S. Reference Credenza area.

In addition to those unpublished lists, the Family History Library is acquiring an ever-growing number of published passenger lists such as Ira A. Glazier, ed. and Michael Tepper, asst. ed., *The Famine Immigrants,* 7 volumes (Baltimore, Md.: Genealogical Publishing Co., 1983-1986). Although the names appearing in these volumes also appear in the Filby-Meyer index, the user is advised to check *The Famine Immigrants* as the lists are published in their entirety. Of course, the optimal approach is to check the films of the original lists.

A useful guide if you know the name of the ship your ancestor arrived on is the *Morton-Allen Directory of European Passenger Steamship Arrivals* (New York: Immigration Information Bureau, Inc., 1931) (FHL# 973/V3m/1980). This book lists all passenger ships arriving in New York (1890-1930), Philadelphia, Boston, and Baltimore (1904-26).

Land and Property Records

Land records are often the earliest records available for a given area, predating court and church records. They provide two types of evidence for the genealogist. First, they often state relationship patterns, especially when a group of heirs jointly sell some inherited land. Second, they place individuals in a specific time and place.

Various types of land records exist, not all of which are available at the Family History Library. Deeds are the backbone of American land records. They are usually located at the county level and generally indexed alphabetically according to the name of the grantor (seller) and grantee (buyer). The Family History Library has recorded thousands of county and city deed records. These are cataloged according to locality.

The second major category of land records are grants or patents. Over 5 million federal grants have transferred land to individuals in various parts of the United States. The Family History Library has very few federal land grant records. These are maintained at the Bureau of Land Management, 350 South Pickett Street, Alexandria, VA 22304 for public domain states east of the Mississippi and states bordering the Mississippi in the West. Records for the western states are in the various BLM state offices.

The Washington National Records Center at 4205 Suitland Road, Suitland, MD 20409 houses military or bounty land files, homestead applications, and private land claims. These homestead applications are especially valuable because they will include copies of naturalization papers if the applicant was not a native-born American. It is necessary to have the legal description of the property before these applications can locate the desired records.

The original thirteen colonies and various other states, i.e., Hawaii, Kentucky, Maine, Tennessee, Texas, Vermont, and West Virginia have many records in the Family History Library collection. They are cataloged under the appropriate state, e.g., **Virginia/Land and Property.**

A third major type of land record is private land claims. These are of two basic types. The first involved official recognition by the United States government of certain land grants made by the earlier French, Spanish, and British governments in areas acquired after the American Revolution.

"Private land claims" may also refer to the claims presented directly to Congress for private relief. While the Family History Library has very few of these records, it has Philip McMullin, ed., *Grassroots of America* (Salt Lake City: Gendex, 1972) (FHL# 973/R2m), an index to *The American State Papers, Public Lands,* (Washington, D.C.: Gales and Seaton, 1832-61). The McMullin index lists the names of individuals who presented claims before Congress between 1789-1837 together with the volume and page number necessary to locate the claim in the papers.

The Family History Library does have microfilms of many private claims records in Louisiana and New Mexico stemming from grants made when these areas were ruled by France and Spain. These are cataloged **[State]/Land and Property.**

Another important type of land record concerns bounty land awarded for military service. See *Military Records* below.

Tax Records

Property taxes rank among the oldest known forms of taxation, predating income taxes by thousands of years. Many of the most famous enumerations of medieval and early modern times such as the Domesday Book were compiled for purposes of taxation. Land tax records in eighteenth- and early nineteenth-century America can be crucial for genealogical success, especially in the South which has far fewer vital records than New England. They are cataloged under the county, for example, **Virginia/Dinwiddie/Taxation.**

Military Records

Military records can be classified according to three basic types:

Service Records:

Include enlistment and discharge papers, muster rolls, prisoner of war lists, and death reports. The amount of information in these records varies greatly. In the colonial wars (1675-1763) they usually list only the name of the soldier and the unit in which he served. By the time of the Civil War, regimental muster rolls often list the soldier's age, physical description, place of enlistment, exact place of birth (meaning county and state in the United States, state or county in Europe, sometimes the exact village) and the date of discharge or death. Thus, these muster rolls can be of exceedingly high genealogical value.

But to use these records, one must know the state the soldier lived in and the unit served in. The Family History Library has indexes to compiled military service records from 1775-1902, covering the Revolutionary War, 1784-1811, War of 1812, Indian Wars, Mexican War, Civil War, Spanish-American War, and the Philippine Insurrection. The Civil War records include indexes to all Union states as well as indexes to veteran reserves and Confederate government troops.

The Family History Library has microfilmed service records of soldiers who served in the American army during the Revolutionary War, and for the years following the war, 1784-1811. The Family History Library does not have the compiled service records of the War of 1812. They are available only at the National Archives.

In the case of the Mexican War, the Family History Library has microfilms of compiled service records for some, but not all states who furnished troops for that conflict. The same situation holds true for Union and Confederate compiled service records in the Civil War.

Users of the Family History Library's collection in Salt Lake City or one of its Family History Centers should consult Marilyn Deputy et al., eds., *Register of Federal United States Military Records,* 3 vols. (Salt Lake City, Genealogical Library, 1985-86) (FHL# 973/M2de) for the call numbers of the appropriate films. Be aware that this register's list of the state regimental muster rolls is not complete. Thus one should always check the appropriate state, for example, **Missouri/Military Records.**

Pension Records:

The Family History Library has microfilm copies of the Revolutionary War pension files. But for most of the other wars, only the indexes are available. An exception to this generalization is the pension records of the Mormon Battalion in the Mexican War.

Bounty Land Records:

These consist of applications for land offered c.1788-1855 as a service benefit. The genealogical information contained is similar to that in the pension records.

The Family History Library possesses microfilms for the bounty land applications of the Revolutionary War and the bounty land warrants for the War of 1812. See *Register of Federal United States, Military Records,* Volume I for the appropriate call numbers. In addition, the Family History Library has microfilms of state bounty land warrants. One example is: Virginia; 31 reels beginning FHL# 0029821. Virginia awarded land to soldiers who served in state units as well as continental units.

A useful series of books for coping with the complexities of Federal Bounty Land Grants is Clifford Neal Smith, *Federal Land Series,* especially volume 2 subtitled *Federal Bounty Land Warrants of the American Revolution, 1799-1835* (Chicago: American Library Association, 1973) (FHL# 973/R23s/Vol. 2).

No discussion of bounty land warrants would be complete without some mention of the Loyalist claims. The British government made a commendable effort to compensate Loyalists for their losses. The Family History Library has 189 reels of microfilm of American Loyalist claims, covering the years 1730-1835 filmed at the Public Record Office in London. These consist of bundles of material arranged by state and Canadian provinces. Abstracts of Bundles 1-35 and 37 have been published. See Peter Wilson Coldham, *American Loyalist Claims,* Volume 1 (Washington, D.C.: National Genealogical Society, 1980) (FHL# 973/R2cp/Vol. 1).

Miscellaneous Military Records:

Draft records do not fit into the three categories of

military records already discussed. At present, the Family History Library is acquiring microfilms of the World War I draft registration cards. But the project has not progressed far enough for microfilm numbers to be issued.

For additional military records not available in the Family History Library, the reader should consult the *Guide to Genealogical Research in the National Archives,* (Washington, D.C.: National Archives and Records Service, 1982) (FHL# REF/973/A3usn). Copies of service and pension records can be obtained by writing to the National Archives and asking for form NATF 80.

In addition to the various unpublished military records available, the Family History Library contains a number of important published works including a complete set of War Department, *The War of the Rebellion* 70 vols. (Washington, D.C.: Government Printing Office, 1880-1901) (FHL# 973/M29u/Ser. 1, 2, 3, and 4; also available on microfilm 0845353-0845426).

A useful compilation is *Published U.S. Military Sources in the Genealogical Library* (Salt Lake City: Genealogical Library, 1980) in the Credenza Collection, no call number.

Native American Records

For many Americans of European descent, genealogy is a pastime – for some a passion. But proof of ancestry is not crucial to their material well being, except in questions of inherited property. For native Americans, proof of Indian ancestry is necessary for full tribal citizenship. The federal records which document that ancestry are voluminous and complex.

Space forbids extensive discussion of all the various types of records concerning native Americans in the Family History Library. They are listed in the locality catalog under the **United States/Native Races,** or under **/[State]/Native Races.** The collection contains a sizable number of secondary works describing the history and customs of various tribes. In regard to unpublished records, the most important part of the collection consists of 692 reels containing the various tribal census enumerations from 1885 to c.1940.

A brief discussion of these enumerations including the Family History Library call numbers can be found in E. Kay Kirkham, *Our Native Americans and Their Records of Genealogical Value,* Volume I (Logan, Utah: Everton Publishers, 1980) (FHL# REF/970.1/K635o). Volume II of this work identifies the Indian tribes enumerated in the 1900 U.S. Census by Family History Library film and page numbers.

In addition, Kirkham's work describes other Indian records available in the Family History Library and elsewhere. The *Guide to Genealogical Research in the National Archives* (previously cited) also contains a chapter on American Indian records. This chapter, while brief, is useful precisely because of its brevity. George J. Nixon's "Records Relating to Native American Research: The Five Civilized Tribes" in Arlene Eakle and Johni Cerny, eds., *The Source* (Salt Lake City: Ancestry Publishing, 1984) (FHL# REF/973/027ts) provides a lucid discussion of records relating to the Five Civilized Tribes of Oklahoma. The bibliography covers a much broader scope.

Naturalization Records

Naturalization refers to the process of granting citizenship to foreign-born residents. Naturalization records can be a key source for finding an immigrant's place of origin, original name, aliases, residence since arrival, birth and marriage dates, etc. They are particularly valuable after 1906, when federal law required much more information than previously.

Naturalization papers fall into three categories. The Declaration of Intention (first papers) are generally the most valuable in terms of genealogical content. The Petition for Naturalization (second papers) are usually of lesser value, at least prior to 1906. After that date, they can be extremely valuable, containing names, birthdates, and birthplaces of children, name of spouse, and spouse's birthplace.

The certificate of naturalization actually issued to the new citizen contains less data than the declaration and the petition. However, it can be valuable because it states the name and location of the court where it was issued and in later years a certificate number. Thus it can lead one to the first and second papers which contain more information.

The laws regarding naturalization have changed over the years. In the nineteenth century, men often declared their intention soon after arriving in the United States. Generally a residence of five years was required before granting of citizenship. But veterans of the Civil War did not have to file a Declaration. Wives and minor children of naturalized men became citizens automatically. After 1922, women no longer gained citizenship automatically by marriage.

Pre-1906 naturalization papers can be difficult to locate as they are scattered among the files of more than 4,000 federal, state, and local courts without any central index. Post-1906 records are indexed at the office of the Immigration and Naturalization Service, Washington, D.C. A copy of an individual's naturalization papers may be obtained from this office using federal form G-641.

The Family History Library catalogs naturalization papers by state, county, or city. But for the New England states (Connecticut, Maine, Massachusetts, New Hampshire, Rhode Island, and Vermont), a Soundex prepared under WPA auspices exists for the naturalization records from 1791-1906, 117 reels starting with FHL# microfilm 1429671. These are cataloged under the state in question, for example, **Rhode Island/Naturalization.**

Most of the naturalization records in the Family History Library pre-date 1906 and are from the eastern half of the United States. However, post-1906 records for certain large cities such as Chicago and New York have been filmed.

For those records not available at the Family History Library, you should write to the county clerk of the county where your ancestor settled. An extremely useful book for determining whether a county has naturalization records for a given time period is James C. and Lila Lee Neagles, *Locating Your Immigrant Ancestor,* 2d ed. (Logan, Utah: Everton Publishers, 1986) (FHL# REF/973/P47n).

If your immigrant ancestor homesteaded land after the Civil War, a copy of his naturalization papers with his homestead entry papers are filed at the National Archives Records Center in Suitland, Maryland. However, you must know the patent number or the legal description of the claim in order to locate the record.

A useful discussion of the history of the naturalization process is John J. Newman, *American Naturalization Processes and Procedures* (Indianapolis: Family History Section, Indiana Historical Society, 1985) (FHL# 973/P4n).

Newspapers

Newspapers offer an excellent source of genealogical information reporting births, marriages, and deaths in the form of obituaries. Beyond that, they mirror the day-to-day life of a community, with insights about family history. Small town and foreign language newspapers often provide better obituaries than big city dailies. Thus, if your ancestor died in a large city, but was buried in a small town, check the small town's newspaper for an obituary. It is likely to be far more detailed.

The same holds true for ethnic newspapers. A big city daily may carry only a one-line death notice of an immigrant, but a foreign language paper may feature a lengthy obituary stating his exact place of birth in Europe.

Denominational newspapers offer another excellent source. Certain denominations featured very complete obituaries of active members. Others limited themselves to obituaries of clergymen, their wives, and teachers.

The Family History Library's current policy precludes the filming of newspapers. However, this was not always the case. Hence, the Family History Library has good newspaper collections for a few states, notably Kentucky and Tennessee. They are listed in the locality catalog under the name of the city.

A useful guide to the newspaper holdings of the Family History Library is Pat Barben, comp. *Register of U.S. Newspapers and Related Holdings in the Genealogical Library* (Salt Lake City, Genealogical Library, 1984) (FHL# REF/973/A3r).

Although the Family History Library's collection of newspaper holdings is not large, it does have a number of reference books concerning newspapers. Perhaps the most useful of these is *Newspapers on Microform* (Washington, D.C.: Library of Congress, 1973, 1978, and supplements) (FHL# REF/011.35/N479). These volumes list newspapers published as early as 1690 which are now on microfilm or some other type of microform in one or more libraries. The holdings of the Family History Library are not included. However, most of these newspapers can be obtained via inter-library loan through a public library.

An older work which should always be consulted in conjunction with the above is Winifred Gregory, ed. *American Newspapers, 1821-1936* (New York: H. W. Wilson, Co., for the Bibliographical Society of America, 1937) (FHL# REF/Q/970/A3bs or microfilm 0430291. This work lists many newspapers which have not yet been microfilmed, listing the years for which holdings exist and the repositories.

Newspaper indexes can be extremely useful. For instance, *The New York Times Obituaries Index 1858-1968* (New York: New York Times, 1970) (FHL# 974.71/-V42n) contains 350,000 names, while the *New York Times Personal Names Index 1851-[present]* (New York: New York Times, n.d.) (FHL# 974.71/B3f) contains many more.

A multi-volume guide to newspaper indexes throughout the United States is Anita Cheek Milner, comp., *Newspaper Indexes: A Location and Subject Guide for Researchers,* 3 vols. (Metuchen, N.J., and London: Scarecrow Press, 1977, 1979, 1982).

Individuals interested in colonial America should consult Clarence Brigham, comp., *History and Bibliography of American Newspapers, 1690-1820,* 2 vols. (Worcester, Mass.: American Antiquarian Society, 1947) (FHL# REF/973/A3bc). The two volumes contain brief historical sketches of almost 2,000 newspapers published in colonial America and list archives and libraries which hold copies of them.

The standard guide to newspapers in print is *Ayer Directory of Publications* (Philadelphia: Ayer Press, annual) (FHL# REF/970/E4ay). The Family History Library also has older editions of this directory, for example, 1886, 1958.

In addition to these general guides, the Family History Library has many specialized newspaper guides. It has state guides for almost twenty states, cataloged under **[State]/Newspapers/Bibliography.**

Another category of specialized newspaper bibliographies are those for ethnic newspapers, cataloged under **United States/Newspapers/Bibliography.**

Periodicals

The Family History Library collections include genealogical and historical periodicals at all levels, from those of national scope such as the *National Genealogical Quarterly* to publications of local genealogical societies. They will be listed in both the Author/Title and the Locality FHLCs. Those of national interest are cataloged under **United States/Genealogy** or **History Periodicals,** while those of more local interest are cataloged under the specific locality. A published guide to genealogical periodicals is the *Genealogical Periodical Annual Index,* (Bowie, Md.: Heritage Books, 1962-date) (FHL# REF/973/B22gp).

Archives and Libraries

While the collection of the Family History Library is

immense, it is by no means all encompassing. One of the worst mistakes a genealogist can make is to assume that if a genealogical problem cannot be solved using the resources of the Family History Library, it is therefore unsolvable. Yet one often hears such sentiments being uttered.

The imaginative genealogist quickly learns to cast his or her net widely. One way to do this is to contact a historical or genealogical society in the area where your ancestor lived. Another approach is to contact the local library. With the ever-growing interest in genealogy, many local reference librarians have acquired considerable expertise in local genealogical and historical source material. Three valuable directories in this regard are:

American Library Directory. New York: R. R. Bowker Co., biannually. (FHL# 973/J54a).

Craig, Tracey Linton. *Directory of Historical Societies and Agencies in the United States and Canada*. 12th ed. Nashville, Tenn.: American Association for State and Local History, 1982. (FHL# 970/H24d).

Meyer, Mary K. *Directory of Genealogical Societies in the U.S.A. and Canada*. 5th ed. Linthicum Heights, Md.: Libra Publications, 1984. (FHL# 970/C44m).

Probate Records

Probate records stem from the process of disposing of an estate after a person's death. There are two basic types: "testate" meaning the person left a valid will, and "intestate" meaning no will existed. Various types of "intestate" papers may thus be created: petitions, bonds, letters of administrations, inventories, and sales.

Guardianships are closely related to probate records and the probate process. They are usually handled by the same court which deals with probate cases.

Probate records rank among the most valuable genealogical records available because they usually state relationships within a family very precisely. To be sure, this is not always the case. A man may leave his estate "to my beloved wife and children" without naming them. But more often than not, their names will be stated, including the married names of daughters.

In some courts, all probate records are indexed together, while in others the wills are indexed separately. In some cases, finding records of the various actions concerning a person who died intestate may require careful reading of the docket or court calendar.

Probate records are extremely valuable in themselves, but can also be valuable as clues for other records, such as land records. A man may leave all his property "to my children" without naming them. But the land records may state the names, especially if one heir buys out the rights of his siblings.

Many early probate records have been transcribed and indexed. However, it is always best to check the original, or at least a microfilm copy of the original. Correctly transcribing old records is often difficult, and errors creep in.

The Family History Library has microfilmed probate records in counties in the southern, eastern, and midwestern states. They are usually cataloged according to the county, although some collections may be listed under the state heading. Not all states use the term probate court, so it is best to check the various types of courts and court records listed. In some counties, only the indexes have been filmed. In many counties, only the more important papers have been microfilmed, not the complete probate packets or case files. Hence, it is necessary to contact the courthouse or hire a local agent to obtain copies of all the papers.

Tax Records

In addition to the land taxes already discussed, other forms of taxes were levied, of which many records have survived. Among the most important was the poll or head tax, levied in colonial and ante-bellum counties and towns on free adult males. What constituted an adult varied over the years. In colonial times, sixteen-year-old males were subject to the poll tax in North Carolina. Later, the minimum was set at twenty-one. Older men were exempt, but again the age varied, at times set at forty-four, but more often it was fifty.

Many individuals were exempted from paying the tax–for example, paupers, ministers, justices of the peace, and of course, women. Still, these lists are valuable genealogical records, and the Family History Library has filmed many of them.

Other tax records of genealogical value are those created by the direct taxes of the federal government levied in 1798, 1814-16, and in the Civil War years of 1862-1866. All of these taxes were prompted by war expenses. Unfortunately, very few records of the 1798 tax and even fewer of the 1814-16 tax appear to have survived. Massive records of the 1862-66 tax have survived and are being filmed by the National Archives. But these are not yet available at the Family History Library.

Tax records are cataloged under the locality in question. A useful summary of tax records appears in William Thorndale "Land and Tax Records," in Arlene Eakle and Johni Cerny, eds., *The Source (*Salt Lake City: Ancestry Publishing, 1984) (FHL# REF/973/D27ts).

Voting Records

In certain situations, notably large cities, voting records have been preserved. These are sometimes indexed or listed by ward and can serve as a complement to census records and city directories. To date, the Family History Library has filmed few of these. However, voting records from some localities have been filmed and are cataloged under **[State]/[County]/[City]/Voting Registers.**

Vital Records

Birth, marriage, and death records rank at the very top of the list of important genealogical records. In the

United States, registration of vital statistics has been left to the states. Thus the inception of vital records varies greatly. Generally speaking, the southern states were the last to require registration of vital statistics. Even in those states which did record (Virginia/West Virginia in 1853) such data in the nineteenth century, enforcement was very sporadic at first and often interrupted during the Civil War.

Birth records:

A birth record usually states the name and sex of the child, date and place of birth, and names of parents and their place of residence. In some states, place of birth of the parents is also stated. Thus, such records become valuable for tracing immigrants to Europe. Also, the name of the midwife or attending physician is typically listed. Post-1900 birth records generally contain more information.

A variant type of birth record is the delayed registration of a birth. Many individuals obtained such documents in the 1940s to prove their eligibility for Social Security benefits, among other reasons. The Family History Library has filmed many of these, especially from the midwestern states.

Birth records are arranged according to locality, but not always by city. For example, the pre-1907 Wisconsin birth records are cataloged under **Wisconsin/Vital Statistics.** But those of Cook County, Illinois are cataloged under **Illinois/Cook County/Vital Records** and **Illinois/Cook/Chicago/Vital Records.**

Marriage records:

Marriage records are usually the first vital records kept in a locality and may predate birth records by more than 200 years. Typically they list the name and age of the bridal couple, the place and date of the marriage, and the names of the officiant, witnesses, and in some areas bondsman.

About 1880, many midwestern states began requiring complete applications for a marriage license. These often contain a great deal of data such as names of parents, exact place of birth, etc. They may be on a separate roll of microfilm than the license itself.

Generally speaking, the various types of records created in the process of marriage include the (1) marriage bond, bann, consent, contract, or application; (2) license; (3) certificate; (4) return or register. The Family History Library has filmed many marriage records and some of them, notably those of pre-1850 Ohio, appear in the IGI. Generally they are cataloged under the county.

Divorce records:

The Family History Library has very few divorce records. Those available are listed in the FHLC under **/Court Records or /Vital Records.**

Death records:

These generally list the name of the decedent, date and place of death, age or date of birth, cause of death, place of burial, names of undertaker, attending physician, and informant. Sometimes the names of parents and spouses are listed. Death records may be far off the mark in regard to birth information. They are often valuable as leads for other records such as obituaries or church records.

Death records are cataloged according to locality. But depending upon the state, they may be listed under the county or the state.

Statewide collections of vital records:

The Family History Library has a number of significant statewide collections and special indexes of vital records for the following states: California, Connecticut, Delaware, Hawaii, Kentucky, Maine, Massachusetts, New Hampshire, New Jersey, North Carolina, Rhode Island, Tennessee, Vermont, Washington, and Wisconsin.

For vital records not available at the Family History Library, one must write the vital statistics office of the state in question, or the county clerk. Current addresses and search fees are listed in *Vital Records in the United States,* compiled by the Family History Library staff on an ongoing basis. No catalog number is available in the Credenza Collection.

Other Records

Other records available in the Family History Library not included in the above discussion are listed in the Family History Library Catalog under the following headings: **Almanacs, Bibliography, Business Records and Commerce, Correctional Institutions, Medical Records, Notorial Records, Occupations, Orphans And Orphanages, and Schools.**

Bibliography

Useful sources not cited with the discussion above include:

Everton, George B., Sr. *The Handy Book for Genealogists,* 7th ed. Logan, Utah: Everton Publishers, 1981. (FHL# REF/973/D27e/1981)

Greenwood, Val. *The Researcher's Guide to American Genealogy.* Baltimore, Md.: Genealogical Publishing Co., 1973. (FHL# 973/D27g).

My thanks to the staff of the American Reference Desk at the Family History Library for their help in answering certain questions. Also the unpublished guide, "Research Outline: United States" prepared by the American Reference staff, has been of great assistance in preparing this chapter.

Chapter 5

United States: New England

Clifford L. Stott

Genealogical source material for the six New England states has long been recognized as the richest in the nation. Early New Englanders were devoted record keepers and preserved a large and diverse body of records, much of which is available for research. The holdings of the Family History Library are particularly strong for New England, as the Genealogical Society of Utah focused very early on collections in this area.

Historical Background

1620	Plymouth Colony established by the Pilgrims, separatists from Church of England.
1622	Commercial settlement founded at Monhegan, Maine.
1623	Commercial enterprises established at Rye, Portsmouth, and Dover, New Hampshire, and Saco, Maine.
1628	Puritans led by John Endicott settle Salem, Massachusetts.
1629	Massachusetts Bay Colony established by royal charter.
1630	Massachusetts Bay Colony strengthened by John Winthrop and 900 English immigrants, mostly Puritans. Expands rapidly.
1636	Rev. Thomas Hooker leads colony from Cambridge, Massachusetts, to Hartford. Beginning of Connecticut Colony. Roger Williams founds Providence, Rhode Island. William Pynchon leads colony from Roxbury, Massachusetts, to Springfield. First English settlement in western Massachusetts.
1636-37	The Pequot War.
1638	New Haven Colony founded. Exeter, New Hampshire, founded by John Wheelwright and group of Antinomian dissenters. Portsmouth, Rhode Island, settled by Antinomian dissenters led by Anne Hutchinson, John Clarke, William Coddington, and others. Disaffected Puritans settle Hampton, New Hampshire.
1639	Newport, Rhode Island, settled by dissenters from Portsmouth.
1641	Massachusetts extends sovereignty over New Hampshire towns.
1642	Colony founded at Warwick, Rhode Island, by Samuel Gorton and other dissenters.
1643	County government begins in Massachusetts with the formation of Suffolk, Norfolk, Essex, and Middlesex counties.
1646	New London, Connecticut, founded. Many settlers from Massachusetts.
1647	The four Rhode Island towns merge under royal charter.
1650-51	Several hundred Scottish prisoners arrive to work in iron works at Lynn and Braintree.
1659	Beginning of the colonization of Nantucket, largely by Essex County, Massachusetts, families, including a number of Quakers.
1662	Connecticut receives royal charter. New Haven and Connecticut colonies merged.
1666	County government commences in Connecticut with formation of Hartford, New Haven, Fairfield, and New London counties.
1675-77	New England devastated by King Philip's War. Veterans eventually receive land grants in Maine, western Mas-

	sachusetts, and New London County, Connecticut.
1679	New Hampshire becomes royal colony, removed from Massachusetts jurisdiction.
1684	Massachusetts charter revoked.
1686-88	Massachusetts, Connecticut, Plymouth, Rhode Island, and New Hampshire united as the Dominion of New England under Sir Edmund Andros.
1688	Stuart monarchy overthrown. Dominion of New England abolished.
1688-97	New Englanders fight French and Indians in King William's War.
1691	Massachusetts receives royal charter, is merged with Plymouth Colony and given jurisdiction over Nantucket and Martha's Vineyard, formerly under New York control.
1703-13	New Englanders fight French and Indians in Queen Anne's War.
1717	Beginning of Ulster immigration to New England.
1744-48	New Englanders participate in King George's War, the third French and Indian war fought on American soil.
1746	The towns of Bristol, Tiverton, Little Compton, Warren, and Cumberland ceded from Massachusetts to Rhode Island.
1755-63	French and Indian War results in termination of French occupation of Canada. Many New Englanders settle in Nova Scotia and Maine.
1760	Approximate beginning of settlement of Vermont by settlers from southern New England. Region claimed by New York and New Hampshire.
1769	Beginning of county government in New Hampshire.
1775-83	Revolutionary War. New England responds with enthusiasm.
1777	Vermont established as an independent republic.
1785	Massachusetts surrenders western lands.
1788	Connecticut, Massachusetts, and New Hampshire ratify constitution.
1790	Rhode Island ratifies constitution.
1791	Vermont admitted to the Union.
1812-15	War of 1812 involves New England soldiers and sailors, although generally unpopular in New England.
1820	Maine admitted to the Union.
1840s	Rise of manufacturing in southern New England induces emigration from Europe and British Isles.
1845-55	Great Famine in Ireland brings hundreds of thousands of Irish into New England, primarily into the cities.
1861-65	Many New Englanders fight for the Union during Civil War.

Settlement and Migration

England's original claim to North America was based on the voyages of John Cabot, the Venetian navigator who explored the New England coast in 1497 and 1498. More than a century elapsed, however, before settlement of this region was attempted. In 1607, as the English settlement of Jamestown was underway in Virginia, a group of merchants and adventurers called the Plymouth Company established a colony on Sagadahoc at the mouth of the Kennebec River in present-day Maine. Other small fishing and trading outposts soon sprang up along the New England coast. But these trading colonies were short-lived and contributed little, if anything, to the permanent settlement of the region except as an encouragement to other groups.

The first permanent settlement in New England began when 102 Separatists arrived at Plymouth harbor in what would later be Massachusetts aboard the *Mayflower* in December of 1620. The Pilgrims, as they became known, had fled first from England to Holland in search of religious freedom and then becoming disillusioned with Dutch life, obtained a grant from the London Company to settle on the James River in Virginia in 1619. Late in 1620, autumn gales drove the 180-ton *Mayflower* far to the north of her intended objective.

Plymouth was successfully colonized; and through the next several decades, the colony expanded across southeast Massachusetts from Cape Cod to the Narragansett Bay. In 1632 Duxbury was founded, followed the next year by Scituate. The Cape Cod towns of Barnstable and Sandwich sprang up in 1638, joined by Yarmouth in 1639 and Eastham in 1649. Others were Hingham (1635), Taunton (1639), Marshfield (1640), Rehoboth (1645), Dartmouth (1652), and Middleborough (1669).

In 1628 a company of English Puritans led by John Endicott arrived at Cape Ann, where a fishing outpost under Roger Conant had been clinging since 1623. Here Endicott and his followers established Salem under a grant from the Council of New England, the successor of the Plymouth Company. A royal charter was granted the following year creating the Massachusetts Bay Company.

The Great Exodus to Massachusetts Bay commenced in 1630, resulting in the arrival of 20,000 Englishmen in the colony before the decade was over. With the ascent of Charles I to the British throne in 1629, the Puritans found themselves exposed to persecution and harsh penalties for their dissenting beliefs. Puritan leader John Winthrop spearheaded the first wave of immigration when his fleet carrying some 900 colonists anchored in Boston harbor in the summer of 1630 and founded the town. The company charter was removed to Massachusetts, and for almost fifty years the colony remained a narrow theocracy almost independent of the Crown.

The population of the Massachusetts Bay colony

under Governor Winthrop soon outstripped its Plymouth neighbor. The decade of the 1630s saw the arrivals of religious dissenters, adventurers, traders, and economically depressed Britons as well.

The bulging population pressed New England frontiers in every direction. From Maine to Plymouth, towns and villages blossomed on the coast, and town after town pushed the frontier west. Lynn, Roxbury, Cambridge, Dorchester, and Watertown were settled by 1631, followed by Ipswich (1633), Newbury (1635), Marblehead (1635), Concord (1635), Dedham (1636), Rowley (1639), Sudbury (1639), Braintree (1640), and Salisbury (1640). By 1636 Puritan settlement had reached the Connecticut River.

Growing towns divided to form new towns. In 1643 Massachusetts was divided into four counties–Suffolk, Essex, Middlesex, and Norfolk (not to be confused with the modern Norfolk County, established in 1793. The original or "old" Norfolk County included Hampton, Dover, Portsmouth, and Exeter, which are now in New Hampshire, besides Salisbury and Haverhill in present-day Massachusetts). With the establishment of New Hampshire as a royal province in 1679, Norfolk County became extinct, and the towns of Salisbury, Amesbury (created in 1666 by a division of Salisbury), and Haverhill were absorbed by Essex County.

Religious disputes and land hunger soon resulted in the settlement of the Connecticut Valley. The Reverend Thomas Hooker led a segment of his congregation from Cambridge to the valley, where they founded Hartford in 1636 near the site of a Dutch trading post. In the same year, mass migrations from Watertown and Dorchester settled Wethersfield and Windsor, and a fort was built at Saybrook at the mouth of the Connecticut River.

Also in 1636, William Pynchon led a group of colonizers from Roxbury to the Connecticut River twenty-five miles north of Hartford and founded the town of Springfield, Massachusetts. By 1639 the Connecticut towns were virtually autonomous, and a charter for the Connecticut colony was granted in 1662.

Dissent continued to plague Massachusetts and Connecticut authorities. In 1656 a party of dissatisfied Puritans left Connecticut to establish Northampton still further north of Springfield. The upper Connecticut Valley saw the settlement of Hadley (1661), Hatfield (1670), Deerfield (1670), Northfield (1673), and Greenfield (1686).

The settlement of New Haven, briefly an independent colony, commenced in 1638 with a group of English Puritan merchants. Besides New Haven, other new towns were Milford (1639), Guilford (1639), Stamford (1641), Branford (1644), and Southhold, Long Island (1640). But the New Haven colony did not thrive. Torn by religious strife and the failure of its commercial enterprises, New Haven was absorbed by the Connecticut colony in 1662.

The "heretical" doctrines of Roger Williams, Anne Hutchinson, and others resulted in the establishment of Rhode Island. Williams founded Providence in 1636 after his banishment from Massachusetts. Anne Hutchinson, John Clarke, William Coddington, and other adherents to Antinomian beliefs settled Portsmouth in 1638. Newport was settled the following year by dissenters from Portsmouth. In 1642, a fourth colony was begun at Warwick by Samuel Gorton, a man previously ejected from Plymouth for his dissenting views.

Despite opposition from Massachusetts, the four Rhode Island towns were merged under a charter from the Earl of Warwick in 1647. Exactly a century later, Massachusetts ceded Tiverton, Little Compton, Bristol, Warren, and Cumberland on the eastern shore of Narragansett Bay to Rhode Island. Many records relating to these towns prior to incorporation with Rhode Island are found in Bristol County, Massachusetts.

From its beginning, Rhode Island was a haven for dissidents from Massachusetts and Connecticut theocracies. In Rhode Island, church and state were separate to a degree unheard of in the older colonies. Virtually all Christian sects were tolerated. Thus, the same independent spirit which led the Puritans to America was responsible for fragmenting the older colonies and pushing settlements across the frontiers at an accelerated pace.

Early settlements in New Hampshire were made in 1623 at Rye, Portsmouth, and Dover. These were largely commercial enterprises; but after the founding of Massachusetts Bay, they were soon overwhelmed by the dominant Puritan influence. In 1638 John Wheelwright and his band of Antinomian dissenters from the Bay colony founded the town of Exeter. Hampton followed later with a migration of disaffected Puritans from Watertown, Newbury, and Dedham.

In 1641 Massachusetts extended sovereignty over the New Hampshire towns, and they became a part of Norfolk County two years later. In 1679 New Hampshire was taken out of Massachusetts control and made a royal province. Until well into the next century settlement of New Hampshire was confined largely to the coastal plain, and there was a considerable movement of settlers between the New Hampshire towns and the neighboring towns of York County, Maine, and Essex County, Massachusetts.

The Maine coast was inhabited by English traders and fishermen from at least 1607. Permanent settlement commenced with the founding of Monhegan in 1622, Saco in 1623, and York soon afterward. Although many Puritans migrated into Maine from Massachusetts Bay and New Hampshire, commercialism, not religion, was the dominant force in Maine's settlement. Dutch merchants and French missionaries also continued to frequent Maine until well into the eighteenth century.

Maine grew slowly. Conflicting land claims, political changes, and brutal attacks by the French and Indians made settlement in Maine unattractive to most. Nevertheless, small villages gradually cropped up along the Maine coast throughout the seventeenth century and at an accelerated pace in the next. The interior was not settled to a great extent until the conclusion of the Indian problem with the end of the French and Indian War in 1763. Maine continued as a province of Massachusetts until it became the twenty-third state in 1820.

The four New England colonies of Massachusetts,

New Hampshire, Connecticut, and Rhode Island were briefly united from 1686 to 1688. In an attempt to tighten imperial control, the Crown repealed the Massachusetts charter in 1684 and instituted the Dominion of New England under Sir Edmund Andros. New York and New Jersey were later brought into the short-lived confederation. Massachusetts strongly resisted the new government, and the dominion form was dropped in 1689 with the overthrow of James II and the Stuart monarchy. Massachusetts authorities hoped for the restoration of the old charter but, in 1691, became a royal colony under William and Mary.

At this time, the Plymouth colony was combined with Massachusetts, which also received jurisdiction for the islands of Nantucket and Martha's Vineyard, formerly under New York control. During the brief existence of the Dominion of New England, many court and probate matters from throughout New England were filed in Boston, making Suffolk County court records essential for some research problems in other colonies.

Although Nantucket and Martha's Vineyard were under New York's jurisdiction until 1691, the islands were inhabited almost exclusively by migrants from New England. Nantucket was first settled by a mass migration from Essex County, beginning in 1659. Many who came to Nantucket were Quakers, a sect severely persecuted in most parts of New England.

Prior to the Revolutionary War, New Englanders were involved in several Indian wars as well as four French and Indian wars. The Pequots, an Indian tribe which inhabited Connecticut east of the Thames River, were almost totally destroyed by the Massachusetts militia in a few fierce battles in 1636-37.

King Philip's War, which exploded across New England in 1675, was the most destructive conflict ever faced by the English colonists. Philip, a sachem of the Wampanoag in Plymouth, attempted to create an alliance among the most powerful tribes in southern New England against the tide of English settlement. Although Philip's confederation was only partially successful, his war ravaged New England for two years. Over 1,000 colonists were killed, and the entire outer perimeter of English settlement was shattered. Many towns were totally destroyed and others severely damaged. Despite these losses, the English recovered; but the power of the southern New England tribes was permanently broken, their confederacy was smashed, Philip was killed, and his family was sold into slavery in the West Indies.

It was the policy of the New England governments to grant free land to the veterans of Indian wars. In this way, much land was distributed in Maine and western Massachusetts. Connecticut provided the town of Voluntown, New London County, for her King Philip's War veterans in 1700. Many Massachusetts soldiers or their descendants received land grants in the so-called Narragansett townships in Maine during the 1730s and moved north. The Massachusetts veterans who fought the Indians at the "Falls Fight" in 1676 were awarded land near present-day Bernardston, Massachusetts, just a few miles from where the battle occurred.

For nearly a century, the British and French fought for control of North America using the Indians as allies. While the English colonized the East Coast, the French had settled the maritime region of Canada and the St. Lawrence Valley, moving down the Ohio and Mississippi valleys in an attempt to contain British westward expansion. Border conflicts arose all along the line, with European wars frequently spilling over into the colonies. As a result, the New England colonists participated in four French and Indian wars.

King William's War, fought intermittently from 1688 to 1697, severely damaged the settlements of Maine, generated Indian massacres in New Hampshire and Massachusetts, and resulted, by 1691, in all but four of the Maine towns being destroyed or abandoned. Queen Anne's War of 1703-13 brought additional destruction to Maine. In the conflict of 1744-48, King George's War, an army of New England provincials captured the French fortress of Louisburg, Nova Scotia, the so-called "Gibraltar of the West." The final French and Indian war lasted from 1755 to 1763 and terminated French occupation of Canada. With the declaration of peace, Indian warfare in New England subsided, causing many New Englanders to migrate into Maine and Nova Scotia.

The seeds of American independence were sown during the French wars. Taxes levied on the colonists to help defray the cost of military operations brought resistance from the colonies, followed by punitive legislation from Britain that threathened to cripple New England trade. Further resistance led to open rebellion. The revolution began in New England on 19 April 1775 with battles at Lexington and Concord. Throughout the conflict, New England sentiment for independence remained high. A large majority of able-bodied men served in the state militias or Continental Army. Local Committees of Safety almost always confiscated the property of Loyalists and Tories; the military rolls, pension, and bounty land records generated by the Revolutionary War are of great value to the New England genealogist.

Permanent settlement of Vermont began about 1760 with large migrations from Massachusetts and Connecticut. Both New York and New Hampshire claimed the area and issued land grants. Massachusetts also granted land in Vermont. Some Vermont records are in the collections of each state. In 1777, Vermonters declared themselves an independent republic and remained such until their admission to the union in 1791. Twenty thousand people resided in Vermont at the commencement of the Revolutionary War, and numbers grew steadily after American independence was secured.

The War of 1812 was generally unpopular in New England, especially in Massachusetts, because it damaged trade. Massachusetts business had already been crippled by the Embargo Act of 1807 and stood virtually dormant throughout the war. Nevertheless, significant numbers of New Englanders served in state militias during this period. Many Vermonters served along the Canadian border. Massachusetts, however, prohibited her troops from leaving the state.

New England was the birthplace of the Abolitionist movement and was strongly pro-Union during the Civil

War of 1861-65. Federal military and pension records of New England Civil War veterans provide much valuable genealogical information.

Prior to the nineteenth century, the New England population was predominantly English Protestant with only fractional minorities, notably a smattering of Irish immigrants, mostly seamen in port cities. In 1650 and 1651, several hundred Scottish prisoners were sent into Lynn and Braintree, Massachusetts, to labor in the iron works. With the revocation of the Edict of Nantes in 1685, a few French Huguenots came to Massachusetts and founded Oxford. Others settled in Boston and elsewhere.

Large numbers of Presbyterians from Northern Ireland came into New England during the eighteenth century. Between 1690 and 1715, over 50,000 Scottish Presbyterians, fleeing poor harvests, rising rents, and religious strife, arrived in Ulster. When their leases in Ireland expired, many emigrated to the colonies. Massachusetts authorities offered the Ulster-Scots cheap lands in Maine and central and western Massachusetts, hoping they would create a buffer between the older towns and hostile Indians. Thus, the Ulster-Scots founded Londonderry, New Hampshire, and Pelham, Massachusetts, and were well represented throughout Rockingham County, New Hampshire, along the Maine coast, and in other areas. Protestant immigration from Northern Ireland continued sporadically until the American Revolution.

Other Europeans appeared in New England during the eighteenth century, but their overall impact was generally small. French-Canadians frequently filtered down into northern New England. Some Hessian mercenaries remained in New England after the Revolution, and a colony of Germans settled in Waldoboro, Maine, in 1753.

The largest influx of immigrants since the Great Exodus of the 1630s occurred between 1845 and 1855, when the Great Famine of Ireland sent almost 2 million exiles streaming into North America. Roughly one-fourth of Ireland's pre-famine population went overseas during this period. Hundreds of thousands found their way into New England, where they congregated primarily in manufacturing centers. Many Irish immigrants who went to Canada eventually arrived in the Champlain Valley of Vermont.

Throughout the nineteenth century, the economy of northern New England remained largely agricultural. But during the 1840s, Massachusetts, Connecticut, and Rhode Island turned dramatically toward manufacturing. Textiles, shoes, machinery, and paper became important products of the mill towns scattered along the rivers of southern New England. Economic booms encouraged immigration from all parts of Europe. By the latter half of the century, all major cities in southern New England claimed large non-English populations.

Others came for other reasons. For example, in the 1890s a large immigration of Portuguese fishermen arrived in southeast Massachusetts, where they established significant communities in New Bedford and Provincetown.

While immigrants were flowing into New England, a constant flow of emigrants came out. New Englanders moved on to New Jersey and Long Island from the earliest dates of settlement. A large migration from southeast Massachusetts and Connecticut came into Dutchess County, New York, during the 1740s. Many New Englanders settled in the Annapolis Valley of Nova Scotia after the deportation of the French Acadians in 1755.

Twelve thousand American loyalists, many of them New Englanders, came into the St. John Valley of New Brunswick during and after the Revolutionary War. After the Revolution, the upper Hudson and Mohawk valleys received a large influx of immigrants from New England. By 1785, the westward migration of New Englanders had reached Ohio. The exodus continued throughout the nineteenth century until New Englanders flooded the Midwest.

New England Library Collection

The published history of New England is voluminous. Valuable local histories exist for most towns, cities, and counties in New England. These are important aids in tracing family migrations from one locality to another. Moreover, many published local histories contain genealogical information available from family members at the time of publication which is now unobtainable. The Family History Library has a very large collection of local history for the New England states. To determine what is available, look under these headings in the Family History Library Catalog (FHLC), locality division: **State/History, State/[County]/History**, and/or **State/-[County]/[Town]/History**, for example: **Massachusetts/ Hampden/ Springfield/History.**

Histories, General

The library has a good selection, but not all, of the major general historical works for the New England states. Some of its more important works are:

Coddington, John Insley. "Migrations from New England to New York and New Jersey." *World Conference and Genealogical Seminar.* Salt Lake City: Genealogical Society of the Church of Jesus Christ of Latter-day Saints, 1969. (FHL# 929.1/W893/I20 or microfilm 897217, item 18)

Holbrook, Stewart H. *The Yankee Exodus: An Account of Migration from New England.* Seattle: University of Washington Press, 1950. (FHL# 973/W21h)

Palfrey, John Gorham. *History of New England.* 5 vols. Boston: Little, Brown & Co., 1882-90. (FHL# 974/H2p or microfilm 928115, items 1-4).

Rosenberry, Lois Kimball Matthews. *The Expansion of New England: The Spread of New England Settlements and Institutions to the Mississippi River, 1620-1685.* 1909; rpt. ed., New York: Russell & Russell, 1962. (FHL# 973/H2r)

Winthrop, John. *A Journal of the Transactions and Occurrences in the Settlement of Massachusetts and Other New England*

Colonies for the Years 1630 to 1644. Hartford: Elisha Babcock, 1790. Several editions. (FHL# 974.4/H2wi)

Connecticut

Andrews, Charles McLean. *The Rise and Fall of the New Haven Colony.* Tercentenary Pamphlet Series no. 48. New Haven: Yale University Press, 1936. (FHL# 974.6/H2c/ser. 48)

Atwater, Edward Elias. *History of the Colony of New Haven to its Absorption into Connecticut, with Supplemental History and Personnel of the Towns of Branford, Guilford, Milford, Stratford, Norwalk, etc.* Meriden, Conn.: Journal Publishing Co., 1902 (FHL# 974/H2ae or microfilm 833384)

Bingham, Harold J. *History of Connecticut.* 4 vols. New York: Lewis Historical Publishing Co., 1962. (FHL# 974/H2bh)

Burpee, Charles W. *The Story of Connecticut.* New York: American Historical Co., 1937. (FHL# 974.6/H2b)

Deming, Dorothy. *The Settlement of the Connecticut Towns*. Tercentenary Pamphlet Series no. 6. New Haven: Yale University Press, 1933. (FHL# 974.6/H2c/ser. 6)

Hollister, Gideon Hiram. *The History of Connecticut from the First Settlement of the Colony to the Adoption of the Present Constitution*. 2 vols. New Haven, Conn.: Durrie and Peck, 1855. (FHL# 974.6/H2h or microfilm 982334, item 2 or 599297, item 1)

Mather, Frederick Gregory. *Refugees of 1776 from Long Island to Connecticut.* Albany, New York: J. B. Lyon, 1913. (FHL# 974.6/H2m or microfilm 164690)

Morrow, Rising Lake. *Connecticut Influences in Western Massachusetts and Vermont.* Tercentenary Pamphlet Series no. 58. New Haven, Conn.: Yale University Press, 1936. (FHL# 974.6/H2c/ser. 58)

Peters, Samuel. *The Reverend Samuel Peters' General History of Connecticut from its First Settlement under George Fenwick to its Latest Period of Amity with Great Britain prior to the Revolution, Including a Description of the Country and Many Curious and Interesting Anecdotes.* New York: D. Appleton and Co., 1877. (FHL# 974.6/H2p)

Trumbull, Benjamin. *A Complete History of Connecticut, Civil and Ecclesiastical, from the Emigration of its First Planters from England in the Year 1630 to the Year 1764 and to the Close of the Indian Wars*. New London, Conn.: H. D. Utley, 1898. (FHL# 974.6/H2t)

Maine

Clark, Charles E. *The Eastern Frontier: The Settlement of Northern New England, 1610-1763.* Hanover, N.H.: University Press of New England, 1983. (FHL# 974/H2cc)

Kershaw, Gordon E. *The Kennebeck Proprietors, 1749-1775: "Gentlemen of Large Property and Judicious Men."* Somersworth, N.H.: New Hampshire Publishing Co. for Maine Historical Society, 1975. (FHL# 974.122/H2k)

Moody, Robert Earle. *The Maine Frontier, 1607 to 1763.* Ann Arbor, Mich.: Michigan University Microfilms, 1980. (FHL# 974.1/H2mr)

Sullivan, James. *History of the District of Maine*. Augusta: Maine State Museum, 1970. (FHL# 974.1/H2sj or microfilm 1036234, item 2)

Sylvestor, Herbert Milton. *Maine Pioneer Settlements.* 5 vols. Boston: W. B. Clarke, 1909. (FHL# 974.1/H2sh or microfilm 1035913, item 3)

Massachusetts

Ames, Azell. *The Mayflower and Her Log, July 15, 1620–May 6, 1621, Chiefly from Original Sources.* Boston: Houghton Mifflin, 1901. (FHL# 974.4/W2a or microfilm 833390)

Banks, Charles Edward. *The English Ancestry and Homes of the Pilgrim Fathers Who Came to Plymouth on the "Mayflower" in 1620, the "Fortune" in 1621, and the "Anne" and the "Little James" in 1623.* 1929; rpt. ed. Baltimore: Genealogical Publishing Co., 1968. Several editions. (FHL# 974/W2be or microfilm 590442)

______. *The Planters of the Commonwealth: A Study of the Emigrant and Emigration in Colonial Times, 1620-1640.* 1930; rpt. ed. Baltimore: Genealogical Publishing Co., 1975. (FHL# 974/W2bf)

______. *The Winthrop Fleet of 1630: An Account of the Vessels, the Voyage, the Passengers and Their English Homes from Original Authorities*. Boston: Houghton Mifflin Co., 1930. Several editions. (FHL# 974.4/W2b or microfilm 924084)

Barber, John Warner. *Historical Collections: Being a General Collection of Interesting Facts, Traditions, Biographical Sketches, Anecdotes, etc. Relating to the History and Antiquities of Every Town in Massachusetts with Geographical Descriptions*. Worcester, Mass.: Dorr Howland and Co., 1840. (FHL# 974.4/H2b or microfilm 370880 or 1000062, item 1)

Barry, John Stetson. *The History of Massachusetts, the Colonial Period.* 3 vols. 1855; rpt. ed., Tucson, Ariz.: W. C. Cox Co., 1974. (FHL# microfilm 1000062, items 2-4)

Bradford, William. *Bradford's History of Plimoth Plantation from the Original Manuscript with a Report of the Proceedings Incident to the Return of the Manuscript to Massachusetts*. Boston: Wright and Potter Printing, 1901. Numerous editions. (FHL# 974.4/H2bw)

Encyclopedia of Massachusetts. 13 vols. Chicago: The American Historical Society, [c.1913]. (FHL# 974.4/D3e or microfiche #6046891)

Hutchinson, Thomas. *The History of the Colony and Province of Massachusetts Bay.* Edited by Lawrence Shaw Mayo. 3 vols. Cambridge: Harvard University Press, 1936. (FHL# 974.4/ H2ht)

Young, Alexander. *Chronicles of the First Planters of the Colony of Massachusetts Bay from 1623 to 1636.* Boston: Charles C. Little and James Brown, 1846. (FHL# 974.4/H2ya)

______. *Chronicles of the Pilgrim Fathers of the Colony of Plymouth from 1602 to 1625.* Boston: Charles C. Little and James Brown, 1844. (FHL# 974.4/H2y)

New Hampshire

Barstow, George. *The History of New Hampshire from Its Discovery in 1614 to the Passage of the Toleration Act in 1819.* Concord, N.H.: I. S. Boyd, 1842. (FHL# 974.2/H2b)

McClintock, John Norris. *History of New Hampshire: Colony, Province, State, 1623-1888.* Boston: B. B. Russell, 1888. (FHL# 974.2/H2m or microfilm 1000197, item 1)

Sanborn, Edwin David. *History of New Hampshire from Its Dis-*

covery to the Year 1830. Manchester, N.H.: J. B. Clarke, 1875. (FHL# 974.2/H2se)

Stackpole, Everett Schermerhorn. *History of New Hampshire*. 4 vols. New York: The American Historical Society, 1916. (FHL# 974.2/H2ses or microfiche 6046852)

Squires, James Duane. *The Granite State of the United States: A History of New Hampshire from 1623 to the Present*. New York: American Historical Co., 1956. (FHL# 974.2/H2s)

Rhode Island

Arnold, Samuel G. *History of the State of Rhode Island and Providence Plantations, 1636-1790*. 2 vols. 1859-60; rpt. ed., Spartanburg, S.C.: Reprint Co., 1970. (FHL# 974.5/H2a or microfilm 1036728, items 3-4)

Chapin, Howard Millar. *Documentary History of Rhode Island*. 2 vols. Providence: Preston and Rounds, 1915-19. (FHL# 974.5/H2ch)

McLoughlin, William G. *Rhode Island, A Bicentennial History*. New York: W. W. Norton & Co., 1978. (FHL# 974.5/H2m)

Vermont

Collins, Edward Day. *A History of Vermont, with the State Constitution, Geological and Geographical Notes, Bibliography, Chronology, Statistical Tables, Maps, and Illustrations*. Boston: Ginn & Co., [c.1903]. (FHL# microfilm 176664)

Crockett, Walter H. *Vermont, The Green Mountain State*. 5 vols. New York: Century History Co., 1921. (FHL# 974.3/H2c or microfilm 1000619)

Goodrich, John Ellsworth. "Immigration to Vermont." *Vermont Historical Society Proceedings* 1908-09: pp. 65-87. (FHL# 974.3 B2v)

Hemenway, Abby Maria. *Vermont Historical Gazetteer*. 5 vols. Burlington, Vt.: The author, 1869-91. (FHL# 974.3/H2ha; also several microfilmings; see FHLC Locality Catalog under **Vermont/History**)

Atlases, Maps, and Gazetteers

Maps and gazetteers are useful for locating extinct places, small communities, farms, property, highways, watercourses, and other features as they have existed historically. (See Figure 5:1.) Besides several works of national scope that apply to New England research, the library contains a number of statewide atlases and gazetteers:

Connecticut

Gannett, Henry. *A Geographical Dictionary of Connecticut and Rhode Island*. 2 vols. in 1. 1894; rpt. ed., Baltimore: Genealogical Publishing Co., 1978. (FHL# 974/E5g or microfiche 6046786)

Maine

Atwood, Stanley Bearce. *The Length and Breadth of Maine*. Orono, Maine: University of Maine, 1977. (FHL# 974.1/E5a)

Chadbourne, Ava Harriet. *Maine Place Names and the Peopling of Its Towns*. Portland, Maine: Bond Wheelwright Co., 1955. (FHL# 974.1/E5c)

136 GAZETTEER OF MASSACHUSETTS.

Burlington is a small agricultural town, of 105 farms, 124 houses, and 626 inhabitants, in the easterly section of Middlesex County, about 10 miles north-west of Boston, with which it has no direct railroad-communication. The nearest station is at Woburn Centre, 3 miles distant. The boundaries are Bedford and Billerica on the north-west, Wilmington on the north-east, Woburn on the east. and Lexington on the south-west. The surface is broken and uneven; and there are conspicuous eminences at the north, centre, and south, from which admirable landscape-views are obtained. The principal rock is calcareous gneiss and sienite; and the trees are maple, oak, walnut, gray-birch, and pine. A beautiful stream called Vine Brook, an affluent of the Shawshine River, winds through the south-west part of the town, affording water-power for mills, and haunt for the disciples of Izaak Walton. Sources of the Ipswich River also originate in the easterly part of the town. The soil is rather light, but, under skilful cultivation, produces good crops of hay, grain, and culinary vegetables. The town has one saw and one grist mill; also mills, owned by Thomas Barr and Company, for printing woollen fabrics. It has one post-office, a public hall and library, five school-districts, and a Congregational church, organized Oct. 29, 1735, and having for its present pastor the Rev. Alfred S. Hudson, installed Dec. 19, 1867.

The Central Village is pleasantly situated on elevated land; and, with good railroad accommodation, Burlington, being in such close proximity to Boston, would doubtless soon become a very populous and prosperous town.

It sent 82 men (a large number for so small a place) into the late war; and 9 of them were lost.

The town was taken from Woburn, and incorporated Feb. 28, 1799. The number of voters is 212; the valuation, $510,537; and the tax-rate, $1.20 per $100.

Samuel Sewall is the present town-clerk.

Figure 5:1 Page from Elias Nason, *A Gazetteer of the State of Massachusetts* (Boston: B.B. Russell, 1874), 136.

Works Progress Administration, Historical Records Survey. *Counties, Cities, Towns, and Plantations of Maine: A Handbook of Incorporations, Dissolutions, and Boundary Changes*. Portland: Maine Historical Records Survey Project, 1940. (FHL# 974.1/E5b or microfilm 009742 or 012251, item 3)

Eckstrom, Fannie Hardy. "Maine Maps of Historical Interest." *Maine Bulletin* 42 (August 1939): ix-xxxv. (FHL# microfilm 1033802, item 2)

Tower, Fred L., comp. *Maine Arrow Guide*. Portland, Maine: Fred L. Tower, 1939. (FHL# 974.1/E6t)

Maine Geographic Names: Alphabetical Finding List. Reston, Va.: U.S. Geological Survey, 1985. (FHL# 974.1/E5u)

Varney, George Jones. *A Gazetteer of the State of Maine*. Boston: B. B. Russell, 1881. (FHL# 974.1/E5v or microfilm 599175, item 2, or microfiche 6046702)

Massachusetts

Nason, Elias. *A Gazetteer of the State of Massachusetts, with Numerous Illustrations on Wood and Steel*. Boston: B. B. Russell, 1874. (FHL# 974.4/E5n or microfilm 547258, item 1, or microfiche 6046886)

New Hampshire

Charlton, Edwin Arzo. *New Hampshire As It Is*. 3 parts. Claremont, N.H.: Tracy and Sanford, 1855. (FHL# 974.2/H2c or microfilm 823666, item 3) Part 2 is a gazetteer.

Farmer, John, and Jacob B. Moore. *A Gazetteer of the State of New Hampshire.* Concord, N.H.: Jacob B. Moore, 1823. (FHL# 974.2 E5f or microfilm 823666, item 2)

Fogg, Alonzo J. *The Statistics and Gazetteer of New Hampshire, Containing Descriptions of All the Counties, Towns, Villages, also Boundaries and Area of the State and Its Natural Resources.* Tucson, Ariz.: W. C. Cox and Co., 1972. (FHL# microfilm 1000197, item 2)

Hayward, John. *A Gazetteer of New Hampshire, Containing Descriptions of all the Counties, Towns, and Districts in the State, also of its Principal Mountains, Rivers, Waterfalls, Harbors, Islands.* Boston: John P. Jewett, 1849. (FHL# 974.2/E5h, microfilm 823666, item 1, or microfiche 6019968)

Town and City Atlas of the State of New Hampshire. Boston: D. H. Hurd and Co., 1892. (FHL# 974.3/E7r)

Rhode Island

Gannett, Henry. *A Geographical Dictionary of Connecticut and Rhode Island.* 2 vols. in 1. 1894; rpt. ed., Baltimore: Genealogical Publishing Co., 1978. (FHL# 974/E5g or microfiche 6046786)

Wright, Marion I., and Robert J. Sullivan. *The Rhode Island Atlas.* Providence: Rhode Island Publications Society, 1982. (FHL# 974.5/E6w)

Vermont

DeLorme, David. *The Vermont Atlas and Gazetteer.* Yarmouth, Maine: David DeLorme and Co., 1978. (FHL# Q/974.3/E7v)

Hemenway, Abby Maria. *Vermont Historical Gazetteer.* 5 vols. Burlington, Vt.: The author, 1869-91. (FHL# 974.3/H2ha; also several microfilmings) Contains much historical and biographical material.

Thompson, Zadock. *History of Vermont: Natural, Civil, and Statistical*. 3 parts. Burlington, Vt.: The author, 1853. (FHL# 974.3/H2t or microfiche 6064850) Part 3 is a gazetteer.

Many gazetteers and atlases exist for individual New England counties. For holdings, see the FHLC Locality Catalog under **[State]/[County]/Gazetteer** or **[State]/-[County]/Maps**, for example, **Connecticut/Hartford/-Gazetteer.**

Hamilton Child has published a gazetteer for each of the Vermont counties, which contains much historical and biographical information as well as geographical details. The library has all of them except Bennington County. They are cataloged under **Vermont/[County]/History** and **Vermont/[County]/Directories.**

The Family History Library has many state and local maps for New England, either in the map case or on microfilm. Check the FHLC under each of following the headings: **[State]/Maps, [State]/[County]/Maps**, or **[State]/[County]/[Town]/Maps**, for example, **Massachusetts/Suffolk /Boston/Maps.**

Cemetery Records

Private individuals and organizations have transcribed gravestone inscriptions of many New England cemeteries. Transcripts also appear in genealogical and historical periodicals, local histories, genealogical collections, and as separate monographs. The Daughters of the American Revolution has surveyed hundreds of cemeteries in New England. (See *Periodicals and Serials* and *Genealogy* below.)

In compliance with a 1902 law, more than 200 Massachusetts towns have published their vital records, including cemetery inscriptions prior to 1850, listed under "Deaths" in each volume. (See *Vital Records* below for cataloging information.) Vermont's vital records index, consisting of vital information from town record books through 1870, contains information from most of the cemeteries in the state. Some cemetery information is also included for a few of the towns in the Maine index to vital records prior to 1892.

A few major collections of New England cemetery records deserve special notice:

Charles R. Hale Collection. 360 reels. See **Connecticut/Cemeteries** for call numbers.

Over 1 million inscriptions abstracted from over two thousand Connecticut cemeteries, alphabetized in one statewide index arranged by town and cemetery (56 reels). The collection also includes marriage and death notices from Connecticut newspapers; master index to the entire collection is on 157 reels.

Nathan Hale Collection. *Index to Maine Cemetery Records.* 210 reels. See FHLC under **Maine/Cemeteries/Indexes**.

Abstracts cemetery inscriptions from all parts of the state onto one statewide index. Groups families together that appear on the same monument or are otherwise obviously connected, along with separate index entries. (See Figure 5:2.)

Maine Veterans Cemetery Records. 15 reels.

Card index to veterans buried in Maine from King Philip's War to World War I; alphabetical by veteran's name.

Brown, Clarence I., comp. Rhode Island Cemetery and Genealogical Records. 2 reels.

Index to Arnold's Rhode Island Vital Records: Rhode Island Cemetery Records. 10 reels.

Anthony Tarbox Briggs Collection. 19 reels.

A card index of cemetery, vital, probate, genealogical, and historical records.

The library also has separate monographs of many New England cemetery records plus sexton records, cemetery plat records, and plat maps. Check the FHLC under **[State]/[County]/[Town]/Cemeteries.**

Census Records

See the discussion of federal census records in Chapter 4, "United States: General." It is worthy of note, however, that New England's federal census records are among the most complete in the nation. Very few schedules have been lost.

A number of colonial and state census returns are also available for the New England states. These vary greatly

8 MAINE CEMETERY RECORDS 13

INSTRUCTIONS: Copy only what is on stone. Write surnames in CAPITALS. Use separate space for Heads of families, Wives and Wives' former husbands (Mrs. John M. (SMITH) BROWN) and children. Note relationship only when on stones. If too many for front, use back side of form. All surnames of Heads of families, Wives' former husbands, Wives' maiden names and children 15 and over should be on separate sheet. Place additional inscriptions and/or comments on back of form. DOUBLE CHECK.

19. Buckfield Quadrangle - Ox
N4415-W7015/15

This is from the stone of: Nathaniel Thomas

SURNAME	FIRST	MIDDLE
(THOMAS	Capt. Nathaniel	

RELATION TO	BORN	DIED
husband of Sally(Thomas)		Sept. 12,1825

AGE		
45 YEARS	MONTHS	DAYS

NAME OF CEMETERY
North Hartford Schoolhouse Yard or Poland Corner Cemetery. No. 19 on quad map.

STREET/ROUTE	TOWN	COUNTY
At 4 corners on road off Route 140, north of Green Acres Inn.	Hartford	Oxford

LOT NUMBER	TYPE MATERIAL	CHECK LOCATION IN CEMETERY
		☐ N. ☒ E. (3rd row) ☐ S. ☐ W. ☐ CENTER

The following names also appear on this stone
NOTE: Indicate with "X" in box for all those on separate sheet

NAME	BORN	DIED	AGE YRS	AGE MOS	AGE DAYS
☒ Sally Thomas		April 8, 1867	86	4	
☐ (ON separate stones)					
☐ Elisha Thomas, son of Nathaniel & Sally Thomas	(town record) Aug. 20, 1820	May 3, 1846	25		
☐ Ichabod, son of Nathaniel & Sally Thomas		May 8, 1827	22		
☐ Clarinda, dau of Nathaniel & Sally Thomas		Mar. 28, 1827	4		24
☐ Lucy, dau of Nathaniel & Sally Thomas		July 11, 1822	7	3	
☐					
☐					
☐					
☐					

MILITARY SERVICE: Corp. in War with England, 1812-1814. Lt. I. Bartlett's Co. Lt. Col. S. Holland's Regt. (p. 223 of Records of Mass. Militia 1812-1814.) Served at Portland.

SIGNATURE	DATE	ORGANIZATION
Mrs. Frank W. Howard	July 16, 1972	DAR records. Vol. 34, sec. 1

Figure 5:2 Sample entry from Nathan Hale Collection, Index of Maine Cemetery Records.

in the quantity and type of information given. Some were compiled for tax purposes, others for military, or other reasons. A few localities commissioned private censuses to be included in local histories or registers, which are similar to city directories. Some individuals and groups have produced reconstructed censuses–actually compiled lists of residents for a particular time period.

To see holdings for a given state, check the FHLC under **[State]/Census/Year.** Censuses compiled for a single town are cataloged under **[State]/[County]/-[Town]/Census.** For all colonial, state, and local census records for New England available in the library, see *State and Special Census Records*, (6 volumes) located on the index tables in the U.S./Canada reference area. Here is a state-by-state listing of non-federal census records available in the library:

Connecticut

1670 Holbrook, Jay Mack, comp. *Connecticut 1670 Census.* Oxford, Mass.: Holbrook Research Institute, 1977. (FHL# 974.6/X2h/1670)

Names of some 2,300 residents (1660-73) reconstructed from thirty-eight different records.

1776 Willard, Josiah. *A Census of Newington, Connecticut, Taken According to Households in 1776.* ed. Edwin Stanley Welles. Hartford: Frederic B. Hartranft, 1909. (FHL# 974.62/N2/X2p or microfilm 823814, item 3)

Newington took this census to determine the state's tax quota for the new Continental Congress; gives the name of every male resident with date and place of birth.

Maine

1881 Census of Kennebec County. 2 reels. (FHL# microfilm 011316-011317)

Lists each person roughly in alphabetical order with name, sex, age, and race.

1906 Daggett, F. E., T. C. Holt, P. I. Lawton, and George A. Sawyer, comps. *The Saco Register with Old Orchard 1906.* Brunswick, Maine: H. E. Mitchell Co., 1906. (FHL# 974.195/S1/H2m)

An every-name listing taken in 1905-06 of Saco and Old Orchard, Maine; similar to a town directory.

Massachusetts

1837 Census of the town of Danvers. (FHL# microfilm 876100, item 9)

Names heads of household, numbers of males and females, age group of persons, and taxables.

1855 State census of Massachusetts. 31 reels.

Names every person; gives sex, age groups of children and adults, state or country of birth, race, occupation, and miscellaneous facts (blind, disabled, etc.).

1865 State census of Massachusetts. 37 reels.

Names every person; gives sex, age, place of birth, marital status, race, registered voter, naturalized voter, occupation, taxables, and miscellaneous personal data. Only the state or country of birth was required, but many census returns include the town of birth, especially when the town was in Massachusetts.

1912 *Register of Towns of Manchester, Essex, Hamilton and Wenham.* Auburn, Maine: Lawton Register Co., 1912. (FHL# 974.45/X2r)

Similar to city directories.

1915 Gettemy, Charles F., comp. *The Decennial Census, 1915.* Boston: Wright & Potter Printing Co., 1918. (FHL# 974.4/X2m)

Statistical census only.

New Hampshire

1776 Holbrook, Jay Mack, comp. *New Hampshire 1776 Census.* Oxford, Mass.: Holbrook Research Institute, 1976. (FHL# 974.2/X2h/1776)

Alphabetically lists 9,348 male residents of New Hampshire in or about 1776; compiled from lists of signers of the New Hampshire Association Test (document opposing British invasion of the colonies) which represents 44-66 percent of New Hampshire households.

1878 Census of Walpole, New Hampshire. (FHL# 974.29/-W1/H2a)

Taken 1 April 1878 and included in George Aldrich, *Walpole As It Was and As It Is* (Claremont, N.H.: Claremont Manufacturing Co., 1880), 389-404. Names every person; gives place and date of birth and relationship to the head of household.

Rhode Island

1747 A Census of the Freemen of 1747 as Found in the Supplement to the Rhode Island Colonial Record. (FHL # microfilm 022390, item 2)

The library's microfilm is virtually illegible–too light to read.

1774 Bartlett, John R., arr. *Census of the Inhabitants of the Colony of Rhode Island and Providence Plantations Taken by Order of the General Assembly in the Year 1774.* Providence: Knowles, Anthony & Co., State Printers, 1858. (FHL# 974.5/X2pb; original manuscript also available: FHL# microfilm 947359, item 1)

Names heads of household, numbers of males and females over sixteen, numbers of males and females under sixteen, and race.

1777 State census of Rhode Island. (FHL# microfilm 947359, item 2).

Also includes a list of men on the alarm list (a military list in response to an alarm) of Westerly and signers of the Test Act. Names heads of household, age groups of males, residence, race, militia status, and whether Quaker. Women are listed if they are the heads of household.

1782 State census of Rhode Island. (FHL# microfilm 022390, item 1)

Microreproduction of a typescript copy of the original (and incomplete) manuscript. Names each head of household; gives age groups of males and females. A published version which uses tax lists to reconstruct the missing manuscript is Jay Mack Holbrook, comp., *Rhode*

Island 1782 Census (Oxford, Mass.: Holbrook Research Institute, 1979). This version does not include North Providence and Smithfield.

1865 State census of Rhode Island. 14 reels.

Names every person; gives sex, age, place of birth, town of birth if born in state, race, nationality, voter status, occupation, Civil War veteran status, remarks, and miscellaneous personal data. Card index available, 24 reels.

1875 State census of Rhode Island. 9 reels.

Names every person, gives relationship, age, sex, date of birth, state or country of birth (town if in Rhode Island), marital status, race, nationality, voter status, occupation, and miscellaneous personal data.

1885 State census of Rhode Island. 12 reels.

Includes name of every person, relationship, sex, age, place of birth, parents' place of birth, marital status, race, citizenship status, voter status, occupation, and miscellaneous personal data.

Vermont

1771 Holbrook, Jay Mack, comp. *Vermont 1771 Census.* Oxford, Mass.: Holbrook Research Institute, 1982. (FHL# 974.3/X3h)

Reconstruction of a 1771 census conducted by New York which then claimed Vermont and had organized the area into the counties of Cumberland and Gloucester, although most settlers considered themselves to be in the New Hampshire grants. Uses available fragments of the original census supplemented by tax lists, petitions, histories, and other Vermont records.

Church Records

The Congregational Church predominated in New England during the seventeenth and eighteenth centuries, although there were significant numbers of Quakers, Episcopalians, Presbyterians, and Baptists. Large numbers of Irish Catholics arrived in New England during the 1800s, later joined by Polish and Italian Catholics. French-Canadian Catholics frequently drifted into northern New England. The nineteenth century also saw large numbers of Methodists, Lutherans, and Jews arrive from Great Britain and Europe.

Records of many individual churches are available in the library. Congregational church records are by far the most numerous. These are accessed in the FHLC Locality Catalog under **[State]/[County]/[Town]/[Denomination or Church]**.

Kirkham, E. Kay. *Survey of American Church Records*. Logan, Utah: Everton Publishers, 1978. (FHL# 973/K2k)

A guide to American church records; identifies many records available at the library and elsewhere.

The library also has microfilmed the Connecticut State Library's collection of some 600 church registers from all parts of the state. Many of these registers have been indexed, the only major state-wide index of its kind for New England:

Connecticut State Library. 69 reels.

Index cards to vital records of Connecticut churches at the Connecticut State Library. The first Thirty-three reels are a statewide index of alphabetized individual slips of paper each containing a record of admission, baptism, marriage, death, or burial. The remaining thirty-six reels are slip indexes to individual churches not integrated into the statewide index. They are arranged alphabetically by town.

Bailey, Frederic W., ed. *Early Connecticut Marriages as Found on Ancient Church Records Prior to 1800.* 7 vols. in one; rpt. ed., Baltimore: Genealogical Publishing Co., 1968. (FHL# 974.6/V25b)

The library has microfilm copies of many private ministerial records, most of them dating from the nineteenth century. Most New England ministers preached to several different congregations during their careers. Their records are therefore usually cataloged under state headings, unless only one congregation is mentioned in the record. Check the FHLC under **[State]/Church Records.**

Among the more than 200 published volumes of Massachusetts vital records are many entries taken from church records. The compilers of these volumes generally included information from church records when the corresponding entry was missing from the town vital records or if the entry differed from the vital records. (See *Vital Records* below.)

Eighty towns participated in the state's project to collect the town vital records in 1892. A few included church records in the abstracts they supplied to the state. (See *Vital Records* below.)

Many genealogical periodicals have printed New England church records. Foremost among them is the *New England Historical and Genealogical Register,* published continuously since 1847. Many other periodicals and some local histories also include church records. (See *Periodicals* below.)

Church records are also included in several private collections, the largest being the National Society of the Daughters of the American Revolution. (See *Genealogy* below.)

Court Records

New England court records vary from state to state and would require a full-length volume to adequately describe their scope. The library's collection of New England court records range from good to sparse. (See also *Probate Court Records* below.)

Connecticut

The following courts have existed in Connecticut: General Court (later known as the General Assembly) – 1636-1784; Supreme Court of Errors – 1784-1965; Particular Court – 1638-65; County Court – 1666-1855; Court of Assistants – 1665-1711; Superior Court (replaced Court of Assistants) – 1711-present; Maritime Court – 1775-87; Court of Common Pleas (replaced County Courts) – 1869-present; Justice of the Peace – 1686-1961; and Town and Borough Courts – 1600s-1961.

The Family History Library has few Connecticut court records. Check the FHLC under **Connecticut/Public Records** and **Connecticut/[County]/Court Records.** They include:

Trumbull, J. Hammond, ed. *The Public Records of the Colony of Connecticut, 1636-1776.* 15 vols. Hartford, Conn.: Case, Lockwood and Brainard, 1850-90.

Volume 1: General and Particular courts, 1636-49; records of the General Court, 1650-65; wills and inventories, 1640-49; and the Code of Law established by the General Court in May 1650. Volume 2: General Court, 1665-77, plus numerous other colonial period and Revolutionary War documents. (FHL# 974.6/N2c or microfilm 908423)

Hoadly, Charles J., ed. *The Public Records of the State of Connecticut.* 7 vols. Hartford, Conn.: Case, Lockwood and Brainard, 1894.

Continues first work. Its documents are not true court records but relate largely to the Revolutionary War and Connecticut statehood. (FHL# 974.6/N2ct or microfilm 944114-944115)

Records of the Particular Court of Connecticut, 1637-1663. Vol. 22 of *Connecticut Historical Society Collections.* Hartford: Connecticut Historical Society and the Society of Colonial Wars in the State of Connecticut, 1928. (FHL# 974.6/B4c/v.22 or microfilm 897077)

Hoadly, Charles J., ed. *Records of the Colony or Jurisdiction of New Haven, from May 1653 to the Union, Together with the New Haven Code of 1656.* Hartford, Conn.: Case, Lockwood, 1858. (GS #974.6/N2n, microfilm 928602, item 1, or 944116, item 2)

Records of Trials in the County Court of New London County, Connecticut, 1661-1700. (FHL# microfilm 005138)

Maine

While the following courts have existed in Maine, the starting and ending dates of many are unknown or questionable: Proprietary Courts - 1635-52, 1661-68; Provincial Courts - 1680-92; County Courts - 1653-present; Court of Common Pleas (replaced by District Court) - 1687-1839; District Courts (replaced by Supreme Court) - 1839-52; Supreme Courts - 1852-present; Justice of the Peace Courts - 1600s-present; Court of Quarterly Sessions - 1687-1700; Court of General sessions (replaced Court of Quarterly Sessions) - 1700-1831; County Commissioners' Court (replaced Court of General Sessions) - 1831-unknown; Superior Courts created for Cumberland and Kennebec counties - 1868; and Municipal Courts (dates unknown).

The Family History Library has few Maine court records. Many early records of Maine are published in:

Province and Court Records of Maine. 6 vols. Portland: Maine Historical Society, 1928. (FHL# 974.1/P2p; vols. 1-5 also on microfilm 982043 and on microfiche 6046855).

Includes York County court records, 1653-1727. Prior to 1760 all of Maine was in York County.

Until 1820 Maine was in the jurisdiction of Massachusetts. Consequently, many papers from the counties of Cumberland, Lincoln, Washington, and York are in Massachusetts county court files volumes 859-930 (index FHL# microfilm 908878). See discussion of Massachusetts court records below.

The library has these court records cataloged under **Maine/[County]/Court Records:**

Androscoggin County. Some court records with deeds, 1854-78. 47 reels. Court attachments 1854-95. Records are mainly from the Supreme Judicial Court and District Court. (FHL# microfilm 010519)

Cumberland County. Justice of the Peace Court, 1829-66 (FHL# microfilm 012620, item 2)

Hancock County. Real estate transfers and court cases, 1931-44 (FHL# microfilm 1033869, item 2)

Lincoln County. Noyes, Benjamin Lake, comp. "Miscellaneous genealogical papers, Deer Isle, Hancock County, Maine." Contains records of the Court of Common Pleas held at Pownalborough, Lincoln County. (FHL# microfilm 1035912, item 14)

Washington County. Supreme Judicial Court records, 1821-92. 15 reels.

Massachusetts

While the following courts have existed in Massachusetts, the starting and ending dates of many are unknown or questionable: General Court - 1620-1865; Court of Assistants - 1630-92; Justice of the Peace Courts - 1630-present; County Courts (also known as Quarter Courts and Inferior Quarter Courts) - 1636-93; Stranger's or Merchant's Court - 1639-84; Superior Court of Judicature (replaced some duties of County Courts) - 1692-1782; Inferior Court of Common Pleas (called Court of Common Pleas, 1782-1859) - 1686-1859; Court of General Sessions of the Peace - 1692-1862; Supreme Judicial Court (replaced Superior Court of Judicature) - 1782-present; Vice-Admiralty Courts - 1700s; and Municipal Courts (dates unknown).

The Family History Library has microfilmed many Massachusetts court records. A few are also in print.

These records pertain to Massachusetts as a whole and are cataloged in the FHLC under **Massachusetts/-Court Records:**

Massachusetts County Court files, 1629-1799. Includes indexes. 1,639 reels.

Consists of some 250,000 papers bound in 1,285 volumes; originated in the county courts, Court of Assistants, Courts of General Sessions, Courts of Common Pleas, and Superior Courts of Judicature. Arranged by counties including those in Maine and New Hampshire which were under Massachusetts jurisdiction.

Shurtleff, Nathaniel B., and David Pulsifer, eds. *Records of the Colony of New Plymouth in New England.* 12 vols. in 10; Boston: William White, 1855-61. (FHL# 974.4/N2n or microfilm 896852-896856 or microfiche 6046893)

Fiche copy omits volumes 9 and 11. For other complete microfilm copies, see FHLC under **Massachusetts/Court Records.**

Records of the Court of Assistants of the Colony of the Massachusetts Bay, 1630-1692. 3 vols. Boston: Rockwell & Churchill Press, 1901-28. (FHL# 974.4/P2re or microfilm 496679, items 4-6)

Shurtleff, Nathaniel B., ed. *Records of the Governor and Company of the Massachusetts Bay in New England*. 5 vols. in 6. Boston: W. White, 1853-54. (FHL# 974.4/N2s or microfiche 6046893)

These court records are cataloged under **Massachusetts/[County]/Court Records:**

Berkshire County. Court of Common Pleas, 1760-1860. 46 reels.

Bristol County. Circuit Court of Common Pleas, 1780-1868, FHL# microfilm 905544, items 1-3. Court of Common Pleas, 1714-1814, 3 reels. Pleas, 1696-1808, 23 reels. Court of General Sessions, 1702-38, FHL# microfilm 899093, items 5-6. Supreme Judicial Court records, 1797-1861, 4 reels.

Essex County. Circuit Court of Common Pleas, 1811-21, 8 reels. County Court Records, 1638-92, 11 reels. County Court records of (Old) Norfolk County including towns of Salisbury, Haverhill, and Amesbury, now in Essex County, 4 reels. Court of Common Pleas, 1782-1811, 1821-59, 29 reels. Court of General Sessions of the Peace, 1692-1796, 5 reels. Inferior Court of Common Pleas, 1686-1783, 2 reels. Inferior Court of Common Pleas, 1749-1782, 4 reels. Inferior Court of Common Pleas, 1686-1726, 5 reels. Quarterly Court records, 1636-41, FHL# microfilm 877461, item 1. *Records and Files of the Quarterly Courts of Essex County, Massachusetts*, 9 vols. (Salem, Mass.: Essex Institute, 1911-75), covers 1636-86, FHL# 974.45/-P2e or microfilm 873951-873954). Superior Court records, 1859-65, 3 reels. Supreme Judicial Court records, 1797-1826, 10 reels. Witchcraft papers, 1655-1750 (also contains records of Court of Assistants, 1673-92, and the Superior Court of Judicature, 1692-95), (FHL# microfilm 877465, item 2).

Franklin County. Court of Common Pleas, 1823-65 (dockets) and 1812-58 (records), 22 reels. Justices Court records, 1790-92 (FHL# microfilm 902898, item 5). Justices Court records and proceedings kept by Henry Bassett, one of the Justices of the Peace for Franklin County, 1816-38 (FHL# microfilm 902898, item 6). Superior Court records, 1859-67, 2 reels (FHL# microfilm 901086-901087). Supreme Judicial Court index and dockets, 1816-88 and records 1816-71, 6 reels.

Hampden County. Court of Common Pleas, 1812-59, 19 reels. Court of General Sessions of the Peace, 1638-1812, 2 reels (This court was held in Springfield, now in Hampden County. Court records remained in Springfield after division of Hampshire County, 1812.)

Hampshire County. County Court, 1677-1728, FHL# microfilm 886420, item 1). Court of Common Pleas, 1783-1853, 26 reels. Court of Common Pleas, 1854-59, 2 reels, FHL# microfilm 892043-892044. Court of Common Pleas, 1852-59, 1 reel, FHL# microfilm 892045. Court of General Sessions of the Peace, 1638-1812, 2 reels. Court of Sessions, 1800-37, 2 reels. Inferior Court of Common Pleas, 1728-83, 8 reels. Court records, 1663-77, "Waste Book of Hampshire County" (the original notes of the clerk prior to recording in official transcipts) FHL# microfilm 014766, item 2.

Middlesex County. Circuit Court of Common Pleas, 1783-1811, 1821-47, 33 reels. Circuit Court of Common Pleas, 1812-21, 9 reels. County Court records, 1649-99, 2 reels. Court of General Sessions of the Peace, 1686-1809, 3 reels. Court of Sessions, 1808-31, FHL# microfilm 892255. Inferior Court of Common Pleas, 1699-1783, 6 reels. Supreme Judicial Court, 1747-1850, 8 reels. Colonial County Court papers and card index, 34 reels.

Nantucket County. Obed Macy Collection, it's cataloged c.1658-1855 (miscellaneous genealogical material including some court records), 4 reels. Court of Common Pleas, 1721-1859, 4 reels. Court of General Sessions of the Peace, 1721-1816, FHL# microfilm 903862.

Norfolk County. Circuit Court of Common Pleas, 1812-20, 5 reels. Circuit Court of Common Pleas, 1793-1811, 1821-58, 20 reels. Superior Court records, 1859, FHL# microfilm 878202, item 3. Supreme Judicial Court, 1764-1859, 8 reels

Plymouth County. Court of Common Pleas, 1702-1859, 15 reels. Court of General Sessions of the Peace, 1686-1817, 3 reels. Plymouth Colony records, court orders, 1633-90, 2 reels, FHL# microfilm 567792-567793). Plymouth Colony records, laws, and early court records, 1623-76, FHL# microfilm 912073, item 2).

Konig, David Thomas, ed. *Plymouth Court Records, 1686-1859*. 16 vols. (Wilmington, Del.: Michael Glazier, Inc., 1978-81), FHL# 974.482/P2p.

Suffolk County. Works Progress Administration. Historical Records Survey, *Abstract and Index of the Records of the Inferior Court of Pleas (Suffolk County Court) Held in Boston, 1680-1698*. (Boston: Historical Records Survey, 1940), FHL# 974.46/P2h or microfilm 823824, item 5. Madeline Connors, comp., "List of Names Compiled from Old Records" (typescript; chronological index of names taken from court files of the Supreme Judicial Court of Suffolk County and list of the indexes to early court files), FHL# microfilm 902789, item 2. Greenough Collection. (microfilm of 1647-1828 records in Suffolk County courthouse) FHL# microfilm 902795, item 1. County Court records, 1680-92, FHL# microfilm 947731. Court of Admiralty, 1718-72, FHL# microfilm 902790. Court of Common Pleas, 1701-1855, 142 reels. Court of General Sessions of the Peace, 1702-1780, 4 reels. Supreme Judicial Court records, 1686-1799, (records of the Superior Court of Judicature, 1686-1781 and Supreme Judicial Court, 1781-99) 62 reels. *Catalogue of Records and Files in the Office of the Clerk of the Supreme Judicial Court for the County of Suffolk*. (n.p., 1890), FHL# microfilm 974.46/A5c or microfilm 908077, item 2. Supreme Judicial Court partitions and executions, 1694-1856, 6 reels. Supreme Judicial Court dockets, 1790-1870, 37 reels. Supreme Judicial Court records, 1800-04, FHL# 946895, item 1-2. Massachusetts Miscellaneous Papers, 1679-1808 (arranged chronologically), 4 reels. Supreme Judicial Court, index to dockets, equity and probate, 1862-70, FHL# microfilm 947289.

Worcester County. Court of Common Pleas, 1784-1859, 56 reels. Court of General Sessions of the Peace, 1731-1862, 12 reels. Inferior Court of Common Pleas, 1731-84, 8 reels. Franklin P. Rice, comp. *Records of the Court of General Sessions of the Peace for the County of Worcester, Massachusetts from 1731-1737*. (Worcester, Mass.: Worcester Society of Antiquity, 1882), FHL# 974.43/B4w/v.5 or microfilm 864091, item 3.

New Hampshire

Because New Hampshire was under Massachusetts jurisdiction until 1679, many early court records are in Massachusetts. While the following courts have existed in New Hampshire, the starting and ending dates of many are unknown or questionable: Court of General

Quarter Sessions of the Peace – 1692-1771; Court of Appeals – 1714-74; Inferior Court of Common Pleas – 1696-1771; Superior Court of Judicature – 1699-unknown; Supreme Judicial Court – 1800s; and Court of Common Pleas – 1771-unknown.

The following New Hampshire court records are cataloged under **New Hampshire/Court Records:**

State Papers of New Hampshire. 40 vols. Concord: State printer, 1867-1943. Volume 40 only. (FHL# microfilm 1033745, item 2, microfiche 6046775)

Volume 40 contains court records, 1640-92.

Court of General Quarter Session. Minutes, 1695-1771. (FHL# microfilm 980828)

Court of General Quarter Sessions. Court Records, 1730-70. 2 reels. (FHL# microfilm 980937-980938)

Colonial Court records, 1638-1772. Index. 207 microfilm reels.

Court papers, 1659-96. 5 reels.

Court records, 1692-1771. 5 reels.

Court records, 1714-74. (FHL# microfilm 984105, items 2-3)

Inferior Court of Common Pleas, 1696-1771. (FHL# microfilm 980829)

Inferior Court of Common Pleas, 1729-70. 9 reels. Superior Court of Judicature, 1699-1771. 2 reels. (FHL# microfilm 980830-980831)

New Hampshire was divided into counties in 1771, and courts were then established in each county. These records are cataloged in the FHLC under **New Hampshire/[County]/Court Records**:

Belknap County. Court judgements, 1841-99. Indexed. 6 reels.

Carroll County. Supreme Judicial Court judgements, 1861-1900. 4 reels.

Cheshire County. Court of Common Pleas, 1771-1859, 10 reels. Superior Court of Judicature, 1772-1855, 6 reels. Supreme Judicial Court, 1813-1902, 8 reels.

Coos County. Supreme Court judgements 1886-1900, 3 reels.

Grafton County. Court of Common Pleas, 1773-1860, 10 reels. Superior Court of Judicature, 1774-1821, 5 reels.

Hillsborough County. Court of Common Pleas, 1782-1859, 8 reels. Superior Court of Judicature, 1772-1827, 6 reels. Supreme Court judgements, 1855-1901, 38 reels. Court of Common Pleas execution of lawsuits, 3 reels.

The records below are cataloged under **New Hampshire/Court Records:**

Merrimack County. Court of Common Pleas, 1840-67. 4 reels. Supreme Judicial Court records, 1840-1875, and Index, 1824-88, 7 reels. Supreme Judicial Court records, 1876-1900, and index, 1890-1900, 16 reels.

Rockingham County. County Court records of (old) Norfolk County, Massachusetts (included Hampton, Exeter, Dover, and Portsmouth, New Hampshire until 1680), 4 reels. Court of Common Pleas, 1772-1819, 4 reels. Superior Court of Judicature, 1774-1820, 1842-53, and Index 1771-1900, 15 reels.

Strafford County. Inferior Court of Common Pleas, 1773-1859, 8 reels. Superior Court of Judicature, 1773-1874, 13 reels. Supreme Judicial Court, 1855-74, 3 reels. Supreme Judicial Court, 1876-1901, 6 reels.

Sullivan County. Court of Common Pleas, 1827-59. 2 reels. Superior Court of Judicature, 1828-55, FHL# microfilm 1005107, item 1. Supreme Court, 1855-1905, 8 reels.

Rhode Island

While the following courts have existed in Rhode Island, the starting and ending dates of many are unknown or questionable: Quarter Court of Freeman – 1636-40 Court of Election – 1640-1854; General Court – 1640-47; General Court of Trials – 1647-1729; Superior Court of Judicature – 1729-98; Supreme Judicial Court – 1798-1843; Supreme Court – 1843-1905; Superior Court – 1905-present; County Courts of Common Pleas – 1729-1898; County Courts of General Sessions – 1729-1838; Courts of Arbitration – 1640-unknown; Justice Courts – 1729-1886; Courts of Magistrates – 1845-86; District Courts – 1886-present; Court of Admiralty – 1653-unknown; Court of Vice-admiralty – 1697-1776; Admiralty Court – 1767-89 (known as Maritime Court 1776-80); Court of Equity – 1741-44; and Municipal Courts (dates unknown).

The Family History Library's collection of Rhode Island court records is relatively small. These records are cataloged in the FHLC under **Rhode Island/Court Records:**

Court of Admiralty. Papers, 1726-1786. 6 reels.

Court of Admiralty. Minute books, 1727-1783. (FHL# microfilm 954916)

Court of Equity, 1741-1743 (FHL# microfilm 954936, item 2)

Rhode Island Court Records: Records of the Court of Trials of the Colony of Providence Plantations, 1647-1670. 2 vols. Providence: Rhode Island Historical Society, 1920-22. (FHL# 974.5/P2r)

Towle, Dorothy S., ed. *Records of the Vice-admiralty Court of Rhode Island, 1716-1752.* 1936; rpt. ed., Milwood, N.Y.: Kraus Reprint, 1975. (FHL# 974.5/P2v)

Petitions to the General Assembly, 1725-1867. Index. 78 microfilm reels.

Supreme Court. Records, Fines, and Recoveries, 1671-1901. 9 reels.

Two Rhode Island county court records have been filmed and are cataloged under **Rhode Island/[County]/Court Records:**

Newport County. Court of Common Pleas, 1730-1881. 15 reels.

Washington County. Court of Common Pleas, 1731-1880. 13 reels.

Vermont

While the following courts have existed in Vermont, the starting and ending dates of many are unknown or questionable: County Courts – 1777-present; Superior Court (dates unknown); Supreme Court (dates unknown); Justice of the Peace Courts – 1786-present; Court of Common Pleas (dates unknown); Court of Quarter Sessions (dates unknown); and Municipal Courts (dates unknown).

Some early court matters were settled at Portsmouth, New Hampshire, or Albany, New York, prior to 1777. New York created Gloucester County in 1770; its 1770-74 court records are published:

The Upper Connecticut: Narratives of Its Settlement and Its Part in the American Revolution. Montpelier: Vermont Historical Society, 1943, Vol. 2, pp. 141-92. (FHL# 974.3/B2vh/v.4)

This two-volume work constitutes Volume 4 of *Collections of the Vermont Historical Society, 10 vols., Montpelier: Vermont Historical Society, 1870-1947.*

The library has court records for only two Vermont counties under **Vermont/[County]/Court Records**:

Bennington County. Miscellaneous county records, 1782-1832. Includes some court records. 2 reels. (FHL# microfilm 027962-027963)

Orange County. Miscellaneous county records, 1770-81. Includes some court records. (FHL# microfilm 028622)

Directories

The Family History Library has a large collection of directories from New England covering towns, counties, and states. State directories are usually business directories only. These, however, can be quite useful when you know an ancestor's occupation. County directories may be business directories, household directories, or a combination of both. They are usually subdivided for each town within the county and are cataloged in the FHLC under both county and major cities in the county. City directories frequently include sections for nearby towns. These, too, are usually cataloged in the FHLC under all major city and town headings.

Directories are, therefore, located in the FHLC under three headings: **[State]/Directories, [State]/[County]/Directories**, and **[State]/[County]/[City]/Directories.**

The majority of the library's directories, particularly the older ones (1700s-1901), are not cataloged in the current FHLC 1987, because they represent recent acquisitions in microform of city and town directories produced by Research Publications. A guide to the collection is:

City Directories of the United States, 1860-1901. Woodbridge, Conn./Reading, England: Research Publications, 1983. (FHL# 973/E43c)

Available in the U.S./Canada reference area. The title is misleading, as the guide includes many works published before 1860.

Genealogy

New England's important genealogical collections can often greatly reduce the time necessary to identify an ancestor. These range from the collections of lineage societies, such as the Daughters of the American Revolution and the Society of Mayflower Descendants, to the private files of various New England researchers.

For complete holdings, check the FHLC under **[State]/Genealogy** or **United States/Genealogy.** (Many collections involve more than one state.) When the collection contains more than one record type it is usually indexed under the record type as well (i.e., **[State]/-Cemeteries** or **[State]/Vital Records,** etc.). Many of the DAR collections are cross-referenced under six or more headings; they can always be accessed under **/Cemeteries.** Except as noted, the following records are cataloged under **[State]/Genealogy** or **United States/-Genealogy:**

New England, General

Bennett, Archibald F. Family Genealogical Records Alphabetically Arranged by Family. 19 reels.

Calef, Frank T. Genealogies of New England Families Descended from a "Mayflower" Ancestor. Card index. 18 reels.

Daughters of the American Revolution collections. Check the Author/Title FHLC under **Daughters Of The American Revolution/ [State or Chapter]** or the Locality FHLC under **[State]/Genealogy** (or **/Bible Records, /Cemeteries, /Vital Records,** etc.).

The DAR collection for each state generally includes cemetery inscriptions, vital records, military records, Bible records, and other record groups compiled into volumes. Arrangement varies from state to state. No central index, but indexes for many volumes. See state-by-state listing below. Note: The DAR Massachusetts collection has not yet been entered on the FHLC; until entered, consult the camera operators reports behind U.S./Canada Reference Desk. Film numbers can be obtained from two large binders describing the contents of each film.

Haug, Gladys Elizabeth, comp. *Early New England Families.* 20 reels. Arranged alphabetically by family. Indexed.

Rider, Fremont, ed. *The American Genealogical/Biographical Index to American Genealogical, Biographical, and Local History Materials.* 143 vols. Middletown, Conn.: Godfrey Memorial Library, 1952-86. (FHL# 973/D22ag) Indexes many New England family histories, the 1790 census, and the genealogical column of the *Boston Evening Transcript.* (See *Newspapers* below.) Arranged alphabetically and is now complete for surnames A-R. New volumes are added annually.

Haseltine Papers. 23 reels. A collection of family histories, vital records, and cemetery records concentrating on Essex County, Massachusetts, and Rockingham County, New Hampshire; includes other areas as well. Some of the records appear only in this collection. Catalogued only in the Author/Title FHLC under Haseltine Papers, where the contents are described in full. No current cross reference in the Locality Catalog.

Woodworth, Emmett Huling, comp. Mayflower Register. 14 reels. Card index arranged alphabetically by family.

Society of Mayflower Descendants (California). 53 reels. Family group records arranged alphabetically by family.

Connecticut

Lucius B. Barbour Collection. 98 reels. Check the FHLC under **Connecticut/Vital Records** for call numbers.

The most important Connecticut collection. Abstracts on separate slips of nearly all Connecticut vital records prior to 1850, arranged alphabetically by surname. Includes typescripts of most Connecticut vital records arranged alphabetically by town. (Since this format blurs the family group format that prevails in most New England town record books, distinguishing between children of persons with the same surname sometimes requires examining the original records.)

Bible Records of Connecticut. 8 reels.

Alphabetical arrangement of family Bible entries from the Connecticut State Library Bible collection. Cataloged under **Connecticut/Bible Records.**

Bowman Collection. 2 reels.

Index cards to Connecticut death notices in Massachusetts newspapers, 1800-1900, alphabetically arranged. Cataloged under **Connecticut/Newspapers.**

Daughters of the American Revolution Collection (Connecticut). 24 reels.

Includes cemetery, church, vital, Bible, and probate records arranged by county. Some volumes indexed. Cataloged under **Connecticut/Collected Works.**

Charles R. Hale Collection. 360 reels.

Collection of death and marriage notices (in separate sections) from over 100 Connecticut newspapers and cemetery inscriptions from over 2,000 Connecticut cemeteries from early period to about 1865 (later in some areas). Dates vary widely. Earliest newspapers from 1764 through 1866. Entries on separate slips filed alphabetically. Indexed. Cataloged under **Connecticut/-Cemeteries, /Newspapers,** and **/Vital Records.**

Lucius M. Boltwood Research Collection. 11 reels.

Includes family records, vital records, and other materials from Connecticut and western Massachusetts, 1650-1850.

Sylvester Judd Manuscripts.

Includes land, vital, and town records from Connecticut and Massachusetts, 1635-1850. Cataloged under Connecticut/Vital Records and **/Town Records.**

Jones, Edward P., comp. *300 Early Families of Connecticut.* 10 vols. 2 reels. (FHL# microfilm 003058 -003059)

Arranged alphabetically by family.

Maine

Daughters of the American Revolution Collection (Maine). 18 reels.

Bible, cemetery, family, land, probate, vital, and other records, collected 1925-72 and arranged by year of submission. Most volumes indexed. Cataloged under **Maine/Cemeteries, /Vital Records, /Genealogy,** etc.

Maine Family Records. 10 reels.

Miscellaneous papers and genealogies, arranged alphabetically by family. Some indexes.

Piscataqua Pioneers. Applications for membership, 1908-1978. 3 reels.

Alphabetically arranged lineage papers of over 1,000 descendants of the first settlers of New Hampshire and Maine. The Society of Piscataqua Pioneers was organized in 1905 by descendants of the early settlers of the Piscataqua Valley, which forms the border between Maine and New Hampshire.

Massachusetts

Catalogue of Manuscripts of the Massachuestts Historical Society. 7 vols. Boston: G. K. Hall & Co., 1969. (FHL# Q/974.4 A3m)

Walter E. Corbin and Lottie S. Corbin Manuscript Collection. 60 reels. See FHLC under **Massachusetts/Genealogy** for call numbers.

Local histories, church records, vital records, Bible records, cemetery records, genealogies and source notes arranged by county and town. Concentrates on families of central and western Massachusetts.

Daughters of the American Revolution Collection (Massachusetts). 43 reels.

Cemetery, vital, Bible, church, land, family, and probate records. Not yet cataloged in the FHLC. Consult camera operators' reports, see the notation under **/Genealogy.**

Johnson, John French. Genealogies and Family Histories of Many Massachusetts and New England Families. 6 reels.

Partial index. Arranged by family.

Genealogical Papers of Harry Gay Fletcher. 2 reels. microfilm

Histories, diaries, inventories, wills, deeds, town records, vital records, and family records. Indexed.

Holliston Historical Society Collections, 1585-1960. 51 vols. 14 reels.

Arranged alphabetically by family.

See also Judd Manuscripts and Lucius M. Boltwood Collection described under Connecticut.

New Hampshire

Daughters of the American Revolution Collection (New Hampshire). 15 reels.

Vital records, cemetery records, church records, historical records, and Bible records arranged by town. Some volumes indexed. Cataloged under **New Hampshire/Cemeteries, /Church Records, /Vital Records, /History,** and **/Genealogy.**

Haseltine Papers. (See *New England, General*).

Piscataqua Pioneers. (See *Maine*)

Provincial and State Papers of New Hampshire. 40 vols. 21 reels. 149 microfiche. Concord, N.H.: State Printer, 1867-1943. (FHL# 974.2/N2nhp, or microfiche 6046775)

Legislative records, Revolutionary War documents, town charters, township grants, probate records, and court records. Cataloged under **New Hampshire/Land and Property.** Microfilm copy is complete. Microfiche contains vols. 8, 11-13, 17-18, 30-40. Shelf copy includes vols. 1-15, 17-32, 34-40.

Rhode Island

Louise Prosser Bates Collection of Genealogical Data of Rhode Island Families. 88 volumes plus index. 23 reels.

Anthony Tarbox Briggs Collection. 19 reels.

Card index of cemetery records, vital records, wills, genealogies, and historical records.

Clarence I. Brown Collection of Rhode Island Cemetery and Genealogical Records. 2 reels. (FHL# microfilm 022473, 002474)

From private and family cemeteries. Cataloged under **Rhode Island/Cemeteries/Indexes.**

Daughters of the American Revolution Collection (Rhode Island). 23 reels.

Cemetery records, pension records, and probate records. Indexed. Cataloged under **Rhode Island/-Cemeteries** and **/Genealogy.**

Durfee, Grace Stafford, comp. Genealogical Records of the Durfee and Stafford and Allied Families. 14 reels. Arranged alphabetically by family.

Vermont

Daughters of the American Revolution Collection (Vermont). 14 reels.

Cemetery, vital, and family records. Arranged by area. Many volumes individually indexed. Cataloged under **Vermont/Collected Works, /Cemeteries, /Census, /Military Records,** and **/Vital Records.**

Daughters of the American Revolution Collection (Vermont). 20 vols. individually indexed. 6 reels.

Bible, church, cemetery, town, vital, family, military, tax, and other records. Cataloged under **Vermont/Bible Records, /Genealogy, /Cemeteries, /Church Records, /Land and Property, /Town Records**, and **/Vital Records.**

State Papers of Vermont. 17 vols. Montpelier: Secretary of State, 1918-69. (FHL# 974.3/B4s)

Includes town charters, petitions, laws, and legislative records.

Genealogical Dictionaries

For well over a century, New Englanders have endeavored to catalog the names of their colonial ancestors. As a result, several genealogical dictionaries are available to the New England researcher today. (See Figure 5:3.) The works of James Savage, John Osborne Austin, Charles Henry Pope, and John Farmer were early standards in the field. The most comprehensive dictionary is:

Noyes, Sybil, Charles Thorton Libby, and Walter Goodwin Davis. *Genealogical Dictionary of Maine and New Hampshire.* 1928-39; rpt. ed., Baltimore: Genealogical Publishing Co., 1983. (FHL# 974/D2n or microfilm 476892, item 1; 599337, item 4; and microfiche 6046621)

This section also includes similar genealogical works of a lesser scope but excludes purely biographical works. Many New England compiled biographies exist and are particularly helpful for prominent individuals. See the FHLC under **[State]/Biography, [State]/County/Biography,** and **[State]/[County]/[Town]/ Biography.** Many town and local histories also contain virtual genealogical dictionaries of the area's early settlers. See, for example, the works of William Richard Cutter, who has compiled several extensive volumes of genealogical and biographical material relating to New England families. The Cutter works are collections of biographies, not a reference to town and local histories.

Genealogical dictionaries and related regional compilations are cataloged in the FHLC under **[State]/-Genealogy.** Here is a state-by-state listing of major works:

New England, General

Austin, John Osborne. *One Hundred and Sixty Allied Families.* 1893; rpt. ed., Baltimore: Genealogical Publishing Co., 1977. (FHL# 974/D2a)

Cutter, William Richard, comp. *New England Families Genealogical and Memorial.* 4 vols. New York: Lewis Historical Publishing Co., 1913-14. (FHL# 974/D2c)

Cutter's voluminous works have been indexed: Norma Olin Ireland and Winifred Irving. (FHL# 974/D2ci or microfilm 1036507, item 6). Do not rely exclusively on Cutter genealogies in research, as they contain numerous errors.

Farmer, John. *A Genealogical Register of the First Settlers of New England.* 1829; rpt. ed. with corrections and additions by Samuel G. Drake, Baltimore: Genealogical Publishing Co., 1969. (FHL# 974/D2f or microfilm 874195, item 2)

Holmes, Frank R. *Directory of the Ancestral Heads of New England Families, 1620-1700.* Baltimore: Genealogical Publishing Co., 1964. (FHL# 974/E4p)

Savage, James. *A Genealogical Dictionary of the First Settlers of New England, Showing Three Generations of Those Who Came before May 1692 on the Basis of Farmer's Register.* 4 vols. 1860-62; rpt. ed., Baltimore: Genealogical Publishing Co., 1969. (FHL# 974/D2s)

Improved and greatly enlarges Farmer, although it contains some errors and omissions.

Connecticut

Cutter, William Richard. *Genealogical and Family History of the State of Connecticut.* 4 vols. New York: Lewis Historical Publishing Co., 1911. (FHL# 974.6/D2c or microfilm 1000146)

Roberts, Gary Boyd, ed. *Genealogies of Connecticut Families from the New England Historical and Genealogical Register.* 3 vols. Baltimore: Genealogical Publishing Co., 1983. (FHL# 974.6/D2g)

Goodwin, Nathaniel. *Genealogical Notes or Contributions to the Family History of Some of the First Settlers of Connecticut and Massachusetts.* Hartford: F. A. Brown, 1856. (FHL# 974/D2g or microfilm 238325)

Hinman, Royal Ralph. *A Catalogue of the Names of the Early*

HULL 359 HUNKING

Taxed Portsm., fisherman, 1713; mariner Newington 1716; Portsm. same yr. when she was recd. into covt. So.Ch.; witn. John Abbott's deed 1717, presum. one of his crew, and two deeds of Wid. Sarah Leavitt 1723; taxed 1727. 9 ch. bp. So.Ch. 1716-1729, incl. **James**, b. Manchester 27 Aug. 1710, m. ab. 1732 Hannah Matthews; **Elizabeth**, bp. 1718, m. 18 Apr. 1735 Thos. Harwood of Chatham, Kent, Eng.; two **Dionysias**. None bp. aft. 1729, tho she had lately had a ch. in 1734, when s. **William** bp. 1716, brot stolen sheep to the ho. to be dressed. See (4), (9).

HUMBER, 1 **Edward**, blacksmith, Salem 1665-72, had sent for his w. in 1669. In 1673 he bot on Smuttinose, where John Short agreed in Nov. to work for him six mo. Sold to John Shute 1675; same yr. as a Shoals fisherman was indebted to Robt. Paine, sr.

2 **HUMPHREY**, Mr., scrivener, Hampton 1645. In 1653 he witn. for Wm. Fifield; depos. Mar. 1653-4 ab. being in Rowley; fined Hampt. Ct. Oct. 1654 for telling a lie, bondsm. Wm. Fifield and John Sanborn. John Philbrook's depos. used in Salem Ct. June 1662, copy by H. H. List 323.

HUMPHREY, principally found in south-eastern England.

1 **JEREMIAH** (also Umfress), Richmond Isl. 1648, pd. wages by R. Jordan. A link with (2) is Thos. Kennedy, a witn. with him to Jordan's deed 3 Mar. 1657-8; Y. D. i. 87. Saco 1658. Lists 21, 244a.

2 **THOMAS**, distiller, Oyster River, Kennebec. Taxed O. R. 1659, recd. inhab. 16 July 1660; O. F. 5 June 1661. He owned near Plum Brook Swamp with no rec. of gr. or purch., and abutted John Ault as late as Nov. 1678. See (1); see also Kennedy. At Kennebec he witn. a Parker deed 17 Dec. 1661, the same day his Head was named in ano. Parker deed. In 1664 swore to an acct. due him from est. of Mrs. Ludecas, whose adm. Jas. Middleton was later his partn. on Kennebec Riv. Jury N. H., 1661, 1663; Gr. j. Casco 1666. Clerk of the Writs for Kennebec, Sagadahoc and Pejepscot 1665; O. A. to King 8 Sept. 1665, Constable same date. Under Mass. he took O. F. in 1674, contin. as Constable and Clerk of Writs, and was made Sergt. for Sagadahoc and Kennebec; Marshal for co. of Devon. Lists 361a, 362b, 356g, 182, 15, 83, 183, 191. M. Hannah Lane (Geo.), 23 Dec. 1665, at Hingham, where one T. H., adult, had been bap. 19 July 1660. Both last found 9 June 1675, acknowl. a deed. Sarah (Hackett) Smith testif. he was k. by Ind. Her fa.'s will 16 Oct. 1688 named her sons, not her: **George**, d. Hingham 17 June 1732, ag. 68. Will names w. Elizabeth (m. 16 Feb. 1686-7) and 6 of 8 ch., giving to Thos. and Wm. his land at Harwich on the Kennebec, yet in 1742 s. John deeded 1/4 of his fa.'s land there 'willed to me.' **William. Ebenezer. Joseph**, Hingham.

HUNKING.

1 **BENTON**, N. H. Probate 1.41. Read Beaton, w. of (2).

2 **HERCULES**, fishing master, Star Isl., and cred. of Stephen Sargent's est. 1649; likely the same bap. at St. Stephens by Saltash, co. Cornwall, 13 June 1604, s. of Hercules, gr. s. of Roger, br. of (6). Fined for not serving on Gr. j. 1650; granted 50 a. in 1652. Com. t. e. s. c. See Boaden(9). Removing to Portsm. he occup. ho. and 50 a. bot in 1652 from Roger Knight, who confirmed to John Hunking 24 Oct. 1671. Selectm. 1658. Lists 301, 323, 324, 326a. If the man of Stonehouse, Plymouth, who m. Christian Leane 16 Sept. 1627, and had daus. Elizabeth and Joan, bp. 27 June 1634, his will 21 Aug. 1659 ment. neither but only w. (unnamed), dau. Ann and her ch. Inv. 6 Sept. 1659, incl. 3 boats, and ho. and stage on Star Isl. he had enjoyed 10 yrs.; sworn to in Essex Ct. by wid. Beaton Hunking 8 Nov. 1659. She m. 2d Wm. Hearl(4). Ch: **Ann** (Agnes), b. ab. 1630, m. John Hunking (3).

3 **JOHN**, Mr., Star Isl., Portsm., poss. an outsider, or relat. to (2) bef. he m. his dau. Ann, who was liv. 1671-2, ±42. List 331c. Star Isl. 1652, selling without lic. Com. t. e. s. c., Shoals, 1660, 1670, 1677. Selectm. Portsm. 1663, 1667-8, 1671. Gr. j. 1669, 1677, 1680, 1681. See Broad(4). Guardian of Benj. Cotton(1) 1679. Master of the ·Endeavor· and owner in other vessels 1681. Com. Ensign 1680, but called Sergt. 1681. Lists 326ac, 330ab, 323, 324, (?47), 305c, 306cd, 331ab, 54, 49, 50, 51, 329. Will 25 Aug. 1681—7 June 1682 names 2d w. Richord (m. by 1679), 6 ch. She m. 2d Geo. Snell; will, resid. in Boston 24 Sept. 1691—23 Apr. 1695 names s. Geo. Littlejohn of Halwel, co. Devon, a sis. in Eng., and gives £10 to step-dau. Elizabeth H. Ch. by 1st w: **John**, b. 2 Mar. 1651-2, d. in Eng. July 1666. **Hercules**, b. 11 July 1656, not in will. **John**, b. 6 Apr. 1660. **Peter**, b. 20 Mar. 1662-3, inher. ho. and land where John Light liv. and 20 a. adj. Wm. Cotton. In 1688, at Barbadoes, bound sudd. to sea, he gave P/A to Rich. Hyat, mercht., Piscataqua, Nich. Hunking a witn. The way for 60 yrs. bet. land of Peter and Elizabeth given them by their fa., ment. in 1721. **Agnes**, b. 2 June 1665; inher. little ho. on Great Isl. adj. Fabes, and a seal ring marked A. H. Poss. she who o. c. No. Ch. 17 Oct. 1708, when Wm.'s w. and ch. bp. **William**,

Figure 5:3 Page from Sybil Noyes, et. al., *Genealogical Dictionary of Maine and New Hampshire.* (1928-39; rpt. ed., Baltimore: Genealogical Publishing Co., 1983), 359.

Puritan Settlers of the Colony of Connecticut. 1 vol. in 2 parts. 1846; rpt. ed., Hartford: E. Gleason, 1946. (FHL# 974.6/D2hra or microfilm 908908, item 2)

The Society of Colonial Wars in the State of Connecticut Register of Pedigrees and Services of Ancestors. Hartford: The Society, 1941. (FHL# 974.6/D2s)

Maine

Little, George Thomas, comp. *Genealogical and Family History of the State of Maine*. 4 vols. New York: Lewis Historical Publishing Co., 1909. (FHL# 974.1/D2L or microfilm 1000058; microfiche 6051259, vols. 1, 3, 4 only)

Noyes, Sybil, Charles Thorton Libby, and Walter Goodwin Davis. *Genealogical Dictionary of Maine and New Hampshire*. 1928-39; rpt. ed., Baltimore: Genealogical Publishing Co., 1983. (FHL# 974/D2n or microfilm 476892. item 1; 599337, item 4; microfiche 6046621)

Prugh, Dallas Wylie, comp. *Piscataqua Pioneers, 1623-1775: Register of Members and Ancestors, 1905-1967.* Somerville Printing Co. for Piscataqua Pioneers, 1969. (FHL# 974/C4p)

The Society of Piscataqua Pioneers was organized in 1905 by descendants of the early settlers of the Piscataqua Valley, which forms the border between Maine and New Hampshire. Part two of this work is a catalog of many of the early settlers of this region.

Pope, Charles Henry. *The Pioneers of Maine and New Hampshire from 1623-1660.* 1908; rpt. ed., Baltimore: Genealogical Publishing Co., 1965. (FHL# 974/D2po)

Massachusetts

Cutter, William Richard. *Genealogical and Personal Memoirs Relating to the Families of Boston and Eastern Massachusetts.* 4 vols. New York: Lewis Historical Publishing Co., 1908. (FHL# microfilm 1035606, item 3)

The library does not have Volume 3.

______. *Genealogical and Personal Memoirs Relating to the Families of the State of Massachusetts.* 4 vols. in 8. New York: Lewis Historical Publishing Co., 1910. (FHL# 974.4/ D2c, microfilm 905528-905529, or microfiche 6051241)

Davis, William Thomas. *Genealogical Register of Plymouth Families.* 1899; rpt. ed., Baltimore: Genealogical Publishing Co., 1975. (FHL# 974.7/d23d or microfilm 1036201, item 23)

Roberts, Gary Boyd. *Genealogies of Mayflower Families from the New England Historical and Genealogical Register.* 3 vols. Baltimore: Genealogical Publishing Co., 1985. (FHL# 974.4/D2gm)

Goodwin, Nathaniel. *Genealogical Notes or Contributions to the Family History of Some of the First Settlers of Connecticut and Massachusetts.* Hartford: F. A. Brown, 1856. (FHL# 974/D2g or microfilm 238325)

Pope, Charles Henry. *Pioneers of Massachusetts*. 1900; rpt. ed., Baltimore: Genealogical Publishing Co., 1965. (FHL# 974.4/D2p, microfilm 924405, item 1, or microfiche 6046669)

Register of the Massachusetts Society of Colonial Dames of America, 1893-1905. Boston: The Society, 1905. (FHL# 974.4/D2n)

Editions for 1917, 1927, and 1944 are also available.

New Hampshire

Genealogical Dictionary of Maine and New Hampshire. See Maine.

Piscataqua Pioneers, 1623-1775: Register of Members and Ancestors, 1905-1967. See Maine.

Pope, Charles Henry. *The Pioneers of Maine and New Hampshire from 1623-1660.* See Maine.

Stearns, Ezra S., comp. *Genealogical and Family History of the State of New Hampshire*. 4 vols. New York: Lewis Publishing Co., 1908. (FHL# 974.2/D2s, microfilm 1000198, or microfiche 6046857)

Library has vols. 1, 2, 4 only in the shelf copy; microform copies are complete.

Rhode Island

Austin, John Osborne. *The Ancestral Dictionary*. Central Falls, R.I.: E. L. Freeman, [c.1891]. (FHL# 974.5/D2aj or microfilm 1035200, item 6).

______. *The Genealogical Dictionary of Rhode Island Comprising Three Generations of Settlers Who Came before 1690.* Albany, N.Y.: Joel Munsell's Sons, 1887. (FHL# microfilm 022257)

For additions and corrections by G. Andrews Moriarty, see *The American Genealogist* 19: 129 (Jan. 1943), 221 (Apr. 1943); 20: 53 (July 1943), 112 (Oct. 1943), 181 (Jan. 1944), 223 (Apr. 1944).

Genealogies of Rhode Island Families from Rhode Island Periodicals. 2 vols. Baltimore: Genealogical Publishing Co. 1983. (FHL# 974.5/D2g)

Immigration Records

Most immigration records for New England consist of passenger arrival lists commencing in the early 1800s. Some colonial passenger lists and lists of immigrants have been located in British records and published (see below). A third class of records consists of lists of immigrants gleaned from a variety of primary and secondary sources. Although not actual immigration records, these published directories of immigrants are sometimes a valuable tool for tracing immigrant ancestors. A helpful work dealing with New England immigrant families is this collection of articles reprinted from the *Register*:

Roberts, Gary Boyd, ed. *English Origins of New England Families from the New England Historical and Genealogical Register.* 6 vols. in two series. Baltimore: Genealogical Publishing Co., 1985. (FHL# 974/D2e)

Most New England immigrants came through the port of Boston, both in colonial and recent times. Others came through New York and arrived in New England by land. Still others came through minor ports in New England such as Providence, New Bedford, and Portland.

Port arrival lists began in Boston in 1820. These records usually state the name of the immigrant, age, sex, occupation, origin, and destination. Frequently, though not always, the last two categories contain no more information than the name of a country. Lists are chronological by vessel and date of arrival.

Here is a list of passenger arrival records for New England ports filmed at the National Archives and available in the Family History Library. They are cataloged in the FHLC Locality Catalog under **[State]/[County]/[City]/Emigration and Immigration.** Most of these records are also included in the binder "U.S. Passengers" found on the index tables in the U.S./Canada reference area. Indexes exist for some port records but not for all years or all ports. Some of the more recently acquired passenger lists are not yet cataloged in the FHLC.

Boston. Passenger lists, 1820-91, and index 1848-91, 397 reels. Passenger lists, 1891-1935, and index 1902-20, 349 reels *New Bedford, Massachusetts.* Passenger lists, 1902-42, indexed 1902-54, 10 reels. (See Figure 5:4.)

Providence. Index books to passenger lists, 1911-34, 15 reels. Passenger lists, 1911-30. 9 reels.

Portland. Passenger lists, 1893-1943, 33 reels. Book indexes to Passenger lists, 1907-30, 12 reels.

The National Archives also has a supplemental index to passenger lists of vessels arriving at Atlantic and Gulf Coast ports (excluding New York) for 1820-74. It includes Boston and New Bedford but excludes lesser New England ports. The index is a card file alphabetically arranged by the name of each immigrant. The microfilm copies at the Family History Library on 188 reels are often very difficult to read. See the binder "U.S. Passengers" at the U.S./Canada reference tables or the FHLC under **United States/Emigration and Immigration/Indexes.**

The Family History Library also has microfilm copies of the National Archives collection of passenger lists at miscellaneous ports on the Atlantic and Gulf Coast and ports on the Great Lakes, 1820-73. These are very minor ports generally with few records. They are not indexed. New England ports in this collection (with their microfilm numbers) follow: Bangor, Maine, 1848–Barnstable, Maine, 1820-26–Bath, Maine, 1825-67–Beaufort, Maine, 1865–Belfast, Maine, 1820-51–Bridgeport, Conn., 1870–Bristol and Warren, R.I., 1820-71 (FHL# 830231); Dighton, Mass., 1820-36–Edgartown, Mass., 1820-70–Fairfield, Conn., 1820-21–Fall River, Mass., 1837-65 (FHL# 830232); Frenchman's Bay, Maine, 1821-27(FHL# 830233); Gloucester, Maine, 1820-70–Hartford, Conn., 1837–Hingham, Mass., 1852–Kennebunk, Maine, 1820-42–Marblehead, Mass., 1820-49 (FHL# 830234); Nantucket, Mass., 1820-67–New Bedford, Mass., 1826-52–Newburyport, Mass., 1821-39–New Haven, Conn., 1820-73 (FHL# 830235); New London, Conn., 1820-47–Newport, R.I., 1820-57 (FHL# 830236); Passamaquoddy, Maine, 1820-59 (FHL# 830237-830238); Penobscot, Maine, 1851 (FHL# 830238); Portland and Falmouth, Maine, 1820-68 (FHL# 830239-830244); Portsmouth, N.H., 1820-61 (FHL# 830245); Providence, R.I., 1820-67 (FHL# 830245-830246); and Salem, Mass., 1865-66–Saybrook, Conn., 1820–Waldoboro, Maine, 1820-33–Yarmouth, Maine, 1820 (FHL# 830246).

Published immigration sources pertaining exclusively or primarily to New England are listed below. Works dealing with the United States in general have been excluded. Many of the general works contain records of New England passengers, but such publications frequently focus on a particular ethnic group or nationality. Consult the FHLC under **United States/Emigration and Immigration.** Most published U.S. immigration sources, including those listed below, have been indexed in:

Filby, P. William, comp., with Mary K. Meyer. *Passenger and Immigration Lists Index: A Guide to Published Arrival Records of about 500,000 Who Came to the United States and Canada in the Seventeenth, Eighteenth, and Nineteenth Centuries.* 3 vols. Detroit: Gale Research Co., 1981. (FHL# 973/W32p)

Five supplements published 1982-86. Vols. 1-4 of supplements are cumulative adding 650,000 names in one alphabetical series. The 1986 supplement is a separate index adding another 125,000 names.

Ames, Azel. *The Mayflower and Her Log, July 15, 1620-May 6, 1621.* Boston: Houghton, Mifflin, 1901. (FHL# 974.4/W2a or microfilm 833390)

An Abstract of the List of Alien Passengers Bonded under the Law of May 10, 1848. 3 vols. Boston: Dutton and Wentworth, 1851. (FHL# microfilm 864089)

Banks, Charles Edward. *The English Ancestry and Homes of the Pilgrim Fathers Who Came to Plymouth on the "Mayflower" in 1620, the "Fortune" in 1621 and the "Anne" and the "Little James" in 1623.* New York: Grafton Press, 1929. (FHL# microfilm 590442 or FHL# 974/W2be--rpt. ed., Baltimore: Genealogical Publishing Co., 1968)

______. *The Planters of the Commonwealth: A Study of Emigrants and Emigration in Colonial Times, 1620-1640.* 1930; rpt. ed., Baltimore: Genealogical Publishing Co., 1975. (FHL# 974/W2bf)

______. *Topographical Dictionary of 2885 English Emigrants to New England, 1620-1650.* rpt. ed., Baltimore: Genealogical Publishing Co., 1957. (FHL# 974/W2ba)

______. *The Winthrop Fleet of 1630: An Account of the Vessels, the Voyage, the Passengers and Their English Homes from Original Authorities.* Boston: Houghton, Mifflin, 1930. (FHL# 974.4/W2b or microfilm 924084, item 3) Several editions.

Bolton, Ethel Stanwood. *Immigrants to New England, 1700-1775.* 1931; rpt. ed., Baltimore: Genealogical Publishing Co., 1966. (FHL# 974/W2b or microfilm 874195, item 3)

Drake, Samuel Gardner. "Results of Some Researches among the British Archives for Information Relative to the Founders of New England in the Years 1858, 1859 and 1860." Boston: *New England Historical and Genealogical Register,* 1860. (FHL# 974/W2d or microfilm 982051, item 4)

Includes an index to passengers. Several reprints.

Hotten, John Camden. *Our Early Emigrant Ancestors: The Original Lists of Persons of Quality.* 1880; rpt. ed., Baltimore: Genealogical Publishing Co., 1968 (FHL# 973/W2h or microfilm 874190, item 1)

COPY of Report and List of the Passengers taken on board the Caledonia of Liverpool whereof John Leitch is Master, burthen 615 tons, and 95 ths of a ton, bound from the Port of Liverpool for Boston

NAMES.	AGE.	SEX.	Occupation, Trade, or Profession.	Country to which they severally belong.	Country of which they intend to become inhabitants.	Remarks relative to any who may have died or left the vessel during the voyage.
William Bradbury	32	Male	Proff. Music	United States	United States	
Mrs Bradbury	30	Female	Lady	"	"	
Emily Maria Bradbury	4	"	"	"	"	
Mary Leanet Bradbury	17 mos	"	"	"	"	
Edward Burstall	40	Male	Merchant	England	Canada West	
Mrs Burstall	24	Female	Lady	"	"	
Mr Pilstone	65	Male	Gentleman	"	Quebec	
Mr Pilstone Jr	19	"	"	"	"	
Mr Elwes	24	"	"	"	Canada West	
Mrs Elwes	23	Female	Lady	"	"	
Mr Thayer	36	Male	Minister	United States	United States	
" J Rice	18	"	Gentleman	"	"	
" McCormick	21	"	"	"	"	
" Dowley	18	"	"	"	"	
" Wilson	40	Male	Farmer	England	England	
" Mantell	24	"	Civil Engineer	"	United States	
Lieut Shafford	19	"	Officer B.A.	"	Canada West	
Mr A. G. Adams	29	"	Merchant	United States	United States	
" C. S. Pearson	36	"	"	England		
Walter Harvey	28	"	"	"		
Wm. Klein	26	"	Servant	"	Canada West	
Mrs Harris	28	Female	Lady	Nova Scotia	United States	
Wm Harris	17 mos	Male		"	"	
John Harris	3	"		"	"	

Figure 5:4 Boston Passenger Arrival List, 26 May 1849.

Important for New England research, although it also includes many lists of passengers going elsewhere.

Tepper, Michael, ed. *Passengers to America: A Consolidation of Ship Passenger Lists from the New England Historical and Genealogical Register.* Baltimore: Genealogical Publishing Co., 1977. (FHL# 973/W3t)

Selected excerpts from the *Register*, 1847-1961.

Whitmore, William H., comp. *Port Arrivals and Immigrants to the City of Boston, 1715-1716 and 1762 and 1769.* Baltimore: Genealogical Publishing Co., 1973. (FHL# 974.46i/W2p)

Putnam, Eben. *Two Early Passengers Lists, 1635-1637: Reprinted from the New England Historical and Genealogical Register, July 1921 with Additions and Corrections.* Baltimore: Genealogical Publishing Co., 1964. (FHL# 973/A1/no.14 or microfilm 874251, item 5)

Boyer, Carl, III, ed. *Ship Passenger Lists: National and New England, 1600-1825.* Newhall, Calif.: Boyer, 1977. (FHL# 973/W3s)

Virkus, Frederick Adams, ed. *Immigrants to America before 1750: An Alphabetical List of Immigrants to the Colonies before 1750 Compiled from Official and Other Records.* 1929-32; rpt. ed., Baltimore: Genealogical Publishing Co., 1965. (FHL# 973/W2v or microfilm 874190, item 5)

Land Records

The Family History Library has microfilmed most of the New England land records prior to 1850. Deeds are by far the most common type of land record, but you should not overlook proprietors' records where they are available. To establish new towns, the various colonies granted large parcels of land to prospective settlers, called proprietors.

The proprietors' records indicate original land ownership prior to the first deeds and often contain information about where these first settlers originated. Frequently the original proprietors were from the same area or town, where meetings were held long before the new town was settled; and proprietors' records include minutes of these meetings. They are cataloged in the FHLC under **[State]/[County]/[Town]/Land and Property.**

Deeds are not recorded uniformly in the various New England states. Connecticut, Rhode Island, and Vermont deeds are recorded in the towns. Massachusetts, New Hampshire, and Maine have county deed registries. When searching for land records it is important to know what county the property was in at the time the instrument was recorded. Counties were often divided to form new counties, but deeds will usually be located in the registry of the county where the property was located at the time it was recorded regardless of where it is presently located. Some exceptions to this rule are noted in Massachusetts and Maine as mentioned below. Similarly, in states where deeds are recorded in the towns, you may need to search the parent town for land transactions occurring in what is now a separate municipality.

Most New England deeds were recorded by town or county clerks in deed books with grantee and grantor indexes. Deeds for a few areas have been published. Below is a state-by-state summary of the Family History Library's deeds collections:

Connecticut

Connecticut deeds are recorded in towns and are cataloged in the FHLC Locality Catalog under **Connecticut/[County]/[Town]/Land and Property.** The library has microfilm copies of almost all Connecticut town deeds to 1850 and is presently acquiring deeds for the period 1850-1900. A few deed books are lost. Below are collected works dealing with land matters:

Colonial Land Records of Connecticut, 1640-1846. 5 vols. 3 reels. (FHL# microfilm 003656-003658)

These are bound vols. of original documents at Connecticut State Library. Includes patents, deeds, and land surveys. Arranged chronologically.

Judd, Sylvester, arr. Connecticut Archives: Indians, 1647-1789. (FHL# microfilm 003624)

Transactions between Connecticut and the Indians.

Robert C. Winthrop Collection, Connecticut Manuscripts, 1631-1794. (FHL# microfilm 003644)

Jurisdiction and land titles, 1631-1716. Indexed.

Maine

The library has microfilm copies of all Maine county deeds from the creation of each county to about 1860 or later. Consult the FHLC under **Maine/[County]/Land and Property.** A few counties have copies of deeds for land originally recorded in the parent county. Major collections and published works relating to Maine lands are:

House, Charles J., comp. *Names of Soldiers of the American Revolution Who Applied for State Bounty under Resolves of March 17, 1835, March 24, 1836, and March 20, 1836, as Appears of Record in the Land Office.* 1893; rpt. ed., Baltimore: Genealogical Publishing Co., 1963. (FHL# 974.1/ M2n)

Revolutionary War Veterans Land Records. 12 reels. Cataloged under **Maine/Land and Property.**

Applications and declarations. House's work is a partial index.

York Deeds. 18 vols. First volume published Portland, Maine: John T. Hull, 1887. Various publishers for next 17 volumes, 1887-1910. (FHL# 974.195/R2m, or microfiche 6046839)

Very important; York County included all of present-day Maine prior to 1760. Covers 1642-1737. Well indexed. Volume 10 omitted from microfiche. Cataloged under **Maine/Land and Property.**

Noyes, Benjamin Lake, comp. *York County, Maine, Unpublished Deeds*. Typescript, 1929. (FHL# microfilm 859059)

Indexed. Covers the period 1733-1800.

Massachusetts

Deeds are recorded in counties in Massachusetts; however, some of the larger counties have more than one deed registry. In a few instances, the deeds of a parent county have been transferred to a county created by a later division, contrary to common practice. See the county-by-county discussion below. For call numbers of county collections consult the FHLC under **Massachusetts/[County]/Land and Property.**

Barnstable County. Created in 1685 from Plymouth Colony, which has deeds prior to 1686. A fire in Barnstable in 1827 destroyed all but one deed book prior to that date. The surviving volume covers 1804-08. The library has complete records on fifty reels from 1827 to 1866, with some older deeds which were re-recorded. Indexed [illegible]

Berkshire County. Created in 1761 from Hampshire County. From 1761 to 1788 all Berkshire County deeds were recorded at Pittsfield. In 1788, three deed registries were created: (1) The Northern District at Adams includes the towns of Adams, Cheshire, Clarksburg, Florida, Hancock, Lanesborough, New Ashford, North Adams, Savoy, Williamstown, and Windsor. 58 reels. (2) The Middle District at Pittsfield includes the towns of Becket, Dalton, Hinsdale, Lee, Lenox, Otis, Peru, Pittsfield, Richmond, Stockbridge, Tryingham, and Washington. All Berkshire County deeds prior to 1788 are retained in this registry. 98 reels. (3) The Southern District at Great Barrington includes the towns of Alford, Egremont, Great Barrington, Monterey, Mount Washington, New Marlborough, Sandisfield, Sheffield, and West Stockbridge. 56 reels.

Also see "Colonial Records and Proprietary Plans: A Compilation of the Proprietors' Lots, Grants, Plantations, and Colonial Records of the Middle, Northern and Southern Districts of Berkshire County." 2 reels. Cataloged under **Massachusetts/Berkshire/Land and Property.**

Bristol County. Created in 1685 from Plymouth Colony. Bristol County has three deed registries. Deeds recorded between 1686 and 1837 are in the Northern District registry at Taunton. In 1837 a Southern District registry was established at New Bedford, and in 1892 a third registry was created at Fall River. The Family History Library has microfilm copies of all Bristol deeds to 1900. The Taunton registry presently includes the towns of Attleborough, Berkley, Dighton, Easton, Mansfield, North Attleborough, Norton, Raynham, Rehoboth, Seekonk, and Taunton. The New Bedford registry includes the towns of Acushnet, Dartmouth, Fairhaven, New Bedford, and Westport. The Fall River registry includes the towns of Fall River, Freetown, Somerset, and Swansea.

The two sub-registries have retained copies of the Taunton registry deeds from 1686 to the establishment of the registry. Each registry has its own index and must be consulted separately in the FHLC Locality Catalog. Bristol deeds are cataloged under **Massachusetts/Bristol/Land and Property.** The Taunton registry includes 353 reels, New Bedford 146, and Fall River 123. Deeds for this area prior to 1686 are at the Plymouth registry.

Dukes County. Created in 1683 by New York. Annexed to Massachusetts in 1695. Deeds begin in 1641, far predating its organization as a county, and are available to 1859. Indexed. 21 reels. Also see proprietors records, 1641-1717, 4 reels.

Essex County. Created in 1643 as an original county. Three deed registries existed in Essex County prior to 1869. The "regular" Essex County deed registry is at Salem, beginning in 1639. Microfilmed through 1866. Indexed 1640-1879. 365 reels. Cataloged under **Massachusetts/Essex/Land and Property.**

A separate registry was maintained at Ipswich 1640-95, primarily for the Ipswich area. 5 vols. Indexed. In 1695 the registry was closed and its records transferred to the Salem registry; however, they are cataloged separately under **Massachusetts/Essex/Ipswich/Land and Property.** 2 reels. (FHL# microfilm 873018-873019)

Records of Old Norfolk County, Massachusetts, (not to be confused with present-day Norfolk County) exist for 1647-1714. Old Norfolk County was largely composed of the towns in present-day Rockingham County, New Hampshire, during Massachusetts's period of jurisdiction over the region but also included that part of present-day Essex County north of the Merrimack River, primarily the towns of Salisbury, Amesbury, and Haverhill.

Although Norfolk technically ceased to exist in 1680 and the Massachusetts towns were annexed to Essex County, some records are dated as late as 1714. The four volumes of Norfolk County records are deposited at the Salem registry but cataloged separately under **Massachusetts/Essex/Land and Property.** 3 reels.

Essex County also has a collection of unregistered deeds for about 1700-1820. (FHL# microfilm 878779)

In 1869 a Northern Registry was established for the towns of Andover, Lawrence, Methuen, and North Andover. Not microfilmed.

Franklin County. Created in 1811 from Hampshire County. Deeds exist from 1787 when a registry of Hampshire County was established at Deerfield. Franklin deeds have been microfilmed for 1787-1867 with indexes to 1889. 129 reels. Earlier records are at Springfield. See Hampden County below.

Hampden County. Created in 1812 from Hampshire County. Deeds for 1636-1867; indexed to 1869. A deed registry was established at Springfield in 1636 when the first settlers arrived in what is now Hampden County, then within the jurisdiction of Middlesex County. In 1662 the area now consisting of the counties of Hampden, Hampshire, Berkshire, Franklin, parts of Worcester, and the towns of Somers and Suffield, Connecticut, was established as Hampshire County with Springfield as the shiretown. The deed registry for the entire region remained at Springfield.

In 1761 Berkshire County was set off with a deed registry at Pittsfield. In 1787 three deed registries were established in Hampshire County: (1) The registry at Deerfield included the towns Ashfield, Bernardston, Buckland, Charlemont, Colrain, Conway, Deerfield, Greenfield, Heath, Leverett, Leyden, Mantague, New Salem, Northfield, Orange, Rowe, Shelburne, Shutesbury, Sunderland, Warwick, Wendell, and Whately; (2) the registry at Northampton included the towns of Amherst, Belchertown, Chester, Chesterfield, Cummington, Easthampton, Goshen, Granby, Greenwich, Hadley, Hatfield, Middlefield, Northampton, Norwich (now Huntington), Pelham, Plainfield, Southampton, South Hadley, Ware, Westhampton, and Williamsburg; (3) the registry at Springfield included the towns of Blanford, Brimfield, Granville, Holland, Longmeadow, Ludlow, Monson, Montgomery, Palmer, South Brimfield (now

Wales), Southwick, Springfield, Tolland, Westfield, West Springfield, and Wilbraham.

The area served by the three registries was approximately equal to the present boundaries of Franklin, Hampshire, and Hampden counties. Hampden County was set off from Hampshire in 1812. The deed registry at Springfield has retained all of its original records dating from 1636, however. Thus, Hampshire County deeds for 1662-1787 are located in the Hampden County deed registry; you must consult the Hampden deeds from Berkshire County lands prior to 1761 and Franklin County lands prior to 1787 even though both counties were created from Hampshire County. 164 reels.

Hampshire County. Created in 1662 from Middlesex County. Deeds collection, 1787-1865. Indexed for 1787-1865. 159 reels. Earlier records are at Springfield. See Hampden County above.

Middlesex County. Created in 1643 as an original county. The Family History Library has filmed all Middlesex County deeds for 1649-1900. Indexed to 1950. Beginning in 1855 a second registry was established at Lowell, but all deeds are at Cambridge. 2,790 volumes of deeds plus indexes. 1,781 reels.

Nantucket County. Created in 1695 from New York. Deeds for 1659-1875. Indexed. 36 reels.

Norfolk County. Created in 1793 from Suffolk County. Deeds for 1793-1890. Indexed. 373 reels.

[Old] Norfolk County. Created in 1643 as an original county. See Essex County above.

Plymouth County. Created in 1685 from Plymouth Colony. "Regular" Plymouth County deeds commence in 1664. Microfilmed through 1900. Indexed 1685-1914. 462 reels.

Numerous other Plymouth County and Plymouth Colony records contain land records. Consult the FHLC under **Massachusetts/Land and Property, Massachusetts/Plymouth/Land and Property**, and **Massachusetts/Plymouth/Plymouth Land and Property** to obtain all references to Plymouth land records. The library also has:

Shurtleff, Nathaniel B., and David Pulsifer, eds. *Records of the Colony of New Plymouth in New England*. 12 vols in 10. Boston: William White, 1855-61. (FHL# 974.4/N2n or microfilm 896852-896856 or microfiche 6046893)

Volume 12 includes colony deeds 1620-51.

Plymouth Colony Records. Deeds. 1620-99. 3 reels.

Plymouth Colony Records. Indian deeds, treasurers' accounts, lists of freemen, 1666-82. (FHL# microfilm 567791)

Proprietors' Records, 1702-15. (FHL# microfilm 417210)

Records of the Colony of New Plymouth, 1643-79. (FHL# microfilm 912074, items 1-3)

Deeds, 1664-99. (FHL# microfilm 912074, items 4-5)

Plymouth Colony Records, Scrapbook, 1636-95. (FHL# microfilm 912073, item 1)

Contains deeds, inventories of estates, guardianship records, bonds, bills of sale, and ships' papers.

Pope, Charles Henry. *The Plymouth Scrap Book: The Oldest Original Documents Extant in Plymouth Archives Printed Verbatim*. Boston: C. E. Goodspeed, 1918. (FHL# 974.4/N2p)

Suffolk County. Created in 1643 as an original county. Deeds are available for 1639-1885. Indexed to 1920. 1,128 reels. An excellent compilation covering the earliest period of Massachusetts deeds is Suffolk Deeds, 14 vols. (Boston: Rockwell and Churchill, 1880-1906). Covers 1629-97. (FHL# 974.46/R2s or microfiche 6046903. Microfiche excludes volumes 3, 8, 12, 13.

Worcester County. Created in 1731 from Suffolk, Middlesex, and Hampshire counties. Deeds for 1721-1866. Indexed 1731-1889. 408 reels.

New Hampshire

All land and probate records for New Hampshire prior to the formation of counties in 1769 and during the Massachusetts administration of the province are centralized in one collection with a master index for 1623-1772. 118 reels. Includes 103 volumes of province deeds for 1641-1771; card index. Cataloged under **New Hampshire/Land And Property**.

The remainder of New Hampshire land records are in the county deed registries. Microfilmed for 1771-1850. Rockingham County deeds prior to 1771 are the New Hampshire province deeds. Rockingham County deeds therefore begin with Volume 100. Belknap County deeds include copies of Strafford County deeds for Belknap land prior to the separation of Belknap from Strafford County in 1840. Coos County has copies of relevant Grafton County deeds prior to 1803. After an 1885 fire scorched the 1839-85 deeds, all decipherable records were transcribed.

For New Hampshire town charters, township grants, and Masonian patent papers, see *Provincial and State Papers of New Hampshire*, 40 vols. (Concord, N.H.: State Printer, 1867-1943), vols. 24-29. 21 reels. (FHL# 974.2/N2nhp or microfiche 6046775. See **New Hampshire/Town Records** for microfilm numbers.

Rhode Island

Deeds in Rhode Island, sometimes called land evidences, are recorded by town. The Family History Library has microfilm copies of all Rhode Island town deeds prior to 1850 except New Shoreham. Cataloged under **Rhode Island/[County]/[Town]/Land and Property**. See also:

Arnold, James N. *The Records of the Proprietors of the Narragansett, Otherwise Called the Fones Record*. Providence: Narragansett Historical Publishing, 1894. (FHL# 974.5/R2p or microfilm 1033805, item 2)

Dougine, Genevieve N., comp. "Index to Rhode Island Land Evidences, 1648-1696." (FHL# microfilm 022254)

Land and Public Notary Records of Rhode Island, 1671-1795. 5 reels.

Proceedings of the General Assembly, 1646-1851. 18 reels.

Includes land transfers and grants.

Worthingon, Dorothy, comp. *Rhode Island Land Evidences*, vol. 1, 1648-96. Providence: Rhode Island Historical Society, 1921. (FHL# microfilm 564389) Reprinted with preface by Albert T. Klyberg. Baltimore: Genealogical Publishing Co., 1970. (FHL# 974.5/R2r/1970)

Vermont

Vermont deeds are recorded at the town level. All Vermont deeds to 1850 and many proprietors' records are available on microfilm at the library. Check the Locality FHLC under **Vermont/[County]/[Town]/Land and Property.** Additional Vermont land records, mostly concerning land grants, are available under **Vermont/Land and Property**. Here is a selected bibliography.

Bogart, Walter Thompson. *The Vermont Lease Lands*. Montpelier: Vermont Historical Society, 1950. (FHL# 974.3/R2b)

Charters Granted by the State of Vermont, 1779-1846. 2 vols. n.p., Vermont: Vermont Public Records Division, 1974. (FHL# microfilm 982539)

Denio, Herbert Williams. *Massachusetts Land Grants in Vermont.* Cambridge, Mass.: John Wilson and Son, University Press, 1920. (FHL# microfilm 824082, item 7)

Reprinted from *Publications of the Colonial Society of Massachusetts* 24 (Mar. 1920):35-99.

Holbrook, Jay Mack. *Vermont's First Settlers*. Oxford, Mass.: Holbrook Research Institute, 1976. (FHL# 974.3/R2h)

Land grants in Vermont 1763-1803, alphabetical by surname of recipient.

State Papers of Vermont. 17 vols. Montpelier: Secretary of State, 1918-69. (FHL# 974.3/B4s)

These volumes have separate titles: Volume 1: *Index to the Papers of the Surveyor-General.* Volume 2: *Charters Granted by the State of Vermont: Being Transcripts of Early Charters of Townships and Smaller Tracts of Land Granted by the State of Vermont.* Volume 5: *Petitions for Land Grants, 1778-1881.* Volume 7: *New York Land Patents, 1668-1786, Covering Land and Included in the State of Vermont.*

Military Records

New England soldiers are included in various record groups and indexes of veterans compiled by the National Archives. The records include service records, pension applications, and bounty land records for 1775-1900. For more information on the library's holdings of National Archives military records, see Chapter 4, "United States: General."

A separate index to Connecticut service records of the Revolutionary War is available in the National Archives collection, 25 reels, alphabetically arranged by the name of the veteran. Consult the FHLC under **Connecticut/Military Records/Revolution, 1775-1783/Indexes.**

The index to service records of volunteer Union soldiers of the Civil War compiled by the National Archives is arranged by state with all New England states represented. These are cataloged under **[State]/Military Records/Civil War, 1861-1865/Indexes** and in *U. S. Military Records*, Volume 1, located on the index tables in the U.S./Canada Reference area. See Chapter 4, "United States: General," for further information.

The library has many additional military records: military histories, service and pension records, bounty land records, and indexes, many of which date from the colonial period. Some New England towns have published lists of their own soldiers in local histories or separate monographs. Find them in the FHLC under **[State]/[County]/[Town]/Military Records.** The library also has many unit histories, particularly of volunteer regiments during the Civil War, cataloged under **[State]/Military Records/[Name and Dates of War].**

Below is a state by state list of the library's major collections and publications of New England military records, excluding National Archives materials. Check the Locality FHLC under **[State]/Military Records, [State]/Military Records/[Name and Dates of War], [State]/Military Records/Indexes**, and **[State]/Military Records/Pensions.**

Connecticut

Catalogue of Connecticut Volunteer Organizations. Hartford: Case, Lockwood, 1864. (FHL# 974.6/M25cc)

Judd, Sylvester, and Connecticut State Library, arrangers. Connecticut Archives. Militia Records. Selected papers, 1678-1820. 18 vols. 3 series. 18 reels.

Each series indexed.

______. Connecticut Archives. Colonial Wars. Selected Papers. 7 reels.

Papers of King Philip's War, 1675-76; King William's War, 1689-97; Queen Anne's War, 1702-12; Eastern Indian War, 1722-25; War with Spain, 1740-42; King George's War, 1744-48; and the French and Indian War, 1755-63. Also includes papers concerning colonial agents in England, 1751-74. Indexed.

______. Connecticut Archives. Revolutionary War. Selected papers, 1763-1820. 3 series. 60 reels.

Series 1: 37 vols., 1763-89. Series 2: 56 vols. Series 3: 6 vols. Indexes for Series 1 and first volume of Series 3 only.

______. Connecticut Archives. War of 1812. Selected Papers, 1812-19. 3 vols. 2 reels. Indexed.

Connecticut Daughters of the American Revolution, comp. *Connecticut Revolutionary Pensioners*. Baltimore: Genealogical Publishing Co., 1987. (FHL# 974.6/M2cr)

Middlebrook, Louis F. *History of Maritime Connecticut during the American Revolution, 1775-1783.* 2 vols. Salem, Mass.: Essex Institute, 1925. (FHL# 974.6/M25m)

Connecticut State Library. Miscellaneous French and Indian War records. Partial index. 2 reels.

Record of Service of Connecticut Men in the[:] I. War of the Revolution, II. War of 1812, III. Mexican War. Compiled by authority of the General Assembly under the direction of the Adjutant-General. Hartford: Adjutant-General's Office, 1889. (FHL# 974.6/M2ca, microfilm 1036328, item 4, or microfiche 6046698)

Adjutant-General's Office, comp. *Record of Service of Connecticut Men in the Army and Navy of the United States during the War of the Rebellion*. Hartford: Case, Lockwood &

Brainard, 1889. (FHL# 974.6/M2c or microfilm 982124, item 1) Also 42-page supplement (FHL# 974.6/M2c supp. or microfilm 982124, item 2)

_____. *Record of Service of Connecticut Men in the Army, Navy, and Marine Corps of the United States in the Spanish American War.* Hartford: Case, Lockwood & Brainard, 1919. (FHL# Q/974.6/M2co, microfilm 1036755, item 1)

Connecticut State Library. Revolutionary War Orderly Books of Regiments and Companies of the Continental Army. Partial index. 8 reels.

_____. Revolutionary War papers and Private Collections. 3 reels.

Maine

Maine military records prior to 1820 are located in Massachusetts records.

Annual Report of the Adjutant General of the State of Maine, 1862-1866, and Supplement, 1861-1866. 5 vols. in 7. Augusta: Stevens and Sayward, 1863-67. (FHL# 974.1/M2mag)

Maine soldiers who served the Union during the Civil War.

Aroostook War: Historical Sketch and Roster of Commissioned Officers and Enlisted Men Called into Service for the Protection of the Northeastern Frontier of Maine from February to May 1839. Augusta: Kennebec Journal Print, 1904. (FHL# 974.1/M2a)

Maine Division of Vital Statistics. Deaths of World War II Veterans of Maine. (FHL# microfilm 010216)

Flagg, Charles Allcott. *An Alphabetical Index of Revolutionary Pensioners Living in Maine.* 1920; rpt. ed., Baltimore: Genealogical Publishing Co., 1967. (FHL# 974.1/M22f)

Hanson, James W., Adjutant General, comp. *Roster of Maine in the Military Service of the United States and Allies in the World War, 1917-1919.* 2 vols. Augusta: n. pub., 1929. (FHL# 974.1/M2ma or microfilm: vol. 1 1036025, vol. 2 1036049, item 1)

Massachusetts

Allen, Gardner Weld. *Massachusetts Privateers of the Revolution.* [Boston]: Massachusetts Historical Society, 1927. Volume 77 of *Massachusetts Historical Society Collections.* (FHL# 974.4/B4m)

Bodge, George Madison. *Soldiers in King Philip's War, Being a Critical Account of That War with a Concise History of the Indian Wars of New England from 1620-1677.* 1906; rpt. ed., Baltimore: Genealogical Publishing Co., 1967. (FHL# 973/M2b)

Higginson, Thomas Wentworth, comp. *Massachusetts in the Army and Navy during the War of 1861-1865.* 2 vols. Boston: Wright & Potter Printing Co., 1895-96. (FHL# 974.4/M25ht or microfilm 238371-238372)

Hambrick-Stowe, Charles E., and Donna D. Smerlas, eds. *Massachusetts Militia Companies and Officers in the Lexington Alarm.* [Boston]: Society of Colonial Wars in the Commonwealth of Massachusetts, 1976. (FHL# 974.4/M2h)

Voye, Nancy S., ed. *Massachusetts Officers in the French and Indian Wars, 1748-1762.* [Boston]: Society of Colonial Wars in the Commonwealth of Massachusetts, 1975. (FHL# 974.4/M2v)

Donahue, Mary E., ed. *Massachusetts Officers and Soldiers, 1702-1722: Queen Anne's War to Dummer's War.* [Boston]: Society of Colonial Wars in the Commonwealth of Massachusetts, 1980. (FHL# 974.4/M2d)

Stachiw, Myron O., ed. *Massachusetts Officers and Soldiers, 1723-1743: Dummer's War to the War of Jenkins Ear.* [Boston]: Society of Colonial Wars in the Commonwealth of Massachusetts, 1980. (FHL# 974.4/M2s)

Doreski, Carole, ed. *Massachusetts Officers and Soldiers in the Seventeenth-Century Conflicts.* [Boston]: Society of Colonial Wars in the Commonwealth of Massachusetts, 1982. (FHL# 974.4/M24d)

McKay, Robert E., ed. *Massachusetts Soldiers in the French and Indian Wars, 1744-1755.* [Boston]: Society of Colonial Wars in the Commonwealth of Massachusetts, 1978. (FHL# 974.4/M2mc)

Adjutant-General, comp. *Massachusetts Soldiers, Sailors and Marines in the Civil War.* 9 vols. Various publishers, 1931-37. 9 reels. (FHL# 974.4/M2ma)

Massachusetts Soldiers and Sailors of the Revolutionary War. 17 vols. Boston: Wright & Potter Printing Co., 1896-1908. (FHL# 974.4/M23m or microfiche 6046890) (See Figure 5:5.)

Fiche excludes Volume 17. Abstracts of service records of Massachusetts and Maine soldiers and sailors from records in the Massachusetts Archives. Not the same records held by the National Archives.

Nason, George W. *History and Complete Roster of the Massachusetts Regiments: Minutemen of '61, who Responded to the First Call of President Abraham Lincoln, April 15, 1861, to Defend the Flag and Constitution of the United States.* Boston: Smith & McCance, 1910. (FHL# 974.4/M2n)

Record of the Massachusetts Volunteers, 1861-1865. 2 vols in 4. Boston: Wright & Potter Printing Co., 1868-70. (FHL# 974.4/M2mar or microfilm 1321031, items 1-2)

Records of the Massachusetts Volunteer Militia Called Out by the Governor of Massachusetts to Suppress a Threatened Invasion during the War of 1812-14. Boston: Wright & Potter Printing Co., 1913. (FHL# Q/974.4 M23ma or microfilm 103395, item 5)

New Hampshire Card Index to Revolutionary War and other Military War Rolls listed in the *New Hampshire State Papers*, vols. 14-17 at the New Hampshire Historical Society. 4 reels.

Civil War Oaths, 1861-1865. 3 reels.

Civil War Service Records, 1860-1865. Card file index arranged alphabetically by name of veteran. 13 reels.

Indian and French Wars and Revolutionary Papers. 4 vols. 2 reels. Includes many original lists from seventeeth and eighteenth centuries.

New Hampshire Pension Records, 1776-1850. 101 vols. 25 reels.

Abstracts of original pension records in National Archives typed by Mrs. Amos G. Draper. Original

510 MASSACHUSETTS SOLDIERS AND SAILORS

BRIGGS, JAMES. 1st Lieutenant, Capt. Elijah Walker's (9th) co., 2d Bristol Co. regt.; list of officers of Mass. militia; commissioned April 26, 1776.

BRIGGS, JAMES. Private, Capt. Francis Cushing's co., Col. John Cushing's (2d Plymouth Co.) regt.; service, 11 days, on an alarm in Dec., 1776; marched to Bristol, R. I.

BRIGGS, JAMES. Private, Capt. Seth Stowers's co., Col. J. Robinson's regt.; enlisted July 1, 1777; service, 6 mos.; enlistment to expire Jan. 1, 1778; reported mustered by James Hatch, Muster Master for Plymouth Co.

BRIGGS, JAMES. Captain, Col. John Bailey's regt.; service from Dec. 10, 1775, to Feb. 1, 1776; roll dated Roxbury; *also*, list of officers of Mass. militia; commissioned Feb. 13, 1776; *also*, Captain of a company raised from Col. Carpenter's regt. in the towns of Dighton, Berkley and Raynham; marched July 31, 1776, to join Continental Army in New York; *also*, receipt for travel allowance given to Col. Cary, dated Chelsea Camp, Aug. 20, 1776; *also*, receipt for wages from Oct. 1, 1776, to Dec. 12, 1776, given to Col. Simeon Cary dated Cortlandt Manor, Dec. 3, 1776; *also*, marched from Dighton Oct. 2, 1777, on a secret expedition to Rhode Island under command of Col. Freeman; discharged Oct. 29, 1777, by Gen. Spencer; service, 28 days; *also*, Col. Jacobs's regt.; an account for wages in addition to Continental wages for 3 mos. 21 days service from July 1, 1778, when detached, to Oct. 12, 1778, when discharged; account includes 42 days subsistence money from Sept. 1, 1778, to Oct. 12, 1778.

BRIGGS, JAMES, Freetown. Private, Capt. Samuel Tubbs's co., Col. Timothy Walker's regt.; muster roll dated Aug. 1, 1775; enlisted May 1, 1775; service, 3 mos. 7 days; *also*, company return dated Oct. 6, 1775; *also*, order for bounty coat or its equivalent in money dated Roxbury, Nov. 20, 1775; *also*, Capt. Benjamin Read's co., Col. Pope's regt.; marched Dec. 8, 1776; service, 6 days, on an alarm at Rhode Island; *also*, Capt. Elijah Walker's co., Col. John Hathaway's regt.; marched from Dighton to Tiverton, R. I., April 23, 1777; service, 20 days; *also*, Capt. Walker's (7th) co., Col. Hathaway's (Bristol Co.) regt., Brig. Gen. Godfrey's brigade; marched to Tiverton, R. I., on the alarm of Aug. 2, 1780; service, 5 days.

BRIGGS, JAMES, Dighton. Private, Capt. Daniel Drake's co., Col. Luke Drury's (Bristol Co.) regt.; enlisted Aug. 23, 1781; arrived in camp Sept. 1, 1781; discharged Dec. 1, 1781; arrived home Dec. 10, 1781; service, 3 mos. 19 days; marched to North River.

BRIGGS, JAMES, Dighton. Private, Colonel's co., Col. Henry Jackson's regt.; Continental Army pay accounts for service from Sept. 10, 1777, to Dec. 31, 1780; *also*, Lieut. Hodijah Bayles's co. of grenadiers, Col. Jackson's regt.; pay roll for Feb., 1778, dated Guelph, Pa.; *also*, pay roll for June, 1778, dated Providence; *also*, Lieut. John Hobby's (1st) co., Col. Jackson's regt.; pay roll for July and Aug., 1778, dated Providence; *also*, pay rolls for Sept. and Dec., 1778, and March and April, 1779, dated Garrison at Pawtuxet; *also*, Colonel's co.; return made up to Dec. 31, 1779, dated Camp at Providence; enlisted Sept. 10, 1777; enlistment, 3 years; reported deserted June 5, 1779; returned Oct. 8, 1779; *also*, Colonel's co., commanded by Lieut. Hobby, Col. Jackson's regt.; pay rolls for April-July, 1780.

BRIGGS, JEDEDIAH. Seaman, brigantine "Rising Empire," commanded by Capt. Richard Whellen; engaged June 12, 1776; discharged Sept. 3, 1776; service, 2 mos. 22 days.

BRIGGS, JEDEDIAH, Berkley. 1st Lieutenant, Capt. James Nicolls's (8th) co., 2d Bristol Co. regt.; list of officers of Mass. militia; commissioned April 26, 1776; *also*, Capt. James Durfee's co., Col. Thomas Carpenter's regt., raised from Brig. Gen. Godfrey's brigade; list of officers of Mass. militia dated Taunton; appointed agreeable to resolve of Sept. 12, 1776; *also*, Capt. Nickols's co., Col. Edward Pope's (Bristol Co.) regt.; marched to Rhode Island on the alarm of Dec. 16, 1776; service, 22 days; roll includes travel to camp at Warren and home again.

Figure 5:5 *Massachusetts Soldiers and Sailors of the Revolutionary War.* 17 vols. (Boston: Wright and Potter Printing Co., 1896-1908), 2:510.

manuscript in library of the Daughters of the American Revolution, Washington, D.C.

Potter, Chandler E. *The Military History of the State of New Hampshire, 1623-1861.* Baltimore: Genealogical Publishing Co., 1972.

Includes many colonial and Revolutionary War muster lists.

Provincial and State Papers of New Hampshire. 40 vols. Concord, N. H.: State Printer, 1867-1943. (FHL# 974.2/-N2nhp with Volume 16 missing; also 21 reels, complete.)

Volumes 14-17 include Revolutionary War rolls of New Hampshire veterans. Volume 30 includes signers of the Association Test, New Hampshire soldiers in Massachusetts Revolutionary War rolls, and New Hampshire pension rolls.

Adjutant General's Office. *Report of the Adjutant General of the State of New Hampshire.* Concord: Amos Hadley, State Printer, 1860-79. (FHL# 974.2 M2n)

The library only has copies of annual reports for 1860-65, 1869-79. Adjutant General's Office, Includes Civil War rolls of New Hampshire soldiers.

Ayling, Augustus D., Adjutant General, comp. *Revised Roster of the Soldiers and Sailors of New Hampshire in the War of the Rebellion, 1861-1866.* Concord, N.H.: I. C. Evans, 1895. (FHL# Q/974.2/M23nh)

Revolutionary Pensioners Records of New Hampshire. 64 vols. Typescript. 26 reels.

Abstracts of pension applications of New Hampshire veterans.

Gilmore, George C., comp. *Roll of New Hampshire Men at Louisburg, Cape Breton, 1745.* Concord, N.H.: Edward N. Pearson, 1896. (FHL# 974.2/M2gg)

Rhode Island

Annual Report of the Adjutant General of the State of Rhode Island and Providence Plantations for the Year 1865. 2 vols. Providence: E. L. Freeman, 1893-95. (FHL# 974.5/ M2r, microfilm 982363, or microfiche 6046949)

Volume 1 is a register of Rhode Island volunteers, 1861-66. Volume 2 is the annual report of the Adjutant General.

Rhode Island State Archives. Card Index to Military and Naval Records, 1774-1805. 18 reels. Arranged alphabetically by veteran.

Chapin, Howard Millar. *A List of Rhode Island Soldiers and Sailors in King George's War, 1740-1748.* Providence: Rhode Island Historical Society, 1920. (FHL# 974.5/-M2ch or microfilm 1425647, item 11)

______. *Rhode Island in the Colonial Wars, A List of Rhode Island Soldiers and Sailors in the Old French & Indian Wars, 1755-1762.* Providence: Rhode Island Historical Society, 1918. (FHL# 974.5/M2c or microfilm 1425576, item 5)

Rhode Island State Archives. Maritime Papers of Rhode Island, 1723-1790. 12 reels. Cataloged under **Rhode Island/Business Records And Commerce**.

Eleven volumes of bonds from masters of vessels, 1756-83; outward and inward entries, colonial war records, 1723-87; letters of marque, 1776-81; 5 volumes of manifests export cargoes, 1775-90; 5 volumes of manifests import cargoes, 1744-87; and registers of vessels and miscellaneous papers. Indexes at the beginning of each volume. Many colonial and Revolutionary War documents.

Rhode Island State Archives. Military Papers, 1730-1765. (FHL# microfilm 954956) Includes muster rolls, accounts, and correspondence.

Rhode Island State Archives. Military Papers of Rhode Island, 1731-1792. 19 vols. 17 reels.

Volumes 1-6: French and Indian War records. Volume 7-19: Revolutionary War records. Indexed at the beginning of each volume.

Rhode Island State Archives. Military Papers. War of 1812, 1792-1794, 1812-1815. 3 vols. 2 reels. Indexes at the beginning of each volume.

Smith, Joseph Jenks. *Civil and Military List of Rhode Island.* 2 vols. Providence: Preston and Rounds, 1900-01. (FHL# 974.5/N2s, microfiche 6046905, microfilms 925437, item 3 for vol. 1 and 925438, item 1 for vol. 2)

Volume 1 includes officers elected by the General Assembly, 1647-1800. Volume 2 includes officers elected by the General Assembly, 1800-50, all Rhode Island officers in the Revolutionary War appointed by Congress, officers in the army and navy to 1850 including volunteer officers in the War of 1812 and the Mexican War, and all officers in the privateer service through 1812.

Vermont

Clark, Byron N., ed. *A List of Pensioners of the War of 1812 with an Appendix Containing Names of Volunteers for the Defence of Plattsburgh from Vermont Towns.* 1904; rpt. ed., Baltimore: Genealogical Publishing Co., 1969. (FHL# 974.3/M2L)

Goodrich, John E., comp. *Rolls of the Soldiers in the Revolutionary War, 1775 to 1783.* Rutland, Vt.: Tuttle Co., 1904. (FHL# 974.3/M2g, microfilm 896961, item 1, or microfiche 6046670)

Report of the Adjutant and Inspector General of the State of Vermont, 1864-1866. 2 vols. Montpelier, Vt.: Walton's Steam Printing Establishment, 1864-66. Includes lists and records of soldiers. (FHL# 974.3/M2a)

Peck, Theodore S., Adjutant General, comp. *Revised Roster of Vermont Volunteers.* Montpelier, Vt.: Press of the Watchman Publishing Co., 1892. (FHL# 974.3/M2va or microfilm 1036000, item 8, or 1000623, item 1)

Johnson, Herbert T., comp. *Roster of Soldiers in the War of 1812-14.* St. Albans, Vt.: Messenger Press, 1933. (FHL# 974.3/M2vr)

Naturalization Records

As early as 1790 Congress passed an act providing for the naturalization of aliens. Immigrants desiring to be naturalized declared their intentions of citizenship in a court of record. After waiting the required residency period, they then petitioned the court for citizenship status, proved that they had fulfilled the residency statute, and took the oath of allegiance. Naturalization records therefore consist of declarations of intentions, affidavits, oaths of allegiance, petitions for citizenship, and final certificates.

The difficulty in using naturalization records is that virtually any court of record in the United States could grant citizenship provided that the immigrant met federal requirements. Immigrants were naturalized in U. S. District Courts, Courts of Common Pleas, county courts, municipal courts, and others, making the search for naturalizations difficult. Furthermore, immigrants were not required to petition for citizenship in the same court in which they filed their original declarations. Therefore, the record of an individual's naturalization may be found in two or more different courts.

After 1906 all naturalization records had to be forwarded to the new Bureau of Immigration and Naturalization in Washington, D.C., thus greatly simplifying the process of locating the records of a particular individual.

The Family History Library has few original New England naturalization records. Fortunately, the Works Progress Administration began a project in the late 1930s to centralize information in the naturalization records of the more than 5,000 federal, state, and local courts. The project was never completed, but the New England states were among the first to be processed and are relatively complete. The records consist of 5"x8" photocopies of naturalization documents and a card index. The index is available on 117 microfilm reels covering 1791-1906. See **United States/New England/Naturalization and Citizenship/ Indexes** or **[State]/Naturalization and Citizenship/Indexes.** For the locations of many New England naturalization records see:

Neagles, James C., and Lila Lee Neagles. *Locating Your Immigrant Ancestor: A Guide to Naturalization Records.* Logan, Utah: Everton Publishers, 1986. (FHL# 973/P47n, in the U.S./Canada Reference area)

The Family History Library has no naturalization records for Connecticut. The library's collections include naturalization records for Androscoggin County, Maine; Middlesex County, Massachusetts; Belknap, Cheshire, Coos, Grafton, Hillsborough, Merrimack, Strafford, and Sullivan counties, New Hampshire; Newport and Washington counties, Rhode Island; and Lamoille and Orleans counties, Vermont. These records primarily cover the late 1800s and are cataloged under **[State]/[County]/Naturalization and Citizenship.**

Newspapers

Newspapers are a valuable source of genealogy and family history, especially for obituaries and notices of marriage and death. The difficulty with using newspapers as a source is that the material is voluminous, and there are few indexes. A handy reference guide to newspaper indexes is:

Milner, Anita Cheek. *Newspaper Indexes: A Location and Subject Guide for Researchers.* Metuchen, N.J./London: The Scarecrow Press, 1977). (FHL# 973/B32m)

The library has several catalogs of U.S. newspapers, held in the U.S./Canada Reference area. See Chapter 4, "United States: General."

The Family History Library has microfilmed few New England newspapers. For holdings see *Register of U. S. Newspapers and Related Holdings in the Family History Library* in the U.S./Canada Reference area (FHL# 973/A3r) and check the Locality FHLC under **[State]/-[County]/[City]/Newspapers.**

A few important collections of newspaper abstracts, indexes, and genealogical clippings available in the library are:

Boston Evening Transcript. Genealogical clippings. 1900-41. 10 reels.

Queries and answers published in the genealogical column of the *Transcript*, largely focused on New England problems. The *Transcript* is indexed in Fremont Rider, ed. *The American Genealogical-Biographical Index to American Genealogical, Biographical and Local History Materials*, 143 vols. (Middletown, Conn.: Godfrey Memorial Library, 1952-86). (FHL# 973/D22ag) Volumes A-R completed. References to articles in the *Boston Evening Transcript* are cited as "Transcript" followed by the date of the edition and the query number.

Charles R. Hale Collection. Marriage and Death Notices from Connecticut Newspapers and Connecticut Cemetery. 360 reels.

Vital data from over 100 Connecticut newspapers to about 1865. Several indexes; separate slips for each marriage and death. Death notices index includes cemetery inscriptions. Cataloged under **Connecticut/Newspapers** and **/Vital Records.**

Hammond, Otis G. *Notices from the New Hampshire Gazette, 1765-1800.* Lambertville, N.J.: Hunterdon House, 1970. (FHL# 974.2/V4h)

Hartford Times. (Hartford, Connecticut.) Genealogical Section, 1912-67. 13 reels. 75 microfiche. (FHL# 973/-D2ha)

Microfiche for 1957-67. The library has scrapbooks for 1918, 1920, 1939, 1941-42, 1945-66. Surname index only for 1912-16, 1956-66. Cataloged under **Connecticut/Hartford/ Hartford/Newspapers** and **Connecticut/Hartford/Hartford/ Newspapers/Indexes.**

Index to the Burlington [Vermont] Free Press in the Billings Library, University of Vermont. 6 vols. Montpelier: Works Projects Administration, Historical Records Survey, 1940-41. (FHL# 974.317/B32h or microfilm 844896, item 3)

Covers 1848-65. Index includes names of individuals and descriptions of the articles.

Index to Hampshire Gazette (Part III, Personal Section). Northampton, Massachusetts. Works Progress Administration, Historical Records Survey, 1939. (FHL# 974.423/N1/B3h)

American Antiquarian Society, comp. *Index to Marriages in the Massachusetts Centinel and the Columbian Centinel, 1784-1840.* 5 vols. Boston: G. K. Hall Co., 1961. (FHL# 974.4/V22i)

______. *Index to Obituaries in the Massachusetts Centinel and the Columbian Centinel, 1784-1840.* 5 vols. Boston: G. K. Hall Co., 1961. (FHL# 974.4/V42i)

Index to Obituaries in Boston Newspapers, 1704-1800. 3 vols. Boston: G. K. Hall Co., 1968. (FHL# 974.46/B1/V28b or microfilm 823596, items 1-3)

Mercy Warren Chapter of the Daughters of the American Revolution, comp. Typed and edited by Mrs. Seth Ames Lewis. *Marriages, Deaths, Ordinations, Probate Records from Newspapers, 1785-1812 in the City Library of Springfield, Massachusetts.* Title varies. (FHL# 974/V2d)

Periodicals and Serials

Since the mid-nineteenth century, periodicals dedicated to the history and genealogy of the region have appeared in print. Although the format and content vary, most genealogical periodicals publish such items as cemetery, church, vital, military, and probate records, compiled family genealogies, historical studies, and genealogical queries and answers. The value of such works is obvious.

The major difficulty in using genealogical periodicals is the lack of indexing or incomplete indexing. To help alleviate this shortcoming, several indexes have been published. None of these indexes covers all periodicals for all periods. Nevertheless, they are an important contribution to research. These are the most useful for New England research:

Index to American Genealogies, with Supplement 1900-1908. 1900; rpt. ed. published by Joel Munsell's Sons with supplement, Detroit: Gale Research Co. 1966. (FHL# 973/D22m in U.S./Canada Reference area).

Indexes surnames treated at length, primarily in family genealogies but also in some periodicals. The 107-page supplement in the back of the book is a separate index and needs to be searched independently.

Jacobus, Donald Lines. *Index to Genealogical Periodicals.* rev., ed. Carl Boyer, III. Newhall, Calif.: Carl Boyer, III, 1983. (FHL# 973/B22j)

Reprints original work published in three volumes in 1932, 1948, and 1953, which covered eighty-five genealogical periodicals through 1952. Indexes only surnames treated extensively (generally the subject of articles). Jacobus excluded works from his index which were already indexed, including the first fifty volumes of the *New England Historical and Genealogical Register* and the first fifty volumes of *Collections of the Essex Institute*. The 1983 reprint contains a list of periodicals included and excluded.

Towle, Laird C., ed. *Genealogical Periodical Annual Index.* 24 vols. Bowie, Md.: Heritage Books, 1962-85. (FHL# 973/B22gp)

Includes all major genealogical periodicals. The 1985 edition includes 10,000 entries from 224 periodicals. Since 1962 a new volume has been issued annually under various editors and compilers. Not cumulative. Indexes only surnames treated at length.

Waldenmaier, Inez, ed. *Annual Index to Genealogical Periodicals and Family Histories, 1956-1963.* 8 vols in 4. Washington: Waldenmaier, 1956-63. (FHL# 973/B2gna or microfilm 982310, items 8-11)

Reprint from Waldenmaier's *Genealogical Newsletter and Research Aids.* Indexes surnames treated at length in a few major New England periodicals. Partially fills gap between Jacobus and Towle.

For further information about genealogical periodical indexes, see:

Sperry, Kip. *A Survey of American Genealogical Periodicals and Periodical Indexes.* Detroit: Gale Research Co. 1978. (FHL# 973/B23s, in U.S./Canada Reference area)

Most genealogical periodical indexes are cataloged in the Locality FHLC under **United States/Genealogy/-Periodicals/Indexes.**

Most of the major genealogical periodicals themselves are cataloged under **[State]/Periodicals, [State]/-Genealogy/Periodicals, [State]/History/Periodicals, [State]/Societies/Periodicals.** Some New England towns, such as Lynn, Dedham, and Topsfield, Massachusetts, have genealogical periodicals cataloged under **[State]/[County]/[Town]/Periodicals.** All genealogical periodicals are also cataloged by title in the Author/Title FHLC. Here are the periodicals and serials of most interest to New England researchers available in the library.

New England, General

The American Genealogist. 1932-to date. Quarterly. (FHL# 973/B2ag)

First eight volumes called *Families of Ancient New Haven* and published separately in four volumes by Donald Lines Jacobus. *The American Genealogist* publishes a variety of well-documented family genealogies and articles as well as miscellaneous documents and records.

New England Historical and Genealogical Register. 1847-to date. Quarterly. 140 vols. Boston: New England Genealogical Society. (FHL# 974/B4ne)

First published by Samuel G. Drake, later by the Society. Contains valuable historical articles, scholarly genealogies, and genealogical records: cemetery, Bible, vital, church, and others for New England towns. Articles on the English origins of early settlers reprinted as: Gary Boyd Roberts, ed. *English Origins of New England Families from the New England Historical and Genealogical Register,* 6 vols. in 2 series (Baltimore: Genealogical Publishing Co., 1985) (FHL# 974/D2e). Every-name index for first fifty volumes; index for volumes 51-110 was drawn primarily from tables of contents of individual volumes.

New York Genealogical and Biographical Record. Quarterly. 115 vols. (1870-). New York: New York Genealogical and Biographical Society. (FHL# 974/B2n)

Contains much information about the New England origins of families who migrated to New York. Surname index for volumes 1-40. Subject index for 1870-1982, compiled by Jean D. Worden, includes 32,000 entries and names of individuals who are the subjects of articles.

Connecticut

Bulletin. (1968-69) Quarterly. Connecticut Society of Genealogists (FHL# 974.6/B2n) Name changed to *The Nutmegger* in 1969.

Bulletin of the Stamford Genealogical Society. (1958-71) Quarterly. Stamford: Stamford Genealogical Society. (FHL# 974.6/B2s) The primary focus is Stamford and Fairfield County. Continued as *Connecticut Ancestry* in 1971.

Collections of the Connecticut Historical Society. (1860-1967) Invervals of publication vary. Hartford: Connecticut Historical Society. (FHL# 974.6/H25c) Mostly historical material.

Connecticut Ancestry. (1971-) Quarterly. Stamford: Stamford Genealogical Society. (FHL# 974.6/B2s) Previously published as *Bulletin of the Stamford Genealogical Society.* Primary focus is on Fairfield County. Separate index volumes to vols. 1-25.

The Connecticut Magazine. (1897-1908) Quarterly. Hartford: The Connecticut Magazine Company. (FHL# 974.6/B2c) Previously published as *Connecticut Quarterly.* Mostly historical articles but some genealogy.

Connecticut Maple Leaf. (1983-) Semi-annual. Rocky Hill: French-Canadian Genealogical Society of Connecticut. (FHL# 974.6/F25c) French-Canadian families in Connecticut.

Connecticut Nutmegger. (1972-) Quarterly. West Hartford, later Glastonbury: Connecticut Society of Genealogists. (FHL# 974.6/B2n) Previously published as *The Nutmegger.*

Connecticut Quarterly. (1895-96) Quarterly. Hartford: The Connecticut Quarterly Co. (FHL# 974.6/B2c) Continued in 1897 as *The Connecticut Magazine.*

The Nutmegger. (1969-72) Quarterly. West Hartford: Connecticut Society of Genealogists. (FHL# 974.6/B2n) Previously published as the *Bulletin.* Continued in 1972 as the *Connecticut Nutmegger.*

Maine

Bangor Historical Magazine. (1885-92) Monthly. Bangor: Benjamin A. Burr. (FHL# 974.1/H25b). Continued as *Maine Historical Magazine* in 1892.

Collections of the Maine Historical Society. (1831-1906) 3 Series. Frequency of publication varies. (FHL# 974.1/H25mc)

Downeast Ancestry. (1977-) Bi-monthly. Machias, Me: The News-Journal. (FHL# 974.1/D25d or microfiche 6019964)

Maine Genealogical Inquirer. (1968-75) Bi-monthly. Gorham and other cities. (FHL# 974.1/D25m) Largely queries and answers.

The Maine Genealogist and Biographer. (1875-78) Quarterly. Augusta: Maine Genealogical and Biographical Society. (FHL# 974.1/D25mg)

Maine Historical and Genealogical Recorder. (1884-98) Quarterly. Monthly 1898. Portland: S. M. Watson. (FHL# 974.1/H25mh)

Maine Historical Magazine. (1892-95) Monthly. Bangor: Charles H. Glass & Co. (FHL# 974.1/H25ba) Previously published as *Bangor Historical Magazine.*

The Maine Seine. (1979-) Bi-monthly. Farmington: Maine Genealogical Society. (FHL# 974.1/D25ms)

Massachusetts

Berkshire Genealogist. (1982-) Quarterly. Pittsfield: Berkshire Family History Association. (FHL# 974/D25bg)

Collections of the Massachusetts Historical Society. (1846-1941) Intervals of publication vary. (FHL# 974.4/B4m)

Collections of the Old Colony Historical Society. (1879-1909) Published irregularly. Taunton: Old Colony Historical Society. (FHL# 974.4/B2o)

Danvers Historical Society Collections. (1913-49) Annual. Danvers: Danvers Historical Society. (FHL# 974.45/-D1/H2dh) Deals primarily with Danvers and Salem, Massachusetts.

Dedham Historical Register. (1890-1903) Annual. Dedham: Dedham Historical Society. (FHL# 974.47/B2d) Deals primarily with Dedham and Norfolk County.

Essex Antiquarian. (1897-1909) Quarterly. Salem, Mass.: Essex Antiquarian. (FHL# 974.45/B2a)

Historical Collections of the Essex Institute. (1859-) Quarterly. Salem: Essex Institute. (FHL# 974.4/B2e) Includes a cumulative index. Focus is on Essex County, Massachusetts.

Historical Collections of the Topsfield Historical Society. (1895-1982) Annual. Topsfield: Topsfield Historical Society. (FHL# 974.45/T1/H25t) Focuses on Topsfield and Essex County.

Library of Cape Cod History and Genealogy. (1912-24) Yarmouth, Mass.: C. W. Swift. Intervals of publication vary. (FHL# 974.492/B4L incomplete, or microfilm 1004003)

Massachusetts Magazine. (1908-18) Quarterly. Salem: Salem Press. (FHL# 974.4/B2mm)

Massog. (1977-) Quarterly. Ashland: Massachusetts Society of Genealogists. (FHL# 974.4/D25ma)

The Mayflower Descendant. (1899-1937, 1985-to date) Quarterly. Boston: Massachusetts Society of Mayflower Descendants. (FHL# 973/D25md; vols. 1-34 on microfilm) Includes records, documents, and articles dealing primarily with southeast Massachusetts with special focus on the *Mayflower* passengers and their descendants. Publication was suspended 1926-29 and 1937-84. Indexes.

The Mayflower Quarterly. (1935-) Quarterly. Plymouth: General Society of Mayflower Descendants. (FHL# 973/D25mq)

Pilgrim Notes and Queries. (1913-17) Monthly (except in the summer). Boston: Massachusetts Society of Mayflower Descendants. (FHL# 974.4/B2p)

Proceedings of the Massachusetts Historical Society. 3 Series. (1791-1957) Boston: Massachusetts Historical Society. Intervals of publication vary. (FHL# 974.4/C4p) Mostly historical. Vols. 1-60 indexed.

Publication of the Colonial Society of Masachusetts. (1895-1982) Intervals of publication vary. (FHL# 974.4/B4cs) Largely historical.

The Register of the Lynn Historical Society. (1898-1931) Annual. Lynn: Lynn Historical Society. (FHL# 974.45/-L2/B5L)

New Hampshire

Collections of the New Hampshire Historical Society. (1824-1939) 1st ed. Concord: Jacob B. Moore, later for the Society by various publishers or by the Society. Intervals of publication vary. (FHL# 974.2/C4hs)

The Genealogist. (1975-) Bi-annual. Manchester: American-Canadian Genealogical Society of New Hampshire. (FHL# 974.2/D25a)

The Granite Monthly. (1877-1919) Monthly. 51 vols. Concord: John N. McClintock. Index in Vol. 37 to vols. 1-34. On microfiche only. 51 microfiche.

The New Hampshire Genealogical Records. (1903-10) Quarterly. Dover: Charles W. Tibbetts. (FHL# 974.2/B2g. Vols. 1-7 or microfilm 014928-014929)

New Hampshire Yesterday: For Researchers in New Hampshire Genealogy and the Life of Her People Yesterday. (1982-) Quarterly. Concord: n.p. (FHL# 974.2/D25n)

Proceedings of the New Hampshire Historical Society. (1874-1908) Concord: New Hampshire Historical Society. Intervals of publication vary. (FHL# 974.2/C4n) Largely historical.

Rhode Island

Rhode Island Historical Society Collections. (1827-1941) Providence: 1st ed. John Miller, later Rhode Island Historical Society. Published occasionally 1827-1902. Quarterly from January 1918 (Vol. 11). (FHL# 974.5/H25r) Continued publication as *Rhode Island History* in 1942.

Rhode Island History. (1942-) Quarterly. Providence: Rhode Island Historical Society. (FHL# 974.5/H25ri) Previously as *Rhode Island Historical Society Collections.*

Rhode Island Genealogical Register. (1978-) Quarterly. Princeton, Mass.: Rhode Island Families Association. (FHL# 974.5/D2ri)

Rhode Island Roots. (1975-) Quarterly. Warwick: Rhode Island Genealogical Society. (FHL# 974.5/D25r)

Vermont

Branches and Twigs. (1971-) Quarterly. Putney: Genealogical Society of Vermont. (FHL# 974.3/B2br)

Collections of the Vermont Historical Society. (1870-1943) Montpelier: Vermont Historical Society. Intervals of publication vary. (FHL# 974.3/B2vh, vols. 9-10 FHL# 974.3/D3v separately numbered vols. 1-2) Cumulative index to volumes 1-10. Largely historical.

Proceedings of the Vermont Historical Society. (1905-43) Quarterly. Montpelier: Vermont Historical Society. (FHL# 974.3/B2v) Continued in 1944 as the *Vermont Quarterly.*

The Vermont Antiquarian. (1902-04) Quarterly. Burlington: The Research Publication Co. (FHL# 974.3/B2va or microfilm 962548, item 2)

Vermont History: The Proceedings of the Vermont Historical Society. (1954-) Quarterly. Montpelier: Vermont Historical Society. (FHL# 974.3/B2v) Previously published as the *Vermont Quarterly..* Primarily historical.

Vermont Quarterly. (1944-53) Quarterly. Montpelier: Vermont Historical Society. (FHL# 974.3/B2v) Previously published as *Proceedings of the Vermont Historical Society.* Continued in 1954 as *Vermont History.*

Probate Records

Probate records consist of a variety of documents. When someone died, his or her property was disposed of by the courts. If the deceased left a will, the document was admitted to probate and recorded in the records of the probate court.

When someone died intestate (without a will), the court appointed an administrator to see that the property was accurately inventoried and distributed as the court directed. The property was usually divided among the heirs with one third going to the widow as her dower. Whether testate or intestate, it was often necessary to sell some of the property to pay the debts of the deceased.

The courts also appointed male guardians for minor children, even if they were living with their mother and residing elsewhere, to handle property matters. Probate records therefore include wills, administrations, bonds, inventories, bills of sale, petitions, accounts, guardianship records, and other documents relating to the property and family of the deceased. They are a valuable resource but are sometimes overlooked by beginning New England researchers who prefer to stay with vital records and published histories.

New England probate records are recorded in the probate books kept by the various courts. Before the establishment of probate courts, probate records were scattered throughout the records of the criminal and civil courts and even appear among land records. During the Andros administration, the probates of all estates valued at over fifty pounds were administered at Boston. Thus the Suffolk County court files contain probate matters for all of New England for 1686-89.

The Genealogical Society of Utah has obtained copies of virtually all extant probate court records for New England through 1850. In some areas, the original documents have also been preserved. Some of these case files have also been microfilmed.

The probate court system is not uniform throughout New England. Some states have county probate courts. Towns and districts are the primary unit in other states. Here is a state-by-state summary of the probate records available:

Connecticut

Probate matters in Connecticut were heard by the General Court, Particular Court, and the county courts until 1698, when four probate districts were created. In 1719, the four original districts were divided to accommodate the increasing population. Division has continued until, by 1984, 131 probate districts represent the 169 towns in the state.

Because of the numerous divisions of districts, many

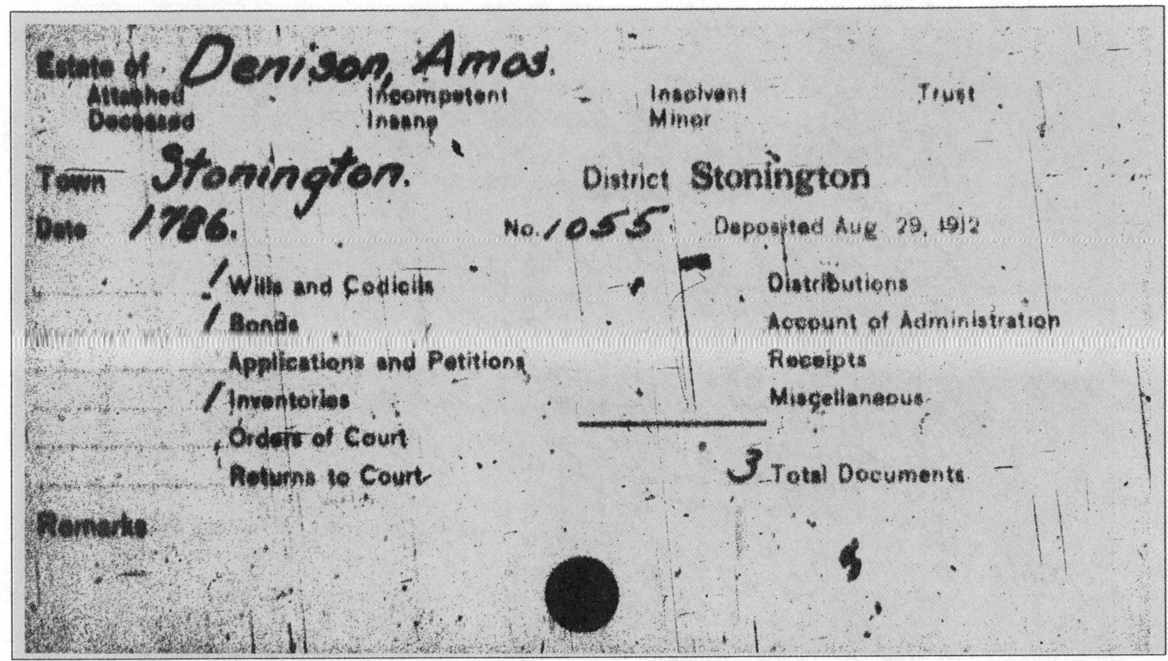

Estate of Denison, Amos.
Attached Incompetent Insolvent Trust
Deceased Insane Minor
Town Stonington. District Stonington
Date 1786. No. 1055 Deposited Aug. 29, 1912
/ Wills and Codicils
/ Bonds
Applications and Petitions
/ Inventories
Orders of Court
Returns to Court
Distributions
Account of Administration
Receipts
Miscellaneous
3 Total Documents
Remarks

Figure 5:6 Sample entry from Index to Connecticut Probate Records.

Connecticut towns have fallen within the jurisdiction of three or more courts. It is therefore necessary to identify the district in which the town of interest fell during the periods being researched. Probate records always remain in the district in which they were originally recorded.

As an example, Groton, Connecticut, was established in 1705 within the New London probate district. In 1766 Groton became a part of Stonington district, and in 1839 it became a separate district. To find the probate districts of each town, see:

Lindberg, Marcia Wiswall. *Genealogist's Handbook for New England Research.* Boston: New England Historic Genealogical Society, 1985. (FHL# 974/D27g)

Kemp, Thomas Jay. *Connecticut Researcher's Handbook.* Detroit: Gale Research Co., 1981. (FHL# 974.6/D23k)

Wright, Norman Edgar. *Genealogy in America.* Salt Lake City: Deseret Book Co., 1968.

The library has microfilms of the original probate books of each Connecticut district through 1850 and at present is collecting Connecticut probate records for 1850-1900. For holdings, consult the Locality FHLC under **Connecticut/[County]/[District]/Probate Records.**

Do not overlook probate case files. They are the original documents from which the probate books were copied. All Connecticut probate district courts have retained these original documents to 1880 in separate packets for each case, arranged alphabetically by surname and district. A statewide card index of the entire collection inventorying the documents in the packet is on 67 reels. It is cataloged under **Connecticut/Probate Records/Indexes.** (See Figures 5:6 and 5:7.)

The case files sometimes contain documents not found in the probate record books. In other cases they may be easier to read, or it may be easier to access the document in the case files because of the excellent index. However, probate books sometimes contain records which have apparently become lost or misfiled. It is therefore necessary to search both the probate books and the case files. The case files are cataloged under **Connecticut/Probate Records**, then by probate district. 1,622 reels.

For an important contribution to Connecticut research, see:

Manwaring, Charles William. *Digest of Early Connecticut Probate Records.* 3 vols. 3 reels. Hartford, Conn.: R. S. Peck, 1904-06. (FHL# 974.6 S2m; Volume 2 is on microfilm only.)

Cataloged under **Connecticut/Probate Records**. Although this work covers only the Hartford probate district, this district heard probate matters from the entire colony during the earliest period. Furthermore, Manwaring extracted these records from a variety of court documents besides standard probate court records, which commenced later. Vol. 1: 1635-1700; Vol. 2, 1720-29; Vol. 3, 1729-50. Every-name index in the back of each volume.

Maine

Maine probate records were kept on a county basis. Until 1760, all of Maine was within the jurisdiction of York County. All York wills to 1760 are included in:

Sargent, William M., ed. *Maine Wills, 1640-1760.* Portland, Maine: Brown Thurston, 1887. (FHL# 974.1/P2s, microfilm 599180, or microfiche 6046701)

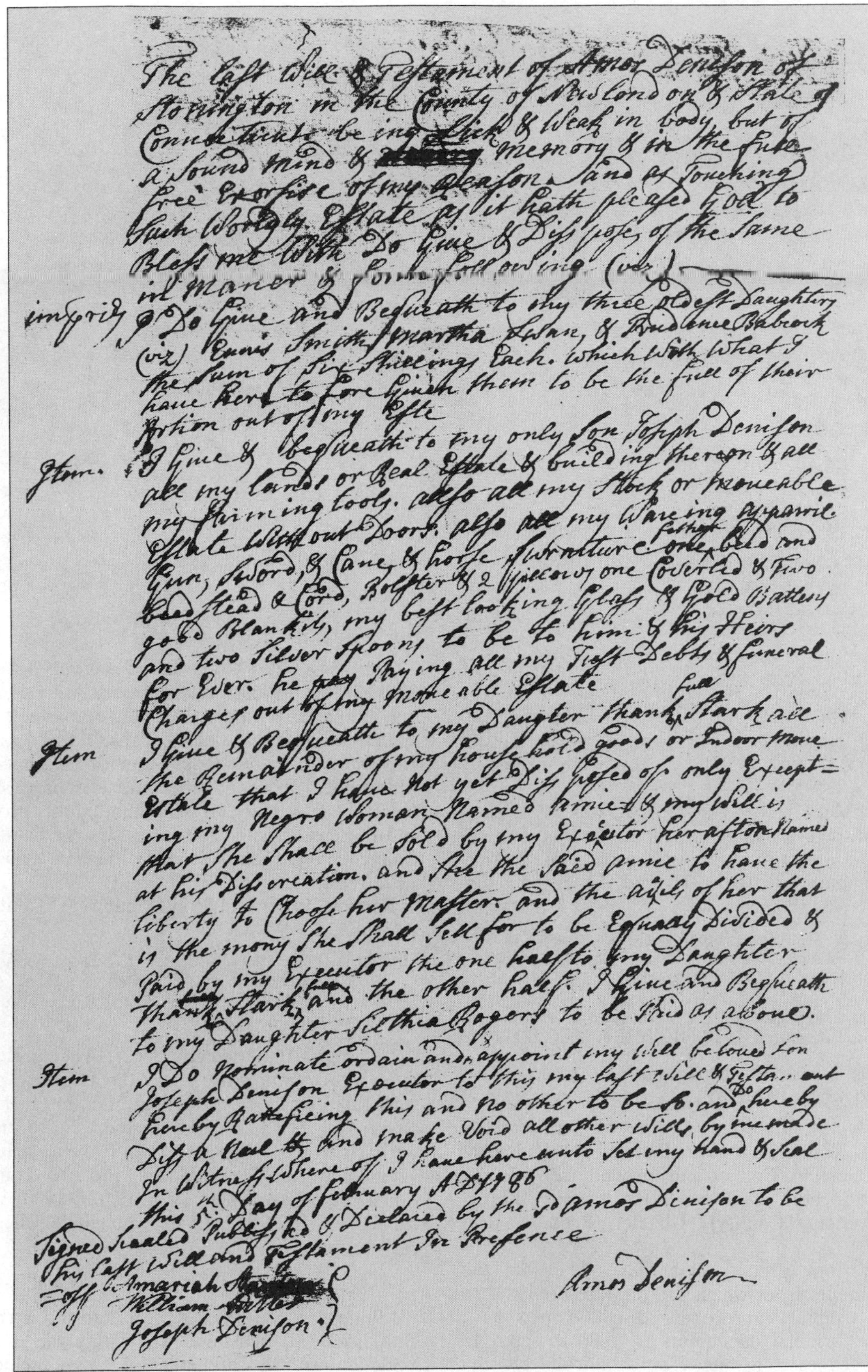

The last Will & Testament of Amos Denison of Stonington in the County of New London & State of Connecticute being Sick & Weak in body but of a Sound mind & [illegible] memory & in the free Exercise of my Reason and as Touching Such Worldly Estate as it hath pleased God to Bless me With Do Give & Dispose of the Same in Maner & form following (viz)

Imprimis I Do Give and Bequeath to my three oldest Daughters (viz) Eunis Smith, Martha Swan, & Prudence Babcock the Sum of Six Shillings Each. which With What I have heretofore Given them to be the full of their portion out of my Estate

Item. I Give & Bequeath to my only Son Joseph Denison all my Lands or Real Estate & building thereon & all my farming tools. also all my Stock or moveable Estate Without Doors. also all my Wearing apparel Gun, Sword, & Cane & horse furniture one feather bed and bedstead & Cord, Bolster & 2 pillows one Coverled & Two good Blankits, my best looking Glass & Gold Buttons and two Silver Spoons to be to him & his Heirs for Ever. he paying all my Just Debts & funeral Charges out of my moveable Estate

Item I Give & Bequeath to my Daughter thankfull Stark all the Remainder of my household goods or Indoor moveable Estate that I have not yet Disposed of only Excepting my Negro Woman Named Amie & my Will is that She Shall be Sold by my Executor hereafter Named at his Discreation. and the Said Amie to have the liberty to Choose her Master. and the avails of her that is the mony She Shall Sell for to be Equally Divided & paid by my Executor the one half to my Daughter thankfull Stark and the other half. I Give and Bequeath to my Daughter Silthia Rogers to be Paid as above.

Item I Do Nominate ordain and appoint my Well beloved Son Joseph Denison Executor to this my last Will & Testament hereby Ratifieing this and no other to be So. and hereby Disannul and make Void all other Wills by me made In Witness Whereof I have hereunto Set my hand & Seal this 5th Day of February AD 1786

Signed Sealed Published & Declared by the Sd Amos Denison to be his last Will and Testament In Presence

Amariah [illegible]
William [illegible]
Joseph Denison

Amos Denison

Figure 5:7 Will of Amos Dennison, Stonington, Connecticut, Probate District #1055.

See also rpt. ed., Baltimore: Genealogical Publishing Company, 1972. Limited to wills; thus administrations, guardianships, division, etc., are excluded.

Original York County probate records have been microfilmed for 1687-1860 (indexes to 1900). 52 reels. Prior to 1687, Maine probate records were kept by the recorder of the province. They are scattered throughout the deeds and court records, both of which are published and indexed for this period. (See *Court Records* and *Land Records* above.)

The Genealogical Society of Utah has microfilmed all extant probate records of each county from the earliest dates to about 1860-1900, with the exception of Knox County, which was not created until 1860. Cumberland County probate records prior to 1908 were destroyed by fire.

Massachusetts

Massachusetts keeps its probate records at the county and has microfilmed all of them. A few counties have also kept their original papers.

In some of the more populous counties, you must locate the probate index, and determine the case number of the probate of interest. Then you must locate this number in the probate docket, which contains an inventory of the various documents in the case with volume and page numbers. When you know the volume and page, you can then find the corresponding film number. The indexes, dockets, and probate books are accessed in the FHLC under **Massachusetts/[County]/Probate Records.**

The least populated counties have indexes at the beginning of each volume. Massachusetts probate records are generally cataloged in the FHLC under **Massachusetts/[County]/Probate Records.** Here are some comments county by county:

Barnstable County. The original papers were burned, but most probate books survived. Records before 1686 are at Plymouth.

Bristol County. Besides the probate books, Bristol County has an excellent set of original papers arranged alphabetically, 1690-1881. Records before 1687 are at Plymouth. Prior to 1746 the Rhode Island towns of Little Compton, Cumberland, Bristol, Warren, and Tiverton were in Bristol County, Massachusetts.

Essex County. Probate records, 1635-81, are published in *The Probate Records of Essex County, Massachusetts, 1635-1681,* 3 vols. (Salem, Mass.: Essex Institute, 1916-20). (FHL# 974.45/P2m or microfilm 1033717, items 1-3. Volume 1 is on film only)

Besides the "regular" series of Essex County probate records, there are four volumes of "Old" Norfolk County probate and deed records. "Old" Norfolk County included the towns of Salisbury, Amesbury, and Haverhill, now in Essex County. Although Norfolk County became extinct in 1680, the registry recorded documents as late as 1714. 3 reels. Consult the FHLC under **Massachusetts/Essex/Probate Records.**

Wills and deeds were also recorded at Ipswich for 1639-95 when the registry was terminated and the records transferred to Salem. 5 vols., 2 reels. Check the FHLC under **Massachusetts-Essex/Ipswich/Probate Records.**

Nantucket County. Probate records begin in 1706, although the county had been populated in the 1660s and was organized in 1695.

Plymouth County. Plymouth probate records per se begin in 1686 and have been microfilmed through 1903. Earlier probate records are located in Plymouth Colony records. Four volumes of wills, 1633-1686, with index are available. 2 reels.

Other important works include:

Sherman, Ruth Wilder, and Robert S. Wakefield, comps., *Plymouth Colony Probate Guide: Where to Find Wills and Related Data for 800 People of Plymouth Colony, 1620-1691.* Warwick, R.I.: Plymouth Colony Research Group, 1983. (FHL# 974.4/P2s)

Contains information from every known Plymouth Colony probate record and every colony resident whose probate was found elsewhere from the landing of the Pilgrims to the merger of Plymouth with Massachusetts in 1691.

Plymouth Colony Wills and Inventories. 3 vols. (FHL# 974.4/P2p)

Typescript collection of probate records extracted from the *Mayflower Descendant.*

Suffolk County. An important published work reprinted from the *New England Historical and Genealogical Register* of records dating 1639-70.

Suffolk County Wills: Abstracts of the Earliest Wills upon Record in the County of Suffolk, Massachusetts. Baltimore: Genealogical Publishing Co., 1984. (FHL# 974.46/P2s) (See Figures 5:8 and 5:9.)

New Hampshire

Probate records in New Hampshire are recorded at the county level. Prior to the formation of counties in 1771, New Hampshire probate records were recorded on a provincial basis and in "Old" Norfolk County, Massachusetts, which had jurisdiction for the four New Hampshire towns of Portsmouth, Hampton, Dover, and Exeter until the county was suspended in 1680. Its records were eventually transferred to Salem, Massachusetts. They are cataloged under **Massachusetts/Essex/Probate Records** as a separate series from the Essex County probate records.

Twenty-six volumes of New Hampshire probate records for 1655-1771 have been microfilmed with a card index. The collection also includes 103 volumes of provincial deeds. 118 reels. Cataloged under **New Hampshire/Probate Records.**

Nine volumes, containing all of the New Hampshire probate records, 1635-1771, are published minus legal phrases, in the *Provincial and State Papers of New Hampshire* series, Volumes 31-39. (See *Genealogy* above.) Sources are "Old" Norfolk, Essex, Suffolk, and Middlesex counties, Massachusetts; York County, Maine; and the provincial court and probate records of New Hampshire. 21 reels. (FHL# 974.2/N2nhn) Cataloged under **New Hampshire/Probate Records.**

After 1771 each county recorded its own probate

YEAR.	NAME.	CASE.	NO.
	Hobart, *cont.*		
1776	Samuel . . .	will	15829
1801	Samuel . . .	administration	21472
1864	Samuel B. . .	will	45574
1874	Samuel B. . .	will	55526
1729	Sarah	will	5871
1741	Sarah	guardianship	7685
1851	Sarah	guardianship	37231
1861	Sarah B. . . .	adoption . .	43619
1890	Sarah B. . . .	will	84808
1879	Sarah C. . . .	will	62857
1801	Seth	guardianship	21545
1737	Solomon . . .	will	6990
1726	Susanna . . .	guardianship	5294
1767	Susanna . . .	guardianship	14028
1689	Thomas . . .	administration	1696
1858	William H. . .	will	41820
1892	William H. . .	administration	89007
	Hobbs		
1860	Alexander . .	administration	42898
1870	Alvah . . .	will	50964
1867	Ann	administration	48277
1867	{ Calista Calistia } . .	administration	47620
1877	Charles . . .	administration	59956
1691	Christopher . .	guardianship	1821
1691	Christopher . .	administration	1822
1826	Daniel. . . .	administration	27896
1891	Edson C. . .	foreign sale .	86844
1893	Elizabeth. . .	administration	93673
1856	Evangeline . .	guardianship	40312
1893	Gertrude W. .	adoption, etc.	93867
1891	Granville J. .	partition . .	86720
1893	Harriet E. . .	partition . .	92365
1850	Henrietta . .	guardianship	36776
1849	Henry A. . .	administration	36516
1848	James	guardianship	35770
1857	James	administration	41392
1728	John	administration	5696
1842	John	administration	33431
1872	John	guardianship	53413
1893	John S. . . .	will	94225
1890	John W. F. .	will	84988
1877	Joseph H. . .	administration	60208
1886	Joseph W. . .	administration	75372
1850	Marietta . . .	guardianship	36777
1892	Mary A. . . .	will	90786
1872	Mary F. . . .	administration	52774
1889	Mary J. . . .	will	82326
1762	Matthew . . .	will	12866
1877	Nellie M. A. .	guardianship	60197

YEAR.	NAME.	CASE.	NO.
	Hobbs, *cont.*		
1851	Robert G. . .	will	37367
1891	Samuel M. . .	administration	88740
1877	William H. . .	guardianship	60197
	Hobby		
1715	Charles, Sir . .	administration	3690
1719	Charles . . .	guardianship	4211
1719	Edward . . .	guardianship	4212
1711	John	will	3351
1741	John	administration	7608
1835	Maria L. . . .	guardianship	30943
1717	Mary	guardianship	3837
1835	Mary M. . . .	guardianship	30944
1871	Nancy . . .	will	51774
1767	Rachel . . .	will	14150
1719	Wensley . . .	guardianship	4213
1743	Wensley . . .	administration	7957
1808	Wensley . . .	administration	23247
1713	William . . .	administration	3494
1719	William . . .	guardianship	4244
1850	William . . .	will	36790
	Hobson		
1825	Moses	administration	27492
1826	Moses	guardianship	27898
	Hoburn		
1699	William . . .	will	2503
	Hockaday Hockardy }		
1748	Edward . . .	will	8938
1860	Robert . . .	administration	42768
	Hockey		
1863	Joseph . . .	will	44976
1885	Mary B. . . .	administration	72951
	Hodgdon		
1866	Ada M. . . .	guardianship	47440
1772	Benjamin . .	will	15130
1776	Benjamin . .	administration	16014
1866	Eliza	administration	47449
1888	Franklin N. .	administration	79043
1885	George M. . .	guardianship	73861
1892	Gertrude L. .	administration	91085
1880	James W. . .	administration	64646
1884	John G. . . .	will	72417
1866	Lewis	guardianship	47440
1877	Lucinda . . .	will	60655
1883	Mary A. . . .	administration	69577
1757	Nathaniel . .	administration	11612
1884	Sarah W. . .	administration	71180
1880	William C. . .	administration	63928
	Hodge, *see also*	**Hodges**	
1883	Clementina . .	administration	70362

(125)

Figure 5:8 Page from Elijah George, *Index to Probate Records of the County of Suffolk, Massachusetts from the Year 1636 to and Including the Year 1893.*

No.	Name	Date	Proceedings	Vol.	Page.
3350	Ann Fisher (Dedham	1711	Will	17	311
			Evidence new series	6	397
			Probate + Letter	17	310
3351	John Hobby	1711	Will	17	309
			Evidence new series	6	397
			Accept^ce of Ex^r.	6	398
			Probate + Letter	17	309
			Inv.	17	425
		1738	Bond (Adm. will &c. d.b.n.) new series	6	398
			Letter	34	172
			Inv	34	179
3352	Bethulea Mighell	1711	Will	17	315
			Evidence new series	6	399
			Probate + Letter	17	314
3353	Elizur Holyoke	1711	Will	17	321
			Evidence new series	6	400
			Acceptance of Ex^r.	6	400
			Probate + Letter	17	320
			Inv.	17	408
			Acct + Division (?) new series	6	401
3354	John Cass (Roxbury	1711	Will	17	325
			Evidence new series	7	167
			Probate + Letter	17	325
			Inv.	17	372
			Acct	17	471
3355	William Sullivant	1711	Bond (Adm) new series	7	167
			Letter	17	326
			Inv.	17	341

Figure 5:9 Probate Docket, Suffolk County, Massachusetts.

records. The library has microfilm copies of all extant records to about 1860. Coos County probate records were destroyed by a fire in 1880.

Rhode Island

Probate records in Rhode Island are recorded by the towns, and earliest probate matters are sometimes scattered throughout the town record books before separate volumes were maintained. The Family History Library has microfilm copies of almost all Rhode Island probate records to about 1850. Probate records for Little Compton, Cumberland, Warren, Bristol, and Tiverton are in Bristol County, Massachusetts, until 1746 when they were ceded to Rhode Island. There are no records for New Shoreham. They are cataloged under **Rhode Island/[County]/[Town]/Probate Records.**

The Anthony Tarbox Briggs Collection contains abstracts of many Rhode Island wills. 19 reels. Cataloged under **Rhode Island/Probate Records**. (See *Genealogy* above.)

Vermont

Vermont probate records are filed by county except in the counties of Bennington, Orange, Rutland, Winham, and Windsor, which are divided into two districts each, listed below with their towns.

Bennington County. Manchester District includes Arlington, Dorset, Landgrove, Manchester, Peru, Rupert, Sangate, Sunderland, and Winhall. Bennington District includes Bennington, Glastenbury, Pownal, Readsboro, Searsburg, Shaftsbury, Stamford, and Woodford.

Orange County. Randolph District includes Braintree, Brookfield, Chelsea, Orange, Randolph, Tunbridge, Washington, and Williamstown. Bradford District includes Bradford, Corinth, Fairlee, Newbury, Strafford, Thetford, Topsham, Vershire, and West Fairlee.

Rutland County. Rutland District includes Brandon, Chittenden, Clarendon, Danby, Ira, Mendon, Middletown Springs, Mount Holly, Pittsfield, Pittsford, Proctor, Rutland, Sherburne, Shrewsbury, Tinmouth, Wallingford, and West Rutland. Fair Haven District includes Benson, Castleton, Fair Haven, Hubbardton, Pawlet, Poultney, Sudbury, Wells, and West Haven.

Windham County. Marlboro District includes Brattelboro, Dover, Dummerston, Guilford, Halifax, Marlboro, Newfane, Somerset, Stratton, Vernon, Wardsboro, Whitingham, and Wilmington. Westminster District includes Athens, Brookline, Grafton, Jamaica, Londonderry, Putney, Rockingham, Townshend, Westminster, and Windham.

Windsor County. Windsor District includes Andover, Baltimore, Cavendish, Chester, Ludlow, Plymouth, Reading, Springfield, Weathersfield, West Windsor, Weston, and Windsor. The Hartford District includes Barnard, Bethel, Bridgewater, Hartford, Hartland, Norwich, Pomfret, Rochester, Royalton, Sharon, Stockbridge, and Woodstock.

The Genealogical Society of Utah has microfilmed all Vermont probate record books to about 1850 with the exception of the Fair Haven District of Rutland County which ends in 1823. Addison County probate records prior to 1824 were destroyed by fire. Vermont probate records are cataloged under **Vermont/[County]/Probate Records** (followed by district if appropriate).

Tax Records

New England tax records are of three basic types: poll (head) tax, real property tax, and personal property tax. These records may be separate or combined. The information on the tax lists varies from place to place and time to time. White males were required to pay poll tax when they reached the age of twenty-one (in some areas, sixteen or eighteen). In some tax lists, fathers were required to pay poll tax for sons between sixteen and twenty-one still living at home.

Real property was not always taxed equally. Improved and unimproved land were taxed differently. The types of personal property taxed varies greatly but was often broken down into categories of livestock, structures, implements, etc. See:

Eakle, Arlene Haslam. *Tax Records: A Common Source with an Uncommon Value.* n.p., 1978. (FHL# 973/R47e)

Thorndale, William. "Land and Tax Records," in Arlene Eakle and Johni Cerny, eds., *The Source: A Guidebook of American Genealogy.* Salt Lake City, Utah: Ancestry Publishing Co., 1984, pp. 235-36. (FHL# 973/D27ts, in U.S./Canada Reference area)

Many early tax lists are found in town record books among minutes of town meetings, vital records, cattle marks, etc. New Hampshire town records are indexed; for other colonies, examine them page by page. Some towns maintained separate tax books. These are cataloged under **[State]/[County]/[Town]/Taxation**. They are excellent supplements to the federal census and often pre-date census records. See *Town Records* below.

The library has a few state-wide collections of tax records for New England:

Maine

Massachusetts General Court. Valuations Committee. Various valuations for 1780-1811, arranged alphabetically by town and surname. 6 reels. Cataloged under **Maine/-Taxation**. Also see *Massachusetts.*

Massachusetts

Massachusetts Department of Archives. Property valuations and taxes, 1760-1771. Contains tax lists from various colonial counties and towns in Massachusetts. Incomplete. 4 reels. Cataloged under **Massachusetts/Taxation**.

Massachusetts General Court. Valuations Committee. Valuations for various years, 1780-92, 1810-11. Arranged by year and alphabetically by town and surname. Some indexes at the beginnings of some volumes. 19 reels. Cataloged under **Massachusetts/Taxation.**

Pruit, Betty Hobbs, ed. *The Massachusetts Tax Valuation List of 1771.* Boston, G. K. Hall & Co., 1978. (FHL# Q/974.4/-R4m)

An excellent work, state-wide, well edited and indexed. Overy thirty columns of information were used to evaluate each taxpayer.

United States. Secretary of the Treasury. Massachusetts and Maine Direct Tax Census of 1798. 20 vols. 18 reels.

Microfilm of original manuscript in the library of the New England Historic Genealogical Society. Record of a federal tax levied to support the war against France. Includes information about owners of property, tenants, relative boundaries, current valuation, number of buildings, etc., arranged by county and town. The records were partially destroyed by fire in the 1840s. Indexes for vols. 1-3. Cataloged under **Massachusetts/Taxation.** Guide to the location of each town in the collection in Michael H. Gorn, *An Index and Guide to the Microfilm Edition of the Massachusetts and Maine Direct Tax Census of 1798* (Boston: New England Historic Genealogical Society, 1979). (FHL# 974/ R2i) Not a name index.

New Hampshire

New Hampshire. Secretary of State. Non-resident tax lists, 1849-1874. 9 reels. Cataloged under **New Hampshire/-Taxation**.

Tax Books, 1727-1788. Inventories of taxes assessed and received from the various towns. Incomplete. Only volume 1 contains actual lists of taxpayers. 1 reel (FHL# microfilm 983686).

Town Records

In New England the town was the primary unit of government, and it is in the records of the towns that New Englanders most frequently appear. The town record books generally include vital records, proprietors' records, town meeting minutes, cattle marks, highway and boundary surveys, tax lists, appointments, election results, etc., including some probate and land records. The various record types are usually kept in separate volumes by town clerks; but in the small towns and in the early days of most settlements, these records were often combined in a single volume. The Genealogical Society of Utah has microfilmed vast numbers of New England town record books – virtually all extant town records of Vermont and New Hampshire through 1850 and the majority of the town records for Maine, Massachusetts, and Rhode Island. Town records are cataloged under **[State]/[County]/[Town]/Town Records**.

An exception has been Connecticut, where the several major collections of vital records made the acquisition of the town record books less imperative, but its town records are presently being filmed though not yet cataloged.

Most New Hampshire town records are included in a statewide, every-name card index to about 1850, alphabetized and arranged by town with volume and page numbers of the original entry noted. Birth and death entries are labeled "F.R." (family record) and marriage entries "M.R." (marriage record). But the large majority of the entries are from town meeting minutes, tax lists, and other records. Index on 111 reels. Check the FHLC under **New Hampshire/Vital Records/Indexes.**

Seven towns not included in the general index are on a separate card index, similar in format: Croydon, Landaff, Lisbon, Meredith, Mount Vernon, New Castle, and Springfield. At least one volume of Springfield town records was omitted in indexing. Check the Author/-Title FHLC under "Index to Seven Towns in New Hampshire." 3 reels.

Vital Records

The town is the primary source of vital records in the New England states. It was the duty of town clerks to record births, marriages, and deaths in the town records. The usual procedure in the seventeenth and eighteenth centuries was for the head of each household to report these events to the clerk after the family was relatively "complete." Thus, families are usually grouped in the original records. Sometimes additional children were reported later, as are many later events such as marriages and deaths.

Vital records were usually kept in separate books; but in the early years of settlement and in many small towns, the vital records mingle with minutes, cattle marks, and other town records. Some vital record books are lost; others are incomplete, as some clerks were less meticulous than others. Check the FHLC under **[State]/[County]/[Town]/Vital Records.**

Here is a state-by-state listing of major collections and peculiarities:

Connecticut

Vital records were recorded in each town from its beginning to the present. A few Connecticut towns have published their vital records. Many vital entries are found in the deed books of the older towns in the state. From 1897 to the present, town clerks have been required to forward copies of current vital records to the State Department of Health at Hartford.

The Family History Library is currently filming Connecticut town vital records and has two major collections of vital records.

1. The most important source is the Lucius B. Barbour Collection of Connecticut vital records prior to 1850 – typescript copies of the vital records of most Connecticut towns alphabetically arranged with an accompanying slip index, each slip containing one entry of birth, marriage, or death, and arranged alphabetically for the entire state. It is sometimes necessary, however, to consult the original vital records to distinguish among the children of different persons of the same name as the alphabetization of the Barbour collection destroys the original family group format. 98 reels. For call numbers, check the locality FHLC under **Connecticut/Vital Records.** (See Figures 5:10 and 5:11.)

2. The Charles R. Hale Collection of vital records consists of all marriages and death notices abstracted from over 100 Connecticut newspapers and tombstone inscriptions from about 2,000 cemeteries. Hale also made statewide slip indexes for marriage and death information, including complete citations of original sources. 360 reels. Cataloged under **Connecticut/Vital Records.**

See also:

Torrey, Almon Clarence. *New England Marriages Prior to*

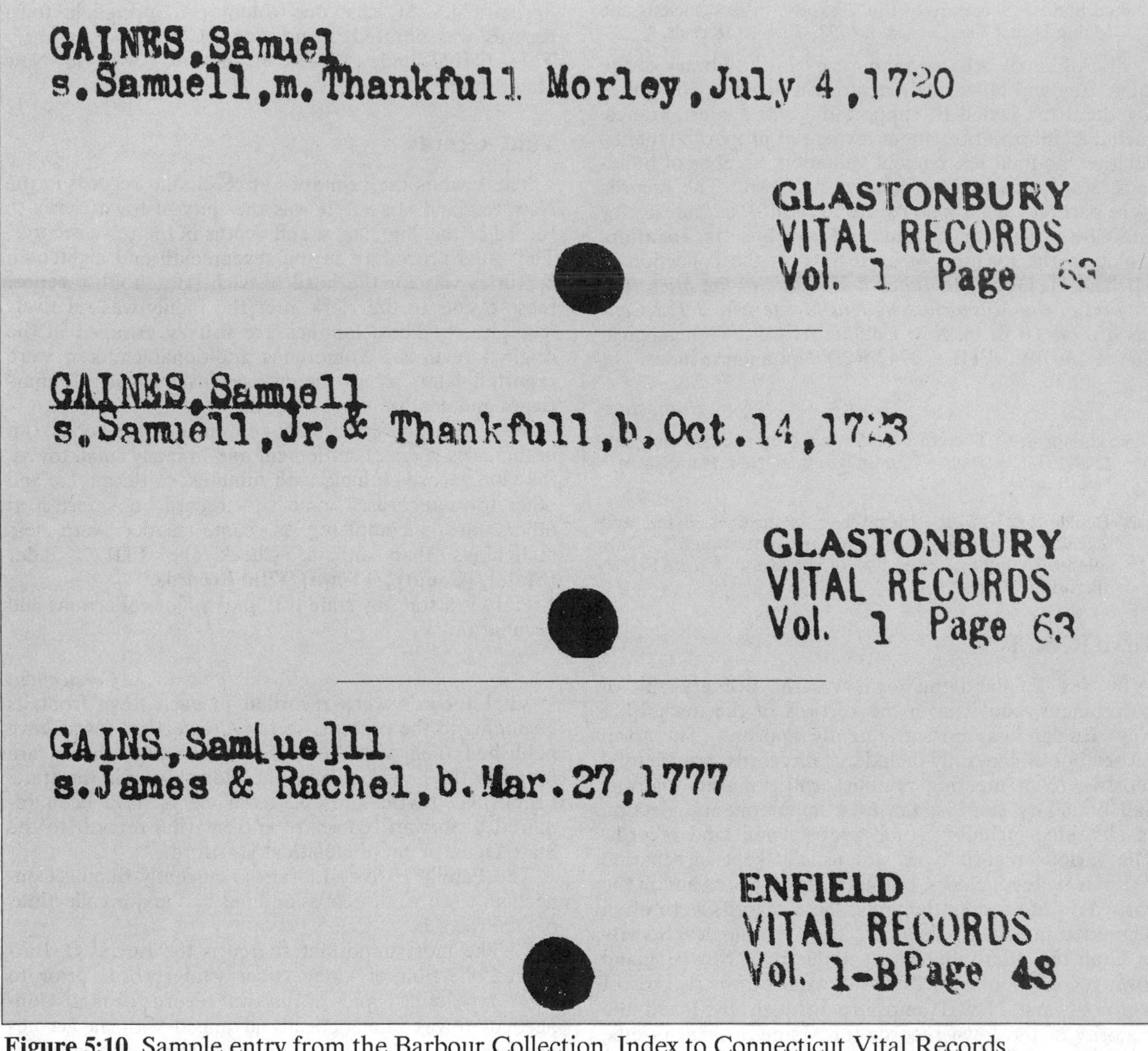
GAINES, Samuel
s. Samuell, m. Thankfull Morley, July 4, 1720

GLASTONBURY
VITAL RECORDS
Vol. 1 Page 63

GAINES, Samuell
s. Samuell, Jr. & Thankfull, b. Oct. 14, 1723

GLASTONBURY
VITAL RECORDS
Vol. 1 Page 63

GAINS, Sam[ue]ll
s. James & Rachel, b. Mar. 27, 1777

ENFIELD
VITAL RECORDS
Vol. 1-B Page 48

Figure 5:10 Sample entry from the Barbour Collection, Index to Connecticut Vital Records.

1700. Baltimore: Genealogical Publishing Co., 1985. (FHL# 974/ V2t)

Includes marriages in vital records and also evidence of marriage from other sources.

Maine

Maine's town clerks keep its vital records, although an 1828 law required county clerks to make a record of marriages performed by the clergy. County records also include some civil marriages. Early Maine vital records are very incomplete. Only five towns have vital records dating from the seventeenth century, and many towns are not included in statewide indexes. In 1864 state law mandated that town clerks forward copies of vital records to the state. Compliance was minimal, and new legislation was enacted in 1892. Since 1892, the State Board of Health has retained copies of birth, marriage, and death records. The state also attempted to obtain abstracts of all pre-1892 town vital records by encouraging town clerks to transcribe vital entries from the record books on individual cards, which were then alphabetized to form a statewide index of vital statistics. Only eighty towns participated.

For holdings, check the FHLC under **Maine/[County]/[Town]/Vital Records**. County marriage records are cataloged under **Maine/[County]/Vital Records**. The library's major collections of Maine vital records, all of them cataloged under **Maine/Vital Records**, are:

238 PROBATE RECORDS. VOL. III,

Right of Mary his wife, and appointed to him by the Executors of the last Will of Edward Stebbing, Decd.

Page 119.

Stebbing, Mrs. Frances, Hartford. Invt. £82-11-02. Taken 23 December, 1673, by Thomas Bull & Robert Webster.

I ffrances Stebbing, Living in Hartford, in the colony of Conecticot, Widdow, being aged and under many weaknesses of body, but having my perfect memory and Understanding, Doe make and Ordain this my last Will and Testament, wherein I give to my Dear and beloved son Mr. John Chester, now living in or neer unto London in old England, the ffull and Just some of Twenty and four pounds Starling; or, if deceased, to his wife and his two Sons John and Sampson Chester, in equal portion, to be paid in Hartford. I give unto my ffowr grand children, Thomas, William, Matthew and Mary Cadwell, fower pounds a pece, to be paid in Currant Country pay into the hands of my Son Thomas Cadwell. I give to my daughter Cadwell all my wearing apparell, both Woolen and Linen. I Constitute Lt. Thomas Bull and James Ensign Executors. 20th May, 1670.

ffRANCES X STEBBING.

Witness: *Thomas Bull.*

Codicil, wherein is given 7 Acres of Land in the South Meadow not before disposed of, it being four score Rod Long and about fourteen Rod and a quarter wide, bequeathed to Thomas, William and Mary Cadwell. And 4 acres more I doe give, two acres of ye said fowre to ye now two youngest children of my son and daughter Matthew and Abigail Cadwell, and the other two acres I leave to the dispose of my two friends in trust, Lt. Bull and Lt. Robert Webster, whom I ordain Executors.

I ffrances Stebbing doe now Rattify the within specified will, dated 20th May, 1670; only the Executors, which I now ordain Lt. Bull and Lt. Robert Webster. And also I now doe bequeath to my daughter Cadwell only my wearing goone, and the rest of my apparell to be divided betwixt ye wife of John Wilson, Mary Day and Mary Cadwell.—12 November, 1673. Also I give to Mr. John Whiting 40s, and my husbands cloak to John Wilson.

Witness: *Eliazer Way,* FFRANCES X STEBBING.
John Wilson.

Court Record, Page 136—20 January, 1673-4: Will exhibited. Proven.

Page 153.

Stedman, Lt. John, Wethersfield. Died December, 1675. Invt. £172-04-08. Taken February, 1675, by Lt. Chester, Ensign Goodrich, John Belden sen., Townsmen. Will dated 11 January, 1675-6.

Figure 5:11 Charles William Manwaring, *A Digest of Early Connecticut Probate Records,* Vol. 1 (Hartford: R.S. Peck, 1904).

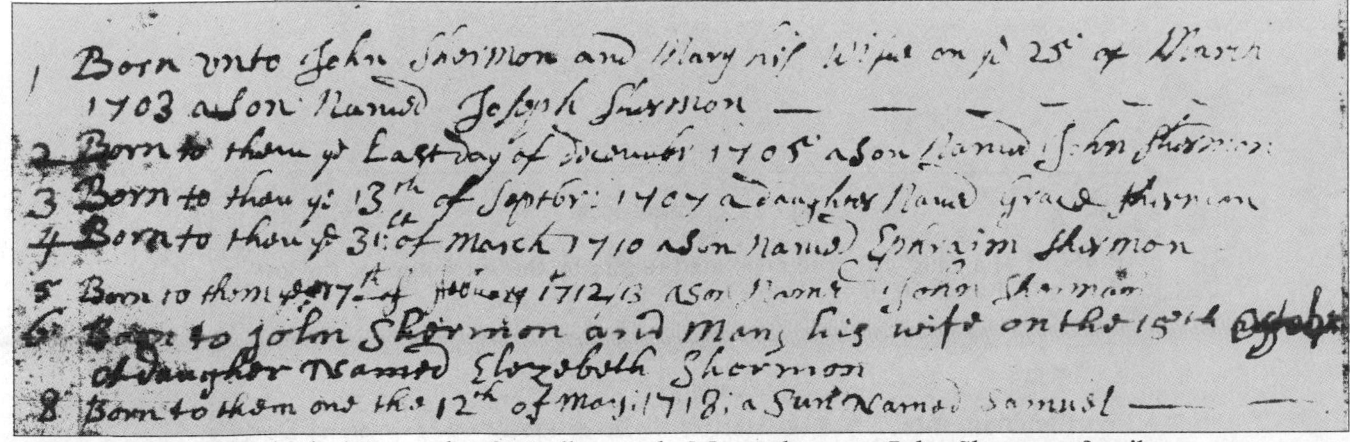
1 Born unto John Shermon and Mary his Wife on ye 25 of March 1703 a Son Named Joseph Shermon — — — — —
2 Born to them ye Last day of December 1705 a Son Named John Shermon
3 Born to them ye 13th of Septbr: 1707 a daughter Named Grace Shermon
4 Born to them ye 31st of March 1710 a Son Named Ephraim Shermon
5 Born to them ye 17th of February 1712/13 a Son Named John Shermon
6 Born to John Shermon and Mary his wife on the 15th of October a daughter Named Elizabeth Shermon
8 Born to them ond the 12th of May 1718 a Son Named Samuel — —

Figure 5:12 Original Vital Records of Marlborough, Massachusetts, John Shermon family.

Maine Division of Vital Statistics. Index to Vital Records prior to 1892 of 80 Maine Towns. 141 reels. Arranged alphabetically by surname and year within the surname.

_____. Index to Vital Records, Bride's Index to Marriages, 1895-1953. 11 reels.

_____. Index to Vital Records, 1892-1907. Arranged alphabetically by surname. 184 reels.

_____. Index to Vital Records, 1907-22. 148 reels.

Maine State Archives. Delayed Returns of Birth, Marriage, and Death, 1670-1891. 109 reels.

Noyes, Benjamin Lake. "Vital Records Copied from Town, Church, and Cemetery Records in Various Towns and Counties of Maine along the Atlantic Seaboard." Typescript. 2 reels. (FHL# microfilm 873738, items 1,2 and 859060, item 4)

Massachusetts

Massachusetts vital statistics are kept in each town. Beginning in 1841, town clerks were required to forward copies of birth, marriage, and death records to the State Registrar of Vital Records. The state collection with indexes has been microfilmed. Birth and marriage records are available 1841-90. Death records are available to 1899. The statewide index covers 1841-1971. 523 reels. Check the FHLC under **Massachusetts/Vital Records** for call numbers.

There is no statewide index to pre-1841 Massachusetts vital records. However, most births and marriages recorded in vital records prior to 1850 have been entered on the International Genealogical Index (IGI). (See Chapter 2.)

In 1902 Massachusetts enacted legislation to encourage the towns in the state to compile and publish their vital records to 1850. About 200 participated, producing a remarkable collection of records. Conforming to the prescribed format, the compilers drew not only from town record books but from court, church, cemetery, and Bible records as well. Volumes are

168 MARLBOROUGH BIRTHS.

SHERMAN, Susanna Frost, d. Micah and Susanna Dennison, Aug. 27, 1800.
Thomas, s. Isaac, bap. May 14, 1797. C.R.I.
William, s. Isaac and Hannah, May 20, 1782.

SHERMON (see Sharmon, Sherman), Elezebeth, d. John and Mary, Oct. 15, —.
[Sherman, C.R.], Ephraim, s. John and Mary, March 31, 1710.
[Sherman, C.R.], Grace, d. John and Mary, Sept. 13, 1707.
John, s. John and Mary, Dec. 31, 1705.
[Sherman, C.R.], John, s. John and Mary, Feb. 17, 1712-13.
Joseph, s. John and Mary, March 25, 1703.
[Sherman, C.R.], Samuel, s. John and Mary, May 12, 1718.

SHORTLIFF, Joseph Henry, s. Joseph and Louisa, May 17, 1822.

SIGOURNEY, John, s. John, bap. July 21, 1776. C.R.I.

SIZE, John, s. John and Thankfull Robins, Nov. 12, 1761.

SLACK, Joel, s. William, bap. Sept. 18, 1768. C.R.I.
Oliver, s. William, bap. Oct. 19, 1766. C.R.I.
Pheebe, d. William, bap. June 10, 1764. C.R.I.

SMITH, Abby Caroline, d. Abner B. and Caroline, Aug. 12, 1843.
Abigail, d. Abner B. and Caroline, Dec. 19, 1841.
Abraham, s. John and Experience, April 13, 1722.
Andrew, s. Edward and Charlotte, May 16, 1822.
Ann, d. Edward and Charlotte, Sept. 17, 1824.
Anna, d. Nathaniel and Lydia, Oct. 16, 1744.
Anne [Anna, C.R.], twin d. Rev. Aaron and Martha, Aug, 22, 1741.
Betsy, d. Jonas and Susanna, March 24, 1785.
Calven, s. John and Rebecca, May 1, 1770.
Calvin, s. Calvin and Ruth H., Aug. 3, 1804.
Calvin, s. Edward and Charlotte, July 24, 1833.
Carolina Mariah, d. Abner B. and Caroline, Sept. 10, 1839.
Caroline, d. Calvin and Ruth H., Sept. 7, 1807.
Catte [Kate, C.R.], d. Nathaniel Jr. and Kezia, Jan. 20, 1753.
Charles, s. Edward and Charlotte, Nov. 30, 1837.
Charles Brigham, s. Abner B. and Caroline, April 27, 1834.
Charlotte, d. Edward and Charlotte, Feb. 6, 1827.
Damarus [Damaris, C.R.], d. Nathanel and Kerziah, Aug. 1, 1751.
David, s. John and Rebecca, May 17, 1772.
David, s. David and Abigail, Aug. 5, 1801.
Edward, s. Jeduthan, bap. Oct. 29, 1797. C.R.I.

Figure 5:13 Published version of *Vital Records of Marlborough, Massachusetts,* John Shermon family.

divided into three sections–births, marriages, and deaths–with vital entries strictly alphabetized and cross-referenced to other surname variants. Alphabetization obliterates the family-group format of the original town vital record books, but the library has copies of both the original records and the published volume for many towns.

A few Massachusetts towns published their vital records prior to 1902, using a variety of formats and inclusive years. Some of these have preserved the original format and chronology of the town record books but added an index. For all Massachusetts town records, check the FHLC under **Massachusetts/[County]/-[Town]/Vital Records**. (See Figures 5.12 and 5.13.)

The library has records for almost all towns. Many Massachusetts vital records are published in the *New England Historical and Genealogical Register* and the *Mayflower Descendant.* For a guide to the location of vital records of each town in the state, see:

Crandall, Ralph J. *Genealogical Research in New England.* Baltimore: Genealogical Publishing Co., 1984, pp. 97-108. (FHL# 974/D27gr)

Includes citations to all Massachusetts vital records in periodicals and other publications.

Massachusetts vital records are also included in the DAR Massachusetts collection. (See *Genealogy* above.) Major vital records collections and publications available in the library are:

Bailey, Frederic W. *Early Massachusetts Marriages Prior to 1800, with Addition of Plymouth County Marriages, 1692-1746.* 3 vols. in 1. 1897-1914 with additions; rpt. ed., Baltimore: Genealogical Publishing Co., 1968. (FHL# 974.4/V2b or microfilm 874201, item 1)

Bowman, Ernest George. *Records of Plymouth Colony: Births, Marriages, Deaths, Burials, and Other Records, 1633-1689.* ed., Nathaniel B. Shurtleff. Baltimore: Genealogical Publishing Co., 1976. (FHL# 974.4/V28s or microfilm 1036208, item 2)

Reprints volume 8 of *Records of the Colony of New Plymouth in New England,* 1857.

Walter E. Corbin and Lottie S. Corbin Manuscript Collection. 60 reels. For call numbers, consult the FHLC under **Massachusetts/Genealogy**.

Includes local histories, church records, vital records, Bible records, cemetery records, genealogies, and source notes, mostly from western and central Massachusetts. Arranged by county and town.

Judd, Sylvester. Manuscripts. 10 vols. 5 reels. Vital records from various towns in Massachusetts.

Massachusetts. Secretary of the Commonwealth. Registrar of births, marriages, and deaths. 523 reels. Includes births and marriages, 1841-90, and deaths 1841-99. Indexed to 1971. Cataloged under **Massachusetts/Vital Records.**

Torrey, Clarence Almon. *New England Marriages Prior to 1700.* Baltimore: Genealogical Publishing Co., 1985. (FHL# 974/ V2t)

Smith, Leonard H., Jr. *Vital Records of Southeastern Massachusetts.* 3 vols. Clearwater, Fla.: n.pub., 1980. (FHL# 974.4/V2v)

A collection of reprints from the *Mayflower Descendant.* Includes vital records of Eastham, Orleans, Middleborough, Wareham, Barnstable, and Sandwich. Index.

New Hampshire

Town clerks keep New Hampshire vital records and forward copies to the State Bureau of Vital Records and Health Statistics in Concord. The state collection includes a statewide card index of vital record abstracts from the town records, 1640-1900, divided into sections for marriages (102 reels), bride's index (17 reels), births (98 reels), deaths (60 reels), and divorces before 1938 (8 reels). The cards are indexed by the first and *third* letters of the surname. For call numbers, consult the locality FHLC under **New Hampshire/Vital Records.**

The library has microfilm copies of nearly all New Hampshire town vital record books to 1850. Many for the southeastern part of the state were beautifully transcribed by Priscilla Hammond. A card index to every name in the town records to about 1850 is available, arranged by surname and thereunder by town in one statewide series. Birth and death entries are labeled "F.R." (family record). Marriage entries are labeled "M.R." (marriage record). Original record books are cited.

This card index is on 111 microfilm reels. Check the FHLC under **New Hampshire/Vital Records/Indexes**.

A few towns are not included in this general index. Springfield, Landaff, Lisbon, Croydon, Mount Vernon, Meredith, and New Castle have a separate card index with a format similar to the general index. Some vital records for Springfield, and perhaps other towns, are not included in the second series, which is a separate card index. 3 reels. This collection is currently cataloged only in the Author/Title FHLC under "Index to Seven Towns in New Hampshire."

Haseltine Papers. 23 reels.

A collection of family histories, vital records, and cemetery records concentrating on Essex County, Massachusetts, and Rockingham County, New Hampshire, and containing some New Hampshire vital records not found elsewhere in the library. Catalogued only in the Author/Title FHLC under Haseltine Papers. No current cross reference in the Locality Catalog or in the old card index.

Torrey, Clarence Almon. *New England Marriages Prior to 1700.* Baltimore: Genealogical Publishing Co., 1985. (FHL# 974/ V2t)

Rhode Island

Rhode Island vital records are kept by the town clerks. Since 1853 copies of vital records have been filed with the State Registrar of Vital Statistics in Providence. The Genealogical Society has microfilmed most of the original town vital record books; they are cataloged under **Rhode Island/[County]/[Town]/Vital Records**. See these collections:

Arnold, James N. *Vital Records of Rhode Island, 1636-1850: A Family Register for the People.* 20 vols. Providence: Narraganset Historical Publishing, 1891-1912. (FHL# 974.5/V2a)

Also on 16 reels and 163 microfiche. For call numbers, check the Locality FHLC under **Rhode Island/Vital Records**. Be aware that Arnold's vital records contain many errors.

Calef, Frank T. "Genealogical Index to Rhode Island Records." n.p., n.d. 42 reels.

Includes many vital records to about 1850, also some cemetery and church records. Index entries are on individual cards with reference citations. Alphabetized statewide by surname but out of order within the surname. For call numbers, check the FHLC under **Rhode Island/Vital Records/Indexes.**

Anthony Tarbox Briggs Collection. 19 reels. A card index of cemetery, vital, probate, genealogical, and historical records. Includes some Rhode Island vital records.

Vermont

As in other New England states, the primary responsibility of recording Vermont vital statistics belongs to the town clerks. Copies of vital records are forwarded to the Division of Vital Records in Montpelier. The library has microfilm copies of all extant town vital records to about 1850 cataloged under **Vermont/[County]/-[Town]/Vital Records.**

The Family History Library has two excellent card indexes to the vital records of Vermont. The first index covers the earliest records through 1870. Town clerks abstracted vital entries, including cemetery information, from the town records on individual cards. Marriage entries were indexed under both bride and groom. These cards have been alphabetized statewide. Early Vermont vital records are very incomplete. Perhaps fewer than half of the births, marriages, and deaths in Vermont were recorded during this period. 287 reels.

The second index, covering 1871-1908, has a similar format. 120 reels. Both are cataloged under **Vermont/Vital Records/Indexes.**

The DAR Vermont collection also includes some vital records. (See *Genealogy* above.)

Bibliography

These reference books may also be helpful:

New England General

Connecticut Society of Genealogists. *Family History in the Northeast.* 2 vols. Hartford: n.p., 1983. (FHL# 974/D27f)

A collection of papers, outlines, and bibliographies presented at the Hartford Conference for Genealogists in the Northeast hosted by the Connecticut Society of Genealogists, 1983.

Crandall, Ralph J. *Genealogical Research in New England.* Baltimore: Genealogical Publishing Co., 1984. (FHL# 974/D27gr)

Reprints with addenda six articles originally published in the *New England Historical and Genealogical Register,* 1976-82.

Glynn, Joseph Martin. *Guide to New England Genealogy.* Newton, Mass.: New England Family History Society, 1982. (FHL# 974/D27gl)

Lindberg, Marcia Wiswall. *Genealogists' Handbook for New England Research.* Boston: New England Historic Genealogical Society, 1985. (FHL# 974/D27g)

Wright, Norman Edgar. *Genealogy in America,* vol. 1. Salt Lake City.: Deseret Book, 1968. (FHL# 973/D27wg)

Includes material for Massachusetts, Connecticut, and Maine. Some material is outdated.

______. *Genealogical Reader: Northeastern United States and Canada.* Provo, Utah: Brigham Young University, 1973. (FHL# 929.173/W934ne in General Reference area, first floor)

Some material is outdated.

Connecticut

Abbe, Elizabeth. *Conneticut Genealogical Research: Sources and Suggestions.* rpt. from *The New England Historical and Genealogical Register,* Vol. 84 (Jan. 1980). (FHL# 974.6/A1/no.24)

A reprint from the *New England Historical and Genealogical Register,* January 1980.

Kemp, Thomas Jay. *Connecticut Researcher's Handbook.* Detroit: Gale Research Co., 1981. (FHL# 974.6/D23k)

Sperry, Kip. *Connecticut Sources for Family Historians and Genealogists.* Logan, Utah: Everton Publishers, 1980. (FHL# 974.6/D23s)

Maine

Fisher, Carleton Edward. "Research in Maine." No. 122. *World Conference on Records and Genealogical Seminar.* Salt Lake City: Genealogical Society of the Church of Jesus Christ of Latter-day Saints, 1969. (FHL# 929.1/-W893/I22 in General Reference area first floor, or microfilm 897217, item 20)

Frost, John E. *Maine Genealogy: A Bibliographical Guide.* Portland, Maine.: Maine Historical society, 1977. (FHL# 974.1/A1/no.31 or microfiche 6046727)

Massachusetts

Bowen, Richard LeBarron. *Massachusetts Records: A Handbook for Genealogists, Historians, Lawyers, and Other Researchers.* Concord, N.H.: Rumford Press, 1957. (FHL# 974.4/D2b)

New Hampshire

Carpenter, Randall C. *Descriptive Inventory of the New Hampshire Collection.* No. 8 in Finding Aids to the Microfilm Manuscript Collection of the Genealogical Society of Utah. Salt Lake City: University of Utah Press, 1983. (FHL# 974.2/A3c)

Towle, Laird C., and Ann N. Brown. *New Hampshire Genealogical Research Guide.* Bowie, Md.: Heritage

Books, 1983. (FHL# 974.2/D27t in U.S./Canada Reference Area)

Rhode Island

Farnham, Charles W. "Rhode Island Colonial Records." No. I-25. *World Conference and Genealogical Seminar.* Salt Lake City: Genealogical Society of the Church of Jesus Christ of Latter-day Saints, 1969. (FHL# 929.1/W893/I25 in General Reference Area first floor, microfilm 897217, item 23, or microfiche 6039409)

Sperry, Kip. *Rhode Island Sources for Family Historians and Genealogists.* Logan, Utah: Everton Publishers, 1986. (FHL# 974.5/D23s)

Vermont

Eichholz, Alice. *Collecting Vermont Ancestors.* Montpelier, Vt.: New Trails, 1986. (FHL# 974.3/D27e)

For additional reference works, check the FHLC under **United States/Genealogy/Handbooks, Manuals; United States/Genealogy/Sources; United States/Genealogy/New England; [State]/Genealogy/Handbooks, Manuals;** and **[State]/Genealogy/Sources.**

Chapter 6

United States: The Mid-Atlantic States

Sheri L. Slaughter

PENNSYLVANIA

Historical Background

Early	Lenni-Lenape Indians inhabit the eastern river valleys, and the Susquehannock live in the lower Susquehanna river basin until the 1670s. William Penn pays scrupulously for land received from Indians. Indians aid white settlers, who use Indian trails during migration.
1643	Johan Björnsson makes first permanent settlement on Tinicum Island in the Delaware River, capital of New Sweden.
1655	The Dutch capture New Sweden and annex it as part of New Netherland.
1664	British capture New Netherland, rename entire region New York.
1681	William Penn receives Pennsylvania as a royal grant.
1682	Philadelphia laid out; Penn arrives in October.
1688	Quakers take stand against Negro slavery.
1701	Penn's Charter of Privileges gives lawmaking power to an elected assembly. It remains in force until 1776.
1718	Penn dies; control of colony goes to second wife and then to his three sons.
1723	Benjamin Franklin comes to Philadelphia.
1754	The French and Indian War begins in Pennsylvania with defeat of Colonel George Washington at Fort Necessity.
1774	Philadelphia site of the First Continental Congress.
1776	Pennsylvania becomes a commonwealth. The British enter Philadelphia 27 September; Washington defeated at Germantown, 4 October.
1787	Pennsylvania becomes the second state to ratify the U.S. Constitution.
1792	First labor union in the United States founded by Philadelphia shoemakers.
1811	Steamboats run from Pittsburgh to New Orleans.
1812	Harrisburg becomes the state capital.
1842	State law passed to impede the capture of fugitive slaves. Pittsburgh and Philadelphia become centers of abolitionist activity.
1861	Pennsylvanians vigorously support the Union, supplying 375,000 men to the Union Army.
1863	The Battle of Gettysburg fought, 1-3 July.
1889	South Fork Dam bursts; Johnstown destroyed; more than 2,000 dead.

There are over 160 titles in the Pennsylvania collection as well as twelve historical periodicals. The following sources may be beneficial in research:

Day, Sherman. *Historical Collection of the State of Pennsylvania.* Philadelphia: G. W. Gorton, [c.1843]. Index. (FHL# 974.8/H2d or microfilm 824413, item 1)

Gordon, Thomas F. *The History of Pennsylvania from Its Discovery by the Europeans to the Declaration of Independence in 1776.* 1829; rpt. ed., Spartanburg, S.C.: Reprint Co., 1967. (FHL# 974.8/H2go/1967 or microfilm 982153, item 1)

Shenk, Hiram H. *Encyclopedia of Pennsylvania.* Harrisburg,Pa.: National Historical Association, 1932. (FHL# 974.8/A7s)

Settlement and Migration

William Penn extended an invitation to Europe's religiously persecuted people to come to Pennsylvania, which he called the Holy Experiment. In response to his advertisement, the Society of Friends came from England, Scotland, Ireland, and Wales. They occupied the area within twenty-five miles of Philadelphia.

Early in the eighteenth century there was a large influx of Rhineland Germans, many of them from religious groups such as the Amish, Mennonites, Schwenkfeldians, Anabaptists, and Dunkards. They settled in the rich farmlands between Philadelphia and the Blue Mountains, a region that came to be known as the Pennsylvania "Dutch" country.

Beginning in about 1718, great numbers of Scotch-Irish arrived and by the 1740s they had settled the mountain valleys beyond the German belt. Also, many people from Virginia, Maryland, and Connecticut settled land that, after boundary adjustments, became part of Pennsylvania.

The major groups did not merge but remained geographically separate, with the English in the east, Germans in the middle, and Scotch-Irish in the west.

With the rapidly advancing mineral and industry developments in the 1800s, tens of thousands of European immigrants came to Pennsylvania including Italians, Poles, Russians, Austrians, Czechs, Hungarians, Swedes, Greeks, French, Norwegians, Danes and Finns.

Pennsylvania Library Collection

Atlases, Maps, and Gazetteers

Maps in the Pennsylvania collection include maps of coal fields, oil and gas fields, railroad access, streams, historic Indian paths, and the early Ohio Valley (1673-1783), to name but a few. The following are practical aids in genealogical research:

Pennsylvania: Minor Civil Divisions, Townships, Cities and Boroughs. Washington, D.C.: Government Printing Office, 1961. (Map Case FHL# 974.8/E7us)

Pennsylvania. Department of Commerce. *Pennsylvania County Outline Maps.* n.p., n.d. [c.1960]. (FHL# 974.8/E7p or microfilm 962819, item 2) These show township boundaries.

Espenshade, Abraham Howry. *Pennsylvania Place Names.* 1925; rpt. ed., Baltimore, Md.: Genealogical Pub. Co., 1970. Index. (FHL# 974.8/E5e/1970 or microfilm 1425647, item 5)

Gordon, Thomas F. *A Gazetteer of the State of Pennsylvania.* Philadelphia: n.pub., n.d. (FHL# 974.8/E5g or microfilm 543662, item 5, or microfiche 6053251)

For a complete list of Pennsylvania maps available at the Pennsylvania State Archives, see the following inventory:

Pennsylvania. Division of Archives and Manuscripts. *Descriptive List of Map Collection in the Pennsylvania State Archives.* Compiled by Martha Simonetti. Harrisburg: Pennsylvania History and Museum Commission, 1976. (FHL# 974.8/E73p)

Cemetery Records

Every county in Pennsylvania except Forest and Venango have cemetery records in the collection. The Daughters of the American Revolution (DAR) have transcribed many cemetery records in Pennsylvania, as well as the following groups of records:

Missionaries and Members of the Eastern States Mission, comp. *Cemetery Records of Pennsylvania.* Typed by the Genealogical Society, 1946. 9 vols., 3 reels. (FHL# 974.8/V3c or microfilm 823929-823931)

Pennsylvania Cemetery Records. Salt Lake City: n.pub., 1941-43. (FHL# 974.8/V3p or microfilm 496937, item 3)

Baldwin, Henry. *The Henry R. Baldwin Genealogical Records.* 87 vols. in 31. Fort Wayne, Ind.: Allen County Public Library, 1983. (FHL# 977.1/D2bh)

Cemetery, church, court records gathered from western Pennsylvania and eastern Ohio 1867-1913. Index by Public Library of Youngstown and Mahoning County. 8 vols. Fort Wayne, Ind.: Allen County Public Library, 1983. (FHL# 977.1/D2bh/Index)

Census Records

The federal census records from 1790 to 1910 are available on microfilm, and there are head of household indexes for 1790-1850. There are every-name indexes for 1850-70 for Allegheny County and Pittsburgh. For 1790 to 1830, part of the censuses are missing. There are no known state census records. Tax lists were taken every seven years beginning in 1779 and continued until 1863 in some counties. For a list of these see:

Clint, Florence. *Pennsylvania Area Key.* Denver: Area Keys, 1976. (FHL# 974.8/D2cf/1976) Area keys have also been published for each county.

Mortality schedules (persons who died within the year before the federal census was taken) are available for 1850, 1860, and 1870. These were compiled by Ronald Vern Jackson (Bountiful: Accelerated Indexing System). (FHL# 974.8/X22p/1850, 974.8/X22p/1860, and 974.8/-X2j/1870)

Church Records

All of the major denominations are represented in Pennsylvania church records, and every county except McKean and Monroe has church records in the collection. For a bibliography and inventories of works concerning the various churches see the following sources, cataloged under **Pennsylvania/Church Records/Archives and Libraries** for film numbers:

Wilkinson, Norman. *Bibliography of Pennsylvania History.* Harrisburg: Pennsylvania History and Museum Commission, 1957. (FHL# 974.8/H2wn)

Historical Records Survey. Works Progress Administration.

Inventory of Church Archives of Pennsylvania's Presbyterian Churches. 24 reels. Salt Lake City: Genealogical Society of Utah, 1967. Index.

______. *Inventory of Church Archives in Pennsylvania.* 72 reels. Salt Lake City: Genealogical Society of Utah, 1977. Original record at Harrisburg, State Archives. Arranged by county, most denominations represented.

Other church records found under the state listings include DAR collections, Reformed, early German, Friends, Welsh Congregationalist, and several miscellaneous reverends' records. A large collection is found in:

Miscellaneous Church and Genealogical Records to 1968 in the Chester County Historical Society. Salt Lake City: filmed by the Genealogical Society of Utah, 1968. 162 microfilm reels. Index. Includes Baptist, Presbyterian, Friends, and others arranged alphabetically. (See FHLC for film numbers.)

Court Records

For a detailed study of Pennsylvania's court records see Sylvester K. Stevens and Donald H. Kent's *County Government and Archives in Pennsylvania* (Harrisburg: Pennsylvania History and Museum Commission, 1947). (FHL# 974.8/N2s) Some of the records listed under the state include Chancery Court 1720-39, Court of Admiralty 1780-88, Habeas Corpus for Negro slaves 1771-87, and eastern district divorce papers 1786-1815. Also of interest are these works:

Pennsylvania. Board of Pardons. *Death Warrants, 1874-1899.* 13 reels. Salt Lake City: Genealogical Society of Utah, 1979. Records at Harrisburg: State Archives.

Pennsylvania. Secretary of the Commonwealth. *Clemency File, 1790-1873; Pardon Books, 1791-1877.* 53 reels. Salt Lake City: Genealogical Society of Utah, 1977-79. Records at Harrisburg, State Archives.

Pennsylvania. Supreme Court. *Court Records for Eastern District, 1736-1896.* 24 reels. Salt Lake City: Genealogical Society of Utah, 1977. Records at Harrisburg, State Archives.

Indexed at beginning of some volumes. Includes warrant of attorney, judgment docket, appearance docket, etc.

Directories

Directories give an annual listing of residents, their addresses, and often occupations. They began as early as 1819 for Philadelphia. Many are on microfilm. Some of the cities with directories in the collection are Reading, Chester, Erie, Lancaster, Wilkes-Barre, and Williamsport to name a few. Polk city directories exist for Pittsburgh 1916, 1941, and 1969. (FHL# Q/974.885/E4ph) and Philadelphia 1935-36 (FHL# Q/974.811/E4cp). Among the directories listed in the FHLC under **Pennsylvania/Directories** are:

Gibson, Gail M. *Pennsylvania Directory of Historical Organizations,* 1970. Harrisburg: n.pub., 1970. (FHL# 974.8/E4p)

Gopsill's Directory of Lancaster, Harrisburg, Lebanon, and York, 1863-1864. 1863; rpt. ed., Tucson, Ariz.: W. C. Cox Co., 1974. (FHL# microfilm 1000559, item 2)

The Pittsburgh and Allegheny Blue Book: A Private Address Directory and Ladies' Visiting and Shopping Guide, Including Prominent Families in Beaver, Beaver Falls, New Castle, Sharon and Washington. Cleveland, Ohio: Mrs. M. B. Haven, 1887. (FHL# 974.8/E4h)

Genealogy

There are over 130 titles in the Pennsylvania collection under **/Genealogy**, thirteen titles under **/Bible Records**, and fifty-five under **/Biography**. The chances are very high that your Pennsylvania ancestors can be located in one of these collections. A surname index is included in Floyd G. Hoenstine, *Genealogical and Historical Research in Pennsylvania* (Hollidaysburg, Pa.: n.pub., 1978). (FHL# 974.8/A3h/1978) Another surname index is in:

Pennsylvania State Library. *General Surname Card Index.* Salt Lake City: Genealogical Society of Utah, 1977. 42 reels. Index to names in genealogical collection at Pennsylvania State Library where information is found. Much of this collection is also on microfilm at the Salt Lake City Family History Library.

Genealogical Society of Pennsylvania. *Family Records, Arranged Alphabetically.* 360 reels. Salt Lake City: Genealogical Society of Utah, 1964. From records at Philadelphia.

For Pennsylvania German genealogies, be sure to search Dr. Albert H. Gerberich's collection cataloged under **Pennsylvania/Genealogy.** Collections of the following groups or individuals should also be checked: DAR, Schuyler Brossman, Chester County Historical Society (five major collections and over 366 reels), Colonial Society of Pennsylvania, Gilbert Cope, Warren S. Ely, the Huguenot Society, Alfred R. Justice, Sophie Seldon Rogers, and Israel D. Rupp. All are cataloged under **Pennsylvania/Genealogical Collections.**

Immigration/Emigration Records

Passenger lists for Philadelphia are available on microfilm for c.1800 to 1906. Indexes are located at the reference table under "Immigration" or in the FHLC under **Philadelphia/Emigration and Immigration.** First check P. William Filby, *Passenger and Immigration Lists Index,* 3 vols. and cumulated supplements for 1982-86 (Detroit: Gale Research Co., 1981), at the reference table. (FHL# 973/W32p) If you do not find your Pennsylvania immigrant, there are twenty-seven additional titles in the Pennsylvania collection to search. Most of these deal with German immigrants and a few are more general. Examples of some of the records are:

Tepper, Michael, ed. *Emigrants to Pennsylvania, 1641-1819: A Consolidation of Ship Passenger Lists from The Pennsylvania Magazine of History and Biography.* Baltimore, Md.: Genealogical Publishing Co., 1975. (FHL# 974.8/W3t) Index.

Herrick, Cheesman A. *White Servitude in Pennsylvania: Indentured and Redemption Labor in Colony and Common-*

wealth. c.1926; rpt. ed., New York: Negro University Press, 1969. (FHL# 974.8/U3h)

Myers, Albert Cook. *Immigration of the Irish Quakers into Pennsylvania, 1682-1750, with Their Early History in Ireland.* 1902; rpt. ed., Baltimore, Md.: Genealogical Publishing Co., 1969. Index. (FHL# 974.8/W2m/1969 or microfilm 1036555, item 43)

Rupp, Israel Daniel. *A Collection of Upwards to Thirty Thousand Names of German, Swiss, Dutch, French, and Other Immigrants in Pennsylvania from 1727-1776.* c.1898; rpt. ed., Baltimore, Md.: Genealogical Publishing Co., 1965. (FHL# 974.8/W2ra/1965 or microfilm 1036690, item 1; and in German on microfilm 496904, item 2) Indexed.

Land and Property Records

Warrants, grants, rent rolls, deeds, and patents were recorded by the office of Master of the Rolls for the province of Pennsylvania. Many of these early records are available on microfilm. Deeds and mortgages were kept by the county Recorder of Deeds, and most of the counties in Pennsylvania have land and property records in the collection. An index to surveys, warrants, and patents is located in the following work:

Pennsylvania. Bureau of Land Records. *Warrant Register 1682-1950.* 10 reels. Salt Lake City: Genealogical Society of Utah, 1976.

The patent books (1676-1960) and original warrants (1676-1960), including purchases from the Indians were filmed by the Genealogical Society of Utah at the Bureau of Land Records in Harrisburg on 234 reels.

Other records in the state collection from the Pennsylvania Land Office are depositions 1683-1881, proof of settlement 1797-1869, caveats 1699-1890, title papers 1784-1852, mortgage records 1687-1820, and applications for warrants 1734-1865 for a total of over 250 reels. From the Pennsylvania Surveyor General there are original surveys 1682-1920 on 499 reels.

Military Records

Pennsylvania's collection contains a large amount of military records. A few from each period of time follow.

Colonial Wars

Pennsylvania Archives. First series, vol. 1. *An index for the names of soldiers and their companies.* A-N: (FHL# microfilm 844571 and O-Z: FHL# microfilm 844572)

Revolutionary War

Pennsylvania. Auditor General's Office. *Revolutionary War Pension File, 1809-1893.* 3 reels. Salt Lake City: Genealogical Society of Utah, 1977.

Pennsylvania. Division of Archives and Manuscripts. Bureau of Archives and History. *Military Abstract Card File for Revolutionary War, 1775-1783.* 42 reels. Salt Lake City: Genealogical Society of Utah, 1978. Arranged alphabetically by soldier's name under four military units.

United States. War Department. *Revolutionary War Rolls.* 138 reels. Washington, D.C.: National Archives, 1957. Penn. Jackets, records of Pennsylvania soldiers, included in FHL# microfilm 830359-830363.

Historical Society of Pennsylvania. *Index to Pennsylvania in the War of Revolution: Battalions and Line.* 10 reels. Salt Lake City: Genealogical Society of Utah, 1966.

War of 1812

Pennsylvania. Auditor General's Office. *War of 1812 Pension Records, 1866-1896.* 27 reels. Salt Lake City: Genealogical Society of Utah, 1977.

Pennsylvania. Bureau of Audits. *War of 1812 Militia Accounts, 1812-1827.* 8 reels. Salt Lake City: Genealogical Society of Utah, 1978.

Mexican War (1846-48)

U.S. Records and Pension Office. *Compiled Service Record of Volunteer Soldiers Who Served in Organizations from the State of Pennsylvania in the Mexican War, 1846-1848.* 13 reels. Washington: National Archives, 1976.

Civil War

Pennsylvania. Adjutant General's Office. *Veterans Name Listing, 1861-1866.* 80 reels. Salt Lake City: Genealogical Society of Utah, 1978.

United States. Adjutant General's Office. *Index to Compiled Service Records of Volunteer Union soldiers Who Served in Organizations from the State of Pennsylvania, 1861-1865.* 136 reels. Washington, D.C.: National Archives, 1965. Arranged alphabetically. (FHL# microfilm 882336-882471)

Native Races

Several worthwhile sources are available on the native races in Pennsylvania. Among them are:

Indian Treaties Printed by Benjamin Franklin, 1736-1762. 1938; rpt. ed., Ann Arbor: University of Michigan, 1963. (FHL# microfilm 1009058)

Sipe, C. Hale. *The Indian Chiefs of Pennsylvania.* 1927; rpt. ed., New York: Arno Press & New York Times, 1971. (FHL# 970.1/Si74i) Indexed.

Naturalization Records

The following naturalization records are available:

1727-75: Oaths of Allegiance are listed in the *Pennsylvania Archives,* second series, Vol. 17. (FHL# microfilm 823999, item 2)

1740-73: *Naturalization Lists, 1740-1773 by the Pennsylvania Supreme Court.* (FHL# microfilm 1032845, item 5-7) Persons Naturalized in the Province of Pennsylvania, 1740-1773, Pennsylvania Supreme Court. (Baltimore, Md.: Genealogical Publishing Co., 1967). (FHL# 974.8/N4p/1967 or microfilm 824000, item 3)

1776: Aliens living in Pennsylvania at the time of the Declaration of Independence were automatically naturalized.

1776-94: New arrivals simply took an oath of allegiance some of which are found in Thompson Wescott, *Names of Persons Who Took the Oath of Allegiance to the State of Pennsylvania between the Years 1777 and 1789*

(1865; rpt. ed., Baltimore, Md.: Genealogical Publishing Co., 1965.) (FHL# 974.8/P4w or microfilm 1033632, item 7) Also see P. William Filby, *Philadelphia, Naturalization Records* (Detroit, Mich.: Gale Research Co., c.1982). (FHL# 974.811/P4p) This is an index to records of aliens' declarations of intention and/or oaths of allegiance 1789-1880 in a variety of Pennsylvania courts.

1793-Present: Naturalizations are kept by county, state, or federal courts. These are available in *Declarations of Intention for the Eastern District of Pennsylvania, 1832-1906*, from the Pennsylvania Supreme Court, 10 reels by year, starting with FHL# microfilm 1017086. *Naturalization Records, 1794-1868, 1871-1872, 1892, 1903,* from the Pennsylvania Supreme Court, 42 reels, and an *Index to Naturalization Records, 1794-1824* (FHL# microfilm 295740). Also consult **Pennsylvania/[County]/Naturalization Records and /Court Records.**

Newspapers

Pennsylvania's first newspaper was the *American Weekly Mercury* published in Philadelphia in 1719. For a thorough listing of Pennsylvania newspapers and where they can be found see Ruth Salisburg, ed., *Pennsylvania Newspapers: A Bibliography and Union List* (Pittsburgh: Pennsylvania Library Association, 1969). (FHL# 974.8/A3s) Also see **Pennsylvania/[County]/Newspapers,** or **/Obituaries.** The state collection includes *Clippings from the Pennsylvania Dutchman, 1949-1953* (FHL# Q/974.8/F2p) and *The Presbyterian Newspaper,* 1879 (FHL# microfilm 504271-504272). The *Philadelphia Recorder* from 1823 to 1831 is on microfilm.

Probate Records

The Constitution of 1776 provided for a Register's office in each county to record the wills. Records kept by the Register include wills, indexes to will books, and executors' and administrators' papers. Other records are inventories, appraisements, and inheritance tax records, 1826 to the present. An orphans' court was established in each county in 1683. The records kept there include minutes, dockets, partition papers (distribution of estate), bonds, inventories and appraisements, appeals, marriage records 1885-present, birth and death records 1893-1905, and adoption records 1925-present. Many of these records are available on microfilm.

All counties in Pennsylvania except Fulton, Lackawanna, Lawrence, Monroe, and Potter have some probate records. For instance, in Allegheny County, will books from 1789 to 1917 are on microfilm and an estate index from 1788 to 1971 is available. In Philadelphia, wills from 1682 to 1916 are available on 327 reels.

The state collection contains miscellaneous records such as Pennsylvania German wills, eastern district escheats 1796-1822, unrecorded wills 1753-79, DAR wills, and miscellaneous county records.

Taxation

Tax records usually began with the origin of the county. Some of the items kept are tax assessment records, maps of assessment districts with property lines, delinquent tax returns, and lists of land sold for taxes. A few of the taxation records are cataloged under the county, but the majority are cataloged under **Pennsylvania/Taxation.** Examples of taxation records are:

Egle, William H. *Returns of Taxables: for counties Bedford(1773-84), Huntingdon (1788), Westmoreland (1783, 1786), Fayette (1785, 1786), Allegheny (1791), Washington (1786), and census for Bedford (1784) and Westmoreland (1783).* Salt Lake City: Genealogical Society of Utah, 1966. (FHL# microfilm 432614)

Pennsylvania. Comptroller General. *Tax and Exoneration Lists, 1762-1801.* 29 reels. Salt Lake City: Genealogical Society of Utah, 1978. Original records in the Pennsylvania State Archives. Arranged by county.

United States. Secretary of the Treasury. *United States Direct Tax of 1798, Tax Lists for the State of Pennsylvania.* 24 reels. Washington, D.C.: National Archives and Records Service, 1962. Arranged by county.

Vital Records

For an inventory of Pennsylvania's vital records see the Historical Records Survey's *Inventory of the Vital Statistics of Most Counties and Towns* (FHL# microfilm 1016402). County registration of births, marriages, and deaths were kept in many cases from 1852 on. See Florence Clint's *Pennsylvania Area Key* for details of each county.

The state's vital record collection consists of such miscellaneous items as: mortality schedules, genealogical records, records of marriages 1885-89, death warrants. marriage licenses 1784-86, and births, marriages, and deaths on file at the State Archives 1852-54.

All but a few counties have vital record information. An example of county vital records is Allegheny with microfilmed birth registers from 1870 to 1912, ministers' returns of marriages 1875-1909, and death registers from 1851 to 1906. Dates and records vary from county to county.

Voting Records

There are no state voting records available in the Pennsylvania collection.

MARYLAND

Historical Background

Early The Piscataway Indians inhabit the area west of Chesapeake Bay; and the Nanticoke, Wicomico, and Assateague settle on

	the lower part of the Eastern Shore. The Susquehanna are also in the area.
1500s	Spanish explore coast of Maryland.
1631	William Claiborne establishes a trading post and small settlement on Kent Island.
1634	Cecil Calvert, the second Lord Baltimore, and 200 settlers establish St. Mary's City under a royal grant.
1649	Provincial assembly passes the Act of Tolerance insuring religious freedom to all believers in Christ.
1689	Protestant rebels, led by John Coode, overthrow the province's Catholic leadership.
1689-1715	Maryland a crown colony with a royal governor.
1694	Anne Arundel Town (later Annapolis) replaces the Catholic-dominated St. Mary's City as the colony capital.
1715	Maryland again made a proprietary province because Charles Calvert, the fifth Lord Baltimore, converts to Protestantism.
1729	Baltimore founded.
1769	The Mason-Dixon line officially recognized as the boundary between Maryland and Pennsylvania.
1776	The province's delegates support independence at the Continental Congress. Maryland's merchant vessels converted to warships.
1788	Maryland ratifies the U.S. Constitution and becomes the seventh state.
1814	Fort McHenry, at the entrance to Baltimore Harbor, is successfully defended against British attack during the War of 1812.
1828	Work begins on the construction of the Chesapeake and Ohio Canal and the Baltimore & Ohio Railroad.
1861	Some Marylanders favor secession, particularly the state's 14,000 slaveholders. Baltimore occupied by federal troops to ensure the state's loyalty to the Union. 50,000 Marylanders fight for the Union and about 22,000 for the Confederacy.
1862	Union forces defeat Confederate forces at Antietam, the bloodiest battle of the Civil War.
1876	Johns Hopkins University opens.

The following sources will be helpful in researching Maryland's history:

Radoff, Morris Leon. *The Old Line State: A History of Maryland.* Annapolis: Hall of Records Commission, 1971. (FHL# 975.2/B4ma/no.16)

Richardson, Hester Dorsey. *Side-Lights on Maryland History: With Sketches of Early Maryland Families.* Baltimore, Md.: Williams and Wilkins, 1913. (FHL# 975.2/H2r)

Walsh, Richard. *Maryland: A History 1632-1974.* Baltimore, Md.: Maryland Historical Society, 1974. (FHL# 975.2/H2wr)

Settlement and Migration

Many early settlers were Catholic, but in 1689 the Church of England (Episcopal) was established. The Act of Toleration attracted a large group of Puritans from Virginia who settled Anne Arundel County. Other religious groups such as Quakers, Lutherans, Dutch Reformed, Presbyterians, Methodists, and Baptists migrated to the state hoping for religious freedom.

Some settlers had large plantations, but most worked smaller tobacco farms, sometimes with the help of indentured servants or black slaves. Settlement was concentrated at first on the Atlantic Coast Plain. Between 1730 and 1740, the Appalachian section farther west in Maryland began to be settled by Scotch-Irish and English immigrants. Large groups of Germans came down from Pennsylvania. Acadians driven from Nova Scotia came to Baltimore in 1755. In the 1790s, more than a thousand French people came to Baltimore, seeking refuge from the riots in Santo Domingo.

From 1817 to 1847, thousands of Irish immigrants came to Baltimore as canal diggers. Later they moved to the Appalachian section to farm and mine. Thousands of Germans fled their homeland after the 1848 Revolution and were given shelter in Baltimore. The rapid increase of Maryland's population resulted in the creation of eleven of her twenty-three counties by 1700 and eight more by 1800.

Maryland Library Collection

Atlases, Maps, and Gazetteers

Maps of Maryland are often included with maps of the other colonies or states, especially with Delaware or Virginia. A few useful aids to research are:

Fisher, Richard Swainson. *Gazetteer of the State of Maryland: Compiled from the Returns of the Seventh Census of the U.S. and Other Official Documents.* New York: J. H. Colton, 1852. (FHL# 975/E5f or microfilm 896649, item 2)

Gannett, Henry. *A Gazetteer of Maryland and Delaware.* Baltimore, Md.: Genealogical Publishing Co., 1976. (FHL# 975/E5g or microfilm 982220, item 3)

Morrison, Russell, et al. *On the Map.* Chestertown, Md.: Washington College, 1983. (FHL# 975.2/E7o) Contains early maps of Maryland.

Cemetery Records

The majority of the cemetery records in Maryland are found under **Maryland/[County]/Cemetery Records**; all the counties except Calvert, Garrett, Kent, and Somerset have cemetery records. The following records in the state collection may be helpful:

DAR Maryland. *DAR Genealogical Records (Family and Cemetery Records, Military Records, etc.).* Compiled and typed by various DAR chapters, arranged by GS, n.pub., n.d. (FHL# 975.2/D2d or microfilm 908909, item 2)

The Maryland Historical and Genealogical Bulletin. Quarterly. Baltimore, Md.: Robert F. Hayes, Jr., 1941-50. (FHL# 975.2/B2ha) Includes many cemetery records.

Turner, Joseph Brown. *Genealogical Collections: Miscellaneous Church, Cemetery, and Vital Records of Delaware, Maryland, and New Jersey.* Salt Lake City: Genealogical Society of Utah, 1948. (FHL# microfilm 006302) Original records at Hall of Records, Dover.

Zacharias, George Merle de Fere. *Inscriptions Copied from Various Graveyards in Virginia, Pennsylvania, and Maryland.* Salt Lake City: Genealogical Society of Utah, 1947. (FHL# microfilm 020366, items 5-6)

Census Records

The 1790-1910 federal census records for Maryland are available on microfilm with indexes for 1790-1850. The census records for 1790-1830 are incomplete, however. There were no state censuses taken in Maryland. The following early and miscellaneous census records may prove helpful:

Brumbaugh, Gaius Marcus. *Maryland Records: Colonial, Revolutionary, County, and Church, from Original Sources.* Baltimore, Md.: Genealogical Publishing Co., 1975. (FHL# 975.2/D29b/1975 or microfilm 1033832, item 1)

Index. Includes provincial censuses, oaths of fidelity, muster rolls, etc.

Carothers, Bettie Stirling. *1776 Census of Maryland.* Lutherville, Md.: B. S. Carothers, [c.1970s]. (FHL# 975.2/X2p/-1776)

Dilts, Bryan Lee. *1890 Maryland Census Index of Civil War Veterans or Their Widows.* Salt Lake City: Index Publishing, 1985. (FHL# 975.2/X22d/1890)

Church Records

Roman Catholics and Anglicans (Protestant Episcopal) were among the earliest settlers, and Quakers settled in Maryland by 1662. Presbyterian, Baptist, Lutheran, and Dutch Reformed churches were established by the mid-1700s. Many of the early records are on microfilm by county. The following records may be useful:

Inventory of the Church Archives of Maryland: Protestant Episcopal Diocese of Maryland. Baltimore, Md.: Maryland Historical Records Survey, 1940. (FHL# 975.2/K2h)

Jacobsen, Phebe R. *Quaker Records in Maryland.* Annapolis: Hall of Records Commission, 1966. (FHL# 975.2/-B4ma/no.14)

Also consult the Brumbaugh records, the DAR collection, and the Turner collection mentioned above under *Cemetery* and *Census Records.*

Court Records

The Circuit Court records for many of the counties contain some vital records, land commission records, and probate records. A good source on the court records available in each county and the dates they cover is:

Radoff, Morris L. *County Courthouses and Records of Maryland.* Annapolis: Hall of Records Commission, 1963. (FHL# 975.2/B4ma/no.12 and no.13)

Included in the state collection are calendar of state papers, proprietary papers, judgements and decrees, patents, orphans' court records, court proceedings, administration accounts, and guardian accounts. The following index is useful:

Passano, Eleanor Phillips. *An Index to the Source Records of Maryland: Genealogical, Biographical, Historical.* Baltimore, Md.: Genealogical Publishing Co., 1967. (FHL# 975.2/D22p/1967)

The following large collections are a few of those cataloged under **Maryland/Court Records:**

Maryland. Court of Appeals. *Judgement and Decrees.* 39 reels. Annapolis: Hall of Records Commission, 1947. Many have indexes. 1788-1891. (FHL# microfilm 012999-013037)

Maryland. General Court. *Judgments.* 25 reels. Annapolis: Hall of Records Commission, 1947. Indexes for most volumes. 1778-1800. (FHL# microfilm 013038-13062)

Maryland. Provincial Court. *Provincial Court Judgments.* 28 reels. Annapolis: Hall of Records Commission, 1947. 1679-1778. (FHL# microfilm 012941-012968)

Directories

The Baltimore City directories for 1863-1901 are on microfilm. For 1914, see *Baltimore, Maryland City Directory, 1914.* Baltimore, Md.: R. L. Polk, 1914. (FHL# Q/975.271/Bl/E4p)

There is also a suburban directory for the Maryland towns adjacent to the District of Columbia (FHL# 975/E4p).

The Maryland Directory. Tucson, Ariz.: W. C. Cox Co., 1974 (FHL# microfilm 1000059, item 2)

Genealogical Collections

Many Maryland families are included in genealogical collections from other states, particularly Delaware, Virginia, and Pennsylvania. Several genealogical collections that should be searched are:

Bell, Annie W. B. *Maryland Genealogies and Historical Recorder.* Washington, D.C.: Burns, 1941. (FHL# 975.2/D25mg)

Hansrote, Hazel Groves. *Genealogical Records of Maryland, Pennsylvania, Virginia, and West Virginia, 18th Century to 1975.* 8 reels. Salt Lake City: Genealogical Society of Utah, 1975. Alphabetically arranged. (FHL# microfilm 984210-984217)

Old Bible Records with Charts and Genealogical Sketches. 12 vols. 4 reels. 1944-67; rpt. ed., Salt Lake City: Genealogical Society of Utah, 1970. Index. (FHL# microfilm 845762-845765)

St. Mary's County Historical Society. *Family Group Records, 1600s to 1900s* and *Family Genealogies in Folders, 1600s to 1900s.* 8 reels. Salt Lake City: Genealogical Society of

Utah, 1976. Two separate record groups, alphabetically arranged by surname. (See FHLC for call numbers)

Immigration/Emigration Records

For microfilm numbers to passenger lists for the port of Baltimore, see the gray binders at the reference table labeled "Immigration" or consult the FHLC under **Maryland/Baltimore (Independent City)/Emigration and Immigration**. There is a Soundex system index for 1832-97 for Baltimore, but the passenger lists themselves begin in 1820. Other miscellaneous immigration records in the state collection are:

Campbell, Penelope. *Maryland in Africa: The Maryland State Colonization Society, 1831-1857*. Urbana: University of Illinois Press, c.1971. (Africa/Mid-East Area FHL# 966.6/H2c) The recolonization of Negroes from Maryland to Liberia and other parts of Africa.

List of Persons Known to Arrive in Maryland on the Ark and the Dove, on March 25, 1634. [c.1980s] (FHL# 975.2/W2L)

From information obtained from Charles County Community College in La Platta.

Newman, Harry Wright. *To Maryland from Overseas*. Annapolis: H.W. Newman, 1982. (FHL# 975.2/W2n)

Includes approximately 1,400 Maryland settlers from 1634 to the early federal period with source documentation, and a list of Jacobite Loyalists sold into white slavery in Maryland.

Skordas, Gust. *The Early Settlers of Maryland: An Index to Names of Immigrants Compiled from Records of Land Patents, 1633-1680*. Baltimore, Md.: Genealogical Publishing Co., 1968. (FHL# 975.2/W2s)

Land and Property Records

Most of the Maryland counties have early land records available on microfilm, including patents, warrants, certificates, and some deeds. In 1781 Maryland gave land to officers and soldiers who served in the Revolutionary War. The names are published in the following work:

Scharf, John Thomas. *History of Western Maryland*. 2 vols. 1882; rpt. ed., Baltimore, Md.: Regional Publishing Co., 1968. (FHL# 975.2/H2s)

For an understanding of Baltimore's wards, read:

Le Fúrgy, William G. *Baltimore Wards, 1797-1978: A Guide*. Baltimore, Md.: Baltimore City Archives and Record Management Office, Department of Legislative Reference, [c.1980s]. (FHL# 975.2/A1/no.57)

Miscellaneous Maryland land records are found in:

Bell, Annie W. B. *Maryland, Early Settlers, Land Records*. Annie Walker Burns Bell, 1936-37. (FHL# 975.2/R2b)

Early Settlers of Maryland, 1633-1680. Typescript at Maryland Historical Society, Baltimore. Salt Lake City: Genealogical Society of Utah, 1949. Index to land records in Maryland. (FHL# microfilm 013158, item 2)

Newman, Harry Wright. *Maryland Revolution Records: Data-Obtained from 3,050 Pension Claims and Bounty Land Applications*. Baltimore, Md.: Genealogical Publishing Co., 1967. (FHL# 975.2/M2n 1967 or microfilm 1036487, item 2)

Also see the Skordas record under *Immigration*.

Military Records

The military records in the Maryland collection, although not as numerous as those for some states, include the following useful sources.

Revolutionary War

McGhee, Mrs. Carl W. *Maryland Revolutionary War Pensioners, War of 1812, and Indian Wars*. Washington, D.C.: n.pub., 1952. (FHL# 975.2/M24m or microfilm 496676, item 6)

United States. War Department. *Revolutionary War Rolls 1775-1783*. 138 reels. Washington, D.C.: National Archives, 1957. Maryland Jackets record of Maryland soldiers, included in FHL# microfilm 830312-830313.

War of 1812

Huntsberry, Thomas. *Western Maryland, Pennsylvania, Virginia Militia in Defense of Maryland, 1805 to 1815. Baltimore, Md.: T. V. Huntsberry, 1983. (FHL# 975.2/M2h)*

Wright, F. Edward. *Maryland Militia, War of 1812*. Silver Spring, Md.: Family Line Publications, 1979. (FHL# 975.2/M2w)

Civil War

United States. Record and Pension Office. *Compiled Service-Records of Confederate Soldiers Who Served in Organizations from the State of Maryland*. 22 reels. Washington, D.C.: National Archives, 1960. Arranged alphabetically under each unit. (FHL# microfilm 1292663-1292684) See index next entry.

United States. Adjutant General's Office. *Index to Compiled Service Record of Confederate Soldiers Who Served in Organizations from the State of Maryland, 1861-1865*. Washington, D.C.: National Archives, 1962. (A-K: FHL# microfilm 821887; L-Z: 821888)

United States. Adjutant General's Office. *Index to Compiled Service Records of Volunteer Union Soldiers Who Served in Organizations from the State of Maryland, 1861-1865*. 13 reels. Washington, D.C.: National Archives, 1962. (FHL# microfilm 881522-881534) Alphabetically arranged.

Native Races

The library has two titles under **Maryland/Native Races.**

McAllister, James A. *Indian Lands in Dorchester County, Maryland: Selected Sources, 1669 to 1870*. Cambridge, Md.: McAllister, [c.1962]. (FHL# 975.227/R2m)

Manakee, Harold R. *Indians of Early Maryland: A Book on Maryland Life*. Baltimore, Md.: Maryland Historical Society, [c.1959]. (FHL# 970.1/M311i)

Naturalization Records

Naturalization records for Maryland appear in provincial court judgments 1685-1777, general court proceedings, county court records, etc. Frederick County has naturalization records for 1799 to 1850 and St. Mary's County has naturalizations from 1900 to 1917. Also cataloged under **Maryland/Naturalization and Citizenship** are:

Brumbaugh, Gaius Marcus. *Revolutionary Records of Maryland.* 1924; rpt. ed., Baltimore, Md.: Genealogical Publishing Co., 1967. (FHL# 975.2/W6b/1967 or microfilm 928174, item 8) Contains patriots' oaths of fidelity and support, 1778. Indexed.

Wyand, Jeffrey A. *Colonial Maryland Naturalizations.* Baltimore, Md.: Genealogical Publishing Co., 1975. (FHL# 975.2/W5w) Indexed.

Newspapers

Lists of Maryland newspapers may be found in:

Hofstetter, Eleanore O. *Newspapers in Maryland Libraries: A Union List.* Baltimore, Md.: Division of Library Development Services, Maryland State Department of Education, 1977. (FHL# 975.2/B22h or microfiche 6046965)

There are abstracts from newspapers in several counties (i.e., marriages and deaths). For instance, under **/Baltimore County/Newspapers**, see:

Hollowak, Thomas L. *Index to Marriages and Deaths in the (Baltimore) Sun, 1837-1850.* Baltimore, Md.: Genealogical Publishing Co., 1978. (FHL# 975.26/B38h)

Also consult the FHLC under **Maryland/Obituaries:**

Barnes, Robert. *Marriages and Deaths from the Maryland Gazette, 1727-1839.* Baltimore, Md.: Genealogical Publishing Co., 1973. (FHL# 975.2/V2b) Indexed.

Probate Records

Probate records and inventories were kept by the orphans' and circuit courts in Maryland. Many of these records are available on microfilm and all of the counties except Garrett and Wicomico have probate records in the Family History Library collection. There are several good indexes to help locate Maryland wills, among them:

Cotton, Jane Baldwin. *Index to Wills of the Colonial Period, 1634-1777.* Annapolis: Hall of Records Commission, 1947. (FHL# microfilm 012859) Also on (FHL# 975.2/-P2m/1967) with a new introduction and additions by James Mosby Magruder.

Cregar, William F. *Index to Maryland Wills.* Typescript at Maryland Historical Society, Baltimore. Salt Lake City: Genealogical Society of Utah, 1949. c.1666 to 1781. (FHL# microfilm 013150, item 2)

Index to Inventories of Estates, 1718-1777. Annapolis: Hall of Records Commission, 1947. (FHL# microfilm 012898)

Cotton, Jane Baldwin, comp. *The Maryland Calendar of Wills.* 8 vols. 1906-28; rpt. ed., Baltimore, Md.: Genealogical Publishing Co, 1968. (Original printing: FHL# 975.2/S2c; rpt. ed.: 975.2/S2c/1968; later edition on microfilm 873762-873764) Wills 1635-1743.

The Maryland Prerogative Court has many records pertaining to wills, including accounts of estates 1718-77 (19 reels), inventories and accounts of estates 1674-1718 (11 reels), inventories of estates 1718-77 (36 reels), testamentary proceedings 1657-1777 (11 reels), and will books 1653-1777 (18 reels).

Taxation

Many of Maryland's taxation records were kept in the proprietary papers. They are available on microfilm for 1636-1785 (FHL# microfilm 012969-012974). Also available are the federal assessments for 1790-1805 for twelve of Maryland's counties, arranged by county (FHL# microfilm 499893-499905). Another source that may be helpful is:

Carothers, Bettie Stirling. *1783 Tax List of Maryland.* Lutherville, Md.: Carothers, 1977. Indexed. (FHL# 975.2/R4c)

Vital Records

Unfortunately there are no state vital statistic registrations available for Maryland. State registration for births and deaths did not begin until 1898, and marriage registration did not begin until 1951. None of these records are available at the Family History Library yet. Substitutions must be made from church, cemetery, and military records, etc. County courts also often recorded vital information. The LDS Church has done some record extraction from early Maryland parishes. They can be found under **Maryland/[County]/Vital Records** or **Maryland/[County]/Church Records**. The following records, compiled from various sources, may be helpful:

Bell, Annie W. B. Maryland Marriage Records. 23 vols. Photocopy of typescript, 1938-39. (FHL# 975.2/V25b or microfilm 873768-873775, or microfiche 6046950) Alphabetically arranged. Mostly 1700s with some late 1600s.

_____. *Maryland Record of Deaths 1718-1777.* Photocopy of typescript, 1936. (FHL# 975.2/V23b or microfilm 924445, item 2)

Barnes, Robert. *Maryland Marriages 1634-1777.* Baltimore, Md.: Genealogical Publishing Co., 1975. (FHL# 975.2/K2bar) Alphabetized by groom's surname with bride index.

_____. *Maryland Marriages 1778-1800.* Baltimore, Md.: Genealogical Publishing Co., 1978. (FHL# 975.2/K2ba)

Chance, Hilda. *Western Maryland Pioneers, Alphabetical Lists of Marriages, Births, and Deaths of 8,000 Early Settlers.* Salt Lake City: Genealogical Society of Utah, 1968. Original record at Pennsylvania Historical Society (Misc. Film Area FHL# microfilm 560192, item 7)

Voting Records

There are no voting registers available for the state of Maryland.

NEW JERSEY

Historical Background

Early	First inhabited by the Lenni-Lenape Indians (Delawares).
1498	John Cabot, English explorer, discovers New Jersey.
1524	Giovanni da Verrazano, Italian navigator, traces and charts the New Jersey coastline.
1609	Henry Hudson's sailors explore Sandy Hook.
1618	The Dutch establish a trading post at Bergen, now part of Jersey City.
1623	Dutch traders establish fort near present site of Gloucester.
1634	English settlers arrive, mostly from New England.
1638-55	Swedes and Finns arrive, dominate area.
1655-64	Dutch dominate. (New Netherland)
1664	Dutch surrender New Jersey to England. John Berkeley and George Carteret become proprietors. Named New Jersey after the English Channel home of Carteret.
1673	Dutch regain possession of New Jersey briefly.
1674	English regain possession. Quakers arrive from England.
1676	New Jersey divided into East Jersey and West Jersey. West Jersey is controlled by Quakers and East Jersey by Carteret.
1702	New Jersey united as a royal colony under the governor of New York.
1738	Lewis Morris, a native of New Jersey, becomes the first royal governor of united New Jersey.
1776	A provincial congress in Burlington declares New Jersey's independence on July 2.
1776-80	More than 100 Revolutionary War battles fought in New Jersey.
1787	New Jersey ratifies the U.S. Constitution, becomes the third state.
1790	Trenton chosen as the state capital.
1791	Paterson founded as America's first planned industrial city.
1844	New Jersey adopts its second constitution.
1846	Slavery permanently abolished.
1860	Becomes the only Northern state not to give Lincoln all of its electoral votes.
1861-65	New Jersey gives 88,000 men to Union Army and spends $25 million in bounty, separation, and death payments.
1876	Thomas A. Edison opens first research laboratory at Menlo Park.

Many good history sources are in the New Jersey collection, including histories of New Sweden, forgotten towns, Jewish settlement, the Finns in New Jersey, and colonial, Revolutionary and Civil War histories. A few helpful sources are:

Barber, John Warner. *Historical Collections of the State of New Jersey.* New York: S. Tuttle, 1844. (FHL# 974.9/H2bj) This contains facts, traditions, biographical sketches, and geographical descriptions of townships.

Brown, William Mawbey. *Biographical, Genealogical, and Descriptive History of the State of New Jersey*. Newark: New Jersey Historical Publishing Co., 1900. (FHL# 974.9/H2bw)

Kull, Irving Stoddard. *New Jersey: A History.* 5 vols. New York: American Historical Society, 1930-32. (FHL# 974.9/H2k)

Settlement and Migration

The early Dutch, Swedish, and English settlers were first attracted to the coast of New Jersey and later moved inland following the many navigable rivers. The migration pattern was from northeast to southwest.

When the English took control in 1664, the territory was opened up to land seekers. Dutch settlements along the Hudson grew with the influx of the British. Puritans from Connecticut founded settlements at Newark, Woodbridge, Piscataway, Middletown, and Shrewsbury. Scotch-Irish came to the eastern counties and English Quakers came to the fertile regions along the Delaware River. Huguenots who fled France in search of religious liberty also settled in New Jersey. The slave trade brought blacks; and the Great Awakening, a democratic religious movement in the colonies during the 1740s, brought immigrant Germans, Welsh, and Belgians to New Jersey.

Many families moved back and forth between New Jersey, New York, and Pennsylvania. New Jersey's position between New York and Philadelphia and between New England and the South made adequate transportation imperative. By 1830, the legislature had chartered more than fifty turnpike companies; about 550 miles of road were built. In 1834 the Delaware and Raritan Canal connected the Delaware and Raritan rivers, providing a short all-water route from New York to Philadelphia.

New Jersey Library Collection

Atlases, Maps, and Gazetteers

A number of helpful maps and gazetteers of the New Jersey area are in the library's collection. These will prove useful for genealogical research:

Clement, John. *A Collection of Maps and Drafts: As Copied from Old Maps and Drafts from Actual Surveying.* Salt Lake City: Genealogical Society of Utah, 1966. 2 reels. Original records at Genealogical Society of Pennsylvania, Philadelphia. (FHL# microfilm 501011, items 3-8, and 501012, item 1)

Gannett, Henry. *A Geographical Dictionary of New Jersey.* 1894; rpt. ed., Baltimore, Md.: Genealogical Publishing Co., 1978. (FHL# 974.9/E5ga)

New Jersey: Minor Civil Divisions, Cities, Towns, Boroughs. Washington, D.C.: U.S. Government Printing Office, 1961. (Map Case FHL# 974.9/E7un)

Maps for 1790, 1810, 1823, 1838, 1857, 1862, 1878, 1884, and 1917 can be found on microfilm 002083.

Cemetery Records

There are several major state cemetery collections for New Jersey as well as listings under **/[County]/Cemetery Records** for every county.

The collection of the New Jersey Bureau of Archives and History in Trenton was microfilmed by the Genealogical Society of Utah in 1969 and is entitled *New Jersey Tombstone Inscriptions.* It is arranged alphabetically on the following reels: A-Co 591271, Co-Gr 591272, Gr-I 591273, I-Ph 593589, Ph-Sto 593590, Sto-Wo 593591, and Wo-Misc. 593592. The Daughters of the American Revolution have extensive cemetery records that are listed alphabetically by town, city, or county. Here are other state collections which may prove useful:

Holland Society of New York. *Cemetery and Geographical File.* Salt Lake City: Genealogical Society of Utah, 1977. 3 reels. (FHL# microfilm 1019527-1019529) Arranged alphabetically.

Matlack, T. Chalkley. *Graveyard Inscriptions, Books 1-14.* Salt Lake City: Genealogical Society of Utah, 1967. (FHL# microfilm 511744, item 2) Includes cemeteries in southwest New Jersey, Pennsylvania, and Delaware.

New Jersey Cemetery Inscriptions. Salt Lake City: Genealogical Society of Utah, 1976. (FHL# microfilm 1005022, item 9) Indexed by the names of the cemeteries and also the names of the individuals.

The Genealogical Society of New Jersey has a collection of over 600 cemeteries, many on microfilm. See **/[County/Cemetery Records**. Many New Jersey cemeteries are on microfilm with Pennsylvania, Delaware, and New York cemetery records.

Census Records

Although the federal census has been taken in New Jersey every ten years beginning in 1790, the entire census copies for 1790, 1810, and 1820 were lost or destroyed, and only the Cumberland County census is available for 1800. There are indexes by heads of households for the 1830-50 censuses.

State censuses were taken every ten years from 1855 to 1915. The returns for some counties are missing for 1855 and 1865, and only the Sussex County census for 1875 survives. The state censuses for 1855, 1865, 1885, and 1895 are on microfilm. There are also mortality schedules available for 1850, 1860, 1870, and 1880. Also consult:

Stryker-Rodda, Kenneth. *Revolutionary Census of New Jersey.* Cottonport, La.: n.pub., 1972. Indexed. (FHL# 974.9/X2r) Taken from tax ratables.

Compendium of Censuses 1726-1905: Together with the Tabulated Record of 1905. Trenton: J. L. Murphy Publishing Co., 1906. (FHL# 974.9/X2n or microfilm 1036501, item 1)

Church Records

The library has several guides to New Jersey church records. Churches are listed in the following directories:

Historical Records Survey. Works Progress Administration. *Directory of Churches in New Jersey.* Newark: The Survey, 1940. (FHL# 974.9/K22h)

An Index to Some Churches in New Jersey, Arranged by Denomination. Salt Lake City: Genealogical Society of Utah, 1971. (FHL# microfilm 855189)

Guides that describe New Jersey church records are in the following:

New Jersey Church Archives. *Guide to Vital Statistics Records in New Jersey.* Newark: Historical Records Survey, 1941. (FHL# microfilm 874039)

Nelson, William. "Church Records in New Jersey." Microreproduction of article in *Journal of the Presbyterian Historical Society*, 1904. Salt Lake City: Genealogical Society of Utah, 1985. (Microfiche FHL# 6010550)

Includes churches of the 1800s and the church records which contain births, marriages, and deaths not likely to be found elsewhere.

The library has inventories from the Church Archives of New Jersey for these denominations: Baptist, Baha'i, Congregational, Evangelical, Presbyterian, and Unitarian. These inventories were prepared by the New Jersey Historical Records Survey Project in the 1940s. Also see **New Jersey/Church Records** for record collections of the DAR, Catholic, Friends, Dutch Reformed, and Lutheran. Every county in New Jersey has listings under **/Church Records.**

Court Records

Of New Jersey's many courts the following have records on microfilm: Court of Common Pleas (marriages, naturalizations, child support, etc.), Orphans' Court (estates and guardianships), Court of Quarter Sessions (desertions, apprenticeship disputes, vice), Chancery Court (mortgage foreclosures, protection of women's estates, legacies in trust), Prerogative Court (estate disputes), and the Supreme Court (estate disputes, treason, murder, appeals).

Many volumes are indexed; other indexes appear under the heading **New Jersey/Court Records/Indexes.** By far the largest collection of records is that of the Chancery Court with about 495 reels. See:

Index of Names to Various Records in Various New Jersey Counties, 1600-1800. 6 reels. Salt Lake City: Genealogical Society of Utah, 1972. (FHL# microfilm 946856-946861)

Alphabetical index of names listed in commissions in military, power of attorney, court appointments, pardons, land agreements, mortgages, warrants, surveys, patents, wills, and marriages.

Indentures Collection Containing Deeds, Bonds, Commissions, etc. of New Jersey Individuals: and Other States, 1600-1900. 16 reels. Salt Lake City: Genealogical Society of Utah, 1970. Microreproduction of original records at Rutgers University. Indexed. (FHL# microfilm 849543-849557 and 849596)

All but five counties in New Jersey have court records in the collection.

Directories

Most of the New Jersey counties have directories of some kind including city or business directories. A few of the cities with directories in book or on microfilm are Atlantic City, Rutherford, Camden, Newark, Jersey City, and Princeton. There is also a farm directory for Burlington County 1900. Cataloged in the FHLC under **New Jersey/Directories** are:

Directory of State Officers, Judges, etc. Prepared by the Laws, Commissions, and Publications Secretary of the Office of the Secretary of State, 1969. (FHL# 974.9/P6n)

Kirkbride, Stacy B. *Kirkbride's New Jersey Business Directory, General Register, and Advertising Medium.* 1850; microreproduction Salt Lake City: Genealogical Society of Utah, 1971. (FHL# microfilm 854584)

Genealogy

There are numerous published genealogies of New Jersey families including over eighty-eight titles under **/Genealogy**, twenty-one under **/Biography**, and twelve under **Bible Records.**

The Charles Carroll Gardner collection consists of three different collections of alphabetically arranged files on northeastern New Jersey families on 63 reels filmed by the Genealogical Society of Utah in 1973. Part of his collection is at the New Jersey Historical Society and part at Rutgers University.

The John Pickens Dornan collection consists of *Collection, Family File*, arranged alphabetically by surname, 37 reels, and *Dornan Collection 1600-1900*, 33 reels with separate index. The original collection is at Rutgers University Library in New Brunswick, and it was filmed by the Genealogical Society of Utah in 1970-71.

Other large collections worth searching are the Elias Budinot Stockton collection, the Gilbert Cope collection (Quaker families), the Genealogical Society of New Jersey collection, the Charles E. Sheppard collection, the Verna Hill Jacob collection, and the DAR collection. All of them are cataloged under **New Jersey/Genealogy Collections.**

Immigration/Emigration Records

The majority of people who moved into New Jersey probably arrived at either New York City or Philadelphia since New Jersey had no major port of entry. Between 1820 and 1892, approximately 11.8 million people passed through the port of entry in New York City; during the same period, 660,000 landed in Philadelphia. Passenger lists from both these ports are available on microfilm. (See the gray binders at the reference table entitled "Immigration" for film numbers).

Also in these binders under "Miscellaneous Ports" are microfilm numbers for several New Jersey ports for various years. Passenger lists are on the following films: Cape May 1828 (FHL# 830232), Little Egg Harbor 1831 (FHL# 830234), Newark 1836 (FHL# 830235), and Perth Amboy 1820-32 (FHL# 830238). For earlier immigrations, see the following sources:

Filby, P. William. *Passenger and Immigration Lists Index.* 3 vols. Detroit: Gale Research Co., 1981. At the U.S./-Canada reference table. (FHL# 973/W32p)

Boyer, Carl, ed. *Ship Passenger Lists: New York and New Jersey, 1600-1825.* Newhall, Ca.: Boyer, 1978. (FHL# 973/-W3sa)

Land and Property Records

Many deeds and mortgages from about 1780 to 1900 have been microfilmed and are listed by county. You may also want to search the following indexes and collections of land records listed under **New Jersey/Land and Property.**

Index to Deeds, Grantor and Grantee, 1670-c.1800. 7 reels. Salt Lake City: Genealogical Society of Utah, 1967-68. Original records at New Jersey State Library, Trenton.

Archives of the State of New Jersey, 1st series, vol. 21. (FHL# microfilm 844443) *Abstracts of East and West Jersey Deeds, 1664-1703.* New Jersey. Western Division. Council of Proprietors.

Surveys. New Brunswick, N.J.: Rutgers University, 1953-55. (Index FHL# microfilm 888803)

New Jersey. Bureau of Archives and History. *Index to Power of Attorney, Surveyors' Reports, Commissions, etc. Referring to Deeds, 1703-1856.* Salt Lake City: Genealogical Society of Utah, 1969. (A-I: FHL# microfilm 542530, and J-Z: 542531)

New Jersey. State Library (Trenton). *East Jersey Deeds, 1667-1783.* 15 reels. Salt Lake City: Genealogical Society of Utah, 1967. (Grantee and grantor index FHL# microfilm 522742)

New Jersey. State Library (Trenton). *West Jersey Deeds, 1677-1854.* 29 reels. Salt Lake City: Genealogical Society of Utah, 1967. (Grantor index FHL# microfilm 460043; grantee index 460044)

Also be sure to check the *Indentures Collection* listed under **/Court Records** and the John Clement records which have Gloucester and other county titles, field books, warrants, and surveys.

Military Records

The New Jersey collection contains hundreds of records from colonial times up through the Spanish-American War (1898). A few records from each period are:

Colonial Wars

New Jersey State Library (Trenton). *New Jersey Wars: Index to Colonial Period, 1665-1774.* Salt Lake City: Genealogical Society of Utah, 1969. (FHL# microfilm 573334, items 1-

4) Includes officers and soldiers of French and Indian War.

Revolutionary War

The library's microfilm collection includes: manuscripts, citations, indexes, pension claims, lists of loyalist officers and men of New Jersey, and records of damages in New Jersey. Most of these are alphabetically arranged or indexed. Among these records are:

Jones, Chester. *New Jersey Revolutionary War Veterans.* 37 reels. Salt Lake City: Genealogical Society of Utah, 1971. Original records at Rutgers University, New Brunswick. Arranged alphabetically.

New Jersey. Adjutant General's Office. *Official Register of the Officers and Men of New Jersey in the Revolutionary War.* 1872; rpt. ed., Baltimore, Md.: Genealogical Publishing Co., 1967. (FHL# 974.9/M23n/1967 or microfilm 908526) Index compiled and revised by James W. S. Campbell, 1965. (FHL# 974.9/M23n/Index)

U.S. War Department. *Revolutionary War Rolls 1775-1783.* (FHL# microfilm 830334-830343)

War of 1812

New Jersey State Library (Trenton). *New Jersey in the War of 1812.* 16 reels. Salt Lake City: Genealogical Society of Utah, 1969. (Index on FHL# microfilm 573337).

New Jersey. Adjutant General's Office. *Records of Officers and Men of New Jersey in Wars, 1791-1815.* 1909; rpt. ed., Baltimore, Md.: Genealogical Publishing Co., 1970. (FHL# 974.9/M25no or microfilm 874048)

Civil War

Adjutant-General's Office, comp. *Records of Officers and Men of New Jersey in the Civil War, 1861-1865.* 2 vols. Trenton: J. L. Murphy, 1876. (FHL# 974.9/M25nr or microfilm 579866, item 2--Index)

Alphabetical Roll of New Jersey Volunteers in Civil War. Salt Lake City: Genealogical Society of Utah, 1969. Original records at New Jersey State Library, Trenton. (A-H: FHL# microfilm 579863; L-P: 579864; Q-W: 579865; W-Z missing)

U.S. Adjutant General's Office. *Index to Compiled Service Record of Volunteer Union soldiers Who Served in Organizations from the State of New Jersey.* 26 reels. Washington, D.C.: National Archives, 1965. (FHL# microfilm 882031-882056)

Also included are 121 microfilm reels of Civil War record books and an index to Civil War pension claims of New Jersey soldiers.

Spanish-American War

Records and an index for the Spanish-American War are available on microfilm.

Native Races

The library has only one volume on native races in New Jersey:

Stewart, Frank H. *Indians of Southern New Jersey.* [c.1932]; rpt. ed., Woodbury, N.J.: Gloucester County Historical Society, 1977. (FHL# 970.1/A1/no.73)

Naturalization Records

Naturalization records in New Jersey are listed under the individual counties, and all counties except Camden have naturalization records on microfilm. The state records are as follows:

New Jersey. Court of Chancery. *Naturalization Records, 1832-1847, 1852, 1856-1858, 1861-1862.* Salt Lake City: Genealogical Society of Utah, 1978. Original records in Bureau of Archives and History, Mercer County. (FHL# microfilm 1022907)

New Jersey. Supreme Court. *Naturalization Records, 17[illegible]-1873; Card index 1761-1860.* Salt Lake City: Genealogical Society of Utah, 1978. Original records in Bureau of Archives and History, Mercer County. (FHL# microfilm 1022906 and 1022908-1022914)

Index to Naturalization, 1700's-1800's. Salt Lake City: Genealogical Society of Utah, 1972. (FHL# microfilm 913176)

Newspapers

The earliest regular newspapers in New Jersey date from about 1778, so for earlier information, search the papers of New York, Philadelphia, or Boston. Extracts from American newspapers relating to New Jersey for 1704-82 are published in chronological order in volumes 11, 12, 19, 20, 24-29, and 31 of the *Archives of the State of New Jersey*, with surname, place, and subject indexes for each volume. They are cataloged in the FHLC under **New Jersey/Newspapers.** See also:

Documents Relating to Revolutionary History of the State of New Jersey. 5 vols. Trenton: John L. Murphy Publishing Co., 1901-17. (FHL# 974.9/B49a/Ser. 2/vols. 1-5) Each volume is indexed.

Cataloged under **New Jersey/Mercer/Trenton/Newspapers/Indexes** is:

New Jersey. Bureau of Archives and History. *Vital Statistics Index from Trenton Newspapers, 1800-1900.* 18 reels. Salt Lake City: Genealogical Society of Utah, 1969. (FHL# microfilm 542512-542529)

Monmouth and Sussex counties also have listings under **/Newspapers.**

Probate Records

All counties in New Jersey have probate records on microfilm. Most of these are in the Orphan's Court records, but also many estate papers have been microfilmed. These range from about 1665 to about 1900.

The state collections contains the following records and indexes:

New Jersey. Department of State. *Record of Wills in New Jersey, 1705-1804.* 27 reels. Salt Lake City: Genealogical Society of Utah, 1968. Original records in New Jersey State Library, Trenton. Index at the beginning of each volume.

New Jersey. Prerogative Court. *Wills, 1823-1906.* 5 reels. Salt Lake City: Genealogical Society of Utah, 1978-79. Original records at New Jersey State Library, Trenton. Miscellaneous wills filed alphabetically.

Index of Wills, Inventories, etc. in the Office of the Secretary of State Prior to 1901. 1912; microreproduction Salt Lake City: Genealogical Society of Utah, 1968. (FHL# microfilm 545437) rpt. ed., 3 vols., Baltimore, Md.: Genealogical Publishing Co., 1969. (FHL# 974.9/P22s/1969) Names arranged alphabetically under each county.

Smeal, Lee, and Ronald Vern Jackson, eds. *Index to New Jersey Wills, 1689-1890, the Testators.* Salt Lake City: Accelerated Indexing System, 1979. (FHL# 974.9/P22a)

Taxation Records

The available tax records from the 1700s to 1822 have been microfilmed and are cataloged by county. These statewide indexes are also available:

Index to County Tax Ratables: Bergen-Sussex Counties, 1778-1822. Trenton: New Jersey State Library, 1956. (FHL# microfilm 802935)

Index to Tax Ratables, 1700's-1800's: Listing of Counties and Townships and Years of Taxes. Salt Lake City: Genealogical Society of Utah, 1972. (FHL# microfilm 913174)

Genealogical Society of Utah, comp. *Register of New Jersey County Tax Ratables, Abstracts and Exempt Lists, 1773 to about 1889.* Salt Lake City: Genealogical Society of Utah, 1965. (FHL# 974.9/R4p or microfilm 599498, item 4, and microfiche 6051263)

Vital Records

To learn when a particular town began keeping birth, marriage, or death records see *Guide to Vital Statistics Records in New Jersey, Vol. 1* (Newark: New Jersey Historical Records Survey, 1941) (FHL# 974.9/V2h or microfilm 874039, items 1-2) The Historical Records Survey began a project of abstracting birth, death, and marriage information on cards; although incomplete, they will probably be useful. They are in:

New Jersey. Historical Records Survey. Works Project Administration. *Birth and Death Records, early to 1900.* 12 reels. Salt Lake City: Genealogical Society of Utah, 1969.

Record of Births, Marriage and Deaths of New Jersey, 1848-1900. 290 reels. Salt Lake City: Genealogical Society of Utah, 1969. Original records at New Jersey State Library, Trenton. Indexed.

The marriage records to 1900 are available on microfilm and are arranged by county for each year. The following records may be helpful for marriages:

New Jersey. Department of Education. Division of State Library of Archives and History. *New Jersey Marriages 1711-1878.* 10 reels. Trenton: Microfilm and Recording Unit, 1966. Alphabetical by surname groups, but not alphabetical within the group. (FHL# microfilm 888701-888710)

New Jersey Marriage Bonds of the 1700's. Salt Lake City: Genealogical Society of Utah, 1966. (A-R: FHL# microfilm 540682; S-Z: 540683)

New Jersey Bureau of Archives and History. Works Project Administration. *Marriage Records 1670-1900.* 24 reels. Salt Lake City: Genealogical Society of Utah, 1969. Alphabetical.

Voting Records

There are no voting records available in the New Jersey collection either on the state or county level.

DELAWARE

Historical Background

Early	Lenni Lenape Indians (Delawares) occupy what is now Delaware.
1609	Henry Hudson, a British explorer with the Dutch West India Company, visits and locates Delaware River.
1610	Samuel Argall, English explorer, names area after the governor of Virginia, Lord De La Warr.
1631	David Pietersen de Vries, of the Dutch West India Company, establishes a camp on Lewes Beach.
1638	Swedes with the New Sweden Company establish first permanent settlement, Fort Christina (present-day Wilmington); introduces the construction of log homes in America. Colony called New Sweden.
1655	Dutch take control of New Sweden, rename it New Amstel.
1664	English seize the settlement, governed as part of the proprietary colony of New York.
1682	Delaware becomes part of Pennsylvania, referred to as the Lower Counties.
1684-1732	Lord Baltimore of Maryland claims southern and western Delaware.
1704	Lower Counties establish independent legislature although Delaware continues to be part of Pennsylvania until 1776.
1776	Slavery prohibited by state law, although it is still practiced until 1865. Delaware adopts a state constitution and moves reluctantly toward independence with the other colonies.
1787	On 7 December, Delaware becomes first state to ratify the U.S. Constitution.
1802	Franco-American industrialist Eleuthere Irenee du Pont de Nemours founds gunpowder factory near Wilmington, beginning Delaware's most important industry, DuPont Chemical Co. (This factory important in War of 1812.)
1861	Delaware sides with the Union during the Civil War but has many Confederate sympathizers.

Many good sources are available for the history of Delaware. A few of them are:

Acrelius, Israel. *A History of New Sweden, or the Settlements on the River Delaware.* 1874; rpt. ed., New York: Arno Press, 1972. (FHL# 974/H2ac/1972 and microfilm 982319, item 2)

Bevan, Wilson Lloyd. *History of Delaware, Past and Present.* 4 vols. New York: Lewis Historical Publishing Co., 1929. (FHL# 975.1/H2b)

Historical and Biographical Encyclopedia of Delaware. Wilmington: Aldine Publishing and Engraving Co., 1883. (FHL# 975.1/D3h)

Settlement and Migration

The early Swedish and Dutch settlers in Delaware were followed by Finnish colonists who came aboard Swedish ships in 1656. While the British had possession of Delaware, a large influx of English people came from Virginia, Maryland, New Jersey, New York, and Europe. Many Scotch-Irish came after 1698 for the right of worshipping in accordance with the Presbyterian faith. Roman Catholics established themselves in northern Delaware as early as 1730, where the first Catholic chapel was built in 1772. More Catholics arrived in 1790, when several French families came seeking refuge from the West Indies uprisings. A flourishing slave trade brought many blacks into Delaware, where by 1790 they constituted 21.6 percent of the state's population.

Although the Lenni Lenape lived quite peacefully among the early European settlers, white settlements began to encroach on their hunting lands, so they gradually moved to Pennsylvania, Ohio, and finally beyond the Mississippi River. Approximately 2,000 Delaware Indians survive today on reservations in towns in Oklahoma, and in Ontario, Canada.

Many early settlers migrated from Delaware into Pennsylvania, Maryland, and New Jersey. By 1749 there was an established migration route from the northeastern states through Philadelphia to Wilmington, Delaware, to Baltimore, Maryland, and south to Virginia. In the 1700s there were several established roads between southern Delaware and Maryland.

After the Civil War, a major demographic change occurred when many of the state's natives left and were replaced by Irish Roman Catholics and Germans. New industries brought additional immigrants by 1920, mainly Italians, Poles, and Russian Jews. After World War II, another population shift occurred with the migration of blacks to urban areas.

Delaware Library Collection

Atlases, Maps, and Gazetteers

Delaware maps for 1790, 1810, 1823, 1857, 1862, 1878, 1884, and 1917 are located on microfilm 002083. Other good sources are:

Gannett, Henry. *A Gazetteer of Maryland and Delaware.* Baltimore, Md.: Genealogical Publishing Co., 1976. (FHL# 975/E5g or microfilm 982220, item 3)

Heck, L. W. *Delaware Place Names.* Washington, D.C.: U.S. Government Printing Office, 1966. (FHL# 975.1/E2h) Excellent for locating towns, rivers, etc.

The National Gazetteer of the United States of America: Delaware 1983. Washington, D.C.: U.S. Government Printing Office, 1984. (FHL# 975.1/E5n)

Cemetery Records

Cemetery records in Delaware are one of the best sources for locating vital information. During the 1930s and 1940s, the Historical Records Survey, under the direction of Walter G. Tatnall, recorded tombstone inscriptions in all three Delaware counties. See **Delaware/[County]/Cemetery Records**. An excellent source is typewritten records of approximately 120 cemeteries of New Castle County, about 175 cemeteries of Kent County, and 500 cemeteries of Sussex County, including family and farm cemeteries (FHL# microfilm 006303). At the beginning of the section for each county, there is an alphabetical list of the town or family cemeteries covered, with page references. Some of the cemeteries only have death dates to about 1925.

The best cemetery record for Sussex County is the Millard F. Hudson collection (FHL# microfilm 006690). It lists 630 cemeteries of Sussex County and is indexed by surname, cemetery, and road.

Census Records

The federal census has been taken in Delaware every ten years beginning in 1790. The 1790 U.S. Census is missing, but it has been reconstructed from tax and assessment lists by Leon deValinger, Jr. and published by the National Genealogical Society in Washington, D.C. It is arranged by county, then by hundred (a political subdivision), and then alphabetically by surnames of the head of families who owned property. (FHL# 975.1/-X2d/1790 or microfiche 6019928 or microfilm 1000156, item 6). The returns for 1800-1910 are available at the Family History Library. Censuses for 1800-70 have been indexed by head of households.

A couple of early census-type records have been reconstructed from tax rolls, etc.:

Jackson, Ronald Vern. *Early Delaware Census Records, 1665-1697.* Bountiful: Accelerated Indexing System, 1977. (FHL# 975.1/X2p)

Hancock, Harold B., ed. *The Reconstructed Delaware State Census of 1782.* Wilmington: Delaware Genealogical Society, 1983. Indexed. (FHL# 975.1/X2r)

Church Records

Church records are another very good source of genealogical information in Delaware. From 1936 to 1942, the Delaware Historical Records Survey copied about 100 volumes of records of individual congregations verbatim; many were indexed. Check the FHLC under **Delaware/[County]/Church Records** and **Delaware/-[County]/[Town]/Church Records**.

In 1942 the Public Archives Commission of Dover

published a valuable aid for finding which churches existed in each town: *Directory of Churches and Religious Organizations in Delaware* (FHL# 975.1/E4h or microfilm 1036702, item 3). The directory is arranged alphabetically by denomination and has two indexes, one listing the churches by town and another by name.

The major denominations in Delaware are Methodist, Episcopalian, Lutheran, Presbyterian, Protestant Episcopal, Methodist Protestant, Welsh Baptist, Quaker, and Catholic.

Court Records

In 1941 the Delaware Historical Records Survey prepared an *Inventory of the County Archives of Delaware: No. 1, New Castle County* (Dover: Public Archives Commission, 1941) (FHL# microfilm 897354, item 2) This volume explains the various courts of Delaware since its settlement and describes the types of court records found in the Delaware counties. Three courts keep records of genealogical value: the Orphans' Court which rules on rights of property, estates, and guardians of minors; the Court of Common Pleas or Chancery Court which hears civil and criminal cases; and the Superior Court which hears suits and appeals brought up from the lesser courts.

Consult the FHLC under **Delaware/[County]/Court Records**. All three counties have Orphan's Court and Chancery Court records on microfilm.

Directories

The Wilmington city directory for 1890 (Tucson, Ariz.: W. C. Cox, 1974) is on FHL# microfilm 1000736. The Polk city directory for Wilmington for 1934 (Salt Lake City: Genealogical Society of Utah, 1985) is on microfilm 1307613, item 10.

Genealogy

If you have Delaware ancestors, the Reverend Joseph Brown Turner, *Genealogical Collection of Delaware Families* (Salt Lake City: Genealogical Society of Utah, 1948) is a top priority in research. It contains about 3,000 genealogies, arranged alphabetically on 29 reels. (FHL# microfilm 006272-006300)

To learn if there is a published biography of your ancestor or a genealogy of your family, see Henry Clay Reed, *A Bibliography of Delaware through 1960* (Newark: University of Delaware Press, 1966). (FHL# 975.1/a3r) Also check the genealogical collections of Maryland, Pennsylvania, and New Jersey, since many of the early families moved back and forth between these states. Check the following sources for more information:

Delaware Bible Records. Newark: DAR, Delaware, 1950. Indexed. (FHL# 975.1/V29d and microfilm 924445, item 1)

Old Bible Records. 4 reels. Salt Lake City: Genealogical Society of Utah, 1970. Charts and general sketches. (FHL# microfilm 845762-845765)

Scott, Kenneth R. *Genealogical Data from the Pennsylvania Chronicle 1767-1774.* Washington, D.C.: National Genealogical Society, 1971. (FHL# 974.811/B38s or microfilm 1035770, item 5) Contains information on 3600 persons' births, marriages, or deaths from Delaware, Maryland, Pennsylvania, and New Jersey.

Immigration Records

Customs passenger lists for Wilmington cover the periods 1820, 1830-31, 1833, 1840-49, indexed on FHL# microfilm 830246. If your ancestors lived in Delaware, they might have arrived at Philadelphia, Baltimore, or other ports. Microfilmed indexes for those ports are available. Look under **[State]/[County]/[City]/Emigration and Immigration**. See also:

Boyer, Carl, ed. *Ship Passenger Lists: Pennsylvania and Delaware, 1641-1825.* Newhall, Calif.: Boyer, 1980. Indexed. (FHL# 973/W3sb)

Land and Property

The early Dutch and Swedish land titles were recognized by the English, but they had to be validated by registration. So in 1682, William Penn required by law that all deeds, grants, or conveyances of land be registered. For a study of Delaware's land records, see *Inventory of the County Archives of Delaware: No. 1, New Castle County.* (FHL# microfilm 897354) See the following indexes to deeds, warrants, and surveys:

Kent County: An alphabetical index to warrants, surveys and some deeds, from the 1600s to about 1860 (FHL# microfilm 006530). A deed index for 1680-1873 (FHL# microfilm 006483). Deed books for 1680-1850, 35 reels (FHL# microfilm 006449-006482).

New Castle County: An alphabetical index to warrants, surveys and some deeds from the 1600s-1890 (FHL# microfilm 006617). Deed indexes for 1640-1873 (FHL# microfilm 006610-006613). Deed books for 1673-1850, 56 reels (FHL# microfilm 006558-006609).

Sussex County: An alphabetical index to warrants, surveys, and some deeds from the 1600s-1870 (FHL# microfilm 006691). A deed index, 1682-1844 (FHL# microfilm 006623). Deed books 1693-1850, 30 reels (FHL# microfilm 006624-006652)

Original Land Titles in Delaware (1646-1679). Wilmington, Del.: Sunday Star Print, [c.1899]. Commonly known as the Duke of York Records. Indexed. (FHL# 975.1/R2o)

Military Records

The Public Archives Commission of Delaware published a five-volume set of Delaware military and naval records entitled *Delaware Archives* (Wilmington, Del.: 1911-16). 3 reels and 19 microfiche. Consult the FHLC for call numbers: Volume 1: colonial period (1744-48, 1754-63); Volumes 2-3: Revolutionary War (1775-84); Volumes 4-5: the War of 1812 (1812-15). Volume 3 indexes Vols. 1-3; Volume 5 indexes Vols. 4-5.

Also see:

United States. War Department. *Revolutionary War Rolls*

1775-1783. 138 reels. Washington, D.C.: National Archives, 1957. Delaware Jackets. (FHL# microfilm 830308-830310)

Ward, Christopher. *The Delaware Continentals, 1776-1783.* Wilmington: Historical Society of Delaware, 1941. (FHL# 975.1/M25wa or microfilm 1000154, item 4)

United States. Adjutant General's Office. *Index to Compiled Service Records of Volunteer Union Soldiers Who Served in Organizations from the State of Delaware, 1861-1865.* 4 reels. Washington, D.C.: National Archives, 1964. Alphabetically arranged. (FHL# microfilm 881617-881620)

Conner, William H. *Delaware's Role in World War II, 1940-1946.* Dover: Delaware Public Archives Commission, 1955. (FHL# 975.1/M25d)

Native American Records

There are two titles cataloged under **Delaware/Native Races:**

Speck, Frank Gouldsmith. *The Nanticoke and Conoy Indians with a Review of Linguistic Material from Manuscripts and Living Sources.* Wilmington: Historical Society of Delaware, 1927. (FHL# 970.3/N158s)

Weslager, C. A. *Delaware's Forgotten Folk: The Story of the Moors and Nanticokes.* Washington, D.C.: Library of Congress, [c.1970s]. (FHL# microfilm 1009062, item 1)

Naturalization Records

The library has few naturalization records for Delaware, since the records to 1906 are generally in the custody of the Bureau of Archives and Records Management. The one available record is:

Delaware. Superior Court. *Naturalization Papers, Transcripts and Originals, A-Z.* Salt Lake City: Genealogical Society of Utah, 1949. (FHL# microfilm 006529)

Newspapers

There are no microfilms available for any of the Delaware papers. You may wish to look for references to Delaware residents in newspapers of Pennsylvania, New Jersey, and Maryland.

Probate Records

The wills to the three counties of Delaware have been fully indexed to 1800:

Kent County: Index for 1680-1948 (FHL# microfilm 006492-006493)

New Castle County: Index for 1682-1885 (FHL# microfilm 006545)

Sussex County: Index for 1682-1948 (FHL# microfilm 006618)

Many of the will books, will abstracts, inventories, and letters of administration are also on microfilm. Consult the FHLC under **Delaware/[County]/Probate Records.**

If your deceased ancestor left minor children, you may want to search the guardian accounts. Those for Kent and Sussex are on microfilm to 1850.

Taxation Records

In 1683 William Penn decreed that public expenses should be paid for by taxing the people. A brief history of taxation in Delaware is contained in *Inventory of the County Archives of Delaware: No. 1, New Castle County*, pp. 231-37 (Dover: Public Archives Commission, 1941) (FHL# microfilm 897354) Tax assessment records, besides giving the names of the persons being taxed, may also give information on their livestock, previous residences, occupations, death dates, land transfers during the year, and taxes on estates. Those available on microfilm from about 1726 to about 1850 are:

Kent County: 1726-77, 17 reels (FHL# microfilm 006494-0064510)

New Castle County: 1738-1852, 6 reels, arranged alphabetically. (FHL# microfilm 006531-006536)

Sussex County: 1767-1850 some undated, 5 reels (FHL# microfilm 006674-006678)

Vital Records

Registration of births was required by the state for a short time from 1861 to 1863. Birth registration began again in 1881, but compliance was loose. It was not until 1913 that all births were required by law to be registered. Some christening records from 1759 to 1890 are indexed on FHL# microfilm 006423. An alphabetical index to the available births from c.1680 to 1913 is on FHL# 006424-006430.

Marriages were registered by the county starting about 1832. Some earlier marriage license bonds have been preserved. Consult the FHLC under **Delaware/Vital Records/Indexes.**

Some death records were recorded beginning about 1855, then again in 1881, but these records were very scattered and incomplete. In 1913, death registration became a law. The following christening, birth, marriage, and death records and indexes are available on microfilm:

Delaware. Bureau of Vital Statistics. *Vital Records: Births 1861-1913; Deaths 1855-1910.* 87 reels. Salt Lake City: Genealogical Society of Utah, 1949. Partial index. (FHL# microfilm 006323-006409)

Delaware. Bureau of Vital Statistics. *Index Cards of Delaware Marriages, Baptisms, Births and Deaths 1680-1913.* 18 reels. Salt Lake City: Genealogical Society of Utah, 1949. (FHL# microfilm 006416-006433)

Delaware. Clerk of the Peace. *Marriage Bonds, 1855-1861 and Marriage Licenses 1889-1894.* Salt Lake City: Genealogical Society of Utah, 1949. (FHL# microfilm 006412)

Cope, Gilbert. *A List of Marriage License Bonds, So Far as They Have Been Preserved in New Castle County, Delaware 1744-1836.* Salt Lake City: Genealogical Society of Utah, 1965. Index. (FHL# microfilm 441415)

Also consult the FHLC under **/[County]/Vital Records** and **/[County]/[Town]/Vital Records.**

Voting Records

There are no voting records for the state of Delaware.

NEW YORK

Historical Background

Early	New York area inhabited by Mohegan, Lenni Lenape, and Wappinger (Algonquian tribes), and Mohawks, Oneida, Onondaga, Cayuga, and Seneca (Iroquoian tribes).
1524	Giovanni da Verrazano in the service of France, sails into New York Harbor.
c.1570	Iroquois Confederacy formed, uniting Iroquois tribes.
1603	Samuel de Champlain with a party of fur trappers explores northern New York.
1609	Henry Hudson sails up Hudson River as far as present-day Albany, claims region for the Netherlands.
1624	Dutch establish Fort Orange (now Albany) and found New Netherland.
1625	New Amsterdam settled by the Dutch on Manhattan Island.
1648-64	Peter Stuyvesant governs New Netherland.
1664	New Amsterdam seized by British; New Netherland renamed New York.
1683	First elected representative assembly adopts a Charter of Liberties.
1689	Jacob Leisler, a German-born merchant, leads a people's rebellion against the aristocracy of landlords.
1755-63	The French and Indian War fought after years of conflict between the British and French over domination of North America.
1771	About half of New York's 186,000 inhabitants of British descent; many loyal to the crown (Tories).
1776	Nearly one-third of Revolutionary War's battles take place in New York, including major conflicts at Saratoga, Oriskany, and Bennington. By the end of the war, half of New York's aristocracy (British sympathizers) have fled to Canada.
1788	New York ratifies the U.S. Constitution, becoming the eleventh state.
1789-90	New York City the temporary national capital. George Washington inaugurated president there.
1800	Most Iroquois and Algonquian lands signed away.
1825	Erie Canal opened.
1839	Anti-rent War leads to end of the manorial system in New York.
1861-65	Most citizens of New York Union sympathizers; one-third of the casualties of the Battle of Bull Run are New York soldiers.
1890-1920	High point of immigration; Ellis Island major point of entry.

The library has over 150 titles cataloged under **New York/History**. Among these are:

Barber, John Warner. *Historical Collections of the State of New York*. New York: S. Tuttle, 1842. (FHL# 974.7/H2b) Contains fact, traditions, biographical sketches, geographical descriptions, maps. Indexed.

Blenz, Beth, ed. *Encyclopedia of New York.* St. Clair Shores, Mich.: Somerset Publishers, 1982. (FHL# 974.7/A5e)

Sullivan, James, ed. *History of New York State, 1523-1927.* 5 vols. New York: Lewis Historical Publishing Co., 1929. (FHL# 974.7/H2s)

Chronology of Ellis Island

1890	Designated immigration station under federal control to replace Castle Garden.
1892	Opened as an immigration station, January.
1897	Buildings burn; no lives lost.
1900	Reopens as a larger immigration station, December.
1907	Peak year; 1 million immigrants, mostly from Russia, Italy, Austria-Hungary, Germany, Ireland, and Poland.
1917-19	Detention center for enemy aliens, a way station for navy personnel, and a hospital for the army.
1919-54	Deportation/immigration center.
1924	Laws and quotas end mass immigration; immigrants inspected in their countries of origin.
1939-46	Part of Ellis Island used as a Coast Guard station.
1941-54	Part used as a detention center for enemy aliens.
1954	Closed in November.
1965	Added by Presidential Proclamation to the Statue of Liberty National Monument.
1976	Opened for visits.

An estimated 12 million immigrants entered the United States through Ellis Island. There are no records in the FHLC listed under Ellis Island; see **New York/New York/Emigration and Immigration.**

Settlement and Migration

After the British took control of New York from the Netherlands, the Dutch settlers were allowed to keep their farms and most of them remained. During the British rule, expansion of settlement occurred west along the Mohawk River and north along the Hudson. Many Puritan families drifted south into New York from Massachusetts and Connecticut. In 1688 Huguenots established New Rochelle, in Westchester County. German Palatines settled along the Hudson, Schoharie, and Mohawk River valleys. Some French settlers moved into the northern part of New York from Canada. Some Spaniards and Portuguese left the uprisings in the West Indies and came to New York.

Boundaries were settled with Connecticut in 1731, and Massachusetts in 1773. When Vermont became a state in 1791, New York lost its claim to the Vermont lands.

In the late eighteenth century, large tracts of land in central and western New York were opened for settlement. The Military Tract, extending from below Ithaca to Lake Ontario, was reserved for veterans of the American Revolution. Many New England farmers moved west into New York at this time.

From 1820 to 1845, large numbers of immigrants from Europe arrived. The Irish formed the largest group, settling in New York City, along the state's canals and along the railroads. German immigrants settled mostly upstate in Buffalo and Rochester. In 1790 when the first federal census was enumerated, New York had 340,120 people; by 1860 that number had grown to 3,880,735.

The state's system of natural waterways, with outlets to the Atlantic Ocean and the Great Lakes, provided means of transportation for the migrating settlers. In 1825 when the Erie Canal was completed, Albany on the Hudson River was connected with Lake Erie. It carried immigrants from New York City to settle on farms in the Midwest. Also by 1825, 4,000 miles of turnpike roads were in use. By 1831 trains were operating from Albany to Schenectady, and by 1852 railroad lines were running to Buffalo and on to Erie, Pennsylvania.

The immigration influx from 1890 to 1920 brought great numbers of eastern and southern Europeans, mainly Russians, Jews, Italians, and Poles. These arrivals found employment in the state's growing industries: steel-manufacturing around Buffalo, the photography industry (Eastman) in Rochester, locomotive plants in Schenectady, and the garment industry in New York City.

As the nation's business, commercial, and artistic center, the state attracted talented and ambitious people from all over the United States. It also attracted large numbers of Southern blacks trying to escape prejudice and poverty. Puerto Ricans began arriving in large numbers in the 1940s. No less than sixty languages can be heard among the residents. Predominating nationalities are Italian, Russian, German, Polish, Irish, Austrian, English, Hungarian, Swedish, Norwegian, Czech, Greek, French, Finnish, and Danish.

New York Library Collection

Atlases, Maps, and Gazetteers

Forty-six maps and many gazetteers are in the New York collection. There are maps of New Netherland 1614-21, early New York 1749, 1755, Lake Champlain 1779, the railroads 1884, the Military Tract, and many more, including:

A Chorographical Map of the Province of New York in North America. 1779; rpt. ed., Paramus, N.J.: Highway Printing, [c.1970s] (Map Case FHL# 974.7/E7cm) Divided in counties, manors, patents, and townships compiled from actual surveys deposited at the Patent Office in New York.

Disturnell, John. *A Gazetteer of the State of New York.* Albany, N.Y.: Disturnell, 1842. (FHL# 974.7/E5d or microfilm 982372, item 4)

New York: Her Counties, Townships and Her Towns. Indianapolis, Ind.: Researchers, [c.1980s]. (FHL# 974.7/-E7nyh) Contains a section of maps and a list of places.

Cemetery Records

Many of New York's cemeteries have been transcribed for publication. Check the FHLC under **/[County]/Cemetery Records** or **/[County]/[Town]/-Cemetery Records.** Cataloged under the state is:

Missionaries and members of the LDS Eastern States Mission, comps. *New York State Cemetery Records*. 23 typescript vols. 8 reels. Salt Lake City: Genealogical Society of Utah, 1940-69. (FHL# 974.7/V22n or microfilm 844624-844631) Indexed in the following:

Patron's Service of the Genealogical Society [of Utah], comp. *Index to Cemetery Records of New York: 1940-1969*. n.p., n.d. (FHL# 974.7/V22n/Index) Alphabetically by county, then alphabetically by cemetery.

Holland Society of New York. *Cemetery and Geographical Files.* 3 reels. Salt Lake City: Genealogical Society of Utah, 1977. (FHL# microfilm 1019527-1019529)

The DAR also has a large collection of records. For cemetery records, consult the FHLC under **New York/Cemeteries** and **/Bible Records.** This DAR Collection contains Bible records, probates, cemetery records, military records, and vital records. (FHL# microfiche 6331487-6331500 and 6332501-6332543) Most DAR collections include a variety of records on the same film or fiche.

Census Records

The federal censuses of New York have been indexed for 1790-1850. State censuses were taken every ten years from 1825 to 1925; the 1885 census was taken in 1892, and no 1895 census was taken. Many of these state censuses are on microfilm, but not for all counties or all years. For instance, Delaware County state censuses for 1855-1905, and Tioga County for 1825-1905 are on microfilm. Check the FHLC under **/County/Census** for a list of holdings. Also see:

Clint, Florence Runyan. *New York Area Key: A Guide to*

Genealogical Records of the State of New York. Elizabeth, Colo.: Keyline Publishers, 1979. (FHL# 974.7/D27c)

For an inventory of census records, see:

Jacobsen, Edna Louise. *An Inventory of New York State and Federal Census Records.* Salt Lake City: Genealogical Society of Utah, 1941. (FHL# microfilm 017137, item 1) Typescript at New York State Library, Albany. Rev. ed., 1956 (FHL# microfilm 908063, item 6)

See the following miscellaneous census records also:

Dilts, Bryan Lee. *1890 New York Census Index of Civil War Veterans or Their Widows.* Salt Lake City: Index Publishing, 1984. (FHL# 974.7/X22dv/1890)

Meyers, Carol M. *Early New York State Census Records, 1663-1772.* Gardena, Calif.: RAM Publishers, [c.1965]. (FHL# 974.7/X28m)

New York. Department of Social Services. *Enumeration of Indians for Payment of Annuities, June 1969: Cayuga Tribe.* Salt Lake City: Genealogical Society of Utah, 1971. (FHL# microfilm 824184, item 3)

Church Records

Church records began in New York as early as the 1600s. They often contain births, baptisms, marriages, deaths, or burial dates, and sometimes parents' names. There may be vestry minutes, financial records, mention of arrivals, and transfers of memberships. The major denominations in New York are Eastern Orthodox, Lutheran, Methodist, Presbyterian, Protestant Episcopal, Dutch Reformed, Roman Catholic, Jewish, Quaker, and Baptist. The original records are at local churches, denominational repositories, societies, and libraries, but many have been microfilmed. Consult the FHLC under **/[County]/Church Records** or **/[County]/[Town]/-Church Records.** The following references cataloged under the state may also prove helpful:

Dutch Reformed Church Record Collection. 38 reels. Salt Lake City: Genealogical Society of Utah, 1977. (begins with FHL# microfilm 1016557) Also contains Lutheran, Episcopal, German Reformed, and French Reformed records in New York and New Jersey.

Historical Records Survey. Works Project Administration. *Guide to Vital Statistics Records of Churches in New York State (Exclusive of New York City).* Albany: The Survey, 1942. (FHL# 974.7/K23h or microfilm 908710)

Historical Records Survey. Work Progress Administration. *Inventory of the Church Archives of New York's Presbyterian Churches, Excluding New York City.* 3 reels. Salt Lake City: Genealogical Society of Utah, 1967. (FHL# microfilm 505559-505561)

Vosburgh, Royden Woodward. *New York Church Records: Vosburgh Collection.* Transcribed by the New York Genealogical and Biographical Society. 61 reels. Salt Lake City: Genealogical Society of Utah, 1955. (FHL# microfilm 017441-017501) Listings by town, then church with years of the records.

Court Records

Most counties in New York have numerous court records in the collection, usually cataloged under the county seat. Examples of the types of records are judgement rolls, court minutes, proceedings of the commissioners, and *Lis pendens*. Some of these date back to the 1600s. Cataloged in the FHLC under **New York/Court Records** are:

Divorce Decrees, 1884-1919. Salt Lake City: Genealogical Society of Utah, 1981. (FHL# microfilm 1301982, item 2) Contains Albany and other New York counties.

Historical Records Survey. Works Project Administration. *Volumes and Unbound Records from: Old Chancery Court, Supreme Court, and Court of Appeals Records in Albany.* Salt Lake City: Genealogical Society of Utah, 1953. (FHL# microfilm 017440)

New York (State) Archives. *List of Pre-1847 Court Records in the State Archives.* Albany: Office of Cultural Education, New York State Education Dept., 1984. (FHL# 974.7/-A1/no.316)

New York. Chancery Court. *Chancery Minutes and Orders, 1701-1847.* 22 reels. Salt Lake City: Genealogical Society of Utah, 1953. Indexed. (FHL# microfilm 017418-017439)

Directories

City directories, county directories, and occupational directories provide clues to residence, occupation, place of work, and possible relatives. They also list churches, cemeteries, and places of business in a given year. See New York City directories, 1822-50 (FHL# 974.71/E4e) and 1843-1900, 23 reels. Consult the FHLC for call numbers. For Polk's New York City 1917 directory, see FHL# Q/974.71/E4pn.

Other cities with directories in the collection are Albany, Buffalo, Ithaca, Queens, Rochester, Syracuse, and Troy, to name a few. Also these specialized directories are in the state collection:

Medical Directory of New York State. New York State Medical Association, 1949. (FHL# 974.7/E4n)

American Agriculturist Farm Directory of Yates, Schuyler, Tompkins and Seneca Counties, New York 1914. 1914; microreproduction, Provo, Utah: Brigham Young University, 1970. Indexed. (FHL# microfilm 812856, item 4)

O'Callaghan, Edmund Bailey. *The Register of New Netherland: 1626-1674.* Albany: J. Munsell, 1865. (FHL# 974.7/E4o or microfilm 874364, item 4)

Genealogy

You have a good chance of finding information on your New York family in one of the many genealogical collections available at the library. There are over eighty-six titles under **New York/Genealogy, /Biography,** and **/Bible Records.** The Daughters of the American Revolution collection contains over fifteen titles alone; see:

Master Index New York State DAR Genealogical Records. New York: DAR, 1972. Photocopy of typescript. Salt Lake City: Genealogical Society of Utah, [c.1970s]. (FHL# 974.7/D22 or microfilm 1206452, item 13)

Several other large collections are:

National Society of the Colonial Dames of America. *Membership Genealogical File*. 105 reels. Salt Lake City: Genealogical Society of Utah, 1977. Indexed by member and ancestor. See FHLC for call numbers.

The Holland Society of New York. *Manuscript and Historical Collection*. 41 reels. Salt Lake City: Genealogical Society of Utah, 1977. Alphabetical. Also: *Compiled Genealogies*. 47 reels. Alphabetical. See FHLC for call numbers.

Eardeley, William A. *Collection on Eastern States Families*. 14 reels. Brooklyn: Long Island History Society, 1960. Alphabetical. (FHL# microfilm 414880-414893)

Jacob, Verna Hill. *Genealogical Research Notes*. 34 reels. Salt Lake City: Genealogical Society of Utah, 1978. Alphabetical files, queries, and correspondence. (FHL# microfilm 1036885-1036918)

Immigration/Emigration Records

New York City has been a major U.S. port of entry since the early days. Very complete passenger lists are available from 1820 to 1943. See the gray binder at the reference table entitled "New York Immigration 1820-1943." Few passenger lists exist before 1819; indexes for that period have been reconstructed from manifests, baggage lists, custom house records, and newspaper lists. From 1600 on, see:

Filby, P. William. *Passenger and Immigration Lists Index.* 3 vols. Detroit: Gale Research Co., 1981. Located at the U.S./Canada reference table.

Other sources to check are:

Bolton, Ethel Stanwood. *Immigrants to New England 1700-1775.* Salem, Mass.: Essex Institute, 1931. (FHL# 974/-W2b)

Coddington, John Insley. *Migrations from New England to New York and New Jersey*. Salt Lake City: Genealogical Society of Utah, 1969. (FHL# microfilm 897217, item 18)

Meyers, Carol M. *Early Immigrants to New Netherland 1657-1664*. Gardena, Calif.: RAM Publishers, 1965. (FHL# 974.7/W2m)

Other records in the New York state collection include immigration of Italians, Irish, Palatines, French, and Puerto Ricans. For the New York City port records, check the FHLC under **New York/New York City/Emigration and Immigration.**

Land and Property Records

Recording deeds was not required until 1810 in New York, and many deeds were not filed until long after they were written. Grantee and grantor, mortgagee, and mortgagor indexes are available on microfilm for most counties, as are the deeds to about 1900. The library has microfilms of deeds from 1630, patents (1664-1912), survey field books (1708-1848), and other records. Indexes are available for most of these records. A helpful general index is:

Calendar of New York Colonial Manuscripts, Endorsed Land Papers in the Office of the Secretary of State, 1643-1803. Albany: Weed, Parsons Co., 1864. (FHL# microfilm 947853)

Contains petitions and warrants for patents, caveats against granting patents, survey requests, warrants and returns, military land grant requests from 1750 on, and certificates of location.

Included in the twenty-seven titles cataloged under **New York/Land and Property** are works on the Indian deeds treaties, Palatines debts, New York alien residents 1825-48, land disputes (caveats), *lis pendens*, Holland Land Company purchases, and landlords and tenants of New York's manorial society (1664-1775).

Military Records

Military enlistment records in New York began with the French and Indian War 1755-63. These lists are indexed (FHL# microfilm 924818 and 924819). These records may contain information on name, age, trade, height, date of enlistment, companies in which served, where born, etc. Other enlistments into the U.S. Army from 1798-1884 are on microfilm in several alphabetical series and contain information similar to that mentioned above. Consult the FHLC under **New York/Military Records/[War].**

Pension file indexes are also on microfilm in alphabetical lists. With the file number, pension records may be ordered from the National Archives. For Revolutionary War records pertaining to New York see:

United States. War Department. *Revolutionary War Rolls 1775-1783*. 138 reels. Washington, D.C.: National Archives, 1957. New York Jackets. (FHL# microfilm 830344-830357)

Roberts, James A., comp. *New York in the Revolution as Colony and State*. 2 vols. Albany: Comptroller's Office, 1898, 1904. (FHL# microfilm 940048, item 2)

Over 45,000 names. Volume 2 has an every-name index including soldiers, American and British prisoners, refugees, claimants for damages, estates confiscated, British Loyalists, and other participants.

For information on Civil War soldiers from New York, see:

United States. Adjutant General's Office. *Index to Compiled Service Records of Volunteer Union Soldiers Who Served in Organizations from the State of New York*. 157 reels. Washington, D.C.: National Archives, 1965. (FHL# microfilm 882057-882213)

Native American Records

The library has fourteen titles under **New York/Native Races**, including works on the Senecas on the Buffalo Creek reservation, the Kanadesaga, Geneva, and Esopus. Three sources are:

Graymont, Barbara. *The Iroquois in the American Revolution.* Syracuse, N.Y.: Syracuse University Press, 1972. (FHL# 970.3/Ir6g)

Kimm, Silas Conrad. *The Iroquois: A History of the Six Na-*

tions of New York. Middleburg, N.Y.: Press of Pierre W. Danforth, 1900. (FHL# 974.7/F3k)

Ruttenber, Edward Manning. *History of the Indian Tribes of Hudson's River*. Albany, N.Y.: J. Munsell, 1872. (FHL# 974.7/F3r)

Naturalization Records

In colonial as well as later times, only citizens could buy or bequeath property, establish a trade, own a ship, or become the master of a ship. In New York, different forms of naturalization occurred beginning in 1664 when the Dutch surrendered to the British. Naturalization records from 1790-1906 might have been kept by any court, or in the Justice of the Peace records. Many of these records are on microfilm by county and sometimes by town. The information given in the record depends on the format used by the clerk. Before 1790 a country or town of origin was rarely given. Oaths of allegiance were the earliest form of naturalization, and they were taken in New York in 1664, 1687, and 1776. Records preserved are in:

Scott, Kenneth R., and Kenneth Stryker-Rodda. *Denizations, Naturalizations, and Oaths of Allegiance in Colonial New York*. Baltimore, Md.: Genealogical Publishing Co., 1975. Indexed. (FHL# 974.7/P4sc)

Another helpful source aside from the county naturalization records is:

Scott, Kenneth R. *Early New York Naturalizations: Abstracts of Naturalization Records from Federal, State and Local Courts, 1792-1840*. Baltimore, Md.: Genealogical Publishing Co., 1981. (FHL# 974.7/P4s)

Newspapers

Consult the FHLC under **New York/[County]/Newspapers**. In New York City, the *New York Daily Times* (1851) became the *New York Times* in 1857. Daily copies from 18 September 1851 to 31 December 1912 are on 431 reels at the Family History Library. For genealogical information from some New York newspapers, see:

Falk, Byron A. *Personal Name Index to the New York Times Index, 1851-1979*. Succasunna, N.J.: Roxbury Data Interface, 1979. (FHL# 974.71/B3f)

Gavit, Joseph. *American Death and Marriages, 1784-1829*. Albany: New York State Library, 1977. (Marriages: FHL# microfilm 1022833; deaths: microfilm 1022834) From sixty-five state newspapers.

Scott, Kenneth R. *Genealogical Data from Colonial New York Newspapers*. Baltimore, Md.: Genealogical Publishing Co., 1977. (FHL# 974.71/D28s)

______. *Genealogical Data from the New York Post-Boy, 1743-1773*. Washington, D.C.: National Genealogical Society, 1970. (FHL# 974.71/B38s)

These two books have different information.

Probate Records

By an 1823 law, all estate probates came under the jurisdiction of the County Surrogate courts. The clerk of the court keeps comprehensive indexes to estates and probate packets. Many county probate records are on microfilm. Wills earlier than 1823 are indexed statewide by name of deceased persons, heirs, witnesses, executors, and administrators.

Fernow, Berthold. *Calendar of Wills on File and Recorded in the Offices of the Clerk of the Court of Appeals, of the County Clerk at Albany, and of the Secretary of State, 1626-1836*. New York: The Colonial Dames of the State of New York, 1896. (FHL# microfilm 416895) Rpt. ed., Baltimore, Md.: Genealogical Publishing Co., 1967. (FHL# 974.7/P28f/1967)

New York Historical Society. *Abstracts of Wills on File in the Surrogate's Office, City of New York, 1665-1800*. New York: The New York Historical Society, 1892-1908. (FHL# microfilm 845296-845302 and 509196)

Scott, Kenneth R. *Genealogical Data from Inventories of New York Estates, 1666-1825*. New York City: New York Genealogical and Biographical Society, 1970. (FHL# 974.7/P28s) Contains residences, occupations, and personal effects. Indexed.

______. *Records of the Chancery Court, Province and State of New York, Guardianships 1691-1815*. New York: The Holland Society of New York, 1971 (FHL# 974.7/P28sc)

The Chancery Court had custody of the guardianship of infants, minors, lunatics, and estates. Names, ages, residences, parents, etc., are often listed. Fully indexed.

Tax Records

From 1850 to 1870, tax lists were filed both in local clerks' and county treasurers' offices, which are usually at the county seat. Many early tax lists, including burgher and freemen lists exist from 1675 on. There are no listings in the FHLC at the state level, but several counties have tax records listed, including probate estate tax files.

Vital Records

The best place to begin looking for information on New York's vital records is:

Historical Records Survey. Works Project Administration. *Guide to Public Vital Statistics Records in New York State, including New York City*. Albany, N.Y.: The Survey, 1942. (FHL# 974.7/V23h, or microfilm 928101, items 1-3, or microfiche 6046676)

Between 1847 and 1852, some school district clerks kept birth, marriage, and death information. Town or county clerks have what remains of those records.

City registration began in Syracuse in 1873, Rochester in 1875, Albany in 1870, Utica in 1873, New York City in 1848, Buffalo in 1878, and Yonkers in 1875. The State Board of Health was founded in 1880 when legislation required birth, marriage, and death records statewide. However, compliance stayed at about 50 percent from 1880-1915. Consult the FHLC under **/[County]/Vital Records** and **/[County]/[City]/Vital Records.** Different works are cataloged under each heading. Many of

New York's vital records are on microfilm.

Early marriages may be found in records transcribed from marriage bonds kept at the Secretary of State's Office in Albany:

Scott, Kenneth R. *New York Marriages Previous to 1784.* 1860; rpt. ed., Baltimore, Md.: Genealogical Publishing Co., 1968. Reprint has supplement with about 500 additional marriage licenses for 1639-1706. (FHL# 974.7/-V28m/1968; 1860: microfilm 514675)

Some births, marriages, and deaths were recorded in town records from 1665 because of a law passed when the English conquered New Netherland. Consult the FHLC under **New York/[County]/[City]/[Town Records].**

Another helpful source if your ancestors were from western New York is:

Bowman, Fred Q. *10,000 Vital Records of Western New York 1809-1850.* Baltimore, Md.: Genealogical Publishing Co., 1985. Indexed. (FHL# 974.7/V2b)

Voting Records

There are no statewide voting records, and only a few counties have poll lists for the 1700s.

DISTRICT OF COLUMBIA

Historical Background

Early	Inhabited by Powhatans, Manahoacs, Susquehannocks, Tockwocks, Nanticokes, and Lenni Lenapes.
1608	First Potomac excursions of Captain John Smith.
1632	Englishman Henry Fleete sails Potomac, trading furs; produces first written description.
1640s	Scots and Irish settle on Potomac at the mouth of Rock Creek. Colonel Ninian Beall and George Gordon, both Scotsmen, become original proprietors of present-day Georgetown.
1662	George Thompson receives a land patent from Maryland for D.C. area.
1741	Georgetown organized as community, incorporated 1789; busy port for tobacco trade.
1749	Alexandria (Virginia) laid out.
1790	Congress designates area on Potomac River between Eastern Branch (Anacostia River) and Connogocheague (approximately ten miles square) permanent seat of U.S. government.
1791	Bill includes Alexandria, Virginia, and area south of Potomac as part of District of Columbia. L'Enfant drafts plan for "City of Washington." Two tracts in limits of territory laid out for towns of Hamburgh and Carollsburgh. Maryland ratified cession of land to the United States for a federal district.
1793	George Washington lays cornerstone of Capitol Building.
1797	John Adams inaugurated. First bridge over Potomac built.
1798	Construction begins on White House.
1800	Government moves from Philadelphia to Washington, D.C. Washington Navy Yard established. Population 14,003.
1801	Thomas Jefferson inaugurated. Congress assumes jurisdiction over the District.
1807	Three Negro freedmen open first black public school at their own expense.
1809	James Madison inaugurated.
1810	Population 24,023.
1814	British burn Capitol, White House, several other public buildings and bridges.
1817	James Monroe inaugurated; occupies reconstructed White House.
1835	Baltimore and Ohio Railroad reaches Washington.
1840	Smithsonian Institution founded.
1846	District territory south of Potomac retroceded to Virginia.
1850	Chesapeake and Ohio Canal completed.
1860	First Japanese delegation to America visits Washington.
1861	Abraham Lincoln inaugurated, orders Washington Militia into federal service. Metropolitan police force organized.
1862	Emancipation Act frees slaves in the District of Columbia and the Territories.
1863	Emancipation Proclamation frees slaves in the Confederate states.
1864	Capital saved from the Confederacy by skirmish at Silver Spring.
1865	Lincoln assassinated at Ford Theater.
1878	Temporary commission government of District, begun in 1874, becomes permanent.
1881	City flooded to six feet; part of Long Bridge washed away; roof of City Hall blown off during heavy windstorm. Garfield assassinated.
1895	Act of Congress merges Georgetown with Washington.

The following sources are suggested for further information on the history of the District of Columbia:

Webb, William B. *Centennial History of the City of Washington in the District of Columbia.* Dayton, Ohio: United Brethren Publishing House, 1892. (FHL# 975.3/-W1/H2w)

Proctor, John Clagett. *Washington, Past and Present: A History*. New York: Lewis Historical Publishing Co., 1930. (FHL# 975.3/W1/H2p)

Truett, Randall Bond. *Washington, D.C.: A Guide to the Nation's Capital.* New York: Hastings House, 1968. (FHL# 975.3/E6t)

Settlement and Migration

While the area of the District of Columbia was part of the Proprietary Colony of Maryland, the land was legally owned by Lord Baltimore to give and sell as he pleased. English, Scots, and Irish were the first to receive land grants in the area. Georgetown and Alexandria became important ports for the booming tobacco industry and as such attracted people anxious to participate in a growing business.

When Washington, D.C., became the seat of government in 1800, the population of the area grew to 14,003 as Congressmen and Senators and their families moved into the city. By 1820 the population had grown to 33,039 as more government jobs were made available and retail businesses grew to accommodate the city. These people came mainly from surrounding states, but also, merchants arrived from European countries.

Later, as the United States established itself as a strong and viable nation, Washington became a melting pot, attracting diplomats, delegations, and immigrants from almost every nation.

District of Columbia Library Collection

Archives and Libraries

Index to Biographies in Local Histories in the Library of Congress. Baltimore, Md.: Magna Carta Book Co., 1979. Card index. 30 reels. Arranged alphabetically. Consult the FHLC for call numbers.

Atlases, Maps, and Gazetteers

Jefferson, Thomas. *A Map of the Country between Albemarle Sound and Lake Erie*. Thomas Jefferson, 1787. (Map Case FHL# 974/ E2j or microfilm 824072, item 7)

Martin, Joseph. *A New and Comprehensive Gazetteer of Virginia and the District of Columbia*. Charlottesville: Martin, 1835. (FHL# 975/E5m or microfilm 897469, item 1)

National Geographic Society (U.S.), Cartographic Division. *Round About the Nation's Capital*. Washington, D.C.: National Geographic Society, 1956. (FHL# Q/975/E7n)

A number of other very good maps and gazetteers are included with the Maryland and Virginia collections.

Cemetery Records

A number of the District's cemeteries inventories have been microfilmed including:

Register of Burials in the District of Columbia Cemeteries, 1847-1938. Salt Lake City: Genealogical Society of Utah, 1971. (FHL# microfilm 887587) Original record at the DAR Library, Washington, D.C.

Paul E. Sluby has transcribed many of the District of Columbia cemetery records for the Columbian Harmony Society, including the Civil War cemeteries of the metropolitan area, the Eastern Methodist Cemetery (Old Ebenezer), and the Old Methodist burial ground in Georgetown. Consult the FHLC under **District of Columbia/Cemeteries.**

Other records in the collection include the Washington Hebrew Congregation interment list from 1856-1911 (FHL# microfilm 1013426, item 5), Rock Creek Cemetery, Glenwood Cemetery, Mount Zion Cemetery and the Washington Congressional Cemetery Association's interment records, 1820-1978. Consult the FHLC under **District of Columbia/Cemetery Records, District of Columbia/Georgetown/Cemetery Records,** and **District of Columbia/Washington/Cemetery Records.**

Ridgely, Helen West. *Historic Graves of Maryland and the District of Columbia.* Baltimore, Md.: Genealogical Publishing Co., 1967 (FHL# 975.2/V22r)

Census Records

The federal census records for the District of Columbia are available for 1800 and 1820-1910 excluding 1890. The entire census of the District in 1810 is missing or destroyed. The years 1820, 1830, 1840, 1850, 1860, and 1870 are indexed. Also available is Ronald Vern Jackson, comp., *1890 District of Columbia Census Index: Special Schedule of the 11th Census Enumerating Union Veterans* (Salt Lake City: Accelerated Indexing System, c.1983). (FHL# 975.3/X22j/1890)

Church Records

The library has these church records: Epiphany, Concordia Lutheran Evangelical, Eckington Presbyterian, First Baptist, Berean Baptist, 15th Street Presbyterian (1st Colored Presbyterian Church), Wesley Methodist, Union Methodist Episcopal, St. John's Parish, and Western Presbyterian. Some baptisms, marriages, and deaths are included in these records. Also worth checking for other churches in the area are these sources:

A Directory of the Churches and Religious Organizations in the District of Columbia, 1939. Washington, D.C.: District of Columbia Historical Records Survey, 1939. Indexed. (FHL# 975.3/W1/E4h or microfilm 1036761)

Inventory of Church Archives in the District of Columbia. Washington, D.C.: Historical Records Survey, 1940. (FHL# 975.3/K2h or microfilm 1036702, items 1-2)

Court Records

United States District Court (District of Columbia). *Record of the U.S. District Court for the District of Columbia as Relating to Slaves, 1851-1863.* Washington, D.C.: National Archives, 1963. (FHL# microfilm 1299307 for emancipation papers; 1299308 for manumission papers and fugitive slave cases)

Walker, Homer A. *Historical Court Records of Washington, D.C.* Washington, D.C.: n.pub., n.d. (FHL# 975.3/-W1/V2w or microfilm 908367, item 4)

Directories

There is a collection of Boyd's city directories for the Washington, D.C. area for 1897-1941; however, each year is not included. (FHL# 975.3 E4bl) See also Polk's 1956 and 1960 city directories (FHL# Q/975.3/-W1/E4p).

Genealogical Collections

There are no major collections of genealogical records for the District of Columbia, but a helpful genealogical research tool is:

Babbel, June Andrew. *Lest We Forget: A Guide to Genealogical Research in the Nation's Capital.* Annandale, Va.: Annandale Stake of the Church of Jesus Christ of Latter-day Saints, 1982. (FHL# 975.3/D27b)

See *Genealogical Collections* under Maryland, Pennsylvania, and Virginia.

Immigration Records

There are no immigration records listed for the District of Columbia. See the immigration records for Maryland (Baltimore), New York, and Philadelphia.

Land and Property Records

The land records from the District of Columbia Recorder of Deeds for 1792-1886 have been microfilmed from the original records in the District of Columbia courthouse and are contained on 694 reels, including a general index to deeds for 1792-1919. Also cataloged under **District of Columbia/Washington/Land and Property** is:

Gahn, Bessie Wilmarth. *Original Patentees of Land at Washington Prior to 1700.* Baltimore, Md.: Genealogical Publishing Co., 1969. Indexed. (FHL# 975.3/K2lg)

For earlier land records see **Maryland/Land and Property.**

Military Records

Records for the militia of the District of Columbia, 1828-32, are available (FHL# microfilm 020449, item 4), as well as the following Revolutionary and Civil War records:

United States. Record and Pension Office. *Compiled Service Records of American Personnel and Members of the Departments of the Quartermaster General Who Served During Revolutionary War.* 5 reels. Washington, D.C.: National Archives, 1972-73. (FHL# microfilm 1004872 and 1025081 to 1025084)

United States. Adjutant General's Office. *Index to Compiled Service Records of Volunteer Union Soldiers Who Served in Organizations from the District of Columbia, 1861-1865.* 3 reels. Washington, D.C.: National Archives, 1964. (FHL# microfilm 881964-881966)

Native Americans, Naturalizations

No records are cataloged under these headings. See the Maryland sections for these records.

Newspapers

The *Daily National Intelligencer* is available, 82 reels, 31 October 1800-1 March 1852. In the beginning the paper was published every other day; later it was published daily. Extracts of marriage and deaths of prominent men and women taken from the *Daily National Intelligencer* 1806-58 are on microfilm 441391, compiled by Frank Willing Leach.

Probate Records

Early probate records may be found cataloged with Maryland records. Available for the District are:

Bell, Mrs. Alexander H. *Abstracts of Wills in the District of Columbia, 1776-1815.* 2 vols. Washington, D.C.: n.pub. 1945-46. (FHL# 975.3/S2b or microfilm 207695) Index. Compiled from records in the office of the Register of Wills.

Daughters of the American Revolution. E. Pluribus Unum Chapter. *Transcripts of Probate Records, 1799-1837.* Salt Lake City: Genealogical Society of Utah, 1972. Index. (FHL# microfilm 907978, item 4)

Record, Abstract of Wills. 4 vols. Municipal Court, Washington, D.C., 1828-37. Includes index. (FHL# 975.3 S2d)

Taxation

Georgetown, Maryland. *Financial Records.* 10 reels. Washington, D.C.: National Archives, 1965. (FHL# microfilm 1024458, 1024472-1024474, and 1024476)

Includes Account books 1801-08, Journals 1857-74, General Ledgers 1822-71, Stock ledgers 1836-64, Day books 1862-69.

Georgetown, Maryland. *Property Tax Records: 1800-20, 1865-79.* 9 reels. Washington, D.C.: National Archives, 1965. Some volumes indexed. (FHL# microfilm 1024464-1024471 and 1024475)

United States. Congress. *Federal Assessment, 1790-1805, Maryland, District of Columbia.* 13 reels. [Baltimore:] Maryland, Hall of Records Commission, 1965. Includes Maryland counties. (FHL# microfilm 499893-499905)

Vital Records

District of Columbia vital records have not been filmed. Substitutions must be made with church, cemetery, and military records.

Records by Jurisdiction **Pennsylvania**	Archives & Libraries	Bible Records	Bibliography	Biography	Business Records/Commerce	Cemeteries	Census 1790-1850 Index	State	County (Other)	Church Directories	Church History	Church Records	Colonization	Correctional Inst.	Court Records	Description/Travel	Directories	Emigration/Immigration	Folklore	Gazetteers	Genealogy	Guardian & Ward	Historical Geography	History	Land & Property	Maps	Medical Records	Military Records	Minorities	Names: Geographical, Personal	Native Races	Naturalization/Citizenship	Newspapers	Obituaries	Occupations	Officials/Employees	Orphans/Orphanages	Periodicals	Poor House, Poor Law	Probate Records	Public Records	Schools	Slavery/Bondage	Social Life/Customs	Societies	Taxation	Town Records	Vital Records
Adams	•					•			•		•	•					•				•			•	•	•		•					•		•					•						•		•
Allegheny				•		•			•		•	•					•				•	•		•		•			•			•		•						•	•	•						•
Armstrong				•		•					•	•			•		•				•			•	•	•		•				•								•								•
Beaver	•			•		•			•		•	•			•		•	•			•	•		•	•	•		•				•								•						•		•
Bedford				•		•			•		•	•			•						•	•		•	•															•		•			•	•		•
Berks	•	•	•	•	•	•			•		•	•			•		•				•			•	•	•	•	•				•	•	•	•	•		•		•	•	•			•	•		•
Blair	•			•	•	•					•	•					•				•			•		•		•		•										•						•		•
Bradford	•			•		•					•	•					•				•			•	•	•		•										•		•					•	•		•
Bucks	•	•		•	•	•			•		•	•			•	•	•	•		•	•	•		•	•	•		•	•			•								•	•				•	•		•
Butler	•					•						•					•				•	•		•	•							•	•		•					•					•			•
Cambria	•			•	•	•						•					•				•			•	•	•						•	•							•		•						•
Cameron						•						•									•	•		•	•	•						•		•						•								•
Carbon				•		•					•	•									•			•		•		•												•								•
Centre	•			•	•	•			•		•	•				•					•			•		•				•			•					•		•								•
Chester	•	•	•	•	•	•			•		•	•			•		•				•			•	•	•		•	•						•					•	•	•				•	•	•
Clarion				•		•					•	•					•				•			•	•								•							•								•
Clearfield				•		•						•					•				•			•		•						•								•								
Clinton				•		•						•									•	•		•	•	•							•							•								•
Columbia				•		•					•	•			•						•	•		•	•	•		•				•								•								•
Crawford				•		•			•			•			•						•	•		•	•	•	•					•						•		•								•
Cumberland				•	•	•					•	•			•		•				•			•	•	•	•	•				•							•	•	•	•				•		•
Dauphin	•			•		•					•	•			•		•				•			•	•	•	•	•					•							•		•				•		•
Delaware	•			•		•					•	•			•		•				•			•	•	•		•				•		•	•				•	•	•			•	•		•	
Elk						•						•			•						•			•	•	•		•				•								•								•
Erie	•			•		•						•			•		•				•			•	•	•		•	•			•						•		•								•
Fayette	•			•		•			•		•	•									•			•	•	•						•		•						•								•
Forest	•			•								•					•				•				•	•						•								•								•
Franklin				•	•	•					•	•			•		•				•			•	•	•		•												•						•		•
Fulton						•						•									•			•		•																						
Greene	•			•		•			•			•			•						•			•	•	•						•								•	•							•
Huntingdon		•		•		•					•	•		•			•				•	•		•	•	•														•								•
Indiana				•		•			•		•	•			•		•				•	•		•	•	•		•				•						•		•					•	•		•
Jefferson				•		•						•					•				•			•	•	•						•								•								•
Juniata				•		•			•			•									•			•	•	•														•		•						•
Lackawanna				•		•					•	•					•				•			•		•																						
Lancaster	•			•		•			•		•	•			•		•				•	•		•	•	•	•	•	•		•		•	•	•		•	•		•	•	•			•	•		•
Lawrence	•			•		•					•	•			•						•			•		•		•																				
Lebanon				•	•	•			•		•	•			•	•	•				•			•	•	•		•	•				•		•					•	•	•				•		•
Lehigh	•		•	•		•					•	•					•				•			•	•			•							•			•		•								•
Luzerne	•			•		•			•		•	•			•		•				•			•	•													•		•					•			•
Lycoming		•		•		•					•	•					•				•			•	•	•														•								•
McKean						•									•						•			•	•			•				•								•	•							•
Mercer				•		•						•			•		•				•			•	•	•		•				•								•		•						•
Mifflin				•		•			•						•						•			•	•	•	•	•				•		•						•	•					•		•
Monroe				•		•			•			•									•			•		•																						•
Montgomery	•			•		•					•	•				•	•				•	•		•	•	•	•	•										•		•		•				•		•
Montour				•		•						•			•						•			•	•	•						•								•								•
Northampton	•			•		•			•		•	•			•		•		•		•			•	•	•		•	•											•	•	•			•	•		•
Northumberland				•		•					•	•			•		•				•			•	•	•		•				•								•						•		•

Records by Jurisdiction — Pennsylvania (cont.)	Archives & Libraries	Bible Records	Bibliography	Biography	Business Records/Commerce	Cemeteries	Census 1790-1850 Index	State	County (Other)	Church Directories	Church History	Church Records	Colonization	Correctional Inst.	Court Records	Description/Travel	Directories	Emigration/Immigration	Folklore	Gazetteers	Genealogy	Guardian & Ward	Historical Geography	History	Land & Property	Maps	Medical Records	Military Records	Minorities	Names: Geographical, Personal	Native Races	Naturalization/Citizenship	Newspapers	Obituaries	Occupations	Officials/Employees	Orphans/Orphanages	Periodicals	Poor House, Poor Law	Probate Records	Public Records	Schools	Slavery/Bondage	Social Life/Customs	Societies	Taxation	Town Records	Vital Records
Perry				•		•					•	•									•			•	•															•						•		•
Philadelphia	•		•	•	•	•			•		•	•			•	•	•	•			•	•	•	•	•	•	•	•				•	•	•	•		•		•	•	•	•			•	•		•
Pike				•		•			•			•					•				•			•		•																•						
Potter		•				•						•			•						•	•		•	•															•								•
Schuylkill				•		•			•		•	•					•				•			•										•						•		•						•
Snyder				•		•					•	•									•			•		•														•						•		•
Somerset				•	•	•			•		•	•			•		•				•			•	•	•	•	•				•	•							•						•		•
Sullivan				•		•			•			•			•						•			•	•	•						•								•								•
Susquehanna				•	•	•			•			•					•				•			•		•														•								•
Tioga		•		•		•			•			•			•		•				•			•	•			•												•								•
Union				•		•			•		•	•					•				•			•		•												•		•		•				•		•
Venango				•							•	•					•				•			•	•							•	•							•								•
Warren	•			•		•						•					•				•			•	•	•		•				•								•								•
Washington	•			•		•					•	•			•		•				•	•		•	•	•		•				•								•	•	•				•		•
Wayne	•			•		•					•	•			•		•				•			•	•	•														•								•
Westmoreland	•			•	•	•			•		•	•					•				•			•	•	•						•	•	•						•						•		•
Wyoming				•		•			•			•			•						•			•	•	•						•	•							•								•
York	•			•	•	•			•		•	•			•	•	•				•	•		•	•	•		•				•	•							•	•	•			•	•		•
Statewide	•	•	•	•	•	•	•			•	•	•	•	•	•	•	•	•	•	•	•		•	•	•	•		•	•	•	•	•	•	•	•	•	•	•		•	•	•	•	•	•	•		•

Records by Jurisdiction

Maryland

	Archives & Libraries	Bible Records	Bibliography	Biography	Business Records/Commerce	Cemeteries	Census:	1776	1790-1850 Index	Soundex 1880-1900-1910	1890 Veterans	(County) Other	Church History	Church Records	Colonization	Court Records	Directories	Description/Travel	Emigration/Immigration	Folklore	Gazetteers	Genealogy	Guardian & Ward	Heraldry	Historical Geography	History	Jewish Records	Land & Property	Law & Legislation	Maps	Military History	Military Records	Minorities	Names, Personal	Native Races	Naturalization/Citizenship	Newspapers	Obituaries	Occupations	Officials/Employees	Periodicals	Politics & Government	Probate Records	Public Records	Schools	Slavery & Bondage	Societies	Taxation	Vital Records
Allegany	•			•		•							•	•		•		•				•	•			•		•	•								•	•					•						•
Anne Arundel	•			•	•	•								•		•	•					•	•			•		•		•			•										•	•		•			
Baltimore						•						•	•	•								•	•			•		•		•							•					•	•					•	•
Baltimore City	•			•		•						•	•	•				•	•			•	•			•	•			•		•										•	•				•	•	•
Calvert												•		•								•				•																	•						•
Caroline				•		•						•		•		•							•			•		•		•		•					•	•					•			•			•
Carroll	•					•							•	•								•	•			•		•									•						•						•
Cecil				•		•						•	•	•		•						•	•			•		•															•		•				•
Charles		•				•						•		•		•						•	•					•	•														•						•
Dorchester		•				•						•		•		•						•				•		•															•						•
Frederick				•		•						•		•		•		•				•	•			•		•					•			•			•				•						•
Garrett	•													•												•															•								
Harford						•						•	•	•		•							•			•		•															•		•			•	•
Howard	•			•		•								•								•	•			•		•													•		•	•					•
Kent														•		•						•	•			•		•				•							•				•						•
Montgomery	•			•		•						•	•	•				•				•	•			•		•		•													•					•	•
Prince George's						•							•	•		•		•				•	•			•		•												•			•					•	•
Queen Anne's						•						•		•									•			•		•															•					•	
Saint Mary's						•						•	•	•		•			•			•	•			•		•		•			•			•							•	•					•
Somerset													•	•		•						•	•			•		•															•						•
Talbot				•		•						•	•	•		•							•			•		•															•						•
Washington	•		•	•		•						•	•	•		•						•	•			•		•		•													•			•			•
Wicomico	•					•								•																																			
Worcester				•		•							•	•		•						•	•			•		•		•													•						•
Statewide	•	•	•	•	•	•		•	•	•	•		•	•	•	•	•	•	•	•	•	•		•	•	•		•	•	•	•	•	•	•	•	•	•	•	•	•	•	•	•	•		•	•	•	•

Records by Jurisdiction

New Jersey

	Almanacs	Archives & Libraries	Bible Records	Bibliography	Biography	Business Records/Commerce	Cemeteries	Census: 1800	Federal: 1830-1850 Index	Deaths 1850-1880	State 1855, 1865, 1885	Soundex Fed. 1880, 1900, 1910	County (other)	Church Directories	Church History	Church Records	Court Records	Description/Travel	Directories	Emigration/Immigration	Gazetteers	Genealogy	Guardian-Ward	Historical Geography	History	Land & Property	Maps	Military History	Military Records	Minorities	Names: Geographical, Personal	Native Races	Naturalization/Citizenship	Newspapers	Obituaries	Occupations	Officials/Employees	Orphans/Orphanages	Periodicals	Politics/Government	Probate Records	Public Records	Schools	Slavery/Bondage	Societies	Taxation	Vital Records
Atlantic			•		•		•						•	•		•			•			•	•		•	•	•		•				•								•	•				•	•
Bergen		•			•		•						•		•	•	•	•	•			•		•	•	•	•		•				•								•	•		•	•	•	
Burlington			•			•	•						•	•	•	•	•		•				•		•	•	•				•		•		•						•	•				•	•
Camden			•		•		•							•	•	•			•			•			•	•	•		•												•	•			•	•	•
Cape May					•	•	•							•	•	•	•					•	•		•	•	•						•						•		•	•				•	•
Cumberland					•		•	•						•	•	•	•		•			•	•		•	•	•		•				•						•		•	•				•	•
Essex					•	•	•						•	•	•	•	•	•	•			•			•	•	•		•	•			•								•	•	•	•		•	•
Gloucester		•	•		•		•						•	•	•	•	•				•	•			•	•	•		•	•	•		•								•	•	•	•	•	•	•
Hudson		•			•		•								•	•			•			•			•	•	•		•				•								•		•	•			•
Hunterdon					•	•	•						•	•	•	•	•					•	•		•	•	•		•				•			•			•		•	•			•	•	•
Mercer					•		•								•	•	•	•	•			•	•		•	•	•		•				•	•			•				•	•	•			•	•
Middlesex				•	•	•	•						•	•	•	•	•		•			•	•		•	•	•		•	•			•								•	•				•	•
Monmouth				•	•		•						•	•	•	•	•		•			•	•		•	•	•		•				•	•	•			•			•	•			•	•	•
Morris		•			•		•						•	•	•	•	•		•			•			•	•	•		•				•								•	•			•	•	•
Ocean		•			•	•	•							•		•	•					•	•		•	•	•				•		•								•	•	•			•	•
Passaic		•			•		•							•	•	•			•			•	•		•	•	•		•				•								•	•			•	•	•
Salem		•			•		•							•	•	•			•			•	•		•	•	•				•		•								•				•	•	•
Somerset					•	•	•						•	•	•	•	•		•			•	•		•	•	•						•								•	•				•	•
Sussex		•			•	•	•							•	•	•	•		•			•			•	•	•						•	•							•	•		•	•	•	•
Union					•	•	•							•	•	•	•		•			•			•	•	•		•	•			•								•	•				•	•
Warren					•		•							•		•	•					•			•	•	•					•	•								•	•				•	•
Statewide	•	•	•	•	•	•	•		•	•	•	•		•	•	•	•	•	•	•	•	•	•	•	•	•	•	•	•	•	•	•	•	•		•	•	•	•	•	•	•	•	•	•	•	•

Records by Jurisdiction

Delaware

	Archives & Libraries	Bible Records	Bibliography	Biography	Cemeteries	Census:	Early: 1665-1697	Reconstruction: 1790	1800-1870 Index	Soundex 1880, 1900, 1910	Church Directories	Church History	Church Records	Court Records	Description/Travel	Directories	Emigration/Immigration	Gazetteers	Genealogy	Guardian & Ward	History	Land & Property	Maps	Military History	Military Records	Minorities	Names/Geographic	Native Races	Naturalization/Citizenship	Occupations	Officials/Employees	Probate Records	Public Records	Societies	Taxation	Vital Records
Kent				•	•								•	•					•	•	•	•							•			•			•	•
New Castle	•				•							•	•	•					•	•	•	•							•	•		•			•	•
Sussex		•			•								•	•					•	•	•	•	•						•	•		•	•		•	•
Wilmington				•	•							•	•			•			•		•													•		•
Statewide	•	•	•	•	•	•	•	•	•	•	•	•	•		•	•	•	•	•		•	•	•	•	•	•	•	•	•		•		•	•	•	•

Records by Jurisdiction

New York

	Archives & Libraries	Bible Records	Bibliography	Biography	Business Records/Commerce	Cemeteries	Census	Church History	Church Records	Court Records	Description/Travel	Directories	Emigration/Immigration	Folklore	Gazetteers	Genealogy	Guardian & Ward	Historical Geography	History	Land & Property	Law & Legislation	Maps	Military History	Military Records	Minorities	Names: Geographical, Personal	Native Races	Naturalization/Citizenship	Newspapers	Obituaries	Occupations	Officials/Employees	Periodicals	Politics/Government	Probate Records	Public Records	Schools	Social Life/Customs	Societies	Taxation	Town Records	Vital Records	Voting Registers
Albany	•	•		•		•	•	•	•	•	•	•				•	•		•	•		•	•		•			•		•					•	•		•			•	•	
Allegany		•		•	•	•	•		•	•		•							•	•						•		•		•					•							•	
Bronx	•			•		•	•	•	•			•				•			•	•						•										•					•	•	
Broome	•			•	•	•	•		•	•	•	•				•	•		•	•		•		•				•	•	•		•			•	•	•		•		•	•	•
Cattaraugus	•			•		•	•		•	•		•				•			•	•		•		•				•				•			•							•	
Cayuga				•		•	•	•	•	•	•	•				•	•		•	•		•						•							•	•	•					•	•
Chautauqua	•			•	•	•	•		•			•				•			•	•		•						•		•					•							•	
Chemung	•			•		•	•		•	•		•							•	•				•				•	•						•	•	•					•	
Chenango		•		•		•	•	•	•	•	•	•			•	•			•	•		•		•				•	•						•	•	•			•	•	•	
Clinton				•		•	•		•	•						•			•	•								•							•	•						•	
Columbia				•	•	•	•	•	•	•		•			•	•	•		•	•		•		•				•				•			•		•					•	
Cortland				•	•	•	•		•	•						•			•	•		•	•	•				•		•		•			•	•	•			•	•	•	•
Delaware				•		•	•	•	•	•						•			•	•		•		•				•							•	•						•	
Dutchess				•	•	•	•	•	•	•	•	•		•		•	•		•	•		•		•		•		•	•	•	•	•			•	•	•			•	•	•	•
Erie	•			•	•	•	•	•	•	•		•				•	•		•	•		•		•				•							•	•			•		•	•	
Essex				•		•	•	•	•	•	•						•		•	•		•		•				•							•	•						•	
Franklin				•		•	•		•	•		•				•	•		•	•		•						•							•							•	
Fulton	•			•		•	•	•	•			•				•			•	•		•		•				•		•					•	•						•	
Genesee				•	•	•	•	•	•	•		•			•				•	•		•		•				•	•	•					•	•	•		•			•	
Greene				•		•	•	•	•	•	•	•				•			•	•		•						•							•	•						•	
Hamilton						•	•		•	•				•					•	•								•							•							•	
Herkimer				•		•	•	•	•	•						•			•	•					•			•							•	•						•	
Jefferson				•		•	•		•	•		•			•	•	•		•	•				•				•		•					•	•	•				•	•	•
Kings	•			•		•	•	•	•		•	•				•	•		•	•		•			•				•	•		•	•		•	•	•	•	•	•	•	•	
Lewis				•		•	•		•	•						•	•		•	•		•						•	•						•	•			•			•	
Livingston				•		•	•		•	•						•	•		•	•		•		•				•							•							•	
Madison				•	•	•	•	•	•	•		•				•	•		•	•				•				•	•	•					•		•		•			•	
Monroe	•			•		•	•	•	•	•	•	•			•	•			•	•		•		•	•			•		•					•	•						•	
Montgomery	•		•	•		•	•	•	•	•	•	•				•			•	•		•		•	•		•	•							•					•		•	
Nassau	•			•		•	•	•	•	•	•	•				•			•	•				•				•		•			•		•	•				•	•	•	
New York	•	•		•	•	•	•	•	•	•	•	•	•			•	•		•	•		•	•	•	•	•		•	•	•	•	•			•	•	•	•	•	•		•	•
Niagara				•		•	•		•	•	•	•				•	•		•	•								•		•					•							•	
Oneida	•			•	•	•	•	•	•	•		•				•	•		•	•		•			•			•							•		•		•			•	
Onondaga	•		•	•	•	•	•	•	•	•		•			•	•			•	•		•	•	•	•			•		•					•	•	•		•	•		•	
Ontario				•		•	•		•	•		•			•	•			•	•		•						•							•	•				•		•	•
Orange	•		•	•		•		•	•	•	•	•				•			•	•		•	•	•				•	•	•		•	•		•	•	•		•	•	•	•	
Orleans				•		•	•		•	•		•			•	•			•	•								•		•					•	•			•				•
Oswego	•			•		•			•	•		•							•	•		•						•		•						•						•	
Otsego	•			•	•	•	•	•	•	•		•				•	•		•	•		•		•				•							•							•	
Putnam				•		•		•	•	•				•		•			•	•		•						•	•						•						•		
Queens		•		•		•		•	•	•	•	•				•	•		•	•		•		•				•		•			•		•	•				•	•	•	
Rensselaer	•			•		•	•	•	•	•		•			•	•			•	•		•						•							•	•	•		•		•	•	
Richmond	•		•		•	•	•	•	•	•	•				•			•	•		•		•	•			•	•	•					•	•	•		•	•		•		
Rockland			•			•	•	•	•	•		•							•	•		•		•				•							•			•				•	
St. Lawrence		•		•	•	•	•	•	•	•		•				•	•		•	•		•		•	•			•								•	•		•	•		•	
Saratoga	•			•		•	•	•	•	•	•	•			•	•	•		•	•		•		•				•				•			•	•	•			•		•	
Schenectady	•	•		•		•	•	•	•	•		•				•			•	•		•		•				•		•		•			•		•		•	•		•	
Schoharie	•			•		•	•	•	•	•		•				•			•	•		•		•				•		•			•		•	•						•	
Schuyler				•		•		•	•			•				•			•	•		•						•							•							•	

Records by Jurisdiction **New York** (cont.)	Archives & Libraries	Bible Records	Bibliography	Biography	Business Records/Commerce	Cemeteries	Census	Church History	Church Records	Court Records	Description/Travel	Directories	Emigration/Immigration	Folklore	Gazetteers	Genealogy	Guardian & Ward	Historical Geography	History	Land & Property	Law & Legislation	Maps	Military History	Military Records	Minorities	Names: Geographical, Personal	Native Races	Naturalization/Citizenship	Newspapers	Obituaries	Occupations	Officials/Employees	Periodicals	Politics/Government	Probate Records	Public Records	Schools	Social Life/Customs	Societies	Taxation	Town Records	Vital Records	Voting Registers
Seneca				•	•	•		•	•	•		•			•	•			•	•		•	•	•				•			•				•	•			•		•	•	
Steuben	•			•		•	•		•	•		•				•			•	•		•		•				•	•						•							•	
Suffolk	•			•		•	•	•	•	•	•					•			•	•			•	•				•		•			•		•	•	•			•	•	•	
Sullivan				•		•	•		•	•							•		•	•				•				•								•				•		•	
Tioga				•		•	•	•	•	•		•			•	•			•	•				•				•		•					•	•						•	
Tompkins	•			•		•	•	•	•	•		•				•			•	•		•		•				•							•	•	•					•	
Ulster	•	•		•	•	•		•	•	•		•			•	•	•		•	•		•		•	•			•	•	•		•			•	•	•	•				•	
Warren				•	•	•	•	•	•	•							•		•	•		•		•			•	•	•		•				•	•							•
Washington	•			•		•	•	•	•			•	•		•	•			•	•								•				•			•		•					•	
Wayne				•	•	•	•	•	•	•	•	•		•	•	•			•	•		•	•					•	•	•	•				•	•	•		•		•	•	•
Westchester				•		•		•	•	•	•	•				•			•	•		•		•		•		•	•	•			•		•	•	•		•	•	•	•	
Wyoming				•		•	•		•	•						•			•	•		•						•							•					•		•	
Yates				•		•	•		•	•		•				•			•	•		•		•				•		•		•	•		•	•						•	

Records by Jurisdiction **District of Columbia**	Archives & Libraries	Biographies	Cemeteries	Census:	1800 Index	1820-1870 Index	Soundex: 1880, 1900, 1910	1890 Veteran Index	Church Directories	Church History	Church Records	Court Records	Description/Travel	Directories	Gazetteers	Genealogy	Historical Geography	History	Jewish History	Jewish Records	Land & Property	Law & Legislation	Maps	Military Records	Newspapers	Obituaries	Officials/Employees	Periodicals	Probate Records	Public Records	Slavery/Bondage	Societies	Taxation
District	•	•	•		•	•	•	•	•	•	•		•	•	•	•	•	•	•	•	•	•	•	•	•	•	•	•	•	•	•	•	•
Washington			•							•	•	•	•	•				•			•				•							•	

Chapter 7

United States: The Old South

Gordon L. Remington

Introduction

Finding a record in the Family History Library Catalog (FHLC) can often be a frustrating experience. Some records are listed under several headings, not all of them obvious places to look. This introduction will:

1. Explain how to locate records which cover more than one state in the Old South.
2. Give general guidelines on locating record groups common to all states to avoid repetition in the state-by-state descriptions which follow.
3. Explain the headings used in the FHLC and on the chart accompanying each state discussion. These headings are presented alphabetically below, just as they appear in the FHLC.

Although the dates each county was created are included on the charts accompanying the discussion of each state's records, records do not always begin in that year. Furthermore, many counties lost records in courthouse fires, for which the Union Army cannot always be blamed.

Most county records in the Old South are available at the Family History Library only to the 1870s and 1880s. Marriage and vital records (births and deaths) sometimes go later.

Library Collection

Bible Records, Cemetery Records

Genealogical material preserved in family Bibles is usually found in collections and listed under the name of the state rather than by county or town. The Daughters of the American Revolution is responsible for many of these collections. Bible records can also be listed under **[State]/Genealogy** and **[State]/Vital Records**, if they are included in collections which can fall under those headings.

The same general principles also apply to cemetery records, except that many more of them are cataloged by town, township, or county.

Business Records

Listed at both state and local level, these records most often include account books and mortuary records. They can also be listed under **/Occupations** and **/Public Records.**

Church History and Church Records

Religious records are usually listed at the local levels. The same record will often be listed under both headings, but some church histories do not contain records.

Court Records

Technically, court records include land, probate, naturalization, and almost any other record created on the county level. In the FHLC, **Court Records** usually refers to minute and order books. These books are usually indexed, but for lawsuits only. An ancestor involved in some other kind of legal transaction would probably not appear in the index.

Naturalization records were seldom kept separately in the states discussed in this chapter. To find them, you must search the court order and minute books page by page.

Description and Travel, Gazetteers

Sources listed under these headings can also be listed under **/History**. Gazetteers are often listed under **/Directories.**

Directories

Directories are usually listed at the city level, but some county and state directories are available. To find Southern directories not listed in the FHLC, consult:

Research Publications. *City Directories of the United States, 1860-1901: Guide to the Microfilm Collection.* Woodbridge, Conn.: Research Publications, 1983. (FHL# 973/E43c)

This guide, which is in the general reference area of the library, lists an 1854 regional business directory under the heading "The South." (microfiche #6044495)

Emigration and Immigration

The library has these immigration records, which relate to more than one state:

United State Bureau of Customs. *Passenger Lists of Vessels Arriving at Miscellaneous Ports on Atlantic and Gulf Coasts and Port on the Great Lakes 1820-1873.* 17 reels. Washington, D.C.: National Archives, 1964. (FHL# microfilm 0830231-0830246).

These lists include ports in Virginia, North and South Carolina, Georgia, and Florida. They are indexed on microfilm FHL# 0418161-0418348.

United States Immigration and Naturalization Service. *Index to Passenger Lists of Vessels Arriving at Miscellaneous Ports in Alabama, Florida, Georgia and South Carolina, 1890-1924.* 26 reels. Washington, D.C.: INS, 1957. (FHL# microfilm 1324938-1324963).

An index for passenger arrivals in Savannah, Georgia, 1906-17 is cataloged under **Georgia/Chatham/Savannah/Emigration and Immigration.**

For general migration in the South, see:

Potter, Dorothy Williams. *Passports of Southeastern Pioneers 1770-1823: Indian, Spanish and Other Land Passports for Tennessee, Kentucky, Georgia, Mississippi, Virginia, North and South Carolina.* Baltimore: Gateway Press, 1982. (FHL# 975 W4p).

Genealogy

Under the heading of **/Genealogy** can be found published genealogies of state and local interest but also compiled and abstracted collections of probate, land, Bible, cemetery, church, and many other records with genealogical significance. Also cataloged under **Genealogy** may be state and local histories which have genealogies published in them. Always check listings in this section to see what compiled and abstracted sources are available for any given area.

History

Works cataloged under **/History** are usually published state and local histories.

Maps

The Family History Library has a large collection of maps and atlases at both the state and local level. The state-by-state discussion mentions only maps that are particularly useful in genealogical research, for example, maps showing watercourses, old boundaries, land grants, etc.

The *Map Guide to the U.S. Federal Censuses* by William Thorndale and William Dollarhide is available for each of the states in this section and can be consulted at the U.S. reference desk.

Medical Records

For Old South research, **/Medical Records** usually refers to lunacy records or registers of physicians, dentists, and druggists. These professional registers can also be listed under **/Occupations**. For the sake of simplicity and consistency, they are listed under Occupations on the charts accompanying the state-by-state discussion. Medical records dealing with lunacy and inebriety, when available, are noted in the Miscellaneous column.

Military Records

Some military records apply to all of the states in the Old South. Two published volumes of early military records are:

Clark, Murtie June. *Colonial Soldiers of the South, 1732-1774.* Baltimore: Genealogical Publishing Co., 1983. (FHL# 975/M29c)

_____. *Loyalists in the Southern Campaign of the Revolutionary War.* Baltimore: Genealogical Publishing Co., 1981. 3 vols. (FHL# 973/F2clm)

Southern soldiers served in the American Revolution, War of 1812, Mexican War, Indian Wars, and the Spanish-American War. The original records are in Washington, D.C. To find the general indexes to help you locate the records, consult:

Deputy, Marilyn J., et al., comps. *Register of Federal United States Military Records: A Guide to Manuscript Sources Available at the Family History Library in Salt Lake City and the National Archives in Washington, D.C.*. 3 vols. Bowie, Md.: Heritage Books, 1986.

Note that the Revolutionary War "jackets," a term you will encounter in the indexes, are the original records from which the compiled service records of Revolutionary War soldiers were made. Since these records are available at the Family History Library, it is possible to sidestep the compiled service record (available only in Washington) if you know the name of your ancestor's captain. The index to the Revolutionary War Rolls, film 830280, will let you locate the name of the captain and his jacket number; then you can consult the original records. The number of jackets and microfilm reels of each are: Georgia – 7 jackets, 1 reel (FHL# 0830311); North Carolina – 23 jackets, 1 reel (FHL# 0830358); South Carolina – 12 jackets, 1 reel (FHL# 0830368); and Virginia – 364 jackets, 23 reels (FHL# 0830371-0830393).

You should also be aware that the U.S. Volunteer Infantry in the Civil War consisted of Confederate P.O.W.s who obtained their freedom by volunteering to serve in Union units which worked away from the front lines.

Since the enlistment oath in the Union Army required a place of birth, valuable genealogical information on soldiers from the Old South might be in these records.

Although the *Register of Federal United States Military Records* is an admirable effort, the headings used to describe the records do not correspond to those used by the National Archives nor in the FHLC.

Minorities, Native Races, Slavery and Bondage

Records under these headings can sometimes overlap. **/Minorities**, the broadest category, includes a wide variety of religious, ethnic, and racial groups. **/Native Races** deals with native Americans (Indians), but some sources under this heading are also listed under **/Minorities.**

Persons of African descent have a special problem locating genealogical records. Original collection efforts focused on European ancestry, and only recently has the library actively collected records relating to Afro-Americans.

If you are tracing black ancestry, look under **/Minorities** for post-Civil War records, under **/Slavery and Bondage** for pre-Civil War records, and also under **/Court Records, /Land and Property, /Occupations,** and **/Public Records.** Marriage records in 1865 and 1866, when included with indentures, usually validate slave marriage contracts after Emancipation. These indentures are usually papers signed by many ex-slaves to continue a working relationship with their former owners.

It takes some real digging and a knowledge of potentially useful record groups to find such sources on black ancestry, but their value is inestimable if they have survived.

Naturalization and Citizenship.

(See Court Records.)

Newspapers and Obituaries

The heading **/Obituaries** usually refers to abstracted or compiled works from particular newspapers. **/Newspapers** usually refers to the original papers, but there is some overlap with obituaries.

Occupations

This heading includes indentures and registers of physicians, druggists, dentists, attorneys, and notaries.

Orphans and Orphanages.

(See Probate Records.)

Probate Records

Included under this heading are not only wills and administrations, but many court records. The FHLC heading **/Guardian and Ward** usually repeats the information contained under **/Probate Records**. The charts accompanying each state incorporate guardian/ward records under Probate Records. **/Orphans and Orphanages** can sometimes overlap with **/Probate Records.** Where this occurs for Old South states, orphan records have been incorporated in the Probate Record column. When orphan records are created separate from the probate of an estate, they are listed in their own column on the state-by-state chart.

Public Records

This heading is a catch-all for records generated by state and local government bodies. It can include town council minutes, state legislature records, and many other records not assigned to any other heading. It can repeat entries which also appear under **/Occupations, /Officials and Employees, /Schools, /Correctional Institutions** (which sometimes include chain-gang records), **/Notarial Records**, and **/Medical Records.** On the charts accompanying each state discussion, a mark in the Public Records column means that you should check all six of these other categories as well.

WEST VIRGINIA

Historical Background

Until 1863, West Virginia was part of Virginia. The dates below are significant in its pre-statehood settlement and development.

1716	Governor Alexander Spotswood's expedition opens up the settlement of Western Virginia.
1728	Germans from Pennsylvania settle at Shepherdstown. Many German and Scots-Irish from Pennsylvania settle on the south branch of the Potomac in following years.
1751	The Colony of Vandalia is proposed for western Virginia but failed.
1754-63	French and Indian War. Most of the scattered settlements in present-day West Virginia were destroyed.
1774	Lord Dunmore's War.
1776	The State of Westylvania proposed; petition denied.
1775-83	American Revolution.
1861	Virginia secedes from the Union; thirty-five of the forty-six delegates from present West Virginia voted against secession.
1861-65	Civil War. Western Virginia strongly Union in sentiment.
1863	West Virginia secedes from Virginia and enters the Union as the thirty-fifth state.
1866	Virginia contests West Virginia's secession,

but the Supreme Court decides in favor of West Virginia, 1871.

Settlement and Migration

Settlement of the area which is now West Virginia commenced in the 1720s, after Governor Alexander Spotswood discovered the Valley of Virginia. Many Indian tribes hunted in West Virginia, and their hostility hindered settlement for over fifty years. It was not until after the American Revolution that settlement began seriously in West Virginia.

Most of the early settlers came from Virginia, but substantial numbers were also from Maryland, Delaware, Pennsylvania, New Jersey, North Carolina, and even New England. Two early works on this period are still useful:

De Hass, Wills. *History of the Early Settlement and Indian Wars of Western Virginia; Embracing an Account of the Various Expeditions in the West, Previous to 1795, etc.* Wheeling, Va.: H. Hoblitzell, 1851. (FHL# 975.4/H2d or microfilm 1033530)

McWhorter, Lucullus Virgil. *The Border Settlers of Northwestern Virginia from 1768 to 1795 Embracing the Life of Jesse Hughes and Other Noted Scouts of the Trans-Allegheny.* Hamilton, Ohio: Republican Publishing Co., 1915. (FHL# 975.4/Dm or microfiche 6046617)

West Virginia quite naturally inherited its basic county structure from Virginia. Consequently, record keeping in both states is very similar up to a point. Many early records pertaining to West Virginia will be found in Virginia.

West Virginia Library Collection

Archives and Libraries

Perhaps the best collection of West Virginia materials is housed at the West Virginia University Library in Morgantown. See:

Hess, James W. *Guide to Manuscripts and Archives in the West Virginia Collection.* Morgantown: West Virginia University Library, 1974. (FHL# 975.4/A5h)

The library also has inventories of special collections housed at West Virginia University Library. A good source for what else is available in West Virginia is:

Stinson, Helen S. *A Handbook for Genealogical Research in West Virginia.* Dallas, Tex: Privately published, 1981. (FHL# 975.4/D27s)

Biography

The Family History Library has several statewide biographies for West Virginia and a few on the county level. Perhaps the most representative statewide biography is:

Comstock, Jim, ed. *Hardesty's West Virginia Counties.* Richwood, W.Va.: J. Comstock, 1973. 8 vols. (FHL# 975.4/H2ha or microfilm 0908974-0908975)

This source is a reprint of late nineteenth-century biographies published in the Hardesty County Atlas series covering twenty-four counties. The series is indexed in:

Comstock, Jim, ed. *The West Virginia Heritage Encyclopedia.* Richwood, W.Va.: J. Comstock, 1976. 25 vols. (FHL# 975.4/ H26w)

This encyclopedia is a useful biographical reference in its own right. The *Supplemental Series* to the *Encyclopedia* (25 vols., FHL# 975.4/H26wa) reprints valuable West Virginia sources, including the Hardesty atlases. The *Supplemental Series* is indexed in the *Encyclopedia* proper.

Cemeteries, Church Records

The Family History Library has extensive cemetery and church records for West Virginia, usually cataloged on the local level. The library also has WPA Historical Records Survey inventories for records of West Virginia Baptist, Episcopal, Methodist Episcopal, Methodist Protestant, and Presbyterian churches in West Virginia. Look under **West Virginia/Church Records** to locate these inventories.

Census

The Family History Library has all of the extant federal censuses for West Virginia from 1870 to 1910. West Virginia census records before 1870 are found under Virginia.

Mortality schedules for the 1850, 1860, 1870, and 1880 censuses are also available. Many county census records have been extracted and published separately. There are no state census records for West Virginia at the Family History Library.

Court Records

At least some court records for every West Virginia county are available at the Family History Library. Consult the FHLC under **West Virginia/[County]/Court Records** to determine the type and extent of court records available.

Early court records for the area which became West Virginia are printed in:

Loveless, Richard William. *Records of the District of West Augusta, Ohio County, and Yohogania County, Virginia: District of West Augusta, Minutes of the Court (1775-1776), Deeds (1775-1776); Ohio County, Minutes of the Court (1777-1780); Yohogania County, Minutes of the Court (1777-1780), Wills (1776-1780).* Columbus, Ohio: State University Printing Dept., 1970. (FHL# 975/P2L or microfilm 1035976).

For court records involving settlers of West Virginia prior to 1776, see Chalkley's *Chronicles of the Scotch-Irish Settlement of Virginia* (fully cited in the Virginia section).

The library also has extensive court records from Monongalia County, which was created in 1776 and at one time covered a substantial area of north central

West Virginia. In addition, many who settled the interior of West Virginia passed through Monongalia County.

The library's microfilm collection includes the minute and order books of various Monongalia County courts and also the original legal papers that were filed in these courts. These records were indexed at the West Virginia University Library, and the microfilm copy is cataloged under **West Virginia/Monongalia/ Court Records/Indexes.** In at least one instance, some cards were not filmed (the names James G. West through Eliza Wilson).

Directories

Many city and county directories are available and cataloged by locality in the FHLC. Wheeling is listed in the Research Publications Catalogue for a few years before 1860, but is not available at the library.

Genealogy

Most West Virginia counties have some material catalogued under **/Genealogy**, but the items vary considerably. Three typical collections are:

West Virginia University Library. *Genealogies.* 10 reels. Salt Lake City: Genealogical Society of Utah, 1961. (microfilm 023244-0232253).

Manuscript genealogies on West Virginia families, many of them unpublished.

Smith, Aubrey O., and Winton A. Rife, comps. *Smith-Rife Collection of New River Genealogy and Local History.* 16 reels. Salt Lake City: Genealogical Society of Utah, 1979. (microfilm 103965-103980)

Includes family Bible records, family sketches, obituaries, cemetery transcriptions, church records, etc., on families in the New River area, south central West Virginia.

Tetrick, Guy W. *Family Records of Harrision County, West Virginia, and Descendants in the United States.* 116 reels. Salt Lake City: Genealogical Society of Utah, 1958. (FHL# microfilm 0163723-0163838)

_____. *Family Sheets: An Uncompleted Survey for a "Genealogical History of Harrison County, West Virginia."* 49 reels. Salt Lake City: Genealogical Society of Utah, 1958. (FHL# 0163848-0163896)

History

There are a number of good state histories for West Virginia under **West Virginia/History.**

Callahan, James Morton. *Semi-Centennial History of West Virginia.* Charleston: Semi-Centennial Commission of West Virginia, 1913. (FHL# 975.4/H2cj).

A good general overview.

Sims, Edgar Barr. *Making a State: Formation of West Virginia Including Maps, Illustrations, Plates and the Acts of the Virginia Assembly and the Legislature of West Virginia Creating the Counties.* Charleston: E. B. Sims, 1956. (FHL# Q975.4/R2s)

A detailed history of West Virginia's organization with maps. Used with land records and maps, it can help you locate a jurisdiction in which your family lived or owned land.

The FHLC lists some sort of county history for every county in West Virginia except Putnam. See **/[County]/History.**

Land and Property Records

The Family History Library has land and property records for every county of West Virginia plus microfilmed records of land grants made by Virginia.

Sims, Edgar B., *Sims Index to Land Grants in West Virginia.* Charleston: Auditor's Office, 1952. (FHL# 975.4/R21w or microfilm 1036828)

Includes grants made by Lord Fairfax, whose Northern Neck Proprietary extended into northern West Virginia.

See Virginia below for information on locating land grants generated by that state in West Virginia before 1863. Remember that all laws regarding Virginia land grants (including military bounty land) applied in West Virginia before 1863.

The West Virginia State Auditor acquired duplicate copies of Virginia land grants. Microfilms of these grants, including those made by West Virginia after 1863, are available at the Family History Library, cataloged under **West Virginia/Land and Property:**

West Virginia State Auditor. *Land Grants, 1748-1912.* 56 reels. Salt Lake City: Genealogical Society of Utah, 1967. (FHL# microfilm 0521685-0521760, 0462935-0462958)

Maps

Sims, Edgar Barr. *Making a State: Formation of West Virginia Including Maps, Illustrations, Plates and the Acts of the Virginia Assembly and the Legislature of West Virginia Creating the Counties.* Charleston: E. B. Sims, 1956. (FHL# Q975.4/R2s)

New Descriptive Atlas of West Virginia. Clarksburg, W.V.: Clarksburg Publishing Co., 1933. (FHL# Q975.4/E3n)

Shows not only roads and watercourses but also the boundaries of magisterial districts, which are sometimes cataloged by county in the FHLC for cemetery and church records.

Military Records

Prior to 1863, soldiers serving from what became West Virginia are found in Virginia military records. Since West Virginia was not extensively settled prior to the American Revolution, relatively few Virginia records apply for that war. Several printed works deal with soldiers who either served from or eventually resided in West Virginia prior to 1863. Among the more valuable are:

Johnston, Ross B. *West Virginians in the American Revolution.* Baltimore: Genealogical Publishing Co., 1977. (FHL# 975.4/ M2j)

Lewis, Virgil A. *The Soldiery of West Virginia: In the French and Indian War, Lord Dunmore's War, the Revolution, the Later Indian Wars, the Whiskey Insurrection, the Second War with England, the War with Mexico, and Addenda Relating to West Virginians in the Civil War.* 1911; rpt. ed, Baltimore: Genealogical Publishing Co., 1978. (FHL# 975.4/M2L)

Soldiers from what is now West Virginia who served in the Confederate Army during the Civil War can be found by consulting the sources listed for Virginia. This index lists the Union soldiers from West Virginia:

United States Adjutant General's Office. *Index to Compiled Service Records of Volunteer Union Soldiers Who Served in Organizations from the State of West Virginia (1861-1865)* 13 rolls. Washington, D.C.: National Archives, 1964. (FHL# microfilm 0881595-0881607)

For information on how to access the original records of West Virginia soldiers from the American Revolution to the Spanish-American War, see *Military Records* in the introduction to this chapter.

The Family History Library has discharge records recorded for many West Virginia counties. These records vary in coverage but can include records of local soldiers from the Civil War through World War II. See the FHLC under **/[County]/Military Records**.

Minorities

The Family History Library has few sources for minorities in West Virginia. A book with outstanding coverage, which includes many Jewish family genealogies, is:

Shinedling, Abraham Isaac. *West Virginia Jewry: Origins and History, 1850-1958.* 3 vols. Philadelphia: M. Jacob, 1963. (FHL# 975.4/F2js)

Newspapers, Obituaries

The Family History Library has a greater variety of local newspapers from West Virginia than from any other state, including Utah, because West Virginia law at one time required copies of the local newspapers to be kept at the county courthouse. When Family History Library crews microfilmed county records, they included the newspapers as well.

Newspapers from the county seats of thirty-nine out of West Virginia's fifty-four counties are consequently available on film at the library. In cases where more than one paper was published in a county, they may also be available. The time span covered varies, but most papers are from the late nineteenth and early twentieth centuries.

West Virginia has few compiled abstracts of obituaries. :

Tetrick, W. Guy *Obituaries from Newspapers of Northern West Virginia, Principally from the Counties of Barbour, Braxton, Calhoun, Doddridge, Gilmer, Harrison, Lewis, Nicholas, Pocohontas, Preston, Randolph, Ritchie, Taylor, Tucker, Tyler, Upshur, Webster, and parts of Marion, Wetzel and Wirt.* Clarksburg, W.Va.: W. G. Tetrick, 1933. (FHL# 975.4/V3t or microfilm 1033974)

Periodicals

Periodicals published by local genealogical societies are cataloged in the FHLC under **West Virginia/Genealogy/Periodicals**. A particularly useful periodical for general historical information on West Virginia:

West Virginia History: A Quarterly Magazine. Charleston: State Department of Archives and History, 1939-to date. (FHL# 975.4/B2wh)

Probate Records

Probate records are available for every county in West Virginia. For an index, see:

Johnston, Ross B., comp. *West Virginia Estate Settlements (1753-1850).* Fort Worth, Tex.: American Reference Publishers, Inc., 1969. (FHL# 975.4/S2j)

Covers pre-1850 estate settlements (wills, administrations, inventories, etc.) for the counties of Hampshire, Berkeley, Monongalia, Ohio, Greenbrier, Harrison, Hardy, Randolph, Pendleton, Kanawha, Brooke, Wood, and Monroe. Reprints a series of articles in the *West Virginia Quarterly*, volumes 17, 20, and 22-24. The book is arranged county by county. A general index has been added to one of the library copies.

Public Records, Schools

Public records, as defined in the introduction, are available for all West Virginia counties except Putnam. Consult the FHLC under **West Virginia/[County]/-Public Records** for holdings in each county.

School records, largely school board minutes, are available for eleven counties.

Societies

The Family History Library has lineage society registers plus microfilms of the application forms for membership in the Sons of the American Revolution for West Virginia from 1927 to 1957. (FHL# microfilm 0163703-0163706)

Taxation

Land tax records are available for every West Virginia county except Putnam and Logan. These are extremely valuable in tracking individuals between census years and in tracing ownership of a piece of property. Although these records are sometimes cataloged under **/[County]/Taxation**, they are most often listed under **/[County]/Land and Property.**

Vital Records

West Virginia counties began keeping records of births, marriages, and deaths consistent with Virginia law in 1853. Civil marriage records are available from the creation date of most counties, barring courthouse fires. West Virginia continued vital registration after it became a state. In many cases, its counties kept records more consistently than Virginia counties during the same period.

The Family History Library has vital records from every West Virginia county except Lincoln and Logan. Many counties' registers begin in 1853 and some after 1863, while many extend well into the twentieth century. For vital records from 1853 to 1860 see:

Vital Statistics, 1853-1860, of West Virginia. 10 reels. Salt Lake City: Genealogical Society of Utah, 1954. (FHL# microfilm 0034484-0034493)

VIRGINIA

Historical Background

1607 First English settlement at Jamestown.

1607-25 Virginia governed by the Virginia Company of London.

1619 African slaves introduced into Virginia.

1621 House of Burgesses established.

1625 Virginia becomes a royal colony.

1652-60 Commonwealth Period in England; Puritans depose Charles I; Virginia's governor, Sir William Berkeley, surrenders Virginia to the rule of Cromwell.

1660 Charles II restored to the English throne; Berkeley reappointed; concentration of political power in the hand of great landowning families alienates "common" people.

1676 Nathaniel Bacon leads rebellion against the royal government, eventually suppressed.

1716 Governor Alexander Spotswood and the Knights of the Golden Horseshoe explore the Valley of Virginia.

1716-56 Migration of Scots, Scots-Irish, and Germans into theValley of Virginia; beginning of dispute between the Up Country and the Tidewater.

1756 Seven Years' (French and Indian) War; many western settlers fight to defend the colony.

1774 Lord Dunmore's War; Shawnee Indians defeated.

1775-81 American Revolution; little action in Virginia until the end of the war when the British surrendered at Yorktown.

1776 First state convention.

1784 Virginia cedes its territory northwest of the Ohio River to the United States.

1788 Virginia becomes the tenth state to ratify the Constitution.

1792 Kentucky is created out of Virginia as an independent state.

1831 Nat Turner's slave rebellion; suppressed.

1861 Virginia secedes from the Union and joins the Confederacy.

1861-65 Civil War; northern Virginia becomes a battleground; many courthouses are burned; Richmond serves as the capital of the Confederacy.

1863 West Virginia secedes from Virginia and joins the Union as a new state.

1866-70 Reconstruction period.

1870 Virginia readmitted to the Union.

Settlement and Migration

Virginia's history is perhaps best known of all the states in the Old South. Beginning with the settlement at Jamestown in 1607, migration to Virginia from Great Britain and a few European countries was continuous until the American Revolution. At the census in 1790, Virginia was the most populous state and geographically the largest.

Settlement patterns in Virginia were of two basic types, tidewater and up country. Tidewater settlements were located extending up along the major rivers. From there, gradual westward migration began up the river valleys toward the interior, greatly encouraged by land grants based on the headright system. (In this system, a person who paid others' passage fees received so many acres per "head"–the exact number of acres varied.) Many of those thus transported were indentured servants who were also able to claim a headright grant once their terms of service had expired.

The best source for the names of early Virginia settlers is:

Nugent, Nell Marion. *Cavaliers and Pioneers: Abstracts of Virginia Land Patents and Grants.* Vol. 1, Richmond, Va.: Dietz Printing Co., 1934; Vols. 2-3, Richmond: Virginia State Library 1977-79. (FHL# 975.5 R2n)

Lists not only the person receiving the land but also the names of those transported. The names of the transported persons do not always appear in provincial land grants, which sometimes indicate just the number of persons involved. In these cases, check the county court records (if they survive) where the land was located.

Westward migration in Virginia faced two barriers. One was the Appalachian Mountains. The other was hostile Indians. In 1716, Governor Alexander Spotswood led an exploration party over the first range of mountains and "discovered" the Valley of Virginia, i.e., the Shenandoah River Valley. The discovery of this valley led to the second migration pattern in Virginia.

Beginning in the 1720s and 1730s, Scots-Irish and German settlers from Pennsylvania made their way down the Valley of Virginia until there were settlements all the way to the North Carolina border. These settlements provided a buffer between the tidewater settlements and the Indians, allowing settlement in the remainder of the

Virginia low country. The Valley of Virginia soon became a common migration route from Philadelphia to the Carolinas, and it was not uncommon for families to stay awhile in Virginia before moving on.

Several compilations of court records from Virginia's frontier counties provide a good source for the names of early settlers:

Chalkey, Lyman. *Chronicles of the Scotch-Irish Settlement in Virginia: Extracted from the Original Court Records of Augusta County, 1754-1800.* 1912; rpt. ed. Baltimore, Md.: Genealogical Publishing Co., 1980. (FHL# 975.5916/F2c or microfilm 0162043-0162044)

Summers, Lewis Preston. *Annals of Southwest Virginia, 1769-1800.* Abingdon, Va.: L. P. Summers, 1929. 1 vol. bound in 2. (FHL# 975.5/H2sl or microfilm 1000631)

______. *History of Southwest Virginia, 1746-1786, Washington County, 1777-1870.* 1903; rpt. ed., Baltimore, Md.: Genealogical Publishing Co., 1966. (FHL# 975.5/H2sLp or microfilm 0162046)

An important aspect of Virginia's organization is the creation of independent cities, meaning that they are not subject to county administration but are the legislative equivalents of counties. Thorough research requires searching the records of independent cities that existed in the ancestral county. Most independent cities originated during the twentieth century, and the Family History Library has few of their records; but some cities date to the early 1800s. The charts accompanying this section are divided into counties and cities to show what is available at the Family History Library.

Four Virginia counties have been completely consumed by independent cities, and the city holds county records. These four counties are listed in the FHLC but under the respective cities:

Nansemond County: see Suffolk Independent City.

Norfolk County: see Chesapeake Independent City. Do not confuse this county with Norfolk Independent City.

Princess Anne County: see Virginia Beach Independent City.

Warwick County: see Newport News Independent City.

Virginia Library Collection

Archives and Libraries

The Virginia State Library in Richmond houses microfilm copies of most county records. Its pre-1870 records were microfilmed in conjunction with the Genealogical Society of Utah.

The handbook below lists Virginia counties and the records available for them. While the Family History Library does not have all of the records listed, the listing is useful for determining whether other records in the state might help on a particular problem:

Schweitzer, George K. *Virginia Genealogical Research.* Knoxville, Tenn.: G. K. Schweitzer, 1982.

Biography

Most of Virginia's statewide biographies deal with "eminent" men. See **Virginia/Biography** in the FHLC for specific titles of interest. Two biographical indexes are worth noting:

Swem, Earl Gregg. *Virginia Historical Index.* 2 vols. bound in 4. Gloucester, Mass.: Peter Smith, 1965. (FHL# 975.5/A4s or microfilm 0485948-0485949)

True, Ransom B., ed. *Biographical Dictionary of Early Virginia, 1607-1660.* 19 microfiche. Richmond: Association for the Preservation of Virginia Antiquities, 1982. (FHL# microfiche 6331352)

Compiled from names found in official colony records before 1660; citations included.

The Swem *Index* is a standard source for Virginia biography, history, and genealogy and is listed under all three headings in the FHLC. It indexes:

Virginia Magazine of History and Biography

William and Mary Quarterly Historical Magazine

Tyler's Quarterly Historical and Genealogical Magazine

Virginia Historical Register and Literary Advertiser

Lower Norfolk County Virginia Antiquary

Hening's Statutes at Large

Calendar of Virginia State Papers and Other Manuscripts

The Family History Library has all of these sources but locating them is sometimes difficult. Shelf copies of the periodicals are incomplete, but missing volumes can be found on microfilm. In most cases, look under **Virginia/Genealogy/ Periodicals**, but for the *William and Mary Quarterly*, look under **/Williamsburg/Periodicals**.

Cemeteries, Church Records

Although Anglicanism was the established church up to the Revolution, Presbyterians, Quakers, Baptists, and Lutherans all settled in Virginia. To locate records, check the FHLC under **/[County]** and/or **/[Town]/-Cemetery Records** and **[County]/[Town]/Church Records.**

Census

The library has all of the extant federal censuses for Virginia from 1810 to 1910. No mortality schedules are available.

The state census enumerations of 1782 and 1785 were published as the *Virginia Heads of Families, 1790* by the State Census Bureau. No other state censuses are available for Virginia at the Family History Library. See **/Taxation** for census substitutes.

Court Records

Court records are one of the most important record groups for Virginia research. The Family History Library has court records (where they have survived) for many Virginia counties. In addition, many court records are in the process of being abstracted and indexed. Indexes found in the order and minute books of the courts are usually to lawsuits only; probates of wills, guardianships, apprenticeships, and naturalizations are not indexed. For holdings, check the FHLC under **/[County]/Court Records.**

Directories

City directories are available for many Virginia cities. Check the FHLC under **/[City]/Directories** for holdings. The Research Publications series has directories for Norfolk and Richmond up to 1901 and an 1859 directory for Petersburg. See introduction to this chapter under *Directories.*

Genealogies

A wealth of genealogical material is available for Virginia. These guides are helpful in locating it:

Stewart, Robert A. *Index to Printed Virginia Genealogies.* 1930; rpt. ed., Baltimore, Md.: Genealogical Publishing Co., 1965. (FHL# 975.5/022s or microfilm 0962558)

Brown, Stuart E. *Virginia Genealogies: A Trial List of Printed Books and Pamphlets.* Berryville: Virginia Book Company, 1967. (FHL# 975.5/0236)

_____, et al. *Virginia Genealogies, Volume 2.* Berryville: Virginia Book Company, 1980. (FHL# 975.5/ D236/v.2)

History

Consult the FHLC under **Virginia/History** and **Virginia/ [County]/History** to find histories of interest among the many that have been published.

Land and Property Records

The Family History Library has extensive land records for Virginia at both the state and local level. Check the FHLC under the name of the county to see if land records have survived and are on film.

In addition to county land records, the library has the following sources:

Virginia Land Offices. *Land Grants, 1690-1862, and Land Surveys, 1786-1854 of Northern Neck.* 34 reels. Richmond: Virginia State Library, n.d. (FHL# microfilm 0029508-0029541)

_____. *Land Patents and Grants, 1623-1921.* 200 reels. Richmond: Virginia State Library, n.d. (FHL# microfilm 0029308-0029507)

_____. *Land Warrants, 1779-1898.* 11 reels. Richmond: Virginia State Library, n.d. (FHL# microfilm 0029638-0029648)

_____. *Miscellaneous Military, Preemption and Land Warrants, Bounties, Surveys, Grants, etc. 1779-1921.* Richmond: Virginia State Library, n.d. (FHL# 0029649-0029663)

_____. *Surveys Upon Which Land Grants Were Issued, 1779-1878; Index to Surveys, 1779-1914.* 92 reels. Richmond: Virginia State Library, n.d. (FHL# microfilm 0029542-0029633)

Nugent's published abstracts of the land patents up to 1732 is cited in the section on *Settlement and Organization.* The Northern Neck Proprietary of Lord Fairfax overlapped with land under the jurisdiction of the province. This border area saw many conflicting claims, and you should check both land-granting entities. See William Thorndale's discussion of Virginia land records in *The Source* (Salt Lake City: Ancestry, Inc., 1984) pp. 251-52 .

Maps

The most useful maps in the library's collection have no film copies and must be ordered from the condensed storage area, due to their size:

Hale, John S. *A Historical Atlas of Colonial Virginia.* Staunton, Va.: Old Dominion Publications, 1978. (Folio Area 975.5/E7hj)

Virginia Department of Highways and Transportation. County Maps. Richmond: The Department, 1977. (Folio Area 975.5/E7v)

Watercourses, essential in locating land grants and property mentioned in deeds, included.

Military Records

The Family History Library has a wealth of information on Virginia soldiers, some printed, some on microfilm, much of it indexed. Some representative items are:

Crozier, William Armstrong. *Virginia Colonial Militia, 1651-1776.* 1905; rpt. ed., Baltimore, Md.: Genealogical Publishing Co., 1965. (FHL# 975.5/M2c)

Gwathmey, John Hastings. *Historical Register of Virginians in the Revolution: Soldiers, Sailors, Marines, 1775-1783.* 1938; rpt. ed., Baltimore, Md.: Genealogical Publishing Co., 1973. (FHL# 975.5/M23g)

The most comprehensive reference for records of Virginians in the American Revolution.

United States Auditor for Interior. *Virginia Half Pay and Other Related Revolutionary War Pension Application Files, ca. 1778-1875.* 9 reels. Washington, D.C.: National Archives, 1972. (FHL# microfilm 1024434-1024442)

United States Adjutant General's Office. *Index to Compiled Service Records of Confederate Soldiers Who Served in Organizations from the State of Virginia, 1861-1865.* 61 reels. Washington, D.C.: National Archives, 1962. (FHL# microfilm 0881395-0881456)

_____. *Index to Compiled Service Records of Volunteer Union Soldiers Who Served in Organizations from the State of Virginia 1861-1865.* Washington, D.C.: National Archives, 1962. (FHL# microfilm 0881594)

_____. *Compiled Service Records of Volunteer Union Soldiers Who Served in Organizations from the State of Virginia, 1861-1865.* 7 reels. Washington, D.C.: National Archives, 1962. (FHL# microfilm 1292638-1292644)

Virginia Adjutant General. *Muster Rolls of the Virginia Militia in the War of 1812, printed 1852, and Pay Rolls of Militia Entitled to Land Bounty, 1851.* 8 reels. Richmond, Va.: Genealogical Society of Utah, 1955. (FHL# microfilm 0029984-0029991)

Virginia Secretary of Military Records. *Confederate Service Records of Virginia.* 10 reels. Richmond, Va.: Genealogical Society of Utah, 1954. 10 microfilm reels. (FHL# microfilm 0029767-0029776)

See the FHLC under **Virginia/Military Records** and **Virginia/[County]/Military Records.** Many Virginia counties have militia records for the Civil War period. The Virginia Regimental Histories Series is partially available at the Family History Library but is cataloged under the name of the author of each volume and not as a whole. Consult the FHLC under **Virginia/Military Records/Civil War 1861-1865.**

Minorities, Slavery and Bondage

In addition to the Scots-Irish and Germans in the Valley of Virginia, there were Germans in what are now Madison and Culpeper counties who were part of the Germanna Colonies, French Huguenots at Manakin in Goochland County and surrounding counties, Scots just about everywhere, and of course, African slaves wherever there was a plantation economy. Works on all of these groups can be found under **Virginia/Minorities** and **/Slavery and Bondage.**

Newspapers

To search the compiled abstracts of marriages and deaths which are available, check the FHLC under the county and/or town of interest. For colonial research, see:

Cappon, Lester J., and Stella F. Duff. *Virginia Gazette Index, 1736-1780.* 2 vols. Williamsburg, Va.: Institute of Early American History and Culture, 1950. (FHL# 975.5/B3v or microfilm 1036212)

The library also has the *Virginia Gazette* on microfilm.

Orphans' Records

Several counties have records of indentured orphans that are separate from court order books, court minute books, and probate records.

Periodicals

In addition to the periodicals mentioned under *Biography*, the library also has:

The Virginia Genealogist. Washington, D.C.: J.F. Dorman, 1957-to date. (FHL# 975.5/B2vg)

Currently the best available for Virginia research. Check the FHLC under **Virginia/[County]/Periodicals** for others.

Probate Records

In Virginia, all probate matters were recorded in the "will books." The Family History Library has probate records for most counties where they have survived. The FHLC may list only "will books" but you should know that they include all probate matters. Use the will books with court records to find material omitted from the will books. For instance, if a will book does not contain guardianship bonds but does include the dates of an estate's probate, administration, or inventory, you can consult the court order books for that time period to see if guardians were appointed for any minor children.

The probate records of many Virginia counties are beginning to be printed and indexed, a great help in making stray names accessible. These printed records will also be cataloged under the name of the county.

Torrence, Clayton. *Virginia Wills and Administrations, 1632-1800: An Index of Wills Recorded in Local Courts of Virginia, 1632-1800, and of Administrations on Estates Shown by Inventories of the Estates of Inventories Recorded in Will and Other Books of Local Courts, 1632-1800.* 1930; rpt. ed., Baltimore, Md.: Genealogical Publishing Co., 1965. (FHL# 975.5/P22t or microfilm 0844943)

The standard index to wills and administrations in Virginia before 1800. Although it contains some errors and should be used cautiously, it is the most comprehensive work of its kind for Virginia.

Public Records

The primary public records of note for Virginia are:

Hening, William W. *The Statutes at Large, Being a Collection of All the Laws of Virginia from the First Session of the Legislature in the Year 1619: Published Pursuant to an Act of the General Assembly of Virginia, Passed on the Fifth Day of February, One Thousand Eight Hundred and Eight.* 1819-23; rpt. ed., Charlottesville: University Press of Virginia, 1969. (FHL# 975.5/P3h or microfilm 0162029-0162040)

Palmer, William P. *Calendar of Virginia State Papers and Other Manuscripts*. Richmond: n.pub., 1875-93. (FHL# 975.5/-N2p; see FHLC for film numbers. Filming not consecutive.)

Taxation

The Virginia State Library in Richmond has fairly complete personal property and land tax records for most counties commencing in 1782. Unfortunately, the Family History Library has only a few of these records. Check the FHLC under **Virginia/[County]/Tax Records.**

Two substitute censuses have been prepared from tax lists and are available at the Family History Library:

Fothergill, August B., and John M. Naugle. *Virginia Taxpayers, 1782-1787, Other Than Those Published by the United States Census Bureau.* 1940; rpt. ed., Baltimore, Md.: Genealogical Publishing Co., 1966. (FHL# 975.5/R4f or microfilm 0874197 or microfiche 6051284)

Schreiner-Yantis, Netti. *A Supplement to the 1810 Census of Virginia: Tax Lists of the Counties for Which the Census is Missing.* Springfield, Va.: N. Schreiner-Yantis, 1971. (FHL# 975.5/R4s)

Vital Records

Virginia began keeping vital records in 1853. Registration for these years appears to have been better than the post-Civil War period, although marriage records were kept up fairly well. Most of the library's collection of Virginia vital records ends in the 1890s. Check the FHLC under **Virginia/[County]/Vital Records**. Many counties also have printed vital records (usually marriages). Slave births *were* recorded prior to 1865 and appear in the county vital records.

NORTH CAROLINA

Historical Background

1584	First exploration by the English.
1585-86	First English colony at Roanoke, mostly soldiers and adventurers, fails after repeated conflict with Indians.
1587	Second colony at Roanoke mysteriously disappears.
1629	Charters to Heath and Clarendon (see South Carolina).
1663-65	See South Carolina chronology; up to 1712, South and North Carolina were the same province.
1677	Culpeper's Rebellion protests proprietary taxes.
1691	One governor selected by the proprietors established over North and South Carolina.
1706	Church of England becomes established religion.
1708-11	Dissenters' Rebellion against Church of England; fails.
1711-13	Tuscarora War; defeat and removal of the Tuscaroras to New York opens up some of the back country.
1712	Separate governors established in North and South Carolina.
1729	Proprietary rule ends; North Carolina becomes a royal province.
1740-75	Many Germans and Scots-Irish immigrate to the West Country from Pennsylvania and the Valley of Virginia down the Great Wagon Road.
1768-71	The Regulators become active in western North Carolina, protesting rule by eastern landowners; epitomizes long struggle between West and East Country in North Carolina.
1775	"Mecklenburg Declaration of Independence" from Great Britain, signed by residents of Mecklenburg County.
1775-83	American Revolution; Loyalists are effectively defeated at Moore's Creek Bridge in 1776, Cornwallis invades in 1780-81.
1784	North Carolina cedes its western territory, now Tennessee, to the United States.
1790-1835	Prolonged contest between western and eastern counties for political power.
1861	North Carolina secedes from the Union.
1861-65	Civil War; North Carolina escapes major conflict
1866-70	Reconstruction period.
1868	North Carolina readmitted to the Union.

Settlement and Migration

North Carolina's first permanent settlements were in the late seventeenth century in the Albemarle Sound area. Early settlement was largely made from Virginia, but Scots-Irish and Germans from Pennsylvania began to settle the western part of the state after the defeat of the Tuscarora Indians in 1713, many Highland Scots settled in the southeastern part of the state, and Quakers from New England, Pennsylvania, and Virginia settled in the central portion from the 1740s onwards. African slaves were brought into North Carolina by those settlers establishing plantations.

The following works are useful sources for some aspects of North Carolina settlement and migration:

Meyer, Duane. *The Highland Scots of North Carolina, 1732-1776.* Chapel Hill: University of North Carolina Press, 1966. (FHL# 975.6/F2me)

Newsome, Albert R., ed. *Records of Emigrants from England and Scotland to North Carolina, 1774-1775.* Raleigh, N.C.: State Department of Archives and History, 1962. (FHL# 975.6/Al/no.30 or microfilm 0908208)

Ramsey, Robert W. *Carolina Cradle: Settlement of the Northwest Carolina Frontier, 1747-1762.* Chapel Hill: University of North Carolina Press, 1964. (FHL# 975.671/H2r)

McBride, B. Ransom. "Migrations As Shown in Powers of Attorney." *North Carolina Genealogical Society Journal* 3 (1977): 1-15, 116-27, 166-72, 233-41; 4 (1978): 52-57, 108-17, 177-87; 5 (1979): 37-42, 165-72; 6 (1980): 48-58, 125-34. (FHL# 975.6/B2s)

Livingston, Virginia Pope. "Some Migrations from Virginia into North Carolina." *North Carolina Genealogical Society Journal* 2 (1976): 122-28, 192-97; 3 (1977): 32-38, 108-13, 182-86, 229-32. (FHL# 975.6/B2s)

Archives and Libraries

The Family History Library has several guides to record repositories in North Carolina. Some examples are:

Crabtree, Beth G. *Guide to Private Manuscript Collections in the North Carolina State Archives.* Raleigh: North Carolina Department of Archives and History, 1964. (FHL# 975.6/A5n)

Crittenden, Charles Christopher, and Dan Lacy, eds. *The Historical Records of North Carolina.* 3 vols. Raleigh: North Carolina Historical Commission, 1938-39. (FHL# 975.6/A5h or microfilm 1036384)

North Carolina Department of Cultural Resources. *Guide to Research Materials in the North Carolina State Archives, Section B. County Records.* 5th rev. ed. Raleigh: North Carolina Department of Cultural Resources, 1977. (FHL# 975.6/A5nc)

North Carolina Historical Records Survey Project, Division of Professional and Service Projects, Works Progress Administration. *Guide to the Manuscripts in the Southern Historical Collection of the University of North Carolina.* Chapel Hill: University of North Carolina Press, 1941. (FHL# 975.6/B4b/v.24/no.2)

Patterson, Alex M., and F. D. Gatton, eds. *The Municipal Records Manual, 1971.* Raleigh: North Carolina Department of Archives and History, 1971. (FHL# 975.6/A5nm or microfilm 0908979)

Trilley, Nannie M., and Noma Lee Goodwin. *Guide to the Manuscript Collections in the Duke University Library.* Durham, N.C.: Duke University Press, 1947. (FHL# 975.6/B5d/ series 27-28 or microfilm 0899894)

For more detailed information on archives and libraries in North Carolina and how to use them, see:

Leary, Helen F. M., and Maurice R. Stirewalt. *North Carolina Genealogy and Local History.* Raleigh: North Carolina Genealogical Society, 1980. (FHL# 975.6/D27n)

Biography

Most compiled biographies in North Carolina are on the state level and usually deal with "leading" or "eminent" men. However, you can find a few county-level biographical sources in the FHLC under **North Carolina/[County]/Biography**. Two statewide biographical sources are worth mentioning:

Ashe, Samuel A'Court, ed. *Biographical History of North Carolina from Colonial Times to the Present.* 8 vols. Greensboro, N.C.: C.L. Van Noppen, 1905-17. (FHL# 975.6/D3a)

Powell, William S., ed. *Dictionary of North Carolina Biography.* 2 vols. Chapel Hill: University of North Carolina Press, 1979. (FHL# 975.6/D3d)

Cemeteries

Like the other states in the Old South, North Carolina has cemetery inscriptions for nearly every county. What distinguishes North Carolina from the other states is the statewide pre-1914 cemetery inscriptions index prepared by the WPA Historical Records Survey. The Family History Library has both the index (listed under **North Carolina/Cemeteries/Indexes)** and the inscriptions (listed under **/[County]/Cemeteries**). A few post-1914 inscriptions are indexed separately in the series.

The pre-1914 cemetery inscriptions are mostly from rural cemeteries. A list of which cemeteries were transcribed is also cataloged under **North Carolina/-Cemeteries.**

Census

The Family History Library has all of the extant federal census records for North Carolina. At this writing, no mortality schedules are available for the censuses between 1850 and 1880, except where they have been extracted on the county level.

A useful reference for pre-1790 census information is:

Register, Alvarett K., trans. *State Census of North Carolina, 1784-1787.* 2d. ed. rev., 1971; rpt. ed., Baltimore, Md.: Genealogical Publishing Company, 1973. (FHL# 975.6/X2r/1784-1787 or microfilm 0897274)

Church Records

Although the Church of England was the established church in North Carolina, many different religious groups settled there in the colonial period including Quakers, Presbyterians, Lutheran, Reformed, Baptists, Moravians, and Methodists.

The records of the Quakers and Moravians have been printed and are available at the Family History Library:

Fries, Adelaide L., ed. *Records of the Moravians in North Carolina.* 11 vols. Raleigh, N.C.: Edwards and Broughton Printing Co., 1922-69 (FHL# 975.6/F2m)

Hinshaw, William W. *Encyclopedia of American Quaker Genealogy, Volume I, Containing Every Item of Genealogical Value Found in All Records and Minutes of the Thirty-Three Oldest Monthly Meetings which Belong, or Ever Belonged, to the North Carolina Yearly Meeting of Friends (Whose Records Are Known to be Still in Existence).* 1936; rpt. ed., Baltimore, Md.: Genealogical Publishing Co., 1969. (FHL# 973/D2hc or microfilm 6051271)

Several denominational histories are also available. Records of individual congregations can be found in the FHLC under **/[County or Town]/Church Records**.

Court Records

Court records in some form are available for most of the North Carolina counties in the Family History Library's collection. Court records can either be the original minute and order books, or transcribed abstracts. Consult the FHLC under **[County]/Court Records** to see what is available. See also *Public Records* below.

Directories

Directories are available for several North Carolina cities in the nineteenth and twentieth centuries. There are no North Carolina directories in the Research Publications series prior to 1901.

Gazetteers

A comprehensive gazetteer of North Carolina place names, including watercourses, is:

Powell, William S. *The North Carolina Gazetteer.* Chapel Hill: University of North Carolina Press,1968. (FHL# 975.6/E5p)

Genealogy

See the FHLC under **North Carolina/Genealogy** for various publications and collections of genealogical material.

The McCubbins Collection. 76 rolls. (FHL# microfilm 0019828-0019903)

This large collection of information on local families is housed at the Rowan County Public Library. As Rowan County at one time covered a substantial portion of western North Carolina, the information is useful for several counties. Check the FHLC under **/Rowan County/Genealogy** for more precise call numbers.

History

The Family History Library has a variety of state and county histories for North Carolina. Check the FHLC under the county or city name to locate histories of interest.

Lefler, Hugh T. *History of North Carolina.* 4 vols. New York: Lewis Historical Publishing Co., 1956. (FHL# 975.6/-H2L)

A good overview of North Carolina history.

Powell, William S., James K. Huhta, and Thomas J., Franham, comps. *The Regulators in North Carolina: A Documentary History, 1759-1776.* Raleigh: State Department of Archives and History, 1971. (FHL# 975.6/H2p)

A good example of a history dealing with a specific and important time period.

Land and Property

The Family History Library has land and property records from every extant county in North Carolina except for Hoke and Scotland counties. See the FHLC under **/[County]/Land and Property.**

The library does not have original land grant records of North Carolina but has the following printed abstracts:

Hofmann, Margaret M. *Province of North Carolina, 1663-1729, Abstracts of Land Patents.* Weldon, N.C.: Roanoke News Co., 1979. (FHL# 975.6/R2hp)

_____. *Colony of North Carolina, 1735-1764, 1765-1775, Abstracts of Land Patents.* 2 vols. Weldon, N.C.: Roanoke News Co., 1982, 1984. (FHL# 975.6/R2hm)

The library also has the Revolutionary War land warrants and grants made to North Carolina soldiers in what is now Tennessee. See Chapter 8, "The New South," for more information. Some state land entries and warrants are available for North Carolina from 1764 to 1833. See the FHLC under **North Carolina/Land and Property.**

Maps

Of the many North Carolina maps in the Family History Library collection, two series are particularly noteworthy. The State Highway Commission maintenance maps, available on microfilm, show watercourses, which are important for locating land grants. See also:

Stout, Garland P. *Historical Research Maps: North Carolina Counties.* 100 maps. Greensboro, N.C.: G. P. Stout, 1973. (FHL# Map Case 975.6/E7s)

_____. *Index.* 5 vols. Greensoboro, N.C.: G. P. Stout, 1975. (FHL# 975.6/E7s)

Medical Records

The Family History Library has some lunacy and inebriety records for a few North Carolina counties. Check **/[County]/Medical Records.** These records may contain family history information.

Military Records

The Family History Library has several published works listing North Carolina soldiers and several indexes that identify North Carolina records maintained in federal archives. These published works and indexes cover the period from the American Revolution to the Spanish-American War. In addition to these records, see county discharge records for local soldiers who served in the armed forces between the Spanish-American War and the Korean Conflict. Check **/[County]/Military Records** to determine the coverage.

The published works available at the library are:

Daughters of the American Revolution (North Carolina). *Roster of Soldiers from North Carolina in the American Revolution: With an Appendix Containing a Collection of Miscellaneous Records*. 1932; rpt. ed, Baltimore, Md.: Genealogical Publishing Co., 1977. (FHL# 975.6/M2d or microfilm 1036687, 1036677, or microfiche 6046553)

Manarin, Louis H., and Weymouth T. Jordan, comps. *North Carolina Troops, 1861-1865: A Roster.* 9 vols. Raleigh, N.C.: State Department of Archives and History, 1966. (FHL# 975.6/M2nc)

_____. *Muster Rolls of the Soldiers of the War of 1812 Detached from the Militia of North Carolina in 1812 and 1814: Published Under Direction of the Adjutant General, 1851.* 1926; microreproduction, Salt Lake City: Genealogical Society of Utah, 1941. (FHL microfilm 0018079)

North Carolina Adjutant General. *Roster of the North Carolina Volunteers in the Spanish-American War 1898-1899.* 1900; microreproduction, Salt Lake City: Genealogical Society of Utah, 1941. (FHL microfilm 0018079)

The indexes to Federal records of North Carolina soldiers are:

United States Adjutant General's Office. *Index to Compiled Service Records of Confederate Soldiers Who Served in Organizations from State of North Carolina, (1861-1865).* 42 reels. Washington, D.C.: National Archives, 1957. (FHL# microfilm 0821768-0821810)

_____. *Index to Compiled Service Records of Volunteer Soldiers Who Served During the Cherokee Removal in Organizations from the State of North Carolina.* Washington, D.C.: National Archives, 1958. (FHL# microfilm 0368686)

______. *Index to Compiled Service Records of Volunteer Soldiers Who Served During the Revolutionary War in Organizations from the State of North Carolina.* 2 reels. Washington, D.C.: National Archives, 1958. (FHL# microfilm 0821595-0821596)

______. *Index to Compiled Service Records of Volunteer Soldiers Who Served During the War of 1812 in Organizations from the State of North Carolina.* 5 reels. Washington, D.C.: National Archives, 1958. (FHL# microfilm 0880838-0880842)

______. *Index to Compiled Service Records of Volunteer Soldiers Who Served During the War with Spain in Organizations from the State of North Carolina, 1898-1899.* 2 reels. Washington, D.C.: National Arhives, 1963. (FHL# microfilm 0821907-0821908)

______. *Index to Compiled Service Records of Volunteer Union Soldiers who Served in Organizations from the State of North Carolina, (1861-1865).* 2 reels. Washington, D.C.: National Archives, 1962. (FHL# microfilm 0881590-0881591)

Minorities

The Family History Library has a number of published works on North Carolina minorities, mostly dealing with Scots. See the FHLC under **North Carolina/Minorities** for specific references.

Native Races

North Carolina is one of the few Southern states with a significant native American population. The reservation rolls (1848-1970) of the Eastern Cherokee Indians and the School Records of the Cherokee Agency are available on microfilm. See the FHLC under **North Carolina/Native Races** for references. In addition, Swain, Robeson, Haywood, and Cherokee counties also have records relating to native Americans.

Newspapers, Obituaries

The Family History Library has a few original newspapers on microfilm for Raleigh and Salisbury and a number of compiled abstracts of newspaper marriage and death notices, mostly on a local level, although some papers were regional and even statewide in coverage. Check the FHLC at the state, county, and city levels under both **/Newspapers** and **/Obituaries**.

Occupations

Several counties have apprenticeship records which were maintained in separate volumes. See the accompanying chart to see if a particular county has records available on microfilm.

Periodicals

The Family History Library has a number of periodicals of genealogical interest:

Journal of North Carolina Genealogy. [n.p.]: W. P. Johnson, 1962-to date. (FHL# 975.6/B2j)

North Carolina Genealogical Society Journal. Raleigh, N.C.: The Society, 1975-to date. (FHL# 975.6/B2s)

North Carolina Historical and Genealogical Records. Forest City, N.C.: C. Griffin, 1932-to date. (FHL# 975.6/B2g)

North Carolina Historical and Genealogical Record. Edenton, N.C.: J. R. B. Hathaway, 1900-03. 3 vols. (FHL# 975.6/D25n or microfilm 1206449)

The North Carolinian: A Quarterly Journal of Genealogy and History. [n.p.]: W. P. Johnson, 1955-61. 7 vols. (FHL# 975.6/B2j). Continued by *Journal of North Carolina Genealogy.*

The library maintains current issues of the periodicals still being published.

Probate Records

The Family History Library has probate records for all extant North Carolina counties except those created after 1851. Check the FHLC under **/[County]/Probate Records** to locate these records.

The two published abstracts of North Carolina probate records prior to 1800 are useful but are incomplete and sometimes in error.

Grimes, J. Bryan. *North Carolina Wills and Inventories Copied from the Original and Recorded Wills and Inventories in the Office of the Secretary of State.* Raleigh, N.C.: Edwards and Broughton Printing Co., 1912. (FHL# 975.6/S2g or microfilm 459632 or microfiche 6051125)

Olds, Fred A. *An Abstract of North Carolina Wills from About 1760 to about 1800. Supplementing Grimes' Abstract of North Carolina Wills 1663 to 1760.* 1925; rpt. ed., Baltimore, Md.: Genealogical Publishing Co., 1978. (FHL# 975.6/P28o or microfilm 0496782)

The Family History Library also has the original will and inventories from which these abstracts were made. Check the FHLC under **North Carolina/Probate Records.**

Public Records

Check the FHLC under **/[County]/Public Records** to locate the wide variety of public records available for each county. See also these statewide sources:

Saunders, William L., comp. and ed. *The Colonial Records of the State of North Carolina.* 30 vols. 10 reels. 1886-1914; microreproduction, Salt Lake City: Genealogical Society of Utah, 1972, 1976. (FHL# microfilm 0874153-0874162)

Clark, Walter, comp. and ed. *The State Records of North Carolina.* 16 reels. Vols. 27-30 in the Saunders series. Salt Lake City: Genealogical Society of Utah, 1972, 1976. (FHL# microfilm 0874163-0874176)

Weeks, Stephen B., comp. and ed. *Index to the Colonial and State Records of North Carolina.* 2 reels. Salt Lake City: Genealogical Society of Utah, 1972, 1976. (FHL# 975.6/N2n/v.27-30 or microfilm 0485942-0485943 or 0944130)

School Records

The Family History Library has school board minutes for many counties. See the accompanying chart and the FHLC under **/County/School Records.**

Taxation

The Family History Library has tax records for many of North Carolina's counties. Check the FHLC under **/[County]/Taxation**. Not comprehensive, but useful for colonial research, is:

Ratcliff, Clarence E. *North Carolina Taxpayers, 1701-1786.* Baltimore, Md.: Genealogical Publishing Company, Inc. 1984. (FHL# 975.6/R4r)

Vital Records

The Family History Library has marriage records for most of North Carolina's counties from the eighteenth century with some registers available into the 1960s and 1970s. Birth and death indexes are also available for many counties. Some of the records themselves have also been filmed. The indexes extend well into the twentieth century. Check the FHLC under **/[County]/Vital Records.**

In addition to these county records, the Family History Library also has:

North Carolina Division of Archives and History. *An Index to Marriage Bonds Filed in the North Carolina State Archives.* 88 microfiche. Raleigh: North Carolina Department of Cultural Resources, 1977. (FHL# microfiche 6330241-6330328 or 6330553-6330640)

Covers from the eighteenth century (beginning dates vary according to county) to about 1868. The Family History Library does not have microfilms of the bonds but has typescript volumes for each county summarizing the information in each bond.

Voting Registers

This heading is somewhat misleading. The voting records available for North Carolina counties at the Family History Library are statistical only and do not include names of voters.

SOUTH CAROLINA

Historical Background

1520	Spaniards from Cuba explore the Carolina coast.
1562	French Huguenots unsuccessfully attempt to establish a colony near present Port Royal.
1629	Charles I grants land between the 31st and 36th parallels to Sir Robert Heath.
1663-65	Charles II makes a second grant to the Earl of Clarendon and Associates; limits of colony extended to 29 south and 36'30" north. Proprietary government established.
1664	Colonists from the Barbadoes briefly settle at Cape Fear.
1670	First permanent English settlement at Albemarle Point.
1680	First settlement on the site of Charleston.
1682	Original three counties created: Berkeley, Craven, and Colleton. Granville County created 1683. These early counties had few formal functions and were used primarily for determining land-grant locations.
1691	One governor established over both North and South Carolina.
1706	Church of England becomes the established religion in the colony.
1712	Separate governors established in North and South Carolina.
1719	Revolution against the Proprietors.
1729	Proprietary government abolished, South Carolina becomes a royal province, separate from North Carolina.
1739	Uprising by African slaves.
1760-61	Cherokees defeated, opening much of the Up Country for settlement.
1775-83	American Revolution; strong Loyalist sentiment in South Carolina. British forces occupy much of the colony until 1781.
1788	South Carolina becomes eighth state to ratify the Constitution.
1790	State capital moved from Charleston to Columbia, the result of struggle between the Up Country and Low Country.
1832	Nullification Convention meets at Charleston; South Carolina is recognized leader of state's rights movement in the South.
1860	South Carolina secedes from the Union.
1861	South Carolina joins the Confederacy.
1861-65	Civil War. As General William Tecumseh Sherman marches through South Carolina, his army burns many county courthouses.
1865-76	Reconstruction period.
1868	South Carolina readmitted to the Union.

Settlement and Migration

Patterns of settlement in South Carolina can be divided into two types. The coastal areas (the Low Country) were primarily settled by Englishmen from Great Britain and the Barbadoes. Following these early settlements, groups of French Huguenots, Dutch, Germans, Swiss, Irish, and Scots made settlements in the coastal area and began to advance into the central part of the state.

Settlement of the Up Country, however, was hindered by Indian attacks until the defeat of the Cherokees in 1761. Then settlers from North Carolina, Virginia, Maryland, Delaware, Pennsylvania, and even New Jersey arrived, many following the Great Wagon Road from Philadelphia through the Valley of Virginia into the Carolinas. These settlers were largely English, German and Scots-Irish. Low Country South Carolinians also moved into the Up Country. African slaves were largely settled in those parts of the state dependent on the plantation economy.

Reference works on many of these early groups can be found in the FHLC under the heading **South Carolina/Minorities**. Some representative works concerning settlement are:

Baldwin, Agnes Leland. *First Settlers of South Carolina 1670-1680.* Columbia: University of South Carolina Press, 1969. (FHL# 975.7/W7b)

"Liste des Francais et Suisses": from an Old Manuscript List of French and Swiss Protestants Settled in Charleston on the Santee and at the Orange Quarter in Carolina Who Desired Naturalization Prepared Probably about 1695-6. 2d ed. 1888; rpt. ed., Baltimore, Md.: Genealogical Publishing Company, 1968. (FHL# 975.7/W2rl or microfilm 1035525)

Revill, Janie. *A Compilation of the Original Lists of Protestant Immigrants to South Carolina 1763-1773.* 1939; rpt. ed., Baltimore: Genealogical Publishing Company, 1968. (FHL# 975.7/W2r or microfilm 0022819).

Stephenson, Jean. *Scotch-Irish Migration to South Carolina, 1772 (Rev. William Martin and His Five Shiploads of Settlers).* Strasburg, Va.: Shenandoah Publishing House, Inc., 1971. (FHL# 975.7/W2s)

Warren, Mary Bondurant. *Citizens and Immigrants: South Carolina, 1768.* Danielsville, Ga.: Heritage Papers, 1980. (FHL# 975.7/D2wm)

Any South Carolina researcher needs to know the various jurisdictions under which records were created in the state's early history. Knowing these jurisdictions is equally important in using the FHLC, which is organized according to *current* county jurisdictions. A detailed and thorough examination of these jurisdictions is:

Schweitzer, George K. *South Carolina Genealogical Research.* Knoxville, Tenn.: G. K. Schweitzer, 1985. (FHL# 975.7/-D27s)

Contains three pages of charts giving the descent of the modern counties from the old districts.

Here is a summary of jurisdictions. Berkeley, Craven, Colleton, and Granville counties were created 1682-83. These counties served only as reference points for locating land grants, since all land and probate records were recorded at Charleston until 1769.

Church of England parishes created in 1706 began keeping records of baptisms, marriages, and burials. Some of these records and the parish vestry survive, and many have been published. Determine where the parish church is today, then look under **/[County]/Church Records.**

In 1769, seven judicial districts were created throughout the state to relieve the inconvenience of registering all land and probate matters at Charleston. In 1785, the number of judicial districts was increased to nine. These nine districts were subdivided into thirty-seven counties the same year. In 1799-1800, these districts and counties were abolished and replaced by twenty-four new districts, which had functions similar to those of counties in other states. In 1868, the name was changed from districts to counties.

All of these jurisdictions created records; sometimes deeds and wills could be recorded on more than one level. As Schweitzer points out, tracking a particular piece of land from the present to the original grant requires consulting the record of every jurisdiction in which that land was located. The same principle applies to locating records in the FHLC. It is necessary to check every jurisdiction under which older records could be located. There is no hard and fast rule where records from abolished districts might be listed. The records could be listed under the state, under the county of the same name which descends from the original district, (Charleston, for instance), or under the county which currently possesses the old district records. Records for Ninety-six District are listed under Abbeville County, for instance.

It should be noted that records have not survived from all districts. Some old districts did not keep records after 1785, leaving that responsibility to the county. Schweitzer's chart is very useful in determining the record situation for any given county or district. If records cannot be found in the FHLC, either they were not filmed by the Family History Library or they do not exist.

South Carolina Library Collection

Archives and Libraries

The Family History Library has a few WPA inventories of records on the county level in South Carolina. Check the FHLC under **/[County]/Archives and Libraries** to locate these works.

Other references, which provide valuable information on what is available in both South Carolina and on microfilm in Salt Lake City, are:

Cote, Richard N. *Local and Family History in South Carolina: A Bibliography.* Easley, S.C.: Southern Historical Press, 1981. (FHL# 975.7/H23)

Valuable for locating family histories in the FHLC, particularly those dealing with a common surname. By knowing which family histories deal with South Carolina families, you can avoid checking all histories of that name. Cote's work also lists all of the surnames included in the Andrea collection. (See *Genealogy* below.)

Moore, John Hammond. *Research Materials in South Carolina: A Guide.* Columbia: University of South Carolina Press, 1967. (FHL# 975.7/A5m)

Includes county records being microfilmed by the

South Carolina Archives. As this work is ongoing, the 1967 edition is somewhat outdated.

Stokes, Allen H., Jr. *A Guide to the Manuscript Collection of the South Caroliniana Library.* Columbia: University of South Carolina Press, 1982. (FHL# 975.7/A3s)

Schweitzer, George K. *South Carolina Genealogical Research.* Knoxville, Tenn.: G. K. Schweitzer, 1985. (FHL# 975.7/-D27s)

Also includes archival and bibliographic information.

Biography

Unlike many northern, midwestern, and western states, South Carolina has few late nineteenth-century biographical compendiums on the county level. Most biographical works are on the state level and are concerned mainly with "eminent" and "leading" citizens. Look under both state and county headings **/Biography** to see what is available.

Census Records

The Family History Library has all of the extant federal census records for South Carolina up to 1910 and state copies of the federal agricultural, industrial, social statistical, and mortality census schedules for 1850 to 1880, but, at this writing, no state censuses. Look under **South Carolina/[County]/Census/[Year]** to see what is available. The FHLC call numbers for the federal censuses are 1294270 through 1294289; the mortality schedules appear on the last three reels. Look for county indexes for various federal censuses under **/[County]/Census.** See the accompanying chart to see which counties have indexes.

Church Records

The Church of England was the established church in colonial South Carolina, but that did not stop Presbyterians, Baptists, Quakers, Jews, and other religious minorities from settling there before 1775. Roman Catholics did not come in large numbers until after 1800. Church records can be located either under **South Carolina/Church Records/[Denomination]** or under **South Carolina/[Town]/Church Records.**

For histories of major denominations, check the FHLC under **South Carolina/Church History.** Since South Carolina Quakers were under the jurisdiction of North Carolina Yearly Meeting, look for information about them under **North Carolina/Church Records.**

Court Records

Like most Southern states, court records are a valuable resource in South Carolina. The Family History Library has a few county court records. See **/[County]/Court Records.** Equity and chancery court records are very important in South Carolina because they deal with disputes over estates. The FHLC often repeats entries for court records under the heading **/[County]/Probate Records,** and vice-versa. Be certain to check both headings for the county of interest.

Directories

City directories are available for Charleston, Columbia, and Spartanburg. Check the FHLC under **/[County]/[City]/Directories.** The directories for Charleston are available from the 1830s onwards and also through the Research Publications directory collection from 1866 to 1901 (FHL# microfilm 1376645-1376657). See *Directories* in the introduction to this chapter.

Genealogy

See *Genealogy* in the introduction to this chapter. Here are representative published works in South Carolina genealogy:

South Carolina Historical Society. *South Carolina Genealogies: Articles from The South Carolina Historical (and Genealogical) Magazine.* 5 vols. Spartanburg, S.C.: Reprint Company, Publishers, 1983. (FHL# 975.7/O2s)

Wooley, James E., ed. *A Collection of Upper South Carolina Genealogical and Family Records.* 3 vols. Easley, S.C.: Southern Historical Press, 1979. (FHL# 975.7/D2c)

Andrea, Leonardo. *Collection of Family Files.* Typescript. 51 reels. Salt Lake City: Genealogical Society of Utah, 1974. Indexed. Consult the FHLC under **South Carolina/Genealogy** for call numbers.

_____, Genealogical Data Folders. 21 reels. Salt Lake City: Genealogical Society of Utah, 1974. (FHL# 0954255-0947477)

Alphabetically arranged, some by first letter or surname only; includes index at front of A's; contains correspondence and miscellaneous genealogical data.

History

For histories of particular counties, check the FHLC under **/[County]/History.** For histories dealing with the whole state, see **South Carolina/History.** Several books deal with various aspects and periods of the state's history. A good general history is:

Snowden, Yates, ed. *History of South Carolina.* 5 vols. Chicago: Lewis Publishing Co., 1920. (FHL# 975.7 H2s)

Immigration

(See *Immigration* in Introduction.)

Land and Property

Records under this heading usually deal with land grants, surveys, deeds, and mortgages. Because of South Carolina's complicated jurisdictional history, locating land and property records can sometimes be difficult. Useful aids to research in this area are:

Jackson, Ronald Vern, ed., et al. *Index to South Carolina Land Grants 1784-1800.* Bountiful, Utah: Accelerated Indexing Systems, Inc., 1977. (FHL# 975.7/R22j)

Langley, Clara A. *South Carolina Deed Abstracts 1719-1772.* Easley, S.C.: Southern Historical Press, Inc., 1983. (FHL# 975.7/R21)

Lucas, Silas Emmett, Jr. *An Index to Deeds of the Province and State of South Carolina 1719-1785 and Charleston District 1785-1800.* Easley, S.C.: Southern Historical Press, 1977. (FHL# 975.7/R2c)

Salley, A.S., Jr., and R. N. Olsberg, eds. *Warrants for Land in South Carolina 1672-1711.* rev. ed., Columbia: University of South Carolina Press, 1973. (FHL# 975.7/R2s)

Although these works are a good introduction to colonial South Carolina land records, the systems of obtaining grants during the proprietary and royal periods were complicated. You should also check court records and records of the Commons House of Assembly, both listed in the FHLC under **South Carolina/Public Records**. The Family History Library has many of the original land records from the colonial period on microfilm, including:

South Carolina Memorials; Registration of Land Grants, 1704-1775 and Index. 9 reels. Salt Lake City: Genealogical Society of Utah, 1950. (FHL# microfilm 0023297-0023305)

South Carolina. Secretary of State. *Royal Land Grants, 1731-1775; Index 1695-1775.* 17 reels. Salt Lake City: Genealogical Society of Utah, 1951. (FHL# microfilm 0022581-0022597)

The judicial districts established in 1769 (see discussion in Settlement and Migration) allowed for local recording of deeds and probates records, but duplicates were still sent to Charleston until 1785. If you are looking for land records between 1769 and 1785, check both jurisdictions.

After 1785, deeds were recorded on the district and county level. The Family History Library has a fairly complete set of deeds from South Carolina counties where they have survived. Note that the deeds listed under **/Charleston County/Land and Property** prior to 1785 include deeds from throughout the state.

Maps, Gazetteers, Atlases

The Family History Library has a number of maps of South Carolina from the colonial period to the present, including some locally published county maps. The State Highway Department maps are by far the most useful. Although they are quite recent, they give the names of watercourses, often essential in locating land grants. Although they are county maps, they are published by the state and are cataloged under **South Carolina/Maps.**

Mills' Atlas of the State of South Carolina 1825. 1825; rpt. ed., Easley, S.C.: Southern Historical Press, 1980. (FHL# 975.7/E7m)

Includes contemporary indexes to watercourses and the names of property owners listed on the individual district maps.

Military Records

Many published works exist for South Carolina soldiers who served in various colonial wars and in the American Revolution. See the FHLC under South Carolina/Military. Some of them are not well indexed and are difficult to use. The more representative and comprehensive printed sources for South Carolina soldiers are:

Ervin, Sarah Sullivan. *South Carolinians in the Revolution: With Service Records and Miscellaneous Data, also Abstracts of Wills, Laurens County (Ninety-Six District) 1775-1855.* 1949; rpt. ed., Baltimore, Md.: Genealogical Publishing Co., 1965. (FHL# 975.7/M2)

Moss, Bobby Gilmer. *Roster of South Carolina Patriots in the American Revolution.* Baltimore, Md.: Genealogical Publishing Company, 1983. (FHL# 975.7/M2m)

South Carolina Historical Commission. *Stub Entries to Indents Issued in Payment of Claims Against South Carolina Growing out of the Revolution*. 11 vols. Columbia, S.C.: Historical Commission, 1910-56. (FHL# 975.7/M2h or microfilm 0824066-0824068 or 6046914)

The Family History Library has several indexes to records of South Carolina soldiers from later wars. These indexes are:

United States Adjutant General's Office. *Index to Compiled Service Records of Volunteer Soldiers Who Served During the War of 1812 in Organizations from the State of South Carolina.* 7 reels. Washington, D.C.: National Archives, 1966. (FHL# microfilm 0882812-0882818)

______ *Index to Compiled Service Records of Confederate Soldiers Who Served in Organizations from the State of South Carolina (1861-1865).* 35 reels. Washington, D.C.: National Archives, 1962. (FHL# microfilm 0881967-0882001)

Every Confederate state has an index to its men who served in the Union Army except South Carolina. A good printed work covering Confederate soldiers from South Carolina is:

Salley, A. S. *South Carolina Troops in Confederate Service*. 3 vols. Columbia, S.C.: The State Company, 1913-30. (FHL# microfilm 0982339)

Contains abstracts of the detailed information often found in service records.

For information on how to access the original records of South Carolina soldiers in the service of the United States from the American Revolution to the Spanish-American War, see *Military Records* in the introduction to this chapter.

For discharge records of soldiers recorded at the county level from 1898 onwards, check the FHLC under **/[County]/Military Records.** These discharge records vary in coverage but can include information on local soldiers from the Spanish-American War, World Wars I and II, and the Korean Conflict.

Minorities

Both original records and printed works are available on such "minorities" in South Carolina as Huguenots, Scots, Jews, blacks, Quakers, and Germans. Check under both state and county headings for church records, immigration records, and records of close-knit ethnic settlements.

Naturalization and Citizenship

A few county records of naturalization in South Carolina are available at the Family History Library for various time periods. The records of U.S. District Court of South Carolina are available from 1790 to 1906 (FHL# microfilm 0929094). See also:

Holcomb, Brent H., comp. *South Carolina Naturalizations 1783-1850.* Baltimore, Md.: Genealogical Publishing Co., 1985. (FHL# 975.7/P4h)

Newspapers and Obituaries

The Family History Library has a few original newspapers on film for Charleston and for some smaller cities and towns. The most genealogically useful records in this category are the abstracts of records of marriage and death from South Carolina newspapers. Some representative titles are:

Holcomb, Brent H., comp. *Marriage and Death Notices from Baptist Newspapers of South Carolina, 1835-1865.* Spartanburg, S.C.: Reprint Company, 1981. (FHL# 975.7/-V2hbm)

______. *Marriage and Death Notices from the Up-Country of South Carolina: As Taken from Greenville Newspapers, 1826-1863.* Columbia, S.C.: B. H. Holcomb, 1983. (FHL# 975.7/V2hbh)

Wilson, Teresa E., and Janice L. Grimes, comps. *Marriage and Death Notices from the Southern Patriot, 1815-1830.* Easley, S.C.: Southern Historical Press, 1982. (FHL# 975.7915/V2w)

The Family History Library has many more similar works on the state and regional level, many of them compiled by Brent Holcomb.

Periodicals

The library has these genealogical and historical periodicals dealing with South Carolina:

The Carolina Genealogist, edited by Mary Bondurant Warren. Danielsville, Ga.: Heritage Papers, 1969-to date. (FHL# 975/B2cg)

South Carolina Genealogical Register. [n.p.]: N. M. Goggans, 1963-to date. (FHL# 975.7/B2cg)

The South Carolina Historical and Genealogical Magazine. Charleston: South Carolina Historical Society, 1900-52. (FHL# 975.7/B2s)

The South Carolina Historical Magazine. Charleston: South Carolina History Society, 1953-to date. (FHL# 975.7 B2s).

The South Carolina Magazine of Ancestral Research. Kingstree, S.C.: Laurence K. Wells, 1973-to date. (FHL# 975.7/-B2sc)

Probate Records

Prior to 1769, all estates were probated in Charleston. The following source is therefore valuable for the entire state:

Charleston Free Library. *Index to Wills of Charleston County, South Carolina 1671-1868.* Baltimore, Md.: Genealogical Publishing Co., Inc., 1974. (FHL# 975.791/S21)

The following published abstracts of probate records cover different portions of the colonial period:

Gregorie, Anne King, ed. *Records of the Court of Chancery of South Carolina 1671-1779.* Washington, D.C.: American Historical Association, 1950. (FHL# 975.7/P2sc or microfilm 6051256)

Holcomb, Brent H. *Probate Records of South Carolina.* Easley, S.C.: Southern Historical Press, 1977. (FHL# 975.7/P2p)

Moore, Caroline T. *Abstracts of the Wills of the State of South Carolina (1670-1784).* Columbia, S.C.: R. L. Bryan Co., 1960-69. (FHL# 975.7/P2m or microfilm 1035622)

______. *Records of the Secretary of the Province of South Carolina, 1692-1721.* Columbia, S.C.: R. L. Bryan Company, 1978. (FHL# 975.7/P28m)

After 1785, the districts and counties became responsible for probating estates. This index will help you to determine if a will exists up to the 1850s:

Houston, Martha Lou. *Indexes to the County Wills of South Carolina.* 1939; rpt. ed., Baltimore, Md.: Genealogical Publishing Company, 1964. (FHL# 975.7/S2wp)

Because of the complexity of South Carolina's early jurisdictions, it is wise to check all possible district and county courts for probate matters. Although wills from the districts were supposed to be sent to Charleston until 1785, each district has some loose wills which were never recorded and sent.

Public Records

A variety of so-called public records exists for South Carolina on both the state and the county level. You will have to check a number of different headings to locate all of these records. (See *Public Records* in the introduction to this chapter.) These records are valuable for colonial research:

The Journal of the Commons House of Assembly. 12 vols. Columbia: Historical Commission of South Carolina, 1951. (FHL# 975.7/N2a or microfilm 6051246)

Records in the British Public Record Office Relating to South Carolina, 1663-1710. 5 vols. Atlanta, Ga.: Foote and Davis Co., 1928-47. (FHL# 975.7/N2h or microfilm 0944131)

Records in the British Public Records Office Relating to South Carolina, 1663-1782. 24 reels. Columbia: South Carolina Department of Archives and History [c.1970s]. (FHL# microfilm 1294103-1294114)

Hendrix, GeLee Corely, and Morn McKoy Lindsay, comps. *The Jury Lists of South Carolina 1778-1779.* Greenville, S.C.: privately printed, 1975. (FHL# 975.7/P2h)

Extremely useful as a substitute census record.

Slavery and Bondage

Like records relating to minorities, records relating to slavery are often listed under other headings. A particularly useful source for tracing slave ancestry in South Carolina is:

Bill of Sales [sic] of Negro Slaves in the Charleston District of South Carolina, 1799-1872. 13 reels. Salt Lake City: Genealogical Society of Utah, 1951. (FHL# microfilm 0023438-0023451)

Taxation and Voting Registers

The Family History Library has tax lists and voting registers for a few South Carolina counties. Check the FHLC under **/[County]/Taxation** and **/[County]/Voting Registers.**

Vital Records

Registration of vital statistics began in 1911 for marriages and 1915 for births and deaths for South Carolina. Charleston and a few other cities began their own registration earlier.

The Family History Library has post-1911 marriage records for a few counties, most of the pre-1911 city vital statistics, and some published records for the early colonial period; but most vital records in the collection are abstracts of newspaper marriages and deaths from the nineteenth century.

All of these records can be found under **South Carolina/Vital Records**, under **/[County]/Vital Records**, or under **/[County]/[City]/Vital Records.**

The Family History Library also has this state marriage record:

South Carolina Marriage Settlements, 1785-1889. 9 reels. Salt Lake City: Genealogical Society of Utah, 1950. (FHL# microfilm 0022512-0022520)

GEORGIA

Historical Background

1732	James Oglethorpe granted a charter to establish Georgia as a refuge for Protestants.
1733	Savannah founded as first English settlement.
1733-63	Constant conflicts with Spanish in Florida; War of Jenkin's Ear marks cooperative/military effort by Georgia, the Carolinas, and Virginia in the invasion of Florida (1739-42).
1733-52	Early settlers included not only Englishmen but Salzburgers, Piedmontese, Scots-Highlanders, Swiss and Portuguese Jews.
1749	First importation of African slaves.
1753	Georgia becomes a royal province.
1775-83	American Revolution; Georgia almost equally divided in sentiment between patriots and loyalists.
1788	Georgia is fourth state to ratify the Constitution.
1802	Georgia cedes its claim to western territories (now part of Mississippi and Alabama) to the United States.
1805-32	Creek and Cherokee Indians cede their lands to Georgia; state land lotteries held to distribute evenly the new land (1805, 1806, 1820, 1821, 1827, 1832).
1813-14	Creek Indian War; Creek Indian Confederacy severely defeated, loses most of its land, and is moved West.
1828-32	Dispute over jurisdiction of Cherokee lands in northwest Georgia eventually leads to the removal of the Cherokees to Oklahoma (Indian Territory).
1861	Georgia secedes from the Union and joins the Confederacy.
1861-65	Civil War; General William Tecumseh Sherman's army burns many county courthouses during its march to the sea.
1866-72	Reconstruction period.
1870	Georgia readmitted to the Union.

Settlement and Migration

Before 1860, Georgia's settlement can be divided into three basic periods. In the first period, from 1733 to 1753, settlement was confined to the coastal areas and along the Savannah River. Georgia was founded as a haven for Protestant refugees from Europe and for imprisoned debtors from England. The first settlers were, therefore, of varied background and included Englishmen, Salzburgers, Piedmontese, Scots-Highlanders, Swiss, and Portuguese Jews.

When Georgia became a royal province in 1753, settlement from Virginia and the Carolinas increased. In the second period from 1753 to 1805, settlement was confined to the area between the Savannah River on the east and the Altamaha and Oconee Rivers on the west. Settlement from the colonies to the north was steady, including a settlement of New Englanders at Midway in 1752; settlers from Europe and Britain also continued to arrive. The powerful Creek and Cherokee Indian nations prevented settlement further west than the Altamaha and Oconee rivers. During this time, the state encouraged settlement by offering headright land grants: each new male settler could obtain a certain number of acres depending on the size of his family, including slaves. See *Land and Property Records* below.

During the third settlement period, Georgia gradually acquired all of the land now contained within its borders through a series of land cessions and annexations commencing in late eighteenth century. This land was given away in state-sponsored land lotteries, the first of which was held in 1805. This method of land distribution attracted many settlers, many of whom obtained lottery land in several different counties, then sold it, and moved on, a process that facilitated settling the western part of the state. The last land lotteries were held in 1832. Up to the time of the Civil War, settlers from the Carolinas and Virginia funneled through Georgia on their way west.

Since the settlement of Georgia was intricately tied up with its land distribution policy, the sources mentioned in Land and Property Records represent much of the information available on early settlers. Other sources include:

Bryan, Mary G. *Passports Issued by the Governors of Georgia, 1785-1820.* Washington, D.C.: National Genealogical Society, 1962-64. (FHL# 975.8/P4b or microfilm 1033943)

Coulter, E. Merton, and Albert B. Saye, eds. *A List of the Early Settlers of Georgia.* Athens: University of Georgia Press, 1949. (FHL# 975.8/W2L or microfilm 0007092)

Jones, George Fenwick, ed. *Henry Newman's Salzburger Letterbooks.* Athens: University of Georgia Press, 1966. (FHL# 975.8/W2j)

Stewart, William C. *Gone to Georgia: Jackson and Gwinnett Counties and Their Neighbors in the Western Migration.* Washington, D.C.: National Genealogical Society, 1965. (FHL# 975.811/W2s)

Many of the land lottery records give a "militia district" as the residence of a winner. For more information, see:

Hitz, Alex M. *Georgia Militia Districts*. N.p.: Georgia Bar Assocation, n.d.. (published in *Georgia Bar Journal*, Feb. 1956). (FHL# 975.8M2h or microfilm 0874300, item 6)

Georgia Library Collection

"Georgia's records are enormous in volume and complex in nature. Time, geography, politics, and patriotism have all contributed in various ways to the creation and preservation of these documents. So much has survived, and so much that has survived is so out of the ordinary and confusing to the average person that many researchers suffer from 'Georgia Shock'–a feeling of being overwhelmed when trying to grasp the basics of research in Georgia."

So wrote Robert S. Davis, Jr., in his excellent guide *Research in Georgia*, p.ix, (see reference under Archives and Libraries), which is primarily concerned with the records available at the Georgia Department of Archives and History in Atlanta. Because the Family History Library has acquired much of its Georgia collection from the Georgia Archives, Davis's "warning" about Georgia records is equally applicable to the collection in Salt Lake City. Because space is limited here, some of the references below will simply refer the researcher to the FHLC. This does not mean that the records so treated are less valuable than others.

Archives and Libraries

The definitive guide to the Georgia Archives is:

Davis, Robert S., Jr. *Research in Georgia: With Special Emphasis on the Georgia Department of Archives and History.* Easley, S.C.: Southern Historical Press, 1981. (FHL# 975.8/D27d)

Since the Family History Library's collection of original county records primarily consists of microfilmed records from the Georgia Archives, Davis's county-by-county breakdown of what is available is extremely valuable in determining what can be obtained in Salt Lake City. *Research in Georgia* enhances the charts accompanying this section by giving detailed dates of availability for the different records in each county.

Bible Records, Cemeteries, and Genealogy

These records are listed together because so many of them are DAR compilations, originals in the Georgia Archives. The main problem with using these records is that the FHLC often does not specify which records are available on each film. A helpful guide to the collections is:

Historical Collections of the Georgia Chapters of the Daughters of the American Revolution. 5 vols. Atlanta: [publisher varies], 1926-49. (FHL# 975.8/A5d or microfilm 8485946)

Most of these records are cataloged under **Georgia/Bible Records**, **/Cemeteries**, and **/Genealogy**. Also check **Georgia/[County]/Cemeteries.**

A number of individuals and other organizations, including the LDS Church, have also compiled Georgia Bible and cemetery records. Two works in this general area are representative of published sources:

Austin, Jeanette H. *Georgia Bible Records.* Baltimore, Md.: Genealogical Publishing Co., 1985. (FHL# 975.8/D2a)

Dorsey, James Edwards, comp. *Georgia Genealogy and Local History: A Bibliography*. Spartanburg, S.C.: Reprint Co., 1985. (FHL# 975.8/D23d)

Use with the FHLC to see what works on Georgia genealogy are available.

Biography

Biographical material is available for a few counties, but most compiled works are at the state level and deal with "leading" and "eminent men." Check the FHLC under **Georgia/Biography** or **/County]/Biography.**

Georgia Department of Archives and History. *Biographical Questionnaires in the Georgia Department of Archives and History.* 15 reels. Salt Lake City: Genealogical Society of Utah, 1962. (FHL# microfilm 0288169-0288183)

Alphabetically arranged biographies of those who served in Georgia public offices and also fought in the Civil War.

Census Records

The Family History Library has all extant federal census records for Georgia from 1820 to 1910, all of the mortality schedules from 1850 to 1880, and this state census material:

Georgia. *State Census Records, 1838-1879.* 2 reels. Salt Lake City: Genealogical Society of Utah, 1957, 1961. (FHL# microfilm 0007010 and 0234619) Partially alphabetical by surname.

Townsend, Brigid S. *Indexes to Seven State Census Reports for Counties in Georgia, 1838-1845.* Atlanta: R. J. Taylor, Jr., Foundation, 1975. (FHL# 975.8/X2pt)

De La Mar, Marie, and Elizabeth Rothstein, comps. *The Reconstructed 1790 Census of Georgia: Substitutes for Georgia's Lost 1790 Census.* 1976; rpt. ed., Baltimore, Md.: Genealogical Publishing Co., Inc., 1985. (FHL# 975.8/X21)

Pre-1820 census materials.

Warren, Mary Bondurant, comp. *1800 Census of Oglethorpe County, Georgia: The Only Extant Census of 1800 within the State of Georgia.* Athens, Ga.: M. B. Warren, 1965. (FHL# 975.8175/X2p/1800)

Church Records

A variety of religious denominations has been represented in Georgia since its founding. The predominant sects in Georgia at one time or another were the Anglicans, Baptists, Presbyterians, and Methodists. The Family History Library has a wide variety of church records for Georgia, both original and transcribed. Check the FHLC under **/[County]/Church Records** to see what is available.

Court Records

Georgia's judicial system had two basic courts at the county level: the Court of the Ordinary and the Superior Court. The Family History Library has most of the records of both of these courts from the 1780s to the late nineteenth century. Some of the functions of the Court of the Ordinary will be found under **/[County]/Probate Records, /Medical Records, /Vital Records, /Schools, /Occupations, /Slavery and Bondage**, and **/Voting Registers.**

See *Research in Georgia* for a breakdown of court records by county and compare to the FHLC to see which records are available at the Family History Library.

Directories

The Family History Library has major directory collections for Savannah and Atlanta, with some directories extending well into the twentieth century. Check the FHLC under **Georgia/[County]/[City]/Directories.** Also check the Research Publications guide for Savannah, Atlanta, and Columbus.

History

A variety of state and county histories are available at the Family History Library. Consult the FHLC for the time period and place of interest.

Land and Property Records

This is perhaps the most important group of records in the Georgia collection at the Family History Library. Space does not permit giving full FHLC references for all of the original records available. Only certain major record groups and printed copies will be highlighted here. Check the FHLC for miscellaneous land records which may be helpful.

Prior to 1777 all land records were recorded at Savannah. For the original records listed below, mortgages and deeds were filmed together. Check the FHLC for the film numbers for the years of interest:

Colonial Records of Georgia, Books of Conveyances, 1750 to 1802. 8 reels. Salt Lake City: Genealogical Society of Utah, 1957. (FHL# microfilm 0158966)

Colonial Records of Georgia, Books of Mortgages, 1755-1822. 4 reels. Salt Lake City: Genealogical Society of Utah, 1957. (FHL# microfilm 0158968)

Beginning in 1756, free male settlers arriving in Georgia were granted land under the headright system, usually 200 acres for the head of the household and fifty acres for each member of his family, including slaves. The Family History Library has microfilms of the original grants and the surveys made on the grants. These records also include bounty land grants for military service:

Georgia Surveyor General. *Headrights and Land Grants of Georgia, 1756-1939.* 61 reels. Atlanta: Georgia Department of State Microfilm Division, 1953-54. (FHL# microfilm 0465071-0465130, 0511955).

In addition to a self-index, a separate index showing counties of locations and acreage is:

Index to the Headright and Bounty Grants of Georgia, 1756-1909. Vidalia, Ga.: Georgia Genealogical Reprints, 1970. (FHL# 975.8/R2i).

Georgia Surveyor General. *Surveyor-General's Records, Headright Surveys.* 19 reels. Atlanta: Georgia Department of State, Microfilm Division, n.d. Index. (FHL# microfilm 464998-465016)

The Family History Library has typescript indexes to the land lotteries of 1805, 1807, 1820, 1821, 1827 and 1832. They are alphabetical by first letter of the surname. If you know only the land lottery district and lot number, it is hard to find the county in which an ancestor lived at the time of the lottery. The Southern Historical Press has reprinted many of these indexes, but unfortunately, the Family History Library does not have all of these reprints (more legible than photoreproductions of typescripts) at this writing. Other indexes currently available are:

Houston, Martha Lou. *Reprint of Official Register of Land Lottery of Georgia, 1827.* 1929, rpt. ed., Baltimore, Md.: Genealogical Publishing Company, 1967. (FHL# 975.8/R2h or microfilm 0159022, 6019971, or 6046976)

Lucas, Silas E. *The 1832 Gold Lottery of Georgia: Containing a List of the Fortunate Drawers in Said Lottery.* Easley, S.C.: Southern Historical Press, 1976. (FHL# 975.8/-R2L)

Wood, Ralph V., and Virginia S. Wood. *The 1805 Land Lottery of Georgia.* Cambridge, Mass.: Greenwood Press, 1964. (FHL# 975.8/R21w)

Extremely valuable as a substitute census because the names of all individuals who drew in the lottery are listed whether they won land or not, and the law required them to have resided in Georgia before 11 May 1802. See *Research in Georgia* for a good discussion of the qualifications for each lottery. Certain family information can be determined by a knowledge of the qualifications.

The grants made, based on land lottery wins, are available. If you can determine the county, district, and lot number from one of the indexes, you may consult the following records to learn exactly where the land was located:

Georgia Surveyor General. *Land Lottery Surveys.* 24 reels. Atlanta: Georgia Department of Archives and History, 1967. (FHL# microfilm 0465017-0465040)

See **Georgia/Land and Property** for other land lottery records. The loose land lottery papers associated with particular counties, districts, and grants have not been microfilmed. Some of these records have been published:

Davis, Robert S., Jr., and Silas E. Lucas, comps. *The Georgia Land Lottery Papers, 1805-1914: Genealogical Data from the Loose Papers Filed in the Georgia Surveyor General Office Concerning the Lots Won in the State Land Lotteries and the People Who Won Them.* Easley, S.C.: Southern Historical Press, 1979. (FHL# 975.8/R2d)

In using the land lottery records, be aware that the counties designated in the lotteries were subdivided into several counties soon after each lottery. Lottery land owned in 1850 may be in a county which did not exist at the time the lottery was held, but the records will still refer to that yet-uncreated county. (See *Maps* below for a helpful guide to this problem.)

Another problem is that the intricate system of numbering lots may seem very exact, but a man could still sell rights to a lot without recording it in the county deed books, or the lot might never be claimed and would revert to the state. Becoming familiar with the irregularities in the system will help to determine the history of a particular piece of land.

Maps

The most important map in the library's Georgia Collection is:

Hall's Original County Map of Georgia: Showing Present and Original Counties and Land Districts. Atlanta: Hall Bros., 1895. (FHL# Map Case 975.8/E7h)

Extremely useful in showing the current counties in which historic land lottery districts were located.

Hemperley, Marion R. *Map of Colonial Georgia, 1773-1777.* N.p.: n.d. 1979. (FHL# Map Case 975.8/E7h)

Shows parish boundaries before 1777. The parishes of colonial Georgia did not function as administrative units, but land grant and tax district references often mentioned the parish of residence.

See the FHLC under **Georgia/Maps** for other helpful maps.

Medical Records

Almost every county in Georgia has a register of physicians, dentists, and/or druggists. These records can be cataloged under **/[County]/Medical Records** or **/Occupations** or both. On the charts accompanying this chapter, Medical Records refers to lunacy records, available for many Georgia counties and often containing family information. The registers of physicians, etc., have been noted under Occupations, but you should check the FHLC under **/[County]/Medical Records** as well.

Military Records

The Family History Library has a large variety of military records relating to Georgia soldiers. Almost every county has Civil War militia records and late nineteenth- and twentieth-century discharge records. The library also has copies of State Militia military commissions, useful in determining the location of militia districts when only the captain's name is known.

The Family History Library also has a substantial number of printed works and microfilm indexes to military records. Those cited below are representative, not complete. Check the FHLC at both the state and county level for further military records:

Henderson, Lillian. *Roster of the Confederate Soldiers of Georgia, 1861-1865.* 6 vols. Atlanta: State Printing Office, 1959-64. (FHL# 975.8/M22h or microfilm 1033660-1033662)

Knight, Lucian Lamar. *Georgia's Roster of the Revolution, Containing a List of the State's Defenders; Officers and Men, Soldiers and Sailors.* 1920; microreproduction Salt Lake City: Genealogical Society of Utah, 1968. (FHL# microfilm 0547588)

United States Adjutant General's Office. *Index to Compiled Service Records of Confederate Soldiers Who Served in Organizations from the State of Georgia, 1861-1865.* 66 reels. Washington, D.C.: National Archives, 1955. (FHL# microfilm 0821700-0821766)

United States Adjutant General's Office. *Index to Compiled Service Records of Volunteer Soldiers Who Served During the Cherokee Disturbances and Removal in Organizations from the State of Georgia, 1836-1839.* Washington, D.C.: National Archives, n.d. (FHL# microfilm 1205402)

______. *Index to Compiled Service Records of Volunteer Union Soldiers Who Served In Organizations from the State of Georgia, 1861-1865.* Washington, D.C.: National Archives, 1962. (FHL# microfilm 0881394)

In addition to these records, the library also has the complete series of Confederate soldiers' and widows' pensions from Georgia. Check the FHLC under **Georgia/Military Records** to locate these records.

Minorities

Check the FHLC under **Georgia/Minorities** to see what (mostly published works) is available. Records of former slaves who wrote indentures to their ex-masters can be found under **Georgia/Occupations.**

Newspapers, Obituaries

The library has a number of published abstracts of marriages and deaths from Georgia newspapers. Located them in the FHLC under **/Newspapers** and **/Obituaries.**

Occupations

See *Medical Records* and *Minorities* above.

Periodicals

The Family History Library has current subscriptions and complete back issues to most major Georgia genealogical periodicals. Check the FHLC under /Genealogy/Periodicals and **/History/Periodicals.**

Probate Records

The Court of the Ordinary handled most probate matters on the county level in Georgia. In addition to wills, administrations, and inventories, you will find annual returns of administered estates, which often mention disbursements to widows and children. These records are available at the library for many Georgia counties.

The best published index to Georgia wills is:

Brooke, Ted O. *In the Name of God, Amen: Georgia Wills, 1733-1860, An Index of Testators to Wills of Georgia Recorded in Colonial Will Books and in Loose Will Collections, 1733-1777 and Wills Recorded or On File in County and State Offices, 1777-1860.* Atlanta: Pilgrim Press, 1976. (FHL# 975.8/S2b or microfilm 1036842)

Georgia colonial wills are cataloged in the FHLC under **Georgia/Probate Records.** The following work is useful in locating intestates but is inconsistent in coverage of time and place:

Austin, Jeanette H. *Georgia Intestate Records.* Baltimore, Md.: Genealogical Publishing Company, Inc., 1986. (FHL# 975.8/ P28a)

Public Records

Public records are available for a number of Georgia counties, but their type and coverage vary. Check the FHLC under **/[County]/Public Records** for the localities you are interested in. The *Colonial Records of Georgia* series is not cataloged as a unit, but as individual volumes, many of them under **Georgia/Public Records** by Allen D. Candler, a compiler.

Schools

Some school records exist for some Georgia counties, often containing the names of students and their parents or guardians. The records appear to relate to poor laws.

Slavery and Bondage

A few counties have registers of slaves brought into the county.

Taxation

Tax digests exist for many counties. These records are extremely valuable because they list all land owned by residents of the county, even if the land is in another county. Lottery land is identified by district and lot number. Other land is identified by watercourse and previous owner. The library has a few published early tax digests.

Vital Records

Marriage records are available from many Georgia counties. Check the FHLC for the time period available for each county. Birth and death records are generally not available. Several compilations of marriage records are available. These compilations are generally organized county by county, alphabetically by name of the groom, with no bride's index. Check the FHLC under **Georgia/Vital Records** to locate these sources.

Voting Registers

These records are available for a number of Georgia counties for the late nineteenth century.

FLORIDA

Historical Background

1513	Florida discovered by Juan Ponce de Leon and claimed for Spain.
1561-64	French Huguenots claim Florida for France.
1565	Spanish found St. Augustine and drive the French out of Florida.
1696	Pensacola founded by the Spanish to claim the west coast of Florida.
1660-1763	Constant friction with English settlements in the Carolinas and Georgia.
1763	Florida ceded to Great Britain at the end of the Seven Years' (French and Indian) War. Provinces of East and West Florida created.
1769	Greeks, Italians, and Minorcans settle New Smyrna.
1776-83	Florida remains loyal to Great Britain during the American Revolution; many Loyalists relocate from other colonies.

1781	Spain, allied with the United States, captures West Florida.
1783	Florida returned to Spain after the American Revolution.
1810	West Florida declares independence from Spain and petitions for admission to the United States.
1812	United States annexes West Florida.
1818	First Seminole War. Andrew Jackson occupies Pensacola.
1819	Spain formally cedes East and West Florida to the United States.
1822	Civil government established.
1832	Some Florida Indians agree to move west.
1836-42	Second Seminole War; Seminole Indians who resisted removal fight for six years before surrendering.
1845	Florida enters the Union as the twenty-seventh state.
1861-65	Civil War; Union forces occupy most of Florida's coastal towns.
1866-77	Reconstruction period.
1868	Florida readmitted to the Union.

Settlement and Migration

For the first 250 years of European occupation, Florida was sparsely settled. Major Spanish outposts existed at St. Augustine and Pensacola, but their major function was to hold the northern border of the Spanish colonial empire against incursions by the French in Louisiana and the British in the Carolinas. Settlement was confined to the coastal areas. Many black slaves escaping from the Carolinas and Georgia found refuge in Florida.

The British, ruling from 1763 to 1783, tried several settlement schemes which mostly failed. New Smyrna was settled by Italians, Greeks, and Minorcans under the auspices of an Englishman who theorized that they were suited to the climate. Unfortunately, most of these settlers had come from the highlands of their native countries, and many died of tropical diseases. Others moved to St. Augustine.

The British divided Florida into East and West provinces and surveyed a trail leading from Pensacola to St. Augustine. During the American Revolution, Florida remained loyal to England and became a haven for Loyalists. As a result of Spain's assistance to the American cause, Florida was returned to Spanish rule in 1783.

From 1783 to 1819 the major settlement occurring in Florida was by Americans in West Florida. These settlers chafed under Spanish Catholic rule and in 1810 declared their independence. They petitioned for admission to the United States and were annexed in 1812. In 1819, Spain formally ceded both East and West Florida to the United States, and settlement by Americans increased. An excellent source for the American territorial period is:

Carter, Clarence Edwin, ed. *The Territorial Papers of the United States, Volumes XXII-XXVI, The Territory of Florida, 1821-1845.* Washington, D.C.: U.S. Government Printing Office, 1956. (FHL# 973/N2udt)

Contains many lists of early settlers taken from petitions.

American Southerners in Florida introduced the plantation economy and black slaves. Descendants of Seminole Indians who refused to surrender after the Seminole War of 1836 to 1842 still live in the interior of Florida. Many other groups are now represented in Florida's population, including refugees from Cuba and from the cold winters of the northeast.

Florida Library Collection

Archives and Libraries

The Family History Library has a number of WPA inventories of federal records in Florida. Check the FHLC under **Florida/Archives and Libraries.** Two useful volumes are:

Florida State Archives, Public Records Unit. *Microfilmed Records of Florida Counties.* Tallahassee: The Archives, 1975-77. (FHL# 975.9/A3f)

Tampa Public Library Special Collections Department and Holdings of the Florida Genealogical Society: Tampa's Oldest School Building Collection, the University of South Florida Partial List, Church of the Latter Day Saints Partial List of the Tampa Branch. Typescript, n.d. (FHL# 975.9/-B4d/no.2)

Biography

The Family History Library has few biographical compendiums on the county level. A representative work on the state level is:

Biographical Souvenir of the States of Georgia and Florida: Containing Biographical Sketches of the Representative Public, and Many Early Settled Families in these States. Chicago: F. A. Battey and Co., 1889. (FHL# 975/D3bg)

The *Biographical Card Index* of the St. Augustine Historical Society, covering English and Spanish records, is available (FHL# microfilm 0967146-0967162 and 0967258)

For other biographies, consult the FHLC under **Florida/Biography** and **/[County]/Biography.**

Business Records and Commerce

When this heading is marked on the Florida chart for this chapter, it may indicate mortuary and funeral home records.

Cemeteries

Most individual cemeteries are listed under the county in which they are located. The Family History Library has statewide collections of cemetery inscriptions made by members of the LDS Church and typed by the library staff. Check the FHLC under **Florida/Cemeteries.**

Census Records

The Family History Library has all extant federal censuses from 1830 to 1910 and indexes to the mortality schedules for the 1850, 1860, 1870, and 1880 censuses.

Spanish censuses taken in 1783, 1786, 1793, and 1814 are contained in:

Shepard, Winifred. *Genealogical Papers.* Salt Lake City: Genealogical Society of Utah, 1977. (FHL# microfilm 1014120)

In addition, see the following censuses taken by the provincial or state governments:

Coker, William S., and G. Douglas Inglis. *The Spanish Censuses of Pensacola, 1784-1820: A Genealogical Guide to Spanish Pensacola.* Pensacola, Fla.: Perdido Bay Press, 1980. (FHL# 975.999/P1/X2c)

Florida, Secretary of State. *Schedules of the Florida State Census of 1885.* 13 reels. Washington, D.C.: National Archives, 1970. (FHL# microfilm 0888962-0888974)

Church Records

Church records can be found in the FHLC under the name of the county or city/town in which they are located. This source is helpful in locating church records:

Historical Records Survey, Division of Professional and Service Project, Works Projects Administration. *Inventory of the Church Archives of Florida.* Jacksonville, Fla.: Historical Records Survey, 1939. (FHL# 973/A5hi or microfilm 0982228)

The Family History Library also has the records of the Catholic cathedral in St. Augustine from 1594 to 1924. These records are particularly useful for research in the Spanish period of Florida. (FHL# microfilm 1015293-1015306)

Directories

Directories for several Florida cities are available at the Family History Library, chiefly from the first half of the twentieth century. Consult the FHLC under the appropriate county and city heading. There are no Florida directories in the Research Publication series available at the Family History Library.

Genealogy

See the FHLC under **Florida/Genealogy** for published works and compiled abstracts of genealogically valuable records. The library also has a Genealogical File Card Index to family records in the Pensacola Historical Museum. Locate in the FHLC under **Florida/Escambia [County]/Pensacola/Genealogy.**

Another useful source for Florida genealogy is:

Byrd, Beverly P. *Genealogy and Local History: A Bibliography.* 5th Suppl. Tallahassee, Fla.: Department of State, Division of Library Services, 1983. (FHL# 975.9/D23b)

History

For overviews of Florida history see:

Cutler, Harry G. *History of Florida, Past and Present, Historical and Biographical.* 3 vols. Chicago: Lewis Publishing Co., 1923. (FHL# 975.9/H2c)

Fairbanks, George R. *Florida, Its History and Its Romance: The Oldest Settlement in the United States, Associated With the Most Romantic Events of American History, Under the Spanish, French, English and American Flags, 1497-1898.* 2d ed. Jacksonville: H. and W. B. Drew, 1901. (FHL# 975.9/H2fa)

Land and Property Records

Florida is the only state discussed in this section which is a Public Domain State, meaning that it was surveyed into townships and sections like most of the Midwest and West. When the United States acquired Florida in 1819, however, standing claims to land resulting from Spanish and British rule needed to be settled. The Spanish appear to have gone through a similar process when they took the province back from Great Britain in 1783.

The Family History Library has the following records which deal with the settlement of land claims from the Spanish and British periods:

East Florida, Governor. *Spanish Land Grant Archives, 1764-1844.* 9 reels. Salt Lake City: Genealogical Society of Utah, 1977. (FHL# microfilm 1020288-1020295)

Historical Records Survey, Division of Professional and Service Projects, Works Projects Administration. *Spanish Land Grants in Florida: Briefed Translations from the Archives of the Board of Commissioners for Ascertaining Claims and Titles to Land in the Territory of Florida.* 5 vols. Tallahassee, Fla.: State Library Board, 1940-41. (FHL# 975.9/-R21hs or microfilm 0897334-0897335)

United States, Commissioners for Ascertaining Claims to Lands and Titles in East Florida. *Land Claims, 1824-1828.* 17 reels. Salt Lake City: Genealogical Society of Utah, 1977. (FHL# microfilm 1020205-1020217, 1020284-1020287)

The Family History Library has a fairly representative collection of deeds on the county level. See **/[County]/Land and Property.** At this writing, the library has no federal land records for Florida.

Military Records

Military records for Florida soldiers are available from the Spanish period to World War II in both original and printed form.

Military records from the Spanish period can be found in:

Espana. Ministerio de La Guerra. *Hojas de servicios militares de America: Floridas y Luisiana, 1787-1794.* 1 reel. Simancas, Espana: Servicio Nacional de Microfilm, 1971. (FHL# microfilm 115653)

Because so many Loyalists from other American colonies sought refuge in Florida during the American Revolution, you should check general sources for loyalists for any mention of a person from Florida. A useful source is:

Siebert, William Henry. *Loyalists in East Florida 1774 to 1785: The Most Important Documents Pertaining Thereto Edited with an Accompanying Narrative*. 2 vols. Deland: Florida State Historical Society, 1929. (FHL# 975.9/B4f/no. 9)

These sources are available for records of Florida soldiers in later wars:

Florida, Board of State Institutions. *Soldiers of Florida in the Seminole Indian-Civil and Spanish-American Wars*. Tallahassee, Fla.: Board of State Institutions, 1903. (FHL# 975.9/M2s or microfilm 0908213)

United States Adjutant General's Office. *Compiled Service Records, Volunteer Soldiers, Florida Indian Wars, 1835-1858*. 63 reels. Washington, D.C.: National Archives, 1979. (FHL# microfilm 1303446-1303500, 1303296-1303297, 1303918-1303923)

_____. *Compiled Service Records of Confederate Soldiers Who served in Organizations from the State of Florida, 1861-1865*. 103 reels. Washington, D.C.: National Archives, 1959. (FHL# microfilm 0880103-0880206)

_____. *Index to Compiled Service Records of Confederate Soldiers Who Served in Organizations from the State of Florida, 1861-1865*. 9 reels. Washington, D.C.: National Archives, 1959. (FHL# microfilm 0880001-0880009)

_____. *Index to Compiled Service Records of Volunteer Union Soldiers Who Served in Organizations from the State of Florida, 1861-1865*. Washington, D.C.: National Archives, 1962. (FHL# microfilm 0821767)

United States National Archives and Records Service. *Introduction to Compiled Service Records of Volunteer Soldiers Who Served in Florida Indian Wars, 1790's-1917*. Washington, D.C.: National Archives Microfilm Publications, [c.1960s]. (FHL# 975.9/A1/no.25 or microfilm 6019538)

United States War Department. *World War II Honor List of Dead and Missing, State of Florida*. Salt Lake City: Genealogical Society of Utah, 1976. (FHL# microfilm 0988193)

Also see *Military Records* in the introduction to this chapter for information about Florida soldiers in the federal armed forces.

The Family History Library has a few military records of various kinds for individual counties, including pension records for Confederate veterans and their widows. Check the FHLC under **/[County]/Military Records**.

Minorities and Native Races

Because of its varied settlement, Florida has seen many different groups. Some representative titles available at the Family History Library are:

Neill, Wilfred T. *The Story of Florida's Seminole Indians*. St. Petersburg, Fla.: Great Outdoors, [n.d.]. (FHL# 970.1/A1/ no. 24 or microfilm 0908862)

Roselli, Bruno. *The Italians in Colonial Florida: A Repertory of Italian Families Settled in Florida under the Spanish (1513-1762, 1784-1821) and British (1762-1784) Regimes; with a Brief Historical Outline and an Appendix on the Contemporary Colonial Press*. 1940; microreproduction Salt Lake City: Genealogical Society of Utah, 1984. (FHL# microfilm 1035661)

Obituaries and Newspapers

The Family History Library has a few compiled obituaries and original newspapers from major cities and towns. See the FHLC under the appropriate county and heading.

Periodicals

The Family History Library has a number of periodicals from Florida's local genealogical societies. Check the FHLC under **/[County]/Genealogy/Periodicals**. The library also has:

The Florida Historical Quarterly. Tampa: Florida Historical Society, 1908+. (FHL# 975.9B2fh)

Probate Records

The Family History Library currently has no general guides or indexes to Florida probate records at the Family History Library, although it has a fairly representative collection of probate records at the county level. See the FHLC under **/[County]/Probate Records.**

Slavery and Bondage

The Family History Library has a few general works on slaves in Florida. Two sources with detailed information are:

Phillips, Ulrich Bonnell, and James David Glunt, eds. *Florida Plantation Records from the Papers of George Noble Jones*. St. Louis, Mo.: Missouri Historical Society, 1927. (FHL# 975.9/R2ph)

United States. House of Representatives. 25th Congress, 3rd Session, 1839. *Document # 225: Negros, &c. Captured From Indians in Florida, &c. Letter from the Secretary of War, Transmitting the Information Required by a Resolution of the House of Representatives of the 28th, Ultimo, Respecting the Disposition of Negros and Other Property Captured from Hostile Indians During the Present War in Florida, &c. Feb. 27, 1839*. Washington, D.C.: n.pub., 1839. (FHL# 970.1/A1/no.33 or microfilm 0962163)

Taxation

The Family History Library has a few county tax records and these state records:

Florida Tax Commission. *Tax Rolls of Florida Counties, Some are Incomplete, 1839-1891*. 66 reels. Salt Lake City: Genealogical Society of Utah, 1956. (FHL# microfilm 0006888-0006953)

Vital Records

Most of the library's vital records for Florida are marriage records kept at the county level. The following reference will help locate vital records not at the library:

Florida Historical Records Survey, Division of Community Service Programs, Works Projects Administration. *Guide to Public Vital Statistics Records in Florida*. Jacksonville: Florida Historical Records Survey, 1941. (FHL# 975.9/A5h or microfilm 1036590 or 6019962)

Records by Jurisdiction

West Virginia

	Archives & Libraries	Bible Records	Biography	Business Records	Cemeteries	Census	Church History	Church Records	Court Records	Directories	Gazetteers	Genealogy	History	Land & Property	Maps	Military Records	Minorities	Naturalization	Newspapers	Obituaries	Occupations	Orphans	Probate Records	Public Records	Slavery & Bondage	Societies	Taxation	Vital Records	Voting Records	Schools
Barbour			•		•	•	•	•	•			•	•	•					•				•	•			•	•		
Berkeley			•		•		•	•	•	•			•	•	•	•			•			•	•	•		•	•	•		
Boone									•			•	•	•		•							•	•			•	•		
Braxton					•				•	•			•	•		•			•				•	•			•	•		•
Brooke			•	•	•				•			•	•	•					•				•	•			•	•		
Cabell			•		•			•	•	•		•	•	•					•				•	•			•	•		
Calhoun					•	•		•	•	•			•	•		•							•	•			•	•		
Clay					•			•	•			•	•	•		•							•	•			•	•		
Doddridge					•	•			•				•	•		•			•	•			•	•			•	•		
Fayette			•	•	•	•			•				•	•		•			•				•	•	•		•	•		•
Gilmer	•		•		•	•			•				•	•		•				•			•	•			•	•		
Grant	•				•			•	•				•	•		•							•	•			•	•		
Greenbrier		•	•	•	•			•	•				•	•		•			•				•	•			•	•		
Hampshire			•	•	•	•		•	•			•	•	•		•			•				•	•			•	•		
Hancock			•		•	•		•	•	•			•	•					•				•	•			•	•		
Hardy					•	•			•				•	•		•							•	•			•	•		•
Harrison		•	•		•		•	•	•	•		•	•	•		•			•	•			•	•			•	•		
Jackson					•				•	•		•	•	•									•	•			•	•		
Jefferson			•	•	•		•		•			•	•	•		•			•				•	•			•	•		
Kanawha		•	•	•	•				•	•			•	•		•			•				•	•			•	•		
Lewis				•	•			•	•	•			•	•									•	•			•	•		
Lincoln	•				•	•			•			•	•	•										•						
Logan		•				•		•	•			•	•	•		•							•	•			•			
Marion	•		•		•	•		•	•	•		•	•	•		•			•				•	•			•	•		
Marshall		•	•		•			•	•	•		•	•	•	•	•			•				•	•			•	•		
Mason			•	•					•			•	•	•		•			•				•	•			•	•		
McDowell					•	•			•			•	•	•		•			•				•	•			•	•		
Mercer			•	•	•	•		•	•	•			•	•		•			•				•	•			•	•		
Mineral		•			•		•	•	•	•		•	•	•		•			•				•	•			•	•		
Mingo			•	•					•				•	•					•				•	•			•	•		
Monogalia			•	•	•			•	•	•		•	•	•		•			•				•	•		•	•	•		
Monroe	•			•	•	•	•	•	•			•	•	•		•			•	•			•	•			•	•		
Morgan				•	•	•			•				•	•		•			•				•	•			•	•		
Nicholas					•	•			•				•	•		•							•	•			•	•		
Ohio				•		•		•	•	•			•	•		•		•	•				•	•			•	•		•
Pendleton	•				•	•		•	•			•	•	•		•				•			•	•			•	•	•	
Pleasants						•		•	•				•	•		•			•				•	•			•	•		
Pocahontas	•	•	•		•		•	•	•			•	•	•					•				•	•			•	•		
Preston			•		•	•	•	•	•		•	•	•	•		•			•				•	•			•	•		•
Putnam	•				•				•					•					•				•					•		
Raleigh			•			•			•			•	•	•		•			•				•	•			•	•		
Randolph	•				•				•			•	•	•		•			•				•	•			•	•		
Ritchie	•				•	•			•			•	•	•					•				•	•			•	•		
Roane					•	•			•			•	•	•		•			•				•	•			•	•		•
Summers					•			•	•				•	•					•				•	•			•	•		
Taylor			•		•	•		•	•				•	•					•				•	•			•	•		•
Tucker		•	•		•				•				•	•		•							•	•			•	•		
Tyler					•	•			•			•	•	•		•			•				•	•			•	•		•
Upshur		•	•		•	•			•				•	•		•			•				•	•			•	•		

Records by Jurisdiction **West Virginia (cont.)**	Archives & Libraries	Bible Records	Biography	Business Records	Cemeteries	Census	Church History	Church Records	Court Records	Directories	Gazetteers	Genealogy	History	Land & Property	Maps	Military Records	Minorities	Naturalization	Newspapers	Obituaries	Occupations	Orphans	Probate Records	Public Records	Slavery & Bondage	Societies	Taxation	Vital Records	Voting Records	Schools
Wayne						•	•		•				•	•		•							•	•			•	•		
Webster			•						•			•	•	•		•			•				•	•			•	•		
Wetzel					•		•	•	•	•		•	•	•		•							•	•			•	•		•
Wirt					•	•			•				•	•		•			•				•	•			•	•		
Wood			•		•	•			•	•			•	•	•	•			•				•	•			•	•		
Wyoming						•			•				•	•		•							•	•			•	•		•

Records by Jurisdiction **Virginia** **Counties**	Archives & Libraries	Bible Records	Biography	Business Records	Cemeteries	Census	Church History	Church Records	Court Records	Directories	Gazetteers	Genealogy	History	Land & Property	Maps	Military Records	Minorities	Naturalization	Newspapers	Obituaries	Occupations	Orphans	Probate Records	Public Records	Slavery & Bondage	Societies	Taxation	Vital Records	Voting Records
Accomack			•			•		•	•			•	•	•		•					•	•	•				•	•	
Albemarle					•			•	•			•	•	•									•	•				•	
Alleghany									•			•	•	•		•							•					•	
Amelia	•							•	•				•	•		•							•					•	
Amherst								•	•					•		•							•					•	
Appomattox					•		•	•																			•	•	
Arlington					•			•	•				•	•	•							•	•				•	•	
Augusta					•		•	•	•	•	•	•	•	•	•	•	•						•					•	
Bath					•			•	•		•		•	•									•					•	•
Bedford					•		•	•	•			•	•	•		•							•					•	
Bland			•						•				•	•									•	•				•	
Botetourt					•	•			•			•	•	•		•							•				•	•	
Brunswick	•							•	•				•	•		•						•	•				•		
Buchanan																											•	•	
Buckingham							•		•			•	•	•										•			•		
Campbell		•			•			•	•			•	•	•									•					•	
Caroline				•					•				•	•									•				•	•	
Carroll					•				•			•	•	•									•						
Charles City								•	•					•		•							•				•	•	
Charlotte							•	•	•			•	•	•									•					•	
Chesapeake			•		•			•	•				•	•	•	•							•				•	•	
Chesterfield	•						•	•	•			•	•	•		•							•					•	
Clarke					•		•	•	•			•	•			•							•			•		•	
Craig						•	•	•	•					•		•							•					•	
Culpeper					•		•	•	•			•	•	•		•							•					•	
Cumberland									•				•										•					•	
Dickenson												•	•															•	
Dinwiddie	•	•	•		•		•	•	•			•	•	•		•							•				•	•	
Elizabeth City					•		•	•	•				•	•									•	•				•	
Essex								•	•			•	•	•		•							•			•		•	
Fairfax	•				•	•	•		•	•			•	•		•							•	•	•		•	•	
Falls Church					•			•					•										•						
Floyd					•			•	•			•	•	•									•					•	
Fluvanna					•		•	•	•			•		•									•					•	
Franklin			•						•			•	•	•	•								•					•	
Frederick					•		•	•	•			•	•	•		•				•			•					•	
Giles						•			•			•	•	•									•	•			•	•	
Gloucester				•			•	•	•			•	•	•													•	•	
Goochland								•	•				•	•	•								•				•	•	
Grayson									•			•		•									•					•	
Greene					•				•				•	•		•							•					•	
Greensville								•	•				•	•									•					•	
Halifax					•			•	•				•	•		•							•					•	
Hanover						•	•	•	•			•	•	•									•	•			•	•	
Henrico				•			•	•	•	•		•	•	•					•			•	•	•			•	•	
Henry			•		•		•	•	•				•	•	•								•				•	•	
Highland					•	•			•				•	•	•								•					•	
Isle of Wight	•				•		•	•	•				•	•									•					•	
James City					•			•				•	•	•	•								•				•	•	

Records by Jurisdiction — **Virginia** Counties (cont.)	Archives & Libraries	Bible Records	Biography	Business Records	Cemeteries	Census	Church History	Church Records	Court Records	Directories	Gazetteers	Genealogy	History	Land & Property	Maps	Military Records	Minorities	Naturalization	Newspapers	Obituaries	Occupations	Orphans	Probate Records	Public Records	Slavery & Bondage	Societies	Taxation	Vital Records	Voting Records
King and Queen					•		•	•	•				•	•									•	•					
King George					•			•	•				•	•		•							•				•	•	
King William									•			•	•	•									•				•		
Lancaster						•		•	•			•		•		•							•					•	
Lee					•				•			•	•	•									•				•	•	
Loudoun					•		•	•	•			•	•	•	•	•		•					•					•	•
Louisa				•			•		•	•			•	•	•		•						•	•			•	•	
Lunenburg					•	•		•	•			•	•	•									•				•	•	
Madison							•	•	•				•	•		•							•					•	
Mathews							•	•				•	•	•									•				•	•	
Mecklenburg		•			•			•	•				•	•		•							•	•			•	•	
Middlesex				•				•	•			•	•	•		•							•	•			•	•	
Montgomery					•				•			•	•	•		•	•						•				•	•	
Nansemond								•	•				•	•		•							•	•			•	•	
Nelson								•	•				•	•		•							•					•	
New Kent		•				•	•	•	•			•	•	•		•							•				•	•	
Norfolk			•		•			•	•				•	•	•	•							•				•	•	
Northampton			•		•			•	•			•	•	•		•						•	•				•	•	
Northumberland						•	•	•	•			•											•					•	
Nottoway			•			•		•	•			•	•	•		•							•					•	
Orange					•			•	•			•	•	•		•							•					•	
Page					•			•	•				•	•									•					•	
Patrick					•				•			•	•	•	•	•							•					•	
Pittsylvania			•		•			•	•			•	•	•	•	•							•				•	•	
Powhatan	•							•	•					•									•					•	
Prince Edward								•	•			•	•	•	•	•							•	•			•	•	
Prince George	•							•	•				•	•		•							•				•	•	
Prince William					•			•	•				•	•									•				•	•	
Pulaski					•			•	•			•		•									•					•	
Princess Anne			•		•			•	•				•	•		•							•	•				•	
Rappahannock						•			•				•	•									•					•	
Richmond								•	•					•									•				•	•	
Roanoke			•		•			•	•	•			•	•		•							•					•	
Rockbridge					•		•		•			•	•	•		•							•			•		•	
Rockingham			•		•	•	•	•	•			•	•	•	•	•							•				•	•	
Russell					•	•			•				•	•									•					•	
Scott			•		•	•			•			•	•	•		•							•	•			•	•	
Shenandoah			•	•	•			•	•			•	•	•		•			•				•					•	
Smyth			•						•				•	•									•					•	
Southampton	•							•	•				•	•		•							•					•	
Spotsylvania					•		•	•	•				•	•		•	•						•	•				•	
Stafford					•		•	•	•				•	•		•	•						•				•	•	
Surry								•	•				•	•		•							•	•			•	•	
Sussex								•	•				•	•													•	•	
Tazewell									•			•	•	•									•				•	•	
Warren							•		•					•		•							•					•	
Warwick					•	•	•	•		•																	•		
Washington					•				•				•	•		•							•				•	•	
Westmoreland							•		•			•	•	•	•								•				•	•	

Records by Jurisdiction **Virginia Counties (cont.)**	Archives & Libraries	Bible Records	Biography	Business Records	Cemeteries	Census	Church History	Church Records	Court Records	Directories	Gazetteers	Genealogy	History	Land & Property	Maps	Military Records	Minorities	Naturalization	Newspapers	Obituaries	Occupations	Orphans	Probate Records	Public Records	Slavery & Bondage	Societies	Taxation	Vital Records	Voting Records
Wise						•			•			•	•	•									•					•	
Wythe					•	•		•	•			•	•	•					•				•				•	•	
Yohagania																													
York						•	•	•	•			•	•	•		•							•				•	•	

Records by Jurisdiction — Virginia Independent Cities	Archives & Libraries	Bible Records	Biography	Business Records	Cemeteries	Census	Church History	Church Records	Court Records	Directories	Gazetteers	Genealogy	History	Land & Property	Maps	Military Records	Minorities	Naturalization	Newspapers	Obituaries	Occupations	Orphans	Probate Records	Public Records	Slavery & Bondage	Societies	Taxation	Vital Records	Voting Records
Alexandria					•			•	•	•			•	•		•							•					•	
Bedford																													
Bristol									•																			•	
Buena Vista																													
Charlottesville	•				•										•													•	
Chesapeake			•		•			•	•				•	•	•	•							•				•	•	
Clifton Forge																													
Colonial Heights																													
Covington													•						•										
Danville																•										•		•	
Emporia																													
Fairfax					•																								
Falls Church					•			•					•										•						
Franklin																													
Fredericksburg			•		•		•	•	•				•	•			•						•					•	
Galax																													
Hampton					•		•	•	•				•	•									•					•	
Harrisonburg			•										•																
Hopewell													•																
Lexington					•																								
Lynchburg					•		•	•	•	•		•	•	•		•				•			•					•	
Manassas																													
Manassas Park																													
Newport News					•	•	•	•																			•		
Norfolk																													
Norton																													
Petersburg			•		•		•		•				•	•		•							•					•	
Poquoson																													
Portsmouth									•	•			•	•									•					•	
Radford																													
Richmond			•		•		•	•	•	•		•	•			•	•		•				•					•	
Roanoke			•					•		•																			
Salem																													
South Boston																													
South Norfolk																													
Staunton	•				•		•	•	•				•	•									•					•	
Suffolk		•			•	•		•				•	•	•										•					
Virginia Beach			•		•			•	•				•	•		•							•	•				•	
Waynesboro					•			•																					
Williamsburg					•		•	•				•	•										•						
Winchester					•		•	•					•																

Records by Jurisdiction — **North Carolina**	Archives & Libraries	Bible Records	Biography	Business Records	Cemeteries	Census	Church History	Church Records	Court Records	Directories	Gazetteers	Genealogy	History	Land & Property	Maps	Military Records	Minorities	Naturalization	Newspapers	Obituaries	Occupations	Orphans	Probate Records	Public Records	Slavery & Bondage	Societies	Taxation	Vital Records	Voting Records	Schools
Alamance				•	•		•	•	•			•	•	•	•	•							•	•		•		•	•	•
Alexander					•		•	•	•				•	•						•	•								•	
Alleghany					•			•	•			•	•	•		•							•	•					•	
Anson		•		•	•	•	•	•	•				•	•		•		•	•				•	•		•		•	•	•
Ashe					•			•	•				•	•								•	•						•	
Avery					•								•	•															•	
Beaufort					•			•	•				•	•		•							•	•		•		•	•	•
Bertie					•			•	•				•	•							•	•	•						•	
Bladen					•	•	•	•	•				•	•									•					•	•	
Brunswick				•	•		•	•					•	•		•							•	•		•		•	•	•
Buncombe					•	•			•			•	•	•	•				•	•	•		•	•					•	
Burke				•	•	•		•	•			•	•	•		•							•	•				•	•	•
Cabarrus					•		•	•	•			•	•	•		•	•				•		•	•		•		•	•	•
Caldwell					•	•		•	•			•	•	•		•							•						•	
Camden			•		•	•	•	•	•				•	•		•					•		•	•		•	•	•	•	•
Carteret					•	•	•	•	•			•	•	•		•							•						•	
Caswell		•	•	•	•	•	•	•	•			•	•	•	•	•						•	•	•		•		•	•	•
Catawba			•	•				•	•				•	•									•			•			•	
Chatham					•			•	•			•		•	•								•	•				•	•	
Cherokee		•			•	•			•				•	•									•						•	
Chowan				•	•		•	•	•				•	•					•			•	•	•				•	•	
Clay					•				•				•	•									•						•	
Cleveland					•	•	•	•	•			•	•	•									•						•	
Columbus					•		•	•	•			•	•	•									•	•					•	
Craven		•			•	•	•	•	•			•	•	•			•		•		•							•	•	
Cumberland		•		•	•	•	•	•	•					•		•			•				•	•				•	•	•
Currituck				•	•				•				•	•							•		•	•				•	•	•
Dare					•				•				•	•									•	•					•	
Davidson					•		•	•	•			•	•	•		•					•		•						•	
Davie					•		•	•	•				•	•	•								•	•		•		•	•	
Duplin					•		•	•	•	•	•		•	•		•					•		•	•		•		•	•	•
Durham	•				•		•	•	•	•			•	•									•	•				•	•	
Edgecomb					•	•		•	•	•		•	•	•		•						•	•	•				•	•	•
Forsyth					•	•	•	•	•				•	•							•		•	•					•	
Franklin					•			•	•				•	•		•							•	•		•		•	•	•
Gaston				•	•		•	•	•				•	•		•					•		•	•		•		•	•	•
Gates		•		•	•			•	•				•	•		•					•	•	•	•		•		•	•	•
Graham					•	•			•				•															•		
Granville					•	•	•	•	•			•	•	•		•							•	•		•		•	•	
Greene					•	•		•	•				•	•									•					•	•	
Guilford			•		•	•	•	•	•	•		•	•	•	•				•				•					•	•	
Halifax			•	•	•	•	•	•	•				•	•		•			•				•	•		•		•	•	•
Harnett					•			•				•		•															•	
Haywood			•		•	•		•	•			•	•	•			•						•					•	•	
Henderson					•	•		•	•				•	•									•						•	
Hertford				•	•		•	•	•				•	•		•					•		•	•		•		•		
Hoke					•			•																					•	
Hyde					•				•			•	•	•							•		•						•	•
Iredell					•		•	•	•			•	•	•		•							•					•	•	

Records by Jurisdiction

North Carolina (cont.)

County	Archives & Libraries	Bible Records	Biography	Business Records	Cemeteries	Census	Church History	Church Records	Court Records	Directories	Gazetteers	Genealogy	History	Land & Property	Maps	Military Records	Minorities	Naturalization	Newspapers	Obituaries	Occupations	Orphans	Probate Records	Public Records	Slavery & Bondage	Societies	Taxation	Vital Records	Voting Records	Schools
Jackson					•	•								•									•						•	
Johnston		•		•	•			•	•					•		•							•	•		•		•	•	•
Jones				•	•	•		•	•					•		•						•	•	•		•		•	•	•
Lee					•		•	•						•		•							•						•	
Lenoir					•	•	•	•	•			•	•	•									•						•	
Lincoln			•	•	•			•	•			•	•	•		•					•		•	•		•		•	•	•
Macon			•		•			•	•				•	•									•						•	
Madison					•				•				•	•									•	•					•	
Martin				•	•	•			•			•	•	•		•						•	•	•				•	•	•
McDowell					•				•					•									•	•					•	
Mecklenburg			•	•	•		•	•	•	•	•	•	•	•	•	•			•		•	•	•						•	
Mitchell					•				•					•															•	
Montgomery				•	•			•	•			•	•	•	•	•							•	•		•		•	•	•
Moore					•	•	•	•	•				•	•	•								•						•	
Nash				•	•	•			•			•		•		•					•		•	•		•	•	•	•	•
New Hanover			•		•			•	•				•	•	•	•	•		•	•			•					•	•	•
Northampton				•	•			•	•			•	•	•		•					•	•	•						•	
Onslow					•	•		•	•			•	•	•		•							•	•				•	•	
Orange				•	•			•	•				•	•	•	•			•				•	•		•		•	•	•
Pamlico		•			•								•	•		•							•						•	
Pasquotank					•		•	•	•				•	•					•		•		•	•			•	•	•	•
Pender			•		•			•	•				•	•		•							•						•	
Perquimans					•				•				•	•							•	•	•	•				•	•	
Person					•			•				•	•	•									•					•	•	
Pitt				•	•		•	•	•			•	•	•		•							•	•		•		•	•	•
Polk								•	•				•	•									•						•	
Randolph					•	•	•	•	•			•	•	•	•	•			•			•	•	•		•		•	•	
Richmond				•	•		•	•	•				•	•		•		•				•	•	•		•		•	•	•
Robeson		•			•			•	•			•	•	•									•	•					•	
Rockingham					•		•	•	•			•	•	•	•	•					•		•	•				•	•	
Rowan			•	•	•	•	•	•	•			•	•	•	•	•	•		•	•			•	•		•		•	•	•
Rutherford			•	•	•	•	•	•	•			•	•	•		•							•	•		•		•	•	•
Sampson					•	•		•	•			•	•	•		•							•	•		•		•	•	•
Scotland							•	•																						
Stanly					•		•	•	•					•									•						•	
Stokes				•	•				•			•	•	•	•	•							•	•				•	•	•
Surry				•	•	•		•	•			•	•	•	•	•						•	•	•				•	•	•
Swain					•	•		•					•	•		•							•		•				•	
Transylvania							•	•	•			•	•	•									•	•	•				•	
Tyrrell					•	•			•					•									•					•	•	
Union			•		•	•	•	•	•				•	•		•							•						•	
Vance					•			•					•	•									•						•	
Wake					•	•	•	•	•	•		•	•	•					•				•						•	
Warren				•	•		•	•	•				•	•		•							•	•				•	•	•
Washington					•		•	•	•				•	•									•						•	
Watauga					•			•	•			•	•	•									•	•				•	•	•
Wayne					•		•	•	•	•		•	•	•		•					•		•	•				•	•	
Wilkes					•	•	•	•	•			•	•	•				•	•											
Wilson					•			•	•					•									•	•					•	

Records by Jurisdiction

South Carolina

County	Archives & Libraries	Bible Records	Biography	Business Records	Cemeteries	Census	Church History	Church Records	Correctional Institutions	Court Records	Description & Travel	Directories	Genealogy	History	Land & Property	Maps	Medical Records	Military History	Military Records	Minorities	Naturalization	Newspapers	Occupations	Obituaries	Officials & Employees	Periodicals	Probate Records	Public Records	Schools	Slavery	Societies	Taxation	Vital Records	Voting Records
Abbeville	•				•		•	•		•			•		•				•								•	•				•	•	
Aiken	•				•			•						•																		•		
Allendale	•				•			•																										
Anderson	•		•		•	•		•	•	•			•	•	•				•		•	•					•	•	•			•	•	
Bamberg																																		
Barnwell					•			•		•				•	•												•						•	
Beaufort					•			•						•	•				•	•														
Berkeley					•			•						•		•											•							
Calhoun		•			•			•																										
Charleston				•	•	•		•		•	•	•	•		•	•			•	•	•	•	•	•			•	•	•	•			•	
Cherokee	•		•		•			•					•	•																			•	
Chester			•		•	•	•	•		•			•	•	•				•		•	•				•	•							
Chesterfield						•	•	•						•								•											•	
Clarendon					•			•					•			•																		
Colleton					•		•	•						•	•												•							
Darlington					•			•						•	•												•					•		•
Dillon	•				•			•						•																				
Dorchester					•									•													•		•					
Edgefield					•	•	•	•		•			•	•	•									•			•				•	•	•	
Fairfield					•	•		•	•	•	•			•	•				•			•	•				•					•		
Florence	•				•			•					•	•														•						
Georgetown					•			•						•	•																	•	•	
Greenville					•	•		•		•			•	•	•							•					•							
Greenwood					•			•					•	•	•																		•	
Hampton								•						•																				
Horry					•	•	•	•					•	•	•											•	•						•	
Jasper	•				•		•	•						•																				
Kershaw					•	•		•		•	•		•	•	•									•			•	•					•	
Lancaster					•			•							•														•			•		
Laurens			•		•	•	•	•		•			•	•	•		•		•						•		•	•				•	•	
Lee	•							•																										
Lexington					•	•		•		•			•		•			•			•	•			•	•	•	•				•	•	•
Marion					•		•	•						•	•	•			•								•						•	
Marlboro					•		•	•		•			•	•	•								•				•	•				•	•	
McCormick	•				•			•						•						•						•							•	
Newberry					•		•	•		•			•	•	•												•							
Oconee	•				•	•	•	•					•	•						•											•		•	
Orangeburg					•	•		•						•	•					•						•	•						•	
Pickens					•	•		•					•	•	•				•		•						•	•					•	
Richland	•		•		•			•				•		•								•					•							
Saluda	•				•			•						•																				
Spartanburg					•	•		•		•		•	•	•	•				•								•							
Sumter					•		•	•		•				•	•	•			•								•					•		
Union			•		•		•	•		•			•	•	•						•						•	•				•		
Williamsburg					•			•		•			•	•	•																		•	
York			•	•	•		•	•					•	•	•		•		•			•		•	•		•	•				•	•	•

Records by Jurisdiction Georgia	Archives & Libraries	Bible Records	Biography	Business Records	Cemeteries	Census	Church History	Church Records	Correctional Institutions	Court Records	Description & Travel	Directories	Emigration/Immigration	Gazetteers	Genealogy	History	Land & Property	Maps	Medical Records	Military Records	Minorities	Naturalization	Newspapers	Obituaries	Occupations	Orphans	Periodicals	Poorhouse	Probate Records	Public Records	Schools	Slavery	Societies	Taxation	Vital Records	Voting Registers
Appling					•	•		•		•					•		•			•					•				•	•	•			•	•	
Atkinson					•			•																					•							
Bacon					•											•																				
Baker						•				•							•			•									•					•	•	
Baldwin					•	•	•	•		•					•	•	•			•	•	•			•				•		•			•	•	
Banks					•			•		•					•	•	•			•									•		•			•	•	•
Barrow					•										•	•													•						•	
Bartow				•	•			•		•					•	•	•			•			•						•					•	•	
Ben Hill																																				
Berrien						•				•							•			•					•				•		•				•	
Bibb					•	•	•	•		•		•			•		•			•					•				•		•		•	•	•	
Bleckley			•		•	•	•	•								•																				
Brantley			•	•	•																															
Brooks						•	•			•						•	•			•					•				•				•	•	•	•
Bryan					•			•		•							•		•	•					•				•	•				•	•	•
Bullock					•	•	•	•		•						•	•			•									•					•	•	•
Burke				•			•	•		•					•	•	•			•			•		•				•	•			•	•	•	•
Butts					•		•	•		•					•	•	•		•	•					•				•			•		•	•	
Calhoun										•							•			•					•				•	•					•	
Camden					•	•	•	•		•						•	•			•		•			•				•	•			•	•	•	•
Campbell (See Fulton)																																				
Candler					•																		•													
Carroll					•	•		•		•					•	•	•			•					•		•		•		•			•	•	
Cass (See Barlow)																																				
Catoosa										•							•			•					•				•	•	•		•		•	
Charlton			•		•					•						•	•			•					•				•	•				•	•	
Chatham	•	•	•	•	•	•	•	•	•	•		•	•			•	•		•	•	•	•	•		•				•	•			•	•	•	•
Chattahoochee			•		•			•		•					•	•	•			•									•		•			•	•	•
Chattooga								•		•							•			•					•				•	•					•	
Cherokee					•	•				•						•	•			•			•		•				•		•			•	•	
Clarke		•	•	•	•	•	•	•	•	•					•	•	•	•	•	•				•	•		•		•	•	•		•	•	•	•
Clay					•					•						•	•			•					•										•	
Clayton					•	•	•	•		•					•	•	•			•					•				•	•	•			•	•	•
Clinch	•		•			•				•						•	•			•			•		•				•	•				•	•	•
Cobb					•			•								•																		•	•	
Coffee					•	•										•																			•	
Colquitt			•	•				•		•						•	•			•					•				•					•	•	
Columbia						•	•	•		•							•			•					•				•	•	•			•	•	•
Cook	•																																			
Coweta					•			•		•					•	•	•			•					•		•		•					•	•	•
Crawford					•	•		•		•							•			•									•					•	•	
Crisp															•	•																				
Dade						•				•							•			•									•						•	•
Dawson								•		•							•			•					•				•						•	
Decatur		•		•	•			•		•	•						•			•					•				•	•	•	•		•	•	•
DeKalb				•			•	•		•		•			•	•	•			•		•	•		•				•	•			•	•	•	
Dodge			•		•					•						•	•			•					•				•				•	•	•	•
Dooly					•	•				•						•	•			•					•				•					•	•	
Dougherty	•									•	•					•	•			•					•				•						•	•

Records by Jurisdiction Georgia (Cont.)	Archives & Libraries	Bible Records	Biography	Business Records	Cemeteries	Census	Church History	Church Records	Correctional Institutions	Court Records	Description & Travel	Directories	Emigration/Immigration	Gazetteers	Genealogy	History	Land & Property	Maps	Medical Records	Military Records	Minorities	Naturalization	Newspapers	Obituaries	Occupations	Orphans	Periodicals	Poorhouse	Probate Records	Public Records	Schools	Slavery	Societies	Taxation	Vital Records	Voting Registers
Douglas										•		•					•			•					•				•	•					•	
Early			•	•	•	•	•	•		•					•	•	•			•									•	•			•	•	•	•
Echols	•					•				•					•	•	•			•					•				•	•	•			•	•	•
Effingham					•	•	•	•		•					•		•			•									•	•	•			•	•	•
Elbert		•			•	•		•		•					•	•	•		•	•	•				•				•	•			•	•	•	
Emanuel					•			•		•					•	•	•			•					•			•	•	•	•	•	•	•	•	
Evans					•											•																				
Fannin										•					•		•			•									•						•	
Fayette		•			•	•	•	•		•					•	•	•			•					•				•	•	•		•	•	•	
Floyd		•		•	•	•	•	•		•					•	•	•		•	•			•						•	•	•		•	•	•	•
Forsyth						•				•					•	•	•			•					•				•				•	•	•	
Franklin					•			•		•						•			•		•			•				•	•				•	•	
Fulton			•		•		•	•		•		•			•	•	•	•		•	•	•	•	•	•				•					•	•	
Gilmer						•				•						•	•			•					•				•	•	•			•	•	•
Glascock						•				•						•	•			•					•				•					•	•	•
Glynn					•	•	•	•		•		•					•			•					•				•	•	•				•	
Gordon										•						•	•			•					•				•		•			•	•	
Grady			•		•		•									•	•																			
Greene							•	•		•						•	•	•		•									•	•	•			•	•	
Gwinnett			•		•	•	•	•		•					•	•	•			•					•				•						•	
Habersham							•			•					•	•	•			•					•				•	•				•	•	
Hall				•	•			•		•						•		•	•					•				•		•				•	
Hancock					•		•	•		•						•			•	•								•	•	•		•	•	•	•
Haralson					•					•					•	•	•			•			•						•	•				•	•	•
Harris						•				•						•	•			•					•				•	•				•	•	
Hart		•			•		•			•						•	•			•									•				•		•	
Heard					•	•				•						•	•			•									•						•	
Henry					•		•	•		•					•	•	•			•			•		•				•	•	•			•	•	
Houston					•		•	•		•						•	•			•			•		•				•					•	•	
Irwin						•				•					•	•	•			•					•				•	•				•	•	
Jackson					•		•	•		•					•	•	•			•					•			•	•			•		•	•	
Jasper					•			•		•					•	•	•			•					•			•	•				•	•	•	
Jeff Davis					•																															
Jefferson	•				•	•		•		•					•	•	•	•		•									•	•	•			•	•	•
Jenkins					•			•									•																			
Johnson					•					•							•			•					•				•	•					•	•
Jones						•				•						•	•			•					•				•		•	•		•	•	
Kinchafoonee (See Webster)																																				
Lamar			•													•																				
Lanier					•		•									•																				
Laurens							•			•					•	•	•			•					•				•					•	•	
Lee	•				•			•		•					•	•	•			•					•				•					•	•	
Liberty			•		•	•	•	•		•						•	•			•					•				•	•	•			•	•	•
Lincoln					•			•		•					•	•	•		•	•					•				•	•	•			•	•	•
Long					•																														•	
Lowndes					•	•				•		•			•	•	•			•									•					•	•	
Lumpkin					•	•				•						•	•			•					•				•	•	•			•	•	
Macon										•					•	•	•			•					•				•		•			•	•	
Madison					•	•		•		•							•	•		•					•				•					•	•	

Records by Jurisdiction **Georgia (Cont.)**	Archives & Libraries	Bible Records	Biography	Business Records	Cemeteries	Census	Church History	Church Records	Correctional Institutions	Court Records	Description & Travel	Directories	Emigration/Immigration	Gazetteers	Genealogy	History	Land & Property	Maps	Medical Records	Military Records	Minorities	Naturalization	Newspapers	Obituaries	Occupations	Orphans	Periodicals	Poorhouse	Probate Records	Public Records	Schools	Slavery	Societies	Taxation	Vital Records	Voting Registers
Marion			•			•				•						•	•			•									•					•	•	•
McDuffie								•		•						•	•			•					•				•	•	•				•	•
McIntosh					•	•		•		•						•	•			•					•				•	•	•		•	•	•	•
Meriwether			•			•				•						•	•			•					•				•				•		•	
Miller					•					•						•	•			•					•				•	•					•	•
Milton (See Fulton)																																				
Mitchell					•					•					•	•	•			•									•	•					•	
Monroe				•	•		•	•		•					•	•	•			•					•				•	•	•		•	•	•	
Montgomery					•			•		•						•	•			•					•				•	•				•	•	•
Morgan				•	•			•		•							•			•	•				•				•	•	•	•	•	•	•	•
Murray						•				•							•			•					•				•	•					•	
Muscogee	•		•		•					•		•				•	•			•		•		•	•				•					•	•	
Newton		•			•	•		•		•					•		•			•			•		•				•					•	•	•
Oconee								•		•							•		•	•					•				•						•	
Oglethorpe					•	•		•		•				•	•	•	•	•		•					•				•	•	•			•	•	•
Paulding					•		•			•						•	•			•					•				•						•	•
Peach					•										•	•																				
Pickens								•		•						•	•			•					•				•				•		•	
Pierce		•			•					•					•	•	•			•					•				•	•	•			•	•	•
Pike					•					•						•	•			•					•				•					•	•	
Polk								•		•							•			•					•				•						•	•
Pulaski		•	•			•	•	•		•					•	•	•		•	•	•				•				•	•	•			•	•	•
Putnam				•	•					•							•			•					•				•					•	•	
Quitman																																				
Rabun					•	•				•						•	•			•									•		•			•	•	
Randolph										•						•	•			•					•				•	•				•	•	
Richmond	•		•	•	•	•	•	•		•					•		•			•			•						•	•	•	•		•	•	
Rockdale							•	•		•							•			•									•		•				•	
Schley					•			•		•							•			•					•				•	•					•	
Screven					•	•	•	•		•					•	•	•			•					•				•	•				•	•	•
Seminole																																				
Spalding										•							•			•					•				•		•			•	•	•
Stephens					•										•	•																				
Stewart			•	•			•			•						•	•			•					•				•					•	•	
Sumter		•			•		•	•		•					•		•			•		•			•				•	•				•	•	•
Talbot		•			•			•		•					•	•	•			•					•				•	•	•			•	•	
Taliaferro					•	•	•	•		•							•			•	•								•	•	•		•	•	•	•
Tattnall					•	•	•	•		•						•	•		•	•					•				•	•	•			•	•	•
Taylor		•								•							•			•					•				•					•	•	
Telfair					•	•	•			•						•	•			•					•				•						•	•
Terrell										•					•	•	•			•					•				•	•				•	•	•
Thomas						•	•	•		•						•	•			•					•				•	•					•	•
Tift			•													•																				
Toombs					•																															
Towns										•					•		•			•					•										•	•
Treutlen					•											•																				
Troup					•	•	•	•		•					•	•	•	•		•									•				•	•	•	
Turner																•																				
Twiggs					•			•							•	•	•																	•		

Records by Jurisdiction — Georgia (Cont.)	Archives & Libraries	Bible Records	Biography	Business Records	Cemeteries	Census	Church History	Church Records	Correctional Institutions	Court Records	Description & Travel	Directories	Emigration/Immigration	Gazetteers	Genealogy	History	Land & Property	Maps	Medical Records	Military Records	Minorities	Naturalization	Newspapers	Obituaries	Occupations	Orphans	Periodicals	Poorhouse	Probate Records	Public Records	Schools	Slavery	Societies	Taxation	Vital Records	Voting Registers
Union										•						•	•			•					•				•				•	•	•	•
Upson			•		•	•		•		•						•	•		•	•					•				•	•				•	•	
Walker					•	•		•		•					•	•	•			•			•		•				•						•	•
Walton					•		•	•		•						•	•			•									•	•			•	•	•	•
Ware			•			•	•	•		•		•				•	•		•	•					•				•	•					•	•
Warren		•		•				•		•					•	•	•			•					•				•	•	•		•	•	•	•
Washington		•			•	•	•	•		•						•	•			•	•								•					•	•	
Wayne			•		•			•		•							•			•					•				•	•			•	•	•	•
Webster										•					•	•	•			•					•				•					•	•	
Wheeler																																				
White			•					•		•						•	•			•		•							•					•	•	
Whitfield										•						•	•	•		•					•				•				•	•	•	
Wilcox					•	•	•			•					•	•	•			•					•				•	•				•	•	•
Wilkes		•		•	•	•		•		•						•	•	•	•	•			•		•			•	•	•	•		•	•	•	•
Wilkinson					•			•							•	•	•			•															•	
Worth					•					•						•	•			•					•				•	•					•	

Records by Jurisdiction

Florida

County	Archives & Libraries	Bible Records	Biography	Business Records	Cemeteries	Census	Church History	Church Records	Court Records	Description & Travel	Directories	Emigration/Immigration	Gazetteers	Genealogy	History	Land & Property	Maps	Military History	Military Records	Minorities	Naturalization	Obituaries & Newspapers	Periodicals	Probate Records	Public Records	Slavery	Societies	Taxation	Vital Records	Voting Registers
Alachua		•			•	•		•	•					•	•	•								•				•	•	
Baker					•											•												•	•	
Bay														•									•	•	•					
Bradford					•			•								•								•				•	•	
Brevard			•		•		•							•	•	•								•				•	•	
Broward			•		•		•																						•	
Calhoun																•								•				•	•	
Charlotte	•																												•	
Citrus																•								•					•	
Clay	•				•											•								•				•	•	
Collier	•														•														•	
Columbia		•			•			•								•								•				•	•	
Dade						•	•				•			•	•	•						•	•	•				•	•	
De Soto											•													•				•	•	
Dixie					•																								•	
Duval	•				•			•	•		•			•	•	•							•	•				•	•	
Escambia	•		•	•	•	•		•	•		•			•	•	•			•		•	•		•				•	•	
Flagler	•				•																			•					•	
Franklin						•									•	•								•				•	•	•
Gadsden					•			•						•		•								•				•	•	
Gilchrist																													•	
Glades															•															
Gulf					•																								•	
Hamilton									•							•								•				•	•	
Hardee	•				•																								•	
Hendry	•																•													
Hernando																•												•		
Highlands																														
Hillsborough	•		•	•	•	•	•	•						•	•	•			•			•		•			•	•	•	
Holmes								•												•				•				•	•	
Indian River					•																								•	
Jackson								•							•	•				•				•				•	•	
Jefferson									•							•								•				•	•	
Lafayette																												•	•	
Lake					•		•	•							•	•								•					•	
Lee										•					•															
Leon	•			•	•		•	•		•		•					•							•	•	•			•	•
Levy		•			•	•								•	•	•								•				•	•	•
Liberty					•											•								•				•	•	
Madison					•			•								•												•	•	
Manatee					•	•			•					•	•	•							•	•				•	•	
Marion					•			•			•					•								•				•	•	
Martin																														
Monroe					•	•						•			•	•					•			•				•		
Mosquito																														
Nassau					•	•		•																•				•	•	
New River (Changed to Bradford 1861)																														
Okaloosa	•				•			•																•						
Okeechobee					•										•														•	

Records by Jurisdiction

Florida (Cont.)

	Archives & Libraries	Bible Records	Biography	Business Records	Cemeteries	Census	Church History	Church Records	Court Records	Description & Travel	Directories	Emigration/Immigration	Gazetteers	Genealogy	History	Land & Property	Maps	Military History	Military Records	Minorities	Naturalization	Obituaries & Newspapers	Periodicals	Probate Records	Public Records	Slavery	Societies	Taxation	Vital Records	Voting Registers
Orange	•		•		•	•								•	•	•								•				•	•	
Osceola				•	•						•																	•	•	
Palm Beach			•		•						•			•	•								•	•					•	
Pasco					•											•												•		
Pinellas	•				•			•			•			•											•					
Polk			•		•			•	•		•			•	•	•								•				•	•	
Putnam														•		•							•	•				•	•	
St. Johns					•	•			•						•	•			•					•				•	•	
St. Lucas																														
St. Lucie						•																		•					•	
Santa Rosa															•								•				•	•		
Sarasota	•		•		•									•	•								•						•	
Seminole					•																		•						•	
Sumter					•				•							•								•				•	•	
Suwannee																•								•				•	•	
Taylor									•							•			•					•				•	•	
Union																•													•	
Volusia					•			•							•	•			•					•				•	•	
Wakulla	•															•									•			•	•	
Walton															•					•				•				•	•	
Washington					•											•								•				•	•	

Chapter 8

United States: The New South

Wendy L. Elliott

Louisiana

Historical Background

1682 M. Robert de la Salle, a French explorer, discovers Louisiana.

1776-83 Loyalists leave the eastern states and move into Louisiana to escape the Revolutionary War.

1803 France cedes the territory to the United States, but the border between Louisiana and Texas was disputed with Spain for several years.

1804 The southern section, with its northern boundary as the thirty-third parallel, becomes the Territory of Orleans. The northern portion becomes Louisiana Territory, including all of present-day Missouri, Arkansas, and the Northwest Territory.

1804 Federal courts are established in the territory.

1805 Louisiana is divided into twelve counties.

1807 The territory is sectioned into nineteen parishes.

1811 The western boundary north of the Sabine River was established. Part of Spanish West Florida was annexed to the area which became Louisiana.

1812 Louisiana becomes the eighteenth state with thirteen parishes and its capital at New Orleans.

1819 The boundary between Louisiana and Texas is settled by treaty, but the points defined were unknown and jurisdictional problems continued until the 1830s.

1820-30 The far western region of the state was part of Neutral Ground between Louisiana and Texas.

1849 The capital is changed from New Orleans to Baton Rouge.

1861 Louisiana secedes from the Union.

1866 Louisiana is readmitted to the United States.

Settlement and Migration

Ownership of the territory of present-day Louisiana was exchanged between Britain, Spain, and France for nearly 300 years, then sold to the United States as part of the Louisiana Purchase in 1803. It is the only state to be organized with parishes rather than counties.

In 1804, the state was divided into two sections. The upper region was designated the District of Louisiana, and the lower area was called the Territory of Orleans. In 1805, Louisiana was organized into twelve counties, while Orleans was divided into nineteen parishes.

Many of Louisiana's earliest settlers were from France and Spain. They settled in the southern section of the state at New Orleans and along the Mississippi River. During the Revolutionary War, many loyalists moved their families from the eastern states to Louisiana. French Acadians from eastern Canada migrated to Louisiana in the nineteenth century. Northern Louisiana was settled mainly by families who had migrated from older southern states.

The boundary between Texas and Louisiana was unsettled for many years. The disputed area, called Neutral Ground, was south of the Sabine River. Jurisdictional conflicts continued for many years although a temporary compromise made in 1806 left the region without governmental supervision, and created a sanctuary for fugitives. An 1819 treaty between Spain and the United States established the present-day boundary, although the line was obscure until the early

1830s. During this period, the borders of Louisiana, Texas, and Arkansas were uncertain.

Louisiana Library Collection

Archives and Libraries

Louisiana Historical Records Survey Project, Division of Professional and Service Projects, Work Projects Administration. *A Guide to the Manuscript Collections in Louisiana.* Baton Rouge: Department of Archives, 1940. (FHL# 976.3/A3g).

Resources in Louisiana Libraries: Public, Academic, Special and in Media Centers; Preliminary Checking Edition. Baton Rouge: Louisiana State Library, 1971. (FHL# 976.3/A3l, or microfiche 6019941, or microfilm 0896543, item 1)

Report of a survey directed by Sue Hefley.

An index to the archives of Spanish West Florida for 1782-1810 is FHL# 976.3/A3a, and a catalog of documents in the Archives General during the Spanish control of Louisiana is available in Spanish (FHL# 976.3/A3p). For additional titles, consult the Family History Library Catalog (FHLC) under **Louisiana/Archives and Libraries** and **Louisiana/Bibliography.**

Bible Records

As for most other states, various chapters of the Daughters of the American Revolution (DAR) have gathered genealogically oriented records. Those for Louisiana are in the collection under various headings including **Louisiana/Bible Records, Louisiana/Cemeteries, Louisiana/Church Records, Louisiana/Genealogy,** and **Louisiana/Vital Records;** some are cataloged under **Louisiana/[County]/[Subheadings].** A mid-South collection of DAR Bible records was published: FHL# 976/V29d.

Biography

Several biographical and historical compilations have been made for Louisiana. Notable in the collection of biographical publications are:

Lawrence, William Francis, and Debra Nance Lawrence. *Biographical Sketches of the European Immigrants of Northeast Louisiana, 1880-1900.* Baton Rouge: Claitor's Publishing, c.1982. (FHL# 976.3/D3lb)

Perrin, William Henry, ed. *Southwest Louisiana: Biographical and Historical.* New Orleans: Claitor's Publishing Division, 1971. (FHL# 976.35/H2p)

Cemeteries

A twenty-two volume compilation of Louisiana tombstone inscriptions was compiled by the Louisiana Daughters of the American Revolution. These have been indexed and microfilmed (FHL# microfilm 0854861-0854863 and 855248-0855250). A number of parish cemeteries are available in the Louisiana Tombstone Inscription series (FHL# 976.3/V22d or microfilm 0194383, 0194385, 0873717-0873720).

For additional listings see **Louisiana/Cemeteries** and **Louisiana/[County]/Cemeteries.**

Census Records

An early census was taken in 1745 for Pointe Coupe and is cataloged under **Louisiana/Pointe Coupe/Census.** A census enumerated in 1774 is included in the fifth volume of Winston DeVille and Jane Guillary Bulliard, trans. & eds. *Marriage Contracts of the Attakapas Post 1760-1803: Colonial Louisiana Marriage Contracts*, 5 vols. (St. Martinsville, La.: Attakapas Historical Association, 1966) (FHL# 976.3/V25da). See also:

DeVille, Winston. *Attakapas Post, the Census of 1771.* Ville Platte, La.: Winston DeVille, [c.1986.] (FHL# 976.3/X2d/1771)

______. *Rapides Post - 1799: A Brief Study in Genealogy and Local History.* Baltimore: Genealogical Publishing Co., 1968. (FHL# 976.3/A1/no.3)

Roberts, Ed, and Mattie M. Somerville, comp. *1810 Census of the Northeast Louisiana Parishes of Ouachita, Catahoula, and Concordia.* Monroe, La.: Northeast Louisiana Genealogical Society, n.d. (FHL# 976.3/A1/no.33)

For additional titles dealing with the pre-statehood period, consult the FHLC under **Louisiana/Census.**

The 1810 and 1820 U.S. censuses have been published. Indexes are available for the 1810, 1820, and 1850 censuses.

Censuses are available through 1910; for census call numbers, see the Registers on the U.S./Canada Reference credenza.

Deiler, John Hanno. *Zur Geschichte der Deutschen Kirchengemeinden im Staate Louisiana.* Salt Lake City: Genealogical Society of Utah, 1981. (FHL# microfilm 1305374, item 4)

Includes a census of New Orleans German schools and foreign inhabitants for 1850-90.

The 1890 census for Union veterans and their widows has been published and a separate index is available. See **Louisiana/Census.** The federal mortality schedules for 1850-80 are available (FHL# microfilm 0422428-0422432).

In 1865, a Civil War tax assessment was made in Louisiana (FHL# 976.3/R4c).

Arranged alphabetically by county, enumeration of ex-Confederate Louisiana soldiers and their widows was made in 1911; see **Louisiana/Military Records/Civil War,** 1861-65 (FHL# microfilm 0483489).

Church History and Church Records

Most church histories in the collection for Louisiana concern the Catholic Church and its administration. See **Louisiana/Church History** and **Louisiana/[Parish]/Church History.**

A brief history of the German church in Louisiana is FHL# microfilm 1305374, item 4. A guide to the microfilm edition of the records of the Louisiana

Diocese 1576-1803 is cataloged under **Louisiana/Church History/Sources.**

The largest collections of Louisiana church records are:

Hebert, Donald J. *Southwest Louisiana Records: Church and Civil Records*, 33 vols. Eunice, La.: The author, c.1974-85. (FHL# 976.35/V2h)

_____. *South Louisiana Records,* 12 vols. Cecilia, La.: The author, 1978. (FHL# 976.3/K2he)

The Daughters of the American Revolution have contributed several compilations of records to the collection. Records of French and nineteenth-century German churches are available. Consult the FHLC under **Louisiana/Church Records** and **Louisiana/[Parish]/-Church Records.** See **Louisiana/Church Records/-Bibliography** for additional guides and inventories.

Court Records

Notable among the court records cataloged under **Louisiana/Court Records** are French Superior Council and judicial records for 1769 to 1804 filmed on 239 reels (FHL# microfilm 1293721-1031280, 1305391-1305394). Records include court records, land transactions, and debt settlements.

Records of the French Superior Court for 1679-1803 are filmed on 82 reels; the microfilm numbers are mixed. Files are numbered according to the date the case was heard by the Cabildo and arranged in numerical order. The first four digits of the file number represent the year, the second two numbers are the month, the third two numbers are the day, and the last two numbers represent the number assigned on the day it was heard. An index to both sets is available (FHL# microfilm 1276244-1276252).

Louisiana chapters of the Daughters of the American Revolution have compiled several groups of records pertinent to Louisiana including court records; see **Louisiana/Court Records.** For additional information see **Louisiana/Court Records/Archives and Libraries** and **Louisiana/Court Records/Indexes.** Many parish court records are available; see **Louisiana/[Parish]/Court Records.**

Emigration and Immigration

Several collections of records concerning emigration and immigration are available. See **Louisiana/Emigration and Immigration.** These include records of Spanish, French, German, Acadians, American colonials, and slaves. Some indexes are in the collection; see **Louisiana/Emigration and Immigration/Indexes.**

Genealogy

Several compilations are available, including those of Louisiana chapters of the Daughters of the American Revolution. See **Louisiana/Genealogy** and **Louisiana/-[Parish]/Genealogy.** For genealogical information on early families in the state, see:

Stanley, Clisby Arthur, comp. and ed. *Old Families of Louisiana.* New Orleans: Harmanson, 1931. (FHL# 976.3/D2a)

Conrad, Glenn R., trans. and comp. *The First Families of Louisiana.* 2 vols. Baton Rouge: Claitor's Publishing Division, 1970. (FHL# 976.3/D2c)

Heard, Elizabeth M., comp. *Family Records, Vol. 8.* Salt Lake City: Genealogical Society of Utah, 1971. (FHL# microfilm 885264, item 4)

Tanquay, Cyprien. *Dictionnaire Genealogique des Familles Canadiennes Depuis la Fondation de la Colonie Jusqu'a Nos Jours.* 7 vols. Montreal: E. Senecal, 1871-90. (FHL# 971/ D2t, or microfilm 0105970-0105972, and 0824131, item 4, and 0908001,item 1)

Genealogical Dictionary of French Canadian families with Louisiana connections; dates from 1608 to 1763. Genealogies of the French in Louisiana and colonies in Louisiana and Canada.

See additional guides under **Louisiana/Genealogy/Bibliography, Louisiana/Genealogy/Dictionaries, Louisiana/Genealogy/Periodicals, Louisiana/Genealogy/Periodicals/Indexes,** and **Louisiana/Genealogy/-Sources.**

History

The FHLC has a section of general titles, then is organized by time periods, for example: **Louisiana/History/to 1803, Louisiana/History/Colonial Period, c.1600-1775, Louisiana/History/Civil War, 1861-65,** and **Louisiana/History/World War, 1914-1918.**

There are also several subject subheadings for history, including **Louisiana/History, Louisiana/History/[Time Periods], Louisiana/History/Bibliography, Louisiana/-History/Chronology, Louisiana/History/Periodicals, Louisiana/History/Reconstruction, Louisiana/History/Sources,** etc.

Several general histories for Louisiana are:

Carter, Clarence Edwin, comp., ed. *The Territorial Papers of the United States: The Territory of Orleans, 1803-1812.* Vol. IX. Washington, D.C.: Government Printing Office, 1941. (FHL# microfilm 874227)

_____. *The Territorial Papers of the United States: The Territory of Louisiana-Missouri, 1806-1814.* Vol. XIV. Washington, D.C.: Government Printing Office, 1946. (FHL# microfilm 874230)

_____. *The Territorial Papers of the United States: The Territory of Louisiana-Missouri, 1815-1821.* Vol. XV. Washington, D.C.: Government Printing Office, 1947. (FHL# microfilm 874231, item 1)

Davis, Edwin Adams. *Louisiana, A Narrative History.* 2d ed. Baton Rouge: Claitor's Book Store, 1965. (FHL# 976.3/H2d)

Davis, Ellis Arthur, ed. *The Historical Encyclopedia of Louisiana.* 2 vols. n.p.: Louisiana Historical Bureau, n.d. (FHL# 976.3/D3d)

Fortier, Alcee. *A History of Louisiana.* 4 vols. New York: Manzi, Joyant, and Co., Successors, c.1903. (FHL# 976.3/H2f)

Gayarre, Charles Etienne Arthur. *History of Louisiana: With City and Topographical Maps of the State, Ancient and Modern.* 3rd ed., 4 vols. New Orleans: A. Hawkins, 1885. (FHL# 976.3/H2g)

Goodspeed, Weston Arthur, ed.-in-chief. *The Province and the States: A History of the Province of Louisiana under France and Spain, and of the Territories and States of the United States Formed Therefrom.* 7 vols. Madison, Wis.: Western Historical Association, 1904. (FHL# 973/H2gw or microfilm 1415262, items 1-7)

Martin, Francois Xavier. *The History of Louisiana, from the Earliest Period.* 2 vols. New Orleans: Lyman and Beardslee, 1827-29. (FHL# 976.3/H2m)

O'Neill, Charles Edwards. *Church and State in French Colonial Louisiana: Policy and Politics to 1732.* New Haven: Yale University Press, 1966. (FHL# 976.3/H2o)

Rushton, William Faulkner. *The Cajuns: From Acadia to Louisiana.* New York: Farrar Straus Giroux, 1979. (FHL# 976.3/F2ru)

Winzerling, Oscar William. *Acadian Odyssey.* Eunice, La.: Hebert Publications, 1981. (FHL# 976.3/H2q)

Land and Property

The library has land and property records for most Louisiana parishes. Called conveyance records, they are cataloged under **Louisiana/[Parish]/Land and Property** and **Louisiana/[Parish]/Notarial Records.** The library lists the conveyances of some counties under **/Land and Property** while the index to these records is cataloged under **/Notarial Records.**

A large collection of judicial records for 1769-1804, during the period of Spanish jurisdictional control, are available. Microfilms of the original records in the Louisiana Historical Center in New Orleans are available; see **Louisiana/Land and Property.**

First Settlers of the Louisiana Territory: Orleans Territory Grants from American State Papers, Class viii, Public Lands. Nacogdoches, Tex.: Ericson Books [distributor]; St. Louis: Ingmire Publications [distributor], c.1983. (FHL# 976.3/R2f) Includes early eastern Louisiana land records.

For the southwest region of the state, see **Louisiana/Land and Property/St. Landry Papers**; the thirty-four microfilm reels contain land sales and grants, promissory notes, marriage contracts, probate records, successions, apprenticeships, donations, and other records for 1766 to 1921.

Historical Records Survey. *Survey of Federal Archives in Louisiana: Land Claims and Other Documents, ca. 1800-1860.* Baton Rouge: Archives and Records Service, n.d. (FHL# microfilm 882922) Includes later records; indexed.

Northern and southern Louisiana land records are included in:

Louisiana Claim Papers, 1810-1875 (Salt Lake City: Genealogical Society of Utah, 1983) (FHL# microfilm 1376146, items 3-5 and 1376147, item 1).

Under **Louisiana/Land and Property/**, see "United States. District Land Office (New Orleans)" for the Southwestern District; "United States. District Land Office (Opelousas)" for the Northwestern District; "United States. District Land Office (Ouachita)" for the district north of the Red River; "United States. District Land Office (St. Helena)" for the Greensburg District; and "United States. District Land Office (Baton Rouge)" for an index to the U.S. Tract Books, 1807-70. Some published or filmed documents in the collection for the Spanish and French periods have been cited earlier under *Court Records*. Additionally, see the chronological arrangement of documents filmed in the State Lands Office in Baton Rouge, FHL# microfilm 1376478, item 5 for 1750-99 and 1376479 for 1799-1837.

Commissioners' records for 1805-1935 (FHL# microfilm 0984803-0984808) are indexed (FHL# microfilm 0984805 and 1094806, item 1). Later state lands office records include soldiers' proofs for 1884-1902. These bounty land grants were made to indigent Confederate soldiers (or their widows) who had been wounded and disabled or killed. Rejected applications are alphabetically arranged, but all others are numerical (FHL# microfilm 1376480-1376483 and 1378035).

See also:

Maduell, Charles R. *Federal Land Grants in the Territory of Orleans: The Delta Parishes.* New Orleans: Polyanthos, 1975. Adapted from *American State Papers, Public Lands, Volume II*, and arranged by counties as they existed in 1812. (FHL# 976.33/R2m)

Pintado, Vincente Sebastian. *Pintado Papers, 1795-1842.* Baton Rouge: Archives and Records Service, n.d. (FHL# microfilm 0882924, item 5-0882926)

Maps

See **Louisiana/Maps** for the several maps in the collection.

Military Records

A few entries are cataloged under **Louisiana/Military History**. Several compilations of records are available; see **Louisiana/Military Records**. An index to the compiled service records of volunteers who served during the War of 1812 from Louisiana is arranged in alphabetical order (FHL# microfilm 0880010-0880012).

An index to compiled service records of Louisiana Confederate soldiers is on FHL# microfilm 0881457-0881487). Louisiana Union Soldiers' compiled service records are included in the collection (FHL# microfilm 0821926-0821929).

Records of Louisiana military are available for these wars: colonial, Revolutionary, Indian, Spanish-American, World War I, War of 1812, and Civil War. See **Louisiana/Military Records/[War]** and **United States/-Southern States/Military.**

Minorities

Under **Louisiana/Minorities**, the card catalog includes titles for Germans, Creoles, Spanish, French, Negroes, Acadians, Chinese, and Yugoslavians. Some records for blacks are also classified under **Louisiana/-Slavery and Bondage.**

Native Races

Two Louisiana Indian histories and one book of tribal records are cataloged under **Louisiana/Native Races.**

Notarial Records

Land (conveyance) records are also cataloged under **Louisiana/[Parish]/Notarial Records**. These are usually identical to those cross-referenced under **Louisiana/[Parish]/Land and Property**. They are arranged chronologically and usually contain indexes. See the FHLC for a complete description.

Probate Records

Usually called "Successions," most of the general Louisiana probate records are those compiled by Chapters of the Daughters of the American Revolution. The *St. Landry Papers,* discussed under *Land and Property* above, include some probate records for southwest Louisiana. The library has probate records for most counties. See **Louisiana/[Parish]/Probate Records.** Some probate records may be cross-referenced under **Louisiana/[Parish]/Guardian and Ward**; these entries should also be reviewed.

Public Records

Voting, bonds, ministers, marriage, sheriff's, conveyances (deeds), and circuit court records are cataloged under **Louisiana/[Parish]/Public Records**. Not all are cross-referenced, so you should review these entries for each parish.

Vital Records

The library's general collection under this heading is mainly comprised of compilations made by the Daughters of the American Revolution. The Orena V. Grant Genealogical Collection includes marriage and cemetery records from Louisiana; see **Louisiana/Vital Records** for a description of it and other available records. The library has vital records for most Louisiana counties; see **Louisiana/[Parish]/Vital Records.**

Some West Baton Rouge marriage records are cataloged under **Louisiana/Baton Rouge/County/Business Records and Commerce.**

Voting Registers

Voter registration records are usually cataloged under **Louisiana/[Parish]/Public Records**. A few can be located under **Louisiana/[Parish]/Voting Registers.**

TENNESSEE

Historical Background

1541	Hernando DeSoto reaches area of southeastern Tennessee, claiming the area for Spain.
1682	M. Robert de la Salle explores the region and claims it for France.
1682-1795	North Carolina claims the area.
1730	Sir Alex Cumming visits Cherokees.
1748	Dr. Thomas Walker explores the area from Augusta County, Virginia.
1756	British establish Fort Loudon on the eastern section of the Tennessee River.
1760	Under the direction of Richard Henderson, several frontiersmen explore the area.
1763	France cedes territory to British in the Treaty of Paris.
1763	Treaty of Hard Labour opens the territory; settlers from North Carolina and Virginia move into present-day Tennessee.
1768	Iroquois Indians cede title to the United States.
1768	First settlement made in northeastern Tennessee (Watauga).
1769	William Bean locates a settlement on Boone Creek near the Watauga River, and Joseph Martin settles in Powell's Valley near the Cumberland Gap.
1778	Permanent settlements in eastern section.
1780	The Cumberland region in middle Tennessee is settled by James Robertson and others.
1784	The Watauga and Cumberland settlements petition North Carolina for benefits of government. Petition denied. Watauga settlers organize an independent state called Franklin.
1785	Constitution for Franklin prepared.
1787	North Carolina denies Franklin's constitution.
1789-95	North Carolina militia creates road from Knoxville to Nashville.
1790	Southwest Territory organized with William Blount as territorial governor.
1795	Second petition for statehood.
1796	Tennessee accepted into the Union as the sixteenth state; Tennessee County was reorganized into Montgomery and Robertson counties.
1805	Area betweeen Tennessee River, Buffalo River, and present-day Tennessee-Alabama border is ceded by treaty.
1807	The Natchez Trace is completed, connecting Lexington, Kentucky, Nashville, and Natchez, Mississippi.

1817 Cherokees cede land in southeastern Tennessee.

1818 The Jackson Purchase obtains western portion of present-day Tennessee from the Chickasaw Indians.

1819 Cherokees cede more land in southeastern Tennessee.

1836 The last section of Cherokee land is ceded.

1861 Tennessee secedes from the Union although many men from its eastern counties fight in the Union army.

1865 Tennessee is the first state to rejoin the Union.

Settlement and Migration

Many of the earliest settlers established themselves along the Holston and Watauga rivers in the Western District of North Carolina, believing themselves to be in Virginia. Botetourt County, Virginia, records include entries for some of these early residents. In 1777, North Carolina organized its western lands first as part of Rowan County and later that same year as Washington County, with jurisdiction to the Mississippi River.

Most of Tennessee's early settlers were from North Carolina and Virginia and were Scots-Irish Presbyterians. Germans from Pennsylvania, Virginia, and North Carolina soon followed. Others arrived in the area from South Carolina. French Huguenots also located in Tennessee. Quakers from the Carolinas moved into eastern Tennessee, but a few years later, after the turn of the nineteenth century, most of these families moved to Indiana and Ohio.

In 1779, French Lick in the central part of the region was settled. The middle section was rapidly settled; and in 1783, Davidson County was established. Revolutionary War soldiers from North Carolina were granted land in middle Tennessee. North Carolina also sold land in central Tennessee for five cents an acre, attracting many settlers.

In 1779-80, the border between Tennessee and Kentucky was surveyed; the boundary which was established was called the Walker Line, but proved to be north of the intended line and was disputed for several years. Kentucky finally accepted this erroneous border in 1820, but some sections of the boundary remained obscure until 1859 when a second survey was conducted. Some settlers in the disputed strip were uncertain in which state they lived, though Tennessee exercised jurisdiction over much more of the strip than Kentucky.

In 1790, North Carolina ceded Tennessee to the United States, and Congress created the Territory South of the Ohio River, designating Knoxville as its capital. By 1795 Tennessee had 60,000 citizens, and in 1796 it became the sixteenth state, but Nashville did not become its capital until 1843.

Tennessee was divided politically during the Civil War. Many people in the eastern counties opposed secession. Of the 145,000 soldiers serving from Tennessee during the war, 30,000 of them were in the Union Army. More battles were fought on Tennessee land than any other state, with the exception of Virginia.

Tennessee Library Collection

Archives and Libraries

Histories and guides are available both in the general collection and under some counties, including inventories to the church archives of Tennessee and some collections of the Tennessee State Library and Tennessee Historical Society. Guides are available for Tennessee county records, manuscripts of the Tennessee Historical Society, Tennessee genealogical records, microfilms, some collections in the Tennessee State Library, and depositories of manuscript collections in the state.

Bible Records

Bible records for Tennessee are cataloged under **Tennessee/Bible Records** and **Tennessee/[County]/Bible Records**. Several groups have compiled Bible records for the state; these include the Historical Records Survey of the Works Projects Administration and heritage societies. Others in the collection are:

Acklen, Jeannette Tillotson. *Tennessee Records: Bible Records and Marriage Bonds.* Baltimore: Genealogical Publishing Co., 1967. (FHL# 976.8/V2a or microfilm 0823813, item 4)

Bible Record Collection, c.1700-1970 of the Tennessee State Library and Archives. Nashville: Filmed by the State Library and Archives, 1974. 5 reels. (FHL# microfilm 0975600-0975604)

Bible Records of Western Kentucky and Tennessee. Fulton, Ky: n.pub., c.1975. (FHL# 976.9/V2f)

Biography

Biographical publications are cataloged under **Tennessee/Biography** and **Tennessee/History** as well as **Tennessee/[County]/Biography.** The records of two Tennessee Baptist ministers have been published: FHL# microfilm 0024523 and 976.8/D3bu) Others include:

Acklen, Jeannette Tillotson, comp. *Tennessee Records: Tombstone Inscriptions and Manuscripts, Historical and Biographical.* Nashville: Cullom & Ghertner, 1933. (FHL# 976.8/V22a or microfilm 1000313, item 2)

Carr, John. *Early Times in Middle Tennessee.* Nashville: R. H. Horsley and Associates, 1958. (FHL# 976.84/D3c or microfilm 1035834, item 5)

Civil War Veterans' Biographical and Genealogical Questionnaires, 1914-1922. Nashville: Tennessee State Library and Archives, 1974. (FHL# microfilm 0975591-0975599)

Crutchfield, James A. *Timeless Tennesseans.* Huntsville, Ala.: Strode Publishers, c.1984. (FHL# 976.8/D3cj)

Draper, Lyman Copeland, comp. *Draper's Biographical Sketches.* Chicago: University of Chicago Library, 1951. Microfilm of originals at the State Historical Society of Wisconsin. (FHL# microfilm 0001750)

Keever, Rosalie Ausmus. *Some Pioneer Preachers and Teachers of Tennessee.* Johnson City, Tenn.: n.pub., 1975. (FHL# 976.8/D3mc)

Memorial and Biographical Record: An Illustrated Compendium of Biography, Containing a Compendium of Local Biography, Including Biographical Sketches of Prominent Old Settlers and Representative Citizens of Part of the Cumberland Region of Tennessee. Easley, S.C.: Southern Historical Press, 1980. (FHL# 976.8/D3me)

Speer, William S., comp. and ed. *Sketches of Prominent Tennesseans: Containing Biographies and Records of Many of the Families Who Have Attained Prominence in Tennessee.* 1 vol in 2. Nashville: A. B. Tavel, 1888. (FHL# 976.8/D3s, or microfilm 0833388, or 0874322, items 1-2)

Temple, Oliver Perry. *Notable Men of Tennessee, from 1833 to 1875: Their Times and Their Contemporaries.* Comp. by Mary B. Temple. New York: Cosmopolitan Press, 1912. (FHL# 976.8/D3t)

Cemeteries

The library has cemetery records for most counties; see the FHLC under **Tennessee/[County]/Cemeteries.** One of the largest collections is that prepared by the Historical Records Project and Historical Records Survey–cemetery records for thirty-nine Tennessee counties. These are not cataloged individually by counties, but under **Tennessee/Bible Records, Tennessee/-Cemeteries, Tennessee/Church Records,** and **Tennessee/Genealogy** (FHL# microfilm 0024527-0024530).

Cemetery records in the vertical files of the Lauderdale County Library in Florence, Alabama, are arranged alphabetically by county (FHL# microfilm 1034008, item 3 and 1034009, item 1). Several collections of Tennessee cemetery relocation projects are represented in the collection. For other collections and publications, see **Tennessee/Cemeteries.**

Census Records

No census records are available for Tennessee prior to 1810. Only two counties have extant censuses for 1810: Grainger and Rutherford. The 1820 federal census is incomplete, containing only the middle and western counties. No East Tennessee counties (except Grainger) censuses have been preserved prior to 1830.

Several counties have published censuses; see **Tennessee/[County]/Census, Printed**. Mortality schedules are available for 1850-80 (FHL# microfilm 0422433-0422437) An index to these records was published in Nashville by Byron Sistler and Associates in 1984 (FHL# 976.8/X2t).

The library has indexes for most federal censuses for Tennessee. Tennessee censuses are published for 1810, 1820, 1830, 1850, 1880, and 1890 Union veterans; see **Tennessee/Census.**

For census call numbers see the Registers on the U.S./Canada Reference credenza. A Soundex has been prepared for the 1880, 1900, and 1910 Tennessee censuses. For information on using a Soundex see Chapter 4, "United States: General Information."

Church History and Records

Only a few counties have church histories, but most Tennessee counties have some church records. Church histories include those for Lutherans, Presbyterians, Methodists, and Baptists; see **Tennessee/Church History** and **Tennessee/[County]/Church History**. See other headings: **Tennessee/Church Records/Inventories,** Registers, Catalogs and **Tennessee/Church Records/Sources.**

Thirty-nine counties are included in the Historical Records Survey of Tennessee church records and are cataloged under **Tennessee/Church Records.** Included in the state's general collection are records for Baptist, Lutheran, and Methodist churches. A valuable collection of church records is:

Sistler, Byron. *Vital Statistics from 19th Century Tennessee Church Records.* Nashville: Sistler, 1979. (FHL# 976.8/-K29s)

Court Records

The library has court records for all but two counties (Hancock and Pickett). County court records are cataloged under **Tennessee/[County]/Court Records.** Under early Tennessee divorce laws, the Tennessee General Assembly granted privileges for *femme sole* and divorces until 1858; divorce petitions and legislative acts granting divorces are available in state court records.

Bamman, Gale Williams, and Debbie W. Spero. *Tennessee Divorces, 1797-1858: Taken From 750 Legislative Petitions and Acts.* Nashville: G.W. Bamman, c.1985. (FHL# 976.8/P2b)

Historical Records Survey. *Survey to Tennessee County Court Records, Prior to 1860, in the Second, Third and Fourth Districts.* Transcript at the State Library, Nashville. Filmed by the Genealogical Society of Utah, 1943. (FHL# microfilm 0024531)

Genealogy

Several valuable genealogical collections are cataloged only under **Tennessee/Genealogy**. Many publications include biographies, genealogy, and history for Tennesseans. Thirty-nine counties are represented in the Historical Records Survey of genealogy and related records. See **Tennessee/Genealogy** for a description of the contents. (FHL# microfilm 0024527-0024530)

The Robertson Topp papers of biographical and genealogical data for 1805-1929 have been microfilmed (FHL# microfilm 0570845-0570849).

See also:

Edwards, Olga Jones, and Izora Waters Frizzell. *The Connection in East Tennessee.* Washington, Tenn.: Pioneer Printers, c.1969. (FHL# 976.8885/D2e and microfiche 6046842)

Ray, Worth Stickley. *Tennessee Cousins: A History of Tennessee People.* Austin, Tex.: W. S. Ray, 1950. Salt Lake City: Genealogical Society of Utah, 1959. (FHL# microfilm 0176661)

Ritchie, Ruth. *Genealogy of Some East Tennessee Families of the Early Nineteenth Century.* Salt Lake City: Genealogical Society of Utah, 1972. (FHL# microfilm 0896897, item 3)

Supplement: FHL# 976.8/D2rr/Supp.

Sneed, Adele Weiss. *Tennessee Genealogical Miscellany: A Compilation of Original Church, Court, and Inn Records, Linking Tennessee with Alabama, Kentucky, North Carolina, and Virginia.* N.p.: n.pub., 1960. (FHL# 976.8/D4d)

The FHLC cataloged several guides to genealogical research in Tennessee under **Tennessee/Genealogy/-Handbooks, Manuals, etc.** and **Tennessee/Sources. Tennessee/Genealogy/Periodicals** catalogs many valuable publications in the collection.

History

The library has many state histories of Tennessee and Tennesseans and most counties. They are cataloged under **Tennessee/History** and **Tennessee/[County]/History.** Goodspeed Publishing Company published several regional histories in 1887, cataloged by either state or county.

Lyman Copeland Draper collected valuable historical and genealogical data which he donated to the Wisconsin Historical Society. These have been microfilmed and a guide has been published. Included in this manuscript series are many records pertaining to early Tennessee. See **Tennessee/History** for a brief description of the contents and film numbers.

Representative of works in the collection are:

Caldwell, Mary French. *Tennessee, The Dangerous Example: Watauga to 1849.* Nashville: Aurora Publishers, c.1974. (FHL# 976.8/H2ca or microfilm 1036376, item 1)

Carter, Clarence Edwin, comp., ed. *The Territorial Papers of the United States: The Territory South of the River Ohio, 1790-1796.* Vol. IV. Washington, D.C.: Government Printing Office, 1953. (FHL# microfilm 874226, item 1)

Folmsbee, Stanley John, Robert E. Corlew, and Enoch L. Mitchell. *History of Tennessee.* 4 vols. New York: Lewis Historical Publishing Co., 1960. (FHL# 976.8/H2fs)

Garrett, William Robertson, and Albert Virgil Goodpasture. *History of Tennessee, Its People and Its Institutions.* Nashville: Brandon Print. Co., 1900. (FHL# 976.8/H2g or microfilm 1425569, item 6)

Gilmore, James Roberts. *The Advance-Guard of Western Civilization.* Spartanburg, S.C.: Reprint Co., 1974. (FHL# 976.8/H2gl or microfilm 0962510, item 5)

Hamer, Philip May. *Tennessee: A History, 1673-1932.* 4 vols. Tucson, Ariz.: W. C. Fox, 1974. (FHL# microfilm 1000311, items 1-4)

Haywood, John. *The Civil and Political History of the State of Tennessee from Its Earliest Settlement Up to the Year 1796: Including the Boundaries of the State.* Nashville: Publishing House of the Methodist Episcopal Church, South, 1891. (FHL# 976.8/H2hj)

McGee, Gentry Richard. *A History of Tennessee from 1663 to 1930.* Rev. and enl. by C. J. Ijams. New York: American Book Co., [c.1930]. (FHL# 976.8/H2m)

Moore, John Trotwood, ed., and Austin P. Foster. *Tennessee, The Volunteer State, 1760-1923.* Chicago: S. J. Clark Publishing Co., 1923. (FHL# 976.8/D3m)

Ramsey, James Gettys McGready. *The Annals of Tennessee to the End of the Eighteenth Century: Comprising Its Settlement, as the Watauga Association, From 1769 to 1777; A Part of North Carolina, From 1777 to 1784; The State of Franklin, From 1788 to 1790; The Territory of the U.S., South of the Ohio, From 1790 to 1796; the State of Tennessee, From 1796 to 1800.* 1853; rpt. ed., N.p.: n. pub., 1967. (FHL# 976.8/H2r or microfilm 0024525, item 1)

Williams, Samuel Cole. *Beginnings of West Tennessee, in the Land of the Chickasaws, 1541-1841.* Johnson City, Tenn.: Watauga Press, 1930. (FHL# 976.8/H2wa or microfilm 1415253, item 12)

Additional titles are cataloged under **Tennessee/History, Tennessee/History/[Specific War], Tennessee/-History/Bibliography, Tennessee/History/Indexes, Tennessee/History/Periodicals,** and **Tennessee/History/-Sources.**

Land and Property

The library has land and property records for most counties cataloged under **Tennessee/[County]/Land and Property.** For state records, see **Tennessee/Land and Property.** Included in the statewide collection are North Carolina land grants in Tennessee, 1778-91. (FHL# 976.8/R2b, 976.8/R21c, or microfilm 0024541)

Grants south of Walker's Line are microfilmed from the originals in the Kentucky Land Office in Frankfort; these are Kentucky grants for land in Tennessee (FHL# microfilm 0272869-0272873). North Carolina Revolutionary War warrants, 1783-1806, are microfilmed on fifteen reels, arranged numerically by warrant number (FHL# microfilm 1013361-1013375).

State land grants for 1775 to 1905 and 1911 are filmed from the originals in the Tennessee State Library and Archives in Nashville. Indexes are included in the 229 reels of microfilm; see the FHLC for a description and film numbers.

Military History and Records

The library has several military histories for Tennessee. See **Tennessee/Military History** and **Tennessee/Military History/[War].** Many military records are available for the Revolutionary War, War of 1812, Mexican War, and Civil War (both Union and Confederate). See **Tennessee/Military Records, Tennessee/Military Records/[War]**, and **United States/Military Records/[War].**

Notable in the collection are the indexes to compiled service records for Union and Confederate soldiers who served in Tennessee organizations. Confederate pension applications for soldiers and widows and indexes to them have been microfilmed. These are arranged in numerical order separately for soldiers and widows.

Probate Records

The library has probate records for most Tennessee counties; see **Tennessee/[County]/Probate Records** and **Tennessee/Probate Records.**

Taxation

The library has tax records for most counties cataloged under **Tennessee/[County]/Taxation.** Tax records have been compiled to replace missing U.S. census records, including:

Creekmore, Pollyanna. *Early East Tennessee Taxpayers*. Easley, S.C.: Southern Historical Press, c.1980. (FHL# 976.8/R4cp)

Curtis, Mary Barnett. *Early East Tennessee Tax Lists*. Fort Worth, Tex.: Arrow Printing Co., 1964. (FHL# 976.8/R4c)

Lucas, Silas Emmett. *Revised Index to Early East Tennessee Taxpayers*. Easley, S.C.: Southern Historical Press, c.1982. (FHL# 976.8/R4cp/Index)

Sistler, Byron. *Index to Early Tennessee Tax Lists*. Evanston, Ill.: Sistler, c.1977. (FHL# 976.8/R4s)

Vital Records

Indexes and records of Tennessee deaths, 1908-12 and 1914-25 are available on 189 reels. Birth records for the state are available on eighty-five reels for 1908-12. They are cataloged under **Tennessee/Vital Records**. Marriage records are registered in each county; The library has marriage records for most counties. They are cataloged under **Tennessee/[County]/Vital Records.**

Also in the state collection are:

Death Records of Tennessee. N.p.: n.pub., 1947. (FHL# 976.8/V23dr or microfilm 0874008, item 3)

Lucas, Silas Emmett. *Marriages from Early Tennessee Newspapers, 1794-1851*. Easley, S.C.: Southern Historical Press, c.1978. (FHL# 976.8/V21)

ALABAMA

Historical Background

1702	First permanent white settlers arrive in Alabama.
1710	Mobile moved to its present location. First permanent settlement established in what is now Alabama.
1719	First shipload of slaves arrives at Dauphin Island.
1763	France cedes area including Alabama to Great Britain in the Treaty of Paris.
1776	To escape from Revolutionary War service, some Georgians move into Alabama.
1783	Planters from Georgia, Virginia, and the Carolinas move into Alabama.
1790	Spain's control over the Tombigbee settlements disputed by the United States government; the area of present-day Mobile and Baldwin counties considered Spanish West Florida. Washington County extended into present-day Mississippi.
1795	United States obtains the rest of northern Alabama from Spain through Treaty of San Lorenzo.
1798	Boundary disputes between Georgia and Alabama. Alabama becomes part of Mississippi Territory.
1802	Georgia cedes land in present-day Alabama and Mississippi.
1804	Area ceded by Georgia annexed to Mississippi Territory.
1805	The Chickasaw, Cherokee, and Choctaw tribes cede part of their land claims in the Alabama region.
1808	Scots-Irish from Tennessee move into the Tennessee Valley district.
1812	Area west of Perdido River added to Mississippi Territory.
1815	Following the end of the War of 1812, settlers move into Alabama from nearby southern states.
1817	Alabama Territory organized from Mississippi Territory; St. Stephens named the capital.
1818	The first territorial legislature meets at St. Stephens. Although it has no inhabitants, Cahaba becomes the new capital.
1819	Huntsville becomes the temporary state capital. Alabama became the twenty-second state on 14 December.
1840	Boundary dispute with Georgia is settled; Alabama's present boundaries established.
1861	Alabama secedes from the Union as a sovereign republic, 11 January. On 8 February, joins the Confederate States of America. Montgomery named the capital.
1868	Alabama readmitted to the Union.

Settlement and Migration

The routes of migration primarily followed Indian trails and water courses. Most first settlements were along the Alabama, Tombigbee, and other rivers in the state. Depending upon who claimed the area at the time, settlers secured land grants from the French, English, and Spanish government.

The first Caucasian settlers of the territory were from Spain and France, founding Mobile in 1702, the first community. Spain and France exchanged control until Great Britain secured the area in the Treaty of Paris in 1763.

Some Georgians moved into Alabama to escape military service during the Revolutionary War. Others followed in 1783 as did settlers from Virginia and the Carolinas. After the turn of the century, others from the Carolinas and Virginia settled in the central section of Alabama. Others from these states moved into western Alabama along the Tombigbee and the Black Warrior rivers. A group of Scots-Irish left Tennessee and settled in the Tennessee Valley district in 1809.

After the War of 1812, immigration into Alabama increased significantly. In 1817, Alabama Territory was organized from Mississippi Territory, with its first capital established at St. Stephens. In 1819, a convention was held in Huntsville to draft a constitution and petition for admission as a state. Alabama became the twenty-second state in 1819 with twenty-two organized counties.

Alabama Library Collection

Archives and Libraries

Among the few records under this heading in the FHLC are the list of newspapers available at Samford University's Library (FHL# 976.1/A1/no. 3) and an inventory of the Episcopal Church Archives, made under the auspices of Work Projects Administration (FHL# 976.1/K2h or microfilm 0897366, item 3). Nine additional listings are cataloged under **Alabama/[County]/Archives and Libraries.**

Since Alabama was under the early jurisdiction of several governments, see those archival records cataloged under **Mississippi/Archives and Libraries, Mississippi/History, Mississippi/History/Sources**, and **Mississippi/History/Sources/Colonial Period ca. 1600-1775**. Included in this collection is a list of inhabitants of Mobile in 1764 (FHL# microfilm 0899981).

Bible Records

County Bible records for Alabama have not been microfilmed, but some are available. Consult the FHLC under **Alabama/Bible Records.** Various families for whom Bible records are available are also included in the catalog under this heading.

Biography

The library has several biographical works for Alabama. Most are cataloged under **Alabama/Biography** or **Alabama/History**. Nearly a dozen are cataloged under **Alabama/[County]/Biography**. Included in those represented in the general section are:

Brewer, Willis. *Alabama: Her History, Resources, War Record, and Public Men from 1540 to 1872.* Montgomery: Barett and Brown, Printers, 1872. (FHL# 976.1/H2b or microfilm 0934818, item 3)

DuBose, Joel Campbell, ed. *Notable Men of Alabama: Personal and Genealogical with Portraits.* Spartanburg, S.C.: Reprint Co., 1976. (FHL# 976.1/D3no or microfilm 1026263, items 1-2)

Garrett, William. *Reminiscences of Public Men in Alabama, for Thirty Years: With an Appendix.* Atlanta, Ga.: Plantation Publishing Company's Press, 1872. (FHL# 976.1/D2g)

Memorial Record of Alabama: A Concise Account of the State's Political, Military, Professional and Industrial Progress, Together with the Personal Memoirs of Many of Its People. Madison, Wis.: Brant and Fuller, 1893. (FHL# 976.1/-H2m or microfilm 0934817, items 1-2)

Moore, Albert Burton. *History of Alabama and Her People.* 3 vols. Chicago: American Historical Society, 1927. (FHL# 976.1/D2m)

Northern Alabama, Historical and Biographical. Birmingham: Smith and DeLand, 1888. (FHL# 976.1/D3n or microfilm 0934818, item 2)

Owen, Thomas McAdory. *History of Alabama and Dictionary of Alabama Biography.* 4 vols. Chicago: S. J. Clarke Publishing Co., 1921. (FHL# 976.1/H2o)

______. *Revolutionary Soldiers in Alabama: Being a List of Names, Compiled from Authentic Sources, of Soldiers of the American Revolution, Who Resided in the State of Alabama.* Baltimore: Genealogical Publishing Co., 1975. (FHL# 976.1/M23a or microfilm 0928157, item 4)

Riley, Benjamin Franklin. *Makers and Romance of Alabama History: Embracing Sketches of the Men Who Have Been Largely Instrumental in Shaping the Policies and in Molding the Conditions in Rapid Growth of Alabama, Together with the Thrilling and Romantic Scenes with Which Our History is Resplendent.* N.p.: n.pub., n.d. (FHL# 976.1/-D3r or microfilm 0845129, item 2)

Cemeteries

The library has some cemetery records for most Alabama counties. See **Alabama/[County]/Cemeteries.** A few records are cataloged under **Alabama/Cemetery Records.**

The most notable in the collection are those cemetery records compiled by various chapters' Genealogical Records Committees of the Daughters of the American Revolution (FHL# microfilm 0835121, item 2 and 850122, item 4) and the many volumes of Alabama records compiled by Pauline Jones Gandrud and Kathleen Paul Jones (FHL# 976.1/D29ja, 976.1/D29j, microfilm 0840512-0840529; 0844382-0844391; 0896958, item 2; 0873764, items 3-4; 1033928, item 3; 0908501, item 4; 0962805, item 2; 0002326; 0002356-0002359; 0002361; 0002363; 0002364; and 0896962, item 2).

Cemetery records in the vertical files of the Lauderdale County Library in Florence are arranged alphabetically by county. (FHL# microfilm 1034008, item 3 and 1034009, item 1)

Census

Pauline Jones Gandrud and Kathleen Paul Jones have compiled and transcribed census records; they are cataloged under **Alabama/Cemeteries** above.

Indexes have been compiled for Alabama's 1810,

1811-19, 1816, 1820, 1821-29, 1830, 1831-39, 1840, 1850, 1855, and 1860 federal, territorial, and state censuses. They are cataloged under **Alabama/Census.** Mortality schedules for 1870 and 1880 were published by the Alabama Department of Archives in 1981 (FHL# microfilm 1405189 for 1870 and 1405190-1405191 for 1880).

They are cataloged under **Alabama/Census.** For census call numbers see the Registers on the U.S./Canada Reference credenza.

A special state census was taken in 1907 of Confederate veterans. These records are cataloged under **Alabama/[County]/Census** or **Alabama/[County]/Military Records.**

Church History

The library has records for several denominations: Lutherans, Baptists, Methodists, and Episcopalians. Check **Alabama/Church History, Alabama/Church Records, Alabama/[County]/Church History,** and **Alabama /[County]/Church Records** for additional information.

A list of the general holdings and manuscripts contained in Samford University's Library is cataloged under **Alabama/Church Records/Bibliography.**

Court Records

Few county court records are available at the Family History Library for Alabama other than those included in the collection of Alabama records compiled by Pauline Jones Gandrud and Kathleen Paul Jones. See discussion under *Cemeteries* above.

Emigration and Immigration

Indexes to passenger lists of vessels arriving at miscellaneous ports in Alabama and other southern states are arranged alphabetically on twenty-six reels (FHL# microfilm 1324938-1324963)

Genealogy

Several compilations of genealogical data have been made for Alabama people and families. They are cataloged under **Alabama/Genealogy** and **Alabama/-[County]/Genealogy.** Two Alabama chapters of the Daughters of the American Revolution collected genealogical data as well as other information (FHL# microfilm 907975, items 2-3 and 893747, item 4).

Works cataloged under **Alabama/Biography** and **Alabama/History** also detail genealogical information.

Some central Alabama families are listed in Flora Dainwood England, *Notes on Central Alabama* (Baltimore, Md.: Genealogical Publishing Co., 1977) (FHL# 976.1/D2ef). Some northern Alabama families are recorded in Mary Novella Gibson-Brittain, *The History and Genealogy of Some Pioneer Northern Alabama Families* (Flagstaff, Ariz.: Northland Press, 1969). (FHL# 976.1/Mm2g).

The Central Alabama Genealogical Society published lineage charts of members in 1977 (FHL# 976.1/D2c), and the Tuscaloosa Genealogical Society published a lineage chart book in 1979 (FHL# 976.1/D2t). Pioneer families are included in James Edmonds Saunders, *Early Settlers of Alabama,* 2 vols in 1 (1899; rpt. ed., Baltimore, Md.: Genealogical Publishing Co., 1969. (FHL# 976.1/-D2s).

Most genealogical periodicals for Alabama are cataloged under **Alabama/Genealogy/Periodicals.** Only three are recorded for specific counties. For genealogical source material, see **Alabama/Genealogy/Sources.**

History

Several valuable histories are cataloged under **Alabama/History** or **Alabama/[County]/History.** Many are cross-referenced under **Alabama/Biography.** For city histories, see **Alabama/[County]/[City]/History.** For periodicals pertaining to Alabama, see **Alabama/-History/Periodicals.**

Records for the colonial and territorial periods are cataloged under **Alabama/History/Sources/Colonial Period** and **Alabama/History/to 1819.**

For historical background, see also:

Barefield, Marilyn Davis. *Old St. Stephen's Land Office Records and American State Papers, Public Lands.* Easley, S.C.: Southern Historical Press, c.1983. (FHL# 976.1/R2ha)

Carter, Clarence Edwin, comp., ed. *The Territorial Papers of the United States: Mississippi Territory, 1798-1817.* 2 vols. Washington, D.C.: Government Printing Office, 1938. (FHL# microfilm 874226, item 2 or 929379)

Elliott, Carl. *Annals of Northwest Alabama.* 2d ed. Northport, Ala.: Hermitage Press, 1965. (FHL# 976.1/H2e or microfilm 0962559, item 1)

Fretwell, Mark E. *This So Remote Frontier: The Chattahoochee Country of Alabama and Georgia.* Tallahassee: Rose Printing Co., 1980. (FHL# 975.8/H2ft)

Lackey, Richard Stephen. *Frontier Claims in the Lower South: Records of Claims Filed by Citizens of the Alabama and Tombigbee River Settlement in the Mississippi Territory for Depredations by the Creek Indians During the War of 1812.* New Orleans: Polyanthos, c.1977. (FHL# 976.1/A1/No. 45)

Pickett, Albert James. *History of Alabama and Incidentally of Georgia and Mississippi, from the Earliest Period.* Sheffield, Ala.: R. C. Randolph, 1896. (FHL# 976.1/H2p or microfilm 924406, item 1)

Starr, Joseph Barton. *Tories, Dons, and Rebels: The American Revolution in British West Florida.* Gainesville: University Presses of Florida, c.1976. (FHL# 975.9/H2st)

Land and Property

The library has some land and property records for more than half the counties of Alabama. Several general records are cataloged under **Alabama/Land and Property;** those for counties are cataloged **Alabama/[County]/Land and Property.**

Some land and property records for Alabama families

are included in Pauline Jones Gandrud and Kathleen Paul Jones's collection, cited under *Cemeteries* above.

Since present-day Alabama was originally under the jurisdiction of Mississippi Territory, review the following:

Carter, Clarence Edwin, comp., ed. *The Territorial Papers of the United States: The Territory of Mississippi, 1798-1817*. Vol. V. Washington, D.C.: Government Printing Office, 1953. (FHL# microfilm 874226, item 2)

First Settlers of the Mississippi Territory. Nacogdoches, Tex.: Ericson Books, n.d. (FHL# 976/R2f)

Land grants to pioneer Alabama families.

Early land office records have been published. These are:

Barefield, Marilyn Davis. *Old Cahaba Land Office Records and Military Warrants, 1817-1853*. Mobile: Old South Print, c.1981. (FHL# 976.1/R2ho)

______. *Old Sparta and Elba Land Office Records and Military Warrants, 1822-1860.* Easley, S.C.: Southern Historical Press, 1983. (FHL# 976.1/R2h)

______. *Old St. Stephen's Land Office Records and American State Papers, Public Lands.* Easley, S.C.: Southern Historical Press, 1983. (FHL# 976.1/R2ha)

______. *Old Tuskaloosa Land Office Records and Military Warrants, 1821-1855.* Easley, S.C.: Southern Historical Press, 1984. (FHL# 976.1/R2b)

Maps

The library has a collection of Alabama State Highway Department maps arranged alphabetically by county name. The maps vary in scale, but sixty-seven counties are included. The microfilm copies are poor (FHL# microfilm 0924104 and 0924105, items 1-17).

Dodd, Donald B. *Historical Atlas of Alabama.* University: University of Alabama Press, [1974]. (FHL# 976.1/E7d)

Map of the State of Alabama. Compiled from Official Records of the General Land Office and Other Sources. Washington, D.C.: A. B. Graham, 1895. (Map case FHL# 976.1/E7ug)

Roberts, Barbara, and Annie Ford Wheeler. *Maps in the Samford University Library: An Annotated List*. Birmingham: N.pub., 1977. (FHL# 976.1781/A3r)

Military History and Records

Historical records concerning Alabama's military can be located in the catalog under several headings: **Alabama/Biography, Alabama/Genealogy, Alabama/-History,** and **Alabama/Military History**. Most are cross referenced. Some military history or records are listed for each county under **Alabama/[County]/Military History.**

The collection includes military history for the Revolutionary War, War of 1812, Indian Wars, Mexican War, and Civil War. Pauline Jones Gandrud and Kathleen Paul Jones's collection, cited under *Cemeteries* above, includes military records, arranged by county.

The compiled service records for Alabama Union soldiers (FHL# microfilm 1276612-1276620) have been indexed (FHL# microfilm 1276611). Catalog entries can be located under **Alabama/Military Records** and **United States/Military Records**. For additional information on United States military records, see Chapter 4, "United States: General."

Compiled service records for Confederate soldiers have also been microfilmed from records in the National Archives, Washington, D.C. (FHL# microfilm 0191669-0191673). An alphabetical index for Confederate soldiers who served in organizations from the state of Alabama is on FHL# microfilm 0821949-0821997. Records of the various Alabama military companies are on FHL# microfilm 0880330-0880837.

Native Races

Records for Indians in Alabama can be located under **Alabama/Minorities** and **Alabama/Native Races.**

Passenger Lists

Lists of passengers arriving at Mobile for 1820-62, and some as late as 1884, are available on microfilm. See the discussion on Passenger Lists in Chapter 17. Mobile ship news for 1821-22 is cataloged under **Alabama/-Mobile/Mobile/Emigration and Immigration** (FHL# 976.122/W2m or microfilm 0873856, item 4).

Probate Records

Most probate records for Alabama are recorded by county and are cataloged under **Alabama/[County]/Probate Records.** The compilation of Alabama records, including probate, by Gandrud and Jones, cited under Cemeteries above, is also cataloged under **Alabama/Probate Records.**

England, Flora Dainwood. *Alabama Source Book.* Selma, Ala.: Coffee Printing Co., 1964. (FHL# 976.1/A42 or microfilm 845163, item 6)

Index to Alabama Wills, 1808-1870. N.p.: n.pub., 1955. (FHL# 976.1/S2d)

Tax Records

Tax lists taken during the Mississippi Territorial period have been compiled and published in Ben Strickland and Jean Strickland, *Washington County, Mississippi Territory 1803-1816* (Milton, Fla.: n.pub., c.1980). These records cover the area which later became the Alabama counties of Baldwin, Clarke, Mobile, Monroe, and Washington. See also **Alabama/Tax Records** and **Alabama/[County]/Tax Records.**

Vital Records

The library has some vital records for every Alabama county. Most of these are marriage registers. The 1850, 1870, and 1880 federal mortality schedules contain records of those who died during the preceding twelve months. These schedules are cataloged under two distinct headings and are not completely cross-referenced: **Alabama/Vital Records** and **Alabama/Census.**

TEXAS

Historical Background

1682	First permanent settlement at Isleta, near present-day El Paso.
1685-1700	Missions and military outposts are established at Nacogdoches, San Antonio, and Goliad.
1718	San Antonio, with a military post and a mission, becomes administrative headquarters.
1727	Province of Texas established; boundaries undefined.
1803	Part of Texas acquired by the Louisiana Purchase.
1806	Border dispute attains temporary compromise in region of Neutral Ground between Texas and Louisiana.
1812	Mexico, including the area of present-day Texas, gains independence from Spain.
1819	United States government accepts the Sabine River as the western boundary of Louisiana Territory.
1820	Arkansas Territory organizes Miller County partially inside Texas.
1821	Stephen Austin establishes the first permanent American settlement at San Felipe de Austin.
1822-35	Robertson's Colony (sometimes called Leftwich Colony and Nashville Colony) settles in north central Texas; most colonists are from Nashville, Tennessee area.
1835	Austin, Colorado, Jasper, Milam, and San Patricio counties organized.
1836	Texas declares its independence from Mexico as an independent republic; the brief war includes the battle of the Alamo. Robertson's Colony divided into thirty counties.
1839	Austin is selected as the capital, succeeding Houston.
1845	Texas becomes the twenty-eighth state after boundaries are defined.
1845-48	Mexican War; Mexico cedes claims to Texas.
1861	Over internal opposition, Texas joins the Confederacy.
1866	Texas rejoins the Union.

Settlement and Migration

Spanish missions and military posts were established beginning in 1682 in present-day Texas. Colonists were sent to San Antonio by the Spanish. Louisiana Catholics were encouraged to emigrate and settle in Texas.

In 1812, Mexico, including the area of present-day Texas, gained independence from Spain. Stephen Austin, who had inherited his father's grant, established a permanent American settlement at San Felipe de Austin. The Republic of Texas encouraged only Roman Catholic immigrants; but over the next twenty years, it allowed American Protestants to enter under specified grantees (impresarios).

Benjamin Edwards was the force behind settling 30,000 Americans in 1836; this group became the motivating factor in the movement for an independent Texas. When Antonio Lopez de Santa Anna declared himself dictator of Mexico, the Americans refused to acknowledge his authority. The brief war established the Republic of Texas as a separate nation in 1836.

Over the opposition of Governor Sam Houston and German settlers, Texas joined the Confederacy. Many families from neighboring Arkansas moved into Texas to escape conflicts and conscription during the Civil War. At the conclusion of the Civil War, the state was readmitted to the Union.

Large groups from Tennessee and Arkansas migrated into Texas beginning as early as 1820. Great numbers from Pennsylvania, Ohio, Kentucky, and Tennessee followed the Natchez Trace into Texas. Families from South Carolina and Georgia migrated overland through Alabama and Mississippi to Texas; others join them from Alabama and Mississippi. Many traveled by ship from the port at New Orleans to Galveston.

Germans flocked to Texas during the 1840s. Galveston was the port of entry, maintaining good records from 1846 through 1871. Several groups of European immigrants settled in Texas, including Czechs and Poles. A large group of Norwegians settled in Waco. During the Depression, the Post Cereal Company offered inexpensive land in west Texas for those who would contract to grow grain for the company's products.

Texas Library Collection

Archives and Libraries

The library has several guides to archives and archival collections. Numerous counties also have archives and libraries. Consult the FHLC under **Texas/Archives and Libraries, Texas/Archives and Libraries/Inventories, Registers, Catalogs, Texas/[County]/Archives and History,** and **Texas/[County]/Archives and Libraries/Inventories, Registers, Catalogs.**

Holley, Edward G., and Donald D. Hendricks. *Resources of Texas Libraries.* Austin: Texas State Library, 1968. (FHL# 976.4/ J5h and Staff book area 021.8/H724r)

Kielman, Chester Valls. *Guide to the Microfilm Edition of the*

Texas Archives. 3 vols. Austin: University of Texas, 1967-71. (FHL# 976.4/A5kc)

______. *The University of Texas Archives, A Guide to the Historical Manuscripts Collections in the University of Texas Library.* Austin: University of Texas Press, c.1967. (FHL# 976.4/A5k)

Bible Records

Few Bible records are available for Texas families. There are only three compilations for Texas counties. Chapters of the Daughters of the American Revolution have published some Bible records, which, with a few more, are cataloged under **Texas/Bible Records.**

Biography

Most Texas biographies are cataloged under both **Texas/History** and **Texas/Biography.** Those for counties are cataloged under **Texas/[County]/Biography.** Other headings which assist in locating biographical material are **Texas/Biography/Indexes** and **Texas/-Biography/Periodicals.** Notable in the collection are:

Biographical Souvenir of the State of Texas: Containing Biographical Sketches of the Representative Public, and Many Early Settled Families. Chicago: F. A. Battey, 1889. (FHL# 976.4/D3bs or microfilm 0547587, 0599230, or 1000596, item 2)

Brown, John Henry. *Indian Wars and Pioneers of Texas.* Easley, S.C.: Southern Historical Press, c.1978. (FHL# 976.4/D3b)

Carrington, Evelyn M., ed. *Women in Early Texas.* Austin: Jenkins Publishing Co., c.1975. (FHL# 976.4/D3ca)

Davis, Ellis Arthur, and Edwin H. Grobe, comps. and eds. *The Encyclopedia of Texas.* Dallas: Texas Development Bureau, c.1900. (FHL# 976.4/D3de or microfilm 1000595, item 3, or microfiche 6045947)

______. *The New Encyclopedia of Texas.* 4 vols. Salt Lake City: Genealogical Society of Utah, 1976. (FHL# microfilm 0962725-0962727 and microfiche 6046992)

Hunter, John Marvin, ed. *The Trail Drivers of Texas.* 2 vols. New York: Argosy-Antiquarian, 1963. (FHL# 976.4/-H2hj)

Memorial and Genealogical Record of Southwest Texas: Containing Biographical Histories and Genealogical Records of Many Leading Men and Prominent Families. 1894; rpt. ed., Easley, S.C.: Southern Historical Press, c.1978. (FHL# 976.4/D3mg)

Pickrell, Annie Doom. *Pioneer Women in Texas.* Austin: E. L. Steck Co., c.1929. (FHL# 976.4/D3p or microfilm 1000608, item 1)

Ray, Worth Stickley. *Original Typewritten Copy of Austin Colony Pioneers.* 3 vols. N.p.: n.pub., n.d. (FHL# 976.4/H2ra)

Sowell, Andrew Jackson. *Early Settlers and Indian Fighters of Southwest Texas: Facts Gathered from Survivors of Frontier Days.* 2 vols. New York: Argosy-Antiquarian, c.1964. (FHL# 976.4/D3s)

Wharton, Clarence Ray. *Texas under Many Flags: Texas Biography.* 5 vols. Chicago: American Historical Society, 1930. (FHL# 976.42/H2v or microfilm 1000594)

Cemeteries

Some tombstone inscriptions are available for the state, but most cemetery records in the collection are cataloged under **Texas/[County]/Cemeteries.** Under **Texas/Cemeteries** are cataloged six volumes compiled and donated by the Daughters of the American Revolution (FHL# 976.4/V22d or microfilm 0897234, and 0897235, items 1-2), and two volumes which include cemetery inscriptions for the Peters Colonists from Kentucky and their descendants (FHL# 976.4/D2y or microfilm 0982346, item 3).

Census Records

A census of the Republic of Texas was taken in 1840. No regular state censuses were taken. Although indexes have been compiled for the 1850 federal census, you should carefully review the census itself, for the indexes are incomplete. The 1850, 1860, and 1870 (part) mortality schedules have been published. The library has the 1890 Civil War Union Veterans' census. For census call numbers, see the Registers on the U.S./Canada Reference credenza. Indexes to many of the census records have been compiled.

Some early census records have been published including:

Carpenter, Mrs. V. K. *The State of Texas Federal Population Schedules, Seventh Census of the United States, 1850.* 5 vols. Huntsville, Ark.: Century Enterprises, c.1969. (FHL# 976.4/X2p or microfilm 0823884, item 1)

Mullins, Marion Day. *The First Census of Texas, 1829-1836: To Which Are Added Texas Citizenship Lists, 1821-1845 and Other Early Records of the Republic of Texas.* Washington, D.C.: National Genealogical Society, 1962. Special publications Number 22. (FHL# 976.4/X2mm or microfilm 0844966, item 1, and 1000607, item 12)

Osburn, Mary McMillan, ed. *The Atascosito Census of 1826.* N.p., n. pub., 1963. (FHL# 976.4/A1/no.40 or 976.4/-A1/no.149)

White, Gifford Elmore. *1830 Citizens of Texas.* Austin: Eakin Press, c.1983. (FHL# 976.4/X2wh)

______. *The 1840 Census of the Republic of Texas.* Austin: Pemberton Press, 1966. (FHL# 976.4/X2w)

Woods, Frances. *1850 Mortality Schedules of Texas.* Austin: The author, 1965. (FHL# 976.4/V23w or microfilm 1000607, item 7)

______ *1860 Mortality Schedules of Texas.* Austin: The author, 1966. (FHL# 976.4/V23wf or microfilm 1000607, item 8)

Church History and Records

The library has church histories for the following denominations under **Texas/Church Histories**: Baptist, Catholic, Lutheran, Christian, Methodist, and Presbyterian. Many more are cataloged under **Texas/[Coun-**

ty]/Church History and **Texas/[County]/Church Records.**

Some territorial period church records for present-day Texas are included in Shirley Chaisson Bourquard, *Marriage Dispensations in the Diocese of Louisiana and the Floridas, 1785-1803* (New Orleans: Polyanthos, 1980) (FHL# 973/K2bg)

Colonization

The papers of Stephen Austin contain several valuable records of early settlers of Texas. Consult the FHLC under **Texas/Colonization** for these and other books on Texas pioneers. Also see the papers concerning Robertson's Colony in Texas under **Texas/Colonization/Sources.** This colony flourished under different names from 1822 to 1835. When Texas became independent in 1836, the area was subdivided into thirty counties.

Emigration and Immigration

Knowing migration patterns into Texas is often necessary to locate the prior place of residence. Many titles are included in the collection under **Texas/Emigration and Immigration**, but only a few are listed under **Texas/[County]/Emigration and Immigration.** See also the Author/Title catalog under **First Settlers** for several books concerning early settlers in Texas counties. Nationalities discussed in separate works are German, Polish, Spanish, Americans, Swedish, and French.

Genealogy

The library has records compiled by the Daughters of the American Revolution, individual authors, and publications. Some are cross-referenced under **Texas/History** and **Texas/Biography.** Also consult the FHLC under **Texas/[County]/Genealogy.**

The library has a number of works cataloged under **Texas/Genealogy/Bibliography**. There are many entries for **Texas/Genealogy/Periodicals**, although the library usually has only one issue of each.

Several helpful guides are cataloged under **Texas/-Genealogy/Sources.**

History

The library has many regional histories as well as county histories. They are cataloged under **Texas/History** and **Texas/[County]/History**. Other headings include **Texas/History/[War]** and **Texas/History/Periodicals.**

Records for disputed areas of Texas are not all filed under Texas. See also **Arkansas/Miller, Arkansas/Gillespie,** and **Oklahoma/Greer** for additional listings.

Barkley, Mary Starr. *A History of Central Texas.* [Austin]: Austin Printing Co., c.1970. (FHL# 976.4/H2ba)

Brown, John Henry. *History of Texas, from 1685 to 1892.* 2 vols. St. Louis: L. E. Daniell, c.1892-93. (FHL# 976.4/H2b or microfilm 1000590, items 2-3)

Connor, Seymour V. *The Peters Colony of Texas: A History and Biographical Sketches of the Early Settlers.* Austin: Texas State Historical Association, 1959. (FHL# 976.4/D3c)

Daniell, Lewis E. *Texas, The Country and Its Men: Historical, Biographical, Descriptive.* [Austin]: n.pub., c.1924. (FHL# 976.4/H2d)

Ericson, Carolyn Reeves, and Frances Terry Ingmire. *First Settlers of the Republic of Texas: Headright Land Grants Which Were Reported as Genuine and Legal by the Traveling Commissioners, January, 1840.* Nacogdoches, Tex.: Carolyn R. Ericson, c.1982. (FHL# 976.4/R3[illegible])

Johnson, Frank W. *A History of Texas and Texans.* 5 vols. Chicago: American Historical Society, 1914. (FHL# 976.4/H2j or microfilm 0547564)

Salter, Anne, and Phyllis Wolf, eds. *The Calendar of the Claude Elliott Collection, 1821-1937.* Austin: n.pub., 1970. (FHL# 976.4/A5s or microfilm 0908751, item 3)

Webb, Walter Prescott, ed. *The Handbook of Texas.* 3 vols. Austin: Texas State Historical Association, 1952-76. Vol. 3: A supplement, edited by Eldon Stephen Branda. (FHL# 976.4/A7h)

Williams, J. W. *Old Texas Trails.* Ed. and comp by Kenneth F. Neighbours. Burnet, Tex.: Eakin Press, c.1979. (FHL# 976.4/H2wj)

Wooten, Dudley Goodall, ed. *A Comprehensive History of Texas, 1685 to 1897.* Tucson: W. C. Cox Co., 1974. (FHL# microfilm 1000591)

Yoakum, Henderson K. *History of Texas, from Its First Settlement in 1685 to Its Annexation to the United States in 1846.* 2 vols. New York: Redfield, 1855. (FHL# 976.4/H2y)

Land and Property

The library has a good collection of land records for the numerous Texas counties under **Texas/[County]/Land and Property.**

See also:

Miller, Thomas Lloyd. *Bounty and Donation Land Grants of Texas 1835-1888.* Austin: University of Texas Press, 1967. (FHL# 976.4/R21m or microfilm 1000608, item 9)

Military Records

The largest collection of military records for Texans is Confederate pension applications. They are arranged in numerical order with an index. The library has the compiled service records for Union and Confederate soldiers arranged in alphabetical order and including records for the Independent Partisan Rangers, Texas Cavalry, and miscellaneous cards, and personal papers. Consult the FHLC under **Texas/Military Records**. See also:

Ingmire, Frances Terry. *Texas Rangers: Frontier Battalion, Minute Men, Commanding Officers, 1847-1900.* 6 vols. St. Louis: Ingmire Publications, c.1982. (FHL# 976.4/M2ift)

_____, comp. *Texas Ranger Service Records, 1830-1846.* St. Louis, Mo.: F. T. Ingmire, c.1982. (FHL# 976.4/M2if)

Mexican War service records for 1845-77 are also available in the library; see **Texas/Military Records.**

Minorities

Minorities included in the collection are Belgians, Germans, Polish, Irish, French, Czechs, American Indians, Ukrainians, blacks, Swedish, Italians, and Mexicans. See also entries cataloged under **Texas/Minorities/Biography, Texas/Minorities/Genealogy, Texas/Minorities/History**, and **Texas/Minorities/Periodicals.**

Native Races

American Indian records can be found in the catalog under **Texas/Native Races** and **Texas/Minorities.** Tribes in Texas included the Arkokosa, Attacapa, Caddo, Coahuiltecan, Comanche, Karankawa, Nacogdoches, Nasoni, Neche, and Tonkawa.

Naturalization

Most naturalization records are cataloged under **Texas/[County]/Naturalization.** Some titles are also cataloged under **Texas/Naturalization.** Passenger lists for Galveston for 1846-71 are available in the collection.

Probate Records

Probate records are usually cataloged under **Texas/[County]/Probate Records.** Most probated matters are under the jurisdiction of the county court, but large populated counties have probate courts.

Vital Records

The largest collection of records for Texas probably falls under the category of **/Vital Records.** Many more have been microfilmed and are available in the library even though they have not been cataloged. One may review the list of these film numbers at the U.S. and Canada Reference Desk by request.

County vital records are cataloged under **Texas/-[County]/Vital Records.** Several other collections are included under **Texas/Vital Records**, including compilations by the Daughters of the American Revolution and others.

MISSOURI

Historical Background

1673	Jacques Marquette and Louis Joliet explore the area.
1682	M. Robert de la Salle claims the region for France.
1700	Catholic mission established at present site of St. Louis.
1735	French settlers from Illinois establish Ste. Genevieve.
1763	France cedes the region to Spain.
1764	St. Louis founded by Pierre Laclede, a French fur trader from New Orleans.
1777	George Rogers Clark and his "Illinois" troops explore area.
1787	First American settlement is made in Ste. Genevieve County.
1790	Settlement in present-day Perry County.
1795	American settlements on Femme Osage creek in Upper Louisiana, present St. Charles County.
1800	Spain cedes region to France in secret negotiations.
1803	France sells Louisiana Territory to the United States, including present-day Missouri.
1805	Missouri becomes part of Louisiana Territory.
1812	Missouri Territory organized with a population of 20,000.
1815	Peace treaties end Indian attacks.
1821	Missouri becomes the twenty-fourth state.
1820	Missouri Compromise passed by Congress, prohibiting slavery in the Louisiana Territory and allowing Missouri to be a slave-holding state.
1854	Congress repeals Missouri Compromise; all territories to decide slave/free status for themselves.
1857	Missouri Compromise declared unconstitutional; Congress has no right to prohibit slavery in the territories.
1861-65	During the Civil War, Missouri's northern counties support the Union, but many in the southern counties support the Confederacy. Several battles fought on Missouri land.

Settlement and Migration

The first migration into Missouri occurred in 1735 when Frenchmen from Illinois settled in Ste. Genevieve County. The first Americans, John Dodge and associates, located there beginning in 1787, followed by Israel Dodge in 1790 and Dr. Jesse Bryan in 1793.

John Moore migrated into present-day Perry County about 1790, and additional American settlements were made north of St. Louis in 1795 in present-day St. Charles County. When the Louisiana Purchase was completed in 1803, most of the inhabitants of present-day Missouri were Frenchmen from the Illinois country. Americans from Kentucky, Tennessee, and Virginia were among the earliest inhabitants. By 1812, St. Louis was a growing American town, and the area had approximately 20,000 residents. Missouri Territory was created by Congress in 1812. In 1821 as a result of the Missouri Compromise of Congress, Missouri became the twenty-fourth state with a population of about 56,000.

The first immigrants to the region of Missouri were French. Later, settlers in Missouri arrived from Kentucky, Virginia, and the Carolinas. Others migrated from Maryland, Pennsylvania, and Tennessee. Although discouraged by constant British-provoked Indian attacks, the settlements endured.

After 1830, a constant flow of immigrants from Europe entered Missouri. Although many Germans settled in St. Louis, Irish, English, Poles, Swiss, Bohemians, and Italians established homes in various sections of the state.

Missouri Library Collection

Archives and Libraries

The library has guides to manuscript collections, vital statistics, church archives, and inventories of the Federal Records Center in Kansas City and western district court records. Consult the FHLC under **Missouri/Archives and Libraries.** County collections are cataloged under **Missouri/[County]/Archives and Libraries.** Under **Missouri/History/Sources,** is a catalog of the manuscripts in the National Library of Spain which deal with Missourians.

Bible Records

The library has only a few county collections of Bible records besides DAR compilations. They can be located in the catalog under **Missouri/Bible Records** and **Missouri/[County]/Bible Records.**

Bibliography

Only three bibliographies are available for Missouri:

Bates, Frederick. *The Life and Papers of Frederick Bates.* 2 vols. St. Louis: Missouri Historical Society, 1926. (FHL# 921.73/B318b)

Records of Frederick Bates, Secretary of Missouri Territory and a Governor of Missouri.

Bibliography of the Ozarks Books. Salt Lake City: Genealogical Society of Utah, 1977. (FHL# or microfilm 0982434, item 4)

Conard, Howard Louis, ed. *Encyclopedia of the History of Missouri: A Compendium of History and Biography for Ready Reference.* 6 vols. New York: Southern History Co., 1901. (FHL# 977.8/H2c or microfilm 1000272-1000273, items 1-2; 0844960, item 1; 0924411, item 1)

Biography

The library has many biographies cataloged under **Missouri/Biography, Missouri/History,** and **Missouri/[County]/Biography.**

Cemeteries

Numerous collections of cemetery records have been compiled for Missouri; almost every county is represented. One collection includes 196 cemeteries arranged in three volumes for fourteen counties. Another contains headstone inscriptions copied from ten counties. Several chapters of the Daughters of the American Revolution have collected Missouri cemetery records. See **Missouri/Cemeteries** and **Missouri/[County]/Cemeteries.**

Census

Censuses available at the Family History Library include a territorial census recorded in the fall of 1817 (FHL# microfilm 0599782, items 1-2) and the 1860 mortality schedule (FHL# 977.8/X2m). The 1890 federal census for Union veterans and their widows is included in the collection. For census call numbers, see the Registers on the U.S./Canada Reference credenza. Indexes have been prepared for Missouri censuses for 1820-50.

Church History and Records

Church histories are available for Baptists, Catholics, Methodists, and Mormons. See **Missouri/Church History.** A few histories are cataloged under **Missouri/[County]/Church History.** See also a small bibliography of manuscript collections of the Missouri Baptist Historical Society (FHL# 977.8/Al/no.47 and 0908038, item 11)

The library has Church records for Baptists, Catholics, and Mormons under **Missouri/Church Records** and church records from most Missouri counties under **Missouri/[County]/Church Records.**

Some church records are included in the John J. Watts Collection (FHL# or microfilm 0485322-0485326). Bibliographies of Baptist and Lutheran records are cataloged under **Missouri/Church Records/Bibliography.**

Court Records

Early court records for St. Louis include both French and Spanish documents for 1766-1816 arranged chronologically (FHL# microfilm 0981650-0981652 and 1005424-1005426). The library has court records for most counties; see **Missouri/[County]/Court Records.**

Genealogy

Several valuable biographies and genealogical collections are cataloged under **Missouri/Genealogy** and **Missouri/Biography.** See also **Missouri/Genealogy/Bibliography, Missouri/Genealogy/Handbooks, Manuals, etc., Missouri/Genealogy/Indexes, Missouri/Genealogy/Periodicals, Missouri/Genealogy/Societies,** and **Missouri/Genealogy/Sources.** Several lineage societies have compiled their records and donated copies to the library.

Notable in the Missouri genealogical collection are:

Bryan, William Smith. *A History of the Pioneer Families of Missouri With Numerous Sketches, Anecdotes, Adventures,*

Etc., Relating to Early Days in Missouri. St. Louis: Bryan, Brand & Co., 1876. (FHL# microfilm 823561, item 1 or 1000307, item 1)

Hodges, Nadine, Mrs. John Vineyard, and Mrs. Howard W. Woodruff, comps. *Missouri Pioneers, County and Genealogical Records*. 7 vols. N.p.: The compilers, 1967. (FHL# 977.8/D2h or microfilm 0496617, items 8-9; 0496618 items, 1-4; 0823774 item 5)

Phillips, Bud. *The New Ozark Cousins; Genealogical Records of over One Hundred Ozark Families*. Bristol, Va.: B. Phillips, 1984. (FHL# 929.273/P541p)

Pompey, Sherman Lee. *Genealogical Notes on the Missourians.* 2 vols. Salt Lake City: Genealogical Society of Utah, 1968. (FHL# microfilm 0564340 or 0564335, item 2)

Watts, John J. *John J. Watts Collection, 1874-1912.* Rolla, Mo.: University of Missouri microfilm lab, 1980. (FHL# microfilm 0485322-0485326)

History

Almost every Missouri county has at least one published history in the collection. Paul C. Nagel, *Missouri: A Bicentennial History* (New York: Norton, c.1977) includes several pages of bibliography about Missouri history. See also **Missouri/History/[War], Missouri/-History/Bibliography, Missouri/History/Chronology, Missouri/History/Periodicals,** and **Missouri/History/-Sources.** Several statewide histories are also included; some have been described under Biography or Genealogy. Others include:

Carter, Clarence Edwin, comp., ed. *The Territorial Papers of the United States: The Territory of Louisiana-Missouri, 1806-1814.* Vol. XIV. Washington, D.C.: Government Printing Office, 1953. (FHL# microfilm 874230)

______. *The Territorial Papers of the United States: The Territory of Louisiana-Missouri, 1815-1821.* Vol. XV. Washington, D.C.: Government Printing Office, 1953 (FHL# microfilm 874231, item 1)

Davis, Walter Bickford, and Daniel S. Durrie. *An Illustrated History of Missouri.: Comprising Its Early Records, and Civil, Political, and Military History from the First Exploration to the Present Time, Including Biographical Sketches of Prominent Citizens.* St. Louis: A. Hall, 1876. (FHL# 977.88/H2d or microfilm 0928064, item 9)

Douglass, Robert Sidney. *Southwest Missouri, A Narrative Account of Its Historical Progress, Its People and Its Principal Interests.* Chicago: Lewis Publishing Co., 1912. (FHL# 977.89/H2d or microfilm 1000278, items 1-2)

Houck, Louis. *A History of Missouri from the Earliest Explorations and Settlements until the Admission of the State into the Union*. 3 vols. Chicago: R. R. Donnelley, 1908. (FHL# 977.8/H2h)

McReynolds, Edwin C. *Missouri, A History of the Crossroads State.* Norman, Okla.: University of Oklahoma Press, c.1962. (FHL# 977.8/H2mc)

Stevens, Walter Barlow. *Centennial History of Missouri (The Center State): One Hundred Years in the Union, 1820-1921.* 6 vols. St. Louis: S. J. Clarke Publishing Co., c.1921. (FHL# 977.8/H2s)

Violette, Eugene Morrow. *A History of Missouri.* Boston: D. C. Heath & Co., c.1918. (FHL# 977.8/H2v)

Williams, Walter, ed. *A History of Northwest Missouri.* 3 vols. Chicago: Lewis Publishing Co., 1915. (FHL# 977.81H2w or microfilm 0824094-0824095, item 1, and 1000279)

______. *A History of Northeast Missouri.* 3 vols. Chicago: Lewis Publishing Co., 1913. (FHL# 977.83/H2w or microfilm 0897427-0897428, item 1, or 1000276)

Land and Property

The library has some land and property records for almost every Missouri county. See **Missouri/[County]/-Land and Property.** Missouri land was issued under several jurisdictions. See also **Missouri/Land and Property** and **Missouri/Land and Property/Indexes** for territory or state land records.

Dunaway, Maxine, comp. *Missouri Military Land Warrants, War of 1812.* Springfield, Mo.: M. Dunaway, c.1985. (FHL# microfilm 0893713, items 1-2)

First Settlers of the Missouri Territory. 2 vols. Nacogdoches, Tex.: Ericson Books, c.1983. (FHL# 977.8/R2f)

Ingmire, Frances Terry. *Citizens of Missouri.* 3 vols. St. Louis: F. T. Ingmire, c.1984. (FHL# 977.8/R2i)

Volume 1 covers 1787-1810. Volumes 2 and 3 contain grants in present states of Missouri, Arkansas, and Oklahoma 1787-1835.

Land Patents, 1800's-Early 1900's. Jefferson City, Mo.: State of Missouri, 1971. (FHL# microfilm 984749-984764)

Index to and records of swamp lands patents, school lands, seminary and saline lands, and 500,000 acre grants.

Register of Lands. *Tax Deeds, 1847-1878.* Jefferson City, Mo.: State of Missouri, 1970. (FHL# microfilm 0984795-0984801)

Recorder of Land Titles. *Record Books, 1795-1808.* Jefferson City, Mo.: State of Missouri, 1970. (FHL# microfilm 0984777-0984779 and 0984906-0984909)

Includes index to French and Spanish land grants, 1795-1812 and Spanish land grants, surveys, and claims. Microfilm of original records. Many dates are mixed. Text in Spanish and English.

United States, General Land Office. *Missouri Land Plats, 1800's.* Jefferson City, Mo.: State of Missouri, 1969. (FHL# microfilm 984742-984748)

Microfilm of original records.

______. *Records of Missouri Swamp Lands: Original Selections, New Selections, and Sales, 1800's.* Jefferson City, Mo.: State of Missouri, 1969. (FHL# microfilm 984820-984898)

Microfilm of original records, arranged by counties.

______. *United States Land Sales in Missouri, 1827-1903.* Jefferson City, Mo.: State of Missouri, 1969. (FHL# microfilm 984765-984776)

Includes index to land sales, 1818-93. Microfilm of original records. Dates are mixed.

Maps

The library has a good collection of maps cataloged under **Missouri/Maps and Missouri/[County]/Maps.**

Military History and Records

History and records are available for the Revolutionary War (cataloged under **/History**), the Civil War (under **/History and Military History**), and the Spanish-American War (under **/Military Records**). Confederate pension applications and soldiers' home admission records are available on FHL# microfilm 1021101-1021127, cataloged under **Missouri/Military Records** and **United States/Military Records.**

Military records for 1812-1904 from the Adjutant General's Office are in the library's collection. FHL# microfilm 1203650 contains the general index for Seminole, Mexican, and Civil wars. The microfilm records for individuals can be located under **Missouri/Military Records**; they are arranged alphabetically and by military units.

Probate Records

The library has probate records for most counties cataloged under **Missouri/[County]/Probate Records** and **Missouri/[County]/Guardian and Ward.**

Vital Records

The library has marriage records for almost every Missouri county cataloged under **Missouri/[County]/Vital Records.** Other vital records, such as birth and death records are available for some counties. Births and deaths were recorded in most Missouri counties during 1883-1907, and the library has many of them.

KENTUCKY

Historical Background

1739 M. Lonqueil and his French troops discover Big Bone Lick in central Kentucky.

1748 Dr. Thomas Walker follows directions given by Samuel Stalnacker to the Cumberland Gap.

1750 Walker leads Loyal Land Company explorers into Kentucky, crossing the Kentucky, Cumberland, and Big Sandy rivers.

1751 Christopher Gist, Ohio Company representative, reaches what is now Clark County.

1763 French and Indian War ends; Ohio River designated as the boundary between the Indians and whites. Kentucky area under jurisdiction of Augusta County, Virginia.

1772 Fincastle County, Virginia, organized; includes all of present-day Kentucky.

1773 McAfee brothers and others survey land on the Salt River.

1774 Harrodsburg established, first permanent settlement in Kentucky. Richard Henderson purchases all land lying between the Ohio, Kentucky, and Cumberland Rivers from the Indians for his Transylvania Company.

1775 Daniel Boone and others build Fort Boonesborough as headquarters for the Transylvania Company.

1776 Simon Kenton and Thomas Williams clear land and plant corn at Kenton's Station. Indian raids force settlers to abandon Hinkston's Station; they move to McClelland's Station. Residents of Boonesborough and Harrodsburg, meeting at Harrodsburg, vote to make Kentucky a county and elect George Rogers Clark and John Gabriel Jones as Assemblymen. Virginia legislature first rejects, then accepts. Kentucky County created from Fincastle County.

1777 Logan's (Asaph's) Station in present-day Lincoln County and a station on Pleasant Run in today's Washington County are completed. McClelland's Station and settlements at Leestown and Danville abandoned. Census is taken at Fort Harrod, Boonesborough, and Logan's Fort.

1778 Indian attacks reduce Kentucky settlements to three. George Rogers Clark selected to lead an expedition against the British posts in Illinois; it helps to secure Kentucky as a territory of Virginia.

1779-80 Courts of Virginia Land Commission are held at St. Asaph's, Louisville, Boonesborough, Harrodsburg, and Bryan's Station.

1780 Most residents of Martin's and Ruddle's Stations are captured by Indians. Robert Patterson begins erecting a fort at site of present-day Lexington. Bryan's Station, five miles northeast, is settled. Kentucky County is divided into three counties: Fayette, Jefferson, and Lincoln.

1781 Fort Jefferson abandoned. Boone's Wilderness Road widened. Kentucky county courts enact a land survey to make available inexpensive land.

1782 Fort Nelson constructed at present-day Louisville. Virginia establishes district of Kentucky.

1783 Supreme Court for the entire district opens at

	Harrodsburg. Land prices reduced and easier terms offered.
1784	Nelson County organized.
1785	Bourbon, Mercer, and Madison counties created. George Rogers Clark and others conclude treaty with Indians. Shippingport settled.
1786	Frankfort, Stanford, and Washington settled.
1788	Mason and Woodford counties organized.
1792	Logan County created. Kentucky becomes the fifteenth state. First post office west of the Allegheny Mountains is established at Danville.
1794	At Battle of Fallen Timbers, U.S. forces crush Indian resistance. First Episcopal Church in Kentucky established at Lexington.
1797	Methodist and Presbyterian camp meetings.
1803	Louisiana Purchase enables Kentuckians to trade down the Mississippi River.
1805	Cherokees cede land in southeastern section of the state.
1812-5	Many men from Kentucky serve in the War of 1812.
1818	Jackson Purchase from Chickasaws adds land in southwestern portion of state.
1845-48	Some Kentuckians give military service during the Mexican War.
1861-65	Kentucky remains neutral only four months. Counties and families are divided. Generally, the center and western regions endorse the Confederacy, while eastern counties support the Union. Kentucky soldiers serve in the Confederate and Union armies.

Settlement and Migration

Early settlers into Kentucky arrived from Pennsylvania, Maryland, Virginia, and North Carolina. Settlements were made in several areas of the state, but most early ones were abandoned because of Indian attacks. Still, settlers kept coming for the rich, fertile land available on inexpensive terms. Many of those who enlisted in Virginia during the Revolutionary War were rewarded with warrants for Kentucky land in lieu of cash.

Richard Henderson, of North Carolina, established a land-dealing organization called the Transylvania Company and purchased from the Indians all the land between the Kentucky, Cumberland, and Ohio rivers to the Cumberland Mountains. He hired Daniel Boone, James Harrod, and others to survey the area. Restrictions imposed by the government in 1775 limited his success.

Already existing settlements were then abandoned because of Indian hostilities. Harrod founded a namesake town, the first permanent settlement in Kentucky in 1774. Boone brought a company from North Carolina through the Cumberland Gap and up the Wilderness Road. They built Fort Boonesborough as headquarters for Henderson's company in 1775.

Simon Kenton, of Fauquier County, Virginia, and others cleared land and planted corn at Kenton's Station in 1776.

That same year, residents from Hinkston's Station, formerly from Pennsylvania, moved to McClelland's Station. Other outposts were built including Leestown near present-day Frankfort, Logan's Station in what is now Lincoln County, and Sandusky's Station in today's Washington County.

A census taken in February 1777 showed that Harrodsburg was populated by eighty-one able-bodied men, four old or infirm men, twenty-four women, twelve children over ten, twelve Negro slaves over ten, fifty-eight white children under ten, and seven black children under ten. At the same time, Boonesborough had forty men and Logan's Station had twenty men.

By 31 December 1777, the Indian attacks were so severe that only three settlements were left: Boonesborough with twenty-two men, Harrodsburg with sixty-five men, and Logan's with fifteen men. On 22 June 1780, most of the residents of Martin's and Ruddle's stations in present-day Bourbon County were captured by raiding Indians, encouraged by British in the Northwest Territory.

Near the settlement at Harrodsburg, four stations were built: Harrod's Boiling Springs, Sandusky's, McGary's, and McAfee's. Four additional settlements expanded from Logan's Station: Whitley's, Worthington's, Field's, and Pitman. A fort was erected at Lexington in 1780. Bryan's Station, five miles northeast, was settled that year and Fort Nelson was built at Louisville in 1782. Additional early stations included Linn's Station on Beargrass Creek, Brashear's on Floyd's Creek, and Sullivan's Station near present-day Louisville.

In December 1781, the widening of the Wilderness Road was completed, making it passable for wagons. Earlier that year, new Virginia legislation made Kentucky land easy to purchase. The dual combination brought thousands into Kentucky.

During the earliest migrations, families from northwest North Carolina traveled through the Blue Ridge Mountains into the lower Valley of Virginia, through the Cumberland Gap, and up the Wilderness Road. The road split and the western portion led to Harrodsburg while the eastern section went to Boonesborough. Other settlements were established by pioneers coming via the Ohio River. Many left from Fort Redstone in present-day Fayette County, Pennsylvania, and followed the Ohio River downstream towards today's Cincinnati. From the Ohio River, some followed the Licking River into northeastern Kentucky. Others followed the Salt River into north central Kentucky, more trailed the Kentucky River south into the interior of the territory, while still others proceeded along smaller tributaries.

Even by 1795, the population was concentrated in the north central region of the state. Eastern and southwestern Kentucky were relatively unsettled until after two treaties were signed with Indians. In 1805, the

Cherokees ceded their claim to southeastern Kentucky; and in 1818 with the Jackson Purchase, the Chickasaws ceded the southwestern portion.

Kentucky Library Collection

Archives and Libraries

The library has several valuable guides to collections of Kentucky records under **Kentucky/Archives and Libraries** as well as **Kentucky/[County]/Archives and Libraries.** A collection in Chicago's Newberry Library about Kentucky is cataloged under **Kentucky/Bibliography.**

Most helpful in the Family History Library's collection are the following:

Clift, Garrett Glenn. *Guide to the Manuscripts of the Kentucky Historical Society*. Frankfort: Kentucky Historical Society, 1968. (FHL# microfilm 467392)

Duff, Jeffrey Michael. *Inventory of Kentucky Birth, Marriage, and Death Records, 1852-1910.* Rev. ed. Frankfort: Archives Branch, Public Records Division, Department for Libraries and Archives, c.1980, 1982. (FHL# 976.9/V23dj)

Griffin, Warren B. *Preliminary Inventory Records of the United States Courts from the Districts of Kentucky: Record Group 21.* Chicago: Federal Records Center, 1968. (FHL# 976.9/A1/no. 156 or microfilm 1036817, item 15)

Hathaway, Beverly West. *Inventory of County Records of Kentucky.* West Jordan, Utah: Allstates Research Co., c.1974. (FHL# 976.9/A5hb)

Kentucky Historical Society: Microfilm Catalog. 2 vols. N.p.: n.pub., c.1975. (FHL# 976.9/A5k)

Bible Records

Julia Hoge Spencer Ardery's extensive collection of Kentucky genealogical records includes family Bible records. Although somewhat difficult to locate in her massive amount of data, the Bible records appear within the alphabetical arrangement of counties. Two volumes have been published, but only volume one has been microfilmed. (Vol. 1: FHL# 976.9/D2a or microfilm 0007850; Vol. 2: 976.9/D2a/Vol.2)

Typescript and manuscript copies of Bible records from Kentucky are on FHL# 0376982 and 318182. Several compilations of Bible records by DAR chapters are on FHL# 855035, item 3-6; 855037, item 7; 855038, item 12; 851646, item 9; and 976.9/D2da.

Bible records are cataloged under **Kentucky/Bible Records** and **Kentucky/[County]/Bible Records.**

Biography

Many biography titles are cross-referenced under **Kentucky/Biography, Kentucky/Genealogy**, and **Kentucky/History.**

Several valuable publications are included in the collection. Histories or biographies with a specific county in the title are cataloged under **Kentucky/[County]/Biography, etc.**

Cemeteries

Many cemetery records for Kentucky have been copied and published in manuscript or book form. The library's large collection of them is cataloged under **Kentucky/Cemeteries and Kentucky/[County]/Cemeteries.**

Julia Hoge Spencer Ardery's Kentucky genealogical notes and records includes tombstone inscriptions within the alphabetical arrangement of counties. The Daughters of the American Revolution have compiled many manuscript collections of Kentucky cemetery records, usually arranged by county (FHL# microfilm 855035, item 5-6; 855036, item 3-5; 855037, item 7; 855038, item 12; and 0907997, items 1-3).

Other statewide collections are:

Coyle, Malle B., and Lorena Eubanks. *Kentucky Cemetery Records.* Lexington: Kentucky Society, Daughters of the American Revolution, 1960. (FHL# 976.9/V22d or microfilm 0873712, items 1-2)

Johnson, Robert Foster. *Wilderness Road Cemeteries in Kentucky, Tennessee, and Virginia.* Owensboro, Ky.: McDowell Publications, c.1981. (FHL# 973/V3j)

Maupin, Judith Anne. *The Kentucky Lake Cemetery Relocation Project.* N.p.: Winchester Print. Co., 1975. (FHL# 976/V22m or microfilm 09288079, item 6)

Census

The earliest census records for Kentucky were destroyed, but compilations of extant tax records replace the missing schedules to some extent. They are cataloged under **Kentucky/Census.** Some counties have compiled censuses cataloged under **Kentucky/[County]/Census.**

Mortality schedules are available for Kentucky. Those of some counties for 1850, and all counties for 1860-80 have been microfilmed from a collection at the Daughters of the American Revolution Library in Washington, D.C. These records, plus an index and abstract for the 1880 schedules, are on FHL# 422419-422427.

Federal censuses are available for 1810 through 1910; for census call numbers, see the Registers on the U.S./Canada Reference credenza. The library also has several indexes for Kentucky censuses. The 1890 Veterans' Schedules for Kentucky are available for Civil War soldiers and their widows.

Bell, Annie Walker Burns. *Third Census of the United States, 1810, State of Kentucky.* 7 vols. Washington, D.C.: Bell, 1933. (FHL# 976.9/X28b or microfilm 0008658-0008659, or 0481054, item 2)

Clift, Garrett Glenn. *Second Census of Kentucky – 1800: A Privately Compiled and Published Enumeration of Tax Payers Appearing in the 79 Manuscript Volumes Extant of Tax Lists of the 42 Counties of Kentucky in Existence in 1800.* Baltimore, Md.: Genealogical Publishing Co., 1966. (FHL# 976.9/X2p)

Heinemann, Charles Brunk. *First Census of Kentucky, 1790.* Baltimore, Md.: Genealogical Publishing Co., 1965. (FHL# 976.9/X2ph or microfilm 1036803, item 6)

Church History and Records

Kentucky is well represented in collections of church records and histories for Baptists, Catholics, Episcopalians, Methodists, Presbyterians, and Shakers.

The Shane Manuscript Collection from the Presbyterian Historical Society in Philadelphia on thirty-six reels includes many valuable Kentucky church records which are not available elsewhere (FHL# microfilm 0498614-0498642, 0506443, 0504267-0504270).

E. E. Barton's Manuscript Collection on ninety-four reels includes church records for Pendleton County (FHL# microfilm 0341195-0341218 and 0358422-0358491). The Draper Collection (see *History*) and the Ardery Collection (see *Cemeteries*) also contain some church records.

Court Records

Many valuable Kentucky court records are cataloged under **Kentucky/Court Records** and **Kentucky/[County]/Court Records.** The Ardery Collection contains early wills copied from courthouse records. (FHL# 976.9/D2a or microfilm 0908282, item 1) The John Marshall Harlan Papers include court dockets and records for 1843-64 and 1907-11 (FHL# or microfilm 0157133-0157138).

Circuit court orders for 1798-1852 are microfilmed sequentially (FHL# or microfilm 0459767-0459768 and 0460284-0460286), Circuit court records for 1807-43 are arranged chronologically (FHL# microfilm 0460538-0460559 and 0459757-0459766). The general cross-index to suits for 1805-1910 is on (FHL# microfilm 460537). District court orders for 1789-1811 and 1834-44 are indexed and chronologically arranged (FHL# microfilm 460287 and 0467314-0467319).

Several publications provide an understanding of Kentucky's early court system, including jurisdiction, organization, and history:

Griffin, Warren B. *Preliminary Inventory Records of the United States Courts from the District of Kentucky.* Chicago: Federal Records Center, 1968. (FHL# 976.9/A1/no. 156 or microfilm 10036817, item 15)

Ireland, Robert M. *The County Courts in Antebellum Kentucky.* Lexington: University Press of Kentucky, c.1972. (FHL# 976.9/P2i)

Richardson, William C. *An Administrative History of Kentucky Courts to 1850.* Frankfort: Kentucky Department for Libraries and Archives, 1983. (FHL# 976.9/P2r)

Tachau, Mary K. Bonsteel. *Federal Courts in the Early Republic: Kentucky 1789-1816.* Princeton: Princeton University Press, c.1978. (FHL# 976.9/P2t)

Genealogy

Several collections, small and large, pertain to Kentucky families and history. The E. E. Barton Collection contains papers arranged somewhat in alphabetical order by surname for northern Kentucky families. These papers include biographies, guardianship, church, and cemetery records, and a marriage index on ninety-four reels (FHL# microfilm 0341195-0341218 and 0358422-0358491).

Several chapters of the Daughters of the American Revolution have compiled genealogical records based upon court records, wills, deeds, Bibles, cemetery inscriptions, and family records. These and other collections are cataloged under **Kentucky/Genealogy.**

Filson Club Publications contain genealogical information for Kentucky residents, but the library has only thirteen of the thirty-three volumes (FHL# 976.9/B4f or microfilm 1033674, items 1-5; 1033675, items 1-3; and 1033676, items 1-3)

The Ardery, Barton, Draper, and Shane collections contain genealogical data for Kentucky families. The Ardery Collection is cataloged under **Kentucky/Genealogy/Sources.** The Barton and Draper Collections are listed under **Kentucky/History.** The Shane Collection is cataloged under **Kentucky/Cemeteries, Kentucky/-Church History, Kentucky/History,** and **Kentucky/Vital Records.** The Barton Collection is also cataloged under **Kentucky/Church Records, Kentucky/Genealogy,** and **Kentucky/Vital Records.**

The library's Kentucky collection of genealogical records has several divisions; see **Kentucky/Genealogy, Kentucky/Handbooks, Manuals, etc, Kentucky/Genealogy/Indexes, Kentucky/Genealogy/Periodicals, Kentucky/Genealogy/Periodicals/Indexes,** and **Kentucky/-Genealogy/Sources.** The periodical collection for Kentucky is excellent.

History

The library has many histories of Kentucky. Historical subject matter is cataloged under **Kentucky/History, Kentucky/History/Bibliography, Kentucky/History/Indexes, Kentucky/History/Periodicals,** and **Kentucky/-History/Sources.** Notable in the collection are:

Chinn, George Morgan. *Kentucky, Settlement and Statehood, 1750-1800.* Frankfort: Kentucky Historical Society, c.1975. (FHL# 976.9/H2ch)

Clark, Thomas D. *Kentucky: Land of Contrast.* New York: Harper & Row, c.1968. (FHL# 976.9/H2ct)

Collins, Lewis, and Richard H. Collins. *History of Kentucky.* 2 vols. rev., enl., and updated to 1874. 1847; rpt. ed., Frankfort: Kentucky Historical Society, 1966. (FHL# 976.9/H2c or microfilm 0924472, and 1000047)

Draper, Lyman Copeland. *Draper Manuscript Collection.* 147 reels. Chicago: University of Chicago Library, [c.1970s]. (FHL# microfilm 0889097-0889243)

History of Kentucky Before the Louisiana Purchase in 1803. Chicago: S. J. Clarke Publishing Co., 1928. (FHL# 976.9/H2hr)

Kerr, Charles, ed. *History of Kentucky.* 5 vols., by William Elsey Connelley and E. M. Coulter. Chicago: American Historical Society, 1922. (FHL# 976.9/H2k or microfilm 1000045-1000046)

Kincaid, Robert Lee. *The Wilderness Road.* Harrogate, Tenn.: Lincoln Memorial University Press, 1955. (FHL# 973/H2k)

Kinkead, Elizabeth Shelby. *A History of Kentucky.* New York: American Book Co., 1896. (FHL# 976.9/H2ka)

Marshall, Humphrey. *The History of Kentucky: Exhibiting an Account of the Modern Discovery, Settlement, Progressive Improvement, Civil and Military Transactions, and the Present State of the Country.* 2 vols. 2d ed. Frankfort: G. S. Robinson, 1924. (FHL# 976.9/H2m or microfilm 0928093, item 3)

Perrin, William Henry. *Kentucky: A History of the State, Embracing A Concise Account of the Origin and Development of the Virginia Colony, Its Expansion Westward, and the Settlement of the Frontier Beyond the Alleghanies, the Erection of Kentucky as an Independent State, and Its Subsequent Development.* 6th ed. Louisville: F. A. Battey & Co., 1887. (FHL# 976.9/H2p or microfilm 0599686, item 1, and 0874362, item 1)

Polk, Johnson E. *A History of Kentucky and Kentuckians: The Leaders and Representative Men in Commerce, History, and Modern Activities.* 3 vols. Chicago: Lewis Publishing Co., 1912. (FHL# 976.9/H2j or microfilm 0496829-496830, item 1, and 1000044)

Land and Property

Land and property records for Kentucky provide excellent finding tools. Early Virginia land grants in Kentucky and most statewide land and property records have been microfilmed and are cataloged under **Kentucky/Land and Property.** County land records have also been microfilmed and can be located under **Kentucky/[County]/Land and Property.** Valuable works are:

Cook, Michael Lewis. *Kentucky Court of Appeals Deed Books.* Evansville, Ind.: Cook Publications, 1985. (FHL# 976.9/R2c)

Jillson, Willard Rouse. *Old Kentucky Entries and Deeds: A Complete Index to All of the Earliest Land Entries, Military Warrants, Deeds and Wills of the Commonwealth of Kentucky.* Louisville: Standard Printing Co., 1926. (FHL# microfilm 1035625, item 3)

_____. *The Kentucky Land Grants: A Systematic Index to All of the Land Grants Recorded in the State Land Office at Frankfort, Kentucky, 1782-1924.* 1 vol in 2. Baltimore, Md.: Genealogical Publishing Co., 1971. (FHL# 976.9/R2j)

Originally published as Filson Club Publications, Number 33 (Louisville: Standard Printing Co., 1925). (FHL# 976.9/B4f/no. 33 or microfilm 00272808 and 1000053, item 2)

Maps

The library has a good selection of state maps and some county maps. See **Kentucky/Maps** and **Kentucky/[County]/Maps.**

Military Records

Because it includes names of many early Kentuckians and others who later obtained land grants in Kentucky, the records of the George Rogers Clark military expedition are an important source. A chronological compilation of names, rank, dates of enlistment and discharge, and payment contains the most complete list of the men who served in the "Illinois Campaign." See:

Harding, Margery Heberling, comp. *George Rogers Clark and His Men: Military Records, 1778-84.* Frankfort: Kentucky Historical Society, n.d. (FHL# 973/M2gr)

The library also has military records for the Revolutionary War, War of 1812, various Indian Wars, Mexican War, Civil War, Spanish-American, and World War I cataloged under **Kentucky/Military Records.** Kentucky Historical Society's index to veterans of American wars from Kentucky has been microfilmed. Each set of war records is arranged alphabetically. Both Confederate and Union soldiers are included.

Probate Records

Most probate records are located in the county and have been microfilmed by the Family History Library. Some Kentucky probate records are cataloged under **Kentucky/[County]/ Guardian and Ward.**

The Ardery Collection contains many early Kentucky wills and probate records for several counties; see **Kentucky/Probate Records.** Chapters of the Daughters of the American Revolution have contributed several compilations to the collection.

See also:

King, Junie Estelle Stewart. *Abstract of Early Kentucky Wills and Inventories, Copied From Original and Recorded Wills and Inventories.* 1933; rpt. ed., Baltimore, Md.: Genealogical Publishing Co., 1969. (FHL# 976.9/S2k or microfilm 0007822, and 0897212, item 5)

Public Records

Cataloged under this heading is a variety of records: petitions, legislative journals, indexes, and notices to citizens. The Elihu Jasper Sutherland Collection includes Kentucky records for 1822-1900. (FHL# microfilm 0809782)

Taxation

Tax records for Kentucky are invaluable for the periods when census enumerations are missing. The library has tax records for all but one Kentucky county. Tax records are arranged by county and usually by districts within the counties. Although one or two years of tax lists may be missing for some counties, most are available from the organization of each county. They are cataloged under **Kentucky/[County]/Taxation.** Some published statewide tax lists are cataloged under **Kentucky/Taxation.**

Vital Records

The library has marriage records for most Kentucky counties cataloged under **Kentucky/[County]/Vital**

Records. Several major collections also contain vital records of Kentucky residents, including the Ardery, Barton, Draper, and Shane Collections. Various chapters of the Daughters of the American Revolution have also compiled vital records for Kentucky families. These statewide or multi-county collections are cataloged under **Kentucky/Vital Records**. Kentucky marriages are published in:

Clift, Garrett Glenn. *Kentucky Marriages 1797-1865.* Baltimore, Md.: Genealogical Publishing Co., 1974. (FHL# 976.9/V25c)

Birth records for 1874-78 are available on eight reels (FHL# microfilm 0174932-0174939). Vital records are included in Hattie Marshall Scott, *Scott's Papers* (N.p.: Kentucky Historical Society, 1953) (FHL# 976.9/P2s) and in William M. Talley, *Talley's Kentucky Papers.* (Fort Worth, Tex.: Arrow Printing Co., 1966) (FHL# 976.9/V2t).

Births and deaths from the Kentucky Bureau of Vital Statistics, available on ninety-two reels, are arranged alphabetically and cover 1911-54 (FHL# microfilm 0209595-0209686).

Arkansas

Historical Background

1686	French establish Arkansas Post.
1763	France cedes large region, including present-day Arkansas, to Spain.
1800	Spain returns the territory to France.
1803	The United States acquires the area with the Louisiana Purchase.
1804	Arkansas under the jurisdiction of Louisiana Territory.
1806	The District of Arkansas is established.
1808	Osage tribe cedes claim to Arkansas lands.
1812	Arkansas becomes part of Missouri Territory; U.S. Government grant allows formation of Cherokee Territory north of the "Upper" Arkansas River.
1813	Arkansas County organized by the territorial legislature for the approximately 1500 white settlers.
1815	After the War of 1812, rate of settlement greatly increases.
1817	Quapaw Indians cede all remaining Indian lands in Arkansas. Cherokee tribe signs treaty and exchanges land.
1819	Arkansas Territory is created, including present-day Oklahoma; capital at Arkansas Post. Cherokee Nation lands becomes Crawford County.
1820	Presbyterian missionaries arrive.
1821	Little Rock designated capital.
1832	Census of Creek Indians.
1835	Census of Cherokees east of the Mississippi River.
1836	Arkansas becomes the twenty-fifth state.
1861	Arkansas joins the Confederate States of America.
1862	Battle of Pea Ridge in Benton County.
1864	Union forces take Little Rock and establish a federal government, but rebel government continues to operate.
1874	Civil disorder over a governorship dispute.

Settlement and Migration

Arkansas originally belonged to the Quapaw, Osage, Choctaw, and Cherokee tribes. Quapaw lands were located between the Red River and the Canadian and Arkansas rivers. Osage lands were north of the Canadian and Arkansas rivers. These lands were ceded to the United States in 1817 and 1808 respectively. In 1817, part of the Cherokee tribe, known as the Old Settlers, signed a treaty exchanging some Cherokee lands for an equivalent area in the Arkansas and White River valleys. The Choctaws agreed to similar arrangements in 1816, 1820, and 1825, ceding their lands north of the Red River.

Prior to the War of 1812, an estimated 1,500 white people were living in the area, most of them near or in Arkansas Post. Following the war, migration into the region increased rapidly, especially after 2,000 acres of Arkansas lands were issued as bounty land for military service.

The Panic of 1837 caused many people to move into Arkansas from Southern and Eastern states. The Gold Rush in California attracted many Arkansas men, most of whom left from Fort Smith to try their luck in the gold fields. To escape conscription and the friction between the federal and rebel governments competing in Arkansas during the Civil War, many Arkansas families moved into Texas. European immigrants were attracted by the rich land located between the Arkansas and White rivers beginning in 1867.

About the turn of the twentieth century, families from northwest Arkansas began moving into Indian Territory (Oklahoma). During this same period, many families left Arkansas to move farther west. After 1900, many families moved to cities in midwest, western, and eastern states.

Many men from Arkansas served in the U.S. Army during the Mexican War. Some of these soldiers received bounty lands prior to 1855. During the Civil War, Arkansas was a Confederate state, but some of its men served in the Union Army. Many of the families of Union men found it necessary to move into Minnesota and Illinois. Most of these families returned after the close of hostilities.

Arkansas Library Collection

Bibliography

Only three titles are included in the collection for Arkansas.

Bibliography of the Ozarks Books. Salt Lake City, Utah: Filmed by the Genealogical Society of Utah, 1977. (FHL# microfilm 982434, item 4)

Morgan, James Logan. *A Survey of the County Records of Arkansas.* Newport, Ark.: Arkansas Records Association, 1972. (FHL# 976.7/A1/no. 66)

Arkansas History Commission. *Bulletin of Information.* Little Rock: n.p., c.1915. (FHL# 976.7/D33a)

Bibliography of biographies in Arkansas newspapers.

Biography

The library has many biographical histories cataloged under **Arkansas/Biography, Arkansas/[County]/Biography,** or **Arkansas/History.** Many titles are in the collection for Arkansas. Also, see the indexes to the biographies prepared by Mrs. Leister E. Presley under the catalog heading **Arkansas/Biography/Indexes.**

The Book of Three States: Notable Men of Mississippi, Arkansas, and Tennessee. Memphis: Tenn.: Commercial Appeal Pub. Co., 1914. (FHL# 976/D3c or 908024, item 2)

Clark, Mrs. Larry P., comp. *Arkansas Pioneers and Allied Families.* N. pub., n.p., c.1976. (FHL# 976.7/D3c or microfilm 1036635, item 4 or fiche 6051363)

Hallum, John. *Biographical and Pictorial History of Arkansas.* Albany: Weed, Parsons, 1887. (FHL# 976.7/H2hb or microfilm 934819, item 1)

Shinn, Josiah Hazen. *Pioneers and Makers of Arkansas.* 1908; rpt. ed., Baltimore, Md.: Genealogical Publishing Co., 1967. (FHL# 976.7/H2s or microfilm 1004960, item 2)

Speer, William S., and John Henry Brown, ed. *The Encyclopedia of the New West: Containing Fully Authenticated Information . . .; Also, Biographical Sketches of Their Representative Men and Women.* Tucson, Ariz.: W. C. Cox Co., 1974. (FHL# microfilm 1000598, item 2)

Thomas, David Yancey, ed. *Arkansas and Its People, A History, 1541-1930.* 4 vols. New York: American Historical Society, 1930. (FHL# 976.7/H2t or microfilm 934821 or fiche 6051359)

Cemeteries

Members of the LDS Church and Daughters of the American Revolution have copied tombstone inscriptions for Arkansas. See **Arkansas/Cemeteries** and **Arkansas/[County]/Cemeteries** for these and additional titles.

Census Records

Although only heads of households are listed, the 1823 and 1829 sheriff's enumerations are available for Arkansas (FHL# 976.7/X2j). The library also has the published territorial census of 1830 (FHL# 976.7/X2p); indexes for the 1820, 1830, 1840, 1850, and 1860 federal censuses; mortality schedules for 1850, 1860, 1870, and 1880 have been published. Several counties have published census records which are cataloged under **Arkansas/[County]/Census.** Federal censuses are available for 1830-1910; for census call numbers, see the Registers on the U.S./Canada Reference credenza.

Bobbie Jones McLane and Capitola Glazner transcribed and edited the *Arkansas 1911 Census of Confederate Veterans*, 3 vols. (N.p.: n.pub., 1977-81) which gives extensive information on veterans and their families (FHL# 976.7/X2m).

Church History and Records

The library has histories of the Baptist, Presbyterian, Disciples of Christ, Episcopal, Catholic, Christian, and Mormon churches cataloged under **Arkansas/Church History** and **Arkansas/[County]/Church History.**

Records are available for the Catholic, Church of Christ, Baptist, Presbyterian, and Methodist churches under **Arkansas/Church Records** and **Arkansas/[County]/Church Records. Arkansas/Collected Works** includes church registers.

Court Records

No statewide court records are available, but most counties have some court records represented in the collection. See **Arkansas/[County]/Court Records.**

Genealogy

Several compilations of genealogical records are available for Arkansas. See **Arkansas/Genealogy, Arkansas/[County]/Genealogy,** and **Arkansas/Collected Works.** A useful collection of genealogical periodicals is cataloged under **Arkansas/Genealogy/Periodicals.**

History

Several volumes of biographical and historical information for Arkansas were published by Goodspeed Publishing Company in 1889; these regional publications contain data concerning the first seventy years of Arkansas and its early families. See **Arkansas/History** or **Arkansas/Biography.**

The disputed Miller County territory is discussed in Skipper Steely, *Six Months from Tennessee: A Story of the Many Pioneers of Miller County, Arkansas . . . .* (Paris, Tex.: Claiborne Wright Historical Assoc. c.1982) (FHL# 921.72/W93s). Records of the disputed Lovely County area are in Lovely Purchase Donation Claims, microfilmed with Spanish land claims and the original tract book and cataloged under **Arkansas/Land and Property** (FHL# microfilm 1302802).

See additional titles cataloged under **Arkansas/History/Civil War, 1861-65, Arkansas/History/Bibliography, Arkansas/History/Handbooks, Manuals, etc.,**

Arkansas/History/Indexes, and **Arkansas/History/Periodicals.**

See also:

Carter, Clarence Edwin, comp., ed. *The Territorial Papers of the United States: The Territory of Arkansas, 1819-1825.* Washington, D.C.: Government Printing Office, 1953. (FHL# microfilm 874233)

______. *The Territorial Papers of the United States: The Territory of Arkansas, 1825-1829.* Washington, D.C.: Government Printing Office, 1953. (FHL# microfilm 874234)

Herndon, Dallas Tabor. *Annals of Arkansas, 1947: A Narrative Historical Edition Revising, Reediting and Continuing a Centennial History of Arkansas, Preserving the Record of the Growth and Development of the State and Chronicling the Genealogical and Memorial Records of Its Prominent Families and Personages.* 4 vols. Hopkinsville, Ark.: Historical Record Association, 1947. (FHL# 976.7/H2h or microfilm 1036013)

Shinn, Josiah Hazen. *Pioneers and Makers of Arkansas.* 1908; rpt. ed., Baltimore, Md.: Genealogical Publishing Co., 1967. (FHL# 976.7/H2s and 934822, item 1)

Land and Property

Early Spanish land claims and the original tract book are on FHL# microfilm 1302802). Early land grants are in *First Settlers of the Missouri Territory,* 2 vols. (Nacogdoches, Tex.: Ericson Books, c.1983) (FHL# 977.8/-R2f). Most Arkansas land records are filed at the county level; see **Arkansas/[County]/Land and Property.** Of special note is:

Christensen, Katheren. *Arkansas Military Bounty Grants (War of 1812).* [Hot Springs]: Arkansas Ancestors, 1971. (FHL# 976.7/ R2c)

Maps

Several single maps and collections of Arkansas maps are cataloged under **Arkansas/Maps.**

Military Records

The Arkansas Board of Pensions allowed pensions for some Confederate soldiers and their widows. Pension records for other war service are available. The library has records concerning service during the Revolutionary War, War of 1812, and the Indian, Mexican, and Civil wars.

The largest collection concerns the Civil War. The compiled service records of Confederate Soldiers who served from Arkansas organizations are microfilmed on 282 reels. See **Arkansas/Military Records/Civil War, 1861-65.**

Native Races

A few records for Choctaw and Cherokee tribes are included in the collection under **Arkansas/Native Races.**

Newspapers

The *Union List of Arkansas Newspapers, 1819-1942: A Partial Inventory of Arkansas Newspaper Files Available in Offices of Publishers, Libraries, and Private Collections in Arkansas* was prepared by the Historical Records Survey, Division of Community Service Programs, Work Projects Administration (Little Rock: Historical Records Survey, 1942) (FHL# 976.7/B3h or microfilm 0897366, item 2). See also **Arkansas/[County]/Newspapers** for newspapers included in the library's collection.

Probate Records

The library has filmed most probate records for most Arkansas counties; see **Arkansas/[County]/Probate Records** and **Arkansas/[County]/Guardian and Ward.**

Taxation

Jackson, Ronald Vern, and Gary Ronald Teeples, eds. *Arkansas Tax Lists: 1819 to 1829.* Bountiful, Utah: Accelerated Indexing Systems, 1978. (FHL# 976.7/R4j)

The library has most counties' tax records; see **Arkansas/[County]/Taxation.**

Vital Records

The DAR made a large compilation of Arkansas vital records. See **Arkansas/Vital Records** and **Arkansas/-[County]/Vital Records.** Most county marriage records have been microfilmed.

Additional vital records for specific counties are cataloged under **Arkansas/[County]/Vital Records.** See also **Arkansas/Vital Records/Newspapers.**

MISSISSIPPI

Historical Background

1541	Hernando DeSoto discovers the Mississippi River.
1541-1699	Spain controls the area of Mississippi.
1699	France begins colonization with the founding of Fort de Maurepas (now Ocean Springs) and a settlement of 200 colonists at Biloxi.
1699-1716	Settlements increase along the Gulf Coast and the Mississippi River.
1716	Fort Rosalie is established on the Natchez bluffs.
1718	French land grants encourage settlements on the Yazoo River, Bay St. Louis, Pascagoula Bay, and at Natchez.
1721	John Law's Mississippi Bubble scheme results

in the immigration of 300 colonists to Natchez.

1722 Law's plan settles about 300 colonists at Pascagoula.

1762 France cedes territory east of the Mississippi River to Spain.

1763 France cedes area to Great Britain at the close of the French and Indian War. British colonization attempts begin.

1776-83 Americans migrate into Mississippi to escape involvement in the Revolutionary War.

1779-81 Spanish control the Natchez District.

1798 American troops occupy Natchez and claim all the territory including present-day Alabama. Congress creates Mississippi Territory with its capital at Natchez.

1803 Louisiana Purchase encourages land boom in Mississippi.

1804 Georgia relinquishes its claim to Mississippi western lands.

1804-12 Mississippi Territory includes all of present-day Mississippi and Alabama.

1817 Mississippi becomes the twentieth state.

1861 Mississippi becomes the second state to secede from the Union.

1865-70 Mississippi under federal military occupation.

1870 Mississippi is readmitted to the Union.

Settlement and Migration

French colonies were established in Mississippi as early as 1699. These were located at Old Biloxi and along the Mississippi River. French colonists settled Natchez in 1716. The area was ceded to Great Britain in 1763, beginning English settlement. Land grants to retired British officers increased migration to the area and also brought Protestant settlements, contrasting with the earlier Catholic colonies established by France and Spain.

During the American Revolution, the Natchez District remained loyal to England and provided a haven for Loyalists from the American colonies. Between 1779 and 1781, Spain controlled the Natchez District; but by 1798, pro-American feelings were prominent, and Congress established the Mississippi Territory with Natchez as the capital.

After the Louisiana Purchase, the Mississippi River was opened for trade from the Northwest Territory to New Orleans. Shortly, a land boom occurred in Mississippi Territory, bringing thousands of pioneers from the older states.

In 1817, the eastern half of Mississippi Territory was organized into Alabama Territory. Later that year, Mississippi became the twentieth state. The Chickasaws ceded their lands in Mississippi in 1821, 1832, and 1836; the Choctaws gave up their claims in 1820, 1830, and 1832. The opening of former Indian lands to settlement and the Panic of 1837 in older states increased migrations into Mississippi.

During the Civil War, Mississippi supplied the Confederation with its president and many soldiers. It withdrew from the Union in 1861, the second state to do so, and did not rejoin until a Reconstruction government was in control of the state in 1870. The corrupt and extravagant practices of this government brought economic desolation to the state.

Mississippi Library Collection

Archives and Libraries

Four volumes of Mississippi provincial archives under Spanish dominion for 1759-93 and three volumes of Mississippi provincial archives under French dominion from 1701-43 will aid early research in Mississippi records. Spanish period records are on FHL# microfilm 0904443-0904444; those for the French period are on FHL# microfilm 0904441-0904442 or 976.2/A5m.

Another group of records relating to the provincial archives under Spanish dominion for 1757-1820 is also available. These records include early Spanish government and military regulations and correspondence (FHL# microfilm 0899972-0899980)

Although not cataloged under **Mississippi/Archives and Libraries,** (see **Mississippi/History/Sources/Colonial Period, ca. 1600-75**), records are extant for the British provincial period 1763-75 (FHL# microfilm 0899981-0899985). French provincial archival records for 1612-63 are cataloged under **Mississippi/History/Sources** (FHL# microfilm 0899957-0899971). Under **Mississippi/Military Records** is cataloged Spanish military archival manuscripts kept by the Minister of War (Ministerio de La Guerra); these cover military service in the Floridas (including Mississippi) and Louisiana for 1787-94 (FHL# microfilm 1156353).

Additional guides and inventories are in the collection; see **Mississippi/Archives and Libraries.**

Bible Records

The Mississippi Genealogical Society publication include Bible records and cemetery inscriptions, particularly volumes 2-10. The library's only other Bible records holdings are for two counties (Lafayette and Washington) plus a DAR publication (FHL# microfilm 913001).

Biography

The library has a few state-wide and county publications of biographies and history. Most state-wide publications contain only biographies of eminent citizens. See **Mississippi/Biography** or **Mississippi/[County]/-Biography.**

Dunbar Rowland, ed., *Mississippi: Comprising Sketches of Counties, Towns, Events, Institutions, and Persons,* 4 vols.

(Atlanta: Southern Historical Publishing Association, 1907); rpt. ed., Spartanburg, S.C.: Reprint Company, 1976. (FHL# 976.2/H2m)

Arranged in cyclopedic form. Volume 3 includes an index.

Cemeteries

The library has some cemetery records for the majority of Mississippi counties. The publications of the Mississippi Genealogical Society are indexed and contain the largest collection of cemetery records for the state. See *Bible Records* above and the library's listings under **Mississippi/Cemeteries** and **Mississippi/[County]/-Cemeteries.** A few small publications are available. Only one set of Daughters of the American Revolution cemetery records is in the collection, but it is indexed (FHL# microfilm 913001).

Census Records

A valuable guide to early residents is Norman Gillis, *Early Inhabitants of the Natchez District* (Baton Rouge: N. Gillis, c.1963) (FHL# 976.1/X2p).

The library also has state census records for 1792-1866, although the information they contain is extremely limited. Abstracts for 1801-45, the Spanish census for 1792, and the censuses for Adams through Holmes County are contained on one reel (FHL# microfilm 0899868). Issaquena County through Simpson County is on another reel, while the last of this collection covers Smith to Yazoo counties (FHL# microfilm 0899869-0899870).

Indexes are available for the federal censuses for 1810, 1830, 1840, 1850, 1860, and 1890. The 1820 and 1830 censuses for the state have been published; see **Mississippi/Census.** The 1850 mortality schedule is in FHL# 976.2/A1/no.5. Bryan Lee Dilts, *1890 Mississippi Census Index of Civil War Veterans or Their Widows* (Salt Lake City: Index Publishing, 1985) (FHL# 976.2/X22d).

Church History and Records

The library has very few church histories or records for Mississippi. Limited histories of Baptists, Lutherans, Presbyterians, and Methodists are cataloged under **Mississippi/Church History** and **Mississippi/[County]/-Church History.**

Inventories of Jewish and Episcopal records were made during the Historical Records Survey in 1940. These indexed volumes are limited but can help locate synagogue and church records (FHL# 976.2/K2hj and 976.2/K2he).

Court Records

The library has court records for most counties cataloged under **Mississippi/[County]/Court Records.** Some state court records are cataloged under **Mississippi/Court Records.** Territorial court records for 1798-1817 are cataloged under **Mississippi/Land and Property** (FHL# microfilm 0904447-0904451).

Notable in the collection are:

King, Junie Estelle Stewart. *Mississippi Court Records, 1799-1835.* Salt Lake City: Genealogical Society of Utah, 1968. (FHL# microfilm 0547551, item 2)

McBee, May Wilson. *The Natchez Court Records: Abstracts of Early Records, 1767-1805.* Greenwood, Miss.: M. W. McBee, 1954. (FHL# 976.2/P2mm)

Mississippi Territorial Land and Court Records. Salt Lake City: Genealogical Society of Utah, 1972. (FHL# microfilm 0904447-0904451)

Genealogy

Several small collections of genealogical records are cataloged under **Mississippi/Genealogy** and **Mississippi/[County]/Genealogy.** Several periodicals are available; see **Mississippi/Genealogy/Periodicals.**

History

More than half of the counties in the state have some published history. Several area histories are cataloged under **Mississippi/History.** See also **Mississippi/History/Periodicals, Mississippi/History/Societies, Mississippi/History/Sources** and other headings for Mississippi history. Note:

Carter, Clarence Edwin, comp., ed. *The Territorial Papers of the United States: The Territory of Mississippi.* 2 vols. Washington, D.C.: Government Printing Office, 1938. (FHL# microfilm 929479 or 874226, item 2)

Claiborne, John Francis Hamtramck. *Mississippi, as a Province, Territory and State, With Biographical Notes of Eminent Citizens.* Jackson: Power & Barksdale, 1880. (FHL# 976.2/H2c or microfilm 1033822, item 6)

Greenwell, Dale. *Twelve Flags–Triumphs and Tragedies.* 3 vols. Ocean Springs, Miss.: D. Greenwell, 1968. (FHL# 976.2/H2g)

Lowry, Robert, and William H. McCardle. *A History of Mississippi: From the Discovery of the Great River by Hernando De Soto, Including the Earliest Settlement Made by the French, under Iberville to the Death of Jefferson Davis (1541-1889).* Jackson: R. H. Henry, 1891. (FHL# 976.1/-H2l)

McLemore, Richard Aubrey, ed. *A History of Mississippi.* 2 vols. Jackson: University & College Press of Mississippi, c.1973. (FHL# 976.2/H2hm)

Rowland, Dunbar. *History of Mississippi, The Heart of the South.* Chicago: S. J. Clarke Publishing Co., 1925. (FHL# 976.2/H2r or microfilm 0844829, item 1; 0844830, item 1; and 1000271, items 1-2)

Land and Property

Early Mississippi land grants are included in the British, French, and Spanish archival materials described under *History*; the collection includes land grants and surveys for 1770-83 (FHL# microfilm 0899984-0899985).

A collection of land grants under Spanish dominion is

described in Winston DeVille, *Louisiana and Mississippi Lands: A Guide to Spanish Land Grants at the University of Michigan* (Ville Platte, La.: Evangeline Genealogical and Historical Society, c.1985) (FHL# 977.4/A3d).

Early land grants and territorial records are included in Clarence Edwin Carter, *The Territorial Papers of the United States: The Territory of Mississippi* (Washington, D.C.: U.S. Government Printing Office, 1938) (FHL# 929479 or 874226, item 2). See also:

Ainsworth, Fern. *Private Land Claims of Mississippi and Missouri.* Natchitoches, La.: by author, n.d. (FHL# 973/R22a)

First Settlers of the Mississippi Territory (Nacogdoches, Tex.: Ericson Books, n.d.) (FHL# 976/R2f)

State Archives. *Mississippi Territorial Land and Court Records, 1798-1817.* Jackson: Mississippi State Archives, n.d. 5 reels. (FHL# microfilm 904447-904451)

Microfilm of original records at the Mississippi State Archives, Jackson, Mississippi. Alphabetically arranged by surname.

Maps

The library has a collection of Mississippi maps cataloged under **Mississippi/Maps.** Two sets of five maps for 1816-73 have been reproduced from original maps in the Mississippi Department of Archives and History (FHL# 976.2/A1/nos. 1, 3).

Military Records

This heading catalogs records about provincial governments as well as military records. Records, lists of pensioners, and abstracts for the Revolutionary War, War of 1812, Mexican War, Civil War (both Union and Confederate), and World War I usually are arranged chronologically.

The collection of Mississippi Confederate veterans' and their widows' pension applications is arranged in alphabetical order (FHL# microfilm 0902556-0904430). Indexes to the compiled service records of Union and Confederate soldiers are arranged alphabetically (Union: FHL# microfilm 0881535; Confederate: 0821838-821882). See also **Mississippi/Military Records, Mississippi/Military Records/[War], United States/-Military Records,** and **United States/Military Records/[War].**

Minorities

Freedmen's Bureau records are microfilmed from the original documents in the National Archives; these include chronologically arranged records of refugees, freedmen, and abandoned lands (FHL# microfilm 0491558-0491565) Registers of freedmen's marriages are on FHL# microfilm 0491557, items 2-5. See **Mississippi/Minorities** and **Mississippi/Slavery and Bondage** for additional titles relating to blacks in the state.

Native Races

A few records of two American Indian tribes (Pascagoula and Choctaw) are cataloged under **Mississippi/Native Races.**

Probate Records

Most general probate records are cross-referenced under **Mississippi/Court Records** and **Mississippi/-Probate Records.**

Most county records are under **Mississippi/[County]/Probate Records.** Some probate records for the state are also cataloged under **Mississippi/[County]/-Guardian and Ward.**

Tax Records

Scattered counties' tax records are listed under **Mississippi/[County]/Taxation.** Tax lists recorded during the Mississippi territorial period are in Ben Strickland and Jean Strickland, *Washington County, Mississippi Territory 1803-1816* (Milton, Fla.: n.pub., c.1980. (FHL# 976/R4s)

Vital Records

The library has several general collections cataloged under **Mississippi/Vital Records.** Many of these are cross-referenced with other subheadings in the catalog. A guide to vital statistics records in Mississippi was prepared by the state's Historical Records Survey, Service Division, Work Projects Administration. (FHL# 976.2/V23h or microfilm 1036275, item 1)

Records by Jurisdiction Louisiana	Archives & Libraries	Atlases	Bible Records	Bibliography	Biography	Cemeteries	Census (Printed)	Church History	Church Records	Civil Registration	Court Records	Directories	Emigration/Immigration	Employment/Occupations	Genealogy	Genealogy/Periodicals	History	Land & Property	Maps	Migration	Military Records	Minorities	Native Races	Naturalizations	Newspapers	Obituaries	Periodicals	Postal	Probate Records	Public Records	School Records	Slavery/Bondage	Societies	Tax Records	Vital Records	Voting Registers	Yearbooks
Acadia						•											•	•											•						•		
Allen	•					•																							•						•		
Ascension							•								•	•		•											•						•		
Assumption	•						•				•							•								•			•			•			•		
Attakaps																																					
Avoyelles					•			•	•						•			•	•										•						•		
Beauregard	•					•																							•						•		
Baton Rouge																																					
Bienville						•			•								•	•											•						•		
Bossier	•					•												•											•						•		
Caddo					•	•			•			•					•	•							•										•		
Calcasieu	•					•	•		•						•			•											•						•		
Caldwell					•												•	•											•						•		
Cameron						•	•				•							•			•								•	•					•		
Carroll																																					
Catahoula							•				•							•											•	•					•		
Claiborne						•			•								•	•			•								•						•		
Concordia							•				•							•											•	•					•		
De Soto						•					•			•			•	•											•					•	•		
East Baton Rouge	•			•			•		•	•		•			•	•	•	•						•					•						•		
East Carroll					•												•	•											•						•		
East Feliciana					•	•	•		•		•			•			•	•											•						•		
Evangeline									•								•		•										•						•		
Feliciana																																					
Franklin						•					•						•	•											•						•		
Grant	•					•			•								•	•																•	•		
Iberia											•						•	•											•	•					•		
Iberville							•				•							•											•						•		
Jackson																		•											•						•		
Jefferson	•					•					•	•						•											•						•		
Jefferson Davis						•																							•						•		
Lafayette	•								•	•	•						•	•											•						•		
Lafourche	•					•					•							•								•			•	•					•		
La Salle																													•						•		
Lincoln						•		•			•				•		•	•											•						•		
Livingston				•		•	•				•						•	•							•				•						•		
Madison																		•																	•		
Morehouse	•																•											•						•			
Natchitoches	•				•	•	•		•		•					•	•	•			•						•		•	•				•	•		
Opelousas																																					
Orleans	•				•	•	•		•	•	•	•	•	•	•	•	•	•	•		•	•		•	•				•	•		•	•		•	•	
Ouachita	•					•		•			•						•	•											•	•					•		
Plaquemines	•						•				•					•		•							•				•						•		
Pointe Coupee							•		•		•		•		•		•	•											•						•		
Rapides						•			•		•						•	•			•								•						•		
Red River						•			•									•											•						•		
Richland						•					•							•											•						•		
Sabine	•	•			•	•	•				•						•	•			•								•						•		
St. Bernard	•					•	•				•	•				•		•	•										•	•					•		

Records by Jurisdiction **Louisiana** (cont.)	Archives & Libraries	Atlases	Bible Records	Bibliography	Biography	Cemeteries	Census (Printed)	Church History	Church Records	Civil Registration	Court Records	Directories	Emigration/Immigration	Employment/Occupations	Genealogy	Genealogy/Periodicals	History	Land & Property	Maps	Migration	Military Records	Minorities	Native Races	Naturalizations	Newspapers	Obituaries	Periodicals	Postal	Probate Records	Public Records	School Records	Slavery/Bondage	Societies	Tax Records	Vital Records	Voting Registers	Yearbooks
St. Charles	•										•							•											•			•			•		
St. Helena						•	•								•			•			•								•						•		
St. James									•								•	•											•						•		
St. John the Baptist					•						•				•		•	•											•	•		•			•		
St. Landry								•	•		•		•		•		•	•						•	•				•	•					•		
St. Martin						•		•	•		•						•	•											•	•				•	•		
St. Mary											•	•					•	•						•					•	•					•		
St. Tammany						•					•						•	•	•															•	•		
Tangipahoa						•	•		•		•				•			•			•				•				•								
Tensas																																					
Terrebonne	•						•					•			•											•									•		
Union									•		•							•											•	•					•		
Vermilion						•					•							•											•						•		
Vernon						•											•	•						•					•						•		
Washington	•						•		•		•							•											•		•	•			•	•	
Webster	•								•								•	•											•						•		
West Baton Rouge							•											•											•	•					•		
West Feliciana							•				•						•	•							•				•						•		
Winn						•					•					•		•											•					•	•		
West Carroll											•							•											•						•		

Records by Jurisdiction — Tennessee	Archives & Libraries	Atlases	Bible Records	Bibliography	Biography	Cemeteries	Census (Printed)	Church History	Church Records	Court Records	Directories	Emigration/Immigration	Employment/Occupations	Genealogy	Genealogy-Periodicals	History	Land & Property	Maps	Medical Records	Military Records	Minorities	Native Races	Naturalizations	Newspapers	Obituaries	Periodicals	Postal	Probate Records	Public Records	School Records	Societies	Tax Records	Vital Records	Voting Registers	Yearbooks
Anderson	•					•	•	•	•	•				•		•	•							•				•	•			•	•		
Bedford	•		•			•	•		•	•			•			•	•		•	•				•				•	•		•	•	•		
Benton						•	•	•		•				•		•	•		•					•				•	•			•	•		
Bledsoe					•	•	•		•	•				•		•	•	•						•				•					•		
Blount	•					•	•	•	•	•				•		•	•			•				•				•	•	•		•	•		
Bradley	•					•	•	•	•	•			•	•		•	•					•	•	•	•			•	•			•	•		
Campbell			•			•	•	•		•				•			•							•				•					•		
Cannon			•			•			•	•						•	•							•				•	•		•		•		
Carroll									•	•			•				•							•				•	•			•	•		
Carter						•	•		•	•					•	•	•											•		•		•	•		
Cheatham	•		•		•	•	•			•			•			•	•			•				•				•	•			•	•		
Chester						•			•	•							•							•				•				•	•		
Claiborne					•	•				•			•			•	•							•				•		•		•	•		
Clay			•			•				•							•							•				•					•		
Cocke						•	•	•	•	•				•		•	•							•				•				•	•		
Coffee			•			•	•		•	•						•	•			•				•				•	•			•	•		
Crockett	•								•	•				•		•	•			•				•				•	•	•			•		
Cumberland						•	•		•	•						•	•							•				•					•		
Davidson					•	•	•	•	•	•	•		•	•		•	•			•	•			•	•	•		•	•	•		•	•		
Decatur									•	•						•	•							•				•				•	•		
De Kalb									•	•						•	•							•				•				•	•		
Dickson						•			•	•			•			•	•			•				•				•	•	•		•	•		
Dyer						•	•			•				•		•	•							•				•				•	•		
Fayette							•		•	•						•	•							•				•			•		•		
Fentress						•	•		•	•						•	•							•									•		
Franklin					•	•	•		•	•						•	•			•				•		•		•		•		•	•	•	
Gibson						•	•			•						•	•							•				•	•			•	•		
Giles			•			•	•		•	•				•		•	•							•				•	•				•		
Grainger			•			•	•			•						•	•							•				•		•		•	•		
Greene						•		•		•						•	•			•				•				•	•			•	•		
Grundy										•						•	•		•					•				•	•	•		•	•		
Hamblen			•			•		•	•	•				•		•	•											•		•		•	•		
Hamilton	•				•	•		•	•	•	•					•	•			•								•	•		•	•			
Hancock																•	•							•											
Hardeman			•		•	•			•	•					•	•	•							•				•				•	•		
Hardin					•		•			•						•	•							•				•	•		•	•	•		
Hawkins						•			•	•			•	•		•	•	•						•				•	•			•	•		
Haywood	•						•		•	•							•			•				•				•	•			•	•		
Henderson			•			•			•	•				•		•	•							•				•		•			•		
Henry						•			•	•				•		•	•			•				•				•	•			•	•		
Hickman			•			•	•			•				•		•	•			•								•	•			•	•		
Houston									•	•			•			•	•		•	•				•				•	•	•		•	•		
Humphreys			•			•	•		•	•				•		•	•											•		•		•	•		
Jackson			•			•	•		•	•				•		•	•							•				•	•			•	•		
Jefferson			•			•	•		•	•			•	•		•	•			•				•				•	•	•		•	•		
Johnson			•			•	•			•			•				•							•				•	•			•	•		
Knox						•	•	•	•	•	•					•	•	•										•	•			•	•		
Lake										•						•	•											•				•	•		
Lauderdale							•		•	•				•		•	•			•				•				•	•			•	•		

Records by Jurisdiction

Tennessee (cont.)

	Archives & Libraries	Atlases	Bible Records	Bibliography	Biography	Cemeteries	Census (Printed)	Church History	Church Records	Court Records	Directories	Emigration/Immigration	Employment/Occupations	Genealogy	Genealogy-Periodicals	History	Land & Property	Maps	Medical Records	Military Records	Minorities	Native Races	Naturalizations	Newspapers	Obituaries	Periodicals	Postal	Probate Records	Public Records	School Records	Societies	Tax Records	Vital Records	Voting Registers	Yearbooks
Lawrence						•	•		•	•			•			•	•								•			•	•		•	•	•		
Lewis							•		•	•						•	•							•				•	•			•	•		
Lincoln			•				•	•	•	•						•	•							•				•		•	•	•	•		
Loudon	•				•	•			•	•						•	•								•			•				•	•		
Macon			•			•			•	•						•																			
Madison	•					•			•	•						•	•											•				•	•		
Marion					•	•				•			•	•		•	•		•									•	•			•	•		
Marshall						•	•		•	•						•	•											•	•			•	•		
Maury					•	•	•	•	•	•	•			•		•	•			•								•	•			•	•		
McMinn					•	•	•	•	•	•						•	•											•	•			•	•		
McNairy						•	•		•	•						•	•											•				•	•		
Meigs							•									•	•			•								•	•			•	•		
Monroe					•	•			•	•				•		•	•											•	•			•	•		
Montgomery			•		•	•	•		•	•	•			•	•	•	•	•	•	•								•	•	•		•	•		
Moore						•				•			•			•	•		•			•						•	•	•		•	•		
Morgan						•	•		•	•				•		•	•	•						•				•	•				•		
Obion			•				•		•	•						•	•											•				•	•		
Overton									•	•				•		•	•							•				•	•			•	•		
Perry							•			•						•	•											•				•	•		
Pickett														•		•																			
Polk						•			•	•						•	•											•				•	•		
Putnam			•			•				•				•		•	•											•			•		•		
Rhea					•	•	•		•	•				•		•	•			•								•		•		•	•		
Roane						•	•	•	•	•				•		•	•		•	•								•	•			•	•		
Robertson	•				•	•	•	•	•	•			•	•		•	•			•								•	•	•		•	•		
Rutherford	•		•			•	•	•	•	•			•	•		•	•			•						•		•	•	•		•	•		
Scott					•		•	•		•						•	•							•				•					•		
Sequatchie			•			•	•		•	•			•			•	•		•									•		•		•	•		
Sevier						•	•		•	•						•	•							•				•				•	•		
Shelby	•				•	•	•	•	•	•	•					•	•				•							•	•		•	•	•		
Smith			•			•	•		•	•			•			•	•		•	•				•				•	•	•		•	•		
Stewart						•			•	•			•	•		•	•		•									•	•	•		•	•		
Sullivan					•	•	•	•	•	•			•	•		•	•	•		•								•	•			•	•		
Sumner			•			•	•		•	•			•	•		•	•		•	•				•				•	•	•		•	•		
Tennessee																																			
Tipton	•					•	•		•	•						•	•											•					•		
Trousdale									•							•																			
Unicoi									•	•						•	•											•					•		
Union					•	•				•						•	•							•				•				•	•		
Van Buren						•	•			•				•		•	•											•				•	•		
Warren							•		•	•						•	•							•				•					•		
Washington						•	•	•	•	•	•			•	•	•	•			•					•			•	•	•	•	•	•		
Wayne (Old)																																			
Wayne							•		•	•						•	•							•				•				•	•		
Weakley						•	•			•				•		•	•							•				•				•	•		
White						•			•	•			•			•	•		•	•								•	•	•		•	•		
Williamson			•			•	•		•	•			•	•		•	•			•					•	•		•	•	•		•	•		
Wilson	•					•	•		•	•				•		•	•			•								•	•	•	•	•	•		

Records by Jurisdiction

Alabama

County	Archives & Libraries	Atlases	Bible Records	Bibliography	Biographies	Cemeteries	Census (Printed)	Church History	Church Records	Court Records	Directories	Emigration/Immigration	Employment/Occupations	Genealogy	Genealogy/Periodicals	History	Land & Property	Maps	Migration	Military Records	Minorities	Native Races	Naturalizations	Newspapers	Oaths of Allegiance	Obituaries	Periodicals	Postal	Probate Records	Public Records	School Records	Societies	Tax Records	Vital Records	Voting Registers	Yearbooks
Autauga					•	•										•				•								•					•			
Baine See Etowah																																				
Baker See Chilton									•																											
Baldwin					•	•										•	•			•													•			
Barbour				•	•	•	•							•		•	•	•		•					•			•					•			
Benton See Calhoun																																	•			
Bibb					•	•	•	•						•		•				•								•	•				•			
Blount				•	•	•			•					•		•	•			•								•	•				•			
Bullock						•										•				•								•					•			
Butler					•	•								•		•				•					•			•					•			
Cabela See Bibb																																				
Calhoun					•	•				•						•	•			•								•					•			
Chambers					•	•		•						•		•	•	•		•								•					•			
Cherokee					•	•									•	•	•			•								•					•			
Chilton				•	•	•			•							•	•			•								•	•				•			
Choctaw						•	•							•		•				•																
Clarke					•	•		•	•					•		•	•			•					•			•					•			
Clay						•														•																
Cleburne					•	•	•	•												•								•					•			
Coffee						•									•	•	•			•								•					•			
Colbert	•				•	•	•	•								•	•			•									•	•			•			
Conecuh	•					•	•									•				•													•			
Coosa							•													•								•					•			
Cotaco See Morgan																																				
Covington							•													•													•			
Crenshaw						•	•										•			•								•					•			
Cullman	•				•	•	•	•	•	•				•		•	•			•								•					•			
Dale						•	•							•		•				•													•			
Dallas					•	•	•	•	•							•				•								•					•			
De Kalb						•	•	•								•	•			•								•					•			
Elmore						•	•									•	•			•								•					•			
Escambia						•	•									•				•													•			
Etowah						•	•				•					•	•			•				•				•					•			
Fayette						•	•	•						•		•								•									•			
Franklin					•		•	•						•		•				•													•			
Geneva						•	•							•		•				•													•			
Greene						•	•		•		•					•				•								•	•				•			
Hale	•					•	•													•								•					•			
Hancock See Winston																																				
Henry						•	•							•		•	•			•					•			•					•			
Houston						•	•									•				•													•			
Jackson						•	•			•				•		•	•			•								•					•			
Jefferson	•				•	•	•		•		•			•		•				•				•		•		•	•		•		•			
Lamar							•													•				•									•			
Lauderdale	•					•	•	•	•	•				•	•	•	•			•								•	•				•			
Lawrence					•	•	•									•				•					•			•					•			
Lee					•	•	•		•					•		•	•			•								•					•			
Limestone						•	•	•								•	•			•												•			•	
Lowndes	•					•	•		•							•	•			•								•					•			

Records by Jurisdiction **Alabama (cont.)**	Archives & Libraries	Atlases	Bible Records	Bibliography	Biographies	Cemeteries	Census (Printed)	Church History	Church Records	Court Records	Directories	Emigration/Immigration	Employment/Occupations	Genealogy	Genealogy/Periodicals	History	Land & Property	Maps	Migration	Military Records	Minorities	Native Races	Naturalizations	Newspapers	Oaths of Allegiance	Obituaries	Periodicals	Postal	Probate Records	Public Records	School Records	Societies	Tax Records	Vital Records	Voting Registers	Yearbooks
Macon						•	•	•	•								•			•								•					•			
Madison						•	•	•	•		•			•		•	•	•		•				•				•					•			
Marengo	•					•	•		•		•									•								•					•			
Marion						•	•										•			•													•			
Marshall						•	•									•	•			•								•					•			
Mobile					•	•	•		•		•	•		•		•	•	•		•								•					•			•
Monroe						•	•		•		•			•		•	•			•								•					•			
Montgomery						•	•				•			•		•	•	•		•				•									•			
Morgan						•	•		•	•				•		•	•			•					•								•			
Perry						•	•		•								•			•								•					•			
Pickens							•		•					•		•				•				•	•			•					•			
Pike						•	•							•		•	•			•					•			•					•			
Randolph							•							•		•	•			•								•					•			
Russell						•	•				•			•		•	•			•								•					•			
Sanford See Lamar																																				
St. Clair						•	•	•		•			•	•		•	•			•								•	•				•			
Shelby						•	•	•	•	•						•				•													•			
Sumter		•				•	•							•						•								•					•			
Talladega	•					•	•													•													•			
Tallapoosa						•	•							•		•	•			•								•					•			
Tuscaloosa					•	•	•	•	•					•		•				•								•		•			•			
Walker					•	•	•									•				•								•	•				•			
Washington					•		•									•	•			•								•					•			
Wilcox						•	•		•											•								•					•			
Winston						•	•	•								•				•													•			

Records by Jurisdiction

Texas

	Archives & Libraries	Atlases	Bible Records	Bibliography	Biographies	Cemeteries	Census (Printed)	Church History	Church Records	Court Records	Directories	Emigration/Immigration	Employment/Occupations	Genealogy	Genealogy/Periodicals	History	Land & Property	Maps	Migration	Military Records	Minorities	Native Races	Naturalizations	Newspapers	Obituaries	Periodicals	Postal	Probate Records	Public Records	School Records	Societies	Tax Records	Vital Records	Voting Registers	Yearbooks
Anderson					•	•			•	•	•			•		•	•						•					•					•		
Andrews						•											•																		
Angelina						•			•	•						•	•	•		•								•					•		
Aransas								•	•	•							•						•					•					•		
Archer						•										•	•																		
Armstrong																•																	•		
Atascosa						•			•	•						•	•						•					•					•		
Austin					•			•		•				•		•	•	•					•		•			•			•		•		
Bailey						•																													
Bandera	•				•	•			•	•						•	•			•			•					•					•		
Bastrop	•				•	•		•		•				•		•	•	•					•										•		
Baylor								•						•		•	•																		
Bee						•			•	•						•	•						•										•		
Bell					•	•					•					•	•			•			•					•	•	•			•		
Bexar	•					•	•	•	•	•	•			•		•	•	•		•	•		•					•	•	•			•		
Blanco					•									•		•	•						•					•					•		
Borden						•										•	•																		
Bosque						•	•			•						•	•						•					•	•				•		
Bowie			•		•	•	•		•		•			•		•			•									•					•		
Brazoria	•						•		•	•						•	•	•										•				•	•		
Brazos					•	•	•	•	•	•						•	•						•					•				•	•		
Brewster						•			•							•																			
Briscoe																																			
Brooks																																			
Brown	•				•	•					•		•	•		•												•					•		
Buchanan																																			
Burleson													•		•	•											•						•		
Burnet					•	•	•			•						•	•						•					•					•		
Caldwell	•				•	•	•	•						•		•	•						•					•					•		
Calhoun	•					•	•		•	•					•		•						•					•					•		
Callahan	•					•										•	•																		
Cameron											•						•						•					•					•		
Camp	•														•												•								
Carson					•											•																			
Cass					•	•		•	•	•					•	•	•											•					•		
Castro						•		•	•							•																			
Chambers						•	•		•								•											•	•				•		
Cherokee			•		•	•	•	•	•	•				•		•	•			•			•		•			•	•		•		•		
Childress					•											•																			
Clay					•	•										•																•			
Cochran																																			
Coke	•					•																										•			
Coleman	•					•		•						•		•							•					•		•			•		
Collin	•		•		•	•	•	•	•	•				•		•	•			•								•					•		
Collingsworth															•																				
Colorado					•	•			•	•				•		•	•						•					•					•		
Comal									•	•							•						•					•					•		
Comanche						•	•		•							•																	•		
Concho					•	•	•	•								•																	•		

Records by Jurisdiction **Texas** (cont.)	Archives & Libraries	Atlases	Bible Records	Bibliography	Biographies	Cemeteries	Census (Printed)	Church History	Church Records	Court Records	Directories	Emigration/Immigration	Employment/Occupations	Genealogy	Genealogy/Periodicals	History	Land & Property	Maps	Migration	Military Records	Minorities	Native Races	Naturalizations	Newspapers	Obituaries	Periodicals	Postal	Probate Records	Public Records	School Records	Societies	Tax Records	Vital Records	Voting Registers	Yearbooks
Cooke						•		•		•					•	•	•						•						•				•		
Coryell					•	•	•		•							•	•	•						•	•			•				•	•		
Cottle															•																				
Crane																																			
Crockett	•																																•		
Crosby															•																		•		
Culberson					•				•							•																			
Dallam																•																			
Dallas					•	•		•	•	•	•			•	•	•		•						•	•	•		•			•	•	•		•
Davis																																			
Dawson																																			
Deaf Smith																																	•		
Delta	•									•				•		•	•											•					•		
Denton	•				•	•			•	•				•		•		•					•					•					•		
De Witt	•				•			•	•	•						•	•						•					•					•		
Dickens					•											•																			
Dimmit									•	•							•						•					•					•		
Donley																•																			
Duval										•							•											•					•		
Eastland					•	•			•							•																			
Ector	•				•	•										•																			
Edwards																																			
Ellis					•	•		•	•	•				•	•	•	•			•			•					•					•		
El Paso	•				•	•			•		•			•	•	•		•						•							•		•		
Encinal																																			
Erath						•	•			•				•		•	•						•					•	•				•		
Falls					•			•	•	•						•	•						•					•				•	•		
Fannin					•	•	•		•	•				•		•	•			•								•	•				•		
Fayette	•						•	•	•	•			•	•		•	•				•		•					•		•			•		
Fisher						•								•		•																			
Floyd																•																			
Foard					•											•																			
Fort Bend						•			•	•					•	•	•						•					•					•		
Franklin							•			•						•	•											•					•		
Freestone					•	•			•	•						•	•											•					•		
Frio						•			•	•						•	•						•					•					•		
Gaines					•									•		•																			
Galveston	•				•	•	•		•	•	•	•				•	•						•	•									•	•	
Garza						•										•																			
Gillespie	•				•	•			•	•						•	•				•		•					•					•		
Glasscock	•																																•		
Goliad	•									•							•											•					•		
Gonzales						•			•							•	•																•		
Gray																																	•		
Grayson					•	•					•					•	•						•					•					•		
Gregg	•					•										•												•					•		
Grimes						•			•							•	•						•					•					•		
Guadalupe	•							•	•	•						•	•						•					•					•		
Hale	•				•									•		•																			

Records by Jurisdiction **Texas** **(cont.)**	Archives & Libraries	Atlases	Bible Records	Bibliography	Biographies	Cemeteries	Census (Printed)	Church History	Church Records	Court Records	Directories	Emigration/Immigration	Employment/Occupations	Genealogy	Genealogy/Periodicals	History	Land & Property	Maps	Migration	Military Records	Minorities	Native Races	Naturalizations	Newspapers	Obituaries	Periodicals	Postal	Probate Records	Public Records	School Records	Societies	Tax Records	Vital Records	Voting Registers	Yearbooks
Hall					•											•																			
Hamilton						•											•						•					•					•		
Hansford																																			
Hardeman					•											•				•													•		
Hardin						•			•	•							•											•					•		
Harris	•				•	•		•	•	•	•			•	•	•	•				•		•			•		•	•				•		
Harrison						•		•						•		•	•								•				•				•		
Hartley																•																			
Haskell					•			•						•		•																			
Hays	•					•		•	•						•	•	•									•		•					•		
Hemphill									•																								•		
Henderson					•	•	•							•	•	•										•						•	•		
Hidalgo	•									•							•											•					•		
Hill					•			•	•	•						•	•							•				•					•		
Hockley					•			•	•																										
Hood	•						•			•				•	•	•	•											•					•		
Hopkins					•			•		•				•		•	•											•					•		
Houston					•	•				•						•	•						•	•	•			•					•		
Howard						•					•					•																			
Hudspeth										•																									
Hunt					•	•	•	•	•	•	•		•	•		•	•			•			•					•	•			•	•	•	
Hutchinson					•											•																			
Irion	•														•																	•			
Jack							•			•						•												•	•			•	•		
Jackson	•				•		•		•	•						•	•						•					•	•				•		
Jasper					•	•	•		•			•				•	•							•				•					•		
Jeff Davis									•																								•		
Jefferson	•					•	•	•	•		•					•	•											•					•		
Jim Hogg																																			
Jim Wells																																			
Johnson					•	•		•	•						•	•												•					•		
Jones													•			•																	•		
Karnes									•	•						•	•				•		•					•					•		
Kaufman					•	•			•	•						•	•											•					•		
Kendall						•		•	•	•					•		•						•					•					•		
Kenedy	•																																		
Kent					•	•								•		•																			
Kerr					•				•	•						•	•											•					•		
Kimble						•								•		•																	•		
King	•															•																			
Kinney									•	•						•	•											•					•		
Kleberg																																			
Knox						•		•																					•						
Lamar	•				•	•	•		•	•						•	•	•					•					•					•		
Lamb					•											•																			
Lampasas						•	•		•																								•		
La Salle					•				•	•						•	•						•					•					•		
Lavaca							•		•	•						•	•				•		•					•					•		
Lee	•				•	•								•		•	•				•							•					•		

Records by Jurisdiction — **Texas (cont.)**	Archives & Libraries	Atlases	Bible Records	Bibliography	Biographies	Cemeteries	Census (Printed)	Church History	Church Records	Court Records	Directories	Emigration/Immigration	Employment/Occupations	Genealogy	Genealogy/Periodicals	History	Land & Property	Maps	Migration	Military Records	Minorities	Native Races	Naturalizations	Newspapers	Obituaries	Periodicals	Postal	Probate Records	Public Records	School Records	Societies	Tax Records	Vital Records	Voting Registers	Yearbooks
Leon					•	•	•								•	•	•			•						•		•				•	•		
Liberty	•					•	•		•	•						•	•											•					•		
Limestone					•		•	•		•						•	•											•				•	•		
Lipscomb																•																	•		
Live Oak										•						•	•			•								•					•	•	
Llano	•					•				•							•											•					•		
Loving																																			
Lubbock				•		•					•					•																			
Lynn						•																											•		
Madison						•																													
Marion	•					•		•	•							•									•			•					•		
Martin																																			
Mason					•		•	•	•					•		•																	•		
Matagorda	•					•	•		•	•					•	•	•								•			•					•		
Maverick										•							•						•					•					•	•	
McCulloch						•																													
McLennan	•				•	•				•	•					•	•						•		•			•					•		
McMullen									•	•						•	•						•					•					•		
Medina									•	•							•						•					•					•		
Menard						•	•									•																	•		
Midland											•				•														•				•		
Milam	•					•	•	•	•							•	•						•					•	•				•		
Mills	•					•																							•				•		
Mitchell						•																													
Montague	•				•	•			•	•						•	•						•					•					•		
Montgomery						•	•		•	•				•	•	•	•								•			•	•			•	•		
Moore						•										•																	•		
Morris																											•								
Motley						•								•		•																			
Nacogdoches	•				•	•	•	•	•	•	•		•	•	•	•	•	•		•					•			•	•	•	•	•	•		
Navarro					•	•		•		•	•		•		•	•	•			•			•					•			•		•		
Navasota See Brazos																																			
Newton	•					•											•			•								•	•				•	•	
Nolan						•										•												•							
Nueces	•								•	•						•	•				•		•					•					•	•	
Ochiltree					•											•																	•		
Oldham	•					•																													
Orange	•					•	•		•	•							•											•					•		
Palo Pinto	•				•	•										•																	•		
Panola					•	•	•	•						•		•	•										•	•					•		
Parker	•				•	•				•					•	•	•						•					•					•		
Parmer					•											•																	•		
Pecos						•			•																								•		
Polk						•	•			•				•		•	•					•			•			•				•	•	•	
Potter					•	•		•			•					•	•												•						
Presidio							•	•	•																										
Rains	•					•										•																	•		
Randall						•	•				•					•																			
Reagan					•											•																•			

Records by Jurisdiction **Texas** (cont.)	Archives & Libraries	Atlases	Bible Records	Bibliography	Biographies	Cemeteries	Census (Printed)	Church History	Church Records	Court Records	Directories	Emigration/Immigration	Employment/Occupations	Genealogy	Genealogy/Periodicals	History	Land & Property	Maps	Migration	Military Records	Minorities	Native Races	Naturalizations	Newspapers	Obituaries	Periodicals	Postal	Probate Records	Public Records	School Records	Societies	Tax Records	Vital Records	Voting Registers	Yearbooks
Real									•																										
Red River						•	•		•	•				•		•	•	•		•			•					•	•				•		
Reeves									•																										
Refugio							•	•	•	•						•	•						•					•					•		
Roberts																																			
Robertson	•				•	•		•		•				•		•	•			•			•					•					•		
Rockwall	•					•				•							•											•					•		
Runnels					•		•							•		•				•								•					•		
Rusk					•		•			•						•	•			•								•							
Sabine	•					•	•		•					•		•	•			•							•	•					•		
San Augustine						•	•	•		•						•	•			•							•	•				•	•	•	
San Jacinto						•										•	•											•					•		
San Patricio										•						•	•						•					•					•		
San Saba					•	•								•		•												•					•		
Schleicher	•				•								•			•												•					•		
Scurry						•										•							•		•								•		
Shackelford	•																												•				•		
Shelby						•	•	•	•					•		•	•			•	•				•		•	•		•			•		
Sherman														•		•																			
Smith						•	•	•			•			•		•	•									•		•				•	•		
Sommervell	•									•						•	•											•					•		
Starr										•							•											•					•		
Stephens	•													•																			•		
Sterling	•															•																	•		
Stonewall						•																											•		
Sutton																																	•		
Swisher						•										•									•										
Tarrant					•	•	•	•	•		•				•	•	•												•				•		
Taylor						•					•					•								•									•		
Terrell					•				•							•																			
Terry						•										•																			
Throckmorton	•																																		
Titus					•	•								•		•												•							
Tom Green						•					•				•	•										•							•		
Travis	•				•	•	•	•	•	•	•			•		•	•						•			•		•					•		
Trinity						•			•					•		•	•			•			•					•					•		
Tyler																•	•											•					•		
Upshur					•	•										•																	•		
Upton	•															•																			
Uvalde	•					•			•	•							•						•					•					•		
Val Verde									•																										
Van Zandt	•				•	•								•	•	•	•									•									
Victoria									•						•	•	•						•						•				•		
Walker						•			•	•						•	•						•					•	•				•		
Waller					•	•			•	•						•	•						•					•					•		
Ward									•							•																	•		
Washington	•				•	•		•	•		•			•		•	•						•					•					•		
Webb									•	•	•					•	•						•					•					•		
Wharton									•	•						•	•						•					•					•		

Records by Jurisdiction **Texas** (cont.)	Archives & Libraries	Atlases	Bible Records	Bibliography	Biographies	Cemeteries	Census (Printed)	Church History	Church Records	Court Records	Directories	Emigration/Immigration	Employment/Occupations	Genealogy	Genealogy/Periodicals	History	Land & Property	Maps	Migration	Military Records	Minorities	Native Races	Naturalizations	Newspapers	Obituaries	Periodicals	Postal	Probate Records	Public Records	School Records	Societies	Tax Records	Vital Records	Voting Registers	Yearbooks
Wheeler									•																										
Wichita						•					•					•												•					•		
Wilbarger					•											•																			
Willacy																																			
Williamson	•					•			•							•	•						•					•	•				•		
Wilson	•								•	•							•				•		•					•					•		
Winkler					•	•			•					•		•																			
Wise	•				•											•	•											•					•		
Wood	•					•								•		•												•					•		
Yoakum																																			
Young	•					•	•									•				•								•							
Zapata										•						•	•						•					•					•		
Zavala										•							•						•					•					•		

Records by Jurisdiction **Missouri**	Archives & Libraries	Atlases	Bible Records	Bibliography	Biographies	Cemeteries	Census (Printed)	Church History	Church Records	Court Records	Directories	Emigration/Immigration	Employment/Occupations	Genealogy	Genealogy/Periodicals	History	Land & Property	Maps	Migration	Military Records	Minorities	Native Races	Naturalizations	Newspapers	Obituaries	Periodicals	Postal	Probate Records	Public Records	School Records	Societies	Tax Records	Vital Records	Voting Registers	Yearbooks
Adair					•	•	•			•						•	•	•		•								•			•		•		
Allen See Atchison																																			
Andrew		•	•		•	•	•		•	•				•		•	•	•					•					•					•		
Arkansas																																			
Ashley																																			
Atchison					•	•	•		•		•					•		•						•									•		
Audrain					•	•	•	•	•	•						•	•			•					•			•					•		
Barry					•	•	•		•							•	•	•		•								•	•			•	•		
Barton						•	•		•	•						•	•											•					•		
Bates					•	•	•		•	•						•	•											•					•		
Benton					•	•	•		•	•						•	•			•								•					•		
Bollinger							•		•	•						•	•									•		•				•	•		
Boone	•				•	•	•	•	•	•	•					•	•	•							•			•					•		
Buchanan					•	•	•		•	•	•			•		•	•							•				•	•			•	•		
Butler					•	•	•			•	•			•	•	•	•											•		•			•		
Caldwell					•		•			•						•	•	•							•			•					•		
Callaway					•	•	•									•	•											•					•		
Camden					•	•	•		•								•											•					•		
Cape Girardeau						•	•	•	•	•	•					•	•	•										•					•		
Carroll					•	•	•		•	•						•	•	•					•					•	•				•		
Carter										•						•	•											•					•		
Cass	•		•		•	•	•		•	•				•		•	•	•										•					•		
Cedar						•	•		•	•						•	•											•					•		
Chariton					•	•	•			•						•	•											•					•		
Christian						•	•		•	•						•	•											•				•	•		
Clark (Old)																																			
Clark						•	•			•					•	•	•			•			•					•					•		
Clay	•				•	•	•	•	•	•				•		•	•							•	•			•		•			•		
Clinton		•			•	•	•		•	•						•	•	•					•					•					•		
Cole	•				•	•	•	•		•	•					•	•							•				•		•			•		
Cooper		•			•	•	•	•	•	•					•		•	•	•										•					•	
Crawford							•			•						•	•			•								•		•			•		
Dade					•	•	•	•	•	•				•		•	•											•					•		
Dallas	•				•	•	•		•	•						•	•											•					•		
Daviess					•	•	•		•	•				•		•	•											•					•		
De Kalb	•				•	•	•		•	•						•	•	•							•			•					•		
Dent					•	•	•			•				•		•	•											•					•		
Dodge																																			
Douglas						•	•		•	•				•		•	•									•		•					•		
Dunklin					•	•	•			•						•	•											•					•		
Franklin					•	•	•	•		•						•	•	•		•								•					•		
Gasconade							•		•	•						•	•	•			•		•									•	•		
Gentry	•				•	•	•		•	•				•		•	•	•						•				•				•	•		
Greene					•	•	•		•	•	•					•	•							•	•			•	•				•		
Grundy					•	•	•		•	•				•		•	•			•								•					•		
Harrison					•	•	•		•							•												•					•		
Hempstead																																			
Henry	•				•	•	•		•	•				•		•	•	•										•					•		
Hickory					•	•	•		•	•						•	•			•								•				•			

Records by Jurisdiction **Missouri (cont.)**	Archives & Libraries	Atlases	Bible Records	Bibliography	Biographies	Cemeteries	Census (Printed)	Church History	Church Records	Court Records	Directories	Emigration/Immigration	Employment/Occupations	Genealogy	Genealogy/Periodicals	History	Land & Property	Maps	Migration	Military Records	Minorities	Native Races	Naturalizations	Newspapers	Obituaries	Periodicals	Postal	Probate Records	Public Records	School Records	Societies	Tax Records	Vital Records	Voting Registers	Yearbooks
Holt	•				•	•	•		•	•	•					•	•	•					•	•				•					•		
Howard					•	•	•			•						•	•											•					•		
Howell					•	•	•			•				•		•	•											•	•	•		•	•		
Iron						•	•		•	•						•	•											•					•		
Jackson	•		•		•	•	•	•	•	•	•			•	•	•	•	•			•			•	•			•					•		
Jasper	•		•		•	•	•		•	•	•					•	•	•			•			•				•	•				•		
Jefferson						•	•			•						•	•	•										•					•		
Johnson	•				•	•	•		•	•						•	•											•					•		
Kinderhook																																			
Knox					•		•		•	•				•		•	•			•				•				•					•		
Laclede					•	•	•		•	•						•	•											•					•		
Lafayette					•	•	•		•	•			•			•	•	•										•					•		
Lawrence (Old)																																			
Lawrence					•	•	•		•	•						•	•							•				•					•		
Lewis						•	•		•	•						•	•			•								•					•		
Lilard																																			
Lincoln					•	•	•			•						•	•											•					•		
Linn	•				•	•	•			•						•	•	•										•					•		
Livingston					•	•	•		•	•						•	•						•					•					•		
Macon	•				•	•	•			•	•					•	•	•							•			•					•		
Madison						•	•	•	•								•											•					•		
Maries					•		•			•						•	•	•										•					•		
Marion					•	•	•		•	•	•					•	•											•					•		
McDonald	•				•	•	•									•	•			•								•				•	•		
Mercer					•		•		•	•						•	•											•					•		
Miller					•	•	•		•	•						•	•											•	•				•		
Mississippi							•			•						•	•											•				•	•		
Moniteau					•	•	•		•	•						•	•											•					•		
Monroe					•	•	•		•	•				•		•	•											•					•		
Montgomery						•	•		•							•	•											•					•		
Morgan					•	•		•	•	•						•	•			•			•					•					•		
New Madrid	•				•	•	•			•				•		•	•											•	•				•		
Newton					•	•	•		•	•				•		•	•								•			•					•		
Niangua																																			
Nodaway					•	•	•		•	•				•		•	•	•		•								•					•		
Oregon						•	•			•				•		•	•						•					•	•				•		
Osage						•	•	•		•						•	•	•										•	•			•	•		
Ozark					•	•	•		•	•				•		•	•											•					•		
Pemiscot						•	•			•			•			•	•									•		•					•		
Perry							•	•	•	•				•	•	•	•				•		•					•					•		
Pettis	•				•	•	•		•	•	•			•		•	•						•					•	•				•		
Phelps					•	•			•	•						•	•											•	•			•	•		
Pike	•				•	•	•			•						•	•											•					•		
Platte	•				•	•	•		•	•				•		•	•						•					•				•	•		
Polk					•	•	•	•	•	•						•	•			•						•		•				•	•		
Pulaski (Old)																																			
Pulaski					•		•			•				•		•	•			•				•				•		•			•		
Putnam					•	•	•		•	•						•	•										•					•			
Ralls					•	•	•							•		•	•											•					•		

Records by Jurisdiction **Missouri** (cont.)	Archives & Libraries	Atlases	Bible Records	Bibliography	Biographies	Cemeteries	Census (Printed)	Church History	Church Records	Court Records	Directories	Emigration/Immigration	Employment/Occupations	Genealogy	Genealogy/Periodicals	History	Land & Property	Maps	Migration	Military Records	Minorities	Native Races	Naturalizations	Newspapers	Obituaries	Periodicals	Postal	Probate Records	Public Records	School Records	Societies	Tax Records	Vital Records	Voting Registers	Yearbooks
Randolph					•	•	•		•	•						•	•											•		•			•		
Ray	•				•	•	•		•	•				•		•	•	•							•			•					•		
Reynolds	•					•	•		•	•							•											•				•	•		
Ripley	•					•	•		•	•							•								•			•					•		
Rives See Henry																																			
St. Charles					•	•	•		•	•				•	•	•	•								•			•					•		
St. Clair					•	•	•		•	•						•	•											•					•		
St. Francois						•	•			•						•	•							•				•					•		
St. Louis	•				•	•	•	•	•	•	•				•	•	•	•		•			•	•				•	•	•		•	•		
St. Louis City	•	•			•	•	•	•	•		•		•	•		•	•	•			•			•		•		•	•	•	•	•	•		
Ste. Genevieve						•	•			•						•	•						•					•	•				•		
Saline			•		•	•	•	•	•	•				•		•	•	•						•	•			•				•	•		
Schuyler					•	•	•			•						•	•											•					•		
Scotland						•	•			•						•	•											•					•		
Scott						•	•			•						•	•			•			•					•					•		
Shannon						•	•			•							•											•					•		
Shelby	•				•	•	•			•						•	•						•					•					•		
Stoddard						•	•							•		•	•											•					•		
Stone						•	•			•							•											•				•	•		
Sullivan					•	•	•		•	•				•		•	•											•					•		
Taney						•	•		•							•	•			•								•		•			•		
Texas					•	•	•			•						•	•											•					•		
Vernon					•	•			•	•						•	•											•					•		
Warren						•	•		•	•						•	•						•					•					•		
Washington					•	•	•		•	•				•		•	•								•			•					•		
Wayne						•	•			•						•	•											•				•	•		
Webster					•	•	•		•	•			•			•	•											•	•				•		
Worth					•					•						•	•											•	•			•	•		
Wright					•	•	•		•	•						•	•	•										•					•		

Records by Jurisdiction **Kentucky**	Archives & Libraries	Atlases	Bible Records	Bibliography	Biography	Cemeteries	Census (Printed)	Church History	Church Records	Court Records	Directories	Emigration/Immigration	Employment/Occupations	Genealogy	Genealogy-Periodicals	History	Land & Property	Maps	Migration	Military Records	Minorities	Native Races	Naturalizations	Newspapers	Obituaries	Periodicals	Postal	Probate Records	Public Records	School Records	Societies	Tax Records	Vital Records	Voting Registers	Yearbooks
Adair					•	•	•	•	•	•						•	•			•								•	•			•	•		
Allen						•	•		•	•			•			•	•			•								•	•			•	•		
Anderson	•		•			•	•		•	•			•	•		•	•			•				•				•				•	•		
Ballard							•		•	•						•	•											•	•			•	•		
Barren					•	•	•	•	•	•				•		•	•											•				•	•		
Bath		•				•		•	•	•						•	•	•		•								•				•	•		
Bell							•			•						•	•							•		•		•				•	•		
Boone		•	•			•	•	•	•	•				•		•	•							•				•	•	•		•	•		
Bourbon		•				•	•	•	•	•				•		•	•	•		•				•				•				•	•		
Boyd						•			•	•	•				•	•							•				•				•	•			
Boyle						•	•		•	•						•	•							•				•			•	•	•		
Bracken		•				•	•		•	•						•	•	•		•								•				•	•		
Breathitt						•	•		•	•							•							•				•				•	•		
Breckinridge	•					•	•	•	•	•							•			•								•				•	•		
Bullitt					•	•	•			•					•	•	•			•								•				•	•		
Butler						•	•	•	•	•			•	•		•	•	•		•				•				•	•			•	•		
Caldwell						•	•			•						•	•											•				•	•		
Calloway			•		•	•	•		•					•		•	•			•								•				•	•		
Campbell		•				•	•		•	•	•			•		•	•	•		•								•	•			•	•		
Carlisle	•					•										•												•				•	•		
Carroll		•								•							•	•										•				•	•		
Carter						•				•						•	•											•				•	•		
Casey						•	•		•	•						•	•											•				•	•		
Christian					•	•	•	•	•	•						•	•			•			•	•	•			•				•	•		
Clark		•				•	•	•	•	•						•	•			•				•				•			•	•	•		
Clay						•	•			•						•	•			•								•				•	•		
Clinton						•	•	•	•	•							•			•								•				•	•		
Crittenden						•	•			•							•											•				•	•		
Cumberland			•			•	•		•	•						•	•			•								•				•	•		
Daviess					•	•	•	•	•	•	•					•	•	•						•				•				•	•		
Edmonson				•			•			•							•											•				•	•		
Elliott							•										•													•		•	•		
Estill						•	•			•						•	•											•				•	•		
Fayette	•	•	•			•	•	•	•	•	•			•		•	•	•		•			•	•	•			•	•	•		•	•		
Fleming		•				•	•		•	•							•			•								•				•	•		
Floyd							•			•				•		•	•											•				•	•		
Franklin				•		•		•	•	•				•		•	•							•		•		•	•	•		•	•		
Fulton			•		•	•	•	•	•	•					•	•	•							•				•				•	•		
Gallatin		•						•	•	•						•	•	•						•				•	•			•	•		
Garrard						•	•	•	•	•				•		•	•	•										•			•	•	•		
Grant						•	•		•	•							•											•				•	•		
Graves		•				•	•		•					•			•	•		•				•	•					•		•	•		
Grayson							•		•	•							•											•				•	•		
Green					•	•	•		•	•						•	•			•						•		•	•	•		•	•		
Greenup						•	•		•	•	•					•	•			•								•				•	•		
Hancock						•	•		•	•							•											•		•		•	•		
Hardin					•	•	•	•	•	•						•	•							•			•	•				•	•		
Harlan							•			•						•	•			•								•				•	•		
Harrison							•		•	•						•	•			•				•				•				•	•		

Records by Jurisdiction **Kentucky** (cont.)	Archives & Libraries	Atlases	Bible Records	Bibliography	Biography	Cemeteries	Census (Printed)	Church History	Church Records	Court Records	Directories	Emigration/Immigration	Employment/Occupations	Genealogy	Genealogy-Periodicals	History	Land & Property	Maps	Migration	Military Records	Minorities	Native Races	Naturalizations	Newspapers	Obituaries	Periodicals	Postal	Probate Records	Public Records	School Records	Societies	Tax Records	Vital Records	Voting Registers	Yearbooks
Hart					•	•	•		•	•			•			•	•			•				•		•						•	•		
Henderson		•			•	•	•			•				•		•	•	•		•				•		•		•				•	•		
Henry		•				•	•		•	•				•		•	•	•		•								•	•			•	•		
Hickman						•	•			•				•	•	•	•							•								•	•		
Hopkins						•	•		•	•				•	•	•	•	•										•			•	•	•		
Jackson										•							•											•				•	•		
Jefferson		•	•	•	•	•	•	•	•	•	•	•			•		•					•			•		•		•	•			•	•	
Jessamine		•			•				•	•						•	•	•										•				•	•		
Johnson					•	•	•		•	•				•		•	•											•		•		•	•		
Josh Bell																																			
Kenton		•	•			•	•	•	•	•	•					•	•	•		•			•					•	•			•	•		
Knott						•	•			•							•											•				•	•		
Knox	•					•	•		•	•					•	•	•			•								•		•		•	•		
Larue						•	•		•	•						•	•											•				•	•		
Laurel	•						•			•						•	•							•		•		•				•	•		
Lawrence							•			•							•			•				•				•		•		•	•		
Lee										•							•											•				•	•		
Leslie										•						•	•											•				•	•		
Letcher							•			•							•											•				•	•		
Lewis			•			•	•		•					•			•											•	•			•	•		
Lincoln						•	•			•						•	•	•		•				•				•				•	•		
Livingston						•	•		•	•				•		•	•											•				•	•		
Logan			•		•	•	•	•	•	•				•		•	•			•	•			•				•		•		•	•		
Lyon						•				•							•											•				•	•		
Madison						•	•	•		•				•			•			•				•				•				•	•		
Magoffin							•			•			•				•											•	•	•		•	•		
Marion						•			•	•						•	•							•				•	•	•		•	•		
Marshall						•	•		•	•						•	•							•				•				•	•		
Martin							•			•							•											•		•		•	•		
Mason			•			•			•	•	•			•		•	•			•								•	•			•	•		
McCracken						•	•		•		•					•	•							•				•				•	•		
McCreary	•																																		
McLean						•	•		•	•							•								•			•				•	•		
Meade	•					•	•			•						•	•			•								•				•	•		
Menifee									•	•							•											•				•	•		
Mercer			•			•	•	•	•	•				•		•	•			•	•			•				•	•	•		•	•		
Metcalfe						•	•			•							•											•				•	•		
Monroe						•	•		•	•				•			•			•								•		•		•	•		
Montgomery							•			•						•	•			•								•				•			
Morgan							•			•						•	•			•								•		•		•	•		
Muhlenberg					•	•	•			•			•	•	•	•	•			•								•	•			•	•		
Nelson		•					•	•	•	•						•	•	•		•					•	•		•	•			•	•		
Nicholas							•		•	•						•	•			•								•		•		•	•		
Ohio						•	•	•	•	•				•		•	•		•								•				•	•			
Oldham		•				•	•			•				•		•	•	•						•				•				•	•		
Owen		•					•		•	•						•	•	•		•								•				•	•		
Owsley							•																									•	•		
Pendleton		•					•	•	•	•						•	•	•								•		•				•	•		
Perry						•	•									•	•											•				•	•		

Records by Jurisdiction **Kentucky (cont.)**	Archives & Libraries	Atlases	Bible Records	Bibliography	Biography	Cemeteries	Census (Printed)	Church History	Church Records	Court Records	Directories	Emigration/Immigration	Employment/Occupations	Genealogy	Genealogy-Periodicals	History	Land & Property	Maps	Migration	Military Records	Minorities	Native Races	Naturalizations	Newspapers	Obituaries	Periodicals	Postal	Probate Records	Public Records	School Records	Societies	Tax Records	Vital Records	Voting Registers	Yearbooks
Pike							•			•				•		•	•											•		•		•	•	•	
Powell							•			•							•															•	•		
Pulaski						•	•	•	•	•						•	•			•								•				•	•		
Robertson										•							•							•				•				•	•		
Rockcastle						•	•	•	•	•							•											•				•	•		
Rowan							•			•							•							•				•				•	•		
Russell						•	•			•						•	•			•								•	•			•	•		
Scott							•	•	•	•						•	•			•				•				•	•			•	•		
Shelby		•			•	•	•	•	•	•			•			•	•	•		•				•				•	•			•	•		
Simpson						•	•		•	•				•		•	•			•								•		•		•	•		
Spencer		•					•		•	•					•		•	•			•							•		•		•	•		
Taylor					•	•	•		•	•					•	•	•											•				•	•		
Todd					•		•		•	•			•			•	•			•				•				•	•			•	•	•	
Trigg						•	•		•	•						•	•			•							•				•	•			
Trimble										•						•	•			•								•		•		•	•		
Union		•							•	•						•	•	•		•								•				•	•		
Warren						•	•		•	•				•			•								•			•	•			•	•		
Washington						•	•	•	•	•					•	•	•			•				•				•	•			•	•		
Wayne					•	•	•	•	•	•				•		•				•								•				•	•		
Webster					•	•	•	•	•	•				•		•	•											•				•	•		
Whitley						•				•				•			•						•	•				•				•	•		
Wolfe									•							•	•							•								•	•		
Woodford		•						•	•	•						•	•	•		•								•		•		•	•		

Records by Jurisdiction — Arkansas	Archives & Libraries	Atlases	Bible Records	Bibliography	Biographies	Cemeteries	Census (Printed)	Church History	Church Records	Court Records	Directories	Emigration/Immigration	Employment/Occupations	Genealogy	Genealogy/Periodicals	History	Land & Property	Maps	Migration	Military Records	Minorities	Native Races	Naturalizations	Newspapers	Obituaries	Periodicals	Postal	Probate Records	Public Records	School Records	Societies	Tax Records	Vital Records	Voting Registers	Yearbooks
Arkansas							•		•	•				•			•			•								•	•	•		•	•		
Ashley							•		•	•							•			•								•					•		
Baxter	•					•				•		•		•		•	•			•								•				•	•		
Benton	•				•	•	•	•	•	•						•	•	•		•			•			•		•			•	•	•		
Boone						•			•	•				•	•	•	•			•			•					•				•	•		
Bradley								•	•							•													•						
Calhoun						•		•	•	•							•			•								•	•			•	•		
Carroll	•				•	•	•		•	•		•		•		•	•			•								•	•		•	•	•		
Chicot									•	•							•			•								•	•			•	•		
Clark							•	•	•	•							•	•		•								•	•			•	•		
Clay									•	•							•			•			•					•	•			•	•		
Cleburne	•					•			•							•	•			•			•					•		•		•	•		
Cleveland	•					•			•																										
Columbia					•	•	•	•	•	•						•	•			•								•					•		
Conway					•		•			•						•	•			•								•				•	•		
Craighead					•	•		•	•	•						•	•			•				•				•	•			•	•		
Crawford					•	•			•	•			•	•		•	•			•			•	•		•		•	•			•	•		
Crittenden										•							•	•		•								•	•			•	•		
Cross					•					•				•		•	•	•		•								•				•	•		
Dallas					•	•	•			•						•	•	•		•								•	•			•	•		
Desha						•	•		•	•							•	•								•		•		•		•	•		
Dorsey See Cleveland																																			
Drew						•	•			•						•	•			•								•	•	•		•	•		
Faulkner	•				•			•		•						•	•			•						•		•	•			•	•		
Franklin									•	•						•	•			•			•					•	•			•	•	•	
Fulton						•	•			•										•								•					•		
Garland						•			•	•	•					•	•			•			•			•		•	•				•		
Grant									•	•							•			•								•	•			•	•		
Greene					•	•	•			•				•		•	•			•								•				•	•		
Hempstead					•		•			•						•	•			•								•	•			•	•	•	
Hot Springs	•					•	•		•	•						•	•			•								•				•	•		
Howard										•						•	•			•								•				•	•	•	
Independence						•	•			•							•			•						•		•	•			•	•	•	
Izard	•				•	•	•			•						•	•			•								•	•			•	•		
Jackson	•					•	•		•	•				•		•	•	•		•			•					•	•		•	•	•		
Jefferson						•	•			•	•					•												•	•				•		
Johnson					•				•	•						•	•			•			•					•	•			•	•		
Lafayette						•	•	•		•						•	•	•		•								•				•	•		
Lawrence						•	•			•							•			•			•					•	•		•	•	•	•	
Lee										•							•			•								•				•	•		
Lincoln							•		•	•				•		•	•			•								•				•	•		
Little River						•			•	•			•			•	•			•								•		•		•	•		
Logan						•			•	•					•		•			•			•					•	•			•	•		
Lonoke						•	•	•	•	•						•	•	•		•			•					•	•			•	•		
Lovely																																			
Madison	•					•	•		•	•					•	•	•			•			•					•	•	•		•	•		
Marion						•	•							•		•	•			•								•				•	•		
Miller					•		•			•	•					•	•	•		•								•	•			•	•		
Mississippi					•	•	•			•						•	•			•								•				•	•		

Records by Jurisdiction **Arkansas** (cont.)	Archives & Libraries	Atlases	Bible Records	Bibliography	Biographies	Cemeteries	Census (Printed)	Church History	Church Records	Court Records	Directories	Emigration/Immigration	Employment/Occupations	Genealogy	Genealogy/Periodicals	History	Land & Property	Maps	Migration	Military Records	Minorities	Native Races	Naturalizations	Newspapers	Obituaries	Periodicals	Postal	Probate Records	Public Records	School Records	Societies	Tax Records	Vital Records	Voting Registers	Yearbooks
Monroe	•					•		•	•	•						•	•	•		•				•				•	•		•	•	•		
Montgomery	•					•				•							•	•		•								•				•	•		
Nevada						•		•	•	•				•			•			•								•		•			•		
Newton					•	•	•			•				•		•	•			•			•			•		•	•			•	•	•	
Ouachita						•		•	•	•					•	•	•			•						•		•	•	•	•	•	•		
Perry						•	•			•						•	•			•								•				•	•		
Phillips						•			•	•							•	•		•								•	•		•	•	•		
Pike						•	•										•			•								•	•			•	•		
Poinsett							•			•							•	•		•								•				•	•		
Polk						•	•			•							•			•			•						•				•		
Pope					•	•	•	•	•	•					•	•	•			•			•		•			•	•			•	•	•	
Prairie						•			•	•						•	•	•		•			•					•	•			•	•		
Pulaski						•		•		•	•					•	•			•			•			•		•	•	•			•		
Randolph					•	•				•	•					•	•			•			•					•				•	•		
St. Francis						•	•		•	•				•		•	•			•								•				•	•		
Saline	•						•			•							•			•			•					•					•		
Scott	•				•	•	•			•				•		•	•			•					•			•				•	•		
Searcy	•					•	•		•	•						•	•			•			•					•				•	•		
Sebastian					•	•	•		•	•	•		•		•	•	•	•		•								•				•	•		
Sevier						•	•		•	•						•	•			•								•	•			•	•	•	
Sharp						•				•				•		•	•									•		•				•	•		
Stone						•			•							•	•			•						•		•	•			•	•		
Union						•		•	•	•	•						•	•		•				•				•	•			•	•		
Van Buren						•				•						•	•			•								•				•	•		
Washington					•	•	•	•	•	•			•	•	•	•	•	•		•			•			•		•	•			•	•		
White						•	•		•	•						•	•			•			•			•		•				•	•		
Woodruff						•	•	•	•	•						•	•			•						•		•	•			•	•		
Yell					•	•	•		•	•					•	•	•			•				•		•		•				•	•		

Records by Jurisdiction — Mississippi	Archives & Libraries	Atlases	Bible Records	Bibliography	Biographies	Cemeteries	Census (Printed)	Church History	Church Records	Court Records	Directories	Emigration/Immigration	Employment/Occupations	Genealogy	Genealogy/Periodicals	History	Land & Property	Maps	Migration	Military Records	Minorities	Native Races	Naturalizations	Newspapers	Obituaries	Periodicals	Postal	Probate Records	Public Records	School Records	Societies	Tax Records	Vital Records	Voting Registers	Yearbooks
Adams						•			•	•	•			•			•											•	•			•	•		
Alcorn						•				•	•			•		•	•											•					•		
Amite	•					•	•			•			•			•	•			•								•					•		
Attala						•				•			•			•	•			•				•	•			•	•				•		
Benton						•											•											•					•		
Bolivar										•						•	•											•					•		
Calhoun																																			
Carroll									•	•						•	•			•								•	•				•		
Chickasaw						•	•			•						•	•											•	•				•		
Choctaw						•				•						•	•							•				•					•		
Claiborne						•	•		•	•						•	•											•					•		
Clarke						•				•						•	•											•					•		
Clay										•							•											•	•				•		
Coahoma										•						•	•											•	•				•		
Colfax																																			
Copiah							•			•							•							•				•					•		
Covington						•				•							•											•	•				•		
De Soto										•							•											•					•		
Forrest	•					•										•	•											•	•				•		
Franklin						•				•							•											•	•			•	•		
George						•										•	•								•			•					•		
Greene						•	•			•							•											•				•	•		
Grenada	•								•	•							•											•	•				•		
Hancock							•			•			•				•						•					•					•		
Harrison						•	•			•	•	•	•			•	•											•		•		•	•	•	
Hinds					•	•	•		•	•						•	•											•					•		
Holmes						•											•											•					•		
Humphreys	•						•			•			•				•											•					•		
Issaquena																																			
Itawamba							•			•					•		•											•	•				•		
Jackson						•				•		•			•	•	•							•				•					•		
Jasper					•	•									•	•							•				•						•		
Jefferson								•	•						•	•								•				•					•		
Jefferson Davis									•																		•					•			
Jones						•	•			•							•										•				•	•			
Kemper					•					•						•	•											•				•	•		
Lafayette			•			•				•						•	•											•	•				•		
Lamar	•					•										•	•											•	•				•		
Lauderdale						•			•	•	•						•							•				•					•		
Lawrence						•	•		•	•						•	•							•				•				•	•		
Leake										•							•											•					•		
Lee						•				•							•											•					•		
Leflore																	•	•				•							•					•	
Lincoln							•										•							•				•					•		
Lowndes						•			•	•						•	•											•	•				•		
Madison						•				•							•											•	•			•	•		
Marion							•			•						•	•			•								•	•			•	•		
Marshall						•			•	•						•	•											•	•				•		
Monroe					•		•		•	•	•					•	•							•				•	•		•		•		

Records by Jurisdiction — Mississippi (cont.)	Archives & Libraries	Atlases	Bible Records	Bibliography	Biographies	Cemeteries	Census (Printed)	Church History	Church Records	Court Records	Directories	Emigration/Immigration	Employment/Occupations	Genealogy	Genealogy/Periodicals	History	Land & Property	Maps	Migration	Military Records	Minorities	Native Races	Naturalizations	Newspapers	Obituaries	Periodicals	Postal	Probate Records	Public Records	School Records	Societies	Tax Records	Vital Records	Voting Registers	Yearbooks
Montgomery										•							•							•				•					•		
Neshoba							•			•							•							•				•					•		
Newton						•	•		•	•						•	•							•				•				•	•		
Noxubee							•		•	•							•			•								•	•			•	•		
Oktibbeha						•	•			•						•	•											•	•		•		•		
Panola						•		•	•	•						•	•											•	•				•		
Pearl River	•					•										•												•					•		
Perry						•	•										•											•				•	•		
Pickering																																			
Pike						•		•	•	•				•		•	•											•					•		
Pontotoc										•						•	•							•				•					•		
Prentiss	•			•	•				•		•	•											•					•							
Quitman						•				•							•											•					•		
Rankin					•	•			•	•						•	•			•								•	•				•		
Scott						•				•							•											•					•		
Sharkey										•							•											•					•		
Simpson					•		•			•						•	•			•								•					•		
Smith						•											•											•					•		
Stone						•																											•		
Sumner See Webster																																			
Sunflower										•						•	•											•	•				•		
Tallahatchie										•							•											•	•				•		
Tate						•				•				•		•	•											•					•		
Tippah	•					•	•	•		•				•		•	•									•		•	•				•		
Tishomingo						•				•				•		•	•			•								•					•		
Tunica	•					•	•		•	•							•											•	•				•		
Union						•											•											•					•		
Walthall	•													•		•												•					•		
Warren						•				•						•	•			•				•				•					•		
Washington			•			•										•	•											•					•		
Wayne						•	•	•		•						•												•				•	•		
Webster										•							•							•				•					•		
Wilkinson							•			•							•						•	•				•					•		
Winston						•			•	•						•	•							•				•	•				•		
Yalobusha						•				•				•		•	•			•								•	•			•	•		
Yazoo										•						•	•											•					•		

Chapter 9

United States: The Midwest

Marlene M. Marino

Ohio

Historical Background

1667 French explorer LaSalle travels throughout region.

1747 Ohio Company of Virginia organized to colonize the Ohio River Valley.

1749 Ohio Land Company formed.

1763 French and Indian War ends, giving Great Britain control of the region.

1772 Moravian Mission founded.

1779 George Rogers Clark defeats English and claims region for Virginia.

1784 Virginia Military Lands set aside to satisfy Virginia soldiers' bounty claims.

1786-1820 Congress Lands in Ohio sold by military officers. Federal government conducts first survey of Seven Ranges, lands west of Ohio River.

1786 Connecticut Western Reserve established for claims of Connecticut residents.

1787 Northwest Territory established.

1787 Ohio Company's purchase. Scotch-Irish from Virginia, Kentucky, and Pennsylvania settle in Marietta.

1787-96 Moravian Lands in Tascarawas County settled by Moravians from Bethlehem, Northampton County, Pennsylvania.

1792 Donation Tract established. Firelands granted by Connecticut.

1794 Symmes Purchase.

1795 Territorial Legislature mandates first divorce law. French Grant sets aside land in Scioto County.

1796 Refugee Tract established in Columbus for Canadian sympathizers with American Revolution.

1799 Ohio Territory created.

1800 Ohio Territorial Census taken (missing). Marietta and Steubenville Federal Land Offices opened.

1801 Chillicothe and Cincinnati Federal Land Offices opened.

1803 Ohio admitted to the Union as the seventeenth state. Ohio Supreme Court convened for first time.

1804 Zanesville Federal Land Office opened.

1808 Canton Federal Land Office opened; 500,000 acres distributed by lottery in November.

1810 First federal census of Ohio. Destroyed by fire during War of 1812.

1827 National Pike (Cumberland Road) reaches Zanesville.

1831 Members of the Church of Jesus Christ of Latter-day Saints (Mormons) move to Kirtland, Lake County, from New York.

1833 National Pike connects Zanesville and Columbus, Ohio.

1836 Five-year Toledo War ends; boundary between Ohio and Michigan settled.

1840 Statute of Descent and Distribution established.

1840s English and Irish immigrate to Ohio to build railroads.

1851 Ohio District Courts established.

1856-57 Ohio statute orders birth records kept. Limited compliance.

1861-65 Ohio soldiers (310,000) fight in Civil War.

1867 Statewide registration of vital records decreed.

	Western Reserve Historical Society founded.
1908	Registration of all birth and death records.

Settlement and Migration

By 1787, Scotch-Irish from Virginia, Pennsylvania, and Kentucky settled in Marietta, Washington County. A group from Bethlehem, Northampton County, Pennsylvania moved into Tuscarawas County during the period 1787 through 1796. New Englanders, mainly from Massachusetts migrated into Marietta, Washington County, in 1788. That same year, Revolutionary War soldiers left Massachusetts and Connecticut, and established new homes in Marietta, Washington County. Also in 1788, individuals and families from Essex County, New Jersey, resettled in Cincinnati, Hamilton County.

Between 1790 and 1791, French from La Havre, Bordeaux, and Nantes, migrated to the United States and settled in Gallipolis, Gallia County. Pioneers from Connecticut moved to the Firelands in the Western Reserve in 1792. Others from Connecticut and Vermont settled in Geauga County in 1795. Families from Standish, Cumberland County, Maine, relocated in 1796 in Withamsville, Clermont County. That same year, immigrants from Scotland migrated to Dayton and Montgomery County.

In 1800, people from Granville, Hampden County, Massachusetts, moved to Granville, Licking County. During the 1800s, Germans originally from York and Lancaster counties, Pennsylvania, moved from the Shenandoah Valley in Virginia, to settle in Cincinnati, Toledo, and Columbus. Others from Kentucky and Virginia settled in Ross County after 1800.

Members of the Welch Community in Cambria County, Pennsylvania, also settled in Granville Township, Licking County, in 1801. The following year, families from New Britain, Hartford County, Connecticut, resettled in Worthington, Franklin County. In 1805, members of the United Society of Believers of Christ's Second Appearing (Shakers) migrated to Lebanon, Warren County.

Between 1814 and 1824 German Lutherans settled New Harmony, Brown County; other Germans relocated in 1817 to Zoar, Tuscarawas County. Beginning in 1818, Welch families settled in Jackson, Meigs, and Scioto counties. Additional members of the Shaker faith established residences in Cleveland, Cuyahoga County in 1822. Before 1825, Scotch-Irish were situated throughout the state.

In 1831, Mormons from New York, relocated in Kirtland, Lake County. Former residents of Hartford, Hartford County, Connecticut, moved to Bath, Summit County in 1840. During the 1840 decade, Englishmen from Staffordshire, settled statewide. Welch families moved to Mahoning, Trumbull, and Summit counties.

Two significant religious groups established numerous Ohio settlements. Presbyterians founded seventeen separate towns between 1784 and 1799. Quakers (Society of Friends) established forty-three Monthly Meetings and settlements between 1801 and 1883. For a comprehensive list of specific Ohio settlements by the two groups, consult:

Kirkham, E. Kay, comp. *A Genealogical and Historical Atlas of the United States of America.* Providence, Utah: Keith W. Watkins and Sons, Inc., c.1976. (FHL# 973/E3k)

In addition to the above immigrant groups, Ohio attracted Chinese, Czechoslovakians, Greeks, Hungarians, Italians, Lithuanians, Mexicans, Poles, Rumanians, Scandinavians, Spanish, and Yugoslavians in large numbers.

Ohio Library Collection

Atlases, Gazetteers, and Maps

Brown, Lloyd A. *Early Maps of the Ohio Valley: A Selection of Maps, Plans and Views Made by Indians and Colonials From 1673-1783.* Pittsburgh, Pa.: University of Pittsburgh Press, c.1959. (FHL# 977.1/E3b)

Kilbourn, John. *The Ohio Gazetteer, Or, Topographical Dictionary Containing a Description of the Several Counties, Towns, Etc.* Columbus, Ohio: J. Kilbourn, 1826 (FHL# 977.1/E5k or microfilm 823667, item 1; or 476928, item 2)

New Topographical Atlas and Gazetteer of Indiana. Evansville, Ind.: Unigraphics, 1975. (FHL# Q/977.245/E3a or microfilm 940201, item 1)

Ohio, Department of Highways. *Individual Maps of Ohio's 88 Counties.* Columbus, Ohio: Ohio Department of Highways, 1969-70. (FHL# 977.1/E7oh)

Ohio, Her Counties, Her Townships and Her Towns. Indianapolis, Ind.: The Researchers, 1982. (FHL# 977.1/-E7g)

Walling, H. F. *Atlas of the State of Ohio from Surveys.* Knightstown, Ind.: Bookmark, 1976 (FHL# Q/977.1/-E7w or microfilm 982071, item 9)

Biography

Over seventy-five regional or statewide biography titles are included in the Ohio collection, cataloged under **Ohio/Biographies.** Additional biography titles are listed under **Ohio/[County Name]/Biography.** Some of the significant compilations include:

The Biographical Cyclopedia and Portrait Gallery with an Historical Sketch of the State of Ohio. Tucson, Ariz.: W. C. Cox Co., 1974. (FHL# microfilm 934863 and 934864, items 1 and 2)

The Biographical Encyclopedia of Ohio of the Nineteenth Century. Cincinnati, Ohio: Galaxy Publishing Co., 1876. (FHL# 977.1/D3bi or microfilm 934862, item 3; or 1425002, item 3)

Cutler, Julia Perkins. *The Founders of Ohio: Brief Sketches of the Forty-Eight Pioneers Who, Under Command of General Rufus Putnam Landed at the Mouth of the Muskingum River on the Seventh of April, 1788, and Commenced the First White Settlement of the Northwest Territory.* Fort Wayne, Ind.: Allen County Public Library, 1983. (FHL# 977.1/H2cu)

Lewis, Thomas William. *History of Southeastern Ohio and the Muskingum Valley, 1788-1928.* Chicago, Ill.: S. J. Clarke

Publishing Co., 1928. (FHL# 977.1/H21 or microfilm 844862, 844863, item 1, or 934869, items 2-4)

Memoirs of the Lower Ohio Valley, Personal and Genealogical with Portraits. Evansville, Ind.: Unigraphic, 1971. (FHL# 977/D3m or microfilm 896538, item 1, or 934870, items 2-3)

Portrait and Biographical Record of the Scioto Valley. Chicago, Ill.: Lewis Publishing Co., 1894. (FHL# 977.15/D3p or microfilm 934873, item 3).

Rust, Orton G. *History of West Central Ohio.* Salt Lake City: Genealogical Society of Utah, 1967. (FHL# microfilm 483648 and 483649, item 1)

Sargent, Martin P. *Pioneer Sketches: Scenes and Incidents of Former Days.* Ashtabula, Ohio: Ashtabula County Genealogical Society, 1976. (FHL# 973/H2sa or microfilm 982340, item 7)

Cemetery Records

Cemetery tombstone inventories are an important part of the Ohio collection. Published cemetery records are listed under **Ohio/[County]/Cemetery Records.** Additional titles are listed under **Ohio/Cemetery Records.**

Members of the LDS Church of Ohio, comp. *Ohio Cemetery Records: Copied by Members of the L.D.S. Church.* Salt Lake City: Genealogical Society of Utah, 1972. (FHL# microfilm 873854, item 7, 873855, items 2-3)

Ohio Cemetery Records: Extracted from the "Old Northwest" Genealogical Quarterly. Baltimore, Md.: Genealogical Publishing, c.1984. (FHL# 977.1/V3oh)

Ohio Society, U.S. Daughters of 1812, comp. *Index to the Grave Records of Servicemen of the War of 1812, State of Ohio.* Lancaster, Ohio: National Society of the United States Daughters of 1812, 1969. (FHL# 977.1/V22u or microfilm 496718, item 15)

Census Records

Federal censuses enumerated Ohio residents every ten years beginning in 1810 through 1910. During the War of 1812, the 1810 census was destroyed by fire. The 1890 census was also burned except for the special enumeration of Civil War veterans and widows. Twenty-seven Ohio State Censuses supplement the federal Ohio schedules. All of the federal and some of the state schedules are available at the Family History Library under **Ohio/Census Records.** Printed schedules for specific counties are listed under county headings.

Carmean, Barbara, comp. *1860 Mortality Schedule, Ohio.* Hillsboro, Ohio: Southern Ohio Genealogical Society, [c.1980s]. (FHL# 977.1/X28m/1860)

Harshman, Lida Flint. *Index to the 1860 Federal Population Census of Ohio.* Mineral Ridge, Ohio: Harshman, c.1979. (FHL# 977.1/X22h/1860)

Jackson, Ronald Vern et al, eds. *Early Ohio Census Records.* Bountiful, Utah: Accelerated Indexing Systems, 1974. (FHL# 977.1/X22e)

United States Census Office. *Ohio Mortality Schedules, 1850.* Washington, D.C.: National Archives, 1972. (FHL# microfilm 978351 and 1005093)

United States Census Office. *Schedule of Persons Who Died During the Year Ending May 31, 1880 for Ohio.* Washington, D.C.: National Archives, 1972. (FHL# microfilm 978352-978354)

Church Records

Every major religion is represented in Ohio, many at a very early date. Presbyterians and Quakers (Society of Friends) played an important part in the early development of the state. In addition, Moravians, Baptists, Methodists, Congregationalists and several reformed groups were early forces in Ohio's settlement. Catholics, Lutherans, Mormons, Disciples of Christ, United Brethren, and other religions migrated in large numbers to Ohio between 1800 and 1850. By 1890, Catholics and Methodists were the largest Ohio religions. Important church histories, statewide collections, and inventories are cataloged under **Ohio/Church Records**, while local records are cataloged under **Ohio/[County]/Church Records.** William Wade Hinshaw indexed and published extracts of Ohio Quaker records and the volumes are an important part of the Ohio church records collection. They are cataloged under the Author/Title segment of the FHLC.

Brien, Lindsay M. *Abstracts from History of the Church of the Brethren in Ohio.* Fort Wayne, Ind.: Allen County Public Library, 1983. (FHL# 977.1/K2bL)

Davis, Eileen A. *Quaker Records of the Miami Valley of Ohio.* Owensboro, Ky: McDowell Publications, c.1981. (FHL# 977.17/F2d)

Denlinger, Carolyn Teach. *Every Name Index for History of the Church of the Brethren, of the Southern District of Ohio.* Clayton, Ohio: Southern Ohio District Church of the Brethren, 1982. (FHL# 977.1/K2d/Index)

Historical Records Survey, Ohio. *Inventory of the Church Archives of Ohio Presbyterian Churches.* Salt Lake City: Genealogical Society of Utah, 1967. (FHL# microfilm 506375- 506380)

Hollenbach, Raymond E. *Private Records of Reverend Eli Keller, 1856-1914.* (Evangelical and Reformed Churches.) Salt Lake City: Genealogical Society of Utah, 1981. (FHL# microfilm 1305843, item 5)

Court Records

While specific courts had jurisdiction over specific types of cases, many matters were recorded in other courts. Examples are early vital records, naturalizations, and military pension applications, which are found in all Ohio courts – even in deed record volumes. Therefore, you should examine the earliest volumes of Court of Common Pleas, Supreme Court, land records, and certainly all volumes titled "Miscellaneous." Over half of all Ohio court records have been microfilmed by the Genealogical Society of Utah and are listed under **Ohio/[County]/Court Records.**

Genealogical Collections

Baldwin, Henry R. *The Henry R. Baldwin Genealogical Records.* Fort Wayne, Ind.: Allen County Public Library, 1983. (FHL# 977.1/D2bh and 977.1/D2bh/Index)

Brien, Lindsay M. *Miami Valley Genealogies.* Salt Lake City: Genealogical Society of Utah, 1971. (FHL# 977.17/D2b or microfilm 859778, item 3-6)

Daughters of the American Revolution. Western Reserve Chapter. *Bible and Family Records.* Salt Lake City: Genealogical Society of Utah, 1972. (FHL# microfilm 901219, item 5)

Fecher, Con J. *Ancestral Portraits of Ohio Settlers: The Ancestral Tree, a Biographical Sketch; Leaves, Limbs and Trunk.* Dayton, Ohio: University of Dayton Press, 1980. (FHL# 977.14/D2f)

Memoirs of the Lower Ohio Valley: Personal and Genealogical with Portraits. Evansville, Ind.: Unigraphic, 1971. (FHL# 977/D3m or microfilm 896538, item 1, or 934870, items 2-3)

The Ohio Surname Index. 64 reels. Columbus: Ohio Historical Society, 1984. (FHL# microfilm 398201-398264)

Summers, Ewing. *Genealogical and Family History of Eastern Ohio.* Salt Lake City: Genealogical Society of Utah, 1984. (FHL# 977.1/D3s or microfilm 962816, item 2, or 934865, item 1)

History

A large collection of histories are cataloged under **Ohio/History** or under **Ohio/[County]/History**. Notable works include:

Cherry, Peter Peterson. *The Western Reserve and Early Ohio.* Akron, Ohio: R. L. Fouse, 1921. (FHL# 977.1/H2c)

Fernow, Berthold. *The Ohio Valley in Colonial Days.* Albany, New York: J. Munsell's Sons, 1890. (FHL# 977/H2f)

Fess, Simeon D. *Ohio: A Four-Volume Reference Library on the History of a Great State.* Fort Wayne, Ind.: Allen County Public Library, 1983. (FHL# 977.1/H2fs)

Hildreth, Samuel P. *Pioneer History: Being an Account of the First Examinations of the Ohio Valley, and the Early Settlement of the Northwest Territory.* Salt Lake City: Genealogical Society of Utah, 1973. (FHL# microfilm 940924, item 2)

Slocum, Charles Elihu. *The Ohio Country Between the Years 1783 and 1815: Including Military Operations That Twice Saved the United States the Country West of the Allegheny Mountains after the Revolutionary War.* Salt Lake City: Genealogical Society of Utah, 1973. (FHL# microfilm 941311 or 931802, item 2)

Upton, Harriet Taylor. *History of the Western Reserve.* Chicago, Ill: Lewis Publishing 1910. (FHL# 977.13/H2u or microfilm 934867, item 2 and 934868, items 1-2)

Land and Property Records

Initial distribution of Ohio lands was unique. Several states and the United States Government claimed portions of the land, and all of these jurisdictions made sizeable land grants and purchases for specific purposes:

1784	Virginia Military Lands satisfied Virginia Military Land Warrants; granted to the actual soldier or a relative. (4,204,000 acres)
1786	Connecticut Western Reserve owned by Connecticut from an original royal grant. (3,366,921 acres)
1786	Congress Lands sold through immediate officers of the government and through Federal Land District Offices.
1786	Seven Ranges Survey sold by government.
1787	Ohio Company's Purchase by individuals from Massachusetts then resold. (1,500,000)
1792	Firelands, also called Sufferer's Lands, granted by Connecticut to Connecticut families who had experienced fire losses during the Revolutionary War. Connecticut law required that the deeds for the Ohio lands be recorded in the town where the original property had been destroyed. (500,000 acres)
1792	Donation Tract set aside to compensate families; 100 acres per man bearing arms to provide protection from Indians for five years. (100,000 acres)
1794	Symmes Purchase. (311,682 acres)
1795,1798	French Grant by Congress to early French settlers who had been cheated by a greedy land company. (2,500,000 acres)
1796	Military Grant set aside by Congress to compensate Continental soldiers and officers in lieu of pay. (2,500,000 acres)
1786-96	Moravian Lands granted to Moravian Brethren of Bethlehem, Pennsylvania. (12,000 acres)
1796-1802	Zane's Tract granted to Ebenezer Zane for building a road between Wheeling, West Virginia, and Maysville, Kentucky.
1798	Refugee Tract set aside by Congress and awarded to British subjects who sympathized with American colonists, then fled to Nova Scotia and Canada. (50,000 acres)
1801	Dorhman's Grant awarded by Congress to Portuguese merchant in Lisbon who assisted the colonists during the Revolutionary War. (23,040 acres)

Subsequent land transactions were recorded on a county level and are cataloged under **Ohio/[County]/Land and Property**. The Family History Library has microfilm copies of the land records for all but five of Ohio's eighty-eight counties. Additional titles relating to land grants and similar transactions are listed under **Ohio/Land and Property**, and include a number of indexes.

Military Records

A large collection of military titles related to service by Ohioans is included in the Family History Library collection. Most are cataloged under **Ohio/Military Records** with a limited number under **Ohio/[County]/Military Records.** Notable titles include:

A List of Ohioans Killed during the Civil War. Salt Lake City: Genealogical Society of Utah, 1962. (FHL# microfilm 285059)

Alphabetical Index to Ohio Official Roster, Mexican War. Salt Lake City: Genealogical Society of Utah, 1959. (FHL# microfilm 195488)

Dailey, Mrs. Orville D. *The Official Roster of Soldiers of the American Revolution Who Lived in the State of Ohio.* Salt Lake City: Genealogical Society of Utah, 1959. (FHL# microfilm 195451)

Diefenbach, Mrs. H. B. *Index to the Grave Records of Soldiers of the War of 1812 Buried in Ohio.* Np. n.pub. nd. (FHL# 977.1/V22d)

Garner, Grace. *Index to Roster of Ohio Soldiers, War of 1812.* Spokane, Wash.: Eastern Washington Genealogical Society, 1974. (FHL# 977.1/M2e)

The Official Roster of the Soldiers of the American Revolution Buried in the State of Ohio. Salt Lake City: Genealogical Society of Utah, 1983. (FHL# 977.1/M23ad or microfilm 385013 or 928143, items 7-8, or microfiche 6046713)

The Official Roster of Ohio Soldiers in the War With Spain, 1898-1899. Salt Lake City: Genealogical Society of Utah, 1959. (FHL# microfilm 195489 or 928567, item 1)

Ohio Adjutant General's Office. *Grave Registration of Soldiers Buried in Ohio.* 92 reels. Salt Lake City: Genealogical Society of Utah, 1958. (FHL# microfilm 182703-182793)

Ohio Adjutant General's Office. *Official Roster of the Soldiers of the State of Ohio In the War of the Rebellion, 1861-1866.* 365 reels. Salt Lake City: Genealogical Society of Utah, 1959-60. (beginning with FHL# microfilm 212908)

Ohio Adjutant General's Office. *Soldiers From Ohio, War of 1812.* Salt Lake City: Genealogical Society of Utah, 1959. (FHL# microfilm 195486-195487)

United States Adjutant General's Office. *Index to Compiled Service Records of Volunteer Union Soldiers Who Served in Organizations from the State of Ohio.* 122 reels. Washington, D.C.: National Archives, 1965. Consult the Family History Library Catalog for call numbers.

Ohio State Archives. *Index to Spanish American War Records.* Salt Lake City: Genealogical Society of Utah, 1959. Alphabetical card index with name of soldier and unit. All variant spellings of surname should be examined. (FHL# microfilm 223771)

United States General Land Office. *Register of Revolutionary War Land Warrants, Act of 1788: Military District of Ohio, 1789-1805.* Washington, D.C.: National Archives, 1967. (FHL# microfilm 847553)

Minorities and Ethnic Groups

Minorities and ethnic groups have played an important part in the history of Ohio. Several black studies and ethnic studies groups have been established in Ohio in the past two decades in particular.

Gerber, David Allison. *Black Ohio and the Color Line, 1860-1915.* Urbana: University of Illinois Press, c.1976. (FHL# 977.1/F2g)

Haller, Stephen E. *Register of Blacks in the Miami Valley: A Name Abstract (1804-1857).* Dayton, Ohio: Wright State University, c.1977. (FHL# 977.17/F2nh)

Maxwell, Fay. *Irish Refugee Tract Abstract Data and History of the Irish Acadians.* Columbus, Ohio: Maxwell Publications, c.1974. (FHL# 977.156/F2lm)

Nitchman, Paul E. *Blacks in Ohio 1880.* Decorah, Iowa: P. E. Nitchman, c.1985. (FHL# 977.1/F2n)

Ohio Adjutant General's Office. *Official Roster of Colored Troops of the State of Ohio in the War of the Rebellion, 1861-1866.* Salt Lake City: Genealogical Society of Utah, 1962. (FHL# microfilm 285025-285030)

Slave Narratives: 1937, Interviews with Ex-Slaves in Ohio. Columbus: Ohio Historical Society, 1974. (FHL# microfilm 1009035)

Smith, Clifford Neal. *Early Nineteenth Century German Settlers in Ohio, Kentucky and Other States.* McNeal, Ariz.: Westland Publications, 1984. (FHL# 973/W25mn/no.20)

Weston, Rubin F. *Blacks in Ohio History: A Conference to Commemorate the Bicentennial of the American Revolution.* Columbus: Ohio Historical Society, c.1976. (FHL# 977.1/A1/no.119)

Naturalization Records

Throughout Ohio Territory and statehood, foreign-born residents were drawn to the state. Naturalization was important to many of the immigrants; after they met residence requirements, they initiated formal proceedings in any court of record: local, district, state, or federal. Microfilmed copies of naturalization applications for approximately sixty of the eighty-eight Ohio counties are listed under **Ohio/[County]/Naturalization and Citizenship.**

Probate Records

On 7 December 1840, Ohio passed the Statute of Descent and Distribution which governed intestate estates. An excellent explanation and chart of the law is included in:

Bell, Carol Willsey. *Ohio Genealogy Guide.* Youngstown, Ohio: Carol Willsey Bell, [c.1984]. (FHL# 977.1/D25/-fc/1984)

Probate and estate records were filed on a county basis, first with the Court of Common Pleas 1797-1855 and with the Probate Court from 1852 to the present. Both are cataloged under **Ohio/[County]/Probate Records.**

Tax Records

As the 1800 Ohio Territorial Census and the 1810 federal census of Ohio were destroyed by fire, the early tax records become very important to early Ohio genealogical research. Tax records are cataloged under both **Ohio/Records** and **Ohio/[County]/Tax Records.**

Bell, Carol Willsey, comp. *The Index to Early Ohio Tax Records.* Akron, Ohio: Esther Weygandt Powell, 1973. (FHL# 977.1/R4op/Index)

Ohio. Auditor of State. *Tax Records of Ohio, 1801-1814.* Salt Lake City: Genealogical Society of Utah, 1967. (FHL# microfilm 522837-522844 and 514124-514129)

Petty, Gerald M., comp. *Index of the Ohio 1825 Tax Duplicates.* Columbus, Ohio: Petty's Press, c.1981. (FHL# 977.1/-R42p)

_____. *Name Index, 1812 Ohio Tax Duplicates.* Columbus, Ohio: n.pub., 1973. (FHL# microfilm 978442-978446 and 1002585-1002589)

_____. *Ohio 1810 Tax Duplicate Arranged in a State-wide Alphabetical List of Names of Taxpayers with an Index of Names of Original Entries.* Columbus, Ohio: Petty, c.1976. (FHL# 977.1/R4p or microfilm 982373, item 4)

Powell, Esther Weygandt, comp. *Early Ohio Tax Records.* Baltimore, Md.: Genealogical Publishing Company, 1985. (FHL# 977.1/R4op/1985)

Vital Records

In 1856-57, an Ohio statute required registration of births. It met with only limited compliance. In 1867, another law requiring the recording of vital records was passed, but again only a limited number of the counties made a serious attempt to document births and deaths. It was not until 1908 and the passage of a third law that vital records were carefully recorded. Marriage records were kept by court clerks until 1949 when statewide registration of marriages occurred. Vital records titles are listed in the collection under **Ohio/[County]/Vital Records.**

An important compilation of death/burial records which supplements the early inconsistent vital records is:

Ohio Adjutant General's Office. *Grave Registration of Soldiers Buried in Ohio.* Salt Lake City: Genealogical Society of Utah, 1958. (FHL# microfilm 182702-182793)

INDIANA

Historical Background

early	Prehistoric Indians called Mound Builders inhabit the region.
1679	French explorer LaSalle travels throughout Indiana.
1720's	French build trading posts at Miami and Ouiatenon.
1731	French found first permanent settlement at Vincennes.
1749	Catholic Church records kept (extant).
1763	End of French and Indian War transfers control of region from France to Great Britain.
1775-83	Revolutionary War. Battle of Vincennes.
1778	George Rogers Clark takes possession of Vincennes, Indiana, for Commonwealth of Virginia.
1787	Indiana included in the newly created Northwest Territory.
1790	Most of Indiana and a part of Illinois formed into Knox County.
1794	Fort Wayne built.
1798	First Baptist Church in state established in Knox County.
1800	Indiana Territory established.
1801	French Swiss immigrants establish a colony in Switzerland County.
1800s	Society of Friends (Quakers) settle in Wayne County.
1804	First land offices established at Vincennes and Kaskaskia.
1805	Michigan Territory separated from Indiana Territory.
1806	Squire Boone, Daniel's older brother, migrates from Kentucky to Harrison County, Indiana.
1808	Shakers establish religious colony sixteen miles north of Vincennes.
1809	Illinois Territory formed from Indiana Territory.
1811	Battle of Tippecanoe.
1813	Corydon becomes the territorial capital.
1814-15	Peace treaties with Indians and Great Britain end War of 1812.
1814	Fire destroys all Knox County records. Frederick Rapp brings Harmony Society Colony to Posey County.
1816	Indiana admitted to Union as nineteenth state. Thomas Lincoln, father of Abraham, brings family from Kentucky to Spencer County.
1818	New Purchase lands attract large numbers of settlers.
1821	Capital of Indiana moved to Indianapolis.
1825	Robert Owen purchases New Harmony, Posey County.
1829	National Road is begun.
1832	Work on Wabash and Erie Canals begins near Fort Wayne toward Lafayette.
1834	National Road reaches Indianapolis.
1849	Federal government gives National Road to the state.
1850s	Influx of settlers by railroad and wagons over the National Road.

1861-65 Morgan's Raiders in Indiana draw national attention during Civil War.

1880s Population rapidly rises due to industrial development throughout state.

1900 Vital record law requires statewide registration of deaths.

1907 Law passed requiring statewide registration of births.

Settlement and Migration

French explorers, beginning with LaSalle in 1669, travelled over major rivers into the region including present-day Indiana, repeatedly exploring the state from south to north. In 1731, the French built the first permanent settlement at Vincennes. French domination continued until 1763 when Great Britain took control after the French and Indian War. Under British control, slow but steady growth occurred.

The southern half of the state, roughly coinciding with the area south of the National Road between Cambridge City and Terre Haute running east to west, was settled at least a generation earlier than the northern half. The Treaty of Greenville in 1795 resulted in the relinquishment of selected Ohio lands. Pioneers from New England, New York, and the South rushed in to settle the lands along the Ohio River in present-day Dearborn and Clark Counties. The early southern settlers were mainly Virginians and Carolinians who came by way of Kentucky over the Wilderness Road, which stretched from Richmond, Virginia, through Kentucky and Ohio. Between 1812 and the 1840s, other settlers, primarily from Virginia and Maryland, followed the National Road and Ohio River into Indiana.

Two noteworthy families migrated to southern Indiana. The first was Daniel Boone's older brother, Squire, who brought his sons and other relatives to Harrison County in 1806. The second was Thomas Lincoln, Abraham's father, who brought his young family from Kentucky to Spencer County about 1816.

In 1801, a colony was established in Switzerland County by a group of French Swiss from the Commune of Chatelard, Vevay, Canton de Vaud, Switzerland.

New Harmony, Posey County, was established in 1814 when Frederick Rapp brought his Harmony Society colony of native Germans from the area of Pittsburgh, Pennsylvania. In 1825, Rapp sold the property to Robert Owen, a Scot, who attempted to settle and govern New Harmony as an economic and social experiment. The experiment failed. Owen gave the land to his sons and returned to Scotland.

Other notable early German settlements occurred at Jasper and Huntingburg in Dubois County and at Saint Meinard in Spencer County.

Northern Indiana, beginning about 1830 when the Miami Indians were forced from the area, was settled primarily by New Englanders and New Yorkers who came via Ohio. Between the 1830s and 1850, German immigrants from the areas of the Rhine and the Weser settled in Allen County. The area of Fort Wayne, Allen County, also attracted large number of Ohioans, Pennsylvanians, and New Englanders. Many of the Allen County settlers arrived by flatboats over the Wabash and Erie canals. The choice southern acreage had been quickly claimed; and beginning about 1825, the original settlers from the South began a heavy migration into Wabash County and the surrounding area in northern Indiana. About 1830, settlers from Vermont settled at Montpelier, Blackford County. Newly arrived immigrants from Holland settled at New Paris (Goshen) in Elkart County on the Michigan border. Throughout the 1800s, large numbers of new arrivals to the United States also settled in Indiana. One of the best treatments of sources for immigration and migration is:

Eakle, Arlene H. "Tracking Immigrant Origins." In Arlene Eakle and Johni Cerny. *The Source: A Guidebook of American Genealogy.* Salt Lake City: Ancestry Publishing Company, 1984, pp. 452-516.

Several religious groups settled significant areas of Indiana. Southern Quakers (Society of Friends), primarily North Carolinians who first settled in Ohio, were attracted to no-slavery Indiana. Quakers soon outnumbered all other religions. Orange County was settled by Quakers in 1811. Tennessee and Carolinian Friends migrated to Wayne and Randolph Counties. Quakers from the Carolinas and Virginia also settled in the Whitewater area of Wayne County early in the 1800s. Shakers colonized an area on the Wabash River some sixteen miles north of Vicennes in 1808. Baptists established a church in Knox County by 1798. Other Baptist groups settled very early in Sullivan and Johnson Counties. Mennonites settled in Goshen.

Annals of Pioneer Settlers of the Whitewater and Its Tributaries, in the Vicinity of Richmond, Indiana from 1804 to 1830. Salt Lake City: Genealogical Society of Utah, 1977. (FHL# microfilm 982387, item 1)

Burns, Lee. *The National Road to Indiana.* Indianapolis, Ind.: C. E. Pauley, [c.1920] (FHL# 977.2/B4/Vol. 7)

Cox, Sandford C. *Recollections of the Early Settlement of the Wabash Valley.* Lafayette, Ind.: Courier Steam Book and Job Printing House, 1860. (FHL# 977.2/H2c or microfilm 1036275, item 5)

Duncan, Robert. *Old Settlers.* Indianapolis, Ind.: Bowen-Merrill, 1894. (FHL# 977.2/B4/Vol. 2)

Dunn, Jacob Piatt. *Documents Relating to the French Settlement on the Wabash.* Indianapolis, Ind.: Bowen-Merrill, 1894. (FHL# 977.2/B4/Vol. 2)

Reed, M. E. *When Did the Pioneers Come to Indiana?* Winamac, Ind.: M. E. Reed, 1970. (FHL# 977.2/A1/no.3 or microfilm 924107, item 9)

Walters, Pauline. *Pioneer Trails and Traces into Montgomery County, Indiana.* Salt Lake City: Genealogical Society of Utah, 1975. (FHL# microfilm 928044, item 7)

Wood, Mary Elizabeth. *French Imprint on the Heart of America: Historical Vignettes of 110 French-Related Localities in Indiana and the Ohio Valley.* Knightstown, Ind.: Bookmark, 1977. (FHL# 977.2/H2w)

Indiana Library Collection

Archives and Libraries

Griffin, Warren B. *Preliminary Inventory, Records of the United States Courts for District of Indiana.* Chicago, Ill.: Federal Records Center, 1967. (FHL# 977.2/A1/no.83 or microfilm 982239, item 10)

Historical Record Survey. Works Progress Administration. *Guide to Public Vital Statistic Records in Indiana.* Indianapolis: Indiana Historical Records Survey, 1941. (FHL# 977.2/A5h or microfilm 874046, item 5, or microfiche 6051202)

Indiana Historical Society. *Preliminary Checklist of Archives and Manuscripts in Indiana Repositories.* Indianapolis: Indiana Historical Society, 1980. (FHL# 977.2/A3p)

Atlases, Gazetteers, and Maps

Baskins, Forester, ed. *Illustrated Historical Atlas of Indiana.* Salt Lake City: Genealogical Society of Utah, 1967. (FHL# Q/977.2/E3i or microfilm 465403)

County and Township Map of the State of Indiana. N.p.: Bradley and Bradley, 1883. (FHL# 977.2/E7b)

Gioe, Joan Colbert, comp. *Indiana, Her Counties, Her Townships and Her Towns.* Indianapolis: The Researchers, c.1979. (FHL# 977.2/A1/no.160)

Henderson, J. O. *Indiana, The Public Domain and Its Survey, 1892.* Indianapolis: Burford, 1893. (FHL# 977.2/A1/-no.158)

New Topographical Atlas and Gazetteer of Indiana. Evansville, Ind.: Unigraphic, 1975. (FHL# Q/977.245/E3a or microfilm 940201, item 1)

Scott, John. *The Indiana Gazeteer, or, Topographical Dictionary.* Indianapolis: Indiana Historical Society, 1954. (FHL# 977.2/E5s)

The Indiana Gazetteer, or Topographical Dictionary of the State of Indiana. Indianapolis: E. Chamberlain, 1849. (FHL# 977.2/E5i)

Biography

A Biographical History of Eminent and Self-Made Men of the State of Indiana. Cincinnati, Ohio: Western Biographical Publishing Company, 1880. 2 vols. (FHL# 977.2/D3b or microfilm 599144 or 973009, item 1, or 1000527, item 2)

Card Index to Memoirs of Methodist Ministers. Salt Lake City: Genealogical Society of Utah, n.d. (FHL# 977/-D3m/Index or microfilm 1036148, item 3)

Dunn, Jacob Piatt. *Indiana and Indianans, An Index.* Indianapolis: Indianapolis Public Library, 1939. (FHL# 977.2/H2d/Index)

Index to Memoirs of the Lower Ohio Valley. Salt Lake City: Genealogical Society of Utah, [n.d.]. (FHL# 977/-D3m/Index or microfilm 1036148, item 3)

Memoirs of the Lower Ohio Valley: Personal and Genealogical with Portraits. Evansville, Ind.: Unigraphics, 1971. (FHL# 977.2/D3m or microfilm 896538, item 1, or 943890, items 2-3)

Memorial Record of Northeastern Indiana. Salt Lake City: Genealogical Society of Utah, 1968. (FHL# microfilm 547501, item 1)

Platt, Lyman, and Jimmy Parker. *Indiana Biographical Index.* Salt Lake City: Genealogical Indexing Associates, 1984. (FHL# microfiche 6331353)

Taylor, Charles W. *Biographical Sketches and Review of the Bench and Bar of Indiana.* Indianapolis: Bench and Bar Publishing Co., 1895. (FHL# 977.2/D3b or microfilm 874393, items 1-2, or 1000527, item 4)

Woollen, William Wesley. *Biographical and Historical Sketches of Early Indiana.* Indianapolis: Hammond, 1883. (FHL# 977.2/D3w or microfilm 1000527, item 3)

Cemetery Records

Members of the LDS Church in Indiana. *Cemetery Records of Indiana.* Salt Lake City: Genealogical Society of Utah, 1972. (FHL# 977.2/V22c or microfilm 873781, items 1-6)

Fox, John H. *Selected Gravestone Inscriptions in Illinois, Indiana and Kansas.* Salt Lake City: Genealogical Society of Utah, 1980. (FHL# microfilm 1292061-1292064)

Census Records

Indiana state censuses were taken for 1801, 1807, 1815, 1857, 1859, 1866, 1871, 1877, 1883, 1889, 1895, 1901, and 1907. The 1807 census is included in the Family History Library collection. The remaining enumerations are available at the Genealogy Division of the Indiana State Library. The 1853, 1865, and 1877 censuses are also available by writing to the county auditors. Federal censuses are available for 1820, 1830, 1840, 1850, 1860, 1870, 1880, 1900, and 1910. The 1850 Mortality Census listing all deaths occurring for the year ending 1 June 1850 is indexed and in the library collection.

The early censuses were taken under difficult conditions, particularly in 1850. Very poor weather at the time of the enumeration frequently made rural roads and trails impassable, and many rural residents were missed. However, the 1850 Agricultural Census was taken at a different time of the year and most, if not all, rural residents were counted.

An ambitious Indiana 1860 Census indexing project is currently underway by Steve Kratz of Salt Lake City. As portions are completed, they are added to the library collection.

Census of Indiana Territory of 1807. Indianapolis: Indiana Historical Society, c.1980. (FHL# 977.2/X2c/1807)

Heiss, Willard, comp. *1820 Federal Census for Indiana.* Indianapolis: Indiana Historical Society, the Genealogical Section, 1966. (FHL# 977.2/X2p/1820)

Indiana State Library, Genealogy Division. *Index to the 1850 United States Federal Census of Indiana.* Salt Lake City: Genealogical Society of Utah, 1970. (FHL# 977.2/X2p/-1850/Index or microfilm 962904-962909)

Volkel, Lowell M., comp. *1850 Indiana Mortality Schedules.* N.p.: L. M. Volkel, c.1971. (FHL# 977.2/X21p)

Church Records

The quality and availability of Indiana church records varies considerably. With the exception of Quaker records, most church records are cataloged under **Indiana/[County]/Church Records** with some under **Indiana/Church Records.**

Quaker records are very valuable to the Indiana researcher. Marriages, births, and deaths were faithfully recorded and preserved, as were certificates of removal and admissions. Familial relationships were clearly stated.

William Wade Hinshaw indexed and published extracts of a large portion of records in seven volumes: Hinshaw, William Wade. *Encyclopedia of American Quaker Genealogy.* Ann Arbor, Mich.: Edwards Brothers, 1936. (FHL# 973/D2he, vol. 1-6 or microfilm 432597-432606)

Many of the families cited by Hinshaw became members of the eighty-six Indiana Monthly Meeting records which are not included in the first six volumes. Willard Heiss compiled volume seven: *Encyclopedia of American Quaker Genealogy: Abstracts of the Records of the Society of Friends in Indiana.* Indianapolis, Ind.: Indiana Historical Society, 1962, Part 1-6. (FHL# 973/D2he, v.7, pt. 1-6). Some unpublished records are available under **Indiana/Church Records (Society of Friends)** and **Indiana/[County]/Church Records (Society of Friends).** The remaining records are in possession of the Friends Historical Library, Swarthmore College, Swarthmore, Pennsylvania 19081.

A Directory of Churches and Religious Organizations in Indiana. Indianapolis: Indiana Historical Records Survey, 1941. (FHL# 977.2/E4h or microfilm 1036694, items 1-2, 3)

Daughters of American Revolution. *Church Records Found in the State of Indiana.* Salt lake City, Utah: Genealogical Society of Utah, 1972. (FHL# microfilm 907993, item 1)

Eby, Lela, comp. *Every Name Index, History of the Church of the Brethren in Indiana by Otho Winger, 1917.* Mill Valley, Calif.: Eby, [c.1970s]. (FHL# 977.2/K21w/Index)

Finney, James Patterson. *Index of Marriage Records, Ohio, Indiana and Kansas 1866-1900.* Salt Lake City: Genealogical Society of Utah, 1969. (FHL# microfilm 599080, item 11)

Heiss, Willard. *A List of All the Friends Meetings That Exist or Ever Have Existed in Indiana 1807-1855.* Indianapolis: John Woolman Press, Inc., 1961. (FHL# 977.2/K2h or microfilm 873680, item 1, or 874197, item 1)

Rudolph, L. C. *Hoosier Zion: The Presbyterians in Early Indiana.* New Haven, Conn.: Yale University Press, 1963. (FHL# 977.2/K2r)

Court and Probate Records

Twenty-eight of the ninety-two Indiana counties suffered courthouse fires. Many after being rebuilt were again destroyed by fire or natural disaster. Extant court and probate records are listed under **Indiana/[County]/Court Records** or **Indiana/[County]/Probate Records.**

Griffin, Warren. *Preliminary Inventory, Records of the United States Courts for the District Court of Indiana.* Chicago, Ill.: Federal Records Center, 1967. (FHL# 977.2/-A1/no.83 or microfilm 982239, item 10)

Smith, Oliver Hampton. *Early Indiana Trials and Sketches.* Cincinnati, Ohio: Moore, Wilstoch, Keys & Co., 1858. (FHL# 977.2/P2s)

Genealogical Collections

Beeson, Cecil, Sr., comp. *Miscellaneous Records of the State of Indiana.* Salt Lake City: Genealogical Society of Utah, 1959. (FHL# microfilm 207694) Bible records, marriages, cemetery records, church records, and wills.

Daughters of the American Revolution. *Bible and Genealogical Records.* Salt Lake City: Genealogical Society of Utah, 1972. (FHL# microfilm 907993)

Daughters of the American Revolution. *Genealogical Records.* N.p.: Indiana DAR, 1950-54. (FHL# 977.2/D4d or microfilm 982125, items 3-5, or 982126, item 1)

Dorrel, Ruth, comp. *Pioneer Ancestors of Members of the Society of Indiana Pioneers.* Indianapolis: Indiana Historical Society, c.1983. (FHL# 977.2/D2do)

Hoosier Family Record Extracts from English Sources. Salt Lake City: Genealogical Society of Utah, 1969. (FHL# 929.273/H792h or microfilm 599342, item 6)

Hughes, LaVerne Anstead. *Letters and Research of Mrs. LaVerne Anstead Hughes.* Salt Lake City: Genealogical Society of Utah, 1959. (FHL# microfilm 201405)

Indiana Historical Society. *Indiana Source Book: Genealogical Material from the Hoosier Genealogist.* Indianapolis: Indiana Historical Society, 1977. (FHL# 977.2/D29h)

McCay, Betty L. *Indiana Ancestors, Index.* Indianapolis: McCay, c.1985. (FHL# 977.2/A1/no.159)

Memoirs of the Lower Ohio: Personal and Genealogical with Portraits. Evansville, Ind.: Unigraphics, 1971. (FHL# 977/D3m or microfilm 896538, item 1, or 934870, items 2-3)

History

Over 100 titles reporting the history of Indiana are included in the collection. Statewide or regional histories are cataloged under **Indiana/History.** Local histories are listed under **Indiana/[County]/History.**

Ball, T. H. *Northwestern Indiana from 1800 to 1900, Or, A View of Our Region Through the Nineteenth Century.* Chicago, Ill.: Donohue & Henneberry, 1900. (FHL# 977.29/H2b or microfilm 1000528, item 4)

Barnhart, John Donald. *The Impact of the Civil War on Indiana.* Indianapolis: Indiana Civil War Centennial Commission, 1962. (FHL# 977.2/H2bj)

Carmony, Donald F. *Handbook on Indiana History.* Indianapolis: Sesquicentennial Commission, 1966. (FHL# 977.2/A1/no.88)

Cockrum, William Monroe. *Pioneer History of Indiana: Including Stories, Incidents and Customs of the Early Settlers.* Oakland City, Ind.: Press of Oakland City Journal, 1907. (FHL# 977.2/H2cu)

Dillon, John Brown. *A History of Indiana.* Indianapolis: Bingham & Doughty, 1859. (FHL# 977.2/H2dj or microfiche 6051127)

Drake, Samuel Adams. *The Making of the Ohio Valley States 1660-1837.* Fairborn, Ohio: Cincinnati Branch of the Family History Library, 1973. (FHL# microfilm 925037, item 5)

O'Flynn, Anna C. *A Brief History of Old Knox, the Mother County.* Salt Lake City: Genealogical Society of Utah, 1972. (FHL# 977.2/H2o or microfilm 874491, item 1)

Roll, Charles. *Indiana: One Hundred and Fifty Years of American Development.* 5 vols. Chicago, Ill.: Lewis Publishing Company, 1931. (FHL# 977.2/H2r)

Whicker, J. Wesley. *Historical Sketches of the Wabash Valley.* Attica, Ind.: J. Wesley Whicker, c.1916. (FHL# 977.24/-H2w)

Land and Property Records

Indiana was a public domain state. The land, usually under two dollars per acre, was frequently sold at public auction. By 1820, the cost of the land was reduced, and $100 could buy eighty acres. Settlers short on cash could purchase the land on installment payments. These attractive terms greatly increased migration into the state.

Once the total purchase was paid in full, the United States government issued a land patent. Six government land office (GLO) land districts were opened and functioned between 1804 and and 1876. They were: Vincennes, 1804; Jeffersonville, 1807; Terre Haute/Crawfordville, 1818 and 1820; Brookville/Indianapolis, 1818 and 1820; Fort Wayne, 1823; and La Porte, 1833.

Many of the original land documents recorded at these offices listed the name of the purchaser, purchase date, price, and land description as well as the purchaser's residence, often outside of Indiana.

Subsequent land sales were recorded in each county and are cataloged under **Indiana/[County]/Land and Property Records**.

Illinois and Wabash Land Company Minutes 1778-1812. Salt Lake City: Genealogical Society of Utah, 1948. (FHL# microfilm 020445, item 5)

Indiana Historical Society. *This Land Is Ours: The Acquisition and Disposition of the Public Domain.* Indianapolis: Indiana Historical Society, c.1978. (FHL# 977/R21)

Lux, Leonard. *The Vincennes Donation Lands.* Indianapolis: Indiana Historical Society, 1949. (FHL# 977.2/B4/Vol. 15/no.4 or microfilm 928192, item 5, or microfiche 6051134)

Waters, Margaret Ruth. *Indiana Land Entries.* Knightstown, Ind.: The Bookmark, 1977. (FHL# 977.2/R2w/1977 or microfiche 6046718)

Wilson, George R. *Early Indiana Trails and Surveys.* Indianapolis: C. E. Pauley, 1919. (FHL# 977.2/B4/Vol. 6/no.3, or microfilm 824286, item 13, or microfiche 6051190)

Military Records

Daughters of the American Revolution. *Roster of Soldiers and Patriots of the American Revolution Buried in Indiana.* Baltimore, Md.: Genealogical Publishing Company, 1968. (FHL# 977.2/M2o/1968 or microfilm 873911, item 1)

Franklin, Charles M. *Indiana, War of 1812 Soldiers: Militia.* Indianapolis: Ye Olde Genealogie Shoppe, 1984. (FHL# 977.2/M2fr)

Funk, Arville L. *Hoosiers in the Civil War.* Chicago, Ill.: Adams Press, c.1967. (FHL# 977.2/M2f)

Nolan, Alan T. *The Iron Brigade: A Military History.* Salt Lake City: Genealogical Society of Utah, 1974. (FHL# microfilm 954251, item 13)

Record of Indiana Volunteers in the Spanish-American War, 1898-1899. Salt Lake City: Genealogical Society of Utah, 1980. (FHL# microfilm 1033588, item 3)

United States Adjutant General's Office. *Index to Compiled Service Records of Volunteer Union Soldiers Who Served in Organizations from the State of Indiana, 1861-1865.* Washington, D.C.: National Archives, 1965. (FHL# microfilm 881722-881807)

Waters, Margaret Ruth, comp. *Revolutionary Soldiers Buried in Indiana (1949), With Supplement* (1954). Baltimore, Md.: Genealogical Publishing Company, 1970. (FHL# 977.2/M2w or microfiche 6046585)

Wolfe, Barbara Schull. *Index of Revolutionary Soldiers of Indiana and Other Patriots.* Indianapolis: Ye Olde Genealogie Shoppe, c.1983. (FHL# 977.2/M22w)

Newspapers

A very limited number of Indiana newspapers are part of the Family History Library collection cataloged under **Indiana/[County]/Newspapers.** One notable entry is:

Miller, John W. *Indiana Newspaper Bibliography: Historical Accounts of All Indiana Newspapers Published from 1804 to 1980 and Locational Information for All Available Copies, Both Original and Microfilm.* Indianapolis: Indiana Historical Society, 1982. (FHL# 977.2/B32m)

Vital Records

Northwest Territorial statutes required the reading of marriage banns fifteen days before the ceremony. The legal age for marriage without parental consent was seventeen for males and fourteen for females. When Indiana Territory was established in 1800, marriage licenses became mandatory. Territorial divorce laws were enacted in 1808. Recordings of births, marriages, and deaths occurred, with various degrees of completeness, on the county level beginning with the formation of the county. The following counties have recorded vital records prior to Indiana statehood: Clark, 1801; Dearborn, 1803; Franklin, 1811; Harrison, 1808; Knox, 1790; Perry, 1814; Posey, 1814; Switzerland, 1814; Warrick, 1813; Washington, 1814; and Wayne, 1811.

Prior to the statewide recording of deaths in 1900, of births in 1907, and of marriages in 1958, many county health offices kept vital records, although they frequently go back no further than 1882. Vital records are listed under **Indiana/[County]/Vital Records.** An on-going program of microfilming Indiana county records constantly adds to the collection.

Indiana Historical Records Survey. Works Progress Administration. *Guide to Public Vital Statistic Records in Indiana.* Indianapolis: Indiana Historical Records Survey, 1941. (FHL# 977.2/A5h or microfilm 874046, item 5, or microfiche 6051202)

Indiana Source Books: Genealogical Material from The Hoosier Genealogist. Indianapolis: Indiana Historical Society, The Family History Section, 1977. (FHL# 977.2/D29h)

Miscellaneous Records of Indiana, 1827-1922. N.p.: n.pub., 1968.) (FHL# microfilm 549290-549300)

Historical Records Survey. Works Projects Administration. *Indexes to Births, Deaths, Marriages and Miscellaneous Records of Indiana Counties.* Indianapolis: Indiana State Library, [c.1970s]. (FHL# microfilm 1266724-1266733, 1266791-1266801, 1299978-1299986, and 1323320-1323328)

MINNESOTA

Historical Background

1634-1763	French missionaries, explorers, and traders occupy area.
1654	French explorers conduct major expeditions into region.
1680	Father Hennepin discovers Falls of St. Anthony.
1689	Region claimed for France by Nicholas Perrot.
1762	Minnesota lands east of Mississippi River ceded to Spain.
1763	Treaty of Versailles gives control of Minnesota west of Mississippi River to Great Britain.
1783	Great Britain transfers control of eastern Minnesota to United States.
1784	The Northwest Company expands fur trading in the region.
1800	Minnesota east of Mississippi River becomes part of Indiana Territory.
1803	The United States obtains western Minnesota through the Louisiana Purchase.
1809	Minnesota land east of Mississippi River becomes part of Illinois Territory.
1812	Southwestern Minnesota becomes part of Illinois Territory.
1817	American Fur Company begins trading in Minnesota.
1818	Northwestern Minnesota obtained from Great Britain by treaty. Minnesota east of Mississippi River included in Michigan Territory.
1819	Minnesota east of Mississippi River becomes part of Crawford County, Michigan. Fort St. Anthony established by U.S. Army.
1823	First steamboat arrives at Fort Snelling.
1834	Western Minnesota included in Michigan Territory.
1835	Minnesota residents included in 1835 Wisconsin Territorial Census.
1836	Wisconsin Territory organized including all of Minnesota.
1837	Several Indian treaties encourage white settlements.
1838	Minnesota west of Mississippi River made part of Iowa Territory.
1840	St. Paul settled.
1846	Iowa statehood leaves Minnesota west of Mississippi River without government.
1847	Minneapolis settled.
1848	Wisconsin admitted to Union, leaving Minnesota east of Mississippi River without government. Federal land office at St. Croix opens; influx of settlers quickly follows.
1849	Minnesota Territory created. Minnesota Historical Society founded.
1850	First federal census of Minnesota taken.
1851	Treaties of Traverse des Sioux and Mendota open territory west of Mississippi River to settlers.
1850s	Thousands of European, Scandinavian, and Canadian immigrants settle.
1854	Rock Island Railroad opened. Influx of settlers follows.
1855	First suspension bridge on Mississippi River joins Minneapolis and St. Anthony.
1857	Minnesota Territory Census.
1858	On 11 May, Minnesota admitted to Union as thirty-second state.
1861-65	Minnesota first state to offer troops to Union Army; 21,982 Minnesotans serve.
1862	Homestead Act encourages new immigration to Minnesota. First railroad between Minneapolis and St. Paul opens.
1870	Third federal census of Minnesota taken, all but thirteen counties lost. Contracted Swedish laborers imported by Northern Pacific Railroad. Counties begin recording vital records.
1889	William W. Mayo and sons found Mayo Clinic in Rochester.
1896	Three-quarters of Red Lake Indian Reservation open for settlement.
1903	Influx of settlers into northern and western sections of Minnesota.
1908	Statewide registration of vital records begins.
1917	State requires registration of all aliens.

Settlement and Migration

Minnesota came under the jurisdiction of four different nations between the 1630s and 1858. Various Indian tribes ruled the area without interference until the 1630s when French explorers, missionaries, and traders arrived. From the 1630s until 1763, the French occupied the region with the Indians. British control over the area lasted from 1763 to 1812, although it faced increasing challenges from the United States. The treaty signed to end the War of 1812 ceded Minnesota to the United States. From 1818 until 1858, the lands of the present-day state were included in Illinois, Michigan, Iowa, Wisconsin, and Minnesota Territories, the determination of jurisdiction frequently depending on whether the land was east or west of the Mississippi River.

Settlers began to arrive about 1837. Between 1837 and 1850, Yankees from New England and the East, many from Maine, migrated to the state, many via Ohio and Wisconsin. French, English, Scottish, Swiss, and French Canadians also filtered into the state in small numbers. In 1850, the entire white population still numbered only 6,077. Between 1850 and 1860, over 166,000 settlers and immigrants, mainly Germans, Scandinavians, and Irish, moved to the state.

Between 1870 and 1880, settlement in western and southwestern areas began. Iron mines in the north attracted Finns, Czechs, Slovaks, and Poles. People from the Balkans and Lithuania immigrated to work in and around the Twin Cities. The 1890 census documented 1,310,000 Minnesota residents, 467,356 of them foreign born. Of those, all but 30,000 were Germans, Scandinavians, or English-speaking immigrants.

Minnesota Library Collection

The Genealogical Society of Utah microfilming and acquisitions project did not begin in Minnesota until 1982. Although state and local record custodians have graciously permitted microfilming of all vital records, the filming process is necessarily slow though the Minnesota collection is steadily growing. The FHLC will almost certainly not reflect complete holdings at any given moment, and you should request a Family History Library reference employee or volunteer to check the call numbers of new acquisitions from the library computer for you.

Archives and Libraries

Historical Records Survey. Work Project Administration. *Guide to Depositories of Manuscript Collections in the United States: Minnesota.* St. Paul: Historical Records Survey, 1941. (FHL# 977.6/A3h or microfilm 1036213, item 31)

Fogerty, James E., comp. *Manuscript Collection of the Minnesota Regional Research Centers.* St. Paul: Division of Archives and Manuscripts; Minnesota Historical Society, 1980. (FHL# 977.6/A3f/no.2)

Jerabek, Esther, comp.. *Check List of Minnesota State Documents, 1858-1923.* St. Paul: Minnesota Historical Society, 1972. (FHL# 977.6/A5j)

Preliminary Guide to the Holdings of the Minnesota Regional Research Centers. St. Paul: Minnesota Historical Society, 1975. (FHL# 977.6/A3f/no.1)

Biography

A growing collection of Minnesota biographical publications is listed under the FHLC heading **Minnesota/-Biography.** Additional titles are listed under **Minnesota/[County]/Biography.**

Burnquist, Joseph Alfred Arner, ed. *Minnesota and Its People.* Chicago, Ill.: S. J. Clarke, 1924. (FHL# 977.6/H2b or microfilm 928372 and 928374)

Castle, Henry Anson. *Minnesota, Its Story and Biography.* Chicago, Ill.: Lewis Publishing Co., 1915. (FHL# 977.6/H2ch or microfilm 1000251, items 1-3)

Commemorative Biographical Record of the Upper Lake Region: Containing Biographical Sketches of Prominent and Representative Citizens and Many of the Early Settled Families. Chicago, Ill.: J. H. Beers, 1905. (FHL# 977/D3u or microfilm 908798, item 1, or 1000252, item 7, or 1000805, item 2)

Illustrated Album of Biography of Southwestern Minnesota. Chicago, Ill.: Occidental Publishing Company, 1889. (FHL# 977.6/D3i or microfilm 1000253, item 1)

Stevens, Hiram F. *History of the Bench and Bar of Minnesota.* Tucson, Ariz.: W. C. Cox Co., 1974. (FHL# microfilm 1000252, items 1-2)

Cemeteries

No major cemetery tombstone inventories are included in the Minnesota collection at this writing. Available cemetery tombstone records are listed under **Minnesota/[County]/Cemetery Records.**

Census Records

Census of Minnesota Territory, June 11, 1849. Salt Lake City: Genealogical Society of Utah, 1972. (FHL# 977.6/-A1/no.3 or microfilm 908224)

Dilts, Bryan Lee, comp. *1890 Minnesota Census Index of Civil War Veterans or Their Widows.* Salt Lake City: Index Publishing, 1985. (FHL# 977.6/X22d)

Finnell, Arthur Louis, comp. *Index to the 1860 Minnesota Mortality Schedule.* Marshall, Minn.: n.pub., 1978. (FHL# Q/977.6/X22i)

Jackson, Ronald Vern, ed *Iowa 1836 Territorial Census.* Bountiful, Utah, c.1973. (FHL# 977.7/A1/no.10)

Jackson, Ronald V., ed. *Minnesota 1870 Census Index.* Salt Lake City: Accelerated Indexing System, c.1979. (FHL# 977.6/X22j/1870) Every-name index.

Jackson, Ronald Vern, comp. *Mortality Schedule Minnesota 1880.* Bountiful, Utah: Accelerated Indexing Systems, 1979. (FHL# 977.6/X2j/1880)

Minnesota Census Bureau. *Schedules of the Minnesota Census of 1857.* Washington, D.C.: National Archives, 1973. (FHL# microfilm 944283-944290)

Minnesota Historical Society. *Minnesota Territorial Census, 1850.* St. Paul: Minnesota Historical Society, 1972. (FHL# 977.6/X2ph/1850)

United States Bureau of Indian Affairs. Consolidated Chippewa Agency. *Agency Records 1876-1953.* Kansas City, Mo.: Federal Record Center, 1979. (FHL# microfilm 1294364-1294366 and 1266699-1266708)

United States Census Office. *Mortality Census Schedules, Minnesota 1850-1880.* St. Paul: Minnesota Historical Society, 1977. (FHL# microfilm 485345-485346)

Wisconsin Territory. *The First Census of the Original Counties of Dubuque and Demoine Iowa Taken in July 1836.* Salt Lake City: Genealogical Society of Utah, 1978. (FHL# microfilm 1022202, items 1-2, or 989450, item 2) Includes Minnesota.

Church Records

Consult the FHLC under **Minnesota/[County]/Church Records.** The records frequently contain christenings, baptisms, marriages, and burials.

Evangelical Lutheran Church. Missouri Synod. Wisconsin Synod. *Kirchenbuch, 1882-1916.* Salt Lake City: Genealogical Society of Utah, 1980. (FHL# microfilm 1293933, item 5) Includes Minnesota.

Lovett, Mrs. Lovell I., comp. *Early Minnesota Church Records, 1856-1913.* Salt Lake City: Genealogical Society of Utah, 1971. (FHL# microfilm 823992, item 4)

Genealogy

Genealogy titles are listed in the Minnesota collection under **Minnesota/[County]/Genealogy** and **Minnesota/Genealogy.** Notable titles include:

Bible, Genealogical, Vital Records and Pioneer Stories of Minnesota. Duluth, Minn.: n.pub., 1946-47. (FHL# 977.6/D2da)

Genealogical Collection of the Daughters of the American Revolution for the State of Minnesota. Salt Lake City: Genealogical Society of Utah, 1985. (FHL# 977.6/D2d or microfiche 6051204)

Pope, Wiley R., and Alissa L. Wiener. *Tracing Your Ancestors in Minnesota.* St. Paul: Minnesota Family Trees, 1980. (FHL# 977.6/D27p/1980)

Sabatke, Linda, ed. *Surname Index, Anoka County Genealogical Society, 1978.* Anoka, Minn.: Anoka County Genealogical Society, 1978. (FHL# 977.6/A1/no.29)

History

The library has many entries cataloged under **Minnesota/History** and **Minnesota/[County]/History.** Notable are:

Berthel, Mary Elizabeth Wheelhouse. *Minnesota Under Four Flags.* St. Paul: Minnesota Historical Society, c.1946. (FHL# 977.6/B4mc/no.1)

Blegen, Theodore C. *Minnesota: A History of the State.* Minneapolis: University of Minnesota Press, c.1975. (FHL# 977.6/H2bt)

Castle, Henry Anson. *Minnesota, Its Story and Biography.* Chicago, Ill.: Lewis Publishing Company, 1915. (FHL# 977.6/H2ch or microfilm 1000251, items 1-3)

Compendium of History and Biography of Central and Northern Minnesota. Salt Lake City: Genealogical Society of Utah, 1978. (FHL# 977.6/D3c or microfilm 1036200, item 13)

Hubbard, Lucius F. et al, eds. *Minnesota in Three Centuries.* New York: Publishing Society of Minnesota, c.1908. 4 vols. (FHL# 977.6/H2m or microfilm 1036696, items 1-4)

O'Brien, Frank George. *Minnesota Pioneer Sketches from the Personal Recollections and Observations of a Pioneer Resident.* Minneapolis, Minn.: H. H. S. Rowell, 1904. (FHL# 977.6/H2o or microfilm 1036209, item 6)

Wasatjerna, Hans R., ed. *History of the Finns in Minnesota.* Duluth: Minnesota Finnish-American Historical Society, c.1957. (FHL# 977.6/F2h)

Land and Property

Minnesota was a public domain state, and the federal government initially sold land. Subsequent land transfers were recorded in county courts. Land and related matters are listed under **Minnesota/[County]/Land and Property.**

Maps

Gamble, W. H. *County Map of Minnesota.* [Philadelphia]: S. Augustus Mitchell, 1874. (FHL# 977.6/E7g)

Government Printing Office. *Minnesota: Minor Civil Divisions, Townships and Villages.* Washington, D.C.: Government Printing Office, 1961. (Map Case FHL# 977.6/E7u)

Pope, John. *A Map of the Territory of Minnesota.* St. Paul: Minnesota Historical Society, [c.1980s]. (Map case FHL# 977.6/E7p)

Rand McNally and Company's Indexed County and Township Map of Minnesota With New and Original Compilations and Index. Chicago, Ill.: Rand McNally, n.d. (Map case FHL# 977.6/E73)

Military Records

Dilts, Bryan Lee, comp.. *1890 Minnesota Census Index of Civil War Veterans or Their Widows.* Salt Lake City: Indexing Publishing, 1985. (FHL# 977.6/X22d)

Minnesota Board of Commissioners on Publication of History of Minnesota in Civil and Indian Wars. *Minnesota in the Civil and Indian Wars, 1861-1865.* St. Paul: Pioneer Press Company, 1891. (FHL# 977.6/H2bc/1891 or microfilm 1033917, item 1)

United States Adjutant General's Office. *Index to Compiled Service Records of Volunteer Soldiers Who Served in Organizations from the State of Minnesota, 1861-1865.* Washington, D.C.: National Archives. (FHL# microfilm 821930-821938)

Minorities and Ethnic Groups

For library holdings consult the FHLC under **Minnesota/Minorities and Ethnic Groups** and **Minnesota/[County]/Minorities and Ethnic Groups.** Important titles include the following:

History of Finns in Minnesota. Duluth, Minn.: Finnish American Historical Society, c.1957. (FHL# 977.6/F2h)

Ljungmark, Lars. *For Sale–Minnesota: Organized Promotion of Scandinavian Immigration 1866-1873.* Chicago, Ill.: Swedish Pioneer Historical Society, c.1971. (FHL# 977.6/W2L)

Mayer, Friedrich. *Neu-Ulm: Kullturhistorische Erzahlung Aus Dem Deutsch-Amerikanischen Leben Verlag des Weftdeutschen.* Barmen, U.: Junglingsbundes, c.1914. (FHL# 977.631/N1/H2m) Germans in New Ulm.

Nordstrom, Byron. *The Swedes in Minnesota.* Minneapolis, Minn.: T. S. Denison, c.1976. (FHL# 977.6/F2s)

Plaut, W. Gunther. *The Jews in Minnesota: The First Seventy-five Years.* New York: American Jewish Historical Society, c.1959. (FHL# 977.6/F2p)

Saucedo, Ramedo J. *Mexican Americans in Minnesota.* St. Paul: Minnesota Historical Society, 1977. (FHL# 977.6/F2sr)

Holmquist, June Drenning, ed. *They Chose Minnesota: A Survey of the State's Ethnic Groups.* St.Paul: Minnesota Historical Society, 1981. (FHL# 977.6/F2t)

Wyman, Mark. *Immigrants in the Valley: Irish, Germans and Americans in the Upper Mississippi Country 1810-1860.* Chicago, Ill.: Nelson-Hall, c.1984. (FHL# 977/H2wm)

Probate Records

All probate matters in Minnesota are recorded by the clerk of the Probate Court and are available from the creation of the county to the present. Estate-related matters are listed under **Minnesota/[County]/Probate Records.**

Vital Records

Statutes mandating the recording of vital records in each county were passed in 1870. An estimated 90 percent of the events were actually recorded. In 1915, the legislature mandated statewide registration of vital records. From 1870 to 1915, the records are listed under **Minnesota/[County]/Vital Records.** Some counties also recorded marriages prior to 1870.

Minnestoa Right of Privacy Laws required that all illegitimate, adoptive, and other births where parentage was not clearly stated be covered before the Genealogical Society of Utah microfilmed the state's birth records. The indexes of each volume may include the original surname on a covered record.

Numerous counties recorded vital records in several volumes for duplicate or overlapping time periods. Due to the state's rural nature, many doctors in small towns kept separate registers which were transferred later to the county clerk. Therefore, when searching for vital records it is important that all vital record volumes for the county and towns be examined.

Ramsey and Hennepin counties kept extensive vital records for residents outside Minneapolis and St. Paul. If a record in not found among county records, Minneapolis and St. Paul records should be examined.

WISCONSIN

Historical Background

1634	French explorer Nicolet reaches Green Bay.
1673	Joliet and Marquette discover the Mississippi River via Wisconsin.
1745	Green Bay becomes Wisconsin's first permanent settlement.
1763	End of French and Indian War transfers control of region from France to Great Britain.
1774	Quebec Province includes Wisconsin.
1783	Treaty of Paris makes Wisconsin part of the United States.
1787	Wisconsin is part of new Northwest Territory.
1792	Northwest Fur Trading Company establishes Wisconsin River area trade.
1809	Wisconsin included in Illinois Territory.
1818	Wisconsin becomes part of Michigan Territory.
1822	Lead mining developed in southwestern Wisconsin.
1827	Fort Winnebago built at Portage.
1830s	Southerners and easterners migrate to lead region. Mining and logging industries attract settlers.
1832	Black Hawk War ends near Prairie du Chien.
1834	Wisconsin public land sales begin.
1836	Wisconsin Territory established.
1840	First Wisconsin Lutheran Church established.
1845	First free school opened.
1846	State Historical Society founded.
1848	Wisconsin becomes the thirtieth state on 29 May.
1851	Railroad opens between Milwaukee and Waukesha.
1854	Republican Party organized at Ripon, Fond du Lac County.
1855	Wisconsin state census.
1856	Reservation lands set aside for Indians.
1871	Worst American fire occurred at Peshtigo, Marinette County.
1875	Wisconsin state census.
1885	Wisconsin state census.

1895 Wisconsin state census.

1905 Wisconsin state census.

1907 Statutes establish statewide registration of vital records.

Settlement and Migration

As early as 1745, some French settled at Green Bay, Brown County. In 1822, Southerners, mainly from Kentucky, Tennessee, West Virginia, and North Carolina moved to the lead regions in Grant, Lafayette, Iowa, western Dane, and Green counties. In 1830, New Yorkers relocated in Kenosha County. During the 1830 decade, others from New York and Pennsylvania settled along Lake Michigan.

In 1836 groups from New England and Ohio moved to new residences along Lake Michigan, and others from Vermont founded a settlement in Waukesha County. The following year, Norwegians migrated to Waukesha and Racine counties, and families from Colebrook, Coos County, New Hampshire, relocated in Beloit, Rock County.

More Norwegians migrated to Wisconsin in 1838; they settled in Jefferson Prairie and Clinton, Rock County. A year after, Germans moved to Milwaukee and Mequon, Ozaukee County. In 1840 immigrants from Glarus, Switzerland, colonized New Glarus, Green County, and Norwegians made additional settlements in the eastern half of Dane County.

Between 1840 and 1870 Irish entered Wisconsin through its lake ports and settled in the lead region and the southwestern portion of the state. In 1844 families from Winterswik, Gelderland, Holland, migrated to Milwaukee. The following year, Dutch from Zeeland founded Oostburg, Sheboygan County, and Dutch from Gelderland, moved to Alto, Fond du Lac County. In 1847 Hollanders migrated to Little Chute, Outgamie County.

By 1850, 96 percent of the state's inhabitants were Yankee-born. During the 1850s, families from Germany settled in Milwaukee; groups from Norway moved to Rock River Valley and Madison, Dane County; and others from Ireland migrated to Milwaukee, Lafayette, Outgamie, Winnebago, Fond du Lac, Walworth, Rock, and Iowa counties.

Hollanders moved to New Amsterdam, La Crosse County, in 1853, and Friesians from Holland founded Friesland, Columbia County in 1861. Before 1870, Danish immigrants settled in Winnebago, Racine, and Dane counties. Between 1870 and 1920, Poles migrated to Steven's Point and Portage County, Pulaski, Brown County, Outgamie County, and Palonia. During the 1890s, Poles settled in Milwaukee.

In 1892 families from Reinwald and Schafer, Russia, moved to Sheboygan, Sheboygan County. Russians from Grimm, settled in Fond du Lac County in 1895. Germans from Russia and others from Jagodnaja Poljana, Volga, migrated to Oshkosh, Winnebago county via Pine Island, New York. Between 1900 and 1920, Swedes settled in Pine Lake, Waukesha County; western St. Croix Valley, Ogema, Price County; Prentice, Price County; and Glen Flora, Rush County.

Former residents of Grimm, Reinwald, Russia, migrated to Racine, Racine County, in 1904. During the 1900s, Italians moved to Milwaukee. In 1910 and 1911 Russian Jews from Dreispitzand other villages of "Bergseite" relocated in Milwaukee. Prior to 1910, families and individuals from Canada, Austria, England, Wales, Scotland, and Poland had settled throughout Wisconsin.

The State Historical Society of Wisconsin, ethnic groups, state and local genealogical societies, and a number of private individuals are cooperating in a program of documenting immigrant ancestral homes and migration patterns. Notable among their compilations are:

Anuta, Michael J. *East Prussians from Russia.* Menominee, Mich.: Anuta, c.1979. (FHL# 947.718/W2a or microfilm 11183504, item 2, in European film area)

Davies, Phillips G. *The Welsh in Wisconsin*. Madison: State Historical Society of Wisconsin, 1982. (FHL# 977.5/A1/-no.85)

Fapso, Richard J. *Norwegians in Wisconsin.* Madison: State Historical Society of Wisconsin, c.1977. (FHL# 977.5/A1/no.54)

Hale, Frederick. *Danes in Wisconsin.* Madison: State Historical Society of Wisconsin, 1981. (FHL# 977.5/A1/no.87)

Knipping, Mark. *Finns in Wisconsin.* Madison: State Historical Society of Wisconsin, c.1977. (FHL# 977.5/A1/no.52)

Kolehmainen, John Ilmari. *Haven in the Woods: The Story of the Finns in Wisconsin.* Madison: State Historical Society of Wisconsin, c.1965. (FHL# 977.5/F3fk)

Lacher, J. Henry A. *The German Element in Wisconsin.* Salt Lake City, Utah: Genealogical Society of Utah, 1966. (FHL# 424852)

Lempereur, Francoise. *Les Wallons d'Amerique du Nord.* Gembloux, Belgique: J. Duculot, S. A., 1976. (FHL# 977.5/W21)

Lucas, Henry S. *Dutch Immigrant Memoirs and Related Writings.* Assen: Van Gorcum & Co., 1955. (FHL# 949.2/W21, in European film area)

Smith, Clifford Neal. *Immigrants to America (Mainly Wisconsin) from the Former Recklinghausen District (Nordrhein-Westfalen, Germany) around the Middle of the Nineteenth Century.* McNeal, Ariz.: Westland Publishing, 1983. (FHL# 973/W2smn, no. 15)

Zeitlin, Richard H. *Germans in Wisconsin.* Madison: State Historical Society of Wisconsin, 1977. (FHL# 977.5/A1/-no.53)

Atlases, Gazetteers, and Maps

A select group of helpful reference materials is available in the Wisconsin collection, cataloged under both **Wisconsin/Atlases, Gazetteers, and Maps**, and under the county headings as well. In addition to the FHLC entries, excellent maps are included in the gray Wisconsin reference notebook kept at the United States and Canada Reference Desk.

Hunt, John Warren. *Wisconsin Gazetteer.* Madison: B. Brown, 1853. (FHL# 977.5/E5h or microfilm 897468, item 2, or microfiche 6051150)

Mitchell, S. Augustus. *County and Township Map of the States of Michigan and Wisconsin.* N.p.: n.pub., 1881. (FHL# 977/E7ms)

Rand, McNally & Company's Indexed County and Township Map of Wisconsin. Chicago, Ill.: Rand McNally & Company, [n.d.]. (FHL# 977.5/E7r)

Robinson, Arthur Howard. *The Atlas of Wisconsin: General Maps and Gazetteer.* Madison: University of Wisconsin Press, c.1974. (FHL# Q/977.5/E3r)

Walling, H. F. *Atlas of the State of Wisconsin.* Salt Lake City: Genealogical Society of Utah, 1978. (FHL# microfilm 1036174, item 2)

Wisconsin State Gazetteer and Business Directory. Detroit, Mich.: R. L. Polk, 1821. (FHL# 977.5/E5p)

Biography

Wisconsin local biographical titles are cataloged under **Wisconsin/[County]/Biography** and **Wisconsin/[County]/Biography/Indexes.** State and regional biographical compilations and indexes are cataloged under **Wisconsin/Biography** and **Wisconsin/Biography Indexes.** Important titles include:

Aikens, Andrew J., and Lewis A. Proctor. *Men of Progress, Wisconsin: A Selected List of Biographical Sketches and Portraits of the Leaders in Business, Professional and Official Life, Together with Short Notes on the History and Character of Wisconsin.* Tucson, Ariz.: W. C. Cox, 1974. (FHL# microfilm 1000804, item 1)

The Blue Book of the State of Wisconsin. Tucson, Ariz.: W. C. Cox, Co., 1974. (FHL# microfilm 1000825, item 1)

Commemorative Biographical Record of the Upper Lake Region: Containing Biographical Sketches of Prominent and Representative Citizens and Many of the Early Settled Families. Chicago, Ill.: J. H. Beers, 1905. (FHL# 977/D3u, or microfilm 908798, item 1, or 1000805, item 2, or 1000252, item 7)

Dictionary of Wisconsin Biography. Madison: State Historical Society of Wisconsin, c.1960. (FHL# 977.5/D3w)

Forrester, George, ed. *Historical and Biographical Album of the Chippewa Valley, Wisconsin.* Chicago, Ill.: A. Warner, 1891-92. (FHL# 977.5/D3f or microfilm 1000805, item 3)

Notable Men of Wisconsin. Tucson, Ariz.: W. C. Cox, 1974. (FHL# microfilm 1000804, item 3)

Quaife, Milo Milton. *Wisconsin: Its History and Its People, 1634-1924.* Chicago, Ill.: S. J. Clarke Publishing Company, 1924. (FHL# 977.5/H2q or microfilm 1036176 or microfiche 6046726)

The United States Biographical Dictionary and Portrait Gallery of Eminent and Self-Made Men: Wisconsin in Volume. Salt Lake City: Genealogical Society of Utah, 1869. (FHL# 977.5/D3a or microfilm 599147, item 2, or 1000800, item 3, or microfiche 6051214)

Usher, Ellis Baker. *Wisconsin: Its Story and Biography, 1848-1913.* Chicago, Ill.: Lewis Publishing Company, 1914. (FHL# 977.5/H2w or microfilm 1036685 and 1036686, items 1-3)

Women's Auxiliary, Historical Society of Wisconsin. *Famous Wisconsin Women.* Madison: Historical Society of Wisconsin, 1971. 6 vols. (FHL# 977.5/D3ws)

Cemetery Records

With few exceptions, cemetery records are cataloged under **Wisconsin/[County]/Cemetery Records.** Two organizations, the DAR Genealogical Records Committee and the Wisconsin State Old Cemetery Society, have on-going projects to record tombstone inscriptions.

Daughters of the American Revolution, Genealogical Records Committee, Wisconsin. *Bible and Cemetery Records, 1700-1940.* Salt Lake City: Genealogical Society of Utah, 1970. (FHL# microfilm 848696, item 7)

_____. *Bible and Cemetery Records, 1800-1940.* Salt Lake City: Genealogical Society of Utah, 1970. (FHL# microfilm 848696, item 6)

_____ *Bible and Cemetery Inscriptions from Wisconsin.* Salt Lake City: Genealogical Society of Utah, 1970. (FHL# microfilm 848696, item 4)

Census Records

Prior to statehood on 29 May 1848, Wisconsin was successively part of Quebec Province, Northwest Territory, Illinois Territory, Michigan Territory, Iowa Territory, and Wisconsin Territory. Therefore, Wisconsin inhabitants were enumerated with the parent territories. In the 1820 and 1830 federal censuses, Wisconsin residents were listed in Brown, Crawford, and Iowa counties, in Michigan schedules. Wisconsin federal schedules are available for 1840, 1850, 1860, 1870, 1880, 1900, and 1910. All are indexed and/or soundexed. In addition, valuable state and territorial censuses were taken in 1830, 1836, 1842, 1847, 1855, 1865, 1875, 1885, 1895, and 1905.

Iowa County Heritage. Dodgeville, Wis.: Iowa County Heritage, c.1967. (FHL# 977.5/B4f/Vols. 1-4) Wisconsin inhabitants listed in Michigan Territory.

Jackson, Ronald Vern. *Territorial Census for 1836.* Salt Lake City: Genealogical Society of Utah, 1974. (FHL# 977.5/B4wc/no.13 or microfilm 924585, item 3, or 1293919, item 1)

Jackson, Ronald Vern, and Gary Ronald Teeples, eds. *Wisconsin Territorial Census, 1838.* Salt Lake City: Genealogical Society of Utah, 1980. (FHL# microfilm 1293919, item 2)

Jackson, Ronald Vern, and Gary Ronald Teeples, eds. *Wisconsin Territory Census, 1842.* Salt Lake City: Genealogical Society of Utah, 1980. (FHL# microfilm 1293919, item 3)

State Historical Society of Wisconsin. *Index to 1850 Federal Census for Wisconsin.* Madison: University of Wisconsin Film Laboratory, 1971. (FHL# microfilm 933599-933634)

_____. *Index to 1860 Federal Census of Wisconsin.* Madison: University Wisconsin Film Laboratory, 1971. (FHL# microfilm 933635-933729)

_____. *Index to 1870 Federal Census of Wisconsin.* Madison:

University of Wisconsin Film Laboratory, 1981. (FHL# microfilm 933730-933859)

United States Census Office. *Schedules of Persons Who Died during the Year Ending 31 May 1880: Wisconsin.* Salt Lake City: Genealogical Society of Utah, 1979. (FHL# microfilm 1032684, item 3-1032686, item 1)

Wisconsin Census Index 1820. Madison: University of Wisconsin Film Laboratory, 1970. (FHL# microfilm 933597, item 1)

Wisconsin Census Index, 1830. Madison: University of Wisconsin Film Laboratory, 1970. (FHL# microfilm 933597, item 2)

Wisconsin Department of State. *Wisconsin State Census, 1855.* Salt Lake City: Genealogical Society of Utah, 1979. (FHL# microfilm 1032686, items 2-4 through 1032689, items 1-4)

______. *Wisconsin State Census, 1875.* Salt Lake City: Genealogical Society of Utah, 1979. (FHL# microfilm 1032689, item 5-1032694)

______. *Wisconsin State Census, 1885.* Salt Lake City: Genealogical Society of Utah, 1979. (FHL# microfilm 1032695-1032704)

______. *Wisconsin State Census, 1895.* Salt Lake City: Genealogical Society of Utah, 1979. (FHL# microfilm 1032705-1032716)

______. *Wisconsin State Census, 1905.* Salt Lake City: Genealogical Society of Utah, 1952. (FHL# microfilm 1020439-1020455, 1020978, 1020991-1020999)

Wisconsin Territory, Secretary. *Wisconsin Territory Census for 1846.* Salt Lake City: Genealogical Society of Utah, 1980. (FHL# microfilm 1293920)

______. *Wisconsin Territory Census for 1847.* Salt Lake City: Genealogical Society of Utah, 1980. (FHL# microfilm 1293921 and 1293922, item 1)

Church Records

Catholics and Lutherans were most widely represented in Wisconsin with smaller numbers of Methodists, Episcopalians, Baptists, Congregationalists, and other religions. Immigrant Catholics and Lutherans settled primarily in large cities. Additional Lutheran congregations and those of other religions were spread throughout the state. Local church records are listed under **Wisconsin/[County]/Church Records** and **Wisconsin/[County]/Church Histories.** Regional and statewide records are under **Wisconsin/Church Records** and **Wisconsin/Church Histories.** Important titles in the collection are:

Historical Records Survey, Wisconsin. *Directory of Churches and Religious Organizations in Wisconsin.* Madison: Historical Records Survey, 1941. (FHL# 977.5/K24h or microfilm 1036193, item 12, or microfiche 6051165)

Evangelical Lutheran Church. Missouri Synod, Wisconsin Synod. *Kirchenbuch, 1882-1916.* Salt Lake City: Genealogical Society of Utah, 1980. (FHL# microfilm 1293933, item 5)

Historical Records Survey, Wisconsin. *A Directory of Catholic Churches in Wisconsin.* Madison: Wisconsin Historical Records Survey, 1942. (FHL# 977.5/K22h or microfilm 908018, item 3)

______. *Guide to Church Vital Statistic Records in Wisconsin.* Madison: Wisconsin Historical Records Survey, 1942. (FHL# 977.5/K23h or microfilm 1036234, item 5)

Peddle, Jean Larson. *The Reverend George Clarence Alborn and His Pastoral Records.* Salt Lake City: Genealogical Society of Utah, 1978. (FHL# microfilm 1027166, item 3)

Court and Probate Records

Probate records including wills, guardianship, administrator or executor bonds and inventories, are recorded by the county clerks, and/or register of probate clerk, and are available from the date the county was created, with the exception of Menominee County which uses the Shawano County Court. Jurisdiction for guardianship and Orphan Court proceedings was shared by the issuing court and the Public Welfare Department at the State Capital.

The register of deeds in each county records all land- and property-related matters and, in many counties, vital records as well. In other counties, the county clerk has responsibility for vital records. The county clerk and/or the clerk of the circuit court have responsibility for divorce and civil court records. To determine jurisdiction and record custodians for specific counties, consult:

The Handybook for Genealogists. Logan, Utah: Everton Publishers, Inc., 1981. (FHL# 973/D27e)

Genealogical Collections

Bay Area Genealogical Society, comp. *Gems of Genealogy.* Green Bay, Wis.: Bay Area Genealogical Society, 1975. (FHL# 977.5/D25gg)

Daughters of the American Revolution, Genealogical Records Committee, Wisconsin. *Miscellaneous Records, Wills, Bible Records, Autobiography, Family Records, Diaries, Etc., 1700-1900.* Salt Lake City: Genealogical Society of Utah, 1970. (FHL# microfilm 848691, item 5)

______. *Roster: Revolutionary War Ancestors, Members Numbers and Supplements, 1891-November 1964.*. Post Washington: Wisconsin State Genealogical Society, 1977. (FHL# 977.5 A1/no.17)

______. *Genealogical Records, 1700-1930.* Salt Lake City: Genealogical Society of Utah, 1970. (FHL# microfilm 848700, item 2)

______. *Wisconsin Genealogical Records, 1800-1930.* Salt Lake City: Genealogical Society of Utah, 1970. (FHL# microfilm 848699, item 3)

Patterson, Betty, ed. *Some Pioneer Families of Wisconsin: An Index.* Madison: Wisconsin State Genealogical Society, 1977. (FHL# 977.5/D22s)

Wisconsin Families: Quarterly Magazine of the Wisconsin Genealogical Society. Milwaukee: Wisconsin Genealogical Society, 1940. (FHL# 977.5/D25w or microfilm 973820, item 2)

History

Clark, James I. *They Called the Land "Ouisconsin."* Madison: Americana Press, c.1957. (FHL# 977.5/A1/no.55)

Current, Richard Nelson. *Wisconsin: A Bicentennial History.* New York: W. W. Norton & Co., c.1977. (FHL# 977.5/H2cr)

Gnacinksi, Janneyne. *Wisconsin: "Meeting Place Of The Waters."* West Allis, Wis.: Janlen Enterprises, 1976. (FHL# 977.5/H2gn or microfilm 1036718, item 9)

Gregory, John Goadby. *Southwestern Wisconsin: A History of Old Crawford County.* Chicago, Ill.: S. J. Clarke Publishing Company, c.1932. (FHL# 977.5/H2g or microfilm 1000806)

_____. *Southeastern Wisconsin: A History of Old Milwaukee County.* Chicago, Ill.: S. J. Clarke Publishing Company, c.1932. (FHL# 977.5/H2gs or microfilm 1036202, items 1-4)

_____. *West Central Wisconsin: A History.* Indianapolis, Ind.: S. J. Clarke Publishing Company, c.1933. (FHL# 977.5 H2gr or microfilm 1036192)

History of Northern Wisconsin. Chicago, Ill.: Western Historical Co., 1881. v. 1 & 2. (FHL# 977.5/H2n or microfilm 1000804, item 4)

McLeod, Donald. *History of Wiskonsan: From Its Early Discovery to the Present Period.* Salt Lake City: Genealogical Society of Utah, 1978. (FHL# 977.5/H2m or microfilm 1036198, item 1)

Quaife, Milo Milton. *Wisconsin: Its History and Its People, 1634-1924.* Chicago, Ill.: S. J. Clarke Publishing Company, 1924. (FHL# 977.5/H2q or microfilm 1036176 or microfiche 6046726)

Strong, Moses McClure. *History of the Territory of Wisconsin, from 1836-1848.* Madison: Democrat Publishing Co., 1885. (FHL# 977.5/H2s or microfilm 1000800, item 2)

Wyman, Mark. *Immigrants in the Valley: Irish, Germans and Americans in the Upper Mississippi Valley, 1830-1860.* Chicago, Ill.: Nelson-Hall, c.1984. (FHL# 977/H2wm)

Land and Property Records

Initially, all lands in Wisconsin, a Public Domain state, were owned by the federal government or by persons who received title from the government. Land titles were filed at one of the eight Government Land District Offices: Mineral Point, 1834-41, 1843-58/Muskaday, 1841-43; Green Bay, 1835-53/Manasha 1853-93; Milwaukee, 1836-55; Hudson, 1849-60/Falls St. Croix, 1860-89; LaCrosse, 1853-89; Steven's Point, 1853-72/Wausau, 1872-1925; Superior, 1833-60/Bayfield, 1860-86/Ashland, 1886-1905; and Eau Claire, 1857-1905.

From the date of a county's creation, later land transfers were recorded with the county register of deeds. These records are cataloged under **Wisconsin/[County]/Land and Property.**

Military Records

Soldiers' and Citizens Album of Biographical Records (of Wisconsin): Containing Personal Sketches of Army Men and Citizens Prominent in Loyalty to the Union. Chicago, Ill.: Grand Army Publishing Co., 1890. (FHL# 977.5/D3s or microfilm 1000801 or 928504, item 2, or 928508, item 1, or microfiche 6051213)

United States Adjutant General's Office. *Index to Compiled Service Records of Volunteer Union Soldiers Who Served in Organizations from the State of Wisconsin (1861-1865).* Washington, D.C.: National Archives, 1965. (FHL# microfilm 882486-882518)

Wisconsin Adjutant General's Office. *Military Records, 1861-1865.* Salt Lake City: Genealogical Society of Utah, 1981. (FHL# microfilm 1311667-1311698)

Minorities

Cooper, Zachary. *Black Settlers in Rural Wisconsin..* Madison: State Historical Society of Wisconsin, c.1977. (FHL# 977.5/A1/no.51)

Davidson, John Nelson. *Negro Slavery in Wisconsin.* Ann Arbor, Mich.: University Microfilms, 1978. (FHL# 977.5/A1/no.48)

Native American Records

Densmore, Frances. *Chippewa Customs.* Washington, D.C.: Library of Congress, [c.1970s]. (FHL# microfilm 1009057, item 1)

Johnes, John Alan. *Winnebago Ethnology.* New York: Garland Publishing Co., c.1974. (FHL# 970.3/W73j)

Lawson, Publius Virgilius. *Story of Oshkosh, His Tribes and Fellow Chiefs.* N.p.: n.pub., c.1950s. FHL# 970.1/-A1/no.62 or microfilm 982236, item 6)

Ourada, Patricia K. *The Menominee Indiana: A History.* Norman: University of Oklahoma Press, c.1979. (FHL# 970.3/M527o)

United States, Bureau of Indian Affairs. *A Census Register of All the Men, Women and Children Coming Within the Sixth Article of the Treaty Made With the Ottawa and Chippewa Nations of Indiana on the 28th of March 1836.* Washington, D.C.: U.S. Bureau of Indian Affairs, 1836. (FHL# Q/970.1 A1/no.4 or microfilm 982330, item 4)

Vital Records

A statute requiring registration of all vital records in Wisconsin was passed in 1907. Prior to that date, records (except births) were kept at the discretion of the individual counties. Some counties recorded vital records from the date the county was formed, but a majority did not begin until about 1870 or even later.

An 1852 statute had required county registration of all current births, and a separate volume was kept for recording births which had occurred prior to 1852. The earliest delayed birth record dates to 1746. In 1878, the 1852 provision was modified to permit recording of births not previously registered. The 1852 law required that a copy of all birth records be sent to the Secretary of State biannually. These records, on 160 reels, are cataloged under **Wisconsin/Vital Records** as are death registrations from about 1862 until 1907.

An extremely valuable index to the pre-1907 vital

records of Wisconsin is the State Birth Index, 41 fiche, beginning microfiche 6331476 for a chronological arrangement and, alphabetically by surname, 38 fiche, beginning with number 6331478. A marriage index for the same period alphabetically arranged by both bride and groom, contains 930,000 names on 77 fiche beginning with number 6331479. A death index, alphabetically arranged by surname, begins on microfiche 6331472 and lists some 435,000 names.

MICHIGAN

Historical Background

1620-40	Champlain, Brule, Nicolet, and other Frenchmen explore the Great Lakes area.
1660s	Marquette, LaSalle, and Joliet explore the Michigan region.
1668	Marquette establishes the first permanent settlement at Sault Saint Marie.
1671	St. Ignace founds a French fort and Jesuit mission.
1701	Detroit founded; two days later, Saint Anne's Church, a log structure, is dedicated.
1734	Land grants given at Fort Pontchartrain (Detroit).
1743	King George's War with the French and Indians.
1754	Outbreak of the French and Indian War.
1763	The British take possession of the area that includes present-day Michigan.
1783	The Treaty of Paris gives control of the region to the United States, although the British keep forces in Michigan until 1796.
1787	The Michigan area becomes part of the Northwest Territory.
1795	The British and Indians cede most Northwest lands.
1796	Small numbers of New Englanders settle in the area.
1800	Eastern Michigan becomes part of Ohio Territory, and most of western Michigan becomes part of Indiana Territory.
1805	Congress creates Michigan Territory; capital located at Detroit. Detroit completely destroyed by fire.
1818	Government Land Office opened at Detroit, making public lands available. Work commences on Erie Canal, bringing many laborers to the region.
1818-36	Large groups of settlers from throughout New England migrate to Michigan Territory.
1825	Erie Canal completed.
1829	Construction of territorial road through Kalamazoo Valley brings New England settlers to Jackson, Calhoun, Kalamazoo, and Allegan counties.
1830	Daily boat line established between Detroit and Buffalo, New York.
1831	Society of Friends (Quakers) organize Adrian Monthly Meeting in Lenawee County.
1834	Territorial census; 82,000.
1836	First railroad built in Michigan connecting Adrian, Lenawee County, and Toledo, Ohio.
1837	Michigan admitted to the Union as the twenty-sixth state.
1840-90	Thousands of European immigrants attracted to the mining and lumber industry camps.
1847	State capital permanently moved to Lansing. Norwegian immigrants settle in Allegan County.
1861-65	90,000 men from Michigan serve in the Civil War. Immigrants arrive in large numbers from the Netherlands, Sweden, Norway, England, Wales, Australia, Poland, Italy, Russia, and the Slavic countries.
1867	Statewide registration of vital records ordered; compliance incomplete until 1915.
late 1800s	Settlers from northeastern United States migrate into the area.
early 1900s	Large numbers of immigrants come from eastern Europe, mainly unskilled workers from Poland, Italy, Russia, Austria, and Hungary.

Settlement and Migration

French/French Canadians

Although French explorers roamed the Michigan region beginning in 1620, it was not until 1668 that the first permanent French settlement was established at Sault Saint Marie. For fifty-nine years, the area called New France attracted few Frenchmen other than trappers/traders, explorers, and soldiers. Such men usually married local Indian women.

Fifty families arrived from France in 1701, settled in Detroit, acquired special land grants, intermarried, worked hard, and prospered. Their descendants eventually developed Michigan's great lumbering industry.

In 1732, Governor General Beauharnois encouraged French and French-Canadian colonization of Detroit. Beginning some two years later, he made a large number of easy-to-acquire land grants to such immigrants.

Until 1783 when the Treaty of Paris was ratified, practically no growth occurred outside of Detroit due to hostile Indians.

New Englanders and New Yorkers

The United States government opened a land office at Detroit in 1818, offering the first public land cheaply for annual installment payments. Numerous settlers from New York and New England flocked to the area. In the same year, labor commenced on the Erie Canal, bringing an influx of workers and their families. Many were recent immigrants into northeastern United States.

On 26 October 1825, the Erie Canal opened connecting Michigan to the Hudson River. Settlers poured into the southern section of the state, continuing until 1836. In 1837, two-thirds of Michigan's population was comprised of New Yorkers and New Englanders.

Ann Arbor, Romero, White Pigeon, Tecumseh, Mt. Clemens, Pontiac, Dexter, Rochester, and Ypsilanti were among the towns established by these settlers. Settlers from Addison County, Vermont, arrived at Sylvan, Washtenaw County, about 1824. Families from Windsor, Vermont, migrated to Prairie Ronde, Kalamazoo County, in 1830. Also in 1830, Vermonters arrived at Bennington, Shiawassee County, and Schoolcraft, Kalamazoo County. Settlers from Royalton, Massachusetts, settled in Monroe County in 1834. Berrien County was settled in 1835 and New Hampshire families moved into Cass County. Vermontville in Eaton County was settled by residents of Bennington, Vermont, and groups from East Poultney and Castleton, Vermont.

The construction of the first railroad in 1836 linking Adrian and Toledo, Ohio, was soon followed by lines running to Buffalo, New York, various Illinois cities (1855) including Chicago (1849), La Porte, Indiana (1851), Port Huron (1851) and Windsor, Ontario (1854). Safe reliable railroad transportation transported a wave of northeastern settlers that did not subside until the late 1800s.

Germans

The first German family settled at Grosse Point, Wayne County, in 1751. However, it was not until 1830-50 that significant German immigration occurred. In 1830, a large German settlement began in Washtenaw County. From 1837 to 1839, immigrants from Ruthen in Westphalia settled in Clinton County, establishing a village called Westphalia. In 1845 settlers came to Frankenmuth, Saginaw County.

In 1848, Michigan sent agents to Germany to encourage immigration. The German Revolution of 1848 prompted large numbers to accept the enticing offers of low-cost fertile land. Travelling and settling in extended family and community groups, many soon wrote other family members and friends, encouraging their immigration. A steady flow of German settlers until 1900 resulted. Between 1880 and 1885, major political and financial problems in Germany also brought many settlers to the areas of Saline in Washtenaw County and Monroe in Monroe County.

Religious dissent within The Netherlands state church in 1845 caused a splinter group called the Successionists. In 1846, under the direction of their pastor, Dr. Albertus Van Raalte, fifty-three people left from Rotterdam, landed at Detroit, and purchased 1,000 acres between the Grand and Kalamazoo rivers, extending to Lake Michigan. They named their new town Holland. A second Dutch immigrant group, 457 strong, soon followed and bought another section of land east of Holland. They named their settlement Zeeland after their home province. Additional Dutch immigrants followed throughout the 1800s, settling primarily in Kalamazoo and Kent counties. The first Dutch immigration to the United States had been during the seventeenth century to New York and New Jersey. In 1847, descendants of these early settlers moved into Michigan, to Cheboygan and Ostego counties, and the surrounding areas and into Ottawa, Allegan, and Kent counties.

Lumber and mining companies sent agents to the Scandinavian countries to recruit laborers accustomed to hard work in harsh winters. The hiring companies paid their passage. Frequently, the men immigrated alone, sending for their families after they had been able to save passage money. A majority lived and worked in the Upper Peninsula, particularly Delta and Dickenson counties. In June 1847, Norwegian settlers independently began to arrive at Laketown and Fillmore in Allegan County. Eventually, significant numbers of Scandinavians lived in Michigan: Finns in Leelanau, Benzie, Manistee, Mason, and Oceana counties; Norwegians in Monroe, Wayne, Manistee, Oceana, and Mason counties; and Swedes in Monroe and Wayne counties and in all the western counties bordering Lake Michigan.

The Irish Potato Famine of 1845 prompted a mass migration to America. The hard-working Irish laborers were eager to accept jobs in Michigan mines and lumber camps. They also built roads, canals, and railroads, and worked in the fast-growing shipping and fishing industries on the Great Lakes. These nomadic occupations did not encourage ethnic colonies of Irish, with perhaps the possible exception of Irish concentrations in settlements along the southeastern counties bordering Lake Huron.

An important publication documenting migration from New England to Michigan containing the names and ancestral homes of 5,000 settlers is:

Flagg, Charles Alcott. *An Index of Pioneers from Massachusetts to the West, Especially the State of Michigan.* Salt Lake City: Genealogical Society of Utah, 1971. (FHL# microfilm 844970, item 4).

Other notable records include:

Florer, Warrem Washburn. *Early Michigan Settlements.* Ann Arbor, Mich.: W. W. Florer, c.1941-53. (FHL# 977.4/-F2gf)

Hammell, George Lee. *Irish Catholic Pioneer Families: Pre-Potato Famin* [sic] *Emigrants.* Salt Lake City: Genealogical Society of Utah, 1973. (FHL# microfilm 926741, item 1)

Lucas, Henry S., comp. *Memorial Souvenir of the Centennial Commemoration of Dutch Immigration to the United States Held in Holland, Michigan.* New York: Netherlands Information Bureau, 1947. (FHL# 977.4/A1/no.57)

Vander Hill, C. Warren. *Settling the Great Lakes Frontier: Im-*

migration to Michigan, 1837-1924. Lansing: Michigan Historical Commission, c.1970. (FHL# 977.4/W2v).

Michigan Library Collection

Archives and Libraries

Hathaway, Richard J., ed. *Directory of Historical Collections of Michigan*. Lansing: Michigan Archivists Association, 1969. (FHL# 977.4/E4h)

Michigan State Library. *Card File Index to Manuscripts in the Vault, Michigan State Library*. Salt Lake City: Genealogical Society of Utah, 1976. (FHL# A-More: microfilm 1001968, Morehouse-Z: 1001969)

Michigan State Library. *Index to Manuscript Materials in the Michigan State Library*. Salt Lake City: Genealogical Society of Utah, 1974. (FHL# A-Ge: microfilm 934555, GA-Z: 934556)

Norris, Joe Lester. *Classified Finding List of the Collections of the Michigan Pioneer and Historical Society*. Salt Lake City: Genealogical Society of Utah, 1977. (FHL# microfilm 1025816, item 2)

Stevens, Wystan, ed. *Directory of Historical Collections and Societies in Michigan*. Ann Arbor, Mich.: Historical Society of Michigan, 1973. (FHL# 977.4/E4s or microfilm 924606, item 13)

Atlases, Gazetteers, and Maps

Blois, John T. *Gazetteer of the State of Michigan*. Detroit, Mich: S. L. Rood, 1939. (FHL# 977.4/E5b or microfilm 897469, item 2, or microfiche 6051130)

Clark, Charles F., ed. *Michigan State Gazetteer and Business Directory for 1863-1864*. Salt Lake City: Genealogical Society of Utah, 1977. (FHL# microfilm 1015815, item 2)

Mitchell, S. Augustus. *County and Township Maps of the State of Michigan and Wisconsin*. N.p.: n.pub., 1881. (FHL# 977/E7ms)

Seltzer, Wayne A. *City and County Directories and Gazetteers at Michigan State Library*. Flint, Mich.: Flint Genealogical Society, n.d. (FHL# 977.4/A3s)

Winchell, Alexander. *Atlas of the State of Michigan*. Salt Lake City: Genealogical Society of Utah, 1977. (FHL# microfilm 982408, item 6)

Biography

Michigan biographical publications are listed under the FHLC heading **Michigan/Biography**. Additional titles containing biographies of residents of individual counties are listed under **Michigan/[County]/Biography.** Important biographical publications in the collection are:

American Biographical History of Eminent and Self-Made Men, Michigan. Cincinnati, Ohio: Western Biographical Publishing Company, 1878. (FHL# 977.4/D3s or microfilm 874387, items 1-2, or 1035727, item 11)

Case, Herbert S., ed. *The Official Who's Who in Michigan*. Munsing, Mich.: H. S. Case, c.1936. (FHL# 977.4/D3c)

Lanman, Charles. *The Red Book of Michigan: A Civil, Military and Biographical History*. Detroit, Mich.: E. B. Smith, 1871. (FHL# 977.4/H21r or microfilm 1425611, item 1)

Loomis, Frances. *Michigan Biography Index*. New Haven, Conn.: Research Publications, c.1973. (FHL# microfilm 485331, items 4-5, or 1303166, 1303167, 1303168)

Memorial Record of the Northern Peninsula of Michigan. Tucson, Ariz.: W. C. Cox Co., 1974. (FHL# microfilm 1000076, item 3)

Men of Progress: Embracing Biographical Sketches of Representative Michigan Men, with An Outline History of the State. Salt Lake City: Genealogical Society of Utah, 1977. Microreproduction of original published Detroit: Evening News Association, 1900. (FHL# microfilm 1015819, item 3)

The Traverse Region, Historical and Descriptive: With Illustrations of Scenery and Portraits and Biographical Sketches of Some of Its Prominent Men and Pioneers. Chicago, Ill.: H. R. Page, 1884. (FHL# 977.4/H2tr or microfilm 924513, item 1)

Vanderlong, Jan B. *A Genealogical Record with Pictures of Frisians Who Became Americans 1809-1980*. Salt Lake City: Genealogical Society of Utah, 1983. (FHL# microfilm 1312836, item 10) Dutch immigration to Michigan.

Cemeteries

A large collection of Michigan cemetery tombstone inventories has been compiled. Statewide collections are listed under **Michigan/Cemeteries.** Additional publications are listed under **Michigan/[County]/Cemeteries.** Among the most significant entries are:

Members of the LDS Church in Michigan. *Cemetery Records of Michigan*. Salt Lake City: Genealogical Society of Utah, 1960-61. (FHL# 977.4/V22c or microfilm 873724, item 5)

Grand Army of the Republic. *Cemetery Index 1800's-1900's*. Salt Lake City: Genealogical Society of Utah, 1976. (FHL# A-G: microfilm 1002419, H-Roskins: 1002420, Roskins-Z: 1002421)

Grand Rapids, Michigan Public Library. *Cemetery Records of Michigan Soldiers, 1770-1930*. Salt Lake City: Genealogical Society of Utah, 1976. (FHL# A-Fri: microfilm 1002021, Fro-Poo: 1002022, Pop-Z: 1002023)

Har-Al, Inc., comp. *Michigan Cemetery Compendium*. Spring Harbor, Mich.: the Compiler, 1979. (FHL# 977.4/V37h)

Michigan Civil War Burial Records. Salt Lake City: Genealogical Society of Utah, 1978. (FHL# microfilm 1036797, item 13) A and B surnames only.

Mohneke, Edward Harvey, comp. *Cemetery Inscriptions, Michigan*. Grand Rapids, Mich.: E. H. Mohneke, 1938-44. (FHL# 977.4/V22m or microfilm 824260, items 3-5)

Census Records

Michigan state censuses were taken in 1837, 1845, 1854, 1864, 1874, 1884, 1894, and 1904. Prior to statehood, eighteen census enumerations were taken in 1710, 1749, 1759, 1760, 1765, 1769, 1773, 1779, 1782,

1789, 1795, 1796, 1805, 1810, 1818, 1821, 1827, and 1833-1834. Few are extant. Federal censuses for Michigan are available for 1820-80. The 1810 and 1890 census were destroyed by fire. Mortality schedules exist for 1850, 1860, 1870, and 1880. A special 1890 census of Civil War veterans and their widows can serve as partial substitute for the destroyed 1890 federal census.

A large collection of censuses relating to Michigan is cataloged under **Michigan/Census.** Additional printed censuses and indexes are accessed under **Michigan/-[County]/Census.**

Dilts, Bryan Lee, comp. *1890 Michigan Census Index of Civil War Veterans or Their Widows.* Salt Lake City: Index Publishing, c.1985. (FHL# 977.4/X22d)

Harlan, Elizabeth Taft, ed. *1830 Federal Census: Territory of Michigan.* Detroit, Mich.: Detroit Society for Genealogical Research, 1961. (FHL# 977.4/X2h/1830 or microfilm 926745, item 1)

Jackson, Ronald Vern, ed. *Michigan 1827 Index Census.* Bountiful Utah: Accelerated Indexing Systems, c.1984. (FHL# 977.4/X22e)

______. *Michigan 1820 Index Census.* Bountiful, Utah: Accelerated Indexing Systems, c.1981. (FHL# 977.4/-X22m/1820)

Russell, Donna Valley, ed. *Michigan Census, 1710-1820: Under the French, British and Americans.* Detroit, Mich.: Detroit Society for Genealogical Research, c.1982. (FHL# 977.4/X2r)

United States Census Office. *Census of Michigan Territory, 1820.* Salt Lake City: Genealogical Society of Utah, 1972. (FHL# microfilm 915334, items 2-3)

Williams, Ethel W., ed. *Michigan Mortality Record for Year Ending June 1, 1850.* Salt Lake City: Genealogical Society of Utah, 1973. (FHL# microfilm 927685, item 1)

Church Records

The Roman Catholic Church dominated Michigan religious life from 1702 when the first church, St. Anne's, was dedicated, through the 1830s. The quest for religious freedom brought many religious groups to the state. Beginning in 1803, the Lutheran Church in Michigan grew rapidly. Soon the Catholic and Lutheran Churches were the major denominations in Michigan.

A Methodist Episcopalian circuit rider conducted services as early as 1803 on the frontier. Membership grew steadily until the separation of the Methodists and Episcopalians around 1815, when separate churches continued to flourish. In 1816, some members of each denomination chose to worship as Presbyterians or Congregationalists, causing further separation from the original church. Today each group has large congregations in Michigan.

The Baptist Church was founded in Pontiac in 1816 by western New Yorkers. A small group of Moravians were living in Michigan during the Revolutionary War. During the mid-1800s, Universalists, Seventh-Day Adventists, Jews, Mormons, and Strangites, among others, settled in Michigan.

Church records listing christening, marriage, and death information are cataloged under **Michigan/-[County]/Church Records.** Regional church records are cataloged under **Michigan/Church Records.** Four important examples are:

Burns, David. *Marriage Register Kept by David Burns of Michigan Conference at Charlotte 1867.* Salt Lake City: Genealogical Society of Utah, 1964. (FHL# microfilm 926741, item 3)

Presbyterian Church, Presbytery of Lake Superior. *Church Records, 1854-1923.* Salt Lake City: Genealogical Society of Utah, 1974. (FHL# microfilm 955792, item 7)

Protestant Episcopal Church Diocese. *Registrar's Records and Confirmations.* Salt Lake City: Genealogical Society of Utah, 1974. (FHL# microfilm 955798, items 2-3)

Records of the Reverend Guilford S. Northrup, Minister of the Gospel. St. John's, Mich.: Clinton County Historical Society, c.1982. (FHL# 977.4/V2r)

Court and Probate Records

Prior to the establishment of Michigan Territory in 1805, one office for recording probate of wills was maintained in Detroit. In 1796, when Wayne County was formed, all legal proceedings were recorded in French and/or English. Prior to the close of the War of 1812, probate and all court records for Michigan were included in Wayne County records. The extant probate files for that time period are cataloged under **Michigan/Wayne County/Probate Records.** Other court records are listed under **Michigan/Wayne County/Court Records.**

Beginning in 1817, new counties were formed, each with independent courts. From that date, all probate and other court records are under county jurisdiction. Such court records are cataloged in the FHLC under **Michigan/[County]/Court Records** and **Michigan/-[County]/Probate Records.** Search the parent county records for all legal transactions prior to the formation of later counties.

Michigan Supreme Court records for the years 1805-57 are cataloged under **Michigan/Court Records.** Each county, at its creation, established a register of deeds to record all land transfers, including mortgages but excluding land contracts.

Michigan Supreme Court. *Court Records 1819-1857: Index to Cases, 1805-1857.* Salt Lake City: Genealogical Society of Utah, 1974. (FHL# microfilm 955819, item 1, 955816-955818)

Genealogy Collections

Daughters of the American Revolution, Genealogical Records Committee, Michigan. *Alice D. Serrell Collection: Abridged From Oakland County Records.* Salt Lake City: Genealogical Society of Utah, 1981. (FHL# microfilm 1311580, item 8; 1311581, item 1)

______. *Genealogical Records.* Salt Lake City: Genealogical Society of Utah, 1973. (Index on FHL# microfilm 926747-926751, 927674-927677)

Hammell Collection. Salt Lake City: Genealogical Society of Utah, 1973. (FHL# microfilm 927697-927701)

Huguenot Society of Michigan. *Applications for Membership in the Huguenot Society of Michigan.* Salt Lake City: Genealogical Society of Utah, 1971. (FHL# microfilm 860658, item 2)

Michigan Genealogical Council. *Centennial Family Certificate Applications.* 81 reels. Salt Lake City: Genealogical Society of Utah, 1983. (FHL# microfilm 1321843-1321948, 1377719-1377725) Includes indexes, lineages, charts, vital records, censuses, and other important documents.

Michigan Pioneer Records, 1800-1900. Salt Lake City: Genealogical Society of Utah, 1973-74. (FHL# microfilm 934548-934554, 926735-926740. Second filming FHL# microfilm 1001970-1001978)

Michigan State Library. *Link Collection.* Lansing: State Library, 1973. (FHL# microfilm 927668-927673, 931411-931416)

Michigan State Library. *Pioneer Family Collection.* Salt Lake City: Genealogical Society of Utah, 1973. (FHL# microfilm 927650-927667, 931417)

Michigan State Library. *Michigan Bible Records, Family Histories.* Salt Lake City: Genealogical Society of Utah, 1981. (FHL# microfilm 1311581, item 2)

Monteith Collection. Salt Lake City: Genealogical Society of Utah, 1950. (FHL# A-L: microfilm 927706, M-T: 927707, U-Z: 927649)

Thomas Collection. Salt Lake City: Genealogical Society of Utah, 1973. (FHL# microfilm 927704-927705)

Western Genealogical Society Surname Index, 1600's-1900's. Salt Lake City: Genealogical Society of Utah, 1976. (FHL# A-Q: microfilm 1002371, R-Z: 1002372)

Williams, Ethel W. *Michigan Family Register.* Salt Lake City: Genealogical Society of Utah, 1981. (FHL# microfilm 1311581-1311582)

History

Fuller, George Newman. *Historica [sic] Michigan, Land of the Great Lakes.* Dayton, Ohio: National Historical Association, 1928. (FHL# 977.4/H2f or microfiche 6051135)

Sheldon, E. M. *The Early History of Michigan from the First Settlement to 1815.* Salt Lake City: Genealogical Society of Utah, 1984. (FHL# microfilm 1035672, item 16)

Tuttle, Charles Richard. *General History of the State of Michigan.* Detroit, Mich.: R. D. S. Tyler, 1873. (FHL# 977.4 H2t or microfilm 1000075, item 1, or 1015815, item 1)

Welch, Richard Warren. *County Evolution in Michigan, 1790, 1897.* Lansing: Department of Education, 1972. (FHL# 977.4/A1/no.7 or microfilm 896902, item 3)

Williams, Ethel W. *The Counties and Townships of Michigan Past and Present.* N.p.: n.pub.: c.1972. (FHL# 977.4/A1/-no.11)

Land and Property

Michigan was included in the Public Domain owned by the federal government. On 26 March 1804, the first land office was opened in Detroit. The deeds, also called patents, and tract books showing the original conveyance of land from the government to private ownership are in the National Archives. These records are not part of the Family History Library collection. Subsequent land transfers are recorded in each county. Only a limited number of county land records are available; consult the FHLC under **Michigan/[County]/Land Records.**

Military Records

Brown, Brig. Gen George H., Adjutant General. *Record of Service of Michigan Volunteers in the Civil War, 1861-1865.* Detroit, Mich.: Detroit Book Press, c.1980s. (FHL# 977.4/M2r)

Grand Army of the Republic. Department of Michigan. *Records of Posts 1876-1945.* Salt Lake City: Genealogical Society of Utah, 1973. (FHL# microfilm 905724-905750, 915894-915919, 927041-927052, 915935-915946)

Katz, Irving I. *The Jewish Soldier from Michigan in the Civil War.* Detroit, Mich.: Wayne State University Press, 1962. (FHL# 977.4/M25k)

Michigan Adjutant General's Office. *Michigan Volunteer Descriptive Rolls, 1861-1866.* 76 reels. Salt Lake City: Genealogical Society of Utah, 1972. (Index FHL# A-O: microfilm 915346, P-Z: 915347, item 1.) See FHLC for call numbers.

Michigan Adjutant General's Office. *Michigan Volunteers, Spanish American War Muster Out Rolls 1898-1899.* Salt Lake City: Genealogical Society of Utah, 1973. (Index FHL# microfilm 915347, item 2, 915489-915492)

Michigan National Guard. *Michigan State Troops and National Guard, 1858-1905.* Salt Lake City: Genealogical Society of Utah, 1973. (FHL# microfilm 915338-915344)

Michigan State Library. *World War I Card Index.* Salt Lake City: Genealogical Society of Utah, 1976. (FHL# microfilm 1001930-1001966)

Miller, Alice Turner. *Soldiers of the War of 1812, Who Died in Michigan.* Ithaca, Mich.: A. T. Miller, 1962. (FHL# 977.4/ M23m or microfilm 844961, item 3)

Soldiers' Home, Grand Rapids, Michigan. *Applications for Admission, 1885-1960.* 75 reels. Salt Lake City: Genealogical Society of Utah, 1972. See FHLC for call numbers.

_____. *History Register of Inhabitants, 1885-1927.* Salt Lake City: Genealogical Society of Utah, 1972. (Index FHL# microfilm 925039, men 915493-915500, women 925038)

United States Adjutant General's Office. *Index to Compiled Service Records of Volunteers Soldiers Who Served from the State of Michigan during the Patriot War, 1838-1839.* Washington, D.C.: National Archives, 1965. (FHL# microfilm 882795)

Vaughan, Coleman C., Secretary of State. *Alphabetical General Index to Public Library Sets of 85,271 Names of Michigan Soldiers and Sailors Individual Records.* Lansing: Michigan Secretary of State, 1915. (FHL# 977.4/ M22a or microfilm 915948)

Welch, Richard Warren, comp. *Michigan in the Mexican War.* N.p.: n.pub., 1967. (FHL# 977.4/M23w)

Native American Records

Before the 1630s when French explorers, traders, and missionaries settled in the Michigan area, all lands were held by the Ottawa, Chippewa, and smaller Indian tribes. The Indian Nations continued to dominate the region until 1763 when the British took possession. Indian conflicts continued intermittently until the close of the War of 1812.

Blackbird, Andrew J. *History of the Ottawa and Chippewa Indians of Michigan.* Ypsilanti, Mich.: n.pub., 1887. (FHL# 970.1/B562h or microfilm 924102, item 9, or 1011853, item 2)

Claspy, Everett. *The Potawatomi Indians of Southwestern Michigan.* Dowagiac, Mich.: n.pub., 1966. (FHL# 970.3/-P848c)

U.S. Bureau of Indian Affairs. *A Census Register of All the Men, Women and Children Coming Within the Sixth Article of the Treaty Made with the Ottawa and Chippewa Nations of Indians on 28 March 1836.* Salt Lake City: Genealogical Society of Utah, 1977. (FHL# Q/970.1/A1/no.4 or microfilm 982330)

Naturalization Records

Declarations, petitions, and other naturalization records prior to 1906 were recorded with the county clerk's office. Very few naturalization records are included in the Family History Library collection. For holdings consult the FHLC under **Michigan/[County]/Naturalization Records.**

Tax Records

Taxation records for 1835 to 1855 are available for only a small portion of Michigan counties. The state censuses serve as a superior substitute for tax records. For the approximate fifteen counties with extant tax records, consult the FHLC under **Michigan/[County]/Tax Records.**

Vital Records

The Michigan Marriage Registration Act, passed in 1805, required registration of all marriages with the clerk of the district court. When counties were formed, the records were transferred to the county clerks. Marriage licenses have only been required since 1887. Statewide registration of vital records began in 1867 with records filed with the State Department of Health in Lansing, Michigan 48914. Prior to 1867, the clerk of the circuit court had jurisdiction of all vital records. A majority of the birth, marriage, and death records filed on a county level are available in the Family History Library collection, cataloged under **Michigan/[County]/Vital Records** with other collections cataloged under **Michigan/Vital Records**. Several noteworthy titles are:

Daughters of the American Revolution. Louisa St. Clair Chapter. *Marriage Records of Early Michigan; Mainly of Detroit, Michigan, 1838-1849.* Salt Lake City: Genealogical Society of Utah, 1873. (FHL# microfilm 973473, item 1)

Death and Marriage Items Reported in the Lansing State Republican, 1855-1860. Lansing: Mid-Michigan Genealogical Society, 1968. (FHL# 977.427/V4d or microfilm 496751, item 2, or 925955, item 1)

deZeeuw, Donald J. *Death and Marriage, Items Abstracted from the Lansing State Republican, 1861-1871: and Some Divorces and Name Changes Noted in the Michigan Territorial and State Laws.* Lansing: Mid-Michigan Genealogical Society, 1978. (FHL# 977.4/A1/no.52 or microfilm 1036010, item 4)

Grand Rapids Public Library. *Brides' Names 1850-1869.* Salt Lake City: Genealogical Society of Utah, 1976. (FHL# microfilm 1002012)

Historical Records Survey, Michigan. *Vital Records from the Detroit Free Press 1831-1868.* Salt Lake City: Genealogical Society of Utah, 1973. (FHL# microfilm 927477-927479)

Michigan Christian Herald. *Michigan Vital Records from the Michigan Christian Herald 1850-1859.* Salt Lake City: Genealogical Society of Utah, 1974. (FHL# microfilm 955799, item 2)

IOWA

Historical Background

1673	Joliet and Marquette explore Iowa region for France.
1762	France cedes part of Louisiana including Iowa to Spain.
1788	First settler, Julien Dubuque, begins mining lead near Dubuque.
1800	Louisiana transferred by Spain to France.
1803	United States acquires Iowa in the Louisiana Purchase.
1808-16	United States Army builds four forts in Iowa.
1808	Illinois Territory established, includes Iowa.
1812-21	Iowa included in Missouri Territory.
1821-37	Wisconsin and Michigan territories include present-day Iowa.
1832	Black Hawk War and Treaty; first Indian Session of eastern Iowa opens lands for settlement.
1833	Settlers from Tennessee, Kentucky, Missouri, Illinois, Ohio, and Indiana establish permanent settlements in Iowa.
1834-36	Counties of Demoine and Dubuque, Iowa, established as part of Michigan Territory.
1836	Wisconsin Territory created, Iowa included. Iowa territorial census. First public land surveys taken.

1838	Iowa Territory created with capital at Burlington; influx of settlers. Iowa territorial census.
1840	Territorial law requires marriage licenses and records. Territorial capital moved to Iowa City.
1840s	Scandinavians, Dutch, Germans, Scots, and Welsh settlers immigrate to Iowa.
1846	Iowa becomes the twenty-ninth state of the Union on 28 December. Mormon migration to Iowa.
1846-57	Iowa City serves as capital.
1850-80	Mass German migration to Iowa.
1850-77	Steamboat industry peak years.
1855	First Iowa railroad links Davenport and Muscatine. State capital changed to Des Moines.
1861-65	Civil War.
1867	Railroad completed across Iowa from Mississippi River to Council Bluffs.
1880	Statewide registration of vital records by counties with copies ordered to the state office.

Settlement and Migration

Prior to 1800 Indians and French were the only residents in Iowa. In 1832 a group from Denmark settled in Lee County. The following year, families and individuals from Kentucky, Tennessee, Missouri, Illinois, Ohio, and Indiana moved into Iowa and established homes throughout the state.

Before 1836, some immigrants from France lived in St. Mary's, Pottawatomie County; Dubuque, Dubuque County; Girard, Clayton County; Bellevue, Jackson County; Montrose, Lee County; Salix, Woodbury County; Woolstock, Wright County; and Gilbertville, Blackhawk County.

Pioneers from Kentucky, Virginia, and Tennessee lived in settlements scattered throughout the state. Families from New England moved to Bradford, Chickasaw County in 1840. Quakers relocated in Salem, Henry County in 1841. During the 1840s immigrants from Scandinavia, Holland, Germany, Scotland, and Wales resided in or near communities scattered over Iowa.

In 1846 Mormons migrated into Decatur, Clark, Union, Cass, and Mills counties and Council Bluffs, Pottawatomie County. The next year, Irish and Germans settled in western Monroe County, while immigrants from Utrecht, Leerdam, Noordeloos, Amsterdam and other cities migrated to Pella, Marion County. Between 1850 and 1880 Germans were scattered throughout the state. In 1854 a large number of families from Ohio settled statewide.

Archives and Libraries

Gilman, Alcys, comp. *Unpublished Genealogies in the Iowa Historical Library*. Salt Lake City: Genealogical Society of Utah, 1984. (FHL# 977.7/A5g or microfiche 6046633)

Historical Records Survey, Iowa. *Guide To Depositories of Manuscript Collections in the United States: Iowa.* Des Moines: Iowa Historical Records Survey, 1940. (FHL# 977.7/A5h)

Atlases, Gazetteers, and Maps

Andreas, A. T. *A. T. Andreas' Illustrated Historical Atlas of the State of Iowa, 1875.* Chicago, Ill.: Lakeside Press, 1875. (FHL# 977.7/E3a or microfilm 908275 or 966233, item 2)

Atlas of the State of Iowa. Salt Lake City: Genealogical Society of Utah, 1974. (FHL# microfilm 966236, item 1)

A Township Map of the State of Iowa. Fairfield, Iowa: Henn, Williams 1855. (FHL# Map Case 977.7/E7h or microfilm 823579, item 10)

Clements, Diane. *Handcart Trail, 1856-1857, Iowa.* Salt Lake City: Deseret Press, c.1978. (FHL# 977.7/E7cd, part 1)

Colton, C. Woolworth. *Township Map of the State of Iowa, 1864.* Salt Lake City: Genealogical Society of Utah, 1974. (FHL# microfilm 960049, item 11)

Hair, James T., comp. *Iowa State Gazetteer.* Chicago, Ill.: Bailey & Hair, 1865. (FHL# 977.7/E4h or microfilm 982200, item 2 or 1024846, item 5)

Ramsey, Guy Reed. *Postmarked Iowa: A List of Discontinued and Renamed Post Offices.* Crete, Neb.: J-B Publishing, c.1976. (FHL# 977.7/E5r)

R. L. Polk and Company. *Iowa State Gazetteers and Business Directory.* Salt Lake City: Genealogical Society of Utah, 1976. (FHL# microfilm 989449, item 9, and 1007937, item 3)

Shambaugh, Benjamin F. *Maps Illustrative of the Boundary History of Iowa.* Salt Lake City: Genealogical Society of Utah, 1976. (FHL# microfilm 989450, item 3)

Biography

Published biographies are cataloged under **Iowa/Biography and Iowa/[County]/Biography.** Important titles include:

Citizens Historical Association. *Biographical Sketches of Iowans.* Salt Lake City: Genealogical Society of Utah, 1976. (FHL# microfilm 985407-985409)

Gue, B. F. *Biographies and Portraits of the Progressive Men of Iowa: Leaders in Business, Politics and the Professions: Together with An Original and Authentic History of the State.* Des Moines: Conaway & Shaw, 1899. 2 vols. (FHL# 977.7/D3b or microfilm 934927, items 2-3)

Iowa State Department of History and Archives. *Biographical Data Collection.* Salt Lake City: Genealogical Society of Utah, 1978. (FHL# microfilm 1023885-1023889, item 1)

Iowa State Department of History and Archives. *Biography Files.* Salt Lake City: Genealogical Society of Utah, 1978. (FHL# microfilm 1023616, item 2-1023619)

A Memorial and Biographical Record of Iowa. Marceline, Mo.: Walsworth Publishing Company, 1978. (FHL# 977.7/-D3m/Vol. 1 or microfilm 1033791, items 2-3)

Morford, Charles. *Biographical Index to the County Histories of Iowa.* Baltimore, Md.: Gateway Press, c.1979. (FHL# 977.7/D32m)

The United States Biographical Dictionary and Portrait Gallery of Eminent and Self-Made Men. Chicago, Ill.: American Biographical Publishing Company, 1878. (FHL# 977.7/-D3u or microfilm 934926, item 5)

Cemetery Records

A large collection of cemetery tombstone inscriptions are included in the Iowa collection cataloged under **Iowa/Cemetery Records** and **Iowa/[County]/Cemetery Records.**

Flake, Marion Stewart. *Cemetery Records of Iowa.* Salt Lake City: Genealogical Society of Utah, 1967. (FHL# 977.7/V22f or microfilm 823732, item 1)

Iowa Cemetery Inscriptions. Salt Lake City: Genealogical Society of Utah, 1980. (FHL# microfilm 1033527, item 8)

Iowa, State Department of History and Archives. *Iowa Cemeteries.* Salt Lake City: Genealogical Society of Utah, 1978. (FHL# microfilm 1023603, items 6-13 through 1023609, items 1-10)

_____. *Iowa Cemetery and Grave Records by Grave Registration Project of the W.P.A. and D.A.R.* Salt Lake City: Genealogical Society of Utah, 1978. (FHL# microfilm 1022211-1022213 and 1023097-1023114, items 1-3)

Iowa War Record Survey. *Graves Registration Division: Iowa Veterans Buried out of State.* Salt Lake City: Genealogical Society of Utah, 1878. (FHL# microfilm 1023908-1023917, items 1-11)

Pompey, S. L. *Civil War Veterans Burials from Various States.* Salt Lake City: Genealogical Society of Utah, 1868. (FHL# microfilm 564336-564341, item 1)

Census Records

Numerous important Iowa territorial and state censuses supplemented the federal censuses which began in 1840 and continued every ten years. Iowa territorial and state censuses were taken in 1836, 1838, 1844, 1846, 1847, 1849, 1851, 1852, 1854, 1856, 1859, 1862, 1865, 1867, 1869, 1873, 1875, 1885, 1895, 1905, 1915, and 1925. Many are missing. Extant censuses in the Iowa collection are listed under **Iowa/Census** and **Iowa/[County]/Census.**

Jackson, Ronald Vern, ed. *Iowa 1836 Territorial Census Index.* Bountiful, Utah: Accelerated Indexing Systems, 1976. (FHL# 977.7/X22j/1836)

Iowa, Executive Council. *Census Register, 1905.* Salt Lake City: Genealogical Society of Utah, 1978 (FHL# microfilm 1026366-1026520)

Iowa Special Census. Salt Lake City: Genealogical Society of Utah, 1978. (FHL# microfilm 1022202, item 3)

Jackson, Ronald Vern. *Iowa 1836 Territorial Census.* Bountiful, Utah: Accelerated Indexing Systems, Inc., c.1973. (FHL# 977.7/A1/no.10)

_____. *Iowa 1838 Territorial Census Index.* Bountiful, Utah: Accelerated Indexing Systems, c.1984. (FHL# 977.7/-X22ji/1838)

_____. *Iowa Census Records 1841-1849.* Salt Lake City: Accelerated Indexing Systems, c.1979. (FHL# 977.7/-X22/1841-49)

Obert, Rowene. *The 1840 Iowa Census.* Salt Lake City: n.pub., 1968. (FHL# 977.7/X2p/1840 or microfilm 844885, item 3)

Church Records

Church records are particularly important to genealogical research as they often predate vital records registrations. Births, christenings, baptisms, marriages, deaths, burials, cemetery records, admissions, removals, and membership lists are often found in the local church records and in regional or state church repositories. Catholic, Methodist, Lutheran, and Baptist churches were predominant in Iowa with smaller groups of Quakers, Mormons, Amish, Mennonites, and Congregationalists.

Church records are cataloged under both state and county headings.

Court and Probate Records

All Iowa court records are cataloged under **Iowa/[County]/Court Records** and **Iowa/[County]/-Probate Records.** Civil and criminal court records were filed with the county clerks. Matters of probate, including wills, administrator or executor bonds, inventories, and guardianships were kept by the clerk of the county district court.

Directories

Directories, especially statewide compilations, are important as they supplement state and federal census, and act as finding aids in genealogical research. Regional and statewide titles are listed under **Iowa/Directories. Local Directories** are listed under **Iowa/[County]/-Directories.**

Business Directory of the Burlington, Cedar Rapids and Northern Railway, 1882-1883. Salt Lake City: Genealogical Society of Utah, 1978. (FHL# microfilm 1024840, item 1)

Farmers of Iowa: A List of Farmers of Each County with Post Offices. Salt Lake City: Genealogical Society of Utah, 1978. (FHL# microfilm 1024846, item 4)

Sopp, Elsie L. *Personal Name Index to the 1856 City Directories of Iowa.* Detroit, Mich.: Gale Research Company, 1980 (FHL# 977.7/D42s)

Genealogical Collections

Cataloged in the FHLC under **Iowa/Genealogy** and **Iowa/[County]/Genealogy** are numerous important publications. Notable titles include:

Charts and Genealogies of Pioneer Families of Iowa. Salt Lake City: Genealogical Society of Utah, 1975. (FHL# 977.7/D2c or microfilm 908960, item 4)

Daughters of the American Revolution, Iowa. *Early Settlers of Iowa.* Salt Lake City: Genealogical Society of Utah, 1972. (FHL# microfilm 907995, item 3)

______. *Revolutionary War Soldiers and Patriots Buried in Iowa.* Marceline, Mo.: Walsworth, c.1978. (FHL# 977.7/-D3d)

Iowa American Revolution Bicentennial Commission. *Century Farm Application.* Salt Lake City: Genealogical Society of Utah, 1879. (FHL# microfilm 1023895-1023902)

Iowa Mennonite Historical Society. *Ancestors of Members of Iowa Mennonite Historical Society.* Salt Lake City: Genealogical Society of Utah, 1976. (FHL# microfilm 989453, item 7)

Iowa State Department of History and Archives. *Fifty Year Iowa Farm Families.* Salt Lake City: Genealogical Society of Utah, 1978. Genealogies of Iowa families who proved constant ownership of a farm for at least fifty years. (FHL# microfilm 1023893 and 1023894)

______. *Biographical Data Collection.* Salt Lake City: Genealogical Society of Utah, 1978. (FHL# microfilm 1023885-1023889 and 1023620)

______. *Family Record Collection.* Salt Lake City: Genealogical Society of Utah, 1978. (FHL# microfilm 1023611-1023616)

Stofferan, Janice. *Northwest Iowa Pioneers.* N.p.: n.pub., c.1978. (FHL# 977.7/D2sa or microfilm 1036275, item 4, and 1036746, item 5)

The Iowa Genealogical Society Surname Index. Des Moines: Iowa Genealogical Society, 1973. (FHL# 977.7/D2i)

History

The library has numerous state and county histories cataloged under **Iowa/History** and **Iowa/[County]/History.**

Allen, Arthur Francis, ed. *Northwestern Iowa: Its History and Traditions, 1804-1926.* Chicago, Ill.: S. J. Clarke Publishing Company, 1927. (FHL# 977.7/H2a or microfilm 823577, 823578 or 934929, items 2-4)

MacBride, Thomas Huston. *In Cabins and Sod-Houses.* Iowa City: State Historical Society, 1928. (FHL# 977.7/H2m or microfilm 924679, item 1)

Parvin. T. S. *Who Made Iowa, or, Who Are the Pioneers and Old Settlers of Iowa: And Their Work in the Making of the State.* Salt Lake City: Genealogical Society of Utah, 1977. Microreproduction of the original published: n.p. n.pub., 1896. (FHL# microfilm 967584, item 6)

Shambaugh, Benjamin. *Biographies and Portraits of the Progressive Men of Iowa: Leaders in Business, Politics and the Professions: Together with an Original and Authentic History of the State.* Des Moines: Conaway & Shaw, 1899. (FHL# 977.7/D3b or microfilm 934927, items 2-3)

Land and Property Records

Iowa was a public land state and therefore, original land disposition was made by the federal government and its agents. State and federal Land Offices were located at fourteen different cities between 1838 and 1910. Iowa land was also distributed to individuals who were authorized to receive military land warrants after the Mexican War.

For publications discussing many of these land dispositions, consult the FHLC under **Iowa/Land and Property**. Subsequent land transfers were recorded by each county recorder beginning with the establishment of the county.

Military Records

Iowa Adjutant General's Office. *Persons Subject to Military Duty, ca. 1862-1910.* 94 reels. Salt Lake City: Genealogical Society of Utah, 1978. See FHLC for call numbers.

Revolutionary War Soldiers and Patriots Buried in Iowa. Marceline, Mo.: Walworth, c.1978. (FHL# 977.73d)

United States Adjutant General's Office. *Index to Compiled Service Records of Volunteer Union Soldiers Who Served in Organizations from the State of Iowa.* Washington, D.C.: National Archives, 1964. (FHL# microfilm 881808-881836)

Minorities and Ethnic Groups

Christensen, Thomas Peter. *A History of the Danes in Iowa.* New York: Arno Press, 1979. (FHL# 977.7/F2c)

Flom, George T. *Chapters on Scandinavian Immigration to Iowa.* Salt Lake City: Genealogical Society of Utah, 1976. (FHL# microfilm 989450, item 7)

Glazewr, Simon. *The Jews of Iowa.* Salt Lake City: Genealogical Society of Utah, 1976. (FHL# microfilm 989450, item 6)

Nelson, O. M. *Swedish Settlements in Iowa: With Biographies of Swedish Men and Women in Des Moines and Vicinity.* N.p.: n.pub., n.d. (FHL# 977.796/F2n)

Van der Zee, Jacob. *The British in Iowa.* Tucson, Ariz.: W. C. Cox Company, 1974. (FHL# microfilm 934926, item 3)

______. *The Hollanders of Iowa.* Salt Lake City: Genealogical Society of Utah, 1976. (FHL# microfilm 989450, item 4)

Wick, Barthinius Larson. *The Amish Mennonites: A Sketch of Their Origins, and of Their Settlement in Iowa, with Their Creed in an Appendix.* Iowa City: State Historical Society, 1984. (FHL# 977.7/F2w)

Vital Records

With the exceptions of Lee and Woodbury counties, no birth or death records were kept in Iowa prior to 1880. From 1880 until 1921, an estimated 50 percent of the births and deaths were actually reported in the state. In 1880, by law, the state required that vital records be recorded with the clerk of each county district court, with a copy sent to the Division of Records and Statistics, State Department of Health, Des Moines, IA 50319. Only a small portion of the county vital records have been microfilmed. For holdings, consult the FHLC under **Iowa/[County]/Vital Records**. For published vital records, see **Iowa/Vital Records**. Many Iowa counties began keeping marriage records beginning with the formation of the county. Those records are also cataloged under the county heading.

ILLINOIS

Historical Background

1670s	French explorers Marquette and Joliet travel throughout Illinois river valleys.
1682	First settlement established at Kaskaskia.
1699	First Catholic mission founded at Cahokia.
1703	Jesuit mission at Kaskaskia founded.
1717	Illinois governed by French from Louisiana.
1719	Fort de Chartres becomes the seat of military and civil government for area.
1763	Great Britain gains control from French at end of French and Indian War.
1778	George Rogers Clark captures Cahokia and Kaskaskia; Illinois organized as a county of Virginia.
1784	Virginia relinquishes her claim to Illinois.
1787	Congress establishes the Northwest Territory which includes Illinois.
1790	St. Clair and Knox counties formed.
1791	Special Act of Congress gives 400 acres to all families residing in Illinois prior to 1788.
1797-1818	Influx of settlers from Kentucky, Virginia, and North Carolina.
1800	Indian Territory, including Illinois, established.
1804	Government Land Office opens.
1809	Illinois Territory, which includes Wisconsin, created. First capital at Kaskaskia.
1810	First federal census. Missing except Randolph County.
1812	War of 1812.
1813	Preemption Act allows pre-1809 settlers to purchase public lands.
1814	First Illinois newspaper, *Illinois Herald,* published at Kaskaskia. Preemption Land Act extended to post-1809 settlers.
1818	Illinois admitted as twenty-first state, with Vandalia as the capital.
1825	Settlers, mainly from New England, migrate to northern Illinois.
1832	Indians defeated in Black Hawk War.
1833	Chicago founded.
1837	Illinois state capital moved to Springfield.
1838	National Road reaches Vandalia.
1839-46	Mormons found Nauvoo, Hancock County.
1842	First train reaches Springfield.
1848	Illinois and Michigan Canal completed.
1860	One-fourteenth of all immigrants landing at New York migrate to Illinois.
1861-65	Civil War.
1871	Three and one-half square mile section of Chicago destroyed by fire.
1877	Registration of vital records by counties ordered.
1916	Statewide registration of vital records mandated by law.

Settlement and Migration

During 1682 Kaskaskia Island was settled by the French, and two years later, additional French pioneers from New Orleans joined the settlement. French immigrants established Fort Chartres in 1720. Between 1765 and 1820 there was an influx of Southerners who migrated to southern Illinois via Kentucky. Many fled during Indian hostilities, but returned later.

The period of 1800 and 1820 brought additional Southerners from North Carolina, Virginia, and Kentucky and others from the Mid-Atlantic states of Maryland and Pennsylvania into southern Illinois. Between 1815 and 1825 English immigrants settled the southern section of the state, and in 1818 two hundred English migrated to Edwards County.

Fifty-three Norwegians, migrated via New York to Fox River, Illinois, and New Englanders moved into the northern sections of the state in 1825. During the 1830s, newly arrived immigrants from Ireland, Poland, Germany, Italy, Sweden, and Russia established new homes in northern Illinois around Lake Michigan. Also during that decade pioneers from Vermont established Greengarden, Will County; Vermonters settled at Wheatland Village in Sangamon County and in Fremont, Lake County, and founded Virgennes, Jackson County. New Hampshire and Vermont settlers established Bureau and Putnam counties. In 1832 DuPage County attracted a colony from Benson, Vermont.

Norwegians settled LaSalle County and Chicago in Cook County in 1836. Between 1839 and 1848 Mormons from Missouri built the city of Nauvoo in Hancock County. Many Swedish immigrants moved to Chicago, from 1846 through 1880. Former residents of Zuid-Holland established South Holland in Cook County in 1847, and two years later, colonists from Krabbenden, Holland, founded Roseland, Cook County.

Prior to 1850 two hundred Virginia families settled in Edgar County. In 1850 Vermonters moved to New Rutland, LaSalle County. During the decade of the 1850s, a potato famine in Ireland motivated many Irish to emigrate to the United States. Many moved to northern Illinois. Many of these Irish immigrants worked for the railroad and road-building companies, following the available jobs. From 1875 through 1920 Irish immigrants continued to settle in the region around Lake Michigan.

Although many early Illinois families migrated westward, Southern settlers, including some Germans, moved to southern Illinois, particularly Union County, prior to 1800. Many were forced out of the area for a few years by hostile Indians but returned when it was safer. There they prospered; but in the 1820s, a large group migrated together to Crawford and Washington counties in Arkansas. While many members of this colony put down permanent roots in northwestern Arkansas, others migrated into northeastern and central Texas in the 1830s and 1840s, where the families are still represented today.

Illinois Library Collection

Archives and Libraries

Cassady, Theodore J. *Illinois State Archives, Guide to Records Holdings.* N.p.: n.pub., 1964. (FHL# 977.3/A5c or microfilm 1036658, item 7)

Guide to Depositories of Manuscript Collections in Illinois. Chicago, Ill.: Historical Records Survey Project, 1940. (FHL# 977.3/A5gd)

Illinois State Historical Library. *Alphabetic Catalog of the Books, Manuscripts, Maps, Pictures and Curios of the Illinois State Historical Library.* Springfield: Phillips, 1900. (FHL# 977.3/C4h/Vol. 5 or microfilm 982308, item 3)

Illinois State Historical Society Library. *Index to Transactions of the Illinois State Historical Society and Other Publications of the Illinois State Historical Society.* Springfield: The Library, 1953. (FHL# 977.3/C4h or microfilm 982308, item 1-2)

Illinois State Historical Library and Society. *General Index to Collections, Journals, Publications, 1899-1928.* Quincy, Ill.: Royal Printing, 1930. (FHL# 977.3/C4ha or microfilm 982342, item 1)

Pease, Theodore Calvin. *The County Archives of the State of Illinois.* N.p.: n.pub., n.d. (FHL# microfilm 381798)

Atlases, Gazetteers, and Maps

Adams, James N. *Illinois Place Names.* Springfield: Illinois State Historical Society, 1968. (FHL# 977.3/E5s or microfiche 6051287)

Beck, Lewis Caleb. *A Gazetteer of Illinois and Missouri.* New York: Arno Press, 1975. (FHL# 977/E5b or microfiche 6010063 or microfilm 1036690, item 6)

Illinois Guide and Gazetteer. Chicago, Ill.: Rand McNally, c.1969. (FHL# 977.3/E5i)

Map of Illinois Divided into Townships. N.p.: United States Geological Survey, 1943. (FHL# 977.3/E7d)

Mitchell, S. Augustus. *County and Township Map of the State of Illinois.* N.p.: n.pub., 1979. (FHL# 977.2/E7m)

Peck, J. M. *A Gazetteer of Illinois in Three Parts.* Philadelphia: Grigg and Elliott, 1837. (FHL# 977.3/E5p or microfilm 897008, item 3)

Biography

Biographical publications comprise a large part of the general Illinois collection and are cataloged under **Illinois/Biography** or **Illinois/[County]/Biography**, depending on their scope.

Bateman, Newton. *Historical Encyclopedia of Illinois.* Tucson, Ariz.: W. C. Cox, 1974. (FHL# microfilm 825559 or 934973, items 2-3)

_____. *Historical Encyclopedia of Illinois with Commemorative Biographies.* Tucson, Ariz.: W. C. Cox, 1974. (FHL# microfilm 1000173, items 3-4)

The Biographical Encyclopedia of Illinois of the Nineteenth Century. Tucson, Ariz.: W. C. Cox, 1974. (FHL# microfilm 1000172, item 1)

Conger, John Leonard. *History of the Illinois River Valley.* Chicago, Ill.: S. J. Clarke Publishing Company, 1932. (FHL# 977.3/H2c or microfilm 1000171)

Encyclopedia of Biography of Illinois. Chicago, Ill.: Century Publishing and Engraving Company, 1892-1910. (FHL# 977.3/D3e)

In Memoriam, Founders and Makers of Illinois, A Memorial History of the State's Honored Dead. Chicago, Ill.: S. J. Clarke Publishing Company, n.d. (FHL# 977.3/D3i)

The United States Biographical Dictionary and Portrait Gallery of Eminent and Self-Made Men, Illinois Volume. Tucson, Ariz.: W. C. Cox, 1974. (FHL# microfilm 1000172, item 2)

Cemetery Records

Inventories of cemetery tombstone inscriptions are cataloged under **Illinois/Cemetery Records** and **Illinois/[County]/Cemetery Records.** Notable titles include:

Cemetery Records of Illinois. Salt Lake City: Genealogical Society of Utah, 1972. 3 vols. (FHL# 977.3/V22g or microfilm 824272-824274, items 2-4)

Daughters of the American Revolution, Illinois. *Cemetery Records.* Salt Lake City: Genealogical Society of Utah, 1972. (FHL# microfilm 907987, item 3)

Gill, James V., ed. *Illiana Research Report.* Danville, Ill.: Illiana Genealogical Pub., c.1966. (FHL# 977.3/V2ig)

Sargent, Samuel S., comp. *Cemetery Relocations by the U.S. Army Corps of Engineers in Illinois, Iowa, Missouri, Arkansas.* St. Louis, Mo.: St. Louis Genealogical Society, 1977. (FHL# 977/V22s)

Soldiers' Burial Places in State of Illinois for Wars 1774-1898. 31 reels. Salt Lake City: Genealogical Society of Utah, 1975. (FHL# microfilm 1001183-1001211)

Walker, Harriet J. *Soldiers of the American Revolution Buried in Illinois.* Salt Lake City: Genealogical Society of Utah, 1973. (FHL# 977.3/V22wh or microfilm 908831, item 3)

Census Records

Federal censuses of Illinois were taken every ten years beginning in 1810. The 1810 federal census was destroyed except for Randolph County. The 1890 census was also destroyed. Illinois state censuses were taken in 1810, 1818, 1820, 1825, 1830, 1835, 1840, 1845, 1855, and

1865. The state censuses for 1810-55 are indexed and available on microfilm in the Illinois collection.

Frederick, Nancy Gubb. *The 1880 Illinois Census Index: Soundex Code 0-200-0-240, The Code That Was Not Filmed.* Evanston, Ill.: Frederick, 1981. (FHL# 977.3/X2f)

Illinois Secretary of State. *1855 State Census of Illinois.* Salt Lake City: Genealogical Society of Utah, 1975. (FHL# microfilm 976178, item 11, through 976186, and 976670-976673, and 977062-977063)

Jackson, Ronald Vern. *Illinois 1825 State Census Index.* Bountiful, Utah: Accelerated Indexing Systems, c.1984. (FHL# 977.3/X2j/1825)

_____. *Illinois 1835 State Census Index.* Bountiful, Utah: Accelerated Indexing Systems, c.1984. (FHL# 977.3/-X2j/1835)

Mortality Schedules of Illinois, 1850-1880. (Illinois): Records Management Division, Secretary of State's Office, 1967. (FHL# microfilm 1421024-1421030)

Name Index to Early Illinois Records. (Includes Census). Springfield: Illinois State Archives 1975. (FHL# microfilm 1001592-1001801)

Norton, Margaret Cross, ed. *Illinois Census Returns, 1810-1818.* Baltimore, Md.: Genealogical Publishing Company, 1969. (FHL# 977.3/B4i/Vol. 24 or microfilm 897331, item 2)

Volkel, Lowell M., comp. *Illinois Mortality Schedule, 1860.* Indianapolis, Ind.: Heritage House, 1979. (FHL# 977.3/X2i)

Church Records

Church records often pre-date public records, not only documenting events but frequently establishing familial relationships. Local church records are cataloged under **Illinois/Church Records** and **Illinois/[County]/Church Records.** In 1850, Methodists were the largest religious group in Illinois, followed by Baptist, Presbyterians, Roman Catholics, Lutherans, and Congregationalists.

Abstracts of the Records of the Society of Friends of Vermillion Quarterly Meeting in Vermillion Grove, Illinois. Danville, Ill.: Illiana Genealogical and Historical Society, 1970. (FHL# 977.3/K2a)

American Baptist Historical Society. *The Records of American Baptists in Illinois and Related Organizations.* Rochester, N.Y.: The American Baptist Historical Society, c.1982. (FHL# 977.3/K2ab)

Eby, Lela, comp.. *Every Name Index Church of the Brethren in Southern Illinois.* Mill Valley, Calif.: Eby, c.1970s. (FHL# 977.3/A1/no.159 or microfilm 982409, item 1)

_____. *Every Name Index, Brethren in Northern Illinois and Wisconsin.* Mill Valley, Calif: Eby, n.d. (FHL# 977/-A1/no.3 or microfilm 928370, item 7)

Historical Records Survey, Illinois. *Inventory of the Church Archives of Illinois, Presbyterian Church in the United States of America Presbytery of Cairo.* Salt Lake City: Genealogical Society of Utah, 1977. (FHL# 977.3/K2hp or microfilm 1036527, item 4)

Methodist Episcopal Church. Illinois Conference. Paloma Circuit. *Church Records, 1861-1892.* Salt Lake City: Genealogical Society of Utah, 1974. (FHL# microfilm 965272, items 4-5)

Court and Probate Records

The clerk of each Illinois county circuit court is responsible for recording all business, chancery, civil, criminal, divorce, guardianship, insanity, naturalizations, and probate matters. After 1848, divorces were filed with the chancery clerk of the circuit court, who also became responsible for all chancery actions. The clerk of the probate court's duties evolved to handle all estate, guardianship, and probate matters.

Court and probate titles are cataloged under **Illinois/[County]/Court Records** and/or **Illinois/[County]/Probate Records.**

Directories

Hawes, George W. *Illinois State Gazetteer and Business Directory for 1858-1859.* Salt Lake City: Genealogical Society of Utah, 1974. (FHL# microfilm 961869, item 2)

Illinois Central Directory, 1869. Salt Lake City: Genealogical Society of Utah, 1975. (FHL microfilm 969494, item 3)

Genealogical Collections

Albrech, Mrs. E. Julius, comp. *Alphabetical List of Ancestors and their Descendants and the Alphabetical List of Members and their Ancestors.* Salt Lake City: Genealogical Society of Utah, 1972. (FHL# 977.3/D2a or microfilm 908533, item 1)

Champaign County Historical Archives. *Family Files.* Salt Lake City: Genealogical Society of Utah, 1978. (FHL# microfilm 1026779-1026786 and 1027162-1027265)

Chatten, Mrs. Melville C., comp. *Roll of Revolutionary Ancestors, State of Illinois.* Salt Lake City: Genealogical Society of Utah, 1972. (FHL# Q/977.3/D2d or microfilm 874478, item 1-3)

Daughters of the American Revolution, Cooksville, Illinois. *Cemetery, Church and Family Records of Illinois.* Cooksville, Ill.: n.pub., 1941. (FHL# 977.3/D2ce)

Lunde, Mrs. O. B., comp. *Illinois State Genealogical Society Surname Index.* Decatur: Illinois State Genealogical Society, 1981. (FHL# 977.3/D2L)

Ross, Harvey Lee. *An Index to the Early Pioneers and Pioneer Events of the State of Illinois.* Havana, Ill.: n.pub., 1985. (FHL# 977.3/D2r/Index)

Volkel, Lowell M., comp. *Illiana Ancestors.* Danville, Ill.: Illiana Genealogical Publishing Company, 1966. (FHL# 977.3/D2v)

History

Numerous titles detailing the history of Illinois are in the state's collection under **Illinois/History.** Notable titles include:

Alvord, Clarence Walworth, comp. *The Illinois Country, 1673 to 1818.* Springfield: Illinois Centennial Commission, 1920. (FHL# 977.3/B4ic/Vol. 1)

Bateman, Newton, comp. *Historical Encyclopedia of Illinois.* Chicago, Ill.: Munsell Publishing Company, 1921. (FHL# 977.3/D3bh or microfilm 1035737, item 6)

Buck, Solon Justus. *Illinois in 1818.* Springfield: Illinois Centennial Commission, 1917. (FHL# 977.3/B4ic/Vol. 6)

Conger, John Leonard. *History of the Illinois River Valley.* Chicago, Ill.: S. J. Clarke Publishing Company, 1932. (FHL# 977.3/H2c or microfilm 1000171)

Howard, Richard P. *Illinois, A History of the Prairie State.* Grand Rapids, Mich.: William B. Eerdmans Publishing Company, c.1972. (FHL# 977.3/H2hr)

Illinois, Secretary of State. *Counties of Illinois: Their Origin and Evolutions, with Twenty-three Maps Showing the Originals and the Present Boundary Lines of Each County.* Springfield: State Journal Company, 1919. (FHL# 977.3/A1/no.80 or microfilm 924090, item 11)

Matson, Nehemiah. *Pioneers of Illinois, Containing a Series of Sketches Relating to Events that Occurred Previous to 1813: Also Narratives of Many Thrilling Incidents Connected with the Early Settlement of the West, Drawn from History, Tradition and Personal Reminiscences.* Salt Lake City: Genealogical Society of Utah, 1970. (FHL# microfilm 496645, item 1)

Pease, Theodore Calvin, comp. *The Frontier State, 1818-1845.* Springfield: Illinois Centennial Commission, 1918. (FHL# 977.3/B4ic/Vol. 2)

Land and Property Records

Initial land claims in Illinois were issued under the Northwest Territory. Subsequent transactions were filed with counties from the time of their formation. Consult the FHLC under **Illinois/Land and Property Records** and **Illinois/[County]/Land and Property Records.**

Carlson, Theodore Leonard. *The Illinois Military Tract: A Study of Land Occupation, Utilization and Tenure.* Urbana: University of Illinois Press, 1951. (FHL# 977.3/R2c)

Illinois and Wabash Land Company Minutes, 1778-1812. Salt Lake City: Genealogical Society of Utah, 1948. (FHL# microfilm 020445, item 5)

United States, General Land Office. *Federal Land Records: Tract Books of Illinois, 1826-1873.* Springfield: Office of the Secretary of State, Record Management Division, 1966. (FHL# microfilm 899766-899784)

______. *Federal Land Records: Transactions of the Locations of Military Warrants on Which Patents Have Issued under the Acts of Congress Passed on and since the Sixth of May, 1812 for Illinois; 1817-1819.* Springfield: Office of the Secretary of State, Record Management Division, 1966-1968. (FHL# microfilm 882927-882929 and 899785, items 1-3)

Volkel, Lowell M. *Shawneetown Land District Records 1814-1820.* N.p.: n.pub., 1978. (FHL# 977.3/R2s)

War of 1812 Bounty Lands in Illinois. Thomson, Ill.: Heritage House, 1977. (FHL# 977.3/R2w or microfilm 1035624, item 7, or microfiche 6051272)

Military Records

Prior to 1900, Illinois men served in the Revolutionary War, early Indian wars, War of 1812, Black Hawk War, Mexican War, Civil War, and the Spanish-American War. Many important military records are included in the Illinois collection, cataloged under **Illinois/Military Records** and **Illinois/[County]/Military Records.** A majority of the records have been indexed.

Fighting Men of Illinois: An Illustrated Historical Biography. Tucson, Ariz.: W. C. Cox, 1974. (FHL# microfilm 934978, item 2)

Illinois Adjutant General's Office. *Record of the Services of Illinois Soldiers in the Black Hawk War, 1831-1832, and the Mexican War, 1846-1848.* Springfield: H. W. Q. Rokker, 1882. (FHL# 977.3/M23i or microfilm 924557, item 2, 934968, item 3, or microfiche 6051257)

Illinois Department of Veterans' Affairs. *Veterans' National Cemetery Records, Illinois.* Salt Lake City: Genealogical Society of Utah, 1981. (FHL# microfilm 1308571 and 1308572)

Illinois Soldiers' and Sailors' Home at Quincy: Admissions of Mexican War and Civil War Veterans. Thomson, Ill.: Heritage House, 1975. (FHL# 977.3/M2i)

Illinois Veterans' Commission. *Honor Roll, State of Illinois.* Salt Lake City: Genealogical Society of Utah, 1971. (FHL# microfilm 824064, item 3)

Platt, Lyman De. *Commission Records, Illinois State Militia, 1834-1855.* Salt Lake City: Genealogical Society of Utah, 1973. (FHL# 977.3/A1/no.62; in LDS Area, 977.3/-A1/no.62 or microfilm 908142, item 9)

Roster of Revolutionary War Soldiers and Widows Who Lived in Illinois Counties. Salt Lake City: Genealogical Society of Utah, 1972. (FHL# 977.3/A1/no.11 or microfilm 873822, item 12)

Soldiers and Patriots Biographical Album: Containing Biographies and Portraits of Soldiers and Loyal Citizens in the American Conflict, Together with the Great Commanders of the Union Army, Also a History of the Organization Growing Out of the War. Tucson, Ariz.: W. C. Cox, 1974. (FHL# microfilm 1000173, item 1)

Soldiers' Burial Places in State of Illinois for Wars 1774-1898. Salt Lake City: Genealogical Society of Utah, 1975. (FHL# microfilm 1001183-1001211)

United States Adjutant General's Office. *Index to Compiled Service Records of Volunteer Union Soldiers Who Served in Organizations From the State of Illinois, 1861-1865.* 101 reels. Washington, D.C.: National Archives, 1964. (FHL# microfilm 881621-881721)

Walker, Harriet J., comp. *Soldiers of the American Revolution Buried in Illinois.* Salt Lake City: Genealogical Society of Utah, 1973. (FHL# 977.3/V22wh or microfilm 908831, item 3)

Vital Records

Laws mandating the recording of Illinois vital records in each county were passed in 1877. Vital records from 1877 to 1919, when statewide registration was instituted, are found in the office of the county clerk. The records are cataloged under **Illinois/[County]/Vital Records.** The counties of Cass, Cook, Hardin, Lake, Macon, Madison, Massac, McLean, Monroe, Moultrie, Ogle, Pulaski, Scott, Shelby, Stark, Union, Vermillion, Warren, White, Williamson, and Woodford have birth and death records pre-dating 1877. Almost all Illinois counties have marriage records from the date of the creation of the county.

Records by Jurisdiction Ohio	Archives & Libraries	Bible Records	Bibliography	Biography	Business Records	Cemeteries	Census	Church History	Church Records	Court Records	Directories	Emigration/Immigration	Gazetteers	Genealogy	Guardian-Ward	History	Historical Geography	Land & Property	Maps	Medical Records	Military Records	Minorities	Native Races	Naturalization	Newspapers	Obituaries	Occupations	Orphans	Periodicals	Poor House Records	Probate Records	Public Records	Schools	Slavery & Bondage	Societies	Taxation	Town Records	Vital Records	Voting Records
Adams	•	•		•		•	•	•	•					•		•		•	•												•		•			•		•	
Allen	•	•		•		•	•		•	•	•			•	•	•		•	•		•			•							•	•	•			•		•	•
Ashland	•			•		•	•		•	•	•			•		•		•	•																•			•	
Ashtabula				•	•	•	•	•	•		•			•		•		•	•					•							•					•		•	
Athens				•		•	•			•	•			•	•	•		•	•		•			•				•		•	•		•			•		•	
Auglaize				•		•			•	•	•			•		•		•	•		•			•						•	•		•					•	
Belmont	•			•		•			•	•	•			•		•		•			•			•				•		•	•					•		•	
Brown	•			•		•		•	•	•	•			•		•		•			•			•				•		•	•		•			•		•	
Butler		•		•		•	•	•	•	•	•			•	•	•		•	•												•					•		•	
Carroll				•		•	•		•	•				•	•	•		•	•					•							•					•		•	
Champaign		•		•	•	•			•	•				•		•		•	•		•			•				•		•	•					•		•	•
Clark		•		•		•			•	•	•			•	•	•		•	•	•	•			•			•	•		•	•	•				•		•	
Clermont	•	•		•		•	•			•				•	•	•		•			•			•							•		•			•		•	
Clinton		•		•		•		•	•	•	•			•		•		•			•	•		•	•	•	•	•		•	•					•		•	•
Columbiana				•		•	•	•	•	•	•			•	•	•		•	•	•	•									•	•	•				•		•	
Coshocton				•		•	•		•	•					•	•		•	•					•		•					•					•		•	
Crawford				•		•		•	•		•			•		•		•	•		•			•	•						•	•				•	•	•	
Cuyahoga	•	•		•		•		•	•	•	•			•	•	•		•	•			•		•	•						•	•			•	•		•	
Darke		•		•		•	•	•	•	•	•			•		•		•	•					•	•			•		•	•					•		•	
Defiance		•		•	•	•			•	•				•	•	•		•	•					•						•	•							•	
Delaware		•		•		•	•	•	•	•	•			•		•			•		•									•	•					•		•	
Erie				•		•				•	•			•	•	•		•			•			•							•	•				•		•	
Fairfield				•		•	•		•	•	•			•		•		•	•					•						•	•					•		•	
Fayette	•	•		•	•	•	•		•		•			•		•		•			•			•		•				•	•					•		•	
Franklin	•	•		•		•	•	•	•	•	•			•	•	•		•	•		•	•		•		•	•			•	•		•			•		•	
Fulton				•		•		•	•					•	•	•		•	•	•	•	•		•	•	•	•				•	•	•					•	
Gallia		•				•	•		•	•	•			•		•		•	•		•			•						•	•					•		•	
Geauga	•			•	•	•			•	•				•	•	•		•	•		•			•	•		•				•	•	•		•	•		•	
Greene				•		•			•	•	•	•		•		•		•	•		•	•		•		•		•		•	•	•		•		•		•	
Guernsey				•	•	•	•	•	•	•	•			•		•		•	•		•	•		•						•	•					•		•	
Hamilton	•	•		•		•	•	•	•		•			•	•	•		•	•		•	•		•	•						•	•	•		•	•		•	•
Hancock	•			•		•	•	•	•	•	•			•		•		•			•			•						•	•					•		•	
Hardin		•		•		•	•	•		•	•				•	•		•	•	•	•			•							•	•				•		•	
Harrison				•					•					•	•	•		•	•						•		•				•					•		•	
Henry				•		•			•	•				•		•	•	•	•		•			•						•	•	•	•			•		•	
Highland				•		•	•		•		•				•	•	•	•	•		•	•		•	•	•					•						•		•
Hocking				•		•			•	•	•					•		•	•		•			•	•						•	•				•		•	
Holmes				•		•	•		•	•	•			•		•		•	•		•	•		•			•				•		•			•		•	
Huron				•		•	•	•	•	•	•			•	•	•		•		•	•			•	•						•	•				•		•	
Jackson	•					•		•	•	•						•		•	•					•							•		•						
Jefferson				•		•		•	•	•	•			•	•	•		•	•					•	•		•				•		•			•		•	
Knox	•			•	•	•	•		•	•	•			•	•	•		•	•					•	•						•					•		•	
Lake	•	•		•	•	•	•	•	•	•	•			•	•	•		•	•					•	•		•		•		•	•	•		•	•		•	•
Lawrence						•	•		•	•	•			•	•	•		•			•			•						•	•					•		•	
Licking				•		•	•	•	•	•	•			•	•	•		•	•			•		•							•					•		•	
Logan				•		•		•	•	•	•			•	•	•		•			•	•		•				•		•	•		•	•		•		•	•
Lorain	•			•		•	•		•	•	•			•		•		•	•							•			•		•					•		•	
Lucas	•	•		•		•		•	•	•	•			•	•	•		•				•									•					•		•	
Madison	•	•		•		•		•	•	•	•			•	•	•		•	•		•			•						•	•		•			•		•	

Records by Jurisdiction — Ohio (cont)	Archives & Libraries	Bible Records	Bibliography	Biography	Business Records	Cemeteries	Census	Church History	Church Records	Court Records	Directories	Emigration/Immigration	Gazetteers	Genealogy	Guardian-Ward	History	Historical Geography	Land & Property	Maps	Medical Records	Military Records	Minorities	Native Races	Naturalization	Newspapers	Obituaries	Occupations	Orphans	Periodicals	Poor House Records	Probate Records	Public Records	Schools	Slavery & Bondage	Societies	Taxation	Town Records	Vital Records	Voting Records
Mahoning	•	•		•	•	•		•	•	•	•			•	•	•		•	•		•			•		•				•	•		•			•	•	•	
Marion		•		•	•	•		•		•	•			•	•	•		•	•		•			•							•					•		•	
Medina				•		•			•	•	•			•	•	•		•	•												•				•	•		•	
Meigs				•		•			•	•	•					•	•	•	•					•						•	•					•		•	•
Mercer				•		•		•		•				•	•	•		•						•							•	•				•		•	
Miami				•		•		•	•	•	•			•	•	•	•	•	•		•			•				•		•	•			•		•		•	•
Monroe						•	•		•	•				•	•	•		•	•		•			•						•	•					•		•	
Montgomery	•		•	•	•	•	•	•	•	•	•			•	•	•		•	•	•	•	•		•				•		•	•	•			•	•		•	
Morgan				•		•			•	•						•		•	•		•			•							•					•		•	
Morrow				•		•			•	•				•		•		•						•														•	
Muskingum				•		•			•	•	•			•	•	•		•	•		•			•							•	•				•		•	
Noble		•		•		•				•				•	•	•		•	•		•					•					•	•						•	
Ottawa				•		•			•	•						•		•	•		•			•		•					•	•	•					•	
Paulding				•					•						•	•		•	•		•			•							•							•	
Perry				•	•	•		•	•	•				•	•	•		•	•		•			•				•		•	•					•		•	
Pickaway		•		•		•	•		•	•	•			•		•		•										•		•	•					•		•	
Pike	•					•	•		•	•				•		•		•												•	•					•		•	
Portage		•		•		•	•	•	•	•				•	•	•		•	•					•	•	•				•	•		•			•		•	
Preble				•		•	•	•	•					•		•		•	•		•			•	•	•				•	•					•		•	
Putnam				•		•		•	•	•				•	•	•		•	•		•									•	•		•			•		•	
Richland				•		•		•	•	•	•			•	•	•		•	•		•									•	•	•				•		•	
Ross	•			•		•			•	•	•			•		•		•	•		•	•		•	•						•	•				•		•	
Sandusky				•		•		•	•	•	•					•		•	•					•		•					•					•		•	
Scioto	•			•		•	•			•	•					•		•	•					•	•					•	•					•		•	
Seneca	•			•		•		•	•	•	•					•		•			•			•		•				•	•	•				•		•	
Shelby				•		•		•	•	•	•			•		•		•	•		•			•						•	•					•		•	
Stark	•	•		•		•	•	•	•	•	•			•	•	•		•	•					•	•						•					•		•	
Summit	•	•		•		•		•	•	•	•			•	•	•		•	•		•			•							•		•		•	•		•	
Trumbull	•	•		•		•	•	•	•	•	•			•	•	•		•	•		•			•	•	•					•		•					•	
Tuscarawas				•		•		•	•	•			•	•	•	•		•	•			•		•							•	•	•			•		•	
Union				•		•			•	•				•	•	•		•			•									•	•					•		•	
Van Wert				•		•				•	•			•		•		•			•			•							•		•			•		•	
Vinton				•		•			•					•		•		•	•					•							•							•	
Warren		•		•		•		•	•	•	•			•		•		•	•			•		•						•	•		•			•		•	
Washington	•	•		•	•	•	•	•	•	•	•	•		•	•	•		•	•		•			•	•	•				•	•	•	•		•	•		•	•
Wayne		•		•		•	•	•		•	•			•	•	•		•	•			•		•							•	•	•		•	•		•	
Williams				•					•	•	•	•			•	•		•	•		•									•	•					•		•	
Wood				•		•	•	•	•	•	•			•	•	•		•			•			•							•	•	•			•		•	
Wyandot				•		•				•	•			•		•		•	•		•			•							•	•						•	

Records by Jurisdiction — Indiana	Archives & Libraries	Bible Records	Bibliography	Biography	Business Records	Cemeteries	Census	Church History	Church Records	Court Records	Directories	Emigration/Immigration	Gazetteers	Genealogy	Guardian-Ward	History	Historical Geography	Land & Property	Maps	Medical Records	Military Records	Minorities	Native Races	Naturalization	Newspapers	Obituaries	Occupations	Orphans	Periodicals	Poor House Records	Probate Records	Public Records	Schools	Societies	Taxation	Town Records	Vital Records	Voting Records
Adams				•		•	•									•															•						•	
Allen	•				•	•	•	•	•	•	•	•					•		•	•		•	•				•			•		•	•				•	
Bartholomew			•	•	•	•	•		•						•		•	•		•		•		•	•					•							•	
Benton				•			•									•																						
Blackford	•			•	•	•	•			•	•		•	•		•		•	•		•				•	•					•				•		•	
Boone	•			•		•		•	•		•					•		•	•		•			•							•						•	
Brown				•	•	•										•								•							•						•	
Carroll				•		•	•	•	•					•		•		•	•												•				•		•	
Cass				•		•	•		•		•			•		•			•		•				•						•						•	
Clark				•		•	•		•	•				•		•		•			•										•	•					•	
Clay	•			•				•	•		•	•		•		•		•						•							•						•	
Clinton				•	•	•	•		•		•			•		•		•	•																		•	
Crawford				•			•							•		•		•				•		•							•						•	
Daviess				•		•		•	•							•			•												•						•	
Dearborn				•		•		•	•	•	•			•		•		•	•		•			•		•					•				•		•	
Decatur				•	•	•		•		•				•		•		•	•		•										•						•	
De Kalb				•		•	•	•						•		•		•	•																		•	
Delaware	•			•		•	•				•					•		•	•												•						•	
Dubois				•			•		•		•					•		•													•						•	
Elkhart				•		•	•	•	•		•			•		•										•											•	
Fayette				•		•	•	•		•				•		•		•	•												•						•	
Floyd				•	•	•			•							•		•													•						•	
Fountain				•		•	•			•				•		•		•						•							•						•	•
Franklin				•		•		•	•	•				•		•		•	•					•		•					•	•					•	
Fulton	•			•		•	•	•	•							•		•	•													•	•				•	
Gibson				•		•			•		•			•		•		•	•						•						•	•			•		•	
Grant				•		•			•		•			•		•		•	•		•	•			•						•						•	
Greene	•			•		•	•		•					•		•		•	•					•		•					•						•	
Hamilton						•	•		•		•			•		•		•						•							•						•	
Hancock				•			•			•				•		•		•	•		•			•							•				•		•	
Harrison		•		•		•	•			•				•		•		•	•		•	•		•	•						•	•	•		•		•	
Hendricks				•		•	•		•	•				•		•		•	•					•						•	•	•	•		•		•	•
Henry				•		•	•		•		•					•		•	•										•								•	
Howard	•			•			•	•	•		•					•															•						•	
Huntington				•		•	•		•					•		•		•	•												•	•					•	
Jackson				•	•	•			•					•	•	•		•	•			•		•			•				•						•	
Jasper				•		•	•	•	•							•																					•	
Jay	•			•		•	•		•					•		•		•	•							•											•	
Jefferson				•	•	•	•	•	•	•	•			•		•		•			•	•		•			•	•		•	•	•			•		•	•
Jennings				•	•	•		•	•							•		•	•			•		•		•	•				•	•					•	
Johnson		•		•		•	•	•	•	•	•			•		•		•	•					•		•					•						•	
Knox	•	•		•	•	•	•	•	•	•	•			•		•		•	•			•		•							•	•	•				•	
Kosciusko				•	•	•	•	•	•					•		•		•	•		•			•		•					•	•		•		•	•	
Lagrange				•		•	•		•	•						•		•	•						•	•	•				•		•				•	•
Laporte	•			•		•	•	•	•	•				•		•			•												•						•	
Lake				•	•	•	•				•			•		•																•	•				•	•
Lawrence				•	•	•	•									•		•	•					•							•	•			•		•	
Madison				•		•	•	•	•		•					•			•							•											•	
Marion	•			•	•	•	•	•	•	•	•			•		•		•	•		•	•		•	•						•	•	•	•	•		•	

Records by Jurisdiction

Indiana (cont.)

	Archives & Libraries	Bible Records	Bibliography	Biography	Business Records	Cemeteries	Census	Church History	Church Records	Court Records	Directories	Emigration/Immigration	Gazetteers	Genealogy	Guardian-Ward	History	Historical Geography	Land & Property	Maps	Medical Records	Military Records	Minorities	Native Races	Naturalization	Newspapers	Obituaries	Occupations	Orphans	Periodicals	Poor House Records	Probate Records	Public Records	Schools	Societies	Taxation	Town Records	Vital Records	Voting Records
Marshall	•			•		•	•								•		•			•																			•	
Martin				•		•	•	•	•							•		•					•									•					•		
Miami	•			•		•	•	•							•		•		•	•																		•	
Monroe	•			•	•	•	•	•	•	•						•		•	•	•	•	•		•		•					•	•	•		•		•	
Montgomery				•	•	•	•	•	•		•			•		•		•	•					•							•			•			•	
Morgan	•			•		•	•		•		•			•		•			•																		•	
Newton				•			•									•																					•	
Noble				•		•	•							•		•		•	•		•					•					•						•	
Ohio				•		•	•	•								•		•	•		•			•							•						•	
Orange				•		•	•	•	•	•				•		•		•				•		•			•				•	•	•				•	
Owen				•		•	•	•	•							•		•	•		•			•							•				•		•	
Parke		•		•		•	•	•	•					•	•	•		•	•			•			•						•						•	
Perry				•			•	•						•		•		•						•			•				•	•					•	
Pike				•		•	•		•		•			•		•		•	•												•	•					•	•
Porter				•		•	•	•		•			•		•			•												•	•					•		
Posey	•			•		•	•		•		•			•		•		•	•			•			•						•						•	
Pulaski				•		•	•									•																		•			•	
Putnam				•		•	•	•	•					•	•	•		•	•					•			•				•		•				•	
Randolph				•			•	•	•		•					•		•	•			•			•												•	
Ripley				•		•	•	•		•				•		•		•	•					•			•				•						•	
Rush				•	•	•	•	•	•					•		•		•	•													•					•	
St. Joseph	•			•		•		•	•		•			•		•			•			•							•		•	•					•	
Scott				•		•	•		•			•				•		•	•					•							•	•					•	
Shelby	•			•		•	•	•	•					•		•		•						•	•						•				•		•	
Spencer				•		•		•	•							•		•	•												•						•	
Starke				•		•	•							•		•																						
Steuben				•		•	•									•					•																•	
Sullivan				•		•			•		•			•		•		•	•		•			•							•						•	
Switzerland	•					•		•	•							•		•	•		•			•							•						•	
Tippecanoe	•			•		•	•	•	•	•	•			•		•		•	•		•			•	•						•				•		•	
Tipton	•			•		•	•		•							•																					•	
Union				•		•	•		•					•		•																					•	
Vanderburgh	•			•		•		•	•		•			•		•		•	•												•	•	•				•	
Vermillion						•	•	•	•		•		•	•		•		•														•					•	
Vigo				•		•	•		•	•	•		•	•		•		•	•				•	•						•	•						•	
Wabash				•		•	•	•	•					•		•																					
Warren				•		•	•		•							•		•	•						•						•	•					•	
Warrick	•			•		•	•	•	•					•		•		•	•												•	•					•	
Washington				•		•	•		•					•		•		•	•			•		•		•		•			•	•					•	
Wayne				•		•	•	•	•		•	•		•		•		•	•		•			•							•	•					•	
Wells	•			•			•									•			•							•											•	
White				•		•	•		•							•		•	•																•			
Whitley				•			•									•		•	•																•		•	

Records by Jurisdiction

Minnesota

	Archives & Libraries	Bible Records	Bibliography	Biography	Business Records	Cemeteries	Census	Church History	Church Records	Court Records	Directories	Emigration/Immigration	Gazetteers	Genealogy	Guardian-Ward	History	Historical Geography	Land & Property	Maps	Medical Records	Military Records	Minorities	Native Races	Naturalization	Newspapers	Obituaries	Occupations	Orphans	Periodicals	Poor House Records	Probate Records	Public Records	Schools	Societies	Taxation	Town Records	Vital Records	Voting Records
Aitkin	•						•																															
Anoka	•			•		•					•					•																						
Becker				•										•		•																						
Beltrami	•										•																											
Benton	•					•																																
Big Stone	•																																					
Blue Earth	•		•	•				•			•					•		•						•							•						•	
Brown				•												•			•							•					•						•	
Buchanan							•																															
Carlton									•																													
Carver				•		•										•																						
Cass	•			•												•																						
Chippewa	•			•			•									•																						
Chisago							•	•	•							•																•	•				•	
Clay						•			•		•																											
Clearwater																																						
Cook																																						
Cottonwood							•	•	•							•		•	•												•							
Crow Wing				•	•						•					•																						
Dakota	•			•		•					•					•					•																	
Dodge	•			•		•			•	•						•		•													•	•					•	
Douglas	•															•																						
Faribault	•		•						•							•																						
Fillmore	•			•		•		•	•	•				•		•		•						•							•						•	
Freeborn	•															•		•													•						•	
Goodhue	•			•				•	•		•					•															•						•	
Grant	•															•																						
Hennepin				•		•		•	•		•					•		•	•																		•	
Houston									•							•		•						•							•						•	
Hubbard	•																																					
Isanti								•																														
Itasca							•									•																						
Jackson	•			•			•												•																			
Kanabec	•						•																															
Kandiyohi				•		•										•		•																			•	
Kittson								•						•																								
Koochiching																																						
Lac Qui Parle				•		•										•		•			•																	
Lake																																						
Lake of the Woods																																						
Le Sueur				•					•							•															•						•	
Lincoln	•								•							•		•													•						•	
Lyon				•		•			•							•																						
McLeod				•												•																						
Mahnomen																																						
Marshall	•																		•																			
Martin	•			•														•													•							
Meeker	•			•					•							•																						
Mille Lacs	•						•									•																						

Records by Jurisdiction **Minnesota (cont.)**	Archives & Libraries	Bible Records	Bibliography	Biography	Business Records	Cemeteries	Census	Church History	Church Records	Court Records	Directories	Emigration/Immigration	Gazetteers	Genealogy	Guardian-Ward	History	Historical Geography	Land & Property	Maps	Medical Records	Military Records	Minorities	Native Races	Naturalization	Newspapers	Obituaries	Occupations	Orphans	Periodicals	Poor House Records	Probate Records	Public Records	Schools	Societies	Taxation	Town Records	Vital Records	Voting Records
Morrison	•										•					•																						
Mower				•		•			•					•		•		•			•																•	
Murray	•						•												•																	•		
Nicollet	•					•										•		•													•						•	
Nobles	•			•		•										•																						
Norman						•										•																						
Olmsted	•			•		•										•																						
Otter Tail	•			•		•										•																						
Pennington											•																											
Pine									•																													
Pipestone	•																																•					
Polk									•		•					•																						
Pope						•																																
Ramsey	•			•	•			•	•		•					•		•	•												•						•	
Red Lake																																						
Redwood	•			•												•		•													•						•	
Renville	•			•																																		
Rice	•															•					•												•					
Rock	•					•																									•							
Roseau																			•																			
St. Louis				•					•		•					•													•									
Scott	•					•					•					•		•																			•	
Sherburne	•																																					
Sibley								•	•																												•	
Stearns	•			•		•		•	•		•					•																		•				
Steele				•												•																						
Stevens																																						
Swift																																						
Todd																•																						
Traverse	•																																					
Wabasha	•			•												•		•																			•	
Wadena																																						
Waseca				•			•									•		•						•							•						•	
Washington	•			•		•			•		•	•				•			•																		•	
Watonwan				•					•																													
Wilkin																																						
Winona								•			•					•		•																				
Wright	•					•			•					•		•			•																			
Yellow Medicine	•			•		•										•																						

Records by Jurisdiction

Wisconsin

	Archives & Libraries	Bible Records	Bibliography	Biography	Business Records	Cemeteries	Census	Church History	Church Records	Court Records	Directories	Emigration/Immigration	Gazetteers	Genealogy	Guardian-Ward	History	Historical Geography	Land & Property	Maps	Medical Records	Military Records	Minorities	Native Races	Naturalization	Newspapers	Obituaries	Occupations	Orphans	Periodicals	Poor House Records	Probate Records	Public Records	Schools	Societies	Taxation	Town Records	Vital Records	Voting Records
Adams				•		•	•	•										•	•							•											•	
Ashland											•					•					•												•				•	
Bad Ax																																						
Barron	•			•		•	•		•							•								•													•	
Bayfield							•									•						•															•	
Brown				•			•	•	•		•			•		•																					•	
Buffalo	•			•			•		•							•		•						•							•						•	
Burnett						•	•		•															•	•												•	
Calumet							•	•						•		•																					•	
Chippewa						•	•	•	•							•		•	•					•							•						•	
Clark				•			•		•							•								•													•	
Columbia				•		•	•	•	•							•		•							•												•	
Crawford				•		•	•									•			•																		•	
Dallas																																						
Dane	•			•		•	•	•	•	•	•					•		•						•							•						•	
Dodge				•		•	•	•	•							•		•						•													•	
Door				•		•	•									•			•																		•	
Douglas		•				•	•				•			•		•		•						•													•	
Dunn				•		•	•		•					•		•			•					•													•	
Eau Claire				•		•	•	•	•		•					•		•	•					•							•				•		•	
Florence				•		•	•																			•											•	
Fond du Lac				•			•	•			•					•			•					•							•						•	
Forest						•	•																			•											•	
Grant				•		•	•	•	•							•		•																			•	
Green				•		•	•		•							•																					•	
Green Lake				•		•	•																			•											•	
Iowa				•			•									•		•																			•	
Iron							•																														•	
Jackson				•		•										•		•											•								•	
Jefferson				•		•	•				•					•		•	•												•						•	
Juneau				•		•	•		•									•								•			•								•	
Kenosha				•		•	•				•					•																					•	
Kewaunee				•			•				•					•			•		•																•	
La Crosse	•			•		•	•	•	•		•					•		•						•		•			•		•		•				•	
Lafayette				•			•	•								•		•																			•	
Langlade				•		•	•									•										•											•	
Lincoln				•		•	•	•			•					•										•							•	•			•	
Manitowoc				•	•	•	•	•			•			•		•		•	•			•		•													•	
Marathon	•			•			•		•		•					•								•													•	
Marinette				•			•	•			•					•																					•	
Marquette				•		•	•		•																	•											•	
Menominee																																						
Milwaukee	•			•		•		•	•	•	•	•		•		•		•	•			•							•	•				•			•	
Monroe	•			•			•				•			•		•		•	•					•					•	•							•	
Oconto				•			•		•							•																					•	
Oneida				•			•	•			•					•										•											•	
Outagamie	•			•		•	•	•			•			•		•			•							•											•	
Ozaukee				•			•									•		•						•						•							•	
Pepin							•									•																					•	

Records by Jurisdiction — Wisconsin (cont.)	Archives & Libraries	Bible Records	Bibliography	Biography	Business Records	Cemeteries	Census	Church History	Church Records	Court Records	Directories	Emigration/Immigration	Gazetteers	Genealogy	Guardian-Ward	History	Historical Geography	Land & Property	Maps	Medical Records	Military Records	Minorities	Native Races	Naturalization	Newspapers	Obituaries	Occupations	Orphans	Periodicals	Poor House Records	Probate Records	Public Records	Schools	Societies	Taxation	Town Records	Vital Records	Voting Records
Pierce						•	•		•							•			•					•	•									•			•	
Polk						•	•		•				•			•		•						•	•									•			•	
Portage				•		•	•	•	•							•			•							•											•	
Price				•			•		•							•		•																				
Racine				•			•				•					•					•																	
Richland				•		•										•																					•	
Rock				•			•	•	•		•			•		•		•	•															•			•	
Rusk	•						•											•																			•	
St. Croix				•		•	•	•	•							•		•	•					•	•	•							•	•			•	
Sauk				•		•	•		•					•		•		•	•		•																•	
Sawyer							•		•							•		•						•													•	
Shawano				•		•	•									•										•											•	
Sheboygan	•			•			•	•	•		•			•		•								•													•	
Taylor							•		•									•																			•	
Trempealeau	•			•		•	•	•	•							•																					•	
Vernon				•			•	•								•		•	•																		•	
Vilas				•					•							•																					•	
Walworth				•		•	•							•		•																					•	
Washburn						•	•		•					•		•					•			•	•												•	
Washington				•		•	•									•		•																			•	
Waukesha	•		•	•			•	•	•		•			•		•		•			•	•				•	•						•				•	
Waupaca				•		•	•									•										•											•	
Waushara				•		•	•																			•											•	
Winnebago				•		•	•				•					•		•						•		•							•				•	
Wood				•		•	•		•							•		•							•	•								•			•	

Records by Jurisdiction

Michigan

	Archives & Libraries	Bible Records	Bibliography	Biographies	Business Records	Cemeteries	Census (Printed)	Church History	Church Records	Court Records	Directories	Emigration/Immigration	Gazetteers	Genealogy	Guardian/Ward	History	Historical Geography	Land & Property	Maps	Medical Records	Military Records	Minorities	Native Races	Naturalizations	Newspapers	Obituaries	Occupations	Orphans	Periodicals	Poor House Records	Probate Records	Public Records	School Records	Societies	Tax Records	Town Records	Vital Records	Voting Registers
Aishcum																																						
Alcona						•												•													•						•	
Alger	•					•			•			•				•																						
Allegan	•	•		•		•	•		•	•				•		•		•	•		•					•					•		•	•			•	
Alpena	•				•	•		•	•							•		•						•							•		•				•	•
Anamicksee																																						
Antrim		•				•												•													•	•					•	
Arenac						•										•		•													•						•	
Baraga	•			•		•												•													•						•	
Barry				•		•	•									•	•	•	•		•										•	•	•				•	
Bay	•			•		•	•				•			•		•		•			•										•						•	
Benzie						•	•	•	•	•						•		•			•										•						•	
Berrien				•		•		•	•		•					•		•	•		•												•				•	
Bleeker																																						
Branch				•		•			•		•					•		•	•		•				•						•	•	•				•	
Calhoun	•			•	•	•			•	•	•					•		•	•							•					•	•	•		•		•	•
Cass				•		•								•				•								•					•				•		•	
Charlevoix						•				•						•		•						•							•	•					•	
Cheboygan	•					•		•								•		•													•		•				•	
Cheonquet																																						
Chippewa						•	•		•		•							•													•				•		•	
Clare						•				•						•		•	•												•						•	
Clinton				•		•	•	•						•		•		•																•			•	
Crawford						•												•													•						•	
Delta	•					•			•		•							•						•							•						•	
Des Moines																																						
Dickinson						•	•									•		•						•							•						•	
Eaton				•	•	•	•		•	•				•		•		•			•				•						•	•		•	•		•	•
Emmet						•	•		•	•	•							•													•	•			•		•	
Genesee	•			•		•	•		•		•			•	•	•	•	•	•														•		•		•	
Gladwin						•												•																				
Gogebic																		•				•		•													•	
Grand Traverse	•			•		•			•	•	•			•		•		•			•										•	•					•	
Gratiot				•	•	•	•	•	•					•		•		•								•			•		•	•					•	
Hillsdale				•		•	•							•		•		•												•	•	•	•	•	•	•		
Houghton				•		•	•				•							•													•						•	
Huron				•			•		•		•							•													•	•					•	
Ingham		•		•		•	•		•		•			•		•		•	•		•					•					•	•			•	•	•	•
Ionia				•		•	•	•	•		•			•		•		•	•				•	•	•	•				•	•			•	•	•		
Iosco	•					•	•							•		•		•	•												•	•					•	
Iron	•					•												•													•	•					•	
Isabella				•		•	•		•					•		•		•								•					•	•				•	•	
Isle Royal																																			•			
Jackson	•			•		•	•	•	•	•	•			•		•		•	•		•			•							•	•	•				•	
Kalamazoo				•	•	•	•		•	•	•			•		•		•	•	•	•			•	•	•					•	•					•	
Kalkaska						•																				•											•	
Kanotin																																						
Kautawauliet																																						
Kaykakee																																						

Records by Jurisdiction **Michigan (cont.)**	Archives & Libraries	Bible Records	Bibliography	Biographies	Business Records	Cemeteries	Census (Printed)	Church History	Church Records	Court Records	Directories	Emigration/Immigration	Gazetteers	Genealogy	Guardian/Ward	History	Historical Geography	Land & Property	Maps	Medical Records	Military Records	Minorities	Native Races	Naturalizations	Newspapers	Obituaries	Occupations	Orphans	Periodicals	Poor House Records	Probate Records	Public Records	School Records	Societies	Tax Records	Town Records	Vital Records	Voting Registers
Kent				•		•	•	•	•		•					•		•	•					•		•							•				•	
Keweenaw						•	•									•		•			•			•							•						•	
Lake						•												•													•	•					•	
Lapeer				•		•	•		•					•		•		•			•										•	•		•			•	
Leelanau						•			•	•						•		•			•			•							•	•					•	
Lenawee				•		•	•	•	•		•			•		•					•																•	
Livingston				•		•	•		•		•					•		•	•		•												•				•	
Luce						•												•													•					•		
Mackinac					•	•	•		•	•	•					•		•													•		•					
Macomb				•		•	•		•					•		•		•	•										•		•	•	•		•	•		
Manistee				•			•	•	•	•	•					•		•	•				•								•					•		
Manitou																																						
Marquette	•			•	•		•				•							•													•					•		
Mason				•	•	•	•		•					•		•		•			•	•				•					•		•	•		•		
Mecosta				•		•	•									•		•			•															•		
Meegisee																																						
Menominee						•	•				•							•													•	•				•		
Michilimackinac																																						
Midland				•		•	•				•					•		•	•					•							•	•				•		
Mikenauk																																						
Missaukee						•												•													•						•	
Mensoe				•		•			•					•		•	•	•														•	•		•	•		
Montcalm				•	•	•	•	•	•	•				•		•		•						•		•						•	•	•	•		•	•
Montmorency						•			•																												•	
Muskegon	•			•		•				•				•		•		•	•					•		•					•						•	
Neewago																																						
Newaygo				•		•	•							•		•		•			•				•	•											•	
Notysekago																																						
Oakland				•		•		•	•	•				•		•		•	•						•	•					•	•	•	•	•		•	
Oceana				•		•	•									•																•						
Ogemaw						•												•	•												•						•	
Okkudd																																						
Ontonagon						•	•							•		•		•													•	•					•	
Oscesla				•		•	•	•						•		•		•	•		•										•						•	
Oscoda						•												•													•						•	
Oscwola								•	•																													
Otsego						•												•													•						•	
Ottawa	•			•		•	•		•					•		•		•	•												•	•			•		•	
Presque Isle								•								•		•													•						•	
Reshkauto																																						
Roscommon						•												•													•	•					•	
Saginaw	•			•		•	•	•	•					•		•		•			•		•									•			•		•	
St. Clair				•	•	•	•	•	•					•		•		•													•						•	
St. Joseph				•	•	•	•		•							•			•		•					•										•	•	•
Sanilac				•		•	•		•							•		•			•											•	•				•	
Schoolcraft						•	•									•																						
Shawano																																						
Shiawassee				•		•	•		•					•		•		•			•			•	•	•					•	•					•	
Tonadagana																																						

Records by Jurisdiction **Michigan** (cont.)	Archives & Libraries	Bible Records	Bibliography	Biographies	Business Records	Cemeteries	Census (Printed)	Church History	Church Records	Court Records	Directories	Emigration/Immigration	Gazetteers	Genealogy	Guardian/Ward	History	Historical Geography	Land & Property	Maps	Medical Records	Military Records	Minorities	Native Races	Naturalizations	Newspapers	Obituaries	Occupations	Orphans	Periodicals	Poor House Records	Probate Records	Public Records	School Records	Societies	Tax Records	Town Records	Vital Records	Voting Registers
Tuscola				•		•	•		•					•		•		•			•										•	•					•	
Unwattin																																						
Van Buren				•		•	•		•					•		•		•													•						•	
Webassee																																		•				
Washtenaw	•			•		•	•		•							•		•			•		•									•					•	•
Wayne	•			•		•	•	•	•		•	•				•		•	•		•	•		•	•						•	•			•	•		
Wexford						•				•	•					•		•													•							

Records by Jurisdiction

Iowa

County	Archives & Libraries	Bible Records	Bibliography	Biographies	Business Records	Cemeteries	Census (Printed)	Church History	Church Records	Court Records	Directories	Emigration/Immigration	Gazetteers	Genealogy	Guardian/Ward	History	Historical Geography	Land & Property	Maps	Medical Records	Military Records	Minorities	Native Races	Naturalizations	Newspapers	Obituaries	Occupations	Orphans	Periodicals	Poor House Records	Probate Records	Public Records	School Records	Societies	Tax Records	Town Records	Vital Records	Voting Registers
Adair				•		•			•							•		•	•		•			•							•							
Adams				•		•										•			•						•												•	
Allamakee				•		•			•		•					•			•												•							
Appanoose	•			•		•	•		•	•			•			•		•	•		•	•			•						•						•	
Audubon				•							•					•			•												•						•	
Benton				•	•	•	•	•	•		•		•	•		•		•	•		•			•	•	•					•	•	•	•	•		•	•
Black Hawk				•		•	•	•	•	•	•			•		•		•	•					•							•		•				•	
Boone				•		•	•		•		•	•		•		•		•	•		•			•							•						•	
Bremer						•			•	•	•					•		•	•					•	•	•		•			•						•	
Buchanan				•	•	•	•		•		•			•		•			•		•			•							•			•			•	
Buncombe																																						
Buena Vista						•			•							•		•	•																		•	
Butler				•							•			•		•			•												•						•	
Calhoun				•					•							•		•	•												•						•	
Carroll				•			•									•			•												•						•	
Cass				•												•			•																		•	
Cedar				•			•		•	•	•				•	•		•	•					•		•					•		•	•			•	
Cerro Gordo				•		•	•		•		•					•			•						•	•					•						•	
Cherokee	•			•			•	•								•		•																			•	
Chickasaw				•	•	•	•	•	•	•						•		•	•		•			•							•		•		•		•	
Clarke				•		•		•	•	•						•		•	•		•			•	•		•				•	•		•	•		•	
Clay				•		•	•									•			•																			
Clayton				•				•		•	•			•		•			•												•		•				•	
Clinton				•		•			•		•		•			•		•	•					•							•	•					•	
Crawford				•												•			•						•	•											•	
Dallas	•			•		•	•			•						•		•	•												•						•	
Davis				•	•	•			•	•						•		•	•		•			•		•					•						•	
Decatur				•	•	•	•	•	•	•						•		•		•	•										•	•					•	
Delaware				•												•			•												•						•	
Des Moines	•			•		•		•	•	•	•					•		•	•		•	•		•	•						•	•	•				•	
Dickinson				•												•			•																		•	
Dubuque	•			•		•	•		•		•		•			•			•												•						•	
Emmet				•			•			•	•					•			•																			
Fayette				•		•	•		•							•		•	•					•							•	•	•		•		•	
Floyd				•		•			•		•			•		•			•																		•	
Fox																																						
Franklin	•			•		•	•							•		•			•																		•	
Fremont				•		•	•				•					•			•																		•	
Greene				•			•									•		•	•						•						•		•				•	
Grundy				•		•			•	•	•			•		•		•	•															•			•	
Guthrie				•		•			•							•			•						•												•	
Hamilton				•					•		•				•	•		•	•		•			•							•				•		•	
Hancock								•	•							•			•													•						
Hardin						•			•	•				•		•		•	•		•			•		•											•	
Harrison				•		•					•					•			•																		•	
Henry				•		•	•	•	•	•	•			•		•		•	•					•							•		•				•	
Howard										•						•		•	•					•							•						•	
Humboldt						•			•						•	•		•	•		•			•							•						•	
Ida	•			•												•			•			•															•	

Records by Jurisdiction **Iowa (cont)**	Archives & Libraries	Bible Records	Bibliography	Biographies	Business Records	Cemeteries	Census (Printed)	Church History	Church Records	Court Records	Directories	Emigration/Immigration	Gazetteers	Genealogy	Guardian/Ward	History	Historical Geography	Land & Property	Maps	Medical Records	Military Records	Minorities	Native Races	Naturalizations	Newspapers	Obituaries	Occupations	Orphans	Periodicals	Poor House Records	Probate Records	Public Records	School Records	Societies	Tax Records	Town Records	Vital Records	Voting Registers
Iowa	•		•			•		•	•	•						•		•	•					•	•	•					•		•	•			•	
Jackson	•			•					•		•		•			•			•												•						•	
Jasper	•			•		•	•	•		•	•			•		•		•	•		•			•		•					•						•	
Jefferson	•			•	•	•	•	•	•	•	•			•		•		•	•	•	•			•	•						•		•	•	•		•	
Johnson				•		•		•	•		•			•		•		•		•											•	•	•	•	•		•	•
Jones				•				•	•	•	•					•			•						•						•						•	
Keokuk				•		•	•	•	•							•		•	•							•					•			•			•	
Kishkekosh																																						
Knox																															•						•	
Kossuth							•		•							•			•																			
Lee				•	•	•	•	•	•	•	•			•		•		•	•	•	•			•	•	•			•		•	•	•		•		•	
Linn				•		•	•	•	•	•	•			•		•		•	•		•		•	•	•	•					•	•	•	•			•	
Louisa				•		•	•		•	•						•		•	•					•							•						•	
Lucas				•	•	•	•									•		•	•					•							•						•	
Lyon				•					•		•					•			•												•						•	
Madison				•		•		•	•	•	•			•		•		•	•					•							•	•					•	
Mahaska				•	•	•		•	•					•		•		•	•						•	•					•		•				•	
Marion				•		•		•	•		•			•		•		•	•	•				•							•	•	•		•		•	
Marshall				•		•	•	•	•	•	•			•		•		•	•			•		•							•						•	
Mills				•												•			•																		•	
Mitchell				•							•					•			•																			
Monona								•						•		•			•																		•	
Monroe				•	•	•		•	•							•		•	•												•		•				•	
Montgomery	•			•			•		•		•					•			•																		•	
Muscatine				•		•		•	•	•	•			•		•		•	•					•							•						•	
O'Brien				•										•		•			•		•										•						•	
Osceola	•			•												•			•																		•	
Page				•		•	•	•			•			•		•		•	•												•						•	
Palo Alto							•									•			•																			
Plymouth				•		•			•		•				•	•		•	•		•	•		•							•						•	
Pocahontas						•		•	•		•			•		•		•	•												•						•	
Polk	•			•	•	•	•		•	•	•					•		•	•					•		•					•		•	•			•	
Pottawattamie				•		•	•	•	•	•	•				•	•		•	•							•						•	•		•		•	
Poweshiek				•		•		•	•							•		•	•					•		•					•						•	
Ringold	•			•	•	•			•		•			•		•			•			•									•						•	
Risley																																						
Sac				•					•							•		•	•			•		•							•						•	
Scott				•		•		•	•		•			•		•		•						•							•						•	
Shelby				•		•			•							•		•	•																		•	
Sioux															•	•			•					•							•						•	
Slaughterter																																						
Story				•		•	•		•		•				•	•		•	•					•							•						•	
Tama				•	•	•	•	•	•		•			•		•		•	•		•		•								•		•	•	•		•	
Taylor	•			•		•	•		•		•			•		•			•		•										•				•		•	
Union				•		•	•		•		•					•		•	•						•												•	
Van Buren				•	•	•	•	•	•	•	•	•	•	•		•		•	•		•			•	•	•			•		•	•	•	•	•		•	
Wahkaw																																						
Wapello				•		•	•	•	•		•					•		•	•					•							•	•	•	•			•	
Warren				•		•	•	•		•	•			•		•		•	•		•										•		•	•	•		•	

Records by Jurisdiction **Iowa (cont.)**	Archives & Libraries	Bible Records	Bibliography	Biographies	Business Records	Cemeteries	Census (Printed)	Church History	Church Records	Court Records	Directories	Emigration/Immigration	Gazetteers	Genealogy	Guardian/Ward	History	Historical Geography	Land & Property	Maps	Medical Records	Military Records	Minorities	Native Races	Naturalizations	Newspapers	Obituaries	Occupations	Orphans	Periodicals	Poor House Records	Probate Records	Public Records	School Records	Societies	Tax Records	Town Records	Vital Records	Voting Registers
Washington				•		•		•	•	•				•		•		•	•		•			•							•		•				•	
Wayne				•	•	•	•	•	•							•		•	•	•	•					•					•	•	•	•			•	
Webster				•					•		•				•	•		•	•					•							•						•	
Winnebago						•			•							•			•						•												•	
Winneshiek				•				•	•	•	•					•		•	•			•		•	•						•	•					•	
Woodbury	•			•		•		•	•		•					•			•												•						•	
Worth																																						
Wright																															•						•	

Records by Jurisdiction Illinois	Archives & Libraries	Bible Records	Bibliography	Biography	Business Records	Cemeteries	Census	Church History	Church Records	Court Records	Directories	Emigration/Immigration	Gazetteers	Genealogy	Guardian-Ward	History	Historical Geography	Land & Property	Maps	Medical Records	Military Records	Minorities	Native Races	Naturalization	Newspapers	Obituaries	Occupations	Orphans	Periodicals	Poor House Records	Probate Records	Public Records	Schools	Slavery & Bondage	Societies	Taxation	Town Records	Vital Records	Voting Records
Adams				•		•	•	•	•	•				•		•		•	•		•			•	•	•					•		•			•		•	
Alexander				•		•	•		•		•					•		•			•			•							•	•					•		
Bond				•		•	•			•				•		•		•						•							•							•	
Boone		•		•							•			•		•																						•	
Brown	•			•	•	•					•			•		•			•		•															•			
Bureau				•	•	•			•		•					•																						•	
Calhoun				•		•	•				•			•		•		•			•			•							•							•	
Carroll	•			•		•	•		•							•					•																		
Cass				•		•	•				•					•		•	•		•				•													•	
Champaign	•			•	•	•			•	•	•			•		•		•	•					•	•	•					•		•		•			•	
Christian				•		•	•	•	•		•		•			•		•			•			•							•							•	
Clark	•	•				•	•	•	•					•		•		•			•				•	•			•		•		•		•			•	
Clay				•		•		•	•	•						•		•			•			•		•					•							•	
Clinton				•			•	•				•		•		•		•				•		•							•							•	
Coles				•		•	•		•		•			•		•		•	•		•			•			•				•					•		•	
Cook	•	•		•	•	•	•	•	•		•			•		•		•	•		•	•		•	•	•	•		•		•		•		•		•	•	•
Crawford				•		•	•	•	•		•			•		•		•	•												•							•	
Cumberland	•				•	•	•							•		•																						•	
Dane																																							
De Kalb				•		•	•	•	•		•			•		•		•	•					•														•	
De Witt	•			•		•	•	•	•	•	•			•		•		•			•			•	•						•							•	
Douglas	•			•		•	•		•							•		•	•		•			•	•						•							•	
Du Page	•		•	•		•	•	•	•		•			•		•			•												•		•		•			•	
Edgar						•	•		•		•					•		•	•					•							•	•						•	
Edwards						•	•	•	•					•		•		•			•			•	•	•					•				•			•	
Effingham	•			•		•	•		•		•			•		•		•			•			•		•					•							•	
Fayette				•		•	•		•		•			•		•		•						•							•							•	
Ford				•				•	•					•		•		•	•					•							•		•					•	
Franklin						•	•		•		•			•		•		•			•			•					•		•							•	
Fulton				•		•	•	•	•		•		•			•			•																				
Gallatin						•	•		•		•					•		•	•					•							•	•				•		•	
Greene				•		•							•			•		•			•			•							•							•	
Grundy				•			•				•					•																							
Hamilton						•	•	•	•	•	•					•		•						•							•					•		•	
Hancock				•		•	•	•	•	•	•			•		•		•	•		•			•	•	•					•	•	•			•		•	•
Hardin				•		•	•				•					•		•							•	•					•		•			•		•	
Henderson				•	•	•	•		•		•					•		•	•					•	•	•					•							•	
Henry				•		•	•	•	•		•					•			•		•															•			
Iroquois				•		•	•		•					•		•		•	•		•			•					•						•			•	
Jackson	•			•		•	•	•	•	•	•					•		•						•							•		•					•	
Jasper				•		•	•			•						•		•						•							•							•	
Jefferson				•			•		•		•					•		•	•																			•	
Jersey				•		•										•		•	•					•							•							•	
Jo Daviess	•				•	•	•	•			•					•		•			•				•														
Johnson		•		•		•		•	•	•				•		•		•							•	•					•		•					•	
Kane	•			•		•	•				•					•																	•			•			
Kankakee				•		•		•			•			•		•			•		•								•									•	
Kendall				•		•	•									•		•																		•		•	
Knox	•			•		•	•				•		•	•		•		•	•		•	•		•	•				•		•					•		•	

Records by Jurisdiction — Illinois (cont.)	Archives & Libraries	Bible Records	Bibliography	Biography	Business Records	Cemeteries	Census	Church History	Church Records	Court Records	Directories	Emigration/Immigration	Gazetteers	Genealogy	Guardian-Ward	History	Historical Geography	Land & Property	Maps	Medical Records	Military Records	Minorities	Native Races	Naturalization	Newspapers	Obituaries	Occupations	Orphans	Periodicals	Poor House Records	Probate Records	Public Records	Schools	Slavery & Bondage	Societies	Taxation	Town Records	Vital Records	Voting Records
Lake				•		•	•	•			•					•		•			•				•													•	
LaSalle				•		•	•		•		•			•		•		•	•		•																	•	
Lawrence				•		•	•	•	•							•		•													•							•	
Lee				•			•		•		•					•						•																•	
Livingston				•		•		•			•					•		•	•		•			•							•							•	
Logan	•			•	•	•	•		•		•			•		•			•					•							•				•			•	
Macon				•		•	•	•	•	•	•			•		•		•	•		•			•						•	•		•		•	•		•	
Macoupin	•			•		•	•		•		•			•		•		•													•							•	
Madison				•		•	•	•	•		•	•	•	•		•		•			•	•		•							•			•				•	
Marion				•		•	•		•							•		•						•	•						•							•	
Marshall				•			•									•		•																	•				
Mason				•	•	•		•	•		•			•		•		•	•					•							•							•	
Massac				•		•	•	•	•	•						•		•						•							•					•		•	
McDonough				•		•	•		•		•			•		•		•			•				•	•					•							•	
McHenry	•			•		•			•		•			•		•			•																			•	
McLean				•		•	•	•	•		•			•		•		•	•		•								•				•		•			•	
Menard				•		•	•		•		•			•		•		•						•							•				•			•	•
Mercer				•		•										•																							
Monroe				•	•	•			•							•		•						•							•						•		
Montgomery				•		•	•	•	•		•			•		•		•	•					•							•							•	
Morgan	•			•		•	•		•		•			•		•		•	•		•			•							•							•	
Moultrie				•		•	•		•									•	•		•			•					•		•		•					•	
Ogle	•			•		•	•		•		•			•		•					•					•												•	
Peoria	•			•		•	•				•			•		•			•		•										•				•	•		•	
Perry				•		•	•		•	•						•		•						•							•							•	
Piatt	•			•		•	•	•	•									•			•			•	•						•							•	
Pike	•			•	•	•	•	•			•			•		•		•	•					•							•							•	
Pope				•		•	•	•	•	•						•		•			•			•							•	•			•			•	
Pulaski				•		•	•	•								•		•			•			•							•							•	
Putnam				•			•		•							•		•	•																				
Randolph		•		•		•	•	•	•	•	•			•		•		•	•			•		•	•						•	•						•	•
Richland				•		•	•			•						•		•						•							•				•	•		•	
Rock Island	•			•		•					•			•		•		•	•		•			•	•	•			•		•								
St. Clair	•			•	•	•	•	•	•		•	•	•	•		•			•		•	•		•							•	•						•	
Saline	•					•	•	•	•	•	•					•		•													•		•					•	
Sangamon	•			•	•	•	•		•		•		•	•		•		•	•		•			•		•					•				•	•		•	•
Schuyler				•	•	•	•		•		•			•		•		•	•		•			•							•							•	
Scott	•		•	•			•		•					•		•		•	•		•			•	•						•							•	
Shelby	•			•		•	•	•	•		•			•		•		•	•		•			•					•		•					•		•	
Stark				•			•									•		•						•							•							•	
Stephenson	•			•		•	•	•	•		•			•		•		•	•																			•	
Tazewell				•		•	•				•			•		•		•	•		•			•							•							•	
Union				•		•	•		•	•						•		•	•		•	•		•		•					•					•		•	
Vermilion	•			•		•	•	•	•		•					•		•	•		•			•		•					•					•		•	
Wabash						•	•		•		•			•		•		•							•						•								
Warren				•		•	•				•					•		•	•					•							•		•					•	
Washington				•		•		•								•																						•	
Wayne				•		•	•		•							•									•													•	
White				•		•	•	•	•							•		•						•							•							•	

Records by Jurisdiction **Illinois** (cont.)	Archives & Libraries	Bible Records	Bibliography	Biography	Business Records	Cemeteries	Census	Church History	Church Records	Court Records	Directories	Emigration/Immigration	Gazetteers	Genealogy	Guardian-Ward	History	Historical Geography	Land & Property	Maps	Medical Records	Military Records	Minorities	Native Races	Naturalization	Newspapers	Obituaries	Occupations	Orphans	Periodicals	Poor House Records	Probate Records	Public Records	Schools	Slavery & Bondage	Societies	Taxation	Town Records	Vital Records	Voting Records
Whiteside				•		•	•	•								•		•			•				•	•				•	•	•				•		•	
Will	•			•		•	•		•		•			•		•			•		•								•		•		•			•			
Williamson			•			•		•	•		•		•	•		•		•			•			•							•							•	
Winnebago				•		•	•				•					•			•																			•	
Woodford				•		•			•		•			•		•		•	•		•	•		•							•							•	

Chapter 10

United States: The Northern Plains States

Wendy L. Elliott

OKLAHOMA

Historical Background

1803	Louisiana Purchase brings most of the area of Oklahoma under the jurisdiction of the United States with the exception of the panhandle strip.
1803	Oklahoma comes under the jurisdiction of Indiana Territory.
1812	The region is reorganized and Oklahoma becomes part of Missouri Territory.
1817	A trading post on the Grand River becomes the first white settlement.
1818	First Protestant Church (Methodist) is organized at Pecan Point.
1819	The territory of Arkansas, including present-day Oklahoma, is organized from the southern part of Missouri Terrritory.
1820-28	Arkansas claims a wide strip of eastern Oklahoma; it is organized into Crawford and Millercounties, Arkansas.
1824	First post office established in Miller County.
1830	U.S. Congress passes Indian Removal Act. Indians from the Five Civilized Tribes (Seminole, Creek, Chickasaw, Cherokee, and Choctaw) are forcibly relocated among the native Arapaho, Caddo, Cheyenne, Comanche, Kiowa, Osage, Pawnee, and Wichita.
1854	Indian Territory, by treaty, comprises the present state of Oklahoma except the Panhandle.
1866	New treaties negotiated with the Five Civilized Tribes allow freed Negroes to own land.
1866-83	Many more tribes relocated into Oklahoma: the Sac, Fox, Apache, Kansas, Shawnee, Pottawatomie, Pawnee, Nez Perce, Ponca, Otoe, Missouri, Iowa, and Kickapoo.
1889	Fifty thousand prospective homesteaders rush to stake claims during the "Run of 1889."
1890	The region is divided into Indian Territory and Oklahoma Territory.
1890	Territorial government established for most of the Cherokee Strip and unassigned land in the center of Oklahoma.
1890	First capital is located at Guthrie in Logan County.
1890	Seven counties organized and assigned numbers rather rather than names; Indian Territory still has no county form of government.
1891	The "Run of 1891" opens land formerly belonging to the Iowa, Sac, Fox, and Pottawatomie tribes.
1892	Arapaho and Cheyenne lands are opened for settlement.
1893	The Dawes Commission is established to negotiate treaties for land. The Cherokee Outlet, and the Tonkawa and Pawnee lands opened (50,000 settlers claimed 6.5 million acres on the first day).
1896	A court decision and an Act of Congress settle the disputed area claimed by both Texas and Oklahoma. Greer, Jackson, and Harmon counties annexed to Oklahoma.
1900	Federal census taken for Indian Territory and Oklahoma Territory.

1901 Kiowa, Apache, Wichita-Caddo, and Comanche lands are opened.

1907 Oklahoma becomes the forty-sixth state.

1910 Federal government takes the first unified Oklahoma census.

1910 State capital moved from Guthrie to Oklahoma City.

Settlement and Migration

Before the Oklahoma Territory was opened for white settlement, many residents leased land from the Indians. Because there were no official depositories or county clerks during this early period, the respective Indian Agencies hold the records. Most of the territory's first white settlers obtained their lands through homestead claims. The federal government holds these records.

Migrations from Illinois, Iowa, and Kansas settled in the west and northwest portions of Oklahoma. Groups from Arkansas, Missouri, and Texas helped establish the southern and eastern sections. The first railroad into Oklahoma Territory was constructed in 1887, providing easier access from Topeka, Kansas, to Purcell and making possible the settlement of Guthrie and Oklahoma City.

Although county clerks record births and deaths, certificates are available only from the State Department of Health. Marriage, divorce, probate, and civil court records are available from the county clerk of the court for the appropriate county. The county clerks or registrars of deeds also maintain land and property records.

Oklahoma Library Collection

Archives and Libraries

The Family History Library Catalog (FHLC) has several helpful sources:

Blessing, Patrick Joseph. *Oklahoma: Records and Archives.* Tulsa, Okla.: University of Tulsa Publications in American Social History, No. 1, c.1978. (FHL# 976.6/A3b)

Foreman, Grant. *A Survey of Tribal Records in the Archives of the United States Government in Oklahoma.* n.p., n.d. (FHL# 970.1/F76ls, 976.6/A5f, or microfilm 0908208, item 8)

Gibson, Arrell Morgan. *A Guide to Regional Manuscript Collections in the Division of Manuscripts,* University of Oklahoma Library. Norman: University of Oklahoma Press, 1960. (FHL# 976.6/H2g)

Historical Records Survey, Works Progress Administration, Division of Women's and Professional Projects. *A List of the Records of the State of Oklahoma.* Oklahoma City: Historical Records Survey, 1938. (FHL# 976.6/A5h)

Keene, Mrs. H. H. *A Guide to Manuscripts in the Library of the Thomas Gilcrease Institute of American History and Art.* Tulsa, Okla.: Thomas Gilcrease Institute of American History and Art, 1969. (FHL# 976.6/A3k)

Cemeteries

Most Oklahoma counties have composite or partial lists of cemetery inscriptions made by WPA, DAR, and LDS groups. These lists are cataloged under **Oklahoma/[County]/Cemeteries**. General Oklahoma cemetery records in the collection include:

Biggerstaff, Inez Boswell, comp. *Some Tombstone Inscriptions from Oklahoma-Arkansas-Louisiana-Mississippi and Texas.* Typescript by Inez Boswell Biggerstaff, n.p., c.1955. (FHL# 976/V22b)

Carselowey, James Manford. *Indian Territory Notes.* Typescript by James Manford CarseLowey, 1973. (FHL# 976.6/A1/no.9 or microfilm 0940013, item 5)

Cheek, John Carl, comp. *Selected Tombstone Inscriptions from Alabama, South Carolina and Other Southern States.* n.p., c.1970. (FHL# 973/V22cj)

Gray, Ralph D. *Grey's Cemetery Records: Cemetery Records from . . . Texas; . . . Arkansas; . . . Montezuma, La Plata, Colorado, Washita, Oklahoma, and Comanche Counties, Oklahoma.* Fort Worth, Texas: American Reference Publishers, Inc. c.1968. (FHL# 973/V22g)

Mills, Madeline (Siekman), and Helen R. Mullenax. *Relocated Cemeteries in Oklahoma and Part of Arkansas-Kansas-Texas.* n.p.: 1974. (FHL# 976.6/V22m or microfilm 0928142, item 5)

Oklahoma Cemetery Records. Kingfisher, Okla.: Daughters of the American Revolution, Captain Warren Cottle Chapter, 1969. (FHL# 976.6/V22d or microfilm 0496552, item 7)

Tyner, James W., and Alice Tyner Timmons, comps. *Our People and Where They Rest.* Microreproduction. Salt Lake City: Genealogical Society of Utah, 1980. (FHL# microfilm 1290833, items 6-10 and 1290834, items 1-4)

Census Records

Special collections of Oklahoma census records are available at the Family History Library. Censuses for the Cherokee Nation were enumerated in 1880 (FHL# microfilm 989204) and 1896 (FHL# microfilm 989203, item 2). Also see:

An Index to the 1890 United States Census of Union Veterans and Their Widows in Oklahoma and Indian Territories: Including Old Greer County and Soldiers Stationed at Military Installations in the Territories (Section I), Also an Index to Records from the Oklahoma Union Soldiers' Home Including Civil War Veterans and Their Dependents... Oklahoma City: Oklahoma Genealogical Society, 1970. Oklahoma Genealogical Society Special Publication No. 3. (FHL# 976.6/M2o or microfilm 0496937, item 1).

Ellsworth, Carole, and Sue Emler, comps. *1900 U.S. Census of the Cherokee Indian Nation, Indian Territory.* Gore, Okla: Oklahoma Roots Research, 1982. (FHL# 976.6/X2e/1900)

Oklahoma Genealogical Society. *A Compilation of Records from the Choctaw Nation, Indian Territory.* Oklahoma City: Oklahoma Genealogical Society, c.1976. (FHL# microfilm 1206500 or 0488191)

_____. First Territorial Census of Oklahoma, 1890. Oklahoma

City: Oklahoma Historical Society, c.1961. (FHL# microfilm 0227282)

Woods, Frances. *Indian Lands West of Arkansas (Oklahoma): Population Schedule of the United States Census of 1860.* Salt Lake: Arrow Print Co., 1964. (FHL# 976.6/X2p/1860 or microfilm 1000357, item 1)

Church History

Only two church histories related to Oklahoma are included in the Family History Library's general collection, one Methodist and the other Roman Catholic. However, others are available in the FHLC under **Oklahoma/-[County]/Church History**.

Church Records

For church records, see **Oklahoma/[County]/Church Records**. Only one is cataloged at the state level:

Young, Gloryann Hankins. *Oklahoma's Ministers' Licenses–Haskell, Latimer, Le Flore Counties, 1875-1941.* Wister, Okla.: G. H. Young, 1984. (FHL# 976.6/P22y)

Genealogy

The library has a few genealogical collections, including the state genealogical society's surname index and Western Oklahoma Historical Society's history of western Oklahoma. Several genealogical periodicals are available, cataloged in the FHLC under **Oklahoma/-Genealogy/Periodicals**. Also check under **/[County]/-Genealogy/Periodicals** for periodicals devoted to a single county.

History

The library has many histories of Oklahoma, before and after statehood, many including histories of native Americans. Some of the histories cataloged at the state level are actually regional histories. For county or city histories, see **Oklahoma/[County]/History** and **Oklahoma/[County]/[City]/History**. Additional titles are also listed in these subdivisions under **Oklahoma/History: Archives and Libraries, Inventories, Registers, Catalogs, and Periodicals.**

Chapman, Berlin Basil. *The Otoes and Missourias, A Study of Indian Removal and the Legal Aftermath.* Oklahoma City: Times Journal Publishing Co., c.1965. (FHL# 970.3/-Ot6c)

Douglas, Clarence Brown. *The History of Tulsa, Oklahoma: A City with a Personality: Together with a Glimpse Down the Corridors of the Past into Old Indian Territory, The Five Civilized Tribes, the Creek Nation, Tulsa Recording District and Tulsa County, How Oklahoma was Created and Something of the Builders of a Commonwealth.* 3 vols. Chicago: S. J. Clarke Publishing Co., 1921. (FHL# 976.686/-11/D3d)

Gard, Wayne. *The Chisolm Trail.* Norman: University of Oklahoma Press, 1976. (FHL# 976/H2gw)

Gittinger, Roy. *The Formation of the State of Oklahoma (1803-1906).* Berkeley: University of California Press, 1917. (FHL# 976.6/H2gi)

Hall, Ted Byron. *Oklahoma Indian Territory.* Fort Worth, Tex.: American Reference Publishing, 1971. (FHL# 976.6/H2ht)

Hill, Luther B. *A History of the State of Oklahoma, with the Assistance of Local Authorities.* Chicago: Lewis Publishing Co., 1908. (FHL# 976.6/H2h or microfilm 1000353, items 1-2, or microfiche 6051224)

Litton, Gaston L. *History of Oklahoma at the Golden Anniversary of Statehood.* New York: Lewis Historical Publishing Co., 1957. (FHL# 976.6/D31)

McReynolds, Edwin C. *Oklahoma: The Story of Its Past and Present.* Rev. ed., Norman: University of Oklahoma Press, 1971. (FHL# 976.6/H2mc)

Thoburn, Joseph Bradfield. *Oklahoma, A History of the State and Its People.* Tucson, Ariz.: W. C. Cox, 1974. (FHL# microfilm 1000353, items 3-5)

Wilson, Charles Banks. *Indians of Eastern Oklahoma Including Quapaw Agency Indians.* Afton, Okla.: Buffalo Publishing Co., 1956. (FHL# 970.1/W692)

Land and Property

A few land records have been recorded and indexed by the Stillwater and Muskogee chapters of the Daughters of the American Colonists.

Daughters of the American Colonists. Stillwater and Muskogee Chapters (Oklahoma). *Miscellaneous Records.* Manuscript, n.p., 1980. (FHL# 976.6/D2m).

Some land and property records are available for the Concho Agency, Bureau of Indian Affairs, 1891-1915 (FHL# microfilm 1026683-1026686, 1026695, items 3-4, 1026691, item 4, and 1028498, item 3). See also:

Ericson, Carolyn and Frances Ingmire. *First Settlers of the Missouri Territory.* 2 vols. Nacogdoches, Tex.: Ericson Books, 1983 (FHL# 977.8/R2f).

Includes a few land grants made under Missouri Territorial jurisdiction.

Maps

The Family History Library has several maps for Oklahoma before and after statehood. See **Oklahoma/-Maps** for maps of the whole state or of a particular region or territory. To assist in identifying places, the following gazetteer can be located in the FHLC under **Oklahoma/Names,Geographical**:

Shirk, George H. *Oklahoma Place Names.* Norman: University of Oklahoma Press, 1965. (FHL# 976.6/E3s or microfilm 1035624, item 8)

Military Records

The collection includes military records from the territorial period through the twentieth century.

Oklahoma Board of Pension Commisioners. *Confederate Pensions Applications for Soldiers and Sailors.* Oklahoma City: Archives and Records Division, Oklahoma Department of Libraries, n.p.: n.d. (FHL# microfilm 10011529 - 1001548).

The first two reels contain an index and minutes of the Board of Commissioners, 1915-19. A separate index to Confederate pension applications for the state of Oklahoma is available:

Index to Applications for Pensions from the State of Oklahoma, Submitted by Confederate Soldiers, Sailors, and Their Widows. Oklahoma City: Oklahoma Genealogical Society, 1969. Oklahoma Genealogical Society Special Publication No. 2. (FHL# 976.6/M24o or microfiche 6046932)

Several good military histories in the collection may provide additional information. Check the FHLC under **Oklahoma/Military History.**

Native Americans

The FHLC lists native American records under **Oklahoma/Minorities, Oklahoma/Native Races, Oklahoma/Census,** and **Oklahoma/Land and Property.** Numerous Eastern Cherokee applications to the U. S. Court of Claims are cataloged under **/Minorities.** These records were taken from the Guion Miller enrollment lists but include packets of information that are not included in Miller's. Some Cherokee births and deaths abstracted from newspapers and the 1880 and 1900 censuses can be located under **Oklahoma/Native Races** where you will also find reference to Creek and Seminole Indian census cards with an accompanying index. See also:

Baker, Jack D. *Cherokee Emigration Rolls, 1817-1835.* Oklahoma City: Baker Publishing Co., c.1977 (FHL# 970.3/-C424be)

Campbell, John Bert. *Campbell's Abstract of Creek Indian Census Cards and Index.* Muskogee, Okla: Phoenix Job Printing, 1915. (FHL# 970.3/C861c or microfilm 0989199, item 1)

Cook, Fredrea Marlyn Hermann. *Forgotten Oklahoma Records: Cherokee Land Allotment Book.* Cullman, Ala: Gregath Company, 1981. (FHL# 970.3/C424co)

_____. *Campbell's Abstract of Seminole Indian Census Cards and Index.* Muskogee: Oklahoma Printing, 1925. (FHL# 970.3/Se52c)

Griswold, Gillett. *The Fort Sill Apaches: Their Vital Statistics, Tribal Origins, Antecdents.* Fort Sill, Okla: G. Griswold, 1958-61. (FHL# microfilm 0928251, item 8)

Miller, Guion. *Records Relating to Enrollment of Eastern Cherokee, 1908-1910.* Washington, D.C.: National Archives, 1967. 12 reels. (FHL# microfilm 0830434-0830445)

_____. *Eastern Cherokee Applications, August 29, 1906 - May 26, 1909.* Washington, D.C.: National Archives Publications, 1981. 348 reels. (See FHLC for microfilm call numbers)

Oklahoma Genealogical Society. *A Compilation of Records from the Choctaw Nation, Indian Territory.* Oklahoma City: Oklahoma Genealogical Society, c.1976. (FHL# microfilm 1206500 or 0488191)

United States Commission to the Five Civilized Tribes. *Enrollment of the Five Civilized Tribes: Dawes Commission, 1896-1909.* Muskogee, Okla: Filmed by the Bureau of Indian Affairs, 1961. 74 reels. (FHL# microfilm 1022497-1022535, 1022102-1022122, and 1023029-1023048)

_____. *The Final Rolls of Citizens and Freedmen of the Five Civilized Tribes in Indian Territory.* Washington, D.C.: Government Printing Office, c.1907. (FHL# 970.1/Un3c or microfilm 0908371, item 2, or 0962366, item 1)

Tribal records for the Pottawatomie consist of chronologically arranged tribal identification numbers, dates of birth and death of tribal members, and an alphabetical list of tribal members. Genealogies of the Kickapoo Indians are indexed.

Bureau of Indian Affairs records are available for many of the Oklahoma Indian Agencies for varying dates. These valuable records include census, vital statistics, family registers, annuity rolls, land and property records. Records included are for the Kiowa, Osage, Cheyenne, Arapaho, Apache, Comanche, Wichita, Caddo, Cherokee, Shawnee, Kaw, Quapaw, Seneca, Miami, Seneca-Cayuga, Delaware, Wyandotte, Ottawa, Modoc, Nez Perce, Kaskaskia, Peoria, Piankashaw, Choctaw, Chickasaw, Creek, Seminole, Iowa, Kickapoo, Pottawatomi, Otoe-Missouri, Pawnee, Ponca, Tonkawa, Sac, and Fox. These are cataloged in the FHLC under **Oklahoma/Native Races/[Agency].**

Under **Oklahoma/Native Races/Vital Records**, the FHLC lists a good collection of vital records for several Indian tribes.

Carter, Kent, comp. *Preliminary Inventory of the Records of the Osage Indian Agency, Bureau of Indian Affairs.* (Record Group 75), Fort Worth, Tex.: Federal Archives and Records Center, 1977. (FHL# 970.1/A1/no.84)

Foreman, Grant. *A Survey of Tribal Records in the Archives of the United States Government in Oklahoma. n.p., n.d. (FHL# 970.1/F761s, 976.6 A5f, or microfilm 0908208, item 8)*

Slack, C. T. *Genealogies of the Kickapoo Indians.* n.p., n.d. Microfilm of original 6 volumes and index loaned for filming. Salt Lake City: Filmed by the Genealogical Society of Utah, 1976. (FHL# microfilm 0928361)

United States Commission to the Five Civilized Tribes. *Enrollment of the Five Civilized Tribes: Dawes Commission 1896-1909.* Muskogee, Okla: Filmed by the Bureau of Indian Affairs, 1961. 74 reels. (FHL# microfilm 1022497-1022535, 1022103-1022122, and 1023029-1023048)

Wilson, Charles Banks, comp. *Indians of Eastern Oklahoma Including Quapaw Agency Indians.* Afton, Okla: Buffalo Publishing Co., c.1956. (FHL# 970.1/W692)

Wright, Muriel Hazel. *A Guide to the Indian Tribes of Oklahoma.* Norman: University of Oklahoma Press, 1951. (FHL# 970.1/M934g)

Probate Records

Some probate records are available for a few counties. Check the FHLC under **Oklahoma/[County]/Probate Records.** In 1806, the District of Arkansas was created in the Territory of Louisiana, embracing most of present-day Oklahoma. See:

Louisiana (Territory) Probate Court. *Probate Records, 1808-1812.* Salt Lake City: Filmed by the Genealogical Society of Utah, 1975. Microreproduction of manuscript. (FHL# microfilm 0978542, item 5)

Muskogee Area Office Agency records for 1883-1945 are available, including the index file to heirs of the Five Civilized Tribes (FHL# microfilm 1205785). School and vital records are also listed under this heading for the Pawnee Agency.

Wever, Opha Jewell. *Probate Records 1892-1902, Northern District Cherokee Nation*. 2 vols. Winita: Northeast Oklahoma Genealogical Society, 1982-1983. (FHL# 976.6/-P2w)

Vital Records

Statewide registration of births and deaths began in 1908, but records were inconsistently registered for several years. Some marriage records are available at the county level for the territorial period. No state-wide vital records are available in the FHLC, but some records are available for various counties. These are cataloged under **Oklahoma/[County]/Vital Records.** Some tribal vital records are cataloged under **Oklahoma/Native Races/Vital Records.** Also a few vital records are listed under **Oklahoma/Obituaries.** Several publications may be helpful:

Bode, Frances Murphy. *Oklahoma Territorial Weddings.* Geary, Okla.: Pioneer Book Committee, 1983. (FHL# 976.6/ V2bf)

Bogle, Dixie. *Cherokee Nation Births and Deaths, 1884 1901.* Utica, Ky.: McDowell Publications, 1980. Sponsored by the Northeast Oklahoma Genealogical Society. (FHL# 970.3/C42bo)

Cook, Mrs. John P., comp. *Collection of Oklahoma Bible and Family Records*. Assembled by Daughters of the American Revolution Chapters of Oklahoma, n.p., 1954. (FHL# 976.6/V2d or microfilm 0873998, item 1)

Massey, Lynda Stout. *Index to Marriages of Oklahoma India Territory.* Compiled from Book One, Atoka, Oklahoma. n.p., 1980. (FHL# 976.61/V3n)

Oklahoma Genealogical Society. *A Compilation of Records from the Choctaw Nation, Indian Territory.* Oklahoma City: Oklahoma Genealogical Society, 1976. (FHL# microfilm 1206500 or 0488191)

Tiffee, Ellen. *Oklahoma Marriage Records, Choctaw Nation Indian Territory*. n.p.: n.d. (FHL# 976.6/V2t)

KANSAS

Historical Background

1803	Kansas becomes a United States possession with the Louisiana Purchase.
1821	Santa Fe Trail established through Kansas.
1827	Fort Leavenworth established.
1843	John C. Fremont begins exploration of lands suitable for route of the Union Pacific Railroad.
1854	Rev. Joseph Meeker opens Baptist mission in what is now Franklin County and publishes its first newspaper (in English and Cherokee).
1854	Stephen A. Douglas proposes bill to establish the Kansas and Nebraska territories. Kansas becomes a territory 30 May 1854
1854	Massachusetts Emigrant Aid Company incorporated to form colonies to settle the new territories.
1854	Indian tribes removed from Kansas Territory and resettled in the new Indian Territory.
1855	First territorial census.
1860	Second territorial census.
1861	Kansas enters the Union as thirty-fourth state.
1861	Kansas State Militia organized.

Settlement and Migration

Land companies, religious groups, immigrant groups, and residents of other states made up the largest segment of early Kansas settlers. Some of the most active land companies in Kansas brought foreign-born settlers into the state. These include:

1. The Swedish Agricultural Company: formed in Chicago in 1868; settled in Saline and McPherson counties.
2. Galesburg Colonization Company: formed in Illinois in 1868; also settled in Saline and McPherson counties.
3. Scandinavian Agricultural Society: formed in 1869 and settled in Riley and Pottawatomie counties.
4. Swedish Colonization Company: formed in 1887; settled large colonies of Swedish Lutherans in Wallace, Logan, Greeley, Sherman, Thomas, Trego, Marion, and Morris counties.
5. Excelsior Cooperative Colony of Kansas: formed in London by Scots and English to settle colonies mainly in Nemaha County. Also known as Mutual Land Emigration and Cooperative Colonization Company.
6. Kansas Land and Emigration Company: formed in 1869 by John Wormald; purchased 32,000 acres between the Republican River and Chapman Creek.
7. Welsh Land and Emigrant Society of America: formed in 1870 in New York and settled in Lyons County.

Organized colonies from other states also contributed to settling Kansas. South Carolina, Kentucky, and Tennessee sent colonies between 1861 and 1869. A second group of Kentuckians migrated to Cowley County in 1869, and a small colony from Tennessee followed later. Another group from Kentucky settled in McPherson County in 1873. A Massachusetts colony established Edwards County in 1873, and a group from Connecticut settled on government lands in Osborne and Smith counties that same year. The Soldiers' and Sailors' Free Homestead colony was established in McPherson County; and other veterans' colonies were founded later in Meade, Osborne, Barton, Anderson, and Republic counties.

The majority of settlers in Kansas were German and Irish. They settled in colonies but were found in every county as single families migrating west. Other nationalities settling in Kansas between 1860 and 1900 included Norwegians, Danes, Swedes, Bohemians (Czechs), Scots, English, Welsh, French, and Russians.

Religious groups also settled in Kansas. Quakers arrived in noticeable numbers around 1875 to settle in Rich and Osborne counties. River Brethren escaped religious persecution in Germany and settled in Franklin County. Dunkards and German Baptists settled Saline, Ellsworth, Russell, Osborne, Barton, and Lincoln counties. Church of the Brethren members migrated to central and western Kansas in 1878. A small schismatic Mormon group, later called Bickertonites, settled in Stafford County in 1875. Mennonites from southern Russia settled in Marion, Harvey, McPherson, Reno, Barton, and Butler counties.

Kansas Library Collection

Archives and Libraries

Decker, Eugene Donald. *A Selected, Annotated Bibliography of Sources in the Kansas State Historical Society Pertaining to the Civil War.* Emporia, Kans.: State Teachers College, 1961. (FHL# PBA/no.1107)

Historical Records Survey, Works Progress Administration. *Guide to Public Vital Records in Kansas.* Topeka: Kansas Historical Records Survey, 1942. (FHL# 978.1/V2h)

Biography

The library has a large collection of Kansas biographical publications. See the FHLC under **Kansas/Biography.** Additional titles containing biographies of residents from individual counties are listed under the county biography heading following the state's general listings. Notable among the state biographical publications in the collection are:

Andreas, A. T. *History of the State of Kansas.* 1883; Rpt. ed. Marceline, Mo.: Walsworth Publishing Co., 1976. (Original FHL# 978.1/H2hi, or 1000031; reprint FHL# 978.1/H2hi/1976)

Connelley, William Elsey. *A Standard History of Kansas and Kansans.* Chicago: Lewis Publishing Co., 1918. (FHL# 978.1 H2c or microfilm 1000029)

Tuttle, Charles Richard. *A New Centennial History of the State of Kansas.* Madison, Wis.: Inter-state Book Company, 1876. (FHL# 978.1/H2t or microfilm 1036377, item 2)

The United States Biographical Dictionary: Kansas Volume. Chicago and Kansas City: S. Lewis and Co., 1879. (FHL# 978.1/D3u or microfilm 0874388, items 1-2)

Cemeteries

Cemetery tombstone inventories are still being compiled in Kansas. Published inscriptions are listed under **/[County]/Cemeteries.**

Pompey, Sherman L. *Civil War Veterans' Burials from Various States.* Salt Lake City: Genealogical Society of Utah, 1968. (FHL# microfilm 0564337, items 1-2)

Includes a section on veterans buried in Kansas.

Census

Kansas took a state census enumeration midway between the federal census years beginning with the 1855 Kansas Territorial Census. The library has mortality schedules for 1860, 1870, and 1880, along with indexes to the early territorial censuses.

Heiss, Willard C., ed. *The Census of the Territory of Kansas, February, 1855.* Knightstown, Ind.: Eastern Indiana Publishers, 1968. (FHL# 978.1/X/1855)

Territorial Census of 1855. Topeka: Kansas State Historical Society, 1951. (FHL# microfilm 0570188)

Topeka Genealogical Society, comp. *The Mortality Schedule of the Territory of Kansas, 1860.* n.p.: 1973. (FHL# 978.1/X2m/1860 or microfilm 0897418, item 1)

Robertson, Clara Hamlett. *Kansas Territorial Settlers of 1860 Who Were Born in Tennessee, Virginia, North Carolina and South Carolina.* Baltimore: Genealogical Publishing Company, 1976. (FHL# 978.1/H2ro)

Kansas Secretary of State. *State Census of 1865.* 9 reels. Topeka: Kansas Historical Society, 1951. (FHL# microfilm 0570189-0570197)

Kansas State Board of Agriculture. *State Census of 1875.* 23 reels. Topeka: Kansas State Historical Society, 1951. (FHL# microfilm 0570198-0570220)

_____ *State Census of 1885.* 151 reels. Topeka: Kansas State Historical Society, 1969-70. (FHL# microfilm 0975699-0976088)

_____. *State Census of 1895.* 202 reels. Topeka: Kansas State Historical Society, 1953-58. (FHL# microfilm 0570221- 0570416)

Church Records

Church records of christenings, marriages, and burials are generally listed in the FHLC under **/[County]/Church Records.** An exception, cataloged under **/Church History** is:

Jesuit Mission and College Records, 1832-1967. 2 reels. Topeka: Filmed by the Kansas State Historical Society, 1967. Microfilm copy of handwritten and typewritten original and transcribed records in the archives of St. Mary's College, St. Marys, Kans. (FHL# microfilm 0590422-0590423)

Includes some school records, baptisms and marriages, biographies, diaries, communions, confirmations, and lists of Indian heads of families, Indian society members, Indian- and Non-Indian members of fraternities and societies.

Genealogy

Check the FHLC under **Kansas/Genealogy** and **/[County]/Genealogy** for a complete list of genealogical publications. Worth noting is this bibliography of early Kansas history and genealogy:

Critz, Lalla Campbell, ed. *Kansas, the Formative Years.* Fort Worth, Tex: The Magazine of Bibliographies, 1972. (FHL# 978.1/A1/no.30)

Historical Geography

Baughman, Robert W. *Kansas in Maps*. Topeka: Kansas State Historical Society, 1961. (FHL# 978.1/E7br)

Socolofsky, Homer E. *Historical Atlas of Kansas*. Norman: University of Oklahoma Press, 1972. (FHL# 978.1/E3s)

History

Over forty titles detail the history of Kansas in the library's collection. See also:

Blackmar, Frank W., ed. *Kansas: A Cyclopedia of State History, Embracing Events, Institutions, Industries, Counties, Cities, Towns, Prominent Persons, Etc. . . . With a Supplementary Volume Devoted to Selected Personal History and Reminiscence.* 3 vols. Chicago: Standard Publishing Co., c.1912. (FHL# 978.1/H2ka or microfilm 1000027 and 100028)

Owen, Jennie Small, annalist, and Kircke Mechem, ed. *The Annals of Kansas, 1886-1925, in Two Volumes*. 2 vols. Topeka: Kansas State Historical Society, 1954, 1956. (FHL# 978./H2o or microfilm 1036385, items 2-3)

Tuttle, Charles Richard. *A New Centennial History of the State of Kansas: Being a Full and Complete Civil, Political and Military History of the State, from its Earliest Settlement to the Present Time*. Madison, Wis: Inter-State Book Co., 1876. (FHL# 978.1/H2t or microfilm 1036377, item 2)

Land and Property

The federal government initially sold or granted the land of Kansas to settlers. Land transferred after the initial patent was registered by deed at the county level. Land and property records in Kansas are not yet microfilmed; however, published land records and abstracts are listed in the FHLC under **Kansas/[County]/Land And Property**. See also the few general sources listed under **Kansas/Land And Property**.

An early compilation of some early homestead entries is included with description of homestead laws and practices.

Homestead Guide of Kansas and Nebraska. Ann Arbor, Mich.: University Microfilms International, 1970. (microfilm of original published: Waterville, Kans.: F.G. Adams, 1873). (FHL# microfilm 1303173)

Sobotka, Margie. *Nebraska, Kansas Czech Settlers*. n.p. Whippoorwill, c.1980.(FHL# 987/F2so)

Includes the land each male settler owned or rented, his occupation, and his birthplace. Covers forty-five Nebraska and eleven Kansas counties.

Maps, Gazetteers, and Atlases

The library has a large collection of Kansas maps. Among the most useful are:

Baughman, Robert W. *Kansas in Maps.* Topeka: The Kansas State Historical Society, 1961. (FHL# 978.1/E7br)

Carman, J. Neale. *Foreign-Language Units of Kansas.* Lawrence: University of Kansas Press, 1962. (FHL# 978.1/F2c)

Gamble, W. H. *County and Township Map of the States of Kansas and Nebraska.* Philadelphia: n.p., c.1974. (FHL# 978/E7g)

______. *County and Township Map of the States of Kansas and Nebraska*. Philadelphia: n.p. c.1882. (FHL# 978/E7g/1882)

The Official State Atlas of Kansas. n.p.: Kansas Council of Genealogical Societies, 1982. (FHL# Q Area/978.1/E7o)

Identification of places can be made in:

Rydjord, John. *Kansas Place-Names.* Norman: University of Oklahoma Press, 1972. (FHL# 978.1/E2r)

Military Records

Kansas became a state just before the Civil War began, and its early residents participated in that war either as Union Army soldiers or Kansas State militiamen. Some important genealogical resources for Kansas related to that war are:

Decker, Eugene Donald. *A Selected, Annotated Bibliography of Sources in the Kansas State Historical Society Pertaining to Kansas in the Civil War.* Emporia, Kans.: State Teachers College, 1961. (FHL# P.B.A. no.1107 in unassigned book area)

John Haupt Chapter, Daughters of the American Revolution. *Index to the Kansas Militia in the Civil War.* Topeka, Kans.: The Chapter, 1979. (FHL# 978.1/M221)

Pompey, S. L. *An Honor Roll of Kansas Civil War Veterans.* Kingsburg, Calif.: Pacific Specialists, 1972. (FHL# 978.1/A1/no.12 or microfilm 0874332, item 8)

United States Adjutant General's Office. 10 reels. *Index to Compiled Service Records of Volunteer Union Soldiers Who Served in Organizations from the State of Kansas (1861-1865).* Washington, D.C.: National Archives, 1965. (FHL# microfilm 0881746-0881837)

Minorities

The library has a number of published works dealing with ethnic minorities in Kansas. For example, see:

Billdt, Ruth. *Pioneer Swedish-American Culture in Central Kansas.* Linsborg, Kans.: Linsborg News-Record, 1965. (FHL# 978.1/ F2sb)

Carman, J. Neale. *Foreign-Language Units of Kansas.* Lawrence, Kans: University of Kansas Press, 1962. (FHL# 978.1/F2c)

Juhnke, James C. *A People of Two Kingdoms: The Political Acculturation of the Kansas Mennonites.* Newton, Kans.: Faith and Life Press, c.1975. (FHL# 978.1/F2mj)

Schaefer, Lisa. *They Came to Kansas: A Report.* Microfilm of typescript. Salt Lake City: Genealogical Society of Utah, 1978. (FHL# 978.1/A1/no.22)

A report on the Mennonites who left Russia in 1874 and settled in Kansas in 1875.

Sobotka, Margie. *Nebraska, Kansas Czech Settlers*. n.p.: Whippoorwill, c.1980. (FHL# 978/F2so)

Native Races

Kansas territory originally belonged to the Indian tribes that were relocated to Indian Territory in 1854. Records of Indian activities in Kansas after that date include missionary journals, school records and school censuses, agency books, vital records, land records, and probate records. See FHLC headings **Kansas/Native Races, /Probate Records, /Vital Records, /Minorities,** and **/Land Records.** See also:

Haskell Institute. *School Records, 1884-1953.* Fort Worth, Tex: Filmed by the National Archives, 1978. 7 reels. (FHL# microfilm 1205530, item 1, 1249896-1249899, 1028529-1028530)

Jesuit Mission and College Records, 1832-1967. Topeka, Kan: Filmed by the Kansas State Historical Society, 1967. Microfilm copy of handwritten and typewritten original and transcribed records in the archives of St. Mary's College, St. Marys, Kansas. 2 reels. (FHL# microfilm 0590422 and 0590423)

Pratt, John Gill. *John G. Pratt Papers, 1834-1899 in the Kansas State Historical Society.* Topeka: Filmed by the Kansas State Historical Society, c.1970. 13 reels. (FHL# microfilm 0812758-0812769 and 0824280, item 2)

Vital Records

Kansas vital records have not been filmed. Substitutes for these valuable research tools include mortality schedules for 1860, 1870, and 1880, cataloged in the FHLC under **Kansas/Vital Records.** Published vital records of Kansas counties are listed under **/[County]/Vital Records.** Also note:

Pantle, Alberta, comp. *Marriage Notices from Kansas Territorial Newspapers, 1854-1861.* Cheney, Kans.: Midwest Historical and Genealogical Society, c.1980. Reprinted with permission of the *Kansas Historical Quarterly*, Vol. 21, Summer 1955. (FHL# 978.1/A1/no.114 and 978.1/B2k)

NEBRASKA

Historical Background

1541-1803	Area claimed alternatively by French and Spanish.
1803	United States acquires jurisdiction of Nebraska area by the Louisiana Purchase.
1807	United States purchases Black Hawk Territory.
1810	First white settlement made at Bellevue.
1812	Area of Nebraska becomes part of Missouri Territory.
1813	First white man travels through the Platte Valley.
1821	The area becomes Indian Territory.
1823	Bellevue, on the Missouri River, becomes the earliest settlement in present-day Nebraska.
1833	Pawnees cede their lands south of the Platte River.
1834	Area of Nebraska is partitioned into three sections and placed under the jurisdiction of Arkansas Territory, Michigan Territory and the state of Missouri. Baptist mission established at Bellevue.
1841	Migration to Oregon passes through Nebraska.
1847	Mormons establish new trail across Nebraska. Presbyterians build mission house and school at Bellevue.
1850s	Some California gold rushers settle in Nebraska. Germans settle in Nebraska area.
1853	Omaha settled.
1854	First territorial census. Indian treaties cede most land west of Missouri River. Nebraska Territory established; includes Montana, most of Wyoming, northeast Colorado, and western North and South Dakota.
1855	Second territorial census shows a population of 4,494.
1856	Third territorial census.
1857	Pawnee cede remaining lands except reservation. Germans settle at what becomes Grand Island.
1860	Fourth territorial census.
1863	Scandinavians and others homestead.
1865	Union Pacific Railroad lays track in Nebraska.
1867	Nebraska becomes thirty-seventh state.
1870	First federal census since statehood.
1870s	German-Russians (descendants of Germans who settled in southern Russia during the eighteenth century) settle area of Lancaster and surrounding counties.
1880	Second federal census.
1885	First state census.
1890	Third federal census; only military schedule remains.

Settlement and Migration

Nebraska was a major path of travel to the West for thousands of individuals and families during the mid-nineteenth century. The Oregon Trail, running along the Platte River, replaced the longer and more difficult Missouri River path and became the highway of American westward expansion.

The earliest settlers scattered along the Missouri River in the eastern section of Nebraska for the first few years. A German settlement in the west on the Platte River became Grand Island. By 1867, settlements had been established over one hundred miles along the South Platte. More than 75 percent of the territorial population was American-born in 1860. These early Nebraska residents represented a flow of migration from New England and the Mid-Atlantic states across the Old Northwest. The states that contributed substantial numbers of settlers, in this order, were Ohio, New York, Pennsylvania, Illinois, Iowa, Indiana, and Missouri.

Foreign-born settlers also found their way into Nebraska. Germans formed the largest group, over 25 percent of the total. English and Irish followed closely with nearly 25 percent each. Sixty percent of those living in Omaha and Douglas County were foreign-born. Fifty-one percent in Platte and Madison counties were foreign-born, while 49 percent of those in nearby Kearney County, 33 percent of Dakota County, and 25 percent of Otoe County residents were born outside of the United States. Hall County was predominantly German but was sparsely settled.

Since the formation of each county, county clerks have been responsible for maintaining records of birth, marriage, death, probate, and wills. Land and property records are under the jurisdiction of the register of deeds of the respective counties. After 1904, birth and death records have been maintained by the State Bureau of Vital Statistics which also became responsible for marriage records in 1909.

Nebraska Library Collection

Archives and Libraries

The Family History Library has inventories of records in various depositories for Nebraska. Check the FHLC under **Nebraska/Archives and Libraries.** Included among the holdings are as follows:

Diffendal, Anne P., comp. *A Guide to the Newspaper Collection of the State Archives, Nebraska State Historical Society.* Lincoln: Nebraska State Historical Society, 1969. (FHL# 978.2/B33n/no.4/1969)

Hons, Fred W., and Delbert A. Bishop, comps. *Preliminary Inventory Records of the United States District Court for the District of Nebraska: Record Group 21.* Kansas City, Mo: Federal Records Center, 1967. (FHL# 978.2/A1/no.18)

Nebraska Historical Records Survey Project, Division of Professional and Service Projects, Works Projects Administration. *Preliminary Edition of Guide to Depositories of Manuscript Collections in the United States-Nebraska.* Lincoln, Neb.: The Survey, 1940. (FHL# 978.2/A3hg or fiche 6019929 or microfilm 0962706, item 1)

Nebraska State Historical Society, State Archives. *A Guide to the Manuscript Division of the State Archives, Nebraska State Historical Society.* Lincoln: The Nebraska State Historical Society, 1974. (FHL# 978.2/A3n/no.5)

Schmidt, William F., comp. *A Guide to the Archives and Manuscripts of the Nebraska State Historical Society.* Lincoln: The Nebraska State Historical Society, 1965. (FHL# 978.2/A3n/no.1 or microfilm 1036244, item 3)

Also see *Societies* below.

Atlases, Gazetteers, and Maps

The FHLC has several references for each of these three categories. Check under **Nebraska/Atlases, Nebraska/Gazetteers,** and **Nebraska/Maps.** The library has a good collection of Nebraska maps and a few county maps. See listings under **Nebraska/[county Name]/-Maps.**

The notable collection below is cataloged under **Nebraska/Historical Geography/Maps:**

Nimmo, Sylvia. *Maps Showing County Boundaries of Nebraska, 1854-1925.* Papillion, Nebr.: n.p., 1978. (FHL# 978.2/-E7m)

Bible Records

Most genealogical records kept in family Bibles for Nebraska are listed in the FHLC under **Nebraska/Bible Records.** Douglas County is the only smaller unit with a separately listed collection of Bible records.

Biography

Biographies appear in the FHLC under **Nebraska/-Biography** and **Nebraska/[County]/Biography.** Some may also be located under **/History** and **/[County]/Biography.** Several in the collection are notable:

Baldwin, Sara Mullin. *Nebraska, Biographical Sketches of Nebraska Men and Women of Achievement.* Hebron, Nebr.: Baldwin Co., 1932. (FHL# 978.2/D3ba)

A Biographical and Genealogical History of Southeastern Nebraska: Embellished with Portraits of Many Well Known People of This Section of the Great West Who Have Been and Are Prominent in History and Development. Chicago: Lewis Publishing Co., 1904. (FHL# 978.2/D3bi or microfilm 1000181, items 1-2)

Compendium of History, Reminiscence and Biography of Western Nebraska: Containing a History of the State of Nebraska . . . Containing Biographical Sketches of Hundreds of Prominent Old Settlers and Representative Citizens. 2 vols. Chicago: Alden Publishing Co., 1909. (FHL# 978.2/H2c or microfilm 1000181, item 3) Partial index contained in Volume 1.

Edmunds, A. C. *Pen Sketches of Nebraskans with Photographs.* Lincoln: R & J. Wilbur, 1871. (FHL# 978.2/D3e or microfilm 1000182, item 2)

Nebraskans, 1854-1904. Omaha: Bee Publishing Co., 1904. (FHL# 978.2/D3e or microfilm 0908204, item 3 and 1000182, item 5)

Sheldon, A. E. *Semi-centennial History of Nebraska: Historical Sketch.* Lincoln: Lemon Publishing Co., 1931. (FHL# 978.2/H2se or microfilm 1000178, item 3)

Sobotka, Margie. *A History of Czechs in Nebraska.* Microfilm of manuscript submitted by Mrs. Nettie L. McCartney Urban. Salt Lake City: Genealogical Society of Utah. 1979. (FHL# microfilm 982106, item 2)

Shumway, Grant L., ed. *History of Western Nebraska and Its People: Banner, Box Butte, Cheyenne, Dawes, Deuel, Garden, Kimball, Morrill, Scotts, Bluff, Sheridan, and Sioux Counties; A Group Often Called the Panhandle of Nebraska*. 3 vols. Lincoln, Neb.: Western Publishing and Engraving Co., c.1921. (FHL# 978.29/H2s and microfilm 1000182, item 1)

Cemeteries

Tombstone inventories are still being compiled in Nebraska. Published inscriptions are listed in the FHLC under **Nebraska/Cemeteries** and **Nebraska/[County]/Cemeteries.**

Census

Territorial censuses are cataloged under **Nebraska/Census.** A few county census enumerations are listed under **Nebraska/[County]/Census.**

Cox, E. Evelyn, comp. *1854, 1855, 1856 Nebraska Territory Census.* 3 vols. in 1. n.p., 1977. (FHL# 978.2/X2p/1854-1856, microfilm 1036024, item 2, and fiche 6051283)

______. *1870 Nebraska Census.* 3 vols. Ellensburg, Wash.: Ancestree House, 1979-80. (FHL# 978.2/x2c/1870)

______, comp. *1860 Nebraska Territory Census*. Ellensburg, Wash: n.p., 1973. (FHL# 978.2/X2pa/1860 and microfilm 0924579, item 1)

Eastern Nebraska Genealogical Society, comps. *1885 Nebraska Mortality Schedule.* Fremont, Nebr.: Eastern Nebraska Genealogical Society, c.1980. (FHL# 978.22/X2n/1885)

James, Jane Emerson. *Eighth Census of the United States, 1860 Nebraska Territory Mortality Schedules.* Huntsville, Ark.: Century Enterprises, 1972. (FHL# 978.2/A1/no.19, microfilm 0982310, item 3, and fiche 6051181)

Nebraska Superintendent of Census. *Schedules of the Nebraska State Census of 1885*. Washington, D.C.: National Archives, 1961. 56 reels. (FHL# microfilm 0499529-0499584)

United States Bureau of Indian Affairs. *Winnebago Agency Census Records, 1869-1929*. Kansas City, Mo.: Federal Archives and Records Center, 1977. 7 reels. (FHL# microfilm 1015904-1015910)

United States Census Office. *Nebraska Territory 1860 Federal Census Schedules of Inhabitants, Persons Who Died During Year, Production of Agriculture and Industry, Social Statistics*. Kansas City: Archives Branch of the Federal Records Center, 1969. 2 reels. (FHL# microfilm 1025171 and 1025172)

______. *Nebraska 1880 Federal Census Schedules of Products of Agriculture and Industry, Persons Who Died During the Year, and Defective, Dependent and Deliquent Classes.* Kansas City: Archives Branch of the Federal Records Center, 1969. 12 reels. (FHL# microfilm 1025175-1025186)

Church History

Church histories are listed under **Nebraska/Church History** and under **Nebraska/[County]/Church History**. Histories of several denominations are represented. Some church records are enumerated under **Nebraska/[County]/Church Records.** Grand Island Presbyterian Church's are cited under **Nebraska/Genealogy.**

Genealogy

Several genealogical collections are available for Nebraska, listed under **Nebraska/Genealogy** and **Nebraska/[County]/Genealogy.** Several collections were compiled by Nebraska Chapters of the Daughters of the American Revolution. For genealogical periodicals, see listings under **Nebraska/ Genealogy/Periodicals** and **Nebraska/[County]/Genealogy/ Periodicals.**

Sittler, Melvin E. *Sittler Index of Surnames: For Which Information Has Been Abstracted From the [Lincoln] Nebraska State Journal, May 1873-Dec. 1899.* 4 vols. Lincoln, Nebr.: Lincoln-Lancaster County Genealogical Society, c.1983. (FHL# 978.2293/D22si)

This index is compiled from the 70,000 cards in the collection of the Lincoln-Lancaster County Genealogical Society. Data on the cards was abstracted from *The Nebraska State Journal* for 1873-99 and contains birth, death, marriage, pension, and other records.

United States Bureau of Indian Affairs, Winnebago Agency. *Family Registers, 1871, 1902-1907*. Kansas City, Mo.: Federal Archives and Records Center, 1977. (FHL# microfilm 1015911, items 12-16)

History

Over twenty titles deal with Nebraska's history, including a few county histories. However, most are listed under **Nebraska/History** in the FHLC. Also, included in the library's collection are two history journals, cataloged under **Nebraska/History/Periodicals.**

Land and Property

Few land and property records are available for Nebraska. Most concern the Winnebago Agency of the Bureau of Indian Affairs and include land transactions for the Santee, Ponca, Omaha, and Winnebago tribes.

A Homestead Guide of Kansas and Nebraska. Ann Arbor, Mich.: University Microfilms International, 1970. Microfilm of original published: Waterville, Kans.: F. G. Adams, 1873. (FHL# microfilm 1303173)

Contains a list of some homesteaders and description of homestead laws and practices.

Maps, Gazetteers, and Atlases

Maps can be accessed under **Nebraska/Maps**. To identify places in Nebraska, see also:

Fitzpatrick, Lillian L. *Nebraska Place-Names: Including Selections From the Origin of Place-Names of Nebraska by J. T. Link*. ed. with an introduction by G. Thomas Fairclough. Lincoln: University of Nebraska Press, 1960. (FHL# 978.2/E5f)

Perkey, Elton. *Perkey's Nebraska Place Names*. Lincoln: Nebraska State Historical Society, 1982. (FHL# 978.2/E5f)

Military Records

The library has a few state and federal publications on Kansas military records.

Allen, John C. *Rosters of Soldiers, Sailors, and Marines of the War of 1812, the Mexican War, and the War of the Rebellion, Residing in Nebraska 1 June 1891. Nebr.: State Journal Co., Printers, 1892. Reprinted Lincoln, Neb.: Nebraska State Genealogical Society, 1985. (FHL# 978.2/M2n or microfilm 0844966, item 4, or fiche 6010064)*

Dudley, Edgar S. *A Roster of Nebraska Soldiers from 1861 to 1869: Compiled From Books, Records and Documents on File in Office of Adjutant General of State*. Salt Lake City: Filmed by the Genealogical Society of Utah, 1958. Microreproduction of original published: Hastings, Nebr.: Wigton and Evans, 1888. (FHL# microfilm 0164034, item 2).

______, comp. *Roster of Nebraska Volunteers From 1861 to 1869*. Salt Lake City: Filmed by the Genealogical Society of Utah, 1963. Microfilm of original published: Hastings, Nebr.: Wigton and Evans, 1888. (FHL# microfilm 0370881)

Roster of Nebraska Soldiers. Salt Lake City: Filmed by the Genealogical Society of Utah, 1958. Microreproduction of original published: Omaha, Nebr.: Klopp, Bartlett, and Co., 1888. (FHL# microfilm 0164034, item 1)

United States Adjutant General's Office. *Index to Compiled Service Records of Volunteer Union Soldiers Who Served in Organizations From the Territory of Nebraska, 1861-1865.* Washington, D.C.: National Archives, 1965. 2 reels. (FHL# microfilm 0821905 and 0821906)

United States Bureau of Indian Affairs. Winnebago Agency. *Winnebago and Omaha Indians in World War I.* Kansas City, Mo.: Federal Archives and Records Center, 1977. (FHL# microfilm 1015934, item 8-9)

Minorities

Under the heading **Nebraska/Minorities**, you will find:

Irving, John Treat. *Indian Sketches: Taken During an Expedition to the Pawnee Tribes, 1833.* John Francis McDermott, ed. Norman: University of Oklahoma Press, 1955. (FHL# 970.3/ P289)

Reprints the first American edition, 1835, with "new matter from 1888," introductory material, additional details, and anecdotes.

Luebke, Frederick C. *Immigrants and Politics: The Germans of Nebraska, 1880-1900.* Lincoln: University of Nebraska Press, 1969. (FHL# 978.2/F2gl)

Rife, Janet Warkentin. *Germans and German-Russians in Nebraska: A Research Guide to Nebraska Ethnic Studies.* Nebr.: Center for Great Plains Studies, University of Nebraska-Lincoln: Nebraska Curriculum Development Center, University of Nebraska-Lincoln, 1980. (FHL# 978.2/F23r)

Rosicky, Rose. *A History of Czechs (Bohemians) in Nebraska.* Evansville, Ind.: Unigraphic, Inc., 1977. (FHL# 978.2/F2r or microfilm 1036170, item 1)

Sobotka, Margie. *Nebraska, Kansas Czech Settlers.* n.p. Whipporwill, c.1980. (FHL# 978/F2so)

Works Projects Administration in Nebraska, sponsored by the Omaha Urban. *The Negroes of Nebraska: League Community Center.* Lincoln: Woodruff Printing Co., 1940. (FHL# 978.2/F2n)

Native Races

Several collections of records pertaining to the Winnebago Indians and annuity rolls for the Omaha, Winnebago, Ponca, Flandreau, and Santee tribes are available under **Nebraska/Natives Races.** See also **Nebraska/Census, Nebraska/Minorities, and Nebraska/Land and Property.** Native American records are cataloged under various headings. For instance, marriage records for Spotted Tail (Rosebud) Agency are located under **Nebraska/Land and Property,** Pawnee historical sketches are under **Nebraska/Minorities,** and Winnebago Agency probate records are under **Nebraska/Probate Records.**

United States Bureau of Indian Affairs. Winnebago Agency. *Agency Records, 1859-1924.* Salt Lake City: Filmed by the Genealogical Society of Utah, 1978. Microfilm of originals at the Omaha Indian reservation, Macy, Nebraska. 2 reels. (FHL# microfilm 1028441 and 1028442)

These records include marriages; census rolls; land allotments; Presbyterian Church records of baptisms, marriages, deaths; and a tribal index for 1880 to 1904.

Newspapers

A few titles concerning Nebraska newspapers are located under **Nebraska/Newspapers** and **Nebraska/-[County Name]/Newspapers.** See also:

Diffendal, Anne P., comp. *A Guide to the Newspaper Collection of the State Archives, Nebraska State Historical Society.* Lincoln: n.p., 1977 (FHL# 978.2/B33n/no.4)

Nebraska State Genealogical Society. *Nebraska Newspaper Abstracts: A Computer Index to Names and Events Abstracted From Selected Nebraska Newspapers.* Vol. 1. 1870 Series. Alliance, Nebr.: Nebraska State Genealogical Society, 1983. (FHL# 978.2/B32n)

Probate Records

Only Winnebago Agency probate records are available:

United States Bureau of Indian Affairs. Winnebago Agency. *Probate Records, 1885, 1895-1940.* Kansas City, Mo.: Federal Archives and Records Center, 1977. 15 reels. (FHL# microfilm 1015912-1015927, item 2)

Societies

Guides to the archives and manuscripts of the Nebraska State Historical Society are cataloged, not under **/Archives**, but under this listing. Society publications appear in the FHLC under **Nebraska/Societies/Periodicals.**

Vital Records

No statewide vital records are available except for native Americans. See:

Cline, Martha Adamson. *Golden Weddings of Nebraskans.* Lincoln: M. A. Cline, c.1986. (FHL# 978.2/V2c)

Nebraska Historical Records Survey. Works Projects Administration. *A Guide to Public Vital Statistics Records in Nebraska*. Lincoln: Historical Records Survey, 1941. (FHL# 978.2/V23h, or microfilm 0874077, item 3, or microfiche 6046710)

United States Bureau of Indian Affairs. Winnebago Agency. *Vital Statistics: Births, Marriages, and Deaths, 1863-1947.* Kansas City, Mo.: Federal Archives and Records Center, 1977. (FHL# microfilm 1015911, items 1,4-11).

Some county records are cataloged under **Nebraska/[County]/Vital Records.** For names abstracted from the *Nebraska State Journal* and a computer index to names and vital events abstracted from selected Nebraska newspapers, see **Nebraska/Vital Records/Indexes.** Some Spotted Tail (Rosebud) Agency marriage records are listed in the FHLC under **Nebraska/Land and Property.**

SOUTH DAKOTA

Historical Background

1682-1803	South Dakota area claimed alternatively by France and Spain.
1803	Most of South Dakota area included in the Louisiana Purchase.
1803-20	South Dakota area under the jurisdiction of Missouri Territory.
1804-06	Lewis and Clark pass through the Dakotas as they explore the Louisiana Purchase.
1817	Fort Pierre becomes the first permanent settlement.
1836	South Dakota included in the 1836 Iowa Territorial Census.
1857	Settlers from adjoining states establish homes and farms.
1859	Vermillion and Yankton are established.
1861	Dakota Territory is created, including North and South Dakota, most of Montana, and part of Wyoming.
1863	Homestead Act brings numerous settlers to territory.
1874	Gold discovered in the Black Hills.
1875	Settlers enter western part of territory.
1878-87	Great Dakota Boom. Free land and expanded rail service bring many settlers into the area east of the Missouri River.
1887	Territory divided into North and South Dakota.
1889	South Dakota becomes fortieth state. Sixty-six of sixty-nine counties are established.

Settlement and Migration

Unlike the opening of Oklahoma, few people waited anxiously to rush across the forty-third parallel to settle Dakota Territory. The nation's involvement in the Civil War and problems with the Indians occupied people's attention and caused those who pushed for the organization of Dakota Territory to wonder if their efforts were wasted.

Most first settlers located in counties along the Missouri slope. Almost 500 settlers, excluding government employees and fur traders, lived in the southeastern part of the territory. Natives of Minnesota and Wisconsin, they had traveled by covered wagon across northern Iowa or through southern Minnesota to reach Dakota Territory. Yankton, Vermillion, Bon Homme, and Elk Point were the leading settlements. Fertile land on the Missouri bottom between the Vermillion and James rivers attracted a number of Norwegian settlers.

The New York Colony was the largest group to settle in the Dakotas. Encouraged by the passing of the Homestead Law of 1862, officers of the "Free Homestead Association of Central New York" visited the Dakotas and chose to settle near Yankton on the James River. Nearly a hundred families traveled by train to Marshalltown, Iowa, and then came overland for four weeks by covered wagon. Only thirty families remained with the colony after arrival.

Norwegians, a large portion of the Dakota Territory population along the Missouri, became the dominant Scandinavian element and played a key role in South Dakota's settlement up the Big Sioux Valley to Lincoln and Minnehaha counties. Swedish immigrants began settling in the Clay County area in 1868. They were followed by a large Danish colony that numbered several hundred families within twenty years of their arrival in Turner County.

An 1869 group, consisting primarily of Bohemians who formed an immigration company in Chicago and other eastern cities, established Czech communities in western states and territories. The first such immigrants settled in Lakeport along the Fort Randall military road.

German-Russians, descendants of Germans who had settled in southern Russia during the eighteenth century, began arriving in 1873. Several thousand settled in Bon Homme, Hutchinson, Turner, and Yankton counties. They preserved their culture, social customs, language, religious practices, and educational system in Dakota Territory. Most were members of the Mennonite and other faiths that objected to military service.

Dakota Territory representatives formed a five-member immigration bureau to compete with other territorial governments in recruiting new immigrants. They met trains at Chicago, steamboats at New York, Philadelphia, Montreal, and Quebec, and canvassed residents in the Upper Mississippi Valley. Most of the Scandinavians recruited during the immigration bureau's existence settled near Fargo.

When gold was discovered in the Black Hills in 1874, towns sprang up in record numbers. Nearly ten thousand people arrived in the Black Hills between 15 November 1875 and 1 March 1876. From Custer, miners spread out to establish mining camps and townsites like South Deadwood, North Deadwood, Ingleside, Chinatown, Cleveland, Fountain City, Elizabethtown, and Montana City, all of them later consolidated into Deadwood.

The railroad brought about the greatest boom in Dakota Territory population between 1878 and 1887. Most settlers were of American stock from nearby states. Sixty percent of those living in South Dakota in 1900 had been born in Iowa, Wisconsin, Minnesota, and Illinois. Those states were also the previous residences of many of Dakota Territory's foreign-born. Special trains were made up at towns in the upper Mississippi Valley region to move neighbors into the Dakotas.

But others came directly from Europe. A large colony of Welsh immigrants from Welsh farming communities in Wisconsin established themselves at Edmunds County. Dutch people from Holland settled in Douglas County during the early 1880s. The second wave of German-Russians arrived in 1884 and settled Roscoe, Hosmer, and Eureka.

South Dakota Library Collection

Archives and Libraries

Only one title is cataloged under South Dakota/Archives and Libraries, but see **South Dakota/History.**

Rylance, Daniel, ed. *Guide to the Microfilm Edition of the Dakota Territorial Records.* Grand Forks, N.Dak.: Orin G. Libby Manuscript Collection, University of North Dakota, 1969. (FHL# 978/N2r)

South Dakota University. American Indian Research Project. *Oyate Iyechinka Woglakapi: The People Speak for Themselves; an Oral History Collection, Volumes I-IV.* Vermillion, S.Dak.: Institute of Indian Studies, c.1970. (FHL# 970.1/So87o)

Atlases, Gazetteers, and Maps

Numerous South Dakota maps are available in the U.S. Map Case and on microfilm for use at center libraries. Here is a sample of the collection:

R. L. Polk and Company, *Northwestern Gazetteer: Minnesota, North and South Dakota and Montana Gazetteer and Business Directory.* St. Paul: R. L. Polk, 1914. (FHL# 973/E4p)

Johnson, A. J. *Johnson's Nebraska, Dakota, Idaho and Montana.* New York: Johnson and Ward, 1865. (FHL# Map Case 973/E7j)

Map of the State of South Dakota: Compiled from the Official Records of the General Land Office and Other Sources. Washington: A. B. Graham Photo Litho., 1901. (FHL# Map Case 978.3/E7ug/1901)

Census Records

Territorial censuses were taken in 1836, 1870, 1880, 1885. A state census was taken in 1905. Indian censuses varied in date according to the agency but are available for dates between 1874 and 1948. For specific holdings, check the FHLC under **South Dakota/Census**, and see these published sources below with their helpful indexes.

Dakota Territory Census Office. *Partial South Dakota Portion of the 1885 Dakota Territory Census Population Schedules.* Pierre, S.Dak.: South Dakota State Historical Society, 1971. (FHL# microfilm 1405268-1405269)

Jackson, Ronald Vern, ed. *Iowa 1836 Territorial Census.* Salt Lake City: Accelerated Indexing Systems, 1973. (FHL# 977.7/A1/no.10)

Includes present states of Iowa, Wisconsin, Minnesota and parts of North and South Dakota.

Shambaugh, Benjamin F. ed., *The First Census of the Original Counties of Dubuque and Demoine (Iowa) Taken in July, 1836.* Salt Lake City: Genealogical Society of Utah, 1978. Microreproduction of original published: Des Moines: Historical Department of Iowa, 1897-98. (FHL# microfilm 1022202, items 1-2 or 0989450, item 2)

South Dakota Commissioner of Labor Statistics. *Partial South Dakota 1895 Census Population Schedules.* Pierre, S.Dak.: South Dakota State Historical Society, 1971. (FHL# microfilm 1405183)

Church Records

While specific South Dakota church records in the collection are few, those included are listed under **South Dakota/[County]/Church Records,** while histories of denominations are cataloged in the FHLC at the state level under **South Dakota /Church History.**

Genealogy

Several titles for Native Races are cataloged under **South Dakota/Genealogy.** For genealogical and historical publications see **South Dakota/Genealogy/Periodicals.**

Daughters of the American Revolution. *Miscellaneous Genealogical Records from South Dakota.* Salt Lake City: Genealogical Society of Utah, 1971. (FHL# microfilm 855209, items 1-2)

Miners, Mary S., comp. *Lineages (Numbers 1 to 201) From October 20, 1957: Chartered by the General Society of Mayflower Descendants to December 5, 1975.* n.p.: Society of Mayflower Descendants, South Dakota, 1975. (FHL# 978.3/C4m)

History

Among a small collection of South Dakota histories are the following titles:

Hyde, C. W. G. *History of the Great Northwest and Its Men of Progress: A Select List of Biographical Sketches and Portraits of the Leaders in Business, Professional, and Official Life.* Minneapolis: Minneapolis Journal, 1901. (FHL# 977/D3h)

Kingsbury, George Washington. *History of Dakota Territory*. 5 vols. Chicago: S. J. Clarke Co., 1915. (FHL# microfilm 1000584-1000586)

Volumes 4 and 5 contain biographical sketches.

Schell, Herbert Samuel. *History of South Dakota*. Lincoln: University of Nebraska Press, 1968. (FHL# 978.3/H2s)

Land and Property Records

South Dakota was a public-land state with eight districts established to handle the transfer of land. When a settler met the requirements for purchase or homesteading, these offices issued a patent or first-title deed, transferring the land from government to private ownership. Patent records are available at the Montana Bureau of Land Management Office in Billings.

Subsequent transfer of property was recorded by deed at the county level. None of South Dakota's county records have been microfilmed, and the only land and property records available at the Family History Library pertain to various Indian agencies. These listings appear under **South Dakota/ Land And Property.**

Military Records

Residents of the Dakota Territory were involved in countless Indian wars and skirmishes during the nineteenth century. Few military records exist of these Indian conflicts. They also served in the Union Army during the Civil War, for which the following source will be helpful.

United States Adjutant General's Office. *Index to Compiled Service Records of Volunteer Union Soldiers Who Served in Organizations from the Territory of Dakota (1861-1865)*. Washington, D.C.: National Archives, 1964. (FHL# microfilm 881616)

Minorities

Only five titles are cataloged under **South Dakota/-Minorities**; two pertain to Native Races.

Dvorak, Joseph A., comp. *History of the Czechs in the State of South Dakota: Memorial Book*. Tabor, S.Dak.: Czech Heritage Preservation Society, 1980. (FHL# 978.3/F2d)

Rath, George. *The Black Sea Germans in the Dakotas*. Freeman, S.Dak.: Pine Hill Press, 1977. (FHL# 978/F2r and microfilm 1036735, item 2)

Riley, Marvin P. *The Hutterite Brethren: An Annotated Bibliography with Special Reference to South Dakota Hutterite Colonies*. Brookings: Rural Sociology Department, Agricultural Experiment Station, S.Dak. State University, 1965. (FHL# 978.3/F23r or microfilm 1036251, item 6)

Native Races

Native American records comprise the largest portion of the library's South Dakota collection. The collection includes family trees, military records, ration records, census enumerations, tribal council records, adoptions, agency records, newspapers, vital records, school records, and annuity rolls. Check the FHLC under **South Dakota/Native Races, Census, Schools, Vital Records, Military Records, Minorities, Public Records, Periodicals, Names-Personal, and Land and Property.**

Representative works are:

United States Bureau of Indian Affairs. Pine Ridge Agency. *Census Records, 1874-1932*. Kansas City, Mo.: Federal Archives and Records Center, 1976. 6 reels. (FHL# microfilm 1014634-1014635, 1002754-1002757)

_____. Rosebud Agency. *List of Indian Names*. Salt Lake City: Genealogical Society of Utah, 1976. (FHL# microfilm 1012658, item 4)

_____. Standing Rock Agency. *Land Records, 1906-1921*. Kansas City, Mo.: Federal Archives and Records Center, 1977. 2 reels. (FHL# microfilm 1021935, item 3, 1204875, items 1-5)

_____. *Indians of the Dakotas*. Washington, D.C.: U.S. Government Printing Office, 1968. (FHL# 970.1/A1/-no.11)

Probate Records

Probate and estate records in the South Dakota collection also pertain to native Indians. Check the FHLC under **South Dakota/Probate Records.**

Vital Records

Births, marriages, and deaths have been registered and forwarded to the State Department of Health in Pierre since 1905. Local county clerks have kept marriage records from the formation of each county. However, none of South Dakota's vital records have been microfilmed.

Some sources containing vital information are included in the Family History Library's collection for South Dakota, notably the Bureau of Indian Affairs records for most South Dakota agencies. Marriage records have been published for some counties. See also:

Merrick, Velda, comp. *Mortality Records: Persons Who Died in the Year ending 31 May 1880, Dakota Territory*. Typescript. Salt Lake City: Genealogical Society of Utah, 1953. (FHL# microfilm 0020156)

Sargent, Dorothy A. Daskam. *Vital Records in South Dakota Newspapers, 1973-1975*. Salt Lake City: Genealogical Society of Utah, 1974-76. 4 reels. (FHL# microfilm 0962178, 0973006, 0908987, 0928220)

NORTH DAKOTA

Historical Background

1682-1803 The area is claimed alternatively by France and Spain.

1803 The United States acquires, with the Louisiana

	Purchase, most of the territory which would become North Dakota.
1803-20	The area is under the jurisdiction of Missouri Territory.
1812	Scots and Irish families from Canada settle in Pembina.
1818	The United States acquires the northeast corner of North Dakota from Great Britain. The 49th parallel is established as the northern boundary.
1823	Pembina settlers return to Canada
1836	Iowa Territorial Census includes North Dakota.
1850	Minnesota Territorial Census includes Pembina County, North Dakota.
1851	The region is opened for settlement.
1857	Census taken of Pembina County.
1860	First census taken in the area of North Dakota.
1861	Dakota Territory is created, including North and South Dakota, most of Montana and part of Wyoming.
1863	The Homestead Act brings numerous settlers into the area.
1864	The Wyoming-Montana area is separated from Dakota Territory and organized as Montana Territory.
1867	First county, Pembina, is organized.
1870	First territorial census.
1871	Pembina Land Office opens. Bureau of Immigration is created by the Territorial Legislature.
1873	Territorial government divides area east of Missouri River into twenty-seven counties. North and South Dakota are separated into two territories.
1874	Pembina Land Office is moved to Fargo and a second office is opened at Bismarck.
1877	Dakota Territory closes its Bureau of Immigration.
1878	Great Dakota Boom begins.
1880	First North Dakota territorial census.
1885	Second North Dakota Territorial census.
1889	North Dakota becomes the thirty-ninth state.
1915	First state census.

Settlement and Migration

As land filled and population increased in the eastern United States, Americans moved west, seeking new and better opportunities. When the federal government provided ways to obtain relatively inexpensive land, the demand for it was high. The Pre-emption, Homestead, and Timber-Culture acts brought settlers from the east coast and foreign lands.

Two local developments also boosted settlement in the region of North Dakota: railroad construction and the rapidly expanding flour mills in Minneapolis. New-process milling created new markets for wheat farmers, and newly constructed railroad lines made the Red River Valley the chief supplier of that market.

Other factors helped to settle the empty Dakota grasslands. Eastern states were filling up, and land values were rising. Capitalists, railroad companies, and land speculators touted the vast prairie land, advertising its availability and lack of rock and tree to hinder the plow. Two additional events also coincided: the locust population was depleted, and higher-than-average rains provided needed moisture to raise crops.

Norwegians flocked to the territory between 1878 and 1890. During the spring of 1882, immigrants from many countries and states booked hundreds of railway cars, waiting to move to Dakota. Special trains were arranged to handle the crowd, but many settlers crossed the prairie on foot to reach this new land of opportunity. Towns grew rapidly, especially along railroad lines.

Many settlers arrived in colonies, usually consisting of fifty to one hundred families. A colony from Lansing, Michigan, settled in McIntosh County; a German-Russian colony of fifty families arrived in Morton County. Germans settled around Bismarck and the southern tier of counties. Seventy-five Dutch families settled in Emmons County, while an Iowa colony was established in Logan County, and one hundred Polish families made their home in Kidder County.

Norwegians, scattered throughout the state, formed the largest group of immigrants. By 1890, the foreign-born made up 43 percent of North Dakota's population. Of these, 32 percent were from Norway, 28 percent were from Canada, 11 percent were from Germany, 10 percent were from England and Ireland, 7 percent were from Sweden, and 5 percent were from Russia. Immigrants from Denmark, Iceland, Poland, Holland, and Czechoslovakia also found their way into Dakota.

Many immigrants had come from Minnesota, Iowa, or Wisconsin. Minnesota's Fillmore and Houston counties had been home to many Norwegian immigrants who settled in North Dakota, as had St. Ansgar and Decorah, Iowa; and Rock Prairie, Muskego, and Koshkonong, Wisconsin. Most immigrants from Canada were Scottish or French in origin.

Of the 57 percent of American-born residents of Dakota Territory in 1890, 14 percent had been born in Minnesota, 11 percent in Wisconsin, 7 percent in New York, 5 percent in Iowa, and 4 percent from Michigan, Illinois, and Ohio. Additionally, many other states were represented.

Clerks of the district court in each county, have, from the creation of each county, kept death, civil, court, divorce, and probate records. But the state registrar is the best source to issue certified copies of death records and the only source for certified copies of birth records.

Registration of births and deaths was required between 1893 and 1895 and then from 1899 to the present, but it was not until 1923 that registration can be considered complete.

Marriage records are issued by the county judges of the various counties. Since 1925, the state registrar also has copies of marriage records and a state-wide index. Land and property records are in the custody of the Register of Deeds in the various counties.

North Dakota Library Collection

Atlases, Gazetteers , and Maps

A fair sampling of North Dakota maps, including both Dakota Territory and state maps, is available. Atlases, maps, and gazetteers are arranged alphabetically following the North Dakota heading in the FHLC. Several maps, dated 1865 and later, in A. J. Johnson's series, are included in the collection and cataloged under **North Dakota/Maps.**

Johnson, A. J. *Johnson's Nebraska, Dakota, Idaho and Montana*. N. p. Johnson and Ward, 1865. (FHL# 973/E7j)

Johnson and Ward. *Johnson's Minnesota and Dakota*. n.p.: n.d. (FHL# 973/E7jm or microfilm 0940022, item 11)

North Dakota Map. Chicago: Rand McNally, 1902. Reprint of map originally published in 1895. (FHL# 978.4/E7r or microfilm 0982155, item 9)

Polk, R. L and Co. *Northwestern Gazetteer*. St. Paul: R. L. Polk and Company, 1914. (FHL# 973/E4p)

Sherman, William C. *Prairie Mosiac: An Ethnic Atlas of Rural North Dakota*. Fargo: North Dakota Institute for Regional Studies, 1983. (FHL# 978.4/F2s)

Williams, Mary Ann Barnes. *Origins of North Dakota Place Names*. (FHL# 978.4/E5w or microfilm 1036251, item 2)

Archives and Libraries

Historical Records Survey, Works Projects Administration. *Abstract and Check List of Statutory Requirements for County Records*. Bismarck: The Historical Records Survey, 1949. (FHL# 978.4/A3h or microfilm 1036400, item 12)

Oihus, Colleen A., comp. *A Basic Subject Guide to the Orin G. Libby Manuscript Collection: Chester Fritz Library, University of North Dakota*. n.p., 1979. (FHL# 978.4/A3o)

Bibliography

Bibliographies provide guides to reference material, not necessarily in the FHLC, but available in other repositories.

Smeall, J. F. S. *North Dakota Literature*. Grand Forks, N.Dak.: Chester Fritz Library, University of North Dakota, 1979. (FHL# 978.4/A3r)

This work contains a reference guide to North Dakota history compiled by Dan Rylance.

University of North Dakota. *University of North Dakota Theses and Dissertations on North Dakota, 1895-1971*. Grand Forks: University of North Dakota, c.1972. (FHL# 978.4/A3u)

Biography

A limited collection of North Dakota biographical publications is available at the Family History Library. Biographies compiled at the state-wide level are listed under **North Dakota/Biography.** Titles focusing on a single county are listed under **North Dakota/[County]/Biography.** A few of the state biographical publications in the collection are:

Holley, Frances Chamberlain. *Once Their Home: or, Our Legacy From the Dahkotahs; Historical, Biographical, and Incidental From Far-off Days, Down to the Present*. Tucson: Ariz.: W. C. Cox, 1974. (FHL# microfilm 1000589, item 5)

Hyde, C[ornelius] W[illiam] G[illam], and William Stoddard, eds. *History of the Great Northwest and Its Men of Progress: A Select List of Biographical Sketches and Portraits of the Leaders in Business, Professional and Official Life*. Minneapolis: Minneapolis Journal, 1901. (FHL# 977/D3h or microfilm 0962338, item 1)

Lounsberry, Clement Augustus. *North Dakota History and People, Outlines of American History*. 3 vols. Chicago: S. J. Clarke, 1916. (FHL# 978.4/H21c or microfilm 0982024, items 1-3, and 0934860).

White, Hugh L., ed. *Who's Who for North Dakota: A Triennial, a Biographical Dictionary*. Bismarck: North Dakota State Historical Society, 1954. (FHL# 978.4/D3w)

Cemeteries

Cemetery tombstone inscriptions are still being compiled in North Dakota, and published inscriptions are listed under **/[County]/Cemeteries.** Only two state-wide compilations are available:

Glasgow, Libby, and Troy Branch Genealogical Committees of the LDS Church. *Cemetery Records of North Dakota*. Typescript, 1967. (FHL# 978.4/V22c or microfilm 0824257, item 2 or fiche 6051313)

Fargo Genealogical Society. *North Dakota Cemeteries*. Fargo, N.Dak.: Fargo Genealogical Society, 1972. (FHL# 978.4/V22f, or microfilm 0928261, and 0928262, items 1-2)

Census Records

Territorial censuses for 1836, 1850, 1860, 1870, 1880, and 1885 are also available. Iowa's 1836 Territorial Census includes part of North Dakota:

Jackson, Ronald Vern, ed. *Iowa 1836 Territorial Census*. Salt Lake City: Accelerated Indexing Systems, c.1979. (FHL# 977.7/A1/no.10)

______. *North Dakota 1880 Mortality Schedule*. Salt Lake City: Accelerated Indexing Systems, c.1984. (FHL# 978.4/X2j/1880)

______. *North Dakota, Dakota Territorial 1885 Mortality Schedule*. Bountiful, Utah: Accelerated Indexing Systems, c.1984. (FHL# 978.4/X2j/1885)

North Dakota Assessor. *Census of North Dakota of 1925: Bottineau, Bowman, Burke and Burleigh Counties*. Bismarck, N.Dak.: Filmed by State Historical Society of North Dakota, n.d. (FHL# microfilm 1433999)

Shambaugh, Benjamin F. ed., *The First Census of the Original Counties of Dubuque and Demoine (Iowa) Taken in July, 1836*. 1897-98; microreproduction Salt Lake City:

Genealogical Society of Utah, 1978. (FHL# 977.7/-A1/no.10 or microfilm 1022202, items 1-2)

Other census collections are available for the Bureau of Indian Affairs. These include enumerations of males over eighteen in 1889, and yearly lists for 1876 through 1881, 1893-98, and 1903-39.

Church History

Histories of the Presbyterian, Catholic, Brethren, Lutheran, and Episcopal churches are included in the library collection. Church records listing christening, marriage, and burial data are generally found under **North Dakota/[County]/Church Records.**

Genealogy

Few collections of genealogical records, family histories, Bible records, biographical collections, pedigree or lineage book collections are available at the Family History Library for North Dakota. Those which are available are narrow in subject matter and contain limited information. Three examples are:

Aberle, George P. *Pioneers and Their Sons: One Hundred Sixty Five Family Histories*. 2 vols. Vol. 2 subtitle: *One Hundred Twenty Family Histories*. Bismarck: Tumbleweed Press, 1980. (FHL# 978.3/D3a or microfilm 1035608, items 1-2)

Graber, Arthur. *Swiss Mennonite Ancestors and Their Relationship from 1775*. Freeman, S.Dak.: Pine Hill Press, 1980. (FHL# 973/F2gra)

One genealogical periodical is available:

North Central North Dakota Genealogical Record, vol. 1 issue 1 (Summer 1978). Minot, N.Dak.: Mouse River Loop Genealogical Society, 1978. (FHL# 978.4/D25n)

Library's consecutive holdings of this publication begin with Issue 2 (Spring 1979). Issues 2-8 are on microfilm only. (FHL# microfilm 1421601, items 1-7)

History

Several good histories for Dakota Territory and North Dakota are included in the library's collection. See the FHLC under **North Dakota/History** and **North Dakota/[County]/History.** Some subheadings for **North Dakota/History**, include **20th Century, Archives and Libraries, Bibliography,** and **Inventories, Registers, Catalogs**. Selected histories are:

Compendium of History and Biography of North Dakota Containing a History of North Dakota: Embracing an Account of Early Explorations, Early Settlement, Indian Occupancy... and a Concise History of Growth and Development of the State, Also a Compendium of Biography of North Dakota. Chicago: George A. Ogle & Co., 1900. (FHL# 978.4/-D3c, microfilm 0934861, item 1, and 0982021, item 1)

Crawford, Lewis Ferandus. *History of North Dakota and North Dakota Biography.* Chicago: American Historical Society, 1931. (FHL# 978.4/H2c or microfilm 1036393)

History of the Red River Valley, Past and Present. by various writers. 2 vols. Grand Forks, N.Dak.: Herald Printing Co., Chicago: C. F. Cooper, 1909. (FHL# 973/H2hrr or microfilm 0962337, items 1-2, and 1000254, items 1-2)

Holley, Frances Chamberlain. *Once Their Home: or Our-Legacy From the Dahkotahs; Historical, Biographical, and Incidental from Far-off Days, Down to the Present.* Tucson: Ariz.: W. C. Cox, 1974. (FHL# microfilm 1000589, item 5)

Lounsberry, Clement Augustus. *Early History of North Dakota: Essential Outlines of American History*. Washington, D.C.: Liberty Press, 1919. (FHL# 978.4/H21 or microfilm 1036397, item 1)

Robinson, Elwyn B. *History of North Dakota*. Lincoln: University of Nebraska Press, 1966. (FHL# 978.4/H2r)

Periodicals in the North Dakota collection include:

State Historical Society of North Dakota. *Collections.* 7 vols. Bismarck: State Historical Society of North Dakota, 1906-1925. (FHL# 978.4/B2h or microfilm 0547583, item 2 and 0982478, item 12)

Continued by *North Dakota Historical Quarterly*.

______. *North Dakota Historical Quarterly: Collections of the State Historical Society of North Dakota.* Vol. 1 (Oct. 1926). Bismarck: State Historical Society of North Dakota, 1926. (FHL# 978.4/B2ha)

Land and Property

The only records available for North Dakota are from the Bureau of Indian Affairs.

United States Bureau of Indiand Affairs. Standing Rock Agency. *Land Records, 1906-1921.* Kansas City, Mo.: Federal Archives and Records Center, 1977. 2 reels.(FHL# microfilm 1021935, item 3 and 1204875, items 1 through 5).

Native American Records

Two native American records are cataloged under **Minorities** and **/Land and Property** and 1873-1939 censuses are under **/Census**. Standing Rock Agency birth, marriage, death, and probate records are also available; see **North Dakota/Probate** and **North Dakota/Vital Records.**

However, most records about North Dakota Indians are under **/Native Races.**

Some histories are included in the collection. The United States Bureau of Indian Affairs records are arranged by agency in alphabetical order. The Fort Berthola Agency records cover the years 1885-1951 and include birth, marriage, death, census, school, adoption, probate, and military records.

Fort Totten Agency records include most of these categories. Only a list of employees, records concerning rations and adoptions, and historical data and tribal council records are listed for the Standing Rock Agency under **/Native Races.** Turtle Mountain Agency records include census, birth, marriage, death, probate, census, school, military, and payroll.

Probate Records

The only probate records available for North Dakota

are those under the authority of the Bureau of Indian Affairs for the Standing Rock Agency. They are cataloged in the FHLC under **North Dakota/Probate Records.**

Vital Records

Only vital records for the Standing Rock Indian Agency are listed in the **North Dakota/Vital Records** collection. However, some vital records preserved at the county level are listed under **North Dakota/[County]/Vital Records.** Usually these are collections of genealogical records from family Bibles or cemetery headstone inscriptions.

Records by Jurisdiction

Oklahoma

County	Archives & Libraries	Atlases	Bible Records	Bibliography	Biography	Cemeteries	Census (Printed)	Church History	Church Records	Court Records	Directories	Emigration/Immigration	Employment	Genealogy	Genealogy/Periodicals	History	Land & Property	Maps	Migration	Military Records	Minorities	Native Races	Naturalizations	Newspapers	Obituaries	Periodicals	Postal	Probate Records	Public Records	School Records	Societies	Tax Records	Vital Records	Voting Registers	Yearbooks
Adair																	•											•					•		
Alfalfa																•												•					•		
Atoka	•					•	•							•		•												•					•		
Beaver					•									•		•																			
Beckham	•							•								•							•										•		
Blaine					•	•			•					•		•						•	•					•					•		
Bryan					•	•			•		•			•		•																	•		
Caddo						•	•									•						•											•		
Canadian						•					•			•											•								•		
Carter						•					•			•		•				•			•		•					•			•		
Cherokee	•					•	•	•	•	•	•						•							•				•		•			•		
Choctaw																																			
Cimarron	•																																•		
Cleveland					•	•										•									•								•		
Coal										•							•											•					•		
Comanche						•			•		•			•		•																	•		
Cotton																												•					•		
Craig					•	•		•	•	•				•		•	•											•		•			•		
Creek									•							•						•								•					
Custer																•																			
Day																																			
Delaware						•										•									•			•		•			•		
Dewey														•		•												•					•		
Ellis						•										•																			
Garfield						•		•			•			•	•	•								•	•										
Garvin																•																			
Grady											•																	•					•		
Grant					•			•																											
Greer					•											•																	•		
Harmon																													•				•		
Harper					•											•														•					
Haskell	•					•			•	•						•	•											•	•				•		
Hughes						•																											•		
Jackson						•																													
Jefferson																												•					•		
Johnston					•											•																			
Kay						•			•		•					•												•		•			•		
Kingfisher						•								•		•								•									•		
Kiowa					•											•	•															•	•		
Latimer									•	•																		•					•		
Le Flore					•	•	•	•	•						•	•	•					•						•					•		
Lincoln	•					•				•						•																			
Logan	•					•				•	•					•	•						•					•					•		
Love																									•								•		
Major						•			•							•												•					•		
Marshall																																			
Mayes	•																							•				•		•			•		
McClain					•										•	•																	•		
McCurtain					•						•					•						•													

Records by Jurisdiction **Oklahoma (cont.)**	Archives & Libraries	Atlases	Bible Records	Bibliography	Biography	Cemeteries	Census (Printed)	Church History	Church Records	Court Records	Directories	Emigration/Immigration	Employment	Genealogy	Genealogy/Periodicals	History	Land & Property	Maps	Migration	Military Records	Minorities	Native Races	Naturalizations	Newspapers	Obituaries	Periodicals	Postal	Probate Records	Public Records	School Records	Societies	Tax Records	Vital Records	Voting Registers	Yearbooks
McIntosh	•					•																•						•		•			•		
Murray					•									•		•																			
Muskogee	•					•	•		•		•											•						•					•		
Noble						•			•				•				•						•					•	•				•		
Nowata																•	•											•					•		
Okfuskee																												•					•		
Oklahoma						•		•	•		•					•	•	•										•							
Okmulgee						•		•	•					•		•	•											•	•				•		
Osage						•					•																								
Ottawa						•					•					•	•	•							•			•		•			•		
Pawnee																														•					
Payne					•	•					•					•	•								•			•					•		
Pittsburg	•					•					•											•	•	•				•	•	•			•		
Pontotoc						•		•						•	•	•												•					•		
Pottawatomie						•					•					•	•													•			•		
Pushmataha	•																						•					•					•		
Roger Mills					•	•																			•								•		
Rogers														•		•												•					•		
Seminole																																			
Sequoyah						•	•							•		•												•	•	•			•		
Stephens																																			
Texas																																			
Tillman					•	•			•							•																			
Tulsa					•	•		•		•	•					•	•						•					•					•		
Wagoner					•											•												•					•		
Washington						•					•					•												•					•		
Washita						•			•							•		•																	
Woods					•	•			•						•	•												•					•		

Records by Jurisdiction

Kansas

Kansas	Archives & Libraries	Atlases	Bible Records	Bibliography	Biography	Cemeteries	Census (Printed)	Church History	Church Records	Court Records	Directories	Emigration/Immigration	Employment	Genealogy	Genealogy/Periodicals	History	Land & Property	Maps	Migration	Military Records	Minorities	Native Races	Naturalizations	Newspapers	Obituaries	Periodicals	Postal	Probate Records	Public Records	School Records	Societies	Tax Records	Vital Records	Voting Registers	Yearbooks
Allen				•	•	•			•							•	•																•		
Anderson						•			•							•										•									
Atchison					•	•			•			•				•		•																	
Barber																•																	•		
Barton						•												•		•				•	•										
Bourbon	•					•					•					•																			
Brown				•	•				•							•	•					•													
Butler					•	•	•	•	•		•					•												•					•		
Calhoun																																			
Chase						•										•																			
Chatauqua						•										•		•																	
Cherokee	•				•	•			•		•			•	•	•	•						•								•		•		
Cheyenne																																			
Clark						•		•	•					•		•																			
Clay					•	•			•					•		•		•															•		
Cloud					•	•	•																										•		
Coffey						•										•																			
Comanche					•											•																			
Cowley					•	•	•		•		•					•	•	•												•					
Crawford					•	•		•			•			•	•	•	•																•		
Davis See Geary																																			
Decatur					•	•										•																	•		
Dickinson					•	•		•																	•								•		
Doniphan						•	•		•		•					•	•	•		•								•				•	•		
Douglas					•	•			•						•	•														•					
Edwards						•		•			•					•														•					
Elk					•	•										•																			
Ellis					•	•		•			•					•		•			•												•		
Ellsworth						•										•																			
Finney						•		•			•					•																		•	•
Ford						•	•	•	•		•					•	•								•					•			•		
Franklin	•				•	•			•		•																								
Geary					•	•	•		•		•					•		•																	
Gove	•					•		•							•																				
Graham	•														•																				
Grant						•									•									•											
Gray	•					•	•						•		•		•			•					•			•				•			
Greeley																																			
Greenwood	•					•			•						•																				
Hamilton						•									•																				
Harper						•			•						•			•																	
Harvey						•				•					•									•									•		
Haskell						•																													
Hodgeman						•									•																				
Jackson							•																												
Jefferson					•																														
Jewell						•			•						•								•									•			
Johnson	•				•	•			•	•				•	•			•																	
Kearny					•										•																				

Records by Jurisdiction **Kansas** (cont.)	Archives & Libraries	Atlases	Bible Records	Bibliography	Biography	Cemeteries	Census (Printed)	Church History	Church Records	Court Records	Directories	Emigration/Immigration	Employment	Genealogy	Genealogy/Periodicals	History	Land & Property	Maps	Migration	Military Records	Minorities	Native Races	Naturalizations	Newspapers	Obituaries	Periodicals	Postal	Probate Records	Public Records	School Records	Societies	Tax Records	Vital Records	Voting Registers	Yearbooks
Kingman						•				•			•		•																	•			
Kiowa					•	•									•																				
Labette						•	•		•						•														•			•			
Lane															•																				
Leavenworth					•	•			•	•					•					•												•			
Lincoln								•							•	•						•										•			
Linn					•				•					•	•																	•			
Logan						•																													
Lyon						•			•	•					•										•										
Madison																																			
Marion					•		•		•	•					•																				
Marshall					•	•			•						•																				
McGhee																																			
McPherson					•	•			•	•					•						•							•				•			
Meade							•								•																				
Miami																																			
Mitchell					•	•			•				•	•				•					•				•				•	•			
Montgomery	•				•	•				•				•	•													•				•			
Morris	•					•												•																	
Morton																																			
Nemaha					•	•			•						•																				
Neosho					•	•									•									•									•		
Ness						•							•		•										•					•					
Norton						•								•	•																				
Osage	•					•		•	•				•	•	•			•															•		
Osborne						•	•		•					•	•		•																•		
Ottawa						•							•		•								•										•		
Pawnee															•																		•		
Phillips	•					•	•		•				•																				•		
Pottowatomie					•	•	•			•					•																		•		
Pratt						•									•																		•		
Rawlins									•						•																				
Reno						•	•			•				•	•														•				•		
Republic							•								•																		•		
Rice							•		•						•																		•		
Riley					•	•	•	•		•			•	•	•										•								•		
Rooks					•	•	•	•	•				•		•																				
Rush						•									•										•										
Russell						•	•								•																		•		
Saline					•	•	•	•	•	•					•			•			•												•	•	
Scott						•							•		•																				
Sedgwick					•	•	•		•	•		•			•			•															•		
Seward	•				•	•	•			•					•																				
Shawnee	•				•	•	•		•	•				•	•			•		•								•					•		
Sheridan																																			
Sherman						•							•		•																		•		
Smith						•	•																										•		
Stafford															•																				
Stanton						•																													

Records by Jurisdiction **Kansas (cont.)**	Archives & Libraries	Atlases	Bible Records	Bibliography	Biography	Cemeteries	Census (Printed)	Church History	Church Records	Court Records	Directories	Emigration/Immigration	Employment	Genealogy	Genealogy/Periodicals	History	Land & Property	Maps	Migration	Military Records	Minorities	Native Races	Naturalizations	Newspapers	Obituaries	Periodicals	Postal	Probate Records	Public Records	School Records	Societies	Tax Records	Vital Records	Voting Registers	Yearbooks
Stevens															•																				
Sumner					•	•			•						•			•																	
Thomas						•				•			•		•																				
Trego						•																													
Wabaunsee					•	•	•		•							•																			
Wallace						•										•																			
Washington					•	•										•																			
Wichita						•	•		•																									•	
Wilson					•	•	•				•				•	•	•	•						•	•			•				•	•		
Woodson					•											•										•									
Wyandotte	•				•				•		•					•		•																	

Records of Jurisdiction Nebraska	Archives & Libraries	Atlases	Bible Records	Bibliography	Biography	Cemeteries	Census (Printed)	Church History	Church Records	Directories	Emigration/Immigration	Employment	Genealogy	Genealogy/Periodicals	History	Land & Property	Maps	Migration	Military Records	Minorities	Native Races	Naturalizations	Newspapers	Obituaries	Periodicals	Postal	Probate Records	Public Records	School Records	Societies	Tax Records	Vital Records	Voting Registers	Yearbooks
Adams					•	•				•				•	•																		•	
Antelope									•						•																			
Arthur																																		
Banner					•								•		•																	•		
Blaine																																		
Boone													•		•				•															
Box Butte						•								•	•									•							•	•		
Boyd															•																			
Brown															•		•																	
Buffalo					•					•				•	•	•													•			•		
Burt													•		•																			
Butler					•	•			•								•																	
Cass					•	•		•							•									•	•									
Cedar									•																									
Chase																																•		
Cherry						•								•	•																			
Cheyenne										•				•																				
Clay					•	•			•						•																			
Colfax															•		•																	
Cuming															•		•															•		
Custer						•	•							•	•																			
Dakota						•							•		•																			
Dawes								•	•	•				•		•																		
Dawson						•				•					•									•										
Deuel													•	•	•																			
Dixon						•							•	•	•																			
Dodge						•		•	•	•					•		•															•		
Douglas			•		•	•			•	•			•	•	•		•			•					•			•				•		
Dundy																																		
Fillmore					•									•	•																			
Franklin					•	•																						•						
Frontier						•									•																			
Furnas					•	•									•								•											
Gage					•	•		•	•	•	•			•	•																			
Garden						•								•																				
Garfield															•																			
Gosper	•																																	
Grant														•		•																•		
Greeley	•					•									•																			
Hall						•			•	•					•																			
Hamilton					•	•				•					•	•	•		•				•	•					•			•		
Harlan					•	•									•																			
Hayes													•		•	•																		
Hitchcock																																		
Holt						•								•	•																			
Hooker						•								•								•												
Howard	•																																	
Jefferson								•	•	•				•	•																	•		
Johnson					•		•		•					•									•											

Records of Jurisdiction Nebraska (cont.)	Archives & Libraries	Atlases	Bible Records	Bibliography	Biography	Cemeteries	Census (Printed)	Church History	Church Records	Directories	Emigration/Immigration	Employment	Genealogy	Genealogy/Periodicals	History	Land & Property	Maps	Migration	Military Records	Minorities	Native Races	Naturalizations	Newspapers	Obituaries	Periodicals	Postal	Probate Records	Public Records	School Records	Societies	Tax Records	Vital Records	Voting Registers	Yearbooks
Jones																																		
Kearney					•	•	•						•																					
Keith																																		
Keya Paha																																		
Kimball													•																					
Knox						•																												
Lancaster					•	•							•		•	•	•		•	•			•											
Lincoln					•	•	•		•	•			•	•	•	•	•		•															
Logan															•																			
Loup	•														•																			
Madison								•	•	•					•																			
McPherson																																		
Merrick	•														•																			
Morrill					•	•							•		•																	•		
Nance													•		•																			
Nemaha														•	•																			
Nuckolls					•	•									•																			
Otoe					•	•		•	•	•			•		•		•												•					
Pawnee					•	•				•				•																				
Perkins							•								•																			
Phelps					•					•																								
Pierce																																		
Platte						•		•	•	•					•																	•		
Polk					•				•						•																			
Red Willow					•	•				•					•	•																		
Richardson					•		•			•			•	•	•																		•	
Rock																																		
Saline						•								•	•																			
Sarpy									•							•	•												•			•		
Saunders					•				•						•		•			•														
Scotts Bluff					•	•		•		•			•	•	•								•	•			•					•		
Seward	•				•	•									•																			
Sheridan						•							•		•																	•		
Sherman																																		
Sioux														•																				
Stanton															•																			
Thayer									•						•														•			•		
Thomas						•								•																				
Thurston									•																							•		
Valley													•		•																			
Washington						•				•					•		•															•		
Wayne					•										•																	•		
Webster	•				•	•									•																			
Wheeler																																		
Winnebago Indian Reserv.																																		
York					•					•					•					•									•					

Records by Jurisdiction **South Dakota**	Archives & Libraries	Atlases	Bible Records	Bibliography	Biography	Cemeteries	Census (Printed)	Church History	Church Records	Court Records	Directories	Emigration/Immigration	Employment	Genealogy	Genealogy/Periodicals	History	Land & Property	Maps	Migration	Military Records	Minorities	Native Races	Naturalizations	Newspapers	Obituaries	Periodicals	Postal	Probate Records	Public Records	School Records	Societies	Tax Records	Vital Records	Voting Registers	Yearbooks
Armstrong See Dewey																																			
Aurora																																			
Beadle									•		•					•							•	•	•										
Bennett	•																	•																	
Bon Homme																																			
Brookings					•			•	•																										
Brown											•				•	•									•										
Brule																•																			
Buffalo	•																•																		
Butte						•					•																								
Campbell																•																			
Charles Mix																																			
Clark	•													•		•																			
Clay					•					•						•		•			•														
Codington											•																								
Corson																																			
Custer																																			
Davison											•																								
Day																																			
Deuel							•															•			•								•		
Dewey																																			
Douglas						•			•																										
Edmunds									•																										
Fall River																•																			
Faulk	•				•											•																			
Grant																										•									
Gregory																																			
Haakon	•													•																					
Hamlin																																			
Hand																																			
Hanson																																			
Harding																																			
Hughes																•	•								•					•					
Hutchinson							•		•																										
Hyde																•	•																		
Jackson	•													•																					
Jerauld						•										•																			
Jones														•		•																			
Kingsbury						•												•																	
Lake																																			
Lawrence					•	•					•					•														•			•		
Lincoln									•																										
Lyman														•																					
Marshall																																			
McCook								•																											
McPherson									•																										
Meade						•										•																			
Mellette	•													•		•																			
Miner	•										•																								

Records by Jurisdiction — South Dakota (cont.)	Archives & Libraries	Atlases	Bible Records	Bibliography	Biography	Cemeteries	Census (Printed)	Church History	Church Records	Court Records	Directories	Emigration/Immigration	Employment	Genealogy	Genealogy/Periodicals	History	Land & Property	Maps	Migration	Military Records	Minorities	Native Races	Naturalizations	Newspapers	Obituaries	Periodicals	Postal	Probate Records	Public Records	School Records	Societies	Tax Records	Vital Records	Voting Registers	Yearbooks
Minnehaha					•						•					•	•									•							•		
Moody									•																	•				•					
Pennington	•					•					•					•									•			•		•	•		•		
Perkins																																			
Potter					•											•																			
Roberts																•																			
Rusk																																			
Sanborn									•							•																			
Shannon																																			
Spink						•																											•		
Stanley														•		•																			
Sully																																			
Todd																																			
Tripp																																			
Turner					•		•		•							•																			
Union																•																			
Walworth																•																			
Washabaugh	•																																		
Washington																																			
Yankton											•																								
Ziebach																																			

Records by Jurisdiction

North Dakota

	Archives & Libraries	Bible Records	Biography	Cemeteries	Census (Printed)	Church History	Church Records	Court Records	Directories	Genealogy	Genealogy/Periodicals	History	Land & Probate	Maps	Migration	Military Records	Minorities	Native Races	Naturalizations	Newspapers	Obituaries	Periodicals	Probate Records	Public Records	School Records	Societies	Tax Records	Vital Records	Voting Registers
Adams																													
Barnes				•		•			•			•		•														•	
Benson												•		•															
Billings																													
Bottineau												•					•												
Bowman																													
Buffalo																													
Burke										•		•																	
Burleigh									•	•												•	•					•	
Cass				•			•		•	•		•																	
Cavalier						•						•																	
Dickey												•																	
Divide												•																	
Dunn												•										•							
Eddy																													
Emmons										•		•																	
Foster																													
Golden Valley	•																												
Grand Forks	•								•																				
Grant																													
Griggs							•																						
Gringras																													
Hettinger												•																	
Kidder												•																	
La Moure												•																	
Logan				•								•																	
McHenry			•									•																	
McIntosh				•								•																	
McKenzie												•																	
McLean			•									•																	
Mercer	•																												
Morton									•			•																	
Mountrail			•									•																	
Nelson									•		•																		
Oliver																													
Pembina							•			•		•																	
Pierce												•																	
Ramsey														•															
Ransom			•									•																	
Renville			•				•					•													•				
Richland																										•			
Rolette										•		•																	
Sargent																													
Sheridan												•																	
Sioux																													
Slope				•																									
Stark									•			•																	
Steele												•		•															
Stutsman									•					•															

Records by Jurisdiction **North Dakota (cont.)**	Archives & Libraries	Bible Records	Biography	Cemeteries	Census (Printed)	Church History	Church Records	Court Records	Directories	Genealogy	Genealogy/Periodicals	History	Land & Probate	Maps	Migration	Military Records	Minorities	Native Races	Naturalizations	Newspapers	Obituaries	Periodicals	Probate Records	Public Records	School Records	Societies	Tax Records	Vital Records	Voting Registers
Towner				•			•			•				•														•	
Traill							•					•																	
Walsh										•		•																	
Ward				•					•																			•	
Wells												•																	
Williams	•		•									•		•															

Chapter 11

United States: The Mountain States

Johni Cerny

COLORADO

Historical Background

1803	Louisiana Purchase includes the northeastern part of Colorado, with the Arkansas River later fixed as the general dividing line with the Spanish Territory.
1806	Zebulon M. Pike leaves St. Louis with a small exploring party and reaches Pueblo 23 November.
1818	Madiero Gonzales Lupton, a Spanish employee of the American Fur Company, establishes one of the first trading posts on South Platte River.
1829	Four Bent brothers construct a large fort near the present city of La Junta, one of the most successful trading posts founded in eastern Colorado.
1838	Colonel Cerean St. Vrain builds a trading post on the South Platte River; it becomes an important link in a chain extending from Laramie to Bent's Fort.
1840	Town of Pueblo begins with the establishment of a "buffalo farm" to supply buffalo to eastern zoos.
1858	Gold is discovered near Cherry Creek by a group of Georgia prospectors. The first tent and log cabin communities are established near Denver. "Territory of Jefferson" provisionally established to seek territorial status.
1866	Congress passes bill proposing to admit Colorado to statehood. President Andrew Johnson vetoes the bill because Colorado's constitution is illegal.
1870	During 1860s, population increases by only 5,000 because of gold "bust" and a series of Indian wars. 1870 census shows a territorial population of 39,864. The first railroads, the Denver Pacific and the Kansas Pacific, reach Denver. Territory again begins to grow rapidly.
1873	New gold and silver discoveries are made in the San Juan mountains.
1876	Colorado is admitted to the Union as the "Centennial State."

Settlement and Migration

Early Spanish explorers were the first mountain men in Colorado, but their economic enterprise was short lived and dismally documented. They were followed by Frenchmen and early American explorers in the 1800s who left scant record of their activities until 1821 when Mexico broke from Spain during the Mexican Revolution. Up until that date, the western slope of the Rocky Mountains was part of the Spanish empire, and all trade with foreigners was illegal. Mountain men flourished in western Colorado only between 1824 and 1845, but two decades was long enough to open the land to settlement.

The United States acquired eastern and central Colorado under the terms of the Louisiana Purchase. The western portion of the state was annexed after the Mexican War.

Between 1840 when fur trade ended and 1859 when the placer miners started to arrive, numerous exploration parties probed the area looking for railroad routes, overland trails, cattle trails, and suitable places to establish settlements.

Gold was discovered in the mountainous country below South Pass, near present-day Denver, in 1858, the same year prospectors struck gold in Nevada. Midwestern and eastern newspapers exaggerated Colorado gold strikes and people poured into the area by the thousands. By June of the following year, the Pike's Peak area had more than 100,000 prospectors, most of whom would be disappointed.

Colorado Library Collection

The Family History Library has no microfilmed records of Colorado counties, and most of the Colorado collection consists of printed and secondary publications. See the county charts accompanying this chapter for the publications on specific counties.

Archives and Libraries

Historical Records Survey, Colorado. *Guide to Vital Statistics-Records in Colorado*. 2 vols. Denver: Historical Records Survey, 1942. (FHL# 978.8/A7c or microfilm 897482, items 9 and 10)

Griffin, Walter R. *A Comprehensive Guide to the Location of Published and Unpublished Newspaper Indexes in Colorado Repositories*. Denver: State Historical Society of Colorado, c.1972. (FHL# 978.8/A1/no. 24)

Bibliography

Wynar, Bohdan S., ed. *Colorado Bibliography*. Littleton, Colo.: Libraries Unlimited for the National Society of Colonial Dames, 1980. (FHL# 978.8/A3c)

Biography

The Family History Library has twenty books devoted to or containing biographical information about early Colorado residents:

Baker, James Hutchins, ed. *History of Colorado*. 5 vols. Denver: Linderman Co., Inc. 1927. (FHL# 978.8/H2co and microfilm 962125)

Ferril, William Columbus, ed. *Sketches of Colorado in Four Volumes*. Denver: Western Press Bureau Co., 1911. (FHL# 978.8/D3s)

______. *Portrait and Biographical Record of the State of Colorado: Containing Portraits and Biographies of Many Well Known Citizens of the Past and Present.* 2 vols. Chicago: Chapman Publishing. 1899. (FHL# 978.8/D3p or microfilm 1000142)

Census

Colorado numbers among the few states that took a state census enumeration midway between the 1880 and 1890 federal enumerations. Since the 1890 federal census was destroyed by fire, the 1885 Colorado state census is invaluable.

Colorado Census Bureau. *Schedules of the Colorado State Census, 1885*. 8 reels. Washington: National Archives, 1949. (FHL# microfilm 498503-498510)

Church Records

There are some church records in the Colorado collection; however, available titles represent a broad spectrum of religions, some of them for churches in towns or counties. See **Colorado/Church Records** for available titles.

Colonization

Willard, James Field. *Experiments in Colorado Colonization, 1869-1872: Selected Contemporary Records relating to the German Colonization Company and the Chicago-Colorado, St. Louis-Western and Southwestern Colonies.* Boulder: University of Colorado Historical Collections, Vol. 3. Colony series, Vol. 2, 1926. (FHL# 978.8/W7w)

Directories

______. *The Rocky Mountain Directory and Colorado Gazetteer for 1871*. 1870; rpt. ed., Tucson, Ariz.: W. C. Cox. 1974. (FHL# microfilm 1000143, item 4)

Gazetteers

Gannett, Henry. *A Gazetteer of Colorado.* Washington, D.C.: Government Printing Office, 1906. (FHL# 978.8/E5g or microfilm 967327)

Genealogy/Bibliography

Clint, Florence Runyan. *Colorado Area Key: A Comprehensive Study of Genealogical Records Sources of Colorado.* Denver: Eden Press. 1968. (FHL# 978.8/H2cf)

Genealogy/Periodicals

The Colorado Genealogist. Denver: Colorado Genealogical Society. 1939-1987. 48 vols. (FHL# 978.8/B2eg)

Genealogy/Sources

Jenkins, Myra Ellen. *Tracing Spanish-American Pedigrees in the Southwestern United States.* Salt Lake City: Genealogical Society of Utah, 1969. (FHL# 929.1/W893/F14a or microfilm 897215, item 34)

History

The library has forty titles dealing with Colorado state and local history. See **Colorado/History** for a complete list of titles available.

Eichler, George R. *Colorado Place Names.* Boulder, Colo.: Johnson Publishing, 1980. (FHL# 978.8/E2e)

Hall, Frank. *History of the State of Colorado.* 4 vols. Chicago: Blakely Print Co. 1889-95. (FHL# 978.8/H2ha)

Stone, Wilbur Fiske, ed. *History of Colorado.* 4 vols. Chicago: S. J. Clarke Publishing Co., 1918-19. (FHL# 978.8/H2sw)

Land and Property

Part of Colorado was included in the New Mexico Territory until 1861. Thus, New Mexico land grants are critical in early Colorado research.

U.S. Bureau of Land Management. *Miscellaneous Archives Relating to New Mexico Land Grants, 1695-1842.* Albuquerque: University of New Mexico Library, 1955-57. (FHL# microfilm 1016947-1016948)

Includes proceedings, declarations, deliberations, accounts, and letters.

Secretary's Office, New Mexico (Territory). *Records of Land Titles, 1847-1852.* Albuquerque: University of New Mexico Library. 1955-57. (FHL# microfilm 1016950, item 1)

Includes registers of land titles kept by the Secretary of the Territory.

Surveyor-General's Office, New Mexico (Territory). *Record of Private Land Claims Adjudicated by the U.S. Surveyor General, 1855-1890.* Albuquerque: University of New Mexico Library, 1955-57. (FHL# microfilm 1016950, item 2-4-1016974)

Includes Old Grant Docket, docket of private land claims, index by report number, file records of private land claims, and eight volumes of land claims records.

Twitchell, Ralph E. *The Twitchell Archives, 1685-1898.* Albuquerque: filmed by the University of New Mexico Library, 1955-57. (FHL# microfilm 1016940-1016945)

Includes land disputes, appeals, land grants, wills, judgments, mine claims, inventories, and municipal ordinances.

Maps

The library has an excellent collection of Colorado maps. See **Colorado/Maps** for a complete list of holdings. Of particular note are:

Colorado County Maps. (No formal title, publisher, or date of publication.) (FHL# 978.8/E7cm)

A series of county maps showing their boundaries at the times of various legislative assemblies between 1861 to 1911.

Ebert, Frederick J. *Map of Colorado Territory.* n.p., n.d. (FHL# 978.8/E7e)

United States Geological Survey. *Topographic Maps of Colorado.* Washington, D.C.: Geological Survey, 1890-1965. (FHL# 978.8/E7us)

Includes 1,441 maps.

Military

United States Adjutant General's Office. *Index to Compiled Service Records of Volunteer Union Soldiers Who Served in Organizations from the Territory of Colorado, 1861-1865.* Washington, D.C.: National Archives, 1964. (FHL# microfilm 821998-822000)

Minorities and Native Races

The few records available for minorities and native races deal primarily with Indian tribes. See **Colorado/Minorities** and **Colorado/Native Races** for a complete list.

Newspapers

While the library has few Colorado newspapers, an excellent research aid is:

Oehlert, Donald E. *Guide to Colorado Newspapers, 1859-1963.* Denver: Bibliographical Center for Research, 1964. (FHL# 978.8/B3o or microfilm 1000145, item 4)

Vital Records

Works Progress Administration. *Guide to Vital Statistics Records in Colorado.* 2 vols. Denver: Colorado Historical Records Survey Division. 1942. (FHL# 978.8/A5h or microfilm 897482)

IDAHO

Historical Background

1805	Meriwether Lewis and William Clark explore Idaho.
1810	Missouri Fur Company establishes Fort Henry on the Snake River.
1819	Jerome County is created.
1834	Fort Hall is founded in what is now Bingham County. It becomes the junction of several trails leading west.
1846	Great Britain cedes its claim to Idaho under the terms of the Webster-Ashburton Treaty.
1848-53	Idaho is part of the Oregon Territory.
1853	Northern Idaho made part of Washington Territory; southern Idaho remains in Oregon Territory.
1855	Mullan, named for pioneer Joseph Mullan, founded where the wagon road crossed the Coeur d'Alene Mountains.
1859-63	Southern Idaho also becomes part of Washington Territory.
1860	Mormons found Franklin, Idaho's first permanent settlement. Gold discovered on Orofino Creek.
1862	First efforts to create a territorial organization for Idaho at Oro Fino, a mining town located east of Lewiston.
1863	Congress passes the Organic Act creating the Territory of Idaho. It includes Montana until 1864 and Wyoming until 1868.
1890	Idaho becomes the forty-third state on 3 July.

Settlement and Migration

Lewis and Clark made their historic entry into Idaho on 12 August 1805; and for a half century after their departure, numerous fur-trading companies operated in the area. The North West Company built Idaho's first trading post at the site of the present town of Hope in 1809. However, as fur-trading declined in the area, trappers moved on, leaving little to document their presence over several decades.

Missionaries, miners, and farmers settled Idaho. Several Protestant missionaries found their way to Idaho before 1850. A group of Mormons founded Idaho's first permanent settlement at Franklin, thinking they were still within Utah boundaries. The Utah-Idaho boundary-line survey of 1872, however, proved that Franklin was in southern Idaho.

Throughout the 1860s, Idaho's gold rush, much exaggerated by reports, brought in a flood of prospectors. It began in 1860 in the Snake River valley where mining camps flourished at Orofino and Pierce City. Merchants set up shop in Lewiston to outfit mining expeditions. Other prospectors moved to the South Fork of the Clearwater River and established a camp at Elk City.

Salmon River valley mining successes brought people from California, Oregon, the Missouri Valley, and points further east into the upper Snake River valley during 1862. By 1863, 20,000 miners were searching for gold in Idaho.

Gold discoveries along the Boise River in 1863 set off a new stampede and saw the establishment of mining camps at Placerville, Centerville, and Idaho City. Merchants and farmers followed to settle in fertile mountain valleys nearby.

Farmers and cattlemen, both Mormons and non-Mormons, established settlements throughout southeastern Idaho. Idaho became a separate territory in 1863. By 1880, over 32,000 people lived in Idaho Territory, and in the next ten years its population reached 88,548. Idaho became a state in 1890, and its population had virtually doubled by 1900 when it reached 161,772.

Idaho Library Collection

Archives and Libraries

The library's holdings are limited to a copy of the shelf list of the Idaho Genealogical Library and an inventory of the holdings of the Salmon River Genealogical Library. However, a few titles are cataloged under **Idaho/[County]/Archives and Libraries.**

Biography

The library has several historical and biographical publications for Idaho. Most biographies are cross referenced under **Idaho/History.** Notable in the collection are:

Sketches of the Inter-Mountain States: Together with Biographies of Many Prominent and Progressive Citizens Who Have Helped in the Development and History-Making of This Marvelous Region, 1847-1909, Utah Idaho, Nevada. Salt Lake City: Salt Lake Tribune, 1909. (FHL# 979/D3s or microfilm 1000614, item 1)

Wiggins, Marvin E., comp. *Mormons and Their Neighbors: An Index to Over 75,000 Biographical Sketches from 1820 to the Present.* 2 vols. Provo, Utah: Harold B. Lee Library, Brigham Young University, c.1984. (FHL# 978/D32w)

Cemeteries

Many tombstone inscriptions have been copied and compiled by committees under the auspices of the Mormons and DAR chapters. Check the Family History Library Catalog (FHLC) under **Idaho/Cemeteries** and **Idaho/[County]/cemeteries.** A compilation which includes cemetery records for Idaho is:

Tracy, LaMar. *Cemetery Records for Utah, Idaho, and Wyoming.* Salt Lake City: Genealogical Society of Utah, 1969. (FHL# microfilm 0599288-0599291)

Census

Territorial census and mortality schedules have been published for 1870 and 1880 (FHL# 979.6/X2pa and 979.6/X2p respectively). U.S. censuses are available on microfilm for 1870 through 1910. A Soundex (phonetic index) has been prepared for the 1900 U.S. census and for all households with children ten years old and younger in 1880.

Church History and Records

The only denominations represented in the general Idaho collection are Methodists, Church of the Brethren, and the German Reformed Church. There are many Mormon records for Idaho, discussed in Chapter 1.

Directories

Directories are available for Idaho Territory, Pocatello, and the broader region. Check the FHLC under **Idaho/Directories** and **Idaho/[County]/Directories.**

History

Some titles under the **Idaho/Biography** and **Idaho/Genealogy** are cross-referenced under **/History.** Histories of specific counties are cataloged under **Idaho/[County]/History.** Notable in the collection are:

Beal, Merrill D. *History of Idaho.* 3 vols. New York: Lewis Historical Publishing Co., 1959. (FHL# 979.6/H2b)

Defenbach, Byron. *Idaho, the Place and Its People: A History of the Gem State from Prehistoric to Present Days.* 3 vols. Chicago: American Historical Society, Inc., 1933. (FHL# 979.6/H2d)

French, Hiram Taylor. *History of Idaho: A Narrative Account of Its Historical Progress, Its People, and Its Principal Interests.* 3 vols. Chicago: Lewis Publishing Co., 1914. (FHL# 979.6/H2f or microfilm 1000164, items 2-4)

History of Idaho: The Gem of the Mountains. 4 vols. Chicago: S. J. Clarke Publishing Co., 1920. (FHL# 979.6/H2h or microfilm 1000165 and 0908926, item 1)

An Illustrated History of the State of Idaho: Containing a His-

tory of the State of Idaho from the Earliest Period of Its Discovery to the Present Time, Together With Glimpses of Its Auspicious Futures; Illustrations . . . and Biographical Mention of Many Pioneers and Prominent Citizens of Today. 4 vols. in 2. Chicago: Lewis Publishing Co., 1899. (FHL# 979.6/h2ih or microfilm 0924569, item 2, and 1000164, item 1)

Land and Property

Few land records are available for Idaho. See **Idaho/[County]/Land and Property.** Also of interest may be:

Thousands of Idaho Surnames: Abstracted from Rejected Federal Land Applications. Portland: Genealogical Forum of Portland, Oregon, c.1980. (FHL# 979.6/R2t)

Maps

The library has several maps of Idaho. Check the FHLC under **Idaho/Maps.**

Minorities

Minorities cataloged in the FHLC for Idaho include Basques, Jews, Indians, and members of the Church of the Brethren; see **Idaho/Minorities.**

Native Races

Indian tribes represented in the Idaho collection are Coeur d'Alene, Nez Perces, Bannock, and Shoshone. Indian agency records are available for Fort Hall and northern Idaho. They include twentieth-century marriage licenses, land records, medical ledgers, annuity payrolls, employment, heirship records, school records, and money ledgers.

An 1894 census of the Bannock and Shoshone tribes is cataloged under **Idaho/Native Races**, but the 1919-33 census records for the Coeur d'Alene Agency are cataloged under **Idaho/Census**. Also, birth and death records for the Coeur d'Alene Agency between 1918 and 1935 are cataloged under **Idaho/Vital Records** with no entry under **/Native Races.**

Obituaries

A large collection of obituaries has been indexed and microfilmed (FHL# microfilm 0821636-0821699). See **Idaho/Obituaries** for a description of the alphabetical listings.

Tax Records

Only territorial tax records for 1865 and 1866 are available (FHL# microfilm 1024432).

Vital Records

An alphabetical marriage license card index has been compiled from civil records by various Mormon wards and branches and organized by the Family History Library; it is cataloged under **Idaho/Vital Records/Miscellaneous** (FHL# microfilm 0820155, item 2-0820173).

MONTANA

Historical Background

1803	Eastern Montana is included in the Louisiana Purchase.
1805	Members of the Lewis and Clark expedition explore parts of Montana.
1808	Fur trappers build a log hut on the Kootenai River near present-day Jennings, Montana.
1829	The American Fur Company builds Fort Union.
1846	Great Britain cedes its claim to western Montana under terms of the Oregon Treaty. The American Fur Company builds Benton.
1862	Gold is discovered southeast of Butte.
1863	Montana is designated part of Idaho Territory.
1864	Montana becomes a territory.
1866	Ranching begins in Montana when Nelson Story arrives from Texas with a thousand longhorns.
1867-77	Major Indian wars.
1870s	Farmers begin to settle Montana.
1880	The Utah and Northern Railroad reaches Butte.
1889	Montana becomes the forty-first state in the Union.

Settlement and Migration

People began to arrive in Montana in significant numbers during the 1863 gold rush. Settlers and prospectors staked claims along the Snake River early, leaving hundreds of late-comers little choice but to travel Mullan Road in their search for a new lode. Bannock City and Alder Gulch were established first, followed by Virginia City which boasted a population of 4,000 who provided support activities to those working the Alder Gulch lode to extract $30 million worth of gold between 1864 and 1867.

John Cowan, a Georgia prospector, struck gold at a place he called Last Chance Gulch, and a mining camp called Helena sprang up on the site. Since it lay on the trade route between Fort Benton and Bannock and Virginia City, it developed into one of Montana's commercial centers.

Merchants and farmers, keen on making profits by providing merchandise and supplies to miners and mining-related industries, arrived quickly. The need for some form of government was soon apparent, and the Montana Territory was created in 1864 with Virginia City as its capital.

By 1870, Montana's population consisted of 18,306 whites, 1,949 Chinese, and 183 Negroes. The Bureau of Indian Affairs estimated the Indian population at 19,300. Professionally, 8,030 were miners, 2,111 were farmers or cattlemen, and 1,233 were involved in trade and transportation. Helena, the territory's largest city, had a population of 3,106.

Montana's settlement was tied to the "Dakota Boom" of 1878-85 when the Great Northern Railroad brought thousands from Europe and the Mississippi Valley states to homestead the Dakotas and support the railroad with supply and maintenance activities. While Dakota boomed, Montana and its other bordering states grew slowly. Farmers began drifting into Montana in the 1870s, but when the Northern Pacific crept westward from the Dakotas through Montana Territory, newcomers began to follow the railroad.

In 1880, 39,159 people lived in Montana. The territory gained nearly 100,000 settlers during the next decade and boasted a population of over 132,000 in 1890.

With increased population came the creation of new counties and population centers. Montana became a public-domain state and its first Government Land Office opened at Helena in 1867. By 1880, Montana had 2,694 farms, an increase of nearly 2,000 over the number existing in 1870. Montana's bid for statehood was approved and it was admitted to the Union, along with North Dakota, South Dakota, and Washington, in an "Omnibus Bill" adopted in November 1889.

Montana Library Collection

Biography

Most biographical titles are also cataloged under **Montana/History**. Useful examples are:

Progressive Men of the State of Montana. 1 vol. bound in 2. Chicago: A. W. Bowen & Co., n.d. [c.1975]. (FHL# 978.6/D3p and microfilm 1000176)

Hyde, Cornelius William Gillam. *History of the Great Northwest and Its Men of Progress: A Select List of Biographical Sketches and Portraits of the Leaders in Business, Professional and Official Life.* Minneapolis: Minneapolis Journal, 1901. (FHL# 977/D3h and microfilm 0962338, item 1)

Cemeteries

Check the FHLC under **Montana/Cemeteries** and **Montana/[County]/Cemeteries.** A notable source is:

Lewistown Genealogy Society. *Montana Cemetery Records.* Salt Lake City: Genealogical Society of Utah, 1982. (FHL# microfilm 1035938, item 2)

Preceding the inscription records is an index which lists the cemeteries within each county in the central section of the state.

Census

Census enumerations available for Montana include the 1860 census of Washington Territory which includes the Bitter Root Valley and Ponderay Mountains which are not in Montana (FHL# 978.6/A1/no.8), the 1860 and 1870 Montana territorial censuses (indexed), and the 1900 U.S. Census with a phonetic index (Soundex). Census records for the state's numerous Indian tribes are cataloged under **Montana/Native Races.**

Church History and Records

Denominations included in the Montana section of the FHLC are Mennonites, Church of the Brethren, Jesuits, Methodists, and Catholics. See **Montana/Church History** and **Montana/Church Records** in the FHLC.

Historical Records Survey, Works Progress Administration. *Inventory of the Vital Statistics Records of Church and Religious Organizations in 1942.* (FHL# 978.6/V2hi or microfilm 1036415, item 3, and microfiche 6046711)

History

Several titles are included in the collection under **Montana/History** and **Montana/[County]/History.** Those with a state emphasis include:

Burlingame, Merrill G. *A History of Montana.* 3 vols. New York: Lewis Historical Publishing Co., 1957. (FHL# 978.6/H2b)

Hamilton, James McClellan. *History of Montana from Wilderness to Statehood.* Portland, Oregon: Binfords & Mort, [c.1970]. (FHL# 978.6/H2h)

Sanders, Helen Fitzgerald. *A History of Montana.* 3 vols. Chicago: Lewis Publishing Co., 1913. (FHL# 978.6/D3s and microfilm 1000174, items 2-4)

Stout, Tom. *Montana, Its Story and Biography: A History of Aboriginal and Territorial Montana and Three Decades of Statehood.* 3 vols. Chicago: American Historical Society, c.1921. (FHL# 978.6/H2s and microfilm 1000175)

Maps

The library has a large map collection for Montana; these include several territorial and state maps covering the period 1838 to 1968.

Minorities

Included under **Montana/Minorities** and **Montana/Native Races** are Indian tribal records. The Cheyenne, Blackfoot, and Flathead tribes are listed under **/Minorities** along with histories of the Church of the Brethren and Mennonites.

Native Races

The largest collection of records in one FHLC category for Montana are those listed under **/Native Races.** Records exist for the following Indian agencies: Billings Area Office, Blackfeet *(sic)* Agency, Crow Agency, Flathead Agency, Fort Belknap Agency, Fort Peck Agency, and Northern Cheyenne Agency which was also called the Tongue River Agency and Reservation.

Types of documents included in these records are welfare rolls, census records, vital records, land claims, heirship data, ledger sheets, military service records, social security information, mission records, annuity records, school and student records, wills, family registers, employment records, welfare applications, money ledgers, and miscellaneous records.

Vital Records

Most vital records for Montana are those also cataloged under **Montana/Native Races**. However, see also:

Index to Vital Statistics from Bozeman, Montana Newspapers, 1870-1910. Bozeman: Collections Division of the Renne Library at Montana State Univeristy. Filmed by the Genealogical Society of Utah, [c.1975]. (FHL# microfilm 1035604, item1)

A collection of vital statistics taken from the *Avant-Courier* and *Republican Courier*. (FHL# microfilm 1035604)

Historical Records Survey, Works Progress Administration. *A Guide to Vital Records for Montana*. Bozeman, Mont.: Montana State College, 1941. (FHL# 978.6/V2h or microfilm 1036403, item 7, and microfiche 6046712)

Walker, Elaine. *Northwest Notebook.* Post Falls, Idaho: Genealogical Reference Builders, c.1975 (FHL# 979 V2w)

NEVADA

Historical Background

1775	Spanish missionary Francisco Garces, en route to California, becomes the first European to enter Nevada.
1801	Esmeralda County established with its seat at Goldfield.
1825	Fur trapper Peter Skeen Odgen of Hudson's Bay Company discovers the Humboldt River.
1830	The old Spanish Trail across Nevada, part of the route from Santa Fe to Los Angeles, is pioneered by William Wolfskill.
1833	The California Trail from Utah, which crossed the Sierra Nevada mountains, is pioneered by Joseph R. Walker.
1843-45	John C. Fremont makes a series of explorations in Nevada.
1848	The United States acquires Nevada through the Treaty of Guadelupe Hildago which ended the war with Mexico. Nevada was then a part of California, known as the Washoe Country.
1849	Nevada's first permanent settlement established at Mormon Station, now Genoa, by H. S. Beatie.
1850	Most of Nevada is included in the newly organized Utah Territory.
1851	Utah legislature creates Carson County, including all the settlements in the western area. The inhabitants petition Congress to annex them to California.
1859	A rich silver deposit, the Comstock Lode, is discovered near Virginia City, touching off a rush.
1861	Utah Territory is divided; the western portion is designated Nevada Territory.
1864	Nevada is admitted to the Union as the thirty-sixth state.

Settlement and Migration

Spaniard explorers were the first trailblazers through the Great Basin and what would later become Nevada. They were followed by fur trappers who stayed in the area as late as 1843 before finally accepting the fact that the Great Basin held little promise as a fur-trapping region.

Before the trappers departed, at least three different emigrant parties had passed through the Great Basin. One, leaving the Missouri River in May 1844, blazed a trail over the Truckee or Donner Pass a year before John C. Fremont followed the same path and established an alternate route into California from the Humboldt Sink.

A few emigrant parties passed through Nevada between 1841 and 1845; but from 1846 on, the trickle of emigrants to California became a flood. Supply centers sprang up along the trail, with Nevada's first trading post of any substance established at present-day Genoa in Carson Valley in 1850, the same year Congress established Utah's territorial boundaries as including all but the southern tip of Nevada. Brigham Young was appointed territorial governor.

Squatters attempted to organize the Carson Valley area, but the Utah government established Carson County as a judicial district of the territory and granted it one representative to the Utah Territorial Legislature. Orson Hyde, one of the Twelve Apostles of the Mormon church, was appointed probate and county judge to organize the county.

An April 1855 church conference decided to send missionaries or settlers to Carson Valley and the area which later became Clark County. The second party left Salt Lake City on 10 May 1855 and arrived in what was then a part of New Mexico Territory and would become Las Vegas, Nevada, on 14 June 1855.

Non-Mormons in the area were discontented with Mormon government, and a group petitioned the California government to annex Carson County to California.

Mormon control weakened, then ended in 1857 when the impending Utah War impelled Brigham Young to recall Carson Valley Mormons in the early fall of 1857.

The next series of Nevada settlements came after 1859 and the discovery of the Comstock Lode in Virginia City, mid-way between Reno and Carson City. Nevada's population prior to 1860 was about 6,000, but the 1861 territorial census showed a population of 16,374 persons exclusive of Indians and emigrants. Most of the newcomers were miners and became residents of Nevada when it became a state in 1864.

From 1859 to 1880 the history of Nevada is the history of the Comstock Lode. Once word spread of the richest of all silver mines, people began the trek to the Washoe District. Well-to-do speculators from Nevada City arrived first and staked claims along the entire Comstock Lode between Gold Canyon and Six Mile Canyon. Routes from California were packed with miners who prospected around Davidson Mountain and established another tent city in Virginia City that was a thriving metropolis within four years. Businesses sprang up, newspapers were established, and everyone flourished in supporting the 15,000 people needed to mine the lode.

Prospectors who couldn't afford the heavy equipment needed to get the ore out of the mountains moved on to other areas of western Nevada. Strike after strike was reported through 1860. Nevada Territory petitioned for statehood with fewer than 20,000 inhabitants, which was far below the standard expected by Congress. However, Nevada argued that any state with mines producing nearly $25 million annually would attract a huge population shortly, and Lincoln's support won them statehood on 31 October 1864.

Settlement around Davidson Mountain exploded in 1873 when four miners combined efforts as the Consolidated Virginia and began boring through the mountain to reach the Big Bonanza, the richest lode in the history of mining. Its discovery brought more wealth and settlement to Virginia City until 1890 when the boom ended.

Nevada Library Collection

The Family History Library has not filmed Nevada county records; thus the Nevada collection primarily consists of printed and secondary sources that are useful to researchers.

Bibliography

Spiros, Joyce V. Hawley. *Genealogical Guide to Arizona and Nevada.* Gallup, N. M.: Verlene Publishing, 1983. (FHL# 979/D23s)

Biography

History of Nevada. 1881; microreproduction, Tucson, Ariz.: W. C. Cox, 1974. (FHL# microfilm 1000194, item 2)

See **Nevada/Biography** for additional titles.

Census Records

The library has census indexes and mortality schedules for Nevada between 1860 and 1910. See **Nevada/Census** for a complete listing.

Church Records

Episcopal Church. Diocese of Utah. *Episcopal Register of the Bishop of Utah, 1899-1946.* Salt Lake City: Genealogical Society of Utah, 1975. (FHL# microfilm 908728)

Some baptisms, marriages, burials, and confirmations are for eastern Nevada.

Historical Records Survey, Works Project Administration. *Inventory of the Church Archives of Nevada, Protestant Episcopal Church.* Reno, Nev.: Historical Records Survey, 1941. (FHL# 979.3/K2he or microfilm 1036524, item 2)

———. *Inventory of the Church Archives of Nevada, Roman Catholic Church.* Reno, Nev.: Historical Records Survey, 1941. (FHL# 929.3.K2hc and microfilm 1036527, item 7)

Directories

Kelly, J. Wells. *First Directory of Nevada Territory.* rpt. ed., Tucson, Ariz.: W. C. Cox Co., 1974. (FHL# microfilm 1000196, item 2) Microreproduction of original published: Los Gatos, Calif.: Talisman Press, 1962.

Lee, Joyce C. *Genealogical Prospecting in Nevada: A Guide to Nevada Directories.* n.p.: Nevada Library Association, 1984. (FHL# 979.3/A1/no. 29)

Gazetteers

Averett, Walter R. *Directory of Southern Nevada Place Names.* n.p.: W. R. Averett, 1962. (FHL# 979.3/E5a)

History

The library's collection of Nevada histories is extensive. See **Nevada/History** for a complete list. It includes:

Elliott, Russell R. *History of Nevada.* Lincoln: University of Nebraska Press, 1965. (FHL# 973.3/H2e)

Maps

The Nevada map collection includes a significant number of early Utah and Nevada Territorial maps. Check the FHLC under **Nevada/Maps** for a complete list.

Military Records

United States Adjutant General's Office. *Index to Compiled Service Records of Volunteer Union Soldiers Who Served in Organizations from the State of Nevada, 1861-1865.* Washington, D.C.: National Archives, 1965. (FHL# microfilm 0821939)

Minorities

Titles cataloged under **Nevada/Minorities** pertain to

Chinese, Yugoslavians, American Indians, blacks, and Serbo-Croatians.

Names, Geographical

Leigh, Rufus Wood. *Nevada Place Names: Their Origin and Significance.* Salt Lake City: Deseret News Press, 1964. (FHL# 979.3/E2L)

Native Races

The library's collection of publications and films about Nevada's native races includes tribal rolls, employee records, and allottees. See **Nevada/Native Races** for a complete list of holdings on this subject. See also **Nevada/Schools** and **Nevada/Vital Records** for additional listings.

Newspapers

Lingfelter, Richard E. *The Newspapers of Nevada: A History and Bibliography, 1854-1979.* Reno: University of Nevada Press, 1984. (FHL# 979.3/B3L)

Vital Records

Mortality records, miscellaneous births, marriages, deaths, and inventories of territorial documents are some of the subjects covered in this record category. See **Nevada/Vital Records** for exact listings.

WYOMING

Historical Background

1805	Lewis and Clark pass through Wyoming while exploring land acquired in the Louisiana Purchase.
1807	John Colter, a fur-trapper and member of the Lewis and Clark expedition, explores the Yellowstone area.
1824	Start of annual trading rendezvous near the headwaters of the Wind, Bighorn, Snake, Green, or Sweetwater rivers in west central Wyoming
1834	Fort Laramie, the area's earliest supply stop, is established to accommodate emigrants bound for Oregon, California, or Utah who would pass though during the 1840s.
1843	Fort Bridger is established for the same purpose.
1860	Pony Express route goes through Wyoming.
1869	Territorial Legislature gives women the right to vote.
1869	Union Pacific Railroad crosses Wyoming.
1890	Wyoming becomes the 44th State on July 10th.

Settlement and Migration

Routes through Wyoming played an important role in its settlement. Emigrants bound for Oregon, California, and Utah began the trek through Wyoming during the 1840s. The principal route followed the North Platte River to Fort Laramie, which was a fur-trade supply depot from 1834 to 1849 and an Army post from 1849 to 1890. From Fort Laramie, the route continued along the North Platte to present-day Casper, then followed the Sweetwater River to the Continental Divide at South Pass.

West of the South Pass, the trail split. Some travelers went southwest to Fort Bridger, built in 1842 by Jim Bridger and Louis Vasques. Beginning in 1844, more people used the Greenwood Cutoff, later known as the Sublette Cutoff or Sublette Road, which by-passed Fort Bridger to the south and went due west. In 1859 the new Lander Road, pioneered by Frederick W. Lander, drew part of the traffic bound for Oregon. Several others branched from these three major routes west of South Pass.

Most of people who traveled through central Wyoming were headed for California or Utah rather than Oregon. Many used a more southerly route, the Overland Trail, between 1862 and 1868, and, to a lesser extent, as late as 1900. By 1850, stagecoaches routinely passed through Wyoming, followed by the Pony Express in 1860 and the first transcontinental telegraph in 1861.

These thousands of overland travelers spent less than a month in Wyoming and left little besides ruts, names and dates on trailside cliffs, a few place names, and some graves. Wyoming's early population consisted of Indians and those few residents at the forts and inns.

Wyoming's development began in 1867 when speculators laid out Cheyenne and Laramie along the Union Pacific Railroad's right of way in southern Wyoming. Wyoming's 1868 population was more than 16,000; but when railroad construction ended in 1869, the territory showed a population of 8,014. The 1870 census enumerated 9,118 inhabitants in Wyoming. Ten years later the population had reached 20,789 – over half living in seven towns along the Union Pacific. Wyoming was made a separate territory in 1868.

When the railroad failed to increase emigration to Wyoming, promoters unsuccessfully tried to attract new settlers. Wyoming's hoped for cattle boom did not bring the hundreds of thousand of people that farming brought to states just to the east. All other western territories and states were growing faster than Wyoming, despite the 1862 Homestead Act and the Desert Land Act of 1877.

When Wyoming became a state in 1890, it was home to 62,555 people. Ten years later the population had increased by 30,000.

Wyoming Library Collection

The Family History Library has not microfilmed Wyoming county records. Most of the Wyoming collection thus consists of printed and secondary sources; however, holdings of a specific county are noted in the charts accompanying this chapter.

Archives and Libraries

Bolger, Eileen. *Preliminary Inventory of the Records of the Bureau of Land Management, Wyoming.* Denver: Federal Archives and Record Center, 1983. (FHL# 978.7/R2b)

Biography

Chaffin, Lorah B. *Sons of the West: Biographical Accounts of Early-day Wyoming.* Caldwell, Ida.: Caxton Printers, Ltd., 1941. (FHL# 978.7/H2c)

Peterson, C. S. *Men of Wyoming.* Denver: n.pub., 1915. (FHL# 978.7/D3b or microfilm 1000827)

A national newspaper reference book containing photographs and biographies of over 300 male residents of Wyoming.

Census Records

Jackson, Ronald Vern, Scott Rosenkilde, and W. David Samuelson eds. *Wyoming 1860 Territorial Census Index.* Bountiful, Utah: Accelerated Indexing Systems, Inc., 1984. (FHL# 978.7/X22j)

Jackson, Ronald Vern, and Gary Ronald Teeples, eds. *Wyoming 1870 Territorial Census Index.* Bountiful, Utah: Accelerated Indexing Systems, 1978. (FHL# 978.7/X2j)

Jackson, Ronald Vern, ed. *Wyoming 1880 Census Index.* Bountiful, Utah: Accelerated Indexing Systems, 1980. (FHL# 978.7/X22w)

Church Records, Indexes

Historical Records Survey, Works Project Administration. *Guide to Vital Statistics Records in Wyoming: Church Archives.* Cheyenne, Wyo.: Wyoming Historical Records Survey, 1942. (FHL# microfilm 906119)

Gazetteers

Urbanek, Mae. *Wyoming Place Names.* Boulder, Colo.: Johnson Publishing Co., 1967. (FHL# 978.7/E2u)

Genealogy

Spiros, Joyce V. Hawley. *Genealogical Guide to Wyoming.* Gallup, N. M.: Verlene Publishing, 1982. (FHL# 978.7/D27sp)

History

At least sixteen titles in the Wyoming collection deal with state and local history. See the FHLC listing **Wyoming/History** for a complete inventory.

Beard, Frances Birkhead, ed. *Wyoming from Territorial Days to the Present.* Chicago: American Historical Society, 1935. FHL# 978.7/H2be or microfilm 1000827, items 1-3)

Larson, Taft Alfred. *History of Wyoming.* Lincoln: University of Nebraska Press, 1965. (FHL# 978.7/H2Lt)

Maps

The library has a number of excellent early Wyoming maps. See **Wyoming/Maps** for a complete list of maps not noted below.

Bishop, Loren C. *Maps of Wyoming Trails, Roads, Migration Routes and Forts.* Cheyenne: Wyoming State Archives and Historical Dept., 1963. (FHL# 978.7/E7b)

Map of the Oregon Territory of the United States. St. Louis: Edward Hutawa, 1843. (FHL# 979/E7h)

Shows the various trading depots or forts occupied by the British Hudson Bay Company during the period of northwestern fur trade.

Military Records, Civil War, 1861-65

United States Adjutant General's Office. *Index to Compiled Service Records of Volunteer Union Soldiers Who Served in Organizations from the Territory of Nebraska, 1861-1865.* Washington, D.C.: National Archives, 1965. (FHL# microfilm 821905-821906)

Native Races

See **Wyoming/Native Races** for a complete listing of titles pertaining to Wyoming's Indian population. Most of the titles are dated between 1889 and 1943.

Vital Records

Jackson, Ronald Vern, et al., eds. *Wyoming 1880 Mortality Schedule.* Bountiful, Utah: Accelerated Indexing Systems, 1983. (FHL# 978.7/X2jw/1880)

UTAH

Historical Background

1824 Trapper James Bridger discovers the Great Salt Lake while searching for the source of the Bear River.

1846 1,600 Mormons under the leadership of Brigham Young leave Illinois. By fall, 12,000 are camped on the banks of the Missouri on Indian land at a place they name Winter Quarters.

1847 The first party of wagons leave Winter Quarters in the spring and make a new road west along the north bank of the Platte River. They reach Fort Laramie in early June and the Great Salt Lake Valley on 24 July. Settlements at Salt Lake City, Bountiful, Centerville, and Ogden begin.

1848 By the Treaty of Guadelupe Hildago, officially ending the Mexican War, Mexico cedes its western territories, including Utah, to the United States.

1849	Perpetual Emigrating Fund established to loan converts world-wide money to come to the Great Salt Lake Valley. Fort Utah established on the shores of Utah Lake. State of Deseret organized with Brigham Young as governor, including Utah, Arizona, Nevada, and parts of New Mexico, Colorado, Wyoming and California.
1850	Congress creates the Territory of Utah. Lehi and Provo established in Utah Valley, Nephi and Manti in San Pete Valley.
1851	Fillmore established in the valley of the Sevier River; exploration of southern Utah begins.
1852	Under Brigham Young's direction, a company settles San Bernardino in California near Cajon Pass.
1854	Small outposts settled along the "Mormon Corridor" through Nevada.
1856	First handcart company of immigrants arrives in the Salt Lake Valley; two more companies arrive safely but a final thousand people in two companies are caught in early Wyoming blizzards, and over 200 perish before rescue expeditions reach them. Handcart emigration discontinued after 1861.
1890	Polygamy officially prohibited by Church President Wilford Woodruff, clearing the way for statehood.
1896	Utah admitted to the Union as the forty-fifth state.

Settlement and Migration

The story of Utah's settlement begins with the foundation, in 1830, of the Church of Jesus Christ of Latter-day Saints by Joseph Smith in New York. A continually growing but controversial group, thanks to a strong missionary program and an appealing theology of restoration, they moved from New York to Ohio and Missouri, and finally founded Nauvoo in Illinois. Thousands of converts from the United States and Europe increased Nauvoo's population, and by 1844 it was the largest city in Illinois.

Their neighbors, however, feared Joseph Smith's growing economic and political power and were offended by rumors of polygamy, then practiced secretly by selected leaders. Joseph Smith and his brother, Hyrum, were killed by a mob in nearby Carthage on 27 June 1844.

After a respite, Brigham Young, president of the Quorum of the Twelve Apostles, ordered an exodus west, had the city evacuated, and established Winter Quarters on the banks of the Missouri opposite Council Bluffs, Iowa, during the spring and summer of 1846. By fall, the temporary city held 12,000.

Brigham Young led the first company west in mid-April 1847, making their own trail north of the Platte. The first group reached Fort Laramie in early June and entered the Great Salt Lake Valley, where they would settle permanently, on 24 July 1847. Thousands of converts and members followed; Mormon settlements dotted the landscape from California to Idaho, Montana, Wyoming and, by the 1880s, Mexico and Canada.

The majority of those crossing the plains were British and Scandinavian. Fewer converts came from Continental Europe, Australia, and South Africa. British immigration took place between 1849 and 1885, and 1899 and 1925. Continental Europeans arrived at varying times between 1853 and 1932, with the majority arriving between 1853 and 1886.

Largely because of the issue of polygamy, the church had a stormy relationship with the federal government and federal territorial authorities, resulting in increasingly harsher laws, and increasingly punitive judicial enforcement. Many plural wives or husbands went on "the Underground" to escape federal marshals, some for years. Hundreds of men, and some plural wives who refused to testify against their husbands, served penitentiary sentences. The discorporation of the church and the escheatment of its property were among the pressures that finally resulted in the public announcement in 1890 that the church would not sanction marriages contrary to the laws of the country.

Utah Library Collection

Utah records fall in two categories: (1) those created by state and local jurisdictions, and (2) those created by the Church of Jesus Christ of Latter-day Saints, some of which have no geographic relationship to Utah. The latter collection is discussed separately in Chapter 1. Since the Family History Library is located in Utah and Mormons first colonized the state and still constitute a majority of the population, the library's Utah collection eclipses that of the other five mountain states collectively.

Biography

The library has thirty-four biographical titles in its Utah collection. In addition to the titles listed below, check the FHLC under **Utah/Biography.**

Esshom, Frank. *Pioneers and Prominent Men of Utah.* 1913; rpt. ed., Salt Lake City, Utah: Western Epics, Inc., 1966. (FHL# 979.2/D3e/1966 or microfilm 1000617)

Jenson, Andrew. *Latter-day Saint Biographical Encyclopedia.* 4 vols. Salt Lake City: A. Jenson History Co., 1901-36. (FHL# 920.0792/J4531 or microfilm 410869-410871, 547256)

A compilation of biographical sketches of Latter-day Saints, both male and female.

Portrait, Genealogical, and Biographical Record of the State of Utah. Chicago: National Historical Record, 1902. (FHL# microfilm 446501)

Utah Pioneer Biographies, 1935-1964. Salt Lake City: filmed by the Genealogical Society of Utah, 1977. (FHL# microfilm 982281-982305)

Handwritten and typed biographies compiled by hundreds of Utah pioneers and their families.

Cemeteries

A significant number of Utah cemeteries have been inventoried and are cataloged in the FHLC under **Utah/Cemeteries** or **/[County]/Cemeteries**.

Census Records

The Utah census collection includes indexes for censuses taken between 1850 to 1890 and some printed census schedules. See the FHLC under **Utah/Census** for a complete list of holdings.

Kearl, J. R., Clayne L. Pope, and Larry T. Wimmer. *Index to the 1850, 1860, and 1870 Censuses of Utah.* Baltimore: Genealogical Publishing Co., 1981. (FHL# 979.2/X2k or microfiche 6051336)

Dilts, Bryan Lee. *1856 Utah Census Index.* Salt Lake City, Utah: Index Publishing, 1983. (FHL# 979.2/X22d)

An every-name index.

Church History

Most titles in the Utah church history collection pertain to the LDS Church. See **Utah/Church History** for a complete list.

Works Progress Administration. Historical Records Survey. *Inventory of the Church Archives of Utah.* 3 vols. Salt Lake City: Utah Historical Records Survey, 1940. (FHL# 979.2/K2h)

Episcopal Church. Diocese of Utah. *Episcopal Register of the Bishop of Utah, 1899-1946, 1951-1967.* Salt Lake City: filmed by the Genealogical Society of Utah, 1975. (FHL# microfilm 908728)

Contains confirmations, baptisms, marriages, and burials.

Directories

See the FHLC under **Utah/Directories** for the library's complete holdings. Notable is:

Culmer, H. L. A. *Utah Directory and Gazetteer.* 1879; microreproduction, Salt Lake City: Genealogical Society of Utah, 1967. (FHL# microfilm 481064, item 2)

Emigration and Immigration

Foreign and domestic immigration played an important role in the settlement of Utah between 1847 and 1900. The library's Utah collection has a wealth of emigration-immigration microfilms and publications cataloged under **Utah/Emigration and Immigration**. See also Chapter 1, "LDS Church Records."

Alder, Douglas Dexter. *The German-Speaking Immigration to Utah, 1850-1950.* M.A. thesis, University of Utah, n.d. (FHL# 979.2/W2a)

A statistical tabulation from government and church reports and narrative of a century of immigration.

Genealogical Society of Utah. *Names of Persons and Sureties Indebted to the Perpetual Emigrating Fund Company from 1850-1877.* 1877; microreproduction, Salt Lake City: Genealogical Society of Utah, 1950. (FHL# microfilm 025686)

Gazetteers

Sloan, E. L. *Gazetteer of Utah and Salt Lake City Directory.* Salt Lake City: Salt Lake Herald Publishing Company, 1874. (FHL# 979.2/E4s)

Genealogy

The library's collection of Utah genealogy material is vast. See Chapter 2 of this book for detailed information about the major collections (i.e., Family Group Records Archives, International Genealogical Index, and Ancestral File to name a few). See also Chapter 1, and FHLC heading **Utah/Genealogy**.

Bennett, Archibald F. *Family Genealogical Records.* Salt Lake City, Utah: filmed by the Genealogical Society of Utah, 1967. (FHL# microfilm 476963-476965, 483542-483557)

Microfilm of manuscripts in the LDS Church Historian's Office; includes index.

History

The library has a substantial collection of Utah histories cataloged under **Utah/History** and **Utah/[County]/History**. See also Chapter 1, "LDS Church Records," for a more complete list of titles.

The **Utah/History** listings include autobiographies, diaries, geographic histories, gazetteers, directories, genealogical and biographical records, military history, atlases, newspapers, Indian War pension records, historical magazines and quarterlies, and addresses, in addition to histories. Many of these subjects are not also cataloged under their specific subject headings.

Whitney, Orson Ferguson. *History of Utah.* 4 vols. Salt Lake City: G. Q. Cannon and Sons, 1892-1904. (FHL# 979.2/H2w or microfilm 928185-928187, 1036340)

Includes a history of the state's founders, accounts of early Spanish and American explorations, the advent of the Mormon pioneers, the establishment and dissolution of the provisional government of the state of Deseret, and the subsequent creation and development of the territory. Published before statehood in 1896.

Maps

See the FHLC under **Utah/Maps** for a complete list of the library's map holdings for the state, as well as:

Moffat, Riley Moore. *Printed Maps of Utah to 1900.* Santa Cruz, Calif.: Western Association of Map Libraries, 1981. (FHL# 979.2/E33m)

An annotated cartobibliography.

Greer, Deon C., Klaus D. Gurgel, Wayne L. Wahlquist, Howard A. Christy, and Gary B. Peterson. *Atlas of Utah.*

Provo, Utah: Brigham Young University Press, 1981. (FHL# 979.2 E7a)

Military Records

See the FHLC under **Utah/Military Records** for complete list of the large collection of Utah military records beginning with the pioneer period and extending through World War II.

United States Adjutant General's Office. *Index to Compiled Service Records of Volunteer Union Soldiers Who Served in Organizations from the Territory of Utah.* Washington, D.C.: National Archives, 1964. (FHL# microfilm 1292645)

United States War Department. *Utah Territorial Militia Muster Rolls, 1849-1870.* Salt Lake City: filmed by the Genealogical Society of Utah, 1966. (FHL# microfilm 485554-485558) Original records at the State Capitol Building, Salt Lake City.

United States War Department. *World War I Service Records of Utahns.* Salt Lake City: filmed by the Genealogical Society of Utah, 1966. (FHL# microfilm 485733-485750)

Originals in the Utah State Archives in Salt Lake City.

Minorities

Cataloged in the FHLC under **Utah/Minorities** are sources dealing with Germans, American Indians, Jews, Basques, Swedes, and Slavs.

Native Races

Records under the **Utah/Native Races** heading in the FHLC include membership rolls, census enumerations, school records, and superintendency records. See also **/Native Races/Cemeteries, /Native Races/Church History, /Native Races/Genealogy, /Native Races/Periodicals, /Native Races/Vital Records, Utah/Land and Property, Utah/History, Utah/Schools,** and **Utah/Census.**

Newspapers

Holley, Robert P., ed. *Utah's Newspapers – Traces of Her Past.* Salt Lake City: Marriott Library, University of Utah, 1984. (FHL# 979.2/A3un)

Includes "Checklist of Utah Newspapers" compiled by Dennis McCargar and edited by Yvonne Stroup.

Obituaries

Church of Jesus Christ of Latter-day Saints, St. George Branch Library. *Obituary Card Index.* Salt Lake City: filmed by the Genealogical Society of Utah, 1976. (FHL# microfilm 1058731-1058738)

An index to newspaper clippings for the *Deseret News and Telegram, Salt Lake Tribune,* and *Arizona Republic* for 1950-65 editions, plus some from 1928.

Church of Jesus Christ of Latter-day Saints. *Obituary Index to the Salt Lake Tribune and Deseret News.* Salt Lake City: Church Historian's Office, 1971. (FHL# microfilm 821636-821699)

Microfilm copy of card file.

Public Records

Utah State Commission. *Utah Commission Minutes, 1882-95.* Salt Lake City: filmed by the Genealogical Society of Utah, 1966. (FHL# microfilm 497714-497416)

Microreproduction of original minutes produced prior to statehood, but designated as produced by the Utah State Commission.

Vital Records

Genealogical Society of the Church of Jesus Christ of Latter-day Saints. *Miscellaneous Marriage Records Index.* Salt Lake City: filmed by the Genealogical Society of Utah, 1972. (FHL# microfilm 820155, item 2-820173)

Contains names of persons compiled from marriage license records of various Utah counties, Franklin and Lemhi counties in Idaho, and Lincoln County, Wyoming. Arranged alphabetically by the surnames of both bride and groom.

LDS Church Records Collection

You should not skip this section even if you are not a member of the Church of Jesus Christ of Latter-day Saints. Many special collections created by the LDS Church contain information about millions of people who were not affiliated with the church during their lifetime. LDS Church records also contain data about people who were affiliated with the church for a period of time, either as members or non-members.

The Church of Jesus Christ of Latter-day Saints has created enormous numbers of records since its founding in 1830. Because of its emphasis on genealogical research, the church has developed some of the largest genealogical collections in existence. LDS records can be divided into three categories: (1) membership records, (2) historical records, and (3) ordinance records.

The majority of LDS records are easily accessed by using special registers located near the information desk on the main floor of the Family History Library. See *Register of LDS Church Records* by Laureen R. Jaussi and Gloria D. Chaston (Salt Lake City: Deseret Book Company, 1968) (FHL# 289.3/J327r) located at the LDS Register Table. These same authors have written *Fundamentals of Genealogical Research,* 2d ed. rev. (Salt Lake City: Deseret Book, 1972) which offers detailed information about LDS sources (FHL# 289.3/J327f/-1972).

Membership Records

Following the organization of the LDS Church in 1830, wards and branches were created as local congregations. Membership records contain information about the baptism and rebaptism of church members, as well as birth information and parentage. The type and amount of information varies from record to record. Standard membership forms were not used until 1877; thus, a variety of formats existed during the early period. Membership books were used between 1830 and 1941; membership cards were used from 1941 to 1973 (not available to the public); and membership records were then computerized (not available to the public). Unfortunately, there is no comprehensive index to early membership records, and you must know a member's residence before you can locate a record.

Form E (Form 42 FP) Annual Reports 1907-1972/73 is a separate record of vital statistics and religious ordinances. They are on microfilm and can usually be found at the end of a ward's or branch's membership records.

Church membership records created prior to 1941 cannot be accessed without knowing the name of the ward or branch to which a member belonged. Identifying that ward or branch is possible but time consuming since the process involves examining a number of indexes created from ordinance and historical records. These indexes may be used to identify the ward or branch someone attended or will lead you to the original records that may offer the needed information:

The Nauvoo Baptisms for the Dead Card Index is an alphabetical listing of deceased individuals who were baptized by proxy between 1840 and 1845 in Nauvoo, Illinois. A second index lists the name of the heir or proxy involved in the religious ordinance. (FHL# microfilm 183375)

The Endowment House Baptisms for the Dead Index is an alphabetical listing of deceased individuals who were baptized by proxy between 1855 and 1876 at the Endowment House in Salt Lake City, Utah. A second index lists the name of the heir or proxy involved in the religious ordinance. (FHL# microfilm 118381 or 1149524)

The Early Church Information Card Index is an alphabetical listing of people affiliated with the LDS Church between the 1830s and the turn of this century, compiled from various sources, including newspapers, tombstone inscriptions, early church records, ward records, and early civil records. Information recorded on each index card varies. (FHL# microfilm 820136-820147)

The Utah Immigration Card Index, more commonly known as the *Crossing the Plains Card Index,* is an alphabetical card index listing the names of pioneer immigrants who crossed the plains between 1847 and 1868. Information includes name, age, date of arrival in the Salt Lake Valley, name of pioneer company, date of departure, name of ship, and source of information. (FHL# microfilm 0298440-0298442)

The European Emigration Card Index, more commonly called the *Crossing the Ocean Index,* is an alphabetical index of those who emigrated from Great Britain and Europe to the United States as participants in the LDS Church emigration program. Cards list names of emigrants, number of people in the group, age, nationality or country of departure, date of departure, name of ship, port of arrival in the United States or place of settlement in the Salt Lake Valley, date of arrival, and source of information. (FHL# microfilm 298431-298439)

The Membership Card Index, more commonly called *Minnie Margett's File,* is a partial index to early LDS Church members. It indexes over 400 wards and branches, most of which were located in Great Britain. It is arranged in three sections: (1) cards listing ward, branch, conference (the current equivalent of a mission district), and stake records which are included in the main index, (2) cards arranged alphabetically by locality with incomplete names, (3) a surname index to information extracted from ward and branch records. Time period covered is uncertain, but most records are dated between 1830 and 1900. (FHL# microfilm 0415443-0415457)

The Scandinavian Membership Card Index is a card index to early LDS membership records created between 1850 and 1910 for Sweden, Denmark, and Norway. Index cards include the member's name, birthdate, birthplace, date blessed, date baptized, emigration date, excommunication date (where relevant), and source of information. (Card index is located on Level B-1 in the Scandinavian Area of the main library. See reference librarian for assistance.)

The Patriarchal Blessing Card Index contains an individual's name, birthdate, birthplace, parents, date of blessing, place of blessing, biblical lineage, name of patriarch, and the volume and page number of the original blessing given to LDS members between 1833 to 1972. (FHL# microfilm 392631-392696 or microfiche 001-008 located at the LDS Reference Desk)

The Deceased Member File consists of membership records of members who have died since 1841. Records include extensive genealogical information about the deceased, as well as address prior to death; citizenship; name, birthdates, and birthplaces of spouse and children and their spouses, and former spouse. (FHL# microfilm 884001-884392 for 1941-74 and 884393-884420 for 1974-75)

The Missionary Card Index is a card index listing those who served as LDS missionaries between 1830 and 1963. Each card includes the missionary's name, the mission in which he/she served, the date of being called or departure, and some biographical information about those who served prior to 1896. (See *Register of LDS Records* for call numbers.)

The Obituary Card Index is a card index to obituaries printed in Salt Lake City newspapers through 1970. Cards list the name of the deceased, death date, name and date of the periodical, the page or section number where the obituary appeared, and possibly some biographical information. (FHL# microfilm 821636-821699)

The Card Index to Pedigree Charts is the key to the contents of approximately 18,000 pedigree charts compiled by LDS Church members during the 1920s. Not all of the collection is indexed; the remainder of the sheets were filmed in alphabetical order by the name of the first person listed on each pedigree chart. (FHL# microfilm 0820089-0820115)

Historical Records

The LDS Church compiled a census of its members periodically from 1914 to 1960. They contain the name of each person in the household, age, sex, and place of birth. Church census records for 1914-35 have been combined into one collection which has been microfilmed in alphabetical order.

The Missionary Card Index lists information about members who served full-time missions for the LDS Church. Each card contains the missionary's name, birthdate, birthplace, parents, mission area, departure date, return date, and name of ward and stake from which the missionary departed. (See *Register of LDS Records* for call numbers.)

Biographies

LDS Church members have long been encouraged to keep personal diaries and prepare personal and family histories. Assistant Church Historian Davis Bitton has compiled *Guide to Mormon Diaries and Autobiographies* (Provo, Utah: Brigham Young University Press, c.1977), a bibliography of journals, diaries, autobiographies, memoirs, and first-person accounts. (FHL# 016.2893/-B549g) Other LDS biographical works include:

Jenson, Andrew. *Latter-day Saint Biographical Encyclopedia.* 4 vols. Salt Lake City: The Andrew Jenson History Co., 1906-36. (FHL# microfilm 0410869-0410871, 0547256)

Emigration and Immigration

Over 90,000 immigrants entered the Salt Lake Valley between 1847 and 1887. Pioneers born in the United States were members of wagon companies or handcart companies, while foreign immigrants made long ocean voyages before linking up with a Mormon immigration company in Iowa. The church set up a shipping agency in England to charter ships and a receiving company on the frontier to organize immigrants into companies for the trip to Salt Lake City.

Some card file indexes have been discussed already in the section on *Indexes.* Others include:

Card File of LDS Church Immigration to Utah, a file compiled by the Historical Department of the LDS Church. It consists of cards arranged chronologically by date of immigration and name of the captain of the immigrating company, then alphabetically by name of the individual members of the company. This collection is similar to the *Utah Immigration Card Index.* (FHL# microfilm 029440-0298442)

Emigration Registers of the British Mission, compiled by the LDS Church agent at Liverpool, 1849-85. A second group of registers covers 1899-1925. Registers list the departure date; passengers' names, ages, sex, residence, marital status, occupation, country or nationality; name of ship, and destination port. (FHL# microfilm 025690-025695)

Emigration Registers of Continental Europe. These registers contain names of immigrants who emigrated as members of the LDS Church to Utah from Denmark, Norway, Sweden, Germany, Switzerland, Belgium, Hungary, and Holland between 1853 and 1932. Sometimes these emigrants appear also in the *Emigration Registers of the British Mission* mentioned above. Both registers include the same genealogical information. One of the best books about the handcart pioneers is LeRoy R. Hafen and Ann Hafen, *Handcarts to Zion* (Glendale, Calif.: Arthur H. Clark Co., 1960) (FHL# 973/H2hz).

Ordinance Records

The bulk of the Family History Library's ordinance records are summarized in the Temple Index Bureau cards and its companion, Family Group Record Collection, both of which are discussed at length in Chapter 2. Early temple records have been microfilmed and include registers from the following places or temples: Ordinances performed at the Lima Branch in Illinois; Nauvoo Temple Ordinances (Nauvoo, Illinois, 1845-46); Endowment House Records (Salt Lake City, 1855-89); St. George Temple Records (St. George, Utah, from 1884); Manti Temple Records (Manti, Utah, from 1888); and Salt Lake Temple Records (Salt Lake City, from 1893).

See *Register of LDS Records* by Jaussi and Chaston, cited above, for call numbers for the records discussed here and many others.

Records by Jurisdiction Colorado	Archives & Libraries	Atlases	Bible Records	Bibliography	Biography	Cemeteries	Census (Printed)	Church History	Church Records	Court	Directories	Emigration/Immigration	Genealogy	Genealogy-Periodicals	History	Indexes	Land & Property	Maps	Migration	Military	Minorities	Native Races	Naturalization	Newspapers	Obituaries	Periodicals	Probates & Estates	Schools	Societies	Tax Records	Vital Records	Voting Registers	WPA Inventories
Adams						•			•		•																						
Alamosa					•	•		•	•																								•
Arapahoe	•					•					•				•																•		•
Archuleta						•		•																•									
Baca									•																								
Bent					•				•		•				•																		•
Boulder					•	•	•	•	•		•		•	•										•	•						•		
Chaffee					•	•		•	•		•				•																•		
Cheyenne						•																											
Clear Creek					•	•																											
Conejos					•			•	•																								•
Costilla						•			•								•																•
Crowley									•						•																		
Custer						•		•	•																								
Delta									•	•																							
Denver (City)					•	•		•	•	•				•			•						•								•		
Dolores									•																								
Douglas						•																											
Eagle						•																											
Elbert																																	
El Paso						•		•	•		•				•				•						•						•	•	
Fremont					•	•																											•
Garfield											•				•																		
Gilpin					•	•									•																•		
Grand																																	
Gunnison						•			•		•				•																		
Hinsdale															•																		
Huerfano						•			•		•				•																		
Jackson																																	
Jefferson	•				•	•				•	•		•		•		•											•	•		•	•	
Kiowa																																	
Kit Carson											•																						
Lake											•																						
La Plata									•		•																						
Larimer						•			•	•	•				•																		•
Las Animas									•		•				•																		
Lincoln					•										•																		
Logan					•	•			•						•																		•
Mesa									•		•																				•		
Mineral															•																		
Moffatt						•																											
Montezuma						•			•						•																		
Montrose									•						•																		
Morgan						•					•																		•				•
Otero									•																•								
Ouray						•			•																								
Park						•																											
Phillips						•																											•
Pitkin											•				•																		

Records by Jurisdiction **Colorado** (cont.)	Archives & Libraries	Atlases	Bible Records	Bibliography	Biography	Cemeteries	Census (Printed)	Church History	Church Records	Court	Directories	Emigration/Immigration	Genealogy	Genealogy-Periodicals	History	Indexes	Land & Property	Maps	Migration	Military	Minorities	Native Races	Naturalization	Newspapers	Obituaries	Periodicals	Probates & Estates	Schools	Societies	Tax Records	Vital Records	Voting Registers	WPA Inventories
Prowers						•			•		•																						•
Pueblo	•					•		•	•		•		•		•																		
Rio Blanco																																	
Rio Grande									•																								
Routt															•																		
Saguache									•																								
San Juan						•			•																								
San Miguel						•			•																								
Sedgwick																																	•
Summit																																	
Teller						•			•								•																
Washington						•					•				•																		•
Weld																																	
Yuma																																	•

Records by Jurisdiction **Idaho**	Archives & Libraries	Atlases	Bible Records	Bibliography	Biography	Cemeteries	Census (Printed)	Church History	Church Records	Court Records	Directories	Emigration/Immigration	Genealogy	Genealogical Periodicals	History	Indexes	Land & Property	Maps	Migration	Military	Minorities	Native Races	Naturalization	Newspapers	Obituaries	Periodicals	Probate & Estates	Public Records	Schools	Societies	Tax Records	Vital Records	Voting Registers	WPA Inventories
Ada						•			•		•		•		•		•	•														•		
Adams						•							•																			•		
Alturas																																		
Bannock					•	•		•			•		•		•										•							•		
Bear Lake					•	•		•	•		•		•		•																	•		
Benewah						•									•																	•		
Bingham	•				•	•		•			•		•		•																	•		
Blaine						•									•																			
Boise						•							•										•				•			•	•	•	•	
Bonner						•																										•		
Bonneville					•	•		•	•		•		•		•												•							
Boundary						•																										•		•
Butte						•			•				•												•									
Camas						•																												
Canyon						•		•	•		•				•			•					•				•					•		
Caribou					•	•		•			•		•		•																	•		
Cassia					•	•					•		•		•										•							•		
Clark																																		•
Clearwater						•																												
Custer					•	•									•																			
Elmore						•																										•		
Franklin					•	•		•	•				•		•		•	•						•		•		•				•		
Fremont	•				•	•			•				•		•																			
Gem											•																							
Gooding						•					•																							
Idaho						•	•								•																	•		
Jefferson					•	•		•			•				•																			
Jerome											•																		•					
Kootenai						•					•				•		•										•					•		•
Latah					•	•		•					•	•	•			•														•		
Lemhi					•	•									•																			•
Lewis						•									•																			
Lincoln					•										•																	•		
Madison						•		•			•			•	•														•					
Minidoka					•	•					•		•		•																	•		•
Nez Perce						•					•				•																	•		•
Oneida					•	•			•	•	•		•		•																	•	•	
Owyhee					•	•					•				•														•		•			
Payette											•																							
Power					•					•					•																			•
Shoshone						•								•																	•			
Teton						•		•																										•
Twin Falls						•					•																							
Valley						•							•		•																			
Washington						•					•																							

Records by Jurisdiction **Montana**	Archives & Libraries	Atlases	Bible Records	Bibliography	Biography	Cemeteries	Census (Printed)	Church History	Church Records	Directories	Emigration/Immigration	Genealogy	Genealogy-Periodicals	History	Indexes	Land & Property	Maps	Migration	Military	Minorities	Native Races	Naturalization	Newspapers	Obituaries	Periodicals	Probate & Estate	Public Records	Schools	Societies	Tax Records	Vital Records	WPA Inventories
Beaverhead										•																						•
Big Horn					•		•			•		•		•					•						•			•				
Blaine						•																										
Broadwater																																
Carbon						•								•																		
Carter																																
Cascade					•	•				•			•	•												•					•	
Chouteau						•																									•	
Custer										•				•																		
Daniels														•																		
Dawson										•				•																		
Deer Lodge										•				•																		
Fallon												•		•																		
Fergus						•			•	•		•		•									•								•	
Flathead					•	•				•			•											•								•
Gallatin										•																				•		
Garfield																																
Glacier												•							•													
Golden Valley														•																		
Granite									•	•																						
Hill																																
Jefferson																																
Judith Basin						•				•		•		•									•								•	
Lake						•																										•
Lewis & Clark									•	•																		•				
Liberty																																
Lincoln						•								•																		•
Madison						•																									•	•
McCone												•		•																		
Meagher																																
Mineral																																
Missoula						•			•	•				•																	•	
Musselshell																																
Park										•		•		•																		
Petroleum																							•									
Phillips																																
Pondera						•						•		•																		
Powder River					•									•																		
Powell																																
Prairie																																
Ravalli						•	•			•				•										•							•	•
Richland										•																						
Roosevelt																																
Rosebud										•				•											•			•				
Sanders										•																		•				•
Sheridan														•																		
Silver Bow										•				•												•					•	•
Stillwater																																
Sweet Grass														•																		

Records by Jurisdiction — **Montana** (cont.)	Archives & Libraries	Atlases	Bible Records	Bibliography	Biography	Cemeteries	Census (Printed)	Church History	Church Records	Directories	Emigration/Immigration	Genealogy	Genealogy-Periodicals	History	Indexes	Land & Property	Maps	Migration	Military	Minorities	Native Races	Naturalization	Newspapers	Obituaries	Periodicals	Probate & Estate	Public Records	Schools	Societies	Tax Records	Vital Records	WPA Inventories
Teton						•																									•	
Toole																																•
Treasure																																
Valley						•				•																						
Wheatland																																
Wibaux						•																										
Yellowstone						•				•		•		•					•									•			•	

Records by Jurisdiction — **Nevada**	Archives & Libraries	Atlases	Bible Records	Bibliography	Biography	Cemeteries	Census (Printed)	Church History	Church Records	Court	Directories	Emigration/Immigration	Employment	Genealogy	Genealogy-Periodicals	History	Indexes	Land & Property	Maps	Migration	Military	Minorities	Native Races	Naturalization	Newspapers	Obituaries	Periodicals	Probate & Estate	Public Records	Schools	Societies	Tax Records	Vital Records	Voting Registers	WPA Inventories
Carson						•					•														•						•				•
Churchill						•	•				•																	•					•		
Clark						•		•	•		•					•										•							•		
Douglas						•																											•		•
Elko						•										•																			•
Esmeralda																•																			
Eureka						•																													•
Humbolt						•																												•	
Lander						•				•																									
Lincoln					•									•		•																	•		
Lyon						•															•											•	•	•	
Mineral						•																											•		•
Nye						•										•																			•
Ormsby						•																									•				
Pahute						•																													
Pershing						•										•																			
Roop																																			
Storey						•					•					•																	•		
Washoe					•	•					•				•	•									•								•	•	•
White Pine						•					•			•		•								•	•								•		

Records by Jurisdiction

Wyoming

County	Archives & Libraries	Atlases	Bible Records	Bibliography	Biography	Cemeteries	Census (Printed)	Church History	Church Records	Court Records	Directories	Emigration/Immigration	Genealogy	Genealogy-Periodicals	History	Indexes	Land & Property	Maps	Migration	Military	Minorities	Native Races	Naturalization	Newspapers	Obituaries	Periodicals	Probate & Estates	Public Records	Schools	Societies	Tax Records	Vital Records	WPA Inventories
Albany						•			•		•		•				•			•					•			•	•	•		•	
Big Horn					•	•								•		•						•				•				•			
Campbell													•		•																		
Carbon					•					•						•		•														•	
Converse					•	•							•		•																	•	
Crook										•			•		•		•	•										•				•	
Fremont						•					•			•			•			•								•				•	
Goshen															•																		•
Hot Springs																																	
Johnson					•						•				•		•				•							•				•	
Laramie					•	•			•		•		•		•		•												•				•
Lincoln						•							•		•																		•
Natrona						•				•	•				•		•			•									•			•	
Niobrara					•	•							•																				
Park																																	•
Platte								•							•																		•
Sheridan						•					•				•		•											•					•
Sublette						•							•																				
Sweetwater						•				•	•														•								
Teton						•									•																		
Uinta					•	•			•						•		•			•								•					•
Washakie															•																		
Weston																	•											•					•

Records by Jurisdiction

Utah

	Archives & Libraries	Atlases	Bible Records	Bibliography	Biography	Cemeteries	Census (Printed)	Church History	Church Records	Court Records	Directories	Emigration/Immigration	Genealogy	Genealogy-Periodicals	History	Indexes	Land & Property	Maps	Migration	Military	Minorities	Native Races	Naturalization	Newspapers	Obituaries	Periodicals	Probate & Estate	Public Records	Schools	Societies	Tax Records	Vital Records	Voting Registers	WPA Inventories
Beaver					•	•			•	•					•		•						•				•		•			•		
Box Elder					•	•		•	•	•			•		•		•	•				•	•	•			•	•	•			•	•	•
Cache	•					•		•			•		•		•		•	•					•	•	•		•	•	•	•	•	•		
Carbon						•			•	•					•		•									•	•	•				•		•
Daggett						•				•					•		•										•	•				•		•
Davis						•	•	•	•				•		•												•					•		•
Duchesne					•	•		•					•		•												•					•		
Emery					•	•	•								•		•						•				•			•		•		•
Garfield					•	•									•												•				•	•		
Grand					•	•	•								•												•					•		•
Iron						•	•	•	•	•	•				•		•					•					•				•	•		
Juab						•									•								•				•			•	•	•		
Kane					•	•		•		•					•												•					•		
Millard						•			•	•					•		•						•				•			•	•	•		
Morgan					•	•			•	•			•		•												•			•		•		•
Piute						•				•																	•							
Rich					•	•		•						•	•																•	•		
Salt Lake	•				•	•	•	•	•	•	•	•	•		•		•	•		•				•	•	•	•	•	•	•	•	•		
San Juan						•				•					•			•				•					•					•		
Sanpete					•	•	•	•		•			•		•		•									•	•			•	•	•		•
Sevier					•	•		•	•	•			•		•		•			•			•				•	•			•	•		
Summit						•					•			•	•		•			•							•				•	•		
Tooele					•	•	•	•	•	•	•		•		•					•		•					•				•	•		•
Uintah					•	•									•																•	•		•
Utah	•				•	•	•	•	•	•	•		•	•	•		•	•				•	•				•		•		•	•		•
Wasatch					•	•									•		•			•												•		•
Washington					•	•		•	•	•	•		•		•		•	•		•		•		•		•	•				•	•		
Wayne						•				•					•		•			•			•				•	•			•	•		
Weber				•	•	•	•	•	•	•	•		•		•		•	•						•	•				•	•	•	•	•	

Chapter 12

United States: The Southwest

Wendy L. Elliott

ARIZONA

Historical Background

1539	First European explorers enter area of present-day Arizona.
1651	Southern Arizona called Pimeria Alta; under jurisdiction of Sonora and Spain.
1687	Spanish Catholic missionaries teach Arizona Indians.
1742	The presidio of Terrenate is established to protect missions in Pimeria Alta.
1775	The presidio of Santa Cruz is organized.
1776	The presidio of Tubac is established, near Tucson and the mission at San Xavier del Bac; region is reorganized as the Interior Provinces.
1787	Sonora becomes part of the Western Interior Provinces.
1792	The Eastern and Western Interior Provinces are reunited.
1820	Self-government begins in the towns.
1821	The area of present-day Arizona is under the ownership and control of Mexico.
1824	Union of the provinces of Sonora and Sinaloa is decreed; they are organized as the Internal State of the West.
1831	Departments of Arizpe and Horcasitas become the state of Sonora; capital at Hermosillo.
1831	Federal system of government adopted.
c.1830-40	Much hostile activity by Apache Indians.
1837	Other areas of Sonora become a department.
1846	General Stephen Kearny marches across the territory south of the Gila River.
1846-47	Mormon Battalion "constructs" a road to San Diego.
1847	Sonora becomes a state under Mexican control, with a governor and legislature at Ures; federal system again established.
1848	Treaty which ends War with Mexico establishes the international boundary at the Gila.
1848	U.S./Mexican disputes in the international border area.
1848	Many Arizona Mexicans join the California Gold Rush, reducing the population so sharply that the rest take refuge from the Apaches at Tucson.
1850	Beginning of Mormon colonization in Arizona area.
1851	Arizona north of the Gila River is organized under the territory of New Mexico for administrative purposes.
1851	Area on north and south of the Gila River is organized as Dona Ana County, in the Territory of New Mexico.
1852	A small group of Mexican soldiers reoccupy Tubac.
1853	Gadsden Purchase obtains territory south of the Gila River for the United States.
1856	United States dragoons replace Mexican troops at Tucson, and possession of the Gadsden Purchase region is effected.
1863	Arizona Territory is organized including the western section of the Gadsden Purchase.
1865	First capital at Prescott.
1864-67	Three censuses of Arizona Territory.

1867	Capital moved to Tucson.
1870	Territorial census.
1877	Capital relocated at Prescott.
1880	U.S. census.
1887	County record-keeping begins.
1889	Capital established at Phoenix.
1900	U.S. census.
1909	Statewide control of vital records is organized.
1910	U.S. census.
1912	Arizona becomes the forty-eighth state.
1941-45	Relocation camps constructed to intern Japanese Americans.

History and Settlement

Hopi, Navajo, and Apache tribes resided in the northern section of today's Arizona. The first Europeans in the area were Spaniards, exploring the area during the sixteenth century. The region was under Spanish control until 1821, when it came under the jurisdiction of newly independent Mexico. It was not until the conclusion of the Mexican War in 1848 that the territory came under control of the United States.

In 1863, during the Civil War, Arizona Territory was organized. Its first capital was located at Prescott from 1865 to 1867; in 1867 it was moved to Tucson. Another change was made in 1877 when the capital was relocated at Prescott for twelve years. In 1889, the capital was established at Phoenix where it has remained.

Over the years, many bloody battles were fought in Arizona, including Indian conflicts and Civil War battles. The mining communities saw many strikes and skirmishes, particularly between management and workers. Later, difficulties arose between the sheep and cattle ranchers.

When the area was taken from Mexican control at the close of the Mexican War (1845-48), few settlers lived in the region. Little settlement was made during the next fifteen years, except for a few Mormon colonies in the north part of the state beginning in 1850. When Arizona Territory was organized in 1863, the population was small. By 1870, fewer than 10,000 residents were in the area; but in the next forty years, the population of Arizona Territory increased twenty-fold.

The state retains a high percentage of those with Mexican ancestry. Other foreign-born groups represented within the state's population include in order: Canadian, English and Welsh, Germans, Russians, Italians, Poles, Austrians, Swedes, Greeks, Irish, Scots, Yugoslavs, and Czechoslovakians.

Arizona Library Collection

Archives and Libraries

Few guides or inventories of archival collections for Arizona are included in the Family History Library Catalog (FHLC). A guide to vital records prepared by the Work Projects Administration is FHL# 979.1/A1/no. 5. See also:

Colley, Charles C. *Documents of Southwestern History: A Guide to the Manuscript Collections of the Arizona Historical Society*. Tucson: Arizona Historical Society, [c.1972]. (FHL# 979.1/A5c)

Several valuable books which are cataloged under other headings are:

Beers, Henry Putney. *Spanish and Mexican Records of the American Southwest: A Bibliographical Guide to Archive and Manuscript Sources*. Tucson: University of Arizona Press, 1979. (FHL# 973/A3bh)

An informative discussion of the original records and their present locations.

Twitchell, Ralph Emerson. *The Twitchell Archives, 1685-1898.* Albuquerque: University of New Mexico Library, 1955-57. 6 reels. (FHL# microfilm 1016941-1016945; indexed on microfilm 1016940)

Microfilm of original Spanish records in the office of the Surveyor-General, land grant requests, land disputes, appeals, land grants, wills, and records at the U.S. Bureau of Land Management, Santa Fe, N.M. Text in Spanish and English. New Mexico Territory included Colorado until 1861 and Arizona until 1863.

See also a compiled directory of churches and religious organizations in the state. (FHL# 979.1/K22a or microfiche 6051298 or microfilm 0908038, item 1)

Bibliography

A small collection of Arizona bibliography has been compiled in two publications:

Powell, Donald M., comp. *Arizona Gathering: A Bibliography of Arizoniana, 1950-1959.* Tucson: Arizona Pioneers' Historical Society, [c.1960]. (FHL# 979.1/A3p)

Arizona Gathering II, 1950-1969. Tucson: University of Arizona Press, [c.1973]. (FHL# 979.1/A3pa)

Spiros, Joyce V. Hawley. *Genealogical Guide to Arizona and Nevada.* Gallup: Verlene Publishing, [c.1983]. (FHL# 979/D23s)

Biography

Carl Hayden's typescript biographical files are arranged in alphabetical order. 15 reels. (FHL# microfilm 1000464-1000478).

Biographical material is also included in most of the historical works pertaining to the state. See **Arizona/-Biography** or **Arizona/History**.

Notable in the collection are:

Peplow, Edward Haddock. *History of Arizona.* 3 vols. New York: Lewis Historical Publishing Co., 1958. (FHL# 979.1/H2p)

Portrait and Biographical Record of Arizona: Commemorating the Achievements of Citizens Who Have Contributed to the Progress of Arizona and Development of Its Resources. Chicago: Chapman Publishing Co., 1901. (FHL# 979.1/D3p and 979.1/D3p/Index)

Wiggins, Marvin E. *Mormons and Their Neighbors: An Index to Over 75,000 Biographical Sketches from 1820 to the Present.* 2 vols. Provo, Utah: Harold B. Lee Library, Brigham Young University, [c.1984]. (FHL# 978/D32w)

Census Records

An 1831 census of Arizona and Sonora was taken. (FHL# 979.1/X22i). Pre-territorial censuses were enumerated in 1801 and 1852 for Pimeria Alta, district of Altar, Sonora. (FHL# 979.1/X2s/1801 and 979.1/-X2se/1852). The 1860 territorial census for New Mexico includes Arizona under Arizona County. (FHL# 979.1/X2pa or 934829, item 1). Special territorial censuses were enumerated in 1864, 1866, and 1867. (FHL# 979.1/X2p/1864 or 897437, item 5; FHL# 979.1/X2p/-1866 or 928107, item 1; FHL# 979.1/X22j/1867).

Indexes for the 1860 and 1870 censuses and mortality schedules and for the 1864, 1866, 1867, 1870, and 1880 territorial censuses have been compiled; for call numbers see **Arizona/Census** and **Arizona/Census/Indexes.** Note that some indexes are listed under **Arizona/Census** in the catalog. An index was compiled by the Southern Arizona Genealogical Society for the territorial census of 1880. 4 reels. (FHL# microfilm 1323378-1323381). A phonetic index (Soundex) was compiled for the territorial census of 1900. For census call numbers see the Registers on the U.S./Canada Reference credenza. For information on using a Soundex and the 1900 U.S. Census for Arizona see Chapter 4, "United States: General."

Church History and Church Records

Several church histories are available; these include those for Indian missions sponsored by various denominations, Catholic missions in the old Southwest, and Mormon colonies; see **Arizona/Church History**. A few additional histories and records can be located in the catalog under **Arizona/[County]/Church History** and **Arizona/[County]/Church Records.**

Genealogy

Some collections and a few periodicals are included in the FHLC. The former Spanish-American Mission of the LDS Church collected and compiled family group records (FHL# microfilm 0940001-0940006); see **Arizona/Genealogy** for a description of the contents. Some genealogical records have been compiled by the DAR and other heritage socities. Genealogical records of the first Arizona volunteer infantry are also accessible (FHL# 979.1/M2u).

Temple, Thomas Workman. *Sources for Tracing Spanish-American Pedigrees in the Southwestern United States: California and Arizona.* Salt Lake City: Genealogical Society of Utah, [c.1969]. (FHL# 929.1/W893/F14b, or microfiche 6039366, item 2, or microfilm 0897215, item 35)

History

Only mission records for the Spanish settlements in the Gadsden Purchase region have survived. For historical background and an informative discussion of the extant records see the citation for Beers under *Archives and Libraries* above. Additional titles have been cataloged under **Arizona/History, Arizona/History/[Name of War], Arizona/History/Bibliography, Arizona/History/Indexes, Arizona/History/Periodicals**, and **Arizona/History/Sources** as well as these same subheadings for **Arizona/[County]/History.**

See also:

Bancroft, Hubert Howe. *History of Arizona and New Mexico 1530-1888.* Albuquerque: Horn & Wallace, 1962. (FHL# 979/H2ba)

Farish, Thomas Edwin. *History of Arizona.* 8 vols. San Francisco: Filmer Bros. Electrotype Co., n.d. (FHL# 979.1/H2f)

Peplow, Edward Hadduck. *History of Arizona.* 3 vols. New York: Lewis Historical Publishing Co., 1958. (FHL# 979.1/H2p)

Wachholtz, Florence, comp. *Arizona the Grand Canyon State: A History of Arizona.* 2 vols. Westminster, Colorado: Western States Historical Publishers, 1975. (FHL# 979.1/H2a)

Land and Property

No state or county land records are included in the collection. A few titles are cataloged under **Arizona/-Land and Property.** Some records pertaining to Arizona Territory before and after it became a U.S. possession are included in records of New Mexico land grants and land titles (FHL# microfilm 1016947-1016950, item 1). The largest collection of land records for Arizona are those for private land claims adjudicated by the U.S. Surveyor General for 1855-90 (FHL# microfilm 1016950, items 2-4 through 1016974) and 1891-1903 (FHL# microfilm 1016975-1016996).

Some land records are included in *The Twitchell Archives, 1685-1898;* see entry under *Archives and Libraries.*

Maps

Only two maps are cataloged under **Arizona/[County]/Maps**; the majority of the collection is cataloged under **Arizona/Maps.** Several pre-Arizona Territory maps are included as well as postal and army maps.

Military History and Records

Records included in the FHLC under this heading cover frontier military posts, Confederate States of America's Arizona Cavalry, Civil War veterans' burials from Arizona Territory, indexes to the compiled service records of Confederate and Union soldiers who served in organizations from Arizona Territory, and the Gila River Relocation Center.

Minorities

Specified in the collection are records for Pueblo, Navajo (also spelled in the FHLC as Navaho), and Zuni tribes; Japanese relocation; and Slavs. The time periods with separate entries include Spanish missionaries, contemporary, the Spanish era from 1767-1821, World War II, and Arizona's territorial period. See also catalog entries under **Arizona/Native Races.**

Native Races

Included under this heading are records for the Southwestern Indian tribes in general, as well as the Apache, Zuni, Hopi, Maricopas, Havasupai, Navajo, and Pima tribes. The Pima Agency Census records for 1909-40 are cataloged under **Arizona/Native Races/Census.** Additional titles cataloged under this heading are **Arizona/-Native Races/Church History, Arizona/Native Races/-Genealogy, Arizona/Native Races/Periodicals, Arizona/Native Races/Schools, Arizona/Native Races/-Vital Records,** and **Arizona/[County]/Native Races.**

Newspapers

For a complete list of the library's holdings, consult the FHLC under **Arizona/Newspapers, Arizona/-Obituaries,** and **Arizona/Periodicals.**

Probate Records

The library has some probate records for Pima County (FHL# microfilm 844408, item 4) but virtually no others.

Vital Records

Of Arizona's current fourteen counties, the FHLC includes vital records for only six; two of the six are represented only by city records, not those for the entire county. Some titles are cataloged under **Arizona/Vital Records** and **Arizona/[County]/Vital Records.** See also:

Arizona Death Records: An Index Compiled from Mortuary, Cemetery, and Church Records. 3 vols. Tucson: Arizona State Genealogical Society, 1976-82. (FHL# 979.1/V3a or microfiche 6019995)

Includes cemeteries in all fourteen Arizona counties.

Deaths in Arizona Territory, Year Ending May 31, 1870. Typescript, n.p., 1947. (FHL# 979.1/A1/no.1 or microfilm 0824078, item 12)

Federal Mortality Census of Arizona, 1870-1880: and Related Indexes in the Custody of the Daughters of the American Revolution. Microreproduction of original by the National Archives. Salt Lake City: Genealogical Society of Utah, 1962. (FHL# microfilm 0422410)

Voting Registers

The library has no voter registration lists at the state level and county voting records only for Yavapi County.

CALIFORNIA

Historical Background

1540-1792	Explorers from Mexico, Spain, Russia, and England visit California.
1769	First permanent settlement is made at San Diego by Spaniards.
1770	Spaniards travel north from San Diego and build a presidio at Monterey.
1770-1823	Twenty-one Spanish missions are established.
1774	A land route, the Anza Trail, is opened from Sonora to California.
1777	San Jose is founded.
1782	A settlement is made at Los Angelos and a presidio is erected at Santa Barbara.
1796	A United States sailing vessel reaches the coast.
1804	Upper California becomes an independent province under a governor at Monterey.
1812	Russians construct Fort Ross, north of Bodega Bay.
1822	California comes under Mexican control after Mexico gains its independence from Spain.
1822	Spanish rule in upper California ends.
1822	Upper California becomes a territory and is combined with Lower California under one governor under Mexico.
1825	Capital is moved to San Diego from Monterey.
1830	The Californias are separated again; capital returns to Monterey.
1836	Some Californians rebel against Mexican control.
1839	John A. Sutter organizes the "Kingdom of New Helvetia" in the Sacramento River Valley.
1841	First wagon train of settlers leaves Missouri for California.
1841	Sutter buys Fort Ross from Russians.
1846	During the Mexican War, American military forces seize Monterey, San Francisco, Sonoma, and Sutter's Fort. Later that year American forces take possession of Los Angeles.
1848	Treaty terms cause Mexico to cede California to the United States following the end of the Mexican War.
1848	Gold found at Sutter's Fort precipitates the California Gold Rush of 1849.
1849	State constitutional convention meets at Monterey.
1850	California becomes the thirty-first state.

History and Settlement

California was under Spanish control until 1822 when the Mexican government began its administration. In 1812, Russians had built a fort in northern California but gave up the adventure in 1841. At the close of the Mexican War (1846-48), Mexico ceded much of its western territory, including California, to the United States. Two years later, California was admitted to the Union as the thirty-first state.

Spanish settlements and missions were erected all along the coast at distances of about one day's travel. Spanish colonization was primarily along the coast rather than inland.

Americans from other states traveled overland in significant numbers beginning in 1841. When gold was found in the Sacramento Valley at Sutter's Fort, the population jumped from 15,000 to 250,000. Fortune seekers from every other state in the Union and a multitude of countries flocked to California.

Immigrants to California include, in numerical order, Mexico (particularly in Southern California), Canada, Italy, England and Wales, Russia, Germany, Sweden, Ireland, Scotland, Poland, Austria, France, Denmark, Norway, Switzerland, Portugal, Greece, Yugoslavia, Hungary, Netherlands, Spain, Finland, Czechoslovakia, Rumania, Lithuania, Belgium, China, and Japan.

During the early years of California's statehood, Chinese immigrants moved into Northern California. During the early twentieth century, many Japanese arrived. When massive erosion and windstorms turned Oklahoma, Kansas, and Arkansas into a dust bowl during the Depression years, many families packed up and migrated to California, a majority settling in the San Joaquin and Sacramento valleys.

During World War II, the Japanese-Americans living in California were relocated to Arizona and Utah. After the close of the war, many returned to California.

Microfilming of public and private records for California is currently in process. Continue to check new versions of the FHLC for the latest additions to the collection.

California Library Collection

Archives and Libraries

Several guides to archival collections for California are included in the FHLC. Notable among these are:

Beers, Henry Putney. *Spanish and Mexican Records of the American Southwest.* Tucson: University of Arizona Press, 1979. (FHL# 973/A3bh)

Buglio, Rudecinda Lo. *Survey of Prestatehood Records: A New Look at Spanish and Mexican-Californian Genealogical Records.* Monograph delivered at Salt Lake City, World Conference on Records, 1980. Salt Lake City: Genealogical Society of Utah, 1980. (FHL# 929.1/W893/1980)

Directory of Archival and Manuscript Repositories in California. Redlands, Calif.: Beacon Printery, 1975. (FHL# 979.4/-E4so or microfilm 1036038, item 3)

Sanders, Patricia. *Searching in California: A Reference Guide to Public and Private Records.* Costa Mesa, Calif.: ISC Publications, [c.1982]. (FHL# 979.4/J5s or microfilm 1033954, item 3)

Biography

Many biographical works are represented in the collection, often focusing on particular regions, counties, subjects, or time periods. All but a few counties have at least one biographical reference included in the collection. Consult the FHLC under **California/Biography** or **California/County/Biography**. Some titles are also included under **California/History** and **California/Biography/Indexes**.

For lists of inhabitants in California during Spanish control, see:

Bancroft, Hubert Howe. *California Pioneer Register and Index, 1542-1848, Including Inhabitants of California, 1769-1800 and List of Pioneers: Extracted from The History of California by Hubert Howe Bancroft.* Baltimore: Regional Publishing Co., 1964. (FHL# 979.4/D3bh, microfiche 6051337, or microfilm 1000137, item 1)

______. *Register of Pioneer Inhabitants of California, 1542 to 1848: An Index to Information Concerning Them in Bancroft's History of California, Volumes I-V.* n.p., n.d. (FHL# 979.4/D3ba or microfilm 0908065, item 3)

James Miller Guinn authored a number of publications concerning California, including a history of the state and biographical collections for the inhabitants of various areas. Consult the FHLC under **California/Biography** or **California/History**.

See also:

Burdette, Robert Jones, ed. American Biography and Genealogy: California. 2 vols. Chicago: Lewis Publishing Co., n.d. (FHL# 979.4/D3b)

Hunt, Rockwell Dennis, ed. *California and Californians.* 4 vols. Chicago: Lewis Publishing Co., 1932. (FHL# 979.4/H2h or microfilm 1000092, items 1-4)

Men of California: Western Personalities and Their Affiliations. 2 vols. San Francisco: Pacific Art Co., 1901. (FHL# 979.4/D3m)

Cemeteries

The FHLC contains an excellent collection of cemetery records for the state. Most counties have compilations of tombstone inscriptions represented. In addition, an assortment of regional and state series are available, including an eleven-volume set of California cemetery records (FHL# 979.4/V22l, or microfilm 087068, items 1-3, or microfilm 0874075-0874077, item 1). California chapters of the Daughters of the American Revolution have compiled seventeen volumes of cemetery records for the state, arranged by county and date. (FHL# microfilm 0558288-0558290). Descriptions of these and many other titles can be accessed under **California/Cemeteries** and **California/[County]/Cemeteries.**

Census Records

An incomplete 1790 census for California has been compiled. (FHL# 979.4/A1/no.67 or microfilm 1036747, item 6). Decennial U.S. censuses are available for the state for 1850-80 and for 1900 and 1910; call numbers are available in the U.S. Census reference books in the U.S./Canada reference area. Indexes have been prepared for the 1850 and 1860 U.S. censuses. The 1852 California state census is available on nine microfilm reels (FHL# microfilm 0909229-0909234 and 0558285-0558287); both sets should be reviewed. For census call numbers see the Registers on the U.S./Canada Reference credenza.

Dilts, Bryan Lee, comp. *1860 California Census Index: Heads of Households and Other Surnames in Households Index.* Salt Lake City: Index Publishing, 1984. (FHL# 979.4/X22d/1860)

Pompey, Sherman Lee. *Missourians in the San Francisco, California Death Records, 1848-1863: [and] Missourians in the 1870 Mortality Census Records of California [and] Missourians in the Death Records of Marysville, Yuba County, California, 1870-1900.* n.p., n.d. (FHL# 979.4/V23ps or microfilm 0823651)

Some censuses are available for California native races; these are the 1928 and 1935 records for the Sacramento Agency, Bureau of Indian Affairs and United States Bureau of Indian Affairs census records for Roseburg, Greenville, and Tule River Agencies for 1897-1940. See **California/Census.**

Church History and Church Records

Most famous of the California churches are its twenty-one Spanish missions established prior to statehood. Many histories of these missions and missionaries are included in the collection. Other denominations represented in the FHLC are Mormon, Catholic, Methodist, and Presbyterian. A few cities and counties also have church histories or records cataloged.

Mission registers, including baptismal, marriage, and burial records for 1776-1912 are included for the Santa Barbara Mission (FHL# microfilm 0913165-0913169) and for the San Luis Obispo Mission for 1772-1906 (FHL# microfilm 0913300-0913302 and 0909228, items 2-3).

An index to the baptismal records for the Santa Clara Mission for 1777-1855 is available (FHL# 979.4/-Al/no.1 and microfilm 1036271, item 26) as well as an alphabetical list of the California Mission vital records. (FHL# microfiche 6047009 and microfilm 1307621, item 4)

Court Records

California courts are divided into three jurisdictional levels: municipal courts, superior courts, which have original jurisdiction in some cases and hear cases on appeal from municipal courts, and the State Supreme Court. The library has an index to transcripts of court cases in the state archives (FHL# microfilm 978914), an index to records of appellate court cases 1900-30 (FHL# microfilm 0978910-0978011), and an index to records of Supreme Court cases 1850-1930 (FHL# microfilm 0978908-0978909).

Directories

A fair collection of city directories is included in the FHLC for California under **California/Directories, California/[County]/[City]/Directories,** and **California/[County]/Directories.**

Emigration and Immigration

Most emigration and immigration records for the state are arranged in the FHLC under **California/Emigration And Immigration.** Only two cities and one county have records under this listing. Records and histories of Spanish, Australian, New Zealand, Chilean, German, Japanese, and Swiss-Italian people in the state are available. See also **California/Ethnology.**

Genealogy

A few county and city genealogical records are available, but most are cataloged under **California/Genealogy,** including several compilations for DAR and similar heritage societies. The library has complete runs of many genealogical and historical periodicals. See also:

Burdette, Robert Jones, ed. *American Biography and Genealogy: California.* 2 vols. Chicago: Lewis Publishing Co., [c.1910s]. (FHL# 979.4/D3b)

Northrup, Marie E. *Spanish-Mexican Families of Early California: 1769-1850.* 2 vols. New Orleans: Polyanthos, [c.1976]. (FHL# 979.4/F2n).

Parker, J. Carlyle. *Sources of Californiana: From Patron to Voter Registration.* Salt Lake City: Genealogical Society of Utah, [c.1969]. Paper presented at World Conference on Records and Genealogical Seminar; includes a seven-page bibliography. (FHL# 929.1/W893/I34, microfilm 0897217, or microfiche 6039417)

Temple, Thomas Workman, II. *Sources for Tracing Spanish-American Pedigrees in the Southwestern States: California and Arizona.* Salt Lake City: Genealogical Society of Utah, [c.1969]. (FHL# 929.1/W893/F14b, or microfilm 0897215, or microfiche 6039366, item 2)

History

The library has histories for all but four counties (Alpine, Calaveras, Glenn, and Marin), plus several state and regional histories.

Bancroft, Hubert Howe. *History of California.* 6 vols. San Francisco: A. L. Bancroft & Co., 1884-90. (FHL# 979/B4b/-vols. 18-23)

Eleven volumes of California regional and county history and biography were compiled by James Miller Guinn; see **California/History** for description and call numbers.

Separate works are cataloged for these periods:

Spanish, Mexican, Territorial, Gold Rush, American, and Eighties Boom.

Ethnic groups covered include Russians, Swedes, Jews, and Indians.

Several subdivisions should also be noted: **California/History/[Time Period], California/History/Bibliography, California/History/Indexes, California/History/Periodicals,** and **California/History/Sources.**

See also:

Caughey, John Walton. *California.* New York: Prentice-Hall, 1946. (FHL# 979.4/H3cj)

Cleland, Robert Glass. *A History of California: The American Period.* New York: Macmillan, [c.1922]. (FHL# 979.4/H2cl)

Hittel, Theodore Henry. *History of California.* 2 vols. San Francisco: N. M. Stone, 1898. (FHL# 979.4/H2ht)

Hunt, Rockwell Dennis. *California and Californians.* 4 vols. Chicago: Lewis Publishing Co., 1932. (FHL# 979.4/H2h)

Land and Property

Some land and property records are available at the county level. Spanish Archives land records have been microfilmed (FHL# microfilm 0978889-0978900; indexed on microfilm 0978888). A few additional titles are also cataloged under this heading.

Maps

A large collection of California maps is available under the headings **California/Maps** and **California/-[County]/Maps.**

Military History and Military Records

Several titles are included in the FHLC for California military history and records. Periods covered are the Civil War, the Mariposa Indian War, Indian Wars, Mexican War, Civil War, and World War I. An index to and records of California military organizations (1800-1917) are available on microfilm (FHL# microfilm 0981527-0981561). A separate filming includes Californians who served in World War I (FHL# 1001765-1001780; indexed on microfilm 1001454). Records for men who served in the Spanish military from 1786 to 1800 are filmed (FHL# microfilm 1156334-1156342). An index to the compiled service records of volunteers who served during Indian wars and disturbances 1815-58 (FHL# microfilm 0882753-0882794) and volunteer Union soldiers 1861-65 (FHL# microfilm 0881609-0881615) are arranged in alphabetical order.

Minorities

The library has a large collection of records pertaining to minorities in California. The catalog includes entries for Indians, blacks (cataloged as Negroes), Swedes, Spanish-Mexican, Japanese, Chinese, Hindus, Jews, Yugoslavs, Chileans, Russians, Germans, Poles, Italian-Swiss, Basques, British, French, Irish, Slavs, Portuguese, Greek, Welsh, and Armenians.

Native Races

Ethnic groups included under this heading include Indians, Japanese, Chinese, and Hindus. Indian tribes represented are Cahuilla, Modoc, Washo, Paiute, Tule, and Hoopa. Agency records include census, birth, death, school, medical, land, employment, and probate. Agencies with microfilmed records are Tule River, Sacramento, Hoopa Valley, Fort Bidwell, Yuma, Greenville, Roseburg, Round Valley, and Walker River.

Some records of the state's missions and mission histories are also cataloged under **California/Native Races.**

Naturalization and Citizenship Records

Declarations for 1846-1903 have been microfilmed in chronological order (FHL# microfilm 0977767-0977770 northern district and 1249797-1249840 southern district). The library has naturalization records for only two counties and one city.

Vital Records

The library has vital records for every county except Imperial, Kings, Lassen, Merced, San Benito, San Mateo, and Siskiyou. For call numbers, consult the FHLC under **California/[County]/Vital Records.**

Voting Records

The library has voting registers for every county but Imperial, Kings, and Riverside. Called the Great Registers, many of those microfilmed cover approximately thirty years (1867-98). For descriptions and call numbers, consult the FHLC under **California/[County]/Voting Registers.**

NEW MEXICO

Historical Background

1540	Spaniards enter the area of present-day New Mexico.
1598	Led by Juan de Onate Franciscans and soldier-colonists found the first European settlement at San Gabriel.
1599	Acoma Pueblo is the last Indian pueblo to be conquered.
1610	Capital is established at Santa Fe.
1680-92	The only united Pueblo Rebellion occurs against the Spanish; temporarily successful. Most surviving Spaniards flee to Santa Fe and Albuquerque. Indian

	governors rule New Mexico for twelve years.
1692	Spanish army accepts submission of the pueblos.
c.1697	Laguna Pueblo is established as a result of the revolt.
1692-1821	New Mexico remains the northern frontier outpost of New Spain.
1821	New Mexico becomes a territory when Mexico gains its independence from Spain.
1822	The Santa Fe Trail is created by traders from Missouri and other midwestern states.
1836	Reorganization of Mexican administration; New Mexico becomes the Department of New Mexico; two subdivisions *(prefecturas)* created.
1844	A third *prefectura* is organized.
1846-48	Mexican War; New Mexico ceded to the United States.
1846	The Army of the West enters New Mexico.
1850	New Mexico Territory is established.
1853	Gadsden Purchase adds a large tract of land in southwestern New Mexico and Arizona.
1854	Office of Surveyor-General is created to adjudicate Spanish-Mexican land titles.
1861	Colorado Territory organized from New Mexico. Confederate forces invade New Mexico in an attempt to secure California's gold fields and sever the Southwest from the Union.
1862	Southerners defeated near Glorieta Pass by U.S. Army regulars and New Mexico militia.
1863	New Mexico loses additional land when Arizona Territory is created.
1866	Gold is discovered first at Pinos Altos.
1869	Silver is discovered at Silver City.
1877	San Juan Valley is settled by farmers and stockmen.
1880s	Speculation in land grants and public domain lands becomes a national scandal.
1890	Wells tap artesian springs of the Pecos River.
1891	Pecos Irrigation Project organized to develop the Pecos River Valley.
1891	The Court of Private Land Claims created to settle disputed claims.
1903	All land grant claims are adjudicated.
1912	New Mexico becomes the forty-seventh state.
1913	The Sandoval Decision makes native Americans wards of the government.

History and Settlement

When Mexico secured its independence from Spain in 1821, the New Mexico region fell under Mexican jurisdiction until 1846 and the arrival of the United States Army at Santa Fe. This period was troubled, due mostly to problems in Mexico City. In 1836, a complete reorganization of administration subdivided the area into two departments, called *prefecturas*.

The departmental plan was unpopular, resulting in a revolution in 1837, but central authorities continued to ignore New Mexico's problems. Indian problems intensified. The newly formed Republic of Texas threatened to invade in 1841. As a result, the Mexican national government closed New Mexico's ports of entry during 1844 and 1845.

The Army of the West entered New Mexico in 1846 without resistance, taking possession of Santa Fe on 18 August where the acting governor officially surrendered New Mexico to the United States. U.S. occupation of its new territory was generally peaceful. In 1847, nationalists and Taos Pueblo Indians banded together and attacked the Anglo-Americans and Mexican families at Taos and Turley's Settlement. Another uprising occurred at Mora and was subdued by U.S. troops under Colonel Sterling Price and a mountain man militia company.

The area came under the control of the United States at the close of the Mexican War in 1848. The Territory of New Mexico was created in 1850, including the present-day states of Colorado and Arizona until 1861 and 1863, respectively. The Gadsden Purchase of 1854 added some additional land to New Mexico.

During the Civil War, Confederate troops invaded the territory but were defeated by Union and state militia combined.

Gold and silver were discovered soon after the end of the Civil war, thus bringing many miners and land speculators into the territory. Sheep and cattle raisers also flourished there.

Both Mexican and Spanish overlords had awarded land grants, creating many disputed titles, adjudicated by special American courts and offices between 1891 and 1903. After sixty-two years as a Territory, New Mexico was admitted to the Union in 1912 as its forty-seventh state.

New Mexico Library Collection

Archives and Libraries

The FHLC includes several inventories and guides to archives and library collections. For the Mexican period (1821-48), see *Calendar of the Microfilm Edition of the Mexican Archives of New Mexico, 1821-1848,* sponsored by the National Historical Publications Commission, Santa Fe: New Mexico Records Center, 1970 (FHL# 978.9/A5j and microfilm 0962164, item 1). See also:

National Historical Publications Commission. *Calendar to the Microfilm Edition of the Spanish Archives of New Mexico, 1621-1821.* Santa Fe: New Mexico Records Center, 1968. (FHL# 978.9/A5n and microfilm 0908040, item 5)

———. *Calendar to the Microfilm Edition of the Territorial Archives of New Mexico: A Microfilm Project Sponsored by the National Historical Publications Commission.* [1850-1912], Santa Fe: Records Center and Archives, 1974. (FHL# 978.9/A5m)

Eighteen reels of microfilm contain records in the Spanish Archives of New Mexico for 1621-1821 (FHL# microfilm 0581463-0581478). See also:

Chavez, Angelico. *Archives, 1678-1900.* Washington, D.C.: Academy of American Franciscan History, [c.1957]. Publications of the Academy of American Franciscan History, Bibliographical series, Vol. 3. (FHL# 978.9/D2ca)

Some valuable archival publications cataloged under other headings include:

Beers, Henry Putney. *Spanish and Mexican Records of the American Southwest.* Tucson: University of Arizona Press, 1979. (FHL# 973/A3bn)

Twitchell, Ralph Emerson. *The Spanish Archives of New Mexico: Compiled and Chronologically Arranged with Historical, Genealogical, Geographical, and Other Annotations, by Authority of the State of New Mexico.* 2 vols. [Cedar Rapids, Iowa]: Torch Press, 1914. (FHL# 978.9/A2t or microfilm 0845276)

Additional inventories and guides are cataloged under **New Mexico/Archives and Libraries.** No archival collections are available at the county level.

Bibliography

Only one bibliography is listed in the catalog, but Beers, cited above, contains a seventy-page Southwest bibliography of primary and secondary sources; many items pertain to New Mexico. See also:

Shelton, Wilma Loy. *Checklist of New Mexico Publications, 1850-1953.* [Albuquerque]: University of New Mexico Press, 1954. (FHL# 978.9/A3sh)

Biography

Biographical works include:

Peterson, C. S., comp. *Representative New Mexicans: The National Newspaper Reference Book of the New State, Containing Photographs and Biographies of Over Four Hundred Men Residents of New Mexico.* Denver: C. S. Peterson, 1912. (FHL# 978.9/D3p)

Twitchell, Ralph Emerson. *The History of the Military Occupation of the Territory of New Mexico From 1846 to 1851 by the Government of the United States: Together with Biographical Sketches of Men Prominent in the Conduct of the Government During that Period.* Tucson: W. C. Cox, 1974. (FHL# microfilm 1000222, item 3)

______. *The Twitchell Archives, 1685-1898.* Albuquerque, N.M.: Filmed by the University of New Mexico Library, 1955-57. 6 reels. (FHL# microfilms 1016940-1016945)

Microfilm of original at the U.S. Bureau of Land Management, Santa Fe, New Mexico. Text is in English and Spanish. New Mexico Territory included Colorado until 1861 and Arizona until 1863. This collection includes Spanish records in the office of the Surveyor-General; land grant requests, disputes, appeals, and grants; and wills, judgements, mine claims, inventories, and municipal ordinances.

Wiggins, Marvin. *Mormons and Their Neighbors: An Index to Over 75,000 Biographical Sketches from 1820 to the Present.* 2 vols. Provo, Utah: Harold B. Lee Library, Brigham Young University, [c.1984]. (FHL# 978/D32w)

Cemetery Records

A few compilations are cataloged under **New Mexico/Cemeteries** and **New Mexico/[County]/Cemeteries.**

Census Records

Spanish and Mexican censuses have been indexed and compiled by Virginia Langham Olmsted, *Spanish and Mexican Censuses of New Mexico, 1790, 1823, 1845.* (Albuquerque: New Mexico Genealogical Society, [c.1981]). (FHL# 978.9 X2ov). All items except names are in English.

Territorial censuses for New Mexico include 1850 and 1860 and cover the present-day states of Colorado and Arizona. Indexes have been compiled for 1850 and 1860. For census call numbers see the Registers on the U.S./Canada Reference credenza. The 1890 special census of New Mexico veterans is available. A 1930 census for the Navajos in the Shiprock area is available. See also:

New Mexico Census of 1885. Albuquerque: filmed by the Golightly-Payne-Coon Co., 1957. 2 reels. (FHL# microfilms 0016610 and 0016611)

Church History and Church Records

The library has a church history for only one county, but most counties have some church records either for the county or its major city. Histories of Christian Navajo and Zuni tribes, missions in the state, Mormon settlements, and ecclesiastical history are available.

Church records include those for Franciscan (Catholic) and Methodist churches. The majority of the collection for the state is cataloged under **New Mexico/[County]/Church Records** and **New Mexico/-[County]/[City]]/Church Records.**

Court Records

The U.S. Court of Private Land Claims, which adjudicated disputed claims from 1891 to 1903, created a great number of records, available on twenty-two reels (FHL# microfilm 1016975-1016996).

Genealogy

A few collections of genealogical records compiled by chapters of the Daughters of the American Revolution (DAR) are available. See **New Mexico/Genealogy, New Mexico/[County]/Genealogy, New Mexico/Genealogy/-Periodicals,** and **New Mexico/Genealogy/Sources.**

For a guide to the state's genealogical records see:

Spiros, Joyce Verlene Hawley. *Handy Genealogical Guide to*

New Mexico. Gallup: Verlene Publishing, [c.1981]. (FHL# 978.9/D27s or microfiche 6051310)

History

Several histories include historical and biographical sketches. A few county and city histories are included. Beers, cited under *Archives and Libraries* above, includes some history of the state. See also:

History of New Mexico: Its Resources and People. 2 vols. Los Angeles: Pacific States Publishing Co., 1907. (FHL# 978.9/H2h, or microfilm 844902, item 1, or 1000217, item 2)

Twitchell, Ralph Emerson. *The Leading Facts of New Mexico History*. 5 vols. Cedar Rapids, Iowa: Torch Press, 1911-17. (FHL# 978.9/H2t or microfilm 1000218)

______. *The Twitchell Archives, 1685-1898.* 4 reels. Albuquerque: University of New Mexico Library, 1955-57. (FHL# microfilm 1016941-1016945; indexed on microfilm 1016940)

Land and Property

Diaz, Albert James. *A Guide to the Microfilm of Papers Relating to New Mexico Land Grants.* Albuquerque: University of New Mexico Press, 1960. University of New Mexico Publications, Library Series no. 1. (FHL# 978.9/R2d).

A guide to microfilmed papers relating to New Mexico Land Grants.

Ebright, Malcolm. *The Tierra Amarilla Grant: A History of Chicanery*. Santa Fe: Center for Land Grant Studies, [c.1980]. (FHL# 978.952/R2e)

Includes list of the first settlers of Tierra Amarilla.

Miscellaneous Archives Relating to New Mexico Land Grants, 1695-1842. Albuquerque: University of New Mexico Library, 1955-57. (FHL# microfilms 1016947 and 1016948)

Microfilm of originals in the U.S. Bureau of Land Management, Santa Fe, New Mexico. Text in Spanish. Includes proceedings, declarations, deliberations, accounts, and letters.

Private land claim records have been microfilmed (indexed on FHL# microfilm 1016950, items 2-4; records are microfilm 1016951-1016974). For additional titles, see **New Mexico/Land and Property** and **New Mexico/-[County]/Land and Property**. Also consult the FHLC under **New Mexico/Military History, New Mexico/History/Periodicals,** and **New Mexico/History/Sources.**

Maps

The library has several maps dated between 1846 and 1970, including maps of the various governmental periods.

Military Records

Included in this category, are records for the Confederate Army, Spanish military service in America, collections in the Spanish Archives of New Mexico records, Mexican War service records, state Adjutant General Office records, Civil War veterans' burials, and indexes to compiled service records of Union soldiers.

Minorities

This record classification includes some records which should have been cataloged under **/Native Races**, including Navajo, Zuni, Ute, and Mescalero tribal records. Also included under this heading are records for Italians and Mexicans.

Native Races

The library has records for the following tribes: Comanche; Zuni; Taos; Mescalero, Mimbres, and Jicarilla Apache; Navajo; Hopi; and Acoma. History and records of the Southwest, New Mexican Plains, and the Rio Grande Valley Indians are also included.

Especially valuable are the birth, death, and other records of the Bureau of Indian Affairs, United Pueblos Agency for 1919-44 (FHL# microfilm 1266698, items 9-10); Zuni Indian Agency (FHL# microfilm 1266698, items 3-8); Southern Pueblos Agency (FHL# microfilm 1266685-1266687; 1249703-1249708, items 1-3); Northern Pueblos Agency files (FHL# microfilm 1275626, item 5; 1275627-1275632); Jicarilla Agency records (FHL# microfilm 1275623, item 21; 1275624-1275626, items 1-2, and 1276727, items 2-4); and Eastern Navajo Agency records (FHL# microfilm 1249708, items 4-5; 1266696-1266698, items 1-2).

See also entries cataloged under **New Mexico/Minorities.**

Newspapers

Several newspapers and two newspaper bibliographies are available for the state. Birth, marriage, and death notices from El Paso newspapers through 1885 have been published (FHL# 976.496/E1/B3b). Notable bibliographies are:

Grove, Pearce S., Becky J. Barnett, and Sandra J. Hanses, eds. *New Mexico Newspapers: A Comprehensive Guide to Bibliographical Entries and Locations.* Albuquerque: University of New Mexico Press, 1975. (FHL# 978.9/B33g or microfiche 6046704)

Stratton, Porter A. *The Territorial Press of New Mexico, 1834-1912.* Albuquerque: University of New Mexico Press, [c.1969]. (FHL# 978.9/B3s or microfilm 0896539, item 1)

Probate Records

The library has few probate records except some for McKinley County. See **New Mexico/Probate Records** for holdings.

Vital Records

Some marriage records of the state of New Mexico for 1880-1920 have been published (FHL# 978.9/V25d or microfilm 0908289, item 1, and 0928026, item 4). Most vital records for New Mexico's Indian population are cataloged under **New Mexico/Native Races.**

Records by Jurisdiction **Arizona**	Archives & Libraries	Atlases	Bible Records	Bibliography	Biography	Cemeteries	Census (Printed)	Church History	Church Records	Directories	Emigration/Immigration	Employment	Genealogy	Genealogy-Periodicals	History	Indexes	Land & Property	Maps	Migration	Military	Minorities	Native Races	Naturalization	Newspapers	Obituaries	Periodicals	Probate & Estate	Public Records	Schools	Societies	Tax Records	Vital Records	Voting Registers	WPA Inventories
Apache						•		•																					•					
Cochise						•				•			•	•	•													•						
Coconino															•							•		•										
Gila										•			•		•								•					•				•		
Graham	•				•	•			•	•					•																			
Greenlee																																		
Maricopa	•					•		•	•	•				•	•					•	•	•			•				•			•		•
Mohave						•	•			•																								
Navajo	•				•	•		•	•	•			•		•													•	•			•		
Pima	•								•	•					•					•							•					•		•
Pinal																																		
Santa Cruz							•		•																									•
Yavapai			•		•	•		•	•	•					•																•	•	•	
Yuma						•		•										•				•										•		

Records by Jurisdiction California	Archives & Libraries	Atlases	Bible Records	Bibliography	Biography	Cemeteries	Census (Printed)	Church History	Church Records	Court	Directories	Emigration/Immigration	Genealogy	Genealogy-Periodicals	History	Indexes	Land & Property	Maps	Migration	Military	Minorities	Native Races	Naturalization	Newspapers	Obituaries	Periodicals	Probate & Estates	Public Records	Schools	Societies	Tax Records	Vital Records	Voting Registers	WPA Inventories
Alameda					•	•		•	•		•				•		•	•							•			•				•	•	•
Alpine						•																										•	•	
Amador					•	•					•		•	•	•		•	•						•			•		•	•		•	•	
Butte					•	•					•			•	•																	•	•	
Calaveras					•	•												•														•	•	
Colusa										•	•				•																	•	•	
Contra Costa					•	•					•				•		•											•				•	•	
Del Norte					•										•																	•	•	
El Dorado					•	•					•			•	•																	•	•	
Fresno					•	•			•		•		•	•	•			•			•											•	•	•
Glenn						•																										•	•	
Humbolt							•	•			•			•	•					•											•	•	•	
Imperial					•			•			•				•																			
Inyo						•			•						•												•				•	•	•	
Kern					•	•			•		•		•	•	•												•				•	•	•	•
Kings					•						•				•																			
Lake					•	•									•																•	•	•	
Lassen						•									•																		•	
Los Angeles	•				•	•	•	•	•		•		•	•	•		•	•	•	•	•	•	•	•		•	•			•	•	•	•	•
Madera											•			•	•												•					•	•	
Marin					•	•	•				•			•	•												•					•	•	•
Mariposa					•																											•	•	
Mendocino					•	•	•		•					•	•		•															•	•	
Merced					•	•			•		•				•		•										•					•	•	
Modoc						•									•																		•	
Mono						•																						•				•	•	•
Monterey					•	•		•	•		•			•	•		•															•	•	•
Napa					•	•					•				•																	•	•	
Nevada						•							•		•			•														•	•	
Orange	•			•	•	•	•	•	•					•	•		•	•												•		•	•	
Placer						•						•	•														•					•	•	
Plumas															•		•			•							•					•	•	
Riverside					•	•					•		•	•	•																	•		
Sacramento	•				•	•		•			•	•	•	•	•		•	•					•		•		•	•		•	•	•	•	•
San Benito					•	•			•		•				•		•																•	
San Bernardino					•	•		•	•		•			•	•			•														•	•	
San Diego	•				•	•	•	•	•		•		•	•	•		•	•			•					•	•		•	•	•	•	•	•
San Francisco	•				•	•		•		•	•	•		•	•		•	•			•		•	•	•		•			•		•	•	•
San Joaquin					•	•	•		•		•				•			•						•			•					•	•	
San Luis Obispo					•	•	•		•		•			•	•		•														•	•	•	•
San Mateo					•	•					•				•											•							•	•
Santa Barbara	•				•	•		•	•		•			•	•												•					•	•	
Santa Clara	•				•	•			•		•		•	•	•			•								•	•		•			•	•	•
Santa Cruz					•	•			•		•				•		•										•					•	•	
Shasta					•	•			•		•			•	•									•			•					•	•	
Sierra					•	•									•																	•	•	
Siskiyou					•	•									•																		•	
Solano					•	•					•			•	•			•									•					•	•	
Sonoma					•	•		•			•			•	•		•					•										•	•	

Records by Jurisdiction **California** (cont.)	Archives & Libraries	Atlases	Bible Records	Bibliography	Biography	Cemeteries	Census (Printed)	Church History	Church Records	Court	Directories	Emigration/Immigration	Genealogy	Genealogy-Periodicals	History	Indexes	Land & Property	Maps	Migration	Military	Minorities	Native Races	Naturalization	Newspapers	Obituaries	Periodicals	Probate & Estates	Public Records	Schools	Societies	Tax Records	Vital Records	Voting Registers	WPA Inventories
Stanislaus					•	•			•	•	•			•	•												•					•	•	
Sutter					•	•					•		•	•	•																	•	•	
Tehema						•									•			•														•	•	
Trinity					•	•									•												•					•	•	
Tulare					•	•	•				•			•	•			•														•	•	
Tuolumne					•				•		•			•	•		•															•	•	
Ventura					•				•		•		•	•	•											•						•	•	
Yolo					•	•	•				•				•		•	•									•					•	•	
Yuba					•	•	•			•					•		•										•					•	•	

Records by Jurisdiction — New Mexico	Archives & Libraries	Atlases	Bible Records	Bibliography	Biography	Cemeteries	Census (Printed)	Church History	Church Records	Directories	Emigration/Immigration	Employment	Genealogy	Genealogy-Periodicals	History	Indexes	Land & Property	Maps	Migration	Military	Minorities	Native Races	Naturalization	Newspapers	Obituaries	Periodicals	Probate & Estates	Public Records	Schools	Societies	Tax Records	Vital Records	WPA Inventories
Bernalillo						•			•	•					•									•								•	•
Catron																																	
Chaves						•			•	•					•		•															•	
Colfax						•			•						•									•								•	•
Curry									•	•																						•	
De Baca																																	
Dona Ana									•	•														•								•	•
Eddy						•			•	•					•																	•	•
Grant						•			•	•														•									•
Guadalupe						•																											
Harding									•																								
Hidalgo									•																								•
Lea									•	•			•		•									•									
Lincoln						•			•						•					•				•									
Los Alamos																																	
Luna									•	•														•									
McKinley										•					•								•			•	•		•			•	
Mora						•			•															•									•
Otero						•			•																							•	•
Quay						•				•																						•	
Rio Arriba									•								•							•									
Roosevelt						•			•	•					•																	•	
Sandoval									•						•																		
San Juan					•	•				•					•					•												•	
San Miguel									•	•														•									•
Santa Fe								•	•						•									•									•
Sierra									•															•									
Socorro									•															•									
Taos								•	•						•		•							•									
Torrance									•															•									•
Union									•						•									•									•
Valencia									•																							•	

Chapter 13

United States: Pacific Northwest and Hawaii

Marlene M. Marino

OREGON

Historical Background

1579 Sir Francis Drake sails the coast of southern Oregon and northern California, names the region "New Albion."

1765 The name Oregon first used by Major Rogers, spelled "Ouragon."

1775 Spanish navigator, Bruno Heceta, sights mouth of Columbia River but does not enter. Later explorers search for it until 1792.

1778 Captain James Cook sails the Oregon coast.

1788 The *Northwest America,* first ship built in the Pacific Northwest, is launched at Nootka Sound.

1792 Captain Robert Gray, U.S. Navy, rediscovers the Columbia River. English navigator, Lt. William Broughton, sails up the Columbia River for 100 miles and claims entire region for England.

1805 Lewis and Clark expedition reaches the mouth of the Columbia River; Fort Clatsop built.

1810 Unsuccessful attempt for settlement at Oak Point made by Winship brothers.

1811 Astoria founded by John Jacob Astor, first American trading post in the Pacific Northwest.

1819 Treaty between the United States and Spain fixes the present southern border of Oregon.

1820s French-Canadian fur traders settle French Prairie north of Salem on the Willamette River.

1824 Dr. John McLoughlin builds Fort Vancouver and moves headquarters of the Hudson Bay Company from Astoria to the fort.

1834 Methodist colony established at Willamette Valley, Clackamas County.

1836 Presbyterians settle Walla Walla area around Pendleton.

1837-38 Catholics arrive in region.

1840 Influx of settlers.

1842 Oregon Institute established at Salem.

1842-43 First wagon train over the Oregon Trail through present-day Wyoming and Idaho arrives in Oregon.

1843 Willamette settlers at Champolg organize a provisional government.

1846 "Oregon Compromise" makes the 49th parallel the boundary between Great Britain and the United States in Oregon Territory. Barlow Road opens from The Dalles to Oregon City. Oregon's first newspaper, *The Oregon Spectator,* begins at Oregon City.

1847 First regular mail service. Oregon's first private school founded at Portland.

1848 Oregon Territory established. Abraham Lincoln declines governorship.

1849 Oregon counties begin recording marriages.

1850 State capital moved to Salem. Oregon territorial census. Congress passes the Oregon Donation Land Law.

1851 Gold discovered on Jackson Creek in Jackson County. Rogue River Indian War fought in Oregon and northern California.

1852 Gold seekers raise population from 12,000 to 38,000.

1853 Oregon Territory divided and Washington Territory created.

1859 First Oregon rail service begins. Oregon enters the Union as the thirty-third state, losing all lands not included in present-day Oregon.

1860 Pony Express established.

1861 First telegraph line to the Pacific completed.

1862 First Oregon divorce laws enacted.

1863 Idaho Territory created from eastern Oregon.

1872 Modoc Indian War fought in Oregon and northern California.

1903 Statewide registration of vital records implemented.

1912 Oregon adopts women's suffrage.

Migration and Settlement

Between 1811 and 1814 John Jacob Astor and his Scottish-American followers founded Astoria, Clatsop County. French-Canadian fur traders, who married local Indian women, lived in French Prairie, north of Salem during the 1820s.

In 1824, Dr. John McLoughlin arrived in present-day Vancouver.

Bostonians, led by Nathaniel J. Wyeth, settled Sauvie Island, Multnomah, and Columbia counties in 1832 through 1834. In 1834 Jason Lee and a group of Methodists organized settlements at French Prairie and Mission Bottom (near Salem) and Willamette Valley, Clackamas County. That same year Americans traveled through California and founded a community in theWillamette Valley.

In 1836 Presbyterians arrived in Walla Walla and Pendleton, Umatilla County. Two years later French-Canadian Roman Catholics established themselves in St. Paul, St. Louis, Willamette Valley, and Oregon City, Clackamas County. In 1839 and 1840, pioneers from Peoria, Illinois, arrived in Yamhill and Marion counties. Emigration societies organized settlements in 1842 and 1843; about 1,137 pioneers from north and east-central Ohio, Michigan, Illinois, Indiana, Missouri, Pennsylvania, Massachusetts, Iowa, and Kentucky settled throughout the state. In 1843 1,000 persons from St. Clair County, Missouri arrived in north and east-central Oregon. Five years later Congregationalists settled Tulatin Plains (Forest Grove) and Oregon City, Washington and Clackamas counties.

In 1852 gold seekers primarily from Missouri, Illinois, Ohio, Indiana, Kentucky, New York, Iowa, Tennessee, Pennsylvania, and Virginia (in that order) arrived in Jackson County which included the present county of Josephine. Mormons settled Fort Lemhi, now Lemhi County, Idaho, in 1855. "Mercer Girls" from Lowell, Massachusetts, in 1862, migrated to Oregon and Washington to begin careers as teachers and wives.

Bowen, William Adrian. *The Willamette Valley: Migration and Settlement on the Oregon Frontier.* Seattle, Wash.: University of Washington Press, 1978. (FHL# 979.53/X4b)

Wagons West. Salt Lake City, Utah: Genealogical Society of Utah, 1976. (FHL# microfilm 430056, item 3)

Oregon Library Collection

Archives and Libraries

Guide to Depositories of Manuscript Collections In the United States: Oregon-Washington. Portland: Oregon Historical Records Survey, 1940. (FHL# 979.5/A1/no.9 or microfilm 908038, item 9)

Guide to Genealogical Material in the Oregon State Library. Portland: Historcal Records Survey, n.d. (FHL# 979.5/-A5gL)

Guide to Manuscript Collections of the Oregon Historical Society. Portland: Historical Records Survey, 1940. (FHL# 979.5/A5h or microfilm 908038, item 8)

Historical Records Survey, Works Progress Administraton. *Material in the Oregon State Archives Loaned By the Genealogical Records Committee, Oregon Society, Daughters of the American Revolution.* Portland: Oregon Historical Records Survey, 1940. (FHL# 979.5/A5s)

Oregon Historical Society. *Oregon Historical Society Microfilm Guide: 1973.* Portland: Oregon Historical Society, 1973. (FHL# 979.5/A3o)

Atlases, Gazetteers, and Maps

Brown, Erma Skyles. *Oregon County Boundary Change Maps, 1843-1916.* Lebanon, Oreg.: End of Trail Researchers, 1970. (FHL# 979.5/E7b)

Habersham, Robert A. *J. K. Gill & Company's Map of Oregon.* Photocopy of original map. Portland: J. K. Gill, 1878. (Map case FHL# 979.5/E7h)

Habersham's Sectional and County Map of Oregon: Compiled From the Most Recent U.S. Government Maps and Surveys. Photocopy of original map. Portland: J. K. Gill, 1874. (Map case FHL# 979.5/E7g)

Highsmith, Richard M. *Atlas of the Pacific Northwest: Resources and Development.* Corvallis: Oregon State University Press, c.1968. (FHL# Q/979/E3h)

Johnson's Washington and Oregon. N.p.: Johnson & Browning [c.1860s]. (Map case FHL# 979/E7j)

Preuss, Charles. *Map of Oregon and Upper California: From the Surveys of John Charles Fremont and Other Authorities.* Photocopy of original map. Washington: n.pub., 1848. (Map case FHL# 979/E7p)

Map of the Oregon Territory. Photocopy of original map. N.p.: n.pub., 1841. (Map case FHL# 979/37um)

Map of the Oregon Territory: Exhibiting the Various Trading-Depots or Forts Occupied By the British Hudson Bay Company, Connected With the Western and Northwestern Fur Trade. St. Louis, Mo.: Edward Hutawa, 1843. (Map case FHL# 979/E7h)

Mitchell, S. Augustus. *County and Township Map of Oregon and Washington.* Philadelphia, Pa.: n.pub., [c.1881]. (Map case FHL# 979/E7m)

Oregon Country, 1819-1890. Eugene: Oregon Genealogical Society, [c.1979]. (FHL# 979.5 A1/no.40)

Preston, Ralph N. *Historical Oregon: Overland Stage Routes, Old Military Roads, Indian Battle Grounds, Old Forts, Old Gold Mines*. Corvallis, Oreg.: Western Guide Publishers, c.1972. (FHL# 979.5/E3h)

R. L. Polk and Company. *Oregon and Washington Gazetteer and Business Directory, 1909-1910*. Tucson, Ariz: W. C. Cox Company, 1974. (FHL# microfilm 1000367, item 1)

Biography

A large collection of Oregon biographical publications supplements the limited Oregon collection. Biographical titles are listed under **Oregon/Biography** with additional titles listed under **Oregon/[County]/Biography.**

Brandt, Patricia. *Oregon Biographical Index*. Corvallis: Oregon State University, 1976. (FHL# 979.5/D3b/Index)

Gaston, Joseph. *The Centennial History of Oregon, 1811-1912: With Notice of Antecedent Explorations*. Chicago, Ill.: S. J. Clarke Publishing Company, 1912. (FHL# 979.5/H2g or microfilm 1000359)

Hawthorne, Julian. *The Story of Oregon: A History with Portraits and Biographies*. Salt Lake City: Genealogical Society of Utah, 1964. (FHL# microfilm 372513)

Portrait and Biographical Record of the Willamette Valley, Oregon: Containing Original Sketches of Many Well Known Citizens of the Past and Present. Chicago, Ill.: Chapman Publishing Company, 1903. (FHL# 979.53/D3p or microfilm 1000365, item 1)

Portrait and Biographical Record of Western Oregon: Containing Original Sketches of Many Well Known Citizens of the Past and Present. Tucson, Ariz.: W. C. Cox, 1974. (FHL# microfilm 1000362, item 1)

Reminiscences of Southern Oregon Pioneers. N.p.: n.pub., [c.1970s]. (FHL# microfilm 1266790)

Interviews of 132 Douglas county residents during 1938 and 1939.

Who's Who in Oregon: Biographical Dictionary of Men and Women Who Are Building a State. Tucson, Ariz.: W. C. Cox, 1974. (FHL# microfilm 1000368, item 10)

Cemetery Records

A majority of cemetery tombstone inventories are cataloged in the FHLC under **Oregon/[County]/Cemetery Records** with the remainder under **Oregon/-Cemetery Records.**

Of vital importance to Oregon genealogical research is the ambitious *Oregon Cemetery Survey* (Salem: Oregon Department of Transportation, 1978) (FHL# 979.5/V340 or microfilm 1033848, item 4, or microfiche 6051231). This volume includes maps, descriptions, locations, and other pertinent data relating to all known cemeteries in Oregon. Two other publications of special importance are:

Daughters of the American Revolution. *Genealogical Collection*. Salt Lake City: Genealogical Society of Utah, 1971. (FHL# microfilm 857012-857039 and 862001-862002, and 858639, and 893732, item 1)

Oregon Cemetery Records. Salt Lake City: Genealogical Society of Utah, 1956-61. (FHL# 979.5/V22p or microfilm 824258, item 3, and 824259, item 1)

Census Records

In 1841, approximately 400 Americans lived in the Oregon region. Significant rapid growth is evidenced in the various early territorial and state census enumerations taken in 1842, 1845, 1852, 1853, 1854, 1855, 1856, 1857, 1858, 1859, 1865, 1885, 1895, and 1905. Only portions of of some enumerations are extant. Federal censuses began with the Oregon territorial census in 1850 and continued every ten years. The 1890 census was destroyed by fire, and all census enumerations after 1910 are protected by right-of-privacy laws. Federal mortality schedules for Oregon are available for 1850, 1860, 1870, and 1880. Notable census publications include:

Dilts, Bryan Lee, ed. *1870 Oregon Census Index*. Salt Lake City: Index Publishing, c.1985. (FHL# 979.5/X2do)

Jackson, Ronald Vern, ed. *Oregon 1850 Territorial Census Index*. Bountiful, Utah: Accelerated Indexing Systems, 1978. (FHL# 979.5/X2j/1850)

Jackson, Ronald Vern, ed. *Oregon 1860 Census Index*. Salt Lake City: Accelerated Indexing Systems, c.1984. (FHL# 979.5/X22o/1860)

______. *Oregon Census Records, 1841-1849*. North Salt Lake, Utah: Accelerated Indexing Systems, c.1984. (FHL# 979.5/X22o/1841-49)

Pioneer Families in Oregon Territory, 1850. Oregon State Archives Bulletin No. 3, Publication No. 17, David C. Duniway, State Archivist. Portland, Ore.: Oregon State Archives, [c.1980s].(FHL# 979.5/X2pa)

Pioneer Families of the Oregon Territory, 1850. Salem: Oregon State Library, 1951. (FHL# 979.5/B4o/no.3/1951) 2nd ed. published 1961.

Provisional and Territorial Census Records of Oregon, 1842-1859. Salem: Oregon State Archives, 1970. (FHL# microfilm 899786, items 1 and 2)

United States Bureau of the Census. *1850 Census of Oregon*. Northridge, Calif.: San Fernando Valley State College, 1972. (FHL# Q/979.5/X2pb/1850 or microfilm 908211, item 3)

Church Records

Religious groups significantly influenced the populating of Oregon. During Oregon's territorial days, four religions founded independent settlements and churches. In 1834, Methodist missionaries led the settlement of the Willamette Valley and Clackamas County.

First Presbyterians, under the leadership of Marcus Whitman, established churches in the Walla Walla and Pendleton area in 1836. The same denomination colonized Corvallis in Benton County.

In 1835 Reverend Samuel Parker, a Congregationalist missionary, followed by the Reverends Elkanah Walker, Cushing Eells, and A. B. Smith in 1838, settled at and built churches in Forest Grove in Washington County and Oregon City in Clackamas County.

Father Francis Blanchet and Modeste Demers, French-Canadian Roman Catholics, founded missions at St. Paul and St. Louis in the Willamette Valley and Oregon City in Clackamas County, and Roseburg in Douglas County.

The United Presbyterian Church was established in Linn County, first in Brownsville in 1849 and Oakville in 1855. Each of these four churches grew steadily and by 1900 were found throughout the state. Other religions well represented in Oregon at early dates include Baptists, Lutherans, Episcopalians, Christians or Disciples, and Quakers.

Oregon church records are cataloged in the FHLC under **Oregon/Church Records** and **Oregon/[County]/Church Records**. See also works listed under **Oregon/Church History** and **Oregon/[County]/Church History:**

Beebe, Ralph K. *A Garden of the Lord: A History of Oregon Yearly Meetings of Friends Church*. N.p.: n.pub., c.1968. (FHL# 979.5/K2b)

Directory of Churches and Religious Organizations, State of Oregon. Portland: Oregon Historical Records Survey, 1940. (FHL# 979.5/E4h or microfiche 6051178)

Dryden, Cecil Pearl. *Give All to Oregon: Missionary Pioneers of the Far West.* New York: Hastings House, [1968]. (FHL# 979.5/H2dp)

Inventory of the Church Archives of Oregon Presbyterian Churches. Salt Lake City: Genealogical Society of Utah, 1967. (FHL# microfilm 505564)

Court Records

Each county clerk has responsibility for recording and maintaining files of probates, adoptions, guardianships, name changes, divorces, state hospital commitments, civil and criminal actions, miscellaneous licenses, marriages, naturalizations to 1920, and military lists. Such records usually date from the creation of the county.

Portland city records predate county records and should be examined for all persons who resided in Washington, Clackamas, and Multnomah counties.

Some counties have elected to send their court records to the Oregon State Archives in Salem, the staff of which is extremely accommodating to in-person research or written requests for photocopies of all records, including court documents. All available court records which are not restricted by privacy laws are cataloged in the FHLC under **Oregon/[County]/Court Records.**

Directories

A Complete List of Both Active and Inactive Members of the [Oregon] State Bar (Corrected to September 1, 1937). Tucson, Ariz: W. C. Cox Company, 1974. (FHL# microfilm 1000368, item 9)

Knight, William H. *Handbook Almanac for The Pacific States: An Official Register and Business Directory, 1863.* Tucson, Ariz: W. C. Cox Company, 1974. (FHL# microfilm 1000121, item 3)

Langley, Henry G. *The Pacific Coast Business Directory for 1871-1873.* San Francisco, Calif.: H. H. Langley, 1871. (FHL# 970/E4p)

McKenney's Pacific Coast Directory for 1883-1884. San Francisco, Calif.: L. M. McKinney & Co. 1882. (FHL# 970/E4m)

Members of the Legislature, State of Oregon, 1860-1949. Oregon State Archives Bulletin No. 2, Publication No. 14. Salem: Oregon State Library, 1949. (FHL# 979.5/A1/no.49 or microfilm 430056, item 2)

Oregon State Directory, 1881. Tucson, Ariz: W. C. Cox Company, 1881. (FHL# microfilm 1000366, item 5)

R. L. Polk and Company. *Oregon and Washington Gazetteer and Business Directory, 1909-1910.* Tucson, Ariz: W. C. Cox Company, 1974. (FHL# microfilm 1000367, item 1)

Genealogical Collections

Clark, Keith. *Terrible Trail: The Meek Cutoff, 1845.* Caldwell, Idaho: Caxton Printers, 1966. (FHL# 979.5/H2ck)

Peckham, Willie May, ed. *Eighty-Six Ancestral Charts, 1170 Surnames.* Salem, Oreg.: Willamette Valley Genealogical Society, c.1983. (FHL# 979.5/ D2e or microfiche 6019902)

Genealogical Forum of Portland, Oregon. *Genealogical Material in Oregon Donation Land Claims.* Portland,Ore: Genealogical Forum of Portland, 1957-75. (FHL# 979.5/R2g or microfilm 823831, item 7, or microfiche 6051173, items 4-16)

Goodrich, Mrs. George R., comp. *Oregon State Roster of Ancestors.* N.p.: n.pub., 1982. (FHL# 973/D2do)

Gurley, Lottie LeGett, comp. *Genealogical Material in Oregon: Provisional Land Claims, Abstracted Volumes I-VIII, 1845-1849.* Portland: Genealogical Forum of Portland, 1982. (FHL# 979.5/R2gL)

Oregon Memorial of Citizens of the United States and-Miscellaneous Information: Census Records for 1843, Tax Rolls, Newspaper Clippings of Oregon Pioneers, Government Documents on the Boundary Line Between the British and U.S. Territories in Northwestern America. Salt Lake City: Genealogical Society of Utah, 1966. (FHL# microfilm 430055, item 3)

Smith, Fern, comp. *Genealogical Data Copied from the "Pacific Christian Advocate" (Published In Oregon) for the Years 1864-1890.* Salt Lake City: Genealogical Society of Utah, 1963. (FHL# microfilm 369746-369747 and 365234)

National Society of Daughters of American Colonists, Klamath Chapter. *Southern Oregon Records.* N. p.: n. pub., n.d. (FHL# 979.5/D2s)

History

Bailey,.Barbara Ruth. *Main Street, Northeastern Oregon: The-Founding and Development of Small Towns.* Portland: Oregon Historical Society, c.1982. (FHL# 979.5/H2b)

Bancroft, Hubert Howe. *History of the Northwest Coast, 1543-1846.* New York: Arno Press, McGraw-Hill, 1967. (FHL# 979/B4b/Vol.27 or microfilm 982471, items 6 and 7)

______. History of Oregon. Salt Lake City: Genealogical

Society of Utah, 1979. (FHL# microfilm 1036279, items 1 and 2)

Carey, Charles Henry. *History of Oregon*. Chicago, Ill.: Pioneer History Publishing Company, 1922. (FHL# 979.5/H2cc or microfiche 6046590)

Clarke, S. A. *Pioneer Days of Oregon History*. Portland: J. K. Gill, 1905. (FHL# 979.5/H2cs)

Gray, W. H. *A History of Oregon, 1792-1849*. Tucson, Ariz: W. C. Cox Company, 1974. (FHL# microfilm 1000358, item 1)

Hines, Harvey K. *An Illustrated History of the State of Oregon*. Chicago, Ill.: Lewis Publishing Company, 1893. (FHL# 979.5/H2hh or microfilm 1000358, item 2)

Lang, Herbert O. *History of the Willamette Valley*. Salt Lake City: Genealogical Society of Utah, 1985. (FHL# microfilm 1321001, item 2)

Wojcik, Donna M. *The Brazen Overlanders of 1845*. Portland: Wojcik, c.1976. (FHL# 979.5/H3w or microfilm 982206, item 3 or microfiche 6051286)

Land and Property Records

Oregon was one of the thirty Public Land States. After the official land survey, individuals were able to purchase land from the federal government. Land records for the territorial period, 1845-49, were filed with the territorial recorder and are indexed and on file at the Oregon State Archives.

Donation land claims recorded the distribution of government lands and contain valuable genealogical information including year and place of birth, date and place of marriage, given name of wife, record of migration to Oregon, settlement of the land, citizenship, and names of witnesses and those who testified on behalf of the settler. Donation land claims through the Oregon City and Roseburg Land Offices have been abstracted and indexed and are available in the Family History Library collection.

Public Land Offices were opened in the following towns: Oregon City, pre-1855 to 1905; Winchester, 1855-59; Roseburg, 1860-unknown closing date; Burns, 1889-1925; Le Grande, 1867-1925; Linkville, 1873-77; Lakeview, 1877-unknown closing date; The Dalles, 1875-unknown closing date; and Portland, 1905-25. Subsequent land records, including deeds and mortgages were recorded in each county, beginning at the creation of the county.

Index of Oregon Donation Land Claims. Portland: Genealogical Forum of Portland, 1953-57. (FHL# 979.5/R2g/Index)

United States Land Office, Oregon. *Oregon and Washington Donation Land Files, 1851-1903*. Washington, D.C.: National Archives, 1970. (FHL# microfilm 1028543)

Military Records

Gantenbein, C. U., comp. *The Official Records of the Oregon Volunteers in the Spanish War and Philippine Insurrection*. Salem, Oreg.: J. R. Whitney, State Printer, 1903. (FHL# 979.5/M2o or microfiche 6051175)

Myers, Jane. *Honor Roll of Oregon Grand Army of the Republic, 1881-1935*. Cottage Grove, Oreg.: Cottage Grove Genealogical Society, c.1980. (FHL# 979.5/-A1/no.53)

Pekar, M. A. *Soldiers Who Served in the Oregon Volunteers: Civil War Period, Infantry and Cavalry*. Portland: Genealogical Forum of Portland, 1961. (FHL# 979.5/-A1/no.16 or 979.5/M2p or microfilm 928088, item 8, or 928082, item 6 or microfiche 6051234)

Pompey, S. L. *Civil War Veteran Burials from California, Nevada, Oregon and Washington Regiments Buried in Colorado*. Independence, Calif.: Historical and Genealogical Publishing Company, c.1965. (FHL# 978.8/M2ps)

United States Adjutant General's Office. *Index to Compiled-Service Records of Volunteer Union Soldiers Who Served in Organizations from the State of Oregon, (1861-1865)*. Washington, D.C.: National Archives. (FHL# microfilm 821947)

Weatherford, Mark V. *Rogue River Indian War*. N.p.: n.pub., n.d. (FHL# 979.5/M25w)

Minorities and Ethnic Groups

A small number of publications documenting Oregon minorities and ethnic groups are included in the Family History Library collection and are cataloged under **Oregon/Minority and Ethnic Groups** with additional titles listed under county headings.

McCullogh, Flavina Maria. *The Basques in the Northwest: A Dissertation*. San Francisco, Calif.: R. and E. Research Associates, 1975. (FHL# 979/A1/no. 3 or microfilm 940048, item 4)

The Quakers in Oregon. Salt Lake City: Genealogical Society of Utah, 1966. (FHL# microfilm 430055, item 6)

Skarstedt, Ernst Teofil. *Oregon och Dess Svenska Befolkning*. Seattle, Wash.: Tryckt hos Washington Printing Company, 1941. (FHL# 979.5/F2s)

Wong, Karen C. *Chinese History in the Pacific Northwest*. N.p.: n.pub., c.1972. (FHL# 979/F2cw)

Native American Records

Coleman, Arthur D. *Wise-Tong Pioneers of Clackamas, Oregon*. Provo, Utah: J. G. Stevenson, c.1965. (FHL# 979.541/H2c)

Curtin, Jeremiah. *Myths of the Modocs*. New York: Blom, 1971. (FHL# 970.3/M721c)

Drucker, Philip. *Cultures of the North Pacific Coast*. San Francisco, Calif.: Chandler Publishing Company, c.1965. (FHL# 970.1/D84c)

Haines, Francis. *The Nez Perces, Tribesmen of the Columbia-Plateau*. Norman: University of Oklahoma Press [c.1955]. (FHL# 970.3/N499h)

Murray, Keith A. *The Modocs and Their War*. Norman: University of Oklahoma Press, [1969]. (FHL# 970.3/-M721m)

Ruby, Robert H. *The Cayuse Indians, Imperial Tribesmen of Old Oregon*. Norman: University of Oklahoma Press, 1975. (FHL# 970.3/E318r)

______. *The Chinook Indians and Traders of the Lower Columbia River.* Norman: University of Oklahoma Press, c.1976. (FHL# 970.3/C441r)

Sauter, John. *Tillamook Indians of the Oregon Coast.* Portland: Binfords and Mort, [c.1974]. (FHL# 970.3/T461s)

Stern, Theodore. *The Klamath Tribe, The People and Their Reservation.* Seattle: University of Washington Press [1970]. (FHL# 970.3/K662s)

Strong, Thomas Nelson. *Cathlamet on the Columbia: Recollections of the Indian People and Short Stories of Early Days in the Valley of the Lower Columbia River.* Portland: Binfords and Mort, n.d. (FHL# 979.546/H7s)

United States Bureau of Indian Affairs. Chemawa Indian School. *Vital Statistics and Student Records, 1883-1947.* Salt Lake City: Genealogical Society of Utah, 1978. (FHL# microfilm 1028472-1028473 and 1028496-1028497)

United States Bureau of Indian Affairs, Grand Ronde-Siletz Agency. *School Records, 1892-1945.* Salt Lake City: Genealogical Society of Utah, 1978. (FHL# microfilm 1025311-1025312)

United States Bureau of Indian Affairs, Klamath Agency. *School Records, 1920-1952. Salt Lake City: Genealogical Society of Utah, 1978.* (FHL# microfilm 1028453-1028454)

______. *School Records, 1889-1950.* Salt Lake City: Genealogical Society of Utah, 1978. (FHL# microfilm 1028443-1028445, item 1)

United States Bureau of Indian Affairs, Portland Area Office. *Civil Information 1864-1951.* Salt Lake City: Genealogical Society of Utah, 1978. (FHL# microfilm 1028470, item 5)

______. *Heirship and Probate Information, 1887-1952.* Salt Lake City: Genealogical Society of Utah, 1978. (FHL# microfilm 1028461, item 2-1028470, item 1)

______. *Tribal Census Information 1877-1952.* Salt Lake City: Genealogical Society of Utah, 1978. (FHL# microfilm 1028458, item 2, and 1028459, item 1)

United States Bureau of Indian Affairs, Umatilla Agency. *Heirship Records, 1894-1939.* Salt Lake City, Utah, 1977. (FHL# microfilm 1024224)

______. *School Records, 1889-1947.* Salt Lake City: Genealogical Society of Utah, 1977. (FHL# microfilm 1024205, item 2-1024206)

______. *Vital Records, 1889-1932.* Salt Lake City: Genealogical Society of Utah, 1978. (FHL# microfilm 1024205, item 1)

United States Bureau of Indian Affairs, Warm Springs Agency. *Agency Records, 1879-1952.* Salt Lake City: Genealogical Society of Utah, 1978. (FHL# microfilm 1021379-1021385 and 1022004)

Zucker, Jeff. *Oregon Indians: Culture, History and Current Affairs, An Atlas and Introduction.* Portland: Oregon Historical Society, c.1983. (FHL# 979.5/F3z)

Newspapers

A limited number of Oregon newspapers are included in the collection under **Oregon/[County]/Newspapers.** One notable publication is *Oregon Newspapers on Microfilm* by Rory Funke (Eugene: University of Oregon Library, 1980) (FHL# 979.5/B3o). This volume lists the name and locality of all microfilmed newspapers and their availability for interlibrary loan.

Vital Records

Births, marriages, and deaths have been recorded with the Vital Statistics Section, Oregon State Health Division, Portland, since 1907 and for the city of Portland since 1880. In 1862, laws mandating the registration of marriages and divorces were passed. In compliance, county clerks filed the original with the county office and sent the information on a special state form to the State Board of Health.

Prior to the 1907 mandate, some counties chose to record vital records occurring in their county. Vital records are cataloged in the FHLC under **Oregon/Vital Records** and **Oregon/[County]/Vital Records.**

WASHINGTON

Historical Background

1573	Spanish explorers sail the Pacific Coast.
1578	Sir Francis Drake explores the West Coast.
1775	Bruno Heceta and Juan Francisco de Bodega y Quadra land at Point Grenville, the first Caucasians to set foot on Washington soil.
1778	British captain James Cook sails the northwest coast to the Arctic Ocean. George Vancouver explores the Washington Coast and Puget Sound; claims possession for England.
1792	Captain Robert Gray discovers Gray's Harbor and the Columbia River, named for his ship.
1793	Sir Alexander MacKenzie is the first man to cross North America to the Pacific Ocean.
1804-06	Lewis and Clark reach Washington and the Pacific Ocean.
1807-12	North West Company explorer David Thompson establishes posts in Washington, Idaho, and Wyoming.
1810	Spokane House, a British-Canadian fur-trading post, is built at Spokane.
1811	First American settlement built near Spokane by John Jacob Astor's Pacific Fur Company.
1813	Astoria captured by British during War of 1812.
1814	War of 1812 ends; Astoria returned to the United States.
1818	Great Britain and the United States agree to

	joint occupation of the Oregon region including Washington.
1824	Russia and England agree to 54°40' as northern boundary of the Oregon Country.
1830-40	Settlers from Wisconsin, Minnesota, and Canada migrate to Washington.
1832	Nathaniel Wyeth's first party arrives at Columbia. Captain Benjamin Bonneville arrives at Fort Walla Walla.
1833	Fort Nisqually on Puget Sound established by Archibald McDonald.
1836	Marcus Whitman establishes a mission near Walla Walla.
1838	Mission built at Spokane by Reverends Cushing Eells and Elkanah Walker. First Catholic missionaries arrive. Puget Sound Agricultural Company established.
1840s	Wagon train refused entry to Oregon because a black, George W. Bush, accompanies them. The group founds Tumwater, Washington.
1841	Hudson Bay Company brings settlers from the Red River to Cowlitz and Fort Nisqually.
1842	Fort Nisqually transferred to the Puget Sound Agricultural Company. Cowlitz Farm established by same Company.
1843	Influx of settlers into the Oregon Region including Washington.
1845	Michael T. Simmons leads a group that settles at the head of Puget Sound.
1846	U.S.-Great Britain treaty establishes Washington's boundary at 49th parallel. Levi Smith settles at present site of Olympia. J. Borst and Sidney Ford settle at Centralia.
1847	Whitman massacre; Cayuse War.
1848	Oregon Territory created including Washington. Methodists colonize Vancouver.
1849	Vancouver made military headquarters for the Pacific Northwest.
1850	Washington included in the Oregon Territorial Census.
1851	Arthur Denny leads Illinois settlers to Seattle.
1852	Methodists establish a settlement at Olympia. First settlement on Bellingham Bay. The *Columbia*, first Washington newspaper, founded.
1853	Methodist group arrives in Seattle. Washington Territory created 2 March.
1854	First Washington Territorial Legislature session. First federal court held in Washington Territory.
1855-58	Indian wars.
1859-62	Military road from Walla Walla to Fort Benton built.
1860	Washington territorial census. Gold discovered in Idaho. Walla Walla becomes outfitting center for miners.
1861	First territorial university built at Seattle.
1863	Idaho Territory created with present state boundary.
1864	First "Mercer Girls" arrive from New England to become wives and schoolteachers.
1866	Ninety-five members of second Mercer party arrive at Seattle.
1869	First bank in Washington Territory organized in Walla Walla.
1870	Washington territorial census.
1872	Railroad from Walla Walla to the Columbia River started.
1880	Census of Washington territorial residents.
1883	Northern Pacific-Oregon Railway completes transcontinental railroad line to the east.
1889	Washington admitted as forty-second state, 11 November.
1890-1900	Apple industry introduced.
1893	Great Northern Railway completed to Seattle.
1897	Klondike Gold Rush in Alaska attracts many Washington residents.
1900	Federal census. First automobile seen in Seattle.
1907	Statewide registration of births and deaths required.
1910	Federal census.
1916	Boeing Airplane locates in Seattle.
1917	U.S. enters World War I. Fort Lewis rebuilt as a training center.
1918	91st Division from Washington sent overseas.
1968	Statewide registration of marriages mandated.

Settlement and Migration

Until Washington Territory was divided from Oregon Territory in 1853, settlement and migration patterns were identical and are outlined in the discussion on Oregon above.

Numerous factors influenced the settlement of Washington after 1853, including improved trails, roads, railroads, and steamboats. Gold, discovered in southern Oregon and Idaho, attracted an influx of settlers from eastern states but also from Washington Territory. Due to its geographic location on the safely navigable Columbia River, Walla Walla soon became the primary mining outfitting town in the Pacific Northwest. Occupations and businesses that supported the mining industry quickly sprang up in the area, including farmers, ranchers, merchants, hotels and restaurants, liveries and blacksmith shops.

The various military forts in the territory protected pioneer families; therefore, the fertile acreage was quickly claimed and developed as farms, ranches, and orchards. Lumber was also an important natural resource; and settlers, mainly from the northern Midwest, soon provided the necessary skilled labor.

As early as the 1840s, blacks were attracted to Washington, a free state and relatively unprejudiced. In the early 1840s, a wagon train of settlers was refused permanent settlement in Oregon if George W. Bush, a black man, remained with them. The members of the train, grateful to Bush for his many kindnesses during the arduous trek, refused to enter Oregon without him and instead went to Washington where they founded Tumwater. Following the Civil War, particularly in the 1880s and 1890s, blacks from the South migrated to Washington and its vocational opportunities.

The several national depressions/recessions from the 1890s through the late 1930s encouraged many families in economic straits to move to Washington where military, airplane, lumbering and farming industries were relatively prosperous.

Washington Library Collection

Archives and Libraries

Genealogical Resources in Washington State: A Guide to Genealogical Records Held at Repositories, Government Agencies, and Archives. Olympia: Secretary of State, Division of Archives and Records Management, 1983. (FHL# 979.7/A3g)

Historical Records Survey, Works Progress Administration. *Guide to Depositories of Manuscript Collections in the United States: Oregon-Washington*. Portland: Oregon Historical Records Survey, 1940. (FHL# 979.5/A1/no.9 or microfilm 908038, item 9)

Historical Records of Washington State: Records and Papers Held at Repositories. [Olympia]: Washington State Historical Records Advisory Board, 1981. (FHL# 979.7/A3hi or microfiche 6051177)

University of Washington Library. *The Dictionary Catalog of the Pacific Northwest Collection of the University of Washington Libraries, Seattle*. Boston, Mass.: G. K. Hall & Co., 1972. (FHL# 970/A3w)

Atlases, Gazetteers, and Maps

Colton's Map of Oregon, Washington, Idaho, British Columbia and Montana. New York: J. H. Colton, 1860. (Map case FHL# 979/E7co)

Highsmith, Richard M. *Atlas of the Pacific Northwest: Resources and Development*. Corvallis: Oregon State University Press, c.1968. (FHL# Q/979/E3h)

Index to Topographical Maps of Washington. Washington, D.C.: U.S. Geological Survey, 1974. (Map case FHL# 979/E7ug)

Preston, Ralph N. *Early Washington: Overland Stage Routes, Old Military Roads, Indian Battle Grounds, Old Forts, Old Gold Mines*. Corvallis, Ore.: Western Guide Publishers, c.1974. (FHL# Q/979.7/E3e)

R. L. Polk and Company. *Oregon and Washington Gazetteer and Business Directory, 1909-1910*. Tucson, Ariz.: W. C. Cox Co., 1974. (FHL# microfilm 1000367, item 1)

Watson, Gaylord. *Watson's New County, Railroad and Sectional Map of Washington and Oregon*. N.p.: n.pub., 1875. (FHL# 979/E7w)

Biography

A large collection of Washington biographical publications are cataloged under **Washington/Biography**, with additional titles under **Washington/[County]/Biography**. Significant efforts to collect, document, and publish Washington pioneer biographies by state and local historical-genealogical societies regularly add to the library collection.

Hawthorne, Julian. *History of Washington, The Evergreen State, From Early Dawn to Daylight*. New York: American Historical Publishing Company, 1893. (FHL# 979.7/H2hj)

Hines, Harvey K. *An Illustrated History of the State of Washington: Containing . . . Biographical Mention of . . . Its Pioneers and Prominent Citizens*. Chicago, Ill.: Lewis Publishing Company, 1893. (FHL# 979.7/D3h)

History of the Pacific Northwest: Oregon and Washington. Portland: North Pacific History Company, 1889. (FHL# 979/H2hp or microfilm 1000361, items 1-2)

Hunt, Herbert. *Washington West of the Cascades: Historical and Descriptive, the Explorers, the Indians, the Modern*. Tucson, Ariz.: W. C. Cox, 1974. (FHL# microfilm 1000638, items 1-3)

Who's Who in Religious, Fraternal, Social, Civil and Commercial Life on the Pacific Coast. Tucson, Ariz.: W. C. Cox, Co., 1974. (FHL# microfilm 1000645, item 4)

Who's Who in Washington State: A Compilation of Biographical Sketches of Men and Women in the Affairs of Washington State. Tucson, Ariz.: W. C. Cox, 1974. (FHL# microfilm 1000645, item 5)

Cemetery Records

Few compilations of statewide inventories of cemetery tombstone inscriptions exist for Washington. Those available are cataloged in the FHLC under **Washington/[County]Cemetery Records**. Many more tombstone inscriptions for specific cities or counties have been made and are cataloged under **Washington/[County]/Cemetery Records**. Other compilations have been included in genealogical records which are cataloged under **Washington/Genealogical Collections**. Two publication titles of note are:

Cemetery Records of Washington. Salt Lake City: Genealogical Society of Utah, 1972. (FHL# 979.7/V22p or microfilm 824354, item 4-824256, item 1)

Pompey, S. L. *Burial List of the Members of the First Washington Territory Infantry*. Kingsburg, Calif.: Pacific Specialties, 1972. (FHL# 979.7/A1/no.14)

Census Records

The residents of Washington were first enumerated with the 1850 Oregon Territorial Census and were included in the U.S. federal censuses taken in 1860, 1870, and 1880 as Washington Territory residents. The 1860 census included what later became Idaho Territory, with small sections of Montana and Wyoming. Missing from the 1860 census are the counties of Benton, Columbia, San Juan, Snohomish, and Stevens. Counties missing from the 1870 census include Benton, Columbia, and San Juan. Mortality censuses for Washington Territory are available for 1860, 1870, and 1880.

State censuses were taken in 1871, 1883, 1885, 1887, 1889, and 1892.

Jackson, Ronald Vern. *Washington Territory Census Index, 1850 Census Extracted From the 1850 Oregon Census.* (FHL# 979.7/X2j/1850)

Pompey, S. L. *The 1860 Census Records of Sawamish, Scamania, Wahkiahumo Counties, Washington Territory.* Bakersfield, Calif.: Historical and Genealogical Publishing Company, 1966. (FHL# 979.7/X2p/1860)

Stucki, J. U. *Index to the First Federal Census Territory of Washington (1860).* Huntsville, Ark.: Century Enterprises Genealogical Services, 1972. (FHL# 979.7/A1/no.1)

United States, Bureau of Indian Affairs, Portland Agency Office. *Tribal Census Information, 1877-1952.* Salt Lake City: Genealogical Society of Utah, 1978. (FHL# microfilm 1028458, item 2 and 1028459, item 1)

United States, Bureau of Indian Affairs, Tulalip Agency. *Census Records, 1980-1929.* Salt Lake City: Genealogical Society of Utah, 1978. (FHL# microfilm 1124295)

United States, Bureau of Indian Affairs, Yakima Agency. *Census Records, 1880-1952.* Salt Lake City: Genealogical Society of Utah, 1977. (FHL# microfilm 1022003-1022010)

United States, Bureau of the Census. *1850 Oregon Territorial Census.* Lebanon, Oreg.: End of Trail Researchers, 1970. (FHL# 979.5/X2p/1850 or microfilm 897219, item 3)

Jackson, Ronald Vern, ed., *Washington 1850 Mortality Schedules*. Bountiful, Utah: Accelerated Indexing Systems, c.1984. (FHL# 979.7/X2w/1850)

_____., *Washington 1860 Territorial Census Index.* Salt Lake City: Accelerated Indexing Systems, 1979. (FHL# 979.7/X22w/1860)

_____., *Washington 1880 Census Index.* Bountiful, Utah: Accelerated Indexing Systems, 1980. (FHL# 979.7/X22w/1880) Every-name index.

_____., *Washington 1870 Territorial Census Index*. Salt Lake City: Accelerated Indexing Systems, 1979. (FHL# 979.7/X22w/1870) Every-name index.

Church Records

A majority of the church record publications are cataloged under **Washington/Church Records.** Several major denominations were responsible for early settlement and the development of Washington. Church histories, sometimes including membership rolls and other records, are listed under **Washington/Church History** and **Washington/[County]/Church History.**

Guide to Church Vital Statistic Records in Washington. Washington, D.C.: Washington Historical Records Survey, 1942. (FHL# 979.7/V2hm)

Nichols, M. Leona. *The Mantle of Elias, The Story of Father Blanchet and Demers in Early Oregon*. Portland: Binfords and Mort, c.1941. (FHL# 979/V26n or microfilm 372495)

Court and Probate Records

In Washington, law and equity actions fall under the jurisdiction of the county Superior Court. Probate and estate-related matters plus guardianship actions are heard by the county Superior Court. Divorce actions are presented before the Family Court, a department of the County Superior Court. All divorce records prior to 1 January 1968 are filed and maintained by the individual county offices while post-1968 actions are filed with the state.

All land dispute actions and transfers of title are maintained by the County Auditor Department of the County Superior Court. All court records are cataloged under **Washington/[County]/Court Records.**

Directories

Knight, William H. *Handbook Almanac for the Pacific States: An Official Register and Business Directory, 1863.* Tucson, Ariz.: W. C. Cox Co., 1974. (FHL# microfilm 1000121, item 3)

Langley, Henry G. *The Pacific Coast Business Directory for 1871-1873.* San Francisco, Calif.: H. G. Langley, 1871. (FHL# 970/E4p)

McKenney's Pacific Coast Directory for 1883-1884. San Francisco, Calif.: L. M. McKenney & Co., 1882. (FHL# 970/E4m)

R. L. Polk and Company. *Oregon and Washington Gazetteer and Business Directory*. Tucson, Ariz.: W. C. Cox Co., 1974. (FHL# microfilm 1000367, item 1)

Genealogical Collections

Daughters of the American Revolution, Walla Walla Chapter (Washington). *Bible Records from Washington*. Salt Lake City: Genealogical Society of Utah, 1963. (FHL# microfilm 376988, item 2)

Daughters of the American Revolution (Washington). *Family Records of Washington Pioneers.* N.p.: Daughters of the American Revolution of the State of Washington, 1977-78. (FHL# 979.7/D2d/Vol. 47)

_____. *Genealogical Collection*. Salt Lake City: Genealogical Society of Utah, 1970. (FHL# microfilm 848702-848710 and 849485-849493)

Genealogical Resources in Washington State: A Guide to Genealogical Records Held at Repositories, Government Agencies, and Archives. [Olympia]: Secretary of State, Division of Archives and Records Management, 1983. (FHL# 979.7/A3g)

Hamilton Computer Service. *Index to Queries, March 1975-December 1979, from Eastern Washington Genealogical Society.* Park City, Utah: n.pub., 1980. (FHL# 979.7/D22i)

Horne, J. Arthur. *Latter-day Saints in the Great Northwest.* Seattle, Wash.: Graphic Art Press, 1968. (LDS book area FHL# 979.7/K2h)

Patchen, Lee D. *Inland Empire Genealogical Miscellany.* Salt Lake City, Utah: Genealogical Society of Utah, 1968. (FHL# microfilm 599311, item 1)

Seattle Genealogical Society (Washington). *Ancestral Lineages, Second Book.* Salt Lake City: Genealogical Society of Utah, 1965. (FHL# microfilm 438339)

Smith, Fern. *Genealogical Data Copied from the "Pacific Christian Advocate."* Salt Lake City: Genealogical Society of Utah, 1963. (FHL# microfilm 369746-369747 and 365234)

Swart, Shirley, comp. *Index to Washington State Daughters of the American Revolution, Volume 1, 1931-1932 through Volume 52, 1979-1980.* Yakima, Wash.: Yakima Valley Genealogical Society, 1983. (FHL# 979.7/D22i)

Tacoma Genealogical Society, comp. *Bible Records: Records From Twenty-Nine Bibles, Containing One Hundred Ninety Family Names.* Tacoma, Wash.: Tacoma Genealogical Society, 1963. (FHL# 979.7/V29t or microfilm 1036741, item 2)

Told by the Pioneers. N.p.: Works Progress Administra

tion, 1938. (FHL# 979.7/H2t or microfilm 928247, item 2)

History

Atwood, A. *Glimpses in Pioneer Life on Puget Sound.* Tucson, Ariz.: W. C. Cox, 1974. (FHL# microfilm 1000645, item 1)

Avery, Mary Williamson. *Washington: A History of the Evergreen State.* Seattle: University of Washington Press, 1967. (FHL# 979.7/H2am)

Bancroft, Hubert Howe. *History of the Northwest Coast, 1543-1846.* New York: Arno Press, McGraw-Hill, 1967. (FHL# 979/B4b/Vol. 27 or microfilm 982471, items 6-7)

_____. *History of Washington, Idaho and Montana.* Salt Lake City: Genealogical Society of Utah, 1985. (FHL# 979/B4b/Vol. 31 or microfilm 982473, item 6)

Hines, Harvey K. *An Illustrated History of the State of Washington.* Chicago, Ill.: Lewis Publishing Company, 1893. (FHL# 979.7/D3h or microfilm 1000637, item 1)

History of the Pacific Northwest: Oregon and Washington. Portland: North Pacific History Co., 1889. (FHL# 979/H2hp or microfilm 1000361, items 1-2)

Hull, Lindley M. *A History of Central Washington.* N.p.: n.pub., 1929. (FHL# 979.7/H2h)

Johansen, Dorothy O. *Empire of the Columbia: A History of the Pacific Northwest.* New York: Harper, 1957. (FHL# 979/H2j)

Lockley, Fred. *History of the Columbia River Valley from the Dalles to the Sea.* Chicago, Ill.: S. J. Clarke Publishing Company, 1928. (FHL# 979/H2lf or microfilm 1000362, items 2-4)

Preston, Ralph N. *Early Washington: Overland Stage Routes, Old Military Roads, Indian Battle Grounds, Old Forts, Old Mines.* Corvallis, Oreg.: Western Guide Publishers, c.1974. (FHL# Q/979.7/E3e)

Land and Property Records

Washington's 68,192 square miles is one-quarter the size of Texas, yet larger than any eastern state. Congress endeavored to pass laws both to attract settlers to sparsely populated states and to distribute land fairly to such settlers.

Congress appropriated the lands and monies needed to distribute and govern the donation land grants in the territories of Florida, New Mexico, Oregon, and Washington. The federal government granted a "donation" of free land–320 acres to each single man and 640 to each married man–to anyone who would settle in Oregon Territory by 1 December 1850. The free land included, of course, the present state of Washington.

Terms of the donation required that the land would be homesteaded for a minimum of four years. In 1853, the residency requirement was cut to two years. In 1854, Congress passed another act providing the same donation land grant to Washington Territory settlers. Both acts expired in December 1855 after thousands of eager settlers had taken advantage of the generous government offers.

Donation entry files for Oregon and Washington are filed separately in the National Archives. Contained in the completed files is a Notification of the Settlement of Public Land and a Donation Certificate. This document is germane to early Washington genealogical research as it shows the description of the land; name of the entryman; his residence at the time of notification; his citizenship; the date and place of his birth; and, if married, the given name of his wife; and their date and place of marriage.

A large portion of the donation land claim files have been indexed and/or abstracted. Washington entries can be found in *Abstracts of Washington Donation Land Claims, 1855-1902* (Washington, D.C.: National Archives, 1951) (FHL# microfilm 418160).

Subsequent land transfers are filed with the county auditor, County Superior Court. Land records are cataloged under **Washington/[County]/Land and Property Records**.

Military Records

Pompey, S. L. *Burial List of the Members of the Washington Territory Infantry.* Kingsburg, Calif.: Pacific Specialties, 1972. (FHL# 979.7/A1/no.14)

_____. *Civil War Veteran Burials from California, Nevada, Oregon and Washington Regiments Buried in Colorado.* Independence, Calif.: Historical and Genealogical Publishing Company, c.1965. (FHL# 978.8/M2ps)

_____. *Civil War Veteran Burials from the Arizona Territory, Nebraska, Nevada, New Mexico, Oregon, Utah, and the Washington Territory.* Salt Lake City: Genealogical Society of Utah, 1975. (FHL# microfilm 908986, item 2)

United States, Adjutant General's Office. *Index to Compiled-Service Records of Volunteer Union Soldiers Who Served in Organizations from the Territory of Washington, 1861-1865.* Washington, D.C.: National Archives, 1965. (FHL# microfilm 821948)

Minorities and Ethnic Groups

Dahlie, Jorgen. *A Social History of Scandinavian Immigration, Washington State, 1895-1910*. New York: Arno Press, 1980. (FHL# 979.7/F2d)

Skarstedt, Ernst Teofil. *Washington och dess Svenska Befolkn ing*. Seattle: Washington Publishing Company, 1908. (FHL# 979.7/F2s) Swedes in Washington.

Stine, Thomas Ostenson. *Scandinavians on the Pacific, Puget Sound*. N.p.: n.pub., c.1980. (FHL# 979.7/F2sc)

Wong, Karen C. *Chinese History in the Pacific Northwest*. N.p.: n.pub., c.1972. (FHL# 979/F2cw)

Native American Records

Blumhagen, Helen. *Newspaper Clippings, Yakima Indians, Yakima, Washington*. Salt Lake City: Genealogical Society of Utah, 1958. (FHL# microfilm 182307)

Eells, Myran. *The Twana, Chemakum, and Klallam Indians of Washington Territory*. Seattle, Wash.: Shorey Bookstore, 1974. (FHL# 970.1/A1/no.74)

Goddard, Pliny Earle. *Indians of the Northwest Coast*. New York: Cooper Square Publishing, 1972. (FHL# 970.1/-G54li)

United States, Bureau of Indian Affairs, Colville Agency. *Vital Statistics, Birth, Marriages, Divorces and Deaths, 1909-1943*. Salt Lake City: Genealogical Society of Utah, 1977. (FHL# microfilm 1020973-1020976)

United States, Bureau of Indian Affairs, Portland Agency Office. *Family Index Cards, 1938-1950*. Salt Lake City: Genealogical Society of Utah, 1978. (FHL# microfilm 1028470, item 4 and 1028471)

_____. *Heirship and Probate Information, 1887-1952*. Salt Lake City: Genealogical Society of Utah, 1978. (FHL# microfilm 1028461, item 2-1028470, item 1)

_____. *Vital Statistics, 1912-1952*. Salt Lake City: Genealogical Society of Utah, 1978. (FHL# microfilm 1028459, item 2-1028561, item 1)

United States, Bureau of Indian Affairs, Puyallup Agency. *Miscellaneous Records, 1902-1921*. Salt Lake City: Genealogical Society of Utah, 1978. (FHL# microfilm 1024302-1024303)

United States, Bureau of Indian Affairs, Taholah Agency. *Birth and Death Records, 1894*. Salt Lake City: Genealogical Society of Utah, 1978. (FHL# microfilm 1025317-1025320)

United States, Bureau of Indian Affairs, Yakima Agency. *Census Records, 1880-1952*. Salt Lake City: Genealogical Society of Utah, 1978. (FHL# microfilm 1022003-1022010)

_____. *Vital Statistics, Birth, Marriages, Deaths, 1895-1950*. Salt Lake City: Genealogical Society of Utah, 1977. (FHL# microfilm 1022014-1022019)

Vital Records

Births and deaths after 1 July 1907 are recorded with the State Department of Health, Bureau of Vital Statistics, P.O. Box 709, Olympia, WA 98504 as are marriages after 1 January 1968. Births and deaths prior to 1907 were recorded with the county auditor, county seat, with the exception of events which occurred in the cities of Spokane, Seattle, and Tacoma. The City Health Department of each of the three cities independently recorded births and marriages taking place in the cities with no duplicates sent to the counties.

The Family History Library has microfilmed copies of Washington birth, marriage, and death records. However, records for some years are incomplete as inventoried in the Family History Library Catalog.

Historical Records Survey, Washington. *Guide to Public Vital Statistics in Washington*. Seattle: Washington Historical Records Survey, 1941. (FHL# 979.7/V2h or microfiche 6051171)

Patchen, Lee D. *Inland Empire Genealogical Miscellany*. Salt Lake City: Genealogical Society of Utah, 1968. (FHL# microfilm 599311, item 1)

Washington, Bureau of Vital Statistics. *Birth Certificates, 1907-1952. Index to Birth Certificates, 1907-1959*. 211 reels. Olympia: Bureau of Vital Statistics, 1960. Consult the FHLC for call numbers.

_____. *Death Certificates, 1907-1952. Index to Death Certificates, 1907-1959, 1960-1979*. 466 reels. Olympia: Bureau of Vital Statistics, 1959-60. Soundex. Consult the FHLC for call numbers.

_____. *Delayed Birth Certificates, 1936-1953*. 65 reels. Olympia: Bureau of Vital Statistics, 1959. Soundex. Consult the FHLC for call numbers.

ALASKA

Historical Background

1728	Captain Vitus Bering, a Dane serving in the Russian navy, sails the strait that now bears his name.
1741	Bering's second expedition lands on Alaskan Islands.
1759	Russian Orthodox settlers colonize Fox Island.
1774-78	French, Dutch, Bostonians, Portuguese, and English hunt and trade in Alaska.
1778	Hudson Bay Company established in Alaska. Captain James Cook explores the Alaskan coastline and Cook Inlet.
1783	First permanent white settlement made on Kodiak Island by Russian fur traders.
1784	Russian Orthodox missionaries convert hundreds of Alaskan natives.
1791	British Captain George Vancouver explores and surveys Alaskan coast, names Puget Sound and surrounding landmarks.
1799	Russian-American Company obtains a fur-trade charter from Russia.

1801	Numerous Russian settlements established.
1802	Hingit Indians massacre Russian settlers at Sitka and destroy the town.
1802-03	Sitka rebuilt by Aleksandr A. Baranof.
1806	Capital moved from Kodiak to Sitka.
1824	Russians grant equal trading rights to Americans.
1824-25	Through treaties with the United States and England, Russia agrees to 50 degrees 40' latitude as Alaska's southern boundary.
1867	United States purchases Alaska, 375,296,000 acres, from Russia; Alaskan residents become United States citizens.
1880	Federal census.
1880s	Alaskan Federal District Courts established.
1881	Gold discovered at Juneau.
1884	Congressional laws establish a federal court.
1897-98	Klondike and Alaska Gold Rush begins.
1902	Catholic nuns establish hospitals and schools.
1903	International Commission settles dispute between the United States and Canada over the Alaskan boundary.
1912	Alaska becomes a United States Territory with a Territorial Legislature.
1913	Registration of births, marriages, and deaths mandated.
1935	United States government begins a project to relocate 200 farming families to the Matanuska Valley near Anchorage.
1950	Statewide registration of Alaskan divorces implemented.
1959	Alaska admitted as the forty-ninth state on 3 January.

Settlement and Migration

Prior to the mid-1700s, only Eskimos (Aleuts) and a few other small Indian tribes lived in Alaska. The first recorded Caucasians to explore Alaska were Captain Vitus Bering's crew members in 1741. A group of Russian Orthodox settlers established a temporary settlement at Fox Island in 1759. In 1783, Russian fur traders established Alaska's first permanent white settlement on Kodiak Island. From 1783 until about 1883, other small Russian settlements were founded.

During the same time period, a myriad of explorers, hunters, traders, and fishermen moved throughout the region. A majority of these adventurers were French, Dutch, Americans (mainly Bostonians), Portuguese. and English.

Cruelty by the Russian leaders at Sitka toward the natives led to the massacre and destruction of the village in 1802. Quickly rebuilt, Sitka became the predominant Alaska town, and in 1806 became the capital.

Responding to increased American and English fur trade, Russia granted equal trading rights in 1824-25. Russia suffered economically in the process; and therefore, on 30 March 1867, the United States purchased Alaska for $7.2 million.

The late 1800s brought small discoveries of gold and, in 1881, a major one, attracted a large number of adventurers. In 1897-98, the Alaska Gold Rush doubled the number of Alaska residents. The gold rush began to subside about 1910; and by 1920, the population had dropped from 64,000 to 55,000. The years from 1920-30 saw population growth of only 4,000.

The United State's Great Depression in the 1930s caused a small migration to Alaska. The government transported 200 destitute farming families from Michigan, Minnesota, and Wisconsin to the Matanuska Valley near Anchorage.

Another interesting influx of settlers from the "lower forty-eight" occurred in 1942 when thousands of workers rushed to Alaska for the promise of large wages and steady work building the 1,523-mile Alaska Highway which promised security during World War II. The ambitious project was completed in eight months; and the next year, some 140,000 United States military personnel were stationed in Alaska. Many remained to make permanent homes after the close of the war. The population rose from 59,000 in 1930 to 129,000 in 1950. The expectation of a romantic, adventurous lifestyle attracted another 171,000 settlers between 1950 and 1970.

Alaska Library Collection

Archives and Libraries

A Guide to the Russian Holdings in the Alaska Historical Library. Juneau, Alaska: Alaska Division of State Libraries, 1971. (FHL# 979.8/A1 no.2)

Ulibarri, George S. *Documenting Alaskan History: Guide to Federal Archives Relating to Alaska.* Fairbanks: University of Alaska Press, c.1982. (FHL# 979.8/A3u)

Atlases, Gazetteers, and Maps

A number of notable publications documenting Alaskan places and maps are cataloged in the FHLC under **Alaska/Gazetteers** and **Alaska/Maps.** Titles referencing local historical geography are found under **Alaska/[District]/Gazetteers and Maps.**

Alaska. N.p.: National Geographic Society, n.d. (Map case FHL# 979.8/E7ng)

Alaska: Compiled from the Official Records of the General Land Office, U.S. Coast and Geodetic Survey, Geological Survey, Canadian and Other Sources. N.p.: United States General Land Office, 1906. (FHL# 979.8/E7us)

Alaska. Department of Community and Regional Affairs. *Map of the State of Alaska: Showing Organized Boroughs and Cities, Unincorporated Communities, and Regional Attendance Areas.* N.p.: n.pub., 1980. (Map case FHL# 979.8E7a)

Close-up: U.S.A.: Alaska. Washington, D.C.: National Geographic Society, 1975. (FHL# 979.8/E7c/1975)

Index to Topographical Maps of Alaska. Washington, D.C.: United States Geological Survey, 1974. (FHL# 979.8/-E7un)

Mitchell, Samuel Augustus. *Northwestern America Showing the Territory Ceded by Russia to the United States.* N.p.: n.pub., 1867. (FHL# 979.8/E7m)

Orth, Donald J. *Dictionary of Alaska Place Names.* Washington, D.C.: Government Printing Office, 1967. (FHL# 979.8/E5o)

National Geographic Magazine Map of Alaska. Washington, D.C.: National Geographic Society, c.1914. (FHL# 979.8/E7n/1914)

Biography

Only two biographical publications are included in the current Family History Library collection under this heading.

Alaska Bar Association and Sketch of Judiciary. San Francisco, Calif.: Sanborn, Vail & Co., 1901. (FHL# 979.8/D3a or microfilm 908987, item 5)

Hinckley, Ted C. *Alaskan John G. Brady: Missionary, Businessman, Judge, and Governor, 1878-1918.* Columbus, Ohio: Published for Miami University by the Ohio State University Press, c.1982. (FHL# 921.73/B729h)

Cemetery Records

Cemetery tombstone inscription records are listed under **Alaska/[District]/Cemetery Records** with one exception: *Alaska's Kenai Peninsula Death Records and Cemetery Inscriptions* (Kenai, Alaska: Kenai Totem Tracers, c.1983) (FHL# 979.83/V3k).

Census Records

Alaskan territorial censuses were taken in 1870, 1872, 1876, 1878, 1880, 1881, 1885, 1887, 1889, 1890-95, 1900, 1904-07, and 1910. The enumerations taken in 1880, 1900, and 1910 are included with the federal census for those years. The remaining censuses in some cases reflect only part of the territorial residents and are available only for some districts. *Alaska Census Records, 1870-1907* by Ronald Vern Jackson (Bountiful, Utah: Accelerated Indexing Systems, c.1976), (FHL# 979.8/X2j/Index) provides a comprehensive index for all censuses of the time period. Alaskan census publications are cataloged in the FHLC under **Alaska/Census Records** and **Alaska/[District]/Census Records.**

Church Records

Members of the Russia Orthodox Church settled Fox Island as early as 1759 and remained the predominant church in Alaska until 1900. In 1784, Russian missionaries formally organized a church in Alaska. The library has microfilmed copies of these records from 1816-1936.

Catholic missionaries were also active. In 1902, the Sisters of Providence arrived to establish schools and hospitals in Nome, Fairbanks, and Anchorage. The Moravians, Quakers and Presbyterian Evangelical Covenant Church of America, among others, were also represented in Alaska.

The Alaska Department of Vital Statistics has an extensive collection of Alaskan church records which are mixed with civil, government, and vital records. Therefore, church records are cataloged in the FHLC under **Alaska/Church Records, Alaska/[District]/Church Records and Alaska/Vital Records.**

Dorosh, John. *Index to Baptisms, Marriages and Deaths in the Archives of the Russian Orthodox Greek Catholic Church in Alaska, 1816-1886.* Washington, D.C.: Library of Congress, 1973. (FHL# microfilm 944197, items 1-3)

Index to Baptisms, Marriages and Deaths in the Archives of the Russian Orthodox Greek Catholic Church in Alaska, 1890-1899. Washington, D.C.: Library of Congress, 1973. (FHL# microfilm 944197, item 4)

Directories

Alaska Directory and Gazetteer, 1934-35. Seattle, Wash.: Alaska Directory Company, n.d. (FHL# 979.8/E4a)

McKenney's Pacific Coast Directory for 1883-1884. San Francisco, Calif.: L. M. McKenney & Co., 1882. (FHL# 970/E4m)

Langley, Henry G. *The Pacific Coast Business Directory for 1871-1873.* San Francisco, Calif.: H. G. Langley, 1871. (FHL# 970/E4p)

R. L. Polk and Company. *Polk's 1923-1924 Alaska-Yukon Gazetteer and Business Directory.* Tucson, Ariz.: W. C. Cox Company, 1974. (FHL# microfilm 934824, item 2)

The Alaska-Yukon Gold Book: A Roster of the Progressive Men and Women Who Were the Argonauts of the Klondike Gold Stampede. Seattle, Wash.: Stampede Association, c.1930. (FHL# 970/H25o)

History

Armstrong, Terence E. *Russian Settlement in the North.* Cambridge: University Press, 1965. Scott Polar Research Institute Special Publication Number 3. (European area FHL# 957/H2a)

Bancroft, Hubert Howe. *History of Alaska, 1730-1885.* Salt Lake City: Genealogical Society of Utah, 1975. (FHL# microfilm 940009, item 1)

Brown, John W. *An Abridged History of Alaska.* Seattle, Wash.: n.pub., 1909. (FHL# 979.8/H2b)

Chevingny, Hector. *Russian America: The Great Alaskan Venture,1741-1867.* New York: Viking Press, c.1965. (FHL 979.8/H2c)

DeArmond, Robert N. *Alaska, 1867-1959.* Anchorage: Alaska Historical Commission, 1981. (FHL# 979.8/H2da)

Gibson, James R. *Imperial Russia in Frontier America: The Changing Geography of Supply of Russian America, 1784-1867.* New York: Oxford University Press, c.1976. (FHL# 979.8/H2g)

Harris, A. C. *Alaska and the Klondike Gold Fields: Containing a Full Account of the Discovery of Gold*. Salt Lake City: Genealogical Society of Utah, 1978. (FHL# microfilm 1036076, item 4)

Hulley, Clarence Charles. *Alaska, 1741-1953*. Portland, Oreg.: Binfords & Mort, [c.1953]. (FHL# 979.8/H2h)

Hunt, William R. *Alaska, A Bicentennial History*. New York: W. W. Norton and Co., n.d. (FHL# 979.8/H2hu)

Sherwood, Morgan B. *Alaska and Its History*. Seattle: University of Washington Press, c.1967. (FHL# 979.8/H2s)

Stacey, John F. *To Alaska for Gold*. Fairfield, Wash.: Ye Galleon Press, 1973. (FHL# 979.8/H2sj)

Wharton, David. *The Alaska Gold Rush*. Bloomington, Ind.: Indiana University Press, [c.1972]. (FHL# 979.8/H2w)

Wickersham, James. *Old Yukon: Tales, Trails and Trials*. Tucson, Ariz.: W. C. Cox, 1974. (FHL# microfilm 934824, item 1)

Land and Property Records

As a Public Land state, Alaska was first owned by the government and transferred by various means to private individuals. Three Federal Land Sales Offices serviced Alaskan land sales, Indian allotments, and homesteads: Juneau, 1902-23; Nome, 1907-present; and Sitka, 1885-1902. A majority of Alaskan land is still government-owned with some 239 million acres designated for national monuments and conservation sites.

All applicants for federal land must be United States citizens and at least twenty-one years of age to be entitled to one homesite, one headquarter site, and/or one trade and manufacturing site.

Private citizens can acquire state-owned lands through several programs. An applicant must be eighteen years old and must have been an Alaskan resident for at least one year. State land disposals occur each spring and fall by lottery, auction, and homestead and homesite programs.

The limited land-related titles in the Family History Library collection are cataloged in the FHLC under **Alaska/Land and Property Records** and **Alaska/[District]/Land and Property Records.**

Native American Records

Census of Unalaska and Aleutian Villages, Alaska, March 1878. Salt Lake City: Genealogical Society of Utah, 1973. (FHL# Q/979.8/X2p/1878 or microfilm 908376, item 3)

Drucker, Philip. *Cultures of the North Pacific Coast*. San Francisco, Calif.: Chandler Publishing Company, c.1965. (FHL# 970.1/D84c)

Giffen, Naomi Musmaker. *The Roles of Men and Women in Eskimo Culture*. Washington, D.C.: Library of Congress, [c.1970]. (FHL# microfilm 1009060, item 3)

Goddard, Pliny Earle. *Indians of the Northwest Coast*. New York: Cooper Square Publishers, 1972. (FHL# 970.1/-G541i)

Oquilluk, William A. *People of Kauwerak, Legends of the Northern Eskimo*. Anchorage: Alaska Methodist University, c.1973. (FHL# 970.3/E544o)

Rink, Hinrich Johannes. *The Eskimo Tribes, Their Distribution and Characteristics Especially in Regard to Language*. Denmark: Kommissionen for Videnskahelige Undersogelser; Gronland, Meddelelser Om Gronland, n.d. (FHL# 970.3/E544r)

Spencer, Robert F. *The North Alaska Eskimo: A Study in Ecology and Society*. Washington, D.C.: Smithsonian Institution Press, 1969. (FHL# 970.1/Sm69b/no.171)

United States, Bureau of Indian Affairs. *Indians, Eskimos and Aleuts of Alaska*. Washington, D.C.: Government Printing Office, 1968. (FHL# 970.1/A1/no.8)

United States, Bureau of Indian Affairs, Juneau Agency. *School Records, 1927-1952*. Salt Lake City: Genealogical Society of Utah, 1979. (FHL# microfilm 1030793-1030801)

Naturalization Records

In 1867, when Alaska was purchased from Russia, by collective naturalization all residents became citizens of the United States. Subsequent naturalizations to 1906 were recorded by Alaska district courts. Beginning in 1906, all naturalizations were standardized and recorded by the Bureau of Immigration and Naturalization.

Vital Records

State registration of births, marriages, and deaths began in 1913 and divorces in 1950. Vital records are cataloged in the FHLC under **Alaska/[District]/Vital Records**, and in some cases also contain church records.

Alaska's Kenai Peninsula Death Records and Cemetery Inscriptions. Kenai, Alaska: Kenai Totem Tracers, c.1983. (FHL# 979.83/V3k)

HAWAII

Historical Background

0-750	Polynesians, travelling in giant canoes, arrive in Hawaii.
1200	Tahitians migrate to the Hawaiian islands and take control of them from the descendants of early Polynesians.
1500s	Spanish, Dutch, and Japanese explorers visit Hawaii.
1758	Kamehameha I, first Hawaiian monarch, born.
1778	British Navy captain James Cook discovers and names the "Sandwich Islands."
1786	First trading ships arrive from Oregon on way to China.
pre-1790	Western immigrants from various nations settle in Hawaii.

1790-1810	King Kamehameha I unifies the islands.
1819	King Kamehameha I dies, 8 May. U.S.-based Board of Commissioners for Foreign Missions sends eleven Protestant missionary companies to Hawaii.
1820	Protestant missionaries from New England arrive and convert islanders to Christianity.
1827	Roman Catholic missionaries arrive.
1830	First Hawaiian land records kept.
1831	Roman Catholic missionaries forced to leave the islands by Protestant missionary leaders.
1830-90	Settlers and laborers, mainly from Asia with a few from Europe and the United States, immigrate to Hawaii.
1835	First Quakers immigrate. Ladd and Company starts first permanent sugar plantation.
1839	French blockade Honolulu until island government grants religious freedom to Catholics.
1840	Hawaiian kingdom adopts first constitution.
mid-1800s	Thousands of whaling ships stop in Hawaii for supplies on way to Alaskan whaling grounds.
1850	Mormon missionaries arrive from California.
1853	Incomplete vital records kept by Department of Education.
1855	Methodist missionaries arrive.
1862	Church of England (Anglican) established in the islands.
1866	Episcopalian missionaries establish church and missionary activities.
1878	Portuguese and South Sea Island laborers arrive in large numbers.
1881	Norwegian and German laborers arrive.
1885	Japanese laborers arrive. Hawaiian pineapple industry begins importation of sweet pineapple plants from Jamaica.
1887	United States given exclusive rights to use Pearl Harbor as a naval station.
1894	Islanders establish the Republic of Hawaii, with Sanford B. Dole as president.
1896	Registration of vital records recorded by Research and Statistics, State Department of Health
1898	Hawaii annexed to the United States and Sanford Dole serves as governor.
1900	Hawaiian Territory established. Federal census.
1901	Government physicians serve as local registrars of vital records.
1903	The Hawaiian Legislature petitions Congress for statehood.
1906-07	Russian and Spanish laborers arrive.
1927	First airplane flight from mainland to Hawaii.
1941	Japanese attack Pearl Harbor; United States enters World War II.
1951	Law mandating Hawaiian divorce registration implemented.
1957	First telephone cable from mainland to Hawaii.
1959	Statehood granted 21 August making Hawaii the fiftieth state.

Settlement and Migration

Sometime between the birth of Christ and A.D. 750, Polynesians travelling in giant canoes ventured across the ocean, landing eventually at the islands now called Hawaii. These small, shy and peace-loving people lived in comfortable harmony until about 1200 when the more aggressive Tahitians migrated to the islands and quickly seized control.

In the 1500s, Spanish, Dutch, and Japanese explorers stopped at the islands; but it was not until 1778 that serious explorations by British Navy Captain James Cook occurred. Captain Cook immediately named the land the Sandwich Islands in honor of the Earl of Sandwich. Within a dozen years, western immigrants from various nations had migrated and were living throughout the major islands of the chain. Between 1790 and 1810, King Kamehameha I, the first Hawaiian monarch, united the islands and established political and social control.

From 1786 until 1819, visitors to the islands were mainly crews of trading ships who stopped off for supplies on the long vogages to and from the mainland to the Orient. In 1819, the United States-based Board of Commission for Foreign Missions eleven companies to Hawaii. In 1820, these Protestant missionaries converted the islanders to Christianity.

Seven years later, Roman Catholic missionaries arrived and began proselyting activities. Their efforts, however, were met with much opposition. Only four years later, Protestant missionary leaders forced them to leave the islands and many of their native converts were imprisoned. In 1839, the French blockaded Honolulu until the Hawaiian government granted religious freedom to the Catholic converts and missionaries.

The years 1830 to 1890 brought an influx of settlers and laborers, mainly from Asia with others from Europe and the United States. Their migration to the islands helped develop the Hawaiian sugar industry which was introduced in 1835. A second wave of laborers arrived beginning in 1878 with Portuguese and South Sea Islanders, Norwegian and Germans in 1881, and Japanese in 1885, which coincided with the introduction to the Hawaiian pineapple industry; and in 1906-07 when Russian and Spanish laborers were brought to the islands.

Religions also significantly influenced the settlement of Hawaii. In addition to the Protestants and Catholics, Quakers in 1835 and Mormons in 1850 established churches and small colonies. Missionaries of the Methodist Church in 1855, Church of England (Anglican) in 1862, and the Episcopalian Church in 1866 influenced migration to and the lifestyle of the islands.

Hawaii has the most racially and ethnically diverse

population of any state. This is evidenced in Hawaii's population statistics: 33%, white; 24.8%, Japanese; 3.9%, Filipino; 12%, Hawaiian; 5.8%, Chinese; 1.8%, black; 1.1%, Korean; 1.08%, Samoan; and 12.31%, mixed and other.

Hawaii Library Collection

Archives and Libraries

The Bernice P. Bishop Museum in Honolulu, founded in 1889, is the oldest museum and library in Hawaii. The Bishop Museum serves as a principal research repository and research center and continues to document history and genealogy in the Hawaiian Islands.

Lai, Vi. *Hawaii Chinese History Center Library Holdings.* Hana Hawaii Chinese History Center, 1977. (FHL# 996.9/-A1/no.16)

Luster, Arlene D. C. *A Directory of Libraries and Information Sources in Hawaii and the Pacific Ocean.* Honolulu: Hawaiian Library Association, 1972. (FHL# 996.9/J54L)

Atlases, Gazetteers, and Maps

Atlas of Hawaii. Honolulu: University Press of Hawaii, n.d. (FHL# 996.9/E3h)

C. S. Hammond and Company. *Map of Hawaii: Showing the Relative Position of the Islands Comprising the State of Hawaii.* New York: C. S. Hammond and Company, n.d. (FHL# 996.9/E7h)

Lindsey, Jesse H. *District and County Guide of the Territory of Hawaii.* Salt Lake City: Genealogical Society of Utah, 1973. (FHL# 996.9/E5L and microfilm 924462, item 3)

Territory of Hawaii: Map. Washington, D.C.: General Land Office, 1923. (FHL# 996.9/E7u/1923)

United State Board of Geographic Names. *Hawaiian Islands: Official Standard Names Approved by the U.S. Board on Geographic Names.* Salt Lake City: Genealogical Society of Utah, 1984. (FHL# 996.9/E5u or microfilm 1033989, item 1)

Biography

An important collection of Hawaiian biographical publications is cataloged in the FHLC under **Hawaii/Biography** and **Hawaii/[County]/Biography.**

DeFreitas, Joaquim Francisco. *Portuguese-Hawaiian Memories*, 1930. Salt Lake City: Genealogical Society of Utah, 1982. (FHL# microfilm 505972)

Hawaiian Records. N.p.: n.pub., n.d. (FHL# microfilm 888994)

Hilleary, Perry. *Men and Women of Hawaii.* Honolulu: Business Consultants, 1954. (FHL# 996.9/D3emw)

Protestant Episcopal Church. *Missionary District of Honolulu. Book of Remembrance.* Salt Lake City: Genealogical Society of Utah, 1979. (FHL# microfilm 1031811)

Siddall, J. W., ed. *Men of Hawaii.* Honolulu: Honolulu Star-Bulletin, n.d. (FHL#996.9/D3m or microfilm 1000163)

Cemetery Records

A limited number of cemetery tombstone inscription inventories are available in the library collection. Cemetery publications are cataloged in the FHLC under **Hawaii/Cemetery Records.** Two compilations of note are:

Hawaii Cemetery Records. Salt Lake City: Genealogical Society of Utah, 1977. (FHL# 996.9/V22h or microfilm 982174, items 4-5)

Zabriskie, George Olin. *Tombstone Inscriptions from the Royal Mausoleum.* Salt Lake City: Genealogical Society of Utah, 1974. (FHL# 996.9/A1/no.1 or microfilm 962324, item 19)

Census Records

Hawaii was annexed to the United States in 1898; in 1900, Hawaii Territory was created. Therefore, Hawaiian residents were enumerated in the United States federal census for the first time in 1900. The 1910 federal census also documents Hawaiian individuals and families, but subsequent enumerations are protected by right-of-privacy laws.

Territorial and state censuses were taken in 1866, 1878, 1890, and 1896. Records were compiled from school census, population schedules, tax lists, births, and deaths for 1840-66. The 1878 schedule includes only the Islands of Hawaii and Oahu. The 1896 census includes only Oahu and Honolulu, which were enumerated separately.

Hawaii, Bureau of Customs. *Census File, 1840-1866.* Salt Lake City, Utah: Genealogical Society of Utah, 1976. (FHL# microfilm 1009896, items 1-2)

_____. *Census File, 1847-1896.* Salt Lake City: Genealogical Society of Utah, 1976. (FHL# microfilm 1009896, items 3-4)

_____. *Census Records, 1878-1896.* Salt Lake City: Genealogical Society of Utah, 1977. (FHL# microfilm 1010681-1010688)

Schmidt, Robert C. *The Missionary Censuses of Hawaii.* Honolulu: Department of Anthropology, Bernice Pauahi Bishop Museum, 1973. (FHL# 996.9/X2s)

Church Records

Hawaii's "melting pot" includes not only diverse racial and ethnic groups, but also the myriad religious denominations described in the historical discussion.

The earliest reference to Quakers was made in 1835 when Mr. Daniel Wheeler conducted a service on the island.

Although Mormon Sam Brannon stopped at the Hawaiian Islands in 1846 on his way from New England to California, it was not until 12 December 1850 that twelve LDS missionaries were sent on proselyting missions to Hawaii. Mormon settlements were begun in the "City of Joseph" in the Palawai Valley on Lanai; and in 1865, the LDS Church purchased Laie, Oahu. Today, Mormons outnumber all other Protestant religions.

The Methodist Church sent missionaries to establish churches and converts in 1855. In 1862, the Church of England (Anglican) began activities on the islands, followed by Episcopalians in 1866. In 1881, the German Lutheran Church of Liehue was built. Seventh-day Adventists Abraham LaRue and Henry Scott arrived in Oahu and began to sell literature in 1883. When the first Japanese laborers arrived in 1887, they introduced and practiced five forms of Buddism. In 1898, Japanese immigrants built the first Shinto shrine in Hilo.

Although the Jewish Benevolent Society was established in Hawaii in 1910, it was not until 1950 that the first synagogue was built. Presbyterian missionaries were again sent to Hawaii in 1912. Three years later, the Korean Christian Church was built on Liliha Street in Honolulu. J. C. McDonald, a Southern Baptist, began work in Hawaii in 1926. Jehovah's Witnesses were activated on the islands in 1934. In 1944, the Church of God in Christ was founded in the islands. In 1944, the Church of God, was introduced in Honolulu as was the First Assembly of God in 1947. In 1960, some sixteen years after activities began in Hawaii, the Church of God in Christ built churches on Oahu and Kaui.

Today, one-third of the Hawaiian residents are Catholics, 30 percent are Protestant, 20 percent are Buddhist, and the remaining 17 percent worship in other denominations.

Church records are particularly important in Hawaiian genealogical research as they often pre-date the keeping of vital records and often provide familial relationships. They are cataloged in the FHLC under **Hawaii/Church History, Hawaii/Church Records, Hawaii/[County]/-Church Records**, and **Hawaii/[County]/Church History.**

Church of Jesus Christ of Latter-day Saints, Hawaii Mission. *Index of Hawaiian Church Membership Records.* Honolulu: Bell and Howell for the Historical Department of the Church of Jesus Christ of Latter-day Saints, 1970. (FHL# microfilm 1002715 and 1205745-1205747 and 1249988-1249992)

Court and Probate Records

Hawaii is unique among the states in being divided into four counties governed by popularly elected mayors and county council members, with a fifth county administered by the State Department of Health. Hawaiian jurisdictional courts include the supreme court, intermediate appellate courts, circuit courts, district courts, family courts, and land courts.

Probate, law, divorce, criminal, admiralty, and equity case records for the circuit courts are available, 1845-1900. Supreme Court cases before 1900 are included with the circuit court records. Reference material prepared by the Family History Library U.S. and Canada Reference Staff and kept in notebook form at the reference counter specify Hawaiian probate and other court records are on file with the Hawaiian Archives as itemized below:

First Circuit Court (Oahu) Probate, 1845-99; divorce, 1851-95; law, 1848-92; equity, 1851-1907; criminal, 1854-92; minute books, 1848-1900.

Second Circuit Court (Maui, including Molokai) Probate, 1849-1917; divorce, 1848-1915; civil, 1848-1916; criminal 1848-1914.

Third and Fourth Circuit Courts (Hawaii) Probate, 1849-1904; divorce, 1854-1905; civil, 1850-96; equity, 1898-1914; law, 1894-1904; criminal, 1853-1904; minute books, 1850-1943.

Fifth Circuit Court (Kauai) Probate, 1851-1914; divorce, 1852-99; law, 1851-99; criminal, 1851-99; minute books, 1818-1960.

Later court records and indexes remain with their respective courts.

All Hawaiian court record titles are cataloged in the FHLC under Hawaii/Court Records or **Hawaii/[County]/Court Records** and/or **Hawaii/[County]/Probate Records.** One notable title is Hawaii Circuit Court, *Divorce Records, 1849-1915* (Salt Lake City: Genealogical Society of Utah, 1977) (FHL# microfilm 1015620-1015652).

Directories

Directory of Honolulu and the Territory of Hawaii. Honolulu: Polk-Husted Directory Co., 1917. (FHL# 996.9/E4ph or microfilm 962960)

The Hawaiian Kingdom Statistical and Commercial Directory and Tourists' Guide. 1877, rpt. ed., Salt Lake City: Genealogical Society of Utah, 1979. (FHL# microfilm 1036963, item 4)

Emigration and Immigration

Alcantara, Ruben R. *The Filipinos in Hawaii.* Honolulu: Social Science Research Institute, University of Hawaii, 1972. (FHL# 996.9/A3f)

Distribution of Japanese Immigrants, 1892-1894. Salt Lake City: Genealogical Society of Utah, 1977. (FHL# microfilm 1017122, items 7-8)

Hawaii, Board of Immigration. *Chinese Arrivals, 1847-1880.* Salt Lake City: Genealogical Society of Utah, 1977. (FHL# microfilm 1002792)

Hawaii, Chinese Bureau. *Card Index To Chinese Passports, 1884-1898.* Salt Lake City: Genealogical Society of Utah, 1977. (FHL# microfilm 1002791)

______. *Chinese Entry Permits, 1888-1898.* Salt Lake City: Genealogical Society of Utah, 1977. (FHL# microfilm 1002789, item 2-1002790)

______. *Chinese Work Permits, 1895-1897.* Salt Lake City: Genealogical Society of Utah, 1977. (FHL# microfilm 1002808-1002809)

______. *Departures of Chinese From Hawaii, 1852-1900.* Salt Lake City: Genealogical Society of Utah, 1977. (FHL# microfilm 1002793)

______. *Index to Entry Permits for Chinese Minors, 1891-1898.* Salt Lake City: Genealogical Society of Utah, 1977. (FHL# microfilm 1002789, item 1)

Hawaii, Collector of Customs. *Ships' Passenger Manifests, 1843-1900.* 72 reels. Salt Lake City: Genealogical Society of Utah, 1976-77. See FHLC heading **Hawaii/Emigration and Immigration** for call numbers.

Hawaiian Sugar Planters Association, Bureau of Labor and Statistics. *Passenger Manifest of Filipino Contract Laborers*. 85 reels. Salt Lake City: Genealogical Society of Utah, 1977-78. See FHLC heading **Hawaii/Emigration and Immigration** for call numbers.

Hawaiian Sugar Planters Association. *Shipping Lists, 1909-1914.* Honolulu: Remington Rand, 1960. (FHL# microfilm 989212-989213)

Judd, Bernice. *Voyages to Hawaii before 1860. (Volume 1. Chronological List of Vessels, Volume 2. Index of Vessels and Persons)*. Honolulu: University Press of Hawaii, c.1974. (FHL# 996.9/W3j)

Mark, Diane Mei Lin. *The Chinese in Kula: A Recollection of a Farming Community in Old Hawaii.* Honolulu: Hawaii Chinese History Center, c.1975. (FHL# 996.9/H2md)

Nordyke, Eleanor C. *The Peopling of Hawaii.* Honolulu: University Press of Hawaii, c.1977. (FHL# 996.9/W2n)

Patterson, Wayne K. *The Korean Frontier in America: Immigration to Hawaii, 1896-1910.* Ann Arbor, Mich.: University Microfilms International, 1979. (FHL# 996.9/F2p)

Portugal. Consulado General (Hawaii). *Ship Passenger Lists, 1878-1913.* Salt Lake City: Genealogical Society of Utah, 1977. (FHL# microfilm 1017125)

Genealogical Collections

The library has a sizeable collection of Hawaiian genealogical records. A significant number are printed in foreign languages, including Hawaiian, many of which include English translations. Consult the FHLC under **Hawaii/Genealogical Collections** and **Hawaii/[County]/Genealogical Collections.** Notable titles include:

Births Mai Oahu. Salt Lake City: Genealogical Society of Utah, 1977. (FHL# microfilm 1015619, item 5) Microfilm of original records at the Hawaii State Archives.

Includes financial reports, sales agreements, correspondence, genealogies, land leases, and miscellaneous records.

Cartwright, Bruce. *Some Aliis of the Migratory Period.* Honolulu, Hawaii: Bishop Museum, 1933. (FHL# 996/B4bo/Vol.10/no.7)

Cole, William A. *The Cole-Jensen Collection.* Salt Lake City, Utah: Genealogical Society of Utah, 1984. (FHL# microfilm 1358001-1358009)

Includes oral genealogies and other genealogical information of the Polynesian people from the Pacific Islands.

Descendants of New England Protestant Missionaries to the Sandwich Islands (Hawaiian Islands) 1820-1900: An Alphabetically Arranged Copy of Births, Marriages and Deaths from the Records of the Hawaiian Mission Children's Society Library, Honolulu, Hawaii. Honolulu: Privately Printed, Hawaiian State Regent, National Society of Daughters of the American Revolution, 1984. (FHL# 996.9/D2d)

Alphabetically arranged copy of births, marriages, and deaths from the records of the Hawaiian Mission Children's Society Library, Honolulu.

Dynasty of Kamehamela. Salt Lake City: Genealogical Society of Utah, 1977. (FHL# microfilm 1014417, item 6) Microfilm of original records at the Hawaii State Archives.

Freitas, Joaquim Francisco de. *Portuguese Hawaiian Memories.* N.p.: n.pub., [c.1940s]. (FHL# 996.9/D2f)

Genealogy and Index, Volume 1-2. Salt Lake City: Genealogical Society of Utah, 1977. (FHL# 1015619, items 7-9) Microfilm of general collection of genealogies at the Hawaii State Archives.

Hawaiian Charts. Salt Lake City: Genealogical Society of Utah, 1959. (FHL# microfilm 194117)

Includes information on migration and relationship of Polynesian peoples. Comparative genealogy of Nanaulu and Ulu people.

Hawaiian Records. N.p.: n.pub., n.d. (FHL# microfilm 888994) Includes genealogies of leading chiefs, newspaper clippings, biographies, and genealogies of Hawaiian families.

He Buke Huauhau Alii No Na Alii O Hawaii Nei, 1890. Salt Lake City, Utah: Genealogical Society of Utah, 1977. (FHL# 1015618, item 3)

Includes history and genealogy of Lahui Hamaka of Hawaii.

He Buke Oia Io Kuauhua Alii. Salt Lake City: Genealogical Society of Utah, 1977. (FHL# microfilm 1015618, item 7) A book of "truths" about Hawaiian kings.

Kala Kana Collection from Hawaiian Archives. Salt Lake City: Genealogical Society of Utah, 1958. (FHL# microfilm 164678-164679)

Kamakau, Samuel Manaiakalani. *The Genealogy of Kumuhonua To Wakea.* Salt Lake City: Genealogical Society of Utah, 1977. (FHL# microfilm 1014417, item 9)

Kumulipo Genealogy. Salt Lake City: Genealogical Society of Utah, 1977. (FHL# microfilm 1015619, item 12)

Lindsey, Henry K. *Henry K. Lindsey Collection.* Salt Lake City: Genealogical Society of Utah, 1982. (FHL# microfilm 1308916-1308919)

Includes English genealogy, Hawaiian genealogy, family group records, and pedigree charts.

Luke, William K. *Luke Clan of Hawaii.* Honolulu: Chinese History Center, [c.1970s]. (FHL# 996.9/A1/no.18)

McKenzie, Edith Kawelohea. *Hawaiian Genealogies Extracted from Hawaiian Language Newspapers.* Honolulu: University Press of Hawaii, c.1983. (FHL# 996.9/D2m)

Mookupuna Ma Mele O Kapiolani Ma Kalakauna. Salt Lake City: Genealogical Society of Utah, 1977. (FHL# microfilm 1015619, item 3)

Contains genealogy and songs of King Kalakaua.

Nupepa Kuokoa. Honolulu: University of Hawaii Library: Archives of Hawaii, n.d. (FHL# microfilm 1020698-1020729) Genealogies and files in the Bernice P. Bishop Museum.

Ona Kuaukau O Ka Hanau Ana O No Alii Ane Ua Kanaka.

Salt Lake City: Genealogical Society of Utah, 1977. (FHL# microfilm 1015618, item 6)

A list of chiefs' children and their genealogies.

Papa Kuhikuhi Moo O Kumuhonua. Salt Lake City: Genealogical Society of Utah, 1977. (FHL# microfilm 1015619, item 1) Index and genealogical lines from the beginning of the world.

Pukui, Mary Kawena. *Hawaiian Genealogies*. Laie, Oahu Island, Hawaii: College of Hawaii, 1964. (FHL# microfilm 365227)

History

Alexander, Mary Charlotte. *The Story of Hawaii*. New York: American Book Company, c.1912. (FHL# 996.9/H2al)

Alexander, William DeWitt. *A Brief History of the Hawaiian People*. New York: American Book Company, 1899. (FHL# 996.9/H2a)

Blackman, William Fremont. *The Making of Hawaii*. New York: A.M.S. Press, 1977. (FHL# 996.9/H2bL)

Emerson, O. P. *Pioneer Days in Hawaii*. New York: Doubleday Doran & Co., 1928. (FHL# 996.9/H2e or Oceania Collection microfilm 1083301, item 3)

Greer, Richard A. *Hawaii Historical Review: Selected Readings*. Honolulu: Historical Society, 1969. (FHL# 996.9/-H2gr or microfilm 962329, item 2)

Jarves, James Jackson. *History of the Hawaiian or Sandwich Islands*. Salt Lake City: Genealogical Society of Utah, 1985. (Oceania Collection FHL# microfilm 1425609, item 4)

Kuykendall, Ralph Simpson. *Hawaii: A History from Polynesian Kingdom to American Commonwealth*. New York: Prentice-Hall, 1948. (FHL# 996.9/H2K)

Morris, Robert J. *The Crossroads of the Pacific: The Development of Multicultural Families in Hawaii*. Salt Lake City: Genealogical Society of Utah, 1980. (FHL# 929.1/-W893/1980/Vol. 10/Part 9)

The Hawaiian Islands. Honolulu: Printshop Co., Ltd., 1930. (FHL# 996.9/B4ht)

The Hawaiian Journal of History. Honolulu: Hawaiian Historical Society, 1967. v. 1-5 (FHL# 996.9/B2h)

Land and Property Records

Hawaii, located in the central Pacific Ocean, is comprised of eight main islands and 124 islets, reefs, and shoals. Earliest recorded distribution of land occurred about 1830; and by 1860 most of the desirable government land had been sold, mainly to natives, with one-twentieth of all public land sales set aside for educational purposes. Through lease or sale, gradually a majority of the Hawaiian acreage came under control of corporations and wealthy planters and ranchers. As an example, 353,714 acres were granted and/or sold to only five individuals. By 1862, three-quarters of all property on Oahu was held by non-natives. In 1896, there were only 6,327 landowners, or 5.8 percent of the entire population. On 21 August 1959, when Hawaii was admitted as the fiftieth state, 16.1 percent of all land was owned by the Hawaiian government.

Prior to 1849, land transfer records for all islands were kept by the Bureau of Conveyances. Familial relationships were frequently included in the files. The Family History Library has records of the Registrar of the Bureau of Conveyances from 1844 to 1900 including: grantor's index book, 1845-1961; recorded deeds, 1845-1961; land court transfer certificates of title; document and land court maps which are called the file plan; liens; and private abstractors.

The Hawaiian Board of Commissioners to Quiet Land Titles documented special actions between 1848 and 1852. These files are of particular genealogical interest as ownership and transfer of all land had to be documented, including familial relationships, back to the Grand Mehele in 1848 and original royal patents. Arranged geographically, *Index to Awards* (FHL# 996.9/-R2h) serves as an index to these records.

Subsequent land transfers were recorded with the Bureau of Conveyances in each county.

Hawaiian land record titles are cataloged in the FHLC under **Hawaii/Land and Property Records** and **Hawaii/[County]/Land and Property Records.**

Chinen, Jon J. *Original Land Titles in Hawaii*. N.p.: n.pub., c.1961. (FHL# 996.9/R2c)

_____. *The Great Mahele: Hawaii's Land Division of 1848*. Honolulu: University Press of Hawaii, [c.1958]. (FHL# 996.9/A1/no.9)

Hawaii, Department of Land and Natural Resources. *Award Books, 1836-1855*. Salt Lake City: Genealogical Society of Utah, 1964. (FHL# microfilm 571189-571200)

_____. *Patents upon Confirmation of Land Commissioners, 1847-1961*. Salt Lake City: Genealogical Society of Utah, 1964. (FHL# microfilm 571201-571219)

Hawaii, Registrar of Bureau of Conveyances. *Deeds and Other Records, 1844-1900*. Honolulu: Department of Land and Natural Resources, [c.1970s]. (FHL# microfilm 986118-986246)

Naturalization Records

Naturalization records for Hawaii from 1844 until 1894 and other miscellaneous records are on file with the State Archives and may also be found at the office of the county clerk. Naturalization records are cataloged under **Hawaii/Naturalization Records** and **Hawaii/[County]/-Naturalization Records.**

Hawaii, Department of the Interior. *Letters of Denization, 1846-1898*. Salt Lake City: Genealogical Society of Utah, 1977. (FHL# microfilm 1017113, items 1-4, 6)

_____. *List of British Subjects Who Received Special Rights of Citizenship (c.1892-1898)*. Salt Lake City: Genealogical Society of Utah, 1977. (FHL# microfilm 1017113, item 5)

Hawaii, Supreme Court. *Naturalization Records, 1874-1904*. Salt Lake City: Genealogical Society of Utah, 1977. (FHL# microfilm 1015654)

Newspapers

Index to Birth, Marriages and Deaths in Hawaiian Newspapers Prior to 1950. Salt Lake City: Genealogical Society of Utah, 1977. (FHL# microfilm 1002818-1002823)

Mookini, Esther T. *The Hawaiian Newspapers*. Honolulu: Topgallant Publishing Company, 1974. (FHL# 996.9/B3m)

Nupeka Kuokoa. Honolulu: University Press of Hawaii Library; Archives of Hawaii, n.d. (FHL# microfilm 1020698-1020729)

Probate Records

Hawaiian Islands, Circuit Court. *Probate Records, 1845-1900: Indexes 1814-1917.* 141 reels. Salt Lake City: Genealogical Society of Utah, 1977.

Vital Records

Christian missionaries brought vital record keeping to Hawaii. The first Christian marriage occurred in 1822. Evidently they regularized the unions of their converts by mass marriages for a fee that involved the donation of produce. Two thousand marriages were solemnized in the twelve months following June 1830 and four thousand more during 1832 and 1833.

Civil records began in Hawaii in 1853 but are incomplete before 1896. From 1853 until 1896, vital records were kept by the Department of Education. In 1896 the responsibility was transferred to the Research and Statistics Office, State Department of Health. In 1901, government physicians served as the local registrars of vital records. Delayed birth certificates were filed with the Lieutenant Governor's Office from 1901 to 1963. Missionary and church records contain many vital records which often pre-date the keeping of state vital statistics. See **Hawaii/Church Records** for titles.

Many adoptions prior to 1915 were recorded in the files of the Bureau of Conveyances, both state and county offices.

Civil vital records are cataloged in the FHLC under **Hawaii/[County]/Vital Records** and **Hawaii/Vital Records.**

Hawaii. Chinese Bureau. *Certificates of Hawaiian-Born Children of Chinese Parentage, 1893-1898*. Salt Lake City: Genealogical Society of Utah, 1977. (FHL# microfilm 1002810, item 2)

Hawaii (Kingdom). Department of Health. *Birth Records and Transcripts, 1896-1903 and Indexes 1896-1909*. 11 reels. Salt Lake City: Genealogical Society of Utah, 1978. See FHLC heading **Hawaii/Vital Records** for call numbers.

Hawaii (Territory). Department of Health. *Death Registers 1896-1903 and Index 1896-1909.* 17 reels. Salt Lake City: Genealogical Society of Utah, 1978. See FHLC heading **Hawaii/Vital Records** for call numbers.

______. *Delayed Birth Registrations, c.1859-1903 and Index c.1859-c.1938.* 70 reels. Salt Lake City: Genealogical Society of Utah, 1978-79.

Index to Birth, Marriages and Deaths in Hawaiian Newspapers Prior to 1950. Salt Lake City: Genealogical Society of Utah, 1977. (FHL# microfilm 1002818-1002823)

Records by Jurisdiction **Oregon**	Archives & Libraries	Bible Records	Biography	Business Records	Cemeteries	Census	Church History	Church Records	Court Records	Directories	Emigration/Immigration	Gazetteers	Genealogy	History	Land & Property	Maps	Military Records	Minorities	Native Races	Naturalization	Newspapers	Obituaries	Orphans	Periodicals	Probate Records	Public Records	Schools	Societies	Taxation	Town Records	Vital Records	Voting Records
Baker			•		•	•				•			•	•	•																	
Benton	•		•		•	•				•			•	•			•														•	
Champoeg																																
Clackamas			•		•	•				•			•	•	•	•			•	•				•	•						•	
Clark																																
Clatsop	•				•	•	•	•		•				•																	•	
Columbia					•	•				•				•							•			•							•	
Coos	•		•		•	•				•				•	•						•	•			•						•	
Crook			•		•					•																					•	
Curry			•		•	•								•											•							
Deschutes										•																						
Douglas					•	•		•	•					•	•		•								•						•	
Gilliam			•			•								•													•				•	
Grant			•		•	•								•																	•	
Harney					•																											
Hood River	•																															
Jackson				•	•	•				•			•	•										•			•				•	
Jefferson										•																					•	
Josephine	•					•				•			•	•																	•	
Klamath	•		•		•					•				•											•						•	
Lake			•		•																										•	
Lane	•		•		•	•	•	•		•				•			•							•				•			•	
Lincoln					•									•																		
Linn	•		•		•	•	•	•		•			•	•															•	•	•	
Malheur			•		•					•				•																		
Marion					•	•				•			•	•			•				•						•				•	
Morrow	•		•		•	•				•				•																		
Multnomah	•		•		•	•				•			•	•		•		•							•	•					•	
Polk					•	•							•	•																	•	
Sherman			•		•					•				•																	•	
Tillamook	•				•	•								•																	•	
Umatilla	•		•		•	•				•	•		•	•				•													•	
Umpquo																																
Union					•	•				•				•																	•	
Wallowa																																
Wasco					•	•				•			•	•																	•	
Washington	•				•	•	•			•																					•	
Wheeler			•		•																											
Yamhill			•			•				•			•	•																	•	

Records by Jurisdiction — **Washington**	Archives & Libraries	Bible Records	Biography	Business Records	Cemeteries	Census	Church History	Church Records	Court Records	Directories	Emigration/Immigration	Gazetteers	Genealogy	History	Land & Property	Maps	Military Records	Minorities	Native Races	Naturalization	Newspapers	Obituaries	Orphans	Periodicals	Probate Records	Public Records	Schools	Societies	Taxation	Town Records	Vital Records	Voting Records
Adams	•				•									•																		
Asotin	•									•				•																		
Benton	•				•	•				•			•	•																	•	
Chelan	•		•		•	•				•				•								•										
Clallam										•				•																	•	
Clark					•	•		•		•				•	•	•															•	
Columbia					•	•								•							•										•	
Cowlitz	•					•				•			•	•		•								•								
Douglas														•						•												
Ferry			•										•	•																		
Franklin					•					•				•												•					•	
Garfield	•													•																		
Grant					•					•				•																		
Grays Harbor					•	•		•		•																					•	
Island					•											•																
Jefferson					•	•								•																	•	
King	•		•	•	•	•	•			•			•	•		•												•			•	
Kitsap			•		•					•			•	•																		
Kittitas			•			•				•			•	•																		
Klickitat			•		•	•								•																	•	
Lewis	•				•	•		•		•			•								•										•	
Lincoln	•				•					•			•	•																		
Mason					•					•																						
Okanogan			•											•																		
Pacific			•		•	•							•	•							•											
Pend Oreille	•				•																											
Pierce		•	•	•	•					•			•	•	•	•	•									•					•	
San Juan					•																											
Skagit	•		•		•					•				•																		
Skamania					•																•	•									•	
Snohomish	•		•		•					•				•		•			•												•	
Spokane	•		•		•	•				•			•	•	•						•				•		•				•	
Stevens	•		•		•	•								•																		
Thurston			•					•		•			•	•														•			•	
Wahkiakum					•								•	•							•											
Walla Walla			•		•	•				•			•	•																	•	
Whatcom			•	•						•			•	•																		
Whitman			•		•	•		•					•	•			•	•														
Yakima	•		•		•	•	•			•			•	•	•					•		•		•	•			•			•	

Records by Jurisdiction **Alaska**	Archives & Libraries	Bible Records	Biography	Business Records	Cemeteries	Census	Church History	Church Records	Court Records	Directories	Emigration/Immigration	Gazetteers	Genealogy	History	Land & Property	Maps	Migration	Minorities	Native Races	Naturalization	Newspapers	Obituaries	Orphans	Periodicals	Probate Records	Public Records	Schools	Societies	Taxation	Town Records	Vital Records	Voting Records
Aleutian Islands				•		•																						•			•	
Anoktuvuk Pass													•																			
Anchorage					•					•																						
Arctic Village													•						•													
Auke Bay										•																						
Cordova																•																
Douglas					•					•																						
Fairbanks				•	•					•			•																	•		
Fort Richardson					•																											
Haines					•																											
Iliamm																•																
Juneau					•			•		•				•																		
Karluk																•																
Ketchikan										•																						
Knik					•																											
Nome					•																											
Palmer					•																											
Petersburg													•								•											
Point Barrow						•																										
Point Hope																																
Seward													•																		•	
Sitka				•	•		•																									
Skagway					•																											
Wainwright																																
Wrangell					•																					•						
Yakutat														•																		
Yukon-Koyukuk										•				•																		

Records by Jurisdiction **Hawaii**	Archives & Libraries	Bible Records	Biography	Business Records	Cemeteries	Census	Church History	Church Records	Court Records	Directories	Emigration/Immigration	Gazetteers	Genealogy	History	Land & Property	Maps	Migration	Minorities	Native Races	Naturalization	Newspapers	Obituaries	Orphans	Periodicals	Probate Records	Public Records	Schools	Societies	Taxation	Town Records	Vital Records	Voting Records
Hawaii					•		•	•					•	•				•													•	
Islands of:																																
Honolulu.				•		•	•		•	•			•		•		•			•										•		
Kalawao																																
Kauai					•			•		•			•													•					•	
Maui					•		•	•		•			•	•																	•	
Mokupuni														•																		
Oahu													•																		•	

Chapter 14

Dominion of Canada

William L. Arbuckle

The importance of historical knowledge of the area where your ancestors lived cannot be overemphasized. It provides a framework for understanding the events which affected the lives of your ancestors, such as what led them to settle there, where they likely came from, and why they moved on to another area.

Historical background helps put flesh on the bones of the genealogical skeleton of names, dates, and places. It also provides you with an understanding of what records were created and why, thus allowing you to evaluate these records more accurately. For instance, it was much easier for individuals to be omitted from a census record than for them to escape the tax appraiser.

An excellent and concise history of Canada and each of its provinces can be found in *The Encyclopedia Americana* (New York: Americana Corporation, 1986).

Some of the most important historical events are listed below. Others will be noted in the sections on the various provinces.

Historical Background

1608	Champlain establishes a French Colony at Port Royal (now Annapolis Royal), Nova Scotia.
1623	British settle in Nova Scotia.
1670	Hudson Bay Company chartered by Great Britain.
1713	Treaty of Utrecht gives Acadia to the British.
1755-58	French defeated by the British; many French settlers are deported to France, Louisiana, and the American colonies.
1763	New France (Quebec) turned over to the British.
1774	The Quebec Act establishes the early province of Quebec.
1783	Large groups of Loyalists migrate to Canada.
1784	Nova Scotia is divided into three provinces: New Brunswick, Nova Scotia, and Cape Briton Island.
1791	The Constitutional Act divides the early province of Quebec into Upper Canada (Ontario) and Lower Canada (Quebec).
1841	The Act of Union reunites Upper and Lower Canada into the Province of Canada as Canada West (Ontario) and Canada East (Quebec).
1867	The British North America Act establishes the Dominion of Canada, consisting of Ontario, Quebec, New Brunswick and Nova Scotia.
1870	Northwest Territories Act transfers Rupert's Land and the Northwest Territory to Canada.

Local histories can provide valuable information on what churches were in the area and when they were founded. They can also give extensive information on local families and the origins of pioneers. An important guide to printed local histories is William F. E. Morley's *Canadian Local Histories to 1950: A Bibliography* (Canada: University of Toronto Press, 1967). (FHL# 971/A3m).

Sources of local history will be found in the Locality Family History Library Catalog (FHLC) under **Canada/History** and under the various provinces, **/Ontario/History** and under smaller governmental divisions such as **Ontario/York/Toronto/History.**

Settlement and Migration

The early settlement of Canada resulted from the emigration of French and British pioneers from the Old World. At the time of the American War of Independence, large numbers of Loyalists, perhaps 20,000 persons, moved to the Atlantic Provinces, Quebec and Ontario. Migration in the early period was largely dependent on waterways–the St. Lawrence River with its tributaries and the Great Lakes. In the early part of the nineteenth century, improvements of the waterways were made by the construction of canals. The Welland Canal from Lake Erie to Lake Ontario was completed in 1832. The Rideau Canal from Kingston to Ottawa was opened the same year.

The development of the railroad system further facilitated transportation and migration. The St. Lawrence and Atlantic Railroad was completed from Montreal to Portland, Maine, in 1853. The Great Western Railroad from Niagara to Detroit was opened in 1854. The Grand Trunk Railroad extended the line from Portland to Montreal to Toronto in 1856. It was not until 1885 that the Canadian Pacific Railroad facilitated travel from the Atlantic to the Pacific coasts through the Prairie Provinces to Vancouver.

The discovery of gold along the Fraser River in British Columbia in 1858 brought about the migration of thousands of miners from California to that area. As many as 3,000 left northern California alone. Further discoveries of gold in the Cariboo area in 1862 and along the Klondike River in 1896 contributed many settlers to Western Canada.

In the early part of the nineteenth century, land companies and development schemes of individuals contributed much to the settlement of Quebec, Ontario, and the Prairie Provinces. The Canada Land Company under John Galt obtained over a million acres in the Huron tract along Lake Huron, resulting in the cities of Guelph, Galt, and Godrich. The British American Land Company formed about 1832 encouraged settlement in the Eastern Townships of Quebec. Colonel Thomas Talbot sponsored pioneers to the Lake Erie Country. Thomas Douglas, fifth Earl of Selkirk, helped Scottish tenants displaced by the highland clearance program to settle in Prince Edward Island and Ontario in 1803 and in the Red River area of Manitoba in 1812.

The population of what is now Canada in 1760, at the end of the French regime, was about 75,000 souls. By 1871 this had increased to about 3.7 million. In 1951 the population was 13.8 million.

Information on the settlement and migration patterns can be found in the Locality FHLC under **Canada/-Emigration and Immigration**, and under **Canada/-Minorities.**

Canada Library Collection

Archives and Libraries

The Public Archives of Canada are maintained at 395 Wellington Street, Ottawa, Ontario KIA ON3.

The records held by this archive are divided into two classes, the Record Groups and the Manuscript Groups. The Record Groups are primarily those documents created by agencies of the Dominion Government, such as records of the Northwest Mounted Police (RG-18). A guide to the content of these Record Groups is, Public Archives of Canada, *General Guide Series* (Ottawa, Ont.: The Archives 1983).

An inventory of the Manuscript Groups has been published in eight volumes, Public Archives of Canada, Manuscript Division. *Preliminary Inventory* (Ottawa, Ont.: The Archives, 1971). (FHL# 971/A5gim).

Of particular value in finding manuscript material not held by the library is *Union List of Manuscripts in Canadian Archives* (Ottawa, Ont.: The Archives, 1975) with supplements. (FHL# 971/A3cp).

A guide to the location of Canadian Archives is Association of Canadian Archivists, *Directory of Canadian Records and Manuscripts Repositories* (Ottawa, Ont.: The Association 1977). (FHL# 971/E4d) Many of these archives are listed in *American Library Directory*, 38th ed. (New York: R. R. Bowker Co., 1985). (FHL# 973/J54a).

Atlases, Maps, and Gazetteers

A knowledge of the geographical location of your ancestor's residence is essential to locating the records pertaining to his or her life and family. You must know the province, district, county, township, or parish in order to locate the ancestor in the census, deeds, probate records, and church records. You must also understand the development and changes in governmental divisions which control these records. It is also helpful to locate the area on a map in order to know what districts are adjacent to the area where your ancestor lived. You may have found your ancestor in the 1851 Census of Storemont County, Ontario, but his or her marriage record of 1828 will be found in the Eastern District marriage register.

One of the most helpful gazetteers is Peter Alfred Crosby's *Lovell's Gazetteer of British North America* (Montreal, Ont.: John Lovell and Son, 1881). (FHL# 971/E51 or microfilm 844905).

An excellent atlas of Canada with an index to populated places and an index to physical features such as lakes and rivers is *Canadian Gazetteer Atlas* (Canada: Macmillan of Canada, 1980). (FHL# 971/E7cg). Atlases, maps, and gazetteers can be found in the Locality FHLC under **Canada/Atlases** and **Canada/Maps**, and **Canada/Gazetteers.**

Cemetery Records

Cemetery records of Canada are primarily transcriptions taken from tombstones. Very few sexton records, burial records, or mortician records are available. Cemetery records usually contain the person's name, date of death, and date of birth or age. They may also give relationships such as "Mary Jones, age 62, wife of Thomas McKenzie." In Canada, more than in the United States, tombstones give the place of origin of immigrants such as "Thomas McKenzie of Portree, Scotland, age 68 died July 16, 1873."

Two sources of Canadian cemetery records were collected by branches of the LDS Church, *Cemetery Records of Canada* (Salt Lake City: Canadian Mission, 1956). (FHL# 971/V22t or 874019). Also *Cemetery Records of Ontario* (Salt Lake City: Genealogical Society of Utah, 1947). (FHL# 971.3/V3ce or microfilm 823644-823648 and 874379 and 1035565 or microfiche 6046793).

Although the title of the last source does not indicate the scope of these seventeen volumes, they contain records from Quebec, Alberta, and British Columbia in addition to many from Ontario. There is an index to the cemeteries in this collection listing the province, county, and name of the cemetery indicating the volume and page where the records can be found.

Census Records

The Dominion of Canada was formed in 1867 and consisted of Ontario, Quebec, New Brunswick, and Nova Scotia. The first comprehensive census of the Dominion was taken in 1871. Other censuses of the individual provinces were taken at various dates before 1871. The extant census records of Canada are available on microfilm up to and including the census of 1891. The content of the early censuses and years available differ for each province and will be discussed under each province heading.

The 1871 and later censuses provide the following information: name of every family member, sex, age, place of birth, religion, national origin, occupation, and marital status. A guide to extant census records of Canada is Thomas A. Hillman, *Catalogue of Census Returns on Microfilm 1666-1881* (Ottawa, Ont.: Public Archives of Canada, 1981). (FHL# 971/X23c).

Most of the census records of Canada can be found in the Canadian Census Register prepared by the Family History Library. There are three of these registers: one includes the census records through 1871; another is for the 1881 census; and another for 1891. The 1881 and 1891 censuses can be found in the Locality FHLC under **Canada/Census.** The records of the 1871 census and earlier censuses can be found in the Locality FHLC under **[Province]/Census.**

Church Records

Church records may include minutes of meetings concerned with the business of the church, receipt of new members, discipline, financial matters, as well as births, baptism, confirmations, marriages, deaths, or burials. Church records often contain lists of members giving date of membership and where the person was previously a member. Baptism records usually give the date of birth and date of baptism, parents' names and sponsors' names. Marriage records give the date of the marriage and sometimes the fathers' names for both the bride and groom. Lists of the witnesses of the wedding are often included. Death records give the date of death or burial, sometimes the age of the deceased, and relationship, i.e., "Mary Jones, age 64, wife of Thomas Smith." Canadian church records often give the origin of an emigrant when he is first entered in the church register. This is especially true of Roman Catholic churches.

The present church membership of Canada is approximately as follows: 43 percent Roman Catholic, 19 percent United Church, 15 percent Church of England, 7 percent Presbyterian, 4 percent Baptist, and 3 percent Lutheran.

A guide to church records at the Public Archives of Canada is *Checklist of Parish Registers* (Ottawa, Ont.: Public Archives of Canada, 1981). (FHL# 971/K23p). This guide provides the microfilm numbers of the Public Archives of Canada The films can be borrowed on interlibrary loan from the Public Archives of Canada through your local public library, *not* through branches of the Family History Library, Church of Jesus Christ of Latter-day Saints.

Another guide to church records at the Public Archives of Canada is John E. Coderre and Paul A. LaVoie's *Parish Registers Held at the Public Archives of Canada* (Ottawa, Ont.: Ontario Genealogical Society, 1980). (FHL# 971/K23c or microfilm 1036008, item 6). An excellent source of information on Canadian church records and denominational Archives is the "how to" book by Angus Baxter, *In Search of Your Roots* (Toronto, Ont.: Macmillan of Canada, 1978). (FHL# 971/-D25ba). This book gives the names and addresses of the various denominational archives in the several provinces. It also lists church records by name and location giving their content as to birth, marriage, and death and where the records are located in Canada.

Some church records of Canada have been put into the International Genealogical Index (IGI) by the controlled extraction program of the LDS Church, especially those of Nova Scotia and New Brunswick. To determine what church records have been extracted, search the parish and vital records list of the IGI under Canada. The records are listed by province, name of church and location.

Many church records of Canada are still held by the original churches. To locate the addresses of present day churches, consult the Locality FHLC under **Canada/-Church Directories** and **Canada/Church Directories/-Yearbooks.**

Court Records

The types of court records available differ with each province. In general they include probate court records concerned with the distribution of a deceased person's estate, criminal court records, and higher court or appellate court records. The library has large collections of probate court records, but very few of the other types. The probate court records include wills and intestate settlements. These often give the date of death, spouse's name, residence, occupation, and names of the decedent's children or heirs.

These records are found in the Locality FHLC under **[Province]/[District]/Court Records** or **[Province]/-[District]/Probate Records** such as **Ontario/Brant/-Probate Records.**

Directories

Directories include personal names of people who lived in a specific place or names of people with a common occupation, such as ministers or doctors or lawyers.

Occupational directories are valuable because they list the place of residence of the person and often give some biographical information. Locality directories are valuable because they are usually printed annually. An ancestor can be found listed in the same city directory for several years. You may have reason to believe he died there. By consulting the city directories, you may learn about when he died by noting the last year of the directory in which he was listed. They may also tell you when an ancestor arrived or left a given place.

An index to many occupational and "Who's Who" type directories of Canada is *Biographical and Genealogical Master Index* (Detroit, Mich.: Gale Research Co., 1980) second edition with supplements. (FHL# 016.92/G131). This index is also available in microfiche and may be found in most larger public libraries and universities.

A directory of the entire Dominion of Canada was published in 1871, *Lovell's Canadian Dominion Directory* (Montreal, Ont.: John Lovell, 1871). (FHL# 971/E4l or microfilm 856124 and 856125 or microfiche 6046766). An index to this directory has been prepared by the library for the letters A and B (FHL# microfilm 908001, item 2 and 982370, item 4 and 928566, item 3). No index to the entire directory is available for the remaining part of the alphabet. The directory is arranged by province, thereafter alphabetically by name of the town. A separate index to the section for Newfoundland is available (FHL# 971.8/E3p).

Directories are listed in the Locality FHLC under **Canada/Directories.**

Genealogical Collections and Biography

Genealogical collections can be very helpful because they represent the research work done by others and therefore can often save you much time. However, because the research was done by others and because the sources from which the information was taken are often not cited, it is important that you verify the accuracy of the information.

Compiled histories of Canada families are included in the general collection of family histories of the library. These are listed in the surname section of the FHLC alphabetically by surname. Often histories of British or United States families include branches of the family in Canada.

An excellent large collection of biographical information on individual persons is *Dictionary of Canadian Biography* (Canada: University of Toronto Press, 1966-82), eleven volumes (FHL# 971/D3d).

Although somewhat out of date, a good inventory of compiled family histories at the Library of Parliament in Ottawa is Katherine Minne de Varennes's *Annotated Bibliography of Genealogical Works at the Library of Parliament* (Ottawa, Ont.: The Author, 1963). (FHL# 971/A5d or microfilm 962272, item 2).

An index to persons and families found in local histories is David Marshall Howard's *Index to People Listed in Histories of Nova Scotia, Ontario, Prince Edward Island, and New Brunswick* (Calgary: Calgary Branch Genealogical Society, 1981). (FHL# 1402447 to 1402449). This index is divided into separate sections for each province. At the beginning of each section, a list of sources consulted is given. The indexes are on 3 x 5 cards and give the title of the source, the page number, and name of the person or family and where in the province they were living.

An inventory of family histories at the Public Archives of Canada can be found in Manuscript Group 25 in volume 4 of the previously cited *Preliminary Inventory* of the archives. (FHL# 971/A5gim).

Two excellent handbooks on how to do Canadian genealogy are the previously cited book by Angus Baxter, *In Search of Your Roots* (FHL# 971/D25ba) and Eric Jonasson's *The Canadian Genealogical Handbook,* 2nd ed. (Winnipeg, Manitoba: Wheatfield Press, 1978). (FHL# 971/D27j).

Emigration and Immigration

The two main ports of entry into Canada before 1900 were Halifax, Nova Scotia, and Quebec City, Quebec. The records of these ports are available at the library on microfilm, Quebec Officer of Customs, *Passenger Lists* (Ottawa, Ont.: Public Archives of Canada, 1973). (FHL# microfilm 889440-889467). The records for the port of Halifax are Halifax Officer of Customers, *Passenger Lists* (Montreal: Public Archives of Canada, 1973). (FHL# microfilm 889429-889439). The records for Quebec City cover 1865 to 1900. Those for Halifax include 1881 to 1899. The records up to 1908 are at the Public Archives of Canada. Access to records after 1908 is quite limited.

Very few passenger lists before 1865 exist. Many of these have been published and are indexed in P. William Filby, ed., with Mary K. Meyer, *Passenger and Immigration Lists Index,* 1st ed. with supplements (Detroit: Gale Research Co., 1981). (FHL# 973/W32p). There is also an index to the names of ships that arrived in Quebec and Halifax Public Archives of Canada, *Halifax and Quebec Passenger Lists Index* (Ottawa, Ont.: Public Archives of Canada, n.d.). (FHL# microfilm 874104, items 1-5).

There is no comprehensive index to Canadian passenger lists. Two sources of Scottish emigrants not indexed by P. William Filby are Donald Whyte, *A Dictionary of Scottish Emigrants to Canada before Confederation* (Toronto, Ont.: Ontario Genealogical Society, 1986). (FHL# 971/F2wd) and David Dobson, *Dictionary of Scottish Settlers in North America 1625-1825,* 6 vols. (Baltimore, Md.: Genealogical Publishing Co., 1984-86). (FHL# 970/W2d).

An important source of information concerning Canadians who emigrated to the United States through Erie County, New York, is Allen E. Jewitt, *Naturalization Records: Canadian Extracts,* 3 vols. (Hamburg, N.Y.: The Author, 1984). (FHL# 974.796/W22j).

A bibliography of printed sources of emigrant lists to Canada is P. William Filby, *Passenger and Immigration Lists Bibliography 1538-1900* (Detroit, Mich.: Gale Research Co., 1981) with supplement. (FHL# 973/W33p).

A manuscript list of passengers from Southern Ireland is *Miscellaneous List of Passengers Who Embarked at Cove [of Cork, Ireland] 1823-1828*, MS at Public Archives of Canada (Salt Lake City: Genealogical Society of Utah, n.d.). (FHL# microfilm 394002).

During the second half of the eighteenth century, the British government was concerned about the large numbers of citizens emigrating from the British Isles. Lists of outgoing passengers were kept giving name, age, occupation, place of residence, reason for emigrating, and destination. Some of these records are at the Public Record Office, London, and are included in the class of records known as Colonial Office and Treasury Office. These records are described in George A. Neville's *Passenger List Resources at the Public Archives of Canada* (Ottawa, Ont.: Ottawa Branch, Ontario Genealogical Society, 1976). (FHL# 971/A1#37 or microfilm 1036008, item 7).

The records of persons going to Canada have been extracted by the Public Archives of Canada and microfilmed, Public Archives of Canada, *Miscellaneous Lists of British Emigrants to Canada* (Montreal, Ont.: Public Archives of Canada, 1948). (FHL# microfilm 393997). These lists include the time period 1773 to 1784.

Emigration records can be found in the FHLC under **Canada/Emigration and Immigration.** Information about the emigration and settlement of various ethnic groups can be found in the FHLC under **Canada/Emigration and Immigration** and under **Canada/-Minorities.**

Land and Property Records

The records of land and property in Canada differ in each province and will be discussed under each province heading. No general records for the entire dominion exist.

Land records can be helpful in establishing the specific location within a district where your ancestor lived. They can also indicate when he or arrived or left. They may provide relationships, i.e., when a father gives land to his son.

Military Records

The Canadian military establishment before 1870 primarily consisted of regiments of the British army stationed in Canada. Usually at least two regiments were stationed there. These were reinforced by additional regiments during times of strife. They were also supplemented by local units of the militia. Many Canadians served in British regiments while they were stationed in Canada.

The British army was withdrawn from Canada in 1871. The major military engagements of Canada were the French and Indian Wars or the Seven-Years War, the American War of Independence, the War of 1812, the McKenzie Rebellion of 1837, the Fenian Raids of 1866-70 (also known in the United States as the Patriot's War), the Northwest Rebellion of 1885, the Boer War of 1899, and World War I of 1914-18. About 5,000 troops, mostly militia, were involved in the Northwest Rebellion. Canada provided about 7,000 troops for the Boer War, and over 400,000 Canadian troops served overseas in World War I. During the American Civil War, Great Britain had about 11,000 troops stationed in Canada.

The following is a list (by number and regimental name) of British regiments stationed in Canada during the French and Indian war: 1st-The Royal Scots; 15th-East York, Reg't; 17th-Royal Leicestershire; 22nd-Cheshire Regiment; 27th-Inniskilling Regiment; 28th-North Gloucestershire; 34th-Cumberland Reg't.; 35th-Royal Sussex Reg't.; 40th-2nd Somersetshire; 42nd-The Black Watch; 43rd-Monmouthshire Light Inf.; 44th-East Essex Reg't.; 45th-Nottinghamshire Reg't.; 46th-South Devonshire Reg't.; 47th-Lancashire Reg't.; 48th-Northamptonshire Reg't.; 53rd-Shropshire Reg't.; 58th-Rutlandshire Reg't.; 60th-King's Royal Rifle Corps; 73rd-Perthshire Reg't.; and 78th-Rosshire Buffs.

A list of the British regiments stationed in North America during the America War of Independence can be found on pages 150-51 of Edward E. Curtis, *The Organization of the British Army in the American Revolution* (New York: AMS Press, 1969). (FHL# 973/M2ce or microfilm 1036128, item 12).

The British army regiments which saw service in the War of 1812 can be found in L. Homfray Irving, *Officers of the British Army in Canada 1812-1815* (Welland, Ont.: Tribune Print, 1908). (FHL# 971/M23i or microfiche 6010043). A list of Canadian veterans of the War of 1812 is Eric Jonasson, *Canadian Veterans of the War of 1812* (Winnipeg: Wheatfield Press, 1981). (FHL# 971/M2c).

The following is a list (by number and regimental name) of British regiments involved in the McKenzie Rebellion of 1837: 1st-Grenadier Guards; (no number)-Coldstream Guards; 7th-Queen's Own Hussars; 1st-The Royal Scots; 11th-North Devonshire Reg't; 56th-West Essex Reg't.; 85th-The King's Light Infantry; and 93rd-Sutherland Highlanders.

A list of the officers and men who were killed in this rebellion can be found on pages 391-95 in Public Archives of Canada, *Report 1904* (Ottawa: Public Archives of Canada, 1904). (FHL# 971/A2c).

British military records at the Public Archives of Canada are described in the Public Archives of Canada, *General Inventory, Manuscripts* (Ottawa, Ont: Public Archives of Canada, 1976). (FHL# 971/A5gim). The records of the Admiralty Office, London are in MG-12. Those of the War Office, London are in MG-13 and are found in Volume 2 of the inventory.

Some of these records are available on microfilm at the Family History Library. They form part of RG-8 or the old "C" series. Look in the Subject FHLC under **American Loyalists/Great Britain/Army.**

Muster Rolls 1777-1783 (Ottawa, Ont.: Public Archives of

Canada, 1969). (FHL# microfilm 928940- 928947) An index to these records is available at the Public Archives of Canada.

The Regimental Description Books (W025) of the Royal Canadian Rifles (1841-70) are in Vols. 632-34 (FHL# microfilm 859520). The records of soldiers of this unit who received pensions are in W097, Vols. 782 and 1186-94. They are arranged alphabetically and are on microfilm at the library (see Reg. 942/M2a, page 58).

The applications for pensions for widows and children of Loyalist Officers are in W042-59-63 and are on microfilm at the library (See Reg. 942-M2a page 19).

An excellent article on Canadian military records is Eric Jonasson's "An Introduction to Military Records" in *Families* 24, no. 4 (1981): 261-83. (FHL# 971.3/B2f).

A word of caution here is appropriate to the researcher using British army records. The army was reorganized in 1881 and many regiments were assigned new numbers. For further information, the reader is referred to *Military Records* in Chapter 15, "England and Wales."

Some additional outstanding sources must be cited:

Dornbush, C. E. *The Canadian Army 1855-1955 Regimental Histories and a Guide to the Regiments.* Cornwallville, N.Y.: The Author, 1957. (FHL# 971/M25d)

Paterson, Thomas W. *Canadian Battles and Massacres.* Altona, Manitoba: D. W. Friesens and Sons, Ltd., 1977. (FHL# 971/M2p)

Coleman, Emma L. *New England Captives Carried to Canada 1677-1760.* Portland, Maine: Southworth Press, 1925. (FHL# 971/W2c)

Grenville, John H. *Searching for a Soldier in the British Army or Canadian Militia.* Fort Henry, N.Y.: The Author, 1976. (FHL# 971/A1/no.51 or microfilm 1321223, item 2)

Morris, David A. *The Canadian Militia.* Erin, Ont.: Boston Mills Press, 1983. (FHL# 971/M2md)

Minorities, Ethnic Groups, and Native Races

Information about the various ethnic groups and minorities can be found in the Locality section of the FHLC under **Canada/Minorities** and **Canada/Native Races.** The classification in the FHLC of "Minorities" includes any group which had a common characteristic such as national or ethnic origin or religious affiliation.

A guide to ethnic sources is Andrew Gregorovich, *Canadian Ethnic Groups Bibliography* (Toronto, Ont.: Dept. of the Provincial Secretary and Citizenship of Ontario, 1972). (FHL# 971/A3ce).

Very few records exist which deal exclusively with specific minority groups, except for native races. This group of records will be found in the Locality FHLC under **Canada/Minorities** and **Canada/Native Races.**

Naturalization

British immigrants were not required to be naturalized before 1949. Very few naturalization records exist prior to 1865. The library has no Canadian naturalization records.

Newspapers

Newspapers can be a very helpful source of birth, marriage, and death information as well as other details about the life of an ancestor. If the date of death is known, searches can be made to locate an obituary which may provide the decedent's birthdate, place of birth, parents' names, and the names of survivors.

A guide to newspaper holdings of Canadian libraries is *Union List of Canadian Newspapers Held by Canadian Libraries* (Ottawa, Ont.: National Library of Canada, 1977). (FHL# 971/B35u).

A source of current addresses for Canadian newspapers is *The IMS '84 Ayer Directory of Publications* (Fort Washington, Pa.: IMS Press, 1984). (FHL# 970/B34a).

A guide to what newspapers are on microfilm and where these films can be found is *Newspapers in Microform, Foreign Countries* (Washington, D.C.: Library of Congress, 1973). (FHL# 011.35/N479f). A guide to the newspapers that were published in Canada is Winifred Gregory, *American Newspapers 1821-1936*, 1937; rpt. ed. (New York: Kraus Reprint, 1967). (FHL# 970/B33a or microfilm 430291).

The following sources are printed abstracts of births, marriages, and deaths taken from newspapers which, for the most part, were printed in Ontario. However, they include events and people from the other provinces and even foreign countries.

Wilson, Thomas B. *Ontario Marriage Notices.* [1836-1856] Lambertville, N.J.: Hunterdon House, 1982. (FHL# 971.3/B3w)

Reid, William D. *Marriage Notices of Ontario.* [1813-1854] Lambertville, N.J.: Hunterdon House, 1980. (FHL# 971.3/B3r)

_____. *Death Notices of Ontario.* [1810-1849] Lambertville, N.J.: Hunterdon House, 1980. (FHL# 971.3/V4r)

McKenzie, Donald A. *Death Notices from the Christian Guardian 1836-1850.* Lambertville, N.J.: Hunterdon House, 1982. (FHL# 971.3/V4m/vol.1)

_____. *Death Notices from the Christian Guardian 1851-1860.* Lambertville, N.J.: Hunterdon House, 1984. (FHL# 971.3/V4m vol.2)

_____. *More Notices from Methodist Papers 1830-1857.* Lambertville, N.J.: Hunterdon House, 1986. (FHL# 971.3/V2m)

Birth, Marriage, Deaths - Christian Messenger. [1854-1874] 10 vols. Hamilton: Hamilton Branch, Ontario Genealogy Society, n.d. (FHL# 971.3/V28b or microfilm 908997, item 2 and 1033961, item 7)

Periodicals

Periodicals are extremely valuable sources of information to the genealogist. They contain family histories and transcripts of church records, cemetery records, inhabitant lists, census records, tax lists, and other records not otherwise available to the researcher. Many of these periodicals of Canada have been indexed by the library. The index is to types of records, not to people. For example, if you are looking for the cemetery records of Baker Hill Baptist Church in Vaughan Township, Ontario, they can be found in *Canadian Genealogist* Vol. 1 page 41 (1979). The index to Canadian periodicals is Ernie Syke, *Supplementary Index to Canadian Records,* 3 vols. (Salt Lake City: Genealogical Society of Utah, 1985) (FHL# 971/D22si or microfilm 1421714).

Some of the major Canadian periodicals are listed below:

Canadian Genealogist. (1979-to date). Generation Press, 172 King Henry's Blvd., Agincourt, Ont. M1T 2v6. (FHL# 971/D25cg)

Lost in Canada. (1975-to date). Joy Reisinger, ed. and pub., Sparta, Wis. 54656. (FHL# 971/B21c)

The Icelandic Canadian. (1942-to date). 358 Ross Avenue, Winnipeg, Manitoba R3A OL4. (FHL# 971/B2i)

French Canadian and Acadian Genealogical Review. (1968-to date). Quebec: Centre Canadien des Recherches Genealogiques. (FHL# 971/B2f)

Acadiensis. (1971-to date). Fredericton: Department of History, University of New Brunswick. (FHL# 971/B2n)

Probate Records

This group of records includes the records generated by the courts pursuant to the settlement of a decedent's estate. They include wills, administrators' and executors' bonds, and accounts and their appointments. They also include the division of real estate among the heirs and the appointment of guardians. These records will be discussed in greater detail under each province.

Tax Records and Voting Lists

Tax records include lists of persons in a given community giving the amounts of tax assessed. Very few of the records are available at the library.

Voting lists show the names of people who voted in a community. Both the tax records and voting lists are included in municipal records. They are found in the Locality FHLC under the **/[Province]/[County]/-[Township]** or **[Province]/[Municipality]**.

United Empire Loyalists

During the time of the American War for Independence, many British citizens in the colonies did not sympathize with Samuel Adams and his zealous "band of rebels." Although they disapproved of Britain's policies toward the colonies such as the trade regulations, the Stamp Act, and lack of representation in the British Parliament, they did not consider independence from the mother country to be a suitable solution.

These people who remained loyal to the Crown suffered greatly, both in the colonies and in Canada. They were called Tories by their neighbors and were considered traitors to the cause of independence.

Committees of safety were established to insure that they did not undermine the revolutionary effort. Many of these Loyalists fled their homes to take refuge in Canada or the British West Indies, or they returned to the British Isles. It is estimated that as many as 40,000 Loyalists fled the colonies and settled in Canada. The colonial governments confiscated their land and property.

The flight of the Loyalists began before the outbreak of hostilities and continued, to some extent during the war. The major exodus occurred after peace was established.With the assistance of the British Fleet at New York City, some 30,000 refugees were transported to Nova Scotia. Many of these settled in what is now New Brunswick, along the St. John River.

About 6,000 Loyalists settled in the old province of Quebec. They assembled at Sorel at the mouth of the Richelieu River and were later settled on lands in the Niagara peninsula of present-day Ontario, along the St. Laurence River, southwest of Montreal, and at the eastern end of Lake Ontario. New York, New Jersey, and Pennsylvania provided the greatest numbers of Loyalists.

The British government assisted the Loyalist settlers by giving them land. Grants were made not only to the head of the family, but also to each of his sons and daughters.

In 1783 the American Claims Commission was established by the British government to hear claims for compensation of losses submitted by the Loyalists and to adjudicate these claims based on real evidence and sworn testimony. This commission sat at London, England; Halifax, Nova Scotia; St. John, New Brunswick; Montreal, Ontario; Quebec City, Quebec; and Jamaica, British West Indies. The records generated by this commission form an extremely important source of data about Loyalists. The records often give the former residence of the claimant, his age, and some information about his family.

The original claims consist of loose papers grouped into bundles and are housed at the PRO in London. They form Audit Office A013. Originally these claims were filed according to former residence of the claimant, thus we have New York bundles, New Jersey bundles, etc.

This system disintegrated as the claims multiplied. Thus we have miscellaneous bundles. These claims were abstracted and recorded in bound volumes forming Audit Office A012. The records of A012 are valuable because some papers and entire claims of A013 were lost. The only record now preserved of some claims is the abstracts in A012.

Another collection of related documents is contained in Treasury Office T79 in 151 bundles at the Public Records Office. The library does not have the records of T79. The records of A012 and A013 can be found in the Subject FHLC under American Loyalist Claims. The books in A012 are on microfilms FHL# 1401467-1401498. The bundles are on microfilms FHL# 366694-366883. All three sets of records are indexed. The index to the books is FHL# microfilm 162010, item 1. The index to the bundles is item 2 of the same film. The index to T79 is item 3 of the same film.

A printed index to A012 and A013 is Clifford S. Dwyer, *Index Series I and II, American Loyalist Claims*

(Funiak Springs, Fla.: Ram Publishing, 1985). (FHL# 973/R2d and 973/R2da). Series I of these indexes is A012. Series II is A013.

Peter Wilson Coldham has abstracted and published the records from the first thirty-seven bundles in *American Loyalist Claims, Vol. I* (Washington, D.C.: National Genealogical Society, 1980). (FHL# 973/R2cp).

Probably no subject of Canadian genealogy has more extensive literature than the United Empire Loyalists. Below are cited only the more outstanding references. Other useful sources can be found in the Subject FHLC under **American Loyalists.** The reader is also referred to the previously cited sources in this chapter under Canadian military records, RG8 or the old "C" series.

The researcher with Loyalist ancestry is faced with a two-fold problem. He or she must not only search the records generated in Canada, but also those produced in the American colony where the ancestor lived. For that reason, sources from both sides of the border are cited below.

Palmer, Gregory, ed. *A Bibliography of Loyalist Source Material in the United States, Canada, and Great Britain.* Westport, Conn.: Meckler Publishing with American Antiquarian Society, 1982. (FHL# 973/F23b1)

_____. *Biographical Sketches of Loyalists of the American Revolution.* Westport, Conn.: Meckler Publishing, 1984. (FHL# 973/F2slba)

Toronto Branch, the United Empire Loyalists' Association of Canada. *Loyalists Lineages of Canada 1783-1983.* Agincourt, Ont.: Generation Press, 1984. (FHL# 971/D21)

Sabine, Lorenzo. *Loyalists of the American Revolution.* 2 vols. Baltimore, Md.: Genealogical Publishing Co., Inc., 1979. (FHL# 973/F2slb)

Clark, Murtie, J. *Loyalists of the Southern Campaign.* 3 vols. Baltimore, Md.: Genealogical Publishing Co., Inc., 1981. (FHL# 973/F2clm)

Scott, Kenneth. *Rivington's New York Newspaper, Excerpts from the Loyalist Press, 1773-1783.* Binghampton: The New York Historical Society, 1973. (FHL# 974/H2r)

Cruikshank, Ernest A. *The King's Royal Regiment of New York.* rpt. ed., Toronto: Ontario Historical Society, 1984. (FHL# 971/M2ce)

Yoshpe, Harry B. *The Disposition of Loyalist Estates in the Southern District of the State of New York.* New York: Columbia University, 1939. (FHL# 974.7/R2y)

Kelby, William. *Orderly Book of the Three Battalions of Loyalists.* New York: New York Historical Society, 1917. (FHL# 928188, item 2)

Tyler, John W. *Connecticut Loyalists.* New Orleans, La.: Polyanthos, 1977. (FHL# 974.69/R2t)

Siebert, Wilbur H. *Loyalists in East Florida 1775-1785.* 2 vols. DeLand: Florida State Historical Society, 1929. (FHL# 975.4/B4f#9)

Stark, James H. *The Loyalists of Massachusetts and the Other Side of the American Revolution.* Boston: J. H. Stark, 1810. (FHL# 547196 item 1)

Maas, David E. *Divided Hearts, Massachusetts Loyalists, 1765-1790.* Published by New England Historical Society, 1980. (FHL# 974.4/F2m)

Jones, Edward A. *The Loyalists of Massachusetts.* Baltimore, Md.: Genealogical Publishing Co., 1969. (FHL# 974.4/D3je/1969)

Mitchell, Robert G. *Loyalists Georgia.* Ann Arbor, Mich.: University Microfilms, Inc., 1964. (FHL# 975.8/H2ml)

Peck, Epaphroditus. *The Loyalists of Connecticut.* Ann Arbor, Mich.: University Microfilms, Inc., 1978. (FHL# 974.6/H2c Ser. 31)

Jones, Edward A. *The Loyalists of New Jersey.* Newark: New Jersey Historical Society, 1927. (FHL# 974.9/C4n/vol.10 or microfilm 1036367, item 3)

Hancock, Harold B. *The Delaware Loyalists.* Wilmington: Historical Society of Delaware, 1940. (FHL# 975.1/F21 or microfilm 1000154, item 3)

DeMond, Robert O. *The Loyalists in North Carolina During the Revolution.* Durham, N.C.: Duke University Press, 1940. (FHL# 975.6/F2d)

Vital Records

This group includes records of birth, death, and marriage generated by the provincial governments of Canada. Each province has custody of its own records. None of the provincial vital records are available at the library. The content, availability, and beginning dates differ with each province.

Some records kept by the counties or districts before provincial registration began are available at the library. These will be presented under each province heading.

Of special value to the researcher are two collections of vital records concerning Canadians in Erie County, New York:

Jewitt, Allen E. *Buffalo, Erie County, New York Birth Records: Canadian Parentage Extracts.* [1875-1882] 3 vols. Hamburg, N.Y.: The Author, 1984. (FHL# 974.797/V2ja)

_____. *Early Canadian Marriages in Erie County, New York 1840-1890.* 12 vols. Hamburg, N.Y.: The Author, 1982. (FHL# 974.796/V2j)

MARITIME PROVINCES

Historical Background

1604-05	De Monts and Champlain establish a temporary colony near Annapolis Royal.
1621	British attempt first colonization.
1686	Ninety French Acadian families locate at Point Royal.
1713	Treaty of Utrecht cedes Acadia to the British.
1720	Three hundred French settlers establish a colony at Charlottetown, Prince Edward Island.

1749 Halifax settled by the British; large migration of New Englanders.

1755-58 The British defeat the French; many Acadians expelled.

1763 Cape Breton and Prince Edward Island annexed to Nova Scotia.

1769 Prince Edward Island separated.

1783 About 20,000 Loyalists arrive in Nova Scotia.

1784 Cape Breton Island and New Brunswick separated.

1820 Cape Breton rejoined to Nova Scotia.

1815-50 About 55,000 immigrants come to Nova Scotia, mostly Scots and Scotch-Irish.

1867 Nova Scotia joins the confederation which formed the Dominion of Canada.

1873 Prince Edward Island joins the Confederation.

The maritime provinces consist of Nova Scotia, New Brunswick, Prince Edward Island, and Newfoundland. Settlement began with the French primarily in 1686. This continued until the British achieved control of the area at the end of the French and Indian War. At that time, most of the French were expelled and deported to France and Louisiana. Many later returned. The British government sent out about 2,500 immigrants in 1749 to settle in the area of Halifax.

About 1,500 German Protestants were located at Lunenburg as part of the British settlement policy. In 1755 the great influx of New Englanders began. They settled on the lands of the exiled French in the Minas Basin and in the Annapolis River valley and along the coast of the Bay of Fundy. By 1775, the New Englanders made up about 12,000 of the total 17,000 population. Some New Englanders also settled at the mouth of the St. John River in what was to become New Brunswick and on Prince Edward Island.

Another immigrant group consisted of the Ulster and Yorkshire settlements in the Cobequid area numbering about 1,800 by 1775. The Scottish settlement began in 1779 with the landing of 200 Highlanders at Pictou. The American War of Independence contributed another large group of emigrants about 1783. Perhaps as many as 30,000 Loyalists settled in the Atlantic provinces.

NOVA SCOTIA

The province is divided into eighteen counties. These are further divided into townships. The townships are divided into lots. Records can be found in the Locality FHLC under **Nova Scotia/[Subject]** or under **Nova Scotia/[County]/[Subject]** or under the names of smaller divisions. There are also entries in the FHLC under **Nova Scotia/Cape Breton Island.**

Archives and Libraries

The Provincial Archives are located at Halifax. An inventory of its holdings has been published, Public Archives of Nova Scotia, *Inventory of Manuscripts in the Public Archives of Nova Scotia* (Halifax, Nova Scotia: The Archives, 1976). (FHL# 971.6/A5p or microfilm 1036635, item 2). Of special interest are RG12 listing census records, RG27 contains military records, and vital records are listed in RG32. Extensive genealogical information on persons and families is listed in MG1. Church records are found in MG4.

Biography

Three important collections are listed below. Additional sources can be found in the FHLC under **Nova Scotia/Biography.**

Marble, Allan E. *Nova Scotians at Home and Abroad.* Windsor, N.S.: Lancelot Press, 1977. (FHL# 971.6/D3m)

Wright, Esther C. *Planters and Pioneers.* (Hantsport, N.S.: Lancelot Press, 1978. (FHL# 971.6/D2w)

Hebert, Donald J. *Acadians in Exile.* Cecilia, La.: Hebert Publications, 1980. (FHL# 971.6/D2h)

Cemetery Records

Cemetery records are listed in the Locality FHLC under **Nova Scotia/Cemetery Records** and under each of the counties and smaller governmental divisions.

Census Records

Census and census-type records for the following years are available at the Family History Library:

1770. Richard, Bernice C. *Nova Scotia 1770 Census.* Chicago: Chicago Genealogical Society, 1972. (FHL# 971.6/A#18 or microfilm 982213, item 6)

1770-1851. *Census Records and Pole Tax Rolls for Nova Scotia.* Salt Lake City: Family History Library, 1983. See FHLC for call numbers.

1811-18. Harvey, D. C., comp. *Holland's Description of Cape Breton Island.* Halifax: Public Archives of Nova Scotia, 1935. (FHL# 971.6/A1#26 or microfilm 6017740 or 1035587, item 1)

1818-27. Dunlap, Allan C. *Census of Nova Scotia.* Halifax: Public Archives of Nova Scotia, 1979. (FHL# 971.6/X2d or microfilm 6046789)

1851. Halifax and Kings County (FHL# microfilm 1376190-1376191). Indexed in Jackson, Ronald Vern, et al. *1851 Nova Scotia.* Salt Lake City: Accelerated Indexing Systems, Inc., 1986. (FHL# 971.6/X22n)

1861, 1871. All counties: Consult FHLC under **Nova Scotia/-Census.**

1881, 1891. All counties: Consult FHLC under **Canada/Census.**

Church Records

These records can be found in the Locality FHLC under **Nova Scotia/Church Records** and under each of the counties and towns. Additional records are listed in MG4 of the *Inventory of Manuscripts* of the Provincial Archives cited previously.

Emigration and Immigration

Records of this type can be found in the Locality FHLC under **Nova Scotia/Emigration And Immigration**. In addition to the passenger lists cited previously in this chapter under Dominion of Canada, *Immigration,* the following are outstanding sources:

Rieder, Milton P., ed. *The Acadian in France*. Metaire, La.: n.pub., 1967. (FHL# 9744/W2r or microfilm 924094, item 2-4)

Bill, Winthrop P. *The Foreign Protestants*. Toronto, Ont.: University of Toronto Press, 1961. (FHL# 971.63/F3b)

Crowell, Fred E. *New Englanders in Nova Scotia*. Cambridge, Mass.: New England Historical Genealogical Society, 1979. (FHL# microfilm 1402829)

Huling, Ray Greene. *The Rhode Island Emigration to Nova Scotia*. Toronto, Ont.: Canadian House, 1984. (FHL# 971.6/W2h)

Immigration Records of Nova Scotia 1819-1902. Salt Lake City: Family History Library, 1984. (FHL# microfilm 1376183-1876184)

Smith, Leonard H. *A Directory of Immigrants to Nova Scotia*. Clearwater, Fla.: Owl Books, (1985-to date). (FHL# 971.6/W26s) Continuing publication.

Jehn, Janet. *Acadian Exile in the Colonies*. Covington, Ky.: The Author, 1977. (FHL# 973/F2je)

Gazetteers, Maps, and Atlases

These are found in the Locality FHLC under each of the above headings as **Nova Scotia/Maps** and under the counties and towns. A helpful gazetteer is Charles B. Ferguson, *Place-Names and Places of Nova Scotia* (Belleville, Ont.: Mika Publishing Co., 1976). (FHL# 971.6/E5f or microfilm 982210, item 1). Another important gazetteer is Canadian Board of Geographical Names, *Gazetteer of Canada: Nova Scotia* (Ottawa, Ont.: Queen's Printer, 1961). (FHL# 971.6/E5c or 6046788).

Genealogy

A useful guide to genealogical research in Nova Scotia is Terrence M. Punch, *Genealogical Research in Nova Scotia*, 3rd ed. (Halifax, Nova Scotia: Petheric Press, 1983). (FHL# 971.6/D27p). Some major sources are listed below:

Centre Acadian Collection Genealogique. Salt Lake City: Family History Library, 1983. (FHL# microfilm 1319970-1319975) Indexed on FHL# microfilm 1378699 and 1378700.

Genealogy File of Beaton Institute of Cape Breton College. Salt Lake City: Family History Library, 1983. (FHL# microfilm 1376154-1376,162)

Hebert, Donald J. *Acadians in Exile*. Cecilia, La.: Hebert Publications, 1980. (FHL# 971.6/D2h)

Howard, David M. *Nova Scotia Families*. Salt Lake City: Family History Library, 1985. (FHL# microfilm 1035714-1035716)

Stayner Collection. Salt Lake City: Family History Library, 1983. (FHL# microfilm 1376187-1376404; an interrupted series of numbers; see FHLC)

Marble, Allan E. *A Catalogue of Published Genealogies of Nova Scotia Families*. 2d ed. Halifax: Nova Scotia Historical Society, 1984. (FHL# 971.6/D23m)

Land and Property

Land records of Nova Scotia may be classified into two types: land grants from the government to individuals and deeds of transfer from one person to another. The major collection of land grant records is Department of Crown Lands, *Land Records* (Salt Lake City: Family History Library, 1983). Consult the Locality FHLC under **Nova Scotia/Land and Property/Nova Scotia Department of Crown Lands** for film numbers.

There are two sets of these records. Both sets are listed together in the Family History Library. The index to the larger first set is listed first. The index to the smaller set is on FHL# microfilm 1378276. These indexes give the name of the person receiving the grant and the year of the grant. The records are arranged by year then alphabetically within each year by the name of the grantee. Sometimes the grantee was a representative of several people, each of whom received part of the land. Each person is listed in the index with a reference to the name of the principal representative under whose name the grant is filed.

Additional records for land grants can be found for some counties in the FHLC under **Nova Scotia/[County]/Land and Property.**

The deeds for each of the counties can be found in the FHLC under **Nova Scotia/[County]/Land and Property**. Indexes are available for each county. The indexes are listed with the deeds.

Military Records

Most of these records are at the Public Archives of Canada. The reader is referred to the section of this chapter under **Canada/Military Records.**

Minorities

Much helpful information on the settlement and immigration of minority groups can be found in the locality FHLC under **Nova Scotia/Minorities** and under **Nova Scotia/Church History**, and under **Nova Scotia/Emigration and Immigration.**

Periodicals

The publication of the Nova Scotia Genealogical

Society is *The Nova Scotia Genealogist*, (1983-to date). Armdale, Nova Scotia. (FHL# 971.6/D25n).

Probate Records

Probate records consist of wills or testaments, letters of administration, letters testamentary, probate acts of the court, and original loose estate papers. For some counties, the library has microfilm copies of wills recorded at the office of the recorder of deeds as well as those recorded in the probate office. The method of using these records differs with each county. For some counties, there is a general index to the probate court records which gives references for each type of record. In other counties there is an index to wills and an index to estate papers. In others each volume of wills is indexed at the front of the book. Some counties filed the estate papers alphabetically.

These records can be found in the FHLC under **Nova Scotia/[County]/Probate Records.**

United Empire Loyalists

The reader is referred to the records cited previously in this chapter under *Canada, United Empire Loyalists* and to the section under *Canada, Military Records*. In addition to these, the following will be found useful:

Gilroy, Marion. *Loyalists and Land Settlement in Nova Scotia.* Halifax, Nova Scotia: Public Archives of Nova Scotia, 1980. (FHL# 971.6/R2g or microfiche 6046551 or microfilm 844514, item 3)

Peerson, Jean. *The Loyalist Guide.* Halifax, Nova Scotia: Public Archives of Nova Scotia, 1983. (FHL# 971.6/A3p)

Vital Records

Records of birth, marriage, and death kept at the county level of government are available at the library on microfilm for every county of Nova Scotia.

The death records include the time period 1864 to 1877. There is no index to these records. They are arranged by county. There are two entries in the FHLC for the county vital records. Both entries are found under **Nova Scotia/Vital Records.** The indexes to births and marriages are found under **Nova Scotia/Vital Records/Indexes.**

The first set of birth records are the original returns sent in by the local recorders. They were transcribed to form the second set of records. The index to births applies to the second or transcribed record. This second set of vital records includes the births and deaths for 1864 to 1877 and marriages to 1918. They are found in the FHLC under **Nova Scotia/Vital Records** and have the title "Nova Scotia Board of Statistics of Marriages, Births, and Deaths, Vital Records 1864-1877, 1918."

The index to marriages has two parts. The first part is not alphabetical. It is arranged by county and covers the period 1853 to 1864. The second part is alphabetical and has a separate index for each county covering the period 1864 to the early 1900s.

This second part of the marriage index applies to both sets of marriage records. The marriage records to which the first index applies can only be found in the set of marriage records for 1849 to 1918.

In addition to the official records of birth, death, and marriage, there is a printed extract of vital records taken from Nova Scotia newspapers covering the period 1769-1834: Terrance M. Punch, *Nova Scotia Vital Records from Newspapers* (Halifax, Nova Scotia: Nova Scotia Historical Society, 1978-to date). (FHL# 971.6/V29p).

NEW BRUNSWICK

Archives and Libraries

The provincial archives are located at Fredericton. An inventory of manuscripts has been published: Ann B. Rigby, *A Guide to the Manuscript Collections in the Provincial Archives of New Brunswick* (Fredericton, New Brunswick: The Archives, 1977). (FHL# 971.5/A5r or microfilm 1036745, item 5). This inventory includes valuable genealogy collections and data on persons and families.

Another important repository is the New Brunswick Museum at St. John. An inventory of their holdings has been published: *Inventory of Manuscripts* (St. John, New Brunswick: The Museum, 1967). (FHL# 971.5/A2n or microfilm 1036725, item 3).

Biography

Biographical sources are listed in the FHLC under **New Brunswick/Biography.** Much additional information can be found in local histories listed in the FHLC under the name of the county, town, or district.

Cemeteries

These records are found in the FHLC under **New Brunswick/Cemeteries** and under each of the counties and towns. A large collection of cemetery records may be found in Volume 5 of James Hannay, *Reports on Archives* (Salt Lake City: Family History Library, n.d.). (FHL# microfilm 824498, item 2).

The first part of this film is a description of church records, mostly Anglican, as they existed in 1908. These church records were not then at the archives, but were in local custody. The second part of the film has been spliced on and is backwards. The researcher must turn to the end of the film where the list of cemeteries and indexes is found.

Census Records

Census records are available for the years 1851 through 1891. The records for 1891 and 1881 are found in the FHLC under **Canada/Census.** The records for 1851 to 1871 are found in the FHLC under **New Brunswick/Census.**

The 1851 census of New Brunswick is being printed by

the Provincial Archives. Those available at this time in the library are listed below:

Albert: FHL# 971.531/X2f

Charlotte: FHL# 971.533/X2n or microfiche 6010520

St. John: FHL# 971.532/X2n or microfiche 6010521

Sunbury: FHL# 971.543/X29h

Victoria: FHL# 971.553/X2J

Westmoreland: FHL# 971.523/X2n or microfiche 6010522

York: FHL# 971.551/X2s

There is also an index to the entire 1851 census of New Brunswick: Ronald Vern Jackson et al., *New Brunswick 1851* (Salt Lake City: Accelerated Indexing System, 1986). (FHL# 971.5/X22n).

Church Records

Church records will be found in the FHLC under **New Brunswick/Church Records** and under each of the counties and towns. A helpful list of church records is found in the guide to Canadian research by Angus Baxter, *In Search of Your Roots* (Toronto, Ont.: Macmillan of Canada, 1978). (FHL# 971/D25ba). Another helpful guide to church records is found in Appendixes A and B in the guide to genealogical research in New Brunswick by Robert A. Fellows, *Researching Your Ancestors in New Brunswick Canada* (N.p.: n.pub., 1979). (FHL# 971.5/-D27f or microfiche 6051366).

Emigration and Immigration

Several early passenger lists can be found in the FHLC under **New Brunswick/Emigration and Immigration**. Other sources will be cited in this chapter under *United Empire Loyalists*. Some information on Irish emigrants during the famine period can be found in J. Elizabeth Cushing et al., *A Chronicle of Irish Emigration to St. John, New Brunswick 1847* (St. John, New Brunswick: The New Brunswick Museum, 1979). (FHL# 971.532/s1/W2c). An indexed group of records for passengers arriving at St. John during the period 1816 to 1837 can be found in the FHLC under **New Brunswick/St. John/St. John/Emigration and Immigration**: Provincial Secretary, *Passenger Lists for New Brunswick, 1816-1837* (Fredericton, New Brunswick: Provincial Archives of New Brunswick, 1984). (FHL# microfilm 1412362-1412368).

Gazetteers, Maps, and Atlases

These records are found in the FHLC under **New Brunswick/Gazetteers** or **New Brunswick/Maps** and under each of the counties. One of the most helpful of these is *Gazetteer of Canada: New Brunswick* (Ottawa, Ont.: Board of Geographical Names, 1978). (FHL# 971.5/E5c). Another useful work which also gives former names of places and changed names is Alan Rayburn, *Geographical Names of New Brunswick* (Ottawa, Ont.: Department of Energy, Mines and Resources, 1975). (FHL# 971.5/E5r).

Genealogy

Genealogy data can be found in the FHLC under several entries: **New Brunswick/Genealogy, New Brunswick/Minorities**, and in works on local history. Two important collections are the following: David R. Jack, *Biographical Data Relating to New Brunswick Families* (St. John, New Brunswick: MicRo Ltd., 1980). (FHL# microfilm 1276610) and David R. Jack, *Pre-Loyalist Biography* (Fredericton, New Brunswick: The Archives, 1971). (FHL# microfilm 944026). Other sources will be cited in this chapter under United Empire Loyalists.

A valuable guide to research in New Brunswick is the previously cited work by Robert A. Fellows, *Researching your Ancestors in New Brunswick Canada* (FHL# 971.5/D27f or microfiche 6051366).

Land and Property

Several groups of records concerning land grants can be found in the FHLC under **New Brunswick/Land and Property**. Generally speaking, however, only one set of records need be searched. The other sets of records were combined by the Provincial Archives about 1978 to form a new series of records. The new series is found in the FHLC under **New Brunswick/Land and Property** titled "New Brunswick Crown Land Office: Land Petitions 1783-1857." The records are indexed giving the grantee's name and the year of the grant. The grants are arranged by year, then alphabetically.

The province is divided into fifteen counties. Deeds of transfer are available for each county with indexes. The deeds of all counties are located at the Provincial Archives. The library has deeds for some counties as indicated on the chart for New Brunswick. There are many entries in the FHLC under **New Brunswick/[County]/Land and Property** for records filmed at the New Brunswick Museum at St. John. These records are only a few single original deeds and do not represent the deeds of the county recorder's office.

Military Records

Some military records will be found in the FHLC under **New Brunswick/Military Records.** The reader is referrd to the section of this chapter under *Canada, Military Records*.

Minorities

Many sources of information about the various groups who settled in New Brunswick can be found in the FHLC under **New Brunswick/Minorities** and under **New Brunswick/Native Races.** Other sources include local histories.

Periodicals

The New Brunswick Genealogy Society publishes a *News Letter* four times a year including queries and articles about New Brunswick sources for research. Its address is New Brunswick Genealogy Society, Box 3235 Station "B", Fredericton, New Brunswick E3A 5G9.

Probate Records

The library has probate records for each county of the province except Kent County. The probate records of Kent County were destroyed by fire. The probate records can be found in the FHLC under **New Brunswick/[County]/Probate Records.**

United Empire Loyalists

In addition to sources cited in this chapter under *Canada, United Empire Loyalists,* the reader will find the following useful:

Wright, Esther. *The Loyalists of New Brunswick.* Fredericton, New Brunswick: n.pub., 1955. (FHL# 971.5/F2w or microfilm 1415252, item 1)

Hill, Isabel L. *Some Loyalists and Others.* Fredericton, New Brunswick: n.pub., 1977. (FHL# 971.5/D3h)

Dubeau, Sharon. *New Brunswick Loyalists.* Agincourt, Ont.: Generation Press, 1983. (FHL# 971.5/D3d)

Bell, D. G. *Early Loyalists/Saint John.* Fredericton, New Brunswick: New Ireland Press, 1983. (FHL# 971.532/-S1/N2b)

Jack, D. R. "New Brunswick Loyalists of the War of the American Revolution." *New York Genealogical and Biographical Record* 35:35, 87, 165, 277; 36:27, 185, 287; 37:11, 131, 209, 303; 38:10, 140, 171, 251; 39:14, 187, 243; 40:23, 115. (FHL# 974/B2n)

Vital Records

The library has microfilm copies of marriage records for twelve of the fifteen counties in this province. These include the time period of about 1806 to 1888. They can be found in the FHLC under **New Brunswick/[County]/Vital Records.** The records for Charlotte, Kent, Kings, Northumberland, Westmoreland, and York counties are listed in the FHLC under **New Brunswick/Vital Records.**

Some marriage records for Charlotte, Sunbury, Westmoreland, and York counties will be found in the FHLC under **New Brunswick/Kings/Vital Records.** These are also records of coroner's inquests for some counties.

The New Brunswick Genealogy Society is publishing a series of books of vital records extracted from newspapers. Thus far it has reached twelve volumes covering the period 1784 to 1850: *New Brunswick Vital Statistics from Newspapers* (St. John, New Brunswick: The Society, 1982). (FHL# 971.5/V2nb). Another important collection of vital records was compiled by Louise Manny, *Collection of Deaths and Marriages* (Salt Lake City: Family History Library, 1971). (FHL# microfilm 856128 to 856135).

PRINCE EDWARD ISLAND

The library has a very limited collection of records for Prince Edward Island. Therefore, the following represents only the most helpful sources available at the library.

Cemetery Records

Daley, Marie. *Gravestone Inscriptions.* N.p.:, n.pub., n.d. (FHL# 971.7/V3d)

Some other cemetery records can be found in the FHLC under **Prince Edward Island/[County]/[Town].**

Census

1728	Blanchard, Joseph-Henri. *Histoire des acadiens de L'ile du Prince-Edourd.* 3rd ed. N.p.: Societe Saint-Thomas d'Aquin, 1976. (FHL# 971.7/H2b)
1798	Ibid. (FHL# microfilm 1036744, item 11)
1841	*Census of Prince Edward Island – 1841.* N.p.: Public Archives of Canada, 1967. (FHL# microfilm 899938)
1848	*Census of Prince Edward Island – 1848.* Salt Lake City: Family History Library, 1977. (FHL# microfilm 1036755, item 13)
1861	*Census of Prince Edward Island – 1861.* N.p.: Public Archives of Canada, 1967. (FHL# microfilm 899939-899943)
1881	See the section in this chapter on *Canada, Census.*
1891	See the section in this chapter on *Canada, Census.*

Church Records

The records of several Roman Catholic churches can be found in the FHLC under **Prince Edward Island/Church Records** and under **Prince Edward Island/[County]/[Town]/Church Records.**

Directories

An index to the 1871 Dominion Directory of Prince Edward Island has been prepared by the library: *Index to the 1871 Dominion Directory of Canada for the Province of Prince Edward Island* (Salt Lake City: Family History Library, 1985). (FHL# 971/E42a/Vol. 2).

Emigration and Immigration

Some sources of information have been cited in the section on **Nova Scotia/Emigration** and **New Brunswick/Emigration.** These may be helpful for immigrants to Prince Edward Island. Also the following, *Prince Edward Island Ship Passenger Lists* (Salt Lake City: Family History Library, 1978). (FHL# microfilm 1036774, item 8).

Gazetteers and Maps

These are listed in the FHLC under **Prince Edward Island/Gazetteers** and under **Prince Edward Island/-Maps** and under each of the three counties. A helpful gazetteer is *Gazetteer of Canada–Prince Edward Island* (Ottawa, Ont.: Permanent Committee on Geographical Names, 1965). (FHL# 971.7/E5c).

Genealogy

Some collections of genealogy concerning specific areas on the island can be found in the FHLC under the headings of **/Genealogy** or under **/History**, or **Prince Edward Island/[County]/[Town]/Genealogy.**

A helpful guide to research in Prince Edward Island is *Family History in Prince Edward Island* (N.p.: The Prince Edward Island Heritage Foundation, 1981). (FHL# 971.7/D27j).

History

Many entries can be found in the FHLC under **Prince Edward Island/History** and under the names of the counties and towns. These often include information on early settlers and genealogy.

Master Name Index

This is the major reference tool for research on island families. The sources indexed include census, church records, marriage bonds and licenses, land petitions, passenger lists, newspapers, cemetery records, and many other sources. This index is on 60 reels of microfilm and can be found in the FHLC under **Prince Edward Island/Genealogy/Indexes.**

Probate Records

The probate records of the entire province from 1807 to 1900 are on microfilm at the library. There is an index to wills. The volumes of letters of administration and letters of probate are indexed at the front of each volume. These records are found in the FHLC under **Prince Edward Island/Probate Records.**

United Empire Loyalists

A useful source is *An Island Refuge*, Orlo Jones and Doris Hasdlam, eds. (N.p.: Abegeweit Branch UEL Association, 1983). (FHL# 971.7/H2i).

NEWFOUNDLAND

The library has a very limited collection of records for this province. Some of the more helpful sources are listed below.

Census Records

Early Census Records of St. John's. Salt Lake City: Family History Library, 1982. (FHL# microfilm 1033848, item 8)

Biography and Genealogy

Matthews, K. *A Who Was Who Engaged in the Fishery Industry of Newfoundland 1660-1840.* St. John's, Newfoundland: The Author, 1971. (FHL# 971.8/U2m)

Seary, E. R. *Family Names of the Island of Newfoundland.* St. John's: Memorial University of Newfoundland, 1977. (FHL# 971.8/Dr6S)

Directories

An index to the 1871 *Dominion Directory* of Newfoundland has been prepared by the library: FHL# 971/E42a Vol. 1.

Gazetteers

Gazetteer of Canada–Newfoundland. Ottawa, Ont.: N.p.:, 1968. (FHL# 971.8/E5c)

Military Records

The pension records of soldiers who served in the Royal Newfoundland Companies are in Great Britain War Office, *Soldiers Documents* (Salt Lake City: Genealogical Society of Utah, 1971), 97 volumes, 1164 to 1170, for the time period 1760 to 1872. They are arranged alphabetically and are on films FHL# 861818 to 861841 see: Reg. 942/M2a page 28 or microfilm 990313, item 5.

Vital Records

Howard, Mildred. *Vital Statistics from Newspapers of Newfoundland.* Sydney, Nova Scotia, The Author, 1980. (FHL# 971.8/V2h).

QUEBEC

Historical Background

1534	Jacques Cartier lands on the Gaspe Peninsula and claims the land for France.
1603	Samuel de Champlain rediscovers New France.
1617	First settlers at Quebec City.
1629	British capture Quebec City.
1632	Quebec City restored to France.
1642	Montreal founded.
1759	Wolfe defeats Montcalm and captures Quebec City for the British.
1763	New France ceded to Great Britain.

1774 The Quebec Act establishes the early province including the coast of Labrador and parts of Michigan, Wisconsin, Ohio, Indiana, and Illinois.
1783 The Treaty of Paris limits the southern boundary and cedes the area south of the Great Lakes to the United States.
1791 The early province is divided into Upper Canada (Ontario) and Lower Canada (Quebec).
1806 First French language newspaper published.
1825 Lachin Canal opened.
1837 "Patriots" rebellion led by Louis Joseph Papineau.
1841 Act of Union unites Upper and Lower Canada, forming the province of Canada with Canada East (Quebec) and Canada West (Ontario).
1849 Parliament buildings destroyed by fire.
1867 The province of Quebec (Canada East) is formed as part of the confederation.
1876 Railway completed from Halifax to Quebec City.

The population of Quebec in 1754 was about 55,000. In 1901 the population was about 1.6 million, with 80 percent French and 17 percent British.

Archives

There are two locations for the Archives of Quebec, one at Montreal and one at Quebec City. There are now eight branches of the archives. For a list of the regional branches and the counties they cover, see Michael Langlois, *Cherchons nos ancetres* (Montreal, Quebec: Federation Quebecoise Du Loisir Scientifique, 1980). (FHL# 971.4/D271) and *Etat general des archies publiques et privees* (Quebec: Ministere des Affaires Culturelles, 1968). (FHL# 971.4/A5G or microfiche 6046879).

Other guides and inventories of archival material can be found in the FHLC under **Quebec/Archives.**

Biographies

Two collections of biographical information about Baptist ministers and laymen in Quebec can be found in the FHLC under **Quebec/Biographies.**

A helpful source concerning the settlers of the eastern townships is C. M. Day's *Pioneers of the Eastern Townships* (1863; rpt. ed., Montreal, Quebec: Page-Sangster Inc., 1973). (FHL# 971.46/D3d or microfilm 564367, item 3).

Lebel, Gerard. *Nos Ancetres: biographies d'ancetres* 2d ed. Quebec: La Revue, Sainte Anne de Beaupre, 1983). (FHL# 971.4/D31)

Census Records

There are many early census records for this province from the mid-1600s forward. Some of these are for limited areas. Most give only the head of the household between 1731 and 1842. The records from 1851 forward list all members of the family. The early records up to and including 1871 can be found in the FHLC under **Quebec/Census.** The records for 1881 and 1891 are found in the FHLC under **Canada/Census.**

Cemetery Records

Very few cemetery records of Quebec are held by the library. Some, mostly Protestant, can be found in the FHLC under the name of the county, parish, or town.

Church Records

The library has a very large collection of original Roman Catholic church records on microfilm as well as printed and indexed abstracts. There are also large collections of printed abstracts covering specific areas and time periods. Genealogical research in Quebec depends heavily on indexed and abstracted marriage records. Three extensive marriage indexes are listed below.

The Loiselle index covers the time period 1642 to 1963 and includes over a million marriages from 520 parishes. The index cards give the names of the bride and groom, the date of the marriage, and the name of the parish. If neither the bride or groom are widowed, the parents' names are given. If one of the party was widowed, it is necessary to find the record of the first marriage to obtain the parents' names. At the beginning of each reel of film is a list of the parishes indexed and a list of the abbreviations used.

The Revest index includes about a quarter million marriages in the period 1670 to 1972. The parishes indexed are in the Notarial Districts of Joliette, Saint-Jerome, Mont-Laurien, and Sorel, and two parishes in Richelieu.

The index is arranged first alphabetically by maiden name of the bride. Within the maiden name of the bride, the index is alphabetical by surname of the groom. Similar information is included on each entry as in the Loiselle index.

The third index includes records from the counties of Drummond, Sherbrooke, Stanstead, Richmond, Wolfe, Compton, Nicolet, Arthabaska, Megantic, and Frontenac. It includes marriages from the beginning of the parish registers up to 1970. It is arranged alphabetically by groom's surname and then by bride's maiden name.

These marriage indexes can be found in the FHLC under **Quebec/Church Records**. There is a guide to these indexes available at the library (Research Outline B982). These indexes, although quite extensive, are by no means complete. Other helpful sources are listed below.

Tanguay, Cyprien. *Dictionnaire genealogique des familles Canadiennes depuis la fondation de la colonie jusqu'a nos jours.* 1871; rpt. ed., Montreal: Editions Elysee, 1975. (FHL# 971/D2t or microfilm 105970-105972 or microfiche 6016466-6016495)

LeBoeuf, J. Arthur. *Complement au dictionnaire genealogique tanguay.* 3 vols. Montreal: Societte Genealogique

Canadienne-Francaise, 1957-64. (FHL# 971/D2t/suppls. 1-3 or microfilm 823824, items 1 and 2, and 496430, item 4)

Dictionnaire National Des Canadiens-Francais. 3 vols. Montreal: Institut Genealogique Drouin, 1977. (FHL# 971/D2i)

Jette, Rene. *Dictionnaire des familles Canadiennes des origines a 1730*. Montreal: Les Presses de l'Universite de Montreal, 1983. (FHL# 971.4/D2jr)

Talbot, Eloi-Gerard. *Genealogie Des Familles Originaires Des Comtes De Montomagny, L'islet, Bellechasse*. 16 vols. Chateau-Richer, Que.: The Author, n.d. (FHL# 971.4/D2t or microfilm 1006138 and 1006139 [vols. 1-10])

______. *Genealogie: Charlevoix-Saguenay*. 6 vols. Chateau-Richer, Que.: The Author, n.d. (FHL# 971.4/D2ta)

______. *Recueil de Genealogie: Beauce-Dorchester-Frontenac 1625-1946*. 11 vols. Beauceville, Que.: College du Sacre-Colur, 1949-55. (FHL# 971.4/D2tr or microfilm 844887 to 844889)

Repertoire des actes de bapteme, meriage, sepulture et des recensements du Quebec ancien. 30 vols. Montreal: Presses de l'Universite de Montreal, 1980. (FHL# 971.4/K22r). A guide to this is found in the supplement.

Protestant marriages, baptisms, and burials in the St. Francois Judicial District including the counties of Compton, Richmond, Stanstead, Wolfe, Sherbrooke and parts of Frontenac and Arthabaska can be found in the FHLC under **Quebec/Church Records.**

Emigration and Immigration

In addition to the records for the ports of Quebec City and Halifax cited previously in this chapter under *Canada, Emigration and Immigration*, some earlier records can be found in the FHLC under **Quebec/Emigration and Immigration.**

Gazetteers, Maps, and Atlases

These are found in the FHLC under each of the above headings, **Quebec/Gazetteers**, and under **Quebec/-[County]/Maps.**

Two very useful gazetteers are *Repertoire Toponymique Du Quebec* (Quebec, Commission de Toponymie Conseil evecutif Quebec, 1979) (FHL# 791.4/E5r) and Harmisdas Magnan, *Dictionnaire Historique et Geographique Des Paroisses, Missions et Municipalities De La Province De Quebec* (Arthabaska, Quebec: L'Imprimerie D'Arthabaska, 1925). (FHL# 971.4/E5m or microfilm 6016524-6016528).

Genealogy

Some genealogy sources have been cited previously in this section under *Biography* and under *Church Records*. Additional sources are cited here. A helpful guide to Quebec research is Ronald J. Auger's *Tracing Ancestors Through the Province of Quebec and Acadia to France* (Salt Lake City: Genealogical Society of the Church of Jesus Christ of Latter-day Saints, 1969). (FHL# 929.1/-W891/F6 or microfiche 6039358). Two other helpful guides to Quebec research are Jeanne Gregoire, *A la recherche de nos ancetres* (Montreal, Que.: Guerin, 1974) (FHL# 971.4/D27g) and Michael Langlois, *Cherchons nos ancetres* (Sillery, Que.: Federation Quebecoise du Loisir Scientifique, 1980). (FHL# 971.4/D271).

Bergeron, Adrien. *Le grand arrangement des acadiens au Quebec de 1625-1925*. 8 vols. Montreal: Editions Elysee, 1981. (FHL# 971.4/D3ba)

Godbout, Archange. *Vicilles familles de France en Nouvelle-France*. Quebec: Centre Canadien de recherches genealogiques, 1976. (FHL# 971.4/D2g)

Land and Property

Some land grants are listed on *List of Land Grants Made by the Crown 1763 to 1890* (Salt Lake City: Family History Library, 1964). (FHL# microfilm 413121 to 413122). The Seigniories grants are published in *Seigniories Grants 1674-1760* (Quebec: Quebec Legislature, 1853). (FHL# 971.4/R2s or microfilm 1036410, item 10, or microfiche 6046787).

Some additional land records can be found in the FHLC under **Quebec/Land and Property** and under each of the counties. The library has no seigneurial records.

Minorities

Records concerning the various ethnic and religious groups and their settlement in Quebec can be found in local histories and in the FHLC under **Quebec/-Minorities** and **Quebec/Native Races.**

Notarial Records

These records include marriage contracts, land transactions, and probate records. A long-term program for microfilming these records is in process by the library. These records will be found in the FHLC under **Quebec/Notarial Records.** The records are grouped by judicial districts which do not coincide with county boundaries.

Periodicals

Only a few outstanding periodicals are listed below. Others will be found in the FHLC under **Genealogy/Periodicals.**

L'Ancetre: Bulletin de la Societe de Genealogie de Quebec. 1974-to date. Quebec: La Societe. (FHL# 971.4/B2an)

Connections: Quebec Family History Society. 1978-to date. Pointe Claire, Que.: The Society. (FHL# 971.4/D25c)

L'Entraide genealogique: Organ official de La Societe Genealogique des Cantons de L'Est. 1978-to date. Sherbrooke, Que.: La Societe. (FHL# 971.4/D25e)

Memoires de la Societe Genealogique Canadienne-Francaise. 1944-to date. Montreal: La Societe, 1944. (FHL# 971/C45; Vols. 1-26 indexed)

United Empire Loyalists

The sources listed below will be found helpful.

Missisquoi Loyalist Legacies: Vol. 14. Stanbridg East, Que.: Missisquoi Historical Society, 1976. (FHL# 971.462/-B4ma)

Day, C. H. *Pioneers of the Eastern Townships*. N.p.: Page-Sangster, 1973. (FHL# 971.46/D34 or microfilm 564367, item 3)

Illustrated Historical Atlas of the Eastern Townships. 1881; rpt. ed., N.p.: Cumming Publishing, 1980. (FHL# Q971.4/E7i)

Flowers, A. D. *The Loyalists of Bay Chaleur*. Vancouver, B.C.: Precise Instant Printing, 1973. (FHL# 971.478/H2f)

Vital Records

Since 1679 the local Catholic priests were required to send copies of their records to the local civil archives, Palais de Justice. In 1760 this system was extended to include Protestants. The library has these records up to 1877. They can be found in the FHLC under **Quebec/-[County]/[Town or Parish]/Church Records.**

There is also a collection of marriage bonds for the period 1799 to 1842 with an index: *Nominal Card Index for the Lower Canada Marriage Bonds* (Salt Lake City: Genealogical Society of Utah, 1981). The bonds can be found in the FHLC under **Quebec/Civil Registration/Lower Canada Marriage Bonds** on four reels of microfilm. The index is on FHL# microfilm 1276179-1276180.

ONTARIO

Historical Background

1615	Samuel de Champlain and Etienne Brule explore southern Ontario.
1668	First Hudson's Bay Company station, Rupert's House, established on James Bay.
1673	Frontenac founds Cataragué near present site of Kingston.
1759	British capture Fort Niagara.
1763	Ontario becomes a British territory by the Treaty of Paris.
1783	About 10,000 United Empire Loyalists arrive; first land grants made.
1788	Southern Ontario divided into four districts: Hesse, Lunenburg, Mecklenburg, and Nassau.
1791	The province of Canada formed, making Lower Canada (Quebec) and Upper Canada (Ontario).
1792	The four original districts changed Hesse to Western, Lunenburg to Eastern, Mecklenburg to Midland, and Nassau to Home.
1796	Seat of government moves to York (now Toronto).
1812	War of 1812-14 with United States.
1815	Many immigrants arrive from Scotland and a large number settle in Lanark County.
1820-50	Large numbers of British immigrants arrive through the port of New York by way of the Erie Canal.
1841	Upper and Lower Canada are united to form the Province of Canada with Canada East (Quebec) and Canada West (Ontario).
1843	Parliament House burns, destroying many records.
1844	Old districts are abolished and counties are organized to perform their duties.
1857	Ottawa becomes the capital of Canada.
1867	Confederation to form Dominion of Canada.

The population of Ontario in 1840 was 430,000 people, mostly British. By 1867, at the time of the Confederation, the population had increased to about 1.5 million. In 1901 the population of Ontario was about 2.2 million.

Archives and Libraries

The provincial archives are located at Toronto. No general guide to the holdings of the archives has been published. A guide to the Regional Collection of the University of Western Ontario has been published: *Catalogue* (London, Ont.: The University of Western Ont., 1977). (FHL# 971.3/A5s).

Biography

Several important sources will be found in the FHLC under **Ontario/Biography.** Two outstanding sources are cited below.

Canadian Baptist Historical Society. *Biographical File.* 14 reels. Salt Lake City: Family History Library, 1969. See FHLC for call numbers.

Elliot, Noel M., ed. *People of Ontario.* 3 vols. London, Ont.: Genealogical Research Library, 1984. (FHL# 971.3/D22p) An index to people and families in censuses, county atlases, and histories and local histories.

Cemetery Records

Most cemetery records of Ontario will be found in the FHLC under the name of the city, village, or township in which the cemetery is located or for larger collections, under the name of the county. A large collection in seventeen volumes is *Cemetery Records of Ontario* (N.p.: n.pub, n.d.). (FHL# 971.3/V3cl or 6046793). This collection has an index to the cemeteries included but not to the names of people.

Census Records

There are various lists of inhabitants of specific places in Ontario dating from the latter half of the 1700s, but there is no general guide to locating them. The census records of Augusta Township in Grenville County for the years 1796, 1806, 1813, and 1824 are at the library on FHL# microfilm 182225.

The 1842, 1848, 1850, 1851, 1861, and 1871 census records of Ontario can be found in the FHLC under **Ontario/Census.** The records before 1861 are not complete for the entire province. The records for the 1881 and 1891 censuses of Ontario can be found in the FHLC under **Canada/Census.**

Some indexes are available for some of the censuses of Ontario for specific areas, but no complete index to the entire province is available for any census year. These indexes can be found in the FHLC under **Ontario/Census/Indexes** and under the names of the county or township to which they apply, such as **Ontario/Elgin/Malahide.**

The 1871 census is being indexed (transcribed) and published by the Ontario Genealogy Society as volumes are completed. A province-wide index is planned.

A valuable part of the census records is the agricultural schedules. These list the name of the land, land owner, and give the number of horses, etc., owned and the amount of beans produced, etc. The acres of land owned is given with its location by lot and concession number. These schedules are available at the library for some parts of the 1851 and 1861 censuses. The lot and concession numbers are important in using the land records.

Church Records

Most church records of Ontario will be found in the FHLC under the name of the county, township, or town where the church was located. The records of some churches that include larger areas can be found in the FHLC under **Ontario/Church Records.**

Court Records

The judgement dockets of the Court of Queen's Bench 1821 to 1881 and the records of the Supreme Court 1881 to 1937 are available at the library on FHL# microfilm 851369-851371. These records are indexed at the beginning of each volume. They include judgments of the Courts of Queen's Bench, Common Pleas, and Chancery.

Emigration and Immigration

In addition to the sources cited in this chapter under *Canada, Emigration and Immigration*, some records can also be found in the FHLC under **Ontario/Emigration and Immigration.** These consist primarily of records concerned with bonus funds given to emigrants 1862 to 1897. Some of these records are indexed and some are arranged alphabetically.

Gazetteers, Maps, and Atlases

These sources can be found in the FHLC under **Ontario/Gazetteers**, etc. and under the names of the counties. Many valuable county atlases are available at the library. These often give the names of land owners printed on the maps of the townships showing the land they owned.

Two very valuable aids to identifying places in Ontario are listed below.

Department of Mines and Technical Surveys. *Gazetteer of Canada - Ontario.* Ottawa.: The Department, 1962. (FHL# 971.3/E5c)

Carter, Floreen E. *Place Names of Ontario.* London, Ont.: Phelps Publishing Co., 1985. (FHL# microfiche 6332553)

Genealogy

Several important sources will be found in the FHLC under **Ontario/Genealogy.** Some valuable sources of information on early settlers are listed below.

Chadwick, Edward M. *Ontarian Families.* 2 vols. Toronto: Ralph, Smith and Co., 1895-98. (FHL# microfilm 1036587, item 10)

Pioneer Life on the Bay of Quinte. 1904; facsim. ed. Belleville, Ont.: Mika Publishing Co., 1976. (FHL# 971.3/D2p/1976 or microfilm 1033975)

Pringle, J. F. *Lunenburg, or the Old Eastern District.* 1890; rpt. ed., Belleville, Ont.: Mika Silk Screening Ltd., 1972. (FHL# 971.3/H21/1972 or microfilm 874425, item 4)

Canniff, William. *Settlement of Upper Canada.* 1869; rpt. ed., Belleville, Ont.: Mika Silk Screening, Ltd., 1971. (FHL# 971.3/H2c/1971 or microfilm 908363)

Herrington, Walter S. *History of the County of Lennox and Addington.* Toronto: Macmillan and Co. of Canada, 1913. (FHL# 971.359/H2h)

Cooper, C. W. *Frontenac, Lennox and Addington.* Ottawa, Ont.: Canadian Heritage Publications, 1980. (FHL# 971.3/H2cw)

A useful source of general help for the Ontario researcher is Don Wilson's compilation of *Readings in Ontario Genealogical Sources* (Ontario: Ontario Genealogical Society, 1978). (FHL# 971.3/D27c).

An excellent guide to genealogical research in Ontario which is currently being revised is Brenda D. Merriman's *Genealogy in Ontario: Searching the Records* (Ontario: Ontario Genealogical Society, 1985). (FHL# 971.3/-D27m).

Land Records

The land records of Ontario can be one of the most helpful sources of information to the family historian. They can also be one of the most difficult and confusing records to the user. Originally the province was divided into four districts. These original four districts were further divided from time to time, producing twenty districts by 1845. The district offices were responsible for most municipal and judicial functions. Although counties had been formed as early as 1792, their function was primarily as electoral divisions. The governmental responsibilities were gradually transferred from the districts to municipal councils and the districts were abolished in 1849.

The land of the original districts was surveyed into townships of more or less rectangular shapes. The boundaries of these townships have remained essentially constant, except for dividing some into two halves such as East and West or Upper and Lower or North and South. The counties were formed by aggregates of these townships. When new counties were formed, entire townships were taken from older counties; or if a township was divided, it was the East-West or Upper-Lower type of division. An excellent discussion of the districts and counties of Ontario with maps and charts is Eric Jonasson's "The Districts and Counties of Southern Ontario," *Families* 20, no. 2 (1981): 91-102 (FHL# 971.3/B2f). It will often be necessary for the researcher to determine the district or districts to which a given township originally belonged. Reference to the above article by Jonasson will be found helpful.

When the townships were originally surveyed, they were laid out in more or less rectangular shapes and divided into concessions by parallel lines running from one side of the township to the other. These concessions were further divided into lots of about 200 acres. The concessions and lots were assigned numbers or letters. Often irregular or triangular areas resulted which are called a gore.

The land records which are available at the library will be described below.

Ontario Archives Land Records Index (Ontario: Computrex, Ltd. 1979) is an index to the names of the original owners of the land, usually obtained by grant. This index includes the period 1780s to 1910 and has two parts, an index to names of people and an index by township. The name index is on FHL# microfiche 6330425-6330477. The township index is on FHL# microfiche 6330478-6330552. The index gives the following information when available: name of person, residence, location of land by township, lot, and concession, a date code (explained below), date of transaction, transaction type code (explained below), type of grant code (see below), type of lease/sale (see below), and archival reference. This index is derived from three groups of records at the Provincial Archives of Ontario, the Crown Land Papers, "RG-1", the Canada Company Papers, "C.C." and the Peter Robinson Papers, "MS-12." None of these records are at the Family History Library. The original records usually do not contain very much additional information of value to the genealogist. The most useful aspect of this index is to locate an individual on a specific piece of land, to date his or her arrival on the land, and to determine how he or she obtained the land.

The codes used in describing individual date identities are: 1-Location; 2-Assignment; 3-Patent; 4-Lease; 5-Sale; 6-Contract; 7-Deed; and 8-Order-in-Council.

The codes used in describing indivudual types of grants are: OR-Old Regulations; NR-New Regulations; FF-Full Fees; UE-United Empire Loyalist; SUE-Son of United Empire Loyalist; DUE-Daughter of United Empire Loyalist; MC-Military Claimant; COMM-Heir and Devisee Commission; M-Military; ME-Military Emigrant; LB-Land Board; FR-Peter Robinson Settler; SE-Scotch Emigrant; AA-Gratuitous (Hardship Grant); and V-Veteran (Fenian or Boer Wars).

The codes used in describing individual transaction types are: FG-Free Grant; L-Lease; S-Sale; and A-Assignment.

The codes used for describing individual types of leases or sales are: CL-Clergy Reserves; CR-Crown Reserves; SCH-School Reserves; and I-Indian Lands.

The Petitions for land grants are a rich source of genealogical information. The petitions (1791-1867) to Executive Council are at the Public Archives of Canada in Ottawa (RG1; L1 and L3). The index to these records is Public Archives of Canada, Index to Upper Canada Land Records in RG1 Series L1 and L3 (Ottawa: Public Archives of Canada, 1977. (FHL# microfilm 1205476-1205502). It may be found in the FHLC under **Ontario/Land and Property/Indexes.**

Another set of petitions to the Commissioner of Crown Lands (1827-60) is at the Provincial Archives of Ontario at Toronto in RG1 series C-1-1. These records are on microfilm at the library and are arranged alphabetically. They may be found in the FHLC under **Ontario/Land and Property**. Another set of records in this group is series C-1-2. These consist mostly of petitions of military claimants for service in the American Revolution and the War of 1812. They cover the period 1796 to 1844 and are included in the FHLC with the previously cited records.

Another set of records found in the FHLC with the above two sets are the records of C-1-3 listed as "fiats." These are the Orders-in-Council 1796 to 1804 for the Loyalist land grants. These are the Order in Council records used by William D. Reid in preparing his book *The Loyalists in Ontario* (FHL# 971.3/V2r), referred to later in this chapter under *Loyalists.*

Another set of land records which supplements the previously described records is the *Township Papers* which are at the library on 552 rolls of microfilm. These records may be found in the FHLC under **Ontario/Land and Property**. They include the time period of about 1783 to 1870. They are arranged alphabetically by name of the township. Within the township they are arranged by concession and lot number. In towns and villages they are arranged alphabetically by name of locatee.

The Heir and Devisee Commission records resulted from the establishment of this Commission in 1797 to resolve disputes and claims for ownership of land arising when the applicant for a deed was not the person to whom the land was originally assigned. These records are rich in genealogical information, especially concerning Loyalists and their heirs.

The records are divided into two sets and are found in the FHLC under **Ontario/Land and Property**. The first set is arranged by name of the district where the land was located. Within each district, the location certificates are arranged more or less alphabetically by surname of the original grantee. These records usually show the first transfer of the property and are useful in determining the second proprietor. The name of the second proprietor is necessary for using the second set of these records.

The second set of records is indexed by name of the second or later claimant to the land. The index to this set of records is on FHL# microfilm 1313779-1313782. Although William D. Reid used these records in the preparation of his book *Loyalists in Ontario*, much additional information may be found in the original records.

The district land office recorded patents when the land granted to an individual actually became his or her property. Subsequent transfers of the land to new owners were recorded as deeds. Mortgages and their discharge, and quit claim deeds were also recorded. When the counties evolved, this function was performed by the county land office. There are also deeds recorded at the township level and often separate sets of deed records for towns and villages.

The deeds of some districts, counties, townships, or towns occasionally have a *General Index* by name of grantor and grantee. Occasionally no general index exists, but separate indexes are found in each volume of deeds. There is usually an *Abstract Index* to deeds. These indexes are arranged first by township or village then by concession and lot number. They give a chronological account of the transactions pertaining to each lot with numbers referring to the deed (memorial) concerned.

The indexes and deeds can be found in the FHLC under **Ontario/[County]/Land and Property** or under the name of the township or town such as **Ontario/Norfolk/Charlotteville/Land and Property.**

The researcher will realize from the above discussion of land records the importance of identifying the land by township, lot number, and concession number. This identifying information may be obtained from searching the *Archives of Ontario Land Index*, the *Petitions*, the *Township Papers,* the *Heir and Devisee Commission* records, or the *General Indexes* to county and township deeds. Another source of this information is the agricultural schedules of the 1851 and 1861 censuses. The county atlases and histories may provide the necessary information. Many of these are indexed in the previously cited *People of Ontario* by Noel M. Elliot, ed. (FHL# 971.3/D22p).

Military Records

In addition to those cited in this chapter under *Canada, Military* and *United Empire Loyalists*, the following will be found helpful:

Read, Colin. *The Rising in Western Upper Canada 1837-8.* Toronto, Ont.: University of Toronto Press, 1982. (FHL# 971.3/H2r)

Periodicals

Some of the most helpful periodicals are:

Families. 1962-to date . Waterloo, Ont.: Ontario Genealogical Society. (FHL# 971.3/B2f)

The Ontario Register. 1968-to date. T. B. Wilson. (FHL# 971.3/B2or)

Western Ontario Historical Notes. 1942-to date. London, Ont.: University of Western Ontario. (FHL# 971.3/B2w)

Ontario Historical Society Papers and Records. 1899-1937. Toronto: The Society. (FHL# 971.3/B2o)

Probate Records

Most probate records will be found in the FHLC under the names of the counties, thus: **Ontario/[County]/Probate Records.** Wills which resulted in the distribution of land to the heirs were recorded at the land office as well as in the records of the surrogate court. Reference should also be made to the records cited previously in this section under *Ontario, Court Records*.

Another collection of probate records is the Upper Canada (Ontario) Court of Probate on forty-one reels of microfilm, 1793-1859. These are found in the FHLC under **Ontario/Probate Records.** Under this same heading in the FHLC will be found the probate registers of some of the old District Probate offices.

United Empire Loyalists

Cited below are only the most important sources dealing specifically with Ontario. The reader is referred to the section under *Ontario, Genealogy*. Additional sources will be found in the FHLC under **Ontario/-Minorities.**

Cruikshank, E. A. *The Settlement of the United Empire Loyalists on the Upper St. Lawrence and Bay of Quinte in 1784.* 1934; rpt. ed., Toronto, Ont.: Ontario Historical Society, 1964. (FHL# 971/H2u or microfilm 897095, item 3)

Reid, William D. *The Loyalists in Ontario*. Lambertville, N.J.: Hunterdon House, 1973. (FHL# 971.3/V2r or microfilm 823823 or microfiche 6046758)

The Old United Empire Loyalist List. 1885; rpt. ed., Baltimore, Md.: Genealogical Publishing Co., Inc., 1976. (FHL# 971.3/H2u/1976 or microfilm 982355, item 12)

Turner, Larry. *Voyage of a Different Kind*. Belleville, Ont.: Mika Publishing Co., 1984. (FHL# 971.3/H2t)

Vital Records

The registration of marriages in Ontario was provided for by law in 1793. The clergy sent copies of their marriage records to the old district clerks of peace. This system was improved by further legislation in 1857. This latter act resulted in the county marriage registers which were still dependent on the returns of ministers sent in to the clerk's office. This system continued until 1869 when the registration of births, marriages and deaths was taken over by the provincial government.

The district marriage registers of twelve districts are on microfilm at the library. They can be found in the

FHLC under **Ontario/Vital Records.** Notably absent from this collection are the registers of the Eastern and Western Districts. These can be found in the periodical *The Ontario Register* (FHL# 971.5/B2or), cited previously. *Eastern District Marriage Register* (Ottawa: Public Archives of Canada, 1967) can also be found on FHL# microfilm 928968, item 7.

The county marriage registers can also be found in the FHLC under **Ontario/Vital Records.** These are being abstracted and indexed by W. E. Britnell, *County Marriage Registers of Ontario* (Agincourt, Ont.: Generation Press, 1979-in process). (FHL# 971.3/V22m).

Ontario Registrar General, *Marriage Bonds* (Ottawa: Public Archives of Canada, 1963) for 1803-45 are on microfilm at the library. (FHL# microfilm 332403-332417) They have been abstracted and indexed by Thomas B. Wilson, *Marriage Bonds of Ontario* (Lambertville, N.J.: Hunterdon House, 1985). (FHL# 971.3/V29w).

Some coroner's inquest records are also available at the library. These can be found in the FHLC under **Ontario/Vital Records** and under the names of the counties such as **Ontario/Huron/Vital Records.**

THE PRAIRIE PROVINCES

Historical Background

1670	Hudson Bay Company formed.
1794	Fort Augusta established (later Edmonton).
1812	Thomas Douglas, fifth Earl of Selkirk, sponsors settlement by Scottish and Irish settlers along the Red River.
1843	British Columbia established as a royal province.
1858	British Columbia becomes a crown colony.
1866	Colonies of British Columbia and Vancouver united.
1869	Dominion of Canada purchases Rupert's Land from Hudson Bay Company.
1869-70	Reil Rebellion.
1870	Manitoba enters confederation.
1871	British Columbia enters confederation.
1873	Northwest Mounted Police organized.
1875	Northwest Territory Act and Homestead Act.
1876-78	Treaty with Indians for rights to Northwest Territory.
1882	Alberta and Saskatchewan become provinces.
1905	Alberta and Saskatchewan enter confederation.

Settlement and Migration

The prairie provinces consist of Manitoba, Saskatchewan, Alberta, and British Columbia. For purposes of this chapter, the Yukon and Northwest Territories are included.

This area of Canada was originally included in the lands granted to the Hudson Bay Company. The early settlement resulted from the fur trade, the discoveries of gold and other mining activities, and later by agricultural development. Settlement resulted from migration from the eastern provinces, from the United States, and from Great Britain and Europe. The population is largely British with major contributions by French Canadians from Quebec and by emigrants from Germany, Ukrainia, Iceland, Russia, and other European countries. The area was very sparsely populated until the latter part of the nineteenth century. The major growth in population occurred during the period from about 1880 to 1915.

The library has a very limited collection of research material for the prairie provinces. The reader is here reminded that many general sources cited in this chapter under the Dominion of Canada will be helpful for research in the western provinces. These provinces are divided into judicial districts and land registration districts rather than counties. Therefore, records will be found in the FHLC under the name of the province and under the name of the place. Maps showing the boundaries of the judicial districts and the land registration districts can be found in the previously cited book by Eric Jonasson, *The Canadian Genealogical Handbook* (FHL# 971/D27j).

The library has no provincial vital records of the western provinces. It is difficult to obtain copies of the original records from the provincial offices except from Manitoba, which sends photocopies. The abstracts furnished by the other provinces usually contain only a minimum of information. The cause of death is obliterated on a death certificate.

ALBERTA

Archives and Libraries

The Provincial Archives are located at Edmonton. Several inventories to the holdings of the archives will be found in the FHLC under **Alberta/Archives.**

Biographical and Local History

The library has a large collection of provincial and local histories. These will be found helpful although many of them are not indexed or not well indexed.

Cemetery Records

Some cemetery records will be found in the FHLC under **Alberta/Cemeteries**, but most will be found under the name of the place where the cemetery is located.

Census

The 1891 census of Canada includes Alberta and can be found in the FHLC under **Canada/Census.**

Church Records

Some Roman Catholic church records can be found in the FHLC under the name of the town or place where the church was located. Many church records of Alberta are available at the Provincial Archives.

Gazetteers and Maps

Several helpful maps are listed in the FHLC. The following gazetteers will be useful:

Holmgren, Eric J., and Patricia M. Holmgren. *2,000 Place Names of Alberta.* Saskatoon, Sask.: Western Producer Prairie Books, 1976. (FHL# 971.23/E5h)

Mordon, Ernest G. *Community Names of Alberta.* Lethbridge, Alta.: University of Lethbridge, 1973. (FHL# 971.23/-E2m)

Periodicals

Relatively Speaking. 1972-to date. Alberta Genealogical Society. (FHL# 971.23/B2r)

Vital Records

The FHLC has no vital records of Alberta.

BRITISH COLUMBIA

Archives

The Provincial Archives are located at Victoria. No inventory of their holdings is available at the library.

Biography and Local History

Many compilations of local history are available at the library. These frequently include biographical information on early settlers and genealogy.

Cemeteries

Some cemetery records will be found in the FHLC under **British Columbia/Cemeteries.** Most cemetery records are listed in the FHLC under the name of the town or place.

Census Records

The 1881 and 1891 Censuses are available at the FHLC and include British Columbia. The 1881 census has been indexed in Lorne W. Maine, *Index to the 1881 Canadian Census of British Columbia* (Vancouver, B.C.: The Author, 1981). (FHL# 971.1/X22m).

Church Records

Some church records will be found in the FHLC under **British Columbia/Church Records**, but most are listed under the name of the town or place.

Directories

The library has a significant number of directories for various areas of the province.

Gazetteers, Maps, and Atlases

Several helpful sources will be found in the FHLC under each of these headings. Two helpful gazetteers are the following:

Akrigg, George P. V. *1001 British Columbia Place Names.* Vancouver, B.C.: Discovery Press, 1973. (FHL# 971.1/-E5o)

Board of Geographical Names. *Gazetteer of Canada: British Columbia.* Ottawa, Ont.: Board of Geographical Names, 1953. (FHL# 971.1/E5c)

Periodicals

The British Columbia Genealogist. 1971-to date. British Columbia Genealogical Society. (FHL# 971.1/B2g)

This society has a large collection of indexed cemetery records and other sources which they will search for a fee. Contact the British Columbia Genealogy Society, P.O. Box 94371, Richmond, British Columbia V6Y 2A8.

Vital Records

The death and marriage registers of the Stikine District (1975 to 1932) are on FHL# microfilm 990523.

MANITOBA

Archives

The provincial archives are at Winnipeg. No printed guide to the holdings of the archives is available at the FHLC.

Biography and Local History

The library has a large collection of provincial and local histories which often contain much biographical information and family history. These may be found in the FHLC under **Manitoba/History** and under the names of the towns.

Cemetery Records

These are found in the FHLC under the name of the town where the cemetery is located.

Census Records

The Hudson Bay Company censuses of 1831-56 and the 1870 Census are on microfilm FHL# 1375923. Eric Jonasson has indexed the early census in *Surname Index to the 1870 Census of Manitoba and Red River* (Winnipeg: Wheatfield Press, 1981). (FHL# 971.27/X22j).

The 1881 and 1891 censuses can be found in the FHLC under **Canada/Census**. The 1881 census has been indexed by Ronald V. Jackson, et al. *1881 Manitoba* (Salt Lake City: Accelerated Indexing System, 1986). (FHL# 971.27/X22m).

Church Records

Most of these records will be found in the FHLC under the name of the town where the church was located. A few are listed under **Manitoba/Church Records.**

Gazetteers

Board of Geographical Names. *Gazetteer of Canada–Manitoba.* Ottawa: Board of Geographical Names, 1955. (FHL# 971.27/E5c or microfilm 897323, item 3)

Genealogy

The publication of the Manitoba Genealogy Society is *Generations,* 1976-to date. (FHL# 971.27/B2g) This society has a large collection of indexed cemetery records and other valuable sources which it will search for a fee. Contact Manitoba Genealogical Society, P.O. Box 2066, Winnipeg, Canada R3C 3R4.

Probate Records

The library is presently microfilming the Surrogate Court records and estate files of the judicial districts. These records can be found in the FHLC under **Manitoba/Probate Records.**

Vital Records

The library has no provincial vital records. The Manitoba Genealogy Society has indexed and abstracted vital records from newspapers for 1859-91: *An Index of Marriage and Death Notices from Manitoba Newspapers* (Winnipeg: Context Publications, 1986). (FHL# 971.27/V22i).

SASKATCHEWAN

Archives

The Provincial Archives are located at Regina. No general inventory of the holdings is available.

Biography and Local History

The library has a large collection of local histories which often contain much valuable information on persons and families.

Census Records

The 1891 census includes Saskatchewan and may be found in the FHLC under **Canada/Census.**

Cemetery Records

A large collection of indexed cemetery records made by the Saskatchewan Genealogy Society is available at the library (FHL# microfilm 1378991-1378998). Other records will be found under the name of the town where the cemetery is located.

Church Records

Most church records will be found in the FHLC under the name of the town. Some are listed under **Saskatchewan/Church Records.**

Gazetteers

Gazetteer of Canada: Saskatchewan. Ottawa, Ont.: Board on Geographical Names, 1957). (FHL# 971.24/E5c or microfiche 6051270)

Genealogy

The *Bulletin* of the Saskatchewan Genealogy Society is available at the library (FHL# 971.25/B2sa). A guide to research was prepared by the Saskatchewan Archives Board: *Exploring Family History in Saskatchewan* (Regina: The Archives, 1983). (FHL# 971.24/D27h).

Land Records

The homestead records (1870-1930) are available at the library with indexes. They may be found in the FHLC under **Saskatchewan/Land and Property.**

THE YUKON AND NORTHWEST TERRITORIES

The library has some gazetteers, directories, and local histories for these territories. The 1881 and 1891 censuses include the territories and are available at the library on microfilm. See FHLC under **Canada/Census.** There is an index to the first by Ronald V. Jackson, et al., *1881 Northwest Territories* (Salt Lake City: Accelerated Indexing System, 1986). (FHL# 971.92/-X22n).

Please note that there are excellent research outlines available for Canada in general and the provinces, compiled by Family History Library staff members, which should not be overlooked when doing research.

Records by Jurisdiction

Nova Scotia

Counties	Cemeteries	Census	Church History	Church Records	Genealogy	History	Land & Property	Maps	Probate Records	Town Records	Vital Records
Annapolis	•		•	•	•	•	•	•	•	•	•
Antigonish	•		•	•	•	•	•	•	•	•	•
Cape Breton	•	•	•	•	•	•	•	•	•	•	•
Colchester	•		•	•	•	•	•	•	•	•	•
Cumberland	•		•	•	•	•	•	•	•	•	•
Digby	•		•	•	•	•	•	•	•	•	•
Guysborough	•		•	•	•	•	•	•	•	•	•
Halifax	•	•	•	•	•	•	•	•	•	•	•
Hants	•			•	•	•	•	•	•	•	•
Inverness	•	•		•	•	•	•	•	•	•	•
Kings	•		•	•	•	•	•	•	•	•	•
Lunenburg	•			•	•	•	•	•	•	•	•
Pictou	•	•		•	•	•	•	•	•	•	•
Queens	•			•	•	•	•	•	•	•	•
Richmond	•	•		•	•	•	•	•	•	•	•
Shelburne	•			•	•	•	•	•	•	•	•
Victoria	•			•	•	•	•	•	•	•	•
Yarmouth	•			•	•	•	•	•	•	•	•

Records by Jurisdiction

New Brunswick

Counties	Cemeteries	Census	Church History	Church Records	Deeds	History	Marriage Records	Maps	Probate Records	Quit Rent	Taxation	Voting Records
Albert	•	•			•	•	•	•	•	•	•	•
Carleton	•		•									
Charlotte	•	•		•		•	•		•			
Gloucester			•	•	•	•	•		•	•		
Kent	•			•	•	•	•		•	•		
Kings	•			•			•	•	•	•		
Madawaska				•		•	•		•			
Northumberland				•		•	•		•		•	
Queens	•		•	•		•	•		•	•	•	•
Restiqouche				•			•		•			
St. John	•	•	•	•	•		•	•	•		•	
Sunbury	•	•	•	•		•	•		•			•
Victoria	•	•	•	•					•			
Westmorland	•	•		•	•	•	•	•	•	•	•	
York	•	•	•									•

Records by Jurisdiction

Quebec

	Archives	Biography	Cemeteries	Census	Church History	Church Records	Civil Registration	Genealogy	History	Maps	Notarial Records	Protestant Records
Aritibi					•	•		•				
Argenteuil			•		•			•			•	
Arthabaska					•	•					•	
Bagot					•	•			•		•	
Beauce		•			•		•	•				
Beauharnois					•	•		•				
Bellachasse					•	•	•					
Berthier					•	•						
Bonaventure					•			•			•	
Brome	•				•	•	•	•	•	•	•	
Chambly					•	•	•	•				
Champlain		•			•	•		•			•	
Charlevoix-East					•	•	•					
Charlevoix-West					•		•					
Chateauquay				•	•			•		•		
Chicoutimi		•		•	•							
Compton		•			•	•		•	•	•	•	
Deux-Montangnes					•			•	•			
Dorchester		•			•		•	•				
Drummond					•	•		•	•			
Frontenac		•			•		•			•	•	
Gaspe-East					•	•	•	•			•	
Gaspe-West					•	•	•	•				
Gatineau			•		•	•	•	•				
Hull		•	•		•		•					
Huntingdon					•			•	•			
Iberville				•	•	•	•	•				
Île de Montréal	•	•		•	•	•	•	•	•	•	•	
Île Jésus						•				•		•
Île de Madeleine						•	•				•	
Joliette						•		•	•			
Kamouraska		•				•	•	•	•			
Labelle						•						
Lac St. Jean		•				•	•		•			•
Laprairie					•	•	•		•			
L'Assomption						•	•				•	
Levis				•		•	•		•			
L'Islet						•	•	•	•			
Lotbinière			•			•	•		•			
Maskinongé						•	•		•			
Mantane						•	•		•			
Matapédia						•	•		•			
Mégantie			•			•	•	•				•
Missisquoi		•			•	•	•	•	•	•	•	•
Montcalm					•	•			•			
Montmagny						•	•	•	•			
Montmorency						•	•	•	•	•		
Napierville						•	•					
Nicolet						•	•	•	•			

Records by Jurisdiction — Quebec (cont.)	Archives	Biography	Cemeteries	Census	Church History	Church Records	Civil Registration	Genealogy	History	Maps	Notarial Records	Protestant Records
Papineau			•			•	•		•			•
Pontiac			•			•	•		•			•
Pontneuf					•	•	•	•				•
Quebec		•		•	•	•	•	•	•	•		•
Richelieu					•	•	•	•	•			
Richmond				•		•	•		•	•	•	•
Rimouski						•	•	•	•			•
Rivier du Loup						•	•		•			
Rouville						•	•			•		
Saguenay						•	•	•	•			
St. Hyacinthe				•	•	•	•	•	•			•
St. Jean						•	•		•		•	•
St. Maurice						•	•	•	•			•
Shefford		•				•	•		•	•	•	•
Sherbrooke		•		•	•	•	•		•		•	•
Soulanges					•	•	•					
Stanstead			•	•		•	•	•	•	•	•	•
Temiscaminque						•	•					
Temiscouata						•	•		•			
Terrebonne						•	•		•	•		
Vaudreuil			•		•	•	•					•
Vercheres				•		•	•		•			
Wolfe			•	•	•	•	•		•		•	•
Yamaska		•				•	•		•			

Records by Jurisdiction — Ontario	Atlases	Biography	Cemeteries	Church Records	Court Records	Deeds	Directories	Genealogy	History	Maps	Patents	Probate Records	Taxation	Township Records	Vital Records	Voting Registers
Algoma District			•	•					•			•				
Brant	•	•	•	•		•	•	•	•	•	•	•	•	•	•	•
Bruce	•	•	•	•		•	•	•	•	•	•	•	•	•	•	
Carleton	•	•	•	•	•	•	•	•	•	•	•	•	•	•	•	
Cochrane District			•	•					•			•				
Dufferin		•	•	•		•			•	•		•	•	•		
Dundas	•	•	•	•		•			•	•	•	•			•	
Durham	•		•	•		•	•		•	•	•	•			•	
Elgin	•	•	•	•	•	•	•	•	•	•	•	•	•	•	•	
Essex	•	•	•	•		•	•	•	•	•	•	•	•	•	•	
Frontenac	•		•	•		•			•	•		•			•	
Glengarry	•		•	•		•			•	•		•				
Grenville	•		•	•		•		•	•	•		•			•	
Grey	•	•	•	•		•	•	•	•	•		•	•	•	•	
Haldimand	•		•	•		•	•		•							
Haliburton		•				•			•	•		•				
Halton	•		•	•		•	•		•	•		•	•	•	•	
Hastings	•		•	•		•			•	•		•			•	
Huron	•	•	•	•		•	•		•	•		•	•	•	•	•
Kenora District				•					•			•				
Kent	•	•	•	•	•	•			•	•	•	•	•	•	•	
Lambton	•	•	•	•		•		•	•	•		•	•	•	•	•
Lanark	•		•	•		•			•	•		•	•	•	•	
Leeds	•	•	•	•		•		•	•	•		•	•		•	
Lennox & Addington	•	•	•	•		•			•	•		•			•	
Lincoln	•		•	•		•	•	•	•	•		•	•	•	•	
Manitoulin District				•												
Middlesex	•	•	•	•	•	•	•		•	•		•	•	•	•	•
Muskoka District			•	•					•	•						
Nipissing District				•					•	•						
Norfolk	•		•	•	•	•	•	•	•	•	•	•	•	•	•	•
Northumberland	•		•	•		•			•	•	•	•			•	
Ontario	•		•	•		•			•	•		•			•	
Oxford	•		•	•		•	•		•	•		•	•	•	•	•
Parry Sound District			•	•					•	•						
Peel	•		•	•		•	•	•	•	•		•	•	•	•	•
Perth	•		•	•		•			•	•		•	•	•	•	•
Peterborough	•	•	•	•		•			•	•		•			•	
Prescott	•			•		•			•	•		•	•		•	
Prince Edward	•	•	•	•		•			•	•		•			•	
Rainy River District			•	•					•			•				
Renfrew			•	•		•			•	•	•	•	•		•	
Russell	•		•	•		•				•		•			•	
Simcoe	•	•	•	•		•	•		•	•		•			•	
Stormont	•		•	•		•		•	•	•		•	•		•	
Sudbury District				•					•	•						
Thunderbay District			•	•					•							
Timiskaming District				•					•							
Victoria				•		•			•	•		•			•	

Chapter 15

England and Wales

Paul C. Reed, Johni Cerny, and Wendy L. Elliott

Historical Background

Early	Britons inhabit the island.
c.1000B.C.	Celts arrive in Britain.
c.100B.C.	Belgae settle in Britain.
57B.C.	Julius Caesar invades Britain.
c.410	Romans forced out of Britain.
c.415-500	Celts forced into western section of the island as the Angles, Jutes, and Saxons arrive in Britain and settle in East Anglia, Kent, Sussex, Wessex, Northumberland, and Mereia. Saxon heptarchy is established.
603	St. Augustine meets with Welsh bishops and Christianity begins to spread through the Saxon kingdoms.
c664	Death of the Briton Cadwallader ends Saxon and Celtic battle for supremacy in England. Celts retreat to modern day Wales and remain independent.
787	Danes descend on England.
867-878	Danes (Vikings) overrun and settle in Northumbria, East Anglia, Mercia, and Wessex, one by one and Danish law is established.
871-899	Alfred the Great defeats the Danes to rule in southwest England.
c.950	Saxons, Danes, and Jutes unite politically and are called Anglo-Saxons.
1066	Normans, led by William the Conqueror, conquer England and inaugurate vast changes.
1081	William the Conqueror invades Wales.
1086	Domesday Book, a census, is compiled.
1094	Welsh revolt against Norman invaders.
1097	William the Conqueror invades Wales again.
1134	People of Wales revolt again.
1204	British lose provinces of Anjou and Normandy to the French.
1215	King John is forced to sign the Magna Carta, granting national liberties.
1223-1301	Rights granted by the Magna Carta are confirmed.
1277-84	England conquers Wales.
1295	The Model Parliament organized.
1296	Scotland is defeated by English.
1337	The Hundred Years War begins.
1348-51	Black Plague ravages Britain; high mortality results in social reform for feudal laborers. Outbreaks continue every 15 years or so until the 1600s.
1362	English becomes the official language.
1381	Peasants revolt in London, resulting in the abolition of serfdom.
1497	John Cabot sails from England to Newfoundland to begin exploration of North America.
1529	Church of England established by Henry VIII.
1534	Church of England acknowledges the British monarch as "Supreme Head" of the Church of England.
1535	Parliamentary representation is given to Wales.
1536	Act of Union effects alliance of Wales and England.
1538	Henry VIII orders parish registers to be kept; partial compliance.
1553	Protestant persecution begins.

1559 During Elizabeth I's rule, the Church of England is again supreme.

1562 Elizabeth I supports French Huguenots.

1562 Slave trade with Africa begins.

1563 Persecution of Catholics increases.

1574 Last feudal vassals are freed from required labor for a master.

1584 English colonization begins at Roanoke, Virginia.

1588 British navy defeats the Spanish Armada.

1597 Poor Law is passed and parish becomes responsible for administration of it.

1610 Plantation system is established in Ulster, Ireland, allowing the seizure of Irish property.

1618 Beginning of the Thirty Years' War.

1620 Pilgrims form colony in Massachusetts.

1630 Puritans emigrate to New England.

1642-49 Civil War is fought to decide supremacy of Parliament or monarch; Parliament wins.

1649-60 The Commonwealth, headed by Oliver Cromwell, rules Britain.

1650s Society of Friends (Quakers) founded and expanded.

1665 Black Plague ravages London.

1666 London fire destroys large areas of city.

1672-74 War with Holland.

1682 William Penn organizes Society of Friends (Quaker) colony in Pennsylvania.

1701 Parliament passes the Act of Settlement.

1707 Parliament passes the Act of Union which establishes political union between England and Scotland.

1713 Treaty of Utrecht establishes supremacy of Britain in North America.

1715 Scottish Jacobites revolt.

1730s Methodists successfully proselyte in England.

1739 Britain declares war on Spain.

1755-63 Seven Years' War with France; France loses claims to overseas possessions.

1761 Canal is constructed between Worsley and Manchester; additional canals follow.

c.1763 Industrial Revolution begins in England.

1776 American colonies declare their independence.

1783 Revolutionary War in America ends; British lose vast colonial possessions in North America.

1793-1812 Napoleonic Wars continue for nearly twenty years.

1800 Parliament passes the Act of Union with Ireland.

1807 Slave trade with Africa is forbidden by law.

1812 United States declares war on Britain. British fight on two fronts: in Europe and in North America.

1814 Treaty of Ghent ends the War of 1812. United States secures hold on vast North American territory, but Britain maintains claim to Canada.

1818 Border between Canada and the United States is established as the 49th parallel.

1819 Manchester Massacre occurs.

1819 A British settlement is established in Singapore by the East India Company.

1824 First Burmese War begins and British take Rangoon.

1829 Catholics allowed freedom of worship.

1830 Agitators demand reform measures for workers.

1832 Upper-middle class men enfranchised for first time, doubling the number of voters.

1834 New law to aid the poor is passed by Parliament, and an educational system is established through Britain.

1834 Friction between China and Britain develops.

1836 Railway building booms, influencing the size and prosperity of towns.

1836 People's Charter organizes the first national working-class movement, demanding universal suffrage and elections by ballot.

1837 Vital statistics registration begins.

1838 First British-Afghan War begins.

1839 First Opium War begins between China and Britain.

1841 Britain declares sovereignty over Hong Kong.

1842 Treaty settles border dispute between Canada and United States.

1843-5 Maori revolts against British in New Zealand.

1846 Irish potato famine forces thousands to emigrate.

1849 British forces defeat Sikhs; Punjab is annexed by treaty.

1851 Immigrants to England from Scotland and Ireland; English move to United States, New Zealand, South Africa, and Australia.

1853 Peace is achieved between England and Burma.

1856 Britain annexes part of India and establishes Natal as a crown colony.

1857 Peace is achieved between England and Persians, but Britain captures Delhi, defeats Chinese navy, and with France conquers Canton.

1858 British declare peace in India.

1870 Married Women's Property Acts gives married women control of their property

	rights, whether obtained before or after marriage.
1874	British annex Fiji Islands.
1877	Rule over India established as Queen Victoria is proclaimed Empress of India.
1881	Britain loses Transvaal in Treaty of Pretoria.
1882	British occupy Egypt.
1884	Universal male suffrage for men over twenty-one.
1899	Boer War begins.
1900-01	Boxer uprisings occur in China.
1900	British claim Orange Free State and Transvaal, capture Pretoria and Johannesburg.

Settlement and Migration

England

Many aspects of early English immigration and migration are outlined in the above chronology. Migrations from others parts of the British Isles into England was easy and frequent at various periods. Uncomplicated movements between England and Scotland during the thirteenth century became difficult as conflicts between the two increased. Flemish weavers migrated to England during the thirteenth century. Welsh emigrants arrived in England during the Middle Ages and continued to migrate there through the centuries.

In the late sixteenth century, Irish peasants and beggars migrated to England, where a special Act of Parliament was passed in 1572 to authorize Irish repatriation shows. Wars in Ireland continued to promote emigration to the English ports of London, Liverpool, and Bristol. Irish colonies were formed in London.

During the early part of the seventeenth century, increased migration between England and Scotland was renewed. Beginning in 1603, many Scots left their homeland and moved to London, and, by 1707, larger groups of Scots headed for England, influenced by the lack of opportunity and poverty in Scotland. Some difficult Scottish surnames were Anglicized during these periods.

During the eighteenth century, immigration to England from Ireland continued to increase until it peaked during the Potato Famine in 1845-47. Later, this migration lessened as the Irish headed for the United States and Australia.

Refugees from political or religious strife also fled to England from several European countries. During the 1560s, persecution of Protestants in France drove thousands of French Huguenots to England, many of whom only remained a short period before emigrating to North America. Although France's policy towards its Protestants changed several times over the next few decades, emigration to Great Britain continued. The greatest numbers of French Huguenots arrived in England after 1685 when the Edict of Nantes was revoked. These French families settled in London, Westminster, Chelsea, Greenwich, Hammersmith, Hoxton, Islington, Bristol, Barnstaple, Bideford, Plymouth, Stonehouse, Dartmouth, and Exeter.

Other Protestants fled persecution in the Germanic provinces. Protestant Dutch and Flemings moved to England between 1540 and 1640. Many Dutch families settled in Norwich and London.

Jews settled in several English towns including London, Norwich, Lincoln, Canterbury, and York prior to 1290. Sephardic Jews fleeing the Spanish Inquisition arrived in England. By the 1730s, there were as many Ashkenazic as Sephardic Jews, and by the 1770s, the Ashkenazic far outnumbered their Sephardic brethren.

During the reign of Elizabeth I, a system of plantation by private enterprise was inaugurated to settle Britons in Ireland. Others were sent to Ireland to oversee and manage the rebellious Irish. Under James I, the plantation method was used to encourage Scottish Presbyterians and Englishmen to settle in Ulster. By 1622, over eight thousand families had migrated from England to Ulster under the Plantation system. Another large English emigration to Ireland occurred after Cromwell's confiscation of Irish property in 1652.

As the industrial revolution developed, individuals and families left the farmlands and rural villages for new homes in the cities. They moved to large towns and cities where jobs were available in the industrial and manufacturing companies.

Beginning in 1585, thousands of Britons emigrated to the colonies of Canada and America. Others migrated to Bermuda, Barbados, and the West Indies. In 1607, the first enduring settlement was made by Englishmen at Jamestown, Virginia. Pilgrims, religious refugees from Leyden, and others from England established colonies at Plymouth Bay in 1620. Puritans from the West Country, under the leadership of Rev. John White of Dorchester, left England for North America and settled at Massachusetts Bay in 1624. Hundreds followed over the next few years.

Quakers, members of the Religious Society of Friends, began leaving England in the 1650s. Some settled in New England, but because of persecution, most did not remain, but moved to more tolerant colonies. After 1681 when the Crown granted William Penn a large tract of land, the largest majority of Friends migrated to Pennsylvania.

Baptists from England joined Thomas Hooker in Rhode Island. Catholics settled in Maryland. Convicts were transported from Britain to America and Australia between 1787 and 1871. Under General Oglethorpe, Georgia was established as a penal colony for imprisoned debtors and others. Tasmania and New South Wales in Australia received as many or more convicts. Thousands of Royalist prisoners were sent to Barbados between 1645 and 1650. Other political prisoners were transported to Virginia after 1679 and the West Indies after 1685.

After Canada was obtained from the French at the conclusion of the Seven Years War in 1763, migrations to Nova Scotia and New Brunswick increased. By 1775, there were approximately fourteen thousand British residents, and by 1785, their numbers had increased to nearly thirty thousand.

About nine million individuals left Great Britain for the United States between 1815 and 1912. During this same period, about three million migrated to Canada. Between 1815 and 1840, nearly sixty thousand emigrated for Australia while about ten thousand moved to South Africa.

Wales

Wales is basically rural, sprinkled with small clusters of settlements and framed by its early tribal settlement patterns in the regions of fertile soil. Celtic monasteries were established soon after the collapse of the Roman Empire. An Anglo-Norman feudal system was initiated at the end of the thirteenth century. Because of political conditions and Welsh resistance, this system with its traditional villages was successfully established only along the eastern and southern borders.

Castle towns were introduced in Wales after the Norman Conquest of 1066. The Industrial Revolution six hundred years later provided a greater impetus to the creation of towns in Wales. Mining activities greatly increased the number of urban settlements around its two coal fields. Towns in South Wales developed as the steel and tinplate industries evolved and as coal shipping ports were established.

Migration began into Wales from the lowlands in Britain and continental Europe prior to the Roman invasion. Some Scandinavian invasions were made along the coastline; these were followed by those of Anglo-Saxons and Anglo-Normans along the borderlands between Britain and Wales.

England and Wales Library Collection

The majority of records in the English and Welsh collection were created at the local level by church and civil parishes and include parish registers (lists christenings, marriages, and burials), Bishops' Transcripts (transcribed duplicates of the original parish registers), Boyd's and Phillimore's marriage indexes, and Parish Register Print-outs. (Each of these record sources is discussed in detail under the heading *Church Records* later in this chapter.) Since these four sources are the most heavily used in English and Welsh research, a chart at the end of this chapter lists each parish within its county and denotes which of the four records is available for that parish in the Family History Library's collection.

Archives and Libraries

The library has a large number of titles under this heading in addition to those listed below: (See FHLC heading **England** or **Wales/Archives and Libraries** for a complete list.)

Collins, Lydia, comp. *Marriage Licenses: Abstracts and Indexes in the Library of the Society of Genealogists.* 2d ed. rev. London: The Society of Genealogists, 1983. (FHL# 942/K23c/1983)

Sims, Richard. *A Manual for the Genealogist, Topographer, Antiquary, and Legal Professor.* London: E. Avery, 1888. (FHL# 942/A2s, 929.1/Si58m, or microfilm 0599813, item 1)

Descriptions of public records, parochial and other registers, wills, county and family histories, and heraldic collections in public libraries.

Stevens, Henry, comp. *An Analytical Index to the Colonial Documents of New Jersey, in the State Paper Offices of England.* New York: Published for the Society by D. Appleton and Co., 1858. (FHL# 974.9/P2s or microfilm 1035899, item 3)

Thorpe, Thomas. *Description Catalogue of the Original Charters, Royal Grants, and Donations.* London: n.p., 1835 (FHL# 942/A5tho)

Archives and Libraries/Directories

Gibson, J. S. W. *Bishops Transcripts and Marriage Licenses, Bonds and Allegations.* Plymouth, England: Federation of Family History Societies, 1981. 2d rev. ed., 1983. Library has both editions. (FHL# 942/K23b and 942/K23b/1983)

Gibson, J.S.W., and Pamela Peskett. *Record Offices: How to Find Them.* Plymouth, Devon: Federation of Family History Societies, 1981. 2d rev. ed., 1983. Library has both editions. (FHL#942/J54g and 942/J54g, 1983)

Hutton, Barbara, and J. M. Wood. *Library Resources in Wales and Monmouthshire.* London: Library Association, 1967. (FHL# 942.9/J54l)

Library Association. *Libraries in the United Kingdom and the Republic of Ireland.* London: Library Association, 1975. (FHL# 942/A5lu)

A classified listing of all public libraries and selected academic polytechnic, national, government, and special libraries.

Archives and Libraries/Inventories, Registers, Catalogs

The library has a large collection of titles under this heading in the Family History Library Catalog (FHLC). This representative list of titles should be useful:

Analytical Catalogue of English Record Society Publications. Cambridge: Chadwyck-Healey, 1982. (FHL# 942/A3c)

Lists the title and price of more than 1300 volumes.

Bouwens, B. G. *Wills and Their Whereabouts.* London: n.p., 1939. (FHL# microfilm 1405482, item 10)

Catalogue of the Heralds' Visitations. London: S. & R. Bentley, 1825. (FHL# 942/D23bm or 0873528, item 5)

Includes references to many valuable genealogical and topographical manuscripts in the British Museum.

Cox, Jane. *The Records of the Prerogative Court of Canterbury and the Death Duty Registers.* London: Public Record Office, 1980. (FHL# 942.1/L1/U2cn)

A provisional guide, pending preparation of a more

complete guide to be published as a Public Record Office handbook.

Gibson, J. S. W. *Census Returns, 1841-1881 on Microfilm: A Directory to Local holdings.* 4th ed. Plymouth, England: Federation of Family History Societies, 1982. (FHL# 942/X2gi/1982)

______. *Unpublished Personal Name Indexes in Record Offices and Libraries: An Interim List.* Solihull, West Midlands: Federation of Family History Societies, 1986. (FHL# 942/A3gi)

List of India Office Records. Tumba, Sweden: International Documentation Centre A.B., 1976. (FHL# Asia Fiche Area 6031168-6031346)

Microreproduction of seventeen volumes of guides to the records in the India Record office, London, England. Includes records of consultations, proceedings, catalogs, factory records, general records, marine records, and reports.

Lists of Manor Court Rolls in Private Hands. London: Manorial Society, 1907-10. (942/A3lm)

"...being a series of indexes to the dates of such of those records as are in the possession of private individuals, or in the custody of the Stewards of Manors to which the rolls relate, or in that of corporate bodies, as distinguished from those Court Rolls which are preserved in the Public Record Office, the British Museum Library, and other public depositories of collections of manuscripts and other documents of antiquarian interests."

Public Record Office. *Lists of Non-Parochial Registers and Records in England and Wales, in the Custody of the Registrar General of Births, Deaths and Marriages.* Salt Lake City: Genealogical Society of Utah, 1964. (FHL# microfilm 0355544)

______. *Public Record Office Catalogue of Microfilm.* London: Public Record Office, 1967. (FHL# 942/A3p)

Microfilm of original records at the London Public Record Office.

Society of Genealogists (London). *Library Catalogue.* 9 reels. Salt Lake City: Genealogical Society of Utah, 1965. (FHL# microfilm 0417936-0417944)

Original card catalog of the Society of Genealogists in London. Includes family histories, county records, foreign titles, almanacs, military, marine, and mercantile records.

Bibliography

Among the lengthy list of bibliographic works, the following titles will be useful:

Kaminkow, Marion J. *A New Bibliography of British Genealogy.* Baltimore, Md.: Magna Charta, 1965. (FHL# 942/A3k)

Los Angeles County Public Library. *Card Index File, England.* Salt Lake City: Genealogical Society of Utah, n.d. (FHL# microfilm 0889254-0889257)

Microreproduction of typescript.

Biography

The library has sixty-nine biographical titles in its England collection. These will be useful to Americans tracing English immigrants and everyone researching medieval families:

Beltz, George Frederick. *Memorials of the Most Noble Order of the Garter, from Its Foundations to the Present Time.* London: W. Pickering, 1841. (FHL# 942/D3bel or microfilm 0824475, item 3)

Includes the history of the order, biographical notices of the knights in the reigns of Edward III and Richard II, the chronological succession of the members.

Burke, Sir John Bernard. *The Knightage of Great Britain and Ireland: A Concise View of Knighthood and Its Various Order, with Historical and Biographical Details.* Rev. ed. London: Edward Churton, 1842. (FHL# 942/D22bk or microfilm 0896641)

Chalmers, Alexander. *The General Biographical Dictionary.* Rev. ed. 32 vols. London: J. Nichols, 1812. (FHL# 920.042/C353g)

Historical and critical account of the lives and writing of "the most eminent persons in every nation; particularly the British and Irish." Each volume indexed separately. Volume 32 includes a general index. In alphabetical order.

Dictionary of Welsh Biography Down to 1940. London: n. pub., 1959. (FHL# GEN REF 942.9/K2da or Brit Fiche Area 6026369)

Gould, William, ed., with Laurence Urdang Associates. *Lives of the Georgian Age, 1714-1837.* New York: Barnes & Noble Books, 1978. (FHL# 942/D3liv/1714-1837)

Hoffman, Ann. *Lives of the Tudor Age, 1485-1603.* New York: Barnes & Noble Books, 1977. (FHL# 942/D3liv/1485-1603)

Riddell, Edwin, ed., with Laurence Urdang Associates. *Lives of the Stuart Age, 1603-1714.* New York: Barnes & Noble Books, 1976. (FHL# 942/D3liv/1603-1714)

Wagner, Henry. *Pedigrees of Huguenot Families and Materials.* London: Spottiswoode & Ballantyne, 1926. (FHL# 942/A1/no. 102)

Biography/Dictionaries

Stephen, Leslie, and Sidney Lee, eds. *Dictionary of National Biography.* 63 vols. London: Smith, Elder, 1885-1900. (FHL# 920.042/D561n or microfiche 6051261)

For other biographical titles, consult the FHLC under: **England** or **Wales/Biography, England** or **Wales/Biography/Dictionaries, England** or **Wales/Biography/Dictionaries/Periodicals, England** or **Wales/Biography/Indexes, England/Biography/Yearbooks.**

Business Records and Commerce

Titles under this heading discuss England's business history, economic and social history, industries, guilds, mining, navigation, mercantile, and other related subjects. All of the titles are histories, with a few bibliographic compilations. See the FHLC heading **England** or **Wales/Business Records and Commerce, England** or **Wales/Business Records and Commerce/Bibliography, England** or **Wales/Business Records and Commerce/-History, England** or **Wales/Business and Commerce/-Inventories, Registers, Catalogs.**

Cemeteries

Most cemetery records consist of transcribed tombstone inscriptions taken from local burial sites, cemeteries, and church graveyards. The library has more parish registers, which also list burial dates, than cemetery records. Consult the FHLC under **England** or **Wales/[County]/[Town/Parish]** for the library's local holdings and **England** or **Wales/Cemeteries** for collections of epitaphs, discussions about monumental brasses and inscriptions, histories of monuments, and miscellaneous inscriptions.

Census Records

England has enumerated its population every ten years since 1801, except for 1941. The first census of genealogical value was taken in 1841 in England and Wales. Privacy laws prohibit the release of census schedules until 100 years after the enumeration; thus, the 1881 census is the latest available for public use.

Census Returns of Great Britain, 1841 on 365 reels covers England, Wales, the Isle of Man, and the Channel Islands. It includes the following information about those enumerated: name of place (parish, hamlet, village, town, borough, etc.); some street or house numbers; names of persons present in the household when the census was taken (however, relationship to the head of the household is not stated); age and sex, ages for those above fifteen are rounded down five years, thus, someone listed as age thirty-five could have been between thirty-five and thirty-nine (those over sixty are sometimes rounded down ten years); occupation, profession, or rank; birthplace (people born in the county of enumeration have a notation "yes," if born elsewhere in England or Wales, "no," and if born in Scotland, Ireland, or other foreign country the name of the country if given); and enumerators' marks: / is entered at end of household; // is entered at the end of each building.

For call numbers to this census, see *Register of Great Britain Census, 1841* (Salt Lake City: Genealogical Society of Utah, 1967) located at the British Register Tables and the "Street Index, 1841 Census of England and Wales," 3 vols. located at the same table.

The 1851, 1861, 1871, and 1881 enumerations, taken the first week in April, are included in the library's collection and give the following information: name of place: parish, hamlet, village, town, borough, etc.; number or name of house, street, road, etc. (house numbers in rural areas are omitted at times); names of those present in the household when the census was taken; relationship of each person to the head of household; marriage status; age and sex; occupation, profession, or rank; birthplace (the place and county are listed for birthplaces in England and Wales, if elsewhere, the country is listed); and notations of physical and mental debilities (1871).

Census Office. *Census of England, Wales, and the Channel Islands, 1851.* 1370 reels. Salt Lake City: Genealogical Society of Utah, 1949-58. 1370 reels.

_____. *Census of England, Wales, and the Channel Islands, 1861.* London: Filmed by the Public Record Office, n.d.

Not cataloged in the March 1987 edition of the FHLC. See *Alphabetical Index to 1841-1881 Census of England, Wales, Isle of Man, and Channel Islands.* (FHL# Brit Ref Table 942/X2pi). Center libraries have this computer print-out on microfiche; however, no microfiche call numbers are currently available. See the Center Director for guidance. As a further challenge, this census was microfilmed in reverse order starting with the last page of each district.

_____. *Census of England, Wales, and the Channel Islands, 1871.* Salt Lake City: Genealogical Society of Utah, n.d.

Not listed in the March 1987 edition of the FHLC. See *Alphabetical Index to 1841-1881 Census of England, Wales, Isle of Man, and Channel Islands.* (FHL# Brit Ref 942/X2pi or microfiche available at center libraries. No microfiche call numbers currently available. See the Center Director for guidance).

_____. *Census of England, Wales, and the Channel Islands, 1881.* London: Public Record Office, 1982.

Not listed in the March 1987 edition of the FHLC. See index of call numbers (unpublished computer print-out) "Alphabetical Index to 1841-1881 Census of England, Wales, Isle of Man, and Channel Islands," January 1987. (FHL# British Register Table 942/X2pi, BRIT BOOK AREA, or microfiche available at center libraries). No microfiche call numbers currently available. See the Center Director for guidance.

Church of Jesus Christ of Latter-day Saints, Genealogical Department. *Census Surname Index Register.* Salt Lake City: British Reference Section, 1985. No call number. See British Register Table.

Lists all parishes and those census years for which an index is available. A red star by microfilm numbers listed in the "Alphabetical Index to the 1841-1881 Census of England, Wales, Isle of Man, and Channel Islands" indicates that a surname index exists for that parish. Call numbers are included in the *Census Surname Index Register.*

Consult the FHLC under **England/Census/1851/Indexes** for the contents included in "Census of 1851 Street Addresses: An Index to Streets and Other Addresses Used in the 1851 General Census of England," an unpublished register (FHL# BRIT REF/Q/942/X2ib/-1851).

A similar street index exists for the 1861 census (no call number, located at the British Register Table), 1871 census, 16 vols., (FHL# 942/X2ce), and the 1881 census, 21 vols., (FHL# BRIT REF/Q/942/x22r).

Consult the FHLC under **England/Census/[Year]/-Indexes** for other titles.

Census – Handbooks, Manuals, Etc.

Boreham, John M. *The Census and How to Use it.* Essex, England: Essex Society for Family History, 1983. (FHL# 942/X27b)

McLaughlin, Eve. *The Censuses, 1841-1881, Use and Interpretation.* Solihull, West Midlands: Federation of Family History Societies, 1985. (FHL# 942/X27m)

Church History

Adair, John Eric. *Founding Fathers: The Puritans in England and America.* London: J. M. Dent, 1982. (FHL# 973/-K2a)

Black, Kenneth MacLeod. *The Scots Churches in England.* Edinburgh: William Blackwood and Sons, 1906. (FHL# 942/K2bk)

Burrage, Champlin. *The Early English Dissenters, 1550-1641.* 2 vols. 1912; microreproduction, Salt Lake City: Genealogical Society of Utah, 1974. (FHL# microfilm 0990481, item 5 and 0990482, item 1)

Currie, Robert. *Churches and Churchgoers: Patterns of Church Growth in the British Isles since 1700.* Oxford: Clarendon Press, 1977. (FHL# 942/K2cg)

Davis, J. *History of the Welsh Baptists from the Year Sixty-three to the Year One Thousand Seven Hundred and Seventy.* Gallatin, Tenn.: Church History Research and Archives, 1982. (FHL# 942.9/K2da)

Dodd, A. H. *The Background of the Welsh Quaker Migration to Pennsylvania.* Salt Lake City: Genealogical Society of Utah, 1970. (FHL# microfilm 0832243, item 5)

Microreproduction of original.

Royal Commission on the Historical Monuments of England. *An Inventory of Nonconformist Chapels and Meeting-houses in Central England.* London: Her Majesty's Stationer's Office, 1986. (FHL# 942/K2nc)

Leary, William, and John Vickers, comps. *A Methodist Guide to Lincolnshire and East Anglia.* Bognor Regis, West Sussex: World Methodist Society British Section, 1984. (FHL# 942/K2lw)

Mackennal, Alexander. *The Story of the English Separatists.* London: Congregational Union of England and Wales, 1893. (FHL# 942/K2mac or microfilm 1426149)

Norman, Edward. *Roman Catholicism in England: From the Elizabethan Settlement to the Second Vatican Council.* Oxford: Oxford University Press, 1986. (FHL# 942/K2ne)

Pattison, S. R. *The Religious Topography of England.* London: The Religious Tract Society, n.d. (FHL# 942/K2pa)

Consult the FHLC under **England** or **Wales/Church History, England** or **Wales/Church History/Periodicals,** and **England** or **Wales/Church History/Sources** for a complete list of holdings on this subject.

Church Records

The parish is the smallest unit of both church and civil administration in England and Wales. In some parts of England, ancient parishes had jurisdiction over a large geographical area. Administration within large parishes became cumbersome as the population increased and divisions within those parishes, called chapelries, were made to perform christenings, marriages, burials, and other sacraments. Chapelry records were forwarded to the parish where, in some parishes, they were copied into one register; others were maintained separately.

The FHLC will refer you to the parish under which the records are cataloged if they are not cataloged under the chapelry itself; however, you should look for entries under both the parish and chapelry to find complete holdings.

Parish registers, bishops' transcripts, and marriage licenses are the three church records that offer the most genealogical information. Thomas Cromwell, vicar general to Henry VIII, ordered that every marriage, christening, and burial in a parish be recorded beginning 5 September 1538.

Sixty years later under Queen Elizabeth I, parishes were ordered to copy the early entries from paper onto parchment, but a loop-hole in the directive allowed some scribes to copy only those entries made after 1558 when her rule began. As a result, many parish registers begin in 1558. Transcripts of the registers made the previous year were to be sent to the bishop within a month after Easter beginning in 1597. Most parishes, but not all, stopped forwarding bishops' transcripts until 1837 when civil registration began.

The library has a separate register for Welsh Bishops' Transcripts (FHL# British Register Table 942.9/V27b). It lists the parish/locality, volume, years covered, and microfilm numbers.

Both parish registers and bishops' transcripts have gaps due to fire and loss, but sometimes you can use one to fill gaps by the other. It's a good idea to check both whenever possible. The only time when most parishes failed to maintain registers was from 1648 to 1660, the Commonwealth period.

Lord Hardwicke's Marriage Act of 1754 required that all marriages be performed in the parish church or parochial chapelry except those involving Jews and Quakers. All other marriages performed by Nonconformists and Roman Catholics were considered illegal. The act also demanded that all marriages be preceded by the posting of banns or by licensing, that minors obtain parental consent, and that registers of banns be kept.

The Genealogical Department of the Church of Jesus Christ of Latter-day Saints began extracting baptisms and marriages from English and Welsh parish registers during the 1960s for inclusion in the International Genealogical Index (IGI) (see Chapter 2 of this book for a complete discussion of the IGI). Those parishes included in the extraction program are listed in the *Parish and Vital Records Listing* that accompanies each copy of the IGI (no call number). A printed copy of the *Listing* is available at the British Reference Desk. Parish register print-outs were available in bound volumes until 1978. After that date, print-outs were produced on microfilm only. The early printed copies have been microfilmed and are cataloged in the FHLC under the heading **England** or **Wales/[County]/[Parish]/Church Records-Indexes.**

Baptisms. Information recorded in English parish registers varies from place to place, but generally, pre-1812 baptism entries give the name of the child, the father's name, the mother's name, and the date of the baptism. Some registers offer the father's occupation, the parents' residence, and the child's birth date.

Printed forms used after 1812 list eight baptisms per page and include the child's given name, the parents' given names, father's surname, occupation, residence, and sometimes address, and the name of the person who baptized the child.

Marriages. Generally, marriage entries made prior to 1754 give the names of those being married, the date of the ceremony, and sometimes a notation of residence or parentage. After 1754, printed marriage registers give the names of those being married, prior marital status, the parishes they attend, and the groom's occupation. Each entry is signed by the couple, two or more witnesses, and the minister. It will also indicate if the marriage was by license or banns.

Few original marriage licenses remain in existence today; however, registers of licenses and banns have survived and can be searched for additional information. Here is a sample entry:

> *Oakley, Sussex. Banns Published between Godfrey Paine, bachelor of this parish and Sarah Lacey, of this parish, spinster, on three Sundays in January 1814.*

Marriage allegations are sworn statements attesting to the fact that canon law has been observed and that no legal impediment exists to the proposed marriage. Two bondsmen were required to post securities; usually one was the groom and the other a relative. Allegations give the names of the bride and groom, their marital status, ages, occupations, places of residence, and the place they were married. All social classes are found in license and allegation registers.

Welsh Marriage Bonds and Allegations is a register guide compiled by the Cataloging Department in 1968. It includes the parish/locality, years covered, and film number.

A very useful index to marriage records was compiled under the direction of Percival Boyd, an English genealogist, between 1925 and 1955. He and his associates compiled an index of every marriage (where possible) (an estimated 7 million marriages, approximately 15% of the total number of marriages performed nationwide) in 4,200 parishes in England between 1538 and 1837.

Boyd's work is arranged in three series, each of which must be searched. The first series is arranged in order of county. Series two is nationwide. After Boyd died in 1955 there were still over a million entries that had not been included in the first two series. The Family History Library Staff arranged them alphabetically and microfilmed them. See FHLC heading **England/[County]/Church Records-Indexes** for first series holdings and call numbers. See FHLC heading **England/Church Records-Indexes** for series two and three.

A helpful guide showing which parishes within each county have been indexed and the time period they cover is "A Key to Parishes Included in Boyd's Marriage Indexes," compiled by Claire T. Wells of the British Reference Department, located in the British Reference Area of the Family History Library (FHL# 942/K22b or microfilm 0874304, item 2). It is not listed in the FHLC.

William Phillimore Watts Phillimore produced transcripts of marriage records which are completely indexed. See *Phillimore's Parish Register Series of Marriages and Some Banns in England and Ireland Arranged in Counties* compiled by Ronald Cunningham for the Genealogical Society in 1977 (FHL# 942/V25ph or microfilm 0990269, item 2) for a complete guide to the library's Phillimore collection and call numbers.

The *Register of Marriage Indexes for Great Britain* (FHL# 942/K23rm) is another handy guide compiled by the library staff in 1985. It lists marriage indexes compiled by individuals other than Phillimore and Boyd and explains how to order index searches from England.

Burials. English burial entries prior to 1812 offer limited information, usually the name and burial date only. With so little information, it is sometimes difficult to identify the deceased well enough to establish a firm relationship to a family. When printed registers came into use in 1812, clergy began recording residence and age at death.

Parish registers, bishops' transcripts, parish register print-outs, and Boyd's Marriage Indexes are listed under each parish. Consult the FHLC under **England** or **Wales/[County]/[Parish]/Church Records** for titles and call numbers. Charts following this chapter designate those parishes for which the library has any or all of the above four record groups.

Those in England and Wales who belonged to a denomination other than the Church of England were called Nonconformists – a blanket term which included Roman Catholics, Baptists, Congregationalists (also called Independents, Presbyterians, Unitarians, Quakers, Jews, and Methodists). The Church of England was predominant in England, but over half the population of Wales was Nonconformist.

On the whole, most Nonconformist denominations kept very few and poor records, except for Quakers and Jews. Lord Hardwicke's Act of 1754 requiring all Christian marriages except for Quakers to be performed in a parish was designed to eliminate unregistered marriages and to force other denominations to register births and burials as well. Thus, between 1754 and 1836 all marriages except those of Quakers and Jews had to be performed by Church of England clergy to be legally recognized.

All Nonconformist records were supposed to have been forwarded to the Registrar General in 1837; however, the Catholics sent only seventy-nine registers and the Quakers refused to send theirs until 1857. Other denominations were more compliant, but even so there are missing registers for every group. They were transferred to the Public Record Office. The library has a microfilm copy of every Nonconformist register at the Public Record Office. Consult the FHLC under **England** or **Wales/[County]/[Parish]/Church Records** for listings of Nonconformist records.

Some Welsh bishops' transcripts and other church records are cataloged under **Wales/Church Records**.

Civil Registration

All births, marriages, and deaths occurring in England and Wales after 1 July 1837 were required to be registered with the state within six months of the event. Not everyone immediately complied with the law, especially those living in rural areas. Thus, it is not unusual to find some events unrecorded. The country was divided into regions, registration districts, and sub-districts to facilitate registration. There were 623 registration districts in 1851.

The library does not have copies of any original birth, marriage, or death certificates in its collection, but it has a microfilm copy of the complete index covering 1837 through 1980. At the main library, you can obtain applications for birth, marriage, and death certificates at the British Reference Desk, enter information included in the index, and send it to the Registrar General at St. Catherine's House, London, with the required search fee. For a smaller fee, the library will forward it. Since fees depend on currency exchange rates, they change frequently but are posted at the British Reference Desk. All certificates must be paid for at the time the request is made.

Civil Registration Indexes exist for each quarter's records and are strictly alphabetical by surname. Researchers must be creative in determining all surname spelling variants. The index gives the person's name (surname first), registration district, volume number, and page number, all of which are required to order a certificate. It is important to cross-check the marriage indexes for the bride and groom to make certain the volume and page numbers match.

For help in using the indexes and determining which county or counties is represented in each volume number, see *A Guide to the Arrangement of the Registration Districts Listed in the Indexes to the Civil Registration of England and Wales,* rev. ed. (Salt Lake City: Genealogical Department, 1977). (FHL# 942/V2icr/1977, microfilm 0990269, item 4, or microfiche 6020287, item 2). Some registration districts are difficult to read in the original index and the guide, compiled by the library staff, is useful in interpreting handwritten entries. Beginning in 1866, the death indexes list the age of the deceased.

Entries are grouped according to the time the event was registered, not the date of the event. Some events were registered more than a year later after they occurred. A professional rule of thumb is to search up to three years after the event. If you have any reason to suspect that family information about a person's dates may be incorrect, expand the search several years earlier as well as later. Certificates will list the exact date of the event as it was given to the registrar.

See also "Index to Civil Registration Births 1907-1980, Deaths and Marriages 1904-1980" for the call numbers of films added to the collection after 1977. This volume is available at the British Register Table (no call number).

Registrar General. *Index to the Civil Registration of Births, Marriages, and Deaths for England and Wales, 1837-1980.* 1316 reels. Salt Lake City: Genealogical Society of Utah, 1978-86.

For film numbers, consult the FHLC under **England** or **Wales/Civil Registration-Indexes.** Also helpful is the Genealogical Department's *Guide to Genealogical Society Film Numbers for the Index to Civil Registration of England and Wales, 1837-1907* (Salt Lake City: Genealogical Department, 1977). (FHL# 942/V22c).

For other civil registration holdings, such as births, marriages, and deaths at sea, consult the FHLC under **England** or **Wales/Civil Registration**.

Court Records

Since the Norman Conquest (1066), England and Wales have created more court records than any other civilization in history; however, only a small percentage of those records are available outside of the Public Record Office in London. England functioned under the common-law system, meaning that branches of the government, including the court system, developed without preformulated design. There is no comprehensive guide to English court records, but the following guide will explain briefly the court system's development, organization, and records:

General Registrar. *Guide to the Contents of the Public Record Office.* 3 vols. London: Her Majesty's Stationery Office, 1963. (FHL# Ref 942/A2pg)

Volume 1 includes records of the Exchequer, Court of King's Bench, Justices Itinerant, Assize, and Gaol Delivery, etc., Clerks of Assize, Central Criminal Court, Court of Common Pleas, Alienation Office, Supreme Court of Judicature, Court of Requests, Court of Star Chamber, Court of Wards and Liveries, Palace Court, King's Bench Prison, Fleet Prison, and Marshalsea Prison, High Court of Admiralty, High Court of Delegates, Judicial Committee of the Privy Council in Appeals from Ecclesiastical and Admiralty Courts, Court of Bankruptcy, Principality of Wales, Palatinate of Chester, Palatinate of Durham, Palatinate of Lancaster, Duchy of Lancaster, Court of Honour of Peveril, Office of Queen Anne's Bounty, Copyright Office, Stationer's Hall, Special Collections, Key to Regnal Years with Chronological Index to Statutes Cited in the Text, Index of Persons and Places, Index of Subjects.

Volume 2 is a guide to State and Departmental Papers.

Volume 3 is a guide to Documents Transferred 1960-1966.

Some court records have been transcribed and are available at the library, along with miscellaneous calendars, indexes, and general information. See FHLC heading **England** or **Wales/Court Records** and **England** or **Wales/Court Records – Indexes.** The library continues to acquire microfilm copies of English and Welsh court records which include poor law records, civil suits between commoners, and other miscellaneous actions involving commoners and upper classes. Because they offer information about the common people they are important to genealogical research. Most of these records are being cataloged and are yet to appear in the FHLC. Those already cataloged can be located under the FHLC heading **England** or **Wales/[County]/Court Records.** See also **Wales/Court Records – Indexes.**

Directories

Among a sizeable number of English and Welsh directories, the following are particularly useful:

District Register Offices in England and Wales. East Yorkshire, England: Family History Society, 1985. (FHL# 942/-E4ew)

London Kalendar or City and Court Register. London: Printed for H. Woodfall, n.d. Issued in several editions, some volumes on microfilm, including 1752, 1756, 1765, 1775 and intermittent years from 1779 to 1862. (FHL# 942/E4cc or microfilm 0924276-0924285 and 0990338, item 1)

Norton, Jane E. *Guide to the National and Provincial Directories of England and Wales, Excluding London, Published before 1856.* London: Offices of the Royal Historical Society, 1950. (FHL# 942/C4rg/no. 5)

Royal National Commercial Directory of North and South Wales, Monmouthshire, Shropshire and the Cities of Bristol and Chester. Manchester, England: Isaac Slater, 1880. (FHL# 942/E4na or microfilm 0845456, items 1-2)

Consult the FHLC under **England** or **Wales/Directories** for additional titles.

Emigration and Immigration

Ashton, Elwyn T. *The Welsh in the United States.* Hove: Caldra House, 1984. (FHL# 973/F2ae)

Dodd, A. H. *The Character of Early Welsh Emigration to the United States.* 2d ed. Cardiff: University of Wales Press, 1957. (FHL# 973/A1/no. 139 or microfilm 1036619, item 12)

Letters from Welsh Emigrants to America, 1843-1922. Salt Lake City: Genealogical Society of Utah, 1970. (FHL# microfilm 0829054, item 3)

Microfilm of National Library of Wales manuscript number 19331E.

Emigration and Immigration – Bibliography

A First List of References Relating to Emigration from Wales to the United States of America. Salt Lake City: Genealogical Society of Utah, 1978. (FHL# 1036629, item 2)

Banks, Charles Edward. *The English Ancestry and Homes of the Pilgrim Fathers.* 1929; rpt. ed., Baltimore, Md.: Genealogical Publishing Company, 1968. (FHL# 974/W2be/1968)

______. *The Planters of the Commonwealth: A Study of the Emigrants and Emigration in Colonial Times, 1620-1640.* 1930; rpt. ed., Baltimore, Md.: Genealogical Publishing Company, 1975. (FHL# 944/W3bf, 1975)

______. *Topographical Dictionary of 1885 English Emigrants to New England, 1620-1650.* 1937; rpt. ed., Baltimore, Md.: Genealogical Publishing Company, 1981. (FHL# 974/W2ba/1981)

Published from notes after Banks's death. It was not intended to be his final product and must therefore be used as a finding tool only.

Church and Civil Records, c.1400-1864. 39 reels. Salt Lake City: Genealogical Society of Utah, 1981-82.

Includes settlement examinations and lists of French emigrés. See **England/Emigration and Immigration** for call numbers.

Coldham, Peter Wolson. *Bonded Passengers to America.* 9 vols. in 3. Baltimore, Md.: Genealogical Publishing Company, 1983. (FHL# 973/W3c)

Hargreaves-Mawdsley, R. *Bristol and America, A Record of the First Settlers in the Colonies of North America, 1654-1685.* 1929; rpt. ed., Baltimore, Md.: Genealogical Publishing Company, 1970. (FHL# 973/W3b/1970)

Hotton, John Camden. *Our Early Emigrant Ancestors: The Original List of Persons of Quality, Emigrants, Religious Exiles, Political Rebels, Serving Men Sold for a Term of Years, Apprentices, Children Stolen, Maidens Pressed, and Others Who Went from Great Britain to the American Plantations, 1600-1700.* 1880; rpt. ed., Baltimore, Md.: Genealogical Publishing Company, 1982. (FHL# 973/W2h, 1968)

Gazetteers

See also **England** or **Wales/Names, Geographical.**

Bartholomew, John. *Gazetteer of the British Isles.* 9th ed. Edinburgh: Bartholomew, 1943. (FHL# 942/E5ba/1943)

Cassell's Gazetteer of Great Britain and Ireland. 6 vols. London: Cassell, 1894-98. (FHL# BRIT REF 942/E5ca or microfilm 0599360-05990361 and 0924936, items 1-2)

Lewis, Samuel. *A Topographical Dictionary of Wales.* 2 vols. London: S. Lewis, 1833. (FHL# 942.9/E5l/1833, microfilm 0599780, items 2-3, or microfiche 6026723)

The library also has 1838, 1840, 1844, 1848, and 1850 editions. See FHLC heading **England** or **Wales/Gazetteers** for call numbers.

Wilson, John Marius. *The Imperial Gazetteer of England and Wales.* Edinburgh: A. Fullarton, c.1870. (FHL#942/E5i, microfilm 0897325-0897327, or microfiche 6020308-6020327)

See FHLC heading **England** or **Wales/Gazetteers** for other titles included in the collection.

Genealogy

The library has an enormous collection of titles for this subject that pertain to England and Wales. See Chapter 28, "Medieval Families," for a discussion of titles available for that time period. English and Welsh family histories are listed in the Surname FHLC. Also see:

Ancient Welsh Pedigrees. Aberystwyth: Reproduction Systems,

1970. Microfilm of manuscript number 1388 at the National Library of Wales. (FHL# microfilm 0827882, item 1)

Bartrum, Peter C. *Welsh Genealogies, 300-1400.* [Cardiff]: University of Wales Press, c.1980. (FHL# microfiche 6025561-6025616)

Glenn, Thomas Allen. *Welsh Founders of Pennsylvania.* 2 vols. in 1. 1911-13; rpt. ed., Baltimore, Md.: Genealogical Publishing Company, 1970. (FHL# 974.8/F2g/1970)

Howard, Joseph Jackson, and Frederick Arthur Crisp. *Visitation of England and Wales.* 14 vols. London: Frederick Arthur Crisp, 1896-1921. (FHL# 942/D23hn or microfilm 0824457-0824461)

Manuscripts of Genealogical Value in the National Library of Wales. 48 reels. Salt Lake City: Genealogical Society of Utah, 1959. (FHL# microfilm 0250407-0250430)

See also **England** or **Wales/Genealogy–Bibliographies, England** or **Wales/Genealogy–Directories.**

Genealogy–Handbooks, Manuals, Etc.

FitzHugh, Terrick V. H. *The Dictionary of Genealogy.* Totowa, N.J.: Barnes and Noble Books, 1985. (FHL# BRIT REF 942/D26f)

Gardner, Davis Ensign, and Frank Smith. *Genealogical Research in England and Wales.* 3 vols. Salt Lake City: Bookcraft, 1956-64. (FHL# 929.142/G172g)

Hamilton-Edwards, Gerald Kenneth Savery. *In Search of Welsh Ancestry.* London: Phillimore; Baltimore, Md.: Genealogical Publishing Company, 1986. (FHL# 942.9/D27h)

These are only a few of the many titles on this subject. See **England** or **Wales/Genealogy–Handbooks, Manuals, etc.** for a complete list. Other titles related to genealogy are cataloged under **England** or **Wales/Genealogy–Indexes, England** or **Wales/Genealogy–Inventories, Registers, Catalogs, England** or **Wales/Genealogy-Periodicals**, and **England** or **Wales/Genealogy–Sources.**

Genealogy–Indexes

Index to Welsh Genealogies. Salt Lake City: Genealogical Society of Utah, 1950. (FHL# microfilm 0104370, item 5)

Microfilm of manuscript number 1890 at the National Library of Wales.

Handwriting

Bowen, John T. *Welsh: A Course for Beginners.* New York: David McKay, 1960. (FHL# 942.9/A8b)

Contains lessons, keys to exercise, tables of parts of speech, a map of Wales, a Welsh-English vocabulary list, and an index.

Heraldry

Burke, Sir John Bernard. *The General Armory of England, Scotland, Ireland and Wales.* London: Harrison, 1884. (FHL# 942/D24b/1884)

Fox-Davies, Arthur Charles. *A Complete Guide to Heraldry.* 1909; rpt. ed., New York: Bonanza Books, 1978. (FHL# 942/D6fo)

Wagner, Sir Anthony Richard. *Heraldry in England.* London: The King Penguin books, 1946. (FHL# 942/D6wag)

A brief introduction to heraldry for the beginner.

See also **England** or **Wales/Heraldry** for a complete list of holdings. The content of most heraldry books is similar; browse through the collection to find a book that suits your needs.

History

The library has a vast collection of English and Welsh historical titles. It is important to check FHLC heading **England /[County]/History** for references to the collection created as *The Victoria Histories of the Counties of England,* one of which was written for each English county. Wales is not included. Yorkshire's entry, for example, would be:

Page, William, ed. *The Victoria History of the County of York.* 3 vols. London: A. Constable, 1907-13. (FHL# 942/H2vy or microfilm 0908359-0908360, item 1)

Here are some representative titles, but see **England** or **Wales/History** for a complete list:

Caradoc of Lhancarvan. *The History of Wales: Comprehending the Lives and Succession of the Princes of Wales from Cadwalader the late King.* London: Printed for John Sener, 1702. Photocopy of the original. (FHL# 942.9/H2ca)

Dodd, A. H. *A Short History of Wales: Welsh Life and Customs from Prehistoric Times to the Present Day.* London: B. T. Batsford, c.1972. (FHL# 942.9/H2dah)

Evans, E. D. *A History of Wales, 1660-1815.* Cardiff: University of Wales Press, c.1976. (FHL# 942.9/H2wh)

Jones, Gareth Elwyn. *Modern Wales: A Concise History, 1845-1979.* Cambridge: Cambridge University Press, 1984. (FHL# 942.9/H2jg)

Owen, G. Dyfnallt. *Elizabethan Wales: The Social Scene.* Cardiff: University of Wales Press, 1964. (FHL# 942.9/-H2ow)

Roderick, A. J. *An Outline Course in Medieval Welsh History with Bibliography.* London: Historical Association, 1967. (FHL# 942.9/A1/no. 6)

See also **England** or **Wales/History–Bibliography, England** or **Wales/History–Chronology, England** or **Wales/History–Indexes, England** or **Wales/History–Inventories, Registers, Catalogs, England** or **Wales/History–Periodicals,** and **England** or **Wales/History–Sources.**

Land and Property

Land and property records are not used widely in British research, perhaps because they are not generally available. Two sets of tax records are valuable to the researcher: (1) the hearth tax records, made between 1662 and 1674, arranged by place, and listing the number of hearths for which the householder was taxed; and (2) the land tax redemption office quotas and assessments records created between 1798 and 1914, but listing only landowners. Since it was an unpopular tax, many evaded the tax and their names do not appear in the records.

Many medieval court and taxation records are cataloged in the FHLC under the **/Land and Property**; thus, you should check all three headings for applicable titles.

Most of the entries in the FHLC for **Wales/Land and Property** are not national in scope but deal with county or local jurisdictions. See those headings for a complete list of holdings.

Maps

The library has an extensive collection of national maps; however, county maps are most useful to the genealogist. See **England** or **Wales/[County]/Maps** and **England** or **Wales/[County]/[City/Town/** or **Parish]**. On the British Register Table is an untitled and uncataloged binder containing lists of maps that may or may not appear in the FHLC.

Merchant Marine

Private shipping companies created merchant marine records. They are not as complete or informative as Royal Navy records and deal primarily with seamen and ships. Merchant marine operations were required to keep muster rolls beginning in 1747. These rolls include names of seamen and others employed on the ship, their place of residence, and the date they signed onto the ship.

"Merchant Marines," an unpublished guide prepared by the British Reference staff in 1979, is located at the British Register Table. It includes explanations and flow charts that will guide you through merchant marine records.

Among the library's holdings are:

Board of Trade, Mercantile Marine Department. *Agreements and Crew Lists of British Merchant Vessels, 1857-1860.* 1748 reels. Ashridge Park, Hertford: Genealogical Society of Utah, 1970-74.

See **England/Merchant Marine** for call numbers. Original records in the Public Record Office, Ashridge Park, Hertfordshire. Includes names of ships and crewmen's service records, with an alphabetical and numerical index to ships.

Trinity House Petitions, c.1787-1854. 57 reels. Salt Lake City: Genealogical Society of Utah, 1964. (FHL# microfilm 0395554-0395610)

Original records in possession of the Society of Genealogists, London. An alphabetical listing of those who applied for a pension between 1787 and 1854.

See also **England** or **Wales/Merchant Marine-Bibliography, England** or **Wales/Merchant Marine-History.**

Military Records

Military records in England and Wales consist mainly of Army and Navy records. Prior to 1640, England would call men to perform military service as need arose, but a standing army was established after that year. It was not until 1707 that the army included men from all of the British Isles. Until 1855 the army was without central coordination; thus, a standardized record-keeping system did not exist.

You must know the exact name of the regiment in which a person served to search the applicable record group. Only between 1873 and 1900 can searches be made without knowing the regiment.

Commissioned officers generally came from the upper classes and were required to purchase a commission. Enlisted soldiers were commoners. Both groups served for life or until discharged or retired. They are found in the following military records: soldiers' documents, regimental description and succession books, muster books and pay lists, army lists, records of officers' services, and certificates of birth, baptism, marriage, and death, to name a few.

Some navy records are dated as early as 1660, but the majority start in the 1700s. They include ships' musters, service engagement books, warrant officers and seamen's services, bounty papers, and officer's papers.

The library has two registers that are helpful in locating British military records:

"Army Records: A Guide to Finding Soldiers in the Army and Militia Records," was compiled by the British Reference Staff in 1978. It tells you how to find the name of a regiment, the name of a soldier, and how to locate and search the various military records. An uncataloged and unpublished guide, it is located in a binder on the British Register Table.

"Militia Records," also prepared by the British Reference Staff (no date or call number) discusses militia records and records of officers. It is located at the British Register Table.

Once you know the soldier's regiment, the following military records and others will be useful in obtaining more information:

Admiralty of Great Britain. *Continuous Service Engagement Books (Adm. 139), 1853-1896.* 923 reels. Salt Lake City: Genealogical Society of Utah, 1973.

See **England/Military Records** for call numbers. Original records in the Public Record Office, Ashridge Park, Hertfordshire. These books give the date and place of birth, physical characteristics on entry, and a summary of the service of each rating (rank). Also includes an alphabetical index of surnames, giving the individual's continuous service number.

War Office. *Artillery Records of Services of Non-commissioned Officers and Men of the Royal Artillery and the Royal Horse Artillery, 1765-1906.* 107 reels. Salt Lake City: Genealogical Society of Utah, 1971.

See **England/Military Records** for call numbers. Consists of description books, records of service, registers of marriages and baptisms, registers of deceased soldiers, and miscellaneous records of transfers and pension records. Original records in the Public Record Office, London. Service records contain the name, age description, place of birth, trade, dates of service and promotion of each soldier, with the dates of marriage and discharge or death.

_____. *Certificates of Birth, Baptisms, Marriage and Death, 1776-1881, with Bundles of Similar Certificates, 1755-1908.* 156 reels. Salt Lake City: Genealogical Society of Utah, 1971.

See **England/Military Records** for call numbers. Original records in the Public Record Office, London. Include wills, administrations, statements of services and personal papers of officers and their families, alphabetically arranged.

_____. *List of Records of Disbanded Militia Regiments for Transmission to the Custody of the Master of the Rolls.* 141 reels. Salt Lake City: Genealogical Society of Utah, 1973-74. See **England/Military Records** for call numbers.

_____. *A List of the General and Field Officers as They Rank in the Army, 1754-1778.* 28 vols. London: Printed for J. Millan, n. d. (FHL# microfilm 0852023-0852031)

Microfilm of printed volumes, some updated with handwritten changes and additions, located in the Public Record Office, London, and in the Genealogical Society of Utah.

_____. *A List of the Officers of the Army, 1779-1878.* 100 vols. London: n. pub., 1779-1878.

Microfilm of printed volumes, some updated with handwritten changes and additions, located in the Public Record Office, London; the Archives Office of Tasmania, Hobart; and the Genealogical Society of Utah. See **England/Military Records** for call numbers.

_____. *Record of Officers Services, 1771-1919.* 96 reels. Salt Lake City: Genealogical Society of Utah, 1973.

Microfilm of manuscript W.O. 76 in the Public Record Office. See **England/Military Records** for call numbers. Contains lists of different ranks held by officers with date and place of birth, marriage, and children.

_____. *Registers of Out-pensioners of the Army and of the Militia, 1759-1863.* 13 reels. Salt Lake City: Genealogical Society of Utah, 1971.

Original records filmed at the Public Record Office, London. See **England/Military Records** for call numbers.

_____. *Royal Artillery Service Documents of Soldiers (W.O. 97), 1760-1854.* 125 reels. Salt Lake City: Genealogical Society of Utah, 1972. 125 microfilm reels.

Original records filmed at the Public Record Office, London. See **England/Military Records** for call numbers. Contain name, age, birthplace and trade or occupation on enlistment, service record, including any decorations, and the reason for discharge or pension.

_____. *Soldiers' Documents, 1760-1900.* 1256 reels. Salt Lake City: Genealogical Society of Utah, 1971.

Original records in the Public Record Office, London. See **England/Military Records** for call numbers. Arranged by regiment and include the militia to 1854.

_____. *War Office Registers, [Late 1700's-1900].* 202 reels. Salt Lake City: Genealogical Society of Utah, 1971.

Original records at the Public Record Office, London. See **England/Military Records** for call numbers. Include commission, appointments, descriptions, returns of service, casualties, half pay, pensions, and gratuities.

See also **England/Military Records – Army, England/MilitaryRecords – Bibliography, England/-MilitaryRecords – Directories, England/Military Records – Handbooks, Manuals, etc., England/Military Records – History, England/Military Records – Indexes, England/Military Records – Inventories, Registers, Catalogs, England/Military Record – Law and Legislation, England/Military Records – Periodicals,** and **England/Military Records – Sources.**

Names, Personal

Welsh people used patronymics until the sixteenth century when they began to take surnames. For an excellent guide to Welsh surnames see:

Morgan, T. J. *Welsh Surnames.* Cardiff: University of Wales, 1985. (FHL# 942.9/D4m)

English surnames derived differently than Welsh; the best discussion currently available is:

Bardsley, Charles Wareing Endell. *A Dictionary of English and Welsh Surnames.* 1901; rpt. ed., Baltimore, Md.: Genealogical Publishing Company, 1967. (FHL# 942/D4b or microfilm 0856106, item 2)

See **England/Names, Personal** for additional titles.

Naturalization and Citizenship – Indexes

Denization and Naturalization Lists, 1801-1873. Salt Lake City: Genealogical Society of Utah, 1970. (FHL# microfilm 0824514, item 2)

Originals in the Public Record Office, London, Class C, 66 patent rolls in the records of the Chancery Court, England.

Records give names of persons who obtained acts of naturalization from the legislature during 1801-1900 (dates given in the title are incorrect), certificates of naturalization, and index to names.

Page, William. *Letters of Denization and Acts of Naturalization for Aliens in England, 1509-1800.* 4 vols. Lymington, England: [Huguenot Society of London], 1893-1932. (FHL# 942.1/L1/B4h or microfilm 0824513-0824514, item 1)

Newspapers

Since newspapers are printed locally, they are cataloged in the FHLC under **England** or **Wales/[County]/Newspapers** or **England** or **Wales/[County]/[City** or **Town]/Newspapers.**

Nobility

See Chapter 28, "Medieval Families," for a discussion of this subject and the library's collection. See also

England or **Wales/Nobility, England** or **Wales/Nobility-Genealogy,** and **England** or **Wales/Nobility-History.**

Occupations

Guilds in England and Wales are similar to unions in the United States. People had to belong to a guild to work in a particular field or occupation. Guild records are found on a national level, but also on a county basis. See **England** or **Wales/Occupations** and **England** or **Wales/[County]/Occupations.**

Public Record Office. *Apprenticeship Books of Great Britain from the Records of the Board of Commissioners.* 34 reels. Salt Lake City: Genealogical Society of Utah, 1970.

Original records at the public Record Office, London. See **England/Occupations** for call numbers.

______. *Apprenticeship Books (Indexes) of Great Britain from the Records of the Board of Commissioners, [1710-1811].* 15 reels. Salt Lake City: Genealogical Society of Utah, 1965.

Microfilm of original records at the Guildhall Library, London. See **England/Occupations-Indexes** for call numbers.

Periodicals

The library has a large collection of English historical and genealogical periodicals on a national and local level. See **England** or **Wales/Periodicals, England** or **Wales/Periodicals-Bibliography, England** or **Wales/-Periodicals-Directories, England** or **Wales/Periodicals-Genealogy, England** or **Wales/Periodicals-History,** and **England** or **Wales/Periodicals-Indexes** for the long list of holdings.

Probate Records

Before you can search English or Welsh wills effectively, you will need to understand the organization of ecclesiastical and probate jurisdictions.

English wills were proved in Ecclesiastical Courts prior to 1858. After that date the country was divided into civil probate districts and records created in those districts have been housed at the Principal Probate Registry, Somerset House, Strand, London WC2R 1LP. However, it's the pre-1858 wills that are used the most by genealogists and family historians.

It is difficult to determine which court had jurisdiction over a probate matter during the pre-1858 period because of the complexity of the Ecclesiastical Courts system. The following is a brief analysis of how the Church of England is organized:

Parish-the smallest unit in the system, headed by a vicar or rector.

Rural Deanery-a geographical area consisting of approximately twelve parishes, headed by a rural dean.

Archdeaconry-comprised of a number of rural deaneries, headed by an archdeacon.

Diocese-comprised of several archdeaconries, headed by a bishop.

Province-comprised of several Dioceses, headed by an archbishop. (Until 1920 there were two archbishop-one in Canterbury and the other in York. The Archbishopric of Wales was created in 1920.)

Probate courts served all of the divisions of the Church of England outlined above. The courts involved include:

Peculiars-the smallest probate division, consisting of one parish, several parishes spread over a vast area, a manorial court, universities and colleges, cities, and towns.

Rural Deans-only exercised probate jurisdiction when commissioned by the archdeacon or bishop.

Archdeacon's Courts-exercised jurisdiction if the property involved was within the boundaries of a single Archdeaconry. If the property did not exist within one Archdeaconry, the Bishop exercised jurisdiction.

Bishop's Diocesan or Consistory Courts-granted probates where property involved was in more than one archdeaconry, but within the same diocese.

Archbishop's Courts-two courts granted probate when property was located in more than one diocese:

The Prerogative Court of Canterbury (PCC) granted probates in all counties not covered by the Prerogative Court of York (PCY). Estates with property in more than one province were under the jurisdiction of the PCC, as were the estates of those who died overseas. People of social status and wealth often used the PCC rather than the lower court with jurisdiction.

The Prerogative Court of York (PCY) granted probates in Cheshire, Cumberland, Durham, Lancaster, Northumberland, Nottingham, Westmorland, and York.

Understanding these jurisdictions is challenging to the novice researcher; however, the Genealogical Society has prepared a series of guides to English probate jurisdictions county by county. These guides are located in binders at the British Register Table.

Each English county binder has a map showing probate boundaries and a table of probate jurisdictions that will lead you to the courts that had jurisdiction over probates. This table will also tell you the order in which the courts should be searched. Each volume includes a glossary of abbreviations and terms, a list of printed probate records for the county at the library, a summary of filmed records, and a detailed description of each microfilm included under the court headings. Here is an example of how they are cataloged:

Church of Jesus Christ of Latter-day Saints. *Hand List of Probate Jurisdictions in Essex and Filmed and Printed Probate Records Pertaining to Essex in the Genealogical Society Library, Volume 12.* Salt Lake City: The Genealogical Society of Utah, 1970. (FHL# REGISTER 942/S2ha, #12)

Welsh probate jurisdictions are treated in a single binder at the British Register Table. Another binder deals with the Prerogative Court of Canterbury which has had probate jurisdiciton over all of England and Wales since 1858. These binders contain the same sources as the English binders.

The only probate records kept on a national basis before 1858 were those created by the Prerogative Court of Canterbury. After 1858 all courts were consolidated into the Principal Probate Registry.

See "Register of Great Britain Principal Probate Registry Calendar of Wills and Administrations, 1858-1957," compiled by the British Reference Staff in 1964 at the British Register Table (FHL# 942/S2cp). This is only an index, but the original records are being filmed and will be available in the future. Until then, they can be obtained from the Principal Registry of the Family Division, Somerset House, The Strand, London WC2R 1LP, England for between $2 and $3. Payments should be made to the H. M. Paymaster General in pound sterling.

The Family History Department of the Church of Jesus Christ of Latter-day Saints is abstracting every name appearing in original Welsh wills for all probate courts from their beginning to 1858. The entire project is on microfiche, divided by court and year. It includes an index of testators by parish or town, an index of testators by surname, and a separate index by given name, an abstract of each will, a general index by surname, and a general index of males by given name.

The abstracts themselves give the name of the testator, the call number of the film, residence, date of probate, occupation, will number, date of death, persons and places mentioned in the will, relationship to the testator, occupation and residence of those mentioned, properties mentioned, executors, bondsmen, witnesses, and other information.

See **England** or **Wales/Probate Records** for a list of other probate-related titles. See also **England** or **Wales/Probate Records – Dictionaries, England** or **Wales/Probate Records – Handbooks, Manuals, etc., England** or **Wales/Probate Records – Indexes, England** or **Wales/Probate Records – Inventories, Registers, Catalogs,** and **England** or **Wales/Probate Records – Sources.**

Public Records

Titles cataloged under this heading include police activities, prisons, statutes, state papers, and indexes of patentees, among others. See **England** or **Wales/Public Records, England** or **Wales/Public Records – Bibliography, England** or **Wales/Public Records – Handbooks, Manuals, etc., England** or **Wales/Public Records – History,** and **England** or **Wales/Public Records – Indexes.**

Taxation

As early as 1290, Englishmen paid a tax to the crown recorded in subsidy rolls. The first major nationwide tax was the hearth tax, which listed all heads of households and the number of fireplaces/heated rooms in their homes. The tax began in 1662 and was phased out due to unpopularity in 1689. It was followed by the window tax from 1696 to 1851, but few records for this tax exist today. Various taxes followed; however, the library has few tax records for the later periods.

To locate English tax records at the library, see **England** or **Wales/Taxation** or **England** or **Wales/-[County]/Taxation** first. Many hearth tax lists are published in periodicals; the published sources are listed in "An Inventory of Genealogical Sources in the English Collection of the Family History Library, Salt Lake City." The guide, undated and uncataloged, is located in the British Reference Area. See Chapter 28, "Medieval Families," for an additional discussion of how to use this guide.

England
* COUNTY / SHIRE

PARISH	PARISH REGISTERS	BISHOPS' TRANSCRIPTS	BOYD'S MARRIAGE INDEX	PR PRINT-OUTS
BEDFORD*				
Ampthill	•	•		•
Arlesey	•	•		•
Aspley Guise	•	•		•
Astwick	•	•		•
Barton-in-the-Clay	•	•		•
Battlesden	•	•		•
Bedford	•	•	•	•
Biddenham	•	•		•
Biggleswade	•	•		•
Billington	•	•		
Biscott	•			
Bletsoe	•	•		•
Blunham	•	•		•
Bolnhurst	•	•		•
Bromham	•	•		•
Caddington	•	•		•
Campton	•	•		•
Cardington	•	•		•
Carlton	•	•		•
Chalgrave	•	•		•
Chellington	•	•		•
Clapham	•	•		•
Clifton	•	•		•
Clophill	•	•		•
Cockayne-Hatley	•	•		•
Colmworth	•	•		
Cople	•	•		•
Cranfield	•	•		•
Crawley-Husbourne	•	•		•
Dunstable	•	•		•
Dunton	•	•		•
East Hyde	•			
Eaton-Bray	•	•		•
Eaton-Solon	•	•		•
Edworth	•	•		•
Egginton	•	•		•
Elstow	•	•		•
Eversholt	•	•		
Eyworth	•	•		•
Farndish	•	•		
Felmersham	•	•		•
Flitton	•	•		•
Flitwick	•	•		•
Goldington	•	•		•
Great Barford	•	•		•
Harlington	•	•		•
Harrold	•	•		•
Hawnes	•	•		•
Heath and Reach	•			
Henlow	•	•		•
Higham-Gobion	•	•		
Hockliffe	•	•		•
Holcutt	•	•		•
Holwell		•		
Houghton-Conquest	•	•		•
Houghton-Regis	•	•		•
Kempstone	•	•		•
Kensworth	•			
Keysoe	•	•		
Knotting	•	•		•
Langford	•	•		
Leighton-Buzzard	•	•		•
Lidlington	•	•		•
Little Barford	•	•		•
Little Slaughton	•	•		•
Lower Gravenhurst	•	•		•
Luton	•	•		•
Marston-Moretaine	•	•		•
Maulden	•	•		•
Melchbourne	•	•		•
Meppershall	•	•		•
Millbrook	•	•		•
Milton-Bryant	•	•		•
Milton-Ernest	•	•		•
Moggerhanger	•	•		
Nether & Upper Dean	•	•		•
Northill	•	•		•
Oakley	•	•		•
Odell	•	•		•
Pavenham	•	•		•
Pertenhall	•	•		•
Potsgrove	•	•		•
Potton	•	•		•
Puddington	•	•		
Pulloxhill	•	•		•
Ravensden	•	•		
Renhold	•	•		•
Ridgmont	•	•		•
Riseley	•	•		•
Roxton	•	•		•
Salford	•	•		•
Sandy	•	•		•
Sharnbrook	•	•		•
Shefford	•			
Shelton	•	•		•
Shillington	•	•		•
Silsoe	•	•		•
Souldrop	•	•		•
Southill	•	•		•
Stagsden	•	•		
Stanbridge	•	•		•
Steppingley	•	•		•
Steventon	•	•		•
Stopsley		•		
Stotfold	•	•		•
Streatley	•	•		•
Studham	•	•		•
Sundon	•	•		•
Sutton	•	•		•
Tempsford	•	•		•
Thurleigh	•	•		•
Tilbrook		•		
Tilsworth	•	•		•
Tingrith	•	•		•
Toddington	•	•		•
Totternhoe	•	•		
Turvey	•	•		•
Upper Caldicott	•			
Upper Gravenhurst	•	•		•
Upper Stondon	•	•		•
Warden	•	•		•
Westoning	•	•		•
Whipsnade	•	•		•
Wilden	•	•		•
Willington	•	•		•
Wilshampstead	•	•		•
Woburn	•	•		•
Woburn-Sands	•			
Wootten	•	•		•
Wrestlingworth	•	•		•
Wymington	•	•		•
Yielding	•	•		•
BERKSHIRE*				
Abingdon	•	•		•
Aldermaston	•	•		•
Aldworth	•	•		•
Appleford	•	•		•
Appleton	•	•		•
Arborfield	•	•		•
Ardington	•	•		•
Ashampstead	•	•		•
Ashbury	•	•		•
Aston Tirrold	•	•		•
Aston-Upthorpe	•			
Avington		•		
Barkham		•		

England

* COUNTY / SHIRE

PARISH	PARISH REGISTERS	BISHOPS' TRANSCRIPTS	BOYD'S MARRIAGE INDEX	PR PRINT-OUTS
Basilden	•	•		•
Beech-Hill	•			
Beedon	•	•		
Beenham	•	•		•
Besselsleigh		•		
Binfield	•	•		•
Bisham	•	•		•
Blewberry	•	•		•
Boxford		•		
Bradfield	•	•	•	•
Bray	•	•		•
Bright-Walthan	•	•		•
Brightwell		•		
Brimpton		•		
Buckland	•	•		•
Bucklebury		•		
Burghfield	•	•		•
Buscot	•	•	•	•
Catmore		•		
Chaddleworth	•	•		
Charney	•	•		
Cheveley	•	•		•
Childrey	•	•		•
Chilton		•		
Cholsey	•	•		•
Clewer	•	•		•
Coleshill	•			•
Compton	•			•
Compton-Beauchamp				•
Cookham	•			•
Cumnor	•			
Denchworth	•			•
Drayton	•			
Dudcott	•			•
Earley	•			
East Challow	•	•		•
East Garston	•	•		•
East Hanney	•		•	
East Hendred	•	•		•
East Ilsley		•		
East Lockinge	•	•		•
East Shefford	•	•		•
East Hampstead	•			•
Eaton Hastings	•	•		•
Enborne	•	•		•
Engelfield	•	•		•
Faringdon				•
Farnborough	•	•		•
Fawler	•	•		

PARISH	PARISH REGISTERS	BISHOPS' TRANSCRIPTS	BOYD'S MARRIAGE INDEX	PR PRINT-OUTS
Fernham	•	•		
Finchampstead	•	•		•
Frilsham	•	•		•
Fyfield		•		
Garford	•	•		•
Great Coxwell	•			•
Great Faringdon	•	•		•
Greenham	•	•		•
Hagbourne	•	•		•
Hampstead-Norris	•	•		•
Harwell		•	•	
Hatford		•		
Hinton-Waldrist	•	•		•
Hungerford	•	•		•
Hurley	•	•		•
Hurst	•	•		•
Idstone	•			
Inkpen	•	•		•
Kingston-Bagpuize	•	•		•
Kingston-Lisle		•	•	•
Kintbury		•		
Lambourn	•	•		•
Leckhampstead		•		•
Letcombe-Bassett		•		
Letcombe-Regis	•	•		
Little Coxwell	•			•
Little Whittenham	•	•		•
Long Whittenham	•	•		•
Longcott	•	•		•
Longworth	•	•		•
Lyford	•			
Maidenhead	•			•
Marcham	•	•		•
Midgham	•	•		
Milton	•	•		•
Mortimer				•
Moulsford	•	•		•
New Windsor	•	•		•
Newbury	•	•		•
North Fawley		•		
North Hinksey	•	•		
North Moreton	•	•		•
Oare	•	•		•
Old Windsor	•	•		•
Padworth	•	•		•
Pangbourn	•	•		•
Peasemore	•	•		•
Purley	•	•	•	•
Pusey		•		

PARISH	PARISH REGISTERS	BISHOPS' TRANSCRIPTS	BOYD'S MARRIAGE INDEX	PR PRINT-OUTS
Radley	•	•		
Reading	•	•		•
Remenham	•	•		•
Ruscombe		•		
Sandhurst	•	•		•
Shaw-Cum-Donnington		•		
Shellingford	•	•		•
Shinfield	•	•		•
Shottesbrook		•		
Shrivenham	•	•		•
Sonning		•		
Sotwell	•	•		
Southhinksey	•	•		•
South Moreton	•	•		•
Sparsholt	•	•	•	•
Speen		•		
Stanford-Dingley	•	•		•
Stanford-in-the-Vale	•	•		•
Steventon	•	•		•
Streatley	•	•		
Sulham	•	•	•	•
Sulhampstead-Abbotts	•	•		•
Sulhampstead-Bannister	•	•		•
Sunninghill	•	•		•
Sunningwell	•	•		•
Sutton-Courtney	•	•		•
Swallowfield	•	•		•
Thatcham	•	•		•
Theale		•		
Tidmarsh	•	•		
Tilehurst	•	•		•
Touchen-End	•			
Uffington	•	•		•
Ufton	•			•
Upton	•	•		•
Wallingford	•	•		•
Waltham-St. Lawrence	•	•		•
Wantage	•		•	•
Warfield	•			•
Wargrave	•	•		
Wasing	•	•		•
Water-Oakley				•
Welford	•	•		•
West Challow	•	•		•
West Hanney	•	•	•	•
West Hendred		•	•	
West Ilsley	•	•		•
West Shefford	•	•		•
West Woodhay	•	•	•	•

England

* COUNTY / SHIRE

PARISH	PARISH REGISTERS	BISHOPS' TRANSCRIPTS	BOYD'S MARRIAGE INDEX	PR PRINT-OUTS	PARISH	PARISH REGISTERS	BISHOPS' TRANSCRIPTS	BOYD'S MARRIAGE INDEX	PR PRINT-OUTS	PARISH	PARISH REGISTERS	BISHOPS' TRANSCRIPTS	BOYD'S MARRIAGE INDEX	PR PRINT-OUTS
White Waltham	•	•		•	Dorney	•		•		Lillingstone-Lovell	•			
Wickham	•	•		•	Dorton	•				Linchlade	•			
Winkfield		•			Drayton-Parslow	•	•		•	Little Horwood	•	•		
Winterbourn	•	•		•	Dunton	•			•	Little Kimble	•			
Wokingham	•	•		•	Eddlesborough	•		•		Little Missenden			•	
Woodley and Sandford	•			•	Edgecott	•			•	Little Woolstone	•			•
Woolhampton		•			Ellesborough	•			•	Long Crendon	•			
Wootton		•			Eton	•			•	Long Marston	•			
Wytham	•	•			Farnham-Royal	•				Loughton	•			•
Yattendon	•	•		•	Fenny-Stratford	•			•	Ludgershall	•			
BUCKINGHAM*					Fingest	•		•		Maids-Moreton	•			
Addington	•			•	Foxcott	•				Marsh-Gibbon	•			
Adstock	•				Fulmer	•		•		Marsworth			•	
Akeley-Cum-Stockholt	•				Gayhurst	•			•	Medmenham	•			•
Amersham	•		•		Grandborough	•	•		•	Mentmore	•		•	•
Ashendon	•			•	Great Hampden	•			•	Milton-Keynes	•			•
Aston-Abbots	•	•		•	Great Horwood	•			•	Monks-Risborough	•			
Aston-Clinton			•		Great Kimble	•			•	Moulsoe	•		•	
Astwood	•			•	Great Linford	•				Mursley	•			
Aylesbury	•			•	Great Marlow	•			•	Nether or Lower Winchendon	•			•
Barton-Hartshorn	•				Great Missenden	•	•		•	Nettleden	•			
Beachampton	•				Great Woolstone	•			•	Newport-Pagnell	•		•	•
Beaconsfield	•	•		•	Grendon-Underwood	•				Newton-Longville	•			•
Bledlow	•				Grove	•		•		North-Marston	•			
Bletchley	•			•	Halton	•				Oakley	•			•
Bow-Brickhill	•			•	Hambleden				•	Olney	•			•
Bradenham	•		•	•	Hardmead	•				Padbury	•			
Brill	•				Hardwicke	•				Penn	•			
Broughton	•		•	•	Hartwell	•		•		Pitstone	•		•	
Buckingham	•			•	Haversham	•			•	Preston-Bisset	•			
Burnham			•		Hawridge	•	•		•	Prestwood	•			
Chalfont-St. Giles	•		•	•	Hedgerley	•		•		Princes-Risborough	•			
Chalfont-St. Peter			•		Hedsor	•		•		Quainton	•		•	
Chearsley	•				Hillesden	•				Radclive	•			
Cheddington	•		•		Hitcham	•		•		Radnage	•			
Cheneys	•		•	•	Hitchenden	•		•		Ravenstone	•			•
Chesham	•		•	•	Hoggeston	•			•	St. Leonard	•			
Chesham-Bois	•				Horton				•	Saunderton	•			
Chetwode	•			•	Iver	•	•		•	Shenley	•			•
Chicheley			•		Iverheath	•				Sherrington	•		•	
Chilton	•				Ivinghoe	•		•		Simpson	•			•
Choulesbury	•			•	Lane End	•				Slapton	•		•	
Clifton-Reynes	•				Langley-Marish	•			•	Soulbury	•		•	•
Cold Brayfield	•				Lathbury	•		•		Stantonbury	•			
Colnbrook	•			•	Latimer	•			•	Stewkley	•			•
Cublington	•				Lavendon	•				Stoke Goldington	•			
Datchet	•			•	Leckhampstead	•			•	Stoke Hammond	•			
Denham			•		Lee	•				Stoke Poges	•		•	•
Dinton	•				Lillingstone-Dayrell	•				Stone	•		•	

England

* COUNTY / SHIRE

PARISH	PARISH REGISTERS	BISHOPS' TRANSCRIPTS	BOYD'S MARRIAGE INDEX	PR PRINT-OUTS
Stony Stratford				•
Swanbourne	•			•
Taplow			•	
Tattenhoe	•			
Thornborough	•			
Thornton	•			•
Tingewick	•			
Turville			•	
Twyford	•			
Upton	•			
Waddeston	•			•
Walton	•			•
Walton-Stratford	•			
Wavendon	•			•
Wendover	•		•	•
West Wycombe	•			
Westbury			•	
Weston Underwood	•			
Wexham	•			
Waddon	•			
Willen	•			•
Wing	•		•	•
Wingrave				•
Winslow	•	•		
Wooburn			•	•
Wootton-Under-Wood	•			•
Woughton-on-the-Green	•			•
Wycombe	•		•	•
CAMBRIDGE*				
Abington-in-the-Clay	2			•
Arrington	•			
Ashley-Cum-Silverley	•			
Babraham	•			
Balsham	•			
Barrington				•
Bartlow	•			
Bassingbourne	•			•
Benwick	•			
Bottisham	•			
Bourn	•			
Boxworth	•		•	
Brinkley	•			•
Burrough-Green	•			•
Burwell	•			•
Caldecote	•		•	
Cambridge	•		•	•
Carlton-Cum-Willingham	•			
Castle-Camps	•			
Caxton	•	•		•

PARISH	PARISH REGISTERS	BISHOPS' TRANSCRIPTS	BOYD'S MARRIAGE INDEX	PR PRINT-OUTS
Chatteris	•			•
Cherry-Hinton	•			
Chesterton	•		•	
Cheveley	•			
Coates	•			
Comberton	•			
Conington	•		•	
Cottenham	•			
Coveney	•			•
Croxton	•		•	•
Croydon-Cum-Clapton	•			•
Ditton-Wood	•			
Doddington	•			
Downham	•			•
Drydrayton	•		•	
Dullingham	•			
Duxford	•		•	
East Hatley	•			•
Elm	•			
Elsworth	•		•	
Eltisley	•		•	•
Ely	•			•
Fen-Drayton	•		•	
Fordham	•			
Foulmire	•			•
Foxton	•	•		
Friday Bridge	•			
Fulbourn	•			
Gamlingay	•			•
Girton			•	
Grantchester	•			
Graveley	•		•	
Great Abbington	•			•
Great Eversden	•			•
Great Shelford	•			
Great Wilbraham	•			
Guilden-Morden				•
Guyhirn	•			
Haddenham	•			
Hardwicke	•			
Harston	•			
Haslingfield	•	•		•
Hatley-St. George	•			•
Hauxton	•			
Hildersham	•			•
Hinxton	•			
Histon	•		•	
Horningsea	•			
Horseheath	•			

PARISH	PARISH REGISTERS	BISHOPS' TRANSCRIPTS	BOYD'S MARRIAGE INDEX	PR PRINT-OUTS
Ickleton	•			•
Impington	•		•	
Isleham	•			
Kingston	•			
Kirtling	•			
Knapwell	•		•	
Leverington	•			
Linton	•			•
Little Abington	•			
Little Eversden	•			
Little Gransden	•	•		•
Little Shelford	•			•
Little Wilbraham	•			
Little Port				•
Littlington	•			•
Lolworth			•	
Longstaton-All Saints	•		•	
Longstaton-St.Michael	•		•	
Longstow	•			•
Madingley	•		•	
Manea	•			
Melbourne	•			•
Meldreth	•	•		•
Mepal	•			
Milton			•	
Newton	•			
Oakington			•	
Orwell	•			•
Over			•	
Pampisford	•			
Papworth-St.Agnes			•	
Papworth-St.Everard	•		•	•
Parson-Drove	•			
Rampton	•			•
Sawston	•			•
Shepreth	•			•
Shudycamps	•			
Soham	•			•
Stapleford	•			
Steeple Morden	•			•
Stechworth	•			
Stow-Cum-Quy	•			
Stuntney	•			•
Sutton	•			
Swaffham-Prior	•			
Swavesey	•		•	
Tadlow	•			•
Taversham	•			
Thetford	•			•

England
* COUNTY / SHIRE

PARISH	PARISH REGISTERS	BISHOPS' TRANSCRIPTS	BOYD'S MARRIAGE INDEX	PR PRINT-OUTS
Thorney	•			•
Thriplow	•			
Toft	•		•	
Wendy	•			
West Wickham	•	•		
Westley-Waterless	•			•
Whaddon	•			•
Whittlesley	•			•
Whittlesford	•			
Willingham			•	
Wimblington	•			
Wimpole	•			
Wisbeach	•			•
Wisbeach-St.Mary	•			
Witcham	•			
CHESHIRE*				
Acton	•			•
Adlington	•			•
Alderley			•	
Astbury	•			•
Bebington				•
Bidstone	•			•
Birkenhead	•			•
Bosley			•	
Bramhall	•			•
Bromborough	•			•
Bruera				•
Capesthorpe			•	
Cheadle	•			•
Chelford	•		•	•
Chester	•			•
Christleton			•	
Compstall	•			•
Davenham	•			•
Disley	•		•	•
Eastham	•			•
Frodsham				•
Gawsworth	•		•	•
Great Bubworth	•			•
Guilden-Sutton	•			•
Handley	•			
Harthill	•			
Hazelgrove				•
Heaton-Norris	•			•
Heswall	•			•
Knutsford	•			•
Little Leigh				•
Lower Peover				•
Lymm	•		•	•

PARISH	PARISH REGISTERS	BISHOPS' TRANSCRIPTS	BOYD'S MARRIAGE INDEX	PR PRINT-OUTS
Macclesfield				•
Marple	•		•	•
Marthall	•			•
Marton	•		•	
Middlewich	•			•
Mobberley	•			•
Mottram-In-Longdendale	•	•		•
Nantwich	•			•
Nether-Peover	•			
Northenden				•
Northwich	•			•
Over-Peover	•			•
Pott Schrigley			•	
Poynton			•	
Prestbury	•		•	•
Rotherne	•			
Sandbach	•			•
Siddington			•	
Staleybridge	•			•
Stockport	•		•	•
Taxal			•	
Upton	•			•
Wallasey	•			•
Waverton	•			
Weaverham	•			
Whitegate	•			•
Wilmslow	•			•
Witton	•			•
Wybunbury	•			•
CORNWALL*				
Advent		•	•	•
Alternon	•	•		•
Antony	•	•		•
Blisland	•	•	•	•
Boconnoc	•			•
Bodmin	•	•	•	•
Bolventor	•			•
Botusfleming	•	•	•	•
Boyton	•	•	•	•
Breage	•	•	•	•
Broadoak	•			•
Budock	•		•	•
Callington		•		•
Calstock		•		•
Cambourne	•	•	•	•
Camelford		•	•	•
Cardinham	•	•	•	•
Carharrack				•
Colan	•	•	•	•

PARISH	PARISH REGISTERS	BISHOPS' TRANSCRIPTS	BOYD'S MARRIAGE INDEX	PR PRINT-OUTS
Constantine	•	•	•	•
Cornelly	•	•	•	•
Crantock	•	•	•	•
Creed	•	•	•	•
Crowan	•	•	•	•
Cubert	•	•	•	•
Cuby		•	•	•
Cury	•	•		•
Davidstow		•	•	•
Duloe	•	•		•
Egloshayle	•		•	•
Egloskerry	•	•	•	•
Endellion	•	•	•	•
Falmouth	•			•
Feock	•			
Forrabury	•	•		•
Fowey	•	•	•	•
Germoe	•	•	•	•
Gerrans	•		•	•
Gorran	•	•	•	•
Grade	•	•	•	•
Grampound			•	
Gulval	•	•	•	•
Gunwalloe	•	•		•
Gwennap	•	•	•	•
Gwinear	•	•		•
Gwithean	•	•	•	•
Hayle	•			
Helland	•	•	•	•
Helston	•	•	•	•
Illogan	•	•		•
Jacobstow	•	•	•	•
Kea	•	•	•	•
Kenwyn	•	•	•	•
Kilkhampton	•	•	•	•
Ladock	•	•	•	•
Lamorran	•	•		•
Landewednack	•	•	•	•
Landrake	•		•	•
Landulph	•	•	•	•
Laneast	•	•	•	•
Lanherne			•	•
Lanhydrock	•		•	•
Lanivet	•	•	•	•
Lanlivery	•	•	•	•
Lanreath	•	•		•
Lansallos	•	•		•
Lanteglos-By-Fowey	•	•		•
Launcells	•	•	•	•

England

* COUNTY / SHIRE

PARISH	PARISH REGISTERS	BISHOPS' TRANSCRIPTS	BOYD'S MARRIAGE INDEX	PR PRINT-OUTS	PARISH	PARISH REGISTERS	BISHOPS' TRANSCRIPTS	BOYD'S MARRIAGE INDEX	PR PRINT-OUTS	PARISH	PARISH REGISTERS	BISHOPS' TRANSCRIPTS	BOYD'S MARRIAGE INDEX	PR PRINT-OUTS
Launceston	•	•	•	•	Pillaton	•	•	•	•	St. Keverne	•	•	•	•
Lawhitton	•				Poughill	•	•	•	•	St. Kew	•	•	•	•
Laycock				•	Poundstock	•	•		•	St. Keyne	•	•		•
Lesnewth	•	•	•	•	Probus	•	•	•	•	St. Mabyn	•	•	•	•
Levan	•	•	•	•	Quethiock	•	•		•	St. Martin	•			•
Lewannick	•	•	•	•	Rame	•	•		•	St. Martin-In-Meneage	•	•	•	•
Lezant	•		•	•	Redruth	•	•	•	•	St. Mawgan-In-Pyder		•		•
Linkinhorne	•	•	•	•	Roche	•	•	•	•	St. Mellion	•	•	•	•
Liskeard	•	•		•	Ruan-Lanihorne	•	•	•	•	St. Merryn	•		•	•
Little Petherick	•		•	•	Ruan-Major	•	•	•	•	St. Mewan	•	•		•
Lostwithiel	•	•	•	•	Ruan-Minor	•	•	•	•	St. Michael-Penkevil	•	•	•	•
Ludgvan	•	•	•	•	St. Agnes			•	•	St. Minver	•	•	•	•
Luxulion	•	•	•	•	St. Allen	•	•	•	•	St. Neot	•	•		•
Mabe	•			•	St. Anthony-In-Menage	•	•	•	•	St. Nighton				•
Madron	•	•	•	•	St. Anthony-In-Roseland	•			•	St. Pinnock		•		•
Maker	•	•		•	St. Austell	•	•		•	St. Sampson	•	•	•	•
Manaccan	•	•	•	•	St. Blazey	•	•		•	St. Stephen's	•	•	•	•
Marazion	•				St. Breock	•		•		St. Stephen's-By-Saltash		•		•
Marham Church	•	•	•	•	St. Breward	•	•	•	•	St. Stephen's-In-Brannel	•	•	•	•
Mawgan-In-Meneage	•	•	•	•	St. Buryan	•	•	•	•	St. Stithians	•	•	•	•
Mawgan-In-Pyder	•		•	•	St. Cleer	•	•	•	•	St. Teath		•	•	•
Mawnan	•	•	•	•	St. Clement	•	•	•	•	St. Thomas the Apostle		•		•
Menheniot	•	•	•	•	St. Clether	•	•	•	•	St. Tudy	•	•	•	•
Merther	•	•		•	St. Columb-Major	•	•	•	•	St. Veep	•	•		•
Mevagissey	•	•		•	St. Columb-Minor	•	•	•	•	St. Wenn	•	•	•	•
Michael-Carhayes		•		•	St. Dennis	•	•	•	•	St. Winnow	•		•	•
Michaelstow	•		•	•	St. Dominick	•	•		•	Sancreed	•	•	•	•
Minster	•	•		•	St. Enddor	•	•	•	•	Scilly Islands	•			•
Morvah	•	•	•	•	St. Erme	•	•	•	•	Sennen	•	•	•	•
Morval	•	•		•	St. Erney				•	Sheviock	•	•	•	•
Morwinstow	•	•	•	•	St. Erth	•	•	•	•	Sithney	•	•	•	•
Mousehole	•	•		•	St. Ervan	•		•	•	South Petherwin	•		•	
Mullion	•	•		•	St. Eval	•		•	•	Southill		•		•
Mylor	•		•	•	St. Ewe	•	•	•	•	Stoke-Climsland		•		•
Newlyn	•	•	•	•	St. Feock	•	•		•	Stratton	•	•	•	•
North Petherwyn		•			St. Gennys	•	•		•	Talland	•	•		•
North Tamerton	•	•		•	St. Germans	•			•	Tintagel	•	•	•	•
Northill	•	•		•	St. Gerrans				•	Towednack	•	•	•	•
Otterham		•	•	•	St. Giles-On-The-Heath		•			Tregony	•		•	•
Padstow	•	•	•	•	St. Gluvias	•		•	•	Tremayne	•	•	•	•
Par	•			•	St. Hilary	•	•	•	•	Treneglos	•	•	•	•
Paul	•	•	•	•	St. Issey	•		•	•	Tresmeer	•	•		•
Pelynt	•	•		•	St. Ive				•	Trevalga		•	•	•
Pendeen	•			•	St. Ives	•	•	•	•	Truro	•	•		•
Perranarworthal	•	•	•	•	St. John		•		•	Tywardreath	•	•	•	•
Perranuthnoe	•	•	•	•	St. Juliot	•	•	•	•	Uny-Lelant	•	•	•	•
Perranzabuloe	•		•	•	St. Just		•		•	Veryan	•	•	•	•
Phillack	•	•	•	•	St. Just-In-Penwith	•		•	•	Warbestow	•	•	•	•
Philleigh	•	•	•	•	St. Just-In-Roseland	•	•	•	•	Warleggon	•	•	•	•

England

* COUNTY / SHIRE

PARISH	PARISH REGISTERS	BISHOPS' TRANSCRIPTS	BOYD'S MARRIAGE INDEX	PR PRINT-OUTS	PARISH	PARISH REGISTERS	BISHOPS' TRANSCRIPTS	BOYD'S MARRIAGE INDEX	PR PRINT-OUTS	PARISH	PARISH REGISTERS	BISHOPS' TRANSCRIPTS	BOYD'S MARRIAGE INDEX	PR PRINT-OUTS
Week-St. Mary	•	•	•	•	Cross-Canonby		•		•	Ivegill	•	•		•
Wendron	•	•	•	•	Crosthwaite	•	•		•	Keswick		•		•
Whitston		•		•	Culgaith		•		•	Kirk-Andrews-Middle-Quarter		•		•
Whitstone	•				Cumrew	•	•		•	Kirk-Andrews-Upon-Esk	•	•		
Withiel	•		•	•	Cumwhitton	•	•		•	Kirk-Bride		•		
Zennor	•	•	•	•	Dacre		•		•	Kirk-Linton		•		•
CUMBERLAND*					Dalston	•	•		•	Kirkbride				•
Addingham		•		•	Dean		•		•	Kirkland		•		•
Aikton	•	•		•	Dearham		•		•	Kirkoswald		•		•
Ainstable	•	•		•	Distington	•	•		•	Lamplugh		•		•
Allhallows		•		•	Drigg		•		•	Lanerlost	•	•		•
Allonby		•		•	Eaglesfield		•		•	Langwathby		•		•
Alston	•			•	Edenhall		•		•	Lazonby	•	•		•
Arlecdon		•		•	Egremont	•	•		•	Little Clifton		•		•
Armathwaite		•		•	Embleton		•		•	Lorton		•		•
Arthuret		•		•	Ennerdale	•	•		•	Low Holme				•
Aspatria		•		•	Eskdale		•		•	Lowes-Water	•	•		•
Bampton-Kirk	•	•		•	Farlam	•	•		•	Maryport		•		•
Bassenthwaite		•		•	Faugh Fenton				•	Matterdale	•	•		•
Beaumont		•		•	Flimby		•		•	Melmerby		•		•
Beckermet-St. Bridget		•		•	Garrigill	•			•	Midgeholm	•			
Beckermet-St. John		•		•	Gilcrux		•		•	Millom		•		•
Bewcastle	•	•		•	Gilsland	•	•		•	Moresby		•	•	•
Blackford	•			•	Gosforth		•	•	•	Mosser		•		•
Blindbothel		•		•	Grange		•			Muncaster	•	•		•
Blindcrake, Isell & Redmaine				•	Graysouthen				•	Mungrisdale		•		•
Bolton		•		•	Great Boughton				•	Nenthead	•			•
Bootle		•		•	Great Clifton		•		•	Nether-Denton	•	•		•
Borrowdale		•		•	Great Orton				•	Nether-Wasdale	•	•		•
Bowness		•		•	Great Salkeld		•		•	Newlands		•		•
Brampton	•	•		•	Greysouthen		•			Newton-Arlosh		•		•
Bridekirk	•	•		•	Greystoke	•	•		•	Newton-Regny		•		•
Brigham		•		•	Greystone		•			Nichol Forest	•	•		•
Bromfield		•		•	Grinsdale		•		•	Orton		•		
Burgh-By-Sands	•	•		•	Haile		•		•	Ousby		•		•
Buttermere		•		•	Harrington		•	•	•	Penrith		•		•
Caldbeck		•		•	Hayton		•		•	Plumbland		•		•
Cammerton		•		•	Hensingham		•		•	Plumpton-Wall	•	•		•
Carlisle	•	•		•	Hesket-In-The-Forest		•		•	Ponsonby		•		•
Carlisle-St. Cuthbert		•			Holme-Cultram		•		•	Raughton-Head		•		•
Carlisle-St. Mary		•			Holme-Eden		•		•	Renwick		•		•
Castle-Carrock	•	•			Holme-St. Cuthbert		•		•	Rockcliff	•	•		•
Castle-Sowerby		•		•	Holme-St. Paul		•			Rosley		•		
Cleator		•		•	Houghton		•		•	St. Bees	•	•		•
Cleator-Moor		•			Hutton-In-The-Forest	•	•		•	St. John Castlerigg & Wythburn		•		
Cockermouth		•		•	Ireby		•		•	St. John's-In-The-Vale		•		•
Corney		•		•	Irthington	•	•		•	Scaleby		•		•
Croglin	•	•		•	Irton		•		•	Scotby	•			•
Crosby-Upon-Eden		•	•	•	Isell		•		•	Sebergham		•		•

England

* COUNTY / SHIRE

PARISH	PARISH REGISTERS	BISHOPS' TRANSCRIPTS	BOYD'S MARRIAGE INDEX	PR PRINT-OUTS
Setmurthy		•		•
Skelton	•	•		•
Stanwix		•	•	•
Stapleton		•		•
Talkin				•
Thornthwaite		•		
Threlkeld		•		•
Thursby		•		•
Thwaites		•		•
Torpenhow		•		•
Uldale		•		•
Ulpha		•		•
Upper Denton	•	•		
Upperby		•		
Waberthwaite		•		•
Walton		•		•
Warwick		•		•
Wasdale-Head		•		•
Watermillock		•		•
Westward		•		•
Wetheral		•		•
Whicham		•		•
Whinfell		•		•
Whitbeck		•		•
Whitehaven		•		•
Wigton		•		•
Workington		•	•	•
Wreay	•	•		•
Wythop		•		•
DERBYSHIRE*				
Alfreton	•	•	•	•
Alkmonton		•		•
Allestree	•	•	•	•
Alsop-Le-Dale and Eaton	•	•	•	
Alvaston	•	•	•	•
Ashborne	•	•	•	•
Ashford	•	•		•
Ashover	•	•		
Aston-Upon-Trent	•	•	•	•
Atlow	•	•		•
Ault-Hucknall		•	•	•
Bakewell	•	•	•	•
Bamford		•		
Barlborough		•		•
Barlow				•
Barrow-Upon-Trent				•
Barton-Blount	•	•		•
Baslow	•	•		•
Beard		•		

PARISH	PARISH REGISTERS	BISHOPS' TRANSCRIPTS	BOYD'S MARRIAGE INDEX	PR PRINT-OUTS
Beauchief-Abbey			•	
Beeley	•	•	•	•
Beighton		•	•	•
Belper		•		•
Biggin	•	•		•
Blackwell		•		•
Bolsover	•	•		•
Bonsall	•	•		•
Boulton	•	•	•	•
Boylstone	•	•		•
Brackenfield		•		•
Bradbourne	•	•		•
Bradby	•			
Bradley	•	•		
Brailsford	•	•	•	•
Brampton	•	•		•
Brassington	•	•		•
Breadsall	•	•	•	•
Breaston	•	•	•	•
Brimington	•	•		•
Broughton-Church	•	•	•	•
Burbage	•	•		
Buxton	•	•	•	•
Calke	•	•		•
Calow	•			
Carsington	•	•		•
Castleton	•	•		•
Chaddesden		•	•	•
Chapel-En-Le-Frith	•	•	•	•
Chellaston	•	•	•	•
Chelmorton	•	•		•
Chesterfield	•	•		•
Chilcote		•		•
Church-Gresley	•	•		•
ChurchWilne				•
Claycross				•
Clifton Campville		•		
Clifton with Compton	•			
Clown	•	•		•
Codnor	•	•		•
Cotmanhay	•			•
Coton-In-The-Elms	•			•
Crich	•	•		•
Cromford	•	•		•
Croxhall	•			•
Cubley				•
Dalbury-With-Lees	•	•		•
Dale Abbey		•	•	•
Darley	•	•	•	•

PARISH	PARISH REGISTERS	BISHOPS' TRANSCRIPTS	BOYD'S MARRIAGE INDEX	PR PRINT-OUTS
Darley-Abbey		•		•
Denby	•	•	•	•
Derby	•	•	•	•
Derwent		•		•
Dethwick	•	•		•
Dore	•	•		•
Doveridge	•	•		•
Draycott	•			•
Dronfield	•	•	•	•
Duffield	•	•	•	•
Earl-Sterndale	•	•		•
Eckington		•		•
Edale	•	•		•
Edensor	•	•		•
Edlaston-With-Wyaston	•	•		•
Egginton	•	•		•
Elmton-With-Cresswell		•		•
Elton		•		•
Elvaston	•	•	•	•
Etwall	•	•	•	•
Eyam		•		•
Fairfield	•	•	•	•
Fenny-Bentley	•	•		•
Findern		•		•
Foremark	•	•	•	•
Glossop		•	•	•
Great Barlow		•		•
Great Longstone	•	•		•
Hallam-Kirk	•	•	•	•
Handley	•			
Hartington	•	•		•
Hartshorn		•		•
Hathersage	•	•		•
Hayfield		•		•
Hazelwood	•			
Heage	•	•		•
Heanor	•	•	•	•
Heath		•	•	•
Hognaston	•	•		•
Holbrook	•	•		•
Holmesfield	•	•		•
Hope	•	•	•	•
Hopwell	•			•
Horsley		•	•	•
Hulland	•	•		•
Ibstock				•
Ilkeston	•	•	•	•
Ironville		•		
Kedleston	•	•	•	•

England

* COUNTY / SHIRE

PARISH	PARISH REGISTERS	BISHOPS' TRANSCRIPTS	BOYD'S MARRIAGE INDEX	PR PRINT-OUTS	PARISH	PARISH REGISTERS	BISHOPS' TRANSCRIPTS	BOYD'S MARRIAGE INDEX	PR PRINT-OUTS	PARISH	PARISH REGISTERS	BISHOPS' TRANSCRIPTS	BOYD'S MARRIAGE INDEX	PR PRINT-OUTS
Killamarsh		•		•	Quarndon	•	•	•	•	Tupton				•
King's Sterndale	•	•			Radbourne	•	•			Turnditch	•	•		•
Kirk-Ireton		•	•	•	Ravenstone		•		•	Twyford	•	•	•	•
Kirk Langley	•	•	•	•	Repton	•	•	•	•	Upper Langwith	•	•		•
Kniveton	•	•		•	Riddings		•		•	Walton-Upon-Trent	•	•	•	•
Leighton Low		•			Ridgeway		•		•	Wardlow	•			
Lichfield		•			Ripley		•		•	Wessington	•	•		
Litchurch		•			Risley	•	•	•	•	West Hallam	•	•	•	•
Little Eaton	•	•		•	Rosliston	•	•		•	Weston-Upon-Trent	•	•	•	•
Little Longstone		•			Rowsley	•				Whittington		•		•
Littleover	•	•		•	St. Michaels			•		Whitwell	•	•		•
Long Eaton	•	•		•	St. Peter			•		Willesley		•		•
Long Lane	•	•			Sandiacre	•	•	•	•	Willington		•	•	•
Longford	•	•	•	•	Sawley	•	•	•	•	Wilne	•	•	•	•
Lullington	•	•		•	Scarcliff	•	•		•	Wingerworth	•	•		•
Mackworth	•	•	•	•	Scropton		•		•	Winster		•		•
Mapperley	•	•		•	Shardlow	•	•	•	•	Wirksworth	•	•		•
Mappleton	•	•		•	Sheldon	•	•	•	•	Woodthorpe				•
Marston-Montgomery		•		•	Shirebrook	•				Wormhill	•	•		•
Marston-Upon-Dove	•	•		•	Shirland	•	•	•	•	Yeavely		•		•
Matlock		•	•	•	Shirley	•	•		•	Youlgreave		•	•	•
Measham	•	•		•	Shottle and Postern	•				**DEVON***				
Melbourne		•	•	•	Smalley	•	•	•	•	Abbots-Bickington	•			•
Mellor		•	•	•	Smisby		•	•	•	Abbotsham	•			•
Mickleover	•	•		•	Snelston		•	•	•	Abbotskerswell				•
Middleton	•	•		•	Somersall-Herbert		•		•	Alphington	•			•
Middleton-Stony		•		•	South Normanton		•		•	Alwington	•			•
Monyash	•	•		•	South Wingfield	•	•	•	•	Arlington	•			•
Morley	•	•	•	•	Spondon	•	•	•	•	Ashburton	•			•
Morton	•	•	•	•	Stanley		•	•	•	Ashcombe	•			•
Mugginton	•	•		•	Stanton-By-Bridge		•	•	•	Ashford	•			•
Netherseal		•		•	Stanton-By-Dale		•	•	•	Ashwater	•			•
Newbold	•				Stapenhill	•	•		•	Atherington	•			•
Newhall	•	•		•	Staveley	•	•		•	Axminster		•		•
Newmills		•		•	Stretton				•	Axmouth	•			•
Newton Solney	•	•		•	Stretton-En-Le-Field		•		•	Axlesbeare	•			•
Norbury	•	•		•	Sudbury		•		•	Beaford	•			•
Normanton	•	•		•	Sutton-Cum-Duckmanton		•		•	Beer	•			•
Normanton-Temple		•		•	Sutton-On-The-Hill	•	•		•	Belstone	•			•
North Wingfield	•	•		•	Swadlincote	•				Berry-Pomeroy	•			•
Norton		•	•	•	Swarkeston	•	•	•	•	Berrynarbor	•		•	•
Ockbrook	•	•	•	•	Taddington and Priestcliff		•		•	Bickleigh	•			•
Osmaston	•	•		•	Tansley	•	•		•	Bideford	•			•
Parwich	•	•	•	•	Thorpe	•	•		•	Bishop-Morchard	•			•
Peak Forest	•	•		•	Tibshelf		•		•	Bishops-Nympton	•			•
Pentrich		•	•	•	Ticknall	•	•	•	•	Bishops-Tawton	•			•
Pilsey	•				Tideswell	•	•		•	Black Torrington	•			•
Pinxton	•	•		•	Tissington	•	•		•	Bow				•
Pleasley	•	•		•	Trusley	•	•		•	Bradford	•			•

England
* COUNTY / SHIRE

PARISH	PARISH REGISTERS	BISHOPS' TRANSCRIPTS	BOYD'S MARRIAGE INDEX	PR PRINT-OUTS	PARISH	PARISH REGISTERS	BISHOPS' TRANSCRIPTS	BOYD'S MARRIAGE INDEX	PR PRINT-OUTS	PARISH	PARISH REGISTERS	BISHOPS' TRANSCRIPTS	BOYD'S MARRIAGE INDEX	PR PRINT-OUTS
Bradworthy	•			•	Dunchideock	•			•	Kilmington	•			•
Bampford-Speke	•			•	East Anstey	•			•	Kingsbridge	•			•
Branscombe				•	East Down	•			•	Kingkerswell			•	
Bratton-Fleming	•			•	East Putford	•			•	Kingotoignton	•			•
Braunton	•			•	East Teignmouth				•	Kingston	•			•
Brendon	•			•	East Worlington	•			•	Knowstone	•			•
Bridford	•			•	Ermington	•			•	Landkey	•			•
Bridgerulf			•		Exeter	•	•		•	Langtree		•		•
Brixham	•			•	Exminster	•			•	Lapford	•			•
Broad-Clist	•			•	Faringdon	•	•	•	•	Linton	•		•	•
Broadhempston	•			•	Farway	•			•	Little Hempston	•			•
Buckerell	•			•	Feniton	•			•	Little Torrington	•	•		•
Buckfastleigh	•			•	Filleigh				•	Little Ham	•			•
Buckland-Brewer	•			•	Fremington	•			•	Luffincott	•			•
Buckland-Filleigh	•			•	Frithelstock	•			•	Lympston	•			•
Buckland-Monachorum	•			•	Georgeham	•			•	Malborough	•			•
Bulkworthy	•			•	Gidleigh	•			•	Mamhead	•	•		•
Burlescombe	•			•	Halberton	•			•	Mariensleigh	•	•		•
Burrington	•			•	Halwell	•			•	Martinhoe	•	•	•	•
Butterleigh	•			•	Harberton	•			•	Marwood	•			•
Cadbury	•			•	Harford	•			•	Marytavy	•			•
Cadeleigh	•			•	Harpford	•			•	Meeth	•	•		•
Chagford	•			•	Hartland				•	Membury	•	•		•
Challacombe			•		Hatherleigh	•	•		•	Merton	•	•		•
Chardstock				•	Heanton-Punchardon	•			•	Meshaw	•			•
Charles	•			•	Heavitree	•			•	Milton-Abbot	•			•
Cheriton-Fitzpaine	•			•	Hemyock				•	Milton-Damerel	•	•		•
Chittlehampton	•			•	Hennock	•			•	Modbury	•			•
Chivelstone	•			•	High Bickington	•	•		•	Molland	•			•
Chulmleigh	•			•	High Hampton	•	•		•	Monk-Okehampton	•	•		•
Churston-Ferrers	•			•	Highweek	•	•		•	Monkleigh	•			•
Clannaborough	•			•	Hittisleigh	•	•		•	Moreton-Hampstead	•			•
Clawton	•			•	Holbeton	•	•		•	Musbury	•	•		•
Clayhanger	•			•	Hollacombe	•	•		•	Nether Exe	•	•		•
Clist-Honiton	•			•	Holsworthy	•	•		•	Newton-Abbot	•			•
Clist-Hydon	•			•	Honiton	•			•	Newton-Ferrers	•			•
Clist-St. George	•			•	Horwood	•			•	Newton-Poppleford	•			•
Coffinswell	•			•	Huish	•			•	Newton-St. Cyres	•			•
Coldridge	•			•	Huntsham	•			•	Newton-St. Petrock	•	•		•
Combepyne	•			•	Huntshaw	•			•	Newton-Tracey	•			
Cookbury	•			•	Iddesleigh	•			•	North Bovey	•			•
Cornwood	•			•	Ide	•			•	North Leigh	•			•
Cotleigh	•			•	Ideford	•			•	North Molton	•			•
Countisbury	•		•	•	Ilfracombe	•			•	North Petherwin	•			•
Creacombe	•	•		•	Ilsington	•			•	Northam	•			•
Dittisham	•	•		•	Ipplepen			•		Nymet Rowland	•			•
Dolton	•	•		•	Kenn	•			•	Oakford	•			•
Dowland	•			•	Kenton	•			•	Offwell	•			•
Down-St. Mary	•			•	Kerswell				•	Okehampton	•	•		•

England

* COUNTY / SHIRE

PARISH	PARISH REGISTERS	BISHOPS' TRANSCRIPTS	BOYD'S MARRIAGE INDEX	PR PRINT-OUTS	PARISH	PARISH REGISTERS	BISHOPS' TRANSCRIPTS	BOYD'S MARRIAGE INDEX	PR PRINT-OUTS	PARISH	PARISH REGISTERS	BISHOPS' TRANSCRIPTS	BOYD'S MARRIAGE INDEX	PR PRINT-OUTS
Otterton	•			•	Stoke-Damerel	•			•	Woolborough				•
Ottery-St. Mary	•			•	Stoke-Fleming	•	•		•	Woolfardisworthy	•	•		•
Paignton	•			•	Stoke-Gabriel	•			•	Yarcombe	•			•
Pancrasweek	•			•	Stoke-Rivers	•			•	Yarnscombe	•			•
Parkham	•			•	Stokeinteignhead	•			•	Yealmpton	•			•
Parracombe	•			•	Stokenham	•			•	Zeal-Monachorum	•	•		•
Pennycross	•			•	Sutcombe	•	•		•	**DORSET***				
Petton	•			•	Swimbridge	•			•	Abbotsbury		•	•	
Pinhoe			•		Sydenham-Damerel	•			•	Admiston		•		
Plymouth	•		•	•	Talaton	•			•	Aff-Puddle		•		
Plympton-Earls	•			•	Tedburn-St. Mary	•	•		•	Allington		•	•	
Plympton-St. Mary	•			•	Teigngrace	•			•	Almer		•		•
Plymstock			•		Teignmouth	•	•		•	Alton-Pancras		•	•	
Plymtree	•			•	Tetcott	•			•	Anderson		•		
Poltimore	•	•		•	Thelbridge	•			•	Arne		•		
Poughill	•	•		•	Thornbury	•	•		•	Ashmore	•			
Powderham	•			•	Thorverton	•	•		•	Askerswell		•	•	
Rattery	•	•		•	Throwleigh	•	•		•	Batcombe		•		
Rewe	•	•	•	•	Tiverton	•	•		•	Beaminster		•	•	•
Ringmore	•			•	Topsham	•			•	Beer-Hackett	•			•
Roborough	•			•	Tor-Moham	•			•	Bellchalwell		•		
Rockbeare	•			•	Totnes	•			•	Bere-Regis		•		
Rose Ash	•			•	Trentishoe	•		•	•	Bettiscombe		•	•	
St. Budeaux	•			•	Twitchen	•			•	Bincombe		•		
St. Giles-In-The-Wood	•			•	Uffculme	•		•	•	Blandford-Forum		•		
Salcombe-Regis	•	•		•	Ugborough	•			•	Blandford-St. Mary		•		
Sandford	•			•	Uplowman	•			•	Bloxworth		•		
Seaton	•			•	Upottery	•			•	Bothenhampton		•	•	
Sheepstor	•	•		•	Upton-Helions	•	•		•	Bournemouth		•		
Sheepwash	•	•		•	Upton-Pyne	•	•		•	Bourton		•		
Sherwell	•			•	Ven-Ottery	•			•	Bradford-Abbas		•		
Shillingford-St. George	•			•	Weare-Gifford	•			•	Bradford-Peverell	•	•		•
Shobrooke	•			•	Wembury	•			•	Bradpole		•	•	
Sidbury	•	•		•	Werrington	•	•	•	•	Bridport		•		•
Sidmouth	•	•		•	West Anstey		•		•	Broadmayne		•		
Silverton	•	•		•	West Down	•			•	Broadway		•		
Slapton	•	•		•	West Leigh	•			•	Broadwinsor		•	•	
South Bovey	•			•	West Putford	•	•		•	Brownsea		•		
South Huish	•			•	West Worlington	•			•	Bryanstone		•		
South Molton	•	•		•	Whimple	•			•	Buckhorn-Weston		•		
South Tawton	•			•	Whitstone	•			•	Buckland-Newton		•		
Sowton	•			•	Widecombe-In-The-Moor				•	Buckland-Ripers		•		
Spreyton	•			•	Widworthy	•			•	Burstock		•	•	
Starcross	•			•	Wigan				•	Burton-Bradstock		•	•	
Staverton	•			•	Willand	•	•		•	Cann		•		
Stockland		•			Winkleigh	•			•	Castleton		•		
Stockleigh-English	•			•	Witheridge	•		•	•	Catherston-Leweston		•		
Stockleigh-Pomercy	•			•	Withycombe-Rawleigh	•			•	Cattistock	•	•	•	•
Stoke Canon	•	•		•	Woodbury	•			•	Caundle-Bishop	•	•		•

England

* COUNTY / SHIRE

PARISH	PARISH REGISTERS	BISHOPS' TRANSCRIPTS	BOYD'S MARRIAGE INDEX	PR PRINT-OUTS
Caundle-Marsh		•		
Caundle-Purse		•		
Caundle-Stourton		•		
Cerne-Abbas		•	•	
Cerne-Nether			•	
Chalbury				•
Chardstick		•	•	
Charlton-Marshall		•		
Charminster		•	•	
Charmouth		•	•	•
Cheddington		•	•	
Chettle		•		
Chideock		•	•	
Chilcombe		•		
Chilfroome		•	•	
Church-Knowle		•		
Compton-Abbas		•	•	
Compton-Vallence		•		
Coombe-Keynes		•		
Corfe-Castle		•		•
Corfe-Mullen		•		
Corscombe		•	•	
Cranbo		•		
Dewlish		•		
Dorchester	•	•	•	•
Durweston		•		
East Chelborough		•	•	
East Holme		•		
East Lulworth		•		•
East Stower			•	
Edmondsham		•		
Evershot		•		
Farnham		•		
Fifehead-Magdalen		•		
Fifehead-Neville		•		
Fleet		•	•	
Folke		•		
Fontmell		•		
Fordington		•	•	
Frampton		•		
Froome-St. Quinton		•		
Froome-Vauchurch		•	•	
Gillingham		•		
Godmanstone			•	
Great Canford		•		•
Grimstone	•			•
Halstock			•	
Hawkchurch			•	
Haydon	•			•

PARISH	PARISH REGISTERS	BISHOPS' TRANSCRIPTS	BOYD'S MARRIAGE INDEX	PR PRINT-OUTS
Hermitage	•			•
Hinton-St.Mary		•		
Holnest		•		•
Holwell		•		
Hook		•	•	
Horton		•		
Ibberton		•		
Iwerne-Courtnay		•		
Iwerne-Minster		•		
Iwerne-Steepleton		•		
Kimmeridge		•		
Kingstone		•		
Kingston-Magna		•		
Langton-Herrington		•	•	
Langton-Long-Blandford		•		
Langton-Matravers	•	•		•
Lillington		•		
Little Bredy		•		
Litton-Cheney		•	•	
Loders		•	•	
Long Bredy		•		
Long Critchell		•		
Longburton	•	•		•
Lydlinch		•		•
Lyme-Regis		•	•	
Lytchett-Matravers		•		
Lytchett-Minster		•		
Maiden-Newton		•	•	
Mapperton			•	
Marnhull	•			•
Marshwood			•	
Melbury-Bubb		•		
Melbury-Osmond		•		
Melbury-Sampford		•		
Melcombe-Horsey		•		
Melcombe-Regis		•		
Melplash		•		
Milbourn-St. Andrew		•		
Milton Abbas		•	•	
Mintern-Magna		•		
Mosterton			•	
Nether Compton		•		
Netherbury		•	•	
North Poorton			•	
North Wooten	•			•
Overcompton		•		
Owermoigne	•			•
Piddlehinton	•			•
Piddletown			•	

PARISH	PARISH REGISTERS	BISHOPS' TRANSCRIPTS	BOYD'S MARRIAGE INDEX	PR PRINT-OUTS
Pilsdon			•	
Poorstock			•	•
Portisham			•	
Preston			•	
Radipole		•		
Rampisham			•	
Ryme-Intrinsica			•	
Shillingstone				•
Shipton George		•	•	
South Perrott			•	
Stalbridge			•	
Stoke-Abbot			•	
Stratton			•	•
Studland		•		
Sturminster-Marshall	•			•
Swanage				•
Swyre			•	
Symondsbury			•	
Tarrant-Hinton	•			•
Thorncombe			•	
Thornford	•			
Toller-Fratrum			•	
Toller-Porcorum	•		•	•
Upper Cerne			•	
Walditch			•	
Wambrook	•		•	
West Chelborough		•	•	
West Chickerell		•	•	
West Compton Abbas		•		
West Fordington		•		
West Knighton		•		
West Lulworth		•		
Whitchurch-Canonicorum			•	
Wimborne-Minster				•
Winford-Eagle			•	
Woodsford				•
Wootten-Fitzpaine			•	
Wraxall			•	•
Wyke-Regis			•	
Yetminster			•	
DURHAM*				
Aycliffe				•
Barnard-Castle	•			•
Billingham	•			•
Bishop Middleham				•
Boldon	•			
Brancepeth				•
Brigham	•			
Castle-Eden	•			•

England

* COUNTY / SHIRE

PARISH	PARISH REGISTERS	BISHOPS' TRANSCRIPTS	BOYD'S MARRIAGE INDEX	PR PRINT-OUTS
Chester-Le-Street	•			•
Cockfield	•			
Coniscliffe	•			•
Dalton Le Dale	•			•
Denton	•			•
Durham	•			•
Easington	•			
Ebchester	•			
Edmond Byers	•			•
Egglescliffe	•			
Elton	•			
Embleton	•			
Escomb	•			•
Esh	•			•
Gainford	•			•
Gateshead	•			•
Great Aycliffe	•			•
Great Stainton	•			•
Greatham	•			
Grindon	•			•
Hamsterley	•			
Haughton-Le-Skerne	•			•
Heworth	•			•
Houghton-Le-Spring	•			•
Hunstanworth	•			•
Hurworth	•			•
Jarrow	•			•
Lanchester	•			•
Long Newton	•			
Low Dinsdale	•			•
Medomsley	•			•
Merrington	•			
Middleton-In-Teesdale	•			
Middleton-St. George	•			•
Monk-Hesleton	•			•
Monk-Wearmouth	•			•
Muggleswick	•			
Norton	•			•
Pittington	•			
Redmarshall	•			
Ryton	•			•
Sadberge				•
St. AndrewAcukland	•			•
St. Helen Auckland	•			•
Seaham	•			•
Sedgefield	•			•
Sockburn	•			
South Sheilds	•			•
Staindrop	•			•
Stanhope	•			•
Sunderland	•			•
Tanfield	•			•
Trimdon	•			•
Washington	•			•
Whickham	•			•
Whitburn	•			
Whorlton	•			•
Winston	•			•
Witton Gilbert	•			
Witton-Le-Wear	•			
Wolsingham	•			
ESSEX*				
Abberton		•		
Aldham		•		
Alphamstone	•	•		•
Alresford	•			•
Althorne	•			•
Ardleigh		•		
Ashdon	•		•	•
Asheldham		•		
Ashen		•		
Ashingdon		•	•	
Aveley		•		
Barking		•		
Barnston		•		
Basildon		•		
Beaumont-Cum-Moze	•			
Belchamp Otten		•		
Belchamp Walter	•	•		•
Berden		•		
Berechurch	•	•		•
Birch		•		
Birdbrook		•		
Black Notley		•		
Blackmore	•	•		•
Bobbingworth	•	•		•
Bocking	•			•
Boreham		•		
Borley	•	•		•
Bowers-Gifford	•	•		
Boxted			•	
Bradfield	•	•		
Bradwell	•	•		
Brightlingsea		•		•
Broomfield		•		
Broxted		•		
Bulmer	•	•		•
Bulphan		•		
Bumpstead-Helion		•		
Bumpstead-Steeple	•	•		
Bures-Mount		•		
Burnham		•		
Burstead		•		
Buttsbury	•	•		•
Canewdon		•		
Castle-Hedingham	•	•		•
Chadwell		•		
Chapel		•		
Chelmsford		•	•	
Chickney	•	•		•
Chignal-St. James	•			•
Chignal-Smealey	•	•		
Chigwell	•	•		•
Childerditch	•	•		•
Chingford		•		
Chrishall	•			•
Clavering	•	•		•
Coggeshall		•		
Colchester	•	•		•
Cold Norton	•	•		•
Colne	•			
Colne-Engaine		•		
Colne-Wakes		•		
Colne-White	•	•		•
Copford	•	•		•
Corringham		•		
Cranham		•		
Creeksea		•		
Cressing	•	•		
Dagenham		•		
Danbury		•		
Debden		•		
Dengie		•		
Doddinghurst	•	•		•
Dover-Court		•		
Downham		•		
Dunton		•		
Earls Colne				•
East Ham		•		
East Hanningfield	•	•		•
East Horndon	•	•		•
East Mersea	•	•		
East Tilbury	•	•		
Easthorpe		•		
Elmdon	•	•		•
Elmstead	•	•		•
Elsenham	•			•

England

* COUNTY / SHIRE

PARISH	PARISH REGISTERS	BISHOPS' TRANSCRIPTS	BOYD'S MARRIAGE INDEX	PR PRINT-OUTS
Epping	•	•		•
Fairsted	•	•		•
Farnham		•		
Faulkbourn	•	•		•
Finchingfield		•		
Fobbing		•		
Fordham		•		•
Foxearth		•		
Frating	•			•
Frinton		•		
Fryerning	•	•		
Fyfield	•	•		•
Gestingthorpe	•	•		•
Goldhanger		•		
Good Easter	•			
Gosfield		•		
Grays Thurrock		•		
Great Baddow		•		
Great Bardfield		•		
Great Bentley	•	•		•
Great Braxted		•		
Great Bromley	•	•		•
Great Canfield	•	•	•	•
Great Chesterford	•			•
Great Coggeshall		•		•
Great Dunmow		•		
Great Easton		•		
Great Hallingbury	•	•	•	
Great Henny	•	•		•
Great Holland		•		
Great Horksley		•	•	
Great Leighs		•	•	
Great Maplestead		•		
Great Oakley	•	•		•
Great Parndon		•		
Great Saling		•		
Great Sampford		•		
Great Tey		•		
Great Totham		•		
Great Wakering		•		
Great Waltham	•	•		•
Great Warley		•		
Great Wigborough	•	•		•
Great Yeldham	•			•
Greenstead	•	•		•
Hadleigh		•		
Hadstock	•			•
Halstead		•		
Hampton Court		•		

PARISH	PARISH REGISTERS	BISHOPS' TRANSCRIPTS	BOYD'S MARRIAGE INDEX	PR PRINT-OUTS
Harlow		•		
Hatfield-Broad-Oak	•			
Hatfield-Peverel		•		
Hawkwell		•		
Hazeleigh	•	•		•
Hempstead		•		
High Easter	•	•		
High Laver	•	•		
High Ongar		•		
High Roothing		•		
Hockley	•	•		•
Hornchurch	•			•
Hutton		•		
Ingatestone	•			•
Ingrave		•		
Inworth		•		
Kelvedon	•	•		•
Laindon		•		
Lamarsh	•	•		•
Lambourne	•	•		•
Langdon-Hills	•			•
Langford		•		
Langham		•		
Latton	•	•		
Layer-Breton		•		
Layer-De-La-Hay		•		
Laver-Marney		•		
Lexden	•			•
Leyton		•		
Lindsell		•		
Liston		•		
Little Baddow				•
Little Bardfield		•		
Little Braxted	•	•		•
Little Bromley	•			•
Little Burstead		•		
Little Canfield		•		
Little Chesterford	•	•		•
Little Clacton		•		
Little Dunmow		•		
Little Easton	•	•		
Little Hadham		•		
Little Hallingbury		•		
Little Holland		•		
Little Horksley	•		•	•
Little Ilford	•			•
Little Laver	•	•		
Little Leighs		•	•	
Little Maplestead		•		

PARISH	PARISH REGISTERS	BISHOPS' TRANSCRIPTS	BOYD'S MARRIAGE INDEX	PR PRINT-OUTS
Little Oakley		•		
Little Parndon		•		
Little Sampford	•	•		
Little Stambridge		•		
Little Thurrock		•		
Little Totham		•		
Little Wakering		•		
Little Waltham		•		
Little Warley		•		
Little Wigborough	•	•		•
Little Yeldham	•	•		•
Loughton	•	•		•
Magdalen-Laver	•	•		•
Maldon		•		
Manewden		•		•
Margaretting	•	•		
Marks-Tey	•	•		•
Markshall		•		
Mashbury	•	•		•
Mersea		•		
Messing		•		
Middleton		•		
Mistley	•	•		•
Moreton	•	•		•
Mountnessing	•	•		•
Mundon	•	•		•
Navestock			•	
Nazeing	•	•		
Netteswell	•	•		
Nevendon		•		
Newport		•		
North Benfleet		•		
North Fambridge		•		
North Shoebury		•		
North Weald-Bassett		•		
Norton-Mandeville		•		
Ongar	•	•		•
Orsett	•	•		•
Ovington		•		
Paglesham		•		
Panfield		•		
Pattiswick		•		
Pebmarsh		•		
Pentlow		•		
Pitsea		•		
Prittlewell	•			•
Purleigh		•		
Quendon		•		
Rhinham		•		

England

* COUNTY / SHIRE

PARISH	PARISH REGISTERS	BISHOPS' TRANSCRIPTS	BOYD'S MARRIAGE INDEX	PR PRINT-OUTS
Ramsden-Bellhouse		•		
Ramsden-Crays		•		
Rawreth		•		
Rayne		•		
Rettondon		•		
Rickling		•		
Ridgwell		•		
Rivenhall	•	•		
Rochford		•		
Romford	•			•
Roothing Abbots		•		
Roothing Aythorp	•	•		•
Roothing Beauchamp		•		
Roothing Leaden	•	•		•
Roothing Margaret	•	•		•
Roxwell	•		•	•
Runwell		•		
St. Lawrence	•			
St. Lawrence Newland		•		
St. Osyth		•		
Salcott		•		
Sandon	•	•		
Shalford		•		
Sheering		•		
Shelley		•		
Shellow-Bowells	•	•		•
Shenfield		•		
South Benfleet		•		
South Hanningfield	•	•		
South Ockendon		•		
South Shoebury		•		
South Weald		•		•
Southminster	•	•		
Springfield		•		
Stambourne	•	•		•
Stanford-Le-Hope		•		
Stanford-Rivers	•	•		•
Stanstead-Mountfichet		•		
Stanway		•		
Stapleford-Abbots		•		
Stapleford-Tawney	•	•		•
Stebbing		•		
Steeple		•		
Stifford	•	•		•
Stock	•	•		•
Stondon-Massey		•		
Stow-Maries		•		
Streethall	•			•
Sturmere		•		

PARISH	PARISH REGISTERS	BISHOPS' TRANSCRIPTS	BOYD'S MARRIAGE INDEX	PR PRINT-OUTS
Sutton		•		
Tendring		•		
Terling		•		•
Thaxted	•	•		•
Thorrington	•			
Thoydon-Bois		•		
Thoydon-Mount	•	•		•
Thonon-Garnon		•		
Thundersley		•		
Tilbury-Fort		•		
Tilty	•			•
Tollesbury		•		
Tolleshunt-D'Arcy		•		
Tolleshunt-Knights	•	•		•
Tolleshunt-Major		•		
Toppesfield	•	•		•
Twinstead		•		•
Ugley		•		
Ulting		•		
Upminster		•		
Vange		•		
Waltham-Abbey	•			
Walthamstow			•	
Wendon-Lofts	•	•		•
Wennington		•		
West Bergholt		•		
West Ham		•		
West Hanningfield	•	•		•
West Horndon		•		
West Mersea	•	•		
West Tilbury	•	•		
Wethersfield	•	•		•
White Notley	•	•		•
White Woothing	•	•		
Wickford		•		
Wickham Bishops	•	•		•
Wickham St. Paul	•			
Widdington		•		
Widford		•	•	
Willingale-Doe	•	•		•
Willingale-Spain		•		
Wimbish	•	•		•
Wivenhoe		•		
Woodham-Ferris		•		
Woodham-Mortimer	•	•		•
Woodham-Walter	•	•		•
Wormingford		•	•	
Wrabness		•		
Writtle		•		

PARISH	PARISH REGISTERS	BISHOPS' TRANSCRIPTS	BOYD'S MARRIAGE INDEX	PR PRINT-OUTS
GLOUSCESTER*				
Abinghall	•	•		•
Acton-Turville	•	•	•	•
Adlestrop		•		•
Alderley	•	•	•	•
Alderton	•	•		•
Aldsworth	•	•		•
Alkerton				•
Alstone	•		•	•
Alvington	•		•	•
Apney-Crucis	•	•	•	•
Apney-Down				•
Apney-St. Mary		•		•
Apney-St. Peter		•		•
Arlingham	•	•		•
Ashchurch	•	•	•	•
Ashelworth	•	•		•
Ashton-Under-Hill	•	•		•
Aston-Blank	•	•	•	•
Aston-Somerville	•	•	•	•
Aston-Sub-Edge	•	•	•	•
Avening	•	•	•	•
Awre	•	•		•
Badgeworth				•
Badington	•	•		•
Badminton		•	•	•
Bakewell		•		
Barnsley	•	•		
Barnwood	•	•		•
Batsford	•	•	•	•
Baunton	•	•		•
Beckford	•	•		•
Berkeley	•	•	•	•
Beverstone	•	•	•	•
Bibury		•		
Bishops-Cleeve		•	•	•
Bisley	•	•		•
Blaisdon	•	•		•
Blakeney	•			•
Bledington	•	•		•
Boddington		•		•
Bourton-On-The-Hill	•	•		•
Bourton-On-The-Water		•	•	•
Boxwell-With-Leighterton		•	•	•
Bream	•			•
Brimpsfield	•	•		•
Bristol	•			•
Broadwell	•	•	•	•
Brockthrop		•	•	•

England

* COUNTY / SHIRE

PARISH	PARISH REGISTERS	BISHOPS' TRANSCRIPTS	BOYD'S MARRIAGE INDEX	PR PRINT-OUTS
Brockworth	•	•		•
Bromsborrow	•	•	•	•
Buckland	•	•	•	•
Bulley	•	•		•
Cam		•	•	•
Chaceley	•			•
Charfield		•		•
Charlton-Abbots	•	•		•
Charlton-Kings	•	•	•	•
Chedworth	•	•	•	•
Cheltenham	•	•		•
Cherrington		•	•	•
Childs-Wickham	•	•	•	•
Chipping-Campden	•	•		•
Churcham	•	•		•
Churchdown		•		•
Cirencester		•		•
Clifford-Chambers	•		•	•
Coaley		•	•	•
Coates		•		•
Coleford	•			
Colesborne	•	•		•
Coln-Rogers	•	•	•	•
Coln-St. Aldwin	•	•		•
Coln-St. Denis	•	•		•
Compton-Abdale		•		•
Condicote		•		•
Corse	•	•		•
Cowley		•		•
Cranham	•	•		•
Cromhall-Abbots		•		•
Cubberley		•	•	•
Daglingworth		•		•
Deerhurst	•	•		•
Didbrook		•		•
Didmarton		•	•	•
Dorsington	•		•	•
Dowdeswell		•		•
Driffield		•		•
Dumbleton	•	•		•
Duntisborne-Abbots		•	•	•
Duntisborne-Rouse		•	•	•
Dursley		•	•	•
Dymock		•	•	•
East-Leach-Martin		•		•
East-Leach-Turville		•		•
Eastington		•	•	•
Eastleach				•
Ebrington	•	•	•	•
Edge				•
Edgeworth		•	•	•
Elkstone	•	•	•	•
Elmore	•	•		•
Elmstone-Hardwicke		•		•
English-Bicknor	•	•		•
Evenlode	•			•
Fairford	•	•	•	•
Farmcote	•			•
Farmington		•		•
Filton			•	
Flaxley	•	•		•
Forthampton		•	•	•
Frampton-Upon-Severn	•	•		•
France-Lynch	•			•
Fretherne	•	•		•
Frocester		•	•	•
Gloucester	•	•		•
Great Barrington	•	•		•
Great Rissington	•	•	•	•
Great Shurdington		•		•
Great Washburne	•	•		•
Great Whitcombe	•	•		•
Guyting Power	•	•	•	•
Guyting Temple	•	•	•	•
Hampnett	•	•		•
Hampton-Maisey		•		•
Hanham				•
Hardwicke	•	•	•	•
Harescombe		•	•	•
Haresfield		•		•
Harnhill		•		•
Hartpury		•	•	•
Hasfield		•	•	•
Hatherley-Down		•		•
Hatherop	•	•	•	•
Hawkesbury	•	•	•	•
Hawling	•	•		•
Hazleton	•	•		•
Hempstead		•		•
Hewelsfield	•	•		•
Higham				•
Highnam	•			
Hill		•	•	•
Hinton-On-The-Green				•
Horsley	•	•	•	•
Horton		•	•	•
Huntley	•	•	•	•
Iccomb			•	•
Ilmington	•			•
Kemerton		•	•	•
Kempley	•	•		•
Kempsford	•	•		•
Kingscote		•	•	•
Kingstanley	•	•	•	•
Lasborough			•	
Lassington	•			•
Lechlade		•		•
Leckhampton		•		•
Leigh	•	•		•
Leonard-Stanley	•	•	•	•
Lidney	•	•		•
Little Barrington	•	•		•
Little Dean	•	•		•
Little Rissington		•	•	•
Little Sodbury		•		•
Little Washbourne	•			•
Longborough		•		•
Longhope		•		•
Longney	•	•		•
Lower Lemington	•	•	•	•
Lower Slaughter			•	
Lower Swell	•	•	•	•
Lydney				•
Maisemore	•	•	•	•
Marston-Sicca	•	•	•	•
Matson	•	•	•	•
Mickleton	•	•	•	•
Minchinghampton	•	•	•	•
Minsterworth	•	•	•	•
Miserdern		•		•
Mitcheldean	•	•	•	•
Moreton-In-The-Marsh	•	•	•	•
Moreton-Valence	•	•		•
Naunton		•		•
Newent	•	•		•
Newington-Bagpath		•		•
Newland	•	•		•
Newnham		•		•
North Cerney	•	•		•
North Nibley	•	•		•
Northleach	•	•		•
Norton		•		•
Notgrove	•	•		•
Nymphsfield	•	•	•	•
Oddington		•		•
Old Sodbury		•	•	•
Oldbury-On-The-Hill		•	•	•

England

* COUNTY / SHIRE

PARISH	PARISH REGISTERS	BISHOPS' TRANSCRIPTS	BOYD'S MARRIAGE INDEX	PR PRINT-OUTS	PARISH	PARISH REGISTERS	BISHOPS' TRANSCRIPTS	BOYD'S MARRIAGE INDEX	PR PRINT-OUTS	PARISH	PARISH REGISTERS	BISHOPS' TRANSCRIPTS	BOYD'S MARRIAGE INDEX	PR PRINT-OUTS
Oldbury-Upon-Severn	•	•	•	•	Stanton	•	•	•	•	Winson		•		
Oldland				•	Stanway				•	Winstone		•	•	•
Olveston			•		Staunton	•	•		•	Withington	•	•		•
Owlpen	•	•	•	•	Staverton		•		•	Wollastone		•	•	
Oxenhall	•	•		•	Stinchcombe		•	•	•	Woodchester	•	•	•	•
Oxenton		•		•	Stone		•	•	•	Woolstone		•		•
Ozleworth		•	•	•	Stonehouse	•	•	•	•	Wormington		•	•	•
Painswick	•	•	•	•	Stow-On-The-Wold	•	•		•	Wotton-Under-Edge		•		•
Pauntley	•			•	Stratton	•	•		•	Yanworth	•	•		•
Pebworth		•		•	Stroud	•	•		•	Yate		•		•
Pitchcombe	•	•		•	Sudenley-Manor	•			•	**HAMPSHIRE***				
Poulton		•			Sutton-Under-Brails			•		Abbots-Ann	•			
Prestbury	•		•	•	Swindon		•	•	•	Aldershot	•		•	•
Preston		•		•	Syde		•		•	Alresford	•			
Quedgeley	•	•	•	•	Taynton	•	•		•	Alton	•			
Quenington	•	•		•	Teddington	•				Alverstoke	•			
Quinton	•	•	•	•	Tetbury	•	•	•	•	Amport	•		•	
Randwick		•		•	Tewkesbury	•	•		•	Andover	•			•
Rangeworthy		•		•	Thornbury	•	•	•	•	Ashe	•			
Redmarley				•	Tibberton	•	•		•	Basing	•		•	
Rendcombe	•	•	•	•	Tidenham	•	•		•	Basingstroke	•		•	
Ressington-Wick		•	•	•	Tirley	•	•	•	•	Baughurst			•	
Rockhampton		•		•	Toddenham		•	•	•	Beauworth	•			
Rodborough	•	•	•	•	Toddington		•		•	Bedhampton	•			
Rodmarton		•		•	Tormarton	•		•	•	Bentley	•		•	•
Ruardean		•		•	Tortworth		•	•	•	Bentworth			•	
Rudford	•	•		•	Tredington				•	Bighton	•			
St. Briavels		•		•	Turkdean	•	•	•	•	Binstead	•			
Saintbury	•	•	•	•	Twining		•	•	•	Bishops-Sutton	•			
Salperton	•	•		•	Tytherington		•		•	Bishops-Waltham	•			
Sandhurst	•	•		•	Uley	•	•	•	•	Blendworth	•			•
Sapperton	•	•		•	Upleadon	•	•		•	Boarhunt	•			
Saul	•	•	•	•	Upper Slaughter		•	•	•	Boldre	•		•	
Seven Hampton	•	•	•	•	Upper Swell	•	•		•	Bonchurch	•			
Shepscombe				•	Upton St. Leonard		•		•	Bossington	•			
Sherbourne	•	•		•	Walton-Cardiff		•			Botley	•			
Shipton-Moyne	•	•	•	•	West Littleton	•			•	Bourne-St. Mary			•	
Shipton-Oliffe	•	•		•	Westbury-On-Severn	•	•		•	Brading			•	
Shipton-Sollars	•			•	Westcote			•		Bramdean	•			
Siddington		•		•	Weston-Birt		•	•	•	Bramley	•		•	
Side	•		•	•	Weston-Sub-Edge	•	•	•	•	Bramshaw	•	•		•
Siston	•			•	Weston-Upon-Avon	•	•	•	•	Bramshott	•			
Slimbridge		•	•	•	Whaddon		•	•	•	Bransgore	•			
Snowshill		•	•	•	Wheatenhurst		•		•	Brockenhurst	•			
Sodbury-Chipping		•	•	•	Whittington		•	•	•	Broughton	•			
South Cerney	•	•		•	Wickwar		•	•	•	Brown-Candover	•			
Southrop		•	•	•	Willersey	•	•	•	•	Bullington			•	
Spoonbed				•	Winchcombe	•	•	•	•	Burghclere			•	
Standish		•	•	•	Windrush	•	•		•	Buriton	•			

England

* COUNTY / SHIRE

PARISH	PARISH REGISTERS	BISHOPS' TRANSCRIPTS	BOYD'S MARRIAGE INDEX	PR PRINT-OUTS
Burley	•			
Calbourne			•	
Candover-Preston			•	
Carisbrooke	•			
Catherington	•			•
Chalton	•			•
Cheriton	•			
Chilworth	•			
Christchurch	•			
Church-Oakley	•		•	
Clanfield	•			•
Clatford-Goodworth	•			
Cliddesden	•		•	
Colemore	•			•
Combe			•	
Compton	•			
Cove	•			•
Cowes	•			•
Crawley	•		•	
Crondall	•		•	
Crookham	•			
Deane	•		•	•
Dogmersfield			•	
Droxfield	•			
Droxford	•			
Dummer	•		•	
Durley	•			
East Dean	•			
East Meon	•			
East Stratton	•			
East Tisted	•			
East Tytherley	•			
East Wellow	•			•
East Woodhay			•	
East Worldham	•			•
Eastrop			•	•
Eling			•	•
Elvetham			•	
Empshot	•			
Eversley			•	
Ewhurst			•	
Ewshott	•			
Faccombe			•	
Fareham	•			•
Farleigh-Wallop	•			
Farlington	•			•
Farnborough	•		•	
Fawley	•			
Fordingbridge	•			•

PARISH	PARISH REGISTERS	BISHOPS' TRANSCRIPTS	BOYD'S MARRIAGE INDEX	PR PRINT-OUTS
Foxcott				•
Freemantle	•			
Freshwater			•	
Froxfield	•			
Froyle	•			
Gatcombe	•			•
Godshill	•			•
Gosport	•			
Grateley	•			
Greatham	•			
Hambledon	•			
Hampstead-Marshall	•	•		•
Hannington			•	
Hartley-Mauditt	•			•
Hartley-Wespall	•		•	
Hartley-Wintney			•	
Havant	•			
Hawkley	•			
Hawley	•			
Hayling	•			•
Headley	•			
Heckfield			•	
Herriard	•			
Highclere			•	
Hinton Admiral	•			
Hinton-Ampner	•			
Holdenhurst	•			
Holybourne	•			
Hordle				•
Houghton	•			
Hunton	•		•	
Hursley	•			
Hurstbourne-Priors			•	
Hurstbourne-Tarrant			•	
Hyde				
Idsworth	•			•
Itchin-Abbas	•			
Kilmiston	•			
Kingsclere	•	•		•
Kingsley	•			
Kingsworthy			•	
Knights Enham	•		•	•
Laverstoke			•	
Linkenholt	•		•	
Litchfield			•	
Lockerley	•			
Long Sutton			•	
Lyndhurst	•			

PARISH	PARISH REGISTERS	BISHOPS' TRANSCRIPTS	BOYD'S MARRIAGE INDEX	PR PRINT-OUTS
Maplederwell			•	
Mattingley	•			
Medstead	•			
Micheldever	•			
Millbrook	•			•
Minstead	•			•
Monk-Sherborne	•			•
Monxton			•	
Mottisfont	•			
Mottiston	•			•
Nately-Scures			•	
Nately-Up				
Newham			•	
Newport			•	•
Newton-Near-Newbury			•	
Niton			•	
North Baddesley	•			
North Hayling	•			•
North Waltham	•		•	
Northwood	•			
Nursling	•			
Odiham	•		•	
Old Alresford	•			
Overton			•	
Ovington	•			
Pamber	•			
Penton-Mewsey			•	
Popham			•	
Porchester	•			•
Portsea	•			
Portsmouth	•		•	
Priors-Dean	•			•
Quarley	•			
Ringwood	•			
Rockbourne	•			
Romsey	•			
Ropley	•			
Rotherwick	•		•	
Rowner	•		•	
Rownhams	•			
Ryde	•			•
St. Lawrence	•			
St. Mary-Extra	•			
Selbourne	•			•
Shalden	•			•
Shanklin	•			
Sherborne-St. John	•		•	•
Sherfield-English	•			
Sherfield-Upon-Lodden	•		•	

England

* COUNTY / SHIRE

PARISH	PARISH REGISTERS	BISHOPS' TRANSCRIPTS	BOYD'S MARRIAGE INDEX	PR PRINT-OUTS
Shidfield	•			
Shirley	•			
Silchester			•	
Sopley			•	
South Hayling	•			
South Stoneham	•			
South Warnborough			•	
Southampton	•	•		
Southwick	•			
Steventon	•		•	•
Stockbridge	•			
Stoke-Charity	•		•	
Stratfieldsaye	•		•	
Stratfield-Turgis	•		•	
Swanmore	•			
Tadley	•		•	
Tangley			•	
Titchborne	•			
Tufton	•		•	
Tunorbury	•			
Tunworth	•			
Upper Clatford	•			
Upton-Gray	•			
Vernham-Dean	•		•	
Warblington	•			•
Warnford	•			
Weeke	•			
West Meon	•		•	
West Tisted	•			
West Tytherley	•			
West Worldham	•			•
Westend	•			
Weston	•			
Weston-Patrick	•			
Weyhill			•	
Whitchurch	•		•	
Whitsbury	•			
Whitwell			•	
Wickham	•			
Widley	•			•
Wield	•			
Winchester	•		•	
Winchfield			•	
Winnall	•			
Winslade	•		•	
Wolverton			•	
Wonston	•		•	
Woodmancott			•	
Wootton-St. Lawrence	•		•	

PARISH	PARISH REGISTERS	BISHOPS' TRANSCRIPTS	BOYD'S MARRIAGE INDEX	PR PRINT-OUTS
Worting			•	
Wymering	•			•
Yateley	•		•	
Yaverland			•	
HEREFORD*				
Abbeydore	•	•		
Aconbury	•	•		
Allensmore	•	•		
Almeley	•	•		
Ashperton	•	•		
Aston	•			
Aston-Ingham	•			•
Avenbury	•			
Aymestry	•			
Bacton	•			
Ballingham	•			
Bartestree	•	•		
Birley	•	•		
Bishops-Frome	•	•		
Bishopstone	•	•		
Blakemere	•	•		
Bodenham	•	•		
Bosbury	•	•		•
Boulstone	•	•		
Brampton-Abbotts	•	•		
Brampton-Bryan		•		
Bredenbury	•	•		
Brewardine	•	•		•
Breinton	•	•		
Bridge-Sollars	•	•		•
Bridstow	•	•		
Brilley	•			
Brimfield		•		
Brinsop	•	•		
Brobury	•	•		
Brockampton	•	•		
Bromyard	•	•		
Burghill	•	•		
Burrington	•	•		
Byford	•	•		
Byton	•	•		
Callow	•	•		
Canon-Frome	•	•		
Canon-Pyon		•		
Castle-Frome		•		
Clehonger	•	•		
Clifford		•		
Clodock	•	•		•
Coddington		•		

PARISH	PARISH REGISTERS	BISHOPS' TRANSCRIPTS	BOYD'S MARRIAGE INDEX	PR PRINT-OUTS
Collington	•			
Colwall	•	•		
Crasswall		•		
Credenhill	•	•		
Croft	•	•		
Cusop		•		
Dewsall	•			
Dilwyn	•	•		
Dindor	•	•		
Donnington	•			•
Dormington	•			
Dorstone	•	•		
Downton	•	•		
Dulas	•	•		•
Eardisland	•	•		
Eardisley	•	•		
East and West Cradley	•	•		
Eaton-Bishop	•			
Edvin Ralph	•	•		
Elton	•			
Eskley		•		
Evesbatch	•			
Ewyas-Harold	•			
Eye	•	•		
Eyton		•		
Fawley	•			•
Felton	•	•		
Ford	•			
Fownhope	•	•		•
Foy		•		
Ganarew	•	•		
Garway	•	•		
Goodrich		•		
Grafton		•		
Grendon-Bishop	•	•		
Hampton-Bishop	•	•		
Hardwick		•		
Harewood	•	•		•
Hatfield	•	•		
Hentland	•	•		
Hereford	•	•		
Hide		•		
Holm	•	•		
Holmer	•	•		
Hope-Mansell	•	•		
Hope-Under-Dinmore	•	•		
How-Caple		•		
Humber		•		
Huntington	•	•		

England

* COUNTY / SHIRE

PARISH	PARISH REGISTERS	BISHOPS' TRANSCRIPTS	BOYD'S MARRIAGE INDEX	PR PRINT-OUTS
Kenchester	•	•		
Kenderchurch	•	•		
Kentchurch	•	•		
Killpeck	•	•		
Kimbolton		•		
Kings-Caple		•		
Kings-Pyon	•	•		•
Kingsland	•	•		
Kingstone		•		
Kington	•	•		
Kinnersley	•			
Knill	•	•		
Lancillo				•
Laysters	•	•		•
Lea	•	•		
Ledbury	•	•		•
Leinthall-Starkes	•	•		
Leintwardine	•	•		
Leominster		•		
Letton	•	•		
Lingen	•	•		
Linton		•		
Little Birch	•	•		
Little Cowarne	•	•		
Little Dewchurch	•	•		
Little Hereford	•	•		
Little Marcle	•	•		
Llancillo	•	•		
Llandinabo		•		
Llangarren	•	•		
Llanrothall	•			
Llanwarne	•	•		
Long Grove	•			
Lower Bullingham		•		
Lucton	•	•		
Lugwardine	•	•		•
Lyonshall	•	•		
Mansell-Gamage	•	•		
Mansell-Lacy	•	•		
Marden	•	•		
Marstow	•	•		
Michaelchurch-Eskley		•		
Middleton-On-The-Hill		•		
Moccas	•	•		
Monkland		•		
Monnington-Upon-Wye		•		
Mordiford		•		
Moreton-Jefferies	•	•		•
Moreton-Upon-Lugg	•	•		
Much Birch	•			
Much Cowarne	•			
Much Dewchurch	•			
Much Marcle	•	•		
Munsley	•			•
Newton		•		
Norton-Canon	•	•		•
Ogle-Pritchard	•	•		
Oldcastle		•		
Orcop	•	•		
Orleton		•		
Pembridge	•			
Pencombe	•	•		
Pencoyd	•	•		•
Peterchurch		•		
Peterstow	•	•		
Pipe-Cum-Lyde	•	•		•
Pixley		•		
Preston-Upon-Wye		•		
Preston-Wynne	•	•		
Puddlestone		•		
Putley		•		
Richards-Castle	•	•		
Ross	•	•		
Rowlstone	•	•		•
St. Devereux	•	•		
St. Margaret	•	•		•
St. Weonards	•	•		
Sarnesfield	•	•		•
Sellack	•	•		•
Shobdon	•	•		
Sollershope		•		
Stanford Bishop	•	•		
Stanton-Upon-Arrow	•	•		
Staunton-Upon-Wye	•	•		
Stoke-Bliss		•		
Stoke-Edith	•	•		
Stoke-Lacy	•	•		
Stoke-Prior	•	•		
Stretford	•	•		
Stretton-Grandsome	•	•		
Stretton-Suginas	•	•		
Sutton-St. Michael	•	•		
Sutton-St. Nicholas	•	•		
Tarrington	•	•		
Tedstone-Delamere		•		
Tedstone-Wafer	•	•		
Thornbury	•	•		
Thruxton	•	•		
Tiberton		•		
Titley	•	•		
Tretire-With-Michaelchurch	•	•		
Turnastone		•		
Ullingswick	•	•		
Upper Bullingham	•	•		
Upper Kingsham	•	•		
Upper-Sapey		•		
Upton-Bishop	•	•		
Vowchurch		•		
Wacton	•	•		
Walford		•		
Walterstone	•	•		
Wellington	•	•		
Welsh-Bicknor		•		
Welsh-Newton	•	•		
Weobly	•	•		
West Hide	•			
Weston-Beggard	•	•		
Weston-Under-Penyard	•	•		
Whitbourne		•		
Whitchurch	•	•		
Whitney	•	•		
Wigmore	•	•		
Willersley	•	•		
Winforton	•	•		
Withington	•	•		•
Wolferlow	•	•		
Woolhope	•	•		
Wormbridge	•	•		
Wormsley	•	•		
Yarkhill	•	•		•
Yarpole	•	•		
Yazor	•	•		
HERTFORD*				
Abbotts-Langley	•	•		
Albury	•	•	•	•
Aldenham	•	•		•
Anstey	•	•		
Ardeley	•	•	•	•
Ashwell	•	•		•
Aspeden	•	•		
Aston	•	•		
Ayott-St. Lawrence	•	•		•
Ayott-St. Peter	•	•		•
Baldock	•	•		
Barkway	•			
Barley	•	•	•	
Barnet	•	•		•

England

* COUNTY SHIRE

PARISH	PARISH REGISTERS	BISHOPS' TRANSCRIPTS	BOYD'S MARRIAGE INDEX	PR PRINT-OUTS	PARISH	PARISH REGISTERS	BISHOPS' TRANSCRIPTS	BOYD'S MARRIAGE INDEX	PR PRINT-OUTS	PARISH	PARISH REGISTERS	BISHOPS' TRANSCRIPTS	BOYD'S MARRIAGE INDEX	PR PRINT-OUTS
Bayford	•	•		•	High Wych	•				Sarratt	•	•		•
Bengeo	•	•	•	•	Hinxworth	•	•		•	Sawbridgeworth	•	•		
Bennington	•	•	•	•	Hitchin	•	•		•	Shenley	•	•		•
Berkhamstead-St. Mary	•	•		•	Hoddeson	•				Shephall	•	•	•	
Bishops-Stortford	•				Holwell	•				Standon	•	•		
Bovington	•	•	•		Hunsdon				•	Stanstead-Abbotts	•			
Braintfield	•	•		•	Ickleford	•	•		•	Stanstead-St. Margaret	•	•		
Braughin	•				Ippollitts	•	•	•	•	Stapleford	•	•		•
Brent-Pelham	•				Kelshall	•	•		•	Stavenage	•	•		•
Broxbourne	•				Kensworth	•	•	•		Sunnyside	•			
Buckland	•	•			Kimpton	•	•		•	Tewin	•	•		•
Buntingford	•				Kings-Langley	•	•		•	Therfield	•	•		•
Bushey	•	•	•	•	Kings-Walden	•	•		•	Thorley	•			
Bygrave	•	•		•	Knebworth	•	•	•		Throcking	•	•		•
Caldecote	•	•		•	Layston	•	•			Thundridge	•	•		
Cheshunt	•	•			Letchworth	•	•	•	•	Totteridge	•	•	•	•
Chipperfield	•				Lilley	•	•		•	Tring	•	•	•	•
Clothall	•	•		•	Little Anwell	•				Walden-St. Paul's	•	•		
Codicote	•	•			Little Berkhampstead	•	•	•		Walkern	•	•	•	•
Colney-Heath	•				Little Gaddesden	•	•		•	Wallington	•	•		•
Colney-St. Peter	•				Little Hadham				•	Waltham-Cross	•			
Cottered	•	•		•	Little Horwood	•	•			Ware	•	•		
Datchworth	•	•	•	•	Little Munden	•	•		•	Watford	•	•		•
Digswell	•	•		•	Little Wymondley	•	•			Watton	•	•		•
East Barnet	•	•			Long Marston	•	•		•	Watton-At-Stone	•		•	
Eastwick	•		•		Meesden	•				Welwyn	•	•		
Elstree	•	•	•	•	Missenden	•	•		•	West Hyde	•			
Essendon	•	•		•	Newnham	•	•		•	Westmill	•	•		•
Flamsted	•	•		•	North Mimms	•	•		•	Weston	•	•		
Flaunden	•	•	•	•	Northaw	•	•		•	Wheathampstead	•	•		•
Frogmore	•				Norton	•	•			Widford	•			
Furneux Pelham	•				Offley	•	•	•	•	Wiggington	•	•		•
Gilston	•		•		Pelham-Stocking					Willian	•	•		•
Granborough	•				Pirton	•	•		•	Wormley	•	•		
Graveley	•	•	•	•	Puttenham	•	•	•	•	Wyddiall	•	•		
Great Amwell	•	•			Radlett	•				**HUNTINGDON***				
Great Berkhampstead	•	•	•	•	Radwell	•	•		•	Abbots-Ripton	•	•		
Great Gaddesden	•	•		•	Redbourn	•	•		•	Alconby-Weston	•	•		
Great Hadham	•				Reed	•				Alwalton	•	•		
Great Hormead	•		•	•	Rickmansworth	•	•	•	•	Bluntisham	•	•		
Great Munden	•	•		•	Ridge	•	•		•	Botolph-Bridge	•	•		
Great Wymondley	•	•		•	Royston	•	•		•	Brington	•	•		
Harpenden	•	•		•	Rushden	•	•		•	Buckworth	•	•		
Hatfield	•	•		•	Sacomb	•	•			Bury			•	
Hemel-Hampstead	•	•	•	•	St. Albans	•	•		•	Bythorn	•	•		
Hertford	•	•		•	St. Peter	•	•		•	Chesterton	•	•		
Hertingfordbury	•	•		•	St. Stephen's	•	•		•	Conington	•	•		
Hexton	•	•		•	Sandon	•	•		•	Coppingford	•	•		
High Cross	•				Sandridge	•	•			Diddington	•			

England

* COUNTY / SHIRE

PARISH	PARISH REGISTERS	BISHOPS' TRANSCRIPTS	BOYD'S MARRIAGE INDEX	PR PRINT-OUTS
Earith	•			
Elton	•			
Farcett	•			
Fen-Stanton	•			
Fletton	•			
Glatton	•	•		
Godmanchester	•	•		
Great Gidding	•			
Great Gransden	•			
Great Paxton	•	•		
Great Staughton	•			
Great Stukeley	•	•		
Haddon	•	•		
Hail-Weston	•	•		
Hartford	•	•		
Hemingford-Abbots	•	•		
Hilton	•	•		
Holme	•	•		
Holywell-Cum-Needingworth	•	•		
Houghton	•	•		
Huntingdon	•	•		
Keyston	•	•		
Kimbolton	•	•		
Kings-Ripton	•	•		
Leighton-Bromswold	•	•		
Little Gidding	•			
Little Paxton	•	•		
Little Raveley			•	
Little Stukeley	•	•		
Molesworth	•	•		
Newton-Water		•		
Offord-Cluny	•	•		
Offord-Darcy	•	•		
Old Weston	•	•		
Orton-Longville	•	•		
Orton-Waterville	•	•		
Ramsey			•	
Sibson	•	•		
Southoe	•	•		
Standground	•	•		
Steeple Gidding	•	•		
Stibbington	•	•		
Stow	•	•		
Swineshead	•			•
Toseland	•			•
Upton		•		
Upwood	•			
Winwick	•	•		
Wistow			•	

PARISH	PARISH REGISTERS	BISHOPS' TRANSCRIPTS	BOYD'S MARRIAGE INDEX	PR PRINT-OUTS
Woodwalton	•	•		
Wyton	•	•		
Yaxley	•	•		
Yelling	•	•		
KENT*				
Acrise	•			
Addington	•			
Aldington	•			
Allhallows	•			
Allington	•			
Ash	•			
Aylesford	•			•
Barham	•			
Barming	•			
Beaksbourne	•			•
Bearsted	•			•
Beckenham	•			
Bexley	•			
Birchington	•			•
Birling	•			
Borden	•			•
Boughton-Under-Blean	•			•
Boxley	•			•
Brasted	•			
Brenchley	•			•
Bromley	•	•		
Brookland	•			
Burham	•			
Canterbury	•			•
Capel	•			
Chalk	•			
Charing	•			
Charlton-Near-Dover			•	•
Charlton-Near-Woolwich	•			
Chartham	•			
Chatham	•			
Chelsfield	•			
Cheriton	•			
Chevening	•			
Chiddingston	•			
Chilham	•			•
Chiselhurst	•			
Chislett	•			•
Cowden	•			
Cranbrook	•			
Crayford	•			
Cuxton	•			
Darenth	•			
Dartford	•			•

PARISH	PARISH REGISTERS	BISHOPS' TRANSCRIPTS	BOYD'S MARRIAGE INDEX	PR PRINT-OUTS
Davington	•			•
Denton (Near Dover)	•			
Ditton	•			
Dover	•			•
Downe	•			
East Farleigh	•			•
East Malling	•			
East Peckham	•	•		
East Wickham	•			
Eastwell	•			
Edenbridge				•
Elmsted	•			
Elmstone	•			•
Eltham		•		•
Erith	•			•
Eynesford	•		•	
Farnborough	•			
Farningham	•			
Faversham	•			
Folkestone	•			•
Frittenden	•			
Gillingham	•			
Godmersham	•			
Goodnestone (Near Sandwich)	•			•
Gravesend	•			•
Greenwich	•			•
Hadlow	•			
Halden	•			
Halling	•			
Halsted	•		•	
Harbledown	•			•
Harrietsham	•			•
Hastingleigh	•			
Hayes	•			
Hever	•			
High Halstow	•			
Higham (Near Rochester)	•			•
Hoo (Near Rochester)	•			
Hoo (Near Strood)	•			
Horsemonden	•			
Horton-Kirby	•			•
Hunton	•			
Ifield	•			
Igtham	•			
Isle of Grain	•			
Iwade	•			
Keston	•			
Kingsdown	•		•	
Kingstone	•			•

England

* COUNTY / SHIRE

PARISH	PARISH REGISTERS	BISHOPS' TRANSCRIPTS	BOYD'S MARRIAGE INDEX	PR PRINT-OUTS	PARISH	PARISH REGISTERS	BISHOPS' TRANSCRIPTS	BOYD'S MARRIAGE INDEX	PR PRINT-OUTS	PARISH	PARISH REGISTERS	BISHOPS' TRANSCRIPTS	BOYD'S MARRIAGE INDEX	PR PRINT-OUTS
Knockholt	•				Stoke	•			•	Bolton-Le-Moors	•			•
Lamberhurst	•		•		Stone	•			•	Bradshaw	•			
Lee	•	•		•	Strood (Near Rochester)	•				Brathay		•		
Leigh	•				Sundridge	•				Brindle	•			•
Lewishaw	•	•		•	Sutton-At-Home	•				Broughton-In-Furness	•	•		•
Leybourne	•				Swanley	•				Broughton (Near Preston)	•			
Linton	•				Sydenham	•	•		•	Burnley	•			•
Little Chart	•			•	Teston	•				Burton-Wood	•			•
Longfield	•				Trottersclife	•				Bury	•			•
Lullingstone	•			•	Tudeley	•				Cartmel	•	•		•
Lyminge	•		•		Tunbridge	•			•	Cartmell-Fell	•	•		
Lympne	•				Tunbridge-Wells	•				Caton	•			•
Malling (West)	•				Warehorne	•				Chadderton				•
Meopham	•				Wateringbury	•				Cheetham	•			
Mereworth	•				West Farleigh	•		•		Childwall	•			•
Mersham	•				West Peckham	•				Chipping	•			•
Milton-Next-Gravesend	•				Westerham			•		Chorley	•			•
Milton-Next-Sittingbourne	•				Westwell	•				Chorlton-Cum-Hardy	•			•
Nettlestead	•				Whitstable	•				Chorlton-Upon-Medlock	•			•
New Romney	•				Willesborough	•		•	•	Church	•			•
Newenden	•			•	Wilmington	•			•	Claughton	•			•
Newington	•		•		Wingham	•				Clitheroe	•			•
Nonington	•			•	Witchling			•		Cockerham	•			•
North Cray	•				Womenswould	•			•	Colne	•			•
Northfleet	•				Woolwich	•	•		•	Colton	•	•		•
Offham	•				Wouldham	•				Coniston	•	•		•
Orpington	•			•	Wrotham	•				Croston	•	•		•
Otford	•				**LANCASHIRE***					Dalton-In-Furness	•	•		
Penshurst	•			•	Ainsworth	•			•	Darwen	•			
Plaxtol	•	•			Aldingham	•	•		•	Deane	•			•
Postling	•				Altham	•			•	Dendron		•		
Ridley	•		•		Ardwick	•				Denton	•			•
Rochester	•			•	Ashton-In-Mackerfield	•			•	Didsbury	•			•
Ryarsh	•			•	Ashton-Under-Lyne	•			•	Downham	•			•
St. Lawrence	•				Ashworth	•			•	East Broughton		•		
St. Mary Cray	•				Astley	•			•	Eccles	•			•
St. Paul's Cray	•				Atherton	•			•	Eccleston (Near Chorley)	•			
St. Peter	•			•	Aughton (Near Ormskirk)	•			•	Eccleston (Near Croston)	•			•
Saltwood	•				Bacop	•			•	Edenfield	•			•
Sevenoaks	•				Bedford	•			•	Egton-With-Newland	•	•		
Shipbourne	•			•	Billinge	•			•	Ellel	•			•
Shirley	•				Birch (Near Manchester)	•			•	Ellenbrook	•			
Shoreham	•				Birch (Near Middleton)	•				Euxton	•			•
Shorne	•				Bispham	•			•	Everton	•			
Sidcup	•				Blackburn	•			•	Farnworth (With Bolton)	•			•
Snodland	•				Blackley	•			•	Farnworth (With Prescot)				•
Southfleet	•				Blackrod	•			•	Farnworth (With St. Helens)	•			
Stanstead	•				Blawith	•	•		•	Finsthwaite	•	•		•
Staplehurst			•		Bolton	•			•	Flixton	•			•

England

* COUNTY / SHIRE

PARISH	PARISH REGISTERS	BISHOPS' TRANSCRIPTS	BOYD'S MARRIAGE INDEX	PR PRINT-OUTS	PARISH	PARISH REGISTERS	BISHOPS' TRANSCRIPTS	BOYD'S MARRIAGE INDEX	PR PRINT-OUTS	PARISH	PARISH REGISTERS	BISHOPS' TRANSCRIPTS	BOYD'S MARRIAGE INDEX	PR PRINT-OUTS
Flookburgh		•			Liverpool	•			•	Salford (Near Manchester)	•			
Formby	•			•	Longton				•	Samlesbury	•			•
Garstang	•			•	Lowick	•	•		•	Satterthwaite	•	•		•
Garston	•				Lund				•	Scorton	•			
Goosnargh	•			•	Lytham	•			•	Seathwaite	•	•		•
Gorton	•			•	Maghull	•			•	Sephton	•			•
Grange (Near Cartmel)		•			Manchester	•			•	Shaw	•			•
Great Eccleston				•	Melling (Near Hornby)	•			•	Shireshead				•
Great Harwood	•			•	Melling (Near Maghull)	•			•	Smithills	•			
Great Sankey	•			•	Middleton (Near Manchester)	•			•	Stalmine	•			•
Gressingham	•			•	Middleton (Near Oldham)	•			•	Standish	•			•
Hale	•			•	Milnrow	•			•	Staveley		•		
Halsall	•			•	Mossley	•			•	Stretford	•			•
Halton	•			•	Mossley Hill				•	Swinton	•			•
Hambleton	•			•	Newchurch	•			•	Tarleton				•
Haslingden	•				Newchurch-In-Pendle	•			•	Tatham	•			•
Haverswaithe		•			Newchurch-In-Rossendale	•			•	Tatham-Fell	•			•
Hawkshead	•	•		•	Newton	•			•	Thornley-With-Wheatley	•			•
Heapey	•			•	North Meols	•			•	Tockholes	•			
Heapley	•				Northen	•			•	Todmorden	•			
Heaton-Mersey	•				Oldham	•			•	Torver	•	•		•
Heaton-Norris	•				Ormskirk	•			•	Tottington	•			•
Hey				•	Over Kellet	•			•	Tunstall	•			•
Heysham	•	•		•	Over Wyresdale	•			•	Turton	•			•
Heywood	•			•	Overton				•	Ulverston	•	•		•
Higham-Booth-With-West-Close-Booth	•				Padiham	•			•	Unsworth	•			•
Hindley	•				Peel	•			•	Upholland	•			•
Hoghton				•	Pendleton (Near Salford)	•				Urswick	•	•		•
Holcombe	•				Pennington (Near Ulverton)	•	•		•	Walney		•		
Hollinfare	•				Penwortham	•			•	Walton-Le-Dale	•			•
Hollinwood	•			•	Pilling	•			•	Walton-On-The-Hill	•			•
Hoole	•			•	Plumpton-Wood	•			•	Warrington	•			•
Hornby	•			•	Poulton-Le-Fylde	•			•	Warton (Near Kirkham)		•		
Horwich	•			•	Prescot	•			•	Warton (Near Lancaster)	•			•
Hulme	•				Preston	•			•	West Derby	•			•
Huyton	•			•	Prestwich	•			•	West Houghton	•			•
Kersley	•				Radcliffe	•			•	Whalley	•			•
Kirkby	•			•	Rainford	•			•	Whittington	•			•
Kirkby-Ireleth	•	•		•	Ribchester	•			•	Whittle-Le-Woods				•
Kirkdale	•				Ringley	•			•	Wigan	•			•
Kirkham	•			•	Rivington	•			•	Winwick	•			•
Lancaster	•			•	Rochdale	•			•	Woodland and Heathwaite		•		
Langho	•				Royton	•			•	Woodplumpton	•			
Lees	•				Rufford	•			•					
Leigh	•			•	Rusland	•	•							
Leyland	•			•	St. Helens	•			•	**LEICESTER***				
Lindale	•				St. Michael-On-Wyre	•			•	Ad-Kettleby		•	•	•
Little Hulton	•			•	Salesbury	•			•	Alexton				•
Little Lever	•			•	Salford	•			•	Anstey		•	•	•

England

* COUNTY / SHIRE

PARISH	PARISH REGISTERS	BISHOPS' TRANSCRIPTS	BOYD'S MARRIAGE INDEX	PR PRINT-OUTS
Appleby	•	•		•
Arnesby	•	•		•
Ashby-De-La-Zouch	•	•		•
Ashby-Folville	•	•		•
Ashby-Magna	•	•		•
Ashby-Parva		•	•	•
Ashfordby	•	•	•	•
Aston-Flamville	•	•		•
Aylestone		•	•	•
Bagworth		•		•
Barkby	•	•	•	•
Barkestone		•	•	•
Barlestone	•	•		•
Barrow-Upon-Soar		•	•	
Barsby	•	•		•
Barton-In-The-Beans		•		•
Barwell	•	•		•
Beeby		•	•	•
Belgrave	•	•	•	•
Belton		•		•
Billesdon	•	•		•
Birstall	•	•	•	•
Bitteswell		•	•	•
Blaby		•	•	•
Blackfordby		•		•
Blaston		•		•
Borrough-Hill	•			
Bottesford	•	•	•	•
Branston	•	•	•	•
Braunstone	•	•	•	•
Breedon-On-The-Hill	•	•		•
Brentingby	•	•	•	
Bringhurst		•		•
Brookesby		•	•	
Broughton-Astley		•		•
Bruntingthorpe		•		•
Buckminster		•	•	•
Burbage	•	•		•
Burrough		•	•	•
Burton-Lazars		•	•	•
Burton-Overy		•		•
Cadeby		•		•
Carlton		•		•
Carlton-Curliew	•	•		•
Castle-Donington		•		•
Catthorpe		•	•	•
Chadwell			•	
Church-Langton		•		
Clawson		•	•	•
Claybrooke	•	•	•	•
Coalville		•		•
Cold-Overton		•	•	•
Cold-Orton		•		•
Congerston	•	•	•	•
Cosby		•		•
Cossington		•	•	•
Coston		•	•	•
Cottesbach		•		•
Countesthorpe		•		•
Cranoe		•		
Croft	•	•		•
Croxton-Keyrail	•	•	•	•
Dadlington	•	•		•
Dalby-On-The-Wolds	•	•	•	•
Desford	•	•		•
Diseworth		•		•
Dishley-Cum-Thorpacre		•		•
Donisthorpe				•
Dunton-Bassett	•	•		•
Earl-Shilton		•		•
East Norton		•		•
Eastwell		•	•	•
Eaton		•	•	•
Edmondthorpe		•		•
Enderby	•	•		•
Evington		•	•	•
Fenny-Drayton	•	•		•
Fleckney		•		•
Foston		•		•
Foxton	•	•		•
Freeby		•	•	•
Frisby-On-The-Wreak	•	•	•	•
Frolesworth		•	•	•
Gaddesby		•	•	•
Galby		•		•
Garthorpe	•	•		•
Gilmorton	•	•	•	•
Glenfield	•	•	•	•
Glenn Magna		•	•	•
Glooston		•		•
Goadby	•	•		•
Goadby-Marwood		•	•	•
Great Ashby				•
Great Bowden		•		•
Great Dalby		•	•	•
Great Easton		•		•
Great Sheepy		•		•
Grimston	•	•	•	•
Groby				•
Gumley		•		•
Hallaton		•		•
Harby		•	•	•
Harston	•	•	•	•
Hathern	•	•		•
Heather		•		•
Higham-On-The-Hill	•	•		•
Hinckley	•	•		•
Hoby	•	•	•	•
Holt				•
Holwell		•		•
Horninghold		•		•
Hose		•	•	•
Hoton		•	•	•
Houghton-On-The-Hill		•	•	
Hugglescote	•	•		•
Humberstone	•	•	•	•
Hungerton		•	•	•
Husbands-Bosworth	•	•		•
Ibstock		•		•
Ilston-On-The-Hill	•	•		•
Isley-Walton		•		•
Kegworth	•	•		•
Keyham		•	•	•
Kibworth-Beauchamp		•		•
Kilby		•		•
Kimcote	•	•		•
Kings-Norton		•		•
Kings-Pyon				•
Kirby-Bellars		•	•	•
Kirby-Muxloe	•	•	•	•
Kirby-Mallory		•		•
Knaptoft	•	•		
Knighton	•	•	•	
Knipton	•	•	•	•
Knossington		•	•	•
Langton-Thorpe		•		
Langton-Tur		•		•
Laughton		•		•
Leicester	•	•		•
Leire		•	•	
Little Bowden	•	•		•
Little Dalby		•	•	•
Lockington	•	•		•
Loddington		•	•	•
Long Whatton	•	•		•
Loughborough		•		•
Lowesby		•	•	•

England
* COUNTY / SHIRE

PARISH	PARISH REGISTERS	BISHOPS' TRANSCRIPTS	BOYD'S MARRIAGE INDEX	PR PRINT-OUTS
Lubbenham	•	•	•	•
Lutterworth		•	•	•
Market-Bosworth	•	•		•
Market-Harborough	•	•		•
Markfield	•	•		•
Medbourne	•	•		•
Melton-Mowbray	•	•	•	•
Misterton		•	•	•
Mountsorrel	•	•	•	•
Mowsley		•		•
Muston		•	•	•
Nailstone		•		•
Narborough		•		•
Nether-Broughton		•	•	•
Nether Seal				•
Newbold-Verdon		•		•
Newton-Harcourt		•		•
Newton-Linford	•	•		•
Normanton-Le-Heath		•		•
North Kilworth		•		•
Norton-Juxta-Twycross	•	•		•
Noseley		•		
Oadby	•	•	•	•
Oaks		•		
Oakthorpe		•		
Orton-On-The-Hill	•	•		•
Osgathorpe		•		•
Ouston		•	•	•
Over Seal				•
Packington	•	•		•
Peatling-Magna	•	•		•
Peatling-Parva		•		
Peckleton	•	•		•
Pickwell		•	•	•
Plungar		•	•	•
Prestwold		•	•	•
Primethorp				•
Queeniborough		•	•	•
Quorndon	•	•	•	•
Ragdale	•	•	•	
Ratby	•	•	•	•
Ratcliffe-Culey		•		•
Ratcliffe-On-The-Wreake	•	•	•	•
Rearsby	•	•	•	•
Redmile		•	•	•
Rotherby	•	•	•	•
Rothley		•	•	•
Saddington		•		•
St. Giles		•		
St. Margaret	•			
Saltby		•		•
Sapcote	•	•		•
Saxby	•	•	•	•
Saxelby	•	•	•	•
Scalford		•	•	•
Scraptoft		•	•	•
Seagrave		•	•	•
Seal				•
Sewstern			•	
Shackerstone	•			•
Sharnford	•		•	•
Shawell		•		•
Shearsby	•	•		•
Sheepshed				•
Sheepy-Magna	•	•		•
Shenton		•		•
Shepshed	•	•		•
Sibson	•	•	•	•
Sileby	•	•	•	•
Skeffington	•	•		•
Slawston		•		•
Smeeton-Westerby		•		•
Snarestone		•		
Somerby	•	•	•	•
South Croxton	•	•	•	•
South Kilworth	•	•		•
Sproxton		•		•
Stanton-Stoney	•	•		•
Stanton-Under-Barndon		•		
Stapleford	•	•	•	•
Stathern	•	•	•	•
Stockerston		•		
Stoke-Golding	•	•		•
Stonesby		•		•
Stonton-Wyville		•		
Stoughton		•	•	•
Stretton-Magna		•	•	
Stertton-Parva		•		•
Sutton-Cheney		•		•
Sutton-In-The-Elms				•
Swepstone		•		•
Swinford		•		
Swithland		•	•	•
Syston		•	•	•
Theddingworth		•		•
Thornton	•	•		•
Thorpe-Arnold		•	•	
Thrussington		•	•	•
Thurcaston	•	•	•	•
Thurlaston	•	•		•
Thurmaston	•	•	•	•
Thurnby		•	•	•
Tilton		•	•	•
Tugby		•		
Twycross	•	•		•
Twyford		•	•	•
Waltham-On-The-Wolds		•		•
Walton				•
Walton-On-The-Wolds	•	•	•	
Wanlip	•	•	•	•
Wartnaby		•	•	•
Welham		•		•
Whetstone	•	•		•
Whitwick		•		•
Wigston-Magna		•	•	
Willesley	•			
Willoughby-Waterless	•	•		•
Wimeswold		•	•	
Wistow		•		
Withcote		•	•	
Witherly	•	•		•
Woodhouse		•	•	
Woodhouse-Eaves		•		
Worthington		•		
Wycomb and Chadwell		•		•
Wyfordby		•	•	
Wymondham		•	•	
LINCOLN*				
Aby		•		•
Addlethorpe	•	•	•	•
Aisthorpe	•	•		•
Alford	•	•	•	•
Algakirk	•	•		•
Alkborough		•		•
Althorpe	•	•		•
Alvingham	•	•		•
Amcotts	•			•
Ancaster	•	•		•
Anderby	•	•	•	•
Anwick	•	•		•
Apley	•			•
Appleby	•	•		•
Asgarby (Near Horncastle)		•		•
Asgarby (Near Sleaford)	•	•		•
Ashby	•			
Ashby-By-Partney		•		•
Ashby-De-La-Laund	•			•

England

* COUNTY / SHIRE

PARISH	PARISH REGISTERS	BISHOPS' TRANSCRIPTS	BOYD'S MARRIAGE INDEX	PR PRINT-OUTS
Ashby-Puerorum		•		•
Ashby-With-Fenby	•	•		
Aslackby	•	•		•
Asterby	•	•		•
Aswarby	•	•		
Aswardby		•		•
Aubourn	•	•	•	•
Aunsby	•	•		•
Authorpe	•	•		•
Aylesby	•	•		•
Bag Enderby	•			
Bardney	•	•		•
Barholm	•	•		•
Barkstone	•	•	•	•
Barlings	•	•		•
Barnetby-Le-Wold		•		•
Barnoldby-Le-Beck	•	•		•
Barrow-Upon-Humber	•	•		•
Barrowby	•	•	•	•
Barton	•			•
Barton-Upon-Humber	•	•		•
Bassingham	•	•	•	•
Bassingham-Cum-Westby	•			
Bassingthorpe	•	•		•
Baston	•	•		•
Baumber	•	•		•
Beckingham	•	•		•
Beelsby	•	•		•
Beesby-In-The-Marsh	•			•
Belchford		•		•
Belleau	•	•		•
Belton (Near Epworth)	•	•		•
Belton (Near Grantham)	•	•		•
Bennington	•	•		•
Benniworth		•		•
Bicker	•	•		•
Bigby	•	•		•
Billingborough	•	•		•
Billinghay	•	•		•
Bilsby	•	•	•	•
Binbrook		•		•
Biscathorpe		•		•
Bishop-Norton	•	•		•
Bitchfield	•	•		•
Blankney	•	•		•
Bloxholm	•	•		•
Blyborough	•	•		•
Blyton	•	•		•
Bolingbroke	•	•		•

PARISH	PARISH REGISTERS	BISHOPS' TRANSCRIPTS	BOYD'S MARRIAGE INDEX	PR PRINT-OUTS
Bonby		•		•
Boothby	•	•	•	•
Boothy-Graffo				•
Boothby Pagnell	•	•		•
Boston	•	•		•
Bottesford	•	•		•
Boultham	•	•	•	•
Bourn	•	•		•
Braceborough	•	•		•
Bracebridge	•	•	•	•
Braceby	•	•		•
Bradley	•	•		•
Branston	•	•		•
Bratoft	•	•		•
Brattleby		•		•
Brauncewell-With-Dunsby		•		•
Brigsley	•	•		•
Brinkhill		•		•
Brocklesby	•	•		•
Bromby				•
Brothertoft	•	•		•
Broughton	•	•		•
Broughton-Brant	•	•		•
Broxholme	•	•		•
Bucknall		•		•
Bullington		•		•
Burgh-In-The-Marsh	•	•		•
Burgh-Upon-Bain	•	•		•
Burton-By-Lincoln	•	•		•
Burton-Coggles	•	•		•
Burton-Gate		•		•
Burton-On-Stather				•
Burton-Pedwardine	•	•		•
Burton-Upon-Stather	•	•		•
Burwell	•	•		•
Buslingthorpe	•	•		•
Butterwick	•	•		•
Bytham-Castle	•	•		•
Cabourne	•	•		•
Cadney-Cum-Housham	•	•		•
Caenby	•	•		•
Caistor	•	•		•
Calceby	•	•		•
Calcethorpe		•		•
Cammeringham	•	•		•
Candlesby		•		•
Canwick	•	•		•
Careby	•	•		•
Carlby	•	•		•

PARISH	PARISH REGISTERS	BISHOPS' TRANSCRIPTS	BOYD'S MARRIAGE INDEX	PR PRINT-OUTS
Carlton-Castle	•	•		•
Carlton-Le-Moorland	•	•	•	•
Carlton-Scroop	•	•		•
Carrington		•		•
Cawkwell		•		•
Cawthorpe		•		
Caythorpe	•	•		•
Chapel-Mumby		•		•
Chapel-St.Leonards	•			•
Claxby (Near Alford)		•	•	•
Claxby (Near Market-Rasen)	•	•		•
Claxby (Near Normanby)				•
Claxby-Pluckacre		•		•
Claypole	•	•	•	•
Claythorpe		•		•
Clee	•	•		•
Cleethorpes	•	•		
Clixby		•		•
Coates	•	•		•
Cold-Hanworth		•		•
Coleby (Near Lincoln)	•	•		•
Colsterworth	•	•		•
Coningsby	•	•		•
Conisholme	•	•		•
Corby	•	•		•
Corringham	•	•		•
Covenham-St. Bartholomew	•	•		•
Covenham-St. Mary	•	•		•
Cowbit	•	•	•	•
Cranwell		•		•
Creeton		•		•
Croft	•	•		•
Crowland	•	•		•
Crowle	•	•		•
Croxby		•		•
Croxton	•	•		•
Cumberworth	•	•	•	•
Cuxwold		•		•
Dalby		•	•	•
Dalderby		•		•
Deeping-Fen		•		•
Deeping-Market	•	•		•
Deeping-St. James	•	•		•
Dembleby	•	•		•
Denton		•	•	•
Digby		•		•
Doddington	•	•	•	•
Donington	•	•		•
Donington-Upon-Bain		•		•

England

* COUNTY / SHIRE

PARISH	PARISH REGISTERS	BISHOPS' TRANSCRIPTS	BOYD'S MARRIAGE INDEX	PR PRINT-OUTS
Dorrington		•		•
Dowsby	•	•		•
Driby	•	•		
Dunholm	•	•		•
Dunsby (Near Bourn)	•	•		•
Dunston		•		•
Eagle	•	•	•	•
East Allington	•	•		•
East Barkwith	•	•		•
East Halton	•	•		•
East Keal	•	•		•
East Kirkby		•		•
East Ravendale	•	•		•
East Torrington	•	•		•
East Wykeham		•		
Easton	•			
Edenham	•	•		•
Edlington		•		•
Elsham		•		•
Enderby-Bag		•		•
Epworth	•	•		•
Evedon	•	•		•
Ewerby		•		•
Faldingworth	•	•		•
Falkingham	•			
Farforth		•		•
Farforth-Cum-Maidenwell				•
Farlsthorpe		•	•	•
Fenton (Near Lincoln)	•			
Fenton (Near Newark)	•	•		•
Fillingham	•	•		•
Firsby	•	•		•
Fishtoft	•	•		•
Fiskerton	•	•		•
Fleet	•	•	•	•
Flixborough		•		•
Folkingham	•	•		•
Fosdyke	•	•		•
Foston		•	•	•
Fotherby	•	•		•
Frampton	•	•		•
Freiston	•	•		•
Freisthorpe	•	•		•
Friskney	•	•		•
Frithville	•	•		•
Frodingham	•	•		•
Fulbeck	•	•		•
Fulletby	•	•		•
Fulstow	•	•		•

PARISH	PARISH REGISTERS	BISHOPS' TRANSCRIPTS	BOYD'S MARRIAGE INDEX	PR PRINT-OUTS
Gainsborough	•	•		•
Gautby	•	•		•
Gayton-Le-Marsh		•		•
Gayton-Le-Wold		•		•
Gedney	•	•		•
Gedney-Hill	•	•		•
Glentham	•	•		•
Glentworth	•	•		•
Goltho	•	•		•
Gosberton	•	•		•
Goulceby	•	•		•
Goxhill	•	•		•
Grainsby	•	•		•
Grainthorpe	•	•		•
Grantham	•	•		•
Grasby		•		•
Grayingham	•	•		•
Great Carlton	•	•		•
Great Coates	•	•		•
Great Gonerby	•	•	•	•
Great Grimsby	•	•		•
Great Hale	•	•		•
Great Limber	•	•		•
Great Ponton	•	•		•
Great Steeping		•		•
Greatford	•	•		•
Greetham		•		•
Greetwell	•	•		•
Grimoldby	•	•		•
Gunby-St. Nicholas		•		•
Gunby-St. Peter	•	•		•
Habrough	•	•		•
Hacconby	•	•		•
Haceby	•	•		•
Hackthorn	•	•		•
Haddington	•			
Hagnaby (Near Spilsby)		•		•
Hagworthingham		•		•
Hainton	•	•		•
Hallington		•		•
Haltham-Upon-Bain		•		•
Halton-Holegate	•	•		•
Hameringham		•		•
Hannah		•	•	•
Hareby	•	•		•
Harlaxton	•	•	•	•
Harmston	•	•	•	•
Harpswell	•	•		•
Harrington	•	•		•

PARISH	PARISH REGISTERS	BISHOPS' TRANSCRIPTS	BOYD'S MARRIAGE INDEX	PR PRINT-OUTS
Hatcliffe	•	•		•
Hatton	•	•		•
Haugh	•	•		
Haugham	•	•		•
Hawerby-With-Beesby	•	•	•	•
Haxey	•	•		•
Haydor	•	•		•
Healing	•	•		•
Heapham	•	•		•
Heckington	•	•	•	•
Helpringham	•	•		•
Hemingby		•		•
Hemswell		•		•
Hibaldstow	•	•		•
High Toynton	•	•		•
Hogsthorpe	•	•	•	•
Holbeach	•	•		•
Holland-Fen		•		•
Holton-Beckering	•	•		•
Holton-Le-Clay	•	•		•
Holton-Le-Moor		•		•
Holywell-With-Aunby	•	•		•
Honington	•	•		•
Horbling	•	•		•
Horkstow	•	•		•
Horncastle	•	•		•
Horsington		•		•
Hough-On-The-Hill	•	•		•
Hougham	•	•		•
Howell	•	•		•
Humberstone	•	•		•
Hundleby		•		•
Huttoft	•	•	•	•
Immingham	•	•		•
Ingham	•	•		•
Ingoldmells	•	•	•	•
Ingoldsby	•	•		•
Irby-In-The-Marsh	•	•		•
Irby-Upon-Humber	•	•		•
Irnham	•	•		•
Keddington	•	•		•
Keelby	•	•		•
Kelby	•			
Kelstern	•	•		•
Kettlethorpe	•	•		•
Kexby		•		•
Killingholme	•	•		•
Kingerby	•	•		•
Kirkby		•		•

England

* COUNTY / SHIRE

PARISH	PARISH REGISTERS	BISHOPS' TRANSCRIPTS	BOYD'S MARRIAGE INDEX	PR PRINT-OUTS
Kirkby-Cum-Osgoodby	•			•
Kirkby-Green		•		•
Kirkby-Le-Thorpe	•	•		•
Kirkby Under Wood	•	•		•
Kirkby-Upon-Bain				•
Kirkstead	•	•		•
Kirmington		•		•
Kirmond-Le-Mire		•		•
Kirton	•	•		•
Kirton-In-Lindsey	•	•		•
Knaith	•	•		•
Laceby	•	•		•
Langrick-Ville		•		•
Langtoft	•	•		•
Langton-By-Spilsby		•		•
Langton-By-Wragby	•	•		•
Langton-Near-Horncastle	•	•		•
Laughton	•			
Laughton (Near Gainsborough)	•	•		•
Lavington	•	•		•
Lea	•	•		•
Leadenham	•	•		•
Leake	•	•		•
Leasingham	•	•		•
Legbourne		•		•
Legsby	•	•		•
Leverton	•	•		•
Lincoln	•	•		•
Linwood (Near Market-Rasen)	•	•		•
Lissington	•	•		•
Little Bytham	•	•		•
Little Carlton		•		•
Little Cawthorpe				•
Little Coates	•	•		•
Little Grimsby	•	•		•
Little Hale		•		•
Little Ponton		•		•
Little Steeping	•	•		•
Lobthorpe	•			
Londonthorpe	•	•		•
Long Bennington	•	•	•	•
Long Sutton	•	•		•
Louth	•	•		•
Low Toynton	•	•		•
Ludborough		•		•
Luddington	•	•		•
Ludford-Magna		•		•
Ludford-Parva	•			•
Lusby	•	•		•

PARISH	PARISH REGISTERS	BISHOPS' TRANSCRIPTS	BOYD'S MARRIAGE INDEX	PR PRINT-OUTS
Lutton-Bourne	•	•		•
Mablethorpe	•	•	•	•
Mablethorpe-St. Mary		•	•	
Maltby	•			
Maltby-Le-Marsh		•	•	•
Manby (Near Louth)	•	•		•
Manton	•	•		•
Mareham-Le-Fen	•	•		•
Mareham-On-The-Hill		•		•
Markby	•	•	•	•
Marsh-Chapel	•	•		•
Marston	•	•		•
Martin (Near Horncastle)		•		
Martin (Near Lindsey)				•
Marton		•		•
Mavis-Enderby		•		•
Melton-Ross		•		•
Messingham	•	•		•
Metheringham	•	•		•
Middle-Rasen	•	•		•
Midville		•		•
Miningsby		•		•
Minting	•	•		•
Moorby		•		•
Morton (Near Bourne)	•	•		•
Moulton	•	•	•	•
Muckton		•		•
Mumby	•	•	•	•
Navenby	•	•	•	•
Nettleham	•	•		•
Nettleton		•		•
New Sleaford				•
Newton	•	•		•
Newton-By-Toft	•	•		•
Newton-Le-Wold	•	•		•
Newton-Upon-Trent	•	•		•
Nocton		•		•
Normanoby (Near-Spittal-In-the-Street)	•	•		•
Normanby-On-The-Wolds	•	•		•
Normanton	•	•		•
North Carlton		•		•
North Coates	•	•		•
North Cockerington	•	•		•
North Elkington		•		•
North Hyckham		•	•	•
North Kelsey	•	•		•
North Kyme	•			•
North Ormsby		•		•
North Rauceby	•	•		•

PARISH	PARISH REGISTERS	BISHOPS' TRANSCRIPTS	BOYD'S MARRIAGE INDEX	PR PRINT-OUTS
North Reston	•	•		•
North Scarle	•	•	•	•
North Somercotes	•	•		•
North Stoke	•	•		•
North Thoresby	•	•		•
North Willingham	•	•		•
North Witham	•	•		•
Northorpe (Near Gainsborough)	•	•		•
Norton-Disney	•	•	•	•
Old Sleaford				•
Orby		•		•
Osbournby	•	•		•
Osgodby (Near Market-Rasen)		•		•
Owersby	•	•		•
Owmby (Near Market-Rasen)	•	•		•
Owston	•	•		•
Oxcombe		•		•
Panton	•	•		•
Partney	•	•		•
Pickworth	•	•	•	•
Pilham	•	•	•	•
Pinchbeck	•	•	•	•
Potter-Hanworth		•		•
Quadring	•	•		•
Quarrington	•	•		•
Raithby	•	•		•
Raithby-Cum-Maltby		•		•
Ranby	•	•		
Rand	•	•		•
Rasen	•	•		•
Rauceby				•
Redbourne	•	•		•
Repham	•	•		•
Revesby	•	•		•
Riby	•	•	•	•
Rigsby-With-Ailby	•	•	•	•
Rippingale	•	•		•
Riseholme	•	•		
Ropsley	•	•		•
Rothwell		•		•
Roughton	•	•		•
Rowston	•	•		•
Roxby	•	•		•
Ruckland		•		•
Ruskington	•	•		•
Saleby	•	•	•	•
Salmonby		•		•
Saltfleetby-All-Saints	•	•		•
Saltfleetby-St. Clement	•	•		•

England
* COUNTY / SHIRE

PARISH	PARISH REGISTERS	BISHOPS' TRANSCRIPTS	BOYD'S MARRIAGE INDEX	PR PRINT-OUTS
Saltfleetby-St. Peter	•	•		•
Sandtoft			•	
Sapperton	•	•		•
Sausthorpe	•	•		•
Saxby (Near Barton)		•		•
Saxby (Near Lincoln)	•	•		•
Saxelby	•	•		•
Scamblesby	•	•		•
Scampton	•	•		•
Scartho	•	•		•
Scawby	•	•		•
Scopwick		•		•
Scothern	•	•		•
Scotter	•	•		•
Scotton	•	•		•
Scrafield		•		•
Scredington	•	•		•
Scremby	•	•		•
Scrivelsby		•		•
Scunthorpe				•
Searby-With-Owmby	•	•		•
Sedgebrook	•		•	•
Semperingham	•		•	•
Serivelsby	•			
Sibsey	•	•		•
Silk-Willoughby	•			
Sixhills	•	•		•
Skegness	•	•		•
Skellingthorpe	•	•	•	•
Skendleby	•	•		•
Skidbrook	•	•		•
Skillington	•	•		•
Skinnand		•	•	
Skirbeck	•	•		•
Sleaford	•	•		
Snarford	•	•		•
Snelland	•	•		•
Snitterby		•		
Somerby (Near Gainsborough)		•		
Somerby (Near Glanford-Brigg)		•		•
Somerby (Near Grantham)	•	•		•
Somersby	•	•		•
Sotby	•	•		•
South Carlton	•	•		•
South Cockerington	•	•	•	•
South Elkington		•		•
South Ferriby	•	•		•
South Hyckham	•	•	•	•
South Kelsey	•	•	•	•
South Kyme	•	•		•
South Ormsby	•	•		•
South Rauceby				•
South Reston		•		•
South Somercotes	•	•		•
South Stoke				•
South Thoresby	•	•		•
South Willingham	•	•		•
South Witham	•	•	•	•
Spalding	•	•	•	•
Spanby	•	•		•
Spilsby	•	•		•
Spridlington	•	•		•
Springthorpe	•	•		•
Stain		•		
Stainby		•	•	•
Stainfield (Near Lincoln)	•	•		•
Stainton-By-Langworth	•	•		•
Stainton-Le-Vale	•	•		•
Stainton-Market		•		•
Stallingborough	•	•		•
Stamford	•			•
Stamford All-Saints		•		•
Stamford-St. George	•	•		
Stamford-St. John		•		•
Stamford-St. Mary	•	•		
Stamford-St. Michael	•	•		•
Stapleford	•	•	•	•
Stenigot	•	•		•
Stewton	•	•		•
Stickford	•	•		•
Stickney	•	•		•
Stixwould		•		•
Stoke-South	•		•	•
Stow	•	•		•
Stow (Near Gainsborough)		•		
Stragglethorpe	•	•		•
Stroxton	•	•		•
Strubby-With-Woodthorpe	•	•	•	•
Stubton	•	•	•	•
Sturton-Magna		•		•
Sudborough	•			•
Sudbrooke	•	•		•
Sudbrooke (Near Lincoln)				•
Surfleet	•	•	•	
Sutterby		•		•
Sutterton	•	•		•
Sutton-Bridge	•			•
Sutton-In-The-Marsh		•	•	•
Sutton-St. Edmund	•	•		•
Sutton-St. James	•	•		•
Sutton-St. Matthew		•		
Swaby		•		•
Swallow	•	•		•
Swarby	•	•		•
Swaton	•	•		•
Swayfield	•	•		•
Swinderby	•	•	•	•
Swineshead	•	•		•
Swinhope	•	•		•
Swinstead	•	•		•
Syston		•	•	•
Tallington	•	•		•
Tathwell	•	•		•
Tattershall	•	•		•
Tealby	•	•		•
Temple-Bruer	•			
Tetford		•		•
Tetney	•	•		•
Theddlethorpe-All Saints	•	•	•	•
Theddlethorpe-St. Helen	•	•		•
Thimbleby		•		•
Thoresway		•		•
Thorganby		•		•
Thornton		•		•
Thornton-Curtis	•	•		•
Thornton-Le-Fen		•		•
Thornton-Le-Moor	•	•		•
Thorpe-On-The-Hill	•	•	•	•
Thorpe-St. Peter	•	•		•
Threckingham	•	•		•
Thurlby (Near Bourn)	•	•	•	•
Thurlby (Near Newark)	•	•		•
Timberland		•		•
Toft (Lincoln)	•			
Toft-Next-Newton		•		•
Torksey		•		•
Tothill	•	•		•
Toynton-All Saints		•		•
Toynton-St. Peter		•		•
Trusthorpe	•	•	•	•
Tupholme		•		
Tydd-St. Mary	•	•	•	•
Uffington	•	•		•
Ulceby (Near Barton)	•	•		•
Ulceby With Fordington	•	•		•
Upton	•	•		•
Usselby	•	•		•

England

* COUNTY / SHIRE

PARISH	PARISH REGISTERS	BISHOPS' TRANSCRIPTS	BOYD'S MARRIAGE INDEX	PR PRINT-OUTS
Utterby	•	•		•
Waddingham	•	•		•
Waddington	•	•	•	•
Waddingworth	•	•		•
Wainfleet-All Saints	•	•		•
Wainfleet-St. Mary	•	•		•
Waith		•		•
Walcot (Near Rackingham)	•	•		•
Walesby	•	•		•
Walmsgate	•			•
Waltham	•	•		•
Washingborough	•	•	•	•
Welbourn	•	•	•	•
Welby	•	•		•
Well	•	•	•	•
Wellingore	•	•	•	•
Welton	•	•		•
Welton-In-The-Marsh		•		•
Welton-Le-Wold	•	•		•
West Allington	•	•	•	•
West Ashby		•		•
West Barkwith	•	•		•
West Butterwick		•		•
West Deeping	•	•		•
West Halton	•	•		•
West Keal		•		•
West Rasen	•	•		•
West Ravendale	•	•		
West Torrington	•	•		•
Westborough		•	•	•
Weston	•	•	•	•
Whaplode	•	•		•
Whaplode-Drove	•	•		•
Whitton	•	•		•
Wickenby	•	•		•
Wickham	•			
Wigtoft	•	•		•
Wilksby	•	•		•
Willingham	•	•		•
Willingham-Cherry	•	•		•
Willoughby	•	•	•	•
Willoughby-Silk	•	•		•
Willoughton	•	•		•
Wilsford	•	•		•
Wilsthorpe	•	•		
Winceby		•		•
Winteringham	•	•		•
Winterton	•	•		•
Winthorpe	•	•		•
Wispington	•	•		•
Witham-On-The-Hill	•	•		•
Withcall		•		•
Withern	•	•	•	•
Wood Enderby	•	•		•
Woodhall	•	•		•
Woolsthorpe (Near Grantham)		•	•	•
Wooton	•	•		•
Worlaby	•	•		•
Worlaby (Near Glanford-Brigg)				•
Wragby	•	•		•
Wrangle	•	•		•
Wrawby	•	•		•
Wroot	•	•		•
Wyberton	•	•		•
Wyham		•		•
Wyville-With-Hungerton		•		
Yarborough	•	•		•
LONDON*				
All Hallow's, Barking By The Tower	•			
All Hallow's Bread Street Church	•	•		
All Hallow's Honey Lane Church	•			
All Hallow's Lombard St. Church	•			
All Hallow's London Wall Church	•	•		
All Hallow's Staining Church	•	•		
All Hallow's The Great Church	•			
All Hallow's The Less Church	•	•		
Bridewell The Hospital Church	•			
Chapelry of Bridewell Precinct		•		
Christ Church Greyfriers (Newgate St.)	•	•		
Diocese of London	•			
Dionis Backchurch's Church	•			
Holy Trinity, Gough Square	•			
Holy Trinity Minories Church	•	•		
Holy Trinity The Less' Church	•	•		
Parish Church of St. Leonard's	•			
Parish Church of St. Mark	•			
St. Alban Wood Street Church	•	•		
St. Alphage Church (London Wall)	•	•		
St. Andrew By the Wardrobe's Church	•	•		
St. Andrew's Church (Holborn)	•	•		
St. Andrew Hubbard's Church	•	•		
St. Andrew Undershaft's Church	•	•		
St. Ann Blackfrier's Church	•	•		
St. Ann & St. Agnes Church (Aldergate)	•	•		
St. Antholin Budge Row Church	•			
St. Augustine's Church (Watling St.)	•	•		
St. Bartholomew By The Exchange Church	•	•		
St. Bartholomew's Church (Moor Lane)	•			
St. Bartholomew-The-Great's Church	•	•		
St. Bartholomew-The-Less's Church	•	•		
St. Benet Fink's Church	•	•		
St. Benet Gracechurch	•	•		
St. Botolph By Billingsgate Church	•	•		
St. Botolph Without Aldgate's Church	•			
St. Botolph Without Bishopsgate's Church		•		
St. Bride Church (Fleet Street)	•			
St. Christopher-Le-Stock's Church	•	•		
St. Clement Near Eastcheap	•			
St. Dionis Backchurch's Church	•			
St. Dunstan-In-The-East Church	•			
St. Dunstan-In-The-West Church	•	•		
St. Edmund The King's Church	•			
St. Ethelburga Within Bishopsgate	•			
St. Faith Under St. Paul's Church	•			
St. Gabriel Fenchurch's Church	•			
St. George's Church (Botolph Lane)	•			
St. George's Church	•			
St. George The Martyr's Church	•			
St. Giles Without Cripplegate Church	•			
St. Gregory By St. Paul's Church	•			
St. Gregory's Church	•			
St. Helen's Church (Bishopsgate)	•			
St. James' Church	•			
St. James Garlickhithe's Church	•	•		
St. James In The Wall Church	•			
St. John The Baptist Upon Walbrook Church	•	•		
St. John The Evangelist	•			
St. John-Zachary's Church	•	•		
St. Katherine By The Tower's Church	•			
St. Katherine Coleman's Church	•	•		
St. Katherine Cree's Church	•	•		
St. Lawrence Jewry's Church	•			
St. Lawrence Poutney Church	•	•		
St. Leonard's Church (Foster Lane)	•	•		
St. Leonard Eastcheap's Church	•			
St. Leonard's Church (Shoreditch)		•		
St. Magnus the Martyr's Church	•			
St. Margaret's Church		•		
St. Margaret's Church (Lothbury)		•		
St. Margaret's Church (New Fish St. Hill)	•	•		
St. Margret Lothbury's Church	•			
St. Margaret Moses' Church	•			
St. Margaret Patten's Church	•			
St. Martin Ludgate Church	•	•		
St. Martin Urgar's Church	•	•		
St. Martin Outwich's Church	•			
St. Martin Pomeroy's Church	•			

England

* COUNTY / SHIRE

PARISH	PARISH REGISTERS	BISHOPS' TRANSCRIPTS	BOYD'S MARRIAGE INDEX	PR PRINT-OUTS
St. Martin Vintry's Church	•	•		
St. Mary Abchurch's Church	•			
St. Mary Aldermary's Church	•			
St. Mary At Hill's Church	•			
St. Mary Bowthaw's Church	•			
St. Mary's Church	•	•		
St. Mary Colechurch's Church	•	•		
St. Mary Le Bow's Church	•			
St. Mary Magdalene's Church (Milk St.)	•			
St. Mary Magdalene's Church (Old Fish St.)	•			
St. Mary Mounthaw's Church	•			
St. Mary Somerset Church	•			
St. Mary Staining's Church	•	•		
St. Mary The Virgin Church	•			
St. Mary-Woolnoth Church	•	•		
St. Mary Woolchurch Haw		•		
St. Matthew Friday St. Church	•	•		
St. Michael Bassishaw's Church	•	•		
St. Michael's Church (Queenhithe)	•			
St. Michael's Church (Wood St.)	•	•		
St. Michael Cornhill Church	•	•		
St. Michael Crooked Lane Church	•			
St. Michael-Le-Quern's Church	•	•		
St. Michael Paternoster Royal's Church	•			
St. Michael Queenhithe	•			
St. Michael Upon Cornhill	•			
St. Mildred's Church (Bread Street)	•	•		
St. Mildred Poultry's Church	•			
St. Nicholas Acon's Church	•	•		
St. Nicholas Cole Abbey Church	•	•		
St. Nicholas Olave's Church	•			
St. Olave and St. John's Church	•			
St. Olave's Church (Hart Street)	•	•		
St. Olave's Church (Old Jewry)	•	•		
St. Olave's Church (Silver Street)	•	•		
St. Olave Hart Street	•			
St. Oswald's Church		•		
St. Pancras' Church (Soper Lane)	•			
St. Peter Cornhill's Church	•			
St. Peter Le Poer's Church	•			
St. Peter Paul's Wharf Church	•			
St. Peter Upon Cornhill Church	•	•		
St. Peter Westcheap's Church	•	•		
St. Sepulchre (Holborn)	•			
St. Stephen's Church (Coleman St.)	•			
St. Stephen Walbrook Church	•	•		
St. Stephen Walbrook w/ St. Benet Shorehog's Church	•			
St. Swithin's Church (London Stone)	•	•		
St. Thomas Apostle's Church	•	•		
St. Thomas In The Liberty Of The Rolls	•			
St. Vedast Foster Lane Church	•			
Temple Church	•			
MIDDLESEX*				
Acton		•	•	
Ashford		•	•	
Barnet		•		
Barnet-Fryern	•			•
Bethnal Green	•			•
Bow		•		
Brentford		•	•	
Camden-Town	•			
Chelsea	•	•		•
Clerkenwell	•			•
Cowley		•	•	
Cranford		•		
Ealing	•	•	•	•
Edgware		•		
Edmonton	•	•	•	•
Enfield	•		•	•
Feltham		•	•	•
Finchley			•	
Finsbury	•			•
Great Greenford		•	•	
Great Stanmore		•		•
Hackney	•			•
Hadley	•	•		
Hammersmith	•			
Hammondsworth				•
Hampstead		•		•
Hampton			•	
Hannell		•	•	
Hanworth		•	•	
Harefield		•		
Harlington		•	•	
Harmondsworth	•	•		•
Harrow-On-The-Hill	•			•
Hayes	•		•	
Heston		•	•	
Hillingdon			•	
Holborn	•			•
Hornsey	•			
Hounslow	•		•	•
Hoxton	•			•
Ickenham	•	•	•	•
Isleworth	•	•		•
Islington	•	•		
Kensington	•	•		
Kingsbury	•	•		
Knightsbridge	•			
Laleham		•		
Limehouse				•
Little Stanmore		•		
Littleton		•		•
Marylebone	•			•
Mayfair	•			
Monken-Hadley			•	•
Northolt		•	•	
Norwood	•			
Notting-Hill	•			
Paddington	•	•		•
Pentonville	•			•
Perrivale	•			•
Pinner	•	•	•	
Poplar	•			
Ruislip		•		
St.-George-In-The-East	•			
St. Pancras	•			•
Shadwell	•	•		
Shepperton		•		
Shoreditch	•	•		•
Soho	•			•
South Mimms			•	
Southgate	•			
Spitalfields	•			•
Staines	•			•
Stanmore			•	
Stanwell		•	•	
Stepney	•			•
Stoke-Newington	•			
Sunbury	•	•		•
Tedington		•	•	
Tottenham			•	
Tower Hamlets	•			
Twickenham		•	•	
Uxbridge		•	•	
Wapping	•			
West Drayton	•		•	•
Westminster	•			•
Whitechapel	•			
MONMOUTH*				
Abergavenny		•		
Aberystruth		•		
Bassaleg		•		
Beaufort		•		
Bedwas	•	•		•
Bedwelty		•		•
Bettws		•		•

England

* COUNTY / SHIRE

PARISH	PARISH REGISTERS	BISHOPS' TRANSCRIPTS	BOYD'S MARRIAGE INDEX	PR PRINT-OUTS	PARISH	PARISH REGISTERS	BISHOPS' TRANSCRIPTS	BOYD'S MARRIAGE INDEX	PR PRINT-OUTS	PARISH	PARISH REGISTERS	BISHOPS' TRANSCRIPTS	BOYD'S MARRIAGE INDEX	PR PRINT-OUTS
Bettws-Newydd		•		•	Llanthewy-Rytherch		•		•	Roggiett		•		
Bishton		•		•	LLanthewy-Skirrid		•		•	Rumney		•		•
Blaenavon		•			Llanthewy-Vach		•		•	St. Arvans		•		•
Bryngwyn		•		•	Llantillio-Crosseny				•	St. Brides-Netherwent		•		•
Caerwent	•	•		•	Llantrissent		•		•	St. Brides-Wentllooge		•		
Caldicott		•		•	Llanvaches		•			St. Maughans		•		
Chapel-Hill		•		•	LLanvair-Discoed	•	•		•	St. Mellons		•		•
Chepstow		•			Llanvair-Kilgidin		•			St. Pierre		•		
Christchurch		•		•	Llanvapley				•	St. Woolos		•		
Coedkernew		•		•	Llanvetherine				•	Shire-Newton		•		
Cwmcarvan		•		•	Llanvihangel-Crucorney		•			Skenfreth		•		
Cwmyoy		•			Llanvihangel-Llantarnam		•		•	Tintern-Parva		•		
Devaudon		•		•	Llanvihangel-Near-Roggiet		•		•	Tredegar		•		•
Dingestown		•		•	Llanvihangel-Tor-Y-Mynydd		•		•	Tredunnock		•		
Dixton-Newton	•	•		•	Llanvihangel-Ystern-Llewern	•	•		•	Tregare		•		
Goldcliff		•		•	Llanvrechva		•		•	Trelleck		•		•
Goytrey		•		•	LLanwenarth		•		•	Trelleck-Grange				•
Grosmont		•		•	Machen	•				Trevethin	•	•		•
Gwernesney		•			Magor		•		•	Trostrey		•		•
Henllis		•		•	Marshfield		•			Undy		•		•
Ifton		•			Matherne		•			Usk		•		•
Itton		•		•	Michaelstone-Y-Vedw		•		•	Wilerick		•		
Kemeys-Commander		•		•	Mitchel-Troy		•		•	Witson		•		
Kemeys-Inferior		•		•	Monkswood		•		•	Wonastow		•		•
Kilgwrrwg		•		•	Monmouth	•	•		•	**NORFOLK***				
Langstone		•		•	Monnow Over				•	Acle	•		•	•
Llanarth		•		•	Mounton		•		•	Alburgh			•	
Llanbaddock	•	•		•	Mynyddyslwyn		•			Aldoborough	•			•
Llandenny		•		•	Nantyglo		•		•	Aldeby	•			
Llandevand		•		•	Nash		•		•	Anmer			•	
Llandgveth		•			Newchurch		•		•	Antingham	•			
Llandogo		•		•	Newport		•		•	Arminghall	•			
Llanellen		•		•	Newton-Wolves		•		•	Ashby (Near Brundall)	•		•	
Llanfoist		•		•	Oldcastle		•		•	Ashby (Near Buckenham)	•			
Llangattock-Lingoed				•	Panteague	•	•		•	Ashby-With-Oby	•			
Llangattock-Vibon-Avel				•	Penalth		•		•	Ashmanhaugh	•			•
Llangeview		•		•	Penhow		•		•	Ashwicken			•	
Llangibby		•		•	Penrose		•			Attleborough	•			
Llangoven		•			Penterry		•			Attlebridge	•			
Llangua	•	•			Penyclawdo		•		•	Babingley			•	
Llangwm		•		•	Peterson		•			Baconsthorpe	•			
Llanhennock		•		•	Pill-Gwenlly		•		•	Bacton	•			
Llanhiddel		•		•	Pontnewydd		•		•	Bagthorpe				•
Llanishen		•		•	Portscuett		•		•	Bale	•			
Llanllowell		•		•	Raglan		•		•	Barney				•
Llanmartin		•		•	Redwick		•		•	Barningham-Norwood	•			
Llanover		•			Rhymney		•			Barwick			•	
Llansaintfraed		•			Risca		•			Bawsey	•		•	•
Llansoy		•		•	Rockfield		•		•	Beckton	•			

England

* COUNTY / SHIRE

PARISH	PARISH REGISTERS	BISHOPS' TRANSCRIPTS	BOYD'S MARRIAGE INDEX	PR PRINT-OUTS
Bedingham	•		•	
Beechamwell	•			
Beeston	•			
Beeston-Regis	•			•
Beeston St. Lawrence	•			•
Beetley	•			
Beighton	•			
Bergh-Apton	•			
Besthorpe	•			
Bexwell	•			
Billingford (Near Mitford)				•
Billockby	•		•	
Bircham-Tofts			•	
Bixley	•			
Blickling	•			
Blo-Norton	•			
Blofield	•			•
Bodney				•
Booton			•	
Bradeston	•		•	
Bradfield	•			•
Bramerton	•			
Brampton	•			•
Bressingham	•			
Briningham	•			
Brisley	•			
Briston	•			•
Brooke	•			
Broome			•	
Brumstead	•			•
Brundall	•		•	
Buckenham	•			
Burgh-Next-Aylsham				•
Burgh Parva	•			
Burgh-St. Margaret and St. Mary	•			•
Burlingham	•			
Burlingham-St. Andrew	•		•	
Burlingham-St. Peter	•		•	•
Burnham-Deepdale	•			
Burnham-Sutton-Cum-Burnham-Ulph	•	•	•	
Burton-Turf			•	
Bylaugh	•			
Caistor-Next-Yarmouth	•		•	
Caistor-St. Edmunds	•			•
Calthorpe	•		•	
Cantley	•			•
Carleton-Rode			•	
Carleton-St. Peter	•			
Castle-Acre			•	

PARISH	PARISH REGISTERS	BISHOPS' TRANSCRIPTS	BOYD'S MARRIAGE INDEX	PR PRINT-OUTS
Castle-Rising	•		•	
Caston	•			•
Catfield	•			•
Catton	•			
Cawston	•			
Chedgrave	•		•	•
Claxton				•
Clippesby	•			
Coltishall	•			
Congham	•	•	•	
Crimplesham	•			•
Cringleford	•		•	•
Crostwick	•			
Crostwight	•			•
Dersingham	•		•	
Didlington	•			
Dilham	•			•
Diss	•			
Ditchingham			•	
Docking	•	•	•	
Downham	•			
Drayton	•			
Dunston	•			
Dunston-Cum-Doughton			•	
East Barsham			•	
East Bilney	•			
East Bradenham	•			
East Dereham	•			
East Lexham	•		•	
East Rainham			•	
East Rudham			•	
East Ruston	•			
East Somerton	•		•	
East Tuddenham	•			
East Walton	•		•	•
East Winch			•	
Ellingham	•			
Fakenham			•	
Felthorpe	•			
Feltwell	•			
Field-Dalling	•			•
Filby	•		•	
Fincham	•			
Flitcham			•	
Flordon	•			
Foulden	•			
Framingham-Earl	•			•
Framingham-Pigot	•			
Frenze	•			

PARISH	PARISH REGISTERS	BISHOPS' TRANSCRIPTS	BOYD'S MARRIAGE INDEX	PR PRINT-OUTS
Frettenham	•			
Fring	•	•	•	
Garboldisham	•			
Garvestone	•			
Gately	•			
Gayton			•	
Gayton-Thorpe			•	
Gaywood			•	
Geist	•			
Gimingham	•			•
Gissing	•			•
Gorleston	•			
Great Bircham	•	•	•	
Great Cressingham			•	
Great Dunham	•		•	
Great Ellingham	•			•
Great Fransham	•			
Great Massingham			•	
Great Melton			•	
Great Plumstead	•			
Great Ryburg			•	
Great Snoring	•		•	
Great Walsingham	•			
Great Witchingham	•			
Gresham	•		•	•
Gressenhall	•			
Grimstone			•	
Guestwick	•			
Gunthorpe	•			
Hackford-By-Reepham	•			
Haddiscoe	•			
Hainford	•			
Hales	•			
Halvergate		•		
Happisburgh	•			•
Hardingham	•			
Hardley	•			•
Hardwick	•			
Hassingham	•			
Heacham			•	
Heckingham	•			
Hedenham			•	
Helhoughton			•	
Hellesdon	•			
Hemblington	•		•	
Hempstead	•			
Hempstead (Near No. Walsham)	•			
Hemsby	•		•	
Hevingham	•			

England

* COUNTY / SHIRE

PARISH	PARISH REGISTERS	BISHOPS' TRANSCRIPTS	BOYD'S MARRIAGE INDEX	PR PRINT-OUTS	PARISH	PARISH REGISTERS	BISHOPS' TRANSCRIPTS	BOYD'S MARRIAGE INDEX	PR PRINT-OUTS	PARISH	PARISH REGISTERS	BISHOPS' TRANSCRIPTS	BOYD'S MARRIAGE INDEX	PR PRINT-OUTS
Heydon	•				Markshall				•	Ridlington	•			•
Hickling	•		•		Marsham	•			•	Rollesby	•			
Hilgay	•				Martham	•		•	•	Rougham	•			•
Hillington			•		Mattishall	•				Roxham	•			
Hingham	•				Mattishall-Burgh	•				Roydon (Near Diss)	•		•	
Hockering	•				Mautby	•		•	•	Roydon (Near Kings-Lynn)				•
Hoe	•				Melton-Constable	•				Runham	•		•	•
Holkham			•		Mendham	•				Rushall	•			
Holme-Hale	•		•		Middleton			•		Ryston	•			
Holme-Next-The-Sea	•		•	•	Mileham	•				St. John's Maddermarket	•			
Holt	•			•	Morley-St. Botolph	•				Salhouse	•			
Honing	•			•	Morley-St. Peter	•				Sall	•			
Horning	•				Moulton	•				Sandringham			•	
Horningtoft			•		Mundsley	•		•	•	Saxlingham	•			
Horsey-Next-The-Sea	•			•	Narborough			•		Saxlingham-Nethergate	•			
Horsford	•				Narford			•		Saxlingham-Thorpe	•			
Horsham St. Faith	•				New Buckenham	•				Saxthorpe	•			
Horstead			•		New Walsingham	•				Scarning	•			
Howe				•	Newton-Bircham	•		•	•	Sculthorpe			•	
Hunstanton	•				Newton-Flotman	•				Sharrington	•			•
Hunworth	•				North Barsham	•		•		Shelfanger			•	
Igborough	•				North Elmham	•			•	Shelton	•			
Ilketshall-St. Margaret	•				North Lopham	•				Shereford			•	
Ingham	•			•	North Runcton			•		Sheringham	•			
Ingoldisthorpe			•		North Tuddenham	•				Shernborne			•	
Ingworth	•		•		North Walsham	•			•	Shimpling	•			
Itteringham	•				North Wooton			•		Shingham	•	•		
Ketteringham	•				Norwich	•			•	Shipdham	•			•
Kirby-Bedon	•				Oby			•		Shotesham	•			
Knapton	•			•	Old Buckenham	•			•	Sidestrand	•			•
Lammas	•			•	Ormsby-St. Margaret	•		•		Smallburgh	•			•
Langham			•		Outwell	•				Snettisham			•	
Langley	•		•		Oxborough	•			•	South Creake	•		•	
Lessingham	•			•	Oxnead	•				South Rainham			•	
Letheringsett	•			•	Palling	•			•	South Runction	•			
Leziate			•		Panxworth			•		South Ruston	•			
Lingwood	•				Paston	•				South Walsham	•			•
Litcham	•		•		Pentney			•		South Wooton			•	
Little Brandon	•				Pockthorpe	•				Southacre	•		•	
Little Ellingham	•			•	Postwick	•				Southery	•			
Little Fransham	•				Potter-Heigham	•				Southwood	•			
Little Hautbois				•	Pulham-St. Mary-The-Virgin	•				Spixworth	•			
Little Massingham			•		Rackheath	•				Stanhoe			•	
Little Ryburgh			•		Ranworth	•		•		Starston	•			
Little Snoring			•		Redenhall	•				Stockton				•
Longham	•			•	Reedham	•			•	Stody	•			
Ludham	•				Reepham	•				Stoke-Ferry	•			
Mannington	•				Repps-Cum-Bastwick	•			•	Stoke-Holycross	•			
Marham	•				Reymerston	•				Stokesby	•		•	•

England
* COUNTY / SHIRE

PARISH	PARISH REGISTERS	BISHOPS' TRANSCRIPTS	BOYD'S MARRIAGE INDEX	PR PRINT-OUTS
Stow-Bardolph	•			•
Stradsett	•			
Stratton-Strawless	•			
Strumpshaw	•		•	
Surlingham	•			•
Sutton	•			
Swaffham			•	
Swafield	•			•
Swainsthorpe	•			
Swannington	•			•
Swanton-Abbott	•			•
Swanton-Morley	•			•
Syderstone	•		•	•
Tatterford	•		•	•
Tattersett			•	
Taverham	•			
Terrington St. Clement	•			
Thelveton	•			
Thirne			•	
Thorpe-Market	•			•
Thorpe-Next-Haddiscoe	•			
Thorpe-Next-Norwich	•			•
Threxton	•			
Thrigby	•		•	•
Thurlton	•			•
Thurne	•			
Thursford			•	
Thuxton	•			
Thwaite-St. Mary			•	
Tilney-All Saints	•			
Tilney-Cum-Islington	•			
Tittleshall	•			•
Toft-Monks	•			
Toft-Trees			•	
Topcroft	•		•	
Tottenhill	•			
Trimingham	•			•
Trowse	•			
Trunch	•			•
Tunstall	•			
Twyford	•			
Upton	•		•	•
Upwell	•			•
Walcott	•			•
Walsoken	•			
Waterden			•	
Waxham	•			•
Weasenham-All Saints	•			
Weeting-With-Broomhill			•	

PARISH	PARISH REGISTERS	BISHOPS' TRANSCRIPTS	BOYD'S MARRIAGE INDEX	PR PRINT-OUTS
Wellingham	•			
Wells	•			•
Welney	•			
Wendling	•			
Wereham	•			
West Barsham			•	
West Beckham	•		•	•
West Bilney			•	
West Bradenham	•			
West Dereham	•			•
West Harling	•			
West Lexham	•			
West Newton			•	
West Rainham			•	
West Rudham			•	
West Somerton	•		•	•
West Winch	•			
Westacre	•		•	•
Westfield	•			
Westwick	•			•
Wheatacre-All Saints	•			
Whinburgh	•			
Whissonsett			•	
Whitlingham	•			
Whitwell	•			
Wickhampton	•			
Wickmere	•			
Wiggenhall St. Mary				
Magdalen	•			
Wimbotsham	•			
Winfarthing	•			
Winterton	•		•	
Witton (Near Blofield)	•			
Witton (Near Brundall)	•		•	
Wiggenhall St. Mary Magdelen	•			•
Wolverton	•		•	
Wood-Dalling	•			•
Woodbastwick	•		•	
Woodton	•		•	
Wormegay	•			
Wormstead	•			•
Wortwell	•			•
Wramplingham	•			•
Wretton	•			
Wroxham	•			
Yarmouth	•			•
Yaxham	•			
Yelverton	•			
NORTHAMPTON*				

PARISH	PARISH REGISTERS	BISHOPS' TRANSCRIPTS	BOYD'S MARRIAGE INDEX	PR PRINT-OUTS
Abington	•			
Abthorpe	•			
Addington (Great)	•			
Addington (Little)	•			
Ailesworth	•			
Alderton	•			
Apethorpe		•		•
Aynho	•			
Barnack	•			
Broughton	•			
Burton-Latimer	•			
Castor	•		•	•
Clay-Coton	•			•
Colley-Weston	•			
Collingtree	•			
Cranford-St. Andrew	•			•
Cranford-St. John	•			•
Croughton			•	
Deanshanger	•			
Dingley	•			•
Dodford			•	
Duddington		•		•
Easton	•	•		
Evenley	•			
Everdon			•	
Eydon	•			
Farthingstone			•	
Fawsley	•			
Flaxton			•	
Glinton	•		•	•
Greatworth	•			
Gretton		•		•
Harpole			•	
Irchester	•			
Irthlingborough	•			
King's Cliffe	•			•
Kings-Sutton		•		
Lamport			•	
Lilford	•			
Litchborough	•			
Longbuckby	•			•
Marholm	•			•
Maxey	•			•
Milton	•			
Moulton	•			•
Naseby	•			
Nassington		•		•
Newton-Wood		•		•
Northampton			•	

England

* COUNTY / SHIRE

PARISH	PARISH REGISTERS	BISHOPS' TRANSCRIPTS	BOYD'S MARRIAGE INDEX	PR PRINT-OUTS
Northborough	•		•	
Passenham	•			
Paston	•			
Peakirk	•		•	
Peterborough				•
Pilsgate	•			
Pitchley	•			
Rockingham	•			•
Rothwell	•			
Rushton	•			•
Silverstone	•			
Southorpe	•			
Stoke-Albany		•		
Stoke-Bruerne			•	
Stowe-Nine-Churches			•	
Sutton	•			
Sutton-Bassett			•	
Tansor	•			
Thorpe-Achurn	•			
Thorpe-Mandeville	•			•
Titchmarsh	•			•
Upton (Near Northampton)	•			
Wansford	•			
Wellingborough	•			
Westand-By-Welland			•	
Whitfield	•			
Whittering	•			
Wigsthorpe	•			
Yarwell	•	•		•
NORTHUMBERLAND*				
Allendale	•	•		•
Allenton	•			•
Alnham	•			•
Alnwich	•			
Ancroft	•			•
Bamburgh	•			•
Beadnell	•			
Bedlington	•			
Belford	•			•
Bellingham	•			•
Benwell	•			
Berwick-Upon-Tweed	•			
Birtley	•			•
Blanchland	•			•
Bothal	•			•
Branxton	•			
Brinkburn	•			
Byker	•			
Bywell-St. Andrew	•			•

PARISH	PARISH REGISTERS	BISHOPS' TRANSCRIPTS	BOYD'S MARRIAGE INDEX	PR PRINT-OUTS
Bywell-St. Peter	•			•
Cambo	•			
Carham	•			•
Carrshields	•			•
Chatton	•			
Chillingham	•			•
Chollerton	•			•
Corbridge	•			•
Corsenside	•			•
Cramlington	•			•
Dinnington	•			
Doddington	•			•
Earsdon	•			•
Edlingham	•			
Eglingham	•			•
Ellingham	•			•
Elsdon	•			•
Elswick	•			
Embleton	•			
Etal				•
Falstone	•			•
Felton	•			•
Ford	•			•
Gosforth	•			•
Halton	•			
Haltwhistle	•			•
Harbottle				•
Hartburn	•			•
Haydon	•			•
Hebburn	•			•
Heddon-On-The-Wall	•			•
Hexham	•	•		•
Holy Island	•			•
Holystone	•			
Horton	•			•
Howick	•			•
Humshaugh	•			
Ilderton	•			•
Ingram	•			
Kirkharle	•			•
Kirkhaugh	•			
Kirknewton	•	•		•
Kirkwhelpington	•			•
Knaresdale	•			•
Lambley	•			
Lesbury	•			
Long Benton	•			•
Long Framlington	•			
Long Horsley	•			•

PARISH	PARISH REGISTERS	BISHOPS' TRANSCRIPTS	BOYD'S MARRIAGE INDEX	PR PRINT-OUTS
Long Houghton	•			
Lowick	•			
Lucker	•			•
Meldon	•			
Mitford	•			•
Morpeth	•			•
Nether Witton	•			
Newbiggin	•			•
Newbrough	•			
Newburn	•			•
Newcastle-Upon-Tyne	•			•
Ninebanks	•			
Norham	•			•
Ovingham	•			•
Ponteland	•			•
Rennington	•			•
Rock				•
Rothbury	•			•
St. John-Lee	•	•		•
Scremerston	•			•
Seahouses	•			
Shilbottle	•			•
Shotley	•			•
Simonburn	•			•
Slaley	•			
Stamfordham	•			•
Stannington	•			•
Thockrington				•
Tweedmouth	•			•
Tynemouth	•			•
Ulgham	•			•
Walker	•			
Wallsend	•			•
Warden	•			•
Wark	•			
Warkworth	•			•
Whalton	•			
Whitfield	•			•
Whittingham	•			•
Whittonstall	•			•
Widdrington	•			•
Woodhorn	•			•
Wooler	•			•
NOTTINGHAM*				
Adbolton		•		
Alverton				
Annesley		•	•	
Applethorpe		•		•
Arnold		•	•	•

England

* COUNTY / SHIRE

PARISH	PARISH REGISTERS	BISHOPS' TRANSCRIPTS	BOYD'S MARRIAGE INDEX	PR PRINT-OUTS	PARISH	PARISH REGISTERS	BISHOPS' TRANSCRIPTS	BOYD'S MARRIAGE INDEX	PR PRINT-OUTS	PARISH	PARISH REGISTERS	BISHOPS' TRANSCRIPTS	BOYD'S MARRIAGE INDEX	PR PRINT-OUTS
Askham		•	•	•	Eakring		•	•	•	Keyworth		•	•	•
Attenborough		•	•	•	East Bridgford		•	•	•	Kilvington	•	•	•	•
Averham		•	•	•	East Drayton		•		•	Kingston-Upon-Soar		•	•	•
Awsworth		•	•	•	East Leake		•	•	•	Kinoulton		•	•	•
Babworth		•	•	•	East Markham		•		•	Kirby-In-Ashfield		•	•	•
Balderton		•	•	•	East Retford		•		•	Kirklington		•	•	•
Barnby-In-The-Willows	•	•		•	East Stoke		•	•		Kirkton	•	•	•	•
Barnby-Moor					Eastwood		•	•	•	Kneesal		•	•	•
Barton-In-Fabis		•	•	•	Eaton		•		•	Kneeton		•	•	•
Basford		•	•	•	Edingley		•	•	•	Lambley		•	•	•
Beckingham		•	•	•	Edwalton		•	•	•	Laneham	•	•	•	•
Beeston		•	•	•	Edwinstowe	•	•		•	Langar		•	•	•
Bilborough	•	•	•	•	Egmanton		•	•	•	Langford		•	•	•
Bilsthorpe		•	•	•	Elksley		•		•	Laxton	•	•	•	•
Bingham		•	•	•	Elston		•	•	•	Lenton		•	•	•
Bleasby		•	•	•	Elton		•	•	•	Linby		•	•	•
Blidworth		•	•	•	Epperstone		•	•	•	Little Borough		•		•
Blyth	•	•		•	Everton	•	•	•	•	Lowdham	•	•	•	•
Bole		•		•	Farndon		•	•	•	Mansfield	•	•	•	•
Bothamsall	•	•		•	Farnsfield		•	•	•	Mansfield-Woodhouse	•	•	•	•
Boughton		•	•	•	Finningley		•		•	Maplebeck		•	•	•
Bramcote		•		•	Flawborough		•	•	•	Marnham		•	•	•
Broughton-Sulney		•	•		Fledborough		•	•	•	Mattersey		•		•
Bulcote				•	Flintham		•	•		Misson	•	•		•
Bulwell		•	•	•	Gamston	•				Misterton		•		•
Bunny		•	•	•	Gamston (Near Retford)		•		•	Morton (Near Fiskerton)		•	•	•
Burton-Joyce		•	•	•	Gedling	•	•	•	•	Newark		•	•	•
Calverton		•	•	•	Girton		•	•	•	Normanton-Upon-Soar		•	•	
Car-Colston		•	•	•	Gonalstone		•	•	•	Normanton-Upon-Trent		•	•	
Carburton		•		•	Gotham		•	•	•	North Clifton		•	•	•
Carlton		•		•	Granby		•	•	•	North Collingham		•	•	•
Carlton-Upon-Trent		•		•	Greasley		•	•	•	North Leverton		•		•
Caunton		•	•	•	Gringley-On-The-Wall	•		•	•	North Muskham		•	•	•
Clarborough	•	•		•	Grove		•			North Wheatley		•		•
Clayworth	•			•	Halam		•	•	•	Norton		•		
Clifton-With-Glapton		•	•	•	Halloughton		•	•		Norwell		•	•	•
Coddington		•	•	•	Harworth	•	•		•	Nottingham	•	•		•
Colston-Bassett		•	•	•	Hawksworth		•	•	•	Nuthall		•	•	•
Colwick		•	•	•	Hawton		•	•	•	Ollerton	•	•		•
Cossall		•	•	•	Hayton		•	•	•	Ordsall		•		•
Costock		•	•	•	Headon	•	•		•	Orston		•	•	•
Cotgrave		•	•	•	Hickling		•	•	•	Ossington		•	•	
Cotham		•			Hockerton		•	•	•	Owthorpe		•	•	•
Cottam		•	•	•	Holme		•	•	•	Oxton		•	•	•
Cromwell		•	•	•	Holme-Pierrepont		•	•	•	Papplewick	•	•	•	•
Cropwell-Bishop		•	•	•	Hoveringham		•	•	•	Perlethorpe	•	•		•
Cuckney		•		•	Hucknall-Torkad		•	•	•	Plumtree	•	•	•	•
Darlton		•		•	Hyson-Green		•			Radford		•	•	•
Dunham		•		•	Kelham		•	•	•	Ragnall		•		•

England

* COUNTY / SHIRE

PARISH	PARISH REGISTERS	BISHOPS' TRANSCRIPTS	BOYD'S MARRIAGE INDEX	PR PRINT-OUTS	PARISH	PARISH REGISTERS	BISHOPS' TRANSCRIPTS	BOYD'S MARRIAGE INDEX	PR PRINT-OUTS	PARISH	PARISH REGISTERS	BISHOPS' TRANSCRIPTS	BOYD'S MARRIAGE INDEX	PR PRINT-OUTS
Rampton		•		•	Upper Broughton				•	Bicester	•	•		•
Ratcliffe-On-Trent		•	•	•	Upton (Near Southwell)		•	•	•	Binsey	•	•		•
Ratcliffe-Upon-Soar		•	•	•	Walesby	•	•		•	Bix	•	•		•
Rempstone		•	•	•	Walkeringham		•		•	Blackbourton	•	•		•
Rolleston		•	•	•	Warsop	•	•		•	Bladon		•		•
Ruddington	•	•	•	•	Wellow	•	•		•	Bletchington		•		•
Saundby		•		•	West Bridgford		•	•	•	Bloxham		•		•
Scarrington		•	•	•	West Burton		•		•	Bodicott		•		•
Screveton		•	•		West Drayton		•		•	Brightwell-Baldwin		•		•
Scrooby	•	•	•	•	West Leake		•	•	•	Brightwell-Prior		•		
Selston	•	•	•	•	West Markham		•		•	Brightwell-Salome		•		•
Shelford		•	•	•	West Retford		•		•	Broadwell		•		•
Shelton	•	•	•	•	Weston		•	•	•	Broughton		•		•
Sibthorpe		•	•	•	Whatton		•	•	•	Broughton-Poggs		•		•
Skegby (Near Mansfield)	•	•	•	•	Widmerpool		•	•	•	Bucknell	•	•		•
Snenton		•	•	•	Wilford			•	•	Burcott		•		•
South Collingham		•	•	•	Willoughby-On-The-Wolds		•	•	•	Burford	•	•		•
South Leverton		•		•	Winkbourne		•	•		Cassington		•	•	•
South Muskham		•	•	•	Winthorpe		•		•	Caversfield	•	•		•
South Scarle		•	•	•	Wollaton		•	•	•	Caversham		•		•
South Wheatley		•		•	Woodborough		•	•	•	Chadlington				•
Southwell	•	•	•	•	Worksop		•		•	Chalgrove		•		•
Stanford-Upon-Soar		•	•	•	Wysall		•	•	•	Charlbury		•		•
Stanton-On-Wolds		•	•	•	**OXFORDSHIRE***					Charlton-Upon-Otmoor				•
Stapleford		•	•	•	Adderbury		•		•	Chastleton		•		•
Staunton		•	•		Adwell	•	•		•	Checkendon	•	•		•
Staythorpe		•			Albury		•		•	Chesterton		•		•
Stokeham		•		•	Alkerton	•	•		•	Chinnor	•	•		•
Strelley		•	•	•	Alvescott		•		•	Chislehampton		•		•
Sturton		•		•	Ambrosden	•	•		•	Churchill	•	•		•
Sutton		•			Ardley	•	•		•	Clanfield		•		•
Sutton-Bonnington	•	•	•	•	Ascott-Under-Wychwood		•		•	Claydon		•		•
Sutton-Cum-Lound			•	•	Ashampstead		•		•	Clifton-Hampden		•		•
Sutton-In-Ash				•	Asthall		•		•	Cogges		•		•
Sutton-In-Ashfield		•	•		Aston-Rowant	•	•		•	Combe				•
Sutton-Upon-Trent		•	•	•	Aston-Steeple		•			Cornwell		•		•
Syerston		•	•	•	Baldon-Marsh		•		•	Cottesford		•		•
Teversall		•	•	•	Baldon-Toot		•		•	Cowley		•		•
Thorney		•	•	•	Balscott		•		•	Cropredy	•	•		
Thoroton		•	•		Bampton	•	•		•	Crowell	•	•	•	•
Thorpe	•	•	•	•	Banbury	•	•		•	Crowmarsh-Gifford	•	•		•
Thorpe-Bochart		•			Barford-St. John				•	Cuddesden	•			•
Thrumpton	•	•	•	•	Barford-St. Michael				•	Culham	•	•		•
Thurgarton		•	•	•	Barton-Steeple		•		•	Cuxham		•		•
Tollerton		•	•	•	Barton-Westcot		•		•	Deddington		•		•
Treswell	•	•		•	Beckley		•		•	Dorchester	•			•
Trowell		•	•	•	Begbrooke		•		•	Drayton (Near Banbury)		•		•
Tuxford	•	•		•	Bensington	•	•		•	Drayton (Near Wallingford)		•		•
Tythby		•	•	•	Berrick-Salome		•		•	Ducklington		•		

England

* COUNTY / SHIRE

PARISH	PARISH REGISTERS	BISHOPS' TRANSCRIPTS	BOYD'S MARRIAGE INDEX	PR PRINT-OUTS
Dunstew		•		
Easington (Near Thame)		•		•
East Chadlington		•		
Elsfield		•		•
Emmington	•	•		•
Ensham		•	•	•
Enstone	•	•		•
Epwell	•	•		•
Ewelme		•		•
Eye and Dunsden	•			
Fifield (Near Burford)		•		•
Finmere	•	•		•
Finstock		•		
Forest-Hill		•		•
Fringford		•		•
Fritwell	•	•		•
Fulbrook	•			•
Glympton	•			•
Goddington	•			
Great Bourton	•			•
Hampton Gay	•			
Handborough			•	
Headington	•			
Henley-On-Thames	•			
Holton	•			
Iffley	•			
Islip	•			
Kidlington	•			
Kingham	•			
Kirtlington	•			
Lav	•			
Lew		•		•
Lewknor	•	•		
Little Bourton		•		
Little Faringdon		•		
Little Milton		•		
Long Combe		•		
Maple-Durham	•			
Merton	•			
Minster-Lovell		•		•
Mixbury	•			•
Mollington	•	•		•
Newnham-Murren	•			•
Noke	•			
North Aston		•		•
Northmoor			•	
Norton-Brize	•	•		•
Norton-Chipping	•	•	•	•
Oxford	•			•

PARISH	PARISH REGISTERS	BISHOPS' TRANSCRIPTS	BOYD'S MARRIAGE INDEX	PR PRINT-OUTS
Piddington	•			•
Pirton	•		•	
Pishill	•			
St. John-Barford		•		
St. Michael-Barford		•		
Sandford	•			
Sandford-Upon-Thames				•
Sarsden	•			
Shenington	•	•		•
Shifford				•
Shutford	•			
Souldern	•			
South Hinskey	•			
South Weston	•			
Standlake			•	
Stanton-Harcourt			•	
Steeple-Ashton				•
Stoke-Lyne	•			
Stokenchurch	•			•
Stratton-Audley	•			
Sydenham	•			
Thame	•			
Waterperry	•			•
Watlington	•			
Westcott-Barton				•
Westwell	•			
Wheatley	•	•		
Widford		•		
Wolvercote	•			
Wood-Eaton	•			
Wooton			•	
Wroxton		•		
Yarnton			•	
RUTLAND*				
Ashwell		•		
Ayston		•		
Barrowden	•	•		
Belton		•		
Bisbrook		•	•	
Braunston		•		
Brooke		•		
Burley		•		
Caldecott		•		•
Cottesmore		•		
Edith-Weston		•		
Empingham		•		
Essendine	•	•		
Exton		•		
Glaston		•		

PARISH	PARISH REGISTERS	BISHOPS' TRANSCRIPTS	BOYD'S MARRIAGE INDEX	PR PRINT-OUTS
Great Casterton		•	•	
Greetham	•			
Hambleton		•		
Ketton		•		
Langham		•		
Liddington		•		•
Little Casterton	•			
Lyndon		•		
Manton		•		
Morcott		•		
Normanton		•		
North Luffenham	•			•
Oakham	•	•		
Overton-Market		•		
Pickworth		•	•	
Pilton		•		
Preston		•		
Ridlington		•		
Ryhall		•		
Seaton		•		
South Luffenham		•		
Stoke-Dry		•		
Stretton		•		
Teigh		•		
Thistleton		•		
Tickencote		•	•	
Tinwell		•	•	
Tixover		•	•	
Uppingham		•		•
Wardley		•		
Whissendine		•		
Whitwell		•		
Wing		•		
SHROPSHIRE*				
Abdon	•	•		•
Acton-Burnell	•	•		•
Acton-Round	•	•		•
Acton-Scott	•	•		
Adderley	•	•		•
Alberbury	•	•		•
Albrighton (Near Shifnal)	•	•		•
Albrighton (Near Shrewsbury)	•	•		•
Alveley	•	•		•
Ash	•			•
Ashford Bowder		•		
Ashford-Bowdler	•	•		•
Ashford-Carbonell	•	•		
Astley	•	•		•
Astley-Abbotts	•	•		•

England

* COUNTY / SHIRE

PARISH	PARISH REGISTERS	BISHOPS' TRANSCRIPTS	BOYD'S MARRIAGE INDEX	PR PRINT-OUTS
Aston-Botterell	•			•
Atcham	•	•		•
Badger	•			•
Barrow	•			•
Baschurch	•	•		•
Battlefield	•	•		•
Bayston-Hill		•		•
Beckbury	•	•		•
Bedstone	•	•		•
Benthall	•	•		•
Berrington	•	•		•
Bettws	•	•		•
Billingsley	•	•		•
Bishops-Castle	•	•		•
Bitterley	•	•		•
Bolas-Magna	•			•
Boningdale	•	•		•
Bourton	•			•
Brace-Meole	•	•		•
Bridgnorth	•	•		•
Bromfield	•	•		•
Broseley	•	•		•
Broughton	•	•		•
Broughton (Near Wem)				•
Bucknell	•	•		•
Buildwas	•	•		•
Burford	•	•		•
Burwarton	•			
Cainham		•		•
Calverhall		•		•
Cardeston	•	•		•
Cardington	•	•		
Chelmarsh	•	•		•
Cheswardine	•	•		•
Chetton	•	•		•
Chetwynd	•	•		•
Childs-Ercall	•	•		•
Chirbury	•			•
Church-Aston	•	•		•
Claverley	•	•		•
Clee-St. Margaret	•	•		•
Cleobury-Mortimer	•	•		•
Clive	•	•		•
Clun	•	•		•
Clunbury	•	•		•
Clungunford	•	•		•
Cockshutt	•	•		•
Cold Weston	•	•		
Condover	•	•		•
Coreley	•	•		•
Cound	•	•		•
Cressage	•	•		•
Culmington	•	•		•
Dawley	•			•
Dawley-Parva	•	•		•
Deuxhill	•			•
Diddlebury	•	•		•
Ditton-Priors	•	•		•
Donnington		•		•
Dowles	•	•		
Drayton-In-Hales	•	•		•
Drayton-Parva		•		
Duddleston		•		•
Easthope	•			•
Eaton-Constantine	•	•		•
Eaton (Near Church-Stretton)	•			•
Eaton-Under-Heywood	•			
Edgmond	•	•		•
Edgton	•	•		•
Edstaston	•	•		•
Ellesmere	•	•		•
Ercall-Magna	•	•		•
Eyt		•		•
Eyton-Upon-The-Wild-Moors	•			
Farlow	•	•		
Fitz	•	•		•
Ford	•			•
Frodesley	•	•		•
Glazeley	•			•
Great Dawley				•
Great Hanwood		•		•
Great Ness	•	•		•
Greet	•	•		•
Grinshill	•	•		•
Habberley	•	•		•
Hadley		•		•
Hadnall	•	•		•
Halford	•	•		•
Halston (Near Oswestry)	•			•
Hampton-Welsh		•		•
Hanwood	•	•		
Harley	•	•		•
Highley	•	•		•
Hinstock		•		•
Hodnet	•	•		•
Holdgate		•		
Hope Baggot		•		
Hope-Bowdler	•	•		•
Hopesay	•	•		•
Hopstone	•			
Hopton Castle	•	•		•
Hopton In The Hole	•	•		•
Hordley	•	•		•
Hughley	•	•		•
Ightfield		•		•
Kemberton	•	•		
Kenley	•	•		•
Kinlet	•			•
Kinnersley	•	•		•
Knockin	•	•		•
Leaton	•			•
Lee-Brockhurst	•	•		
Leebotwood	•	•		•
Leighton	•	•		•
Lilleshall	•	•		•
Little Drayton				•
Little Ness	•	•		•
Little Wenlock	•	•		•
Llanvair-Waterdine	•	•		•
Llanyblodwell	•	•		•
Llanymynech	•	•		•
Long Stanton	•	•		•
Longdon-Upon-Tern	•	•		•
Longford	•	•		•
Longford (Near Newport)				•
Longnor	•	•		•
Loppington	•	•		•
Loughton				•
Ludford	•	•		•
Ludlow	•	•		•
Lydham	•	•		•
Madeley	•	•		•
Mainstone	•			•
Mawley-Hall				•
Melverley	•	•		•
Middle		•		
Middleton-Scriven	•	•		•
Milson	•	•		•
Minsterley		•		•
Monk-Hopton	•	•		•
Montford	•	•		•
More	•	•		•
Moreton	•			
Moreton-Corbet	•	•		•
Moreton-Say		•		•
Morvill	•	•		
Much Wenlock	•			•

England

* COUNTY / SHIRE

PARISH	PARISH REGISTERS	BISHOPS' TRANSCRIPTS	BOYD'S MARRIAGE INDEX	PR PRINT-OUTS	PARISH	PARISH REGISTERS	BISHOPS' TRANSCRIPTS	BOYD'S MARRIAGE INDEX	PR PRINT-OUTS	PARISH	PARISH REGISTERS	BISHOPS' TRANSCRIPTS	BOYD'S MARRIAGE INDEX	PR PRINT-OUTS
Munslow	•			•	Stockton		•			Almsford	•			•
Myddle	•	•		•	Stockton (Near Bridgnorth)				•	Angersleigh		•	•	•
Neen-Savage	•			•	Stoke St. Milborough	•	•		•	Ash-Priors		•	•	•
Neen-Sollars	•			•	Stoke-Upon-Tern		•		•	Ashbrittle		•	•	•
Neenton	•			•	Stokesay	•	•		•	Ashcott		•		•
Newport	•	•		•	Stottesden	•	•		•	Ashill		•	•	•
Newton (Near Wem)	•	•		•	Stretton-Church	•	•		•	Ashington		•		•
Norbury	•	•		•	Sutton	•				Ashwick		•		•
North Cleobury	•				Sutton-Maddock	•	•		•	Axbridge		•		•
North Lydbury	•	•		•	Sutton (Near Shrewsbury)				•	Babcary		•		•
Norton-In-Hales	•	•		•	Tasley		•		•	Babington		•		•
Oldbury	•	•		•	Tibberton	•	•		•	Backwell		•		•
Onibury		•			Tilstock		•			Badgworth		•		•
Oswestry	•	•		•	Tong	•	•		•	Baltonsborough		•		•
Petton	•	•		•	Trefonen		•		•	Barrington		•	•	•
Pitchford	•	•		•	Tugford	•	•		•	Barrow-Gurney		•	•	•
Pontesbury	•	•		•	Uffington	•	•		•	Barton-St. David		•		
Preen-Church	•	•		•	Uppington	•	•		•	Batcombe		•		•
Prees	•	•		•	Upton-Cresset	•	•			Bath	•	•		
Preston-Gubbals	•	•		•	Upton-Magna	•	•		•	Batheaston		•		
Preston-Gubblas	•				Upton-Waters	•	•		•	Bathford		•		
Preston-Upon-The-Wild-Moors	•	•		•	Wafers Hopton		•		•	Bawdrip		•		
Prior's Lee		•			Wellington	•	•		•	Bedminster		•		
Pulverbatch	•	•		•	Wem	•	•		•	Beer-Crocombe		•	•	
Quatford	•	•		•	Wenlock	•				Bickenhall		•	•	
Quatt	•	•		•	Wentnor	•	•		•	Bicknoller		•	•	
Ratlinghope	•	•		•	West Felton	•	•		•	Bishops-Hull			•	
Rodington		•		•	Westbury	•	•		•	Bishops-Lydeard		•		
Rushbury	•	•			Weston				•	Bleadon	•	•		
Ruyton-Of-The-Eleven-Towns	•	•		•	Weston-Under-Redcastle	•	•		•	Bourton		•		
Ryton	•	•			Wheathill	•	•		•	Bradford		•	•	•
St. Martin's	•	•		•	Whitchurch	•	•		•	Bratton		•		
Selattyn	•	•		•	Whittington	•	•		•	Bridgewater		•		•
Shawbury	•	•		•	Whixhall		•		•	Brimpton		•		
Sheinton	•	•		•	Willey	•	•		•	Broadway		•		•
Shelve	•	•		•	Wistanstow	•	•		•	Brockley		•		
Sheriff-Hales	•	•		•	Withington	•	•		•	Broomfield			•	
Shifnall	•	•		•	Wombridge	•	•			Brushford		•		
Shipton	•	•		•	Woolstaston	•	•		•	Bruton	•			•
Shrawardine	•	•		•	Woore	•			•	Buckland-Denham		•		
Shrewsbury	•	•		•	Worfield	•	•		•	Buckland-St. Mary		•	•	
Sibdon-Carwood	•	•		•	Worthen	•	•		•	Burnett		•		
Sidbury	•	•		•	Wrockwardine	•	•		•	Burham	•			
Silvington		•			Wroxeter	•	•		•	Butcombe		•		
Smethcott	•	•		•	**SOMERSET***					Butleigh		•		
Stanton-Lacy	•	•		•	Aisholt		•	•	•	Cameley		•		
Stanton-Up-The-Heath	•	•		•	Alford		•		•	Camerton		•		
Stapleton	•	•		•	Aller		•	•	•	Cannington		•	•	
Stirchley	•	•		•	Allerton-Chapel		•		•	Castle-Cary		•		•

England

* COUNTY / SHIRE

PARISH	PARISH REGISTERS	BISHOPS' TRANSCRIPTS	BOYD'S MARRIAGE INDEX	PR PRINT-OUTS
Catcott		•		•
Chaffcombe		•		
Charlinch		•	•	
Charlton Adam		•		
Charlton-Adams			•	
Charlton-Mackrell		•	•	
Charlton-Musgrove		•		
Cheddar		•		•
Cheddon-Fitzpaine		•	•	
Chedzoy		•	•	
Chelvey		•		
Chew-Magna		•		
Chew-Stoke		•		
Chewton-Mendip		•		
Chilcompton		•		
Chillington		•		
Chilthorne-Dormer		•		
Chilton-Burtle		•		
Chilton-Cantelo		•		
Chipstable	•	•		•
Christon	•			•
Churchill		•		•
Clapton		•		
Claverton		•		
Clevedon		•		
Closworth		•		
Clutton		•		
Combe-Abbas		•		•
Combe-English		•		
Combe-Florey		•		•
Combe-Hay		•		
Combe-Monckton		•		
Combe-St. Nicholas		•	•	
Compton-Bishop		•		
Compton-Dando		•		
Compton-Pauncefoot		•		
Congresbury	•	•		•
Corfe		•	•	
Cossington		•		
Cothelstone		•	•	
Creech-St. Michael		•	•	
Crewkerne		•	•	•
Cricket-Malherbie		•		
Cricket-St. Thomas		•		
Croscombe		•		•
Crowcombe		•	•	•
Curry-Mallet		•		
Curry-Rivell		•	•	
Dinder		•		•

PARISH	PARISH REGISTERS	BISHOPS' TRANSCRIPTS	BOYD'S MARRIAGE INDEX	PR PRINT-OUTS
Ditcheat		•		
Dodington		•	•	
Donyatt		•		
Doulting		•		
Dowlish-Wake		•		
Downhead (Near Shepton-Mallet)		•		
Drayton		•	•	
Dunkerton		•		
Durleigh		•	•	
Durston	•	•		•
East Bagborough		•		
East Brent		•		
East Cranmore		•		
East Harptree		•		
East Pennard		•	•	
East Quantoxhead		•	•	
Emborrow		•		
Enmore		•	•	
Evercreech	•	•		
Farleigh-Hungerford		•		
Fiddington		•	•	
Fitzhead		•		
Fivehead		•	•	
Forscote		•		
Freshford		•		
Frome		•		
Glastonbury		•		
Goathurst		•	•	
Halse		•	•	
Ham			•	
Hardington		•		
Hatch-Beauchamp		•		
Hawkridge		•		
Heathfield			•	
High Ham		•		•
Hillfarrance		•	•	
Hinton-Blewett		•		
Hinton-St.George		•	•	•
Holcombe		•		
Holford		•	•	
Holton		•		
Horsington	•	•		•
Huish-Champflower		•		
Huish-Episcopi		•	•	
Huntspill		•		
Hutton		•		
Ilchester		•		•
Ilminster			•	
Ilton		•	•	

PARISH	PARISH REGISTERS	BISHOPS' TRANSCRIPTS	BOYD'S MARRIAGE INDEX	PR PRINT-OUTS
Isle-Abbotts		•	•	
Isle-Brewers		•	•	
Keinton-Mandeville		•		
Kenn		•		
Kilmersdon		•		•
Kilmington	•		•	
Kilton		•	•	
Kilve		•	•	
Kingsbury-Episcopi			•	
Kingsdon			•	
Kingston-Seymour	•	•		
Kittisford	•	•	•	•
Langford-Budville			•	
Langport-Eastover			•	
Langridge		•		
Laverton		•		
Leigh-Upon-Mendip		•		
Limington			•	
Long Ashton	•	•		
Long Load			•	
Long Sutton	•	•	•	•
Lopen		•	•	
Lufton		•		
Lullington		•		
Lyncombe and Widcombe		•		•
Maperton		•		
Mark	•			
Marston-Bigott		•		
Marston-Magna		•		
Martock			•	
Meare		•		•
Merriott			•	
Midsomer-Norton		•	•	
Milbourne-Port	•			
Milton-Clevedon	•	•		•
Milton-Podimore			•	
Milverton			•	
Minehead		•		
Misterton		•		
Montacute		•		
Moorlinch		•		
Muchelney		•	•	
Nether Stowey		•	•	
Nettlecombe		•		•
North Barrow		•		
North Brewham		•		
North Cadbury	•	•		•
North Curry		•	•	•
North Perrott		•		

England

* COUNTY / SHIRE

PARISH	PARISH REGISTERS	BISHOPS' TRANSCRIPTS	BOYD'S MARRIAGE INDEX	PR PRINT-OUTS
North Petherton	•			•
North Stoke		•		
North Wootton		•		
Northover		•	•	
Norton-Fitzwarren	•		•	•
Norton-St. Philip		•		
Nunney		•		
Nynehead		•	•	
Oare		•		
Orchard-Portman		•	•	
Orchardleigh		•		
Othery			•	
Otterford			•	
Otterhampton			•	
Over Stowey		•	•	
Pawlett		•		
Pendomer		•		
Penselwood		•		
Pilton		•		•
Pitcombe	•			•
Pitminster		•	•	
Pitney			•	
Portbury		•		
Puckington			•	
Pylle		•		
Queen Camel		•		
Raddington	•	•		•
Rodney-Stoke	•	•		•
Ruishton			•	
Runnington			•	
St. Catherine		•		
St. Michaelchurch	•			•
Sampford-Arundel			•	
Sampford-Brett		•		
Seaborough		•		
Seavington-St. Mary		•		
Shapwick		•		•
Shepton-Beauchamp			•	
Shepton-Mallet		•		•
Shepton-Montague		•		
Shipham		•		
Somerton		•	•	•
South Barrow		•		•
South Brent	•			•
South Brewham		•		
South Cadbury		•		
Spaxton			•	
Stanton-Drew		•		
Stanton-Prior		•		

PARISH	PARISH REGISTERS	BISHOPS' TRANSCRIPTS	BOYD'S MARRIAGE INDEX	PR PRINT-OUTS
Stanton-Fitzpaine		•	•	
Stawell		•		
Stockland-Bristol			•	
Stocklinch-Magdalen		•	•	
Stocklinch-Ottersay			•	
Stogumber		•		
Stogursey		•	•	
Stoke-Lane		•		
Stoke-Pero		•		
Stoke-St. Mary			•	
Stoke-Sub-Hamdon		•		
Stoke-Easton		•		
Stowell		•		
Stowey		•		
Stratton-On-The-Fosse		•		
Street	•			•
Stringston		•	•	
Sutton-Bingham		•	•	
Sutton-Mallett		•		
Swainswick	•			
Swell		•	•	
Taunton			•	
Thorne		•		
Thorne-Falcon			•	
Thorne-St. Margaret			•	
Thurlbear		•	•	
Thurloxton			•	
Timberscombe		•		
Timsbury	•	•		
Tintinhull		•		
Trent		•		
Trull		•	•	
Ubley		•		
Uphill		•		
Upton		•		
Walcot		•		
Walton		•		
Walton-In-Gordano		•		
Wambrook			•	•
Wanstrow		•		
Wayford		•		
Weare		•		
Wedmore	•			•
Wellington		•	•	•
Wellow		•		
Wells	•			•
West Bagborough		•	•	
West Bradley		•		
West Buckland			•	

PARISH	PARISH REGISTERS	BISHOPS' TRANSCRIPTS	BOYD'S MARRIAGE INDEX	PR PRINT-OUTS
West Buckland (Somerset)		•		
West Camel		•		
West Coker		•		
West Cranmore		•		
West Harptree		•		
West Hatch	•		•	•
West Lydford		•		
West Monkton		•	•	
West Pennard		•		
West Quantoxhead		•		
Westbury	•	•		
Weston-Bampflyde		•		
Weston-In-Gordano		•		
Weston-Super-Mare			•	
Wheathill		•		
White Lackington		•	•	
White Staunton			•	
Wilton	•	•		•
Wincanton		•		•
Winford		•		
Winscombe		•		
Winsford		•		
Withiel-Florey		•		
Wiveliscombe		•		•
Wooley		•		
Wraxall		•		
Wraxall (Near Bristol)			•	•
Wrington		•		•
Yarlington		•		
Yatton		•		•
Yeovilton		•	•	
STAFFORD*				
Abbots-Bromley		•		•
Acton-Trussell and Bednall		•		•
Adbaston	•	•		•
Aldridge		•		•
Allstonefield	•	•		•
Alrewas	•	•		•
Alton	•	•		•
Armitage	•	•		•
Ashborne		•		
Ashley	•	•		•
Aston (near Stone)				•
Audley	•	•		•
Bagnall	•			•
Barlaston	•	•		•
Barton-Under-Needwood	•	•		•
Baswick	•	•		•
Betley	•	•		•

England

* COUNTY / SHIRE

PARISH	PARISH REGISTERS	BISHOPS' TRANSCRIPTS	BOYD'S MARRIAGE INDEX	PR PRINT-OUTS	PARISH	PARISH REGISTERS	BISHOPS' TRANSCRIPTS	BOYD'S MARRIAGE INDEX	PR PRINT-OUTS	PARISH	PARISH REGISTERS	BISHOPS' TRANSCRIPTS	BOYD'S MARRIAGE INDEX	PR PRINT-OUTS
Biddulph	•	•		•	Drayton-Bassett		•		•	Kings Bromley		•		•
Bilston	•	•		•	Dunston	•				Kingsley	•	•		•
Blithfield	•	•		•	Eccleshall	•	•		•	Kingston	•	•		•
Blore		•		•	Edial		•			Kingswinford	•	•		•
Bloxwich	•	•			Edingale	•	•		•	Lane-End and Longton		•		•
Blurton and Lightwood-Forest	•	•		•	Elford	•	•		•	Lapley	•	•		•
Blymhill	•	•		•	Elkstone and Warslow		•		•	Leek	•	•		•
Bobbington	•	•		•	Ellastone	•	•		•	Leigh	•	•		•
Bradley	•	•		•	Ellenhall	•	•		•	Lichfield	•	•		•
Bradley-In-The-Moors		•		•	Endon		•		•	Lichfield-St. Michael		•		
Bradley (Near Stafford)		•		•	Enville		•			Longdon	•	•		•
Bramshall		•		•	Entruria	•				Longnor		•		
Brewood	•	•		•	Ettingshall		•		•	Longton				•
Brierley Hill		•		•	Farewell		•		•	Lower Gornall		•		•
Bucknall	•	•		•	Fazeley		•		•	Lower Penn		•		
Burntwood		•		•	Fenton		•		•	Madeley	•	•		•
Burslem	•	•		•	Forebridge (near Stafford)	•				Maer		•		•
Burton-Upon-Trent		•		•	Forton		•		•	Marchington	•	•		•
Bushbury	•	•		•	Fradswell	•	•		•	Marston (Near Stafford)	•	•		•
Butterton				•	Fulford		•		•	Mavesyn-Ridware		•		
Butterton (Near Leek)	•	•			Gayton	•	•			Mayfield	•	•		•
Caldon Canal		•			Gentleshaw		•			Meerbrook		•		•
Calton		•			Gnosall	•	•		•	Milwich		•		•
Cannock	•	•		•	Gratwich	•	•		•	Mowcop	•			
Cannock Wood				•	Great Barr		•		•	Moxley	•			
Castle-Church	•	•		•	Great Haywood		•		•	Mucklestone	•	•		•
Castletown	•				Grindon		•		•	Needwood		•		
Cauldon	•			•	Hammerwich		•		•	Newborough		•		•
Caverswall		•		•	Hamstall-Ridware	•	•		•	Newcastle-Under-Lyne	•	•		•
Cheadle		•		•	Hanbury	•	•		•	Newton				•
Chebsey	•	•		•	Handsworth	•	•		•	Norbury		•		•
Checkley		•		•	Hanford		•		•	Norton-In-The-Moors	•	•		•
Cheddleton	•	•			Hanley	•	•		•	Norton-Under-Cannock		•		•
Chorlton		•		•	Harborne	•	•		•	Oakamoor				•
Church-Eaton	•	•		•	Harlaston		•		•	Oakamore		•		
Clifton-Campville		•		•	Hartshill (Near Stoke-Upon-Trent)	•	•		•	Oakover	•			
Codsall	•	•		•	Haughton	•	•		•	Ogley-Hay	•			
Colton		•		•	Hednesford	•				Onecote		•		
Colwich	•	•		•	High Offley	•	•			Patshull	•	•		•
Coppenhall	•	•		•	Hilderstone		•		•	Pattingham	•	•		•
Coseley		•		•	Himley	•	•		•	Pelsall	•	•		•
Croxall	•	•	•	•	Hints	•	•		•	Penkridge	•	•		•
Croxden	•	•		•	Hixon		•			Penn	•			•
Cubley		•			Horton		•		•	Penn Field		•		
Darlaston (Near Wednesbury)	•	•		•	Ilam		•		•	Penny-Barr				•
Darliston				•	Ingestre		•		•	Pipe-Ridware	•	•		•
Denston	•	•			Ipstones		•		•	Quarnford		•		•
Dilhorne		•		•	Keele	•	•		•	Quarry-Bank	•	•		•
Draycott-In-The-Moors	•	•		•	Kinfare	•	•		•	Ranton	•	•		•

England

* COUNTY / SHIRE

PARISH	PARISH REGISTERS	BISHOPS' TRANSCRIPTS	BOYD'S MARRIAGE INDEX	PR PRINT-OUTS
Rocester	•	•		•
Rolleston		•		•
Rowley-Regis	•			•
Rugeley	•	•		•
Rushall	•	•		•
Rushton		•		•
St. Chad	•			
St. Mary	•			
St. Stephen	•			
Salt				•
Sandon		•		•
Sedgley	•	•		•
Seighford	•	•		•
Shareshill		•		•
Sheen		•		•
Shenstone	•	•		•
Smethwick		•		•
Stafford	•	•		•
Standon	•	•		•
Stoke-Upon-Trent	•	•		•
Stone		•		•
Stonnall		•		•
Stowe	•	•		•
Stramshall				•
Stretton		•		
Stretton (Near Penkridge)	•			•
Swynnerton	•	•		•
Talk-'O-The-Hill		•		•
Tamworth	•	•		•
Tatenhill	•	•		•
Tettenhall	•	•		•
Tettenhall-Wood	•			
Thorpe-Constantine		•		•
Thursfield	•	•		•
Tipton	•	•		•
Tixall		•		•
Trentham	•	•		•
Trysull	•	•		•
Tunstall		•		
Tunstall (near Stoke-Upon-Trent)				•
Tutbury	•	•		•
Upper Arley	•			•
Upper Gornall		•		•
Upper Penn		•		
Upper Tean		•		•
Uttoxeter	•	•		•
Wal		•		•
Walton (Baswick)	•			
Warslow and Elkstones		•		
Waterfall	•	•		•
Wednesbury		•		•
Wednesfield	•	•		•
Weeford	•	•		•
West Bromwich	•	•		•
Weston-Upon-Lizard	•	•		•
Weston-Upon-Trent	•	•		•
Westley-Rocks		•		•
Wetton	•	•		•
Whitgreave	•	•		•
Whitmore		•		
Whittington		•		•
Wichnor	•	•		•
Willenhall		•		•
Wolstanton	•	•		•
Wolverhampton	•	•		•
Wombourn		•		•
Woodhouses		•		
Yoxhall		•		•
SUFFOLK*				
Acton	•			
Akenham	•			
Aldborough	•			
Alderton	•			
Aldham	•			
Aldringham	•			•
Alpheton	•			
Ampton	•			
Ashbocking	•			
Ashby	•		•	
Ashfield	•			•
Aspall	•			
Assington	•			•
Athelington	•			
Bacton	•			
Badwell-Ash	•			•
Bardwell	•			•
Barnardiston	•			
Barnby	•			•
Barnham	•			•
Barrow	•			•
Battisford	•			
Bawdsey	•			•
Baylham	•			
Beccles	•			
Bedfield	•			
Bedingfield	•			
Belstead	•			
Belton	•			
Benacre	•			•
Bentley	•			
Bernardiston	•			
Beyton	•			
Bildestone	•			•
Blaxhall	•			
Blundeston	•			
Blyford	•			
Blythburgh	•			
Botesdale	•			
Boulge	•			
Boxford	•			
Boxted	•			
Boyton	•			
Bradfield-Combust	•			•
Bradfield-St. Clare	•			•
Bradfield-St. George	•			•
Bradwell	•			
Braisworth	•			
Bramfield	•			•
Bramford	•			
Brampton	•			•
Brandeston	•			
Brandon	•			
Brantham	•			•
Bredfield	•			
Brent-Eleigh	•			
Brettenham	•			•
Brightwell	•			•
Brockford	•			
Brockley	•			
Brome	•			
Bromeswell	•			
Bruisyard	•			
Brundish	•			•
Bucklesham	•			
Bungay	•			
Bures-St. Mary	•			
Burgate	•			
Burgh	•			•
Burgh Castle	•			
Burstall	•			•
Bury-St. Edmunds	•			•
Buxhall	•			•
Campsea-Ash	•			
Campsea-Ashe				•
Campsey-Ashe				•
Capel-St. Mary	•			
Carlton	•			•

England

* COUNTY / SHIRE

PARISH	PARISH REGISTERS	BISHOPS' TRANSCRIPTS	BOYD'S MARIAGE INDEX	PR PRINT-OUTS	PARISH	PARISH REGISTERS	BISHOPS' TRANSCRIPTS	BOYD'S MARIAGE INDEX	PR PRINT-OUTS	PARISH	PARISH REGISTERS	BISHOPS' TRANSCRIPTS	BOYD'S MARIAGE INDEX	PR PRINT-OUTS
Carlton-Colville	•				East Bergholt	•				Great Finborough	•			
Cavendish	•			•	Easton	•				Great Glemham	•			
Cavenham	•				Edwardstone	•			•	Great Linstead	•			
Chapel St. Mary			•		Ellough	•			•	Great Redisham	•			
Charsfield	•				Elmsett	•			•	Great Saxham	•			•
Chattisham	•				Elmswell	•				Great Thurlow	•			
Chedburgh	•				Elveden	•				Great Waldingfield	•			•
Chediston	•			•	Eriswell	•			•	Great Welnetham	•			•
Chellesworth	•			•	Erwarton	•				Great Wenham	•		•	•
Chelmondiston	•				Euston	•			•	Great Whelnetham	•			
Chevington	•			•	Exning	•		•	•	Great Wratting	•			
Chillesford	•			•	Eye	•				Groton	•			•
Chilton	•				Eyke	•				Grundisburgh	•		•	•
Chilton (Near Sudbury)	•			•	Fakenham Magna	•				Gunton	•			
Clare	•				Falkenham	•				Hacheston	•			•
Claydon	•				Farnham	•				Hadleigh	•			•
Clopton	•				Felixstow	•			•	Halesworth	•			
Cocksfield	•				Felsham	•			•	Hargrave	•			
Coddenham	•				Finningham	•				Harkstead	•			
Combs	•		•		Flempton	•				Harleston	•			
Cookley	•				Flixton (Near Bungay)	•			•	Hartest	•			
Copdock	•			•	Flowton	•				Hasketon	•			•
Corton	•				Fornham	•				Haughley	•			
Cotton	•				Fornham-St. Genevieve	•				Haveningham	•			•
Covehithe	•			•	Fornham-St. Martin	•				Haverhill	•			
Cowlinge	•				Foxhall	•				Hawkedon	•			
Cransford	•				Framsden	•				Hawstead	•			
Cratfield	•			•	Freckingham	•				Helmingham	•			
Creeting-All Saints	•				Fressingfield	•		•		Hemingstone	•			
Creeting-St. Mary	•				Freston	•			•	Hemley	•			
Creeting-St. Peter	•				Friston	•				Hengrave	•			
Cretingham	•				Fritton	•				Henley	•			
Crowfield	•				Frostenden	•			•	Henstead	•			
Culford	•				Gazeley	•				Hepworth	•			
Culpho	•			•	Gedding	•			•	Herringfleet	•			•
Dalham	•				Gisleham	•				Herringswell	•			
Dallinghoe	•			•	Gislingham	•				Hessett	•			
Darsham	•				Glemsford	•			•	Higham	•			
Debach	•				Gorleston	•				Higham (Near Nayland)	•			•
Debenham	•				Gosbeck	•				Hinderclay	•			
Denham	•			•	Great Ashfield	•				Hintlesham	•			
Denham (Near Bury-St. Edmunds)	•			•	Great Barton	•				Hitcham	•			
Denham (Near Eye)	•				Great Bealings	•			•	Holbrook	•			
Dennington	•				Great Bicet	•				Hollesley	•			•
Denston	•				Great Blakenham	•				Holton	•			•
Depden	•				Great Bradley	•				Holton-St. Mary	•			•
Drinkstone	•				Great Bricett	•				Homersfield	•			•
Dunningworth	•				Great Cornard	•				Honington	•			
Dunwich	•		•		Great Fakenham	•			•	Hoo	•			

England

* COUNTY / SHIRE

PARISH	PARISH REGISTERS	BISHOPS' TRANSCRIPTS	BOYD'S MARRIAGE INDEX	PR PRINT-OUTS	PARISH	PARISH REGISTERS	BISHOPS' TRANSCRIPTS	BOYD'S MARRIAGE INDEX	PR PRINT-OUTS	PARISH	PARISH REGISTERS	BISHOPS' TRANSCRIPTS	BOYD'S MARRIAGE INDEX	PR PRINT-OUTS
Hopton (Near Lowestoft)	•				Little Finborough	•				Old Newton	•			
Hopton (Near Thetford	•				Little Glemham	•				Onehouse	•			
Horham	•				Little Linstead	•				Orford	•			
Horningsheath	•			•	Little Saxham	•			•	Otley	•			
Hoxne	•		•		Little Stonham	•				Oulton	•			•
Hundon	•				Little Thornham	•			•	Ousden	•			
Hunston	•				Little Thurlow	•				Pakefield	•			
Huntingfield	•				Little Waldingfield	•				Pakenham	•			
Icklingham	•			•	Little Welnetham	•			•	Palgrave	•			
Ickworth	•			•	Little Wenham	•		•		Parham	•			•
Iken	•				Little Welnetham	•				Peasenhall	•			•
Ilketshall-St. Andrew	•				Little Wratting	•				Pettaugh	•			
Ilketshall-St. John	•				Livermere-Magna	•				Pettistree	•			•
Ilketshall-St. Lawrence	•				Livermere-Parva	•				Playford	•			
Ilketshall-St. Margaret	•				Long Melford	•				Polstead	•			•
Ingham	•			•	Lound	•				Poslingford	•			
Ipswich	•			•	Lowestoft	•			•	Preston	•			
Ipswich, St. Mary-At-The-Elms	•				Marlesford	•			•	Ramsholt	•			
Ixworth	•				Martlesham	•		•	•	Rattlesden	•			•
Kedington	•				Mellis	•				Raydon	•			•
Kelsale	•			•	Melton	•			•	Rede	•			
Kentford	•				Mendham	•		•	•	Redgrave	•			
Kenton	•			•	Mendlesham	•				Redlingfield	•			
Kersey	•			•	Metfield	•		•		Rendham	•			
Kesgrave	•				Mettingham	•				Rendlesham	•			
Kessingland	•				Mickfield	•		•		Reydon	•			•
Kettlebaston	•				Middleton	•				Rickinghall-Superior	•			
Kettleburgh	•				Milden	•				Ringsfield	•			•
Kirkley	•			•	Mildenhall	•				Risby			•	
Kirton	•				Monewden	•				Rushbrooke	•			•
Knoddishall	•				Monk Soham	•			•	Saxmundham	•			
Lackford	•				Monks-Eleigh	•			•	Semer	•			•
Lakenheath	•				Moulton	•				Shadingfield	•			
Langham	•				Mutford	•			•	Shelland	•			•
Lavenham	•			•	Nacton	•			•	Shelley	•			•
Lawshall	•				Naughton	•				Shimpling	•			
Laxfield	•				Nayland	•				Shipmeadow	•			
Layham	•			•	Nedging	•				Shotley	•			•
Leiston	•				Nettlestead	•				Shottisham	•			
Letheringham	•				Newbourn	•				Sibton	•			
Levington	•			•	Newmarket-All Saints	•				Snape	•			
Lidgate	•				Newmarket-St. Mary	•			•	Soham-Earl	•			
Lindsey	•			•	Newton-Near-Sudbury	•				Soham-Monk	•			
Linstead-Magna	•			•	North Cove	•			•	Somerleyton	•		•	•
Linstead-Parva	•				Norton	•			•	Somersham	•			
Little Bealings	•			•	Nowton	•				Somerton	•			
Little Blakenham	•				Oakley	•				Sotterley	•			
Little Bradley	•				Occold	•				South Cove	•			
Little Cornard	•				Offton	•				South Elmham-All Saints	•			

England

* COUNTY / SHIRE

PARISH	PARISH REGISTERS	BISHOPS' TRANSCRIPTS	BOYD'S MARRIAGE INDEX	PR PRINT-OUTS	PARISH	PARISH REGISTERS	BISHOPS' TRANSCRIPTS	BOYD'S MARRIAGE INDEX	PR PRINT-OUTS	PARISH	PARISH REGISTERS	BISHOPS' TRANSCRIPTS	BOYD'S MARRIAGE INDEX	PR PRINT-OUTS
South Elmham-St. Cross	•	•		•	Tinworth	•			•	Withersdale	•		•	
South Elmham-St. James	•				Tostock	•			•	Withersfield	•			•
South Elmham-St. Margaret	•				Trimley-St. Martin	•				Witnesham	•			
South Elmham-St. Michael	•				Troston	•				Woodbridge	•		•	•
South Elmham-St. Nicholas	•	•		•	Tuddenham	•			•	Woolpit	•			
South Elmham-St. Peter	•				Tuddenham (Near Mildenhall)	•			•	Woolverstone	•			•
Southolt	•				Tuddenham-St. Martin	•				Wordwell	•			•
Southwold	•				Tunstall	•				Worlingham	•			•
Spexhall	•			•	Ubbeston	•				Worlington	•			
Sproughton	•			•	Ufford	•			•	Worlingworth	•			
Stanningfield	•			•	Uggeshall	•				Wortham	•			
Stansfield	•				Walberswick	•				Woverstone	•			
Stanstead	•				Waldringfield	•				Wrentham	•			•
Stanton	•				Walpole	•				Wyverstone	•			
Sternfield	•				Walsham-Le-Willows	•			•	Yaxley	•			
Stoke-Ash	•				Walton	•				Yoxford	•			
Stoke-By-Clare	•				Wangford (Near Halesworth)	•				**SURREY***				
Stoke-By-Nayland	•			•	Wantisden	•				Abinger	•	•		•
Stonham-Aspall	•				Washbrook	•				Addington	•	•		•
Stonham-Earl	•				Wattisfield	•			•	Addlestone		•		•
Stowlangtoft	•				Wattisham	•				Albury	•			•
Stowmarket	•				Wenhaston	•				Alfold	•	•		•
Stowupland	•				West Stow	•			•	Ash	•	•		•
Stradbroke	•				Westerfield	•				Ashtead	•	•		•
Stradishall	•				Westhall	•			•	Bagshot	•	•		
Stratford-St. Andrew	•				Westhorpe	•				Balham	•			
Stratford-St. Mary	•				Westleton	•				Banstead	•	•		•
Stuston	•				Westley	•				Barnes	•	•		•
Stutton	•				Weston	•				Battersea	•			•
Sudbourne	•				Weston-Coney	•				Beddington	•			•
Sudbury	•			•	Weston-Markey	•				Bermondsey	•			•
Sudbury-St. Peters	•				Wetherden	•				Betchworth		•		•
Sutton	•				Wetheringsett	•				Bisley	•	•		
Swefling	•			•	Wetheringsett-Cum-Brockford	•				Bletchingley	•			•
Swilland	•				Weybread	•		•		Botleys and Lyne		•		
Syleham	•		•		Whatfield	•				Bramley	•	•		•
Tannington	•			•	Whepstead	•				Brixton	•			•
Tattingstone	•				Wherstead	•			•	Brixton-St. Matthew	•			
Theberton	•				Whitton-Cum-Thurlston	•				Buckland	•	•		•
Thelnetham	•				Whixoe	•				Burstow	•	•		•
Thetford	•				Wickham-Market	•				Byfleet		•		•
Thorington	•			•	Wickham Skeith	•				Camberwell	•			•
Thorndon	•			•	Wickham Brook	•			•	Capel	•	•		
Thornham-Magna	•				Wilby	•				Carshalton	•	•		•
Thorpe-By-Ixworth	•				Willisham	•				Caterham	•	•		•
Thorpe-Morieux	•				Wingfield	•			•	Chaldon	•	•		•
Thrandeston	•		•		Winston	•				Charlwood	•	•		
Thurston	•				Wissett	•			•	Cheam	•	•		•
Thwaite	•				Wiston	•				Chelsham	•	•		•

England

* COUNTY / SHIRE

PARISH	PARISH REGISTERS	BISHOPS' TRANSCRIPTS	BOYD'S MARRIAGE INDEX	PR PRINT-OUTS
Chertsey	•	•		•
Chessington	•	•		•
Chiddingfold	•	•		•
Chilworth	•			•
Chipstead	•	•		•
Chobham	•	•		•
Clapham		•		•
Claygate	•	•		
Cobham	•	•		•
Coldharbour	•			
Compton	•	•		•
Coulsdon	•	•		•
Cove	•			
Cranley	•	•		•
Crowhurst	•	•		•
Croydon	•			
Deptford	•			•
Dorking	•	•		
Dulwich	•			•
Dunsfold	•			
East Clandon	•	•		
East Horsley	•	•		•
East Molesley	•			•
East Sheen	•			
Effingham	•	•		•
Egham	•	•		
Elstead	•	•		
Englefield Green	•			
Epsom	•	•		•
Esher	•	•		
Ewell	•	•		•
Ewhurst	•	•		•
Farley	•	•		•
Farnham	•	•		
Felbridge	•			
Fetcham	•	•		•
Frensham	•	•		•
Frimley	•	•		•
Gatton	•	•		•
Godalming	•	•		•
Godstone	•	•		•
Graffham	•			
Great Bookham	•	•		•
Guildford	•	•		•
Hambledon	•	•		•
Hascombe	•	•		
Haslemere	•	•		•
Hatcham	•			•
Headley	•			•

PARISH	PARISH REGISTERS	BISHOPS' TRANSCRIPTS	BOYD'S MARRIAGE INDEX	PR PRINT-OUTS
Herne Hill	•			•
Hersham	•			
Holmwood	•			
Horley	•	•		•
Horne	•			•
Horswell	•	•		•
Kennington	•			•
Kew		•		
Kingston-Upon-Thames	•	•		•
Kingswood	•			
Lambeth	•	•		•
Leatherhead	•	•		•
Leigh	•	•		
Limpsfield	•	•		•
Lingfield	•			•
Little Bookham	•	•		•
Littleton	•	•		
Long Ditton	•	•		•
Lower Tooting	•	•		•
Malden	•	•		•
Merrow	•			
Merstham	•			•
Merton	•	•		
Mickleham	•	•		
Milford	•			
Mitcham	•	•		
Mordon	•	•		•
Mortlake	•	•		•
Newdigate	•	•		•
Newington	•	•		•
Norbiton		•		
Normandy	•	•		
Nunhead	•			
Nutfield	•	•		•
Oakwood	•			•
Ockham	•	•		•
Ockley	•	•		
Oxted	•	•		•
Peckham	•			
Penge	•			
Pepperharrow	•	•		•
Petersham		•		
Pirbright	•	•		•
Putney	•	•		•
Puttenham	•	•		•
Pyrford	•	•		•
Redhill	•			
Reighgate	•	•		•
Richmond	•	•		•

PARISH	PARISH REGISTERS	BISHOPS' TRANSCRIPTS	BOYD'S MARRIAGE INDEX	PR PRINT-OUTS
Ripley	•			
Rotherhithe	•			•
Sanderstead	•	•		•
Seal	•	•		
Seale	•			•
Selhurst	•			
Send	•	•		
Shalford	•	•		•
Shere	•	•		•
South Kennington				•
Southwark	•	•		•
Stockwell	•			
Stoke D'Abernon	•	•		•
Stoke-Next-Guilford	•	•		•
Streatham	•	•		•
Summerstown		•		
Surbiton	•			
Sutton	•	•		•
Sutton (Near Croydon)				•
Talworth	•			
Tandridge	•	•		•
Tatsfield	•	•		•
Thames-Ditton	•	•		•
Thornton-Heath	•			
Thorpe		•		•
Thursley	•	•		•
Titsey	•	•		•
Tolworth		•		•
Wallington	•			
Walton-On-The-Hill	•	•		•
Walton-Upon-Thames	•	•		•
Walworth	•	•		•
Wanborough	•			•
Wandsworth	•	•		•
Warlington	•	•		•
West Clandon	•	•		
West Horsley	•	•		•
West Molesley	•	•		•
West Norwood				•
Westcott	•			
Westend	•			
Weybridge	•	•		•
Wimbledon	•	•		•
Windlesham	•	•		•
Wisley	•	•		•
Witley	•	•		•
Woking	•	•		•
Woldingham	•	•		•
Wonersh	•	•		•

England

* COUNTY / SHIRE

PARISH	PARISH REGISTERS	BISHOPS' TRANSCRIPTS	BOYD'S MARRIAGE INDEX	PR PRINT-OUTS
Woodmasterne	•	•		•
Worplesdon	•	•		•
Wotton	•	•		•
Wrecclesham		•		
Wyke	•			•
York-Town	•			
SUSSEX*				
Albourne	•	•		•
Alciston	•			
Aldingborough	•	•		•
Alfold	•			
Alfriston	•			•
Almodington	•			
Amberley	•	•		•
Angmering	•	•		•
Appledram	•	•		•
Ardingly	•	•		•
Arlington	•			•
Arundel	•	•		•
Ash Burnham	•			
Ashington	•			
Ashurst	•			
Balcombe	•	•		•
Barcombe	•	•		
Barlavington	•	•		•
Barnham	•	•		•
Battle	•			
Beckley	•			
Beddingham	•			
Bepton	•	•		•
Berwick	•			
Bexhill	•			
Bignor	•	•		•
Billingshurst	•			
Binderton	•	•		•
Binstead	•	•		•
Birdham	•	•		•
Bishopstone	•			
Blatchington (Near Brighton)	•			
Blatchington (Near Seaford)	•			•
Bodiam	•			
Bolney	•			•
Bosham	•	•		•
Botolph	•			
Boxgrove	•	•		•
Bramber	•			
Brede	•			
Brightling	•			
Brighton	•	•		•

PARISH	PARISH REGISTERS	BISHOPS' TRANSCRIPTS	BOYD'S MARRIAGE INDEX	PR PRINT-OUTS
Broadwater	•			
Buddington	•			
Burpham	•			
Burton	•	•		•
Burwash	•			
Bury	•			
Buxted	•			
Catsfield	•			
Chailey	•			
Chalvington	•			
Chichester	•	•		•
Chiddingly	•			•
Chidham	•			•
Chithurst	•	•		•
Clapham	•			
Clayton	•			
Cliffe	•			
Climping	•	•		•
Coates	•			•
Cocking	•	•		•
Cold-Waltham	•	•		•
Colgate	•	•		•
Compton	•	•		•
Coombs	•	•		•
Cowfold	•	•		•
Crawley	•	•		•
Crawley Down	•	•		•
Crowhurst	•			•
Cuckfield	•	•		•
Dallington	•			•
Danehill	•			
Denton	•			
Didling	•	•		•
Ditchling	•			•
Donnington	•			•
Duncton	•			•
Durrington	•			•
Earnley	•			
Eartham	•			•
Easebourne	•	•		•
East Chiltington	•			
East Dean (Near Chichester)	•	•		•
East Dean (Near Eastbourne)	•			
East Grinstead	•	•		•
East Hoathly	•			
East Lavant	•	•		•
East Marden	•	•		•
East Preston	•	•		•
East Wittering	•			

PARISH	PARISH REGISTERS	BISHOPS' TRANSCRIPTS	BOYD'S MARRIAGE INDEX	PR PRINT-OUTS
Eastbourne	•	•		•
Eastergate	•	•		•
Edburton	•			•
Egdean	•	•		•
Elsted	•	•		•
Eridge Green	•			
Etchingham	•			
Ewhurst	•			
Fairlight	•			
Falmer	•			
Farnhurst	•	•		•
Felpham	•	•		•
Ferring	•	•		•
Findon	•	•		•
Fittleworth	•	•		•
Fletching	•			
Folkington	•			•
Ford	•	•		•
Forest-Row	•			
Framfield	•			
Frant	•			
Friston	•			•
Funtington	•	•		•
Glynde	•			•
Goring	•	•		•
Graffham	•	•		•
Greatham	•			
Guestling	•			
Guildford	•			
Hadlow-Down	•			
Hailsham	•			
Hamsey	•			
Hangleton	•			
Hardham	•	•		•
Hartfield	•			
Harting	•	•		•
Hastings	•			•
Haywards-Heath	•	•		•
Heathfield	•			
Heene	•	•		•
Heighton	•			
Hellingly	•			•
Henfield	•	•		•
Herstmonceaux	•			
Heyshott	•	•		•
Hollington	•			
Hooe	•			
Horsham	•	•		•
Horsted-Keynes	•	•		•

England
* COUNTY / SHIRE

PARISH	PARISH REGISTERS	BISHOPS' TRANSCRIPTS	BOYD'S MARRIAGE INDEX	PR PRINT-OUTS
Houghton	•			
Hove	•			•
Hunston	•			
Hurstperpoint	•	•		•
Icklesham	•			
Iden	•			
Ifield	•			
Iford	•			
Ilford	•			
Iping	•	•		•
Isfield	•			
Itchingfield	•			
Jevington	•			
Keymer	•			
Kingston	•	•		•
Kingston-By-Lenes	•			•
Kingston-By-Sea	•			
Kirford	•			•
Kirdord	•	•		•
Laughton	•			•
Leominster	•	•		•
Lewes	•			•
Linch	•	•		•
Linchmere	•			
Lindfield	•			
Little Hampton	•	•		•
Little Horsted	•			
Littlington	•			
Lodsworth	•	•		•
Lower Beeding	•	•		•
Loxwood	•			
Lullington	•			
Lurgashall	•	•		•
Madehurst	•			
Marden-Up	•			•
Maresfield	•			
Mayfield	•			
Merston	•			
Mid Lavant	•			•
Middleton	•	•		•
Midhurst	•			•
Milland	•	•		•
Mountfield	•			
New Fishbourne	•	•		•
Newhaven	•			
Newick	•			
Newtimber	•	•		•
Ninfield	•			
North Bersted	•			

PARISH	PARISH REGISTERS	BISHOPS' TRANSCRIPTS	BOYD'S MARRIAGE INDEX	PR PRINT-OUTS
North Marden	•	•		•
North Mundham	•			
North Stoke	•	•		•
Northchapel	•			
Northiam	•			
Nuthurst	•			
Ore	•			
Oving	•	•		•
Ovingdean	•			
Pagham	•	•		•
Parham	•			
Patcham	•			
Patching	•			
Peasmarsh	•			
Penhurst	•			
Pett	•			
Petworth	•			•
Pevensey	•			
Piddinghoe	•			
Playden	•			•
Plumpton	•			
Poling	•	•		•
Portfield	•	•		•
Portslade	•			
Poynings	•			
Preston	•			•
Pulborough	•	•		•
Pyecombe	•	•		•
Racton	•	•		•
Ringmer	•			
Ripe	•			
Rodmell	•			
Rogate	•	•		•
Rotherfield	•			
Rottingdean	•			•
Rudgwick	•	•		•
Rumboldswyke	•	•		•
Rusper	•	•		•
Rustington	•	•		•
Rye	•			
Salehurst	•			•
Seaford	•			
Sedlescomb	•			
Selham	•	•		•
Selmeston	•			
Selsey	•	•		•
Shermanbury	•	•		•
Shipley	•	•		•
Shoreham	•			

PARISH	PARISH REGISTERS	BISHOPS' TRANSCRIPTS	BOYD'S MARRIAGE INDEX	PR PRINT-OUTS
Sidlesham	•	•		•
Singleton	•	•		•
Slaugham	•	•		•
Slindon	•	•		•
Slinfold	•	•		•
Sompting	•			
South Bersted	•	•		•
South Malling	•			
South Stoke	•			•
Southease	•			
Southwater	•	•		•
Southwick	•	•		•
Stanmer	•			
Stanstead	•			•
Stedham	•	•		•
Steyning	•			
Stopham	•	•		•
Storrington	•			
Stoughton	•	•		•
Street	•			•
Sullington	•			
Sutton	•	•		•
Tangmere	•	•		•
Tarring-Nevile	•			
Telscombe	•			
Terwick	•	•		•
Thakeham	•	•		•
Ticehurst	•			•
Tillington	•			
Tortington	•	•		•
Treyford	•	•		•
Trotton	•	•		•
Twineham	•			
Uckfield	•			
Udimore	•			
Upwaltham	•	•		•
Upper Dicker	•			
Wadhurst	•			
Walberton	•	•		•
Waldron	•			
Warbleton	•			•
Warminghurst	•	•		•
Warnham	•			
Warningcamp	•	•		•
Wartling	•			
West Chiltington	•	•		•
West Dean (Near Chichester)	•	•		•
West Dean (Near Seaford)	•			
West Firle	•			

England

* COUNTY / SHIRE

PARISH	PARISH REGISTERS	BISHOPS' TRANSCRIPTS	BOYD'S MARRIAGE INDEX	PR PRINT-OUTS
West Grinstead	•			
West Hampnett	•			
West Hoathly	•	•		•
West Itchenor	•	•		•
West Lavington	•	•		•
West Stoke	•	•		•
West Tarring	•			
West Thorney	•	•		•
West Wittering	•	•		•
Westbourne	•	•		•
Westfield	•			
Westham	•			•
Westhampnett	•			
Westmeston	•			•
Whatlington	•			
Wiggonholt	•			
Willingdon	•			
Wilmington	•			•
Winchelsea	•			
Wisborough-Green	•	•		•
Wiston	•	•		•
Withyham	•			
Wivelsfield	•			
Woodmancote	•	•		•
Woolavington	•	•		•
Woolbeding	•	•		•
Worth	•	•		•
Worthing	•	•		•
Yapton	•	•		•
WARWICK*				
Ainsty	•			
Alcester	•			•
Allesley	•	•		•
Alveston	•			•
Amington and Stonydelph	•			
Ansley	•	•		•
Ansty	•	•	•	•
Arden				•
Arley	•	•		•
Arrow	•			•
Ashow	•	•		•
Ashted	•			•
Astley	•	•		•
Aston	•	•		•
Aston-Cantlow	•			•
Atherstone	•	•		•
Atherstone-On-Stour	•		•	•
Attleborough	•			
Austrey	•	•		•
Avon-Dassett	•	•		•
Baddesley-Clinton	•	•		•
Baddesley-Ensor	•	•		•
Baginton	•	•		•
Balsall	•	•		•
Barcheston	•			•
Barford	•			•
Barston	•	•		•
Barton-On-The-Heath	•		•	•
Baxterley	•	•		•
Bearley	•			•
Beaudesert	•			•
Bedworth	•	•		•
Bentley	•	•		•
Berkeswell	•	•		•
Bickenhill	•	•		•
Bidford	•			•
Billesley	•			•
Bilton	•	•		•
Binley	•	•		•
Binton	•			•
Birdingbury	•	•		•
Birmingham	•	•		•
Bishops-Itchington	•	•		•
Bishops-Tachbrook	•	•	•	•
Bishopton	•			•
Bordesley	•			•
Bourton-Upon-Dunsmoor	•	•	•	•
Brailes	•			•
Brinklow	•	•		•
Brownsover	•	•		•
Bubbenhall	•	•		•
Budbrooke	•			•
Bulkington	•	•		•
Burmington	•			•
Burton-Dassett	•	•		•
Burton-Hastings	•	•		•
Butlers-Marston	•		•	•
Caldecote	•	•		•
Calverdon	•			•
Castle Bromwich	•	•		•
Chadshunt	•	•		•
Charlcote	•		•	•
Cherington	•			•
Chesterton	•	•		•
Chilvers-Coton	•	•		•
Church-Lawford	•	•		•
Church-Over	•	•		•
Churchover	•			•
Claverdon	•			•
Clifford-Chambers	•	•		•
Clifton-Upon-Dunsmore	•	•		•
Coleshill	•	•		•
Combrook	•			
Compton-Verney	•			
Compton-Wyniates	•			
Corley	•	•		•
Coughton	•			•
Coventry	•	•		•
Cubbington	•	•		•
Curdworth	•	•		•
Deritend	•			•
Dorsington	•	•		
Dunchurch	•	•		•
Durrington			•	
Eatington	•		•	•
Egbaston	•	•		•
Elmdon	•	•		•
Erdington	•			
Exhall (Near Alcester)	•	•		•
Exhall (Near Coventry)	•	•		•
Farnborough	•	•		•
Fenny-Compton	•	•	•	•
Fillongley	•	•		•
Foleshill	•	•		•
Frankton	•	•		•
Gaydon	•			•
Grafton-Temple	•			•
Grandborough	•	•		•
Great Alne	•	•		•
Great and Little Woodford	•			•
Great Harborough	•	•		•
Great Packington	•	•		•
Grendon	•	•		•
Halford	•		•	•
Hampton-In-Arden	•	•		•
Hampton-Lucy	•			•
Harbury	•	•		•
Hardwick-Priors	•	•	•	•
Hartshill	•			
Haseley	•			
Haselor	•			•
Hatton	•		•	•
Henley-In-Arden	•			
Hill		•		
Hillmorton	•	•		•
Hockley-Heath	•			
Honiley	•	•		•

England * COUNTY / SHIRE PARISH	PARISH REGISTERS	BISHOPS' TRANSCRIPTS	BOYD'S MARRIAGE INDEX	PR PRINT-OUTS	PARISH	PARISH REGISTERS	BISHOPS' TRANSCRIPTS	BOYD'S MARRIAGE INDEX	PR PRINT-OUTS	PARISH	PARISH REGISTERS	BISHOPS' TRANSCRIPTS	BOYD'S MARRIAGE INDEX	PR PRINT-OUTS
Honington	•		•	•	Oversley	•				Walton	•			
Hunningham	•	•		•	Oxhill	•	•		•	Wappenbury	•	•		•
Idlicote	•		•	•	Packwood	•	•		•	Warmington	•	•		•
Ipsley	•			•	Perry-Barr	•	•			Warton	•			
Kenilworth	•	•		•	Pillerton-Hersey	•			•	Warwick	•			•
Keresley	•				Pillerton-Priors	•			•	Wasperton	•			•
Kineton	•			•	Polesworth	•	•		•	Water-Orton	•	•		•
Kingsbury	•	•		•	Preston-Baggot	•				Weddington	•	•		•
Kingston	•	•			Radford	•	•		•	Weethley	•			•
Kinwarton	•			•	Radway	•	•		•	Welford	•	•		•
Knowle	•	•		•	Ratley	•	•		•	Wellesbourne-Hastings	•			•
Ladbrooke	•	•		•	Rowington	•			•	Wellesbourne-Mountford	•			
Lapworth	•			•	Rugby	•	•		•	Weston	•			
Lea-Marston	•	•		•	Ryton-On-Dunsmore	•	•		•	Weston-Under-Weatherly	•	•		•
Leamington	•	•	•	•	St. John Baptist	•				Westwood	•			•
Leamington-Hastings	•	•		•	Salford-Priors	•				Whatcote	•			•
Leek-Wootton	•	•		•	Seckington	•	•		•	Whitchurch	•		•	
Lighthorne	•			•	Sheldon	•	•		•	Whitnash	•	•		•
Lillington	•	•		•	Sherbourne	•			•	Willey	•	•		•
Little Compton		•		•	Shilton	•	•		•	Willington	•			
Little Packington	•	•		•	Shipston-On-Stour	•		•	•	Willoughby	•	•		•
Long Compton	•		•	•	Shirley		•		•	Wilnecote and Castle Liberty		•		
Long Itchington	•	•		•	Shotswell	•	•		•	Wishaw	•	•		•
Lower Shuckburgh	•	•		•	Shottery	•				Witford	•			
Loxley	•			•	Shustoke	•			•	Withybrook	•	•		
Mancetter	•	•		•	Shuttington	•	•		•	Wixford	•			
Marston-Priors	•	•		•	Snitterfield	•		•	•	Wolfhampcote	•	•		•
Marton	•	•		•	Solihull	•	•		•	Wolston	•	•		•
Maxstone	•	•		•	Southam	•	•		•	Wolverton	•			•
Merevale	•	•		•	Sowe	•	•		•	Wolvey	•	•		•
Meriden	•	•		•	Spernall	•			•	Wooton-Wawen	•			•
Middleton	•	•		•	Stivichall	•	•		•	Wormleighton	•	•		•
Milverton	•			•	Stockingford	•	•		•	Wroxnall	•			•
Monks-Kirby	•	•		•	Stockton	•	•		•	Wyken	•	•		•
Morton-Morrell	•				Stoke	•	•		•	Yardley				•
Morton-Baggot	•			•	Stoneleigh	•	•		•	**WESTMORELAND***				
Napton-On-The-Hill	•	•		•	Stratford-Upon-Avon	•	•		•	Ambleside		•		
Nether Whitacre	•	•		•	Stretton-On-The-Foss	•	•		•	Appleby		•		•
New Milverton	•	•			Stretton-Upon-Dunsmore	•			•	Asby	•	•		•
Newbold-Pacey	•			•	Studley	•				Askham	•	•		•
Newbold-Upon-Avon	•	•		•	Sutton-Coldfield	•			•	Bampton	•	•		•
Newton-Regis	•	•		•	Sutton-Under-Brails	•	•		•	Barbon		•		•
Norton-Lindsey	•			•	Tachbrook-Mallory	•				Barton	•	•		•
Nuneaton	•	•		•	Tanworth	•			•	Beetham		•		•
Nuthurst	•	•		•	Tidmington	•		•	•	Bolton	•	•		•
Offchurch	•	•		•	Tysoe	•			•	Brough	•	•		•
Old Milverton	•				Ufton	•	•		•	Brougham	•	•		•
Oldberrow	•			•	Ullenhall	•				Burneside		•		•
Over Whitacre	•	•		•	Upper Shuckburgh		•		•	Burton-in-Kendal		•		•

England

* COUNTY / SHIRE

PARISH	PARISH REGISTERS	BISHOPS' TRANSCRIPTS	BOYD'S MARRIAGE INDEX	PR PRINT-OUTS	PARISH	PARISH REGISTERS	BISHOPS' TRANSCRIPTS	BOYD'S MARRIAGE INDEX	PR PRINT-OUTS	PARISH	PARISH REGISTERS	BISHOPS' TRANSCRIPTS	BOYD'S MARRIAGE INDEX	PR PRINT-OUTS
Casterton				•	Rydal		•		•	Box	•	•		
Cliburn	•			•	Selside	•	•		•	Boyton	•	•	•	
Clifton	•	•		•	Shap	•	•		•	Bradenstoke		•		
Crook		•		•	Soulby		•		•	Bradford	•	•		
Crosby-Garrett	•	•		•	Stainmore		•		•	Bratton	•	•	•	
Crosby-Ravensworth	•	•		•	Staveley	•	•		•	Bremhill	•	•		•
Crosscrake		•		•	Temple-Sowerby		•			Bremilham	•	•		
Crosthwaite and Lyth	•	•		•	Thrimby		•		•	Brinkworth	•	•	•	
Dufton		•		•	Troutbeck	•	•		•	Britford		•	•	
Firbank		•		•	Underbarrow		•		•	Brixton-Deverill		•	•	
Grasmere	•	•		•	Warcop	•	•		•	Broad Blunsdon		•		
Grayrigg	•	•		•	Windemere	•	•		•	Broad-Chalk	•	•		•
Great Musgrave		•		•	Winster		•		•	Broad-Hinton		•		
Great Strickland	•	•		•	Witherslack	•	•		•	Broad-Town		•		
Helsington		•		•	**WILTSHIRE***					Brokenborough		•		
Heversham	•	•		•	Aldbourne	•	•			Bromham	•	•		•
Holme		•		•	Alderbury	•	•			Broughton-Gifford	•	•		•
Hugil		•		•	Alderton	•	•	•		Bulford	•	•	•	•
Hutton (old)	•	•		•	Allcannings	•	•		•	Bulkington	•	•		
Hutton-Roof		•		•	Allington (Near Porton)	•	•	•		Burbage		•	•	
Kendal	•	•		•	Alton-Barnes		•	•		Burcombe		•		
Kentmere		•		•	Alton-Priors		•			Buttermere	•	•		
Killington	•	•		•	Alvesdiston	•	•			Calne	•	•		
Kirby-Longsdale		•		•	Amesbury	•	•			Calstone-Wellington	•	•		
Kirby-Stephen		•		•	Anstey	•	•		•	Castle-Combe		•		
Kirby-Thore		•		•	Ashley		•	•		Castle-Eaton		•	•	
Langdale (Near Ambleside)		•		•	Ashton-Keynes		•			Chapmanslade		•		
Levens		•		•	Atworth	•	•			Charlton (Near Downton)		•		
Long Marton		•		•	Avebury		•			Charlton (Near Malmsbury)		•		
Long Sleddale		•		•	Axford	•	•			Charlton (Near Pewsey)	•	•	•	
Lowther	•	•		•	Barford St. Martin		•			Cherhill	•	•		
Mallerstang	•	•		•	Baverstock		•	•		Chicklade	•	•		
Manserg		•		•	Baydon	•	•			Chilmark		•		
Mardale		•		•	Beeching-Stoke		•	•		Chilton-Foliatt	•	•		
Martindale		•		•	Bemerton	•	•	•		Chippenham	•	•		•
Middleton	•	•		•	Berwick-Bassett	•	•		•	Chisledon	•	•	•	
Milbourne	•	•		•	Berwick-St. James		•			Chitterne-All Saints	•	•		
Milnethorpe		•		•	Berwick-St. John	•	•			Chitterne-St. Mary		•		
Morland	•	•		•	Berwick-St. Leonard	•	•			Chittoe	•	•		•
Murton		•			Biddestone		•			Christchurch-Derryhill				•
Natland		•		•	Bishops-Cannings	•	•	•	•	Christian-Malford		•	•	
New Hutton		•		•	Bishops-Fonthill	•	•			Churton	•	•	•	•
Newbiggin (Near Appleby)	•	•		•	Bishopstone (Near Salisbury)	•	•		•	Chute	•	•		
Old Hutton		•		•	Bishopstone (Near Swindon)	•	•			Chute Forest	•	•		
Ormside		•		•	Bishopstrow	•	•			Clack		•		
Orton		•		•	Blackland	•	•			Cleaverton		•		
Patterdale		•			Blunsdon-St. Andrew		•			Cliffe-Pypard	•	•	•	
Preston-Patrick	•	•		•	Boscombe		•	•		Codford-St. Mary	•	•		
Ravenstonedale		•		•	Bower-Chalk	•	•			Codford-St. Peter	•	•		•

England
* COUNTY / SHIRE

PARISH	PARISH REGISTERS	BISHOPS' TRANSCRIPTS	BOYD'S MARRIAGE INDEX	PR PRINT-OUTS	PARISH	PARISH REGISTERS	BISHOPS' TRANSCRIPTS	BOYD'S MARRIAGE INDEX	PR PRINT-OUTS	PARISH	PARISH REGISTERS	BISHOPS' TRANSCRIPTS	BOYD'S MARRIAGE INDEX	PR PRINT-OUTS
Colerne	•	•	•	•	Farley	•	•			Laycock	•	•		
Collingbourne	•				Fifield-Bavant	•	•			Lea		•		
Collingbourne-Ducis	•	•	•		Figheldean	•	•			Leigh		•		
Collingbourne-Kingston	•	•		•	Fisherton-Anger	•	•			Leigh-Delamere	•	•	•	
Compton-Bassett	•	•			Fisherton-De-La-Mere	•	•			Liddiard-Millicent		•	•	
Compton-Chamberlain		•			Fittleton With Hacklestone		•			Liddiard-Treegooze		•		
Coombe-Bissett	•	•			Fonthill-Gifford	•	•			Liddington	•	•		•
Corsham	•	•			Fosbury	•				Limpley-Stoke		•		
Corsley	•	•			Fovant					Little Bedwin	•	•		
Corston		•			Foxley	•	•			Little Cheverell	•	•		•
Corton		•			Froxfield	•	•			Little Hinton	•	•		
Cricklade	•	•			Fugglestone-St. Peter	•	•	•		Little Langford	•	•		
Crockerton	•	•			Fyfield	•	•		•	Little Somerford	•	•	•	•
Crudwell		•	•		Garsdon		•			Littleton-Drew		•		
Dauntsey	•	•			Great Bedwin	•	•			Long Newnton		•	•	
Derry Hill	•	•			Great Chalfield	•	•			Luckington	•	•	•	
Deverill-Hill	•	•			Great Cheverell	•	•			Ludgershall	•	•		
Deverill-Kingston	•	•	•		Great Somerford	•	•	•	•	Lyneham		•		
Deverill-Longbridge	•	•			Great Wishford	•	•			Maddington	•	•		
Deverill-Monckton	•	•	•		Grittleton	•	•	•		Maiden-Bradley	•	•		
Devizes	•	•	•		Ham	•	•			Malmesbury		•		
Dilton		•			Hankerton	•	•			Manningford-Abbotts		•		
Dilton-Marsh		•			Hannington	•	•			Manningford-Bohun		•		
Dinton		•			Hardenhuish	•	•			Manningford-Bruce		•		
Ditteridge	•	•			Heddington	•	•			Marden	•	•	•	•
Donhead-St. Andrew		•			Hewish		•	•		Marlborough	•	•	•	•
Donhead-St. Mary		•			Heytesbury	•	•	•		Marston		•		
Downtown	•	•			Heywood		•			Marston-Maisey		•		
Draycot-Cerne	•	•		•	Highway	•	•			Martin		•		
Durnford	•	•		•	Highworth	•	•			Melksham	•	•		
Durrington	•	•			Hillmarton	•	•			Mere	•	•	•	
Earl-Stoke	•	•			Hilperton		•			Mildenhall		•		
East Coulston	•	•			Hindon	•	•			Milston	•	•	•	
East Grafton	•	•			Holt	•	•			Milton-Lilbourne	•	•		•
East Grimstead	•	•			Homington	•	•			Minety		•	•	
East Harnham		•			Horningsham	•	•			Monkton-Farleigh		•		
East Kennet		•			Hullavington	•	•			Neston	•			
East Knoyle	•	•	•		Idmiston	•	•	•		Nether Hampton	•	•		
East Lavington	•	•	•	•	Imber	•	•			Netheravon		•		
Easterton		•			Inglesham	•	•			Nettleton		•		
Easton	•	•		•	Keevil	•	•			Newton-Toney	•	•	•	
Easton Grey	•	•			Kellaways		•			North Bradley		•		
Easton-Royal	•				Kemble		•	•		North Newnton		•		
Ebbesborne-Wake	•	•			Kington-St. Michael	•	•	•		North Tidworth	•	•		
Edington	•	•		•	Knook	•	•	•		North Wraxall	•	•		
Eisey	•	•	•		Landford	•	•		•	Norton-Bavant	•	•		
Enford		•			Langley-Burrell	•	•			Norton-Coleparle	•	•	•	
Etchilhampton	•	•		•	Latton	•	•	•		Nunton-With-Bodeham		•		
Everley	•	•			Laverstock	•	•	•		Oaksey	•	•		

England

* COUNTY / SHIRE

PARISH	PARISH REGISTERS	BISHOPS' TRANSCRIPTS	BOYD'S MARRIAGE INDEX	PR PRINT-OUTS	PARISH	PARISH REGISTERS	BISHOPS' TRANSCRIPTS	BOYD'S MARRIAGE INDEX	PR PRINT-OUTS	PARISH	PARISH REGISTERS	BISHOPS' TRANSCRIPTS	BOYD'S MARRIAGE INDEX	PR PRINT-OUTS
Odstock		•			Stanton-Fitzwarren		•			Wilsford (Near Amesbury)	•	•		
Ogbourne-St. Andrew		•			Stanton-St. Bernard		•			Wilsford (Near Pewsey)	•	•		•
Ogbourne-St. George	•	•		•	Stanton-St. Quinton	•	•			Wilton (Near Salisbury)	•	•		
Orcheston-St. George	•	•		•	Stapleford		•			Wingfield		•		
Orcheston-St. Mary	•	•		•	Staverton		•			Winsley	•	•		
Overton	•	•		•	Steeple-Ashton	•	•			Winterbourne-Bassett		•		
Patney	•	•	•		Steeple-Langford	•	•			Winterbourne-Dauntsey		•		
Pertwood		•			Stert	•	•	•		Winterbourne-Earls	•	•		
Pewsey		•			Stockton	•	•	•		Winterbourne-Gunner	•	•		
Pitton	•	•			Stourton	•	•		•	Winterbourne-Monkton		•		
Plaitford		•			Stratford-St. Anthony	•	•			Winterbourne-Stoke	•	•		
Poole-Keynes		•			Stratford-Under-The-Castle		•	•		Wintersnow	•	•	•	
Porton	•	•	•		Stratton-St. Margaret		•			Woodborough		•	•	
Potterne	•	•			Studley		•			Woodford	•	•		
Poulshot	•	•			Sutton-Bengor		•			Wootton-Bassett	•	•		
Preshute	•	•	•	•	Sutton-Mandeville		•			Wootton-Rivers	•	•		
Purton	•	•	•		Sutton-Veney	•	•			Worton	•	•		
Quidhampton	•	•			Swallowcliffe	•	•		•	Wroughton		•		
Ramsbury	•	•		•	Swindon	•	•		•	Wylye	•	•		•
Redlynch		•			Teffont-Evias		•			Yatesbury	•	•		
Road-Hill		•			Teffont-Magna		•			Yatton-Keynell		•	•	
Rodburne		•			Tidcombe	•	•			Zeals	•	•		
Rodborne-Cheney		•			Tilshead	•	•		•	**WORCESTER***				
Rollstone	•	•	•		Tisbury		•			Abberley	•	•		•
Rowde	•	•			Tockenham	•	•			Abberton	•			•
Rushall		•			Tollard Royal		•			Abbots-Morton	•			•
Salisbury	•	•	•		Trowbridge	•	•		•	Acton-Beauchamp	•	•		•
Savernake		•			Tytherton-Lucas		•			Alderminster	•		•	•
Savernake Forest	•	•			Upayon		•			Alfrick	•			•
Seagry	•	•			Upton-Lovell	•	•			Alton				•
Sedghill		•			Upton-Scudamore	•	•			Alvechurch	•			•
Seend	•	•		•	Urchfont	•	•	•		Astley	•	•		
Semington	•	•			Wanborough	•	•			Astwood-Bank	•			
Semley		•			Warminster	•	•			Badsey	•			•
Sevenhampton	•				West Aston		•			Barbourne	•			
Shalbourn	•	•		•	West Cholderton	•	•	•		Bayton	•	•		•
Shaw and Whitley		•			West Dean	•	•		•	Bedwardine-St. John	•			
Sherrington	•	•	•		West Grimstead	•	•			Belbroughton	•			•
Sherston-Magna	•	•	•		West Harnham		•			Bengeworth-St. Peter	•	•		•
Shorncote	•	•		•	West Kington		•			Beoley	•	•		•
Shrewton	•	•			West Knoyle	•	•	•		Berrow	•			•
Slaughterford		•			West Lavington	•	•		•	Besford	•	•		•
Somerford-Keynes	•	•		•	West Wellow	•	•			Bewdley	•			
Sopworth		•	•		Westbury	•	•	•		Birlingham	•			•
South Damerham		•			Westport-St. Mary		•			Birtsmorton	•		•	•
South Marston		•			Westwood-Cum-Iford	•	•		•	Bishampton	•			•
South Newton	•	•			Whaddon		•			Blockley	•			•
South Wraxall		•			Whiteparish		•	•		Bockleton	•			•
Southbroom	•	•	•	•	Wilcot		•			Bordesley	•			

England

* COUNTY / SHIRE

PARISH	PARISH REGISTERS	BISHOPS' TRANSCRIPTS	BOYD'S MARRIAGE INDEX	PR PRINT-OUTS
Bradley	•			
Bransford	•			•
Bredicot	•			•
Bredon	•			•
Bretforton	•	•		•
Bricklehampton	•	•		•
Broadwas	•			•
Broadwaters	•			
Broadway	•			•
Bromsgrove	•			•
Broom	•			•
Broughton-Hackett	•			•
Bushley	•		•	•
Castle-Morton	•			•
Catshill	•			•
Chaddesley-Corbett	•			•
Charlton	•			
Church-Honeybourne-With-Poden	•			•
Church-Lench	•		•	•
Churchill (Near Kidderminster)	•			•
Claines	•			•
Cleeve-Prior	•		•	•
Clent	•			•
Clifton-Upon-Teme	•			•
Cookley	•			
Coston-Hackett	•			•
Cotheridge	•			•
Cowleigh	•			
Crabs-Cross	•			
Cradley	•			•
Croome-D'Abiot	•			•
Croome-Earls	•			•
Cropthorne	•			•
Crowle	•			•
Cutsdean	•			•
Daylesford				•
Defford	•			•
Doddenham	•			•
Dodderhill	•		•	•
Dormston	•			•
Doverdale	•			•
Drakes Broughton	•			
Droitwich	•			•
Dudley	•			•
Eastham	•		•	•
Eckington	•			•
Edvin-Loach		•		
Edwin-Loach	•			
Eldersfield	•			•
Elmbridge	•		•	•
Elmley-Castle	•			•
Elmley-Lovett		•		
Evesham	•	•		•
Fairfield	•			
Feckenham	•			•
Finstall	•			
Fladbury	•		•	•
Flyford-Favel	•			•
Flyford Grafton	•			•
Frankley	•		•	
Great Comberton	•			•
Great Kyre	•	•		•
Great Malvern	•			•
Great Witley	•			•
Grimley	•			•
Hadsor	•			•
Hagley	•			
Halesowen	•			•
Hallow	•			•
Hampton	•			•
Hampton-Lovett				•
Hanbury	•			•
Hanley-Castle	•			•
Hanley-Child	•		•	•
Hanley-William	•	•	•	•
Hartlebury	•			•
Harvington (Near Evesham)	•			•
Hasbury	•			
Heightington	•			
Hill and Moor	•			
Hill-Croome				•
Himbleton	•		•	•
Hindlip	•			•
Hinton-On-The-Green	•	•	•	•
Holdfast	•			
Hollybush	•			
Holt	•			•
Honeybourne-With-Poden				•
Huddington	•		•	•
Inkberrow	•			•
Kempsey	•		•	•
Kidderminster	•			•
Kings Arley	•			•
Kings-Norton	•			•
Kings-Pyon	•			•
Kington	•		•	•
Knighton-On-Teme	•	•		•
Knightwick	•			•
Leigh	•			•
Lenchwick	•			
Lindridge	•			•
Little Comberton	•		•	•
Little Hampton				•
Little Malvern	•			•
Little Witley	•			•
Longdon (Near Tewkesbury)	•			•
Lower Mitton	•			
Lower Sapey	•			
Lulsey				•
Madresfield	•			•
Malvern Link	•			
Mamble	•	•		
Martin-Hussingtree	•			•
Martley	•			
Mathon	•			
Middle Littleton	•			
Moseley	•			
Naunton-Beauchamp	•			•
Newbold	•			
Newland	•			
North Littleton	•		•	
North Malvern	•			
North Piddle	•		•	•
Northfield	•			•
Norton	•			•
Norton-By-Bredon	•			•
Norton-By-Kempsey	•			•
Oddingley	•			•
Offenham	•		•	•
Old Swinford	•			•
Oldbury	•			
Ombersley	•			•
Orleton	•		•	
Overbury	•		•	•
Pedmore	•	•		•
Pendock	•			•
Pensay	•	•		•
Peopleton	•	•		•
Pershore	•			•
Pinvin	•	•		
Pirton	•	•		•
Powick	•			•
Queenhill	•			
Redditch	•		•	
Redmarley-D'Abiot	•			
Ribbesford	•	•		
Ripple	•			

England

* COUNTY / SHIRE

PARISH	PARISH REGISTERS	BISHOPS' TRANSCRIPTS	BOYD'S MARRIAGE INDEX	PR PRINT-OUTS
Rochford	•	•		•
Rock	•	•		•
Romsley	•			•
Rous Lench	•		•	•
Rushock			•	
St. Andrew-Pershore	•			•
St. Kenelm	•			•
Salwarpe	•			•
Sapey-Pritchard		•		
Sedgeberrow	•			•
Severn-Stoke	•			•
Shelsley-Beauchamp	•			
Shelsley-Walsh	•	•		•
Shrawley	•			•
Snead's Green				•
South Littleton	•		•	•
South Middleton	•			
Spetchley	•			•
Stanford-Upon-Teme	•	•		•
Stock and Bradley	•		•	•
Stockton	•	•		•
Stoke-Bliss	•			
Stoke-Prior	•			•
Stone	•			•
Stoulton	•			•
Stourbridge	•			•
Strensham	•			•
Suckley	•			•
Tardebigge	•		•	•
Teddington				•
Tenbury		•		
Throckmorton	•			•
Tibberton	•			•
Tredington	•			•
Upton-Snodsbury	•		•	•
Upton-Upon-Severn	•			•
Upton-Warren	•			•
Warndon	•			•
Welland	•			•
West Malvern	•			•
White Ladies Aston	•			•
Whittington	•			•
Wichenford	•			•
Wick-Near-Pershore	•			•
Wickhamford	•			•
Wolverley	•			•
Worcester	•	•		•
Wribbenhall	•			•
Wychbold	•			•

PARISH	PARISH REGISTERS	BISHOPS' TRANSCRIPTS	BOYD'S MARRIAGE INDEX	PR PRINT-OUTS
Wyre-Piddle	•			•
Wythall	•			
YORK*				
Aberford	•	•		•
Acaster-Malbis	•	•		
Acaster-Selby	•	•		
Acklam	•	•		
Ackworth	•	•		•
Acomb	•	•		•
Addingham	•	•		•
Addle	•	•		•
Adlingfleet		•		
Adwick-Le-Street	•	•		•
Adwick-Upon-Dearne	•	•		•
Agglethorpe	•	•		
Ainderby-Steeple	•	•		•
Airmyn	•	•		
Aislaby	•			
Aldborough	•	•		•
Aldbourough (Near Hill)	•	•		
Aldfield-With-Studley	•	•		
Allerston	•	•		•
Allerthorpe (Near Packlington)	•	•		
Allerton	•			
Allerton-Chapel		•		•
Allerton-Mauleverer	•	•		•
Almondbury	•	•		•
Alne	•	•		•
Alverthorpe	•	•		
Amotherbury	•	•		
Ampleforth		•		
Anston		•		
Appleton-Le-Street	•	•		•
Appleton-Wiske		•		
Ardsley		•		
Arkendale		•		•
Arkengarth-Dale	•	•		•
Arksey	•	•		
Armley		•		•
Armthorpe	•	•		
Arncliffe	•	•		•
Askern		•		
Askham-Bryan	•	•		•
Askham-Richard	•	•		•
Askrigg	•	•		•
Aston-With-Aughton	•	•		•
Attercliffe		•		•
Atwick	•	•		•
Auburn				

PARISH	PARISH REGISTERS	BISHOPS' TRANSCRIPTS	BOYD'S MARRIAGE INDEX	PR PRINT-OUTS
Aughton (Near Selby)	•	•		•
Austerfield	•	•		•
Aysgarth	•	•		•
Ayton	•			•
Badsworth	•	•		•
Bagby	•	•		•
Baildon	•	•		•
Bainton		•		•
Balby-With-Hexthorpe		•		•
Baldersby	•			•
Bardsey	•	•		•
Barlby	•	•		•
Barmby-On-The-Marsh		•		•
Barmby-On-The-Moor	•	•		•
Barmston		•		•
Barnbrough	•	•		•
Barnby-Upon-Don	•	•		•
Barnoldswick		•		•
Barnsley	•	•		•
Barton	•	•		•
Barton-Le-Street	•	•		
Barton (Near Darlington)				•
Barwick-In-Elmett		•		•
Batley	•	•		
Battyeford		•		•
Bawtry		•		•
Beauchief		•		•
Bedale	•	•		•
Beeford		•		•
Beeston		•		•
Bellerby	•	•		
Bempton		•		
Bentham	•	•		•
Bessingby		•		•
Beswick		•		•
Beverley		•		•
Bilbrough	•	•		•
Bilsdale	•	•		•
Bilton (Near Hull)		•		•
Bilton (Near Wetherby)	•	•		•
Bilton (Near York)	•	•		•
Bilton-With-Harrowgate		•		•
Bingley	•	•		•
Birdforth		•		•
Birdsall	•	•		•
Birkby	•	•		•
Birkenshaw		•		•
Birkin	•	•		•
Birstall	•	•		•

England

* COUNTY / SHIRE

PARISH	PARISH REGISTERS	BISHOPS' TRANSCRIPTS	BOYD'S MARRIAGE INDEX	PR PRINT-OUTS
Bishop-Burton		•		
Bishop-Thornton		•		
Bishop-Thorpe	•	•		
Bishop-Wilton	•	•		
Blacktoft	•	•		•
Blyth	•	•		
Bolsterstone		•		
Boltby		•		
Bolton-Abbey	•	•		•
Bolton-By-Rowland	•	•		•
Bolton-Castle				•
Bolton-Cum-Redmire	•	•		
Bolton-Percy	•	•		
Bolton-Upon-Dearne	•	•		•
Bolton-Upon-Swale	•	•		•
Boroughbridge		•		
Bossall	•	•		
Boston-Spa		•		
Bowes	•	•		•
Boynton	•	•		•
Bracewell		•		
Bradfield	•	•		•
Bradford	•	•		•
Brafferton		•		
Braithwell	•	•		•
Bramham	•	•		•
Bramley (Near Leeds)		•		•
Bramwith (Kirk)	•			
Brandesburton	•	•		
Brandsby-With-Stearsby		•		
Brantingham	•	•		•
Brayton		•		
Brearton		•		
Bridlington		•		
Bridlington-Quay		•		
Brighouse		•		
Brignall		•		•
Brodsworth	•	•		•
Brompton (Near Northallerton)	•	•		•
Brompton (Near Sawdon)				•
Brompton (Near Scarborough)	•	•		
Brompton-Patrick	•	•		•
Broomfleet		•		
Brotherton		•		
Brotton	•	•		•
Broughton-In-Airedale		•		
Broughton (Near Stokesley)		•		
Bubwith	•	•		•
Bugthorpe	•	•		

PARISH	PARISH REGISTERS	BISHOPS' TRANSCRIPTS	BOYD'S MARRIAGE INDEX	PR PRINT-OUTS
Bulmer	•	•		
Burgh-Wallis	•	•		
Burley (Near Otley)		•		
Burnby	•	•		
Burneston	•	•		•
Burnsall	•	•		•
Burstwick		•		
Burton-Agnes	•	•		
Burton-Cherry	•	•		•
Burton-Fleming	•	•		•
Burton-Leonard	•	•		•
Burton-Pidsea		•		
Burythorpe	•	•		
Buttercrambe	•			
Butterwick (Near Great Driffield)		•		
Calverly	•	•		•
Campsall	•	•		
Cantley	•	•		•
Carkin				•
Carlton-Miniott		•		
Carlton (Near Skipton)		•		
Carlton (Near Snaith)	•	•		•
Carlton (Near Stokesley)		•		
Carnaby		•		
Castleford		•		
Catterick	•	•		
Catton	•	•		
Catwick		•		
Cawood	•	•		
Cawthorne		•		
Cayton (Near Scarborough)	•	•		•
Chapel-Haddlesey	•			
Chapel-Le-Day	•	•		•
Chapelthorpe		•		
Church-Fenton		•		
Churwell		•		
Clapham	•	•		•
Clayton-With-Frickley		•		•
Cleasby	•	•		•
Cleckheaton		•		
Clifford		•		
Clifford-Cum-Boston	•			
Cloughton		•		
Coatham		•		
Cockayne		•		
Cold-Coniston		•		•
Cold-Kirkby	•	•		
Coley		•		
Collingham	•	•		•

PARISH	PARISH REGISTERS	BISHOPS' TRANSCRIPTS	BOYD'S MARRIAGE INDEX	PR PRINT-OUTS
Conisborough	•	•		
Conistone-With-Kilnsay		•		•
Copgrove		•		•
Copmanthorpe	•	•		
Cottingham		•		
Coverham	•	•		•
Cowesby		•		
Cowgill		•		
Cowick		•		
Cowlam		•		
Cowthorpe	•	•		•
Coxwold	•	•		•
Craike		•		•
Crambe	•	•		
Crathorne		•		
Croft		•		
Crofton	•	•		•
Cropton		•		
Crosstone		•		
Cumberworth		•		
Cundall	•	•		•
Dacre		•		
Dalby-With-Skewsby	•	•		
Dallo-Gill		•		
Danby (With Guisborough)	•	•		•
Danby-Wiske	•	•		•
Darfield	•	•		•
Darnall		•		
Darrington	•	•		•
Darton	•	•		
Deighton	•			
Deighton (Near Northallerton)		•		•
Denby		•		•
Dent	•	•		•
Denton		•		
Dewsbury	•	•		•
Dinnington		•		
Dishforth		•		
Dobcross				•
Doncaster		•	•	
Downholme		•		•
Drax		•		
Driffield		•		
Drighlington		•		
Dringhouses	•	•		
Drypool	•	•		•
Dunnington (Near Hornsea)		•		
Dunnington (Near York)	•	•		
Dunsforth		•		

England

* COUNTY / SHIRE

PARISH	PARISH REGISTERS	BISHOPS' TRANSCRIPTS	BOYD'S MARRIAGE INDEX	PR PRINT-OUTS
Earls-Heaton		•		
Easby (Near Richmond)		•		•
Easington	•			
Easington (Near Guisbrough)		•		•
Easington (Near Patrington)		•		
Easingwold	•	•		•
East and West Lutton	•	•		
East Ardsley	•	•		•
East Cowton	•	•		•
East Harlsey	•	•		•
East Rouncton	•	•		•
East Witton		•		•
Eastrington		•		
Ebberston	•	•		•
Ecclesall		•		
Ecclesfield		•		•
Edlington		•		
Edstone	•			
Egton	•	•		•
Eldon		•		
Elland	•	•		•
Ellenburn		•		
Ellerker		•		
Ellerton-Priory	•	•		
Elloughton		•		
Elsecar		•		
Elstronwick		•		
Elvington	•	•		
Emley	•	•		•
Erringden		•		
Erryholme	•	•		•
Escrick	•	•		
Eskdaleside		•		
Eston	•	•		•
Etton		•		
Everingham	•	•		
Faceby		•		
Fangfoss	•	•		
Farlington		•		
Farndale		•		
Farnham	•	•		•
Farnley (Near Leeds)		•		•
Featherstone		•		•
Feliskirk	•	•		
Felkirk	•	•		•
Fenwick		•		
Ferry-Frystone		•		
Fewston	•	•		•
Filey	•	•		•

PARISH	PARISH REGISTERS	BISHOPS' TRANSCRIPTS	BOYD'S MARRIAGE INDEX	PR PRINT-OUTS
Fimber		•		
Fingall		•		
Firbeck		•		
Fishlake		•		
Flamborough		•		
Flaxton		•		
Flockton	•	•		•
Folkton		•		
Forcett	•	•		•
Foston (Near Thornton)	•	•		
Foston-On-The-Wolds		•		
Foxholes		•		
Fraisthorpe		•		
Frairmere				•
Fridaythorpe		•		
Fulford-Ambo		•		
Full-Sutton	•	•		
Fullneck	•			
Fulwood		•		
Fylingdales		•		
Ganton		•		
Garforth	•	•		•
Gargrave	•	•		•
Garsdale		•		•
Garton		•		
Garton-On-The-Wolds		•		
Gawthorpe		•		
Giggleswick	•	•		•
Gildersome		•		
Gildingwells		•		
Gillamoor		•		
Gilling (Near Richmond)	•	•		•
Gisburn	•	•		•
Glaisdale		•		•
Gleadless		•		
Goathland		•		
Golcar		•		
Goldsborough (Near Knaresborough)	•	•		•
Goodmanham	•	•		
Goole		•		
Goxhill		•		
Greasborough		•		
Great and Little Cowden		•		
Great Ayton	•	•		•
Great Edstone	•	•		•
Great Givendale	•	•		
Great Hatfield		•		
Great Hutton				•
Great Kelk		•		

PARISH	PARISH REGISTERS	BISHOPS' TRANSCRIPTS	BOYD'S MARRIAGE INDEX	PR PRINT-OUTS
Great Langton		•		
Great Ouseburn	•	•		
Great Sandal		•		
Great Smeaton		•		•
Grindale		•		
Grindleton		•		
Grinton	•	•		•
Grosmont		•		
Guisborough		•		
Guiseley	•	•		•
Hackness	•	•		•
Halifax	•	•		•
Halsham	•	•		
Halton-Gill		•		•
Hampswaite	•	•		•
Handsworth		•		
Hanging-Heaton		•		
Hardrow		•		•
Harewood	•	•		•
Harome	•	•		
Harpham	•	•		
Harrogate	•			•
Harswell	•	•		
Harthill		•		
Hartshead	•	•		•
Hartwith	•			•
Harwood-Dale		•		
Hatfield	•	•		
Haukswell	•	•		
Hawes		•		
Hawnby	•	•		•
Haworth	•	•		•
Haxby		•		
Hayton	•	•		
Headingly		•		•
Healaugh	•			
Healaugh (Near Tadcaster)		•		
Heckmondwike		•		
Hedon		•		
Heeley	•			
Helbeck-Lunds		•		
Hellaby	•			
Helmsley		•		
Helmsley-Gate	•	•		•
Helperthorpe	•	•		
Hemingbrough	•	•		
Hemsworth	•			•
Henderskelf		•		
Heptonstall	•	•		•

England

* COUNTY / SHIRE

PARISH	PARISH REGISTERS	BISHOPS' TRANSCRIPTS	BOYD'S MARRIAGE INDEX	PR PRINT-OUTS
Heslerton	•	•		•
Heslington	•	•		
Hessle		•		
Hickleton	•			•
High Hoyland		•		
High Melton	•	•		
High Worsall		•		
Hilston		•		
Hilton		•		
Hinderwell	•	•		•
Hipswell	•	•		•
Hollym		•		
Holme-On-The-Wolds		•		
Holme-Upon-Spalding-Moor	•	•		•
Holmfirth	•	•		
Holmpton		•		
Holtby	•	•		•
Honley		•		
Hook	•	•		•
Hooten-Pagnell	•	•		•
Hooton-Roberts		•		
Horbury	•	•		•
Hornby (Near Bedale)		•		
Hornsea		•		
Horsehouse	•	•		•
Horsforth	•	•		•
Horton-In-Ribblesdale	•	•		•
Horton (Near Bradford)		•		
Hotham		•		
Hovingham	•	•		
Howden	•	•		•
Hubberholme		•		•
Huddersfield	•	•		•
Hudswell		•		•
Huggate	•	•		•
Hull		•		
Humbleton		•		
Hunmanby		•		
Hunsingore	•			•
Hunslet		•		•
Huntington	•	•		
Husthwaite		•		
Hutton		•		
Hutton-Bonville	•	•		
Hutton-Bushel	•	•		•
Hutton-Cranswick		•		
Hutton-Magna	•	•		
Hutton-Wandesley	•			
Huttons-Ambo	•	•		

PARISH	PARISH REGISTERS	BISHOPS' TRANSCRIPTS	BOYD'S MARRIAGE INDEX	PR PRINT-OUTS
Idle		•		
Ilkley	•	•		•
Illingworth	•	•		•
Ingleby-Arncliffe	•	•		•
Ingleby-Greenhow	•	•		•
Ingleton	•	•		•
Keighley	•	•		•
Kellington		•		
Kettlewell		•		
Kexby	•	•		
Keyingham		•		
Kilburn	•	•		•
Kildale		•		
Kildwick	•	•		•
Kilham		•		
Kilnsea		•		
Kilnwick	•	•		•
Kilnwick-Percy	•	•		
Kippax	•	•		•
Kirby-Grindalyth	•	•		•
Kirby-Hill	•	•		•
Kirby-In-Cleveland	•	•		•
Kirby-Knowle		•		
Kirby-Sigston	•	•		•
Kirby-Under-Dale	•	•		
Kirby-Wiske	•	•		•
Kirk-Bramwith		•		
Kirk-Deighton		•		•
Kirk-Ella	•	•		•
Kirk-Hammerton	•	•		•
Kirk-Leatham	•	•		•
Kirk-Leavington		•		
Kirk-Sandall	•	•		
Kirk-Smeaton		•		
Kirkburn		•		
Kirkburton	•	•		•
Kirby-Fleetham	•	•		•
Kirby-In-Malham-Dale	•	•		•
Kirby-Malzeard		•		•
Kirby-Mispearton	•	•		•
Kirby-Moorside		•		
Kirby-Overblow	•	•		•
Kirby-Ravensworth	•	•		•
Kirby-Wharfe		•		
Kirkdale		•		
Kirkheaton	•	•		•
Kirklington	•	•		•
Kirkstall		•		
Knapton (Near Malton)	•	•		

PARISH	PARISH REGISTERS	BISHOPS' TRANSCRIPTS	BOYD'S MARRIAGE INDEX	PR PRINT-OUTS
Knaresborough		•		•
Knottingley		•		
Laith-Kirk		•		
Langtoft		•		
Langton	•	•		
Lastingham		•		
Laughton-En-Le-Morthen		•		
Lawkland	•			•
Laxton		•		•
Leake	•	•		•
Laethly		•		
Leckonfield	•	•		•
Ledsham	•	•		•
Leeds	•	•		•
Letwell		•		
Leven		•		
Levisham		•		
Leyburn		•		
Lightcliffe		•		
Lindley (Near Huddersfield)		•		
Linton (Near Skipton)	•	•		•
Lissett		•		
Little Driffield		•		
Little Ouseburn	•	•		•
Little Ruston		•		
Liversedge		•		
Liverton		•		
Lockton		•		
Lofthouse		•		
Londesborough	•	•		
Long Marston	•	•		•
Long Preston		•		
Long Riston		•		
Longwood		•		
Lothersdale		•		
Loversall		•		
Low Harrogate		•		
Lowthorpe		•		
Luddenden		•		
Lund	•	•		•
Lydgate				•
Lythe	•	•		•
Maltby (Near Rotherham)	•	•		
Malton	•	•		•
Manfield	•	•		•
Mappleton		•		
Marfleet		•		
Marr		•		
Marrick	•	•		•

England

* COUNTY / SHIRE

PARISH	PARISH REGISTERS	BISHOPS' TRANSCRIPTS	BOYD'S MARRIAGE INDEX	PR PRINT-OUTS
Marsden		•		
Marske (Near Guisborough)	•	•		•
Marske (Near Richmond)		•		•
Marton-Cum-Grafton		•		•
Marton-Cum-Moxby		•		
Marton-Le-Moor		•		
Marton (Near Hedon)		•		
Marton (Near Middlesborough)		•		
Marton (Near Skipton		•		
Marsbrough		•		
Masham	•	•		
Melbecks		•		
Melsonby	•	•		•
Meltham		•		
Methley	•	•		
Mexborough		•		
Micklegate	•			
Middleham	•			
Middlesborough	•	•		•
Middlesmoor	•			
Middleton (Near Pickering)		•		
Middleton-Tyas	•	•		•
Middleton-Upon-Leven		•		
Midhope		•		
Millington	•	•		
Mirfield	•	•		•
Mitton	•	•		
Monk-Bretton	•	•		
Monk-Frystone	•	•		•
Monkton-Moor	•	•		
Monkton-Hun		•		•
Morley		•		
Muker	•	•		•
Muston		•		
Myton-Upon-Swale	•	•		•
Naburn	•	•		
Nafferton		•		
Nether Hoyland		•		
Netherthong		•		
New Malton	•	•		
New Mill (Near Huddersfield)		•		
Newton-In-Cleveland		•		
Newton-Kyne	•	•		
Newton (Near Guisborough)				•
Newton-Upon-Ouse		•		
Newton-Wold	•	•		•
Nidd		•		•
Norland		•		
Normanby (Near Pickering)		•		

PARISH	PARISH REGISTERS	BISHOPS' TRANSCRIPTS	BOYD'S MARRIAGE INDEX	PR PRINT-OUTS
Normanton	•	•		•
North Bierley		•		
North Cave	•	•		
North Cowton		•		
North Dalton		•		
North Ferriby		•		
North Frodingham		•		
North Grimstone	•	•		
North Newbald		•		
North Otterington		•		
North Stanley		•		
Northallerton	•	•		•
Norton (Near Malton)	•	•		
Nun-Burnholme	•	•		
Nunkeeling-With-Bewholme	•	•		•
Nunnington	•	•		•
Old Byland	•	•		•
Old Malton		•		
Ormsby	•	•		
Osbaldwick	•	•		
Osmotherley	•	•		•
Ossett		•		
Oswaldkirk	•	•		•
Otley	•	•		•
Ottringham		•		
Oughtibridge		•		
Oulton		•		
Ouseburn				•
Over Silton	•	•		•
Overton (Near York)		•		
Owston		•		
Owthorne		•		
Pannal	•	•		
Pately-Bridge	•	•		•
Patrington	•	•		•
Paull		•		
Penistone	•	•		•
Pickering		•		
Pickhill	•	•		•
Pocklington	•	•		•
Pontefract	•	•		•
Pool		•		
Preston		•		
Pudsey		•		
Raskelf	•	•		
Rastrick		•		
Rathmell		•		
Ravenfield		•		
Rawcliffe (Near Goole)		•		

PARISH	PARISH REGISTERS	BISHOPS' TRANSCRIPTS	BOYD'S MARRIAGE INDEX	PR PRINT-OUTS
Rawdon		•		
Rawmarsh		•		
Redcar		•		
Redhill	•			
Redmire				•
Reighton		•		
Riccall	•	•		•
Richmond	•	•		•
Rillington	•	•		•
Rilston	•	•		•
Ripley	•	•		•
Ripon	•	•		
Ripponden	•	•		•
Rise		•		
Roberton		•		
Rochdale	•			
Rocliffe		•		
Rokeby	•	•		•
Romaldkirk	•	•		
Romanby		•		
Rooss	•	•		
Rosedale	•			•
Rosedale-East-Side		•		•
Rosedale-West-Side		•		•
Rossington		•		•
Rotherham	•	•	•	•
Rothwell	•	•		•
Roundhay		•		
Routh		•		
Rowley (Near Hull)		•		
Roxby	•			
Roxby (Near Whitby)		•		
Royston	•	•		•
Rudby-In-Cleveland	•	•		
Rudston	•	•		•
Rufforth	•	•		
Ryther	•	•		•
Saddleworth	•	•		•
Salton		•		
Sancton		•		
Sand-Hutton (Near Thirsk)		•		
Sand-Hutton (Near York)	•	•		
Sandall-Magna	•			
Sawley (Nea Ripon)		•		
Saxton	•	•		•
Scalby (Near Scarborough)		•		
Scammonden		•		
Scampston	•	•		
Scarborough	•	•		•

England

* COUNTY / SHIRE

PARISH	PARISH REGISTERS	BISHOPS' TRANSCRIPTS	BOYD'S MARRIAGE INDEX	PR PRINT-OUTS
Scawton	•	•		
Scisset		•		
Scorborough	•	•		•
Scrayingham	•	•		
Scruton	•	•		
Sculcoates	•	•		•
Seamer (Near Scarborough)		•		
Seamer (Near Stokesley)		•		
Seaton-Ross	•	•		
Sedburgh	•	•		•
Selby	•	•		•
Sessay	•	•		•
Settle		•		
Settrington	•	•		•
Sewerby-With-Marton		•		
Sharow		•		
Sheffield	•	•		•
Sherburn (Near Leeds)	•	•		•
Sherburn (Near Scarborough)	•	•		
Sheriff-Hutton		•		
Shipley		•		
Shipton (Near Weighton-Market)		•		
Sigglesthorne		•		
Silkstone	•	•		•
Silsden		•		•
Sinnington		•		
Skeffling		•		
Skelbrooke		•		
Skelton (Near Guisborough)		•		
Skelton (Near Ripon)		•		
Skelton (Near York)		•		
Skerne		•		
Skidby		•		
Skipsea		•		
Skipton	•	•		•
Skipton-Upon-Swale		•		
Skipwith	•	•		•
Skirlaugh		•		
Skirpenbeck	•	•		
Slaidburn	•	•		•
Slaithwaite		•		
Sledmere		•		
Slingsby	•	•		
Snainton	•	•		
Snaith	•	•		•
Sneaton		•		
South Cave	•	•		•
South Cliff		•		
South Cowton		•		•

PARISH	PARISH REGISTERS	BISHOPS' TRANSCRIPTS	BOYD'S MARRIAGE INDEX	PR PRINT-OUTS
South Dalton		•		
South Kilvington		•		
South Kirkby		•		
South Milford	•	•		
South Otterington		•		
South Owram		•		
South Stainley	•	•		•
Sowerby-Bridge		•		
Sowerby (Near Halifax)		•		
Sowerby (Near Thirsk)		•		
Speeton		•		
Spennithorne		•		•
Spofforth	•	•		•
Sproatley		•		
Sprotborough	•	•		
Stainburn	•	•		
Stainland		•		
Stainton (Near Tickhill)	•	•		
Stainton (Near Yarn)	•	•		•
Stallingbusk	•	•		•
Stamford-Bridge		•		
Stanley		•		
Stannington		•		
Stanwick-St. John	•	•		•
Startforth	•	•		•
Staveley		•		•
Stillingfleet	•	•		
Stillington		•		
Stockeld	•			
Stockton-On-The-Forest	•	•		
Stokesley	•	•		•
Stonegrave	•	•		
Strensall	•	•		
Sunk-Island		•		
Sutton (Near Hill)		•		
Sutton-On-The-Forest		•		
Sutton-Upon-Derwent	•	•		
Swillington	•	•		•
Swine		•		
Swinton (Near Sheffield)		•		
Tadcaster	•	•		
Tandridge	•			
Tankersley		•		
Terrington	•	•		•
Thirkleby (Near Thirsk)		•		
Thirsk	•	•		•
Thorganby-With-West-Cottingwith	•	•		
Thormanby		•		
Thornaby-On-Tees	•	•		•

PARISH	PARISH REGISTERS	BISHOPS' TRANSCRIPTS	BOYD'S MARRIAGE INDEX	PR PRINT-OUTS
Thorne	•	•		
Thorner		•		
Thornes (Near Wakefield)		•		
Thorngumbald		•		
Thornhill	•	•		•
Thornthwaithe		•		•
Thornton-Dale		•		
Thornton-In-Craven		•		
Thornton-In-Longsdale	•	•		•
Thornton-Le-Street	•	•		
Thornton (Near Bradford)		•		•
Thornton (Near Pocklington)	•	•		
Thornton-Steward	•	•		•
Thornton-Watlass		•		•
Thorp-Arch		•		
Thorpe-Bassett	•	•		•
Thorpe-Salvin	•	•		•
Throapham		•		
Thrybergh		•		
Thurcross	•			
Thurnscoe		•		
Thwing		•		
Tickhill	•	•		
Tickton-With-Hull-Bridge		•		
Tinsley	•	•		
Tockwith		•		
Todwick	•	•		
Tong		•		
Topcliffe (Near Thirsk)	•	•		
Topcliffe (Near Wakefield)	•			•
Tossett		•		•
Tosside		•		
Treeton		•		
Tunstall (Near Patrington)		•		
Ugglebarnby		•		
Ulley		•		
Ulrome		•		
Upleatham		•		
Upper Helmsley	•	•		•
Upper Hopton		•		
Upper Poppleton		•		
Waddington	•	•		
Wadsley		•		
Wadworth	•	•		
Wakefield	•	•		•
Wales	•	•		
Walkington		•		
Walton (Near Wetherby)	•	•		
Walton (Near Wighill)		•		•

England

* COUNTY / SHIRE

PARISH	PARISH REGISTERS	BISHOPS' TRANSCRIPTS	BOYD'S MARRIAGE INDEX	PR PRINT-OUTS
Warmfield		•		
Warmsworth		•		
Warter	•	•		
Warthill	•	•		•
Wath		•		
Wath-Upon-Dearne	•	•		•
Watton		•		
Wawne		•		
Weaverthorpe	•	•		
Weighton-Market	•	•		
Welbury	•	•		•
Well		•		•
Welton		•		
Welwick		•		
Wensley	•	•		•
Wentworth		•		
West Acklam	•	•		•
West Ardsley	•	•		•
West Bretton				•
West Rounceton	•	•		•
West Tanfield		•		•
West Witton	•	•		•
Westerdale		•		
Weston	•	•		•
Westow	•	•		
Wetherby		•		
Wetwang		•		
Wharram	•	•		
Wheldrake	•	•		
Whenby	•	•		
Whiston		•		
Whitby	•	•		•
Whitgift	•	•		•
Whitkirk	•	•		•
Whitwell		•		
Whixley	•	•		•
Whorlton	•	•		•
Wibsey	•	•		•
Wickersley		•		
Wiggington	•	•		
Wighill	•	•		
Wilberfoss	•	•		
Willerby (Near Scarborough)		•		
Willesden		•		•
Wilton (Near Redcar)	•	•		•
Winestead	•	•		•
Winksley		•		
Wintringham	•	•		•
Wistow		•		
Withernsea		•		
Withernwick		•		
Womersley		•		
Woodhouse (Near Huddersfield)		•		
Woodhouse (Near Sheffield)		•		
Woodlesford		•		
Woodsetts		•		
Woolley	•	•		•
Worsborough		•		
Wortley (Near Barnsley)		•		
Wortley (Near Leeds)	•			
Wortley (Near Penistone)		•		
Wragby	•	•		•
Wressell		•		
Wycliffe	•	•		•
Wykeham	•	•		•
Wyton		•		
Yafforth	•	•		•
Yapham	•	•		
Yarm		•		
Yeddingham	•	•		
York	•	•		•

WALES

* COUNTY / SHIRE

PARISH	PARISH REGISTERS	BISHOPS' TRANSCRIPTS	BOYD'S MARRIAGE INDEX	PR PRINT-OUTS
ANGLESEY*				
Aberffraw		•		•
Amlwch		•		•
[illegible]		•		
Beaumaris		•		•
Bodedern		•		•
Bodewryd				•
Bodwrog		•		•
Ceirchiong		•		•
Cerrig-Ceinwen		•		•
Coedana		•		•
Gweredog		•		
Heneglwys				•
Holyhead	•			•
Llanallgo				•
Llanbabo				•
Llanbadrig				•
Llanbedr-Goch				•
Llanbeulan				•
Llandaniel-Fab				•
Llanddausaint		•		•
Llanddona		•		•
Llanddyfnan		•		•
Llandegfan	•	•		•
Llandrygarn		•		•
Llandyfrydog		•		•
Llanedwen		•		•
Llanelian		•		•
Llanerchymedd		•		•
Llanevgrad		•		•
Llanfachreth		•		
Llanfaelog		•		
Llanfaes	•	•		
Llanfaethly		•		•
Llanfair-Matahafrn-Eithaf		•		•
Llanfair-Pwllgwyngyll		•		•
Llanfair-Yn-Enwll		•		
Llanfair-Yn-Ghornwy		•		
Llanfechell		•		
Llanffinan		•		
Llanfflewyn		•		
Llanfigael		•		
Llanfihangel-Esceifiog		•		
Llanfihangel-Tre-'R-Beirdd		•		
Llanfihangel-Tyn-Sylwy		•		
Llanfihangel-Yn-Howyn		•		
Llanfwrog		•		•
Llangadwaladr		•		•
Llangaffo		•		
Llangefni		•		
Llangeinwen		•		•
Llangoed	•	•		
Llangristiolus		•		
Llangwyfan		•		
Llangwyllog		•		•
Llanidan		•		
Llaniestyn		•		
Llanrhwydrys		•		
Llanrhyddladd		•		
Llansadwen	•	•		
Llantrisaint		•		•
Llanwenllwyfo		•		
Llanynghenedl		•		
Llechcynfarwydd		•		
Llechylched		•		•
Newborough-St. Peter		•		
Penmon	•	•		
Penmynydd		•		
Penrhos-Lligwy	•	•		
Pentraeth		•		•
Rhodogeidio		•		
Rhosbeiro		•		
Rhoscolyn		•		•
Rhosybol		•		
Treedraeth	•	•		
Tregayan		•		
Trewalchmai		•		
BRECON*				
Aberyscir			•	•
Alltmawr		•	•	•
Battle			•	•
Brecon		•	•	•
Bronllys		•	•	•
Builth		•	•	•
Callwen		•	•	•
Cantreff		•	•	•
Cathedine		•	•	•
Crickadarn		•	•	•
Crickhowell		•	•	•
Devynock		•	•	•
Garthbrengy		•	•	•
Glasbury	•			•
Gwenddwr		•	•	•
Gyffin		•		
Hay		•	•	•
Illtyd		•		
Llanafan-Fawr		•	•	•
Llanafan-Fechan		•	•	
Llanbedr		•	•	•
Llanddewi-Abergwessin		•	•	
Llanddewi-'R-Clum		•	•	
Llandefailog-Fach		•	•	•
Llandefailog-Tre-Graig		•	•	
Llandefalley		•		•
Llandeilo'R-Fan			•	
Llandilo-Vane		•		•
Llandulas-In-Tyr-Abbot		•		•
Llandyfalle			•	
Llaneliev		•	•	
Llanelly		•	•	•
Llanfaes		•	•	
Llanfeigan				•
Llanfihangel-Fechan				•
Llanfihangel-Abergwessin			•	
Llanfihangel-Bryn-Pabuan		•	•	
Llanfihangel-Cwmdu		•	•	•
Llanfihangel-Nant-Brane		•	•	•
Llanfihangel-Tal-Y-Llyn	•	•	•	•
Llanfilo		•	•	
Llangammarch		•	•	
Llanganten		•	•	•
Llangasty-Talyllyn		•	•	
Llangattock		•	•	•
Llangenny		•	•	•
Llangorse		•	•	
Llangunider		•	•	•
Llangynog			•	
Llanhamlach		•	•	•
Llanigon		•	•	
Llanleon-Vel		•		
Llansaintfraed		•		
Llanspyddid		•	•	•
Llanthetty		•	•	
Llanthew		•	•	•
Llanvigan			•	
Llanvrynach		•	•	
Llanwrthwl		•	•	•
Llanwrtyd		•	•	•
Llanynys		•	•	
Llanywern		•	•	
Llyswen		•	•	•
Llywell		•	•	•
Maesmynis		•	•	•
Mertyr-Cynog		•	•	
Nantddu		•	•	•
Partrishow		•	•	•
Penderyn		•	•	•

WALES

* COUNTY / SHIRE

PARISH	PARISH REGISTERS	BISHOPS' TRANSCRIPTS	BOYD'S MARRIAGE INDEX	PR PRINT-OUTS
Penpont		•	•	
Rhidybriw		•	•	
Talachddu		•	•	
Talgarth		•	•	•
Trallong		•	•	•
Vainor		•	•	•
Ystradefellte	•	•	•	
Ystradgynlais		•	•	•
CARDIGAN*				
Aberporth	•	•		
Aberystwith	•	•		
Bangor		•		•
Bettws-Evan		•		•
Bettws-Leiki		•		•
Blaenpenal		•		•
Blaenporth		•		•
Brongwyn		•		•
Capel-Cynon		•		•
Cardigan		•		
Caron-Uwch-Clawdd		•		•
Caron-Ys-Clawdd		•		
Cellan	•	•		•
Cilcennin	•	•		
Cilie-Aeron	•	•		•
Cydblwyf				•
Dehewid		•		•
Eglwys-Fach		•		•
Eglwys-Newydd	•	•		•
Elerch		•		
Gartheli				•
Garthely		•		
Henfynyw		•		•
Henllan		•		•
Lampeter	•	•		•
Llanafan		•		•
Llanarth		•	•	•
Llanbadarnfawr		•		
Llanbadarn-Fawr		•		•
Llanbadarn-Odwyn				•
Llanbadarn-Trefs-Eglwys	•			•
Llancynfelin		•		•
Llanddeinol		•		•
Llandyssil		•		•
Llanerchayron		•		
Llanfair-Clydogau		•		•
Llanfair-Orllwyn		•		•
Llanfihangel-Geneur-Glynn		•		•
Llanfihangel-Lledrod		•		
Llanfihangel-Y-Croyddin	•	•		•
Llanfihangel-Ystrad		•		•
Llangeitho	•	•		•
Llangoedmore		•		•
Llangorwen		•		•
Llangranog				•
Llangrwyddon		•		•
Llangunllo		•		•
Llangybi		•		•
Llanilar		•		•
Llanina	•	•		•
Llanllwchaiarn		•		•
Llanrhystyd		•		•
Llansaintffraid		•		•
Llanwenog				•
Llanwnen		•		•
Llanychaiarn		•		
Llechryd		•		
Lledrod (Upper & Lower)				•
Lower Gwnnw's				•
Mount		•		•
Nantcwnlle	•	•		•
Penbryn		•		•
Rhostie		•		•
Silian		•		•
Trefilan		•		•
Tregaron		•		•
Tremain		•		•
Troedyraur				•
Upper Gwnnw's				•
Upper Llanddewi-Aberarth		•		•
Upper Llanfihangel-Y-Creuddyn				•
Verwick		•		•
Yspitty-Ystwith				•
Yspytty-Cynfyn		•		•
Yspytty-Ystrad-Meiric		•		•
Yspytty-Ystwith		•		•
CARMARTHEN*				
Abergwilly		•		•
Abernant		•		
Bettwys		•		
Brechfa		•		
Carmarthen	•	•		•
Cenarth		•		
Cil-Y-Maenllwyd		•		
Cilicwm		•		
Conwil-Cayo	•	•		•
Conwil-In-Elfet		•		•
Conwil-In-Elvet		•		•
Cwmamman		•		
Cyffic		•		
Eglwys-Cymmin		•		•
Eglwys-Fair-A-Chyrig		•		
Egremont		•		
Gwynfe		•		
Henllan-Amgoed		•		
Kidwelly		•		•
Kilredin		•		
Landilo-Fawr		•		
Laugharne		•		
Llanarthney		•		
Llanddarog		•		
Llanddausaint		•		
Llandebie		•		
Llandefeilog		•		
Llandilo-Abercowin		•		
Llandilo-Fawr		•		
Llandingat		•		
Llandisilio		•		•
Llandowror		•		
Llandyfeisant		•		
Llanedy		•		
Llanegwag		•		
Llanelly		•		•
Llanfairarybryn	•	•		•
Llanfihangel-Aberbythych	•	•		•
Llanfihangel-Abercowin		•		
Llanfihangel-Ar-Arth	•	•		
Llanfihangel-Cilfargen		•		•
Llanfihangel-Rhos-Y-Corn		•		•
Llanfynydd		•		
Llangadock		•		
Llangain		•		
Llangathen		•		
Llangeler		•		
Llangendeirne		•		
Llangennech		•		
Llaninning		•		
Llanglydwen		•		
Llanguddock		•		
Llangwnnor	•	•		•
Llanllawddog		•		
Llanllwch		•		
Llanllwny		•		
Llannon		•		
Llanpumpsaint		•		•
Llansadurnen		•		
Llansadwrn		•		
Llansawel		•		

WALES

* COUNTY / SHIRE

PARISH	PARISH REGISTERS	BISHOPS' TRANSCRIPTS	BOYD'S MARRIAGE INDEX	PR PRINT-OUTS
Llanstephan		•		•
Llanwinio		•		
Llanwrda		•		
Llanybree		•		•
Llanybyther		•		
Marros		•		
Newcastle-Emlyn	•	•		
Newchurch		•		
Pecarreg		•		
Pembrey		•		
Penboyr		•		
Pencarreg		•		
Pendine		•		
St. Clears	•	•		
St. Ishmael's	•	•		•
Taliaris		•		
Talley		•		
Trelech-Ar-Bettws	•	•		
Upper Tumble				•
Ystradffyn		•		
CARNARVON*				
Aber		•		
Aberdaron		•		
Abererch		•		•
Bangor		•		•
Beddgelert		•		•
Bettws-Garmon		•		
Bettws-Y-Coed		•		
Bodvean				•
Bottwnog				•
Bottwnnog		•		
Bryncroes		•		•
Caerhun		•		
Capel-Curig		•		•
Carngiwich		•		•
Ceidio				•
Clynnog		•		
Conway	•	•		•
Criccieth		•		•
Denio		•		•
Dolbenmaen		•		
Dolwyddelan		•		
Dwygyfylchi		•		•
Edeyrn		•		
Glanogwen		•		
Llanaelhaiarn		•		
Llanarmon		•		•
Llanbeblig		•		•
Llanbedr-Y-Cenin		•		

PARISH	PARISH REGISTERS	BISHOPS' TRANSCRIPTS	BOYD'S MARRIAGE INDEX	PR PRINT-OUTS
Llanbedrog		•		
Llanberis		•		
Llanddeiniolen	•	•		•
Llandegai		•		
Llandegwning		•		•
Llandudno				•
Llandwrog		•		•
Llanengan		•		•
Llanfaglan	•	•		•
Llanfair-Is-Gaer		•		•
Llanfairfechan		•		
Llanfihangel-Bachellaeth		•		•
Llanfihangel-Y-Pennant		•		•
Llangelynin	•			•
Llangian		•		
Llangwnadle		•		
Llangwstennin		•		
Llangybi	•	•		
Llaniestyn	•	•		
Llanllechid		•		
Llanllyfni		•		
Llannor		•		•
Llanrhychwyn		•		•
Llanrug		•		•
Llanwnda	•	•		•
Llanystymdy		•		•
Llysfaen		•		•
Morfa-Nevin		•		
Mylltyern		•		•
Nevin		•		•
Penllech		•		•
Penmachno		•		•
Penmorfa		•		
Pistyll		•		•
Pwllheli		•		
Rhiw				•
Rhiw with Llanfaelrhys		•		•
Trefllys		•		•
Trefriw		•		
Tydweiliog		•		•
Waenfawr		•		
Ynyscynhaiarn		•		•
DENBIGH*				
Abergele	•	•		
Bettws-Abergele		•		
Brymbo		•		
Bryn-Eglwys		•		
Capel-Garmon				•
Cerrig-Y-Druidion		•		

PARISH	PARISH REGISTERS	BISHOPS' TRANSCRIPTS	BOYD'S MARRIAGE INDEX	PR PRINT-OUTS
Chirk		•		
Clocaenog				•
Denbigh		•		•
Derwen		•		•
Efechtyd		•		•
Eglwys-Fach		•		
Erbistock		•		
Gresford		•		
Gwytherin		•		
Gyffylliog	•	•		•
Henllan		•		•
Holt		•		
Isa Clocaenog		•		
Llanarmon		•		
Llanarmon-Dyffryn-Ceirog		•		
Llanarmon-Mynydd-Mawr		•		
Llanbedr-Dyffryn-Clwyd		•		•
Llanddoget		•		
Llanddulas		•		
Llandegla		•		
Lladrillo-Yn-Rhos		•		
Llandyrnog		•		•
Llandysilio		•		
Llanelian		•		
Llanelidan		•		•
Llanfair-Dyffryn-Clwd	•	•		
Llanfair-Talhaiarn		•		
Llanferres		•		•
Llanfwog		•		
Llangadwaladr	•	•		•
Llanganhafal		•		
Llangedwyn		•		
Llangerniew		•		
Llangollen		•		•
Llangwm		•		
Llangwyfan		•		
Llannefydd		•		
Llanrhaiadr-In-Kimnerch		•		
Llanrhaiadr-Yn-Mochnant		•		
Llanrhydd		•		
Llanrwst		•		
Llansaintffraid-Glan-Conway		•		
Llansaintffraid-Glyn-Ceiriog		•		
Llansannan	•	•		•
Llansilin	•	•		•
Llanychan		•		
Llanynys		•		•
Marchwiel		•		
Nantglyn		•		

WALES

* COUNTY / SHIRE

PARISH	PARISH REGISTERS	BISHOPS' TRANSCRIPTS	BOYD'S MARRIAGE INDEX	PR PRINT-OUTS
Pentrevoelas		•		•
Ruabon		•		
Ruthin		•		•
St. George	•	•		•
Ucha Clocaenog		•		
Wrexham		•		
Yspytty		•		
FLINT*				
Bagillt		•		•
Bodfary	•	•		•
Caerwys	•	•		
Cilcen	•	•		•
Cwm		•		
Dymeirchion	•	•		•
Dyserth		•		•
Flint		•		
Gwaenysgor		•		•
Gwernafield		•		•
Halkin		•		•
Hawarden	•			
Holywell		•		•
Hope		•		
Llanasa		•		•
Maylor	•			
Meliden	•	•		•
Mold	•	•		•
Nannerch		•		•
Nerquis		•		•
Newmarket	•	•		•
Northrop				•
Penley		•		
Pont-Blyddyn		•		•
Rhesycae				•
Rhuddlan	•	•		•
St. Asaph	•	•		•
Treddyn		•		
Whitford	•	•		•
Worthenbury		•		•
GLAMORGAN*				
Aberavon	•	•		•
Aberdare	•	•		
Baglan		•		
Barry		•		
Bettws		•		•
Bishopston	•	•		
Blaengwrach		•		
Bonvilston	•	•		•
Briton-Ferry		•		•
Cadoxton		•		•
Cadoxton-Juxta-Barry		•		•
Caerphilly				•
Caira		•		•
Canton		•		•
Cardiff		•		•
Cheriton		•		
Clydach		•		
Cogan		•		•
Colwinstone				•
Cowbridge	•			•
Coychurch		•		•
Coyty		•		•
Dowlais		•		•
Dyffryn		•		
Eglwys-Brewis		•		
Eglwys-Ilan		•		•
Ely		•		
Ewenny		•		
Flemingston	•	•		•
Gelligaer	•	•		•
Gilestown		•		•
Glyn-Corrwg		•		•
Glyntaff		•		
Ilston		•		•
Kenfigg		•		
Kil-Y-Bebyll				•
Kilybebyll		•		
Knelston		•		•
Landough-Juxta-Penarth		•		
Lantwit-Juxta-Neath		•		
Lantwit-Major	•	•		
Lantwit-Vaidre		•		
Lavernock		•		•
Leckwith		•		•
Lisvane		•		
Llanblethian	•	•		•
Llancarvan	•			•
Llandaff		•		•
Llandewy	•	•		•
Llandilo-Talybont		•		
Llandough	•	•		•
Llandough-Juxta-Penarth				•
Llandow		•		•
Llandyfodog				•
Llandyfodwg		•		
Llanedarn		•		
Llanfabon		•		•
Llangafelach	•	•		
Llangan		•		•
Llangeinor	•	•		•
Llangennith		•		•
Llangonoyd		•		•
Llanguick		•		•
Llangyvelach		•		
Llanharan		•		•
Llanhary		•		•
Llanilid		•		•
Llanillterne		•		•
Llanishen		•		•
Llanmadock		•		•
Llanmaes		•		•
Llanmihangel		•		•
Llanrhidian				•
Llanrithan		•		
Llansamlet				•
Llansannor		•		•
Llantrisaint		•		•
Llantrithyd	•	•		•
Llantwit-Major				•
Llanwitfarde				•
Llanwonno		•		•
Llysworney		•		•
Loughor		•		
Loughor Borough				•
Lower Lantwit				•
Maesteg				•
Marcross		•		•
Margam		•		•
Merthyr-Dovan		•		•
Merthyr-Mawr		•		•
Merthyr-Tydvil	•	•		•
Michaelston-Le-Pit		•		•
Michaelston-Super-Avon		•		•
Michaelston-Super-Ely		•		
Monknash		•		•
Mountain-Ash				•
Neath		•		•
Newcastle		•		•
Newton-Nottage		•		
Nicholaston		•		•
Nolton		•		
Oxwich		•		•
Oystermouth	•	•		•
Penarth		•		•
Pendoylan		•		•
Penlline		•		
Penmaen		•		•
Penmark		•		•

WALES

* COUNTY / SHIRE

PARISH	PARISH REGISTERS	BISHOPS' TRANSCRIPTS	BOYD'S MARRIAGE INDEX	PR PRINT-OUTS
Pennard		•		•
Penrice		•		•
Pentyrch		•		•
Peterstone-Super-Ely				•
[illegible]		•		
Peterstone-Super-Ely	•	•		•
Peterstone-Super-Montfm	•			•
Porteynon		•		
Porthkerry		•		
Pyle		•		•
Radyr		•		
Reynoldston		•		
Rhoscilly		•		
Roath		•		
Ruddry		•		
St. Andrew		•		
St. Andrew-Major				•
St. Athan		•		•
St. Brides-Major		•		•
St. Brides-Minor		•		•
St. Brides-Super-Ely		•		•
St. Donats	•	•		•
St. Fagan		•		
St. George		•		
St. Hilary	•	•		
St. Lythan		•		
St. Mary-Hill		•		•
St. Marychurch	•	•		•
St. Nicholas		•		•
Sketty		•		
Skewen		•		
Sully		•		
Swansea	•	•		•
Taibach				•
Tythegston		•		•
Welsh St. Donats	•	•		
Wenvoe	•	•		
Whitchurch		•		
Wick		•		•
Ystradowen		•		
Ystradyfogwd	•	•		
MARIONETH*				
Aberdovey		•		•
Bettws-Gwerfil-Goch		•		
Bontddu		•		
Corris		•		
Corwen		•		•
Dolgelly	•	•		•
Festinog	•	•		

PARISH	PARISH REGISTERS	BISHOPS' TRANSCRIPTS	BOYD'S MARRIAGE INDEX	PR PRINT-OUTS
Gwyddelwern		•		
Llanaber		•		
Llanbedr	•			
Llandanwg	•	•		
[illegible]	•	•		
Llanddwyne		•		
Llandecwyn	•	•		
Llandrillo		•		
Llanegryne		•		
Llanelltyd		•		
Llanenddwyn		•		
Llanfachreth	•	•		•
Llanfair	•	•		•
Llanfawr		•		
Llanfihangel-Glyn-Myeyr	•	•		•
Llanfihangel-Y-Pennant		•		•
Llanfihangel-Y-Traethau	•	•		•
Llanfrothen		•		•
Llangar		•		
Llangelynin	•	•		•
Llangower	•			•
Llansaintffraid-Glyn-Dyfrdwy		•		
Llanuwchllyn		•		
Llanycil	•	•		
Llanymowddwy		•		
Maenwrog	•	•		•
Mallwyd		•		
Pennal		•		•
Penrhyndeudraeth		•		
Talyllyn		•		•
Towyn		•		•
Trawseyndd		•		•
MONTGOMERY*				
Aberhafesp		•		•
Berriew		•		•
Bettws		•		•
Buttington		•		
Carno		•		
Castle-Caereinion		•		
Cemmaes	•			•
Chuchstoke		•		
Darowen		•		•
Garthbeibio		•		•
Guilfield		•		
Hirnant		•		
Hyssington		•		
Kerry		•	•	•
Llanbrynmair	•	•		
Llandinam	•	•		•

PARISH	PARISH REGISTERS	BISHOPS' TRANSCRIPTS	BOYD'S MARRIAGE INDEX	PR PRINT-OUTS
Llandrinio		•		•
Llandysilio		•		
Llandyssil		•		
Llanerfyl		•		•
Llanfair Caereinion		•		
Llanfechan		•		•
Llanfihangel		•		
Llanfihangel-Yn-Ngwynfa				•
Llanfyllin		•		
Llangadean		•		•
Llangurig	•	•		•
Llangyniew		•		
Llangynog		•		
Llanidloes	•	•		•
Llanllugan	•	•		•
Llanllwchaiarn		•		•
Llanmerewig	•	•		•
Llansaintffraid		•		
Llanwddyn	•	•		
Llanwnog	•	•		•
Llanwrin		•		•
Llanwyddelan		•		•
Machynlleth	•	•		•
Manafon		•		
Meifod		•		
Mochdre			•	•
Montgomery		•		
Moughtrey		•		
Newtown	•	•		
Penegoes	•	•		
Pennant		•		•
Penstrowed	•	•		•
Snead	•	•		
Trefeglwys	•	•		•
Tregynon				•
Trelystan		•		
Welshpool		•		•
PEMBROKE*				
Ambelston		•		•
Amroth		•		•
Angle		•		•
Bayvil		•		
Begelly		•		•
Bletherston		•		•
Bosheston		•		•
Boulston		•		•
Brawdy		•		•
Bridell		•		
Burton		•		•

WALES

* COUNTY / SHIRE

PARISH	PARISH REGISTERS	BISHOPS' TRANSCRIPTS	BOYD'S MARRIAGE INDEX	PR PRINT-OUTS	PARISH	PARISH REGISTERS	BISHOPS' TRANSCRIPTS	BOYD'S MARRIAGE INDEX	PR PRINT-OUTS	PARISH	PARISH REGISTERS	BISHOPS' TRANSCRIPTS	BOYD'S MARRIAGE INDEX	PR PRINT-OUTS
Camrose		•		•	Llanhowell		•			Reynoldstone		•		
Carew		•		•	Llanllawer	•	•			Rhoscrowther		•		•
Castellan		•		•	Llanrian		•		•	Robeston-Wathon	•	•		•
Castle-Bythe		•		•	Llanrithan		•		•	Roch		•		•
Castle-Martin		•		•	Llanstadwell		•		•	Rosemarket		•		•
Chapel-Colman		•		•	Llanstinan	•	•		•	Rudbaxton		•		
Clarbeston		•		•	Llantood		•		•	St. Brides		•	•	
Clydey		•		•	Llanwnda	•	•		•	St. Davids		•		•
Cosheston		•		•	Llanycefn		•		•	St. Dogwells	•	•		•
Crinow		•		•	Llanychaer		•		•	St. Edrens		•		•
Crunwear	•	•		•	Llanychlwydog	•	•			St. Elvis		•		•
Dale		•		•	Llawhaden		•			St. Florence		•		•
Dinas	•	•		•	Llysyfran		•		•	St. Ishmaels		•		•
East Walton		•		•	Loveston		•			St. Issells				•
Eglwys-Wrw		•		•	Ludchurch		•		•	St. Lawrence		•		•
Fishguard	•	•		•	Maenclochog		•			St. Nicholas		•		•
Ford		•			Manerdivy		•			St. Petrox		•		•
Freystrop		•		•	Manorbier	•	•		•	St. Twinell		•		
Granston	•	•			Manordeifi				•	Slebech		•		
Gumereston		•		•	Manorowen	•	•			Solva		•		•
Harroldston-St. Issells		•		•	Marloes		•		•	Spittal		•		
Hasguard		•		•	Martlewy		•		•	Stackpole-Elidor		•		•
Haverfordwest	•	•		•	Mathry		•		•	Talbenny		•		
Hays-Castle		•			Meline	•	•			Templeton		•		•
Henry's Moat		•		•	Minwere		•			Tenby		•		•
Herbrandston		•		•	Monachlogddu		•		•	Treffgarn		•		•
Hodgeston		•		•	Monckton		•		•	Uzmaston		•		
Hubberston		•		•	Monington		•			Walwins-Castle				•
Jeffreston				•	Morvil		•		•	Warren		•		
Johnston		•			Moylgrove		•			West Harroldston		•		•
Jordanston		•		•	Narberth	•	•		•	West Robeson		•		•
Kilgerran		•		•	Nash		•		•	West Walton		•		•
Lambston		•		•	Nevern	•	•		•	Whitchurch		•		•
Lampeter-Velfrey		•		•	New Moat		•		•	Whitechurch		•		•
Lamphey		•		•	Newport	•	•		•	Williamston		•		
Lawrenny		•		•	Nolton		•		•	Wiston		•		•
Letterston		•			NorthNewton		•			Wolfsdale				•
LitleNewcastle		•		•	Pembroke		•		•	Yerbeston		•		•
Llandeloy		•		•	Pembroke-Dolk		•		•	**RADNOR***				
Llandewy-Velfrey		•		•	Pembroke-St. Mary		•			Abbeycwmhir			•	•
Llandilo		•			Penally		•		•	Aberdw			•	•
Llandissilio	•			•	Penrith		•			Beguildy	•	•		•
Llanfair-Nant-Gwyn		•		•	Penrydd				•	Bettws-Disserth			•	
Llanfair-Nant-Y-Gof		•			Pontfaen		•		•	Bleddfa		•	•	•
Llanfallteg		•			Prendergast		•			Boughrood		•	•	•
Llanfihangel-Penbedw		•		•	Puncheston		•		•	Bryngwyn		•	•	•
Llanfyrnach		•		•	Pwllcrochan		•		•	Cascob		•	•	•
Llangolman		•			Redbourn		•		•	Cefnllys	•	•	•	•
Llangwm		•			Reynalton				•	Clro		•	•	•

WALES
* COUNTY / SHIRE

PARISH	PARISH REGISTERS	BISHOPS' TRANSCRIPTS	BOYD'S MARRIAGE INDEX	PR PRINT-OUTS
Colva		•		•
Cregizina		•	•	•
Cwm-Toyddwr		•		
Discoed	•	•		
Disserth	•		•	•
Gladestry		•	•	•
Glasbury		•	•	•
Glascwm		•	•	•
Heyop		•	•	•
Knighton		•		
Llananno		•	•	•
Llanbadarn-Fawr		•	•	•
Llanbadarn-Fynydd		•	•	•
Llanbadarn-Garreg		•	•	•
Llanbedr-Painscastle		•	•	•
Llanbister		•	•	•
Llandegley		•	•	
Llandewey-Ystradenny		•	•	•
Llandewyfach		•		
Llandilo-Graban		•	•	
Llandrindod		•	•	
Llanelwedd		•	•	
Llanfihangel-Helygen		•	•	
Llanfihangel-Rydithon		•	•	
Llangunllo		•	•	
Llansaintffraed-In-Elvel			•	
Llansaintfraid Cwmteuddwr			•	
Llanstephan		•		
Llanvareth		•	•	
Llanvihangel-Nantmellan		•	•	
Llanyre		•	•	
Llowes		•	•	
Michaelchurch		•		
Michaelchurch-On-Arrow	•			
Nantmel		•	•	•
New Radnor	•			
Newchurch	•		•	
Norton		•		
Old Radnor	•	•		•
Penybont				•
Pillith		•	•	
Presteigne	•	•		
Rhayader		•	•	
Rhulen		•		
St. Harmon		•	•	
Whitton		•	•	

Chapter 16

Ireland

Johni Cerny and Wendy L. Elliott

Historical Background

Early	Celtic people, called the Pretani or Cruithin, arrive from Britain and locate mainly in east Ulster. The Loiges, another branch of the Cruithin, live in the midlands.
c.500 B.C.	Second group of Celts arrive; branches spread from Antrim to Kerry. Erainn from Britain settle in the south of Ireland, then conquer rest of Ireland.
c.250	Laigin from Armorica in northwestern France arrive in southeast Ireland.
c.50	Gaeil or Goidets migrate from Europe and disembark at the Kenmare River in south Kerry and the Boyne estuary near present-day Drogheda.
c. A.D.432	First Christian missionary, Patrick, arrives at Tara in Meath.
c.450	The main stronghold occupying the site of present-day Ulster is destroyed during war with inhabitants of Northern Ireland.
795	Vikings land near St. Columcille's monastery on Lambay Island.
800-50	Norwegian Vikings plunder Irish monasteries.
845	Thorgils, king of the Norsemen in Ireland, is captured and killed by Maelseachlainn, king of Meath.
853	Danish fleet defeats Norwegians and takes possession at Dublin.
1014	Irish defeat Norwegian and Danish forces at Clontarf.
1066	William the Conqueror becomes king of England.
1169	First Norman settlers arrive in County Wicklow, accompanied by 300 soldiers from southern Wales.
1169	Invaders are turned back by the Danes of Waterford.
1550s	British Queen Mary encourages English settlements.
1600s	English and Scottish settlements are made in Ulster on land confiscated by the British throne.
1603	Thousands from the Scottish lowlands migrate to Ulster and counties Antrim and Down.
1641	Cromwell's army defeats rebellion in Ireland and confiscates property exceeding two and a half million acres.
1652	A list of inhabitants of most of the southern part of County Dublin is assembled.
1654-56	A civil survey is recorded of major landholders and their precedessors of 1641.
c.1659	A census of all large and some small landowners.
1663-66	Hearth money rolls registered for property owners.
1685-1705	French Huguenots seek asylum in Ireland.
1691	Treaty of Limerick penalizes public worship for Catholics and Presbyterians.
1702	Partial lists of male householders for Kilkenny enumerated separately by religious denomination and parish.
1708	Registry of Deeds established.
1709	Over 6,500 Palatines leave war-torn "Germany" and settle in Ireland.
1740	Protestant householders in counties Antrim,

	Armagh, Donegal, Londonderry, and Tyrone are recorded.
1749	A census of most of County Roscommon, part of County Sligo, and nine parishes of County Galway.
1750	Catholic inhabitants of County Tipperary taxed.
1757	Military oaths of allegiance registered.
1766	Rectors of the Church of Ireland record householders by parish, indicating religion and other details. Only records for North Cork and the counties of Limerick, Londonderry, Louth, Tipperary, and Wicklow survive.
1802-83	Census of Protestant parishioners; records of twenty-eight parishes survive.
1821	Population census is enumerated; most volumes destroyed by fire in 1922.
1824-38	Tithe applotments (tax lists) compiled.
1829	Emancipation Act lifts penalties for Catholics and Presbyterians.
1837	Vital registration begins.
1838	Poor Relief for Ireland enacted.
1840s	Great Famine; many emigrate.
1846	Cartographic study of Ireland completed, forms the basis of standardized county boundaries.
1848-64	A householder list compiled of every householder and land owner/renter.
1850	Tenant-Right League founded. Goals: fair rent, fixity of tenure, and free sale.
1851	Government census; few returns survived the 1922 fire.
1852	Tenement Act provides for a uniform evaluation of property for tax purposes.
1858	Probate act changes jurisdiction from the Church of Ireland to the newly established Court of Probate.
1861-71	Censuses taken in 1861 and 1871 are destroyed by order of the government.
1868	Irish Reform Bill passes British Parliament, allows a million more men the right to vote.
1869	Disestablishment Act deprives the Irish Church of property and authority.
1870	Irish Land Act provides protection for tenants.
1898	The administrative counties are formed.
1901	Earliest extant census.
1911	Second surviving census.
1916	Great Easter Rebellion suppressed by British.
1917	Irish Republic adopts a constitution.
1921	By Irish-British treaty, Irish Free State becomes an independent member of the British Commonwealth.
1922	Public Record Office and Four Courts fire destroys many irreplaceable records.
1948	Republic of Ireland Act establishes Ireland as free and separate from Britain.

Settlement and Migration

Celtic migration from Britain began as early as 500 B.C. with invasions into northern and southern Ireland. By 300 B.C., Gallic tribes from present-day Normandy in France added a substantial number of settlements. The early people of Ireland continued to be consistently Celtic until the ninth century when a new ethnic group was added by Viking settlements.

The Danes invaded the land in 853 after defeating the Viking Norsemen. Danish settlers developed commercial trade at Cork, Limerick, Waterford, and Wexford. But constant conflict led to a decisive confrontation in 1014 between the Celts and Danes/Vikings. The united Gaelic military defeated the Norwegian and Danish armies.

After defeating the British in 1066, a century passed before the first Normans migrated to Ireland. Between 1169 and 1172, many of these settlers arrived in County Wexford. From this area, the Normans spread into other areas of Ireland and, by 1250, had settlements in most areas of the island. Welsh immigrants arriving with the Normans eventually contributed settlements.

Queen Mary of Britain encouraged English colonies in Ireland during the 1550s. Using a method of settlement called plantation, English newcomers ousted long-established Irish families in the most fertile areas of the country. Enormous tracts of land in Cork, Kerry, Limerick, Tipperary, and Waterford were confiscated by the English authorities after an unsuccessful rebellion. Land was leased for a penny per acre to those who migrated from England.

In 1598, an Irish rebellion against the English began. Promised Spanish help failed to appear in 1596, 1597, and 1599; assistance in 1601 was too late. After hostilities ceased, King James of Scotland encouraged his subjects to migrate to Ireland by offering unlimited amounts of land at the minimal cost of six pence per acre beginning in 1603.

In 1641, in a desperate attempt to achieve independence, another rebellion began in Ireland. It was put down by Cromwell's forces who confiscated more than 2.5 million acres of Irish lands. By the end of the seventeenth century, a mere 15 percent of Irish land remained in Irish hands. Additionally, in the early 1700s, Ulster lands were confiscated and offered to colonists from England and the Scottish lowlands.

Beginning in the late 1600s, French Huguenots fled religious persecution in their homeland for the relative safety of other countries; some settled in Ireland. The largest group arrived between 1685 and 1705. After a few years, some of the transplanted French Huguenots left for America.

Over 800 Palatinates migrated to Ireland in 1709, but over 200 of these families left Ireland for Britain between April and December 1710.

During the 1840s, thousands of Irish families left their homes for America, driven out by the devastating Irish potato famine. Individuals and families poured into New

York and Boston as well as other American ports. Some arrived at New Orleans and followed the Mississippi River north into the midwestern states.

Between 1881 and 1901, Irish censuses confirm that the Jewish population increased almost ten times. Large migrations from Lithuania, Poland, and Russia increased the numbers significantly during this period.

Irish Records

Irish records of genealogical interest were created within the townland, parish, barony, and county administrative jurisdictions. A thorough understanding of those jurisdictions and Irish historical geography is necessary to use Irish record sources. The *Alphabetical Index to the Townlands and Towns of Ireland* (FHL# 941.5/X2ci or microfilm 476999, or microfiche 6020345-6020353) issued by Ireland's Registrar General (Dublin: Alexander Thom, 1877) is the most comprehensive Irish place-name gazetteer available.

Modern Ireland consists of four provinces which constitute the country's largest administrative jurisdictions : Ulster, Munster, Leinster, and Connacht. Prior to the Norman arrival in 1169, there were five provinces, or ancient political divisions, called "fifths." These jurisdictions became provinces after the English became involved in Ireland's administrative affairs toward the end of the fifteenth century.

From the fifth through the eleventh centuries, monastaries governed church administration in Ireland. By 1152, four ecclesiastical provinces had been created: Armagh, Cashel, Dublin, and Taum. Each ecclesiastical province was headed by an archbishop who supervised twenty-two dioceses. Diocese boundaries followed ancient Irish tribal territorial lines.

The English county/shire system was established in Ireland prior to 1211 and developed into the country's local government jurisdiction. Three shires existed before that date: Dublin, Waterford, and Munster. Waterford encompassed Cork and Munster covered Limerick, Tipperary, and Thomond. Shires were administered by sheriffs who convened courts, collected taxes, maintained highways and bridges, and enforced laws.

There are 273 baronies in Ireland today, each one representing one or more geographic units within a county. Initially, a barony was viewed as a tax unit. Some were named after ancient families or tribes.

Irish parishes are ecclesiastical divisions administered by the church. Each parish has a priest. Initially, early Christian churches established parish boundaries, but they were redefined into civil parishes and parochial parishes during the Reformation. In some instances, a civil parish consisted of one or more parochial parishes which could cross barony and county boundaries. Catholic parishes, however, always observed county boundaries. For civil and Catholic parishes between 1800 and 1900, see:

Lewis, Samuel. *A Topographical Dictionary of Ireland.* 2d. ed., London: S. Lewis, 1847. (FHL# 941.5/E51/1847)

Townlands are the smallest geographic division in Ireland. All larger divisions are groups of its 64,000 townlands. The contemporary townland represents a great variety of units of measurement which were used locally to identify lands, including ancient ploughlands, quarters, cartrons, gneeves, trines, and tates. Tithe applotment (tax) books and later valuations (tax assessments) used the townland as the smallest administrative division.

Ireland Library Collection

Archives and Libraries

The library has a long list of titles offering information about archive and library holdings in Great Britain. The following list includes only a few titles. See Family History Library Catalog (FHLC) heading **Ireland/Archives and Libraries** and **Ireland/Archives and Libraries/Inventories, Registers, Catalogs** for a complete list.

Choille, Breandan MacGiolla. *Sources for Family History in the Public Record Office of Ireland.* Salt Lake City: Corporation of the President of the Church of Jesus Christ of Latter-day Saints, 1980. In Proceedings of the World Conference on Records: Preserving Our Heritage, Vol. 5, British Family and Local History, Part 1, Ser. 402.) See FHLC for call number.

Goodbody, Olive C. *Guide to Irish Quaker Records, 1654-1860.* Dublin: Stationery Office for Irish Manuscript Commission, 1967. (FHL# 941.5/A2q)

Crick, B. R., and Miriam Alman. *A Guide to Manuscripts Relating to America in Great Britain and Ireland.* London: Oxford University Press, 1961. (FHL# 973/A3cg)

Northern Ireland Public Record Office. *Calendar of Government Documents.* 82 reels. Salt Lake City: Genealogical Society of Utah, 1978.

See FHLC heading **Ireland/Archives and Libraries/Inventories, Registers, Catalogs** for call numbers. Contains documents pertaining to bankruptcy guardianship, minute books, crown lands, title deeds, housing, schools, and valuations (taxes).

Public Record Office of Ireland. *Report of the Deputy Keeper of the Records.* Dublin: Stationary Office, 1891. Additional reports 1895, 1899, 1928, 1931, 1936, 1951. See FHLC heading **Ireland/Archives and Libraries** for call numbers.

______. *Inventory of Wills and Administrations, 1612-1900.* 32 reels. Salt Lake City: Genealogical Society of Utah, 1950-51. See FHLC for call numbers.

Includes index to unproved wills, administration bonds, prerogative and diocesan wills from various registers, and original wills, 1630-1900.

Public Record Office of Northern Ireland. *Catalogue of Original Documents and Transcript of Documents on File in the Belfast Public Record Office.* 26 reels. Salt Lake City: Genealogical Society of Utah, 1960. (FHL# microfilm 0258728-0258761)

Report of the Deputy Keeper of the Records. Belfast: Stationery Office, 1929. Additional reports 1924-45, 1946-53, 1938-59. See FHLC heading **Ireland/Archives and Libraries.**

Bibliography

Clare, Wallace. *A Simple Guide to Irish Genealogy.* 3rd ed., revised by Rosemary Folliott. London: Irish Genealogical Research Society, 1966. (FHL# 929.1415/C541s)

Eager, Alan R. *A Guide to Irish Bibliographical Material: A Bibliography of Irish Bibliographies and Sources of Information.* Cornwall: Public Libraries Group Publications, 1980. (FHL#941.5/A3e)

Hayes, Richard J. *Manuscript Sources for the History of Irish Civilization.* 11 vols., 5 reels. Boston: G. K. Hall and Co., 1965. (FHL# microfilm 1440939-1440943)

Magee, Peggy. *Bibliography of Genealogical Sources for the Counties of the Republic of Ireland.* Santa Ana, Calif.: Magee, 1982. (FHL# 942.5/A3c) See FHLC heading Ireland/Bibliography for additional holdings.

Biography

The library collection includes a large number of titles about Irish biography in addition to those noted below. See FHLC heading **Ireland/Biography** for a complete list.

Chalmers, Alexander. *The General Biographical Dictionary.* 32 vols. London: J. Nichols, 1812. (FHL# 920.042/C353g) Arranged alphabetically, each volume indexed.

Crone, John S. *A Concise Dictionary of Irish Biography.* Dublin: Talbot Press, 1928. (FHL# 941.5/D3cr) Rev. ed. Nendeln, Liechtenstein: Kraus, 1970. (FHL# 941.5/-D3cr/1970)

Webb, Alfred. *A Compendium of Irish Biography: Comprising Sketches of Distinguished Irishmen, and of Eminent Persons Connected with Ireland by Office or by Their Writings.* 4 vols. Dublin: M. H. Gill, 1878. (FHL# 941.5/D3 or microfilm 0990292)

Business Records and Commerce

Cullen, L. M. *Merchants, Ships, and Trade, 1660-1830.* Dublin: Gill and Macmillan, 1971. (FHL# 942.5/U3c)

See FHLC heading **Ireland/Business Records and Commerce** for other listings.

Census Records

Irish census schedules are a hodge-podge of record fragments beginning with the 1630 listing of men between the age of sixteen and fifty whom large landlords could produce in the event of armed conflict. While muster rolls are related to military service, this particular roll is considered a census by Irish record-keepers.

The library has the *Index to Muster Roll, 1630* (Salt Lake City: Genealogical Society of Utah, 1984). Microfilm of typescript at the Armagh County Museum, Armagh. (FHL# microfilm 1279356, item 11).

Between 1630 and 1821, Ireland compiled a number of registers, partial censuses, and surveys; however, they are incomplete and not used widely.

Pender, Seamus, ed. *A Census of Ireland, Circa 1659: With Supplementary Material from the Poll Money Ordinances (1660-1661).* Dublin: Stationery Office, 1938. (FHL# 941.5/X29c or microfilm 0923638)

Genison, Groves. *Religious Census of 1766.* Salt Lake City: Genealogical Society of Utah, 1949. (FHL# microfilm 0100173, items 1 and 2)

Microfilm copy of original typescript of the Genealogical Department, Dublin, Ireland. Census returns for counties Tyrone, Londonderry, Antrim, Fermanagh, Tipperary, Longford, Louth, Meath, Kings, Wicklow, Cork, Limerick, Armagh, Dublin, Wexford, and Cavan.

The first comprehensive, nationwide census was authorized on 28 May 1821, but most of it burned at Four Courts in 1922. The library has microfilm copies of original records at the Ireland Census Office, Dublin:

Ireland Census Office. *1821 Census.* 17 reels. Salt Lake City: Genealogical Society of Utah, 1951-69.

Fragments of the census for counties Cavan, Fermanagh, Galway, Meath, and Offaly. See FHLC heading **Ireland/Census/1821** for call numbers.

The 1831 Irish census also burned in the 1922 fire at Four Courts; however, some County Londonderry parishes survived and are in the Public Record Office. Only the 1841 census of Killashandra parish, County Cavan, survived the 1922 fire, all of which were filmed:

Ireland Census Office. *1841 Census.* 8 reels. Salt Lake City: Genealogical Society of Utah, 1969. (FHL# microfilm 0100831-0100838)

Microfilm of original records in the Ireland Census Office, Dublin, of Killashandra Parish, County Cavan.

A sizeable number of original 1851 census returns for parishes in County Antrim survive:

Ireland Census Office. *1851 Census.* 19 reels. Salt Lake City: Genealogical Society of Utah, 1969.

Microfilm of original records in the Ireland Census Office, Dublin, of County Antrim and Drumkeeran parish in County Fermanagh. See FHLC heading **Ireland/Census/1851** for call numbers.

The 1861 and 1871 Irish censuses were destroyed by government order, leaving the 1901 census as the earliest complete enumeration in existence. Arranged by county, district, electoral division, and townland (see *Irish Records* above for Irish geographical divisions), the 1901 census gives the following information: name, age, religion, occupation, ability to read and write, marital status, relationship to householder, county of birth (country if not born in Ireland), and ability to speak English and/or Irish.

Ireland Census Office. *1901 Irish Census.* 1,173 reels. Salt Lake City: Genealogical Society of Utah, 1968.

Microfilm of original records at the Public Records Office in Dublin. See FHLC heading **Ireland/Census** for film numbers.

Census Indexes

British Reference Staff for the Genealogical Department. *Ireland 1901 Census Street Index.* 3 vols. Salt Lake City: Church of Jesus Christ of Latter-day Saints Genealogical

Department, 1982. (FHL# 941.5/X22i or microfilm 0994078, item 2, 1440978, item 9)

Listing of Genealogical Department microfilm numbers for the 1901 Census of Ireland, arranged alphabetically by street name. Includes Belfast, Dublin, Cork, Limerick, Londonderry, and Waterford.

Registrar General of Ireland. *General Alphabetical Index to the Townland and Towns, Parishes, and Baronies of Ireland: Based on the Census of Ireland for the Year 1851.* 1861; rpt. ed., Baltimore: Genealogical Publishing Co., 1984. (FHL# 941.5/X22g)

_____. *Alphabetical Index to the Townlands and Towns of Ireland.* Dublin: Alexander Thom, 1877. (FHL# 941.5/X2ci or microfilm 0476999, or microfiche 6020345-6020353) Photocopy of microreproduction.

Shows the areas of the townlands, county, barony, parish, poor law union, and poor law electoral division in which townlands and towns were situated in 1871. Includes separate indexes of the parishes, baronies, poor law unions, poor law electoral divisions, dispensary districts, petty sessions districts, and parliamentary boroughs of Ireland.

Census/Inventories, Registers, Catalogs

Library Staff of the Genealogical Society, comp. *Register of Ireland Census and Census Substitutes.* Salt Lake City: Church of Jesus Christ of Latter-day Saints Genealogical Department, 1985. (British Register Table FHL# 941.5/X23c)

Church Directories

The Irish Catholic Directory, 1838. Dublin: John Mullany, 1838. (FHL# 941.5/K24i)

Library also has 1862, 1873, 1881, 1889, 1890, 1900, and 1952 editions. Title varies: *Battersby's Catholic Directory, Almanac, and Registry of the Whole Catholic World, The Irish Catholic Directory, Almanac and Registry.* See FHLC heading **Ireland/Church Directories** for complete list of call numbers.

Irish Church Directory and Yearbook. Dublin: Church of Ireland Printing, 1865. (FHL# 941.5/K24icd/1865)

Title and publisher vary for 1875-1960 editions. (1952, 1954 editions FHL# microfilm 0897021, items 3-5; 1875, 1876, 1885, 1886, 1887, 1891, 1892 editions FHL# microfilm 1140983, items 1-7; 1895, 1897, 1910, 1920, 1930, 1940, 1950, 1960 editions FHL# microfilm 1440984, items 1-8).

See FHLC heading **Ireland/Church Directories** for additional holdings.

Church History

A List of the Names of the Popish Priests throughout the Several Counties in the Kingdom of Ireland, 1703. Salt Lake City: Genealogical Society of Utah, 1984. (FHL# microfilm 1279295, item 9)

Microfilm of original manuscript located at the County Leitrim Library, Ballinamore.

Adair, Patric. *A True Narrative of the Rise and Progress of the Presbyterian Church in Ireland.* Belfast: C. Aitchison, 1866. (FHL# 941.5/K2at)

Ball, J. T. *The Reformed Church of Ireland, 1537-1886.* London: Longmans, Green, 1886. (FHL# 941.5/K2b)

King, Robert. *A Primer of the History of the Holy Catholic Church in Ireland from the Introduction of Christianity to the Formation of the Modern Irish Branch of the Church of Rome.* 3rd ed. Dublin: M'glashan, Gill, 1851. (FHL# 941.5/K2k/Vol.2/1851)

Mant, Richard. *History of the Church of Ireland from the Reformation to the Revolution.* 2 vols. 2d ed., London: J. W. Parker, 1841. (FHL# 941.5/K2m or microfilm 0873963, item 2 and 0873964, item 1)

Parish Guide to the Archdiocese of Dublin. Dublin: C. J. Fallon, Ltd., 1958. (FHL# 941.5/K2pg)

Phillips, Randall C. *Irish Methodism.* London: Charles H. Kelly, 1897. (FHL# 941.5/K2prc or microfilm 0990494)

Phillips, Walter Alison, ed. *History of the Church of Ireland: from the Earliest Times to the Present Day.* 3 vols. London: Oxford University Press, 1933. (FHL# 941.5/-K2ph)

Reid, James Seaton. *History of the Presbyterian Church in Ireland.* 3 vols. 2d ed. Belfast: Whittaker, 1853. (FHL# 941.5/K2r/1853 or microfilm 0824282, item 4, and 0824283)

Smiles, Samuel. *The Huguenots: Their Settlements, Churches, and Industries in England and Ireland.* London: J. Murray, 1876. (FHL# 942/K21s or microfilm 0990298, item 3)

Sutcliffe, Joseph. *The History of Methodism Comprising the Life and Labours of Rev. John Wesley, A. M. and the People Under His Care Brought Down to the Present Time.* 4 vols. N.p.: Micro Methods, 1969. (FHL# Vols. 1-2, 1709-79, microfilm 0969920; Vols. 3-4, 1779-1823, microfilm 0969921)

White, B. R., ed. *Association Records of the Particular Baptists of England, Wales, and Ireland to 1660.* 4 vols. London: Baptist Historical Society, 1971-77. (FHL# 942/K2wh or microfilm 1239054, item 8)

The library has a large collection of church histories in the Irish collection cataloged under **Ireland/Church History.**

Church Records

Ireland has been home to people of all faiths; however, the predominant religions have been and still are Catholicism and the Church of Ireland. Huguenots, Quakers, Baptists, Presbyterians (the Scotch-Irish who arrived in 1613, many of whom migrated to America during the eighteenth century), and others created records about their members in Ireland.

Baptisms, marriages, and burials were recorded in local parish registers in Ireland. Catholic records extend back to 1680 in some cities, and registers in some Mayo and Donegal parishes date from 1850. Because of widespread illiteracy, the majority of parish registers date from about 1770. Record-keeping was hampered further by penal laws enacted after the Treaty of

Limerick in 1691 which forbade Catholics and Presbyterians from public worship. Still, a significant number of parish registers and other church records can be used to trace Irish ancestors.

The library has a sizeable collection of Irish church records, but the majority are not yet microfilmed and can be searched only at the parish house or by an agent in Ireland. See FHLC heading **Ireland/Church Records** for holdings not listed below.

Betham, Sir William. *Betham's Genealogical Abstracts of Prerogative Marriage Licenses, 1629-1810.* 16 vols. Salt Lake City: Genealogical Society of Utah, 1969. (FHL# microfilm 0100874-0100875) Handwritten manuscript in the Public Record Office in Dublin.

Catholic Church. *Calender of Rolls of Converts, 1703-1838 and Catholic Qualification Rolls Index, 1793-1796.* 3 reels. Salt Lake City: Genealogical Society of Utah, 1969. (FHL# microfilm 0597103-0597105) Original records at the Public Record Office in Dublin.

Costello, M. A. *De Annatis Hiberniae: A Calendar of the First Fruits' Fees Levied on Papal Appointment to Benefices in Ireland, A.D. 1400-1535.* Dundalk, Ireland: W. Tempest, 1909. (FHL# 941.5/K2i) The library has only Volume 1, Ulster.

Deane, J. L. B. *Church of Ireland Handbook: A Guide to the Organisation of the Church.* Dublin: A. P. C. K, 1962. (FHL# 941.5/K27d)

Goodbody, Olive C. *Guide to Irish Quaker Records, 1654-1860.* Dublin: Stationery Office for Irish Manuscript Commission, 1967. (FHL# 941.5/A2q)

Grovers, Tenison. *Genealogical Collection of Muster Rolls, Householders, Wills, Deeds, Parish Registers.* 54 reels. Salt Lake City: Genealogical Society of Utah, 1959. (FHL# microfilm 0258471-0258524) Original handwritten and typed records in the Public Record Office, Belfast.

Irish Parish Register. N.p.: n.pub., n.d. (British Reference Area FHL# 941.5/K2ip)

Includes a list of counties, parishes, denominations (Roman Catholic, Church of Ireland or Presbyterian), and dates registers begin.

List of Irish Catholic Church Records Filmed in the National Library of Ireland. N.p: n.pub., n.d. (British Reference Area FHL# 941.5/K22r or microfilm 0990442) Lists the dioceses, parishes, record types, and dates covered.

Mettam, Zara. *Northern Ireland Marriages, 18th-19th Century.* 2 vols. Typescript, n.d. (FHL# 941.6/K29m)

Public Record Office of Northern Ireland. *Transcript of Documents on File in the Belfast Public Record Office.* 79 reels. Salt Lake City: Genealogical Society of Utah, 1960.

Original records at the Belfast Public Record Office. See FHLC heading **Ireland/Church Records** for complete list of microfilm numbers. Includes abstracts of wills, leases, bonds, memorials, deeds, militia and commission registers, voters, school registers, rent rolls, genealogical notes, etc.

Simington, Robert C. *The Civil Survey, A.D. 1654-1656.* 10 vols. Dublin: Stationery Office, 1931-45. (FHL# 941.5/R2si or microfilm 0973121-0973124)

Society of Friends (Ireland). *Transcripts of the Records of the Society of Friends, 1858-1949.* Salt Lake City: Genealogical Society of Utah, 1969. (FHL# microfilm 0571399)

Contains births, marriages, and deaths arranged in alphabetical order by years.

See also the FHLC under **Ireland/Church Records** for additional titles.

Church Records/Indexes

Matthews, George F., ed. *Contemporary Index to Printed Parish and Non-Parochial Registers.* London: John Matthews, 1908. (FHL# 942/V26m or microfilm 0496825)

Public Record Office of Ireland. *Index to Diocesan Marriage Licenses of Ireland.* Salt Lake City: Genealogical Society of Utah, 1951. (FHL# microfilm 0100859-0100873)

See also FHLC heading **Ireland/Church Records/Inventories, Registers, Catalogs** for additional holdings.

Civil Registration

Ireland began national registration of births, marriages, and deaths in 1864. The Genealogical Society of Utah has microfilmed a large collection of Irish civil registration records.

General Registry Office. *Births, 1942-1947.* 36 reels. Salt Lake City: Genealogical Society of Utah, 1960.

See FHLC heading **Ireland/Civil Registration** for call numbers.

_____. *Births, 1864-1955.* 1,031 reels. Salt Lake City: Genealogical Society of Utah, 1953-54, 1960-61.

Includes index for 1864-1920. See FHLC heading **Ireland/Civil Registration** for call numbers. Microfilm of original records in Custom House, Dublin.

_____. *Deaths, 1864-1921.* 153 reels. Salt Lake City: Genealogical Society of Utah, 1953.

Microfilm of original records in Custom House, Dublin. Includes index for 1864-1921. See FHLC heading **Ireland/Civil Registration** for microfilm numbers.

_____. *Marriages, 1845-1870.* 334 reels. Salt Lake City: Genealogical Society of Utah, 1953.

Original records in Custom House, Dublin. Includes index for 1845-1921 and marriage records for 1845-70. See FHLC heading **Ireland/Civil Registration** for microfilm numbers.

Northern Ireland General Registry Office. *Births, 1922-1959.* 214 reels. Salt Lake City: Genealogical Society of Utah, 1959.

Original records in Fermanagh House, Belfast. Includes index for 1922-59. See **Ireland/Civil Registration** for microfilm numbers.

_____. *Deaths, 1922-1959.* Salt Lake City: 167 reels. Genealogical Society of Utah, 1959-60.

Original records in Fernamagh House, Belfast. Includes index for 1922-59. See FHLC heading **Ireland/-Civil Registration** for microfilm numbers.

_____. *Marriages, 1922-1959.* 304 reels. Salt Lake City: Genealogical Society of Utah, 1960.

Original records in Fermanagh House, Belfast. See FHLC heading **Ireland/Civil Registration** for microfilm numbers.

Prerogative Marriage Licenses of Ireland, 1629-1858. Salt Lake City: Genealogical Society of Utah, 1949. (FHL# microfilm 0100167, item 3, and 0100168) Handwritten extracts at the Genealogical Department, Dublin.

Civil Registration/Indexes

General Registry Office. *General Index of Births, Marriages, and Deaths Registered in Saorstat Eireann, 1922-1958.* 42 reels. Salt Lake City: Genealogical Society of Utah, 1953.

Original records in the Custom House, Dublin. See FHLC heading **Ireland/Civil Registration/Indexes** for microfilm numbers.

Civil Registration/Inventories, Registers, Catalogs

Church of Jesus Christ of Latter-day Saints Genealogical Department. *Register of Ireland General Registry Office Births, Marriages, and Deaths, 1845-1959.* Salt Lake City: Genealogical Department, 1978. (British Register Table FHL# 941.5/V2vr or microfiche 6020283-6020284)

Typescript list of the library's copies of Irish birth, marriage, and death records from 1845-1959, including call numbers.

Court Records

Ayloffe, Sir Joseph. *Calendars of the Ancient Charters, and of the Welch and Scottish Rolls, Now Remaining in the Tower of London.* London: Printed for B. White, 1774. (FHL# 942/H23a)

Chancery Court and Exchequer Bills. Salt Lake City: Genealogical Society of Utah, 1950, 1959. (FHL# microfilm 0100240, item 5, and 0257820, items 1-2)

Original transcripts in The Castle, Dublin, and the Genealogical Department, Dublin.

Public Record Office. *Calendar of the Justiciary Rolls or Proceedings in the Court of Justiciar of Ireland.* Dublin: Stationery Office. (FHL# 941.5/P2jm) Includes records, 1295-1314.

Description and Travel

The library has a significant collection of guides to traveling in Ireland which describe the country or a region. See library heading **Ireland/Description and Travel** and **Ireland/Description and Travel/Guide Books** for a complete list of titles.

Directories

Irish directories are similar to those produced in the United States and can be grouped into four types: Dublin city directories, directories of provincial towns, country-wide directories, and professional directories.

The Belfast and Provence of Ulster Directory. Belfast: J. A. Henderson, 1852. Vol. 1 (1852) (FHL# 941.6/E4b or microfilm 0908815). Vol. 2 (1854), Vol. 4 (1858-59), Vol. 6 (1863-64), and Vol. 10 (1880) (FHL# microfilm 0908816-0908819)

Business Directory of Belfast and Principal Towns in the Province of Ulster for 1865-66. Belfast: R. W. Wynne, 1865. (FHL# 941.5/E4bd)

Kelly's Directory of Ireland, 1905. London: Kelly Directories, 1905.

Leet, Ambrose. *A Directory to the Market Towns, Villages, Gentlemen's Seats, and Other Noted Places in Ireland.* 2d ed. Dublin: Brett Smith, 1814. (FHL# 941.5/E4Le/1814 or microfilm 099023, item 2)

Thom's Irish Almanac and Official Directory. 37 vols. Dublin: A. Thom, 1844-80. The library has 1851, 1853, 1868 editions. (FHL# 941.5/E4th or microfilm 0990103, item 2, 0990104, item 1, 0990105, item 2, 0990110)

Thom's Official Directory of Ireland. Dublin: A. Thom, 1930. (FHL# 941.5/E4th or microfilm 0990104, item 2, 0990105, item 1)

Thom's Official Directory of the United Kingdom of Great Britain and Ireland. Dublin: Alex Thom, 1901, 1909. Printed annually from 1881. Library has paper copy of 1901 and 1915 editions (FHL# 941.5/E4th); and 1901 and 1909 on microfilm. (FHL# microfilm 0990119-0990120)

Emigration and Immigration

18th Century Ulster Emigration to North America. Belfast: Her Majesty's Stationer's Office for the Public Record Office of Northern Ireland, 1972. (FHL# 941.5/H29ed/no.7)

Adams, William Forbes. *Ireland and Irish Emigration to the New World from 1815 to the Famine.* 1932; rpt. ed., Baltimore, Md.: Genealogical Publishing Company, 1980. (FHL# 970/W2a)

Andrea, Leonardo. *Immigrants from Great Britain to South Carolina, 1763-1773.* Salt Lake City: Genealogical Society of Utah, 1974. (FHL# microfilm 954250, item 10)

Byrne, Stephen. *Irish Emigration to the United States.* 1969; rpt. ed., New York: Catholic Publication Society, 1973. (FHL# 973/B4ai/Vol.10)

Dickson, R. J. *Ulster Emigration to Colonial America, 1718-1775.* London: Routledge and Kegan Paul, 1966. (FHL# 941.5/W2dr)

Ellis, Eilish. *Emigrants from Ireland, 1847-1852: State-aided Emigration Schemes from Crown Estates in Ireland.* Baltimore, Md.: Genealogical Publishing Company, 1977. (FHL# 973/A1, No. 138 or microfilm 1036619, item 3)

Glazier, Ira A., and Michael Tepper, eds. *The Famine Immigrants: Lists of Irish Immigrants Arriving at the Port of New York, 1846-1851.* 4 vols. Baltimore, Md.: Genealogical Publishing Company, 1983-86. (FHL# 974.71/W3f)

Hackett, J. Dominick, and Charles Montague Early. *Passenger Lists from Ireland.* Baltimore, Md.: Genealogical Publishing Company, 1965. Excerpted from *Journal of the American Irish Historical Society,* Vols. 28-29. (FHL# 973/W2he or microfilm 0845449, item 1)

Henchy, Patrick. *Three Centuries of Emigration from the British*

Isles: Irish Emigration to North America for the Past Three Centuries. Salt Lake City: Genealogical Society of the Church of Jesus Christ of Latter-day Saints, 1969. In Proceedings of the World Conference on Records and Genealogical Seminar, Salt Lake City, 1969. (FHL# 929.1/W893, C1-2C)

Lee, Grace Lawless. *The Huguenot Settlements in Ireland.* London: Longmans, Green, 1936. (FHL# 941.5/W2l)

Leyburn, James G. *The Scotch-Irish, A Social History.* Chapel Hill: University of North Carolina Press, 1962. (FHL# 973/F2sl)

Lockhart, Audrey. *Some Aspects of Emigration from Ireland to the North American Colonies between 1660 and 1775.* New York: Arno Press, 1976. (FHL# 970/W2lo)

Marshall, William F. *Ulster Sails West: The Story of the Great Emigration from Ulster to North America in the 18th Century.* Baltimore, Md.: Genealogical Publishing Company, 1977. (FHL# 973/A1/no.137 or microfilm 1036618, item 11)

Myers, Albert Cook. *Immigration of the Irish Quakers into Pennsylvania, 1682-1750, with Their Early History in Ireland.* 1902; rpt. ed., Baltimore, Md.: Genealogical Publishing Company, 1969. (FHL# 974.8/W2m/1969)

O'Donovon, Jeremiah. *Irish Immigration in the United States.* 1864; rpt. ed., New York: Arno Press and the New York Times, 1969. (FHL# 973/B4ai/Vol.34) One volume in a series dealing with immigration to the United States.

Schlegel, D. M. *Passengers from Ireland: Lists of Passengers Arriving at American Ports Between 1811 and 1817.* Baltimore, Md.: Genealogical Publishing Company, 1980. (FHL# 973/W3sp)

Trainor, Brian. *Discovering Ulster Origins Using Letters, Diaries, and Other Family Sources.* Salt Lake City: Corporation of the President of the Church of Jesus Christ of Latter-day Saints, 1980. In Proceedings of the World Conference on Records, Vol. 6, Salt Lake City, 1980. (FHL# 929.1/W893/1980/Vol.6/Pt. 13)

Gazetteers

Bartholomew, John. *Gazetteer of the British Isles.* London: George Newnes, 1904. (FHL# 942/E5ba/1904 or microfilm 0599554) Library also has 9th ed., 1963.

______. *The Survey Gazetteer of the British Isles.* Edinburgh [Scotland]: Bartholomew, 1932. (FHL# 942/E5ba/1932) Library also has 1943 edition.

Carlisle, Nicholas. *A Topographical Dictionary of Ireland.* London: W. Miller, 1810. (FHL# 941.5/E5t or microfilm 0599560)

Cassell's Gazetteer of Great Britain and Ireland. 6 vols. London: Cassell, 1894-98. (FHL# 942/E5ca or microfilm 0599360, items 1-2, 0924936, items 1-2, 0599361, item 2)

County Maps of Ireland: Showing Civil and Catholic Parishes and Baronies. Dublin: The National Library of Ireland, 1974. (FHL# Q/941.5/E3i or microfilm 0962187)

Lewis, Samuel. *A Topographical Dictionary of Ireland.* 3 vols. London: S. Lewis, 1837. (FHL# 941.5/E5l/1847 or microfilm 0496478, items 1-2) Library also has 1847 and 1850 editions.

The Parliamentary Gazetteer of Ireland. 10 vols. Dublin: A. Fullarton, 1844. (BRIT REF FHL# 941.5/E5p or microfilm 0824043-0824045 or microfiche 6020358-6020382)

Registrar General of Ireland. *Alphabetical Index to the Townland and Towns of Ireland.* Dublin: Alexander Thom, 1877. (FHL# 0476999, item 2, or microfiche 6020345-6020353)

Genealogy

Burke, John. *A Genealogical and Heraldic History of the Commoners of Great Britain and Ireland.* 4 vols. London: Published for Henry Colburn by R. Bentley, 1834-38. (FHL# 942/D2bc and 942/D2bc/index; or microfilm 0087947, Vol. 4 only)

Includes . . . "commoners . . . enjoying territorial possessions or high official rank; but uninvested with heritable honors."

______. *A Genealogical and Heraldic History of the Landed Gentry of Great Britain and Ireland.* London: Henry Colburn, 1847. Library has volumes for the following years: 1847-48 FHL# microfilm 0845053-0845054; 1848 microfilm 0845055; 1875 microfilm 0845056-0845058; 1894 microfilm 0994034.

______. *A Genealogical and Heraldic History of the Landed Gentry of Ireland.* London: Harrison, 1904. (FHL# 941.5/D22bu/1904) Library also has 1912 (FHL# 941.5/D22bu/1912) and 1958 (FHL# 941.5/D22bu/1958)

Burke's Peerage. *Burke's Irish Family Records.* London: Burke's Peerage, 1976. (FHL# 941.5/D22bur)

Clare, Wallace. *A Simple Guide to Irish Genealogy.* 3rd ed., revised by Rosemary Ffolliott. London: Irish Genealogical Research Society, 1966. (GEN REF FHL# 929.1415/-C541s)

Lodge, John. *The Peerage of Ireland.* 4 vols. London: W. Johnson, 1754. (FHL# 941.5/D22L) Revised and enlarged by Mervyne Archdall. 7 vols. Dublin: J. Moore, 1972. (FHL# 941.5/D22Lo or microfilm 0908431-0908433)

Piéces Originales. 11 reels. Paris: Biblioteque National, Department des Manuscrits, 1948. (FHL# microfilm 0100803-0100813)

Manuscripts relating to Irish families, thirteenth to eighteenth centuries, collected by Chairebault and Cherin. Manuscripts arranged alphabetically by family surname.

The library also has a several dozen additional titles dealing with genealogy. See FHLC headings Ireland/-Genealogy, **Ireland/Genealogy/Handbooks, Manuals, Etc.**, and **Genealogy/Indexes** for a complete list.

Genealogy/Inventories, Registers, Catalogs

Genealogical Society of Utah. *Major Genealogical Record Sources in Ireland.* Salt Lake City: Genealogical Department of the Church of Jesus Christ of Latter-day Saints, 1974. (FHL# 929.1/G2986gs/Ser. A/no.1/1974) Library also has 1975, 1977, and 1978 editions.

Genealogy Periodicals

The library subscribes to a significant number of Irish genealogy periodicals, most of them published in the United States, London, or Belfast. See **Ireland/Genealogy/Periodicals** for a complete list of holdings.

Genealogy Sources

Denny, H. L. L. *Anglo-Irish Genealogy.* London: The Society of Genealogists of London, 1916. Paper read at the quarterly meeting of the society, 12 May 1916, by W. P. Haskett-Smith. (FHL# 942/D4hs)

Handbook of Irish Genealogy: How to Trace Your Ancestors and Relatives in Ireland. Dublin: Heraldic Artists, 1970. (GEN REF FHL# 929.141/H412h or 929.1415/H412h)

Campbell, R. G. *Scotch-Irish Family Research Made Simple.* Munroe Falls, Ohio: Summit Publications, 1974. (FHL# 941.5/A1/no.26)

Heraldry

Burke, Sir John Bernard. *The General Armory of England, Scotland, Ireland, and Wales: Comprising a Registry of Armorial Bearings from the Earliest to the Present Time.* London: Harrison, 1884. (FHL# 942/D24b/1884)

Fairbairn, James. *Fairbairn's Book of Crests of the Families of Great Britain and Ireland.* 4th ed., rev. and enlarged. 1911; rpt. ed., Baltimore, Md.: Heraldic Book Co., 1968. (FHL# 942/D24fc)

Papworth, John W. *An Alphabetical Dictionary of Coats of Arms Belonging to Families in Great Britain and Ireland.* 1874; rpt. ed., Baltimore, Md.: Genealogical Publishing Company, 1965. (FHL# 942/D24pj/1965)

Swan, Conrad M. J. *Heraldry, Ulster and North American Connections.* Belfast: Ulster-Scot Historical Foundation, 1968. (FHL# 941.5/A1/no.46)

Historical Geography

Bartholomew, John. *Philips' 19th Century County Atlas of Ireland.* Kingston, Canada: Cluny Press, 1984. Reprint of *Philips' Handy Atlas of the Counties of Ireland.* London: George Philip, 1881. (FHL# 941.5/E7ba)

Bullock, L. G. *Historical Map of Ireland.* Edinburgh: J. Bartholomew, n.d. (British Map Case FHL# 941.5/E7bl)

Edwards, Ruth Dudley. *An Atlas of Irish History.* 2d ed. London: Methuen, 1981. (FHL# 941.5/E3br/1981)

History

The library has over 150 titles about Irish history. See **Ireland/History** for a complete list of holdings.

Curtis, Edmund. *A History of Mediaeval Ireland from 1110 to 1513.* Dublin: Talbot Press, n.d. (FHL# 941.5/H2ceh)

Cusack, M. F. *An Illustrated History of Ireland.* 3rd ed. London: Longmans, Green, 1869. (FHL# 941.5/H2cus)

Glasgow, Maude. *The Scotch-Irish in Northern Ireland and in the American Colonies.* New York: G. P. Putnam's Sons, 1936. (FHL# 941.5/H2g)

Joyce, Patrick Weston. *The Origin and History of Irish Names of Places.* 3 vols. 7th ed. Dublin: M. H. Gill and Son, 1901. (BRIT REF FHL# 941.5/E2o/1901)

Mant, Richard. *History of the Church of Ireland from the Reformation to the Revolution.* 2 vols. 2d ed. London: J. W. Parker, 1841. (FHL# 941.5/K2m or microfilm 0873963-0873964)

O'Hart, John. *Irish Pedigrees: Or the Origin and Stem of the Irish Nation.* 2 vols. 1876; rpt. ed., New York: Murphy and McCarthy, 1923. Limited American edition. (FHL# 941.5/D2oha/1923 or microfilm 0924498, item 8) Library has 1876, 1878, and microfilm copy of 1892 edition. See **Ireland/History to 1172** for film numbers.

Wills, James. *The Irish Nation: Its History and Its Biography.* 4 vols. Edinburgh: A. Fullarton, 1870-74. (FHL# 941.5/H2in or microfilm 0990292)

Woodham-Smith, Cecil. *The Great Hunger: Ireland 1845-49.* London: New English Library, 1979. (FHL# 941.5/-H2ws)

See also the FHLC headings **Ireland/History/1172-1603; Ireland/History/Tudors, 1485-1603/Sources; Ireland/History/16th Century; Ireland/History/17th Century; Ireland/History/17th Century/Sources; Ireland/History/18th Century/Sources; Ireland/History/-19th Century; Ireland/History/20th Century; Ireland/-History/Bibliography; Ireland/History/Chronology; Ireland/History/Collected Works; Ireland/History/Indexes; Ireland/History/Inventories, Registers, Catalogs;** and **Ireland/History/Sources.**

History and Maps

Edwards, Ruth Dudley. *An Atlas of Irish History.* London: Methuen, 1973. (FHL# 941.5/E3br)

Land and Property

The Registry of Deeds, located in the King's Inns, Henrietta Street, Dublin, preserves documents involving the transfer of land and property, such as deeds, leases, wills, marriage articles, and business transactions. While some of those records have been microfilmed and others are in printed form, both types are found in the library's Irish collection. Using them, however, requires some knowledge of Irish record keeping and content.

The Irish were not required to register land transactions until 1703 when legislation intended to prevent land from being transferred to Catholics was enacted. Initially, only a few deeds were registered by upper-class, Protestant landholders. The number of deeds registered increased throughout the seventeenth century; and once the Penal Laws were eased in 1778, Catholics also began to register their property.

People living in some counties diligently registered deeds, while those in other counties didn't bother to comply. Most deeds involve transactions between people of the same or nearly the same economic status. Few people owning or leasing small farms registered deeds. Check Richard Griffith, ed., *General Valuation of Rateable Property in Ireland* (commonly called *Griffith's*

Valuation and Tithe Applotment Books) (Dublin: A. Thom, 1848-61).

Griffith's work consists of 157 volumes for which a register lists contents and call numbers for each reel.

Church of Jesus Christ of Latter-day Saints, Genealogical Department Library Staff. *Register of Griffith's Valuation Lists and Tithe Applotment Records.* Salt Lake City: Genealogical Society of Utah, 1982. (Register table FHL#941.5/R23r) Call numbers for original records.

Each county is divided into unions and baronies. Each volume contains an index of the several parishes within each barony. See Lewis's *Topographical Dictionary of Ireland,* cited above under *Gazetteers,* for reference to parishes and baronies. See FHLC heading **Ireland/-Land and Property** for call numbers to *Griffith's Valuations.*

At least an original and one copy of a deed was created. The copy, called a memorial, was forwarded to the Registry of Deeds where it was transcribed and indexed. The original memorials are on file at the Registry of Deeds, but the public uses the transcribed volumes for research. While deeds were supposed to be filed soon after their creation, many years could elapse before the document reached the Registry of Deeds. Deeds are indexed under the date they were registered and not the date they were created.

Registry of Deeds. *Transcripts of Memorials of Conveyances and Wills, 1708-1904.* 2,220 reels. Salt Lake City: Genealogical Society of Utah, 1951.

Original records in Dublin. See FHLC heading **Ireland/Land and Property** for call numbers. Includes surname index, place name index by county, and deeds.

The indexes are difficult to use because there is no grantee index. Before 1833, indexes list only the full name of the grantor, full name of the first grantee, and reference to the location of the deed in the records (volume, page number, and deed number) There is no reference to the property's location. There may be several hundred entries for Patrick Kelly, all of which would have to be examined to identify the property and person of interest. After 1833, the index lists the county in which the property was situated.

The place-name index is arranged by counties, with townland references grouped together by the first letter of their spelling, followed by the barony in which the townland is situated. County indexes created after 1828 are further divided into baronies and one must know the barony to use the record efficiently.

Some indexes are hard to read after centuries of use and others have missing segments. Learning when to use which index can save time. See the following how-to book for a more detailed discussion of Irish land and property records:

Begley, Donal F., ed. *Irish Genealogy: A Record Finder.* Dublin, Ireland: Heraldic Artists Ltd., 1981. (FHL# 941.5/D27b)

An Index of Surnames of Householders in Griffith's Primary Valuation and Tithe Applotment Books. 14 vols. Dublin: National Library of Ireland, 1970. (FHL# 941.5/R22i) Book spine bears title: *Householder's Index.* Microfilm call numbers are: Counties Antrim, Armagh, Carlow, Cavan, #919001; Counties Clare, Cork, Londonderry, #919002; Counties Donegal, Down, Dublin, #919003; Counties Fermanagh, Galway, Kerry, Kildare, Kilkenny, #919004; Counties Laois, Leitrim, Limerick, Longford, Louth, Mayo, Meath, #919005; Counties Monaghan, Offaly, Roscommon, Sligo, Tipperary, #919006; and Counties Tyrone, Waterford, Westmeath, Wexford, Wicklow, #919007.

Other library titles pertaining to Irish land and property records include:

Bateman, John. *The Great Landowners of Great Britain and Ireland.* 4th ed. New York: Augustus M. Kelley, 1970. (FHL# 942/R2b or microfilm 0908379, item 1)

Genealogical Society of the Church of Jesus Christ of Latter-day Saints. *Ireland: Registry of Deeds, Surname and County Index, 1708-1904.* Salt Lake City: Genealogical Society, 1964. (Brit Register Table FHL# 941.5/R2di or microfilm 0599270, item 3)

De Burgh, U. H. Massey. *The Landowners of Ireland.* Dublin: Hodges and Figgis, 1878.

Land and Property/Inventories, Registers, Catalogs

Church of Jesus Christ of Latter-day Saints, Genealogical Department. *Ireland Register of Deeds with Surname and County Indexes, 1704-1929.* Salt Lake City: Genealogical Society of Utah, 1981. (Register table FHL# 941.5/R23c)

Includes instruction for using the registry of deeds and a listing of the Family History Library microfilm numbers for both the indexes and the deed registries.

Church of Jesus Christ of Latter-day Saints, Genealogical Department Library Staff. *Register of Griffith's Valuation Lists and Tithe Applotment Records.* Salt Lake City: Genealogical Society of Utah, 1982. (Register table FHL# 941.5/R23r) Call numbers for the original records.

Law and Legislation

Moleyns, Thomas de. *The Landowner's and Agent's Practical Guide.* 2d ed., Dublin: Shodges, Smith, 1860. (FHL# 941.5/R2mo)

Osborne, R. E. *The Jurisdiction and Practice of County Courts in Ireland in Equity and Probate Matters.* 2d ed. Revised by A. B. Babington. Dublin: E. Ponsonby, 1910. (FHL# 941.5/P3o or microfilm 0873960)

Nicholls, George. *A History of the Irish Poor Law.* New York: A. M. Kelley, 1967. (FHL# 941.5/P3n)

Parnell, Robert. *A Very Full and Complete History of the Penal Laws.* New York: James Sheehy, 1880. (FHL# 941.5/-D3om)

Smythe, Hamilton. *The Law of Landlord and Tenant in Ireland.* Dublin: A Milliken, 1842. (FHL# 941.5/R2sm or 0990026, item 1)

Maps

Atlas of Ireland. Dublin: Royal Irish Academy, 1979. (FHL# Q/941.5/E7at)

Bartholomew's Contoured Road Map of the British Isles. Edinburgh: Bartholomew, 1967. (Map case FHL# 942/E7bar)

Batholomew, John. *Philips' Handy Atlas of the Counties of Ireland.* London: G. Philip, 1881. (FHL# 941.5/E3b)

The Book of Maps of the Dublin City Surveyors, 1695-1827. Dublin: Public Libraries Department, 1983.

Includes a description of the book of maps – a collection of seventeenth-, eighteenth-, and nineteenth-century maps produced by city surveyors and preserved in the archives at City Hall, Dublin.

Gardner, David Ensign, Derek Harland, and Frank Smith. *A Genealogical Atlas of Ireland.* 2d ed. 1964; rpt. ed., Provo, Utah: Stevenson's Genealogical Center, 1972. (FHL# 941.5/E3g)

Compiled from original maps taken from *Philips' Handy Atlas of the Counties of Ireland,* and Lewis's *Atlas Comprising of the Counties of Ireland.*

Lewis, Samuel. *Lewis's Atlas Comprising of the Counties of Ireland and a Map of the Kingdom.* London: S. Lewis, 1846. (FHL# 941.5/E51/1846)

______. *A Topographical Dictionary of Ireland.* 3 vols. London: S. Lewis, 1847. (FHL# 941.5/E51/1847 or microfilm 0496478, items 1-2)

Counties, cities, boroughs, corporate, market and post towns, parishes, and villages with historical and statistical descriptions.

See FHLC heading **Ireland/Maps** for a complete list of map holdings.

Merchant Marine

Lists of Convict Ships with Prisoners' Names from Ireland to Sydney, 1791-1816. Salt Lake City: Genealogical Society of Utah, 1982. (FHL# microfilm 990403, item 8)

Trinity House Petitions, 1787-1854. 57 reels. Salt Lake City: Genealogical Society of Utah, 1964. (FHL# microfilm 0395554-0395610) Original records in the possession of the Society of Genealogists, London.

Military Records

Great Britain, War Office. *Artillery Records of Services of Non-Commissioned Officers and Men.* 107 reels. Salt Lake City: Genealogical Society of Utah, 1971. (FHL# microfilm 0866530-0867582)

Original records in the Public Records Office, London. Includes description books, records of service, registers of marriages and baptisms, registers of deceased soldiers, and miscellaneous records of transfers, pension registers of the Royal Artillery and the Royal Horse Artillery, 1765-1906. Service records give name, age, description, place of birth, trade, dates of service and promotions, and dates of marriage and discharge or death.

______. *List of Records of Disbanded Militia Regiments for Transmission to the Custody of the Master of the Rolls.* 141 reels. Salt Lake City: Genealogical Society of Utah, 1973-74. Original records at the Public Record Office in London.

______. *Soldiers' Documents, 1760-1900.* 1,256 reels. Salt Lake City: Genealogical Society of Utah, 1971.

Original records in the Public Record Office, London. See FHLC heading **Ireland/Military Records** for microfilm numbers.

Includes service documents containing particulars of age, birthplace, trade or occupation on enlistment, service record, decorations, and reason for discharge. Documents are arranged by regiments, 1760-1854; alphabetically for the entire army from 1873-82. Documents dated 1873-82 contain more detailed particulars, such as next of kin, marriage, and children.

See FHLC heading **Ireland/Military Records** for additional holdings.

Names/Geographical

Field, John. *Place-Names: Their Origins and Meanings.* 2d ed. Aylesbury, Bucks: Shire Publications, [c.1971]. (FHL# 942/A1/no.476)

A pocket guide to nearly 900 place-names in England, Ireland, Scotland, and Wales.

Joyce, Patrick Weston. *The Origin and History of Irish Names of Places.* 3 vols. Dublin: Educational Company of Ireland, 1901-20. (FHL# 941.5/E2o/1920 or microfilm 0874330, items 1-2, and 0874331, item 1)

O'Connell, James. *The Meaning of Irish Place Names.* Belfast: Blackstaff Press, [c.1979]. (FHL# 041.5/E20j)

Names/Personal

DeBreffny, Brian. *Irish Family Names: Arms, Origins, and Locations.* Dublin/New York: Gill and Macmillan, 1982. (FHL# 941.5/D4d)

Kelly, Patrick. Irish Family Names. 1939, rpt. ed., Detroit: Gale Research, 1976. (FHL# 941.5/D4k)

See FHLC under **Ireland/Names/Personal** for a full list of titles on this subject.

Newspapers/Bibliography

National Library of Ireland (Dublin). *List of Newspapers on Microfilm.* Typescript, n.d. Microreproduction, Salt Lake City: Genealogical Society of Utah, 1982. (FHL# 941.83/D1/A3n)

O'Kelly, F. *Survey of Newspapers Printed in Ireland before 1801.* N.p.: Irish Committee of Historical Sciences, n.d. (FHL# 941.5/A1/no. 2)

Nobility

Burke, John. *A Genealogical and Heraldic History of the Extinct and Dormant Baronetcies of England, Ireland, and Scotland.* 1841; rpt. ed., Baltimore, Md.: Genealogical Publishing Company, 1977. (FHL# 942/D22bu/1977 and microfilm 0990160)

Burke, Sir John Bernard. *A Genealogical and Heraldic History of the Landed Gentry of Ireland.* 10th ed. Sir Bernard Burke, ed. London: Harrison, 1904. (FHL# 941.5/-D22bu)

______. *The Knightage of Great Britain and Ireland.* Rev. ed. London: Edward Shurton, 1842. (FHL# 942/D22bk or microfilm 0896641, item 4)

Debrett's Illustrated Baronetage. London: Dean, 1868. (FHL# 942/D22did/1868)

Includes the knightage of the United Kingdom of Great Britain and Ireland. Kept in a binder at the refernece table labeled "Baronetage with Knightage."

Debrett's Illustrated Peerage, and Titles of Courtesy, of the United Kingdom of Great Britain and Ireland. London: Dean, 1869. (FHL# 942/D22die/1869)

Dodd, Charles R. *The Peerage, Baronetage, and Knightage of Great Britain and Ireland.* London: Whittaker, 1840. (FHL# 942/D22dod)

The library also has editions for 1851, 1852, 1855, 1857, 1890, 1894, 1907, 1912, 1915, and 1918. See FHLC heading **Ireland/Nobility** for microfilm numbers.

The FHLC also catalogs other books on this subject under **Ireland/Nobility.**

Occupations

Trinity House Petitions, 1787-1854. 57 reels. Salt Lake City: Genealogical Society of Utah, 1964. Original records in the possession of the Society of Genealogists, London.

Periodicals

The library has an extensive collection of Irish periodicals focused on genealogical and historical research cataloged under **Ireland/Periodicals** and **Ireland/Periodicals/Indexes.**

Probate Records

After the Norman invasion until the Probate Act in 1857, Irish wills were proven by the Church of Ireland. A Consistitorial Court presided over by the bishop had jurisdiction over all probate matters when the deceased owned property valued at less than five pounds. When property value exceeded five pounds, the Prerogative Court under the Archbishop of Armagh had jurisdiction.

The Probate Act established a Court of Probate, a principal registry in Dublin and eleven district registries throughout the rest of the country. A law passed in 1867 required that all old wills (any document over twenty years old) be transferred to the Public Record Office where many were lost in the 1922 Four Courts fire. The bulk of Irish wills are filed with memorials at the Registry of Deeds.

Registry of Deeds, Ireland. *Transcripts of Memorials of Conveyances and Wills, 1708-1904.* 2,220 reels. Salt Lake City: Genealogical Society of Utah, 1951. See FHLC heading **Ireland/Probate Records** for call numbers.

See *Land and Property Records* above for discussion on how to use indexes.

Osborne, R. E. *The Jurisdiction and Practice of County Courts in Ireland in Equity and Probate Matters.* 2d ed. revised by A. B. Babington. Dublin: E. Ponsonby, 1910. (FHL# 941.5/P3o or microfilm 0873960, item 1)

Prerogative Wills of Ireland. 11 reels. Salt Lake City: Genealogical Society of Utah, 1950. (FHL# microfilm 01000893-01000903)

Original records in the Public Record Office. Includes General Index for 1536-1858, wills with index from 1644-1858.

Sir Bernard Burke's Collection of Wills for Forming Irish Pedigrees. Salt Lake City: Genealogical Society of Utah, 1959. (FHL# microfilm 02227866-02227900)

Original records in the Belfast Public Record Office. Contains genealogical analyses of wills and administrations in the prerogative court of the Fitzgerald and other families.

Probate Records/Indexes

The Administration Index of the Prerogative Office. Salt Lake City Utah: Genealogical Society of Utah, 1950.. See FHLC for call number.

Original records in the Public Record Office, Dublin. Includes entries of grants of administrations, probates of will, marriage licenses, and notary public faculties, 1596-1858.

Andrea, Leonardo, comp. *Index to Irish Wills, 1617-1831.* Typescript. Salt Lake City: Genealogical Society of Utah, 1974. (FHL# microfilm 0954250, item 11) Includes name, diocese, place, year.

Index to Irish Diocesan Wills, 1536-1859. Salt Lake City: Genealogical Society of Utah, 1950. (FHL# 0100911-0100917)

Originals in the Public Record Office, Dublin.

Index to Prerogative Inventories, 1810-1860. Salt Lake City: Genealogical Society of Utah, 1951. (FHL# microfilm 0100877)

Manuscript in Public Record Office, Dublin.

Phillimore, W. P. W., ed. *Indexes to Irish Wills.* 5 vols. London: Phillimore, 1909. Vols. 3-5 edited by Gertrude Thrift. (FHL# 941.5/S2ph)

Vicars, Sir Arthur. *Index to Prerogative Wills of Ireland, 1853-1810.* Dublin: E. Ponsonby, 1897. (FHL# 941.5/S2v or microfilm 0990303)

Probate Records/Inventories, Registers, Catalogs

Gibson, J. S. W. *A Simplified Guide to Probate Jurisdictions.* Banbury, Oxfordshire: Gulliver Press/Plymouth: Federation of Family History Societies, 1980. (FHL# 942/P23g)

Church of Jesus Christ of Latter-day Saints, British Reference Staff. *Irish Probates Register.* Salt Lake City: Genealogical Society of Utah, 1979. (REF FHL# 941.5/P2gs)

Public Record Office of Ireland. *Inventory of Wills and Administrations, 1612-1900.* 32 reels. Salt Lake City: Genealogical Society of Utah, 1950-51.

Original records in the Public Record Office, Dublin. See FHLC heading **Ireland/Probate Records/Inventories, Registers, Catalogs** for call numbers. Inventory of the records, books, papers of the Prerogative Office with an index to the cause papers, 1670-1810, and Index to Prerogative unproved wills, 1689-1858.

Public Records

General Valuation Office, Ireland. *General Valuation of Rateable Property in Ireland.* Richard Griffith, ed. 157 vols. Dublin: A. Thom, 1848-61. (FHL# Q/941.5/R2g) See FHLC heading **Ireland/Public Records** for call numbers.

Taxation

See *Public Records* above.

Vital Records

General Register Office. *Certified Extracts from the Return of Births, Marriages, and Deaths Made to the Registrar General, 1922-1954.* 8 reels. Salt Lake City: Genealogical Society of Utah, 1960. (FHL# 0232604-0232611)

Original records at Fermanagh House, Belfast.

Chapter 17

Scotland

William L. Arbuckle

Historical Background

550s	Christian era begun by Saints Ninian, Kentigern, and Columba.
1200s	Modern boundaries established.
1411	St. Andreus University established.
1528	Reformation started.
1553	Earliest entry in a parish register.
1560	Scottish Parliament abolishes Roman Catholic Church.
1581	Presbyterian Church formally established.
1600	New Style (Gregorian) calendar becomes effective.
1603	Union of the Crowns.
1610	James VI establishes Episcopal Church in Scotland.
1638	National covenant signed.
1642	Irish rebellion and civil war.
1650	Oliver Cromwell invades Scotland. Many prisoners transported to colonies.
1661	Restoration and Episcopacy reestablished by Charles II.
1691	Presbyterian Church permanently established.
1707	Union with England.
1714	First Jacobite rebellion.
1745	Second Jacobite rebellion.
1782	Highland clearances begin.
1783	Tax on parish register entries, repealed 1793.
1790	Nearly 200,000 people of Scottish origin in the United States.
1801	First official census, 1.6 million people.

Settlement and Migration

The early history of Scotland is one of fierce independence and efforts to resist onslaughts of invading Romans, Norsemen, Anglo-Saxons, and the English. Norse invaders occupied the Orkney and Hebrides Islands.

The rise of Calvanism in the early sixteenth century resulted in the overthrow of the Church of Rome and the establishment of Presbyterianism as the state church. Dissention within the established church resulted in many groups breaking off, then reuniting. The civil war and the invasion of Scotland by Cromwell resulted in many Scots emigrating or being transported to the colonies. The settlement of Scotsmen in Ulster began in the early seventeenth century.

The Highland clearances began in the late eighteenth century and continued into the mid-nineteenth century. They resulted in many Scots being displaced from their homes, and many emigrated to the colonies.

The Industrial Revolution began in the late eighteenth century, resulting in migration to the urban centers. The small farms and home manufacture essentially ended.

An excellent history of Scotland is Henry W. Meikle, *A Short History of Scotland* (Edinburgh: Oliver and Boyd, Ltd., 1961). (FHL# 941/H2brp).

Scotland Library Collection

Archives and Libraries

The National Archives of Scotland are located at General Register House, Edinburgh. The archives consist of Old Register House, containing deeds, court records, land transfer records, government, church, and private archives, and New Register House, containing civil registration, census records, and parish registers. The National Library of Scotland also located at Edinburgh is comparable to the Library of Congress in the United States. Among its private collections are valuable resources on estate papers.

Governmental reorganization in 1975 established regional and district record-keeping archives. Many records pertaining to these regions and districts have been distributed to them from the National Archives. These districts are described by Paul F. Smart in *Genealogical Helper* 32, No. 3 (May-June 1978): 5-11.

Livingston, Matthew. *A Guide to the Public Records of Scotland.* Edinburgh: H. M. General Register House, 1905. (FHL# 941/A51 or microfilm 962301, item 2)

Thomson, J. Maitland. *The Public Records of Scotland.* Glasgow: Maclehouse, Jackson and Co., 1922. (FHL# 941/A5tm or microfilm 874437)

National Library of Scotland Catalogue of Manuscripts Acquired since 1925. Edinburgh: H. M. Stationery Office, 1938. (FHL# 941/A5s) Contains a list of other catalogs of the library.

Scottish Library and Information Resources. Glasgow: Scottish Library Association, 1984. (FHL# 941/J54s/1984)

Biography

Many sources will be found in the FHLC under **Scotland/Biography**. The reader is reminded that many sources cited in Chapter 15 on England also apply to Scotland. There are many sources of a specialized nature such as D. E. R. Watt's *A Biographical Dictionary of Scottish Graduates to* A.D. 1410 (Oxford: Clarendon Press, 1977). (FHL# 941/D3wa) and Alistair and Henrietta Taylor's *Jacobites of Aberdeenshire and Banffshire in the Forty-Five* (Aberdeen: Milne and Hutchison, 1928) (FHL# 941/D3tl or microfilm 6026279).

A collection of biographies of the ministers of the Church of Scotland is Hew Scott's *Fasti Ecclesiae Scoticanae,* 10 vols. (Edinburgh: Oliver and Boyd, 1915-date). (FHL# 941/D3s or microfiche 6026402).

Some general biographical collections are:

Chambers, Robert. *A Biographical Dictionary of Eminent Scotsmen.* 9 vols. Glasgow: Blackie, 1854. (FHL# 941/-D3cr)

______. *Lives of Illustrious and Distinguished Scotsmen.* 8 vols. Glasgow: Blackie and Son, n.d. (FHL# 920.041/C3551 or microfilm 1239087, item 5)

Cemetery Records

Many sources of early tombstone and monumental inscriptions as well as collections from several counties will be found in the FHLC under **Scotland/Cemeteries**. Most cemetery records will be found under the name of the county, parish, or town where the cemetery is located.

Census Records

The first official census was taken in 1801 and gave a population of 1.6 million. Before 1841 the censuses were statistical only. The 1841 census was the first to list each person by name. The name of each family member was given and whether he or she was born in the county of residence. The ages of persons over fifteen were given in multiples of five years. The occupation of the head of the household was also given. No relationships are given.

The 1851 and all later censuses give the following information: name, age, occupation, address, relationship to head of household, marital condition of each person, and exact place of birth, giving county and parish. Birthplaces out of Scotland are usually given only as a country.

The following parts of the 1841 census, listed by parish, are known to be missing: Auchtermuchty, Balmerino, Ceres, Collessie, Creich, Cults, Cuper, Dairsey, Dunbog (district 9 only), Kinghorn (district 10 only), Kinglassie (district 11 only), and Stracathro (district 2 only).

The census records from 1841 through 1891 are available at the library on microfilm and can be found in the Family History Library Catalog (FHLC) under **Scotland/Census**. They are also listed in *Register of the Scottish Census* (Salt Lake City: Family History Library, 1978). (FHL# 941/X2ce/1978 or microfilm 990269 or microfiche 6020420).

The 1851 census has been filmed twice. The second set of film numbers are not listed in the above cited register. These film numbers are listed in the FHLC.

There is no index to persons enumerated in any census of Scotland. There are indexes to the streets of the larger cities giving the enumeration volume numbers and the district numbers where the streets are located in the census. The street indexes follow with their microfilm numbers: 1841, (FHL# 104115, item 1);1851, (FHL# 104115, item 2); 1861, (FHL# 104116); 1871, (FHL# 104117); 1881, (FHL# 203392); and1891, (FHL# 208606).

Scotland is divided into 33 counties and 901 parishes. The parishes are named and have been assigned numbers. Large cities often include several parishes; for instance, Glasgow consists of Glasgow, Barony, and Gorbals. At the advent of civil registration in 1855, the old parishes were established as registration districts. Many new districts were also created. Glasgow then consisted of ten districts.

The census records are arranged first by county then by parish or district in numerical order. The numbers assigned to the parishes and districts can be found in *Index to the Parish Registers in Scotland* (Salt Lake City: Family History Library, 1978). (FHL# 941/E6g or microfilm 599269 or microfiche 6020420, item 2).

The six counties listed below are followed by an older name which may be found in some records: Midlothian/Edinburghshire, Morayshire/Elginshire, Angus/Forfarshire, East Lothian/Haddingtonshire, West Lothian/Linlithgowshire, and Zetland/Shetland.

Church Records

The Established Church of Scotland (Presbyterian) began keeping records of births, deaths, and marriages in the latter half of the sixteenth century. Many registers, however, do not begin until the mid-eighteenth century.

The birth records often give the following information: name of child, date of birth, date of baptism, father's full name, sometimes occupation and residence, mother's full maiden name, and names of witnesses, and whether the child was legitimate.

Marriage records are quite variable in content. They may consist of only the first date the banns were proclaimed and the names of the intended parties. This may be followed by an added date of the actual marriage and the names of witnesses. More complete records may include the names of the parents of the bride and groom, groom's occupation, their residences, and whether either had been married previously.

Records of death or burial are less well kept. They often consist of a date and name of the deceased and the amount of money collected for use of the mortcloth or funeral pall. Married women are occasionally listed under their maiden names without giving the name of their husband.

Two sets of records were usually kept by the parish clerk. One set, the parish registers, contained entries of birth, marriage, and death. The other set, Kirk Session records, were concerned with the government or business of the church and discipline of the congregation. Occasionally the clerk recorded entries of birth, marriage, or death in the Kirk Session books, sometimes for extended periods of time.

Most pre-1855 registers were deposited at New Register House and have been microfilmed twice by the Family History Library. Some Kirk Session records are also available on microfilm at the library. Some church records were not deposited at New Register House and are discussed by J. F. Mitchel in "Registers of Births, Deaths, and Marriages," *The Scottish Genealogist* 14, no. 2 (1967): 25-35 (FHL# 941/B2g).

The records of the Established Church can be found in the FHLC under the name of the parish such as **Scotland/Lanark/Shotts/Church Records.** A guide to these records giving a description of the original records and the film numbers for the first filming was compiled by V. Ben Bloxham, *Key to the Parochial Registers of Scotland,* 2d ed. (Provo, Utah: Brigham Young University Press, 1979). (FHL# 941/K23b).

The first filming of the parish registers in the 1950s had some illegible sections, and some information was obscured by the tight bindings of the original books. In the 1970s the bindings were opened and the records microfilmed again. The film numbers of the second filming may be found in the FHLC under the name of the parish but are not in Bloxham.

Some of the early church records of the parishes of Glasgow have been transcribed. Those for High Church (Glasgow), Barony, Gorbals, and Govan are on microfilm at the library. Consult the FHLC for film numbers under the names of the above listed parishes.

The history of the Established Church is one of dissension, with various groups seceding over questions of church government and forms of worship. These seceding groups, though still Presbyterian, are referred to as nonconformist churches. Some of the records of these churches are available on microfilm at the library. Many of these films are backwards on the spindles, resulting in the identifying title appearing at the end of the record to which it applies. It is therefore necessary to start at the end of the film and work back to the beginning. These records are found in the FHLC under the county and town where the church was located. The library is presently filming this entire collection at Edinburgh.

A list of known registers of nonconformist churches can be found in Donald J. Steel's *Sources for Scottish Genealogy and Family History,* Vol. 12 of the *National Index of Parish Registers* (London: Society of Genealogists, 1970). (FHL# 942/V26ste).

The records of the Reverand John MacMillan, 1706-51, founder of the Reformed Presbyterian Church (Cameronian Society) are available at the library: *Register of the Rev. John MacMillan* (Edinburgh: Lorimer and Chalmers, 1908). (FHL# 941/V2p or microfilm 277980, item 2).

The records of the branches of the Church of Jesus Christ of Latter-day Saints (LDS or Mormon) in Scotland are available at the library on microfilm. They may be found in the FHLC under the county and then the name of the place or town. A guide to these LDS church records is Laureen R. Jaussi and Gloria D. Chaston, *Register of Genealogical Society Call Numbers, Vol. 2* (Provo, Utah: The Genealogy Tree, 1982). (FHL# 979.225/S1/A3j).

Records of the Scottish Episcopal Church (Anglican) are for the most part in local custody. A guide to local churches can be found in *Crockford's Clerical Directory* (London: Church House Publishing, 1975). (FHL# 942/E4c or microfilm 1368350). Some records of this denomination are at Register House in Edinburgh. A list of these registers can be found in the previously cited book by Donald J. Steel, pp. 244-48.

Records of the Roman Catholic Church are mostly in local custody. A guide to local churches is *The Catholic Directory for Scotland* (Glasgow: John S. Burns and Sons, 1985). (FHL# 941/K24ca).

The records of the Society of Friends (Quakers) in Scotland are located at several repositories in Scotland and England. An excellent article by William H. Marwick discussing these records is "Scottish Friends Records," *Scottish Genealogist* 7, no. 3 (1960): 1-10. (FHL# 941/B2g).

Some Scottish Friends records have been extracted by Archibald S. Maxwell, *Scottish Society of Friends, Quakers* (Aberdeen: The Author, n.d.). (FHL# 941/V26q or microfilm 823635). The records of the Aberdeen Monthly Meeting including most of Scotland are also on microfilm (FHL# microfilm 441406, item 3).

Records of the Baptist, Congregational, and Methodist churches are largely in local custody. Directories for these denominations are listed below:

The Scottish Baptist Year Book. Glasgow: Baptist Union of Scotland, 1985. (FHL# 941/K22b)

Congregational Union of Scotland Year Book. Glasgow: Congregational Union, 1986). (FHL# 941/A7c)

An inventory of the church records held at General Register House is *Repertory of Church of Scotland Records, Free, United Presbyterian, United Free, and Other Churches* (Edinburgh: Scottish Record Office, 1983). (FHL# 941/K23sc). See FHLC for film numbers under **Scotland/Church Records/Inventories**. This inventory is divided into sections for different denominations as listed below: CH2 , Church of Scotland; CH3 , Nonconformist; CH10, Society of Friends; CH11, Methodist; CH12, Episcopal; CH13, United Free; CH14, Congregational; CH15, Unitarian; and RH21, Roman Catholic.

The library is in the process of abstracting and indexing the births and marriages from all the parish registers of the Established Church of Scotland. These are known as the OPR Indexes. Thus far, indexes are available for the following counties: Aberdeen, Angus and Dundee City, Banff, Cathness, Clackmannan, Dumbarton, Inverness, Kincardine, Glasgow City, Kinross, Moray, Nairn, Orkney, Ross and Cromarty, Shetland, and Sutherland.

The counties now being indexed but not yet available are: Bute, Fife, Perth, Ayr, Renfrew, Lanark, Argyll, The Lothians, Sterling, and Selkirk.

There are separate indexes to births and marriages. This project does not include deaths and burials. One index is arranged alphabetically by surname, then by given name, then chronologically within the given name. Another index is alphabetical by given name, then chronological within that given name.

The index to births or christenings gives the name of the child, parents' names, date of birth or christening, sex of child, whether birth or christening or adult christening, and place (parish). If the event was not recorded in its proper place chronologically in the parish register, the microfilm frame number is given. The microfilm of the church records used for this index were those of the second (1970-80) filming. Each frame of the film is numbered at the top center of the frame. Dates of christening are usually given, which are useful in finding the original record. The original record should be examined to obtain more information.

The marriage indexes are arranged in the same manner as the birth indexes, having a surname and a given name index. Brides' names are included. The index gives the names of the parties married, date, parish, and frame number if out of order.

The birth and marriage indexes give, in the last column, the batch number and serial sheet number. By reference to the batch number index, the proper film number may be obtained for the original church records.

Another county-wide index to births and marriages which also includes deaths is available. It is not part of the OPR index prepared by the Family History Library but is available on microfilm. This index is for Selkirkshire and is on FHL# microfilm 1067929, item 4.

Civil Registration

The government of Scotland took over the registration of vital records from the Established Church in 1855. A grace period was allowed for people who had neglected to record these events at the proper time in the parish registers. Therefore, a series of neglected entries will often be found in the parish registers after the entries for the year 1854. In addition, the government recorded neglected entries in special registers (FHL# microfilm 103538).

The old parishes were, in most cases, established as registration districts except in the larger cities where several new districts were set up. The districts were all named and numbered. These numbers are essential to using these records. A guide to the names and numbers is found in the previously cited *Index to the Parish Registers in Scotland* (FHL# 941/E6g).

There are yearly indexes arranged in two parts, male and female, with an addendum for omitted names. Where a name was omitted, a stamped cross appears with a note at the bottom of the page stating "Vide Addenda" ("see addenda"). The indexes after 1865 are printed. There are separate indexes for births, deaths, and marriages.

When searching for females, note:

1855-65 marriage indexes are arranged by maiden name in alphabetical order, with the husband's surname in parentheses.

1855-65 death indexes are arranged in alphabetical order under the married surname with the maiden surname in parentheses.

1865-present death indexes are arranged in alphabetical order, once under the maiden surname and once under the married surname. All death indexes after 1865 also give the age of the deceased.

The indexes are available at the library from 1855 to 1955. The original certificates are on microfilm from 1855 to 1875, and 1881, and 1891. The indexes give the full name of the person, the name of the registration district, and the certificate number. The district name must be converted into the district number to find the microfilm numbers of the original certificates. This can be done by consulting the previously cited *Index to the Parish Registers of Scotland* (FHL# 941/E64g). The film numbers for the original records can be found in the FHLC under **Scotland/Civil Registration**. They are also listed in *Register of Births, Marriages and Deaths of Scotland* (Salt Lake City: Family History Library, 1964). (FHL# 941/V2 or microfilm 599269, item 3).

The 1855 registers contain the following information:

Births: Name, sex, place and date, father's full name, occupation, age, birthplace, date and place of parents' marriage, number of other children (living or dead), mother's full name, age, and birth place.

Marriages: Date, place, residence, ages, profession of each, marital condition, number of this marriage, number of children, birthplaces of the couple, parents' names (including maiden name of the mothers), and occupations of both fathers.

Deaths: Name, date, place, occupation, age, sex, where born, how long resided at present address, wife's name, parents' full names, names of all children of dead person, cause of death, place of burial, and informant.

The 1856-61 registers contain the following information:

Births: Name, date, place, father's name, occupation, mother's full name, and informant.

Marriages: Date, place, ages, condition, residence, father's name and occupation, and mother's maiden name.

Deaths: Name, date, place, age, occupation and condition, father's name and occupation, mother's maiden name, and cause of death.

The contents of the registers from 1861 to the present are:

Births: Same as 1856-61 plus date and place of parents' marriage.

Marriages: Same as 1856-61.

Deaths: Same as 1856-61 plus name of spouse.

A large number of these original records have been extracted by the library and entered into the IGI. These are indicated in the FHLC by an "X" following the microfilm number.

There are several special registers, available only at New Register House, Edinburgh. Some follow: marine register of birth and death, 1855 to present; war death register, 1899 to present; stillbirth register, 1939 to present; adopted children register, 1930 to present; air (born or died in an airplane) register of birth and death, 1948 to present; and consular returns of birth, death, and marriages 1914 to present.

Court Records

The court records of Scotland began at the time the central government became sufficiently strong to enforce law and order. The earliest extant records begin about 1478. For a discussion of the court system, see the previously cited *Sources of Scottish Genealogy and Family History* by D. J. Steel (FHL# 942/V26ste).

The legal system evolved over a long period of time, influenced by both Roman law and English common law. Before the Reformation, the Roman Catholic Church had considerable legal authority. It appointed notaries public and administered probate of testaments. The crown also appointed notaries public, administered criminal justice, and established the sheriff court system. The courts consist of a court of session similar to a supreme or appellate court, the commissariot court, sheriff courts, and courts of franchise such as barony courts.

Some early court records of Scotland can be found in the library such as:

Stair Society. *Acta Curiae Admirallatus Scottae. (1557-61).* Publications of the Stair Society, Vol. 2. Edinburgh: The Society, 1937. (FHL# 941/B4st or microfilm 1426033)

______. *Acta Dominorum Concillii 1501-1503.* Publications of the Stair Society, Vol. 8. Edinburgh: The Society, 1943. (FHL# 941/B4st or microfilm 1426040)

______. *Acta Dominorum Concillii et Sessionis 1532-1533.* Publications of the Stair Society, Vol. 14. Edinburgh: The Society, 1951. (FHL# 941/B4st)

The Records of the Justiciary Court Edinburgh 1661-1678. Scottish Historical Society Publications, Vols. 48, 49. Edinburgh: The Society, 1905. (FHL# 941/B4sc)

One of the most valuable court records is the register of deeds, often called the Books of Council and Session because it was kept by the clerk of the court of session.

The register consists of three series. The first covers from 1554 to 1657 in 621 volumes. The second has three concurrent parts, named for clerks Dalrymple, Durie, and Mackenzie. Its 959 volumes cover from 1657 to 1811. The third series covers from 1812 to modern times. Deeds are not concerned with the transfer of land ownership, as they are in the United States, but with the vast material that might be called miscellaneous court records, such as contracts of all kinds including marriages, bills of sale, and agreements – in fact, anything the parties felt worthy of recording or anything requiring by a clause that it be recorded.

The library has no original deeds. It does have the minute books to the first series, the minute books and indexes to the second series, and indexes to the third series up to 1851. The Scottish Record Office is in the process of publishing indexes to these records and to date has produced indexes to the records from 1663 to 1696. For further information on the holdings of the library concerning deeds see *Sasines, Service of Heirs and Deeds Register* (Salt Lake City: Family History Library, 1981). (FHL# Reg./941/R2ss). These records are listed in the FHLC under **Scotland/Land and Property**.

Another important set of court records resulted from a process called horning, which occurred when a creditor was able to obtain judgement against a debtor who had refused to pay a just debt. A messenger of arms made three blasts on a horn and denounced the debtor publicly. These records often provide much valuable information. The library has these records from 1610 to 1620 on microfilm; they are not indexed. For call numbers, consult the FHLC under **Scotland/Land and Property.**

Directories

Directories of the larger cities can be found in the FHLC under the name of the city. Directories for the city of Glasgow are available from 1787 to 1885.

Emigration and Immigration

Scots have been known on the continent since the fifteenth century. They have emigrated to Scandinavia, France, Germany, and Poland as well as Australia and the New World. One of Scotland's most important exports has been its people. They managed other people's businesses, built their factories and industries, and fought their wars. P. William Filby has indexed many printed passenger lists for arrivals in North America in *Passenger and Immigration Lists Index* (Detroit: Gale Research Co., 1981-date, 4 vols.). (FHL# 973/W32p).

Many useful sources concerning internal migration within Scotland and emigration to all parts of the world will be found in the FHLC under **Scotland/Emigration and Immigration**. Some outstanding sources are cited below:

Bailyn, Bernard. *Voyagers to the West.* New York: Alfred A. Knopf, Inc., 1986. (FHL# 973/W2ba)

Adamson, Duncan, and Robin Lobban. *Scottish Population History*. London: Cambridge University Press, 1977. (FHL# 941/X4s)

Dobson, David. *Directory of Scots Banished to the American Plantations 1650-1775*. Baltimore, Md.: Genealogical Publishing Co., Inc., 1983. (FHL# 973/W2dd)

Cameron, Viola Root. *Emigrants from Scotland to America*. Baltimore, Md.: Genealogical Publishing Co., Inc., 1965). (FHL# 973/W2g)

Dobson, David. *Directory of Scottish Settlers in North America*. 6 vols. (Baltimore, Md.: Genealogical Publishing Co., Inc., 1984-date). (FHL# 970/W2d)

Further information on the settlement of Scotsmen in Ulster, Nova Scotia, New England, New York, Canada, Australia, New Zealand, and South Africa can be found in Gerald Hamilton-Edwards, *In Search of Scottish Ancestry*. (Baltimore: Genealogical Publishing Co., 1984). (FHL# 941/D27ham).

Gazetteers and Maps

Several helpful sources will be found in the FHLC under **Scotland/Gazetteers** and **Scotland/Maps**. Some of the most important sources are cited below:

Wilson, John Marius. *The Imperial Gazetteer of Scotland*. 2 vols. London: A. Fullerton, 1900. (FHL# 941/E5w or microfilm 599357 and 599358)

Groome, Francis H. *Ordinance Gazetteer of Scotland*. 6 vols. London: William Mackenzie, 1894. (FHL# 941/E5g)

Findlay, James. *Directory of Gentlemen's Seats*. Edinburgh: W. P. Kennedy, 1843. (FHL# 941/E4d or microfilm 599347, item 3, or microfiche 6026392)

Johnson, James B. *Place Names of Scotland*. 1843. rpt. ed., Wakefield: S. R. Publishers Ltd. 1970. (FHL# 941/E2p)

Parish Maps of Scotland. Salt Lake City: Family History Library, 1979. (FHL# 941/E7ch or microfiche 6026409)

Genealogy and Heraldry

In addition to the previously cited work by D. J. Steel, *Sources for Scottish Genealogy and Family History* (FHL# 942/V26ste), an excellent guide to Scottish genealogy is Gerald Hamilton-Edwards, *In Search of Scottish Ancestry,* 2d ed. (Baltimore, Md.: Genealogical Publishing Co., Inc., 1984). (FHL# 941/D27ham).

Another helpful guide to research is Alwyn James, *Scottish Roots* (Loanhead: Macdonald Publishers, 1981). (FHL# 941/D27j).

A guide to the origins and early references to Scottish surnames is George F. Black's *The Surnames of Scotland* (New York: The New York Public Library, 1946). (FHL# 941/D4b).

A guide to compiled British family histories and its supplement which is also important for Scottish families is George W. Marshall's *The Genealogist's Guide* (Baltimore, Md.: Genealogical Publishing Co., Inc., 1980). (FHL# 929.142/M356g) and the supplement of the same title prepared by J. B. Whitmore (London: Walford Brothers, 1953). (FHL# 929.142/M356g/Supp).

Two guides to compiled histories of Scottish families are:

Stewart, Margaret. *Scottish Family History*. Baltimore, Md.: Genealogical Publishing Co., Inc., 1979. (FHL# 941/A3s)

Ferguson, Joan P. S. *Scottish Family Histories Held in Scottish Libraries*. Edinburgh: Scottish Central Library, 1960. (FHL# 941/D23f)

The ultimate authority in Scottish heraldry is the Lord Lyon King of Arms. Some words of caution are appropriate here concerning the use of arms.

In heraldic law, one is entitled to arms by inheritance if one can prove a direct legitimate male line descent from an ancestor who is himself on official record as being entitled to arms. From this, it follows that not everyone bearing the same surname is entitled to the same arms, for many individuals and families of the same name may bear totally different arms, while others of the same name may have no inherited right to any arms. For further information see *The Coat of Arms* 2, No. 97, N.S. (Spring 1976): 17.

An excellent source on the principles of Scottish heraldry is Thomas Innes, *Scots Heraldry* (Edinburgh: Oliver and Boyd, 1956). (FHL# 941/D6i or microfilm 897027). The clans and tartans of Scotland are well presented in Ian Grimble's *Scottish Clans and Tartans* (New York: Tudor Publishing Co., 1973). (FHL# 941/H2ig). A detailed account of the Scots peerage is Sir James Balfour Paul's *The Scots Peerage,* 9 vols. (Edinburgh: David Douglas, 1904). (FHL# 941/D22p).

For over 150 years the publications of Burke's several accounts of British families have been outstanding. An index to this vast series of publications is *Burke's Family Index* (London: Burke's Peerage Limited, 1976). (FHL# 942/D53b).

History

An excellent and comprehensive history is James Browne's *The History of Scotland: Its Highlands, Regiments and Clans,* 8 vols. (Edinburgh: Francis A. Niccolls and Co., 1909). (FHL# 941/H2b or microfilm 897296 and 897297).

In the late 1790s, Sir John Sinclair compiled *The Statistical Account of Scotland,* 20 vols.; rpt. ed., (Wakefield, England: E. P. Publishing, 1983). (FHL# 941/B4sa or microfiche 6026372). This is a comprehensive account of the history, industry, agriculture, and other aspects of life in each of the parishes of Scotland. These accounts were based on material obtained from local persons at the time, such as parish ministers. They now provide a detailed account of each parish in Scotland, invaluable to the researcher.

Below will be found listed some outstanding histories dealing with specific aspects of life in Scotland:

Richards, Eric. *A History of the Highland Clearances*. London: Croom Helm, 1982. (FHL#941/R4r)

Cowan, Ian B. *The Scottish Reformation*. London: Weidenfeld and Nicolson, 1982. (FHL# 941/K2cow)

Johnston, Thomas. *A History of the Working Class in Scotland*.

Trowbridge: E. P. Publishing, Ltd., 1974. (FHL# 941/U2j)

Logue, Kenneth J. *Popular Disturbances in Scotland 1780-1815.* Edinburgh: John Donald Publishers, Ltd., 1979. (FHL# 941/H21k)

Arnot, Page R. *A History of the Scottish Miners.* London: George Allen and Unwin, Ltd., 1955. (FHL# 941/U2a)

Graham, Henry G. *The Social Life of Scotland in the Eighteenth Century.* London: Adam and Charles Black, 1906. (FHL# 941/H2so)

Lochead, Marion. *The Scots Household.* Edinburgh: Moray Press, 1948. (FHL# 941/H61m)

Land and Property

The registration of land title depends on the office of the notary public. The process of transferring title is known as taking sasine; the word derives from *seize* as, in the United States, a man may be "seized of" (possess) a certain piece of land.

The custom long existed that the grantor and grantee actually stood on the land and the former would hand over soil and stones to the latter. This act was recorded in the notary public's books, which are called the protocol books. The earliest is that of Gavin Ross, starting in 1505. The registration districts for land transfer follow the sheriff court boundaries except for several additional burgh courts set up within the counties. Land transfer could be recorded in the office of the particular district in which the land was located called the "Particular Register"; or it could be recorded in the "general register" at Edinburgh. The general register was also used if the land was not in Scotland.

The library has minute books, indexes, and abridgements of sasines for each county and for the general register at Edinburgh. The sasine records available at the library can be found in the previously cited *Register of Sasines, Etc.* (FHL# 941/R2ss). They are also listed in the FHLC under **Scotland/Land and Property**. A large number of burgh protocol books also record sasines. Those available at the library are listed below with their call numbers:

Linlithgow, 1528-78 FHL# 941/B3sr Vol. 52

Linlithgow, 1546-53 FHL# 941/B4sr Vol. 57

Perth, 1534-52 FHL# 941/B4sr Vol. 65

Edinburgh & Canongate, 1485-1515 FHL# 941/B4sr Vol. 74

Melrose, 1547-1706 FHL# 941/B4sc 2nd series Vol. 13

Melrose, 1605-61 FHL# 941/Brsc 2nd series Vol. 6

Melrose, 1662-76 FHL# 941/B4sc 2nd series Vol. 8

Military Records

Scotland had no regular army or navy before the union of 1707. Forces were raised from time to time as occasion required. A guide to searching army records is Gerald Hamilton-Edwards's, *In Search of Army Ancestry* (London: Phillimore, 1977). (FHL# 942/M2ha).

An inventory of early Scottish muster lists at the Scottish Record Office is *Army Muster Rolls/Scotland 1641-1704* (Edinburgh: Scottish Record Office, 1963). (FHL# Q/941/M2mr or microfilm 874126, item 8). The records inventoried in that list are also at the library on five rolls of microfilm. They are listed in the FHLC under **Scotland/Military Records**. An excellent discussion of early military records is Ronald G. Ball's *Scottish Military and Militia Records Before 1707,* Paper presented at the 1969 World Conference on Records (Salt Lake City: Family History Library, 1969). (FHL# 929.1/W893/C18 or microfiche 6039321).

Some early military records can be found in the following:

Livingston, Alister, ed. *Muster Roll of Prince Charles Stuart's Army 1745-1746.* Aberdeen: Aberdeen University Press, 1984. (FHL# 941.1/M2m)

Terry, Charles S. *Papers Relating to the Army of the Solemn League and Covenant 1643-1647.* Publications of the Scottish History Society, Ser. 2, Vols. 16-17. Edinburgh: The Society, 1917. (FHL# 941/B4sc)

Seaton, Sir Bruce G., and Jean Gordon Arnot. *The Prisoners of the '45.* Publications of the Scottish History Society, Ser. 3, Vols. 13-15. Edinburgh: The Society, 1928. (FHL# 941/B4sc)

Ferguson, James. *The Scots Brigade in Holland 1572-1782.* Publications of the Scottish History Society. Ser. 1, Vols. 32, 35, 38. Edinburgh: The Society, 1899). (FHL# 941/B4sc)

Dalton, Charles. *The Scots Army 1661-1668.* Edinburgh: W. Brown, 1909. (FHL# microfilm 990366)

Histories of the Scottish regiments are:

Barns, R. Money. *The Scottish Regiments.* London: Seeley Service and Co., Ltd., 1960. (FHL# 941/M25b)

Paul, William P. *History of the Scottish Regiments.* Glasgow: M'Kenzie, Vincent and Co., Ltd, n.d. (FHL# 941/M2p)

White, Arthur S. *A Bibliography of Regimental Histories of the British Army.* London: Society for Army Historical Research, 1965. (FHL# 942/A3w)

Murray, Arch K. *History of the Scottish Regiments of the British Army.* Glasgow: Thomas Murray and Son, 1862. (FHL# microfilm 994034)

Hay, George J. *History of the Militia.* London: United Service Gazette, 1905. (FHL# microfilm 994045)

The Scottish regiments of the British Army are listed below. The regiments were named and numbered. In 1881 the army was reorganized and some units were combined and some were assigned new numbers.

The Royal Scots Greys (2nd Dragoons) or 2nd Royal North British Dragoons.

The Scots Guards (3rd Foot Guards).

The Royal Scots (1st Regiment of Foot) Lothian Regiment.

The Royal Scots Fusiliers (21st Regiment of Foot).

The Highland Light Infantry (71st Regiment of Foot) the 74th. (Highlanders) united with 71st.

The King's Own Scottish Borderers (25th Regiment of Foot).

The Queen's Own Cameron Highlanders (79th Regiment of Foot).

The Royal Highland-Black Watch (42nd Foot).

Seaforth Highlanders formed in 1881 by union of 78th Ross-shire Buffs and 72nd Duke of Albany's.

The Gordon Highlanders (92nd Foot) united in 1881 with 75th Sterlingshire Regiment.

Princess Louise's Argyllshire (91st Regiment).

The records of the Scottish regiments are included with those of the British army after 1707.

A guide to the British naval records is N.A.M. Rodger's *Naval Records for Genealogists* (London: Public Records Office, 1984). (FHL# 942/M3r).

A guide to the British army records is *Records of Officers and Soldiers Who Served in the British Army* (London: Public Records Office, n.d.). (FHL# 942/M23gb).

Brief histories of the regiments can be found in Arthur Swinson's *A Register of the Regiments and Corps of the British Army* (London: The Archive Press, 1972). (FHL# 942/M2am).

A guide to British army records at the library is *Army Records* (Salt Lake City: Family History Library, 1978). (FHL# Reg./942/M2a or microfilm 990313, item 5).

The records of soldiers who received a pension are in W097 for the period 1760 to 1900 on microfilm at the library. The Regimental Description and Succession Books (W025) include detailed information on each soldier. They primarily cover the period 1805 to 1850 and are on film at the library. The records of the militia including Scottish units are in W068 on film at the library. Although the Muster Books and Pay Lists (W012) are not available at the Family History Library, an inventory of these records covering the period 1732 to 1878 is available: *Muster Books and Pay Lists,* List and Index Society, Vol. 210 (London: Public Records Office, 1984). (FHL# Q/942/B4pro).

For additional information on the records of the British Army, the reader is referred to the discussion on military records in Chapter 15, "England and Wales."

Newspapers

The library has no newspapers of Scotland. The earliest Scottish newspaper was first published at Leith in 1651, *Mercurius Caledonius.* It was not until 1718 that the *Edinburgh Evening Courant* became the first regular continuous newspaper. A guide to Scottish newspapers is Joan P. Ferguson's *Directory of Scottish Newspapers* (Edinburgh: National Library of Scotland, 1984). (FHL# 941/B3f).

A guide to Scottish newspapers on microfilm, some held by libraries in the United States, is *Newspapers in Microfilm/Foreign Counties* (Washington, D.C.: Library of Congress, 1973). (FHL# 011.35/N479f).

Periodicals

A vast amount of helpful material has been published in a great variety of periodicals. A guide to these sources is Charles S. Terry's *A Catalogue of the Publications of Scottish Historical and Kindred Clubs and Societies* (Glasgow: James Mac Lehose and Sons, 1909). (FHL# 941/A3t or microfilm 990287, item 4). See also the supplement by the same title by Cyril Matheson (Aberdeen: Milne and Hutchison, 1928). (FHL# 941/A3t/1908-27 or microfilm 992823).

The publication of the Scottish Genealogy Society is *The Scottish Genealogist,* 1954-to date (FHL# 941/B2g).

Probate Records

Until the latter part of the nineteenth century, a Scotsman was not able to bequeath land in a will. Testaments distributed only moveable property, such as money, to the heirs. Therefore, many Scots never bothered to prepare a testament. There are many more testaments dative than testaments testamentars. The testament dative is similar to letters of administration and inventories as found in the United States. The granting of letters of administration is known as "confirmation." The testament testementars results from the decedent having prepared a written testament.

Before the Reformation, the Catholic Church administered testaments. Courts were set up along bishop's boundaries resulting in the Commissory Courts. The boundaries of these courts are not related to county boundaries. To use the records of testaments, it is necessary to determine the court of jurisdiction for the parish of interest. This can be done by reference to the previously cited work by Hamilton-Edwards (FHL# 941/D27ham) or by consulting the appendix to this chapter which is an alphabetical listing of parishes giving the Commissariot Court to which it belongs. The jurisdictions of the courts are also given in *Register of Testaments and Commissariot Courts of Scotland* (Salt Lake City: Family History Library, 1972). (FHL# 941/P2gs).

The Scottish Record Society has published indexes up to 1800 for each of the courts. These are given in the previously cited *Register of Testaments.* The microfilm numbers for the records of the Commissariot Courts are also given in that register up to 1823.

In 1823 the boundaries of the Commissariot Courts were made to coincide with county boundaries. In 1876 these courts were abolished, and the administration of testaments was transferred to the Sheriff Courts. Since 1876 a calendar of all confirmations and inventories has been published yearly including all sheriffdoms. These printed calendars are available at the library up to 1936 (FHL# Q/941/P2s).

Abstracts of the records of the Commissariot of Edinburgh 1514-1600 have been published in Francis J. Grant, *The Commissariot Record of Edinburgh/Register of Testaments* (1897; rpt. ed., Wiesbaden, Germany: Kraus Reprint 1968). (FHL# 942/B4b/Vol. 16). The Commissariot of Edinburgh administered testaments from all parts of Scotland as well as for persons who died abroad or overseas.

Although not strictly probate records, the Service of Heirs will be discussed here. Since land could not be bequeathed in a will, the service of heirs provides the legal process by which an heir acquired title to the land other than by sasine. The procedure consisted of a brieve issued from chancery instructing the sheriff to impanel a jury. The jury was to determine what lands the deceased ancestor had and if the claimant was the true heir at law. The verdict of the jury sent back to chancery was known as the retour. It was therefore necessary for the claimant to establish his right to heirship. These records obviously contain a wealth of genealogical information.

The records are essentially complete since 1600. Abstracts of the early records from 1544 to 1699 have been published by T. Thompson, *Inquisitionum ad Capellam Regis Retornatarum Abbreviatio* (N.p.: n.pub., 1811-16). (FHL# Q/941/A2i).

There are decennial indexes or abridgements from 1700 to 1959 available at the library. After 1860, there are annual indexes. The records and indexes are available at the library. They are listed in the FHLC under **Scotland/Land and Property.** They may also be found in the previously cited register *Sasines, Service of Heirs and Deeds* (Salt Lake City: Family History Library, 1981). (FHL# Reg. 941/R2ss). The original records are in Latin before 1848.

Tax Records

The hearth tax of 1690-95 and poll tax 1694-99 are available on microfilm at the library. They may be found in the FHLC under **Scotland/Taxation**. Some tax records have been published as listed below:

Wood, Marguerite. *Edinburgh Poll Tax Returns for 1694.* Publications of the Scottish Record Society, Vol. 82. Edinburgh: The Society, 1951. (FHL# 941/Bsr)

Simple, David. *Poll Tax Rolls of the Parishes of Renfrewshire 1695.* Salt Lake City: Family History Library, 1963. (FHL# microfilm 385260)

Records by Jurisdiction

Scotland

Counties	Biography	Cemetery	Census	Church of Scotland	Civil Registration	Court	Directories	Gazetteers	Genealogy	History	Land & Property	Maps	Non-conformists	Notarial	OPR Index	Probate	Tax
Aberdeen	•	•	•	•	•	•	•	•	•	•	•		•	•	•	•	
Angus	•	•	•	•	•	•	•			•	•		•		•	•	
Argyll		•	•	•	•	•		•	•	•	•	•	•			•	
Ayr	•	•	•	•	•	•	•		•	•	•		•	•		•	
Banff	•	•	•	•	•	•				•	•		•		•	•	
Berwick		•	•	•	•	•			•	•	•		•	•		•	
Bute		•	•	•	•	•			•	•	•	•	•			•	
Caithness	•	•	•	•	•	•			•	•	•		•		•	•	
Clackmannon		•	•	•	•	•			•	•		•		•	•		
Dumbarton	•	•	•	•	•			•	•	•	•	•			•		
Dumfries	•	•	•	•	•	•	•		•	•	•		•			•	
East Lothian	•		•	•	•	•				•	•		•			•	
Fife	•	•	•	•	•	•			•	•	•		•	•		•	
Inverness	•	•	•	•	•	•		•	•	•	•	•	•		•	•	
Kincardine		•	•	•	•	•				•	•		•	•	•	•	
Kincross	•	•	•	•	•	•				•	•	•			•	•	
Kirkcudbright	•	•	•	•	•	•			•	•	•					•	
Lanark	•	•	•	•	•	•	•			•	•		•	•	•	•	
Midlothian	•	•	•	•	•	•	•		•	•	•		•	•		•	
Moray		•	•	•	•	•				•	•				•	•	
Nairn			•	•	•	•				•	•				•	•	
Orkney			•	•	•	•			•	•	•		•		•	•	
Peebles		•	•	•	•	•				•	•		•			•	
Perth	•	•	•	•	•	•		•	•	•	•		•	•		•	
Renfrew		•	•	•	•	•	•		•	•	•		•		•	•	
Ross & Cromarty		•	•	•	•	•		•	•	•	•					•	
Roxburgh		•	•	•	•	•				•	•		•	•		•	
Selkirk		•	•	•	•	•				•	•		•		•	•	
Shetland	•		•	•	•	•			•	•	•		•		•	•	•
Sterling	•	•	•	•	•	•			•	•	•		•			•	•
Sutherland		•	•	•	•	•				•	•				•	•	•
West Lothian	•	•	•	•	•	•		•	•	•	•		•	•		•	•
Wigton	•		•	•	•	•			•	•	•		•			•	•

Records by Jurisdiction

Scotland

Counties	Biography	Cemetery	Census	Church of Scotland	Civil Registration	Court Records	Directories	Gazetteers	Genealogy	History	Land & Property	Maps	Non-conformist Records	ORP Index	Probate Records	Tax Records
County																
Aberdeen	•	•	•	•	•	•	•	•	•	•	•		•	•	•	•
Angus	•	•	•	•	•	•	•			•	•		•	•		•
Argyll												•	•			•
Ayr													•			•
Banff													•	•		
Berwick													•			•
Bute													•			•
Caithness													•	•		
Clackmannan													•	•		•
Dumbarton													•			•
Dumfries													•			•
East Lothian													•			•
Fife													•			•
Inverness													•	•		•
Kincardine													•	•		•
Kincross														•		
Kirkcudbright																
Lanark													•	•		•
Midlothian													•			•
Moray														•		
Nairn														•		•
Orkney													•	•		•
Peebles													•			
Perth													•			•
Renfrew													•			•
Ross & Cromarty														•		
Roxburgh																•
Selkirk																•

Chapter 18

Scandinavia

Sheri E. Slaughter

Scandinavia is a group of five nations that have interdependent histories and many elements of society in common, yet each country is fiercely proud of its own unique identity. Scandinavia is a land of 20 million people and 500,000 square miles (excluding Greenland). It is the "Land of the Midnight Sun" in summer and the "Northern Lights" in winter.

Scandinavia claims the world's first parliament (Iceland, A.D. 930) and also the first woman ever elected to the head of state (the current president of Iceland). Iceland and Finland are republics, Sweden, Denmark, and Norway constitutional, hereditary monarchies. Politically Scandinavia is considered moderate with the Social Democratic party being the largest overall. However, there are eleven parties in Norway and nine in Finland.

The languages of Denmark, Norway, and Sweden all developed from the same root, but modern Icelandic has changed little since pre-Christian times, and it bears about the same relationship to Danish or Norwegian that Anglo-Saxon does to English. Finnish is not related to the other Scandinavian languages at all. It is most closely related to Estonian, and more distantly related to Lapp or Hungarian.

Parts of Scandinavia have been inhabited for 8,000 years; Scandinavians were successful farmers, hunters, potters, and weavers during the Bronze Age (c.1500 B.C. to 500 B.C.). By A.D. 700, much of coastal, southern Scandinavia was settled. Because trade depended on sea travel, the Scandinavians became skilled shipwrights. Around 800, for reasons still subject to speculation, Scandinavians began pillaging, looting, and terrorizing Europe; and the Viking Age began.

The disintegration of the Holy Roman Empire created a power vacuum in Europe, leaving the continent weak and vulnerable. The Vikings took possession of many of these weakened areas. Swedes sailed southeast across the Baltic Sea and founded Varangian (Viking) Russia. Then they continued on across the Black Sea and became the elite bodyguards of the Byzantine emperor. The Norwegians sailed west and south to overpower the Orkney, Shetland, Hebrides, and Faeroe islands. From there they moved on west to Iceland (870), Greenland (982), and North America (1000); and south to parts of Great Britain and Ireland. The Danes sailed west to establish York in eastern England and south to establish Normandy in northern France. About A.D. 844 the Vikings established themselves on parts of the Iberian Peninsula, then sailed around Gibraltar into the Mediterranean about 859, settling along the coast in parts of France and Italy.

The Viking Age was relatively short, lasting from 800 to 1050. By 1300, Christianity began to take hold throughout Scandinavia. The history of each country from then until World War II is discussed later under individual country headings.

Patronymics

Common to all Scandinavian countries and important in genealogical research is the use of patronymics, a naming system which identifies the child as the son or daughter of a certain man. For example, a son of a man named Anders would have the surname Andersson (Swedish) or Anderssen (Danish and Norwegian). Anders' daughter would have the surname Andersdotter (Swedish) or Andersdatter (Danish and Norwegian). Women in Scandinavia kept their maiden names after they married, a custom which was practiced until around 1900.

The patronymic system prevailed until about 1875 when the children in a family started taking their father's surname. (Iceland still uses the patronymic system, and women still keep their maiden names.)

Scandinavian Library Collection

The Family History Library Catalog (FHLC) lists a group of records under **Scandinavia**. These records deal with topics that are common to all the Scandinavian countries. The following sources are helpful and are a good base to begin any Scandinavian research. The FHLC has two files for each Scandinavian country: one has English translations of the records and the other (Foreign Language FHLC) is strictly in the native language.

Chronology

Slaegtskalender, 1600-2050. N.p.: n.pub., [c.1950]. (FHL# 948/A9s)

A guide for determining the dates of the Scandinavian feast days from 1600 to 2050. Parish ministers often recorded vital events by feast day instead of by date.

Emigration and Immigration

There are several good sources included in this section which deal with the Scandinavian population in the United States. Of interest if the Scandinavian ancestor was LDS is:

Clemmons, Aurelia. *Emigration from the Scandinavian Mission, 1853-1886.* 2 vols. Salt Lake City: Aurelia Clemmons, n.d. (FHL# 948/W2ca)

Lists emigrating LDS Church members by conference under each year; includes some entries from the Icelandic Mission.

Another good source for ancestors who settled on the Pacific coast is:

Stine, Thomas Ostenson. *Scandinavians on the Pacific, Puget Sound.* San Francisco, Calif.: R. & E. Research Association, 1968. (FHL# 979.7/F2sc/1968)

Genealogy

The major source here is one that was put together by the research department of the Church of Jesus Christ of Latter-day Saints' Genealogical Society. It consists of genealogical research notes, family group records, pedigree charts, and correspondence between the Research Department and the persons sponsoring the research. Access to the files is provided by indexes to 3,920 reels of microfilm. Instructions on how to use these indexes is on the FHLC microfiche under the heading **Scandinavia/Genealogy**; they include indexes for place names, ancestor's surname, patron's surname, etc.

The Genealogy Society of the Church of Jesus Christ of Latter-day Saints. *Research Department Patron Files, ca.1928-1966, and Indexes.* Salt Lake City: Filmed by the Genealogy Society of Utah, 1965-70, 1976. See FHLS for call numbers.

Another good source is a volume of research papers prepared by various Scandinavian researchers for the World Conference on Records in 1980. It contains articles about using emigration records, a Scandinavian soldier's life, local histories, life in the cities of Denmark, Norway, and Sweden, rural life, and other topics of interest. A copy of this volume, *Scandinavian Family and Local History* (Salt Lake City: Published by the Corporation of the President of the Church of Jesus Christ of Latter-day Saints, 1980), can be purchased at the library. A copy is also kept in the reference area (FHL# 929.1/W893/1980/Vol.8).

One other work that should not be overlooked is:

Christiansen, Henry E. *Searching for Scandinavian Ancestors at the Genealogical Society Library.* Salt Lake City: Genealogical Society of the Church of Jesus Christ of Latter-day Saints, c.1969. (FHL# 929.1/W893/E3 or microfilm 897215, item 4, or microfiche 6039338)

Handwriting

A source that is helpful in deciphering the Gothic script used in most of the early records is:

Johansson, Carl-Erik. *Thus They Wrote: A Guide to the Gothic Script of Scandinavia, Denmark, Norway, Finland, Sweden.* Provo, Utah: Brigham Young University Press, 1970. (FHL# Ref/948/A8j)

History

A good history of the Vikings written in English with twenty-eight illustrations and twenty-eight maps is:

Kendrick, Thomas Downing. *A History of the Vikings.* New York: Charles Scribner's Sons, 1930. (FHL# 948/H2k or microfilm 896938, item 1)

A bibliography of books and articles about the history of Scandinavia in English is:

Oakley, Steward P. *Scandinavian History, 1520-1970.* London: Historical Association, c.1894. (FHL# British Area/942/-H2ha/no.91)

Maps

Several useful maps of the Scandinavian area are kept in the map case:

Map of Scandinavia: Denmark, Finland, Iceland, Norway, Sweden. New York: Scandinavian National Tourist Offices, 1978. (FHL# 948/E7m)

National Geographic Society (U.S.). Cartographic Division. *Northern Europe.* Washington, D.C.: National Geographic Society, 1954. (FHL# Europ. Map Case/-940/E7ng/no.3)

Yonge, Charlotte Mary. *History of Christian Names.* 2 vols. London: Parker and Bourn, 1863. (Folded map of Scandinavia in the front of Vol. 1.) (FHL# Gen Ref Area 929.4/Y8h/1863)

Other subject headings under **Scandinavia** include **/Folklore, /Heraldry, /Names (Personal), /Nobility, /Population, /Religion,** and **/Social Life and Customs.**

For beginning Scandinavian researchers, two useful guides are:

Thomsen, Finn A. *Scandinavian Genealogical Research*

Manual. 3 vols. Bountiful, Utah: Thomsen's Genealogical Center, 1980. (FHL# 948/D27t)

Volume 1 is a Danish-Norwegian language guide and dictionary. Volume 2 is about the handwriting and names of Denmark and Norway. Volume 3 is a guide to Danish and Norwegian genealogical research sources.

Poulsen, Ellyn, and Gay P. Kowallis, ed. *The Scandinavian Genealogical Helper.* 3 vols. Logan, Utah: Everton Publishers, 1969. (FHL# 948/B2s)

Volume 1 discusses Scandinavia in general and major sources in Norway, Sweden, and Denmark. Volume 2 continues the discussion of the records of Norway, Sweden, and Denmark, and Volume 3 is primarily about the probate records of Denmark.

The Family History Department of the Church of Jesus Christ of Latter-day Saints has published brochures for Denmark, Sweden, Norway, Finland, and Iceland in its *Major Genealogical Record Sources* series, Series D. These are available for purchase in the Scandinavian Area Copy Center.

DENMARK

Historical Background

c.800-1050	Danish sailors raid European coastal towns for slaves and booty.
c.950	King Harald Bluetooth unites Denmark and introduces Christianity.
1013-42	Denmark rules England. King Canute II completes the Christianization of Denmark.
1219	Denmark conquers Estonia.
1240s	Civil wars and disputes with north German cities greatly weaken the country.
1380	Denmark and Norway are united under Queen Margrete, wife of King Haakon VI of Norway. (He died that year.)
1388	Queen Margrete is elected ruler of Sweden as well.
1397	Denmark, Norway, and Sweden are united in the Union of Kalmar.
1412	Death of Queen Margrete.
1443	Capital of Denmark transferred from Roskilde to Copenhagen.
1536	Lutheranism becomes the official religion of Denmark during the Reformation and the reign of King Christian III.
1611-60	Denmark fights several wars with Sweden for control of the Baltic Sea, loses much territory.
1661	The Hereditary Autocracy Act ends tax-exemption privileges of the nobility; commoners replace nobles in administrative positions.
1700s	Denmark colonizes Greenland.
1788	Serfdom abolished.
1801-07	Copenhagen bombarded by British fleets during the Napoleonic Wars, destroying the Danish navy.
1814	Denmark cedes Norway to Sweden in the Treaty of Kiel, keeps Greenland and Iceland.
1849	Denmark adopts its first democratic constitution
1864	Denmark loses Schleswig and Holstein to Prussia and Austria.
1900s	Industry, education, and finance flourish.
1914-18	Denmark remains neutral during World War I.
1918	Denmark grants independence to Iceland, which remains under the Danish king until 1944.
1920	North Schleswig returned to Denmark.
1939	Denmark signs a ten-year nonaggression pact with Hitler.
1940-45	Germany occupies Denmark during World War II.
1944	Iceland ends union with Denmark.
1966	Denmark begins a $600 million development program in Greenland.

Settlement and Migration

Denmark is a comfortable, cozy, fertile land with no wilderness and few hills. Its population is about 5 million. Denmark proper consists of the peninsula of Jutland (Jylland) and 483 islands of which 100 are inhabited. The seven main islands are Sjaeland (Zealand), Fyn (Funen), Laaland (Lolland), Falster, Møn (Møen), Langeland, and Bornholm (eighty miles east of Sjaeland in the Baltic Sea). Far to the northwest of Jutland in the Atlantic Ocean, between the Shetland Islands and Iceland, lies a group of about eighteen Danish islands called the Faeroe Islands.

The capital and largest city is København (Copenhagen) on the island of Sjaeland, with a metropolitan population of 1.25 million. Copenhagen celebrated its 800th anniversary in 1967. Less than a fifth of the people live in rural villages or on farms.

The Danes are closely related to the Norwegians and the Swedes. Their written languages are also very similar, but the spoken language sounds quite different. Faeroese, related to Danish, is spoken among the 40,000 inhabitants of the Faeroe Islands.

Denmark's only minority consists of about 30,000 persons of German ancestry who live in southern Jutland, along Denmark's border with West Germany.

Toward the end of the nineteenth century, Denmark, like all industrialized European nations, experienced a pronounced migration of people from the countryside to the towns and larger cities. About 350,000 Danes immigrated to the United States between 1870 and 1920.

The Evangelical Lutheran Church is the official church of Denmark with about 97 percent of the population belonging, but there is complete freedom of worship.

For an introduction to Danish genealogical research, see the following guide at the reference table:

Smith, Frank, and Finn A. Thomsen. *Genealogical Guidebook and Atlas of Denmark.* Salt Lake City: Bookcraft, 1969. (FHL# Ref/948.9/E6s)

Discusses the four major Danish genealogical sources: parish registers, census returns, military levying rolls, and probate records; Danish words and their meanings; personal given names; the gothic alphabet; converting movable feast days to the modern calendar; list of parishes and related areas; map of the counties; sectional maps, etc.

Also at the reference table is a large gray binder labeled *Denmark* that explains how to access the Danish records. It contains sections on archives, census, church records, Copenhagen City, emigration, land records, language, LDS sources (centers), maps, military, research procedures, vocabulary, etc.

Denmark Library Collection

The Family History Library has the largest centralized collection of Danish genealogical records available anywhere for any country of comparable size. Research on Danish pedigrees can thus be conducted with greater ease than in Denmark itself, where the records are dispersed throughout various archives.

Four major sources provide valuable genealogical information: church records, census returns, military levying rolls, and probate records.

The Danish alphabet has three extra letters that come after "z"–"ae," "ø," and "å." Names of counties, parishes, or people that begin with these letters will fall at the end of the alphabet.

Denmark is divided into twenty-four counties or *Amter* in the FHLC. Other jurisdictions are district *(Herred)*, parish *(Sogn)*, and village *(By)*. The Faeroe Islands constitute an independent *Amt* with permission for home rule under the Danish crown.

The Faeroe (Foroyar in their language) have seven *Sysla* (counties) and the records are on a separate microfiche in the FHLC. The primary sources are census returns for the years 1801, 1834, 1840, 1845, 1850, 1855, 1860, 1870, 1880, 1890, 1901, 1906, and 1911 and church records from about 1750 to 1850. One *Sysla* has church records from 1687 to 1878. The Faeroese language is similar to Icelandic and the records are much like the Danish.

Archives and Libraries

The library currently lists forty-one sources under **Denmark/Archives and Libraries** including archive bibliographies, histories, inventories, and periodicals. Archives include the Royal Archives, county, military, province, *Landsarkivet* (regional), Public Records Office, Danish National Archives *(Rigsarkivet)*, and city archives. Lists of holdings, addresses, and research aids, some with English summaries, are also available.

Biography

The library has biographies of members of the Parliament, outstanding Danish personalities, Danish fathers as commemorated by their children, royal surgeons (1660-1848), Danish jubilee teachers (those who taught for fifty years or more), bookdealers, royal foresters (1660-1790), priests (1869-1911), Danish mothers as commemorated by their children, sculptors, farmers from Sjaelland, officers of the Danish army, navy and marines, nobility, scholars, and attorneys (1660-1869). There are also several biographical dictionaries.

Census Records (Folketaellinger)

Census records are available for 1787, 1801, 1834, 1840, 1845, 1850, 1855, 1860, 1870, 1880, 1890, 1901, 1906, and 1911.

Danish census returns began in 1787. The census lists are, as a whole, well preserved, generally complete for the whole country, correct, and dependable, although some names and ages are wrong.

The 1787 and 1801 censuses give the full names of each person in the household including servants and persons who were staying with the family for a short time. Maiden surnames of all women are given as are relationships, ages, titles or profession, marital status (first or subsequent marriage), and residence by parish, street name, and number. Children, including illegitimate children and stepchildren, are listed by birth order.

Consult the FHLC under **Denmark/[County]/Census/[Year]** after which the districts and parishes will be listed with an appropriate film number. Within the parish, the family is located in a village *(By)*, a farm *(gaard)*, or a city *(stad)*.

Types of information recorded in the 1834 and 1840 census returns are the same as above, except that the number of previous marriages is no longer reported.

The 1845 census enumeration was the first to include the place of birth. Other information is similar to the earlier censuses. The 1850 census is the same as 1845.

From 1855 forward, religious affiliation is given in addition to all the other data. From 1870 forward, the gender of each individual is added to the record.

The 1901 census returns add the complete birth date of each person; year of marriage, divorce, or death of spouse; number of living children; number of deceased children including stillbirths; the year a person moved into the parish; and previous place of residence.

The 1906 and 1911 census returns include the full name of each person, sex, relationship in the family, birth date, marital status, and religious affiliation. (Year of marriage or divorce and number of living and dead children are not reported.)

Copenhagen's census records are found in the FHLC under **København/København/Census.** These census records are extremely difficult to access. It is necessary to know the neighborhood and street. Streets are often mentioned in the parish register, so that is the first place to look. The Police Census *(Politiets Mandtaller)* occurred in Copenhagen from 1866-1923. These yearly census records occupy 7,814 reels of microfilm, are filmed alphabetically by street name, and include names of residents and their children over ten, ages, places of birth, relationships, residences, and occupations.

Church Records (Kirkebøger)

Lutheran parish registers date back to as early as 1573 and all are available on microfilm up to as late as 1925 in some cases. Generally they begin around 1645 when laws were passed requiring ministers to record births (christenings), marriages, and deaths (burials). The state church (Lutheran) is still the birth registrar. In 1850, there were 1,853 parishes in Denmark.

The Danish parish registers usually contain the following information: Birth and Christening *(Fødte og Døbte)*: given name of child, sex, date of birth and christening, legitimacy, names of parents, mother's age, names of witnesses at the christening, their places of residence, occupations, and relationships (in earlier records only the father's name is given); Marriage and Engagement *(Copulerede og Trolovede):* names of candidates, ages or dates of birth, residences, occupations, personal or marital status, witnesses, date of marriage or betrothal; Death and Burial *(Døde og Begravede):* name of deceased, dates of death and burial, residence at the time of death, occupation, marital status, age, and cause of death. These records are listed under **Denmark/[County]/[Parish]/Church Records**.

From about 1736 on, Confirmations *(Konfirmerede)* were added to the record. Prior to 1814, they may only give the name and age of the child being confirmed; but after 1814, they usually include the date of birth or christening, the name of one or both parents, and residence. Absolutions, introductions, and communions usually only give the name of the person and the date of the event.

After 1814 the parish registers were on printed forms, so the information may be more complete. Also Arrivals and Removals *(Til og Afgangslister)* were added to the record at that time. These records were mostly kept in rural parishes and include the name of the person arriving at or leaving the parish, former and new places of residence, marital status, sometimes date and place of birth, and relationships. From 1814, general indexes were supposed to be kept in each parish with reference to christenings, confirmations, marriages, deaths, arrivals and removals.

The non-state church congregations whose ordinances and records are accepted by the civil authorities are classified as recognized nonconformists. Recognized nonconformist groups are the Reformed French and German, Jewish, Roman Catholic, and Methodist; some of their records have been microfilmed. Unrecognized nonconformists must register births, marriages, and deaths in the Lutheran Church.

Listed under **Denmark/Church Records** are extracts from parish records, a handbook of church property in Denmark, a list of the various rectories in Denmark, and inventories of various parish registers, LDS (Form E) reports, and LDS branch and ward reports.

Civil Registration (Personregistre)

Civil marriages *(Borgerlige vielser)* were permitted in cities starting about 1851. These records are on microfilm up to 1961 and are listed under the FHLC heading **Denmark/[County]/[City]/Civil Registration**. They contain the names of the bride and groom, residence, occupation, marital status, date of marriage, and sometimes age. Marriages may be registered with the state church or with the local civil authorities.

Since about 1857, deaths could be registered with the church or state. Death certificates *(Dødsattester)* are on microfilm up to about 1933. See FHLC heading **Denmark/[County]/[City]/Civil Registration**. They contain the name of the deceased, age, marital status, occupation, residence, date of death, cause of death (sometimes obliterated on the film). Copenhagen's death certificates are available from 1840 to 1933, filed by district.

Civil registration in the counties of Abenra, Haderslev, and Tønder for births, marriages, and deaths has occurred since 1874 and are available on microfilm to about 1950. For birth records, the name, date and place of birth, sex, parentage, religion, and residence are given. Marriage records will give the names of the bride and groom, dates of birth, parents, religion, residences, names of witnesses, and the date of the marriage. Death records list the name of the deceased, including maiden name for a married woman, residence, name of spouse, date and place of birth, parentage, date and place of death.

From 1800-1847 Copenhagen city had applications *(Blanketregnskaber)* administered by the civil authorities under the direction of the chancery regarding marriages, divorces, burials, and testaments. (These are not yet cataloged in the FHLC but are available on microfilm; check later editions of the FHLC for holdings.) From 1720 to 1868, Copenhagen city also had a Marriage License *(Kopulationsprotokoller)* Index, listing the names of grooms, date of license, and parish in which the marriage was to be performed. These are listed on FHL# microfilm 048119-048124.

The death certificates of Jylland (1857-1932) are catalogued under the country heading of civil registration. Also under the country heading are documents concerning internal affairs, lists of convicts in the Duchy of Holstein (1802-48), drafts and enclosures, lists of persons working for the civil government of Denmark, 1923, and a directory of addresses and telephone numbers of the civil registration offices in Denmark.

Court Records (Tingboger eller retsprotokoller)

Court records from 1564 to 1886 are available on microfilm. These deal with decisions in criminal trials, transfers of real estate, marriage settlements, guardianships, mortgages, teacher applications, and miscellaneous judiciary items. Often names of persons involved, occupations, relationships, and residences are mentioned.

Listed under **Denmark/Court Records** are deeds *(Skøder),* recording of notices, proclamations, appointments and various legal procedures from the *Sjaellandsfars Landsting* (Upper Chamber of Parliament) for 1630-1805. There are also the following records: extracts for Viborgs *Landsting,* duties of the district Sheriff, history of judicial district courts of Copenhagen County 1521-1965, and cases brought before the Sjaellandsfar *Landsting* 1676-1789.

Directories

The following directories are found under the country listing: a business directory of the Duchies of Schleswig-Holstein and the Principality of Lubeck for 1869; a register of county and court officials in Denmark; Denmark's royal and state government officials, 1832-50; directory of Copenhagen and Denmark, 1951; and an address list for Denmark's archives.

For Copenhagen there are directories for street numbers (1872), government officials (1783), and the city of Copenhagen and its suburbs for 1801, 1813, 1827, 1834, 1840, 1845, 1850, and 1855 (on microfiche).

Emigration and Immigration (Udvandringsjournaler)

The emigration records for 1868-1934 are available on microfilm or microfiche. They contain the name of the emigrant, occupation, place of residence, age, destination, and date of embarkation. Copenhagen's registers of emigration are on 776 microfiche. The later years (1934-40) are restricted by laws of privacy and will be released 1 January 1990. Available registers are listed in the FHLC under **Denmark/København/Emigration and Immigration.**

Passport records *(Pasprotokoller)* for 1780-1920 are also available on microfilm and are listed under **Denmark/[County]/[City]/Emigration and Immigration.** They give the name of the person receiving the passport, occupation, former place of residence, destination, and the date of issue.

Other subjects cataloged under **Denmark/Emigration and Immigration** are French emigrants in Denmark, civil registration cards of German refugees in Denmark including vital records, 1945-49; Danish colonization of the Virgin Islands; Danish emigration to America 1868-1914 (with English summaries), Danish Mormon migration, and Danish pioneers and enterprises all over the world. The following English research guides to emigration from Denmark are helpful:

Hvidt, Kristian. *Along the Scandinavian Emigrant Trail: Denmark.* Salt Lake City: Genealogical Society of the Church of Jesus Christ of Latter-day Saints, c.1969. (FHL# 929.148/W893/E1 - 2a or microfilm 897215, item 1, and microfiche 6039337, item 1)

______. *Sources Related to Danish Emigration.* Salt Lake City: Genealogical Society of the Church of Jesus Christ of Latter-day Saints, c.1969. (FHL# 929.1/W893/E14 or microfilm 897215, item 15, or microfiche 6039349)

Ljungmark, Lars. *For Sale–Minnesota: Organized Promotion of Scandinavian Immigration, 1866-1873.* Chicago: Swedish Pioneer Historical Society, c.1971. (FHL# U.S. & CAN/977.6/W21)

Gazetteers, Maps, and Atlases

There are many excellent maps and gazetteers to use as research aids. Among them are:

Trap, J. P. *Denmark.* 32 vols. [Copenhagen]: G. E. C. Gad, 1958-72. (FHL# 948.9/E2t/1958 and on microfiche by county)

Gazetteer of Denmark, Faeroe Islands, and Greenland.

United States. Board on Geographic Names. *Denmark and the Faeroe Islands: Official Standard Names Approved by the U.S. Board on Geographic Names.* Washington, D.C.: Government Printing Office, 1961. (FHL# 948.9/E5u or microfilm 874461, item 3)

Becker, Peter Willemoes. *Dansk Atlas.* Copenhagen: Lokalhistorisk Afdeling, c.1974. (FHL# 948.9/E6bp)

Maps of Denmark with summaries in English.

Bramsen, Bo. *Gamle Danmarkskort.* Copenhagen: Politikens Forlag, 1952. (FHL# Q/948.9/E3b)

Old maps of Denmark with biographical notes of the cartographers.

There are over forty listings under **Denmark/Maps.**

Genealogy

The genealogy records of Denmark consist primarily of family histories. Some of them are Boesen, Borberg, von Wowern, Fabricius, Ryge, Gad, Rohweder, Dinesen, Thura, Sturz, Hvidt, Olrog, Aubert, and Slottved. Most of these are written in Danish. There are also genealogies of nobility and priests. The *printed* genealogies of the nobility *(Adelen)* are the oldest Danish records in the library, dating from the eleventh century to the present and containing names; pedigrees listing their progenitors to the earliest known ancestor; names of spouses and children, dates and places of birth, marriage, and death; and residences, offices, commissions, occupations, and relationships.

The library also has genealogical tables of Haderslev *Amt,* ancestral pedigree charts of the Jens Jensen family, dozens of genealogical handbooks in English, and many genealogy periodicals.

Handwriting

Excellent aids are available to help in reading the paleography of Denmark; two of them are:

Danish-Norwegian Paleography. Salt Lake City: Genealogical Department of the Church of Jesus Christ of Latter-day Saints, c.1976. (FHL# REF/929.1/G286gs/Ser. D/no.16 or microfiche 6030017)

Simon, Georg. *Gotisk Skrift.* Copenhagen: Dansk Historisk Håndbogsforlag, 1977. (FHL# Ref/948.9/G3s)

A handbook of instruction on how to read the Gothic script used in many older Danish documents.

History

The library's numerous works cataloged in the FHLC under **Denmark/History** includes works on Danes in the nineteenth century, historical survey of Danish letters 1250-1505, collected essays concerning various aspects of Danish daily life from 1620-1964, old Danish manor-houses, a history of Danish circuses, history of castles and estates, Danish provincial towns 200 years ago, and a history of museums (with English summaries).

Most of the histories are in Danish, but a few good ones are written in English. Three of those are:

Neilsen, Roger. *Denmark.* Copenhagen: Egmont H. Petersen, 1939. (FHL# 948.9/H2ni) Pictorial history.

Wheaton, Henry. *History of the Northmen: Or Danes and Normans.* London: John Murray, 1831. (FHL# Europe/-940/H2w)

Covers from prehistory to the conquest of England by William of Normandy, 1066.

Worsoe, Hans H. *Life in the Cities of Denmark.* [Salt Lake City]: Corporation of the President of the Church of Jesus Christ of Latter-day Saints, 1980. (FHL# Special Book Area/929.1/W893/1980/Vol. 8/Pt. 4)

There are also many history bibliographies, handbooks, inventories, and periodicals.

Land and Property (Faesteprotokoller og Jordeboger)

Some of the oldest Danish records available are land tenancy records dating from about 1515 and available on microfilm to about 1922. The deed and mortgage records *(Skøde og Panteprotokoller)* date from 1580 and are available on microfilm to about 1945. These records contain the names of persons, residences, and dates of transactions. Deeds often mention relationships and descriptions of property.

Land records are generally cataloged under the county headings but at the national level are land registrations and copyholds of various estates from 1688-1917; German deeds, 1664-68; deeds, 1680-1848; land tenancy records, 1649-79; land registers, 1688-92, 1662-92; drafts and enclosures of deeds, 1680-1719, 1661-79; appraisement notices during a war with Sweden, 1657-63; land tenancy with citizen and tax records, 1660-1771, 1682-1800; farms for officers and military units, 1662-74; royal land tenancy, 1680-1702; royal deeds, 1720-27; deeds issued and obtained by the king, 1535-1765; manor lords and copyholders of the 1600s; cottagers on the island of Sjaelland; and the development of farms and estates.

Copenhagen city land and property records consist of property obligations, 1687-1850; mortgage records, 1653-1862; records of legal ownership, 1800-62; documents calling heirs into probate proceedings, 1697-1855; rental contracts, 1795-1866; deeds and conveyances, 1681-1862; and a register of real estate, houses, lots giving abstracts of deeds with reference to the mortgage book by number and page, c.1730-1927.

Language and Languages

There are several excellent Danish-English and English-Danish dictionaries in the collection. The following are helpful in research:

Schibsbye, K., and H. Kossmann. *Danish-English Dictionary.* Brooklyn, N.Y.: P. Shalom Publishing, Inc., 1967. (FHL# 439.81321/Sch31d/1967)

Perry, Gay, comp. *Danish-English Genealogical Dictionary.* Logan: n.pub., 1965. (FHL# 439.81321/D228k)

Military Records

The military records of Denmark are an extremely valuable genealogical source. These records contain lists of the eligible male rural population from birth to about forty-four years of age in the period from 1789 to 1849. After 1849, the males were enlisted at the age of fourteen and, after 1869, at seventeen.

The earliest military records are the Army Service Records *(Stambøger)* which began as early as 1693 in some places, but generally began in 1765. These contain names of both officers and enlisted men as recorded in regiments, batteries, companies, etc.; age; sometimes date and place of birth; date of death and discharge; place of death; general description of the soldier; previous service; place of enlistment (prior to 1803); and sometimes military levying rolls number. (Available on film to about 1890.)

The army levying rolls *(Laegdsruller)* began in approximately 1789. These records were kept in each parish by civil authorities. The rolls consisted of a complete list of males conscripted or liable to be conscripted in the future from each district. The list was usually compiled every three years, with special supplemental lists of all males born, for the intervening years. It also included all males who moved into the district. These rolls are arranged chronologically by parish and are available on microfilm to approximately 1890 (some as recent as 1930).

Entered on these lists was the conscript's name, age, place of birth, residence, height, old and new serial numbers, unit of service, disabilities, death, exemptions from military service, and father's name (or mother's name, if he was illegitimate). Their names remained on these rolls until they moved from the parish, died, were exempted, or were transferred to the navy. The names of persons born in the cities did not appear in the levying rolls before 1842 because the cities had their own militia until that time. There are no military levying rolls for the county of Bornholm prior to 1850, and the counties of Haderslev, Tønder, and Åbenrå have incomplete rolls.

The navy levying rolls *(Søruller)* began in 1802 and are available on microfilm to about 1893. These rolls are similar to the army levying rolls but consist of three sections: (1) The roll of young men *(ungdomsrulle)* which listed young men from birth to the age when they are able to serve in the Navy. Given on these rolls are the youth's name, his father's name, place of birth, age, sometimes date of birth, a reference to where the father's name is found on other rolls, and the new enrollment number; (2) The active roll *(hovedrulle)*, which contains the names of those men of appropriate age to serve in the navy. They give the name of conscript, place of birth, age, height, marital status, number of children, residence, name of father, parish number, serial number, date and number of seaman's certificate, occupation, if presently at sea, home port of ship, name of captain, expected date of return, and transfer or death; (3) The extra or reserve roll *(extrarulle)*, which lists older men who probably would be asked to serve only in event of a national emergency. Information given on these rolls is similar to the active roll except for the addition of the date when the person was transferred to the extra roll and the reason; former main roll number; and death date (names remain on this roll until death).

These rolls are arranged chronologically by parish and are cataloged in the FHLC by county.

Miscellaneous military records under the **Denmark/-[County]** heading include histories, handbooks of warrant officers, biographies of officers, lists of the Royal Danish Guard, and handbooks of Danish army units.

Minorities

The FHLC lists an index to Jewish deaths in Denmark, 1693-1976, and several other works on Jews. See FHLC heading **Denmark/Minorities** for a complete list of titles.

Names, Geographical

In the Scandinavian Reference section of the library are eight volumes prepared by the Denmark Statsministeriet with lists of place names of the various counties in Denmark. (FHL# Ref/948.9/ B4s, v. 1-8).

Names, Personal

The library has many books on personal names in Denmark and among the various topics are: suggested surnames for changing from patronymics to family names (from 1912); Danish family law including parents, children, and legislation on names; Denmark's personal names, given names, and surnames; naming customs in southwest Jylland throughout 300 years; surnames used in Lolland-Falster from the sixteenth to nineteenth century; and the origin of Danish names.

Pensions

There are numerous titles for pension records covering the 1747-1848 time period. See FHLC heading **Denmark/Pension** for a complete list of titles.

Probate Records (Skifteprotokoller)

Until 1683 when King Christian V established the laws of the present probate system of Denmark, wills were uncommon. However, there are probate records (wills-intestate) as early as 1562 and guardianship records *(Overformynderiprotokoller)* as early as 1573. There are also wills *(testamenter)* generally starting after 1683, all available on microfilm to between 1870 and 1913. Most of these records are indexed (calendars).

The probate records are a valuable genealogical source because it was necessary to list all heirs and their relationships. The following information is usually contained in a probate record: full name of the deceased and last place of residence; sometimes date of death; list of the heirs and their residences at the time of the probate; ages of children; names of the husbands of married female heirs; names of guardians of minors and relationship, if any; name of the guardian for the widow, usually one of her relatives; and an inventory and distribution of property.

Guardianship records give name of deceased, names of heirs, relationships, residences, name of guardian, and sometimes date of birth or christening of the minor.

The probate jurisdictions of Denmark are divided into three main areas: Copenhagen city, other incorporated cities, and rural areas. In rural areas there are county, cavalry, land estate, and district probate jurisdictions. To access probate records, it may be necessary to look in more than one jurisdiction for the desired record.

Cataloged under **Denmark/Probate Records** are listings for miscellaneous probates of public officials and nobility, wills approved through the Chancery Office of Denmark, Iceland, and the West Indies, and probate records of several Cavalry Districts.

Public Records

The public records of Denmark are numerous but of little significance to the genealogist. They consist of correspondence, transactions, drafts, enclosures, journals, and applications of Danish royal and government officials to other officials. Many of these are from the Second and Third Department of the Royal Danish Chancery and date from about 1572 to 1848. These public records are contained on over 3400 reels of microfilm.

Schools (Skoleprotokoller)

School matriculation records in Denmark start as early as 1584 and are available to 1905 on microfilm. These list names of those enrolling in school, inventories, endowments, and teachers' land tenancy records. They also have probate records of headmasters, assistants, and students.

Under **Denmark/Schools** are biographies of Danish students, lists of Danish students (1836, 1856, 1866), and a history of the public schools in Denmark.

Cataloged under **/Copenhagen City/Schools** are vital statistics of boys at parish poor schools 1772-1815; lists of students of Copenhagen University 1611-67; and lists of students who took their examinations and left school from 1880 to 1903.

Social Life and Customs

Among the many library holdings that describe Denmark's social life and customs are books dealing with aspects of Danish daily life from 1620-1964, gypsies in Denmark, family life, the land and the people, and rural home life.

Taxation

There are taxation records cataloged at the national, county, and city levels. These records may start as early as 1660 but are generally not valuable to the genealogist, since they usually state only names, residences, and the amount of tax paid. Taxation records may consist of land tenancy and tax records, taxation lists, cavalry district accounts, estate accounts, contribution tax records, and property tax records. For a better understanding of Denmark's tax records and how they can be used to aid in genealogical research, see:

Jorgensen, A. Harald. *How to Use Court, Land, and Tax Records of Denmark in a Genealogical Program.* Salt Lake City: Genealogical Society of the Church of Jesus Christ of Latter-day Saints, c.1969. (FHL# 929.1/-W893/E13 or microfilm 897215, item 14)

Miscellaneous Danish records are still cataloged in the old card catalog located in the library's European stacks area. Most of the cards have been transfered to the FHLC, but a few remain to be transfered.

FINLAND

Historical Background

100 Ancestors of present-day Finns begin to move inland from the east (probably from between the Volga River and the Ural Mountains in Russia) and from Estonia in the south into territory already occupied by Lapps for thousands of years.

c.800-1050 Finns do not participate in Viking raids but benefit by the growing contact and trade with other colonies.

1000 Three defined Finnish tribes emerge: the Finns in the southwest, the Tavastians in the interior lake district, and the Karelians to the east. No unified government or state exists.

1100s Sweden and Russia struggle for control of Finland.

1200s Finns are converted to Christianity (Roman Catholicism by the Swedes and Eastern Orthodoxy by the Russians).

1216 The Pope confirms Swedish title to Finland, many Swedes settle there, and Swedish becomes the official language.

1362 Finns receive the same rights within the monarchy as the Swedes.

1400-1500s Most of Finland is administered as fiefs by Swedish noblemen, who levy heavy taxes on the people.

1555 Sweden and Russia (Ivan the Terrible) fight over Finland. Finland becomes a Swedish duchy.

1616 Gustavus II Adolphus grants Finland local autonomy and a *Riksdag* (parliament) is established.

1695-97 Crop failure causes a famine; one-fourth of the population dies.

1700s Continual wars and conflicts between Sweden and Russia for control of Finland.

1809 Czar Alexander I occupies Finland, proclaims it a grand duchy of the Russian Empire. The country is ruled by a Russian governor-general, with a puppet senate.

1820 Nationalist awakening; Finnish language revived.

1863 The *Diet* (parliament), which had not met since 1809, is reconstituted. Finnish language is granted equal status with Swedish.

1894-99 Finland loses autonomy, Russian becomes the official language, and a Russian governor is appointed.

1905 A six-day nationwide strike restores much of Finland's self-government.

1906 The Finns create the first parliament elected by *all* adult citizens, including women.

1917 Taking advantage of the Russian Revolution, the Diet votes in favor of independence. Soviet government accepts Finnish sovereignty.

1918 Finnish civil war between the socialists and non-socialists. (Non-socialists won.)

1919 The Diet adopts a new republican constitution. The first president of Finland is elected, Kaarlo J. Ståhlberg.

1939-44 Russia defeats Finland in the Winter War and the Continuation War, separate sections of World War II. Parts of Finland are ceded to the Soviet Union.

Settlement and Migration

Finland is a difficult and resilient land with some 60,000 lakes, 30,000 islands, and nearly three-quarters of the land forested. Its cities and people appear more central European than Scandinavian, but the country functions with Scandinavian efficiency. With a population density of about thirty-six persons per square mile, Finland is one of the most sparsely inhabited countries in Europe. More than two-thirds of the population resides in the south third of the country. Finland has about 5 million people with 500,000 residing in the capital of Helskini.

Finns constitute about 90 percent of the population and persons of Swedish descent about 7 percent. The far north is inhabited by about 4,000 Lapps. Finland also has about 6,000 eastern Europeans and small groups of Jews and Turks.

Approximately 55 percent of the population is rural. Finnish and Swedish are the official languages with more than 93 percent of the people speaking Finnish and about 7 percent speaking Swedish. The Evangelical Lutheran Church is the principal national church, and its members make up more than 90 percent of the population. Freedom of worship is guaranteed to all faiths. The Russian Orthodox Church, still a national church, has sharply declined in numbers since World War II.

Finland Library Collection

A guide to beginning Finnish research is kept at the reference table in the Family History Library in a large gray binder labeled *Finland Misc. Information.* It contains sections on the Archives of Finland, parish information, parishes within each county, maps, emigration, research, and vocabulary.

Finland was a part of Sweden from the twelfth century until 1809. Consequently, early genealogical records for Finland are recorded in both Finnish and Swedish. Many early tax lists, provincial accounts, census, and military records pertaining to areas of Finland are found in the National Archives of Sweden at Stockholm.

Finland is divided into eleven *Laani* (counties) in the FHLC. Ecclesiastical divisions are similar to those in Sweden. The Finnish *Pitäjä is equivalent to the Swedish Socken* (parish). The Finnish *Seurakunta* is like the Swedish *Forsamling* (parish). Both countries have two words meaning "parish." They were used in different parts of the countries during different time periods. Smaller units within the parish are called *pieni kyla* (village), and *tila, maatila* (farm). The parish registers begin about 1648, are written in Swedish until about 1850-60, and are similar to Swedish parish registers.

Censuses *(Henkikirjat)* were taken yearly for census and tax purposes from about 1635. The probate records *(Perukirjat)* are available from as early at 1650 in some areas. They give the name of the deceased, age, sometimes date of death, residence, names of heirs, guardians, relationships, and distributions of real and personal property.

Archives and Libraries

Finland. *Riksarkivet: en Handledning.* Helsingfors: n.pub., 1973. (FHL# 948.97/A35v/no.3/1973)

Guide to the National Archives of Finland.

Krigarkivet: en Handledning. Helsingfors: n.pub., 1977. (FHL# 948.97/A35v/no.9/1977)

Guide to the Military Archives of Finland.

There are fifteen other listings for archives and libraries in the Finnish collection.

Biography

The FHLC lists seventy-four titles under **Finland/Biography** including *Who's Who in Finland*; yearbooks of Swedish folk high schools in Finland; a yearbook of the Society of Finnish Nobility; biographies of Finnish bankers, physicians, members of the Senate, sea captains, soldiers, mayors of Finnish towns in the 1800s, clergy, elementary school teachers, apothecaries, prominent women, lawyers, and businessmen; biographical encyclopedias; family histories, genealogical notes, and obituaries of well-known Finns from 1641 to 1934; migrations from Karelia; and others.

Census Records (Henkikirjat)

The majority of the census records are found under the county listings, but a miscellaneous account containing general documents, transactions, military and ecclesiastical records, provincial accounts, land records and retractions, and verification books including mill and livestock tax lists and census lists from 1635 to 1809, is found under **Finland/Census** on seventeen reels. There is also an inventory of the microfilm copies of the census records in the general archives.

The county census records begin with the provincial accounts (1635-1809) and include land records, retractions, mill, livestock and seed tax lists, tithings, fines, custom revenues, military, and annual census lists. From 1810 to 1860, every fifth year has been microfilmed. Information on these records includes name of the taxpayer, residence, number of children over age fifteen, sometimes ages or year of birth, and sometimes, after 1810, the names of the wife and older children.

Church Records (Kirkonkirja)

Church records (Lutheran Parish Registers) are cataloged under **Finland/[County]/[Parish].** The records available on microfilm at the Family History Library date from the earliest records to roughly 1860. Some parishes are available on microfilm up to around 1900.

The following information can be found on these records: (1) births *(Syntyneet):* names of persons born and christened, dates of birth and christening, parentage, occupations, names of witnesses at christening, places of residence, and legitimacy; (2) marriages *(Vihityt)*: names of bride and groom, marital status, dates of banns and marriage, occupations, residence, and sometimes names of parents or sponsors; (3) deaths *(Koulleet)*: names of deceased, ages, cause of death, occupations, dates of death and burial, and places; (4) miscellaneous: parish minutes, absolutions, misdemeanors, public assistance accounts, transactions of the parsonage, church and private inventories. From about 1700 (generally) the Lutheran parishes also kept a communion and clerical survey records book *(Rippikirjat).* This record contains the population of the parish grouped by families including servants, journeymen, lodgers, etc., names of persons, dates of birth or age, relationships, occupations, altered residences, and places of residence. Later records include places of birth, marriage data, legitimacy of children, marital status, and rating of religious knowledge. These are available to 1860 and later in some parishes.

From approximately 1800 the Lutheran parishes recorded the movement of the membership (*Muuttaneet*). These records list the names of persons arriving at or leaving the parish, former and new places of residence, marital status, sometimes date and place of birth, and relationships. These are available to 1860 and later in some parishes.

The Roman Catholic and Russian Orthodox church records have not been microfilmed nor have cemetery records.

Cataloged under **Finland/Church Records** are many good church histories and the following church records:

Church Record Extracts Guide. Salt Lake City: n.pub., 1953. (FHL# REF/948.97/V23c or microfiche 6054059)

Suomen Kirkko. Pietarin Suomalainen Maarian Seurakunta. *Kirkonkirjojen Kopiot, 1733-1875.* Salt Lake City: Utahin Sukututkinusseuralle kuvannut AB. Rekolid, 1950. (FHL# Europe microfilm 055663, items 1-6)

Contains church record extracts of Pietari Finnish Parish, Maaria Congregation, births (1733-1875), marriages (1733-1833), and deaths (1733-1866).

Civil Registration

Civil records are cataloged in the FHLC under **Finland/[County]/[Parish].** They are general registers of the inhabitants of the parish compiled from different tax documents and other accounts. Civil registration records are not available for all parishes, but those accessible cover approximately 1539-1809.

These records include a collection of genealogical data about the landowner, farms and inhabitants of farms.

Court Records (Oikeuden Paatokset)

Court records date from about 1603 and are available on microfilm to about 1860. They are cataloged by county. Examples of the type of records found are decisions in criminal trials, transfers of real estate, marriage settlements, guardianship records, mortgages, miscellaneous judiciary items, and names and relationships of persons involved.

Directories

The library has a trade directory of Scandinavia, a register of districts and record keepers, and a directory of paper manufacturers.

Emigration and Immigration

There are twenty references in the Finland collection regarding emigration or immigration. Among these are sources about Finnish Americans, Finns in the western Great Lakes region, migration from Finland to North America between the Civil War and World War I, Scandinavian settlements in Australia before World War II, internal migration, Finns in Canada, and the following index of persons from Sweden and Finland who emigrated through Malmö, Sweden, between 1874 and 1939:

Sverige. Poliskammaren (Malmö). *Personregister till Poliskammarens Emigrantlistor, 1874-1891 Samt Emigrantlistor, 1874-1939.* 44 reels. Salt Lake City: Genealogical Society of Utah, 1967-75. Indexed. See FHLC heading **Sweden/-Emigration-Immigration** for call numbers.

Gazetteers, Maps, and Atlases

The collection's many good maps and gazetteers will help locate towns and villages. A few are:

Pauninkoski, P. *Suomen Paikkakuntahakemisto.* Kuopio: Kirjapaino OY Savo, 1949. (FHL# 948.97/E5p or microfilm 824098, item 3) Locality index.

United States. Board on Geographic Names. *Finland: Official Standard Names Approved by the United States Board on Geographic Names.* Washington, D.C.: U.S. Government Printing Office, 1962. (FHL# 948.97/E5f or microfilm 874464, item 1)

Jutikkala, Eino. *Suomen Historian Kartasto.* Porvoo: WSOY, 1949. (FHL# Q/948.97/E3j) Historical maps covering the bronze age to 1939.

Suomi. Maanmittaushallitus. *Finland before 1944.* Helsinki: n.pub., n.d. (FHL# Map Case/948.97/E7su)

Genealogy

The Finland collection includes at least 120 genealogy references, including the following family names: Sursill, Aminoff, Lybecker, Bronsdorff, Colliander, Ståhlberg, Bergendahl, Nixon, Karhula, Luttio, Godenhielm, Granfelt, Topelius, Grotenfelt, Hagfors, Viitavesi, Hjelmman, Launis, Alopaeus, and Pohjanpalo. Consult the FHLC for call numbers.

The collection also includes many records on Finnish nobility.

History

There are thirty-three sources on the history of Finland in the collection, all in Finnish. In addition to general histories, specific histories include statistical information on the Swedish-speaking communities of Finland, estates in Finland, East Karelia and Kola Lapland, agrarian-political, Finnish peasants, history of the Estate of Burgesses of Finland, self-government in Finnish counties and provinces, education of the Finnish bourgeoisie in the 1600s, and contributions of the history of Finland.

For general histories see:

Ottelin, A. K. *Finlands Historia: För Mellanskolor, Flickskolor och Seminarier.* Helsingfors: Söderström, 1947. (FHL# 948.97/H2o/1947)

Palmen, E. G. *Oma Maa: Tietokirja Suomen Kodeille.* 6 vols.

Porvoossa: Werner Söderström Osakeyhtiö 1920-25. (FHL# 948.97/H26p) Historical encyclopedia.

Land and Property (Maakirjat)

Land records in Finland go back as early as 1540. Land records are found in the counties of Häme, Kymi, Lappi, Turku Pori, Uusimaa, and Viipuri. These records, produced by the circuit courts, are available on microfilm from about the year 1700 to 1860 and contain mortgage records, guardian accounts, and marriage settlements.

Cataloged under **Finland/Land and Property** are several works on estates of noble Finns, tax-free purchases in Finland during the reign of Queen Kristina, conditions of land ownership in the northern counties (1550-1750), and land tenancy records of Finland, 1540.

Language and Languages

Many excellent sources are available about the Finnish language. There are Finnish-English and English-Finnish dictionaries, a Finnish-Swedish dictionary, dictionaries of citations, famous quotations, Finnish personal names, Finnish phrases, an orthographic dictionary of modern Finnish, and a map of the language areas in Finland. There is also a statistical report of Southwestern Finland, showing the language distribution.

Military Records (Sotilasasiakirjat)

Finland's military history is long and stormy with many conflicts with Sweden and Russia. As a result, military records make up the bulk of the library's Finnish collection. The library has a number of fine military histories as well as thousands of military records. These records include Mannerheim decorations of honor given to Finnish soldiers 1941-45, biographies of members of the Finnish sharpshooter battalion, Finnish compatriots in the Russian Navy, residences of army officers during Swedish rule, Finnish citizens in Russian military service about 1819-59 and 1888-1901, and others. There are Finnish muster rolls (1565-1874); enlistments (1696-1830); regiment inventories (1620-1723); induction lists (1653-1728), officer service records (1668-1868); and military court records (1689-1811).

Cataloged under **/[County]/Military Records** are general muster rolls, enlistments, payrolls of officers, and accounts for the years between about 1537 and 1845. These records give names of personnel, residence, province of birth, age, death, discharge (varies), and monetary data.

Names, Personal (Nimi)

Because the language used in Finland differs from other Scandinavian languages, Finnish names differ from other Scandinavian names. Patronymics were not used as last names except among the Swedish settlers. The father's given name is often used as the child's middle name. Family names are often taken from locations, descriptions, occupations, etc. There are several good sources that discuss names and name origin in Finland. Among them are:

Finnish Personal Names. Washington, D.C.: Central Intelligence Agency, [c.1980s]. (FHL# 948.97/D4f)

Nimi ja usko: Ortodoksinen Ristimänimiopas. Kuopio: Ortodoksisen Kirjallisuuden Julkaisuneuvosto, 1952. (FHL# REF/948.97/D4n) Russian Orthodox given names.

Sukunimeä Koskeva Lainsäädäntö. Porvoo: WSOY, 1940. (FHL# 948.97/P3s) Surname law in Finland.

Nobility (Aateliskalenterit)

Finnish nobility records start in the fifteenth century, and the library has many. From these records, the following information can be found: the names of those introduced and accepted into the House of Nobility; pedigrees listing their progenitors to the earliest known ancestor; names of spouse and children; dates of birth, marriage, and death; residences; offices and commissions received; occupations; and relationships.

Probate Records (Perukirjat)

The probate records of Finland are cataloged under the county and/or parish. The records for approximately 1650-1860 are available on microfilm. They contain the name of the deceased, ages, sometimes dates of death, residence; names of heirs, guardians; relationships; and distributions of real and personal property.

There are no listings for probate records at the national level.

Public Records (Tilikirjakokoelma)

The public records of Finland began in approximately 1538 and go to about 1809, but as late as 1870 in some counties. The "Old Collection of Accounts" (1538-1634) contains general documents, registers, trial documents, special lists, bailiffs' accounts, names of persons employed in the collection of state taxes, receipts, and residences. The "New Collection of Accounts" (1635-1809) contains general documents, military lists, provincial accounts, land records, census lists, and mill taxes. These records are cataloged by county, but some miscellaneous public records are listed under the country heading.

Schools

The library has numerous school records in the Finland collection. Consult the FHLC under **Finland/School Records, /[County]/School Records**, and **/[County]/[Town or Parish]/School Records**. They include a register of elementary and secondary schools in Finland in 1893, a history of Finnish Folk high schools, a register of the Navigational Schools of Finland, and yearbooks for Swedish folk high schools of Finland.

Social Life and Customs

Family life, work customs, traditional festivities, the history of the social structure, a history of tradesmen, and a history of municipal judges are a few of the topics covered in the sources cataloged under **Finland/Social Life and Customs.**

Societies

Some of the societies represented in the library's collection are the Railroad Association of Finland, 1862-1912, Finnish Journalist Association, Swedish Student Association in Finland, Finnish Literature Society, Finnish Geographical Society, and the Suomalais-Ugrilainen Seura (the Finnish-Ugrian Society, consisting of Siberian tribes).

Taxation

Tax lists were kept in Finland from the early 1600s. Most of these records are cataloged under **/[County]/Taxation,** including:

Maatalouden Veroluettelot. Salt Lake City: Utahin Sukututkimusseuralle Kuvannut AB. Rekolid, 1951. (FHL# microfilm 055723, items 1-2)

Earliest tax lists of livestock and seed of various districts and counties in Finland for 1621-37.

Suomen Tilallis-ja Veroluetteloita Kuudennentoista Vuosisadan Jälkimmäiseltä Puoliskolta. *Mantalregister öfver Finland fran Senare Halften af Sextonde Arhundradet.* Helsingissä Suomal [Finland]: Kirjall, Seuran Kirjapainon Osakeyhtiö, 1904. (FHL# 948.97/B4t/Vol. 3/no.5)

Tax list of Finland during the latter part of the 1600s.

GREENLAND

Historical Background

985 — First explored by Eric the Red, a Norwegian settler in Iceland and the father of Leif Ericson. Icelandic settlements established.

1400s — Settlements vanish; all contact with Greenland lost.

1585 — English navigator John Davis explores the island.

1600s — English explorers Henry Hudson and William Baffin explore the west coast of Greenland.

1721 — Norwegian missionary Hans Egede founds a mission for Denmark at Godthäd, now the capital of Greenland, also known as Nûk.

1800s — Greenland explored and mapped by numerous explorers and navigators.

1921 — Denmark declares Greenland Danish; dispute with Norway over hunting and fishing rights.

1930-33 — British, German, and American expeditions make weather and meteorological observations on the inland ice caps north of the Arctic Circle.

1931 — A strip of land on the east coast is claimed by some Norwegian hunters; their action is recognized by the Norwegian government.

1933 — Permanent Court of International Justice at The Hague invalidates Norway's claim.

1941 — Denmark gives United States right to construct and operate landing fields, radio and meteorological stations, and seaplane facilities. U.S. gets protective custody over Greenland for the duration of World War II.

1951 — A twenty-year pact provides for Danish control of the chief U.S. Naval station in Greenland and for the establishment of jointly operated defense areas.

1953 — Under the new Danish constitution, Greenland becomes an integral part of the Danish monarchy and obtains representation in the national parliament.

1979 — Following a popular referendum, Greenland is granted home rule, governed by a premier.

1982 — Greenlanders vote by a narrow margin to withdraw from the European community.

Settlement and Migration

Greenlanders are a people of mixed ancestry, primarily Inuit (Eskimo) and European, especially Danish-Norwegian. The total population of Greenland in 1981 was 50,643. Nearly all of the people live on the narrow southwest coastal fringe. Although Greenland is the largest island in the world (about 840,000 square miles), nearly 85 percent (708,110 square miles) is ice cap. It has about 100 schools where instruction takes place in both Greenlandic (an Inuit language with some Danish words) and Danish. Thule Air Force Base in the northwest supports a community of American and Danish civilian and military personnel.

Greenland Library Collection

The library collection for Greenland (Grønland) is very limited, but the sources that are available are good ones. Some are written in English, but most are in Danish.

Archives and Libraries

Nordisk arkivnyt. Quarterly. Copenhagen: Rigsarkivet, 1956-to date. (FHL# 948/J55n)

Journal on the archives of Denmark, Norway, Sweden, Finland, and Iceland; includes numerous mentions of Greenland.

Census Records

National censuses are available for 1840, 1845, 1850, 1855, 1860, 1870, 1901, and 1911. These records are all on microfilm.

See FHLC heading **Greenland/Census** for call numbers.

Church Records

The church records of Greenland are contained on one microfilm, FHL# 054133, the parish registers for 1752-1861. Records of births and christenings, confirmations, marriages, deaths, and burials were kept in these registers.

Colonization

Gad, Finn. *The History of Greenland.* Ernst Dupont, trans. 3 vols. 1867-75; rpt. ed., Montreal: McGill-Queen's University Press, 1971-82. (FHL# 998.2/H2gf)

Volume 1: earliest times to 1700, Volume 2: 1700-82, and Volume 3: 1782-1808.

Description and Travel

Two sources are available:

Biggar, Henry Percival. *The Voyages of the Cabots and of the Corte-Reals to North America and Greenland, 1497-1503.* Washington, D.C.: Library of Congress, n.d. (FHL# microfilm 973760, item 1)

Garnett, Eve. *To Greenland's Icy Mountains: The Story of Hans Egede, Explorer, Colonizer, Missionary.* New York: Roy Publishers, c.1968. (FHL# 921.982/Eg2ig)

Gazetteers

Trap, J. P. *Danmark.* 32 vols. [Copenhagen]: G. E. C. Gad, 1958-72. (FHL# 948.9/E2t/1958) In Danish. Greenland is in Volume 30.

History

In addition to the work mentioned under colonization, there is another good history:

Crantz, David. *The History of Greenland.* David Crantz, trans. 2 vols. London: Printed for the Brethren's Society for the Furtherance of the Gospel among the Heathen, 1767. (FHL# 998.2/H2c)

Describes the country, religious and social life of the people. Illustrated with maps and copper-plates.

Maps

Danmark, Geodaetisk Institut. *Kongeriget Danmark.* Copenhagen: Geodaetisk Institut, 1981. (FHL# Map File/-948.9/E7kd/1981) Faerøe Islands and Greenland.

Piors Lomme-Atlas over Danmark og Bilande. Salt Lake City: Genealogical Society of Utah, 1983. (FHL# microfilm 1124575, item 3)

Atlas of Denmark; includes the Faeroes, Greenland, Iceland, and the Danish West Indies.

ICELAND

Historical Background

800s	Visited by Irish monks (Saint Brennan).
850s	Three Norwegian explorers name it Iceland. (Only 1/8 of country is covered by ice.)
871	First permanent settlement by Norwegians Ingolfur Arnarson and Hjorleifur Arnarson at present site of Reykjavik.
871-930	Continual settlement by Norwegians, many fleeing King Harald the Fair-haired's rule. Many bring with them Irish/Scottish (Celtic) wives and servants.
930	Establishment of the world's first parliament "The Althing" and the commonwealth (Republic of Iceland).
1000	Christianity peacefully accepted by vote of the Althing.
1000-1262	Period of great development. The art of story telling developed; sagas written.
1100	Icelandic population 70,000-80,000.
1262	Commonwealth abolished because of Norwegian kings and ambitious priests. Acceptance of Norwegian sovereignty.
1380	Norway and Iceland come under Danish rule.
1402-04	Plague.
1550	Reformation imposed by Danish king. Jon Arason, last Catholic bishop of Iceland beheaded without a trial.
1602	Imposition of trade monopoly by Danish king.
1627	Algerian pirates carry away captives.
1661	Establishment of absolute monarchy in Denmark, acceptance of autocracy in Iceland.
1703	Icelandic population 50,358.
1707-09	Smallpox epidemic kills one-third of population.
1783-84	Eruption of Laki volcano and subsequent earthquakes result in great loss of human life, flora, and fauna. Danish government considers moving population en masse to Denmark.

1800 The Althing dissolved and replaced by High Court at Reykjavik.

1801 Icelandic population 47,000.

1843 The Althing reestablished.

1874 Constitution granted, giving Iceland the power of self-government.

1880 Icelandic population 72,000.

1918 Iceland becomes a sovereign state united with Denmark only by the king.

1944 June 17, Iceland formally proclaimed a republic, independent of Denmark.

1947 Eruption of the volcano Hekla.

1961 Eruption of the volcano Askja.

1963 Eruption of the volcano Surtur, resulting in a large new island off the south coast of Iceland named Surtsey.

1986 Icelandic population 242,000; 97 percent Evangelical Lutheran and 100 percent literate.

Settlement and Migration

Iceland, the land of ice and fire, is 80 percent uninhabited. It is a barren land of petrified lava fields, glaciers, and geysers. It is 500 miles from Scotland and 1,000 miles from Copenhagen. Although it was settled by Norwegian Vikings, they brought with them Irish/Scotch wives and servants, so much of the Icelandic population is of Celtic descent. Iceland has remained isolated from the rest of the world because of its harsh and inhospitable terrain.

With a history of calamities, volcanic eruptions, earthquakes, Spanish and English pirates, famine, smallpox, leprosy, and the plague, few people since the Norsemen have chosen to make Iceland their home. But geography has forged a strong, proud people who prosper in spite of their environment. Although sheep herding and fishing keep some of the population rural, the majority of Iceland's people live in cities. The custom of patronymics persists to this day, as does the custom of the woman keeping her maiden name after marriage. (It is the only Scandinavian country where these customs remain.)

The language of Iceland is virtually unchanged since the time of the Vikings and is one of the few ancient languages still spoken today.

A good place to begin Icelandic research is with:

Jonasson, Eric. *Tracing Your Icelandic Family Tree*. Winnipeg: Eric Jonasson, 1975. (FHL# 949.12/D27J)

Contains chapters on historical background, major Icelandic settlement in North America, genealogical research in North America, genealogical research in Iceland, further helps, and maps.

Also for beginning Icelandic researchers, there is a large gray binder located at the Scandinavian reference table labeled *Miscellaneous Scandinavia–Iceland.* It contains articles about the language, background notes, Icelandic genealogical terms, time tables for the Icelandic sagas, county maps, lists of parishes and archives.

Iceland Library Collection

Some of the oldest records in the Family History Library are contained in the Icelandic sagas which date from the third century. These are the stories and histories of the early Viking period and the Middle Ages. Names of persons, genealogies of families, relationships, and residences are given in these sagas. See FHLC heading **Iceland/History** or **Iceland/Folklore.**

Old documents and correspondence, appointments, names of persons and places of residence are included in the Diplomatarium Islandicum records dating from 834-1570. These are on microfilm at the Family History Library and are found in the FHLC under **Iceland/Court Records.**

Archives and Libraries

The following sources list the national and district archives of Iceland and tell of their holdings:

Olason, Páll Eggert. *Skrá um Handritasöfn Landsbókasafnsins.* 6 vols. Reykjavik: Rikisprentsmidjan utenberg, 1935-70. (FHL# 949.2/A5o) Manuscript collection at the National Library of Iceland.

Viljhalmsson, Bjarni. *I skrá um skjalasöfn syslumanna og sveitarstjórna.* 4 vols. Reykjavik: n. pub., 1973. (FHL# 949.1/A5v) Inventory of records holdings in the Icelandic archives.

______. *Um Thjodskjalasafn Islands og Heradsskjalasöfn.* N.p.: n.pub., 1970. (FHL# 949.1/A1/no.1) National and district archives.

Biography

There are nineteen listings under **/Biography**. These deal with a variety of subjects including sheriffs of Iceland (1262-1915), doctors of Iceland, the history of the drug-stores, lawyers (1736-1963), Icelandic students at the University of Copenhagen, teachers of Iceland, clergy (1000-1930), and learned men (1400-1800). There are also several general biographies of Icelanders and a National Biographical Dictionary containing names of prominent persons with dates and places of birth, marriage and death, occupations, parentage, names of spouse and children from the ninth century to 1940.

Census (Manntal)

The first census of Iceland was in 1703, and it is on microfilm and in print (typescript) at the library. It lists the names of all inhabitants of Iceland, ages, relationships (if any) to head of household, residences, occupations. It is indexed by name of each person, and the volume also has a 1729 census for three counties (Arnes, Hnappadals, and Rangárvalla). (FHL# 949.12/X2m/-1703 or microfilm 073351).

There are also indexed national censuses for 1762,

1801, 1816, 1835, 1840, 1845, 1850, 1855, 1860, 1870, 1880, 1890 and 1901 which include the names of all inhabitants, ages, occupations, residences, relationships, marital status, and sometimes birthplace and religion. The 1901 census also gives the year of marriage, number of children born, whether previously married and year of death of former spouse; year of arrival in parish, and former residence. Indexes are available for 1801 and 1901. See FHLC heading **Iceland/Census** and **Iceland/-Census/Indexes** for call numbers.

Miscellaneous censuses were taken from about 1748 by individual ministers within a parish. These records, called *Salnaregistur* and *Folkstal*, are cataloged with the church records by county, then parish.

Church Records (Ministerial baekur)

The Evangelical Lutheran Church has kept parish registers as early as the 1664 in some parishes, but generally they begin about 1780. All parish records have been filmed and are available to about 1935. The major body of the Iceland collection consist of these parish records. They tell: (1) Births *(Faeddir):* names of persons born and christened, dates of birth and christening, names of parents, father's occupation and residence, names of witnesses at christening and their residence; (2) Marriages *(Hjönaband)*: names of bride and groom, their ages and places of residence, date of marriage, and names of parents or sponsors; (3) Deaths *(Daudir)*: names of the deceased, their dates of death and burial, ages, places of residence at the time of death, occupations, conditions, cause of death; (4) Arrivals *(Innkomnir):* names of persons moving into the parish, ages, relationships when accompanied by other family members, occupations, places of former residence and new residence; (5) Removals *(Burtviknir):* the same information as arrivals with destination given.

In about 1831, confirmations *(Fermingarskyrslur)* were added to the registers. These records are cataloged under **Iceland/[County]/[Parish]/Church Records**.

Clergy lists *(prestar)* go back to 1400 in some cases.

Several good church histories are found in the Icelandic collection including :

Homiliubók: (Icelandic Sermons). Salt Lake City: Genealogical Society of Utah, 1953. (FHL# microfilm 073581, item 1)

Collection of sermons and prayers in Icelandic. English introduction gives a history of Christianity in Iceland and explanation of contents.

The library collection also contains an alphabetical list of the churches in Iceland, 1785-1900, an inventory of Icelandic church records, and LDS Icelandic Mission membership records (1874-1914). See FHLC heading **Iceland/Church Records** for call numbers.

Civil Registration

The library has a register of applications, vital, civil, and probate records for 1800-47 in:

Denmark. *Register of Blanketregnskaber 1800-1847*. Salt Lake City: Genealogical Society of Utah, 1969. (FHL# 948.9/-A6 or microfilm 599136, item 6)

Court Records

Besides the early Diplomatarium Islanicum mentioned previously, the library has Superior and Supreme Court records for the period 1801 to 1919 listed under **Iceland/Court Records.** Other records listed under **/[County]/Court Records** date from 1619 and contain civil and criminal actions with names of persons involved, relationships, if any, to other persons mentioned, places of residence, dates, and personal, legal and moral circumstances.

The Orphan's Court Records *(Yfirfjarradabaekur)* are available on microfilm from 1808 to 1916. They contain the names of orphans and guardians, sometimes names of parents, ages or dates of birth for orphans, residence, and relationships. They are listed under the FHLC heading **/[County]/Orphans and Orphanages.**

For an understanding of Iceland's courts, see:

Vilhjalmsson, Bjarni. *The Court Records of Iceland*. Salt Lake City: Genealogical Society of the Church of Jesus Christ of Latter-day Saints, c.1969. (FHL# 929.1/W893/E17 or microfilm 897215, item 17, or microfiche 6039351)

Directories

The library has a trade directory of Scandinavia which includes Iceland and a commercial and industrial directory of Iceland (1968).

Emigration and Immigration

The emigration and immigration records in the library collection include a short history of the Icelandic settlers in Canada, biographies of the early settlers of Iceland, an index to Icelandic farmers who emigrated to the Americas during 1875-90, a history of the settlements of New Iceland in Manitoba, and LDS Icelandic emigration.

Folklore

The Icelandic sagas (histories), next to the church records, are the largest segment of the Icelandic collection. Among the sagas are Arna-Magnaean manuscripts (A.D. 551), Njal's Saga, Erex Saga Artuskappa, fragments of the Elder and the Younger Edda, Dunstanus Saga, Snorri Sturluson och Eglis Saga, Haroar Saga, Dinus Saga Drambláta, Viktors Saga of Blávus, Trojumanna Saga, and Gibbons Saga. While most of these are written in Icelandic some have been translated into English or have English summaries. For a useful background in the sagas see:

Johnson, Skuli. *Iceland's Thousand Years: A Series of Popular Lectures on the History and Literature of Iceland*. Winnipeg: Icelandic Canadian Club and the Icelandic National League, 1946. (FHL# 949.1/H2j)

Liestøl, Knut. *The Origin of the Icelandic Family Sagas*. Oslo:

n.pub., 1930. (FHL# 949.1/H21 or microfilm 897486, item 3)

Gazetteers and Maps

The following gazetteers and maps will help in locating towns and villages in Iceland:

Póststjórnin. *Baejatal á Islandi.* [Gazetteer of Iceland.] Reykjavik: Isafoldarprentsmidja H.F., 1930. (FHL# 949.1/-E5p/ 1930)

United States. Office of Geography. Board on Geographic Names. *Iceland: Official Standard Names Approved by the U.S. Board on Geographic Names.* Washington, D.C.: Government Printing Office, 1961. (FHL# REF/-949.1/E5u or microfilm 874463, item 1)

Denmark. Geodaetisk Institut. *Ísland.* Copenhagen: Geodaetisk Institut, 1963. (FHL# Map Case/949.1 E7g)

Ísland: Vegir og Vegalendir. N.p.: Oliufélagid Skeljungur, 1964. (FHL# Map File/949.12/E7s) Shell Oil Company map of roads and distances in Iceland.

Other maps are also available.

Genealogy

As mentioned earlier, the Icelandic sagas contain many interesting genealogies preserved by oral traditon. (They are as valuable and reliable as anything dating that early.) Some of these sagas are cataloged under **/Folklore, /Biography,** and **/History,** in addition to those listed under **/Genealogy.** Some of these listings are duplicates.

Under **Iceland/Genealogy** are important genealogical works of Jón Espólin, Olafur Snóksdalin, Pétur Zophoniasson, and Steingrimur Lónsson. Most Icelandic families will be mentioned in one of their works. Other works included are a history of settlements which contains genealogy, a genealogy of parish priest Gisle Johnson (1758-1829), a pedigree of the ancestors and descendants of Porlákur Skúlason (1628) and his wife Kristin Gisladottir, and a genealogy from 765-1900 of Mormon convert John Johannesson. These works also contain Iceland genealogies:

Jonsson, Einar. *Aettir Austfiroinga.* 9 vols. in 4. Reykjavik: Aoalutgefand, 1953-68. (FHL# 949.12/D2j or microfilm 073287-073288)

Sigurjonsson, Arnon. *Asverjasaga.* Reykjavik: Helgafell, 1967. (FHL# 949.1/H2si)

Contains illustrations, facsimiles, genealogical tables, and a map.

Handwriting

See the *Handwriting* in the discussions on Norway and Denmark.

History

See also sources listed under *Biography, Folklore,* and *Genealogy.* These histories are in English.

The Book of Settlements/Landnámabók. Hermann Palsson and Paul Edwards, trans. Manitoba: University of Manitoba Press, c.1972. (FHL# 949.12/ H21a or 1440805, item 5) Early settlers and settlements in Iceland.

Hermannsson, Halldor. *The Periodical Literature of Iceland down to the Year 1874.* Ithaca, N.Y.: Cornell University Library, 1918. (FHL# 949.1/H2h)

Jóhannesson, Jón. *A History of the Old Icelandic Commonwealth: Icelandic Saga.* Haraldur Bessason, trans. Manitoba: University of Manitoba Press, c.1974. (FHL# 949.1/H2jo and microfilm 1440805, item 4) Indexed.

Also see the references under *History* in the discussion on Norway for references to the settlement of Iceland.

Land and Property

Mortgage records *(Vedmalabaekur)* are available on microfilm from 1790 to about 1907. These contain information regarding real estate conveyances, mortgages, agreements, contracts, etc., which will sometimes give genealogical data such as names of persons, residences, and relationships. See FHLC heading **/[County]/Land and Property.**

Cataloged under **Iceland/Land and Property** are these helpful sources:

Bearnson, John Y. *Index of Farms and Villages in Iceland.* Springville, Utah: John Y. Bearnson, [c.1958]. (FHL# 949.1/E2b or microfilm 824238, or microfiche 6054058)

Based on Icelandic books of records Ny-Jarabook and Jardatal A Islandi for the years 1847 and 1848.

Lárusson, Björn. *The Old Icelandic Land Registers.* Lund: C. W. K. Gleerup, 1967. (FHL# 949.1/R21)

Language and Languages

The following references will help the Icelandic researcher in translating records:

Chapman, Kenneth G. *Graded Readings and Exercises in Old Icelandic.* Berkeley: University of California Press, 1964. (FHL# 949.1/A8c)

Cleasby, Richard. *An Icelandic-English Dictionary.* Oxford: Clarendon Press, 1957. (FHL# 439.6321/C581i)

The library also has English-Icelandic and Icelandic-Norwegian dictionaries.

Obituaries

Indexes for registers of people who died in Iceland between 1972 and 1985 are available. Information given includes: name, occupation, residence, marital status, birth date, and death date.

Probate Records (Skiptabaekur)

The probate records of Iceland are available on microfilm from 1717 to 1918. The type of information given in these records is the name of the deceased, heirs, guardians, ages, relationships, places of residence, inventory, valuation, and division of real estate and property.

See FHLC heading **/[County]/Probate Records** for call numbers.

Statistics

The special confirmation records and statistics for all of Iceland from 1831 to 1951 are available on forty reels of microfilm, filmed by the Genealogical Society of Utah in 1953 from manuscripts in the National Records Office in Reykjavik.

Taxation

The Sheriff's Tax Register *(Manntalsbaekur)* contains the names of persons paying taxes, their residences, and the amount of tax paid. These are available on microfilm for 1696 to 1805 and are found in the FHLC under **/[County]/Taxation.**

NORWAY

Historical Background

c.2000 B.C.	Germanic tribes settle along western coast of Norway.
A.D. 800	Norwegian Vikings attack British Isles and islands in the north Atlantic.
c.870	Norwegian Vikings colonize Iceland.
c.900	Harald I (Fairhair) unites Norway.
985	Eric the Red colonizes Greenland.
990s	King Olaf I introduces Christianity in Norway.
1000	Leif Ericson sails to North America.
1000s	Early Olaf II achieves Norwegian unity and firmly establishes Christianity. He becomes Norway's patron saint in 1031.
1130-1240	Civil wars and political confusion.
1217-63	King Haakon IV restores peace.
1300s	Norway's economy largely controlled by north German merchants (Hanseatic League).
1349-50	Bubonic plague kills about half the people of Norway.
1380	Norway united with Denmark.
1536	Norway becomes a Danish province. Lutheranism becomes Norway's official religion.
1600-1700s	Norway's shipping industry (mainly lumber) prospers.
1807	During Napoleonic Wars, Britain ends trade with Norway and blockades trade with Denmark. Many Norwegians starve.
1814	Denmark yields Norway to Sweden but keeps Norway's island colonies. Norway elects an assembly and adopts a constitution, but Sweden refuses to grant Norway independence.
1884	The cabinet of Norway becomes responsible to the parliament instead of the king.
1890s	Norway's merchant fleet becomes one of the largest in the world.
1905	Norway becomes independent. (All but 184 Norwegians vote for independence.)
1914-18	Norway remains neutral during World War I, but its merchant fleets carry cargo for the Allies; Germany sinks about half its ships.
1940-45	German troops occupy Norway during World War II.

Settlement and Migration

Norway, the land of fiords (fjords), has a population of about 4.16 million–500,000 in the capital city of Oslo. About one-third live in rural areas, while only six cities have populations over 50,000.

The Norwegians are closely related to the Danes and Swedes. They also have strong ties with Americans. During the late 1800s and early 1900s, more than 600,000 Norwegians migrated to the United States. No other country except Ireland has provided the U.S. with so many immigrants in proportion to the population.

About 20,000 Lapps live in the far northern parts of Norway. That region also has about 10,000 people of Finnish ancestry. The Evangelical Lutheran Church is the official religion of Norway with about 96 percent of the people belonging.

The Norwegian language has two forms–*Bokmäl* and *Nynorsk*. They are gradually being combined into a single form called *Samnorsk*. *Bokmäl* and *Nynorsk* are similar enough for speakers of each to understand the other. *Bokmäl* is the Norwegian form of Danish and is used in the cities and taught in the schools. It has the same vocabulary and spelling as Danish but is pronounced much differently. *Nynorsk*, created during the mid-1800s as a reaction against Danish influence, is based on the many dialects that developed in the villages during Norway's union with Denmark.

Helpful aids for beginning Norwegian research are located at the reference table:

Smith, Frank, and Finn A. Thomsen. *Guidebook of Norway*. Salt Lake City: Frank Smith and Finn A. Thomsen, n.d. (FHL# 948.1/E6st)

Discusses the three major record sources (church, census, and probate), some Norwegian words and their meanings, personal given names, the Gothic alphabet, converting moveable feast days to the modern calendar, parishes, sectional maps, etc.

Wellauer, Maralyn A. *Tracing Your Norwegian Roots*. Milwaukee, Wis.: Maralyn A. Wellauer, 1979. (FHL# 948/-D27w)

Good introduction to Norwegian research including addresses for correspondence.

Also at the reference table is a large gray binder

labeled *Norway* with articles and aids to help the beginning researcher. It has sections entitled: archives, maps/-atlases/gazetteers, vital records, census, probate, emigration, land and property, tax, court, military, histories, collections, LDS sources (branches), and nobility.

Norway Library Collection

The Family History Library has the largest centralized collection of Norwegian genealogical records available anywhere for any country of comparable size. Research on Norwegian pedigrees can be conducted with greater ease in the Family History Library than in Norway itself, where the records are dispersed throughout various archives.

Of the many printed sources available, the rural histories *(bygdebøker)*, which often devote most of their space to farm history and the genealogies of families, are a major source of information regarding farming communities and their inhabitants. For call numbers, see the gray binder at the Scandinavian reference table labeled *Norway–Farm & Community Histories* compiled by Ruth Ellen Maness (Salt Lake City: LDS Family History Library, 1986).

Among the major sources for research in Norway are the church records, census returns, and probate. The Lutheran parish registers began generally about 1689, the census returns about 1664, and the probate in about 1660.

The use of farm or locality names as the family surname was a common practice in Norway, as well as the use of patronymics. Other surnames found in the church records of Norway are old established surnames, nobility surnames, trade names, and soldier names.

The FHLC catalogs the Norway collection under twenty counties *(fylke)*, including Bergen and Oslo. Norway has nine bishoprics *(bispedømme)*, 560 clerical districts *(prestegjeld)*, and 1,047 parishes *(sogne)*. A *prestegjeld* consists of one or more *sogne.*

Archives and Libraries

The library has eleven works cataloged under this heading, including:

Krag-Rønne, Cato. *AEttegransking: Momenter til en første orintering.* Oslo: Grondahl, 1943. (FHL# 948.1/D27k or microfilm 599521, item 1, or microfiche 6030018-6030020)

Guide to Norwegian genealogical research and archival material.

Nysaeter, Egil. *Norske Arkivkatalogar: Oversikt over Katalogar, Register, mikrofilm, kjeldeutgåver m.m. i offentlege Norske Arkiv.* Oslo: Noregs allmennvitskaplege forskingsråd, 1982. (FHL# REF/948.1/A3na)

Biography

Some of the subjects included among the Norway biographical materials are biographies of 330 Norwegian Army officers from 1628-1885; a history of the city judges in Norway from 1125-1975; biographies of the pharmacists from 1588-1908; biographical sketches of the Goldsmith's Guild for the last hundred years; histories of the kings and queens of Norway for a thousand years; biographical sketches of LDS missionaries to Scandinavia; biographies of some of the men who emigrated to America and became successful businessmen; and three biographical dictionaries.

Census (Manntall og Folketellinger)

Although not exactly a census record, the head tax list of 1664-66 lists all men and boys over twelve living in the rural districts, the farm names, names and ages of owners (including widows), and names and ages of cottagers. If an eligible son was living on his father's farm, the relationship is shown. Not all rural districts have complete sets, but the library has filmed all of those extant. They are cataloged under the **Norway/Census** or **/[County]Census.** This head tax was collected by the local civil authorities.

Clerical authorities also took a more complete census for this same time period. Both censuses should be searched. The civil record is listed first in the FHLC and the clerical record is listed second.

The 1701 military census lists only males in rural districts who were over the age of one year. It includes the farm names, name and ages of the owners, names and ages of sons and servants, and the residences of all unmarried males living away from home. These males were also covered by the census taken in the area where they were residing. Records covering large parts of eastern and southern Norway are missing. These records are cataloged under the country or county heading. Check either heading. The 1801 census records names, position in the household (relationships), age, marital status, and occupation. The records are arranged by county, clerical district, parish and farm, or by county, city, city section, and street number under the country heading. This was Norway's first national census. A printed edition with indexes is also available on microfiche:

Mikrokortutgava av 1801-teljina. Bergen: 1801-prosjektet, Historisk Institutt, Universitetet i Bergen, 1980. (FHL# microfilm 6200701-6201260)

Includes instruction on how to determine clerical district, city section, etc.

The next census of genealogical value did not take place until 1865. It was the first national census to list a place of birth for all persons recorded. This census contains name, residence, status in the family, occupation, sex, marital status, place of birth, religion if not a member of the state church, and other miscellaneous information.

In the counties, each book usually contains the records for one clerical district *(prestegjeld)*. A listing of the farms is given at the beginning of each book with an indication of where the farm can be found within the book.

In the larger cities each parish *(menighet)* may have several books. An alphabetical list of the city streets is given at the beginning of the first book. To find these records, consult the FHLC under **Norway/Census** or **/[County]/[Parish]/Census.**

The 1875 census, which supplies the same information as the 1865 census, has been microfilmed. To find film numbers, see FHLC heading **/[County]/[Parish]/Census** or consult the gray binder labeled *Norway Census* at the Scandinavia reference table. (All other census film numbers are also in this binder.) Thirteen of the twenty counties have been indexed for 1875, and an explanation on how to use these indexes is given in the binder.

The 1900 census contains the person's name, sex, status as resident or temporary resident, position in the family, marital status, occupation, year of birth, place of birth, citizenship, religion, and other miscellaneous information. Those temporarily absent and their locations are also given.

The index lists *(Hoved-og kretslister)* at the beginning of the record are statistical records. They also list the names of the census takers and names of owners of businesses and dwellings and the number of people there. These records are cataloged under **Norway/Census** or **/[County]/[Parish]/Census.**

There are locality indexes for the censuses of 1664-66, 1701, 1801, 1865, and 1875.

Church Records (Kirkebøker)

In 1688, the law of the Lutheran Church prescribed that every minister should register baptisms, marriages, and burials. The majority or registrations did not begin until 1700, although one began as early as 1623. In 1736, confirmations *(Konfirmerte)* and introductions *(Introduserte)* were added to the registers already recording christenings, marriages, and burials. After having a child, a woman was considered "unclean" and she had to be reintroduced to the church by the minister. From 1814 to the present, arrivals *(Innflyttede)*, removals *(Utflyttede)*, and vaccinations *(väksinerte)* were added and introductions dropped.

Information that can be found on these church registers is as follows: Births/christenings *(Døpte)*: given name of child, dates, parents, their occupations, witnesses at the christening, and places of residence of parents; Marriages *(Viede)*: names, conditions (meaning marital status), date of marriage, occupations, residences, and, after 1830, ages, place of birth, and fathers' names; Deaths/burials *(Begravede)*: name of deceased, age, cause of death, occupation, death date, place of death, and, after the late nineteenth century, place of birth; confirmations: name, age (usually fourteen or later), residence, and, after 1814, date of christening and names of parents; Arrivals: name, age, occupation, former residence, and new place of residence; Removals: name, age, occupation, place of residence, and place of destination.

These records are available on microfilm to about 1910 and are cataloged under **/[County]/[Parish]/-Church Records.**

Civil Registration

The civil registration records of Norway are mainly in the larger towns and are usually just death records. For instance, the city of Bergen has death records available from 1821-98, recorded by a judge and clerk. See FHLC heading **Norway/Civil Registration** for a complete list of holdings.

Court Records (Justisprotokoller)

The court records include civil and criminal action and *odelssaker,* which refer to allodial property rights. These records contain names, dates, places, relationships; personal, legal, and moral circumstances; and sometimes information about some of the individuals involved. The years 1650-1700 are on microfilm and are found in the FHLC under **/[County]/Court Records** or **/[County]/-[Parish]/Court Records.** These records are not indexed and should be used in conjunction with mortgage and probate records.

Early Diplomatarium Norvegicum letters and documents dating from 990 to 1700 are listed under **Norway/Court Records**. They include probates, deeds, court records, and real estate conveyances.

Directories

Among the directory listings for Norway are a trade directory of Scandinavia, a directory of the paper manufacturers in Norway, and a street directory showing postal districts for Norway. Listed under **Norway/Postal and Shipping Guides** is a Norwegian place-name index, showing the community, county, zip code, post office name, and telegraph office name. See FHLC heading **Norway/Directories** for other titles.

Emigration and Immigration (Emigrant protokoller)

There are numerous references to Norwegian emigration, primarily dealing with arrivals and destinations in the United States. Thus, many of the sources are kept in the United States area. On microfilm in the Scandinavia area are the emigration records of various Norwegian cities. See FHLC heading **Norway/Emigration-Immigration** or **/[County]/[City]/Emigration-Immigration** for complete holdings.

These records list the name of the emigrant, the emigration number, age, occupation, year and place of birth, residence, destination, and sometimes marital status, ship sailed on, when it sailed, and which state in America was the destination. Cities for which these records were kept are Ålesund in Møre og Romsdal (1852-1923), Bergen (1874-1924), Kristiania (Oslo) (1867-1902), Kristiansand in Vest-Agder (1873-1911), Kristiansund in Møre og Romsdal (1882-1959 and 1837-1909), and Trondheim (1867-1926).

Seventy-eight microfiche of documents from Bergen's Politmeisterarkiv list approximately 99,900 persons who emigrated through Bergen, 1874-1924. This source is indexed by last name and first name.

Additional emigration sources include discussions of Norwegian migration to America, 1825-60, Norwegian immigrant families that came to Iowa, organized promotion of Scandinavian immigration to Minnesota, 1866-73, Norwegians in Canada, Mormon migration from Scandinavia, Norwegian immigrant churches, immigration from Norway to Texas, and emigration from Vega County, Norway.

Gazetteers, Maps, and Atlases

The following gazetteers and maps are helpful genealogical aids:

Norge. 4 vols. Oslo: J. W. Cappelens Forlag, c.1963. (FHL# REF/948.1/E6nc)

United States. Board on Geographic Names. *Norway, Svalbard and Jan Mayen: Official Standard Names Approved by the U.S. Board on Geographic Names.* Washington, D.C.: U.S. Government Printing Office, 1963. (FHL# REF/948.1/E5u or microfilm 874469)

Det Bestes Store Norge Atlas. Oslo: Forlaget Det Beste, c.1983. (FHL# REF/Q/948.1/E7b) Atlas with relief and topographical maps, statistics, and a gazetteer.

Genealogy

The library has over seventy works under **Norway/Genealogy**. Most of these are family histories, biographies, and pedigrees. Some of the family names with genealogical references are Bay, Lange, Berner, Ameln, Daae, Dietrichson, Hartmann, Falsen, Conradi, Sjölund, and Vatshell to name but a few.

There are also numerous genealogy handbooks, manuals, and periodicals that will aid in Norwegian research. These include census records of Norway, church records of Norway, major genealogical record sources in Norway, Norwegian genealogical research techniques prior to 1750, and an introduction to the court records, deeds, mortgage records, probate records, etc., of Norway. The local histories contain hundreds of genealogies cross-referenced in the FHLC under the parish.

Handwriting

Excellent aids are available to help in reading the paleography of Norway. Three are:

Haarstad, Kjell *Gotisk skrift, en tekstsamling.* Trondheim: Tapir, 1981. (FHL# 948.1/G37h) Manual for reading Gothic script.

Kvifte, Gunnar. *Gamle dokumenter–Gotisk Skrift.* Drammen: Harald Lyche & Co., 1945. (FHL# 948.1/G37k)

Guide for learning to read Gothic in land ownership documents.

A guide in English is:

Danish-Norwegian Paleography. Salt Lake City: Genealogical Department of the Church of Jesus Christ of Latter-day Saints, c.1976. (FHL# REF/929.1/G286gs/Ser. D/no.16 or microfiche 6030017)

History

Many good histories of Norway are available, most of them in Norwegian or Danish. Some of the topics covered are: Norway under German occupation, 1940-45; culture, customs, history, fishing, and life along the fjords of western Norway; everyday life in the sixteenth century (a cultural-historical description); sagas of the early kings; and a history of the Norwegian pioneers in Minnehaha County, South Dakota, 1866-96.

A few of the histories with English text are:

Gjerset, Knut. *History of the Norwegian People.* New York: Macmillan, 1915. (FHL# 948.1/H2g)

Du Chaillu, Paul B. *The Viking Age: The Early History, Manners, and Customs of the Ancestors of the English-Speaking Nations.* 2 vols. London: John Murray, 1889. (FHL# 948/H2d)

Stephens, George. *Handbook of the Old-Northern Runic Monuments of Scandinavia and England, Now First Collected and Deciphered.* London and Copenhagen: Williams and Norgate/H.H.J. Lynge, 1884. (FHL# Q/948/-H2sg)

Land and Property (Jordebøker)

The oldest Norwegian documents are the deeds *Diplomatarium Norvegicum,* (Christiania: P.T. Mallings Forlagshandel, 1847-1972. 21 vols.) dating from the twelfth to the seventeenth centuries. (See FHL# 948.1/H2d or microfilm 222646-222689). The library has printed copies. Manorial estate records (Jordebøker) include letters settling land rights of manorial estates, land rental records, tax lists, and miscellaneous documents relating to land transactions. They cover the period 1624-1769 and are cataloged under **Norway/Land and Property.**

Revenue and Expense records *(Lensregnskaper)* for 1570s to 1690s are available on microfilm. These are tax lists, real estate registers, and other material containing names of the owners and cultivators of farms. There are indexes to land rentals and records, containing names, dates, and acreage for 1660-76 on microfilm. Land commissions records for 1661-65 and 1680-91 are also available on microfilm. These records contain ledgers, land rentals, tithes, and various other taxes, mostly listing names and monetary amounts. See FHLC heading **Norway/[County]/Land And property** for call numbers.

Mortgage records *(Pantebøker)* that are available on microfilm cover 1680s-1880s and contain information on real estate conveyances, mortgages, and other encumbrances on property, agreements, contracts, etc., which sometimes give extensive genealogical data. See FHLC heading **Norway/[County]/[Parish** or **[Town]/-Land and Property** for call numbers.

Listed under **Norway/Land and Property** are:

Holmsen, Andreas. *Gård of gods i Norge i eldre tid.* Oslo: Universitetsforlaget, 1981. (FHL# 948.1/R2h) A study of land ownership in Norway, 1600s-1800s.

______. *Gård, Skatt og Matrikkel.* Oslo: Universitetsforlaget, 1979. (FHL# 948.1/R2ha) A study of farms, taxes, and land registers, 1500s-1800s.

Language and Languages

Helpful in Norwegian research is:

Fritzner, Johan. *Ordbog over det Gamle Norske Sprog*. 4 vols. Oslo: Tryggve Juul Møller Forlag, 1954-72. (FHL# 439.823/F9190)

Scavenius, H. *McKay's Modern Norwegian-English, English-Norwegian Dictionary*. New York: David McKay, [c.1953]. (FHL# 439.82321/M192)

Merchant Marine and Military Records

According to an 1803 law, every boy, when he reached sixteen, had to appear before the draft board to be registered, receive a medical examination, and receive a certificate to show that he was registered. These enlistment registers *(Sjøinnrulleringen)* were kept in four groups: (1) sixteen-year-olds, (2) males seventeen to thirty-six, (3) males thirty-six to fifty, and (4) over fifty *("ekstra rullen")*. The men were classified as: (1) able-bodied, (2) not able-bodied, (3) used to the sea, and (4) not used to the sea.

These records vary in detail but usually list given name, surname (father's name), age, birthplace, place of residence, and often body build and hair color. Sometimes the record contains information on the person's previous experiences on a ship. If a man voluntarily enlisted, he was given special privileges. In times of war, all merchant marines were required to serve in the Navy.

The merchant marine and military records of the various towns that kept these enlistments are identical. The time periods that are available on microfilm will vary from town to town. For example Oslo's records cover 1817 to 1910, Drammen's 1860 to 1940, and Drøbak's 1819 to 1892. See FHLC heading **Norway/[County]/[Parish]** or **[Town]/Merchant Marine** or **Military Records**.

Hassløf, Olof, et al. *Ships and Shipyards, Sailors and Fishermen*. Copenhagen: Rosenkilde and Bagger, 1972. (FHL# 948/U2s)

An introduction to maritime ethnology and a history of the merchant marine.

The military records *(Militärprotokoller)* of Norway from 1643 to 1909 are available on microfilm. The early rolls or lists of officers and men will give the name, age, residence, and sometimes place of birth. Eighteenth and nineteenth century rolls give more detailed information, but preservation of these records was not universal. Certain districts or units are missing. Men were recruited on a territorial basis and companies had territorial names. If the dictrict where an ancestor lived is known, his recruiting district should be locatable. See FHLC heading **Norway/Military Records** for call numbers.

Other military records that are currently listed in the FHLC under **Norway/** include various military histories and biographies of Norwegian army and navy officers.

Names, Geographical

The library has eleven listings under this heading, including a listing of the geographical divisions in Norway for the civil, clerical, and judicial departments with populations for each area for 1900, 1920, 1930, and 1946; geography for public schools of Norway, Sweden, etc.; old personal names used in Norwegian place names; estate and farm names in Norway, arranged by the old county names and by township; farm names and their histories from all of Norway; Norwegian place names dictionary; and a history of place names that tells the story of place naming customs.

Names, Personal

Some of the library's thirteen works on this topic discuss laws about personal names in the Scandinavian countries; Norwegian names and their meanings; 2,000 names used in Norway with their origin; Norwegian family names, their origin and variations; and Norwegian naming customs.

Obituaries

The library has an alphabetical list of people who died in Norway between April 1942 and April 1944; obituaries taken from Norwegian newspapers, 1763-1840, and obituaries for 1924; and an alphabetical list by surname, then given name of people who died in Bergen City from 1765-1850.

Probate Records (Skifteprotokoller)

Norwegian probate records commenced in the various probate districts around 1660. By 1685, each county was divided into probate districts and the probates were kept by the district judge *(Sorenskriver)*. Some of the larger towns had their own probate jurisdiction and the records were kept by the town judge *(Byskriver)*. Probate records usually give the name of the deceased, heirs, guardians, relationships, places of residence, inventory, property, land tenure rights, and the division of property.

All of the Norwegian probate records are on microfilm up to about 1900 and are listed in the FHLC under **Norway/[County]/[Town** or **Judicial District]/-Probate Records**. Some indexes (calendars) are available, which usually indicate the date of the probate, the name of the testator, and the parish of residence of the deceased. The probate registers do not cover the estates of all deceased persons, but generally there was a probate when the heirs were not yet of age.

Social Life and Customs

There are numerous sources on the social life and customs in Norway, and these works paint a rich and unique portrait of the country and its people during the earlier years. Some of the topics covered are population changes from 1735 to 1865; unwed mothers and pregnant brides, 1700s-1800s; family life; traditional concepts of death and the dead, 1100s-1900s; and marriage and sexual morality in Norwegian history; and life in the cities.

Taxation (Skattelister)

The library has microfilms of Norwegian tax lists from their commencement in 1645 to 1814. There are surtax lists for cities, rural districts, and ecclesiastical districts that contain names and amount of tax; special tax assessments that list names, financial status, locality, and amount paid; and a levy on capital assets list (1789) that contains farm name, person's name, and amount and type of tax. See FHLC heading **Norway/Taxation** and **Norway/[County]/Taxation** for call numbers.

Under the country heading there is a history of the taxation of the people of Norway by Denmark from 1760-1779:

Sandvik, Gudmund. *Det Gamle Veldet: Norske Finansar 1760-79.* Oslo: Gyldendal Norsk Forlag, 1975. (FHL# 948.1/R4s)

Skattematrikkelen: 1647. Oslo: Universitetsforlaget, 1969. (FHL# 948.1/R4f) 1647 tax register.

SWEDEN

Historical Background

c.6000 B.C.	Earliest identified settlements.
50 B.C.	Swedes begin trading with the Roman Empire.
A.D. 100	Roman historian Tacitus writes about the "Svear," a Scandinavian people. "Sverige" (Sweden) means "land of the Svear."
c.800	Swedish Vikings sail to many parts of the world to acquire wealth by trade and conquest.
829	Christianity first preached in Sweden by Saint Anskar, a Frankish (French) monk. A 200-year struggle between paganism and Christianity begins.
1008	Conversion of Olof Skötkonung, the first Christian king of Sweden.
1249	Sweden conquers much of Finland.
1397	Sweden (Finland), Denmark, and Norway united in the Union of Kalmar for next hundred years.
1523	Gustavus Vasa elected king, Sweden becomes independent, and the Reformation begins in Sweden.
1540	Lutheranism becomes Sweden's official religion.
1611-32	Gustavus (II) Adolphus leads Sweden to victory in the Thirty Years' War; Sweden's new power and possessions throughout Europe lead to continual wars with Denmark, Poland, and Russia.
1709	Swedish power declines after defeat at the Battle of Poltava by Peter the Great of Russia.
1720-72	Age of Freedom. The *Riksdag* (parliament) adopts a new constitution that reassigns many of the crown's powers to itself.
1809	Sweden loses Finland to Russia, king deposed, new constitution passed, position of ombudsman originated to investigate complaints against government departments.
1814	Sweden acquires Norway from Denmark.
1800s	Decline in political power. Sweden economically crippled by the Industrial Revolution in Europe. Agricultural decline, epidemics, wide-spread rural poverty, and crowded, unsanitary cities encourage massive emigration to America which peaks between 1880-1900.
1905	Norway dissolves union with Sweden.
1914-18	Sweden neutral during World War I.
1939-45	Sweden neutral in World War II. In 1943, camps set up for Danish and Norwegian refugees.

Settlement and Migration

The fair-skinned, light-haired Swedes are of Germanic descent and are closely related to the Danes and Norwegians, both in language and heritage. The Lapps, who live in the far north, differ in appearance, language, and way of life from most other Swedes. There are about 10,000 Lapps and 30,000 Swedes of Finnish origin living in the northern part of Sweden.

During the Middle Ages, a large number of German merchants (Hanseatic League) settled in Sweden. Dutchmen and Walloons from Belgium were persuaded to go to Sweden during the sixteenth and seventeenth centuries to help develop the country's iron industry. In the late eighteenth century, a few Jews immigrated to Sweden and a number of Scots settled in Göteborg.

The nineteenth century saw major population shifts. Internal migration occurred as farms failed and workers moved to the slowly industrializing cities. But jobs in the cities were seldom steady, causing workers to move on again. City life in the nineteenth century was deplorable; crowding caused sickness, crime, fires, alcoholism, and poverty. Between 1860 and 1920 more than 500,000 Swedes immigrated to America.

Although Sweden was weakened economically by World War II, it escaped the physical destruction of other European nations. As a result, many Europeans moved to Sweden both during and after the war. Approximately 1 million people have settled in Sweden since the end of World War II. Sweden's population is now about 9 million with over 1 million in the metropolitan area of Stockholm.

About nine-tenths of Sweden's people live in the cities and towns of the south and central part of the country. Almost one-third of the people live in the three largest cities – Stockholm, Göteborg, and Malmö – and their suburbs. About 98 percent of Sweden's population belongs to the Lutheran Church. All Swedes whose parents belong to the Lutheran Church become members automatically at birth.

A helpful place to start Swedish research is with this source located at the reference table and in the Scandinavian area stacks:

Johansson, Carl-Erik. *Cradled in Sweden*. Logan, Utah: Everton Publishers, Inc., 1972. (FHL# REF/929.1485/-J599/c.1972)

Discusses the language, the country (ecclesiastical and civil jurisdictions), names of places, names of persons, the archives of Sweden, fixed and moveable feast days, handwriting, Swedish Mission records of the LDS Church, emigration records, parish registers, clerical survey records, etc. It also contains an alphabetical index of all parishes in Sweden.

Also at the reference table is a large, gray, loose-leaf binder labeled *Sweden* with articles and research aids on archives, census and church records, a clerical survey, emigration, handwriting, jurisdictions, land records, maps, prominent families, probate records, research procedures, etc.

Sweden Library Collection

The Family History Library has the largest centralized collection of Swedish genealogical records available anywhere for any country of comparable size (some 76,000 reels of microfilm plus thousands of printed volumes). Research on Swedish pedigrees can thus be conducted with greater ease there than in Sweden itself, where records are dispersed throughout various archives. All parish records that are found in Regional Archives have been microfilmed and are available.

The Swedish alphabet has three additional letters that come after "z" – "å," "ä," and "ö." In alphabetical lists of counties, parishes, or people, names beginning with those letters will fall at the end of the alphabet.

Administratively, Sweden is divided into counties *(län),* districts *(härad),* and parishes *(socken* or *församlingar).* The twenty-four *län* have changed their borders very little since 1634. *Härad,* with two to twenty parishes each, are judicial units governed by a district chief and a council. There are about 300 of these districts with few border changes in the last couple of centuries. (Other words for districts are *tingslag* and *skeppslag.*) The term *Landskap* refers to the old historical units of provinces, but these are of no significance to the genealogical researcher because they are not used in the jurisdiction or administration of records. Each parish consists of several villages *(byar),* farms *(gårdar, hemman)* and individual houses *(hus*).

Archives and Libraries

Sources cataloged under this heading include genealogical source material in the archives of Malmöhus, Kristianstad, Halland, and Blekinge counties; the bulletin of the Commission for National Inventories of private archives; a bibliography of Scandinavian genealogical material; a short survey of Swedish libraries; a history of the Royal Military Archives (in English); a description of the Swedish National Archives, 1618-1968; an inventory of court records of Swedish cities, 1640-1847; and others.

Biography and Portraits

The library has over 200 biography listings and over 400 listings under **/Biography** in the Swedish collection. Many of these are duplicate listings. One major source is a collection known as Series II: *Biographica,* (Salt Lake City: Filmed by the Genealogical Society of Utah, 1962), containing information on Swedish nobility, military personnel, or other distinguished personalities. In these records are various papers, letters, probates and extracts from other court records, marriage petitions, and releases of minors from guardianship. This collection is arranged alphabetically on 350 reels of microfilm.

Many biographies and portraits of nobility, government officials, priests, and prominent people are in the collection. Other groups of people with biographies are freemasons, postal workers, dentists, bookdealers (1800-1935), teachers (elementary, secondary, university, schools of the deaf), merchants, bookbinders (1460-1880), dairymen, copper-plate engravers (1500-1944), Jews, church musicians, millionaires, men of the Middle Ages, midwives, centenarians, and authors. There are also biographical dictionaries.

The portraits section is much like the biography section except that these volumes contain photographs or engravings of the people as well as biographies. Some of the groups of people in this category are men of the Swedish auto industry; civil service workers of World War II; artists in the theater, musical, and film industry (1500-1942); eminent women; ambassadors; pharmacists; bank officials; physicians (1862-1939); and members of the shoemakers' guild.

Census Records (Mantalslängder)

These records are not really census records, but rather a tax list or verification of taxed or assessed property. Sweden does not have ordinary census returns because the population count was done by the parish ministers in the clerical survey records.

The *mantalslängder* were made annually and can be quite helpful. These records contain the names of persons between fifteen and sixty-three who were supposed to pay a tax called *mantalspenningen.* These records start around 1630 and each year to 1750 is available on microfilm. From 1750-1860, microfilms of the records are available every five years.

Unfortunately, the lists often name only the head of the family and list wife, children, and/or servants without giving names. Also, soldiers were exempt from this tax; the record often indicates only "soldier's wife" without naming either the soldier or the woman. Families of nobility were also exempt until 1810. Information varies widely; but the later the census, the more detailed the information. These records are cataloged under **/[County]/Census Records**.

Under **Sweden/Census Records** (actually tax verification records) are listed the registers of typed indexes to the census records, arranged by county, then by district. The FHLC listing also includes microfilm numbers of the census records. These typescript registers are located at the register table in the Scandinavia Reference Area.

Church Records (Kyrkoböcker)

The Swedish Lutheran Church Law of 1686 made it mandatory for the minister of each of Sweden's 2,500 parishes to keep a record of each person living within the parish and of all ordinances he performed.

Some ministerial records begin as early as 1622. All of these records are on microfilm to around 1860 (some to 1900).

The parish registers contain: (1) Births and christenings *(Födde och Doplängd)*: names of persons born and christened, dates of birth and christening, legitimacy, names of parents, father's occupation and residence, sometimes the age of mother, names of witnesses at the christening and their residence, occupation, and sometimes relationship; (2) Marriages *(Vigde)*: names of bride and groom, their places of residence, date of marriage, sometimes ages and names of parents or sponsors, and information regarding any former marriages; some ministers also made note of the dates of banns *(lysningsbok)*; (3) Deaths and Burials *(Döde och Begravnings)*: names of deceased, dates of death and burial, ages, place of residence at time of death, occupation, conditions, cause of death, and sometimes biographical information, particularly in Västmanland and Kopparberg counties; (4) Confirmations *(Konfirmationslängd)*: names of children, age at confirmation (usually about fifteen), and residence; (5) Arrivals and Removals *(Inflyttningslängd och utflyttningslängd)*: names of persons moving into or out of the parish, beginning around 1800; former residence or destination; dates of arrival or removal; and sometimes marital status and date and place of birth. Sometimes certificates of moving *(Flyttningsattester)* are given; they contain the same information but with more detail.

The most important records for the genealogist in tracing a family's movement are the Lutheran *household examination rolls* (clerical survey records–*Husförhörslängder*), kept by the parish ministers from about 1686 to around 1895 and available on microfilm. These records are listed by parish with the other church records. The ministers visited every household and "examined" each member's knowledge of the scriptures and reading ability. The examinations took place once a year and the new information was recorded in a book that would cover about a five-year period. The records gave information about all members of a household including husband, wife, children, servants, farmhands, aged parents, etc. Information recorded was generally as follows: names (including women's maiden names), dates of birth or ages, place of birth, occupations, relationships, marriage data, dates of death, former places of residency, arrival dates (from where), removal dates (to where), legitimacy of children, marital status, and rating on religious knowledge. The information will vary, especially before 1800.

Under **Sweden/Church Records** are clerical survey abstracts, parish register abstracts, and other miscellaneous church records.

Civil Registration

The civil registration records in Sweden consist of extracts of births, marriages, and deaths taken from church records from 1860-97. These records are found under the county heading only and not by parish. There is an index in the beginning of the birth records that will list the order in which the different parishes appear in the record.

Court Records (Domböcker)

The lowest court in Sweden is the district court *(häradsrätt)* in the counties and city court *(rådhusrätt)* in the cities. Records, decisions, and transcripts of small claims court, civil court, and criminal court are found in these court records. Court proceedings may also include mortgage transactions *(lånehandlingar)*, marriage settlements, guardian accounts *(småprotokoll)*, wills *(testamente)*, and deeds *(lagfart)*. City courts start as early as 1620 in Sweden but generally started around 1660. The Genealogical Society has microfilmed them from their beginnings to 1860. They are cataloged under **/[County]/[District]/Court Records** or under **/[County]/-[City]/Court Records**.

The next higher court is the Royal Circuit Court of Appeals *(hovrätt)*. Sweden has three, each for a certain geographical area. *Svea hovrätt* is the appellate court for eastern and northern Sweden with its seat in Stockholm. *Göta Hovrätt* founded in 1634, with headquarters in Jönköping, was over the western and southern twelve counties until 1820 when the *Hovrätten över Skåne och Blekinge* was formed with jurisdiction over the counties of Malmöhus, Kristianstad, and Blekinge with the headquarters first in Kristianstad and then in Malmö.

Under **Sweden/Court Records**, the records of *Göta Hovrätt* are listed in the FHLC. Other Hovrätt records are found under **/Stockholm/Court Records** and *Hovrätten över Skåne och Blekinge* under **/Malmöhus/Court Records** and **Kristianstad/Court Records.** Hovrätt records include decisions of civil cases, criminal court records, registry of cases, court auditor records, royal letters and resolutions in criminal cases, and orders and decisions and notarial papers in regards to probated estates and taxation. Records for *Gota Hovrätt* (1635-1876), *Svea Hovrätt* (1614-1868), and *Hovrätten över Skåne och Blekinge* (1706-91) are currently in the FHLC. There are also several court inventory sources listed.

Directories

References under this heading include a directory of Central Sweden for 1914, a list of civilian and military officers for 1841-90, a directory of government forest inspectors, forest schools and state administrators for 1945, a directory of state officials of Göteborg City for 1786, a trade directory of Scandinavia (1956), a directory of officials of the Swedish railways in 1924, a directory of local historical societies in 1982, a register of Swedish policemen and constables in 1942, a directory of state officials and personnel of Swedish prisons in 1924, a Swedish business directory for 1948, and a directory of provincial and district physicians and medical institutions for 1890 to 1942.

Stockholm directories exist for 1842, 1890 and 1948. There is also a Stockholm business directory for 1911 and a clerical directory for 1943.

Emigration and Immigration

The major ports of departure from Sweden were Göteborg, Malmö, and Stockholm. Many Swedish people also set sail from Oslo and Trondheim in Norway. The emigration lists of each city have been indexed and are available on microfilm. See FHLC heading **/[County]/[City]/Emigration and Immigration** or **Sweden/Emigration** for a complete list of holdings and call numbers.

There are government, police department, and emigration agency passenger/emigrant lists. These are the specific registrations of persons emigrating from Sweden to various countries, usually the United States. These records usually include names, places of residence or places of birth, ages or dates of birth, destination, relationships of persons traveling as a family unit, date of emigration, marital status, and often reason for emigration.

Indexes to these records cover the following period: Göteborg, 1869-1951; Malmö, 1874-1891; Stockholm, 1851-1947; Stockholm (city), 1865-1904; Trondheim, 1867-1926, and Oslo (Kristiania), 1867-1902.

Other emigration records include the Larsson Brothers & Company Emigration Agency correspondence from 1876-1913 and passport journals from the eighteenth and nineteenth centuries. Both are available on microfilm and contain various information about persons leaving the country.

Under **Sweden/Emigration and Immigration** are also many miscellaneous emigration references including a demographic study of Swedes in Chicago 1846-80 (in English); history of Swedish emigration to Australia; a register of refugees from Finland and Baltic States to Sweden; the background of Swedish immigration 1840-1930 (in English); Swedish passenger arrivals in New York 1820-50 (in English); Swedish Mormon pioneers (in English); emigration statistics and reports; and characteristics of Swedish emigration.

Gazetteers, Maps, and Atlases

Among the helpful gazetteers and maps are:

Generalstabens Litografiska Anstalt (Stockholm). *Svenska Orter, Atlas över Sverige med Ortbeskrivning.* Stockholm: n.pub., 1932. (FHL# REF/948.5/E5so) Swedish topographical dictionary and atlas.

United States. Board on Geographic Names. *Sweden: Official Standard Names Approved by the U.S. Board on Geographic Names.* Washington, D.C.: U.S. Government Printing Office, 1963. (FHL# REF/948.5/E5u or microfilm 874467)

Generalstabens Litografiska Anstalt. *Svenska Kartor Utmärkande Domsago.* Stockholm: Generalstabens Litografisks Anstalt, 1960. (FHL# 948.5/E7gl) Maps of districts and community borders before 1952.

______. *Kommuner och Församlingar, 1960.* Stockholm: Kartografiska Institut, Esselte AB, 1964. (FHL# Map Case/948.5/E7kf) Two maps designating communities and parishes.

Genealogy

The library has over 200 sources cataloged under **Sweden/Genealogy** plus numerous genealogies under county and parish headings. Most of these are family histories. Some of the family names with histories are: Ämark, Anna Lovise Peterson, Samsioe, Nils Larsson (1652) of Jönköpings, Zingmark, Mellgren, Beckman (1390-1918), Behm (1611-1888), Bjuggren, Svedbom, Ludvigsson, Monson (790-1880), Hammarskjöld, Söderhielm, and Danchwardt, to name just a few.

There are many genealogies of nobility and also genealogies for patronymic names such as Jonsson, Pehrsson, Hansson, etc. The numerous genealogical handbooks, indexes, directories, and periodicals also cataloged under this heading will aid the Swedish researcher.

Handwriting

There are many valuable sources to help in reading paleography used in the old Swedish records. Among them are:

Åberg, Alf. *Läsning av Gamla Handstilar.* Stockholm: Genealogiska Foreningen, 1955. (FHL# 948.5/B4gh/no.5 or microfilm 1224950, item 12)

Handskrift-prof, 1500-1800. Stockholm: P. A. Norstedt & Söner, 1891. (FHL# 948.5/A81u or microfilm 599864, item 3) Examples of handwriting from 1500-1800 with explanations.

Many of the genealogy handbooks also contain examples and explanations of handwriting.

History

Some of the historical topics dealt with by the library's Swedish collection include a cultural, commercial, and industrial history of Jönköping, Kalmar, and Kronoberg counties: Swedish history 960-1560; descriptions of peasant dwellings in Sweden; Swedish history c.1100-1960; Swedish folk traditions; economic history; a history of Swedish nobility; a history of Swedish peasants; a history of ancient hunters in the mountains of Sweden (in English); an administrative history of Swedish parishes; a history of Swedish book-printing; a history of the Walloon immigration into Sweden; a historical study of clothes and furniture; a history of festivals in several centuries; a history of Swedish manorial estates; and activities and customs of people in villages. Two histories in English are:

Lundborg, Herman Bernhard. *The Swedish Nation in Word and Picture.* Stockholm: Printed by Hasse W. Tullberg, 1921. (FHL# 948.5/H6L)

Scott, Franklin D. *Sweden, the Nation's History.* Minneapolis: University of Minnesota Press, 1977. (FHL# 948.5/H2sc)

Land and Property (Jordeböcker)

The land and property records of Sweden are usually found within the court records where the mortgage transactions and deeds are recorded. When available, there will be a separate listing under **/[County]/Land and Property**, however. The earliest records start about 1630 and are available on microfilm up to about 1750. Some deeds are available to about 1820.

Since the names of the landowners and tenants, residences, and the valuation of the land are usually the only information given, land records are not of great value in finding genealogical data. Provincial accounts *(Landskapshandlingar)* are available on microfilm for 1541-1605 but list only names and residences of landowner and tenant. See FHLC heading **/[County]/Land and Property.**

Under **Sweden/Land and Property** are several histories of castles and manorial estates, a copy of land records in Göta Royal Circuit Court of Appeals for 1591-1684, and a record of provincial transactions with various tax, estate accounts, annual rents and revenues, and dispositions from 1532-1635.

Language and Languages

Dictionaries in the Swedish collection include a Finnish-Swedish dictionary, a dictionary of old or unusual words, a dictionary of medieval Swedish, a Swedish dialect dictionary, a dictionary of medieval Latin used in early documents in Sweden, and several Swedish-English, English-Swedish dictionaries. A helpful dictionary for the Swedish researcher is:

Nojd, Ruben. *McKay's Modern English-Swedish and Swedish-English Dictionary.* New York: McKay, 1954. (FHL# 439.7321/N699m/1954)

Military Records (Militärhandlingar)

Sweden has not fought in a war since 1814; but before then, its history is one of continual conflicts with Russia, Prussia, Denmark, and Poland. Military records, unfortunately, contain very little genealogical or vital data and should be used only for biographical information about a particular person.

The earliest records are rotations and inductions starting about 1537 and containing the names of military personnel and their residences. The General Muster Rolls began between 1620-80 and are available in the library on microfilm to 1869. They were kept by respective regiments every three to ten years and contain the names of personnel of all ranks, usually the province (not parish) of birth, age (not always reliable), date of death or discharge. (Information varies, sometimes height, years of service, marital status, and if slain on the battlefield are recorded.) Regiments may have been infantry, cavalry or navy in the provinces, or enlisted regiments in the city.

Pension and salary lists give names of officers and noncommissioned officers only and salaries (sometimes names of relatives). These records, as well as muster rolls, Army rotation and induction lists, merit and service records of officers, transactions of the Army Pension Fund, letters of the Military High Command, and military court records are cataloged under **Sweden/-Military Records.**

Under **Sweden/Military Records** are the histories of various regiments and biographical sketches of army and navy officers.

Minorities

The Swedish collection contains works on Jews, Mormons, Walloons, Scots, Swedish Baptists, and other religious minorities.

Names, Personal

Some of the topics cataloged under this heading are Walloon names in Sweden, laws about personal names, Swedish personal names and their meanings, Swedish Christian names at the end of the sixteenth century, historical notes on surnames, and Swedish surnames of the nineteenth century. A helpful English reference book is:

Swedish Personal Names. Washington, D.C.: Central Intelligence Agency, [c.1980s]. (FHL# Staff Area/929.4/-UN4sw)

Nobility (Heraldry) (Riddarhuset)

The records on the nobility of Sweden are the oldest available in the Swedish collection, dating to the fifteenth century. They include the names of those introduced and accepted into the House of Nobility; pedigrees listing their progenitors to the earliest known ancestor; names of spouse and children; dates of birth, marriage, and death; residences, offices, and commissions received; occupations; and relationships.

These records are cataloged under **/Biography, /Genealogy, /Heraldry,** and **/Nobility.** Topics listed include members of the Order of King Carl XIII; armorial of Swedish nobility; history of counts and barons; contributions of nobility to history; coats of arms of Swedish knighthood; heraldry unregistered; and registry of the Swedish Seraphim Order of Knighthood, 1748-1938.

Probate Records (Bouppteckningar)

The probate record is the most important court record to the genealogist. In Sweden, probates are really inventories of property. Court-appointed appraisers would turn the inventory list over to the district or city court to be probated at the next session. (Sessions usually occurred two to four times a year.)

Probate records began as early as 1660 (generally about 1725) and are on microfilm to 1860, but only half have been indexed. These films are cataloged under **Sweden/[County]/[City or District]/Probate Records.**

Probate records may contain all or part of this information: date of inventory; by whom performed, name of deceased, death date of deceased (usually follows a few lines below the date of the inventory), last residence of the deceased, names of the heirs, their ages, their residences, their relationship to the deceased, and the distribution of real and personal property.

Public Records

Public records are numerous, but generally are of greater historical than genealogical value. They include civil accounts, business transactions, diplomatic salary settlements, and tax lists.

Schools

Most of the library's holdings about Swedish schools are histories of various schools throughout Sweden, including Swedish public schools, trade technological schools, Swedish girls' schools, navigational schools, and trade schools for underprivileged children. There is also a chronological list of the students in Uppsala University from 1595 to 1788.

Social Life and Customs

Excellent sources on the social life and customs of Sweden will enhance the genealogist's understanding of the country. A few of the topics mentioned are a study of work tools in rural areas before the industrialism, life in the cities 150 years ago, males and females in Swedish folk traditions, whores in peasant society, and activities and customs of people in a village. Helpful works in English are:

Lorenzen, Lilly. *Of Swedish Ways.* Minneapolis: Dillon Press, Inc., 1981. (FHL# 948.5/H61o)

O'Connor, David E. *The Swedes in Their Homeland, in America, in Connecticut.* Storrs, Conn.: I.N. Thut World Education Center, University of Connecticut, 1983. (FHL# 974.6/F2o)

Taxation (Boskapsräkningar)

Tax lists from 1563 to 1718 are on microfilm and give the names of landowners and tenants. Also see *Census Records* and *Public Records* above.

Church of Jesus Christ of Latter-day Saints. Genealogical Department. *Sweden: Lanskaphandlingar, 1532-1635.* Salt Lake City: Genealogical Society of Utah, 1967. (FHL# 948.5/R41 or microfilm 599277, item 2)

Contains various tax lists, estate accounts, annual rents and revenues, dispositions, and various provincial transactions.

Town Records (Public Records)

These records include the minutes of the magistrates' court and city administration records, usually for the seventeenth and eighteenth centuries.

Records by Jurisdiction **Denmark (Danmark)**	Archives & Libraries	Bibliography	Biography	Business & Commerce	Census	Chronology	Church History	Church Records	Civil Registration	Court Records	Description & Travel	Directories	Emigration/Immigration	Folklore	Gazetteers	Genealogy	Guardian & Ward	Handwriting	Heraldry	History	Land & Property	Language/Dictionaries	Manors/Castles	Maps	Medical Records	Merchant Marine	Military Records	Minorities	Names, Geographical	Names, Personal	Naturalization & Citizenship	Nobility	Obituaries	Occupations	Officials/Employees	Pensions	Periodicals	Poor Houses	Postal & Shipping Guides	Probate Records	Public Records	Schools	Social Life & Customs	Taxation
Country Wide	•	•	•	•	•	•	•	•	•	•	•	•	•	•	•	•		•	•	•	•	•	•	•	•	•	•	•	•	•		•	•	•	•	•	•	•	•	•	•	•	•	•
Counties:																																												
Åbenrå	•		•		•			•	•	•			•		•	•				•	•		•		•		•							•	•	•				•	•	•		•
Ålborg				•	•		•	•	•	•						•	•				•						•	•	•				•	•						•	•	•		•
Århus			•		•		•	•	•	•		•			•	•	•			•	•		•				•		•					•				•		•	•	•	•	•
Bornholm			•		•			•		•					•	•	•			•	•			•	•		•		•		•		•	•							•	•		•
Fredriksborg			•		•			•		•	•		•		•	•	•			•	•			•	•		•	•			•		•	•					•	•	•	•	•	
Haderslev	•		•		•	•	•					•	•				•	•				•		•							•	•					•	•	•	•	•			
Hjørring					•			•	•	•			•			•	•			•	•		•				•	•						•				•		•	•			•
Holbaek					•			•		•	•		•			•	•			•	•				•		•				•		•	•						•	•		•	•
København	•		•		•		•	•	•	•		•	•			•	•			•	•			•	•		•	•			•		•	•				•		•	•	•	•	
Maribo			•		•			•		•					•	•	•			•	•			•	•		•		•		•		•	•						•	•	•		•
Odense	•	•		•	•			•	•	•	•		•		•	•	•			•	•		•		•		•		•				•	•						•	•	•		•
Praestø					•			•	•	•	•					•	•			•	•			•	•		•				•		•	•						•	•			•
Randers					•			•	•	•	•	•	•			•	•			•	•		•	•	•		•		•					•				•		•	•	•		•
Ribe	•				•		•	•		•					•	•	•			•	•		•		•		•							•						•	•	•	•	•
Ringkøbing					•			•	•	•			•			•	•			•	•		•				•		•					•				•		•	•			•
Sjaelland								•												•	•				•									•						•				•
Skanderborg					•			•	•	•		•			•	•	•			•	•		•				•	•	•					•				•		•	•	•		•
Sorø			•		•			•		•			•			•	•		•	•	•			•	•		•	•			•		•	•						•	•	•		•
Svendborg	•	•			•			•	•	•	•		•		•	•	•			•	•		•		•		•		•				•	•						•	•	•		•
Sønderborg	•	•	•		•			•	•	•					•	•				•	•				•		•							•	•					•		•		•
Thisted					•			•	•	•						•	•			•	•						•	•						•						•	•			•
Tønder		•	•	•			•	•	•			•		•	•				•	•				•		•							•	•			•		•	•	•		•	
Vejle			•	•	•			•	•	•	•	•			•	•	•			•	•						•		•					•		•		•		•	•			•
Viborg	•				•			•	•	•		•			•	•	•			•	•		•				•		•		•			•						•	•	•		•

Records by Jurisdiction **Faerøe Islands** Islands	Archives & Libraries	Census: 1801, 1834	Census: 1840, 1845, 1850, 1855, 1860, 1870, 1880	Census: 1890, 1901, 1906, 1911	Church Records	Civil Registration	Gazetteers	Land & Property	Language/Dictionaries	Maps	Probate Records
Eysturoy		•	•	•	•						
Norduroya		•	•	•	•						
Sandoy		•	•	•	•						
Streymoy		•	•	•	•						
Suduroy Nordre		•	•	•	•						
Suduroy Søndre		•	•	•	•						
Vagar		•	•	•	•						
Country wide	•	•	•	•	•	•	•	•	•	•	•

Records by Jurisdiction

Finland (Suomi)

Records by Jurisdiction	Almanacs	Archives & Libraries	Bibliography	Biography	Census	Church History	Church Records	Civil Registration	Court Records	Description & Travel	Directories	Emigration/Immigration	Ethnology	Gazetteers	Genealogy	Guardian & Ward	Handwriting	History	Land & Property	Languages	Law & Legislation	Maps	Military Records	Names, Geographical	Names, Personal	Nobility	Occupations	Officials/Employees	Periodicals	Politics & Government	Postal & Shipping Guides	Probate Records	Public Records	Schools	Social Life & Customs	Societies	Statistics	Taxation	Town Records	Yearbooks
Country wide	•	•	•	•	•	•	•		•	•	•	•	•	•	•	•	•	•	•	•	•	•	•	•	•	•	•	•	•	•	•		•	•	•	•	•	•		•
Counties: (Laani)																																								
First Spelling is Finnish,																																								
Second Spelling is Swedish																																								
Ahvenanmaa - Åland					•		•		•									•					•	•								•	•	•						
Hame - Tavastehus				•	•		•	•	•						•	•		•	•			•	•			•						•	•	•				•		
Kuopio				•	•	•	•	•	•						•			•					•									•	•	•						
Kymi - Kymmene				•	•	•	•	•	•						•			•				•	•									•	•	•	•					
Lappi - Lappland					•		•	•	•									•	•				•	•								•	•	•						
Mikkeli - St. Mickels				•	•	•	•	•	•						•							•	•									•	•	•			•			
Oulu - Uleåborg				•	•		•	•	•						•			•					•				•	•				•	•	•				•		
Turku Pori-																																								
Åbo och Bjørneborg				•	•	•	•	•	•			•			•	•		•	•			•	•			•						•	•	•				•	•	
Uusimaa - Nyland		•		•	•	•	•	•	•						•			•	•	•		•	•	•		•	•	•				•	•	•		•	•	•	•	•
Vaasa - Vasa				•	•		•	•	•			•			•	•		•				•	•	•			•	•				•	•	•	•	•		•		
Viipuri				•	•	•	•		•						•			•	•			•	•		•		•					•	•	•						

Records by Jurisdiction

Greenland (Gronland)

Records by Jurisdiction	Archives & Libraries	Census	Census Bibliography	Church Records	Church Rec.-Inventories	Colonization	Description	Gazetteers	History	Maps	Religion & Religious Life	Social Life & Customs
Country wide	•	•	•	•	•	•	•	•	•	•	•	•

Records by Jurisdiction **Iceland (Islandi)**	Archives & Libraries	Bibliography	Biography	Business & Commerce	Census Indexes	Church History	Church Records	Civil Registration	Court Records	Description & Travel	Directories	Emigration/Immigration	Folklore	Gazetteers	Genealogy	Handwriting	History	Land & Property	Language (Dictionaries)	Law & Legislation	Maps	Medical Records	Names, Geographical	Names, Personal	Occupations	Officials & Employees	Periodicals	Postal & Shipping Guides	Probate Records	Public Records	Religion & Religious Life	Statistics	Yearbooks
Country wide	•	•	•	•	•	•	•	•	•	•	•	•	•	•	•	•	•	•	•	•	•	•	•	•	•	•	•	•	•	•	•	•	•
Counties: (Sysla)																																	
Arnes					•		•																										
Austur-Barðastrandar							•							•																			
Austur-Húnavatns							•																										
Austur-Skaftafells							•																										
Borgarfjarðar							•																										
Dala							•							•																			
Eyjafjarðar							•																										
Gullbringu							•										•				•												•
Hnappadals					•		•																										
Kjósar							•								•																		
Mýra							•																										
Norður-Ísafjarðar							•																										
Norður-Múla							•																										
Norður-Pingeyjar							•																										
Rangárvalla					•		•								•																		
Skagafjarðar						•	•						•		•		•	•															
Snæfellsnes							•																										
Strada			•				•																										
Suður-Múla							•																										
Suður-Pingeyjar							•																										
Vestmannaeyjar			•				•						•	•	•		•										•						
Vestur-Barðastrandar							•																										
Vestur-Húnavatns							•																										
Vestur-Ísafjarðar							•								•																		
Vestur-Skaftafells			•				•																										

Records by Jurisdiction **Norway (Norge)**	Archives & Libraries	Bibliography	Biography	Census, 1664-66	Census	Census Indexes	Centennial Celebrations	Chronology	Church History	Church Records	Civil Registration	Court Records	Description & Travel	Directories	Emigration/Immigration	Folklore	Gazetteers	Genealogy	Handwriting	History	Land & Property	Language/Dictionaries	Law & Legislation	Maps	Merchant Marine	Military Records	Names, Geographical	Names, Personal	Nobility	Obituaries	Occupations	Officials & Employees	Periodicals	Politics & Government	Population	Postal & Shipping Guides	Probate Records	Public Records	Religion & Religious Life	Social Life & Customs	Statistics	Taxation
Country wide	•	•	•	•	•	•	•	•	•	•	•	•	•	•	•	•	•	•	•	•	•	•	•	•	•	•	•	•	•	•	•	•	•	•	•	•	•	•	•	•	•	•
Counties: (Fylke or Amt)																																										
Akershus			•	•	•	•	•		•	•	•	•	•			•		•		•	•				•	•					•						•			•		•
Aust-Agder			•	•	•		•		•	•	•	•				•		•		•	•				•	•											•			•		•
Bergen	•	•	•		•				•	•	•	•	•		•	•		•		•	•			•		•				•	•						•			•		•
Buskerud		•	•	•	•		•		•	•		•	•		•			•		•	•			•	•	•											•		•	•		•
Finnmark					•		•		•	•	•	•		•		•		•		•	•			•													•			•		•
Hedmark			•	•	•		•			•		•			•	•		•		•	•			•							•						•			•		•
Hordaland		•	•	•	•				•	•	•	•			•			•		•	•	•										•	•		•		•			•		•
Møre og Romsdal			•	•	•		•		•	•		•	•		•			•		•	•			•													•			•		•
Nord-Trøndelag			•	•	•		•		•	•		•	•			•		•		•	•																•			•		•
Nordland			•	•	•					•	•	•						•		•	•	•		•											•		•			•		•
Oppland				•	•		•		•	•		•	•		•	•		•		•	•										•						•			•		•
Oslo	•		•	•	•		•		•	•		•	•		•			•		•	•			•	•	•					•		•				•			•		•
Østfold			•	•	•		•		•	•		•	•					•		•	•				•	•					•			•			•			•		•
Rogaland			•	•	•		•		•	•	•	•	•		•	•		•		•	•			•			•					•					•			•		•
Sogn og Fjordane		•		•	•		•		•	•		•				•		•		•	•			•													•			•		•
Sør-Trøndelag	•		•	•	•		•		•	•		•	•		•			•		•	•			•				•			•	•					•			•		•
Telemark			•	•	•		•			•		•			•	•		•		•	•				•	•					•						•			•		•
Troms			•	•	•					•	•	•	•					•		•	•			•													•					•
Vest-Agder		•	•	•	•		•		•	•		•			•	•		•		•	•				•	•					•				•		•			•		•
Vestfold				•	•		•		•	•		•	•					•		•	•			•	•	•											•					•

Records by Jurisdiction

Sweden (Sverige)

	Almanacs	Archives & Libraries	Bibliography	Biography	Business & Commerce	Census	Chronology	Church History	Church Records	Civil Registration	Court Records	Description & Travel	Directories	Emigration/Immigration	Encyclopedias	Folklore	Gazetteers	Genealogy	Guardian & Ward	Handwriting	Heraldry	History	Land & Property	Language/Dictionaries	Maps	Merchant Marine	Military Records	Minorities	Names, Geographical	Names, Personal	Nobility	Occupations	Officials & Employees	Periodicals	Portraits	Postal & Shipping Guides	Probate Records	Public Records	Schools	Social Life & Customs	Societies	Statistics	Taxation	Town Records
Country wide	•	•	•	•	•	•	•	•	•	•	•	•	•	•	•	•	•		•		•	•	•	•	•	•	•	•	•	•	•	•	•	•	•	•	•	•	•	•	•	•	•	
Counties: (Lan)																																												
Blekinge			•	•	•	•		•	•	•	•			•				•	•			•	•		•		•		•			•	•				•	•	•			•	•	
Gotland		•	•		•	•		•	•	•	•	•		•		•		•	•			•	•		•	•	•		•		•	•					•		•				•	•
Gavleborg			•	•		•			•	•	•			•				•	•			•	•		•				•		•	•	•				•	•	•				•	•
Goteborgs och Bohus		•	•	•	•	•		•	•	•	•		•	•			•	•	•			•	•		•		•	•	•		•	•			•		•	•	•	•	•		•	•
Halland			•	•	•	•			•	•	•	•	•	•			•	•	•			•	•		•		•		•					•			•	•	•	•			•	•
Jamtland		•	•	•		•		•	•	•	•		•	•		•		•	•			•	•		•				•		•		•		•		•	•		•			•	•
Jonkoping		•	•	•		•			•	•	•		•	•				•	•			•	•		•		•		•			•					•	•	•				•	•
Kalmar		•	•	•	•	•		•	•	•	•		•				•	•				•	•		•		•		•		•	•	•				•	•	•				•	•
Kopparberg			•	•	•	•		•	•	•	•		•	•				•	•			•	•		•				•		•	•	•				•	•	•				•	•
Kristianstad			•	•	•	•		•	•	•	•		•	•				•	•			•	•		•			•	•			•	•		•		•	•	•	•			•	•
Kronoberg		•	•	•		•			•	•	•			•				•	•			•	•		•		•		•			•					•	•	•				•	
Malmohus		•	•	•	•	•		•	•	•	•	•	•	•				•	•			•	•		•		•	•	•		•	•	•		•		•	•	•	•	•		•	•
Norbotten			•	•		•		•	•	•	•		•	•				•	•			•	•	•	•		•	•	•		•						•	•	•				•	
Skaraborg		•	•	•	•	•			•	•	•		•	•			•	•	•			•	•		•				•			•	•				•	•	•				•	•
Stockholm		•	•	•	•	•		•	•	•	•	•	•	•				•	•			•	•	•	•		•	•			•	•	•		•		•	•	•	•	•		•	•
Sodermanland			•	•	•	•		•	•	•	•		•	•				•	•			•	•		•						•	•					•	•	•				•	•
Uppsala		•	•	•	•	•			•	•	•		•	•		•		•	•			•	•		•			•			•	•	•	•			•	•	•	•			•	•
Varmland		•	•	•		•		•	•	•	•	•	•	•				•	•			•	•		•		•		•		•	•					•	•	•				•	•
Vasterbotten		•	•	•		•			•	•	•		•	•				•	•			•	•	•	•			•	•		•						•	•	•				•	•
Vasternorrland		•	•	•		•		•	•	•	•			•		•		•	•			•	•	•	•				•		•	•	•				•	•	•	•			•	•
Vastmanland			•	•	•	•			•	•	•		•	•				•	•			•	•		•				•		•	•	•				•	•	•	•			•	•
Alvsborg		•	•	•		•		•	•	•	•		•	•				•	•			•	•		•				•		•	•			•		•	•	•	•			•	•
Orebro		•	•		•		•	•	•	•			•				•	•			•	•		•						•	•	•				•	•	•	•			•	•	
Ostergotland		•	•	•	•	•		•	•	•	•		•	•				•	•			•	•		•				•		•	•					•	•	•				•	•

Chapter 19

Germany and Central Europe

Richard W. Dougherty

GERMANY

Historical Background

1517	Martin Luther publishes his ninety-five theses sparking the Reformation.
1545-63	Council of Trent mandates Catholic parish registers.
1555	Peace of Augsburg allows each ruler to determine the religion of his or her subjects.
1550-1600	Catholic Counter reformation regains large areas of central Europe for the Roman Catholic Church.
1618-48	Thirty Years' War devastates many areas of Germany. Ended by Peace of Westphalia which grants part of Alsace to France. Remainder of Alsace comes under French control by 1697.
1687-97	French invasion of the Palatinate.
1710-14	War of the Spanish Succession. Palatines leave for England and America.
1742	Prussia annexes Silesia.
1763	Catherine the Great invites German colonists to settle in South Russia.
1798	French occupy the Palatinate and Rheinland.
1803	Reichsdeputationshauptschluss (Main Conclusion of the Imperial Deputation) dissolves all ecclesiastical principalities, reduces the number of Free Cities to six, and eliminates Imperial Knights.
1806	Dissolution of the Holy Roman Empire and formation of Confederation of the Rhine.
1815	Congress of Vienna organizes German Confederation, awards Rheinland, Westphalia, and a substantial portion of Saxony to Prussia. Bavaria receives the Palatinate.
1834	Creation of the Zollverein (customs union).
1848	Revolution fails; "48ers" immigrate to America.
1864	Danish War results in joint occupation of Schleswig-Holstein by Prussia and Austria.
1866	Seven Weeks' War. Prussia annexes Hanover, Nassau, Hesse-Kassel, Schleswig-Holstein and Frankfurt am Main. Formation of North German Confederation.
1870	Franco-Prussian War.
1871	Proclamation of the New German Empire at Versailles. Annexation of Alsace-Lorraine.
1876	Civil registration of vital events begins throughout empire.
1914-18	First World War; Germany defeated; Second Empire dissolved.
1919	Creation of the German Republic. New state of Thuringia created from seven small principalities. Treaty of Versailles forces Germany to cede Alsace-Lorraine to France; Upper Silesia, most of Posen, and West Prussia to Poland; North Schleswig to Denmark; and three small frontier districts to Belgium. Danzig becomes a free city, Memel is ceded to Lithuania, and the Saarland is to be administered by the League of Nations for fifteen years.
1933	Dissolution of the Weimar Republic and creation of the Third (Nazi) Reich.
1938	Germany annexes Austria and part of Czechoslovakia.

1939	Germany annexes Bohemia and Moravia, Memel, and invades Poland. World War II begins.
1939-45	World War II. Germany defeated.
1945	Potsdam Agreement results in loss of all German territory east of the Oder and Neisse rivers to the Soviet Union and Poland. German inhabitants of these areas (East Prussia, Danzig, Silesia, Eastern Pomerania, and part of Brandenburg) are expelled as are the German-speaking inhabitants of Czechoslovakia.
1949	Creation of the Federal Republic of Germany (West Germany) and the German Democratic Republic (East Germany).

Germany Library Collection

Millions of Americans can recall their immigrant grandparents speaking of the "old country," meaning, of course, the country in Europe where they were born. Paradoxically, many European countries are much younger than the United States, politically speaking. For instance, Czechoslovakia did not become an independent political entity until 1918, 142 years after the birth of the American republic in 1776.

A parallel situation holds for Germany. Prior to the proclamation of the second German Empire at Versailles in 1871, the German Confederation existed between 1815 and 1866. From medieval times until 1806, the major political union in Germany had been the Holy Roman Empire, consisting of hundreds of principalities, some barely large enough to support a knight in his castle. Others, such as Prussia, covered a vast area, at least by European standards.

Since the end of the First World War, Germany, compared to its 1871-1918 status, has suffered a massive loss of territory. One-third of the second empire was annexed by Poland and Russia in 1945. Alsace-Lorraine reverted to French control after the First World War as did northern Schleswig to Denmark. Beyond that, various states in central and eastern Europe expelled their German-speaking inhabitants in 1945 on the grounds that they were a disloyal element.

This means that the ancestral village for many Americans of Germanic descent no longer appears on the map with the same spelling that it had in 1880 when the ancestor lived there. Rather, it might appear in any of ten languages ranging from Russian to French to Danish to Italian.

These basic facts of geography and history, plus the fact that most Germans who emigrated to the U.S. did so in the nineteenth century, led the Family History Library to jettison its system of cataloging its German collection according to the modern name of the locality. *Rather, the German collection is organized according to the political boundaries as they existed between 1871 and 1918* as described in E. Uertecht, comp., *Meyers Orts-und Verkehrs-Lexikon des Deutschen Reichs* (Leipsig und Wien: Bibliographisches Institut, 1912) (FHL# 943/E5mo).

This same arrangement with some modification holds true for the German portion of the International Genealogical Index (IGI). Chapter 2 describes the basic arrangement of the IGI as town, county, and state. Naturally, European countries do not use the exact equivalent, but the Family History Library has organized the IGI so that an acceptable governmental subdivision is recorded in the place of the county. This arrangement differs according to the various German states.

Since the IGI annually becomes a more important source for tracing German immigrants, a basic discussion of its organization seems warranted. Germany is listed within the category of Central Europe. Eight distinct subdivisions exist for Germany, the first called **Germany/Miscellaneous**. This category consists of the eight minor states of Anhalt, Braunschweig (Brunswick), Lippe-Detmold, Oldenburg, Schaumburg-Lippe, Waldeck, Mecklenburg-Schwerin, Mecklenburg-Strelitz, and the Free Cities of Bremen, Hamburg, and Luebeck. In this section, the Minor States and Free Cities fill the category of counties under the country of Germany, e.g., **Germany/Anhalt/Lindau** or **Germany/Bremen/Seehausen**. Hence if an individual stated in the 1870 U.S. census that his or her place of birth was Mecklenburg, you should check the **Germany/Miscellaneous** section of the IGI for a possible entry.

The remainder of the German section of the IGI is organized under the headings of the major states, which are used as the equivalent of countries. Major states, with a list of their subdivisions, cataloged like the equivalent of American states and counties in the IGI, are: Baden, County (Kreis in German, meaning an administrative district): Baden, Freiburg, Heidelberg, Karlsruhe, Konstanz, Loerrach, Mannheim, Mosbach, Offenburg, Villingen, and Waldshut. An entry from Schlechtnau would be listed as **Schlechtnau/Loerrach/-Baden.**

Bavaria, (Bayern) Government District (Regierungsbezirk): Mittelfranken, Neiderbayern, Oberbayern, Oberfranken, Oberpfalz, Pfalz, Schwaben, and Unterfranken. An example would be **Bavaria/Niederbayern/Niedotfingen.** It is important to remember that Bavaria in the nineteenth century, indeed-from 1815 to 1945-ruled an area west of the Rhine River in what is now the German State (Land) of Rheinland-Pfalz. This area, officially Regierungsbezirk Pfalz, Bayern, sometimes appears in the U.S. census tabulations or naturalization papers as Rhenish Bavaria. Equally important, Pfalz translates into English as Palatinate. Hence, this region is the source of many, although by no means all, of the so-called Palatine Germans who settled in New York and Pennsylvania in the eighteenth century. It follows that you should check the Bavarian section of the German IGI for entries concerning these "Palatines."

But "Palatine" came to be a generic term for German in eighteenth-century America. Hence, you must check other portions of the IGI for eighteenth-century German immigrants, i.e., Baden, Hesse-Darmstadt, Wuerttemberg, Prussia, and France (Alsace).

Hesse-Darmstadt/Hessen-Darmstadt, Province (Provinz) Oberhessen, Rheinhessen, and Starkenburg. Example: **Hesse-Darmstadt/Oberhessen/Kirtorf.** Hessen-Darmstadt, sometimes called Ducal Hessen, was distinct from Hessen-Kassel (Cassel) also known as Kurhessen (Electoral Hessen). Thus, an ancestor who listed his or her country of origin as Hesse-Cassel or Cur-Hesse in the 1860 U.S. census would *not* appear in the Hesse-Darmstadt IGI. After 1866, Hessen-Darmstadt was known simply as Hessen, since Hessen-Kassel no longer existed as a separate state. Hence, when Meyers gazetteer lists a locality as Hessen, it means Hessen-Darmstadt.

By far the largest German state, Prussia was divided into administrative provinces *(Provinzen)* which serve as counties in the IGI. These provinces are: Brandenburg, Hannover, Hessen-Nassau, Hohenzollern, Ostpreussen (East Prussia), Pommern (Pomerania), Posen, Rheinland, Sachsen (Saxony), Schlesien (Silesia), Schleswig-Holstein, Westfalen (Westphalia), and Westpreussen (West Prussia). The IGI uses the German names, not these English versions, but they are included here to help the novice genealogist identify the correct province. For instance, Schlesien is often mistaken for Schleswig, when in fact it is the German term for Silesia.

Again, an elementary knowledge of German history helps in using the Prussian portion of the IGI. Prussia acquired part of the kingdom of Saxony at the Congress of Vienna in 1815. The annexed area was called Provinz Sachsen. Hence, the name of an ancestor from this area would not appear in the IGI for Saxony, but rather for Prussia.

Prussia also acquired considerable territory as the result of the Seven Weeks' War of 1866. It annexed the old kingdom of Hanover, which became the Province of Hannover, Schleswig-Holstein, the Duchy of Nassau, and Hessen-Kassel. Hence, ancestors from these areas would all appear in the Prussian IGI.

The same holds true for individuals from those areas of Prussia absorbed by Poland and the Soviet Union, e.g., East Prussia, West Prussia, Posen, parts of Pomerania, Brandenburg, and Silesia.

A typical example of a geographical designation in the Prussian IGI would be **Prussia/Brandenburg/Neuwalde.** In those cases where more than one village of the same name exists in a given province, the *Kreis* (county) designation is added to identify the correct place. For instance, there are at least fourteen Neudorfs in West Prussia. A particular Neudorf would be identified by also listing the *Kreis*, e.g., Elbing. Hence, it would read **Prussia/Westpreussen/Elbing.** This system applies in other states besides Prussia.

Saxony (Sachsen): Government district (Kreishauptmannschaft): Bautzen, Chemnitz, Dresden, Leipzig, and Zwickau. Example: Tannenberg, Chemnitz, Saxony. Only the names of individuals born or married in the old kingdom of Saxony will appear in the Saxony IGI.

Thuringia, (Thuringen): The former duchies serve as the county equivalents: Reuss-Aeltere-Linie, Reuss-Juengere-Line, Sachsen-Altenburg, Sachsen-Coberg-Gotha, Sachsen-Meiningen, Sachsen-Weimar-Eisenach, Schwarzburg-Rudolstadt, and Schwarzburg-Sonderhausen. Example: **Thruingia/Reuss-Aeltere-linie/-Fraureth.** Thus, you should seek an individual whose place of birth appears as Saxe-Weimar in the 1860 U.S. census in the Thuringia IGI rather than that of Saxony. Figure 19:1 shows a sample entry from the Thuringia IGI.

Wuerttemberg: Government district *(Kreis)*: Donaukreis, Jagekreis, Neckarkries, and Schwarzwaldkreis. Example: **Wuerttemberg/Schwartzwaldkreis/Pfulling.**

There is one exception to the general rule that the names of individuals who were born, christened, or married in areas belonging to Imperial Germany 1871 1918 appear in one of the eight sections of the German IGI. That exception is Alsace-Lorraine. Even though this region was part of Germany from 1871-1918, all submissions of names for LDS temple processing from Alsace-Lorraine are recorded in the French IGI.

A second collection of material available in the Family History Library which should be consulted very early in the quest for a German ancestor is the family group records collection (FGRC) in the LDS Archives. This collection predates the IGI, which replaced it in 1969. Some of the data found on these group sheets has been evaluated and included in the IGI, but most of it has not.

The FGRC is not organized according to geographic locality, but alphabetically, according to surname. Hence, there are no specific instructions for seeking a German ancestor apart from those mentioned in Chapter 2 on the FGRC.

Still another LDS source worthy of mention is the Temple Index Bureau (TIB). This name index is not open for general research, but you can request information about a specific individual. TIB entries list the individual's date and place of birth, marriage, and death as well as the names of his or her parents and spouse. This index began in 1921 and is particularly useful for data on individuals whose descendants joined the LDS Church relatively early in the church's history.

Admittedly, neither the FGRC nor the TIB is a part of the German collection as such. Nor is the German section of the IGI, in the strict sense of the word. Yet these indexes, particularly the IGI, are of crucial importance in tracing a German ancestor. Returning to the German collection per se, it seems imperative to explain the arrangement of the catalog. The FHLC is divided into four main sections: Locality, Author-Title, Surname, and Subject. Of these, the Locality section is by far the most important in using the German collection. It begins with an alphabetical list of place names, e.g., **Aachen, Germany/Germany** is cross referenced to **Germany/-Preussen, Rheinland, Aachen.** This means that Aachen is cataloged under the heading of Rheinland, Prussia. Thus, if all you know is the name of the parish with no data on the state or duchy, this portion of the catalog may be useful.

But a word of caution is in order. The list of place names at the beginning of the catalog contains only parishes. It does not list hamlets or villages too small to support a parish church. For instance, if an immigrant's naturalization papers state that he or she was born in Wisborienen, East Prussia, you will not find Wisborienen

REGION: CENTRAL EUROPEAN COUNTRY: GERMANY/THURINGIA AS OF JUN 1984 PAGE 1,954

NAME	SEX: M MALE F FEMALE/H HUSBAND/W WIFE — FATHER/MOTHER OR SPOUSE	SEX	TYPE	EVENT DATE	COUNTY, TOWN, PARISH	B	E	S	SOURCE BATCH	SOURCE SERIAL SHEET
SEMMEN, DOROTHEA										
SEMMEN, DOROTHEA	FRIEDRICH OR FRITZ SCHIECK	W	M	24NOV1674	SACHSEN-WEIMAR-EISENACH,FARNRODA			23DEC1960SL	A457678	1878
SEMMEN, MARTHA ELISABETH	JOHANN FRIEDRICH SCHRAMM	W	M	18OCT1739	SACHSEN-WEIMAR-EISENACH,EISENACH			28MAY1957MT	A458611	0138
*SEMMLER										
SEMMLER, JOHANN GOTTLIEB	JOHANN GOTTFRIED SEMMLER/ANNA SOPHIA HOPFE	M	C	01JUN1803	SACHSEN-ALTENBURG,REICHSTADT	15APR1983SW	22APR1983SW	22APR1983SW	8306780	6
SEMMLER, JOHANNA SOPHIA	JOHANN GOTTFRIED SEMMLER/JOHANNA SOPHIA HOPF	F	C	25FEB1806	SACHSEN-ALTENBURG,REICHSTADT	15APR1983SW	21APR1983SW	22APR1983SW	8306780	6
SEMMLER, JUSTINA	JOHANN GOTTFRIED SEMMLER/ANNA SOPHIA HOPFE	F	C	12NOV1800	SACHSEN-ALTENBURG,REICHSTADT	15APR1983SW	21APR1983SW	22APR1983SW	8306780	6
SEMMELER, MARGARETA	BARTEL SEMMELER/	F	C	27DEC1567	SACHSEN-ALTENBURG,ALTENBURG	11JUN1982JR	26JUL1982JR	06AUG1982JR	8123220	55
*SEMPER										
SEMPER, EMIL	SEMPER/	M	B	23JUN1873	SACHSEN-ALTENBURG,WUSTENHAIN	10JUN1975IF	08JUL1975IF	UNCLEARED	7435227	81
*SENEBALD										
SENEBALD, ANNA CATHARINA	LORENZ SENEBALD/BARBARA HERLING	F	B	01APR1702	SACHSEN-COBURG-GOTHA,MENTERODA	31MAR1971LG	01JUN1971LG	27JUL1971LG	7018219	33
SENEBALD, ANNA CATHARINA	HANS HEINRICH LINSE	W	M	18JAN1724	SACHSEN-COBURG-GOTHA,MENTERODA			27JUL1971LG	7018219	33
=SENF , ** SEE SENFT										
=SENFF , ** SEE SENFT										
*SENFT										
SENF, ALBIN EMIL	FRANZ EDUARD SENF/EMILIE KERSCHER	M	B	16JUL1877	REUSS-JUENGERE-LINIE,GROSSSAARA	28JUN1947	08DEC1982JR	14DEC1982JR	8209720	44
SENF, ANNA CHRISTIANA	JOHANN GOTTLIEB SENF/ANNA MARIA PANZER	F	B	27SEP1781	REUSS-JUENGERE-LINIE,GROSSSAARA	04MAR1972IF	18APR1972IF	26JUL1972IF	7126521	10
SENF, ANNA PAULINE	FRIEDRICH EDUARD SENF/ERNESTINE CHARLOTTE PANZER	F	B	16JUN1864	REUSS-JUENGERE-LINIE,GROSSSAARA	INFANT	INFANT	26JUL1972IF	7126521	4
SENF, CARL FRIEDRICH	JOHANN GOTTLIEB SENF/ANNA MARIA PANZER	M	B	21NOV1782	REUSS-JUENGERE-LINIE,GROSSSAARA	12NOV1955	27JAN1956SG	07AUG1956LG	7126521	10
SENF, CARL FRIEDRICH	CHRISTIANE BERGNER	H	M	18OCT1814	REUSS-JUENGERE-LINIE,GROSSSAARA			01JUL1972IF	7126521	14
SENF, CARL FRIEDRICH	CHRISTIANE BERGNER	H	M	18OCT1814	REUSS-JUENGERE-LINIE,GROSSAGA			07AUG1956LG	A455193	1181
SENF, CARL FRIEDRICH AUGUST	CARL FRIEDRICH SENF/CHRISTIANE BERGNER	M	B	30NOV1814	REUSS-JUENGERE-LINIE,GROSSSAARA	07MAR1972IF	19JUL1972IF	09AUG1972IF	7126521	5
SENFT, CATHARINA	HERMANN EISLEIB	W	M	24MAY1619	SACHSEN-MEININGEN,OBERELLEN			13OCT1983PV	8311923	85
SENFF, DOROTHEA	HANSS SENFF/	F	C	04DEC1611	REUSS-JUENGERE-LINIE,GERA	07AUG1971IF	12NOV1971IF	14APR1972IF	7102019	9
SENF, EDUARD	ERNESTINE PANZER	H	M	06MAY1849	REUSS-JUENGERE-LINIE,GROSSAGA			07AUG1956LG	A455193	1180
SENF, ELISABETH BARBARA	JOHANN VALENTIN SCHULZ	W	M	02NOV1751	SCHWARZBURG-RUDOLSTADT,GRAFINAU ANGSTEDT			09MAR1934SL	A184630	6945
SENF, EMILIE PAULINE	FRIEDRICH EDUARD SENF/ERNESTINE CHARLOTTE PANZER	F	B	10MAY1863	REUSS-JUENGERE-LINIE,GROSSSAARA	INFANT	INFANT	26JUL1972IF	7126521	3
SENF, ERNESTINA BERTA	FRIEDRICH EDUARD SENF/ERNESTINE CHARLOTTE PANZER	F	B	10MAY1858	REUSS-JUENGERE-LINIE,GROSSSAARA	INFANT	INFANT	26JUL1972IF	7126521	2
SENF, ERNESTINE EMMA	FRIEDRICH EDUARD SENF/ERNESTINE CHARLOTTE PANZER	F	B	04JAN1867	REUSS-JUENGERE-LINIE,GROSSSAARA	INFANT	INFANT	26JUL1972IF	7126521	4
SENF, ERNST PHILIBERT	FRIEDRICH EDUARD SENF/ERNESTINE CHARLOTTE PANZER	M	B	27DEC1856	REUSS-JUENGERE-LINIE,GROSSSAARA	INFANT	INFANT	09AUG1972IF	7126521	2
SENF, FRANZ EDUARD	FRIEDRICH EDUARD SENF/ERNESTINE CHARLOTTE PANZER	M	B	08MAR1849	REUSS-JUENGERE-LINIE,GROSSSAARA	12NOV1955	27JAN1956SG	07AUG1956LG	7126521	1
SENF, FRANZ EDUARD	EMILIE THERESE KERTSCHER	H	M	03APR1877	REUSS-JUENGERE-LINIE,WALTERSDORF			29JUN1956SG	A458166	0465
SENF, FRANZ JULIUS	FRIEDRICH EDUARD SENF/ERNESTINE CHARLOTTE PANZER	M	B	15MAY1852	REUSS-JUENGERE-LINIE,GROSSSAARA	07MAR1972IF	19JUL1972IF	09AUG1972IF	7126521	1
SENF, FRIEDRICH EDUARD	CARL FRIEDRICH SENF/CHRISTIANE BERGNER	M	B	04MAR1828	REUSS-JUENGERE-LINIE,GROSSSAARA	12NOV1955	27JAN1956SG	07AUG1956LG	7126521	6
SENF, FRIEDRICH EDUARD	ERNESTINE CHARLOTTE PANZER	H	M	06MAY1849	REUSS-JUENGERE-LINIE,GROSSSAARA			01JUL1972IF	7126521	14

FOR 'Σ', '>', 'ə', '#' SEE PAGE 11 OF INSTRUCTIONS AND REGION FICHE

A = ADULT CHRISTENING B = BIRTH C = CHRISTENING D = DEATH OR BURIAL F = BIRTH OR CHRISTENING OF FIRST KNOWN CHILD M = MARRIAGE N = CENSUS W = WILL ALL OTHERS = MISCELLANEOUS

Figure 19:1 Sample page from the Thuringia section of the International Genealogical Index.

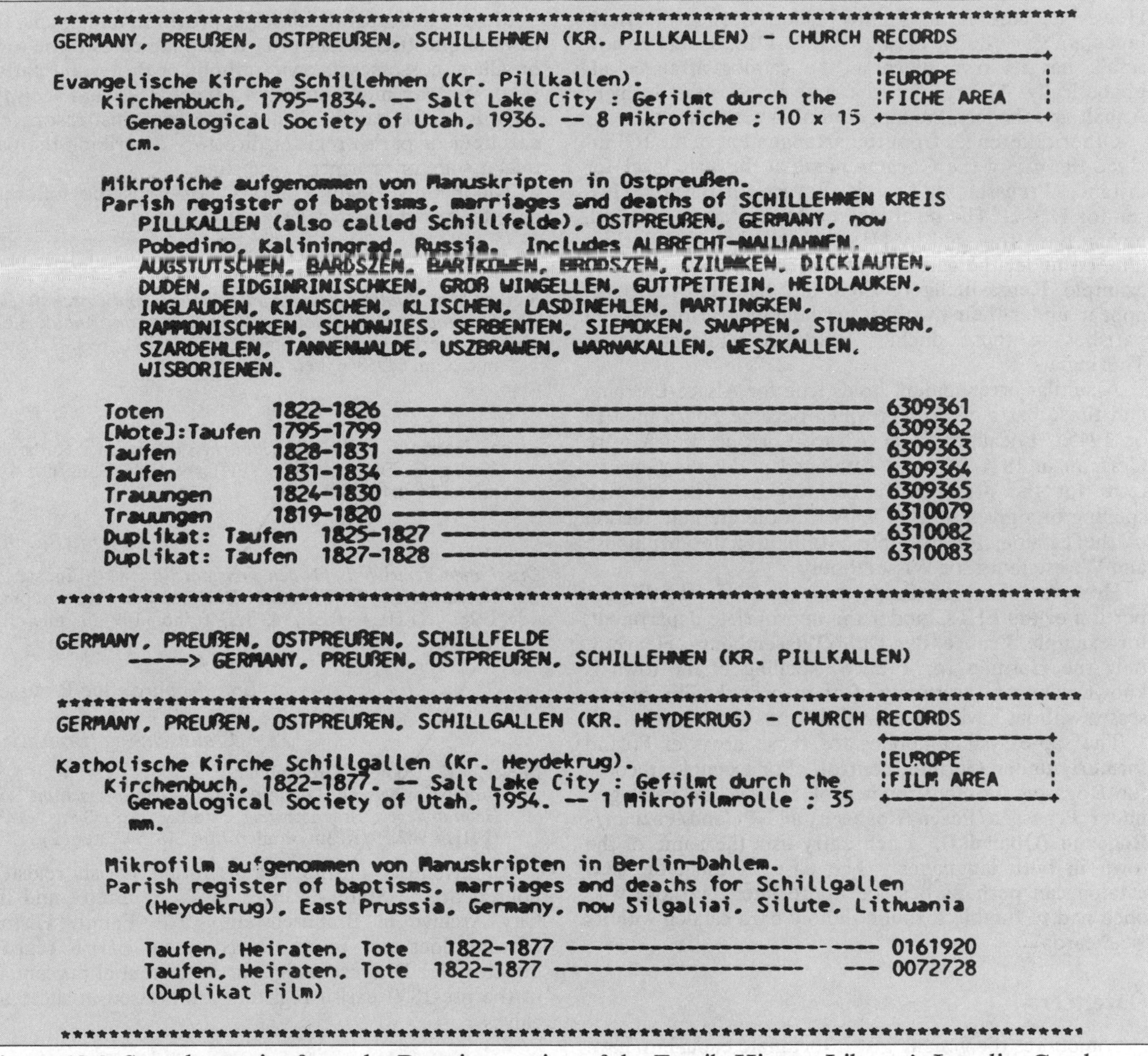

```
*****************************************************************************
GERMANY, PREUßEN, OSTPREUßEN, SCHILLEHNEN (KR. PILLKALLEN) - CHURCH RECORDS
                                                              +-------------+
Evangelische Kirche Schillehnen (Kr. Pillkallen).             :EUROPE       :
   Kirchenbuch, 1795-1834. -- Salt Lake City : Gefilmt durch the  :FICHE AREA :
     Genealogical Society of Utah, 1936. -- 8 Mikrofiche ; 10 x 15 +-------------+
     cm.

   Mikrofiche aufgenommen von Manuskripten in Ostpreußen.
   Parish register of baptisms, marriages and deaths of SCHILLEHNEN KREIS
     PILLKALLEN (also called Schillfelde), OSTPREUßEN, GERMANY, now
     Pobedino, Kaliningrad, Russia.  Includes ALBRECHT-NAUJAHNEN,
     AUGSTUTSCHEN, BARDSZEN, BARTKOWEN, BRODSZEN, CZIUNKEN, DICKIAUTEN,
     DUDEN, EIDGINRINISCHKEN, GROß WINGELLEN, GUTTPETTEIN, HEIDLAUKEN,
     INGLAUDEN, KIAUSCHEN, KLISCHEN, LASDINEHLEN, MARTINGKEN,
     RAMMONISCHKEN, SCHONWIES, SERBENTEN, SIEMOKEN, SNAPPEN, STUNNBERN,
     SZARDEHLEN, TANNENWALDE, USZBRAWEN, WARNAKALLEN, WESZKALLEN,
     WISBORIENEN.

   Toten          1822-1826 ------------------------------------ 6309361
   [Note]:Taufen  1795-1799 ------------------------------------ 6309362
   Taufen         1828-1831 ------------------------------------ 6309363
   Taufen         1831-1834 ------------------------------------ 6309364
   Trauungen      1824-1830 ------------------------------------ 6309365
   Trauungen      1819-1820 ------------------------------------ 6310079
   Duplikat: Taufen  1825-1827 --------------------------------- 6310082
   Duplikat: Taufen  1827-1828 --------------------------------- 6310083

*****************************************************************************

GERMANY, PREUßEN, OSTPREUßEN, SCHILLFELDE
     -----> GERMANY, PREUßEN, OSTPREUßEN, SCHILLEHNEN (KR. PILLKALLEN)

*****************************************************************************
GERMANY, PREUßEN, OSTPREUßEN, SCHILLGALLEN (KR. HEYDEKRUG) - CHURCH RECORDS
                                                              +-------------+
Katholische Kirche Schillgallen (Kr. Heydekrug).              :EUROPE       :
   Kirchenbuch, 1822-1877. -- Salt Lake City : Gefilmt durch the  :FILM AREA  :
     Genealogical Society of Utah, 1954. -- 1 Mikrofilmrolle ; 35 +-------------+
     mm.

   Mikrofilm aufgenommen von Manuskripten in Berlin-Dahlem.
   Parish register of baptisms, marriages and deaths for Schillgallen
     (Heydekrug), East Prussia, Germany, now Silgaliai, Silute, Lithuania

     Taufen, Heiraten, Tote   1822-1877 ------------------------- 0161920
     Taufen, Heiraten, Tote   1822-1877 --------------------  --- 0072728
     (Duplikat Film)

*****************************************************************************
```

Figure 19:2 Sample entries from the Prussian section of the Family History Library's Locality Catalog.

on the list of place names or as a subheading under **Prussia/Ostpreussen**. Through use of a gazetteer, you learn that Wisborienen is part of the parish of Schillehnen. Under the catalog entry for Schillehnen, is Wisborienen – the last of twenty-nine villages listed as part of that parish (see Figure 19:2).

Schillehnen parish represents a somewhat extreme example. Yet it is fairly typical of East Prussia, where parishes tended to be geographically large. But even in Baden in extreme southwestern Germany, a parish may consist of four or five hamlets in addition to the village containing the parish church.

Various aids such as gazetteers and parish register directories will help you solve such problems. These will be discussed later.

After the list of place names at the beginning of the locality section, material is organized alphabetically according to various topics, e.g., **/Emigration And Immigration, /Genealogy, /Heraldry, /Maps, /Occupations, /Periodicals**, etc. On the whole, these tend to be general discussions of the subject. For example, a discussion of legal questions in German family research is cataloged under **/Genealogy**. But sometimes they refer to fairly specific areas; for example, a book about the glassmaking trade in eastern Westphalia is listed under **/Occupations.**

Following the introductory section, the catalog is arranged according to geography, somewhat like the IGI.

However, there is no section called **Germany/Miscellaneous**. Each duchy or state c.1871-1918, no matter how small, has its own place in the catalog arranged alphabetically. Hence, the first state listed is the duchy of Anhalt and the last, the kingdom of Wuerttemberg.

Other differences from the arrangement of the IGI include the use of the German name at the state level, for instance, Preussen for Prussia, Bayern for Bavaria, Hessen for Hesse. The term Hessen-Darmstadt is not used, having been replaced by Hessen. All the small duchies lumped under the category of Thuringia in the IGI, (for example, Reuss-Juengere Linie and Sachsen-Alterberg) appear under their own distinct headings. However, all parishes in these duchies are also cataloged under Thuringia.

A similar arrangement holds true for Alsace-Lorraine and those parts of Prussia which became Polish in 1918 or 1945. Localities from Alsace-Lorraine which were German in 1871-1918 are cataloged under the German term for the area, Elsass-Lothringen. The German spelling of a given locality is used in the German section of the catalog, for example, Mulhausen for Mulhouse and Weissenburg for Wissembourg.

However, these localities also appear in the French portion of the FHLC under the appropriate department, for example, **France/Bas-Rhin/Wissembourg**. Hence, if only the German (or French) spelling of the town is known, you can locate any of its records the library possesses without having to consult various gazetteers.

The same system applies for those areas of Poland formerly under German control. For example, records for Rogasen, Posen Province of Prussia are cataloged under **Preussen/Posen/Rogasen**, and **Poland/Poznan/-Rogozno (Oborniki)**. Each entry lists the name of the town in both languages. The ease of using the new catalog can perhaps best be appreciated by those who once had to fumble through the old card catalog with its "see" cards.

Gazetteers

Sometimes the genealogist is fortunate enough to have the name of the ancestral village or parish and the name of the province or state. In such cases, he or she can simply look for records concerning the parish in the FHLC, note the film or book number, and find or order the desired item.

Regrettably, the quest is not always so easy. Obviously, a detailed discussion of the steps necessary to find the ancestral village in Germany is not possible here. But assuming that the genealogist does possess a valid place name–for example, Wisborienen–the Family History Library possesses several gazetteers and register directories. The most basic of these is the *Meyers Orts–und Verkehrs–Lexikon des Deutschen Reiches* (FHL# 943/-E5mo and microfilm 496640-496641) previously mentioned. Some users will be dismayed to find that Meyers is printed in the old Gothic *Fraktur* type. However, a guide at the beginning of Volume I prepared by the Family History Library staff is of great assistance in using the gazetteer.

Meyers indicates which state, province, and county the town in question belongs to. It also indicates if the town or village possesses its own Catholic or Protestant parish. If so, you can move directly to the FHLC and seek the records of the parish. If not, then you must resort to a gazetteer or parish register directory describing the particular state or province in question.

The Family History Library possesses the following gazetteers and parish register directories:

Anhalt

Starke, Mor. *Statistisches Handbuch der Landwirtschaft Und Geographisches Ortslexikon Vom Herzogtum Anhalt.* Leipzig: Verlag von E. M. Starke, 1879. (FHL# 943.2/E5a or microfilm 0496846, item 4)

Baden

Franz, Hermann. *Die Kirchenbücher in Baden*. Karlsruhe: Verlag G. Braun, 1957. (FHL# 943.46/B3ns/no. 4 or microfilm 0492889)

Bayern (Bavaria)

Ortschaften-Verzeichnis für den Freistaat Bayern. München: J. Lindauersche Universitäts Buchhandlung (Schopping), 1928. (FHL# REF/943.3/B4fr/no. 109 or microfilm 924721)

Brandenburg. See Preussen.

Braunschweig (Brunswick)

Meyer, K. "Die Kirchenbücher," Vol. 1. pp. 1-52. *Braunschweigische Landestelle für Heimatforschung und Heimatpflege.* Braunschweig, Verlag Appelhans, 1939. (FHL# 943.59/K23m or microfilm 1181597, item 2)

An inventory of the Braunschweig parish registers housed at the State Archives in Wolfenhuttel and the City Archive in Braunschweig. The Family History Library does not possess a complete parish register directory for Braunschweig, but a substantial percentage of the pre-1800 parish registers are housed in these archives.

Elsass-Lothringen (Alsace-Lorraine)

Koch, Herbert. "Die Kirchenbücher von Elsass-Lothringen." Vol. 9, pp. 14-61; "Die Kirchenbücher des Reichslandes Elsass Lothringen" Vol. 10, pp. 8-52; *Mitteilungen der Zentralstelle für Deutsche Personen–Und Familien-Geschichte*. Leipzig: H. A. Ludwig Degener, 1911-12. (Vol. 9, FHL# 943/B4m or microfilm 0942890; Vol. 10, microfilm 0942892)

Hannover. See Preussen.

Hessen

Praetorius, Otfried. *Kirchenbücher Und Standesregister für alle Wohnsplatze im Land Hessen*. Darmstadt: Selbstverlag der Historischen Kommission fur das Land Hessen, 1939. (FHL# 943.1/B4ks or microfilm 0495714, item 2)

This directory covers the area known as Hessen-Darmstadt before 1866.

Hessen-Kassel. See Preussen, Hessen Nassau.

Lippe-Detmold

Die Bestände des Staatsarchivs und Personenstandsarchives Detmold. Detmold: Selbstverlag des Staatsarchivs Detmold, 1970. (FHL# 943.55/B4nw/Ser. B/no. 3)

Inventory of the holdings of the State Archive in Detmold. Contains an alphabetical list of parishes in Lippe-Detmold.

Mecklenburg

Mecklenburgs Familiengeschichtliche Quellen. Hamburg: Richard Hermes Verlag, 1936. (FHL# 943.2/A5e or microfilm 0496473, item 8)

Nassau. See Preussen, Hessen-Nassau.

Oldenburg

Ortschafts Verzeichnis des Grossherzogtums Oldenburg. Oldenburg: Druck und Verlag von Ad. Littmann, 1911. (FHL# REF/943.1/E5L or microfilm 0806633)

Ostpreussen (East Prussia). See Preussen.

Pfalz (Palatinate). See Bayern.

Pommern (Pomerania). See Preussen.

Posen. See Preussen.

Preussen (Prussia)

Gemeindelexikon für das Königreich Preussen. 10 vols. Berlin: Verlag des Königlichen Statistischen Landesamts, 1908. (FHL# REF 943/E5kp)

Gemeindelexikon für den Freistaat Preussen. 14 vols. Berlin: Verlag des Preussischen Statistischen Landesamts, 1931-32. (FHL# REF/943/E5fp)

The Family History Library has two sets of gazetteers for Prussia. The first, and more complete one was published in 1908 when Prussia still occupied North Schleswig, Posen, and West Prussia. For this reason it should be consulted first, even though the quality of the print is not as good as the 1932 edition. There is a general index as well as a separate index for each volume, which is easier to use if you know the province. Separate volumes exist for the following provinces in the 1908 edition of the gazetteers: Brandenburg, Vol. 3 (FHL# microfilm 0806635, item 2); Hannover, Vol. 9 (FHL# microfilm 0806634, item 2); Hessen-Nassau, Vol. 11 (FHL# microfilm 1187921); Hohenzollern, Vol. 8 (FHL# microfilm 0806635, item 2); Ostpreussen, Vol. 1 (FHL# microfilm 1187921, item 2); Pommern, Vol. 4 (FHL# microfilm 0806634, item 4); Posen, Vol. 5 (FHL# microfilm 0806634, item 5); Rheinland, Vol. 12 (FHL# microfilm 1187921, item 5); Sachsen, Vol. 7 (FHL# microfilm 0806634, item 3); Schlesien, Vol. 6 (FHL# microfilm 0806635, item 3); Schleswig-Holstein, Vol. 8 (FHL# microfilm 0806635, item 3); Westfalen, Vol. 11 (FHL# microfilm 0806637, item 5); and Westpreussen, Vol. 2 (FHL# microfilm 1187921, item 3).

Reuss-aeltere Linie (Thuringia). See Sachsen Kingdom.

Reuss-juengere Linie (Thuringia). See Sachsen Kingdom.

Rheinland (Rhineland). See Preussen.

Sachsen (Saxony) Kingdom

Schumann, August, comp. *Vollständiges Staats-Post-und Zeitungs Lexikon Von Sachsen.* 13 vols. Zwickau: Im Verlag der Gebruder Schumann, 1825. (FHL# Extra Surveilleance 943.2/E5v or microfilm 0824319-0824325)

Extra surveillance means the original is too fragile for general use. Hence the public must use the microfilm copy.

This gazetteer also includes the minor Saxon duchies which were later consolidated into the Land (State) Thüringen (Thuringia).

Sachsen Altenburg (Thuringia). See Sachsen Kingdom.

Sachsen Coburg-Gotha (Thuringia). See Sachsen Kingdom.

Sachsen Meiningen (Thuringia). See Sachsen Kingdom.

Sachsen Weimar-Eisenach (Thuringia). See Sachsen Kingdom.

Schaumburg-Lippe

Ulmenstein, Christian Ulrich, Freiherr von. "Das Land Schaumburg-Lippe." *Familiengeschichtlicher Wegweiser Durch Stadt und Land.* No. 12, pp. 4-5. Verlag Degener; lnh. Oswald Spahr, Marktschellenberg Berchtesgaden, Nos. 12-16. (FHL 943/B4fw)

Contains a list of the parishes in Schaumburg-Lippe and the dates their various registers commence.

Schlesien (Silesia). See Preussen.

Schleswig-Holstein. See Preussen.

Schwarzburg-Rudolstadt (Thuringia). See Sachsen Kingdom.

Schwarzburg-Sonderhausen (Thuringia). See Sachsen Kingdom.

Thüringingen (Thuringia). See Sachsen Kingdom.

Waldeck. See Preussen, Westfalen.

Westfalen (Westphalia). See Preussen.

Westpreussen (West Prussia). See Preussen.

Wuerttemberg.

Ortschaftsverzeichnis des Koenigsreichs Wuerttemberg. Stuttgart: Druck von W. Kolhammer, 1912. (FHL# REF/943.46/-E5w)

This is by no means a complete list of gazetteers and parish register directories available in the German collection. For instance, there are many parish register directories for individual Catholic dioceses (for example, Münster and Paderborn) or for former Prussian provinces (for example, Pommern and Westpreussen). These are cataloged under the state or provincial localities (for example, **Preussen, Westfalen/Church Records/Inventories, Registers, Catalogs**).

Two gazetteers must be included because they serve a particular purpose, that of determining the present place name of a locality. For as stated earlier, many cities, towns, and villages in Eastern Germany and throughout East Central Europe which once possessed German names now appear only in some other language. Beyond that, the political geography of present-day Germany has undergone fundamental changes since the end of the Second Empire in 1918.

For the present-day names and political affiliations of places which were lost to Germany after World War II, the standard reference is Fritz Müller, *Müllers Grosses Deutsches Ortsbuch*, Part I and II (Wuppertal-Barmen: Post-und Ortsbuchverlag Postmeister A. D. Friedrich Müller, 1958). (FHL# REF/943/E5m/1958 or microfilm 1045448). Part II, pp. 1139 ff. contains the list of German places now in Poland or Russia, and their current Polish or Russian names.

For those parts of Germany that were annexed by other countries after World War I, use:

Kredel, Otto, and Franz Thierfelder. *Deutsch-Fremdsprachiges Ortsnamen-Verzeichnis*. 3 vols. Berlin: Deutsche Verlagsgesellschaft, 1931. (FHL# REF/Q/940/E5kt or microfilm 0583457)

This gazetteer is useful not only for determining present-day names of places which were part of Imperial Germany, but also in other parts of Europe. For example, Laiback, Krain, Austria, is now Ljubljana, Slovenia, Yugoslavia.

Obviously the use of gazetteers implies the use of maps. The Family History Library has a good collection of maps of Germany over the centuries. Two of these warrant special mention–the volume entitled *Maps of the 1871 German Empire* by Larry Jensen and Norman Storrer (Pleasant Grove, Utah: Jensen and Storrer, P.O. Box 502, 1975) (FHL# EUR REF/943/E7s) and *Karte des Deutschen Reiches* (Berlin: Kgl. Prussischen Landes-Aufnahme, 1900), scale 1:100,000 (FHL# microfilm 068814). By using these two sets in conjunction with the gazetteers previously listed, you should be able to locate the ancestral village in question.

Emigration and Immigration

Among the most valuable records in the Family History Library for tracing German and Central European immigrants are migration records. Of these, the Hamburg passenger lists undoubtedly rate as the most important. Bremen (whose lists were almost totally destroyed) and Hamburg were the two chief ports of embarkation for Central and Eastern European emigrants in the nineteenth century. Some estimates maintain that 30 percent of all European emigrants passed through Hamburg between 1859 and 1891.

The Hamburg passenger lists contain the names of virtually all the persons who sailed from that port between 1850 and 1934. They are arranged in chronological order according to the date of departure of the ship. The first page of a given list states the name of the captain, the name of the ship, the flag under which it sailed, and the port of destination. For all passengers, the lists give the name, sex, age, last place of residence, occupation, number of accompanying family members, and destination.

There are but two basic categories of lists. The "direct" lists cover the years 1850-1934 and include those passengers traveling directly from Hamburg to the port of final destination. The "indirect" lists cover the years 1854-1910 and include passengers who were going to stop at an intermediate port (for example, Liverpool) often to change ships before going on to the final destination.

Between 1850-54 and after 1910, the "indirect" lists were combined with the "direct" lists. Since most emigrants sailed directly to their final destination, there are many more "direct" lists (256 reels of microfilm) than "indirect" lists (81 reels).

During their first four years (1850-54), the lists were semi-alphabetically arranged, according to the first letter of the passenger's last name. Hence, all the A's are listed together, all the "B's, C's etc. But they are not internally in precise alphabetical order. For example, Ahrens might precede Adolfs.

Beginning in 1855, the Hamburg authorities no longer tried to arrange the lists themselves in semi-alphabetical order. Rather, they created a semi-alphabetical index similar to the arrangement of the lists from 1850-54, according to the first letter of the surname of the head of the family. Dependents are included but not indexed separately. Two indexes exist, one for the direct lists 1855-1934 (126 reels) and 1855-1910 (12 reels) for the indirect lists. You must check both lists for a given time period.

In addition to these two indexes, the Family History Library possesses a fully alphabetized card index of the direct indexes for 1856-1871, the so-called fifteen-year index (10 reels FHL# microfilm 0884668-0884677). It was compiled by members of the Hamburg, Germany, LDS Branch. This very valuable aid includes name, occupation, age, place of origin, accompanying family members and their ages, the year of departure, whether the family intended to travel directly or indirectly, as well as the page of entry for the family in the original passenger list. Unfortunately, this index is not totally complete for the years covered. Hence, you must check the original direct indexes if the sought-for name does not appear in the fifteen-year index. And of course, it does not include the names on the indirect indexes.

The Wuerttemberg Emigration Registers form a second major collection of migration records. Arranged according to the various *Oberämter* (administrative districts), these documents stem largely from the nineteenth and early twentieth centuries, although a few date to the fifteenth century. These records are largely requests for permission to migrate. The disposition of such requests and documents renouncing citizenship in the kingdom of Wuerttemberg cover internal as well as external migration. Requests to move to another town in Wuerttemberg are found next to requests to emigrate to Russia, other areas in Central Europe, or North America.

Unfortunately, until very recently, no central index existed for this important collection. Unless the researcher knew the particular *Oberamt* the individual come from, he or she faced the formidable task of reading through hundreds of microfilm reels looking for the pertinent entry. Happily, an index is now being prepared by Trudy Schenk and Ruth Froelke. Volumes I, II, and III of *The Wuerttemberg Emigration Index* (Salt Lake City: Ancestry, Inc., 1986) (FHL# 943.47/W22st) have already appeared and more are forthcoming. The index contains the name of the individual, his or her birthdate and place, the name of the *Oberamt*, the date of the emigration application, the destination, and the FHL microfilm number.

Other state emigration indexes possessed by the Family History Library include the Baden Emigration Index filmed at the Landesarchiv in Karlsruhe (13 reels FHL# microfilm 1180095-1180102, 1180209-1180213). As with the Wuerttemberg register, most of the individuals listed in this index left Baden during the nineteenth century, but a few entries concern seventeenth-century emigrants. Item 2b on FHL# microfilm 1180095 consists of the Jewish emigration index from the city of Karlsruhe and environs c.1935-40. It should be stressed that this index is by no means complete; the archive has added many names to it since it was filmed.

A similar index exists for Hessen, that is the old Grand Duchy of Hessen-Darmstadt. It consists of five reels of microfilm containing the names of immigrants who left during the nineteenth century (FHL# microfilm 1124278-1124280 and 1124319-1124320). Again it should be stressed that this index is by no means complete. The Hessen State Archive at Darmstadt has added many names since it was filmed.

Still another index of interest in this regard is the Alsace-Lorraine Emigration Index. See the discussion of French records in Chapter 22.

Various local historians and genealogists have published lists of emigrants from their particular village or district. The Family History Library has acquired many of these which are cataloged according to the locality. Space forbids the listing of every article on the subject. Worth particular mention, however, is the index prepared by Fritz Gruhne for the former Duchy of Brunswick: *Auswanderlisten des ehemaligen Herzogtum Braunschweig 1846 bis 1871. Quellen und Forschugen zur braunschwiegischen Geschichte Nr. 20.* (Wolfenbüttel: Selbstverlag des Braunschweigischen Geschichtsverein, 1971). (FHL# 943.59/H2q/Vol. 20 microfilm 1045468, item 10).

Another series worthy of special mention is *Westfällische Auswanderer im 19 Jahrhundert* (Westphalian Emigrants in the Nineteenth Century) *Beitrage zur Westfalischen Familienforschung*, Vols. 22-24 (Münster: Verlag Aschendorff, 1964-66). Volumes 22-24 consist of emigrants from the *Regierungsbezirk* (governmental district) of Münster, 1800-50 (FHL# 943.55/B5bf/Vol. 22-24) while Volumes 38-39 (FHL# 943.56/D2b/Vol.38-39) list those from *Regierungsbezirk* Minden from 1816-1900.

Military Records

The bulk of military records in the German collection consists of military parish registers of Prussian regiments stationed in garrison towns. These records are recorded under the locality where the unit was stationed, for example, **Preussen/Pommern/Pyritz/Church Records/-Evangelishce Kirche/ Militargemeinde (Military Congregation) Pyritz**. This collection consists of 150 reels of microfilm. In addition, the collection contains lists of Prussian and Wuerttemberg military units and their officers from 1824 to 1899 (29 reels) also FHL# 943/-M23k. Other military records include casualty lists from the First World War, officers diaries, muster rolls of Hessian regiments stationed in America during the Revolutionary War, etc.

A military index of considerable interest to Americans is the *Hetrina Project*, an acronym for *Hessische Truppen in Amerikanisches Unabhanigkeits Kreig* (Hessian Troops in the American War of Independence), Veröffentlichen der Archivschule Marburg Institut für Archivwissensdraft, No. 10 (Marburg Lahn: Staatsarchiv, 1972). (FHL# 943/M2mg). This index includes names, approximate birth dates, places of origin in Germany, with their modern ZIP code number, rank, unit, when entered service, and disposition (for example, killed in action, deserted, returned to Europe, etc.)

Census Records

Unlike the United States, where census records form the backbone of the genealogical endeavor, census records in Germany tend to be rather scattered. A primary reason for this was the fragmented political structure of Germany before 1871. With no central government in existence, no uniform national census akin to the decennial U.S. census was possible. Hence, extant pre-1871 census records are on the state or local level.

The most systematic of these were enumerated in Mecklenburg. The Family History Library has sixty reels of microfilm containing the 1819 census records of Mecklenburg-Schwerin (FHL# microfilm 068874-068933). It also has one reel covering earlier census enumerations in Mecklenburg-Schwerin (1633, 1634, 1677, and 1689) (FHL# microfilm 068934).

Other enumerations were made in various localities,

often for military purposes. These are usually cataloged in the Locality FHLC under the state or town where they were made.

Church Records

Of all the material in the German collection, that of greatest interest to the genealogist is the microfilms of parish registers, now totalling nearly 100,000 reels.

The keeping of *Kirchenbücher* (literally, "church books"), equivalent to parish registers in British usage, generally began in the sixteenth century, although the Family History Library has a few films of material dating from the fifteenth century. Protestant records generally antedate Catholic ones, although the Council of Trent (1545-63) mandated the keeping of parish registers in Catholic churches.

Some Lutheran churches in Saxony possess records dating back to 1540, although the Family History Library has few of these. A similar situation holds true in Wuerttemberg, where the library has a much higher percentage of the available records.

The practice of record keeping in German churches did not really become general in Germany until after the Thirty Years' War (1618-48).

Church records tend to begin somewhat later in the north and east. Many parishes in Mecklenburg began keeping records around 1700, while in the Posen Province of Prussia, Lutheran records often began about 1790. In part, this reflected the settlement of originally Polish areas by German Lutherans.

Typically, German parish registers record baptisms, marriages, and deaths. The baptismal or christening register generally records the christening date, the names of the parents and the child, and the names of the godparents, who very often are close relatives. Generally speaking, the birthdate of the child was not recorded until approximately 1750. However, in earlier centuries a child was typically christened on the day he or she was born or the day following, especially in Catholic regions. So the christening date makes an acceptable substitute for the birthdate.

Marriage records usually contain a great deal of genealogical information. By the mid-eighteenth century, they typically list the full names of the groom and bride, the occupation of the groom, his residence if different from the parish where the ceremony is taking place, the names of his parents, often the names of the bride's parents, or at least that of her father. Widows generally used the surnames of their deceased husbands. Hence, it becomes necessary to find the first marriage entry to learn her maiden surname. Some churches kept a separate register for the proclamation of the banns, which can be quite useful if the marriage register itself has been lost.

Death records often began somewhat later than christening or marriage records. They typically list the name, occupation, age, and cause of death. The age must be treated somewhat skeptically, as it is often incorrect. This is particularly true when the deceased moved in from another parish and the pastor had only oral report to rely upon.

Other church records of interest include confirmation records, first communion records, and penance records. Typically, if the bride were pregnant, the pastor would fine the couple and enter this fact in the church records.

In Wuerttemberg and to some extent in Baden, family books were kept by both Lutheran and Catholic parishes. Usually they only cover the nineteenth century, but in some parishes they date back much further.

These family books or registers typically devote a page to a given nuclear family, i.e., father, mother, and children. It states date and place of birth for all concerned, date of marriage for the parents and for the children if they were married in or near the parish. Death dates for parents and children are recorded, as are the names of the grandparents if known. If a daughter of the family had an illegitimate child, that birth will often be recorded. If one or more of the family emigrated, the pastor would often note this fact in the family book. In short, the family book is an excellent genealogical source. However, human error can creep in, and it is always best to check the entries against the original christening, marriage, and death records.

The Roman Catholic church required that Latin be used in its records until fairly late in the nineteenth century. However, many priests used German or a mixture of Latin and German in the eighteenth century. Protestant pastors also used Latin in the sixteenth and seventeenth centuries but began using German much earlier than the Catholics.

German handwriting further complicates the use of these registers. Latin registers are generally written in the so-called "round hand" which resembles modern handwriting. But most Protestant and Catholic registers written in Germany use the old Gothic script, which can be difficult for the novice. Nevertheless, it can be mastered with effort.

In terms of format, pastors tended to use whatever came to mind. By 1800, a standard format dictated by the diocese or state authorities became fairly standard practice. This generally makes nineteenth-century registers easier to use, although nineteenth-century Gothic script often is more difficult to read than that of earlier centuries.

By 1800, governmental officials realized the value of these records for other reasons than those of the church. Therefore, they began requiring the pastors to begin filling duplicate copies and sending them to the state authorities. The Family History Library has many of these *Duplikaten* which generally run from about 1808 to 1875, when they were superceded by civil registers. Indeed, in some areas of the German Democratic Republic (East Germany) – for example, certain parts of Pommern (Pomerania), Province Sachsen (Saxony), and Brandenburg, Prussia – these transcripts are the only church records in the Family History Library's current holdings. Even in those areas where the library has the original records, the transcripts can be very useful in case the original was lost or is illegible for various reasons.

This leads to the question of the Family History

Library's holdings in the various parts of Germany. Since the microfilming agreements are purely voluntary, holdings depend on the willingness of the each individual archive's officers to have such copies made. In some areas – for example, the Archdiocese of Freiburg in Baden or the Diocese of Augsburg – the attitude of the church authorities has been extremely cooperative. Hence, the library has been able to film better than 95 percent of the available parish registers. In other areas, church or governmental authorities have not been cooperative, and thus the library's holdings are minimal.

Estimating the percentage of the Family History Library's holdings as compared to the total is not easy. The only summary available was made by the Priesthood Genealogy Department in 1982. Hence, it is five years out of date. Beyond that, some of the figures – those of Ostpreussen, for example – were based on preliminary estimates of material which hopefully would arrive from the Central Genealogical Archive of the German Democratic Republic in Leipzig. Unfortunately, not all the available material was released. Thus, it seems best to confine estimates about the extent of the collection to some general observations. As noted above, the Catholic, Protestant, and state authorities in Land Baden-Wuerttemberg have generally been cooperative with the LDS filming program. Hence, the library's holdings of Baden parish registers exceed 95 percent, according to most estimates. The same situation holds true for the Catholic areas of Wuerttemberg and Hohenzollern.

However, the library's holdings of the Protestant parishes in Wuerttemberg are not as great, perhaps 65 percent, according to some estimates. The Lutheran Church in Wuerttemberg is currently filming its parish registers and the Family History Library is purchasing copies as they become available.

A similar situation holds true in Hessen. The Evangelical Church of Hessen-Nassau is filming its own parish registers and selling copies to the Family History Library. It is difficult to cite precise figures, as new films are currently arriving. The 1982 summary listed estimates of 63 percent for Hessen (Hessen-Darmstadt) and 6 percent for Hessen-Nassau. Suffice it to say that the second figure is now much higher – possibly 50 percent.

Bavaria presents greater difficulties. Certain diocesan archives have been filmed – for example, Augsburg and Speyer – while others – for example, Regensburg, Bamburg, and Passau – have not. Nineteenth-century transcripts of parish registers in the Bavarian State Archive in Munich have been filmed but not those at the State Archive in Wuerzburg. In general, the percentage of records from the former Bavarian Pfalz is much higher than for Bavaria as it exists today.

For Alsace-Lorraine, the picture is complicated by the fact that after 1792, civil records superseded church records in France. The library has films of more than 90 percent of these civil registers (1792-1872). In regard to pre-1792 church records, the 1982 summary cited a figure of 60 percent. Filming has continued since that time.

The situation for northern Germany is much more problematical. Catholic church authorities – for example, those in Munster or Hildesheim – have been more willing to allow LDS filming of their archival holdings than the Lutheran *Landeskirche* of Hannover. The dearth of Protestant records has been alleviated somewhat in the past few years through the acquisition of many films of nineteenth-century transcripts housed in the State Archives of Niedersachsen (Lower Saxony).

The holdings of the Family History Library for the smaller north German states – i.e., Braunschweig, Lippe-Detmold, Schaumburg-Lippe, and Oldenburg – are not extensive. It has very few films of parish registers from Braunschweig and Schaumburg-Lippe. The situation for Lippe-Detmold is relatively better, thanks to the cooperation of the Evangelical Archive in Bielefeld. Oldenburg presents a somewhat mixed pattern, as it lies within the jurisdiction of several Catholic dioceses – for example, Münster and Trier. In general, the library has a higher percentage of Catholic records from Oldenburg than Protestant. Overall, its holdings are considerably less than 50 percent of the total.

The Family History Library holds a higher percentage of parish registers from Nordrhein-Westfalen, formed from the former Prussian provinces of the Rheinland and Westfalen than from Niedersachsen, formed from Hannover, Oldenburg, and the minor states listed above. Most estimates rate the percentage of parish registers in Westphalia available on film at 50-60 percent. Figures for the Rheinland run somewhat lower.

In the Free Cities of Bremen, Hamburg, and Luebeck, the possessions of the Family History Library again reflect the attitude of church archival authorities. The percentage of filmed parish registers is lowest in Hamburg, somewhat better in Bremen, and best in Luebeck.

In the adjoining land of Schleswig-Holstein, the percentage of parish registers filmed by the FHLC is highest in that part of Schleswig which was Prussian between 1864-1919 but which reverted to Danish control after World War I. Here the library has microfilms of most of the available records.

In sharp contrast, the Family History Library has relatively little material from the portion of Schleswig-Holstein which remained German apart from some films recently acquired from the Central Archive of the German Democratic Republic in Leipzig. Unfortunately, most of these were made in the mid-1930s when microfilm technology was in its infancy. As a result, many of the pages are illegible.

The city of West Berlin, while geographically surrounded by the GDR, is politically attached to the Federal Republic. Here the library has been able to film a great deal of material including some parish registers from those formerly German areas now controlled by Poland and the Soviet Union, as well as for Berlin itself.

In regard to the GDR proper, with the exception of Mecklenburg, the library has a very few films of original parish registers. However, thanks to a record collecting project undertaken by the National Socialist authorities, over 90 percent of the parish registers of Mecklenburg were stored in an archive at Goslar at the end of World

War II. Hence, the library was able to film the entire collection in 1951.

The dearth of church records from the GDR was alleviated to some extent by an agreement which the library reached with the East German authorities in 1980. This resulted in the library's filming those holdings of the State Archives of the GDR which had genealogical value. Hence, the library acquired a large number of microfilmed transcripts of nineteenth centry church records, plus some copies of original church records. Thus, the library now has better than 50 percent of the nineteenth-century (1808-75) parish register transcripts of the former Prussian province of Saxony. This project also filmed some of the transcripts of that part of Brandenburg lying west of the Oder River as well as some Pomeranian transcripts from what is now Poland.

The library's holdings of church records from the former kingdom of Saxony remain minimal. If transcripts exist, they have not appeared in the library's collection.

The situation is somewhat better for the former Saxon duchies which were combined to form the state of Thuringia in 1919–for example, Sachsen-Meiningen, Sachsen-Altenberg, etc. The regional archives possessed numerous transcripts of church records and some originals. In addition, the library was able to obtain duplicate copies of films made c.1940 of parishes in the region. So while the holdings for Thuringia are by no means complete, the situation has markedly improved in the past four years.

The old Prussian province of Pommern (Pomerania) was divided between the German Democratic Republic and Poland after World War II. That portion lying west of the Oder River (Vor Pommern or Western Pomerania) ranks with the kingdom of Saxony as a barren spot in the German collection. For some reason, the transcripts filmed at the Greifswald State Archive were mostly from that part of Pomerania which is now in Poland. As such, they were a most welcome addition, but the "blank spot" in regard to Western Pomerania remained.

Of course, the original records are still in the parishes or in the Evangelical Archive in Greifswald. But until the Evangelical Church reverses a policy against allowing LDS filming of its records, they will not appear on microfilm in the Family History Library. The same holds true for the small portion of Silesia which remained German after 1945.

Turning to those parts of Germany which are now part of Poland or the Soviet Union, the situation ranges from abysmal to surprisingly good. The worst areas for German Lutheran records are Hither-Pomerania and the part of Brandenburg east of the Oder River. These areas were the scene of bitter fighting in the winter and spring of 1945, and many towns were destroyed. To compound the situation, the German inhabitants of the region were expelled and it was resettled by Poles.

In the confusion which resulted from these cataclysmic events, many parish registers were lost or left in the churches. Visitors to Poland c.1979 reported seeing German records in former Lutheran churches now serving the Polish Catholic populace. In former Posen province, some of the Evangelical records have been deposited in the Archdiocesan Archive of Poznan, where they were recently microfilmed. Hopefully, more will turn up in Pomerania and Brandenburg. The library does have films of a few parish records from that area which have been deposited in Polish State Archives. The one bright spot in Hither-Pomerania is the city of Stettin where the library has dozens of films of the church and civil registers prior to 1945.

The situation in Silesia is markedly better, thanks to a microfilming project undertaken in the 1930s. Pre-1800 Catholic and Evangelical parish registers were microfilmed with the intent of publishing them in book form. Hence, these films consist of a series of right-hand pages filmed in sequence, followed by a series of left-hand pages.

Prior to 1982, the only copies the library possessed of these films were microfiche copies, many of which are illegible. As a result of the agreement reached with the GDR authorities, the library has purchased copies of the original 35mm microfilms from which the fiche were made. The results are variable. Some pages are faint and illegible, but many are surprisingly clear, considering they were filmed in 1935 and 1936.

Hopefully, better copies of many of these Silesian Church records will soon be available. The Family History Department is currently filming the archive of the Archdiocese of Breslau (Wroclaw). Following completion of this project, it will film the holdings of a Protestant parish register archive in former Silesia.

In addition to the films of the pre-1800 registers made at Leipzig, the library acquired films of some nineteenth-century transcripts from the Polish State Archives in the early 1970s. Thus, while its overall holdings of Silesian parish register holdings hardly rank with Mecklenburg, the percentage is surprisingly high, possibly 45 percent, considering the trauma Silesia experienced in 1945.

East Prussia presents a somewhat similar situation. There, too, the pre-1800 parish registers were filmed under National Socialist auspices. Whatever the motive, it resulted in the preservation of records that otherwise would have been lost. As with Silesia, prior to 1982, the only copies of these 1930s films in the library's possession were on microfiche, at best barely legible.

The library obtained copies of some of the original films from the Central Genealogical Archive in the GDR c.1983. However, the GDR authorities stated at the outset of the project that no filming of parish registers in areas now controlled by the Soviet Union (the northern half of East Prussia plus the Memel region of Lithuania) would be permitted.

The result was that less than half of the former area of northern East Prussia is available on film in Salt Lake City. However, parishes in East Prussia tended to be very large, geographically speaking. Hence, parishes where the church building was actually located in what is now Poland may include hamlets now lying within the borders of the Soviet Union. So some areas currently under Russian control are represented by 35mm film.

Beyond that, the Germans managed to evacuate many

of the church records of Königsberg and the Memel region before the Russians occupied it in late 1944. These records were filmed at Berlin-Dahlem in the 1950s. So perhaps 45 percent of the total number of parish registers for East Prussia as it existed in 1914 is available on 35mm film.

West Prussia, much of which was ceded to Poland after World War I to form the so-called "Polish Corridor" presents a surprisingly positive picture in terms of record preservation. Many of the Evangelical and Catholic parish registers were removed to archives in West Germany before the area was overrun by the Red Army. The Family History Department was able to microfilm them in the 1950s. In addition, the library acquired films of nineteenth-century transcripts from the Polish State Archives in the 1970s. Thus, in marked contrast to adjoining Pomerania, the library has film copies of better than 50 percent of the parish registers of West Prussia.

Posen province of Prussia, most of which was ceded to Poland after World War I, presents a somewhat different situation. The Genealogical Department has filmed the archival holdings of the Catholic Archdiocese of Poznan (Posen in German). Hence, the percentage of Catholic parishes preserved on microfilm is quite high. But of course these were largely Polish in their ethnic makeup.

The percentage of Evangelical parish registers available on film is much lower. Some Evangelical registers were deposited in the Poznan archdiocese archive, were filmed during that project. Transcripts of some of the Evangelical parish registers were found in a salt mine at the end of World War II. They were sent back to the old Prussian State Archive in Poznan, where they were filmed in the 1970s.

Civil Registers

Civil registration of births, marriages, and deaths did not begin in Germany as a whole until 1876. However, those areas west of the Rhine River occupied by the French during the Napoleonic Wars began civil registration in 1798. This practice was continued after 1815 when the area reverted to German control. In Alsace-Lorraine, civil registration began in 1792 and continued after 1871 when the area was annexed by the German Empire.

Other areas of Western Germany, for example, Westphalia and Hannover, inaugurated civil registration based upon the French model in 1808. But it lasted only four years and was not resumed until 1874 when civil registration became mandatory throughout Prussia.

Hessen-Kassel required civil registration of marriages as early as 1790, although this requirement was evidently not enforced very thoroughly until 1820 or so.

The library possesses microfilms of a relatively high percentage of the civil registers from the west back of the Rhine. In Alsace-Lorraine the figure exceeds 90 percent. In the Bavarian Palatinate, the Prussian Rhineland, and the Rheinhessen province of Hesse Darmstadt, the percentage is not so high, perhaps 75 percent.

With some exceptions, notably Stettin, the library has not filmed the post-1874 civil registers of Prussia. A major exception is in those areas which are part of present-day Poland. In many areas of Pomerania and Brandenburg, the only vital records available are the civil registers from 1874-77. The later date represents an arbitrary cut-off date of 100 years prior to the time of filming, i.e., 1977. More of these registers will be filmed in the future.

Civil registers rank ahead of parish registers in ease of use by a genealogist who has only a limited knowledge of German. They tend to be written in a standardized format, which is not difficult to decipher.

In addition to parish and civil registers, the German collection has acquired thousands of microfilms of other primary source material discussed below. To use these records, you need a good reading knowledge of German and the capacity to decipher the old Gothic script. Admittedly this poses a problem for many American genealogists, but the information contained in these records is too valuable to be ignored.

Guild Records

Among the more accessible of these records currently under discussion are guild records. Guilds were the forerunners of modern craft unions. In the larger German cities, guilds for every imaginable occupation existed–for example, lace makers, locksmiths, sausage makers, etc.

Usually these records consist of membership lists, financial records and the like. But occasionally they will contain a great deal more than that–for example, the name of the guild member, the place and date of his marriage, the name of his wife and the names and baptismal dates of his children and the names of the godparents. In summary, a virtual family group sheet.

Guild records are primarily useful when pursuing lines in larger towns and cities. They are cataloged according to locality–for example, **/Bayern/Augsburg/Guild Records** or **/Preussen/Sachsen/Magdeburg/Guild Records.** The library has 643 reels of microfilmed guild records from Augsburg alone.

Tax Lists and Other Census Substitutes

Various sources of information about a given family prior to the establishment of parish registers may have survived the ravages of time. Tax lists are one such source. A typical and fairly widespread example is the *Turkensteurliste* (literally Turk Tax list) of 1584. Advancing Turkish armies threatened the Empire. The Emperor called upon the local rulers to enumerate the citizens and their property. The purpose was to generate sufficient information to levy a tax for national defense.

Often such lists have been compiled and published by local historians. The German collection contains a number of these which are cataloged by locality–for example, **/Bayern/Neustadt A/D Haardt/Taxation**.

Other useful census substitutes are residents' lists, citizens' lists, and local military muster rolls. Citizenship was a highly prized status in earlier centuries, for among other things it meant the holder was not obligated to provide service to a landlord. Usually an individual had to take an oath of citizenship before the mayor and the town council. Usually a record was kept of this oath in the *Bürgerbücher* (literally, "citizenship books").

The earliest form of *Bürgerbücher* are lists of citizens dating back to 1130. By the beginning of the nineteenth century in Prussia, they had evolved into detailed entries containing such information as the name of the citizen, date and place of birth, status or profession, whether the individual owned property, whether he had fulfilled his military duty, the date he took the oath of citizenship, the fee paid for the certificate, and remarks.

Obviously these *Bürgerbücher* are extremely important documents for the German researcher. The library attempts to add as many as possible to the German collection. They are cataloged according to locality under the subheading **/Naturalization and Citizenship.**

Legal Records

The bulk of the legal material in the German collection consists of probate and guardianship records. Again they are cataloged according to locality under the subheading **/Probate Records**. The largest single collection is more than 1700 reels of greater Berlin wills covering the years 1616-1932. Generally speaking, reading these documents requires a much better command of German and the old Gothic script than most of the material previously discussed.

Municipal Records

The German collection also contains particularly complete records for the cities of Augsburg, Bavaria, and Speyer, formerly in Bavaria, but now in Rheinland Pfalz. These records are cataloged under the locality under various subheadings–for example, **/Guardian and Ward, /Land and Property, /Medical Records, /Migration Internal, /Notarial Records, /Public Records**, and **/Taxation.**

In general, these records are perhaps of greater interest to the social historian than the genealogist. They require a good reading knowledge of German and the old Gothic script.

Provincial Records

The German collection does not yet contain extensive material at the provincial level with the exception of the former Prussian province of Westpreussen (West Prussia). These records, filmed at the former Prussian State Archive in Berlin-Dahlem, cover a wide range of subjects from the late eighteenth to the early twentieth century. School administrative matters, church-state relationships, and settlement questions are among the subjects covered.

Jewish Records

Given the tragic fate of the Jewish community in Germany, a surprisingly large number of Jewish records have survived. Of course, many synagogue records were destroyed during the Nazi era, especially during the *Kristallnacht* pogrom of 1938. But beginning about 1808 (1798 on the west bank of the Rhine), most German states began requiring Jews to register vital statistics with, depending upon the particular state, the civil registrar or the Catholic or Lutheran pastor. In the latter case, they will be filmed with the church records, usually at the end of the section. A typical example is **/Wuerttemberg/ Michelback (Am Heuchel)/Jewish Records** (FHL# microfilm 1195662, item 14).

The inventory of the German Jewish holdings of the library printed in *Toledot: The Journal of Jewish Genealogy* vol. 2, No. 1 (Summer 1978): 16-25 is now out of date, as the library has recently acquired films of many Jewish records from the Central Genealogical Archive in the DDR in Leipzig.

Secondary Sources

All the material previously discussed has been "primary source" material–church records, civil registers, tax lists, etc. Although such material is usually of immense genealogical value, it was not originally compiled for genealogical purposes.

In addition to this huge collection of primary source material, the German collection possesses an impressive amount of secondary material, i.e., family histories, lineage books, and special collections compiled by local or regional genealogists. These are discussed below.

Local Histories

Local historians in Germany have been active for several decades in compiling and publishing lists of names derived from tax lists, citizens books, emigration records, etc. Space does not permit an enumeration of all the various types of records that their efforts have made available to the genealogist. Suffice it to say that the library makes a continual effort to find such material and purchase or photocopy it.

Information of a purely local nature will appear in the locality catalogue under the city or town and the appropriate subheading–for example, **/Land Records**. Information of a broader scope will be cataloged under the state or province–for example, **/Wuerttemberg** or **/Hannover**, while information of national interest will be cataloged under **Germany/History**, etc.

One particular type of local history warrants special mention, the German *Ortsippenbuch* (local lineage book) series. Originally begun in the late 1930s under the title of *Dorfsippenbücher* (village lineage book), the series was resumed after World War II under the new title. Thirty *Dorfsippenbücher* were published before the war put an end to such work. Over 150 volumes of the *Ortsippenbücher* have been published, a few of which are revised editions of the original *Dorfsippenbücher*.

Basically the books consist of transcriptions of the local parish registers organized alphabetically and chronologically by surname. A typical example is from the *Sippenbuch* of the town of Gochsheim in Baden (Figure 19:3).

Obviously these books are a godsend for the American genealogist who can read German but cannot cope with the old Gothic script. Within a few hours, all the ancestral lines from the village in question can be traced with a minimum of effort.

In addition to the transcribed parish registers, most *Ortsippenbücher* contain a history of the town based upon available records such as tax lists and citizenship oaths. An increasing number list the families who emigrated, the year of emigration, and the destination. Some feature drawings and photographs of local landmarks and notables.

Unfortunately, the available *Ortsippenbücher* cover less than 1 percent of the total villages in Germany. Also they tend to be concentrated in Baden (fifty-two volumes) as of 1985, Ostfriesland (seventeen volumes), and Waldech (twenty-four volumes), with a scattering elsewhere.

German Lineage Book (Deutsches Geschlechterbuch)

In 1934, Dr. Ludwig Finckh prefaced Volume 80 of this series with the statement, "All nations of the earth envy us because of this work. In no other country of the world is there anything similar that can be compared with the *German Lineage Book*." While the statement is no doubt a bit exaggerated, it does suggest that this series is a superb secondary source for German genealogical research.

The subtitle of the series is "Genealogical Handbook of Bourgeois Families," which describes its particular emphasis. It is not oriented toward families of noble or peasant rank, but toward upper middle-class families.

The first volume appeared in 1889, and volume 192 appeared in 1986. The library call number for the series is 943/D2dg followed by the individual volume number. As the title implies, each volume consists of several family histories, beginning with the founder and proceeding to the present generation by means of genealogical tables. If the family possesses a coat of arms, a color plate is usually included, as are various family portraits. A complete surname index is included in each volume covering families who married into the lines under consideration.

Questions have risen as to the reliability of these lineage books. The information used to compile them comes from primary sources–for example, parish and civil registers, probate records, tax lists, etc. In regard to whether they may contain misleading information to disguise Jewish ancestry, Gerhard Jeske of the European Reference Staff at the library points out on page 1 of the *German Lineage Books* that only 42 of the 192 volumes extant were published during the Nazi period.

The library has all of the German lineage books that have been published in book form with the exceptions of volumes 8, 57, 112, and 122 which are on microfilm. Gerhard Jeske has prepared two indexes to the books. The first, a locality index, indicates which areas of Germany are covered by the various volumes. The second lists the surnames of all the families for whom lineages have been compiled since 1889, together with the place of origin of the family, and the volume and page number of the particular book in which the history appeared. This index is available at the European Reference Desk.

The German collection also has two editions (1963 and 1969) of a joint index to the Genealogical Manual of the Nobility and the German Lineage Book *(Stammfolgenverzeichnisse für das Genealogische Handbuch des Adels und das Deutsche Geschlechterbuch)* (Limburg/Lahn: C. A. Starke Verlag, 1963, 1969). (FHL# 943/D2dg/Index/1963, 1969 or microfiche 6053506). This index, which is part of the Family History Center's (Branch Library's) Microfiche Core Collection, explained in Chapter 2, contains the names of all the families for whom lineages have been compiled in both series up to the time of publication.

In addition, the collection has four volumes of an every-name index to the first fifty volumes of the *German Lineage Book* covering A-Reinisch; Wassmannsdorff, Erich *Gesamt Namenverzeichnis umfassend Bank 1-50 Deutsches Geschlechterbuch* (Gorlitz: C. A. Starke Verlag, 1938). (FHL# 943/D2dg/Index/Vols. 1-4). This work is also on microfilm, but the films cannot circulate to branch centers because of copyright restrictions.

The first 125 volumes of the *German Lineage Book* have been microfilmed (FHL# microfilm 491876-491981), but films of volumes published less than fifty-six years ago cannot be circulated because of copyright restrictions.

Periodicals

The library currently has more than 150 periodicals devoted to German and German-American genealogy. More titles are added every year. Again, access poses a problem. How does the researcher find a pertinent article without leafing through dozens of bound periodicals?

Fortunately, indexes exist which can cut this particular Gordian knot. The first of these is *Familiengeschichtliche Bibliographie* edited by Johannes Hohlfeld, Friedrich Wecken, and others (Neustadt/Aisch: Degener Verlag, 1920-1945). (FHL# 943/A3fb). It is part of the Family History Center's (Branch Library's) Core Collection (FHL# microfiche 600820). The first six volumes are on microfilm (FHL# 942936-942938).

The first seven volumes cover German genealogical literature published between 1897 and 1945. Vol. 1 covers 1900-20; Vol. 2, 1921-26; Vol. 3, 1927-30; Vol. 4, 1931-34; Vol. 5, 1935 and 1897-99; Vol. 6, 1936-37; Vol. 7, 1938-45. Section 3 of Volume 6 contains a cumulative index for the entire series from 1897-1937. The German collection also has two later volumes of this index, Vol. 11, covering 1960-62, and Part 1 of Vol. 16 covering 1975-77. Gerhard Jeske has prepared a detailed explanation of this index which is available at the European Reference Desk, entitled *Bibliography of Family History*, photocopy of typescript (Salt Lake City: Family History Library, n.d.), p. 11.

(B a l d u f)

114 Martin Balduf, Bauer, (∞ mit Fraulin 1613). Erwähnt um 1580/1613/1616/1619/1620/1622. A 229/32258/32337. B 66/2864,2868, 2871.

115 ∞...: Peter Friedrich Balduf, Mälzer, u. Maria Walter <T.d. Johann W., Angestellter, u.d. Barbara geb.Ries>, * Heidelberg-Schlierbach 18.6.1896, <∞II s. 1602>.
3 Kdr: Katharina Barbara <116>. - Charlotte <5273>. - Ruth Helga <1374>.

116 ∞ 10.12.1955: Katharina Barbara Balduf <aus 115>, Büroangestellte, * Heidelberg 15.2.1921, <∞I ...>, u. Erich Heinrich Anton Zink <S.d. Heinrich Z., Küfer, u.d. Anna Maria Martha geb. Schmidt>, kaufm.Angestellter, * Karlsruhe 30.5.1924, <∞I ...>.
1 Kd (o-o der Frau): Dieter Richard Walter Karl 31.5.1943, † 8.2.1944.

B a l l u f

117 Hans Balluf (Balduf), Beständer der herrsch.Mühle (Stadtmühle) 1524. A 229/32378. U 1524 Juli 28.

118 ∞...: Melchior Balluf, Ziegler in Bruchsal, kath., u. Katharina Kirchhöfer <T.d. Johann Georg K., Zimmermeister in Heidelsheim, u.d. Katharina geb.Seiband>, * Heidelsheim 6.2.1790, † Gochsheim 19.7.1846.

B a l t e s a r

119 . . . Baltesar, Maurer beim Stadtmühlbau 1690. A 229/32378.

B a p s t

120 Bono-Erben Bapst, U. 16.Jhdt./Reg.Censum.
121 Hans Bapst, * Bauerbach, ∞ in Gochsheim, Erwähnt 1613. A 229/32258.

B a r m e r

121a Konrad Barmer, * Villingen 1906, Vikar in Gochsheim 1934.

B a r t

122 Simon Bart (Bartz)(Barz), Hintersasse, Bader 1679. Erwähnt 1665. A 213 Bd. 152 Nr.30. B 66/2877.

B a r t h

123 ∞ 30.11.1957: Richard Barth <S.d. Adolf B., Zigarrenmacher in Menzingen, u.d. Christiane geb.Dörr>, Eisenbahnassistent, * Menzingen 24.7.1908, u. Herta Ruth Auch <aus 67>, * 8.11.1925. Richard Barth <aus 738>. (o/o).
2 Kdr: Karin Agathe, * Bruchsal 10.12.1958. - Karl-Heinz, * Bruchsal 6.5.1962.

B a r t o s c h

124 ∞ 10.9.1892 in Adler-Kosteletz: Robert Bartosch <S.d. Blasius B., Weber in Weiswasser in Mähren, u.d. Anna geb.Kunisch>, Oberwebmeister, kath., * Mährisch-Rotwasser 2.2.1861, † Gochsheim 25.5.1946, u. Antonia Schwendemann, † Mannheim-Waldhof 12.11.1936.

Figure 19:3 Page from Rudolf Herzer. *Sippenbuch der Stadt Gochsheim, Landkreis Bruchsal in Baden.* (Grafenhausen: Albert Kobeler, 1968), p. 149.

A second major index to German genealogical periodicals is Oswald Spohr, ed., *Familiengeschichtliche Quellen* (Family History Sources) (Leipzig: Degener Verlag, 1926 ff). (FHL# 943/B2fa). Volumes 2-13 are also on microfilm (FHL# 496680-496682). This work is also part of the Branch Library Microfiche Project (FHL# microfiche 600817).

This index contains over 30 million surnames drawn from more than 1,750 sources. Each of the thirteen volumes is a separate index to the periodical literature published during a given time period. Following each surname is a number which refers to the source from which the name was taken. The titles of these sources are listed at the beginning of each volume.

The final periodical index discussed here is *Der Schlüssel: Gesamtsinhaltsverzeichnisse mit Ortsquellennachweis für genealogische heraldische und historische Zeitschriftenreihen* (The Key: Comprehensive Index Including Place Names to Genealogic, Heraldic and Historical Periodicals) (Gottingen: Heinz Reise Verlag, 1950-65). (FHL# 943/D25sc).

This is a more recent index than the first two cited and is much easier for a non-German to use as it is printed in modern type rather than Gothic *Fraktur. Der Schlüssel* covers a far greater area than the current boundaries of Germany. Indeed, it indexes periodicals covering virtually all the German-speaking areas of Europe prior to World War II.

The first four volumes index German language periodicals published prior to World War II. Volume 3 devotes itself to the first sixty-five years of *Der Deutsche Herold,* (1870-1945), the single most important periodical devoted to heraldry in German-speaking Europe.

Volume 5 covers periodicals published in the Federal Republic of Germany (i.e., West Germany) for 1945-60. Volume 6 devotes itself to German language periodicals from Austria and Czechoslovakia. Much of it dates from between the wars, but some pre-dates 1917 when it was all part of the old Austro-Hungarian Empire.

Volume 7 indexes material published from 1961-75. Although most of the periodicals were published in West Germany, many focus on areas no longer inhabited by Germans – for example, Pomerania, the Sudetenland of Czechoslovakia, and the Banat region of Yugoslavia. Volume 8 covers periodicals since 1975.

Clifford Neal Smith and Anna Smith devote several pages to *Der Schlüssel* in their *Encyclopedia of German-American Genealogical Research* (New York and London: R. R. Bowker, 1976). (FHL# 943/D27sp). The various periodicals indexed are categorized according to particular subject matter – for example, heraldry, and geographic area. Gerhard Jeske has also prepared a patron aid explaining *Der Schlüssel* entitled *Der Schlüssel: The Key for Genealogical Research in Germany, Switzerland and Austria*, Patron Aid Service No. 8 (Salt Lake City: Family History Library, 1985). It is located at the European Reference Desk. No call number. Although *Der Schlüssel* is the easiest of the cited indexes to use, it should be consulted in conjunction with the others. For instance, the *German Lineage Book (Deutsche Geschlechterbuch)* is not indexed in *Der Schlüssel* but in Volume 6 of *Familiengeschichtliche Bibliographie*.

Not every periodical cited in these indexes is currently available in the German collection. However, the Family History Library makes every effort to locate and photocopy or microfilm out-of-print German genealogical periodicals. As the collection of microfilmed parish registers grows, so does that of the periodicals.

Academic Records

As the very existence of the *German Lineage Book* indicates, the German upper middle-class has avidly pursued genealogy for more than a century. An excellent source for this social strata, and for the nobility too, are academic records. Matriculation and scholarship lists of the major German universities have been preserved over the centuries.

If you have a Protestant clergyman for an ancestor, the chances of finding his name in a university matriculation list are quite good. Both Lutheran and Reformed confessions required a university education of candidates for the ministry.

Fortunately, many of these matriculation and scholarship lists have been published. A few of these have been cataloged under the general heading of **Germany/Schools.** But most are cataloged under the specific locality where the university is located – for example, **Germany/Preussen/Hessen-Nassau/Marburg/Schools** for the University of Marburg.

Occupations

A somewhat parallel phenomenon to the publishing of university matriculation lists is that of publishing books about occupations – for example, a roster of the members of the Merchants' Association in various towns in Silesia 1658-1912. Perhaps the most widespread of such books are biographical dictionaries of the pastors and teachers of a given area – for example, of the Rheinpfalz from 1585-1621. Some of these are cataloged under the general heading of **Germany/Occupations,** but most are found under the state provincial or local subheading – for example, **/Hessen/Occupations.**

A word of caution is in order here. The catalog is not invariably consistent. For instance, a book listing the pastors and schoolmasters of Rheinhessen 1521-1923 is not cataloged under **/Hessen/Occupations**, but **/Hessen/Church History**. Similarly, a book listing civil servants in Hessen 1820-1933 is cataloged under **Hessen/Officials and Employees.**

Funeral Sermons

Leichpredigte (funeral sermons) constitute an interesting and valuable source which often predates parish registers. Upper-middle and upper-class Lutheran families c.1550-1800 typically printed and distributed copies of the funeral sermons to friends and relatives. These predecessors of modern-day obituaries eulogized the deceased, narrating his or her life and achievements and listing the names of close relatives and ancestors.

Several large collections of these sermons exist, some of which have been published. More often, indexes have been compiled which list the names contained in a given collection. The German collection has some of these cataloged under **Germany/Obituaries, /[State]/**, and/-or **[City]/Obituaries.**

Nobility.

See Chapter 28, "Medieval Families."

Family Histories

Given the intense interest in genealogy which exists in Germany, it is not surprising that many family histories have been published. The Family History Department endeavors to acquire as many of these as possible. They are cataloged alphabetically in the Surname FHLC.

Special Collections

As in other areas of the library, the German collection contains special collections of material which is primarily genealogical in nature. Most of these are local in character and are listed under the appropriate place in the locality catalog.

Two collections are sufficiently broad in size and scope to warrant mention. Beyond that, the first of these, the Brenner collection, merits discussion because, to borrow a phrase from Professor Ronald Smelser, "it represents, graphically, one of the less salubrious uses to which genealogical study can be put."

The collection consists of 674 reels of 16mm (unless otherwise noted, all films are 35 mm) microfilm cataloged under **Germany/Bayern/Mittelfranken/Genealogy/Collected Works.** As the catalog entry implies, the collection is focused in Middle Franconia, i.e., North-Central Bavaria, around the city of Ansbach. The bulk of the collection consists of lineages of families in the region, as well as extensive correspondence among a number of Nazi and governmental offices. Its purpose was to enable individuals to prove they had no Jewish ancestors so they could receive a certificate of genuine German blood *(Ariernachweis)*.

In spite of the nefarious purpose for which it was created, the collection is extremely valuable to the genealogist because it covers an area where the Family History Department has not been able to film the parish registers. The most important part of the collection for the genealogist is thus the first portion, which consists of an alphabetical index (A-We) of family surnames containing vital record information–for example, names, dates of birth and death, place of residence, occupation, names and occupations of parents, and identification of the individual in question as either Aryan or Jew.

Part 3 consists of miscellaneous family information not integrated into Part 1. Part 4 contains marriage records of soldiers stationed in the area in the eighteenth and nineteenth centuries, while Part 5 is a directory of locations in Middle Franconia where research was done. Part 6, an *Erbhofliste* (hereditary farm list) forms a pedigree of families living in the area 200 years or more, reflecting the Nazi philosophy of "blood and soil." Part 7 contains verification data including vital and parish records dating back to the sixteenth century. Part 8 is a pedigree of Heinrich Himmler's family.

The other major collection has been compiled by *Das Institut zur Erforschung Historischer Fuhrungschichten* (The Institute for the Research of Historically Leading Classes) and is titled *Führende Personlichkeiten* (Leading Personalities). It consists of 388 reels of 16mm microfilm (beginning FHL# microfilm 1204024) containing miscellaneous data on personalities ranging from long-deceased German dukes to current Olympic champions–for example, pedigree charts, lineage tables, obituaries, newspaper articles, etc. It is cataloged under **Germany/Hessen/Bensheim/Archives and Libraries.**

Directories

Directories greatly facilitate genealogical research in large cities. The German collection contains city and town directories dating back into the nineteenth century, telephone directories from the present century, etc. These localized directories are cataloged by locality–for example, **Germany/Preussen/Brandenburg/Berlin/Directories.**

In addition to these, the collection contains a host of other directories covering a variety of topics–for example, occupational directories, business directories, etc. Those on a national scope are cataloged under **Germany/Directories**, while those of a state or regional scope appear under the appropriate category–for example, **Germany/Hessen/Directories.**

Encyclopedias, Dictionaries, and other Reference Works

The German collection houses various German language encyclopedias and dictionaries. In addition to standard German-English dictionaries, the library is acquiring many specialized dictionaries which translate local dialects into modern High German. Anyone who has struggled to translate late seventeenth-century parish registers written in the local dialect can appreciate the value of these books. Of wider interest are Latin-German dictionaries which translate Latin words and phrases found in parish registers into German, especially:

Wiedler, Wilhelm, comp. *Latein für den Sippenforscher* (Latin for the Genealogical Researcher) (Görlitz: C. A. Starke, 1939). (FHL# EUR REF/473/W4261).

Miscellaneous

A survey of this length cannot possibly list all the various types of sources, both primary and secondary housed in the German collection. The best approach to finding these is to check all the records listed under a given locality.

AUSTRIA

Historical Background

955	The beginning of an Austrian nation after the victory over the Magyar at Lechfeld.
976-1246	The Babenbergers rule Austria until 1246 when Emperor Frederick II is killed in battle against the Hungarians leaving no male heirs.
1247	An Interregnum, which lasts for about 100 years. After several attempts, the Habsburgs take possession and rule Austria until 1918.
1365	Rudolf I is succeeded by his two brothers, Albert III and Leopold III; serious internal disputes over divisions of Hapsburg territory.
1457-63	A period of strife and civil war between Frederick I and his brother, Albert VI. Albert's death in 1463 allows reunification.
1493	Frederick dies; Maximilian I succeeds to whole Habsburg dominion and greatly expands territorial possessions.
1517	Beginning of the Protestant Reformation in Germany.
1519	Maximilian's grandson, Charles V, already ruler of Spain and the Netherlands, inherits Austria when Maximilian dies. Delegates the government of Austria, Styria, Carinthia, and Carniola to his brother, Ferdinand I, leading to the division of the house of Habsburg into the Austrian and Spanish branches.
1523	Earliest known Roman Catholic Church records in Austria.
1545-63	Council of Trent. Pastors required to keep christening and marriage registers.
1570	Conflicts between the Roman Catholics and Protestants begin as early as 1570; meanwhile, Austria suffers persistent invasions from the Turks.
1618	Beginning of the Thirty Years' War between Roman Catholics and Protestants.
1663-1739	Wars against the Turks. Many church records in eastern Austria destroyed.
1731	Edict of Archbishop Firmian of Salzburg expels 23,500 Austrian Protestants; most settle in East Prussia and Brandenburg.
1740-44	Silesian War. Austria loses Silesia to Prussia.
1741-49	Austria at war with Bavaria, Spain, France, and Saxony.
1772-95	Three partitions of Poland; Austria acquires Galicia.
1781	Emperor Joseph II invites German peasants to settle in Galicia. Tolerance Act gives non-Catholics privilege of keeping duplicate church registers.
1784	A decree of Emperor Joseph II requires that all pastors keep separate registers of christenings, marriages, and deaths.
1798-1815	Napoleonic Wars.
1806	Dissolution of Holy Roman Empire.
1848	Hungarian Revolution.
1859	Loss of Lombardy to Italy.
1866	Austrian-Prussian War; Austria loses Venetia to Italy.
1867	Compromise of 1867 divides Austrian Empire between Austria and Hungary.
1908	Austria annexes Bosnia and Herzegovina.
1914-18	World War I. Austrian-Hungarian Empire dissolved and territory divided among Austria, Czechoslovakia, Hungary, Italy, Poland, Romania, Russia, and Yugoslavia.
1938	German occupation of Austria. Beginning of civil registration in Austria.
1939-45	World War II.
1955	Austria becomes again an independent and democratic state.

Austria Library Collection

Although Austria, Czechoslovakia, and Hungary are now independent sovereign states, prior to 1918 they formed the core of the once vast Austrian-Hungarian Empire. Millions of emigrants left the Empire seeking better fortune in the New World. Today, increasing numbers of their descendants are seeking their ancestral roots in the Old Empire. But all too often they may have only the vaguest idea of just where. If asked they might say "Austria."

This may well be correct as far as it goes. But Austria in 1900 covered a vast area extending from what is now the Soviet Union to the shores of the Adriatic, including half of present-day Czechoslovakia, the southern third of Poland, and a sizable portion of present-day Yugoslavia. Before 1867, it also included all of present-day Hungary, the Slovakian part of present-day Czechoslovakia, a huge portion of present-day Romania lying north and west of the Carpathian Mountains, and Croatia and Slavonia in what is now Yugoslavia (see map, Figure 19:4).

Your first task in using the Central European library holdings is to determine just where your ancestors came from. Sometimes this poses no particular problem. Sometimes it does.

This chapter cannot devote itself to a full-scale discussion of the various American sources for determining European place of origin. Census records, church records, naturalization papers, obituaries, and passenger lists can be of great help in this regard. The 1910 census is particularly useful for immigrants from Austria-Hungary because it lists the language spoken. Hence, if an immigrant was from Austria, but spoke Polish, he or

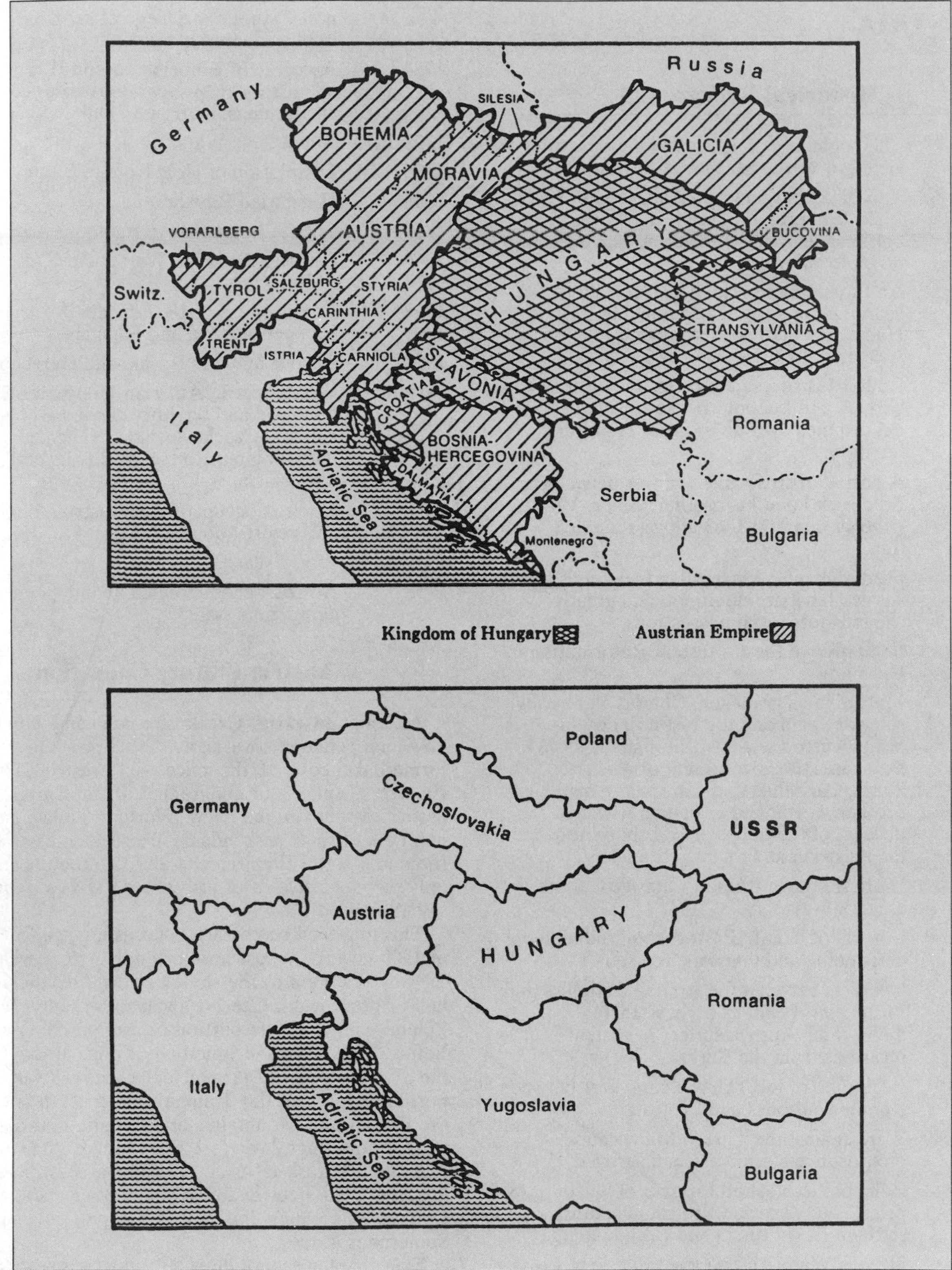

Figure 19:4 Austro-Hungarian Region 1900 and 1946.

she would very likely be from Galicia in present-day Poland.

Unfortunately the International Genealogical Index (IGI), for the countries under discussion, does not yet contain enough names to make it as useful a name-finding tool as the IGI for Germany. Nevertheless, it is still valuable and will become more so in the years to come.

Unlike the German IGI, the Austro-Hungarian IGI is not arranged according to the pre-1918 boundaries. Indeed, the name *Austria-Hungary* is not used in arranging the entries. Rather, the current political designations are used, with one notable exception. Hence, individuals born or married in the former Crownlands of Bohemia, Moravia, and Silesia are entered in the IGI for Czechoslovakia.

Entries from Western Galicia appear in the Polish IGI, while those from Eastern Galicia and the northern part of Bukovina are in the USSR. The Crownland of Carniola forms present-day Slovenia in northern Yugoslavia. Thus, its entries appear in the Yugoslavian IGI as do those from the Crownland of Dalmatia and the annexed areas of Bosnia and Herzegovina.

Trieste, part of Styria and the southern half of Tyrol now belong to or are administered by Italy. Hence, entries from those areas appear in the Italian IGI.

Certain areas belonging to the old kingdom of Hungary form an exception to the rule. Slovakia, Ruthenia, and Transylvania have been assigned to the Hungarian IGI together with contemporary Hungary. From the standpoint of using the IGI as a tool for tracing ancestors, this makes considerable sense. For instance, Slovakian immigrants who were naturalized prior to 1918 would usually list their village, the old Hungarian county, and kingdom of Hungary as their place of origin. Perhaps someday computer technology will permit a cross-listing of entries from the old Austro-Hungarian Empire which will state both the old and new political designations of a given locality.

Entries from areas now known as the Banat may appear in either the Romanian, Hungarian, or Yugoslavian IGI. Croatia, Slavonia, and Fiume have been assigned to the Yugoslavian IGI, but some entries may appear in the Hungarian IGI.

For further discussion of the Polish, Romanian, and Yugoslavian sections of the IGI, see Chapter 20, "Eastern Europe." The Austrian IGI uses Austria as the country, with the administrative state *(Bundesland)* - for example, Tirol or Niederoesterreich - as the county equivalent, followed by the name of the town. If there is more than one place of the same name in a given state, the name of the county *(Bezirkshauptmannschaft)* is added without a comma between the two names - for example, Neusiedl in Neunkirchen Bezirkshaupmannschaft, Lower Austria would appear as **Austria/Niederoesterreich/Neusiedl Neunkirchen.** A word of caution about the Austrian IGI is pertinent here. Because of many border and name changes which have occurred in the old Austro-Hungarian Empire, inconsistencies appear in the IGI. For instance, there are many entries in the Austrian IGI for Kronland Krain, the German spelling of Crownland Carniola. Yet this region is now Slovenia, Yugoslavia. Entries from other Crownlands or provinces of pre-1918 Austria occasionally appear in the Austrian IGI. So it is best to check both the Austrian IGI and those of the successor states, i.e., Poland, Czechoslovakia, Yugoslavia, Italy, and the USSR.

In contrast to the IGI, the FHLC for Austria contains subdivisions from both contemporary and pre-1918 Austria. For instance, the state of Burgenland was part of pre-1918 Hungary, but is now part of Austria. So it appears in the Austrian section of the FHLC, but all entries also appear in the Hungarian section - for example, **Austria/Burgenland/Pilgersdorf** is **Hungary/Vas/Pörgöleny.**

In addition, the Austrian FHLC contains numerous entries listed under the Crownlands or provinces of the old empire - for example, Böhmen (Bohemia), Galizien (Galicia), Küstenland (literally Coastlands, i.e., Trieste, Istria, and Goritz) - which are no longer in Austria proper. Again, these places are listed in both the Austrian FHLC and that of the successor state. For example, **Austria/Galizien/Hyzne** also appears as **Poland/Rzeszow/Hyzne.**

Indeed, the Austrian FHLC contains entries from areas that became Hungarian after 1867 - for example, Croatia, Slavonia, and the Siebenbürgen. But most of the areas which belonged to the kingdom of Hungary including Slovakia do not appear in the Austrian FHLC, but in the Hungarian FHLC. To complicate matters further, separate gazetteers were published for the two halves of the empire c.1905.

Gazetteers

As this discussion makes plain, determining location is of prime importance. Assuming that you have a valid place name but do not know the province, only "Austria," you could look in the fifteen-volume gazetteer of Austria and not find the name of the village because it was in Hungary. Fortunately, the library has a gazetteer compiled in 1845-53, i.e., before the empire was split between Austria and Hungary, and Venetia was lost to Italy:

Raffelsperger, Franz ed. *Allgemeines Geographisch-Statistisches Lexikon aller Osterreichischen Staaten* (General Geographical-Statistical Gazetteer of all Austrian States). Wien: n.pub., 1845-53. (FHL# 943.6/ESr or microfilm 1187928-1187933 or 1186708-1186711)

Admittedly, the Raffelsperger gazetteer is not a panacea. Written in German, it uses some quaint spellings for example, Pohlen for Polen (the German term for Poland). Names of villages in Slovakia are listed only in their Hungarian form for example, *Cziroke-Hoszu-Mezo* for *Dlhé nad Cirochou.* Place names in Carinthia, Carniola, and Istria are all listed under the heading of Illirien, which is the English form of the word Illyria.

Still, for all of its quirks, it is the only gazetteer in the library's collection which covers all of the old Austro-Hungarian Empire. Another positive factor is that it is printed in standard type rather than the old Gothic

Franktur. The European Reference staff has prepared a guide to this gazetteer which explains many of its idiosyncracies. This is an unpublished photocopy of a typescript at the European Reference Desk.

A more systematic and thorough gazetteer for the Austrian half of the old empire is *Gemeindelexikon der in Reichsrate Vertretenen Königreiche und Länder* (Gazetteer of the Crownlands and territories Represented in the Imperial Council), 14 vols. (Wien: K. K. Statistischen Zentralkommission, 1904). (FHL# EUR REF/Q/-943.6/E5g).

It has also been microfilmed: Volume 1: *Gemeindelexikon von Niederösterriech (Lower Austria)*: now in Austria (FHL# microfilm 1187925, item 2). Volume 2: *Gemeindelexicon von Oberösterreich (Upper Austria)*: now in Austria (FHL# microfilm 1187925, item 3). Volume 3: *Gemeindelexikon von Salzburg (Salzburg):* now in Austria (FHL# microfilm 1187925, item 4). Volume 4: *Gemeindelexikon von Steiermark (Styria):* now in Austria and Yugoslavia (FHL# microfilm 1187926, item 1). Volume 5: *Gemeindelixikon von Kärnten (Carinthia):* now in Austria, Italy, and Yugoslavia (FHL# microfilm 1187926, item 2). Volume 6: *Gemeindelexikon von Krain (Carniola)*: now in Yugoslavia (FHL# microfilm 1187926, item 3). Volume 7: *Gemeindelexikon von Küstenland (Istria, Görz and Trieste)*: now in Italy and Yugoslavia (FHL# microfilm 1187926, item 4). Volume 8: *Gemeindelexikon von Tirol and Voralberg (Tyrol):* now in Austria and Italy; Voralberg: now in Austria (FHL# microfilm 1187926, item 5). Volume 9: *Gemeindelexikon von Böhmen (Bohemia):* now in Czechoslovakia (FHL# microfilm 1187927, item 1). Volume 10: *Gemeindelexicon von Mähren (Moravia):* now in Czechoslovakia (FHL# microfilm 924736, item 1). Volume 11: *Gemeindelexikon von Schlesien (Silesia):* now in Czechoslovakia and Poland (FHL# microfilm 1187927, item 2). Volume 12: *Gemeindelexikon von Galizien (Galicia)*: now in Poland and Ukraine (FHL# microfilm 1187928, item 1). Volume 13: *Gemeindelexikon von Bukowina (Bukovina)*: now in Ukraine and Romania (FHL# microfilm 1187928, item 2). Volume 14: *Gemeindelexikon von Dalmatien (Dalmatia):* now in Yugoslavia (FHL# microfilm 1187928, item 3).

This series of gazetteers is based upon the Austrian census of 1900. The gazetteer for each province is organized by political district with place-name index according to standard alphabetical order. However, there is no overall index to the entire series. Hence, you must know the province in which the sought-for place is located. One way to achieve this is to use the Raffelsperger gazetteer as a general index. Another overall index would be the *Verzeichnis der Post und Telegraphien-Amter in Osterreich, Ungarn und in Bosnien-Hercegovina* (Directory of the Post and Telegraph Offices in Austria, Hungary and Bosnia-Herzegovina) (Wien: n.pub., 1910). (FHL# 943.6/E5a or microfilm 887093, item 1). This directory also lists Austrian post offices in Liechenstein and the Levant. While not as complete as the Raffelsperger gazetteer, the political designations correspond to the 1904 gazetteer. Hence, by using the 1910 postal directory and the Raffelsperger gazetteer, you should be able to identify the province in which the parish village lies. Once this is known, the provincial indexes in the 1904 gazetteer should indicate the actual hamlet in question.

Of course, if the province or Crownland – for example, Bohemia or Galicia – is known, then one can turn directly to the 1904 gazetteer. Daniel Schlyter of the European Reference Department has prepared a brief guide for using this gazetteer which is available at the European Reference desk.

The library has an excellent set of maps of the former Austro-Hungarian Empire on a scale of 1:75,000 (FHL# Atlas 943.6/E2am or microfilm 1045395). After determining the location of the place in the 1904 gazetteer, note a large town nearby, typically the equivalent of the county seat. Look for this town on the map key at the beginning of the film. Note the number of the quadrangle in which it appears, and turn the film until said quadrangle appears on the screen.

The best gazetteer for modern-day Austria is *Ortsverzeichnis von Osterreich* (Gazetteer of Austria) (Wien: Osterreichischen Statistischen Zentralamt, 1965). (FHL# 943.6/E5o/ 1965 or microfilm 1181555, item 7). Using it in conjunction with *Auto Atlas Osterreich* (Wien: F & B, 1970) (FHL# EUR REF/943.6/E7f), you should be able to locate virtually any locality in Austria, no matter how small.

As in the German collection, the library has many other gazetteers than those discussed here. Those pertaining to Czechoslovakia and Hungary are treated below.

Emigration and Migration Records

The Hamburg passenger lists discussed under *Germany* above are as important for tracing emigrants from the old Austro-Hungarian Empire as from the German Reich. Hence, they deserve mention here.

While detailed emigration records from various areas of the old empire – for example, Bohemia – are known to exist, for the most part they have not been microfilmed by the Family History Department. One exception is the Vienna passport registers for 1792-1918 (136 reels cataloged under **Austria/Niederösterreich/ Wien (Vienna)/Emigration and Migration**.

Two other sets of migration indexes in the library's collection are worth mentioning. The first is *Ansiedlerkartei nach Galizien* 1782-1805, alphabetized index cards listing individuals from Germany, Bohemia, and Moravia who settled in Galicia between 1782-1805, eighteen reels of 16mm microfilm beginning with FHL# 1326450.

A book based upon this index is Ludwig Schneider, *Das Kolonisationswerk Josefs II in Galizien* (The Colonization Efforts of Emperor Joseph II in Galicia) (Leipzig: n.pub., 1939). (FHL# Q 943.86/W2 or microfilm 1256477, item 1. This work lists names and includes maps of the areas of settlement.

A similar index to settlers in the Banat region of present-day Yugoslavia is *Ansiedlerakten* 1686-1855, which lists settlers from Germany, Switzerland,

Bohemia, and Moravia to the Banat and other areas of Hungary. It consists of thirty-five reels of 16mm film beginning with FHL# 1326419. Both of these sets are cataloged under **/Wien/Emigration and Migration.**

Various works in the collection discuss the fate of the Salzburg Protestants who had the choice of converting to Catholicism or emigrating at the beginning of the eighteenth century. One of particular interest to Americans is Samuel Urlspergh, *Detailed Reports on the Salzburger Emigrants Who Settled in America* (Athens: U. of Georgia Press, 1968). (FHL# 973/W2a).

The library has other studies of emigrants who left given localities. As with the German collection, these records are cataloged according to locality.

Census Records

Although decennial censuses were taken every ten years – for example, 1890 and 1900 – and provided the data for the gazetteer of 1904, they were primarily taken for statistical purposes and are not available in the library. However, the kingdom of Hungary took various censuses in the nineteenth century which have survived. See discussion under *Hungary* below. As for local censuses or census substitutes, these are cataloged under the locality in question.

Parish Registers

St. Stephen's Cathedral in Vienna has the oldest parish registers in contemporary Austria, namely the burial registers of 1523-29 and the marriage registers of 1542-56. The Council of Trent (1545-63) decreed that all Roman Catholic parishes keep records of births and marriages. The implementation of this decree took decades, even centuries.

The oldest extant registers apart from St. Stephen's are found in the Tyrol, Vorarlberg, and the Maritime provinces now belonging to Italy. The Thirty Years' War greatly impeded the keeping of parish registers in Bohemia, Moravia, and Silesia. Hence, most church records of those regions begin in the mid-seventeenth century.

In the outer reaches of the empire, methodical record keeping began much later. The earliest known parish registers in Bucovina date from 1776. In Galicia, the keeping of parish registers did not become mandatory until the decree of Emperor Joseph II dated 20 February 1784 required that all pastors keep vital records. In Austria proper, this decree was not superseded until 1939, when civil registration was inaugurated.

In a sense, this is all moot since the Austrian church authorities have not yet permitted the library to film their records. The net result is that contemporary Austria constitutes a barren spot in the library's collection of European parish registers.

The one exception is Burgenland, which belonged to Hungary prior to 1919. The Genealogical Department filmed transcripts of the Burgenland parish registers deposited in the Hungarian Central Archive in Budapest in the early 1970s. They are cataloged according to the individual locality. The collection also has a scattering of parish registers from other areas, so it is always wise to check the locality catalog before writing off a given parish.

Legal Records

In contrast to the bleak situation concerning church records, the library has numerous legal records from various parts of contemporary Austria, including probate records dating back to the sixteenth century. Of course, using these requires a good command of German and Gothic script. Check the locality catalog under the appropriate place and subheading – for example, **Austria/-Tirol/Brixen/Court Records.**

Land Records

In the process of filming legal records, the Genealogical Department also acquired various land records involving real estate transactions. Some of these date back to the fifteenth century. Again, they are cataloged under the locality and the subheading **/Land and Property.**

Municipal Records

Various municipal records which fall neither into the category of court nor land records have been acquired by the library. A typical example would be the city council records of Bozen, Tirol, now Bolzano, Bolzano, Italy.

Police records might be classified as municipal records. Police authorities in Austria as in Germany require residents to report upon arriving in the city and again upon departure. They contain much data of genealogical interest – for example, names of adults and children, place and dates of birth, last place of residence, current address, intended place of residence, etc. The Austrian collection contains 390 reels of these *Meldezettel* (registration forms) from Vienna covering the years 1850-1920. Hence, if an ancestor resided for a brief period in Vienna before emigrating to the USA, these records could be very useful for determining the actual village of origin.

Another type of municipal record is occupation records. The Conscription Office in Vienna kept so-called *Arbeitsbuch Protokolle* categorizing the local male inhabitants by occupation. The library has 101 reels of these records covering the years 1860-1919.

Civil Registers

Civil registration of vital statistics – i.e., births, marriages, and deaths – began only in 1939 after Austria had been annexed into the greater German Reich. Hence, the library has very few films of civil registers.

One notable exception is the Burgenland, which was a part of Hungary until after the First World War. Hungary began civil registration of vital statistics in 1895. Localities in the Burgenland sent transcripts of their vital records to Budapest where they were microfilmed in the late 1950s.

The other exception is Vienna itself where death records began in 1648. The collection consists of 823 reels of microfilm covering the years 1648-1920. After 1777, they are arranged alphabetically by year.

Supplementing these are eighty-two 35mm reels of hospital death records from 1868-1942. In addition, the library has indexed records of various Vienna cemeteries.

Military Records

The "crown jewels" of the library's Austrian collection are the films of the holdings of the *Kriegsarchiv* (War Archive) of the old Austrian Imperial Army in Vienna – more than 6,400 reels with filming continuing.

The current holdings consist of four major types of records. The largest, consisting of 3,103 reels, contains muster rolls of the various regiments of the Army from c.1740-1820. Subsequent years are currently being filmed.

These records contain the following information: The name of the soldier or officer, his place of birth, age, religion, occupation or profession, and marital status. After 1770, the names of his children are listed.

While an index exists for the Office Corps, no index for the enlisted men has ever been compiled. Therefore, you must know the name of the regiment to find the records of an enlisted man. One way to learn this is through the church records. If a soldier is on active duty, his unit is usually noted in the birth and marriage entries. Even if he is a reservist, his unit is often recorded in the marriage entry.

A less direct method of determining the unit is through Otto Kasparkovitz, *Dislokations-Verzeichnis des K.U.K. Heeres and der K.U.K. Marine* (Distribution Location Directory of the Austro-Hungarian Military and Naval units) (Wien: n.pub., 1969). (FHL# microfilm 1186632, item 1).

This directory shows the location of the regiments at any given period. It helps the researcher determine which regiment or regiments were recruiting in the area of the ancestor's residence during the time period in question. The regiments tended to be garrisoned in the same area and were absent only during actual time of war. They recruited from the surrounding area according to the legal residence of the potential recruit. It follows that the muster reels are not especially useful as a finding tool for enlisted men. However, they do contain valuable genealogical data.

The second major portion of the Austrian War records collection are the *Grundbuchblätter und Stellungslisten,* 1820-1918, (Service Records and Enlistment Orders). Those currently in the Austrian collection cover the years 1820-69. They form the logical continuation of the muster rolls and contain much the same information. However, they are more systematically arranged.

As with the muster reels, the officers are indexed. In the case of the enlisted men, the annual muster list was replaced by an individual sheet for each soldier which was updated by the annual muster. A copy of this record went with the soldier if and when he changed regiments.

An important addendum to the service record is the enlistment orders, which state the exact birthdate of the soldier and the names of his parents through extracts from the parish registers.

After 1869, when universal conscription was established, the service records were no longer kept by regiment but by the state military registration district. The records in the *Kriegsarchiv*, 1869-90 consist primarily of service records for the modern Austrian states. For 1891 to 1900, those still available are located in the archive of the Ministry of the Interior. Most of the post-1869 records of other parts of the empire have been sent to the successor states – for example, Yugoslavia, Poland, Hungary, etc.

An extremely important collection of military records in the library's collection are the *Kopfzettel* (literally head lists) of the *Konscriptionsamt* (conscription office) in Vienna. This collection, 669 reels of 16mm film, is divided into several parts. The largest consists of individual muster sheets of soldiers registered at Vienna arranged alphabetically according to birth year 1865-1900. In other words, all conscripts born in 1865 would be arranged A-Z, as would those for 1866, etc. The information always lists date and place of birth, current occupation, legal residence, regiment, name of wife if married, names of children, and sometimes names of parents and siblings including place and date of birth. Individuals from all parts of the empire are listed, although there is a predominance of individuals in areas relatively close to Vienna – for example, Bohemia, Moravia, Upper and Lower Austria. A few are from more distant areas – for example, Galicia, Hungary, or Croatia.

The second portion of these records consists of an alphabetical list of individuals covering 1760-1880, while the third is a list covering 1861-1900 and 1900-10. None of these lists is grouped according to year of birth, but all are alphabetical.

The fourth part is an alphabetical list of individuals not mustered into service during 1865-71, which, of course, includes the war years of 1866. The fifth set covers foreign males residing in Vienna c.1800-80, while the last consists of alphabetical lists of individuals according to administrative districts in Vienna, for example, 13th *Bezkirk*, 14th *Bezkirk,* etc.

These conscription office lists, unlike the regimental muster reels or service records, are an extremely important finding tool for the genealogist. If there is any reason to suspect that an ancestor spent some time in Vienna before emigrating to the U.S. or elsewhere, you should check these lists. Another set of military records which the library acquired from the *Kriegsarchiv* are the *Dienstbeschreibungen und Qualifikationslisten* (Service Records of Officers and Officials, 1823-1918), which consist of 3,224 reels. They are filed alphabetically and thus constitute an index to the officer corps for the time period covered. They contain much more complete information about a given individual than that contained in the regimental muster reels and service records.

The last set of records from the *Kreigsarchiv* currently available in the library are the *Versorgungswesen* (pension and assistance records), 113 reels, 1773-1920. These are pension records for officers, officials, employees, military widows, and orphans. It is partially indexed. For a helpful source, see:

Blodgett, Steven W. "Great-Grandfather Was in the Imperial Cavalry: Using Austrian Military Records as an Aid to Writing Family History." In Proceedings of World Conference on Records: Preserving Our Heritage, sponsored by the Genealogical Department, Vol 7: *Continental European Family and Local History* (Salt Lake City: Corporation of the President of the Church of Jesus Christ of Latter-day Saints, 1980), Ser. 504. (FHL# 929.1/-W893/1980/vol.7)

Jewish Records

The bulk of the Jewish records in the Austrian collection consists of the Jewish civil registers in Vienna covering the years 1826-1938, 173 reels, indexed. Perhaps civil registers is a misnomer, as they were recorded by leaders of the Jewish community for the civil authorities rather than by the civil authorities themselves. They are cataloged under **Austria/NiederösterReich/Wien/Jewish Records.** In addition, the collection has one reel of birth and circumcision records for Jews in Vienna 1870-1914 (FHL# microfilm 1335317).

Family Histories

As in the German collection, Austrian family histories are cataloged in the surname section of the FHLC.

Periodicals

The library has several sets of periodicals pertaining to Austrian genealogy, the most important of which is *Adler, Zeitschrift für Genealogie und Heraldik* (FHL# 943.6/B2a). The title of this journal has varied over the years. The publisher is *Heraldisch-Genealogische Gesellschaft Adler* (Heraldic and Genealogical Society Adler) (Wien, 1881-date).

This and other Austrian genealogical periodicals have been indexed in Volume 6 of *Der Schlüssel,* previously discussed.

Directories

The library has collected directories of various sorts–for example, city and telephone directories, parish register directories, etc. Check the individual locality–for example, **Wien/Directories.**

School and University Records

As in Germany, university matriculation lists have been compiled and published. In some areas this has been done for secondary schools as well. These are listed under the pertinent locality.

Miscellaneous Records

Various other types of primary records or secondary records derived from them are found in the Austrian collection under the appropriate locality.

CZECHOSLOVAKIA

Historical Background

400-500	Slavic tribes settle the area of the Vltava River valley under the mythical leader Cech whose name became that of his people and the land (Cechy) they settled. It was called Bohemia or Bohmen in Western Europe from the beginning.
500-600	Avars subjugate the Czechs.
620	Legendary chieftain Samo throws off the Avar yoke and establishes his capital near present-day Prague.
658	Death of Samo and disintegration of his empire.
775-800	Rise of the Premyslid dynasty.
833-35	First known Christian church among the Western Slavs built at Nitra Slovakia under the regime of Mojmir I of Great Moravia.
863	Rotislav of Moravia converted to Byzantine Christianity by the missionaries Cyril and Methodius.
885	Pope Stephen V forbids use of the Slavic liturgy and Bohemia and Moravia become Roman Catholic.
896	Moravian Empire defeated by the Magyars. Slovakia comes under Magyar (Hungarian) control until 1918.
900-25	Decline of Moravia and rise of Bohemia.
929	Murder of national hero St. Wenceslas Premyslid by his brother Boleslav the Cruel.
955	Boleslav and Otto the Great decisively defeat the Magyars at the Battle of Lechfeld.
973	Bishopric of Prague established.
1086	Vratislav II crowned king of Bohemia for life by Holy Roman Emperor Henry IV.
1114	Duke of Bohemia becomes Hereditary Cup Bearer of the Holy Roman Emperor. Hereafter, sovereign of Bohemia is an Elector of the empire.
1198	Otakar I crowned King of Ceské Zemé (Bohemia, Moravia, and Silesia) at Mainz.
1212	Otakar I extracts from the Emperor a Golden Bull confirming the royal title of the Premysl house. Simultaneously the emperor renounces his claim to ratify succession and to appoint the bishop of Prague.
1527	Archduke Ferdinand Habsburg of Austria becomes king of Bohemia and Hungary.

1556	Ferdinand invites the Jesuits to settle in Prague.
1579	Publication of vernacular "Kralicka" Bible by the United Brethren.
1618	Defenestration of three of the Emperor's representatives at Hradcany Castle in Prague sparks the Thirty Years' War.
1620	Defeat of Czechs by Catholic Habsburg armies results in total suppression of Protestantism and forced re-Catholicization of the population.
1648	Thirty Years' War ends; Habsburg dynasty in complete control of Bohemia. Keeping of Catholic parish registers on a widespread basis begins in Bohemia, Moravia, and Silesia.
1648-1790	Period of total eclipse of Czech culture.
1790-1848	Rebirth of Czech nationality.
1848	Revolution in Bohemia and subsequent suppression by the Austrian army.
1848-60	Beginning of large-scale Czech migration to the U.S.
1848-1900	Czech cultural revival.
1867	Prussia defeats Austria. Subsequent division of the monarchy into Austria and Hungary.
1867-1900	Increasing political discord between Czechs and Germans in Bohemia.
1867-1914	Hungarians increasingly repressive to Slovaks.
1895-1908	Slovaks emigrate to U.S. in large numbers.
1914-18	World War I. Austro-Hungarian Empire defeated and dissolved.
1918	Creation of Czechoslovakian Republic.
1930-38	Increasing discord among the German-speaking inhabitants of Czechoslovakia.
1938	Munich agreement forces Czechoslovakia to cede Germany area of heavy German concentration (Sudetenland).
1939	Germany occupies remainder of Bohemia and Moravia and sets up Slovakia as a puppet state.
1939-45	World War II. Germany defeated.
1945	Reestablishment of independent Czechoslovakia; Ruthenia taken by USSR.
1945-46	Germans in Czechoslovakia expelled.
1948	Communist party takes over Czechoslovakia.
1951-52	State authorities confiscate church records and place them in regional archives.
1968	Russian troops invade Czechoslovakia and oust liberal Dubcek government.

Czechoslovakia Library Collection

As the historical outline indicates, Czechoslovakia as such only dates from 1918. Yet, paradoxically, the kingdom of the Czechs played an important role in the Holy Roman Empire as early as the twelfth century A.D.

Regrettably, the holdings of the Czech collection in the library are meager. Apart from microfilms of a few German-speaking parishes filmed in 1941 by the *Reichsippenamt* (Reich genealogical office), the collection has almost no films of parish registers in Czechoslovakia.

Paradoxically, Czechoslovakia ranks as one of the easiest countries in Europe to pursue genealogy by correspondence. The Czech government confiscated all the parish registers of the churches in 1951-52 and centralized them in regional archives. The archival staff personnel will search these records and prepare genealogical reports at reasonable rates. However, they must know the exact place of origin to begin research. The difficulties of this task are compounded in Czechoslovakia by the fact that, in the nineteenth century, a given village often had two and sometimes three names, one in German, one in Czech or Slovak, and one in Hungarian. This situation reflected the domination of the country by Austria and Hungary.

Fortunately, the library has reference works which can help you solve this particular problem. The first of these is the International Genealogical Index. As in Austria, the Czech section of the IGI does not yet have enough entries to make it as effective a name-finding aid as the German IGI. Yet it does have enough entries to warrant investigation.

In using the Czech IGI, you must be aware of its peculiarities. The first and most important of these is that it only covers half of present-day Czechoslovakia, notably the old Austrian Crownlands of Bohemia, Moravia, and Silesia. Slovakia, including Ruthenia or Sub-Carpathian Russia, belonged to the kingdom of Hungary and all entries from this area are found in the Hungarian IGI.

In the Czech IGI, Czechoslovakia is used as the country, with the Czech county serving as county equivalent, followed by the town–for example, **Czechoslovakia/Vyskov/Pozorice.**

In Slovakia, Hungary serves as the country or state, with the old Hungarian county (*Megye*) serving as the county equivalent–for example, **Hungary/Trenscen Megye/Stiavnik**. The term *megye* in the IGI entry indicates that the place in question is not in present-day Hungary.

At present, there are very few entries from Slovakia in the Hungarian IGI. The same situation holds true for the Family Group Records Collection (FGRC) and the Temple Index Bureau (TIB). However, there are a few Czech (Bohemian or Moravian) family group sheets in the FGRC, so you should check it at the beginning of the research process.

The Czechoslovakian portion of the FHLC includes all of present-day Czechoslovakia plus Ruthenia which was ceded to the USSR after World War II. At the beginning is a list of alphabetized localities with reference to the appropriate entry–for example, **Baldover/Czechoslovakia** is cross referenced to **Czechoslovakia/Morava/Baldover**.

Hence, the second entry in the FHLC is not the county as in the IGI, but the Czech name of the old Austrian Crownland or province, i.e., Cechy is Böhmen or Bohemia, Morava is Mähren or Moravia, Podkarpatska Rus is Sub-Carpathian Russia or Ruthenia, Slezko is Schlesien or Austria Silesia, while Slovensko is Slovakia.

In the main portion of the Czechoslovakian FHLC, individual entries are cross-referenced–for example, **Czechoslovakia/Cechy/Blatno** is cross-referenced as **Platten/Böhmen/Austria.**

Thus, if you know only the German name of an ancestral village in Bohemia, you should check the Austrian FHLC for possible entries. But if the Czech name of the village is known, then you should check the Czechoslovakian IGI.

The same approach holds true for Slovakian localities. If you know only the Hungarian name for a given locality, then you should check the Hungarian FHLC. For example, Homonna was in the old Hungarian county of Zemplen and is cataloged as **Hungary/Zemplen/Homonna.** But today it is in Slovakia and is cataloged as **Czechoslovakia/Slovensko/Humenne.**

But the library has only a few microfilms of parish registers and other primary genealogical documents from Czechoslovakia. Hence, the vast majority of the small communities in the country are not yet listed in the FHLC. To locate these, you must consult a gazetteer.

Gazetteers

The single most useful gazetteer for modern Czechoslovakia, including the area ceded to the USSR after World War II, is *Administratives Gemeindelexikon der Cechoslovakischen Republik* (Administrative Gazetteer of the Czechoslovak Republic), 2 vols. (Prague: Statistische Staatsamt, 1927-1928). (Vol. 1, FHL# EUR REF/943.7/E5a or microfilm 496719; Vol. 2, microfilm 486720). This gazetteer was published in both a German and Czech version. The library's copy is in German. It is arranged by political district with one index for the entire country. Volume 1 includes all of Bohemia, while Volume 2 covers the rest of the country.

The main index (Vol. 2, pp. 257-32) lists all standard Czechoslovak place names, including most, but not all, German and Hungarian versions. It is alphabetized according to Czech alphabetical order, i.e., "c," "s," and "z" are alphabetized separately from the unmarked versions; also "ch" comes after "h" which means that "sch" comes after "sh."

In addition to the main index, this gazetteer contains six separate indexes listing non-Czechoslovak and obsolete place names not listed in the main index. There are separate indexes for obsolete Czech and Slovak place names as well as for German, Hungarian, Ruthenian, and Polish place names. For example, the Hungarian place name of Cziroka-Hoszu-Mezo is listed on page 323 with its modern Slovakian name of Dlhé nad Cirochou.

One advantage of this gazetteer is that it lists the parish to which a given village belongs on the same page on which the village is listed. A disadvantage is its practice of listing Czech names in reverse order. For instance, Novy Jicin (literally New Jicin) will appear in the main text as Jicin, Novy. Fortunately, it is listed correctly in the index. Hence, this feature is more of a nuisance than a genuine handicap.

A second gazetteer worth noting is the Austrian *Gemeindelexikon* of 1904-06, Vols. 9-11 (FHL# EUR REF/943.6/E5gk or microfilm 1187927 and 0924736). If only the German name of a given locality is known, this gazetteer can be easier to use than the *Gemeindelexikon* published in 1927-28. However, this series of gazetteers covers only those areas of Czechoslovakia which were part of Austria before 1918, i.e., Bohemia, Moravia, and Silesia.

For communities in Slovakia prior to 1918, use Janos Dvorzsak, comp., *Magyarország Helységnévtára* (Gazetteer of Hungary) (Budapest: Havi Fuzetak, 1877). (Vol. 1 with index, FHL# EUR REF/943.9/E5d or microfilm 599564; Vol. 2, microfilm 973041). See Daniel Schlyter, *A Handbook of Czechoslovak Genealogical Research* (Buffalo Grove, Ill.: Genun Pub., 1985) pp. 50-51 for instructions on using this gazetteer. (FHL# 943.7/D27s)

A third gazetteer extremely useful for Slovakia is Milan Majtén, *Nézvy obcí na Slovensku za ostantych dvesto rokov* (Place Names in Slovakia During the Past 200 Years) (Bratislava: Slvenska Adademie Vied, 1972). (FHL# EUR REF/943.73/E2m or microfilm 1181569, item 1). This work is particularly valuable for solving problems caused by villages with names in several languages. The index lists localities in Slovak, Czech, Hungarian, German, Russian, Polish, and obsolete Slovak. It can be useful, when used with the Hungarian gazetteer of 1877, in finding the Hungarian version of a Slovakian place name. Again, see Schlyter's book for instructions on its use.

The library has various other gazetteers concerning Czechoslovakia. These can be useful in explaining the origin of a given place name.

Maps

The military map of the old Austro-Hungarian Empire (FHL# microfilm 1045395) discussed under *Austria* is extremely useful for locating places in Czechoslovakia. However, most of the place names are in German and Hungarian, so it should be used in conjunction with the gazetteers discussed above.

For a modern map of Czechoslovakia, see *Auto Atlas CSSR* (Auto Atlas of the Czechoslovakia Socialist Republic) (Bratislava: Slovenska Kartografia, 1971). (FHL# EUR REF/943.7/E3a). This atlas is reprinted and updated every few years. However, it is copyrighted and cannot be microfilmed.

Emigration and Migration Indexes

While nineteenth-century emigration records of persons from Bohemia are known to exist in Czech archives, none have been microfilmed by the library. However, a substantial percentage of emigrants from what is now Czechoslovakia emigrated through Hamburg. Hence, the Hamburg passenger list indexes should be checked if

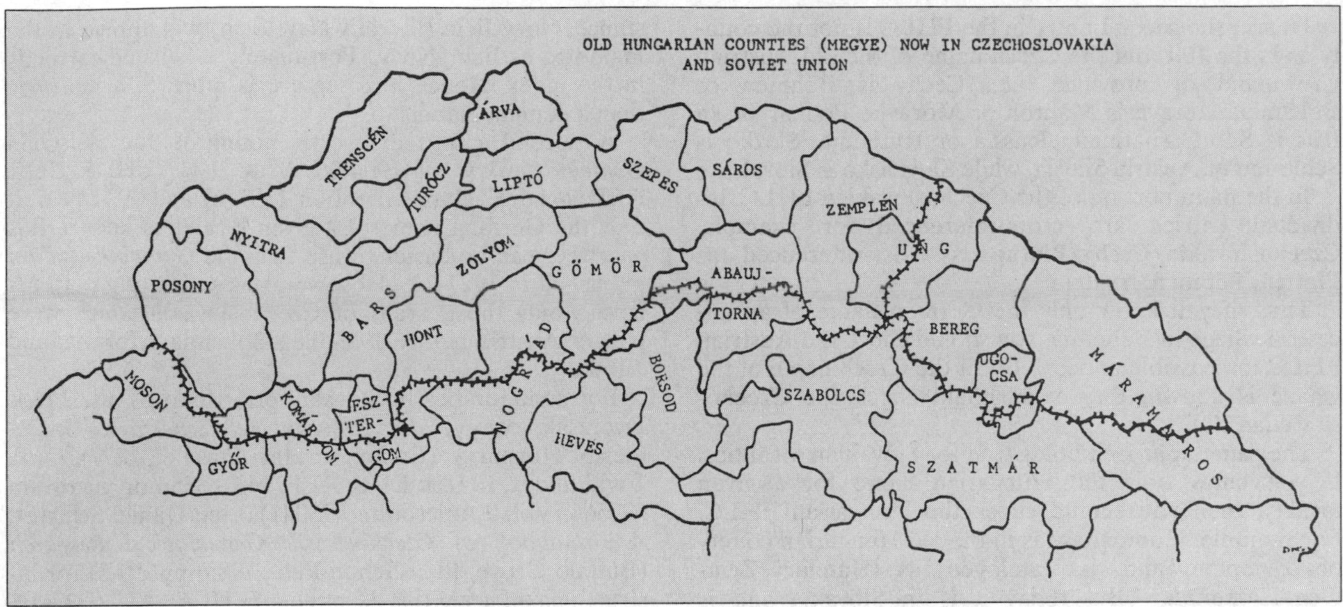

Figure 19:5 Hungarian counties now forming Slovakia and Sub-Carpathian Ruthenia.

the year of emigration is known. Of course, the place of last residence will list a locality as being in Böhmen, Mähren, or Ungarn (the German names of Bohemia, Moravia, or Hungary), and the village names will often be in German or Hungarian. Hence, you must use the gazetteers previously discussed in conjunction with the lists to determine the modern name of the locality.

Other emigration records worth noting are the indexes of settlers in Galicia and the Banat discussed in the Austrian section of this chapter. Many of these people were Germans living in Bohemia and Moravia.

Parish Registers

Czechoslovakia suffered relatively little war damage during World War II. Hence, most church records survived. However, the Czech government has not yet granted the Family History Department permission to film them, so the only parish records available on microfilm are those filmed by the *Reichssippenamt* in 1940-41. These records were recently obtained from the Central Genealogical Archive of the German Democratic Republic in Leipzig. Almost without exception, these registers concern overwhelmingly German parishes in the Sudetenland, the mostly German-speaking border region annexed by the Germans in 1938.

Civil Registers

The library has virtually no civil registers from Czechoslovakia.

Military Records

Since Czechoslovakia belonged to the old Austro-Hungarian Empire, microfilms of the military records from the *Kriegsarchiv* in Vienna contain a great deal of data on officers and enlisted men of Czech or Slovak ethnic stock. As indicated in the section on *Austria*, you must know in which regiment an enlisted man served, as there is no central index.

However, the records of the Vienna Conscription Office have been alphabetized. Turn-of-the-century Vienna acted as a magnet for young men from all over the empire, including many from Bohemia and Moravia.

The Czechoslovakian Archives have not yet given the Family History Department permission to microfilm; consequently, the library has virtually no military records from Bohemia, Moravia, and former Austrian Silesia. However, it does have films of some nineteenth-century muster rolls from Slovakia.

As Slovakia was part of Hungary prior to 1918, these records were stored in Hungarian Archives and were filmed by the library in the 1960s. They are cataloged according to the individual locality–for example, under **Czechoslovakia/Slovensko/Humenne/Military Records.** These military records are an extremely important genealogical source. See the discussion on *Military Records* under *Hungary*, below.

Census Records

The first nominative census in the Czech lands was made in 1651. Various enumerations were made in the following century, usually for military purposes. Although the 1651 census returns are still extant in the Czech Archives, most of the others have been lost. In any event, none are available at the library except the 1770 Census of Staré Mesto Prahka (the old town of Prague) (FHL# 943.71/P3 or microfilm 873665).

In Slovakia, which was part of the kingdom of Hungary, censuses were enumerated according to Hungarian law. The library microfilmed some of the nineteenth-century Hungarian enumerations in the 1960s.

The first of these was the 1828 Hungarian census. This was a land and property census, plus conscription information. The library has returns from virtually all the counties which later became Slovakia and Sub-Carpathian Ruthenia. It is written in Latin and lists only the names of property owners. Film numbers for the various counties are listed in the FHLC under **Czechoslovakia/Census**. The records are arranged by counties and, within the counties, by localities in alphabetical order on 319 reels, only part of which are Slovakian. Hence, you must know which Hungarian counties now form Slovakia and Sub-Carpathian Ruthenia. (See map in Figure 19:5).

The next important census was the 1848 enumeration of the Jews. Returns from the following counties are available: Esztergom, Györ, Komárom, Máramoros, Moson, Trencsen, Turoc and Ung. For the film numbers, check under **Hungary/Census**. This particular census is *not* cataloged under **Czechoslovakia/Census**.

Larger cities and towns in Slovakia were enumerated separately from the counties. Incomplete returns for the following Slovakian towns are available on FHL# microfilm 719823: Eperjes (now Presov), Modor (now Modra), Nagy-Szombat (now Trnava), Szakolcza (now Skalica), and Trenscen (now Trencin). Since this census lists all the members of the family, age, exact place of birth, number of years resided in Hungary, occupation and behavior, it is an extremely valuable genealogical source. For a detailed explanation of its entries, see Schlyter's book, cited above, pp. 85-87.

The next census took place in 1857. Unfortunately, the only Slovakian returns which have been microfilmed are a few towns in the old Hungarian county of Esztergom. This census is cataloged under **Czechoslovakia/Slovensko/Census** on three reels. This census enumerated entire households, lists birth dates and sometimes place of origin. It is written in German and Hungarian.

The last Hungarian census available in the FHLC's collection is that of 1869. It contains considerable information on all the members of a household, including birth dates and birth places. For Slovakia, returns are available for the former Hungarian counties of Zemplen and part of Esztergom on five reels while the returns from Zemplen total 169 reels, most of which concern localities in Slovakia. It is cataloged under **Czechoslovakia/Slovensko/Census**. The places are listed alphabetically according to the original Hungarian place name with the modern Hungarian place name in parenthesis. The modern Slovakian names are in the right hand column. Hence, the first entry is Abara, now Oborin, Slovakia (Slovensko). (See Figure 19:6).

The column headings of this census are in Hungarian and sometimes in Serbo-Croatian or German. See Schlyter, pp. 117-18 for a translation of the headings.

Obviously, this is a major source for anyone who has ancestors from Zemplen county.

Tax Lists

Tax lists were first compiled in 1654 with later enumerations in 1684, 1746, 1757, and 1792. These list only heads of families who owned taxable property or had a trade. The Czechs have published thirty-three volumes of these lists (FHL# 943.7/B4b). They are cataloged under **Czechoslovakia/Land and Property**.

Family Histories

Check the Surname FHLC and the Locality FHLC under **Czechoslovakia/Genealogy**.

Periodicals

The library has a few periodicals pertaining to Czechoslovakia, some of them in German by Sudeten Germans who were expelled from Czechoslovakia in 1945. See **Czechoslovakia/Periodicals**.

Local Histories

The library has a modest collection of local histories. Most of these are Czech with some in German. They are cataloged under the name of the locality.

Jewish Records

Most of the Jewish records of Slovakia are in the State Archive at Bratislava, while those of Moravia, Bohemia, and Silesia were deposited in Prague. As with other records in the Czech archives, they have not been microfilmed. Hence, the only Jewish records currently in the collection are a few local records in Slovakia plus the 1848 Jewish census previously discussed.

Directories

The library has a few business and occupational directories, plus various local directories. See **Czechoslovakia/Directories** as well as under the individual locality.

Archives and Libraries

Of great interest to the genealogist are the directories or inventories of the various regional archives. Among the items listed are the parish registers and the year a particular parish began keeping records. They are cataloged under **Czechoslovakia/Archives and Libraries/-Inventories, Registers, Catalogs.**

Nobility

See Chapter 28, "Medieval Families."

Miscellaneous Records

The library has a few records and secondary sources

```
*************************************************************************************
CZECHOSLOVAKIA, SLOVENSKO - CENSUS
                                                                  +-------------+
Magyar Statisztikai Hivatal.                                      :EUROPE       :
    Népszámlálás, 1869. -- Salt Lake City : Filmre vette a        :FILM AREA    :
      Genealogical Society of Utah, 1970. -- 171 mikrofilmtekercs ; +-------------+
      35 mm.

    Az eredeti iratok mikrofilmrevétele Budapesten a Magyar Országos
       Levéltárban történt.
    1869 census of Zemplén County, Hungary, which is divided now between
       Czechoslovakia and Hungary. Places are listed here alphabetically
       according to the original Hungarian place name. Modern Hungarian
       names are in parenthesis. Modern Czech names are in the right hand
       column.

       Abara                  Oborín ---------------------------------- 0722666
       Agárd (Zemplénagárd) -------------------------------------------- 0722667
       Agyagos                Hlinné ---------------------------------- 0722668
       Agyidócz               Adidovce
       Alsóbereczki
       Alsócsebinye           Nižnie Čabiny
       Alsógolop
       Alsórahócz             Nižní Hraboves ------------------------- 0722669
       Alsójablonka           Nižná Jablonka
       Alsókörtvélyes         Nižny Hrusov
       Alsóolsva              Nižná Ol'šava -------------------------- 0722670
       Alsóregmec
       Alsósitnyicze          Nižná Sitnica
       Aranyospatak           Zlatník
       Arbonyazsadány (Sárazsadány)
       Ardó (Végardó) -------------------------------------------------- 0722671
       Bacska                 Bačka
       Bacskó                 Bačkov
       Barancs                Baranč ---------------------------------- 0722672
       Barkó                  Brekov
       Baskócz                Baškovce
       Bánócz                 Bánovce nad Ondavou
       Bánszka                Banské ---------------------------------- 0722673
       Bekecs
       Berető                 Bracovce -------------------------------- 0722674
       Berzék
       Bély                   Biel'
       Biste                  Byšta ----------------------------------- 0722675
       Bodrogkeresztúr
       Bodrogkisfalud (Bodrogszegi) ------------------------------------ 0722676
       Bodrogolaszi
       Bodrogsára (Sárazsadány) ---------------------------------------- 0722677
       Bodrogszerdahely       Streda nad Bodrogom
```

Figure 19:6 Czechoslovakia, Slovensko – Census entry in the Family History Library Catalog showing the original Hungarian place name with modern Hungarian names in parenthesis and modern Slovakian names in the right hand column.

which do not fit any of the categories described here. Check the individual locality.

Genealogical Research by Correspondence

Because the library's Czechoslovakian collection is still minimal, it is fortunate that Czechoslovakia is one of the easiest countries in the world from which to obtain information by correspondence.

American researchers should submit requests in English to Embassy of the Czechoslovak Socialist Republic, Consular Division, 3900 Linnean Avenue, N.W., Washington, DC 20008. The embassy then transmits these requests to the appropriate regional archive in Czechoslovakia where qualified researchers perform the actual research. Their reports are then sent to the embassy which informs the applicant of the balance due, receives payment, and transmits the report.

Canadian residents should write to Consulate of the Czechoslovakia Socialist Republic, 1305 Pine Avenue, Montreal, Canada H3G 1B2. Persons living outside the USA and Canada should apply directly to the Archival

APPLICATION FOR GENEALOGICAL RESEARCH IN THE FORM OF RUNNING ACCOUNT

ŽÁDOST O VYHLEDÁNÍ NAVAZUJÍCÍCH
GENEALOGICKÝCH INFORMACÍ OBSAHUJÍCÍCH PLNE VÝPISY Z MATRIK

Reference/file number of any previous correspondence with Czechoslovakia Embassy: ___________

1. Name and address of applicant: ___________

2. Name of person to be researched: ___________

Date of birth: ___________

Place of birth (specific town or village): ___________

Further identify the birthplace with the name of the county, the parish or a larger town nearby: ___________

Name of father: ___________

Maiden name of mother: ___________

Religion: ___________

• The most important items are name, date, and place. The date can be a close approximation.

3. Other information available about the person (such as date and place of death, if the death occurred in Czechoslovakia): ___________

4. Relatives of the person being researched. (This is optional but often very helpful.)

a) Husband or Wife

Name: Date of birth: Place:
Date of marriage: Place:

b) Children

Name: Date of birth: Place:

c) Brothers and Sisters

Name: Date of birth: Place:

5. Sources:

□ Please provide birth dates of all brothers and sisters of direct-line ancestors.
Prosím, vyhledejte též narození všech sourozenců přímých předků.

□ Please research direct-line ancestors only.
Prosím, vyhledejte pouze předky přímých linek.

Deposit: $___________ Limit (if any): $___________ Date: ___________

Additional Comments:

Figure 19:7 Application for Genealogical Research Running Account with the Embassy of the Czechoslovak Socialist Republic.

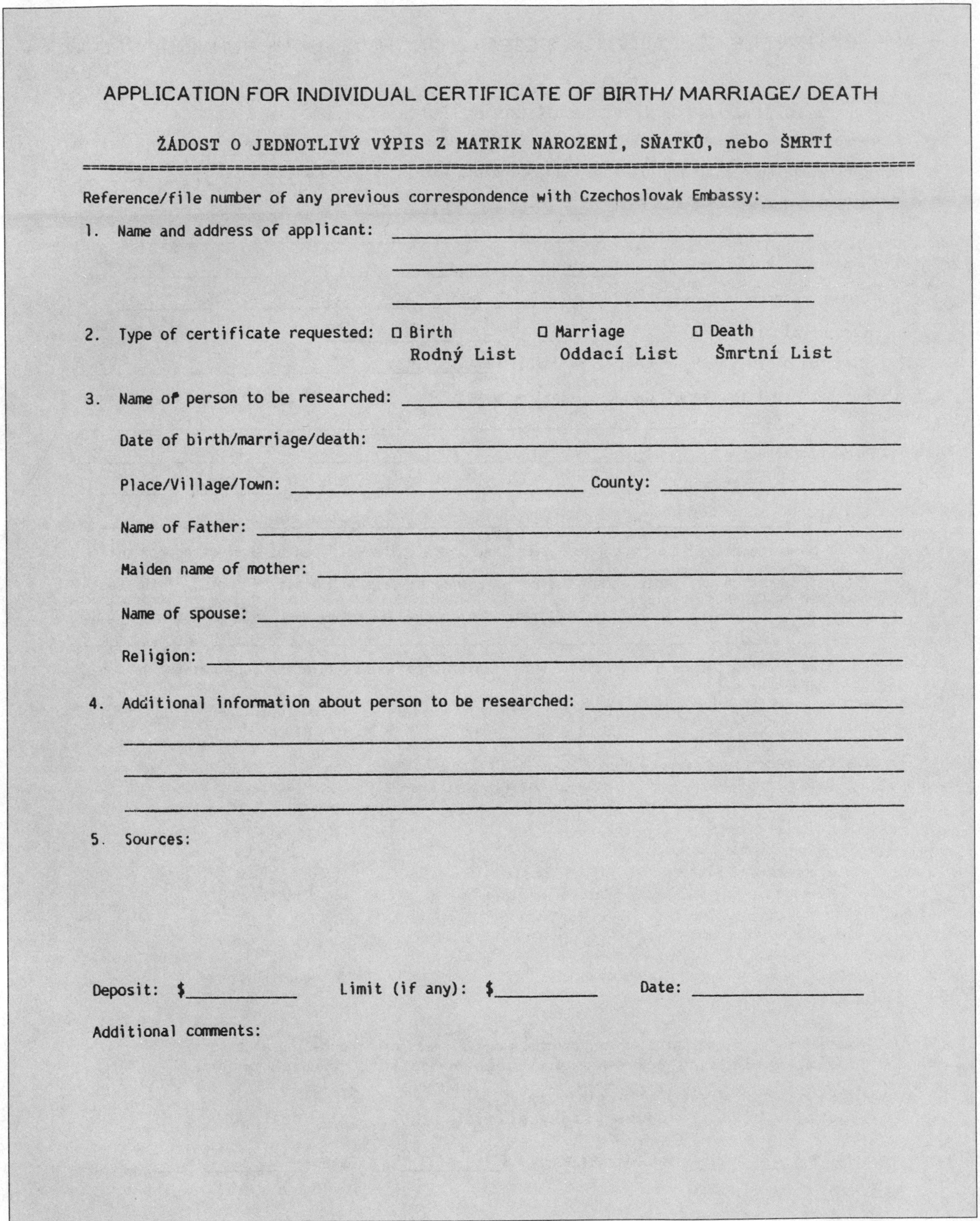

APPLICATION FOR INDIVIDUAL CERTIFICATE OF BIRTH/ MARRIAGE/ DEATH

ŽÁDOST O JEDNOTLIVÝ VÝPIS Z MATRIK NAROZENÍ, SŇATKŮ, nebo ŠMRTÍ

Reference/file number of any previous correspondence with Czechoslovak Embassy: ____________

1. Name and address of applicant: ____________________

____

____

2. Type of certificate requested: ☐ Birth Rodný List ☐ Marriage Oddací List ☐ Death Šmrtní List

3. Name of person to be researched: ____________________

Date of birth/marriage/death: ____________________

Place/Village/Town: ____________ County: ____________

Name of Father: ____________________

Maiden name of mother: ____________________

Name of spouse: ____________________

Religion: ____________________

4. Additional information about person to be researched: ____________

____

____

____

5. Sources:

Deposit: $__________ Limit (if any): $__________ Date: ____________

Additional comments:

Figure 19:8 Application for Individual Certificate of Birth/Marriage/Death from the Embassy of the Czechoslovak Socialist Republic.

Administration of Prague: Archivní Správa, 160 00 Praha 6, Tr. Obrancu miru 133, Czechoslovakia.

The Czech archives cannot begin research without certain basic information. You must provide the name and at least an approximate birth date of the immigrant ancestor. If the ancestor was married before he or she emigrated, it may be possible to begin with the marriage date. *You must give the specific place where the birth or marriage occurred because these records are kept at the local level.* If you do not, your application will be returned to you.

The Czechoslovak Archival Administration provides two types of research reports:

1. Individual birth, marriage, and death certificates written in Czech or Slovak on the forms currently used in Czechoslovakia to record such data. These documents are usually easier to read than the running accounts described below, but they often contain less information. The fee is usually $6 per certificate but may be higher if the research proves difficult or if you provided inaccurate or incomplete information. This type of research is not recommended for extended ancestral research.

2. Genealogical research in the form of a running account from the original registers. The extracted information is usually given in the original language (German, Latin, Hungarian, Czech, or Slovak); but sometimes all information is given in Czech or Slovak. The commentary is given in Czech or Slovak. The fee for research is based upon the time spent at the rate of $12 per hour (subject to change). Photocopies of actual documents cannot be provided.

The chief advantage of the "running account" is that it provides a family history rather than just a list of names. Interesting details such as the house number where a child was born sometimes make it possible to visit the ancestral village and determine which house the family actually lived in. The disadvantage of this format is that sometimes the reports are long and involved and thus confusing to someone unfamiliar with the Czech or Slovak language. But on balance, the advantages of the running account format far outweigh the disadvantages for someone truly interested in family history. For a more complete discussion of the nuances involved in pursuing research in Czechoslovakia by correspondence, see Schlyter, pp. 65-77. Figures 19:7 and 19:8 are samples of the application forms preferred by the Czech Embassy. Simply photocopy the page, fill out the form in duplicate, and send the appropriate fee.

HUNGARY

Historical Background

Late 800s Magyar tribes led by Arpad sweep into the Danube Basin from the east, thus permanently splitting the South Slavs from the other Slavic tribes.

955 Holy Roman Emperor Otto I defeats the Magyars at the Battle of Lechfeld, thus halting their advance into Europe.

975 Arpad's grandson Geza accepts Christianity and begins to organize the Magyar tribes into a unified nation.

1000 Geza's son Istavan (Stephen) makes Roman Catholicism the official religion of his country and invites missionaries from Italy and Germany to propagate the faith. Pope Sylvester II sends him a crown and the title "King of Hungary." He is crowned in the year 1000, according to tradition. After his death, he is sainted.

1241 Devastating invasion by the Mongols kills half the population.

1301 Last member of the Arpad dynasty dies without an heir. Italian House of Anjou succeeds to the throne and rules for next 225 years.

1458-90 Reign of King Mathias. He and his wife Beatrice, Princess of Naples, found Biblioteca Corvina and brings the cultural influence of the Italian Renaissance to Hungary.

Post-1490 Decline of monarchy and rise of the Diet.

1514 Peasant uprising put down by the landlords.

1526 Total defeat of the Hungarians by the Turks at the Battle of Mohacs. King Louis II killed. Crown passes to the Habsburgs until 1918.

1567 Synod at Debrecen adopts a Calvinist confession of faith drafted by Matyas Biro and Peter Melius. Calvinism subsequently becomes an important, though minority, faith in Hungary.

1526-1686 Turkish rule. Central Hungary falls under direct Turkish rule. Eastern Hungary (Transylvania) becomes a Turkish protectorate, which gradually acquires a certain degree of independence. Habsburg control reduced to a long narrow strip on the extreme western and northern edge of the country.

1683 Turks fail to take Vienna. A long period of Turkish decline and retreat begins.

1703-07 Rakoczy rebellion against the Habsburgs results in creation of a temporary republic of Hungary.

1710 Rakoczy defeated and exiled; return of Habsburgs. Hungarian nobility runs internal affairs, thus laying the basis for later Austro-Hungarian dualism.

1718-87 Charles VI, Maria Theresia, and Joseph II encourage mass settlement of Swabian Germans and other non-Magyar peoples in the area of South Hungary left depopulated by the Turks, especially the Banat region.

1740-45	War of Austrian Succession. Hungarian Diet supports Maria Theresia in return for her promise to support the Hungarian Constitution.
1758	Maria Theresia's conciliatory policy toward Hungary results in her assuming the title of Apostolic King of Hungary with papal permission.
1772	György Bessenyci publishes a book in Magyar; first literary use of the language for more than a century. Marks beginning of the Hungarian cultural revival.
1780-90	Joseph II institutes radical changes in the empire, including peasant emancipation in Hungary in 1785.
1790	Opposition by Hungarian nobility forces Joseph to revoke all his reforms in Hungary except the Toleration Patent and the Emancipation of the Serfs.
1790-92	Emperor Leopold pacifies empire without making too many concessions.
1789-1815	French Revolution and Napoleonic Wars.
1815	Congress of Vienna confirms Habsburg supremacy in Central Europe.
1840	Hungarian cultural nationalism revives under Count Stephen Szechenyi.
1848-49	Hungarian Revolution under Louis Kossuth against the Austrians.
1849	Austrians aided by the Russians subdue the Hungarians. Habsburgs reassert control.
1867	Austria weakened by successive military defeats, grants Hungary equal status: Austro-Hungarian Empire.
1878-1913	Two million leave Hungary, mostly for the USA. About 600,000-700,000 were ethnic Hungarians, the rest Slovakians, Ruthenians, Croatians, etc.
1880-1914	Policy of magyarization of Slavs results in growing discontent.
1914-18	World War I. Austro-Hungarian Empire defeated and dissolved.
1919	Short-lived communist regime of Bela Kun suppressed and Admiral Miklos Horthy establishes himself as regent.
1920	Treaty of Trianon reallocates two-thirds of Hungary's land and two-fifths of its population to Austria, Czechoslovakia, Romania, and Yugoslavia.
1940	Hungary allies itself with Nazi Germany and regains part of Slovakia and northern Transylvania.
1941	Hungary enters World War II on the German side.
1944	Horthy government ousted by the Nazis. 500,000 Hungarian Jews sent to concentration camps.
1945	Russian army invasion. Hungarian Republic proclaimed in April.
1946-48	250,000 ethnic Germans expelled from Hungary.
1949	Communists take power under Mathias Rakosi.
1956	Hungarian Revolution suppressed by Soviet tanks. 200,000 Hungarians flee to the West.
Post-1956	Kadar government improves political and economic conditions considerably.

Hungary Library Collection

Of the three successor states to the Austro-Hungarian Empire under discussion, Hungary has been the most cooperative with the Genealogical Department. Hence, the Hungarian collection is much more substantial than that of Austria or Czechoslovakia.

In discussing the organization of the collection, it seems best to begin with the Hungarian IGI. It is not organized to coincide with the boundaries of present-day Hungary but rather with the boundaries of the old, pre-1918 kingdom of Hungary. Hence, entries from areas such as Slovakia, Ruthenia, and Transylvania, which no longer lie within the boundaries of Hungary, appear in the Hungarian IGI.

The county equivalent for such entries is the old Hungarian county or *megye.* To distinguish these historical Hungarian counties from current Hungarian counties, the word *megye* is added in the entry. Hence, an entry from the old country of Maramoros, which now lies partly in the Soviet Union and partly in Rumania, is listed as **Maramoros Megye/Raho**. A county which still exists in contemporary Hungary would not have the *megye* designation – for example, **Heves/Detk/Katholisch** means the entry was in the county of Heves, town of Detk, Catholic parish.

There is a certain amount of overlapping in the IGI. For instance, the old county of Torontal was ceded to Yugoslavia after World War I. Hence, strictly speaking, entries should be in the Yugoslavian IGI. However, one finds entries such as **Torontal Megye/Franzfeld** in the Hungarian IGI. A similar situation occurs in the Austrian state of Burgenland which belonged to Hungary until 1920. So for such areas, it is always best to check all pertinent sections of the IGI, i.e., Hungary, Yugoslavia, Austria, Romania.

The Hungarian FHLC is organized along similar lines, that is, according to the historical counties as they existed before 1918. However, the word *megye* is not used to distinguish the historical counties from modern ones. Usually a given entry will list the various names by which a community was known as well as its present-day jurisdiction. For instance, under **Hungary/Krasso-szoreny/Resicabanya/Church Records**, you will learn that the town was also called Reschitza in German and is now Resita, Caras-Severin, Romania.

At the very beginning of the Locality FHLC is an alphabetical listing of the major towns and villages, i.e., those which were large enough to be parish villages with appropriate cross-references. For instance, Reschitza, Hungary, is cross-referenced to **Hungary/Banat/Reschitza,** and **Hungary/Krasso-szoreny/Resicabanya.**

The Banat was not an old Hungarian county but a geographical region settled by Swabian Germans in the eighteenth century. Most of the Banat now lies in Yugoslavia and Romania. Because the area was so heavily German prior to World War II, the German parishes are cataloged under **Hungary/Banat** and the German name of the village. However, cross-references indicate the Hungarian, Serbian, or Romanian name of the village and its current political jurisdiction.

In Hungary, as with all the countries under discussion, most of the pertinent records are arranged by locality. Hence, you must determine the exact place name. The gazetteer used by the library to catalog the Hungarian collection is Janos Dvorzsak, comp., *Magyaroszag Helységnévtára* (Gazetteer of Hungary) (Budapest: Havi Fuzetek, 1877) (Vol. 1, FHL# EUR REF/943.9/E5d or microfilm 599564; Vol. 2 , microfilm 973041). This gazetteer is also part of the Family History Center's (Branch Library's) Core Collection microfiche 6000840.

It is written in Hungarian and German. Precise instructions for its use are given in English at the beginning of Volume 1. This gazetteer includes all localities of the former kingdom of Hungary prior to 1918. Its chief disadvantage is that all place names are listed in Hungarian or German. Hence, to find the Slovakian name of a given village, use this gazetteer with the Czechoslovakian *Gemeindelexikon* of 1928 discussed in the previous section.

For those with a reading knowledge of German, the Raffelsperger gazetteer of 1845-53 discussed in the Austrian section is somewhat easier to use than the Dvorzsak volume in that it lists all localities in the empire alphabetically with a capsule history of the larger communities. But it is not as comprehensive in its listing of tiny hamlets.

Researchers knowing only English can use *Hungary: Official Standard Names Approved by the U.S. Board on Geographic Names* (Washington, D.C.: Office of Geography, Department of the Interior, 1961). (FHL# EUR REF/943.9/E5U or microfilm 874461). Unfortunately, this gazetteer lists only localities in present-day Hungary.

The collection also contains several other gazetteers which may be useful in certain situations.

Maps

The best series of maps for Hungary are those of the Austro-Hungarian Empire discussed under Austria (FHL# microfilm 1045395). In addition, the collection has individual maps of several old Hungarian counties on FHL# microfilm 1181575, item 2. For modern-day Hungary, see *Auto Atlas* (Budapest: Kartographia, 1975). (FHL# 943.9/E7a/1975).

Emigration and Migration

As with all the countries of Central Europe, the Hamburg passenger lists are a major tool for determining the last place of residence of emigrants from Hungary. See the discussion under Germany. In general, the place names used will correspond with those listed in the Dvorzsak gazetteer of 1877.

After 1897, the New York City passenger arrival lists are indexed and provide an equally valuable source for determining the village of origin. An excellent index to the Germans who settled in the Banat and other regions of Hungary c.1686-1830 are the *Ansiedlerakten* (settlers' documents) discussed under *Austria.* The collection also contains a number of secondary studies written in German concerning this migration. Many of them list emigrants from a given locality or region.

Relatively few treatments of the Hungarian emigration to North America in the late nineteenth and early twentieth centuries exist. An extremely interesting study translated into English is Julianna Puska's *From Hungary to the United States (1880-1914)* (Budapest: Akademiai Kiado, 1982). (FHL# 943.9/W2pj). Her study shows that roughly two-thirds of the emigrants from Hungary were non-Hungarians–that is, Slovaks, Ruthenians, Croatians, ethnic Germans, etc. But in addition to sociological statistics, she provides a vivid picture of the hardships many of the immigrants faced in the new land.

Parish Registers

The library has about 8,000 reels of parish registers from Roman Catholic, Greek Orthodox, Reformed Evangelical Lutheran, Jewish, and smaller denominations. The time span of these records is usually 1700-1895, when civil registration began. However, a few parish registers date from the seventeenth century. The earliest Reformed parish register begins in 1624 in the parish of Kiskomarom as does the Evangelical Lutheran parish of Sopron, while the earliest Roman Catholic record dates from 1633 in the parish of Koszeg. Jewish records start in the nineteenth century.

Some of the parish registers are in fact transcripts, notably from the Burgenland which is now part of Austria. The Hungarian authorities began requiring pastors to send in transcripts in 1827. Hence, these Burgenland registers generally cover 1827 or 1828-95, when civil registration began.

While most of the filmed parish registers in the Hungarian collection come from present-day Hungary, there are some from areas now in Austria, Yugoslavia, or Romania. Many German parish records from the Banat or Transylvania were placed in German archives following World War II, where they were later microfilmed.

Roman Catholic records for Hungarian parishes are generally written in Latin. Those from Hungarian Reformed churches are in Hungarian; parish records in ethnic German areas are generally written in German. Early Jewish records are in German, but later ones are usually in Hungarian.

Most estimates hold that better than 90 percent of the parish registers in present-day Hungary are available on film. In those areas of the historical kingdom of Hungary now in other countries, the holdings are fragmentary. Virtually no parish registers are available from Ruthenia, now part of the Soviet Union.

The same situation holds true for Slovakia. A higher percentage are available from Transylvania, the Banat, and Burgenland, although these are largely German in content.

Civil Registers

Although Hungary began civil registration of vital statistics in 1895, it has not yet permitted the library to film them. The one exception is the Burgenland of Austria under Hungarian control until 1920. Hence, state copies of the registers are housed in the Hungarian State Archives where they were microfilmed.

Census Records

As discussed in the section on Czechoslovakia, parts of at least four different nineteenth-century census enumerations made in Hungary have survived and are available on microfilm:

1. 1828 land and property census. This census was written in Latin and lists only the names of land owners (less than 20 percent of the population). The library has returns for most of the historical kingdom of Hungary including Croatia and Slovakia, but not Transylvania. It is cataloged under **Hungary/Census**. The records are arranged by county and, within counties, by localities in alphabetical order (319 reels).

2. 1848 census of the Jews. This census, written in Hungarian, gives the age of all the members of the household and the specific birth place. As many of those enumerated have moved in from different localities, this information can be extremely useful in extending a line. This census is cataloged under **Hungary/Census Conscriptio Judaeorum 1848.** Returns for individual cities are listed first, followed by the counties. For translations of the columnar headings, see Schlyter, pp. 86-87.

3. 1857 Hungarian census. This was a census of complete households which indicated all members of the household and the relationship to the head. It also lists birth dates, religion, and sometimes place of origin. There are two types of printed forms, one with headings in German and Hungarian, and one with headings in German only.

Returns of this census are currently available from parts of the old Hungarian counties of Csanad, Györ, Esztergom, Sopron, Tolna, Vas, and Zala. The returns from Sopron County are largely from villages now located in Burgenland, Austria. It is cataloged under the individual counties–for example, **Hungary/Esztergom/Census.** Since the library has returns for only two towns in Zala County, they are cataloged under the town, i.e., **Hungary/Zala/Csapi/Census** and **Hungary/Zala/-Ujlak/Census.**

For a translation of the headings, see Daniel Schlyter, *Hungarian Census Returns* (Salt Lake City: Family History Library, 1981). (FHL# 943.9/X27s). This book is also part of the Family History Center (Branch Library) Microfiche Project, microfiche 6000384.

4. 1869 Hungarian census. This census contains information on all members of a household including birth dates and birth places. At present the library has 169 reels from Zemplan County (now mostly in Czechoslovakia) plus fragmentary returns from Estergom, Hajdu, Semogy, and Vas counties. They are cataloged under the individual counties. See the discussion of this census under *Census Returns* in the Czechoslovakia section.

Military Records

The records in the war archive in Vienna concerned units in all parts of the empire. Hence, they contain a great deal of genealogical data on individual soldiers and officers from Hungary. But the problem of accessibility remains. Only the officers' records are alphabetically indexed. Of course, if an ancestor migrated to Vienna, the Vienna Conscription Office records, which are alphabetically indexed, might contain an entry for him.

But in addition to the records from Vienna, the Hungarian collection contains a large number of films of muster rolls compiled by local military districts and stored in regional archives where they were microfilmed. Most of these records date from the nineteenth century, although in some counties they begin as early as 1784, and extend up to 1917. The most complete set is for the city of Budapest itself (1825-1918). They are alphabetically indexed for 1914-18.

They have not survived (or at any rate have not yet been microfilmed) for many counties. For most counties, they are not complete. A typical example is the military district of Homonna in Zemplen County, now part of Czechoslovakia. In this case, the muster rolls have survived for 1873-88, covering the birth years 1853-68. In other words, a young man reported to the conscription office when he was twenty years old. The records are thus arranged by birth year and note such data as name, year of birth, current place of residence, place of birth, name of father, etc.

The genealogical value of such a record becomes apparent if one considers that very often an immigrant would list his ancestral county as his place of birth on his naturalization papers. Given a situation where all you knew was a year of birth and Zemplen County, you might be able to determine the place of birth by searching the muster rolls of the six military districts of Zemplen County for the year he turned twenty. This would involve reading parts of six reels of microfilm as opposed to the 169 reels of the 1869 census returns.

Nobility Records

In addition to the discussion of Hungarian nobility contained in Chapter 28, you should be aware of the extensive records concerning the Hungarian nobility available in the library dating from the seventeenth and eighteenth centuries. They are usually written in Latin and contain patents of nobility, lawsuits to prove nobility, etc. Contents generally include names of the members of the family, place of residence, and the year the family was ennobled. They are arranged by county–for example, **Hungary/Fejer/Nobility.** Within each county they are arranged alphabetically by family.

It should be emphasized that these records are not limited to the higher nobility but also deal with the Hungarian equivalent of English gentry.

Jewish Records

See the discussion of the 1848 Jewish census in *Parish Registers* above.

Directories

As in the other Central European countries, the library has attempted to collect as many city directories as possible, which are cataloged under the locality in question. In addition, the collection contains several occupational directories listing the names of officials and professional people in Hungary from c.1889 to the present. They are cataloged under **Hungary/Directories.**

Archives and Libraries

The collection contains numerous inventories and catalogs of archives in Hungary under **Hungary/Archives and Libraries.** In addition, some archive inventories are cataloged under the regional or county heading.

Genealogical Sources

The library has several important collections of genealogies, primarily of land-owning families. Among the most important are the *Genealogiai tablak* (genealogical charts) which go back to the thirteenth century (53 reels, beginning FHL# microfilm 0722206). This and other collections are cataloged under **Hungary/Genealogy.**

Periodicals

The collection contains a complete set of *A Magyar Heraldikai es Genealogiai Tarsasag Közlönye* (Genealogical and Heraldic Magazine of Hungary) 1883-1950 (Budapest: Magyar Herialdikai es Genealogiai Tarsasag, 1883-1950). (FHL# 943.9/B2t or microfilm 874309-874319), cataloged under **Hungary/Nobility/Periodicals.**

Histories and Encyclopedias

The collection has some books on Hungarian history in English, German, and Hungarian as well as Hungarian encyclopedias. They are cataloged under **Hungary/History.**

Local Histories

Local histories of given communities are cataloged under the locality. The collection has a considerable number of local histories in German describing former German settlements in Hungary as well as local studies in Hungarian. Some of these are of considerable genealogical value.

LDS Records

LDS Church membership records from Hungary covering 1903-14 are found on FHL# microfilm 068727.

Miscellaneous

Other types of records not covered in this survey are available in the collection. They are generally cataloged by locality or county.

Genealogical Research by Correspondence

Except for the areas in Burgenland ceded to Austria after World War I, Hungarian civil registers, which began 1 October 1895, are not available in the library. But certificates of births, marriages, and deaths can be obtained from the Embassy of the Hungarian People's Republic, 3910 Shoemaker Street N.W., Washington, D.C. 20008 for $3 per certificate. Allow two to three months processing time.

Bibliography

A useful discussion of Hungarian genealogical recors available in the library is Suess, Jared H., *Handy Guide to Hungarian Genealogical Records* (Logan, Utah: Everton Publishers, 1980). (FHL# 943.9/D27s).

SWITZERLAND

Historical Background

58 B.C.	Caesar defeats the Helvetii at Bibracte; Roman rule begins.
A.D. c.260	The Germanic Alemanni destroy the city of Aventicum.
c.500	Alemannian settlement begins, the shadow of Frankish power.
c.600	The Christian mission of St. Columbanus and the monks of St. Gall.
800	Charlemagne, king of the Franks, crowned in Rome by Pope Leo III; Switzerland comes under the jurisdiction of the Holy Roman Empire.
c.1200	St. Gottard Pass opened; alpine valleys link the trade routes.
1231	The community of Uri wins important privilege of direct rule by the empire rather than Habsburgs.
1240	Similar status for Schwyz.

1273	Rudolf of Habsburg becomes emperor. Secret alliance between Uri, Schwyz, and Nidwalden.
1291	Death of Rudolf. Uri, Schwyz, Nidwalden (and later Obwalden) conclude their Everlasting Alliance founding the Swiss Confederation.
1315	At Battle of Morgarten Swiss defeat Habsburgs and renew their alliance in the Agreement of Brunnen.
1332	Lucerne joins the confederation.
1339	Berne and the confederates victorious at the Battle of Laupen.
1351	Zürich joins the confederation.
1352	Glarus and Zug also join.
1353	Berne joins.
1386	Battle of Sempach ends in Swiss victory.
1388	Glarus triumphs in the Battle of Näfels.
1393	Covenant of Sempach creates a confederate military agreement. From 1414 Council of Constance meets to deal with Church schism. Confederation expands in north and south, occupying Aargau and Ticino areas.
1436-50	Civil war against Zürich, aided by Austrians and French mercenaries. Confederates win decisive Battle of St. Jakob an der Birs (1444).
1460	Further expansion. Austrians driven out of Thurgau. University founded at Basel.
1476	War against Burgundy. Swiss defeat Charles the Bold at Grandson and Morat.
1481	Covenant of Stans resolves postwar disputes between town cantons and rural cantons. The intervention of Niklaus von Flue results. Fribourg and Solothurn joining the confederation.
1489	Hans Waldmann, burgomaster and dictator of Zürich, arrested, condemned, and executed.
1499	Swabian War. Swiss have de facto independence from the empire.
1501	Basel and Schaffhausen join the confederation.
1513	Appenzell joins creating the Confederation of Thirteen Cantons.
1500-16	Milanese campaigns: victory at Novara (1513), defeat at Marignan (1515), the beginning of neutrality.
1519	Ulrich Zwingli in Zürich; start of the Swiss reformation.
1531	War with the Catholic cantons. Zürich defeated; Zwingli killed.
1536	Calvin in Geneva.
1545-63	Council of Trent; Counter-reformation begins.
1618-48	Thirty Years War. Peace of Westphalia gives legal recognition to Switzerland's independence.
1653	Peasant rising in Switzerland; leaders executed.
1663	Mercenary service agreement with France.
1712	Peace of Aarau resolves further religious conflict.
1749	Rebellion in Bern; rebel leader, Samuel Henzi, executed.
1761	Foundation of the Helvetic Society, dedicated to national regeneration. Members include Johann Heinrich Pestalozzi.
1762	Jean Jacques Rousseau (born Geneva, 1712) publishes *The Social Contract.*
1777	Mercenary agreement with France reaffirmed.
1789	Revolution in France.
1792-93	Massacre of the Swiss Guards in Paris; Louis XVI executed.
1798	The French occupy Vaud, Fribourg, and Solothurn. Berne falls. End of the old confederation.
1798-1803	The Helvetic Republic established.
1803	Napoleon's Mediation Act settles civil strife, establishes Confederation of Nineteen Cantons, including St. Gallen, Aargau, the Grisons, Thurgau, the Ticino, and Vaud.
1815	Napoleon defeated at Waterloo. Congress of Vienna; Geneva, Neuchâtel, and the Valais join Confederation of Twenty-two Cantons. Great powers guarantee Switzerland's territory and recognize its permanent neutrality. Restoration of old practices and reaction excesses of French revolutionary period in Switzerland under Federal Pact of 1814.
1830	July revolution in Paris.
1831	New Liberal constitution in Zürich followed by other cantons.
1841	Religion and politics lead to conflict in Aargau and Lucerne.
1845	Catholic cantons form the Sonderbund.
1847	Civil war between the Confederation and the Catholic Sonderbund.
1848	Revolution in Europe. New federal state organized in Switzerland, with democratic institutions.
1876	Civil registration begins.

Switzerland Library Collection

Switzerland, like the old Habsburg Empire, is a multilingual state, composed of four distinct linguistic groups–German, French, Italian, and Romanish. But there the similarity ends. The Habsburgs were never able to create a true nation out of their polyglot empire. It broke up in 1918 as a result of nationalistic antagonism between its various ethnic groups.

In contrast, Switzerland has forged a true nation, one which has experienced a political stability unique in Central Europe. It has not suffered a major war for 170 years.

This stability reflects itself in the Swiss collection. Unlike the jackdaw's nest of overlapping jurisdictions created by shifting political boundaries characteristic of the rest of Central Europe, the Swiss IGI and FHLC are relatively straightforward.

In the Swiss section of the IGI, Switzerland is the country with the canton serving as the county equivalent followed by the town or parish–for example, Switzerland, Zürich, Kuesnacht. If there is more than one parish by the same name in a given canton, the name of the municipality is added after the canton without any comma between them. Since a substantial number of Swiss joined the LDS Church in the nineteenth century, the Swiss IGI contains many entries.

The same situation holds true for the Family Group Records Collection. Prior to the creation of the IGI, many LDS families of Swiss descent submitted group sheets which are now in the FGRC. Hence, you should check it at the outset of a project.

Unlike most of the countries of Central Europe, the Temple Index Bureau (TIB) collection can be a valuable source for Swiss research. This collection is not open to the public but individuals can request a search of the TIB for a fee of $1 per name.

The Swiss FHLC is organized in a manner similar to the IGI, that is, Switzerland, canton, town or parish. At the very beginning of the Swiss FHLC is an alphabetical list of localities referring the user to the correct entry in the Locality FHLC–for example, **Solgio/Switzerland** is cross-referenced as **Switzerland/Graubunden/Soglio.**

Microfilming has been done canton by canton, and not all cantons have permitted it. To date, the library has filmed records in the following cantons: Appenzell–Ausser Rhoden; Appenzell–Inner Rhoden; Basel–Stadt und Land (city and surrounding area); Geneva; Graubunden; Ura; Luzern; Neuchâtel; St. Gallen; Thurgau; Ticino (Tessin); Uri; Vaud; and Zürich.

In addition, individual cities such as Kussnacht, Canton Schwiez, have permitted filming of their archival holdings.

Thus, the primary source material in the collection comes largely from these cantons. However, the collection has abundant secondary material from many of the cantons which have not yet permitted filming of their archives.

Emigration and Migration

The Hamburg passenger list indexes are not as useful for tracing Swiss immigrants as for other areas of Central Europe. Many eighteenth-century emigrants left via Rotterdam, while those of the nineteenth century left from Le Havre. Many cantons began keeping emigrant registers at the beginning of the nineteenth century, some of which have been indexed. Unfortunately, none of these are yet available in the library collection.

However, the collection does contain a substantial number of secondary works listing emigration from Switzerland to various areas as diverse as Latvia and Brazil. A number deal with emigrants to the USA. They are cataloged under the heading **Switzerland/Emigration and Immigration.**

Atlases and Gazetteers

A major six-volume gazetteer of Switzerland is *Geographisches Lexikon der Schweiz* (Geographical Encyclopedia of Switzerland), (Neuenburg: Gebruder Attinger, 1902-10). (FHL# EUR REF/949.4/E5g or microfilm 599323-599326). This gazetteer is also part of the Family History Center's (Branch Library's) Core Collection microfiche 6053505. As the name and size indicate, this gazetteer contains capsule descriptions of most of the communities in Switzerland.

A more current gazetteer extremely useful for determining the exact location of a general place is *Neue Schweizerisches Ortslexikon* (Gazetteer and Postal Directory for Switzerland) (München: Buches, 1983). (FHL# 949.4/E8s/1983). Earlier editions of this book edited by the late Arthur Jacot are also available in the library. On occasion they may be more helpful than the latest edition. Instructions for use are found in the introduction.

The most current atlas is *Schweiz-Strassenatlas mit Ortsverzeichnis und 35 Stadtplänen* (Switzerland–Road Atlas with Index and 35 City Maps), (Bern: Kümmerly and Frey, 1983) (FHL# EUR REF/949.4/E7s/1980-81). By using this atlas with the *Neue Schweizerisches Ortslexikon* you can usually locate most places in Switzerland.

The library also has several other gazetteers and atlases of Switzerland both on a general and local level.

A rather unique biographical gazetteer is *The Swiss Family Surname Book (Les noms de famille Suisses, Familiennamenbuch der Schweiz, I nomi di famiglia svizzeri)* (Zürich: Polygraphischer Verlag, 1940). (FHL# EUR REF/949.4/D4f or microfilm 441670). This book is part of the Family History Center (Branch Library) Microfiche Project, microfiche 6054507.

This book lists many Swiss family names together with the town or towns in which they originated. The letter "a" following the name of a town indicates the family originated there or lived there prior to 1800. Letter "b" indicates the family first appeared in the town 1800-1900 while "c" means the family moved there after 1901. An "o" after the letter signifies that very few people carried that surname. Precise instructions in English for the use of the book have been inserted prior to the title page in the FHLC's master copy of this book. Obviously this is an exceedingly useful finding aid if the surname in question is not common. It is cataloged under **Switzerland/Names.**

Parish Registers

The earliest-known Swiss baptismal register dates from 26 December 1489 in Pruntrut, Canton Bern. It was kept for only a short time.

In the Protestant areas, especially in cities such as

Zürich and Bern, keeping parish registers began with the Reformation, edicts mandating the keeping of christening records were issued in these cities in the 1520s. In Zürich, Ulrich Zwingli himself ordered them to be kept in 1525 as a means of controlling the Anabaptists. Protestant parishes in the rural areas of Canton Bern began keeping registers c.1540-60. Village churches in other rural areas generally followed suit in the latter half of the sixteenth or at the beginning of the seventeenth centuries.

Catholic record keeping lagged behind the Protestants. The Council of Trent (1545-63) mandated the recording of baptisms and marriages, but inertia at the parish level took years to overcome. The oldest sixteenth-century Catholic register began in 1500 at Beromünster. Generally speaking, Catholic registers began after 1600.

Catholic records were generally written in Latin. Protestant records used German, sometimes German-Swiss, with some Latin influences. As in Germany, the handwriting was in Gothic script or *Fraktur*. For unusual expressions, words, and abbreviations found in Swiss parish registers, see Jared H. Suess, *Handy Guide to Swiss Genealogical Records* (Logan, Utah: Everton Publishers, 1978), pp. 24-25, 64-83. This book, although out of date in regard to the new FHLC cataloging system, is a good survey of the subject.

Recording deaths or burials began much later than baptisms and marriages, often not until the early eighteenth century. By mid-eighteenth century, such records usually stated the age of the deceased (often an approximation). As time passed, record-keepers added more details.

An important addition to the standard birth, marriage, and death registers are the family registers. They resemble the family registers found in Wuerttemberg in that they record on one page a given family followed by their children. Birth, death, and marriage dates are listed, together with the place, if different from the parish in question. On occasion, the parents of the head of the household and his wife are also listed.

A few parishes in Canton Zürich began keeping such registers as early as 1650. More typically they began in the late eighteenth or early nineteenth century. They are a boon to the genealogist when they exist. However, since some of them were compiled much later, they should always be compared against the original entries.

Other types of parish registers include confirmation records and consistory records, which list illegitimate births and sometimes will list the name of the father. Parish registers are cataloged according to the location of the church.

The FHLC's collection includes most of the parish registers in those cantons where they have received permission to microfilm. Filming has not been completed in Jura or Uri. Also, because cantonal boundaries have changed, the collection contains parish registers from cantons such as Aargau which have not permitted filming. So it is best to check the Locality FHLC in all cases.

Population Registers

Population registers *(Bevölkerungsverzeichnisse)* form an extremely important supplement to the parish registers. The government of Zürich decreed in 1634 that pastors should conduct clerical censuses, recording the names and ages of each member of the family. In addition, their degree of religious knowledge was noted.

Since Zürich controlled a larger area than that comprised by the present-day Canton Zürich, these population registers cover parts of Aargau, Appenzell-Ausserhoden, Freiburg, Schaffhausen, St. Gallen, and Thurgau. From 1634 to roughly 1650, these censuses occurred approximately every three years. Many parishes lack records for 1650-70.

In that time period, pastors did not always record the names of the parents of the bride and groom. Thus, these lists which group individuals by families become an indispensable resource for compiling lineages and family histories.

These population registers evolved into the *Haushaltungsrödel* (household census) by the mid-eighteenth century. Further evolution produced the *Bürger Registry* (citizens' register) and, since 1929, the *Familienregister* (family registers) which are now found throughout Switzerland.

The library has filmed many of these population registers and household censuses. Since they were originally taken under church auspices, they are cataloged as church records by locality. A useful index to the population registers is Barbara W. Whiting, comp. *Index to Bevölkerungsverzeichnisse* (Census Records) *of Zürich, Switzerland* (Provo, Utah: Barbara W. Whiting, 1978). (FHL# 949.458/X2w). Despite its title, this index lists many parishes outside the current boundaries of Canton Zürich.

Civil Registers

Civil registration began in Switzerland as a whole on 1 January 1876. The library has not filmed any of these post-1876 records. However, several cantons inaugurated civil registration much earlier. Canton Geneva began keeping civil registers in the eighteenth century, Canton Vaud in 1821, and Canton Basel in 1826. The library has films of these registers up to 1876 (1871 for Basel).

Extracts from later records or from cantons which have not permitted microfilming must be obtained by correspondence with the civil registrar of the community in question.

Notarial Records

In the French- and Italian-speaking areas of Switzerland, notarial records rank as the most important genealogical records after parish and civil registers. Canton Graubünden, which is partly German speaking, also has numerous records of this nature. Notaries made out marriage contracts, property divisions and transfers, testaments, and donations.

The library has films of notarial records from Geneva dating to 1389 and from Graubünden beginning in 1407. Thus, they predate parish registers by almost two centuries in some areas. Notarial records from Ticino and Vaud are also available.

Court Records

Wills, guardianship records, and civil lawsuits all fall under this category. They are cataloged under the appropriate canton and locality.

Municipal Records

In Canton Graubünden, notarial records, court records, minutes of city councils, etc., are all lumped together under the heading **Gemeindeakten** (community documents).

Citizenship Records

A few of these records date from the eleventh century, but most date from the fourteenth century. Many of them have been published in book form, notably for Basel and Baselland and the cities of Bern, Geneva, St. Gallen, Sisach, Thun, Winterthur, Zofingen, and Zürich. Many have been published for smaller cities and towns. See the Locality FHLC.

They can be extraordinarily useful in determining a place of origin, as they usually list the name of the individual obtaining citizenship, the date the event took place, and where the individual came from. After the seventeenth century, they often listed other family data.

Academic Records

The library has published compilations of university matriculation records–for example, for Basel and Geneva. Check the Locality FHLC for published secondary school matriculation records.

Military Records

The library has relatively few military records from Switzerland. A few have been microfilmed on the cantonal level–for example, **/Luzern/Military Records** lists muster rolls from Canton Luzern from 1582-1798.

Genealogical Records

Genealogy has been avidly pursued in Switzerland for centuries. Hence, many published genealogies exist and can be found in the FHLC's collection. See **Switzerland/Genealogy** as well as individual cantons–for example, **/Zürich/Genealogy**. Family histories also appear in the Surname FHLC.

The *German Lineage Book* discussed earlier contains lineages of upper-middle-class Swiss families as well.

Another source worth mentioning is Heinrich Turler, Marcel Godel, and Victor Attinger, *Historische-Biographisches Lexikon der Schweiz* (Historical-Biographical Encyclopedia of Switzerland) (Neuenberg: Victor Attinger, 1921). (FHL# 949.4/D36hb or microfilm 1181541-1181543). This title is part of the Family History Center (Branch Library) Microfiche Project, microfiche 6000184. It contains histories of clans, families, and organizations as well as individual biographies.

Special Collections

Among the many collections of Swiss genealogy available in the library is the Julius Billeter Collection. Billeter was a Swiss genealogist who researched the ancestral lines of many LDS families between 1896-1950.

Opinions differ as to the reliability of Billeter's work. The current consensus among individuals with considerable expertise in Swiss genealogy is that some of Billeter's work was necessarily conjectural. He worked almost exclusively from parish registers. Since seventeenth-century marriage records often did not list the parents of the bride and groom, extending the line was sometimes a matter of choosing between various individuals of the same name and approximately the same age. Inevitably some mistakes were made. Now that the population registers of Canton Zürich and surrounding areas are available for study, the means for correcting some of Billeter's erroneous conjectures are at hand.

Periodicals

The collection contains sets of various Swiss periodicals including *Monatliche Nachrichten Schweizerisher Neuheiten* (Monthly New Bulletin of Switzerland), vols. 1-64. Library has volumes encompassing the years 1750-1813. (FHL# 949.4/B2m or microfilm 1045383-1045389)

Directories and Inventories

For those cantons which the library has not yet microfilmed, archival inventories and directories take on added importance. Those currently in the collection are listed under **Switzerland/Archives and Libraries/Directories**, also **/Inventories.** See also under the individual canton–for example, **Switzerland/Aargau/Archives and Libraries.** Other types of directories can be found under the appropriate locality.

Miscellaneous Records

For record types not specifically mentioned in this survey, see entries under the national, canton, and city headings of the Locality FHLC.

An excellent bibliography of secondary sources, including many periodicals not available in the Family History Library is Martin, Donald J. "Swiss Echos for Genealogists." *Journal of Genealogy.* Vol. 4, No. 3 (March 1979): pp. 12-23. (FHL# 973/B2jg).

LIECHTENSTEIN

Liechtenstein is a tiny principality situated between Austria and Switzerland with a total population of 27,200 in 1984.

The library has filmed the pertinent holdings of the Landesarchiv in Vaduz, the capital. They include parish registers from the seventeenth century to 1977, civil registers from the early eighteenth century, plus court, land, census, and other records of genealogical value.

See the FHLC under *Liechtenstein* for holdings. Liechtenstein is listed as a separate country in the IGI.

BIBLIOGRAPHY

Germany

Arbeitsgemeinschaft ostdeutscher Familienforscher e.v. Herne, ed. *Genealogical Guide to German Ancestors from East Germany and Eastern Europe.* Trans. by Joachim O. R. Nuthack and Adalbert Goertz. Neustadt/Aisch: Degener Verlag, 1984. (FHL# 943.D27gg)

A book of particular interest to a person whose ancestral roots are in those areas of Germany which are now part of Poland and the Soviet Union, or from former German-speaking areas in Central and Eastern Europe.

Hilbig, Frederick Walter. *Bibliography of Research Aids (Maps, Gazetteers, Parish Registers) of Germany and of Neighboring Countries.* Salt Lake City: Genealogical Society of Utah, 1975. (FHL# 943/A3hi)

The subtitle is a bit misleading in that this book lists parish register inventories and directories rather than parish registers as such. Also, it is now somewhat out of date. Nevertheless, it remains useful in that it lists all the parish register inventories in the collection c.1975, together with their call numbers.

Heydenreich, Edward. *Handbuch der Praktischen Genealogie* (Manual of Practical Genealogy). 2 vols. Leipzig: Degener Verlag, 1913. (FHL# 943/D27he/1913)

As Clifford Neal Smith states, "Despite its age and also because of it, this handbook remains without peer. It contains exhaustive bibliographies of the older literature and descriptions of the contents of East German archives, which only recently have become accessible to western genealogists."

Jensen, Larry O. *A Genealogical Handbook of German Research, Volume I.* Rev. ed. Pleasant Grove, Utah: 1978. (FHL# 943/D27j)

This book is part of the Family History Center (Branch Library) Microfiche Project, microfiche 6000366-6000368. This book is easily the best in the field on how to trace a German ancestor and is very closely keyed to the German collection. I highly recommend it for the novice genealogist planning a visit to the library.

Minerva-Handbücher Archiv: Archiv im deutschsprachigen Raum (Minerva-Handbook of Archival holdings in German-speaking Areas). 2 Aufl. Berlin: Walter de Gruyter, 1974. (FHL# 943/A5m/1974)

A useful guidebook to archival holdings for East and West Germany, Austria, Switzerland, Luxembourg, and Liechtenstein. Includes a few in Poland and Czechoslovakia.

Rebbe, Wolfgang, and Eckart Henning. *Taschenbuch für Familiengeschichtsforschung* (Pocketbook for Family History Reseach). 9th ed. Neustadt/Aisch: Degener Verlag, 1980. (FHL# 943/D27r)

Much more substantial than its title implies. It contains an excellent discussion of various genealogical topics-for example, village lineage books, academic records, citizen books, a current list of genealogical periodicals published in Germany and elsewhere, etc. Very useful for the researcher who reads German.

Smelser, Ronald M. with Thomas Dullien, and Heribert Hinrichs. *Preliminary Survey of the German Collection.* Salt Lake City, University of Utah Press, 1979. (FHL# 943/A3s)

Although this book is now out of date in its description of the catalog and its inventory of the holdings, it still ranks as a useful discussion of the collection.

Smith, Clifford Neal, and Anna Piszczan-Czaja. *Encyclopedia of German-American Genealogical Research.* New York and London: R. R. Bowker, 1976. (FHL# 943/D27sp)

A veritable jackdaw's nest of fascinating information culled from both American and European sources. Among its positive qualities is a discussion of the exceedingly complex history of the German-American churches, a subject unduly neglected by most German-American genealogical manuals. While it is definitely not the book to help a novice genealogist find the ancestral village, the experienced researcher will find it extremely useful and interesting.

Finally, mention must be made of the unpublished material prepared by Gerhard Jeske and others of the European Reference Desk at the Family History Library in Salt Lake City. Current plans are to film some of this material for the Family History Center (Branch Library) Microfiche Project.

Austria

Senekovic. Dagmar. *Handy Guide to Austrian Genealogical Records.* Logan, Utah: Everton, 1979. (FHL# EUR REF/943.6/D29s)

Particularly useful for its directory of all the parishes in present-day Austria, indicating when the parish registers began. It also lists branch and ancestral parishes.

Czechoslovakia

Miller, Olga. *Genealogical Research for Czech and Slovak Americans.* Detroit, Mich.: Gale Research, 1978. (FHL# 943.7/D27m)

Particularly strong in its discussion of Czech sources.

Schlyter, Daniel. *A Handbook of Czechoslovak Genealogical*

Research. Buffalo Grove, Ill: Genun Publishers, 1985. (FHL# 943.7/D27s)

A model of what a "how to trace your immigrant ancestor" book should be.

Hungary

Liptak, Eva T. "Family Origins in Eastern Europe: Using the Records of the Genealogical Society. Hungary, Hungarians and Their Records." In Proceedings of World Conference on Records: Preserving Our Heritage, sponsored by the Genealogical Department, Volume 7: *Preserving our Family and Local History,* Ser. 515b. Salt Lake City: Corporation of the President of the Church of Jesus Christ of Latter-day Saints, 1980. (FHL# 929.1/W893/1980)

A useful survey.

Schlyter, Daniel. *Hungarian Census Returns*. Typescript. 21 pp. Salt Lake City: Family History Library, n.d. (FHL# 943.9/X27s)

Contains translations of the headings used in the various Hungarian census returns available in the library.

Switzerland

Martin, Donald J. "Swiss Echoes for Genealogists." *Journal of Genealogy* 4, no. 3 (March 1979): 12-23 (FHL# 973/B2jg)

Contains an excellent bibliography of secondary sources, including many periodicals not available in the library.

Suess, Jared H. *Handy Guide to Swiss Genealogical Records.* Logan, Utah: Everton Publishers, 1978. (FHL# EUR REF/949.4/D27s)

Although out of date in its discussion of the cataloging system, it remains a good survey of the types of genealogical records available in Switzerland.

Records by Jurisdiction

German Empire 1871-1918

States and Provinces	Archives & Libraries	Bibliography	Biography	Census	Church Records	Church Transcripts	Civil Registration	Colonization	Description & Travel	Directories	Emigration & Immigration	Encyclopedias & Dictionaries	Ethnology	Gazetteers	Genealogy	Guild Records	Heraldry	Historical Geography	History	Jewish History/Records	Land & Property	Language	Maps	Military Records	Minorities	Names, Geographic	Names, Personal	Naturalization/Citizenship	Nobility	Obituaries	Periodicals	Probate Records	Public Records	Schools	Social Life & Customs	Societies	Taxation
Anhalt	•					•					•			•					•	•			•	•				•			•	•	•				•
Baden	•				•	•					•			•	•				•	•			•	•							•	•					
Bavaria	•				•	•	•			•	•			•	•	•			•	•			•	•				•			•		•	•			•
Braunschweig	•					•	•				•			•		•			•	•			•	•	•			•			•	•	•				
Bremen	•				•		•				•								•				•	•									•				
Hamburg	•				•		•			•	•					•			•					•	•			•			•						•
Hessen-Darmstadt	•			•	•	•					•				•				•	•			•	•				•			•			•			
Lippe-Detmold	•				•	•	•				•								•	•	•		•		•			•				•	•				•
Luebeck	•				•		•			•				•					•	•			•	•	•						•						
Mecklenburg-Schwern	•			•	•					•				•	•				•	•	•		•	•							•		•	•			
Mecklenburg-Strelitz	•				•					•				•					•	•	•		•	•													
Oldenburg	•			•	•		•			•	•			•	•				•		•		•	•							•			•			
Prussia: Berlin	•			•	•	•	•			•	•			•	•				•	•			•	•	•			•				•	•				
Brandenburg	•			•	•	•	•			•				•	•				•	•	•		•	•	•			•						•			
Hannover	•				•	•	•			•	•			•	•				•	•	•		•	•	•			•									•
Hessen-Nassau	•			•	•	•	•			•	•			•	•					•			•	•	•												
Hohenzollern	•				•					•	•			•																							
Ostpreussen	•			•	•		•			•	•			•	•	•			•	•	•		•	•	•						•		•	•			•
Pommern	•			•	•	•	•							•	•				•	•			•	•				•			•						•
Posen	•				•	•	•			•	•			•	•				•	•			•					•					•	•			
Rheinland	•			•	•	•	•			•				•	•				•	•			•	•				•			•	•					
Sachsen	•					•				•				•	•				•	•	•		•	•							•						
Schlesien	•				•	•	•			•	•			•	•				•	•			•	•													
Schleswig-Holstein	•			•	•	•	•							•	•				•		•		•	•	•						•	•	•	•			•
West Falen	•			•	•	•	•			•	•			•	•				•	•	•		•	•				•			•		•	•			
West Preussen	•			•	•	•	•			•	•			•	•				•	•	•		•	•	•			•					•	•			
Sachsen Kingdom	•									•				•	•				•	•			•					•									•
Schaumberg-Lippe	•									•				•	•					•					•												
Thuringia	•				•	•	•			•				•	•				•	•								•									
Waldeck	•										•			•	•								•									•					
Wuerttemberg	•				•	•					•			•	•				•				•	•	•						•	•	•	•			

Records by Jurisdiction — Austria (since 1918) — States	Archives & Libraries	Bibliography	Biography	Census	Church History	Church Records	Civil Registration	Colonization	Description & Travel	Directories	Emigration & Immigration	Encyclopedias & Dictionaries	Ethnology	Gazetteers	Genealogy	Guild Records	Heraldry	Historical Geography	History	Jewish History/Records	Land & Property	Language	Maps	Military Records	Minorities	Names, Geographic	Names, Personal	Naturalization/Citizenship	Nobility	Obituaries	Periodicals	Probate Records	Public Records	Schools	Social Life & Customs	Societies	Taxation
Burgenland				•	•		•							•					•	•			•														
Kaernten (Carinthia)														•					•				•														
Niederoesterreich					•									•		•			•				•	•													
Oberoesterreich				•										•									•										•				•
Salzburg											•			•					•		•		•					•									
Steiermark				•			•				•			•					•		•		•														•
Tirol											•			•					•				•	•								•					
Voralberg														•		•			•				•														
Wien	•						•				•			•					•	•			•	•								•	•				

Records by Jurisdiction — Czechoslovakia — Regions	Archives & Libraries	Bibliography	Biography	Census	Church History	Church Records	Civil Registration	Colonization	Description & Travel	Directories	Emigration & Immigration	Encyclopedias & Dictionaries	Ethnology	Gazetteers	Genealogy	Guild Records	Heraldry	Historical Geography	History	Jewish History/Records	Land & Property	Language	Maps	Military Records	Minorities	Names, Geographic	Names, Personal	Naturalization/Citizenship	Nobility	Obituaries	Periodicals	Probate Records	Public Records	Schools	Social Life & Customs	Societies	Taxation
Cechy (Bohemia)	•									•	•			•					•		•		•		•												
Morava (Moravia)	•									•	•			•					•		•		•		•												
Podkarpatska Rus														•					•						•												
Slezsko	•									•				•					•		•		•														
Slovensko	•			•						•				•					•				•	•													

Records by Jurisdiction **Hungary** Counties	Emigration	Mil. Muster Rolls	Parish Registers	P.R. Transcripts	Nobility Records	1828 Land Census	1848 Jewish	Census	1857 Census	1869 Census	Genealogy	Secondary Sources	Civil Registration	Jewish Registers
Abauj-Torna			•			•					•	•		•
Also-Feher						•						•		
Arad			•			•								
[illegible]	•		•			•						•		•
Baranya		•	•		•	•		•			•	•		•
Bars						•						•		
Bekes		•	•		•	•		•	•			•		•
Bereg			•			•						•		
Beszterge-Naszod			•											
Bihar			•		•	•		•				•		•
Borsod		•	•		•	•								•
Brasso												•		
Csanad		•	•		•	•		•	•		•	•		•
Csik														
Csongrad		•	•		•	•		•	•			•		•
Esztergom		•	•		•	•		•	•	•		•		•
Fejer			•		•			•						•
Fogaras														
Gomor			•			•					•	•		
Gyor		•	•	•	•	•		•	•	•		•		•
Hajdu			•	•				•		•	•			•
Haromszek														
Heves		•	•		•	•					•	•		•
Hont			•			•					•	•		
Hunyad											•	•		
Jasz-Nagy-Kun-Szolnok		•	•								•	•		•
Kis-Kukullo			•									•		
Kolozs			•											
Komarom				•		•		•	•	•	•	•		•
Krasso-Szoreny				•		•		•						
Lipto						•					•	•		
Maramoros						•		•						
Maro-Torda				•							•	•		
Moson		•	•	•	•	•	•					•	•	•
Nagy-Kukullo														
Nograd		•	•		•	•						•		•
Nyitra						•					•	•		
Pest-Pilis-Kis-Kun		•	•		•	•					•	•		•
Pozsony						•						•		
Saros						•								•
Somogy		•	•		•	•				•	•	•		•
Sopron		•	•	•	•	•			•		•	•	•	
Szabolcs			•		•	•						•		•
Szatmar			•			•					•	•		•
Szeben			•									•		
Szilagy			•									•		
Snolnok-Doboka			•											
Temes	•					•					•	•		
Tolna		•	•		•	•	•							•

Records by Jurisdiction Switzerland Counties	Archives & Libraries	Bibliography	Biography	Census	Church History	Church Records	Civil Registration	Colonization	Description & Travel	Directories	Emigration & Immigration	Encyclopedias & Dictionaries	Ethnology	Gazetteers	Genealogy	Guild Records	Heraldry	Historical Geography	History	Jewish History/Records	Land & Property	Language	Maps	Military Records	Minorities	Names, Geographic	Names, Personal	Naturalization/Citizenship	Nobility	Obituaries	Periodicals	Probate Records	Public Records	Schools	Social Life & Customs	Societies	Taxation
Aargau	•									•				•					•				•														
Appenzell	•					•								•					•				•														
Basel	•			•		•	•				•			•					•				•										•	•			
Bern	•													•					•				•		•												
Fribourg	•													•					•				•														
Geneva						•	•							•					•				•		•							•	•				
Glarus														•					•				•														
Graubuenden						•								•					•		•		•										•	•			•
Jura																							•														
Lucerne	•					•								•									•	•				•					•				•
Neuchatel						•								•									•								•						
Nidwald														•					•				•														
Obwald														•									•														
Sanktgallen						•								•					•				•														
Schaffhausen						•								•					•				•														
Schwyz														•					•				•														
Solothurn														•					•				•														
Thurgau						•								•									•														
Ticino				•		•								•									•									•					
Uri														•					•				•														
Valais														•					•				•														
Vaud	•			•		•	•							•									•									•	•			•	
Zuerich	•			•		•	•			•				•					•				•								•		•				•
Zug	•													•					•				•														

Chapter 20

Eastern Europe

Kory L. Meyerink

ROMANIA

Historical Background

1828	End of Russo-Turkish war sees new Russian governor who makes progressive reforms.
1859	Autonomous "United Principalities of Walachia and Moldavia established.
1864	Emancipation of serfs.
1866	First formal constitution.
1878	End of Russo-Roumanian Turkish war brings complete independence to Romania.
1907	Unsuccessful peasant revolt.
1914	Romania neutral at beginning of World War I.
1918	Romania receives Transylvania, Bessarabia, and Bucovina at end of World War I.
1940	USSR annexes Bessarabia.
1944	USSR liberates Romania from German forces.
1947	King Michael abdicates, Communists seize complete power.

Settlement and Migration

Romania's history has been one of fluctuating boundaries and varying conquerors. While the area has been settled since the first century B.C., it was not an independent state until the 1830s, having been part of the Turkish Ottoman Empire for centuries. Significant portions had also been occupied by Hungary and Russia and remained in their control until 1918. Throughout its long history, Romania has seen very little immigration into its boundaries. In fact, the only significant immigration predates most genealogical materials. Many Germans settled in Transylvania during the Middle Ages at the invitation of the Hungarian kings. Significant numbers of Germans and Hungarians still live in the regions that formerly belonged to the Austro-Hungarian Empire.

Modern Romania is subdivided into thirty-nine districts *(Judetele).* The Family History Library Catalog (FHLC) uses the same subdivisions, where twenty-two districts are represented by at least one entry. In addition, the FHLC also maintains categories for seven former Bessarabian districts which are now in the Ukraine or Moldavia as part of the Union of Soviet Social Republics. (See discussion under the Union of Soviet Social Republics below.) The FHLC includes entries for four non-political regions now or formerly in Romania: Bassarabia [*sic*], Dobrogea, Transylvania [*sic*], and Valachia.

Note that the FHLC lists records dealing with specific places under the current name and jurisdiction of the locality, as well as under jurisdictions dating back to the mid-l800s. Therefore, most Romanian records will also appear in the FHLC under Austria, Hungary, the Ukraine, or Moldavia. See the discussion under USSR regarding cross-filing in the FHLC. The library has not filmed records at any Romanian archives or repositories. However, a small collection has been obtained from other sources including church records from over 200 parishes.

Romania Library Collection

Census

The 1828 Hungarian Census included much of the western, northern, and central areas of modern Romania. This census is available on 319 reels of microfilm and is fully described in the discussion below on Hungary.

Church History

Five books in the collection detail various aspects of church history in Romania, including:

Tichner, Henrietta M. *Roumania and Her Religious Minorities.* London: A. M. Philot, 1925. (FHL# 949.8/k2t)

Church Records

The library has collected records from about 200 churches in areas of Romania that were formerly Hungarian. Most of these are in the old provinces of the Banat and Bucovina with a few from Transylvania. Primarily, the records are from Roman Catholic German and/or Hungarian parishes. They are often written in either language or in Latin. The dates they cover vary greatly. Some begin in the mid-1700s. Many come down to almost 1900 with a few including dates as late as 1940. Very few of the records cover the whole time period in a parish, but they have been, and can be, used for successful research.

Church Records, Inventories

Schmidt, Josef. *Die Banater Kirchenbuecher.* Stuttgart: Bibliothek und Dokumentationsstelle des Instituts für Auslandsbeziehungen, 1979. (FHL# 949.84/K23b)

An inventory of microfilms at the Institute for Foreign Relations in Stuttgart.

Emigration and Immigration

The library has no source records from Romania detailing emigration. However, the collection includes four histories of emigration. Although comparatively few Romanians emigrated, those that did primarily were ethnic Germans and Hungarians, many of whom traveled through the port at Hamburg, Germany. Departure records for that port are available at the library and are discussed in Chapter 5, "Western Europe." For arrival records, see the chapters on United States areas that would include ports, for example, Chapter 18, "United States: New England" for a discussion of Boston port records.

Gazetteers

Gazetteers help the researcher determine the specific town where an ancestor lived and which parish may have recorded his or her vital events. Several useful gazetteers are described in the sections for Germany, Austria, and Hungary below.

Brandtner, Paul. *Ortsverzeichnis der deutschen Siedlungen Grossrumaniens*. Stuttgart: Heimatortskartei für Osteuropa, 1930. (FHL# microfilm 417010)

Directory of German settlements in Romania.

Iordan, Ion. *Indicatorul localitatilor din Romania.* Bucharest: Edistura Academiei Republicii Socialiste, 1974. (FHL# 949.8/E5 or microfilm 1181561)

Modern gazetteer of Romania.

History

Very few local histories are available for Romania. However, the library has about forty books dealing with various aspects of Romanian history. Most are in German or Romanian.

Seton-Watson, R. W. *A History of the Roumanians.* 1934; rpt. ed., n.p.: Archon Books, 1963. (FHL# 949.8/H2w)

Jewish Records

The library has very few records of the Jewish communities in Romania. Some of the towns in the former Hungarian areas in the FHLC include some Jewish references, notably five towns in present-day Bihor district in northwest Romania. These records generally only cover a few years in the second half of the 1800s.

Maps

The library has many good maps of Romania, although the best maps focus primarily on the old Hungarian areas. For detailed military maps, see *Maps* under Austria below.

Iancu, Mihai. *Romania, Ghid-atlas turistic.* Bucharest: Stadion, 1971. (FHL# 949.8/E7i or microfilm 1181609)

Romanian tourist atlas, scale 1:500,000.

Minorities

A dozen books are available in the collection dealing with minorities in Romania. Germans are almost exclusively the subject of these references.

Paikert, G. C. *The Danube Swabians: German Populations in Hungary, Romania, and Yugoslavia, and Hitler's Impact on Their Patterns.* Hague: Martinus Nijhoff, 1967. (FHL# 940/B4s/Vol. 10)

Bibliography

Conover, Helen Field. *The Balkans: A Selected List of References. Vol. 4: Rumania.* Washington, D.C.: n.pub., 1943. (FHL# 949.6/A31)

YUGOSLAVIA

Historical Background

1718	Serbia annexed to Austria-Hungary.
1739	Serbia taken by Ottoman Empire.
1809	Croatia and Dalmatia included in Napoleon's "Illyrian Provinces."
1815	Austria regains Illyrian area.
1878	Austria-Hungary occupies Bosnia and Hercegovina.
1903	New king and liberal constitution in Serbia

	thrusts them to prominence among South Slavs.
1913	End of Balkan wars strengthens Serbia.
1914	Serbian nationalist assassinates Austrian Archduke, precipitating World War I.
1918	New Kingdom of the South Slavs (Yugoslavia) declared.
1941	Germany invades Yugoslavia, divides it up among other Axis powers.
1945	Communist party establishes complete control of Yugoslavia.

Settlement and Migration

Although the country of Yugoslavia has only existed since 1918, the history of the population in that area dates back many hundreds of years, and different countries have exercised control over it throughout history. During recent centuries, its history has been compounded by the continued fighting between the Turkish Ottoman Empire and the Austro-Hungarian Empire. Historically, the Turks held power in the south while the Austrians prevailed in the north and west.

There were no colonization efforts by the ruling powers for several hundred years; but from about 1900 to 1950, a small but steady stream of emigrants left Yugoslavia. Most of these emigrants came from the Austrian and Hungarian areas. Many of the sources discussed under these countries will be applicable to research on Yugoslavian ancestors.

Yugoslavia Library Collection

The FHLC for Yugoslavia uses the present boundaries of the country in describing locations of records. The country is divided into six republics, all of which are represented in the FHLC by some records.

The library has very few primary (source) records for Yugoslavia. Generally, only published works are available. However, there are church records for over 100 parishes in Srbija (Serbia), which formerly belonged to Hungary. The library anticipates receiving some records from Yugoslavian archives in the near future. Check new editions of the FHLC to see if the records needed have been obtained. Many of the books in the collection are written in Serbian or other Balkan languages.

Biography

Kleine slavische Biographie. Wiesbaden, Germany: O. Harrassowitz, 1958. (FHL# 940/D3ks)

A collection of Slavic biographies in German.

Census

The 1828 Hungarian census included portions of present-day Yugoslavia. This census is available on 319 reels of microfilm and is described in the section on Hungary below.

Church Directories

Opci sematizam katolicke crkve u Jugoslaviji. Jagreb: Biskupska Konfrencija Jugoslavije, 1975. (FHL# 949.7/-K220)

Roman Catholic church directory for Yugoslavia, including explanatory notes in English.

Church Records

Although the library has not yet cataloged any church records from Yugoslavia, it has some records from former Hungarian parishes which are now in Yugoslavia: seven parishes in Hrvatska (Croatia), twelve in Slovenija, and 110 in Srbija. These are primarily Roman Catholic registers dating from as early as 1789 to as late as 1895, although most parishes do not have complete records for that time period. The language of the records vary, but it is usually Latin or Hungarian. These parishes were formerly in the area known as the Banat.

Church Records, Inventories

The FHLC catalogs four inventories under this heading to help determine which parish an ancestor attended. See also the Schmidt entry under Romania above and Langheinrich under Poland below.

Emigration and Immigration

The library does not have any original source records dealing with emigration from Yugoslavia, although a card index of emigrants to Germany has been microfilmed, including two reels which list Yugoslavians. See the discussion under Poland for further information. Ship departure lists from Hamburg or USA arrival lists may help document an immigration. Several books are available about Yugoslavian emigration.

Prpic, George J. *The Croatian Immigrants to America.* New York: Philosophical Library, 1971. (FHL# 973/W2p)

Gazetteers

For the largest portion of Yugoslavia, the best historical gazetteers are those for Austria and Hungary. See *Gazetteers* under those countries. Two modern gazetteers are available for current names and boundaries.

Imenik mesta u Jugoslaviji. Beograd: n.pub., 1965. (FHL# 949.7/E5i)

Yugoslavia: Official Standard Names Approved by the U.S. Board on Geographic Names. Washington, D.C.: U.S. Office of Geography, 1961. (FHL# 949.7/E5u or 874462 or microfiche 6053509)

History

Several histories are available for Yugoslavia tracing its development, but the library has no local histories for particular towns or districts.

Clissold, Stephen. *A Short History of Yugoslavia from Early Times to 1966.* Cambridge: University Press, 1968. (FHL# 949.7/H2s)

Maps

The library has a good collection of maps for Yugoslavia. The most detailed are military maps of the Austro-Hungarian Empire, which cover the northern half of Yugoslavia. They are available on microfilm and are described under *Maps* in the section on Austria, Chapter 19.

Jugoslavija auto atlas. Zagreb: Jugoslavenski Leksikografski Zavod, 1973. (FHL# 949.7/E7j)

Minorities

Eight books in the library's collection explore the conditions of minorities in Yugoslavia. Most of them are about Germans, but Jews and Muslims are also treated.

Plautz, Oskar. *Das Werden der deutschen Volksgemeinschaft in Sudslawien.* Novisad: Druckeri-und Verlags-Aktien-gesellschaft, 1940. (FHL# 949.72 F20 or microfilm 1045321)

Bibliography

Horton, John J. *Yugoslavia.* Oxford: Clio Press, 1977. (FHL# 949.7/A3j)

BULGARIA

Historical Background

1396	Second Bulgarian Kingdom ends by Turkish conquest. Turks control Bulgaria for almost 500 years.
1878	Russo-Turkish war ends. Bulgarian Kingdom created as autonomous tributary to Ottoman Empire.
1885	Annexation of eastern Rumelia (southern Bulgaria).
1908	Bulgaria declares complete independence from Ottoman Empire.
1912	First Balkan War yields eastern Macedonia to Bulgaria.
1913	During Second Balkan War, most of Macedonia is lost. Southern Dobrudzha ceded to Romania.
1914	Bulgaria sides with Germany and Austria in World War I.
1940	Southern Dobrudzha ceded back to Bulgaria.
1941	Bulgaria joins Germany and Italy in World War II.
1944	Soviets occupy Bulgaria.
1946	Monarchy abolished, Communist government established.

Settlement and Migration

Various ethnic tribes have lived in Bulgaria since several centuries before Christ. The area has usually been part of the great empires of history-Greek, Roman, Byzantine, and Ottoman-except for two periods before 1400 when independent Bulgarian kingdoms flourished. Except for twenty-two intermittent years and from 1908-1946, the Bulgarians have not been totally independent since 1396. In modern history, there has been little migration in or out of Bulgaria.

Bulgaria Library Collection

The library has no primary records from Bulgaria and has not microfilmed any records in Bulgarian archives. The prospects of future microfilming are very dim. The catalog contains several books of general interest related to Bulgarian research.

The locality section of the FHLC uses the modern boundaries of Bulgaria and its present twenty-eight *okrugs* (districts). Only three districts, however, are represented, with one book each, in the catalog. Several of the books in the catalog are also cataloged for other Balkan or Slavic countries. Few of the sources in the library are in English.

Church Records

The library has no church records for Bulgaria. About 85 to 90 percent of the population belonged to the Bulgarian Orthodox Church (before Communism), which broke off from the Eastern (Greek) Orthodox Church in 1860. Church registers probably began about that time. The parishes may answer a letter of inquiry for baptism or marriage certificates.

Civil Registration

Government registration of births, marriages, and deaths began in 1893. The library has none of these records. They are kept at local registration offices and may be available through correspondence.

Emigration and Immigration

The best available source for information on Bulgarian immigrants is probably the U.S. arrival lists. See the chapters on United States areas that would include each port of interest.

Altankov, Nikolay G. *The Bulgarian Americans.* Palo Alto, Calif.: Ragusan Press, 1979. (FHL# 949.77/W2an)

Gazetteers

U.S. Board of Geographic Names. *Bulgaria: Official Standard Names Approved by the U.S. Board of Geographic Names.* Washington, D.C.: U.S.Government Printing Office, 1959. (FHL# 949.77/E5u or microfilm 874457 or microfiche 6053514)

History

Several books in the collection deal with various aspects of Bulgarian history.

Mishew, D. *The Bulgarians in the Past: Pages from the Bulgarian Cultural History.* Lausanne: Librairie Centrale des Nationalites, 1919. (FHL# microfilm 1181613)

Language and Languages

Bulgaria is a Slavic language and uses the Cyrillic (Russian) alphabet.

Russev, R. *Bulgarian English Dictionary.* New York: Saphrograph Corp., 1969. (FHL# 491.81321/R919b)

Maps

Bulgaria: Motoring Across Bulgaria. N.p.: Tourist Publicity Centre, [c.1979]. (FHL# 949.77/E7b)

Bibliography

Pundeff, Martin V. *Bulgaria: A Bibliographic Guide.* Washington, D.C.: Library of Congress, 1965. (FHL# 949.77/A3p or microfilm 812974)

ALBANIA

Historical Background

1468 Death of resistance leader Prince Skanderbeg allows full Ottoman rule.

1878 End of Russo-Turkish war. Albania parcelled out to other Balkan countries.

1913 End of Balkan Wars, creation of Albania.

1918 Italian and French armies occupy Albania after World War I.

1938 King Zog flees; Italians absorb Albania.

1943-44 Civil War eliminates Axis occupation, brings Communists to power.

1945 Communist government established.

Settlement and Migration

Throughout most of its history, Albania has been subjected to the rule of major empires such as the Roman and Byzantine. Since the 1400s, the Ottoman Turks controlled the area, but many remote areas were semi-autonomous. The Turks brought the Muslim religion and converted two-thirds of the population. The remainder were Roman Catholic or Greek Orthodox.

Very few people have immigrated to Albania; but over centuries of oppressive governments, many Albanians have emigrated. Today there are more Albanians outside the country than within its borders. Many Albanians settled in southern Italy through the eighteenth century. In later years, economic reasons forced many to leave as there was little employment in Albania. These emigrants settled in Western Europe and America.

Albania Library Collection

The library has no primary records for Albania nor has it filmed in any archive in Albania. It is not likely that records will be obtained in the future. The present collection consists of about thirty books, mostly histories, about various aspects of the country.

Church Records

Religion was abolished in Albania in 1967, and few church records are known to have survived. Some Muslim records may be in Turkish archives. The library has no Albanian church records.

Civil Registration

Government registration of vital events began in 1929. The Albanian government has no diplomatic relations with the United States, but requests for documents by nationals of countries with which Albania has good relations may be answered.

Gazetteers

U.S. Board of Geographic Names. *Albania: Official Standard Names Approved by the U.S. Board on Geographic Names.* Washington, D.C.: Government Printing Office, 1961. (FHL# 949.65/E5u and 873794 and 603508)

History

Pollo, Stefanaq. *The History of Albania: From Its Origins to the Present Day.* London: Routledge and Kegan Paul, 1981. (FHL# 949.65/H2ps)

Bibliography

Conover, Helen Field. *The Balkans: A Selected List of References. Vol. 2: Albania.* Washington, D.C.: n.pub., 1943. (FHL# 949.6/A3L)

POLAND

Historical Background

1569	Union of Lublin unites Poland and Lithuania.
1577-82	War with Grand Duchy of Muscovy over Livonia.
1600	War with Sweden.
1629	Truce with Sweden.
1632-34	War with Russia.
1654-67	Polish-Russian War.
1655-60	Polish-Swedish War.
1672	Turks invade Poland.
1686	Peace with Russia.
1702	Swedish invade Poland.
1764	Constitutional reforms.
1772	First partition of Poland by Prussia, Russia, and Austria.
1793	Second partition of Poland by Prussia and Russia.
1795	Final partition of Poland by Prussia, Russia, and Austria.
1797	Poles fight with Napoleon's army.
1807	Establishment of Duchy of Warsaw under Napoleon.
1808	Introduction of the *Code Napoleon*, including civil registration.
1815	Napoleon defeated. Russian Kingdom of Poland founded.
1831	Failed revolution, thousands emigrate.
1848	Failed revolutions in Poland and throughout Europe.
1863	January insurrection fails; stricter Russian controls.
1866-85	Gradual elimination of Polish language from schools.
1898	Anti-Polish laws in Prussian Poland.
1915	Kingdom of Poland occupied by German and Austrian troops.
1918	Independent Poland established.
1939	Germany occupies Poland; beginning of World War II.
1945	Communist government established in Poland; new borders drawn.

Poland Library Collection

The library has a very large collection of material to assist in the search for Polish ancestors, especially Catholic church records, the primary source of genealogical information. However, the researcher must be familiar with certain aspects of Poland's history. Historically, Poland has undergone numerous political changes which constantly affected its boundaries. In fact, for over a century (1795-1916), Poland ceased to exist as an independent country. Three times between 1772 and 1795, large portions of–and eventually all–Polish territory were taken away and given to its three neighbors: the empires of Russia, Prussia, and Austria-Hungary.

It is essential for a researcher to have a good understanding of where a Polish ancestor lived and what jurisdictional changes occurred before, during, and since his or her residence there to use the FHLC effectively.

Often an ancestor residing within boundaries of modern Poland was not Polish, but rather German or Jewish. Other ethnic groups who lived in the borders of modern Poland include Lithuanians, Belorussians, Russians, Ukrainians, Austrians, and Hungarians. (See the relevant sections and chapters for additional research aid.) Poland's neighbors have frequently laid claim to parts of Poland because their ethnic kinsmen were a major (or predominant) segment of the population in certain areas. Thus, Prussia claimed the northern and western areas, Austria-Hungary the southern, and Russia the central and eastern areas. It was along these lines that Poland was partitioned in 1795.

While Prussia and Austria incorporated their portions of Poland into existing provinces, Russia created a separate subordinate government for its Polish lands that went under various names. Usually called the Kingdom of Poland in English (although it did not have the autonomy of a kingdom), it was also known as the Duchy of Warsaw (under Napoleon) or Congress Poland by the Russians.

The Locality FHLC catalogs each town or locality under the national jurisdiction it has today. It also lists each locality under other countries to which it has belonged since the end of the nineteenth century. See the introduction to "Union of Soviet Socialist Republics Library Collection" below for a discussion of cross-filing. However, the FHLC does not consider the "Kingdom of Poland" as part of the Russian Empire for filing purposes. Thus, records for Warsaw, Lublin, and other central and eastern Polish areas are found only under **Poland** in the FHLC.

For areas formerly under Prussian control, look either under the modern Polish province or under **Germany, Preussan** and the applicable province: Ostpreussen, Westpreussen, Pommern, Posen, or Schlesien. Austrian possessions will also be cataloged under the present boundaries or under **Austria, Galicia,** or **Schlesien.** Some areas in southern Poland may also appear under **Hungary** or **Czechoslovakia.**

The FHLC also reflects the 1918-39 boundaries when Poland extended further south and west than today. These areas appear under various USSR republics (notably the Ukraine), but also under the historic Polish province.

The names or spellings of many towns changed with the country of jurisdiction, notably in the German areas. Usually, the FHLC uses the spelling native to the country of the particular portion of the catalog. Thus, towns in Posen appear with their Polish spelling under **Poland** and the German spelling under **Germany**.

In compiling the following survey of the FHLC for Poland, I have considered only the major works and categories, preferably in English where possible, but the FHLC contains other entries. The majority of sources are written in Polish or German; they have been cited where such works were clearly the best in that category.

Archives and Libraries

Several works detailing the holdings of Polish archives are in the library's collection including at least five inventories. The best English discussion is:

Lewanski, Richard Casimir. *Guide to Polish Libraries and Archives*. Boulder, Colo.: East European Quarterly, 1974. (FHL# 943.8J/541 or microfilm 1045441)

Biography

Few immigrant ancestors or their predecessors will be found in compiled biographies in Poland. The library has virtually no local biographical works, but there is one major Polish work on a national scale available.

Polski sownik biograficzny. 19 vols. Krakow: Polska akademia nauk, 1935-74. (FHL# microfilm 1044531-1044549)

Church Directories

If gazetteers do not reveal where an ancestor attended church, church directories will determine what parishes currently exist in the area and often when they were created. The library has directories published in the 1970s for each Roman Catholic diocese. The Evangelical church in Poland is much smaller than it was before World War II. A 1979 yearbook includes a directory of the then-functioning clergy and parishes:

Kosciót Ewangelicki: 1979. Warsaw: Wydawnictwo Zwiastun, 1978. (FHL# 943.8/K24ke or microfilm 1183508)

Church History

Books on church history in Poland are particularly helpful in determining information on Evangelical, Reformed, or smaller Protestant groups. Those available in the collection cover the whole of Poland or specific German or Polish provinces. Some may act as a historical directory, telling what parishes existed during a given time period.

Kneifel, Eduard. *Die evangelish-augburgischen Gemeinden in Polen 1555-1939*. Vierkirchen uber München, Germany: The author, [c.1972]. (FHL# 943.8/K2ka or microfilm 6000812)

Includes short histories of individual parishes. In German.

Church Records

As with all European countries, church records are the primary source of genealogical information for most ancestors in Poland. Virtually every person was baptized, married, and buried by a church. No other record in Poland begins to include everyone in the country. The library has an excellent collection of Polish church records, especially those from the Roman Catholic Church, to which almost every ethnic Pole belonged. Most Germans adhered to the Evangelical or the Reformed Church.

It has been estimated that there are between 7,000 and 8,000 Roman Catholic parishes in Poland. Most researchers, however, are concerned with nineteenth-century records. Despite the anti-church stand of the present Polish government, the Catholic church is very strong in Poland and continues to grow with the population. Therefore, there were fewer parishes during the nineteenth century, probably under 6,000 parishes in the 1880s. The FHLC contains entries from about 4,700 Catholic parishes which means that 80 percent or more of the parishes of Catholic ancestors are represented in the library's collection. These records were microfilmed by the Polish authorities for the Family History Library and, due to Polish rights of privacy laws, seldom, if ever, include records after 1864-70.

Most Catholic records in present-day Poland began in the mid-1700s. In some cases, the records were destroyed or lost or simply are not yet in the archives and, hence, were not filmed for all or part of the time period during which they were kept. Consequently, some parishes are represented in the FHLC by over 100 years of records and others by only a dozen years or less. Many of the early records are written in Latin; but in most areas, Polish was predominantly used by the 1850s. During the last few years of these records (the 1860s), the Russian language and the Cyrillic alphabet appear widely. Parish records for parishes or time periods not in the library's collection are sometimes available through correspondence with the Polish National Archives or directly with the parish.

Ethnic Germans seldom belonged to the Catholic Church. Rather, their records are found in Evangelical or Reformed parishes, chiefly in the five German (Prussian)-Polish provinces. The library has a good collection of these German parishes, but it is far from complete. During and after the two World Wars, most Germans fled from what is today Poland, taking many of their church records with them. These were then stored in numerous "safe" places, but many have not yet come to light. Others have since been deposited in numerous private, church, and government archives in Poland, East, and West Germany. Whenever possible, the Family History Library has microfilmed these records.

This pattern has resulted in varying degrees of coverage for the Prussian provinces. For Posen, the library has records from most German (protestant) parishes while in Silesia, perhaps two-thirds to three-quarters of the parishes are represented. In East and West Prussia, over half of the parishes are in the collection, but in Polish-Pomerania, very few have been found and microfilmed. German parish registers usually begin in the mid-1600s, although some start as early as 1589. Whenever possible, they have been microfilmed to a late date, usually close to 1900. Some are available as recently as 1944.

Records of German parishes for time periods not in the library's collection are hard to find and usually require correspondence with several archives and repositories.

Records of Protestant parishes in the Austrian areas of Poland are not as well represented in the FHLC. However, most Germans in this area were Catholic and were recorded in the now-Polish Catholic registers, many of which are in the library. The library is continually receiving additional church records from Poland. Check the current editions of the FHLC for the parish of interest for newly added holdings. For assistance in using the parish register, consult:

Ortell, Gerald A. *Polish Parish Records of the Roman Catholic Church: Their Use and Understanding in Genealogical Research.* 2nd rev. ed. Buffalo Grove, Ill.: Genun, 1984. (FHL# 943.8/K20)

Church Records, Inventories

Inventories of parish registers attempt to list what parish records are available as of the date of publication, what dates or records they include, and where the records were to be found at the time the inventory was made. Each inventory usually covers a diocese or province. They are useful for determining where parishes were and if records are available. They also usually indicate from which parish a new parish was created. The library has a very good collection of these inventories in both book and microfilm format. They are usually written in German or Polish and are cataloged in the FHLC under **[Country]/[Province]/Church Records, Inventories.**

Langheinrich, Paul. *Verzeichnis der im Archiv für Genealogie befindlichen Originale und Filme von Kirchenbüchern.* N.p.: n.pub., 1953. (FHL# 943/K23v or microfilm 1045486)

An inventory of church records available in the central Archives for Genealogy in Leipzig.

Civil Registration

Civil registration of vital events began in Russian Poland with Napoleon's "Duchy of Warsaw" in 1808 and follow, to a large extent, the format found in French civil registers. See the discussion under *Civil Registration* in Chapter 22, "Western Europe." Mostly, these are records of "non-Christian" people such as Jews, as the church records were considered "semi-official" registration. Sometimes, the civil registers are simply transcripts of church records. The library has a small but growing collection of civil registers from Russian Poland, mainly for 1830 to 1870.

In Prussian Poland, civil registration began in 1874 and was fairly comprehensive. The library has some civil registration records from Ostpreussen province and other areas. Some of these records come up well into the twentieth century.

In the FHLC, civil registration records are cataloged under **Poland/[Province]/[Town]/Civil Registration.** However, not every town was a place of civil registration. The gazetteers discussed under Germany in Chapter 19, and under Poland (see *Gazetteers* below) will tell you which civil registration district a particular town belonged to.

Emigration

Poles have been emigrating from Poland for centuries but not in large numbers until after 1795 when Poland's neighbors annexed the last part of Poland, and the country ceased to exist for 120 years. Poles migrated all over the globe. Some Germans in Poland settled in southern Ukraine (see Union of Soviet Social Republics below), but most left for western Europe or North and South America. Polish emigration grew slowly until the end of the 1800s when more and more left for the United States and other countries.

There appears to have been no systematic, official method of emigration, so there are no government records of "passports" or departures from Poland in the FHLC. There are, however, several other sources for tracking an emigrant.

After the failed revolution of 1831 against Russia, several Poles fled to France. The library has twenty reels of individual dossiers of Polish refugees in France, 1831-70, filmed in Strasbourg. See FHLC heading **Poland/-Emigration-Immigration**. The Prussians deported many Poles and Germans through Bromberg (now Bydgoszcz), Posen, from the 1880s to 1918. The library has sixty-five reels of these records in three different sets cataloged under **Poland/Emigration/Immigration**. The Baden State Archives in Karlsruhe has a card index to immigrants to Germany and missing foreigners in Germany. The library has microfilmed this collection, and four of the seven reels of film contain alphabetical cards of Polish emigrants (FHL# 1125476-1125477 and 118756-118757).

By far the largest number of emigrants from Poland left through the German port of Hamburg. Departure lists for this port are available from 1850 to 1936 and include the emigrant's last residence or place of birth. It has been microfilmed and is partially indexed by the first letter of the surname. See the discussion in Chapter 19 under *Emigration* in the section on Germany.

Soroka, Waclaw W. *Polish Immigration to the United States.* Stevens Point, Wis.: University of Wisconsin-Stevens Point, 1976. (FHL# 973/F2swp)

Gazetteers

The library has several gazetteers that will help locate the town an ancestor lived in and the parish and civil registration district to which it belonged. Using several gazetteers from different time periods and different jurisdictions may be necessary to understand fully the locality being sought. Also see *Gazetteers* under USSR below, and under Germany and Austria in Chapter 19 for other important references.

Alphabetisches Ortsverzeichnis von Russisch-Polen. Berlin: Preussische Verlagsanstalt, 1915. (FHL# Q/943.8/E5g or microfilm 583455)

Bundesanstalt für Landeskunde. *Amtliches Gemeinde-und Ortsnamenverzeichnis der deutschen ostgebiete unter fremder Verwaltung.* 3 vols. Remagen: Bundesanstalt für Landeskunde, 1955. (FHL# microfilm 824243 and 1045449)

Cross indexes German and foreign place names for former German areas of East Europe.

Doubek, F. A. *Verzeichnis der Ortschaften mit deutscher Bevölkerung auf dem Gebiete des polnischen Staates.* Berlin: Publikationstelle, 1939. (FHL# Q/943.8/E5d or microfilm 583455)

Gazetteer of German place names in Poland where the population was 10 percent German or higher in 1939.

Kaemmerer, M. *Müllers Verzeichnis der jenseits der Oder-Neisse gelegenen, unter fremder Verwaltung Stehenden Ortschaften.* Wuppertal: Post-und ortsbuchverlag, 1958. (FHL# 943/E5m/Suppl. 1958)

German place name changes in Poland and Russia after World War II.

Kredel, Otto. *Deutsch-fremdsprachiges Ortsnamenverzeichnis.* Berlin: Deutsche Verlagsgesellschaft, 1939. (FHL# Q/940/E5kt or microfilm 583457)

Gives German place names for all towns once under German jurisdiction but in other jurisdictions after World War I.

Sownik geographiczny krolestwa polskiego i innych krajow stowianskych. 15 vols. Warsaw: Sulimierski i Walewski, 1880-1902. (FHL# 943.8/E5c or microfilm 920957-920972)

Gazetteer of the Russian Kingdom of Poland and neighboring Slavic areas. Includes parish information for most towns.

Spis miejscowosci Polskiej Rzeczypospolitej Ludowej. 4 vols. Warsaw: Wydawnictwo komunikacji i tacznosci, 1967. (FHL# 943.8/E5s or microfilm 844922 or microfiche 6000369-6000383)

Relatively current Polish gazetteer naming the district and civil registration office to which a town belongs.

Genealogy

The library has no major collections of previously compiled genealogies for Polish families with the exception of some noble families. See *Nobility* below. There are, however, a few short handbooks about research in Poland and a number of published lineage books for families in the Prussian provinces. See *Genealogy* in the German section of Chapter 19.

Arbeitsgemeinschaft ostdeutscher Familienforscher. *Genealogical Guide to German Ancestors from East Germany and Eastern Europe.* Neustadt/Aisch, Germany: Degener, 1984. (FHL# 943/D27gg)

Gnacinski, Janneyne Longley. *Polish and Proud: Tracing your Polish Ancestry.* West Allis, Wis.: Janlen Enterprises, 1979. (FHL# 943.8/D27g)

Wellauer, Maralyn Ann. *Tracing Your Polish Roots.* Milwaukee, Wis.: Wellauer, 1979. (FHL# 943.8/D27m)

History

Very few local histories are available for areas within Poland, and those that are do not include much information on specific families. The Family History Library collection, however, includes about seventy histories of Poland in various languages covering different time periods and topics.

Gieysztor, Aleksander. *History of Poland.* 2nd ed. Warsaw: Polish Scientific Publications, 1979. (FHL# 943.8/H2gk)

A thorough treatment of Polish history to 1940 with a helpful bibliography and chronology.

Leslie, R. F., et al. *History of Poland since 1863.* New York: Cambridge University Press, 1980. (FHL# 943.8/H2hp)

Jewish History and Records

The library has a good collection of Jewish records and Jewish histories for Polish areas. Most Jewish records were kept by the civil authorities in compliance with an 1808 law mandating civil registration of all citizens. Prior to 1826, most Jews were included in Catholic parish registers. After that date, separate Jewish civil registers were kept. Most of the library's Jewish collection is for Russian Poland with some from the Prussian provinces.

Very few records are available for the Austrian Polish provinces. Over 400 Polish towns in the FHLC include entries for Jewish records. These records are usually cataloged under the name of the Catholic parish or civil registration district, not under the *shtetl* (hamlets or villages in the Pale) name. Generally, the FHLC will indicate Jewish records are noted under **/[Province]/-[Town]/Civil Registration** or **/Jewish Records.** A few synagogue records may also appear under **/[Province]/-[Town]/Church Records.** The library has very few memorial books or other Jewish sources except for general histories.

Dubnow, S. M. *History of the Jews in Russia and Poland from the Earliest Time to the Present Day.* Philadelphia: Jewish Publication Society, 1916-20. (FHL# 940/F2d or microfilm 1183537)

Language and Languages

Swan, Oscar E. *A Concise Grammar of Polish.* 2nd ed. Lanham, Md.: University Press of America, 1983. (FHL# 491.85/Sw24c)

Stanistawski, Jan. *English-Polish and Polish-English Dictionary.* Philadelphia: David McKay Co., 1946. (FHL# 491.85321st/24e or microfilm 1045473)

Maps

The library has an excellent collection of Polish maps including microfilm copies of detailed Prussian and Austrian military maps. See *Maps* in the discussions of Austria and Germany in Chapter 19.

Atlas geograficzny illustrowany krolestwa polskiego. Warsaw: J. M. Bazewicz, 1907. (FHL# 943.8/E3b or microfilm 873665 or microfiche 6000827)

Illustrated atlas of the Russian Kingdom of Poland including detailed maps of each district *(powiat)*.

Military Records

The Family History Library does not have military records for Poland, but cataloged under this heading for Poland are sixty-eight reels from the Central Immigration Office of Nazi Germany. These records are the genealogical accounts *(Stammblaetter)* of internees in the labor camps of German-occupied Poland. The files are arranged by the registration number of the internee. It includes records on about 300,000 individuals. There is no index.

Minorities

More than two dozen books and sources in the Polish collection discuss various aspects of minorities in Poland. They are written mostly in Polish or German; most of them deal with Jews and Germans in Poland.

Hagen, William W. *Germans, Poles and Jews: The Nationality Conflict in the Preussian East, 1772-1914*. Chicago: University of Chicago Press, 1980. (FHL# 943/F2hw)

Nobility

Most family traditions of a noble Polish ancestor turn out, on investigation, to have little foundation in fact. The library has a good collection of material on Polish nobility which can be used in investigating such cases. See Chapter 28, "Medieval Families."

Periodicals

Very few periodicals are devoted solely to tracing Polish ancestry, but the library has some which deal with research in the Prussian provinces and Polish history. The best genealogical periodical for Polish research is *Polish Genealogical Society Newsletter,* 1979-present, 984 North Milwaukee Ave., Chicago, IL 60622. (FHL# 943.8/D25p).

Bibliography

Hoskins, Janina. *Polish Books in English.* Washington, D.C.: Library of Congress, 1974. (FHL# 943.8/A3h)

Horecky, Paul L. *East Central Europe: A Guide to Basic Publications.* Chicago: University of Chicago, 1969. (FHL# 946/A3h)

UNION OF SOVIET SOCIALIST REPUBLICS

Historical Background

1547	Ivan IV ("the Terrible") crowned first Tsar of all Russians.
1562	Duchy of Courland formed.
1569	Union of Lublin unites Poland and Lithuania.
1590-93	Russo-Swedish War.
1612	Liberation of Moscow from the Poles.
1632-34	Russo-Polish war.
1654-67	Russo-Polish war.
1700	Introduction of new calendar in Russia.
1703	First Russian newspaper printed in Moscow; founding of St. Petersburg.
1721	Estonia and Latvia annexed from Sweden; Peter I adopts title of Emperor.
1722	Keeping of Church registers required.
1763	German settlers begin arriving in Black Sea and Volga regions in response to invitation of Catherine II ("the Great").
1772	First partition of Poland.
1783	Russia annexes Crimea.
1793	Second partition of Poland.
1795	Third partition of Poland joins Belorussia, Courland, and Lithuania to Russian Empire.
1807	Napoleon obtains Poland, creates Duchy of Warsaw.
1809	Finland annexed.
1812	Bessarabia annexed.
1813-15	Russia repels Napoleon's march to Moscow, obtains Duchy of Warsaw, renamed Congress Poland.
1815-1917	Jewish settlement confined to the Pale.
1825	Decembrist revolution fails.
1853-56	Crimean War.
1861	Serfdom abolished.
1867	Sale of Alaska and Aleutian Islands to United States.
1891-99	Trans-Siberian Railroad built.
1904-05	Russian-Japanese War.
1905	Attempted revolution fails.
1914-18	First World War.
1917	Bolshevik Revolution; Communists seize power; Finland becomes independent.
1918	Poland, Lithuania, Estonia, and Latvia receive independence;Bessarabia seized by Romania.
1939-45	World War II.
1939	USSR seizes Lithuania, Estonia, Latvia,

	Western Ukraine, Bukovina, and eastern Poland (Belorussia).
1940	Bessarabia is returned to USSR.
1941	Volga Germans deported to Siberia.
1945	Konigsberg area of East Prussia seized by USSR; Czechoslovakia cedes eastern Galicia (Ruthenia or Carpathian Ukraine) to USSR.

Settlement and Migration

While the USSR has only existed since the 1917 Revolution, Russia can trace its history back to about A.D. 600 when the Novgorod chiefs made their tribe predominant among the various Slavic peoples in eastern Europe. Numerous wars against the Mongols weakened the Novgorod influence and eventually the duchy of Moscow dominated.

Ivan IV ("the Terrible" of the duchy of Moscow) united the Russians as the first Tsar and, with his successors, conquered neighboring regions. In 1721, Peter I ("the Great") established the Russian Empire which reached its maximum size in 1795.

Russia was composed of many ethnic groups, but historically there was little internal migration before the 1750s. Most groups remained in their historic provinces; and in fact, many are still there today. During the mid- to late 1800s, Siberia was settled by volunteers who were given inducements and forced labor. This pattern continued into the 1950s.

Two major ethnic groups had a great effect on settlement and migration and also supplied the greatest number of later emigrants who became the ancestors most researchers seek: the Jews and the Germans.

Jews have been in Russia for centuries, having fled there from Asia and Europe before the Middle Ages. They were not welcome in Russia either and often became the subject of persecution and forced migrations. In 1815, the Pale of Jewish Settlement was established, limiting Jewish residence to a specific area. The Pale was roughly defined as that portion of the Empire west of a line running approximately from Estonia to the Crimea. At various times, thousands of Jews were forced from Moscow, St. Petersburg, and other cities to tiny hamlets *(shtetls)* in the Pale. Various czars authorized pogroms, organized exterminations of the Jewish population in various areas. Despite these problems, by 1900 there were about 5 million Jews in Russia.

Germans started settling along the Volga River in Russia in 1764 in response to Catherine the Great's invitation promising free land, freedom from taxes and military service, and ethnic recognition. These settlers came from all over Germany but especially from the over-populated states of Baden and Wuerttemberg. Others came from the East Prussian and Polish areas.

Soon, other areas were opened to German settlement, notably in the Ukraine. In 1789, German Mennonites were promised religious freedom and founded colonies in the Chortiza district of the Ukraine. In 1803, Germans settled near Odessa and then the Crimea. After Russia obtained Bessarabia from Turkey in 1812, it was opened to German settlement. German settlement in Russia stopped in 1871 when Catherine's manifesto was repealed; within ten years, the colonists' special privileges were revoked. In 1874, compulsory military service was decreed. Before 1914, thousands of Germans and Mennonites had departed for North and South America. Still, in 1900, about 2 million Germans remained in Russia. Between the world wars, famines caused about 200,000 German deaths by starvation. At the end of World War II, about 100,000 Germans escaped through Poland to Germany, but another 250,000 who tried to escape were returned to the Soviet Union and banished to Siberia.

Except for the Germans and some other colonists invited by Catherine and later Alexander I, most migration has been out of Russia due to the oppressive Czarist, and later, Soviet regimes. Baltic peoples and Poles fled in large numbers during the nineteenth century, as did some Ukrainians and other ethnic groups.

Union of Soviet Socialist Republics Library Collection

Research on ancestry in the USSR is very difficult because the Soviet Union does not make records available for research. However, a few sources are available; and for some parts of the USSR, many important records can be searched. There is probably no better available collection of genealogical sources for the Soviet Union than that at the LDS Family History Library. Understanding the scope and nature of the collection and how to use it may make it possible to trace ancestors successfully in areas now in the USSR.

Most of the FHLC listings are for records that deal with areas that did not belong to the USSR before World War II and, in most cases, did not belong to the Russian Empire either. While these records represent only a small fraction of towns in the Soviet Union today, their value for genealogical research is much greater. Most people tracking "Russian" ancestors are not seeking true ethnic Russians. Rather, they descend from the Germans, Slavs, Poles, Austrians, Baltic peoples, and others who lived in what is today Western or European USSR.

Some of these areas are well represented in the library's collection. Specifically, the library has civil or church records for about thirty-six towns in Lithuania, about 100 from the Koenigsberg (now Kaliningrad) area, and over 450 from the Ukraine. Most of the Ukrainian films are for the eastern third of Galicia which Poland received from Austria in 1920 and then ceded to the Soviet Union in 1945.

For the rest of the USSR, the FHLC has few church or civil records. Nevertheless, the FHLC notes several other record types which can aid in the search for an ancestor or may help piece together fragments of family records which describe places and events with which the researcher is not familiar.

In short, the library's USSR collection is very good for

background or overview purposes, but it does not have many of the primary or secondary sources as used in Western European research.

The FHLC uses the current boundaries and present town names in describing the USSR records in the library. However, considerable changes have taken place in Soviet Union names and boundaries. The family and civil records describing an ancestor may have used old spellings, different names, and often a different language than is used today. Therefore, some understanding of the geography and of the political changes is necessary.

Today the Soviet Union is comprised of fifteen Soviet Socialist Republics (SSR), which can be considered similar to a state or province. The FHLC treats them separately with separate microfiche catalogs for each republic and a general one for the USSR containing records and sources (usually reference books) pertaining to the entire country. Ten of the republics have further geographic/political/civil subdivisions similar to a county in the United States, but the FHLC only uses these subdivisions for the republic of Russia, the old center of the empire around the Moscow area.

Properly called the Russian Soviet Federated Socialist Republic (or RSFSR), the FHLC designates this republic **Russia (Republic)**. The RSFSR has five different types of subdivisions with different names and political structures, similar to counties: Autonomous SSRs, Autonomus *Oblasts*, Autonomus *Okrugs* (before 1977 called national *Okrugs*), *Krays,* and *Oblasts.* There are eighty-six of these different divisions in the RSFSR. Presently, the FHLC has records cataloged for twenty-four divisions: three ASSRs, twenty *oblasts*, and the region of Siberia. Five of these twenty-four divisions are included in the FHLC Overview Chart at the end of this section. The other divisions in the RSFSR section of the FHLC have fewer than five items each listed.

For the fourteen republics in which the FHLC does not use a subdivision, the towns for which there are entries appear alphabetically under the general entries for the republic. For example, to find a history of the city of Minsk, you would look under the republic: **Belorussia/Minsk/History**. There are over 700,000 populated places in the Soviet Union. The FHLC has entries for about 800.

Determining the spelling under which a record may be filed can be difficult. The standard reference used by the library's cataloging staff is *USSR and Certain Neighboring Areas.* See full citation under *Gazetteers* below. While this gazetteer contains some cross-references to earlier spellings or foreign versions of a town name, the FHLC also has some "built in" helps. Records for areas formerly belonging to other countries also appear in those countries under the spelling(s) and local jurisdictions they were known by earlier. The catalog description of such records usually briefly outlines the name changes. Thus the records of Galician towns now in the Ukraine also appear under **Austria/Galizien**, and under **Poland/[Province]**-usually Lwow or Tarnopol. Records in Kaliningrad Oblast, RSFSR, are also cataloged under **Prussia/Ostpreussian/Köningsberg**.

Alternate spellings of a place name have "see" references in the FHLC Locality section for the country under which that alternate name or spelling was known.For example, about 1790, several Germans founded a town in eastern Galicia at the invitation of the Austrian Emperor (Kaiser) who then ruled Galicia. They called their village Kaisersdorf. The local ethnic Ukraines and Galicians knew the settlement as Kalinow. Some of the church records ended up in Poland and were microfilmed in 1971. They were cataloged as Kalinow because that is the name the Polish archives used. However, the FHLC contains a cross-reference in its Austrian listings under Kaisersdorf telling the researcher to see **Galizien/ Kalinöw** where the full description is found. The same records are listed in the FHLC under **Poland/Lwöw/Kalinöw** and **USSR/Ukraine/Kalinöw,** but those microfiche do not have a "see" reference under Kaisersdorf since it was only known by that name when it belonged to Austria. The USSR Gazetteer does not mention Kaisersdorf either, but the old Austrian one does (see *Gazetteer* in Austria section in Chapter 19), so the cataloger was able to create the cross-reference.

Because items are also cataloged under countries to which the locality formerly belonged, there is a FHLC microfiche for **Russia (Empire).** Many items in the Family History Library appear only in this listing. They are not found in the general USSR Locality FHLC nor in the divisions for the various republics. Many items in the general USSR collection are not cataloged elsewhere nor under other divisions.

Those works which deal only with Russia or its subdivisions prior to 1917 are generally cataloged under **Russia (Empire).** Examples might be studies of German colonization on the Volga or military histories of the Napoleonic wars. Works dealing with the Soviet Union since the Revolution (1917) are cataloged under USSR. Some sources will be found in both catalog divisions, and of course, specific local records (church records, local histories, etc.) appear in both catalogs under their specific geographic subdivision.

The pre-1917 Russian Empire was divided into 101 provinces (*Guberniya* or *Oblasts*). FHLC listings under **Russian (Empire)** use these provinces as geographic subdivisions. Presently, records are cataloged for thirty-five provinces; Siberia is cataloged as a non-political region. These provinces bear very little geographic similarity to the modern republics, and most of them have different names. Remember that localities in the **Russia (Empire)** section of the FHLC appear under the then-standard spelling/language and the province to which they belonged. Also, many records in the USSR FHLC are for areas that never belonged to the empire and hence are not in the **Russia (Empire)** FHLC, for example, Koenigsberg/Kaliningrad and eastern Galicia.

Of the thirty-six provinces of the empire listed in the FHLC, most have only a few entries. The following subdivisions have a fair collection, including some town or church records: Bessarabia, Courland, Estonia, Kherson, Livonia, Moskva, Sanktpetersburg, and Volhynia.

To locate all available records at the library, carefully consult the general USSR headings, entries cataloged under **Russia (Empire)**, entries cataloged under specific republics, and/or the appropriate previous country for the geographic area of interest. The following general survey of the library's USSR collection is not comprehensive. Only the major reference works, tools, or research collections have been listed. I have given preference to helpful works in English, especially those available on microfilm to branch center libraries or those recently published works which the researcher may find in major research libraries. Where the most valuable sources were non-English, I gave preference to those in common foreign languages like German, French, and Spanish. Researchers with a reading knowledge of Russian, Ukrainian, Polish, etc. will find a wealth of further sources in the FHLC.

Archives and libraries

Grimsted, Patricia Kennedy. *Archives and Manuscript Repositories in the USSR: Moscow, and Leningrad.* Princeton: Princeton University Press, 1972. (FHL# 947/H3gp)

A 1976 supplement was published in Zug, Switzerland, by Inter Documentation. (FHL# 947/H3gp, Supp.).

Biography

Only a minority of ancestors are profiled in standard biographical dictionaries, but on occasion an ancestor or close relative may have been in government service or in some other notable occupation. These sources may also serve to verify or deny a family tradition of nobility. However, very few of these works are in English. See also the section on *Encyclopedias and Dictionaries* (below) for additional biographical information.

Institute for the Study of the USSR, comp. Heinrich E. Schulz, Paul K. Urban, and Andrew I. Lebed, eds. *Who Was Who in the USSR.* Metuchen, N.J.: Scarecrow Press, 1972. (FHL# 947/D3w)

Contains over 5,000 biographies of prominent historical Soviet personalities.

Kleine Slavische Biographie. Wiesbaden, Germany: O. Harrassowitz, 1958. (FHL# 940/D3ks)

A collection of biographies of Slavs. 832 pages. In German.

Russkii biograficheskii slovar. 25 vols. 17 reels. Petrograd: Imperatorskoe Russkoe Istoricheskoe Obschchestvo, 1896-1918. (FHL# microfilm 127812-127828) Russian biographical dictionary.

Church History

Church histories can be helpful in determining migration patterns and the names of parishes in an area where an ancestor lived. Most church histories focus on German Lutheran and Mennonite groups.

Duin, Edgar C. *Lutheranism under Tsars and the Soviets.* 2 vols. Ann Arbor, Mich.: Xerox University Microfilms, 1976. (FHL# 947/K21d)

Toews, John B. *Czars, Soviets and Mennonites.* Newton, Kans.: Faith and Life Press, 1982. (FHL# 947/F2tj)

Church Records

Very few church records are available for the USSR in the Family History Library or elsewhere outside the Soviet Union. Those in the library's collection are cataloged under **/[Republic]/[Parish]/Church Records** or, in the **RSFSR**, under **/Russian (Republic)/[Oblast** or **Autonomous SSR]/[Parish]/Church Records**. Most of the collection's church records are limited to the Ukraine, Lithuania, and RSFSR (Kaliningrad *Oblast*). Church records cataloged under Russia (Empire) are predominantly in the provinces of Bessarabia and Volhynia and deal primarily with German Lutherans and Mennonites. Helpful in locating parishes and their records are church record inventories such as:

Verzeichnis der Kirchenbücher in polnisch and russisch Verwalteten Gebieten Deutschlands. N.p: n.pub., n.d. (FHL# microfilm 492808)

Undated typescript list of parish registers for areas of Germany now under Polish or Russian rule.

Civil Registration

Registration of civil birth, marriage, and death records did not begin in the Soviet Union until after the 1917 revolution. These are maintained in local civil registry offices and have not been microfilmed.

The library has one small collection that may be helpful if the ancestor emigrated from the eastern German provinces to West Germany between about 1949 and 1957. The Archives of the Evangelical Church of Germany in Hanover kept certificates of birth, marriage, death, and confirmation for these post-World War II emigrés. They are arranged alphabetically by the former civil jurisdiction and do not include persons born in the nineteenth century. The thirty-five reels include one for Lithuania (FHL# microfilm 833177), one for Livonia and Estonia (FHL# microfilm 833178) and five for East Prussia which included Koenigsberg (Kaliningrad) (FHL# microfilm 442154-442158)

Emigration and Immigration

Some of the best available sources for tracing an ancestor from the USSR are works dealing with emigration which include lists of inhabitants or emigrants. Such sources may provide the needed documentation for a lineage. Most of these works discuss specific ethnic/religious groups, Germans, Jews, and Mennonites being the most common because they constituted the majority of emigrants. Also see **[Country]/Colonization/** in the Locality FHLC.

Many emigrants from the USSR left for America from the German port of Hamburg where the departure lists recorded their birthplace or last residence. The library has these lists from 1850 to 1934. For further details see *Emigration* under Germany in Chapter 19. New York (and other United States) port arrival records contain similar information beginning in the 1890s. The library has these lists through 1920 with indexes covering 1897-1943. See *Emigration and Immigration* in the New York section of Chapter 6, "The United States: Mid-Atlantic States." Look for additional information in sources cataloged under the state or province where the emigrant ancestors settled.

Epp, Frank H. *Mennonite Exodus: The Rescue and Resettlement of the Russian Mennonites since the Communist Revolution.* Altona, Manitoba: D. W. Friesen, 1966. (FHL# 289.7/Ep7lm or microfilm 1231511) Includes a helpful bibliography.

William, Hattie Plum. *The Czar's Germans: With Particular Reference to the Volga Germans.* Lincoln, Neb.: American Historical Society of Germans from Russia, 1975. (FHL# 947/F2w)

Stumpp, Karl. *The Emigration from Germany to Russia in the Years 1763-1862.* 1972; rpt. ed., Lincoln, Neb.: American Historical Society of Germans from Russia, 1978. (FHL# 943/W2sk microfilm 1183529 or microfiche 6000829)

The primary source for locating Germans in Russia. Includes thousands of names of emigrants to Russia. Often family and church records in America and Canada (or possibly those in the Bessarabia collection when applicable) can carry a lineage back to someone in this book who can then be traced to an original home in Germany. Several maps are also included.

Encyclopedias and Dictionaries

Great Soviet Encyclopedia: A Translation of the Third Edition. 30 vols. New York: Macmillan, 1973. (FHL# 030.47/-G798s)

Gazetteers

Gazetteers for the proper location and period are essential in correctly identifying the place where an ancestor lived. Often the place name in family or government records is garbled or in a foreign language. Many towns may have similar names. See also the *Gazetteer* section under Poland above for important gazetteers covering much of the western USSR including the Baltic states and the former "Duchy of Warsaw" as a part of the Russian empire. Most gazetteers cover an entire country, but some are for provinces or for ethnic groups.

U.S. Board on Geographic Names. *USSR and Certain Neighboring Areas: Official Standard Names Approved by the U.S. Board on Geographic Names.* Washington, D.C.: U.S. Government Printing Office, 1959, rev. ed. 1970. (FHL# 947/E5u or microfilm 928609-928610, 874455-874456 or microfiche 6053504)

The library uses this standard modern gazetteer for the USSR in cataloging Soviet records. For areas previously belonging to different countries, (Poland, Germany, Austria, and Romania) check older gazetteers listed under those countries for other versions of the town name. The following works may help with specific problems or areas:

Cohen, Chester G. *Shtetl Finder: Jewish Communities in the 19th and Early 20th Centuries in the Pale of Settlement of Russia and Poland and in Lithuania, Latvia, Galicia, and Bukovina, with Names of Residents.* Los Angeles, Calif.: Periday Co., 1980. (FHL# 947/F24s or microfilm 1206428)

Meckelein, Wolfgang. *Ortsumbenennungen und Neugründungen in Europaischen Teil der Sowjetunion.* Berlin: Duncker and Humbolt, 1955. (FHL# 947/E5m or microfilm 1187934)

Covers place name changes and new settlements in the Soviet Union as of 1910, 1938, and 1951 with an appendix for East Prussia as of 1953. In German.

Sallet, Richard. *Russian-German Settlements in the United States.* Appendix "Place Names of German Colonies in Russia and the Dobrudja" by Armand Bauer. Fargo: North Dakota Institute for Regional Studies, 1974. (FHL# 973/F2rs)

Seltzer, Leon E., ed. *The Columbia Lippincott Gazetteer of the World with 1961 supplement.* Morningside Heights, N.Y.: Columbia University Press, 1952, 1962. (FHL# 910.3/-C723g)

A helpful, popular source that describes present and former regions, areas, provinces, districts, countries, etc., as well as most medium and all large towns and cities in the world, including brief historical information for larger areas.

Genealogy

Very few compiled genealogies are available for families or areas in the USSR today. Some of the German and many Mennonite families who settled in North America have published small family histories. The *Genealogy* heading in the FHLC for the USSR is almost exclusively devoted to handbooks or works about doing research. Most are in Russian. A brief but helpful English handbook is:

Mehr, Kahlile, and Daniel M. Schlyter. *Sources for Genealogical Research in the Soviet Union.* Buffalo Grove, Ill.: Genun, 1983. (FHL# 947/D27m)

Historical Geography

Gilbert, Martin. *Russian History Atlas.* London: Weidenfeld and Nicolson, 1972. (FHL# 947/E3g)

History

The library has a large collection of Russian histories that are helpful in understanding ancestral settlement and migration patterns. Histories are available for almost each republic and many smaller areas, but they seldom include specific families or individuals. For more detailed treatments of local or ethnic life and history, see the Subject FHLC under **Russia/Social Life and Customs/USSR.**

Riansanovsky, Nicholas V. *A History of Russia.* 2nd ed. New York: Oxford University Press, 1969. (FHL# 947/H2n)

Schreiber, Herman. *Teuton and Slav: The Struggle for Central Europe.* New York: Knopf, 1965. (FHL#940/H2sr).

Seton-Watson, Hugh. *The Russian Empire, 1801-1917.* Oxford: Oxford University Press, 1967. (FHL# 947/H2s)

Stumpp, Karl. *The German-Russians: Two Centuries of Pioneering.* Bonn: Atlantic Forum, 1971. (FHL# 947/F2sa)

Language and Languages

Books about the various languages in the USSR, and particularly Russian-English dictionaries, can aid the researcher in understanding documents found in family files or through research. The library has several such works including:

Pushkarev, Sergei G. *Dictionary of Russian Historical Terms, from the Eleventh Century to 1917.* New Haven, Conn.: Yale University Press, 1970. (FHL# 491.73/P979d)

Segal, Louis. *New Complete Russian-English Dictionary.* New York: G. E. Stechert & Co., 1942. (FHL# 491.7321/-Se37n or microfilm 1183562)

Maps and Atlases

When used in tandem with comprehensive gazetteers, maps can help the researcher learn what towns and/or parishes were near the ancestral home, then search available records for nearby areas. The library has a good collection of maps of the Soviet Union, but most of the detailed ones are printed in Russian. For many areas of western Russia, especially those formerly belonging to Prussian and Austria, the library has microfilms of excellent detailed military maps with German place names. See *Maps* in the sections under Germany and Austria in Chapter 19.

Minorities

The population of the Soviet Union is composed to a large extent of various minorities. Because few ethnic Russians emigrated, most ancestors that researchers are seeking were minorities. The library has many books about minorities, chiefly regarding the history, settlement, or culture of the various German colonies. Other sources are also listed under the specific republics. Also see **USSR/Ethnology, /Church History, /History, /Emigration and Immigration,** or **/Jewish Records** and the same headings under each republic or **Russia (Empire).**

Katz, Zev, ed. *Handbook of Major Soviet Nationalities.* New York: Macmillan, 1975. (FHL# 947/F2h)

Geisinger, Adam. *From Catherine to Khrushchev: The Story of Russia's Germans.* Battleford, Saskatchewan: Marian Press, 1974. (FHL# 947/F2ga)

Koch, Fred C. *The Volga Germans in Russia and the Americas from 1763 to the Present.* University Park: Pennsylvania State University Press, 1977. (FHL# 947/F2Kf)

Frumkin, Jacob, ed. *Russian Jewry, 1860-1967.* 2 vols. New York: Thomas Yoseloff, 1966. (FHL# 947/F2f)

Nobility

Most family stories of Russian nobility before the 1917 Revolution usually have no basis in fact. As a privileged class, nobles had no reason to leave Russia. However, descendants of Russian nobles who left during the revolution may be the easiest of Russian ancestry to trace since many sources have been compiled and published outside the USSR. The library has a fair collection on Russian and Baltic nobility, although many are in Russian or French. For further sources, see Chapter 28, "Medieval Families."

Gmeline, Patrick de. *Dictionnaire de la noblesse russe.* Paris: Editions Contrepoint, 1978. (FHL# 947/D5g)

Dukes, Paul. *Catherine the Great and the Russian Nobility.* Cambridge: Cambridge University, 1967. (FHL# 947/-H2du)

Bibliography

Successful USSR research entails searching all available material, even in obscure places. The following bibliographies contain references to a comprehensive range of aspects of Russian or Soviet life and history. Many of them include references to other books of genealogical value.

Horak, Stephan M. *Junior Slavica: A Selected Annotated Bibliography of Books in English on Russia and Eastern Europe.* Rochester, N.Y.: Libraries Unlimited, 1968. (FHL# 940/A3s)

Long, James. *The German-Russians: A Bibliography of Russian Materials with Introductory Essay, Annotations and Locations of Materials in Major American and Soviet Libraries.* Santa Barbara, Calif.: ABC-Clio, 1978. (FHL# 947/F231)

Maichel, Karol. *Guide to Russian Reference Books.* 3 vols. Stanford, Calif.: Hoover Institution on War, Revolution and Peace, 1962-67. (FHL# 947/A3m)

Selected Sources for Various Republics

Armenia

The library has a small but helpful collection of reference and history books for Armenia, many of them in English. There are also three histories of Armenian families. However, the library has no original source records (church, civil registration, etc.) for Armenia except for a few LDS membership records from the old Armenian mission (1924-28).

Azerbaijan

Maps and histories (in English and Russian) are the only items in the FHLC for this republic.

Belorussia

Histories and geographic aids comprise most of the Belorussia collection, but the library has an archives inventory (see *Estonia* below) as well as church records from six parishes.

Estonia, Latvia, and Lithuania (Baltic states)

Although they are three separate republics and each is listed separately in the FHLC, these republics share a common history, and many library sources apply to all three. Most of the entries for histories, maps, genealogy handbooks, and archive inventories are restated under each heading. In addition, the library has a good collection of materials on Baltic nobility, including documents on the Livonian Knights dating back to the thirteenth century, as well as many printed nobility lineages.

Records for specific towns, cities, and parishes are listed under the respective republic to which they belong. Church records are available for two parishes in Estonia, three in Latvia and thirty-six in Lithuania which were copied from West European archives. Most of the Lithuanian records are for old East Prussian areas around Meinel (Klaipeda). General sources include:

Grimsted, Patricia Kennedy. *Archives and Manuscript Repositories in the USSR: Estonia, Latvia, Lithuania, and Belorussia.* Princeton, N.J.: Princeton University Press, 1981. (FHL# 947/A3gr)

Welding, Olaf. *Deutschbaltische biographisches Lexikon 1710-1960.* Koln: Bohlau Verlag, 1970. (FHL# 947.4/D3w)

Biographical dictionary of Germans in the Baltic states. In German.

Langheinrich, Paul. *Verzeichnis der im Archiv für Genealogie befindlichen Originale und Filme von Kirchenbüchern.* N.p.: n.pub., 1953. (FHL# 943/K23v or microfilm 1045486)

Inventory of church records from eastern European areas in the Archives for Genealogy in Leipzig, East Germany.

Georgia

Histories again make up the majority of the small Georgia collection. There is, however, a small set of evangelical church records, 1900-15 for Tiflis (now Tbilisis).

Kazakhstan and Kirghizia

Four books, all in English, are available on the history and social life of these republics as well as a map of German settlements, and a study of the language.

Moldavia

Histories, maps, and gazetteers are again the focus of this collection; however, parish registers are available for a dozen German Evangelical communities in Moldavia (formerly Bessarabia) from about 1870 to about 1940.

Tadzhikistan, Turkmenistan, and Uzbekistan

The catalogs for these three Asian Soviet republics include a total of seven different entries dealing with histories, maps, language, and the LDS Turkish mission records.

Ukraine

By far the largest collection of genealogical research material for the USSR is Ukrainian church records (mostly Greek or Roman Catholic) from about 460 parishes, mostly in areas that used to be in Galicia, Bukovina, and Bessarabia. Although the FHLC does not catalog by geographic subdivisions for the Ukraine, each town or parish in the catalog is further identified by the addition of the *oblast* (in parenthesis) to which the town belongs. Most towns are in the *oblast* of L'vov, Ternopol, Ivano-Frankovsk, and Odessa. Most of these church records are also cataloged under Austria and Poland or Romania.

The FHLC includes many histories, maps, gazetteers, and emigration references for the Ukraine as well as the Hungarian census of 1828 which included Galicia and other present-day Ukrainian areas. See *Church Records* under Hungary in the Central Europe chapter for more information. Since most Ukrainian ancestors for which researchers are seeking are German settlers, the following may be helpful:

Keller, Conrad. *The German Colonies of South Russia.* 2 vols. Saskatoon, Saskatchewan: n.pub., 1968, 1973. (FHL# 947.7/F2k or microfilm 1181597)

Russia (Republic) or RSFSR

Russia is by far the largest Soviet republic, both in land area and population. Hence, most of the general references in the catalog are also cataloged under USSR or **Russia (Empire).** Major sources have been discussed earlier. Most of the catalog entries for **Russia (Republic)** include records from Kaliningrad *Oblast,* and a few other divisions, Leningrad being the second largest collection. Kaliningrad includes the former East Prussia area of Koenigsberg; registers are available for about 100 parishes. The FHLC includes another fifty localities in Kaliningrad for which the library lacks church records but has tax or land records, or local histories. Kaliningrad records also appear in the FHLC under **Germany/Preussen/Ostpreussen.**

Records by Jurisdiction — **Romania**	Archives & Libraries	Bibliography	Biography	Census	Church History	Church Records	Civil Registration	Colonization	Description & Travel	Directories	Emigration/Immigration	Encyclopedias/Dictionaries	Ethnology	Gazetteers	Genealogy	Handwriting	Heraldry	Historical Geography	History	Jewish History/Records	Land & Property	Language	Maps	Military Records	Minorities	Names, Geographic	Names, Personal	Newspapers-Bibliogr.	Nobility	Obituaries	Occupations	Periodicals	Politics & Government	Population	Social Life & Customs	Societies	Taxation
Romania	•	•	•	•	•	•	•		•		•	•	•	•	•			•	•	•		•	•		•	•	•		•			•	•	•	•		
Regions of:																																					
Drobrogea														•					•						•										•		
Transylvania	•		•		•	•			•		•		•	•	•		•		•				•		•		•		•			•			•		
Valachia																			•																		
Selected Districts:																																					
Arad				•		•																															
Bihor																				•																	
Bistrija Nasaud						•																															
Caras-Severin						•																															
Mures						•																															
Suceava						•					•																										
Timis						•																															

Records by Jurisdiction — **Yugoslavia**	Archives & Libraries	Bibliography	Biography	Census	Church History	Church Records	Civil Registration	Colonization	Description & Travel	Directories	Emigration/Immigration	Encyclopedias/Dictionaries	Ethnology	Gazetteers	Genealogy	Handwriting	Heraldry	Historical Geography	History	Jewish History/Records	Land & Property	Language	Maps	Military Records	Minorities	Names, Geographic	Names, Personal	Newspapers-Bibliogr.	Nobility	Obituaries	Occupations	Periodicals	Politics & Government	Population	Social Life & Customs	Societies	Taxation
Yugoslavia	•	•	•	•	•	•	•		•		•	•		•	•	•	•	•	•		•	•	•		•	•			•			•		•	•		
Republics of:																																					
Bosnai-Hercegovina							•																•									•			•		
Crna Gora															•			•																•			
Hrvat Ska	•				•	•	•				•			•	•	•		•									•								•		•
Makedonija							•						•					•																			
Slovenija	•					•					•			•				•				•	•									•					
Srbija	•	•				•								•	•			•									•		•					•			

Records by Jurisdiction — **Bulgaria and Albania**	Archives & Libraries	Bibliography	Biography	Census	Church History	Church Records	Civil Registration	Colonization	Description & Travel	Directories	Emigration/Immigration	Encyclopedias/Dictionaries	Ethnology	Gazetteers	Genealogy	Handwriting	Heraldry	Historical Geography	History	Jewish History/Records	Land & Property	Language	Maps	Military Records	Minorities	Names, Geographic	Names, Personal	Newspapers-Bibliogr.	Nobility	Obituaries	Occupations	Periodicals	Politics & Government	Population	Social Life & Customs	Societies	Taxation
Bulgaria		•	•						•		•			•					•			•	•		•	•	•		•				•		•		
Okrugs:																																					
Blagoevgrad														•												•											
Burgas																																			•		
Varna																																			•		
Albania		•							•				•	•	•				•			•	•						•						•		

Records by Jurisdiction — Poland's former regions	Archives & Libraries	Bibliography	Biography	Cemeteries	Church Directories	Church History	Church Records	Civil Registration	Colonization	Description & Travel	Directories	Emigration/Immigration	Ethnology	Gazetteers	Genealogy	Handwriting	Heraldry	Historical Geography	History	Jewish History/Records	Land & Property	Language	Maps	Military Records	Minorities	Names, Geographic	Names, Personal	Newspapers-Bibliogr.	Nobility	Obituaries	Occupations	Periodicals	Politics & Government	Public Records	Social Life & Customs	Societies	Taxation
Former Regions:																																					
Halicz														•					•						•												
Lwow							•																														
Nowogrod														•																							
Polesie							•							•																							
Pomorze		•										•		•	•				•				•			•	•										
Slask			•				•							•	•		•		•			•	•		•	•	•		•								
Stanistawow							•																														
Suwatki																																					
Tarnopol							•																														
Wilno							•							•																							
Wotyn						•						•					•		•				•		•				•								

Records by Jurisdiction — Poland and its present districts	Archives & Libraries	Bibliography	Biography	Cemeteries	Church Directories	Church History	Church Records	Civil Registration	Colonization	Description & Travel	Directories	Emigration/Immigration	Ethnology	Gazetteers	Genealogy	Handwriting	Heraldry	Historical Geography	History	Jewish History/Records	Land & Property	Language	Maps	Military Records	Minorities	Names, Geographic	Names, Personal	Newspapers-Bibliogr.	Nobility	Obituaries	Occupations	Periodicals	Politics & Government	Public Records	Social Life & Customs	Societies	Taxation
Poland	•	•	•	•	•	•	•	•	•	•	•	•		•	•		•	•	•	•	•		•		•	•	•		•	•		•			•		
Present Districts:																																					
Biatystok					•		•	•						•												•											
Bydgoszcz	•				•		•	•	•			•		•				•					•		•	•	•							•			
Gdansk			•		•		•	•				•		•					•		•				•		•										
Katowice			•		•		•	•												•			•		•												
Kielce					•		•	•																		•											
Koszalin					•	•	•	•				•		•							•		•														•
Krakow					•		•	•						•							•		•			•											
Lodz					•		•	•				•									•		•						•								•
Lublin					•		•	•											•				•												•		
Olsztyn				•	•	•	•	•				•		•						•			•			•											
Opole			•		•		•	•															•														
Poznan					•	•	•	•	•					•				•	•	•	•		•		•				•	•					•		•
Rzeszow	•				•		•	•													•		•			•											
Szczecin					•		•	•							•				•		•		•														
Warszawa	•				•		•	•		•									•				•			•											
Wroctaw		•			•		•	•															•						•								
Zielona Gora			•		•		•	•							•				•		•		•														

Records by Jurisdiction

U.S.S.R.

	Archives & Libraries	Bibliography	Biography	Church History	Church Inventories	Church Records	Civil Registration	Colonization	Description & Travel	Directories	Emigration/Immigration	Encyclopedias & Dictionaries	Ethnology	Gazetteers	Genealogy	Handwriting	Heraldry	Historical Geography	History	Jewish History/Records	Land & Property	Language	Maps	Military Records	Minorities	Names, Geographic	Names, Personal	Newspapers-Bibliogr.	Nobility	Obituaries	Occupations	Periodicals	Politics & Government	Schools	Social Life & Customs	Societies	Taxation
Russia (Empire)	•	•	•	•				•	•		•	•	•	•	•	•	•	•	•	•	•	•	•	•	•	•	•		•		•	•	•		•	•	
U.S.S.R.	•	•	•	•		•	•		•		•	•	•	•	•	•	•	•	•	•		•	•	•	•	•	•		•			•	•		•	•	
Republics of:																																					
Armenia	•		•	•		•							•		•				•			•	•		•		•					•			•	•	
Azerbaijn				•									•						•				•		•												
Belorussia	•		•	•		•					•			•					•			•	•			•		•				•			•		
Estonia	•	•	•	•		•	•				•			•	•				•		•	•	•	•	•	•			•	•	•						
Georgia				•		•					•		•		•		•		•		•	•	•		•				•								
Kazakhstan								•	•										•				•												•		
Kirghizia																			•			•	•														
Latvia	•	•	•	•	•	•	•				•			•	•		•	•	•		•	•	•		•		•		•	•	•				•		
Lithuania	•	•	•	•	•	•	•				•			•	•		•		•		•	•	•	•	•				•	•	•	•			•		
Moldavia					•	•			•					•					•				•		•								•	•	•		
Tadzhikistan																			•																		
Turkmenistan						•																															
Ukraine	•	•	•	•	•	•		•	•		•	•		•	•				•	•	•	•	•		•	•	•	•	•			•	•	•	•		
Uzbekistan																			•			•															
Russia (R.S.F.S.R.)	•	•		•								•	•	•	•			•	•			•	•		•			•									
Divisions of:																																					
Kalingrad		•		•	•	•	•			•	•			•	•				•	•			•	•		•							•				
Karelia			•			•				•			•						•				•												•		
Leningrad	•		•	•		•				•			•						•					•													
Moskva	•					•													•		•											•					
Siberia								•	•										•			•	•		•										•		

Chapter 21

Southern Europe

Kory L. Meyerink

Southern Europe, or Mediterranean Europe, consists of the major and minor countries which border or are close to the Mediterranean. For the purposes of this chapter, they are Italy, Spain, Portugal, Greece, and the tiny city states of Andorra, Gibraltar, Malta, Monaco, San Marino, and Vatican City. Because of the important similarities in the Family History Library's collection for these countries and the general availability of these countries' genealogical records, this introduction will discuss most of the major record categories. Specific details, when applicable, will follow in the country-by-country section. One major similarity is the relatively small collection in the library for these countries. Virtually no records are available through the Family History Library for the six city states while primary records (church and civil records) are presently available for only a few provinces in the four larger countries. Ninety percent of these records have been obtained in the last ten years, and microfilming is presently underway in Italy, Spain, and Portugal. Eventually, their collections will be among the largest in the library's collection.

However, the finding aids or secondary sources discussed here will generally still be applicable as research aids. The accompanying chart notes the provinces or administrative districts in Italy, Spain, Portugal, and Greece in which substantial microfilming has occurred, thus suggesting where original research can be most profitably pursued. Correspondence may be the best method for research in areas not yet microfilmed.

Southern Europe Library Collection

Archives

Archives abound in Southern Europe. Each province or administrative district has at least one in which older government records are deposited. Most large cities and many towns also have separate archives, as do many church dioceses. In addition, many family archives are scattered throughout these countries, usually containing the records of noble or wealthy families.

The library has inventories, descriptions, and finding aids for various archives in every southern European country except Gibraltar, Andorra, and San Marino. These are usually in the native language, as are most books in the collection, but some are in English. They are helpful in understanding the available records, especially for those areas not yet thoroughly microfilmed.

Biography

Most biographical works in this region are nationwide in scope and profile only major figures. They are of limited value in tracking the typical immigrant ancestor's family, who would usually be middle or lower class. However, for the major countries, the library has several collections of biographies.

Church Records

Church records are one of the two major genealogical tools for research in southern Europe and are becoming increasingly more available. Southern Europe is overwhelmingly Roman Catholic which, until the last century, was the state church in most of these areas. Greece, where the dominant religion is Greek Orthodox, is the only exception.

Some parish registers date from the mid-1500s, but loss and destruction of records in various areas make it impossible to give fixed dates for the beginning of parish registers. However, if a parish has extant records, they will usually date back to at least the end of the 1600s. For the most part, these records have not been centralized or indexed. They are generally available at the local parish, with, in some cases, copies in a local or church archive. Generally the records are written in Latin.

Church records are very similar to those found in the rest of Europe: primarily baptismal, marriage, and burial registers, naming the individual, his or her age, and the parents' names. Confirmation records or clerical surveys (a type of census) will also be found in some areas.

Civil Registration

In southern Europe, civil registration began in the mid- to late-nineteenth century, which is fortunately about a generation or so before most emigrants left these areas. In some areas, they begin earlier. Civil registration here, like most of the rest of continental Europe, was conducted locally, generally the town or municipality. Most of these records remain in the local offices; there are no regional or national indexes. Therefore, it is necessary to know the locality where the family lived before using these records successfully.

Some have been deposited in provincial archives and are being microfilmed. Decennial indexes, like those in Western Europe, do not exist, but usually each year is indexed. These records generally give more information about births, marriages, and deaths than do church records, sometimes including the grandparents of the subjects involved. Thus, even though they began comparatively recently, they can actually move a pedigree back two or more generations at a time.

Therefore, even if you know information about the ancestors who came after civil registration began, you should still look for them in these records.

Emigration and Immigration

Very few source records are available in these countries about emigrants. Except for some very early Spanish records, no emigration or departure lists are known to exist. Documenting immigrant ancestors is best done through U.S. arrival lists which are indexed after 1897 when most southern European ancestors came to America.

The numerous books cataloged in the FHLC under this heading in the various countries are typically studies about emigration, often focusing on a particular time period or group of emigrants. Generally, they are not lists of names of emigrants.

Genealogy

Published genealogies are still relatively rare in this area of Europe. The FHLC lists many such works for the larger countries, but they typically treat only the wealthy, major, or upper-class families. A few collected works are available for some countries. See the country-by-country discussion below. Also cataloged under this heading are genealogical periodicals, and "how to" books, when they are available.

History

These sources in the FHLC are of limited value in tracing a specific ancestor, for they tend to be general histories covering a region or time period. However, they can be very helpful for the researcher in learning about the history of an area, migration patterns and causes, and social information. Many of these are written in the native language; but where possible, I have cited comprehensive English histories.

Nobility

Some of these countries are still monarchies, and prior to 1900 most of them were. Thus, the nobility plays an important part in these countries. The library has an excellent collection of published books on the ancestry of many noble families. There are also many large collections on noble genealogies; this chapter cites only a few per country. Remember that most immigrant ancestors had no noble connections, so these collections should be used with care. For further information, see Chapter 28, "Medieval Families."

Bibliography

For further information on research and records in this area see:

Baxter, Angus. *In Search of Your European Roots.* Baltimore, Md.: Genealogical Publishing Co., Inc. 1985. (FHL# 929.1/B333i)

ITALY

Historical Background

476	Last Roman emperor defeated by German barbarians.
800	Charlemagne crowned emperor of the Romans.
1000s	Rise of independent city states.
1521-59	Spain defeats France for control of Italy.
1700s	Austria controls Italy.
1796	Napoleon conquers Italy.
1815	Congress of Vienna restores Italian states to pre-Napoleon rulers.
1848	Revolution in the Kingdom of the Two Sicilies. Constitution established there and in other Italian states.
1861	King of Sardinia defeats Naples and the Sicilies, creates united kingdom of Italy.
1866	Venetia added to kingdom.
1870	Rome added to kingdom, becomes capital 1871.
1880s	Italy tries to colonize parts of northern Africa without success.

1890s Half a million Italians emigrate yearly to America and elsewhere.

Settlement and Migration

Italy has been inhabited since the earliest historic times. Constant warfare among local groups and with invaders discouraged major immigration into Italy but encouraged many to leave. Overseas migration began in earnest in the late 1800s, when millions began emigrating to the Americas, notably New York. Emigration declined considerably after World War I.

Italy Library Collection

Italy is divided into nineteen regions that are roughly comparable to the historic areas of the country. Each region in turn is subdivided into one to nine provinces, making a total of ninety-one in the country. These provinces are the subdivisions used for most cataloging in the Family History Library Catalog (FHLC). Town records, when available, are listed under the name of the town within the specific province. In addition, a few general sources are listed in the FHLC under the regions when they apply to an area.

While extensive microfilming is currently underway in Italy, the collection is currently centered primarily in two regions: Toscana in West Central Italy with nine provinces, and Abruzzi e Molise in East Southern Italy with five provinces. The accompanying chart indicates which provinces have been thoroughly microfilmed. Since filming has concentrated primarily on the provincial archives, most of the records available are civil registration. Very few church records have been filmed since many remain at the local parishes or are in church archives. Note that most Toscana records are listed in the FHLC under Toscana itself and not under the specific provinces.

Archives and Libraries

Lewanshi, Rudolf J. *Guide to Italian Libraries and Archives.* New York: Council for European Studies, 1979. (FHL# 945/A3L)

Gli archivi di stato al 1952. 2d ed. Rome: Institute Poligrafico dello stato P.V., 1954. (FHL# 945/A3u/1952)

Description of the holdings of various civil registry offices, including amount of war damage.

Biography

Dizionario biografico degli italiani. Rome: Instituto della enciclopedia italiana fondata da Giovanni Treccani, 1960-date. (FHL# 920.045/D639d)

Church Records

Most Catholic registers in Italy begin in the early 1600s, although some begin in the 1500s. The library has few church records. Most remain at the local parish or are in diocesan archives; correspondence is probably the more practical way of doing research in these records. The Family History Library does have a small collection of parish registers of the Waldensians, a small protestant group in the Piedmont area on the French border (Torino province). It also has Catholic records from the province of Parma and some other areas. For help in determining Catholic parish boundarics scc:

Annuario della diocesi d'Italia, 1951. Torion: Marietta, 1951. (FHL# microfilm 780555-780556)

Civil Registration

The government began keeping civil records of births, marriages, and deaths throughout the country in 1869. However, many areas began civil registration earlier. In much of southern Italy, the records date from about 1808. For most of Tuscany, the records begin as early as 1838 while parts of northern Italy have records dating to 1810.

Even those areas with later records are benefitted by the thoroughness of these registers. Often two generations of ancestors are included on the record about an individual. These are the best records to use for nineteenth-century Italian research. The civil registers of other provinces are currently being microfilmed.

Directories

The library has a copy of virtually every province's telephone directories from about the year 1980. For some provinces, these are one of the few records in the library.

Emigration and Immigration

Foerster, Robert F. *The Italian Emigration of Our Times.* 1924; rpt. ed., New York: Arno Press and the New York Times, 1969. (FHL# 973/B4ai/Vol. 22)

Gazetteers

Nuovo dizionario dei comuni e frazioni di comuni con le circonscrizioni amministrative. Rome: Societa Editrice Dizionario Voghera dei communi, 1966. (FHL# microfilm 795216)

Genealogy

Gheno, Antonio. *Contributo alla bibliografia genealogica italiana.* Bologna: Forni Editore, 1971. (FHL# 945/A3g, microfilm 908856)

A bibliography of Italian genealogies.

History

Abbott, John Stevens Cabot. *Italy.* New York: Peter Fenelon Collier, 1900. (FHL# 945/H2a)

Maps

Touring Club Italiano. *Atlante automobilistico.* 3 vols. Milano: Arti Grafiche, 1969-71. (FHL# 945/E7tou)

Nobility

Litta, Pompeo. *Famiglie celebri italiani.* 21 vols. Milano: Paolo Emilio Giusti, 1819-71. (FHL# microfilm 761764-761769)

Bibliography

Stych, F. S. *How to Find Out about Italy.* Oxford: Pergamon Press, 1970. (FHL# 945/A3s)

Spain

Historical Background

711	Moors conquer Spain.
1200s	Various Christian Spanish kingdoms defeat Moors.
1479	Castile and Aragon unite as single kingdom.
1480-1700s	Inquisition persecutes non-Catholics.
1492	Granada conquered by Spain; Columbus discovers America for Spain.
1500s	Spain colonizes much of the North and South Americas.
1588	British defeat Spanish Armada.
1640	Portugal regains independence from Spain.
1714	Spain surrenders much of Italy to Austria.
1783	Spain gains control of Florida.
1808	Napoleon conquers Spain.
1810s	Spanish colonies in South America revolt.
1821	United States obtains Florida.
1898	Spain loses Spanish-America War and several territories including Puerto Rico.

Settlement and Migration

Spain has been inhabited since the earliest times, and there has been little immigration into the country since the Christian kingdoms defeated and expelled the Moslem Moors by the 1200s. In the sixteenth century, Spain was the dominant world power and established numerous colonies, thus encouraging emigration to the southern, central, and western Americas. Prior to the twentieth century, immigration to the United States was relatively small. Those choosing to leave Spain preferred to settle in present or former colonies.

Spain Library Collection

Geographically, Spain is divided into fifteen regions which are very similar to the original smaller kingdoms from which Spain was created in 1492. These regions are further divided into fifty provinces which are the major subdivisions used in the FHLC. Town records, as far as they have been collected and cataloged, are listed under the specific town within the appropriate province in the FHLC. Some references are cataloged under the regions when they apply to a larger area.

Microfilming is currently being done in Spain, and the library has large collections for some provinces; others, however, are sparse. Church records form the bulk of the Spanish collections. The provinces where microfilming has provided a large collection are indicated on the accompanying chart.

Archives and Libraries

Bibliografia de archivos españoles y de archivistica. Madrid: Luis Sanchez Belda, 1963. (FHL# 946/A5s)

Bibliography of the Spanish archives.

Censo. *Guia de archives españoles.* 2 vols. Madrid: Ministerio de Educaion y Ciencia, 1972. (FHL# microfilm 1389046)

Departmental listing of records to be found in various parishes.

Biography

Canals, S. Olives, and Stephen S. Taylor, eds. *Who's Who in Spain.* Barcelona: Intercontinental Book and Publishing Co., 1963. (FHL# 920.046/W62, microfiche 6000789)

Church Records

Church records are the primary source for genealogical research in Spain. Catholic registers go back to at least 1650 in most of Spain, and many registers begin a full century or more earlier. Some, but not many, have been destroyed by nature or through human agency.

The Family History Library is microfilming various diocesan archives. The records are generally being filmed from the earliest dates through the nineteenth century, in several cases to the 1920s and later. Where the parish records needed for research are not listed in the FHLC, correspondence with the parish or archive may be helpful. For a directory of Catholic parishes, see:

Guia de la Iglesia en España. 14 vols. Madrid: Secretariado del Episcopado España, 1954-1976. (FHL# 946/K24i; Vols 1-4 on microfilm 1162424; vol. 6 on 924464)

Civil Registration

Nationwide civil registration began in 1870, although some areas began earlier. Very few of these records have been microfilmed so they are best accessed through correspondence to the local Court of First Instance. The comparatively late date should not discourage researchers, as grandparents are usually included on the birth registers, thus effectively taking the information back to the 1820s.

Emigration and Immigration

Emigration lists are very rare in Spain. The only known lists are of persons sailing to America 1509-1701, but these were primarily persons on government or private business and not immigrants. They have been microfilmed on eleven rolls of microfilm, but are not indexed. See heading **Spain/Emigration-Immigration** in the FHLC for call numbers.

Maduell, Charles R. *Index of Spanish Citizens Entering the Port of New Orleans between January 1840 and December 1865.* N.p.: The author, n.d. (FHL# 976.335/NI/W2m)

Gazetteers

Gonzáles Ponce, Andrés. *Diccionario geografico de correos de España, con sus posesiones de ultramar.* 2 vols. Madrid: D. Manuel Morale Y Rodriguez, 1956. (FHL# 946/E8g or microfilm 599363)

Genealogy

Garcia Carraffa, Alberto. *Diccionario heraldica y genealogico de appellidos españoles y americanos.* 86 vols. Madrid: Nueva Imprenta Radio, 1952-63. (FHL# 980/D24g or Vols. 1-76 on microfilm 035111-035122)

History

Wilberforce, Archibald. *Spain and Her Colonies.* New York: Peter Fenelon Collier, 1900. (FHL# 946/H2wn)

Maps

Atlas geografico de España. 6th ed., rev. and corrected. Barcelona: Editorial 'alberto Margin, 1953. (FHL# Q/946/-E3ag or microfilm 599863)

Nobility

Municio Cristobal, Benito. *Bibliografia heraldico-genealogico nobiliaria de la Biblioteca Nacional de Madrid.* 2 vols. Madrid: Ediciones "Hidalguia," 1958. (FHL# 946/A3mc or microfilm 896895)

Bibliography

Ryskamp, George R. *Tracing Your Hispanic Heritage.* Riverside, Calif.: Hispanic Family History Research, 1984. (FHL# 946/D27r)

PORTUGAL

Historical Background

1143	Portugal becomes independent from the Moors.
1415	Portugal expands into Morocco.
1500	Portugal discovers and claims Brazil.
1580	Spain seizes and incorporates Portugal.
1640	Portugal regains independence.
1755	Major earthquake levels Lisbon, kills about 60,000 people, destroys many records.
1807	Napoleon conquers Portugal.
1811	British expel French.
1822	Liberal constitution grants many freedoms in Portugal; Brazil declares independence.
1861	Plague in Lisbon kills thousands.
1878	Slavery abolished in Portuguese colonies.
1910	Revolution ousts monarchy, establishes republic of Portugal.

Settlement and Migration

Germanic Visigoths invaded Portugal in the fifth century A.D. but were conquered by the Moors in the eighth. Wars against the Moors began in the 1000s by Spanish Christians who eventually were successful. By the mid-1200s, Portugal had ousted the last Moors and was in complete control of the present area of Portugal.

Few immigrants have settled in Portugal, but many emigrants have left since the 1500s to settle its many colonies, including Brazil. The islands of the Açores and Madeira have always been part of Portugal. In the nineteenth century, many people from these overpopulated islands came to America, settling chiefly in Massachusetts, California, and Hawaii.

Portugal Library Collection

Portugal is divided into twenty-two administrative districts which are also used as the major subdivisions in the FHLC. Records for a specific town or locality are listed under that town within its applicable administrative district. Some references, which apply to a broader region, are cataloged under that region – the Açores, for example.

Microfilmed church records form the greatest part of the library's collection with microfilming continuing, primarily in the various district archives. The accompanying chart indicates which districts have been mostly filmed. Note also that the islands themselves are often used as subdivisions in the FHLC to catalog maps and a few other records applying to an island, but not to the district or the group of islands (Açores) as a whole.

Archives and Libraries

Bibliotecas e arquivos de Portugal. 3 vols. Lisboa: Ministerio da Educação Nacional, 1969-73. (FHL# 946.9/A3b)

Biography

Pereira, João Manuel Esteves, ed. *Portugal: diccionário histórico, chorográphico, heráldico, biográphico, bibliográphico, numismático e artistico.* 7 vols. Lisboa: João Romano Torres, 1904-15. (FHL# 946.9/E5p or microfilm 946796-946805)

Church Records

As with Spain, church records are the major source for genealogical research in Portugal and constitute the vast majority of the library's collection. Most parish records begin in the late 1500s or early 1600s and are still usually kept in the local parishes. Microfilmed registers are available for many parishes, and are usually filmed to about 1880.

In addition, the library has seventy-seven reels of microfilm of Inquisition proceedings from Lisbon. Most of these date from the early 1700s.

For help in locating a parish, see:

Anuario católico de Portugal, 1968. 8th ed. Lisboa: Secretariado de Informaçño Religiosa, 1968. (FHL# 946.9/-K24a)

Civil Registration

In some areas, civil registration began in 1832, but it was not officially nationwide until 1878. Even then, it applied only to non-Catholics who were a small minority. Mandatory registration for the entire population began in 1911. The library has not yet microfilmed these records.

Emigration and Immigration

Taft, Donald R. *Two Portuguese Communities in New England.* 1923; rpt. ed., New York: Arno Press and the New York Times, 1967. (FHL# 973/B4ai/Vol. 42)

Gazetteers

U.S. Board on Geographic Names. *Portugal and Cape Verde Islands: Official Standard Names Approved by the U.S. Board on Geographic Names.* Washington, D.C.: U.S. Office of Geography, 1961. (FHL# 946.9/E5u or microfilm 874460)

Genealogy

Moya, Salvador de. *Catalogo de autores genealógicos.* São Paulo, Brazil: Departamento de Cultura, 1937. (FHL# 981/A1/no.15)

Bibliography of Brazilian and Portuguese genealogies.

Dornellas, Affonso de. *História e genealogia.* 14 vols. Lisboa: Livraria Ferin (vols. 1, 2) and Casa Portuguese (vols. 3-14), 1913-24. (FHL# 946.9/H2d)

History

Peres, Damião, ed. *História de Portugal.* 7 vols and supplement. Barcelos, Portugal: Portucalense Editora, 1928-54. (FHL# 946.9/H2ph)

Maps

Mapa de carreteras, España y Portugal. Madrid: Editorial Almaz, 1982. (FHL# 946/E7mc)

Nobility

Gayo, Manoel Jose da Costa Felgueiras. *Nobiliário de familias de Portugal.* 33 vols. Braga, Portugal: Oficinas Graficas da Pax, 1938-42. (FHL# 946.9/D2g)

Bibliography

Mattos, Armando de. *Manual de genealogia portuguese.* Porto: Fernando Machado, 1943. (FHL# 946.9/D27ma or microfilm 896862)

GREECE

Historical Background

1453	Ottoman Empire breaks up Byzantine Empire, absorbs Greece.
1820-70	Civil registration begins in various regions
1822	Greece declares independence.
1829	Greece defeats Turkey in war of independence.
1830	Kingdom of Greece established.
1911-13	Greece fights in Balkan Wars.
1924	Greece becomes a republic.
1935	Monarchy restored.
1967	Army seizes control, king exiled.

Settlement and Migration

Greece is one of the cradles of modern civilization, having been settled before recorded history. Migration into or out of Greece has not been common in the modern era until the late nineteenth century. Then, economic and political pressures encouraged many Greeks to resettle, principally in America and the major cities of Europe.

Greece Library Collection

The library has only recently begun to acquire primary source records from Greece, and the collection is still very small. Greece is divided into ten administrative regions which are similar to historic areas. These ten regions are further divided into fifty-two departments *(nomes)*, which the FHLC uses as its primary subdivisions.

Town records, when available, are filed by the name of the town within the *nome* to which it belongs. A few references are cataloged under the name of the various regions when applicable. The accompanying chart illustrates the sketchy status of the present collection. Beyond the church records available for three *nomes,* the library collection consists mostly of general references.

Many works are in Greek, and the catalog often transliterates them to the Roman alphabet. Rules for transliteration vary, so words, especially place names, appear under a variety of spellings.

Church Records

Church records are the primary source for genealogical research in Greece. The Greek Orthodox Church was the only church in Greece until recently. Many registers begin in 1707; but due to destruction, others are not available until the early 1800s. Most records are still in the individual parish; but some, prior to 1850, have been deposited in departmental archives.

The library has filmed church records prior to 1850 in the *nomes* of Leukada, Kerkyra, and Kykladon. These make up about 90 percent of the library's Greek collection. Correspondence is necessary to research other areas of Greece.

Gazetteers

U.S. Board on Geographic Names. *Greece: Official Standard Names Approved by the U.S. Board on Geographic Names.* Washington, D.C.: Government Printing Office, 1960. (FHL# 949.5 E5u or microfilm 873795 or microfiche 6053510)

Rossiter, Stuart. *The Blue Guides: Greece.* Chicago: Rand McNally, 1973. (FHL# 949.5/E6s)

Although primarily a travel guide, it has a helpful set of maps and good English descriptions of many towns.

History

Heurtley, W. A., et al. *A Short History of Greece, from Early Times to 1864.* Cambridge: University Press, 1967. (FHL# 949.5/H2h)

Language and Languages

Stouriotis, S. D. *Practical Modern Greek, a Self-education for English-Speaking People.* Athens: Margarita Press, 1971. (FHL# 949.5/A8s)

Maps

Greece Maps. N.p.: D. G. Tsopelas, 1981. (FHL# 949.5/-E7gm)

ANDORRA

Historical Background

c.800	Charlemagne drives Moors out of present-day Andorra.
954	Bishop of Urgel of Spain receives Andorra from the Holy Roman Emporer.
1278	Joint sovereignty agreement between Bishop of Urgel and French Count of Foix.
1589	King Henry IV of France, as Count of Foix, rules Andorra with Bishop of Urgel.
1614	Baptismal registers begin.
1694	Marriage and burial registers begin.
1800s	French president replaces king as co-prince of Andorra.
1950s	Increased tourism aids economy and changes occupations of many natives. Keeps many from emigrating.

Settlement and Migration

The original settlers of Andorra are not known but may well have been Charlemagne's troops. The country is nestled in the Pyrenees Mountains between France and Spain. Lack of land to expand into meant that many children of landowners had to move to France or Spain. Thus, more people with Andorran ancestry live outside the country today than within. The present population is about 38,000. Most migration has been to France and Spain.

Andorra Library Collection

Church Records

Seven parishes in Andorra contain all the primary genealogical records available. Roman Catholicism is the state church, under the direction of the Bishop of Urgel, Spain. The records begin in 1614 and are still in the parishes. The library has not filmed these records. However, twenty-four reels are available in the library, which include the sacramental records of the Diocese of Urgel from 1851 to 1876.

Gazetteers

U.S. Board on Geographic Names. *Spain and Andorra: Official Standard Names Approved by the U.S. Board on Geographic Names.* Washington, D.C.: Government Printing Office, 1961. (FHL# 946/E5sa or microfilm 874461)

GIBRALTAR

Historical Background

1309	Spanish capture Gibraltar from Moors.
1333	Morocco recaptures Gibraltar and heavily fortifies it.
1462	Spain regains Gibraltar.
1704	Gibraltar captured by British.
1783	Treaty of Versailles reconfirms British possession.

1830 Gibraltar becomes English crown colony.

1967 99.6 percent of population votes to keep ties to Great Britain.

1969 New constitution declares Gibraltar independent and part of British dominions.

Settlement and Migration

Ever since Spain successfully rid Gibraltar of the Moors, it has wanted control of this strategic "Rock." Britain, however, has remained in control, clearly by the choice of inhabitants. Most of the population is of Spanish ancestry but consider themselves "Gibraltarians" and are heavily influenced by the British.

Settlement in Gibraltar was slow due to the conflicting claims of possession and, beginning in 1704, was mostly British military personnel. Several hundred Spaniards settled there when Spain tightened border restrictions. Emigration from Gibraltar has predominately been to England.

Gibraltar Library Collection

Church Records

The population of Gibraltar is predominately Roman Catholic. However, the library has not yet microfilmed any Catholic records there. The library does, however, have some Church of England records for 1807-12.

MALTA

Historical Background

1530 Emperor Charles V gives Malta to Knights of St. John of Jerusalem.

1798 Napoleon seizes Malta.

1800 British blockade forces French surrender; Malta becomes British protectorate.

1814 Annexed by Britain.

1964 Malta declares independence.

1974 Malta becomes a republic.

Settlement and Migration

Malta sits in a strategic position and has been possessed and settled by many cultures over the years. Many inhabitants are descendants of Moors who lived there a thousand years ago. Many British settled there during the last two centuries. It is very densely populated, but relatively little emigration has taken place, as the British supported the economy fairly well until their withdrawal in the 1970s.

Malta Library Collection

Church Records

The library has no church records from Malta. Most of the population is Roman Catholic, and some parish registers date back to the 1550s. Most are still in the local parishes, and some were severely damaged during World War II.

Genealogy

Gauci, Charles A. *The Genealogy and Heraldry of the Noble Families of Malta.* Malta: Gulf Publishing, 1981. (FHL# 945.85/D5g)

History

Godechot, Jacques. *Histoire de Malte.* Paris: Presses Universitaires de France, 1952. (FHL# 945.85/H2g)

MONACO

Historical Background

900s Otto I, Emperor confers Monaco on house of Grimaldi.

1304 Ranier I becomes first Prince of Monaco.

1524 Monaco under the jurisdiction of Spain.

1641 Monaco under the jurisdiction of France.

1792 Royal line deposed by France.

1814 Sovereignty reestablished.

1815-60 Monaco under rule of kingdom of Sardinia.

1861 Monaco regains independence as French protectorate.

Settlement and Migration

Monaco was settled centuries before Christ, and there have been no major historical influx or decreases due to emigration. It is the second smallest sovereign state in the world, with a population of about 28,000. Most of the present population are recent immigrants from France, Italy, and other European countries drawn there by the political, social, economic, and physical climate.

Monaco Library Collection

Church Records

The state church is Roman Catholic, and there are five parishes in Monaco. Records prior to 1900 are in the Chancellery of the Bishop's Palace. The library has no Monaco church records.

Civil Registration

Civil registration began with French occupation in 1792. For a full discussion of these records, see Chapter 22, "Western Europe." The library has not filmed any civil records in Monaco, but filming in Nice, France, included five reels of films of Monaco civil registers from 1792 to 1813.

History

Labande, Léon-Honoré. *Annales de la principauté de Monaco.* 2d ed. Monaco: Les Editions de l'Imprimerie Nationale de Monaco, n.d. (FHL# 944.949/H21)

SAN MARINO

Historical Background

1250s	Under protection of Montefeltro family of Urbino.
1631	Pope Urban VIII recognizes San Marino's independence.
1862	San Marino places itself under protection of kingdom of Italy.

Settlement and Migration

Traditionally, San Marino was settled about A.D. 400 and has been a democratic republic since about 1000. Situated in a tiny mountain region in the Apennie region of Italy, it has been under the control or protection of several other states at times. It has not attracted many immigrants and presently has a population of only about 22,000. No major exodus has occurred from San Marino, but those who have left usually settle in the surrounding areas of Italy.

San Marino Library Collection

Church Records

San Marino is Roman Catholic, but the records have not been microfilmed by the library. They are available in the local parishes.

Description and Travel (Gazetteers)

Packett, C. Neville. *Guide to the Republic of San Marino.* N.pub.: n.p. n.d. (FHL# 945.49/E6p)

Genealogy

Koller, Fortune. *Livre d'or de la noblesse et du patriciat de Saint-Martin.* Bruxelles: Editions de Feniks, 1963. (FHL# 945.49/D5k)

History

Rossi, Guiseppe. *Storia breve della Repubblica di San Marino.* Lecco, Italy: Editrice Stefanoni, 1964. (FHL# 945.49/H2r)

VATICAN CITY STATE

Historical Background

1815	Congress of Vienna restores Papal States to papal control.
1859	Italo-Austrian war reduces Papal States by two-thirds.
1870	French withdrawal incorporates rest of Papal States in kingdom of Italy.
1871	Kingdom of Italy confines papal sovereignty to Vatican.
1929	Agreement between Italy and papacy creates Vatican City State as sovereign territory within Rome.

Settlement and Migration

Vatican City State is a remnant of the medieval collection of city states, often controlled by the pope, which covered central Italy. Since the creation of the kingdom of Italy (1870), the secular control of the pope has been limited to a small portion of Rome. In 1929, its size was fixed at 108.7 acres; and its current population is about 1,000. The Roman Catholic popes and their entourage have lived in the Vatican for most of the last 1,000 years. Migration in and out of the Vatican has been minimal–principally to and from Rome and the rest of Italy.

Vatican Library Collection

The Family History Library has not collected any primary records from the Vatican. Church records are available by correspondence. The FHLC lists four books about the Vatican, including a history of the Zouaves of the Pope and three archive guides. Particularly helpful is:

Boyle, Leonard E. *A Survey of the Vatican Archives and of Its Medieval Holdings.* Toronto: Pontifical Institute of Medieval Studies, 1972. (FHL# 945.634/A3b)

Records by Jurisdiction

Italy

Provinces	Archives & Libraries	Bibliography	Biography	Cemeteries	Census	Church Directories	Church History	Church Records	Civil Registration	Court Records	Description & Travel	Dictionaries	Directories	Emigration/Immigration	Gazetteers	Genealogy	Heraldry	Historical Geography	History	Land & Property	Language	Maps	Military Records	Minorities	Names, Geographical	Names, Personal	Naturalization	Nobility	Notarial Records	Periodicals	Population	Probate Records	Public Records	Social Life	Societies	Taxation
Italy	•	•	•				•	•			•	•		•	•	•	•		•		•	•		•	•	•	•	•	•	•	•		•	•	•	
Agrigento								•					•																							
Allesandria			•										•			•	•											•								
Ancona			•										•			•																				
Arezzo*									•				•																							
Ascoli Picento											•		•						•																	
Asti													•			•			•																	
Avellino									•				•			•																				
Bari													•			•												•								
Belluno													•																							
Benevento									•				•																							
Bergamo	•		•				•			•			•			•	•		•	•	•					•		•	•			•				
Bologna													•			•	•											•								
Bolzano							•		•	•			•						•	•			•										•			
Brescia							•		•				•			•																				
Brindisi													•			•												•								
Caltanissetta													•																							
Campobasso*									•				•																							
Caserta*													•													•										
Catania													•																							
Catanzaro													•			•												•								
Chieti*									•				•																							
Como													•			•												•								
Cosenza													•																							
Cremona			•										•			•												•								
Cuneo									•				•			•												•								
Enna													•																							
Ferrara			•						•				•			•												•								
Firenze*								•	•		•		•			•			•																	
Foggia*									•				•																							
Forli													•						•									•								
Frosinone									•				•																							
Genova								•					•			•												•								
Gorizia													•																							
Grosseto*									•				•																							
Imperia*									•				•			•	•																			
La Spezia													•															•								
L'Aquila*									•				•																							
Latina*									•				•																							
Lecce													•			•												•								
Livorno*								•	•				•											•												
Lucca*									•							•												•								
Macerta													•																							
Mantova													•						•									•								
Massa Carrara*			•						•				•																							
Matera													•			•			•									•								
Messina								•					•																							
Milano			•				•						•			•			•					•				•								
Modena*									•				•																							

Records by Jurisdiction

Italy (cont.)

Provinces	Archives & Libraries	Bibliography	Biography	Cemeteries	Census	Church Directories	Church History	Church Records	Civil Registration	Court Records	Description & Travel	Dictionaries	Directories	Emigration/Immigration	Gazetteers	Genealogy	Heraldry	Historical Geography	History	Land & Property	Language	Maps	Military Records	Minorities	Names, Geographical	Names, Personal	Naturalization	Nobility	Notarial Records	Periodicals	Population	Probate Records	Public Records	Social Life	Societies	Taxation
Napoli*									•				•			•			•									•								
Novara									•				•			•			•									•								
Padova													•			•	•		•									•								
Palermo	•						•		•				•																							
Parma*						•		•					•			•			•									•				•				
Pavia	•												•			•			•									•								
Perugia*								•					•																							
Pesaro e Urbino													•			•			•									•								
Pescara*									•				•																							
Piacenza								•					•																							
Pisa*									•				•																							
Pistoia*			•						•				•															•								
Pordenone													•																							
Potenza													•																							
Ragusa			•										•																							
Ravenna											•		•						•									•								
Reggio-Emila									•				•																							
Rieti*									•				•																							
Roma	•		•				•	•			•		•			•			•					•				•								
Rovigo													•			•												•								
Salerno							•						•						•									•								
Savona													•			•																				
Siena*									•				•																							
Siracusa			•										•																							
Sondrio													•						•							•										
Taranto													•			•												•								
Teramo*									•				•						•																	
Terni													•																							
Torino*								•					•						•									•								
Trapani			•					•					•						•									•								
Trento														•						•																
Treviso													•						•					•												
Trieste													•						•																	
Udine								•					•			•												•								
Varese													•															•								
Venezia							•	•					•						•					•				•			•					
Vercelli			•										•						•									•								
Verona													•			•			•									•								
Vicenza													•			•			•									•								
Viterbo													•																							

* Indicates that church and/or civil records of the entire province have been microfilmed.

Records by Jurisdiction — Italy Regions	Archives & Libraries	Bibliography	Biography	Cemeteries	Census	Church Directories	Church History	Church Records	Civil Registration	Court Records	Description & Travel	Dictionaries	Directories	Emigration/Immigration	Gazetteers	Genealogy	Heraldry	Historical Geography	History	Land & Property	Language	Maps	Military Records	Minorities	Names, Geographical	Names, Personal	Naturalization	Nobility	Notarial Records	Periodicals	Population	Probate Records	Public Records	Social Life	Societies	Taxation
Abruzzi e Molise													•																							
Bascilicata													•																							
Calabria											•		•									•						•								
Campania													•																							
Emilia Romagna													•						•					•												
Friuli-Venezia Guilia													•			•												•								
Lazio													•																							
Laguria													•																							
Lombardia			•									•	•		•	•			•	•					•			•								
Marche													•																							
Piemonte	•	•	•				•		•				•	•	•	•	•		•			•		•	•	•		•								
Pugie													•			•												•								
Sardegna	•										•		•		•				•									•								
Sicilia			•								•		•		•	•			•	•								•								
Toscana*	•				•				•				•			•			•						•			•								
Trentino-Alto Adige	•		•			•			•				•		•	•	•		•	•		•		•	•	•		•								
Umbria																•			•									•								
Veneto																•			•									•			•					

* Indicates that church and/or civil records of the entire province have been microfilmed.

Records by Jurisdiction

Spain

Provinces	Archives & Libraries	Bibliography	Biography	Cemeteries	Census	Church Directories	Church History	Church Records	Civil Registration	Court Records	Description & Travel	Dictionaries	Directories	Emigration/Immigration	Gazetteers	Genealogy	Heraldry	Historical Geography	History	Land & Property	Language	Maps	Military Records	Minorities	Names, Geographical	Names, Personal	Naturalization	Nobility	Notarial Records	Periodicals	Population	Probate Records	Public Records	Social Life	Societies	Taxation
Spain	•	•	•		•	•	•	•	•	•	•	•	•	•	•	•	•		•	•	•	•	•	•	•	•		•		•	•	•	•	•	•	
Alva*	•					•	•	•			•				•	•	•		•							•		•						•		
Albacete*								•			•								•															•		
Alicante											•																	•								
Almeria											•						•		•			•						•								
Avila	•						•				•								•																	
Badajoz	•						•	•			•								•			•														
Baleares	•										•								•			•						•								
Barcelona*						•		•	•		•					•			•	•		•						•								
Burgos		•	•			•	•	•								•				•																
Caceres	•																		•																	
Cadiz					•						•							•	•									•								
Castellon						•																														
Ciudad Real			•						•		•				•				•				•										•	•		
Cordoba																•		•	•									•								
La Coruna*			•			•		•			•								•														•			
Cuenca											•								•															•		
Gerona*							•	•	•		•			•					•	•		•								•				•		
Granada						•													•									•								
Guipuzcoa*					•	•					•				•	•		•	•			•				•								•		
Huelva																												•								
Huesca	•		•			•													•	•		•														
Jaen						•												•										•								
Leon						•													•			•		•				•								
Lerida*						•														•		•														
Lagrona	•		•			•					•				•	•						•												•		
Lugo*						•					•								•												•					
Madrid	•	•																																		
Malaga						•																						•								
Mallorca	•																					•														
Murcia																			•																	
Navarra*	•										•					•	•		•	•					•			•						•		
Orense						•		•			•								•			•									•					
Oviedo	•					•	•	•			•				•				•			•				•					•					
Palencia						•																														
Pontevedra*						•					•								•												•					
Salamanca*	•					•	•																						•							
Santander	•					•											•		•							•										
Segovia																•	•		•									•								
Sevilla	•					•	•																					•								
Soria																•																				
Tarragona						•			•										•	•		•														
Teruel	•		•			•		•											•			•														
Toledo											•					•	•		•															•		
Valencia	•						•		•							•						•						•								
Valladolid*	•				•	•																						•								
Vizcaya*		•	•			•					•				•	•	•		•			•				•		•						•		
Zamora	•	•	•			•	•												•			•						•								
Zaragoza	•		•			•											•		•	•		•			•											

* Indicates that church and/or civil records of the province have been microfilmed.

Records by Jurisdiction — Spain Regions	Archives & Libraries	Bibliography	Biography	Cemeteries	Census	Church Directories	Church History	Church Records	Civil Registration	Court Records	Description & Travel	Dictionaries	Directories	Emigration/Immigration	Gazetteers	Genealogy	Heraldry	Historical Geography	History	Land & Property	Language	Maps	Military Records	Minorities	Names, Geographical	Names, Personal	Naturalization	Nobility	Notarial Records	Periodicals	Population	Probate Records	Public Records	Social Life	Societies	Taxation
Andalucia			•				•										•											•								
Aragon		•																	•																	
Cataluna			•		•				•							•	•		•		•	•			•	•		•			•				•	
Extremadura																•			•										•							
Galicia	•		•								•					•	•		•							•										
Leon																			•																	
Vascongadas			•											•	•		•		•					•		•								•		

Records by Jurisdiction — Small States of Southern Europe	Archives & Libraries	Bibliography	Biography	Cemeteries	Census	Church Directories	Church History	Church Records	Civil Registration	Court Records	Description & Travel	Dictionaries	Directories	Emigration/Immigration	Gazetteers	Genealogy	Heraldry	Historical Geography	History	Land & Property	Language	Maps	Military Records	Minorities	Names, Geographical	Names, Personal	Naturalization	Nobility	Notarial Records	Periodicals	Population	Probate Records	Public Records	Social Life	Societies	Taxation
Andorra		•						•						•								•														
Gibraltar								•						•																						
Monaco	•								•	•	•		•			•			•									•								
Malta	•						•			•	•					•	•		•									•								
San Marino											•		•			•			•									•			•					
Vatican City	•																						•													

Chapter 22

Western Europe

Kory L. Meyerink

The countries of France, Belgium, Netherlands, and Luxembourg need to be treated together–not because their history, language, or peoples resemble each other but because most of their major record types do. While each country will be treated separately in depth in this chapter, several common links, genealogically speaking, apply to most of these four countries.

Over the last two hundred years (since the rise of Napoleon), similarities have increased. This is particularly true of Belgium and Luxembourg which straddle the cultural and linguistic borders between the French and the Dutch (or Germans) to the extent that two languages are recognized in both countries.

Each country is subdivided into regional areas called provinces in Belgium and the Netherlands, administrative districts or cantons in Luxembourg, and départements (departments) in France. These subdivisions correspond to counties in the United States or Great Britain and are the subdivisions used in the Family History Library Catalog (FHLC) Locality section.

The library catalogs in-coming records by jurisdiction: which jurisdiction created the record or which jurisdiction has the greatest interest in this record? The library has relatively few records of genealogical value at the provincial or departmental level, for most records of interest to the researcher were created at the next smaller jurisdiction, usually called the town in English *(geemente* in Dutch or *commune* in French). The influence of the town on local life and record-keeping is similar to that of the towns in New England. Virtually all records were kept at this local level, for the towns usually had original jurisdiction. As a result, numerous town records are available, cataloged town by town.

Usually, resources from the national or provincial (departmental) level are secondary sources such as histories or books about the topic (for example, archive inventories). Even though these records are not often primary research documents, they are valuable sources for successful research, as this chapter will illustrate.

Naturally, most of the sources (both books and primary records) discussed for these countries will be in one of the native languages: French, Dutch, Flemish, or German. All of these languages have some similarity to English, and the researcher should not shy away from using them. The major primary sources (civil registration and church records) use the same format. Once you understand the format, you can easily search the records.

Throughout this chapter, I cite key references with the same heading under which they appear in the locality section of the FHLC and in the same alphabetical order used by the catalog. Where possible, English sources have been used, but the best collection or treatment of a subject is often in a native language. The FHLC has many more references in most of these categories than I cite. Several minor categories (like heraldry or manors) do not appear at all in this chapter. You should consider this chapter as an introduction to the FHLC, but a thorough use of the FHLC itself and the many sources cited therein will spell the difference between successful research and genealogical "dead ends" for many researchers.

The two major primary sources for genealogical research in Western Europe–civil registration and church records–are similar for all four countries and will be discussed here. Specifics are then addressed under each country.

Western Europe Library Collection

Civil Registration

The coming of Napoleon in the 1790s had an effect on genealogical research as profound as his impact on the political and geographic shape of Europe. Perhaps greater–for the system of civil registration which he instituted is still used by many countries today. He began civil registration as far east as Russian Poland, but it is France and "Benelux" (Belgium, Netherlands, and Luxembourg) that most concerns us now.

Under this system, the government is responsible for recording births, marriages, and deaths for legal purposes, a function previously left to the church. Civil registration began in 1792 in France, in 1795 in southern Netherlands and 1811 in northern Netherlands, and in 1796 in Belgium and Luxembourg.

These records are very complete and include the complete name of each participant, age, residence, birthplace (even on death records), occupation, marital status, and usually the parents' names. Witnesses are required for each registration, and often their relationship to the subject is given. Registration was required for each birth, marriage, or death regardless of race or religious conviction. The compliance rate was very high, so almost all ancestors were recorded.

The country was divided for this purpose into civil registration districts which usually encompassed a local town and the smaller villages or hamlets that were politically linked to the town. The registration office was usually in the district's major town. No state or province-wide indexes to these records exist, so knowing the town or locality where the ancestor lived is necessary.

However, each registration district has indexes which cover ten years of records at a time. These "decennial" indexes are not strictly alphabetical. Usually they are chronological by the first letter of the surname. Registration districts are small enough that decennial indexes are usually quite short; all the names beginning with one letter usually cover only two or three pages. Therefore, it is fairly easy to find all the persons with the same surname in the records of the town for a ten-year period. When you do not know a specific town but know the region or area, you can easily check the indexes for several neighboring towns. Sometimes the birth indexes even include the father's name, making it very easy to put family groups together.

Church Records

Prior to the beginning of civil registration, the national government required churches to keep records of vital events which were made available to the local officials for legal matters. For most areas of Western Europe, parish registers began in the late 1500s regardless of the denomination. While these records do not include as much information as the civil registers, they are more complete than their British or American counterparts and, given the various denominations, seem to cover the vast majority of the local population.

Each local parish kept its own records, and parish, not civil boundaries, determine who was included in which register. However, in all four countries, the parish boundaries for the dominant church are usually identical to or very close to those of the local town and civil registration boundaries. For smaller denominations, you may need to determine the parish by using gazetteers and church inventories described under the specific countries later in this chapter.

These registers are usually written in the native language, although early Catholic registers will be in Latin. Some parishes are indexed (especially in the Netherlands and Belgium); if an index exists, it will be listed as part of the FHLC description of the record.

FRANCE

Historical Background

800	Charlemagne crowned King of France.
987	Hugh Capet crowned King of France.
1302	Philip IV called first States-General (forerunner of Parliament).
1540s	Intense persecution of Protestants.
1598	Edict of Nantes gives limited religious. freedom to Protestants.
1680s	France annexes Alsace.
1685	Edict of Nantes cancelled; 200,000 Huguenots flee France.
1783	France helps United States of America win independence.
1789	French Revolution.
1792	First Republic established.
1804	Napoleon founds First Empire.
1815	Napoleon exiled, Louis XVIII regains throne.
1848	Revolutionists establish Second Republic.
1852	Napoleon III founds Second Empire.
1871	France defeated in Franco-Prussian War; Third Republic begins.
1914	France fights World War I on Allied side.

Settlement and Migration

The Franks and other Germanic tribes invaded the area of modern France in the 400s. Their descendants are the French of today. While boundaries, especially those in the east and north, have shifted greatly over the 1100 years since Charlemagne, France has experienced no major migrations. Persecution of the Huguenots and wars with Germany along the Rhine produced a steady flow of emigrants to America, and elsewhere, from the 1600s to 1900.

France Library Collection

The Family History Library has a large and growing collection of French research materials. In fact, the size of the French collection is second only to Germany (nearly 100,000 reels of microfilm) among continental European countries. The vast majority of this collection consists of primary genealogical sources, civil and church registers, but in some areas, court or notarial records have also been microfilmed. Unfortunately, even this large collection represents only about one-third of the French records available, and the acquisition process seems to be slowing down at present. The library has a fairly complete filming of the major primary sources for thirty-two of France's ninety departments. Most of these thirty-two lie in southeast, northeast, and north-central France. The area around Paris has also been filmed.

For the remaining departments, the collection is very sparse, consisting mainly of secondary sources, background references, or a few scattered church or other records. The FHLC overview chart for France, shown at the end of this chapter, gives a department-by-department listing of microfilmed records. This overview chart will also give the numerous minor records or sources which cannot be described here that have been collected unsystematically for a few departments.

Before the revolution in 1789, France was divided into about forty large provinces. In 1795, as part of Napoleon's domestic reforms, France was divided into nearly 100 smaller and more efficient departments. The number of departments has fluctuated slightly over time due to mergers. The FHLC uses ninety departments and one territory as the primary subdivisions for the French locality catalog.

Records are filed according to their scope or jurisdiction. Most primary records were kept on a town or municipality (commune) basis and are listed under that town within its applicable department in the FHLC. (To locate a town, see *Gazetteers* below.) Works dealing with a larger area are filed under the department itself or **France/General.** The FHLC also uses thirty-three of the old provinces to catalog works such as histories that apply to an entire region. These entries sometimes also appear under the various departments which were created from those provinces. Town or local records are not listed under the old province to which they belonged.

Almost all records in the French FHLC are written in French, although early Catholic church records are in Latin. Where possible in this survey, appropriate English references will also be given. Be aware that, as of 1987, not all French sources have been input into the computer catalog (FHLC). Be sure to check the microfilmed card catalog (MCC) for additional records.

Archives and Libraries

The archival system of France includes the National Archives in Paris as well as archives in each department. Private, church, local, and family archives also exist. When possible, the library has tried to obtain inventories or catalogs from as many archives as possible. The FHL has archival inventories for most department archives.

Departmental archives typically have copies of church registers prior to 1792, civil registration to 1877, and notarial records over 125 years old.

Welsh, Erwin K. *Libraries and Archives in France.* Rev. ed. New York: Council for European Studies, 1979. (FHL# 944 J54w)

Favier, Jean, ed. *Les Archives nationales: état général des fonds.* 4 vols. Paris: Archives nationales, 1978. (FHL# 944 A3f)

Biography

Few local biographical works are available for France, but several books treat individuals of national prominence. Others focus on regional personalities or highly specialized topics such as Protestant ministers in Alsace-Lorraine from the Reformation to the present or the individuals for whom Paris streets were named. Governmental and military figures comprise the majority of persons included in most works.

Biographie moderne, ou, galerie historique, civile, militaire, politique, et judiciaire. 2 vols. Paris: Alexis Eymery, Libraire, et Dulaunay, 1815. (FHL# 920.044/B52m or microfilm 823592)

Haag, Eugene. *La France protestante: l'historie.* 9 vols. Paris: Imprimerie de J. B. Gross, 1846-59. (FHL# 944/D3hg or microfilm 962949-962953).

Biographical sketches of prominent persons in the Protestant movement in France.

Census Records

Beginning in 1836, the French government took national censuses every five years. These records list every person in each household with ages and sometimes birthplaces. Census records are kept in the departmental archives, and some have been microfilmed. A few earlier censuses are available for selected Departments, including a 1590 census for Bas-Rhin department, then part of Alsace. These earlier censuses only list the head of the household.

Church Records

Church records are the primary source of genealogical information prior to 1792. Catholic registers began in the mid-1500s and are still kept today, although some early books have been lost or destroyed over the years. Most registers prior to 1792 have been deposited in departmental archives, while the local parishes maintain later records. Roman Catholicism was the state religion of France prior to the French Revolution, and the vast majority of French were Catholic.

Protestant records have been kept since the 1500s but are very rare outside of Alsace. The records were illegal until 1787, so many Protestants are recorded in Catholic registers. The church records which have been microfilmed are listed in the FHLC under the name of the town where the church was, within the applicable department. Virtually every town was also the home of a Catholic parish.

Almanach ecclésiastique de France, pour l'an MDCCCXII. Paris: Adrien Le Clere, 1812. (FHL# 944/K22a or microfilm 823897)

Catholic church directory for 1812.

Civil Registration

After Napoleon ascended to power, he had the legal system reformed. The *Code Napoleon,* which is still the present French legal system, included civil registration of vital events, beginning in 1792. The local mayor of each town is responsible for maintaining the records. Records prior to 1850 are at the departmental archives. These records have been and are being microfilmed to the early 1870s. Some decennial indexes are available to 1902, filed in the FHLC by the name of the town where the act was registered. These registers are the primary source of genealogical information after 1792.

Court Records

Civil and criminal suits brought before the courts can include important genealogical information. Especially rich sources are land transactions, probate administrations, and paternity acknowledgements. These are kept at local and departmental archives. A few of these records have been microfilmed in the departments where filming has been completed. They appear in the FHLC under the town where the court was established.

Emigration and Immigration

The French have been establishing colonies all over the world for almost four hundred years, some of which still are under French protection. Consequently, the French population has been emigrating to those colonies and elsewhere, notably the United States. Registers of emigration, kept since about 1788, are found in the departmental archives. However, few of these records have been microfilmed.

The FHLC lists several brief records of emigration but most of the listings are studies about emigration and emigrants rather than emigration records. Most nineteenth-century emigrants left through French ports, notably La Harve. The library does not have these lists and probably will not for several more years. U.S. arrival records are the best available source for documenting French emigrants.

An important exception is an emigration record of persons traveling from or through the Alsace region between 1817 and 1866. A card index to these emigration records has been microfilmed on six reels (FHL# 1125002-1125007).

For ancestors leaving Alsace and Lorraine, or moving to or from these areas within France about 1871-72, another source is available. A half-million inhabitants of Alsace and Lorraine, were recorded in 395 lists created by local governments. About 25 percent of these people shortly thereafter moved to America or elsewhere in France. These lists are available on thirteen reels of microfilm (FHL# 787154-787166). For emigration to America before this period see:

Neu, Heinrich. *Elsasser und Lothringer als Ansiedler in Noord America*. In *Jahrbuch der Elsass-Lothringischen Wissenschaftlichen Gessellschaft zu Strassburg.* Strassburg: n.pub., 1930. (FHL# microfilm 1071428)

Gazetteers

Gazetteers are necessary tools in locating a specific town, since the FHLC lists town records according to the department of the town itself. Departmental boundaries are the only significant permanent change in French political geography over the last few hundred years. For boundaries prior to the 1789 revolution, consult:

Mirot, Leon. *Manuel de géographie historique de la France*. 2 vols. Paris: A. et J. Picard, 1947-1950. (FHL# 944/E2m)

For modern France, including departmental maps, see:

Bottin, départements, classement géographique. 4 vols. Paris: Didot-Bottin, 1970. (FHL# 944/E4b/1977)

See also *Maps* below.

Genealogy

Published genealogies of common families are now becoming popular in France, and the library's collection is growing slowly. Those before a generation ago usually deal only with noble families. Such works are listed under **France/Genealogy** in the FHLC. A helpful index or repertory citing the major families covered in most of the available published genealogies is:

Arnaud, Étienne. *Repertoire de généalogies françaises imprimées*. 3 vol. Paris: Berger-Levrault, 1978-82. (FHL# 944/D23a)

Two small collections in the FHLC may also be helpful:

Chaix-d'Est-Ange, Gustav. *Dictionnaire des familles françaises, anciennes ou notables à la fin du XIXe siécle.* 20 vols. Evereux: Hérissey, 1903-29. (FHL# microfilm 661936-661942 and 767586)

Woelmont de Brumage, Henri. *Notices généalogiques.* 8 vols. Paris: Henri Champion and Librarie historique et nobiliaire, 1923-35. (FHL# microfilm 745338-745346)

History

The library has over 150 books on various aspects of French history plus histories for many of the departments. Unfortunately, most of these sources have not been microfilmed for family history center circulation. The vast majority are written in French with some in English or German.

Lévêque, André. *Historie de la civilisation française.* Rev. ed. New York: H. Holt, 1949. (FHL# 944/H2Lb)

Land and Property Records

Until the revolution, land ownership in France generally followed the feudal system; feudal lords generally held large tracts of land in fief from the monarch. Although there were some small freeholders, most were attached to estates, rented land from the lord, and owed goods and services to him. The library has some microfilms of records dating from the fourteenth and fifteenth centuries which include purchases and rentals of land with names and dates of those involved. The original records, including many which have not been filmed, are at the national and departmental archives. However, these records generally include only a small percentage of the population.

Language and Languages

French is a Latin-based language and has contributed thousands of words to the English language, making it one of the easiest languages for American researchers to work with. Since the French Revolution, all records have been kept in French except for those areas (Alsace-Lorraine) which belonged at times to Germany. Records for those areas appear in either French or German. Prior to the revolution, many records were kept in Latin, especially Catholic church registers, with French being used in other records. Besides a good French-English dictionary, the following dictionary of Old French would be helpful:

Godefroy, Frédéric. *Lexique de l'ancien français*. Paris: Librairie Honoré Champion, 1965. (FHL# 447.013/-G542L)

Maps

The Bottin gazetteer of France includes maps of each department. See also:

Dufour, Auguste Henri. *Atlas des départements de la France*. Paris: Logerot J. Gaultier, n.d. (FHL# 944/E7a)

Minorities

Historically, the largest minority in France has been the Huguenots or French Protestants. Most of them left France for America, Switzerland, Germany, Belgium, the Netherlands, or England.

The Huguenot Society of London has published many records, including Huguenot parish records, which are available at the Family History Library. "Assistance records" from Frankfurt am Main, cataloged in the Germany FHLC, also help in locating the original French town of an immigrant Huguenot.

The library also has ninety microfilm reels of French documents arising from the administration of Huguenot property. These records are cataloged by province or region in the FHLC under **France/Minorities.**

Rothrock, George A. *The Huguenots: A Biography of a Minority*. Chicago: Nelson-Hall, 1979. (FHL# 944/F2rg)

Nobility

The library has well over 100 sources on French nobility, most of them published genealogical books. For further information, see Chapter 28, "Medieval Families," which handles royal and noble families. A major source is:

Saint-Allais, Nicolas Viton de. *Nobiliare universel de France.* 21 vols. Paris: Réimprimé à la Librarie Bachelin-Deflorenne, 1872-77. (FHL# 944/D5s or microfilm 661853-863)

Periodicals

Almost every department in France has a local genealogical society which publishes a magazine. These periodicals contain queries, articles on sources, some source records, and compiled genealogies. However, many began publication within the last decade, so the amount of published data is relatively small. The library has copies of some of these periodicals, but they are not available on microfilm.

For further information, contact the Fédération des Sociétés Françaises de Généalogie, d' Héraldique et de Sigillographie, 11 Boulevard Pershing, 78000 Versailles, France.

Bibliography

Bernard, Gildas. *Guide des recherches sur l'historie des families*. Paris: Archives Nationales, 1981. (FHL# 944/-D27b)

Durye, Pierre. *Genealogy: An Introduction to Continental Concepts.* Wilson Ober Clough, trans. New Orleans: Polyanthos, 1977. (FHL# 944/D25d0)

de Tupigny, Jacques Meurgey. *Guide des recherches généalogiques aux archives nationales.* Paris: n.pub., 1956. (FHL# 944/ D2f or microfilm 896889)

NETHERLANDS

Historical Background

1450s	Estates General, early form of Parliament, established, controlled by Philip the Good, Duke of Burgundy.
1454	Great Council established to unify court system between states.
1479	War between Holland and Gelderland begins; devastates much of countryside.
1522	Inquisition instituted in most Dutch states.
1530s	Anabaptists (later called Mennonites) established.
1568	Eighty-year war for independence from Spain begins.
1579	Union of Utrecht consolidates northern provinces.
1588	Republic of the Seven United Netherlands founded.
1602	United East India Company founded.
1609	"Pilgrims" settle in Netherlands; Hudson discovers New Netherland (later New York).
1621	War with Spain resumed.
1623	First Dutch settlements in New Netherland.

1648	Peace of Munster ends eighty-year war; Netherlands officially recognized as an independent state.
1702-13	Third War with France (War of Spanish Succession).
1795	France conquers Netherlands, forms Batavian Republic.
1805	Batavian Republic dissolved, kingdom of Holland created under French rule.
1810	Kingdom of Holland dissolved, annexed to French Empire.
1814	Napoleon defeated.
1815	Southern (or Austrian) Netherlands (now Belgium) becomes part of new kingdom of the Netherlands.
1829	First national census.
1831	Southern Netherlands rebels and establishes kingdom of Belgium (recognized 1839).
1846	Reformed Church dissenters begin emigration to Michigan and Iowa.

Settlement and Migration

Settlements dating to several centuries before Christ have been unearthed in the Netherlands, but little is known of the area before the sixth and seventh centuries A.D. when the Fries, Franks, and Saxons were christianized. Although there has been little immigration after the Frank and Fries tribes settled in the area a few centuries earlier, it has remained one of the most densely populated regions of Europe.

Whenever the Dutch were not fighting conquering countries (Germans, Burgundians, Spanish, then French), they were fighting nature. Many coastal locales were subject to flooding, and the bubonic plague recurred frequently between the fourteenth and seventeenth centuries. Consequently, the population fluctuated wildly from between 1 and 3 million.

Even before they were part of the wide-flung Spanish empire during the sixteenth century, the Dutch have been world travelers. Dutch craftsmen built cities in Sweden and Russia while others settled in the East and West Indies and in North and South America. Today people of Dutch descent are found all over the world, including 6.3 million Americans who claim predominant Dutch ancestry. Given over 350 years of Dutch residence in America, probably more than twice that number have some Dutch ancestors.

Netherlands Library Collection

The Family History Library has an excellent collection of primary source records for the Netherlands as well as outstanding secondary sources to assist the researcher. The scope of the collection makes the Netherlands the easiest Continental country to do research in and one of the best in the entire world. In fact, it is probably faster to do Dutch research in Salt Lake City than anywhere else, including the Netherlands themselves.

In using the FHLC, be aware of potentially troublesome Dutch spellings. The ij combination is treated as one letter, equivalent to a "y" and is filed alphabetically between "y" and "z." Also, certain prefixes to given or place names are disregarded in filing, notably Ter, De, Den, 's, and 't. In each of these cases, find entries by looking for the word following these prefixes.

The library has published an excellent series of research papers on the sources available for each province and other aspects of Dutch research. See the bibliography at the end of the Netherlands section for further details.

Archives and Libraries

The Dutch system of archives includes a Rijks (national or state) Archive and an archives in each of its eleven provinces. In addition, numerous church, private, and family archives exist. The FHLC lists over sixty archive inventories or catalogs, many of them for family archives. For an overview of the state archives holdings, see:

De Rijksarchiven in Nederland: overzicht van de inhoud van de Rijksarchiefbewaarplaatsen. 's-Gravenhage: n.pub. 1953. (FHL# 949.2/A3dr)

Biography

The FHLC lists over two dozen biographical dictionaries for the Netherlands. However, these works usually focus on notable persons or specific occupations, for example, Dutch navigators of the seventeenth century, royal governors, Jewish physicians, or Dutch artists. One six-volume set is the major reference work:

Molhuysen, P.C. *Niew Nederlandsch biografisch Woordenboek.* Leiden: A. W. Sijthoff's Uitgevers-Maatschwappij, 1911-24. (FHL# 949.2/D3m or microfilm 1045431-1045433, microfiche 6053511)

Census Records

Censuses were taken in parts of Holland as early as 1580, but generally they date from 1795. Censuses prior to 1829 (the date of the first federal census) were taken on a local or provincial level. Generally, they are available only to 1850 when they were incorporated into the Population Registers (see below). The Family History Library has filmed most extant pre-1850 census records; and, depending on their scope, they are cataloged either under the province or under a specific town.

Church History

Reitsma, J. *Geschiedenis van de Hervorming en de Hervormde Kerk der Nederlanden.* 3rd ed. Utrecht: Kemink & Zoon, 1916. (FHL# 949.2/K2r)

This work is a history of the Reformation and the Dutch Reformed Church in the Netherlands.

Church Records

Church records are one of the major sources for Dutch research before civil registration began in 1795 for the southern provinces, and 1811 for the northern. For that period, they are the only source which recorded virtually the whole population. Generally, the Roman Catholic Church predominated in the south while the Dutch Reformed Church was the major denomination in the north. Church registers of baptism, marriages, and burials began before 1600 in each province except Overijssel. However, many early books were not complete or have been lost, so not every parish has records dating to the 1500s.

Most of the minor denominations, notably the Mennonites (doopsgezinden), Lutheran, Remonstrant, and Walloon or French Reformed Churches also kept good records. See the Bibliography at the end of this section for research papers that describe the records available for which localities for each denominations. Each provincial research paper acts as a parish gazetteer.

The Family History Library has filmed most available church records. They are listed in the FHLC under the name of the parish which is usually the same as the municipality *(geemente)*. Many church records have been indexed, and these indexes are noted in the FHLC. These indexes combine the information from several parishes for some large cities, facilitating research. The FHLC also has inventories which can help locate church records. Of particular note is this concise repertory which lists each parish, the municipality to which it belongs, the types of church records extant, the years they cover, and the record repository:

Wijnaendts Van Resandt, Willem. *Repertorium DTB.* 2d ed. 's-Gravenhage: Centraal bureau vor Genealogie, 1980. (FHL# 949.2/K2w/1980)

Civil Registration

In the Netherlands, civil registration began by 1811–by 1795 in some southern areas. Prior to 1813 or 1814, the records are kept in French. Decennial indexes begin for the 1813-22 time period and continue at ten-year intervals. Earlier years have one- or two-year indexes. The library has records for virtually every municipality through 1882 and most to 1892. Later records are available if the subject of the record or his/her proven descendent request them in writing from the local municipality.

After about 1813, the records are kept on pre-printed forms. This standardized format plus the indexes makes research in these records fairly easy. To see what records are available for each locality and to see which civil registration municipality it belongs to, see the research papers in the bibliography.

Court Records

Dutch court records contain criminal and civil suits, civil marriages, property transfers, probate records, powers of attorney, and other legal documents. In the Netherlands, some court records date to the 1200s, but the library's collection largely concentrates on the seventeenth to mid-nineteenth centuries.

Despite their rich information, court records are among the least used of Dutch sources because they are seldom indexed, not formatted like church and civil records, often use a more difficult handwriting, and include a smaller segment of the population. Researchers generally use court records to resolve pedigree and biographical problems. Generally, they are cataloged under the municipality or province served by the court.

Emigration and Immigration

The Dutch have always been a sea-going people and established overseas colonies as early as the sixteenth century. Thus, the Dutch have been emigrating all over the world for almost 400 years. The most important and sizeable of their settlements was New Netherlands, later New York, explored in 1609 and permanently settled in 1624.

Very few emigration records exist from those early years. However, the published genealogies of many early Dutch families in America very often begin by locating the immigrant ancestor in Europe. Most eighteenth-century immigrants from continental Europe (the Germans, French, Swiss, and Dutch) left from the Dutch ports of Rotterdam and Amsterdam, but the departure lists have not survived. Nor are American arrival lists available except for those kept in Philadelphia. (See this topic under Pennsylvania in Chapter 6.) New York arrival lists begin in 1820 and are available through 1943 with indexes for 1820-47 and 1897-1943. (See the topic under New York in Chapter 6.)

The Dutch began keeping emigration lists provincially in the 1830s and nationally in 1847. These lists include the emigrant's name, age, marital status, previous residence, destination, and other information. They are available through 1877 on twelve reels of microfilm in the Family History Library. These lists, with the addition of some earlier and later provincial lists, have been abstracted and indexed:

Swierenga, Robert P. *Dutch Emigrants to the United States, South Africa, South America, and Southeast Asia, 1835-1880.* Wilmington, Del.: Scholarly Resources Inc., 1983. (FHL# 949.2/W2s)

Dutch arrivals at U.S. ports have also been indexed to 1880:

Swierenga, Robert P. *Dutch Immigrants in the U.S.: Ship Passenger Manifests, 1820-1880.* 2 vols. Wilmington, Del.: Scholarly Resources, 1983. (FHL# 973/W2sr or microfiche 6200012-35)

In addition, the same author has indexed Dutch arrivals in Quebec passenger lists, 1865-80. The local population registers (see *Population Registers* below) kept in various localities, then nationally, have recorded emigration from the Netherlands since 1850.

Another recommended book in the library's large collection on Dutch immigration is:

Hinte, Jacob von. *Netherlanders in America: A Study of*

Emigration and Settlement in the Nineteenth and Twentieth Centuries in the United States of America. Grand Rapids, Mich.: Baker Book House, 1985. (FHL# 973 W2hj) Translation of the 1928 Dutch edition.

Gazetteers

Several gazetteers will help you determine the specific locality where an ancestor lived so you can then find the records which were generated by a municipality and have been cataloged in the FHLC by the name of that municipality. If you know the province your ancestor came from, then the research paper for that province will help locate towns. The FHLC also lists several other helpful gazetteers:

Aa, Abraham Jacobus van der. *Aardrijkskundig Woordenboek der Nederlanden.* 13 vols. Gorichem: Jacobus Noorduijn, 1839. (FHL# 949.2/E2a or microfilm 496582-590)

Laan, Kornelis ter. *Van Goor's Aardrijkskundig Woordenboek van Nederland.* 3d ed. Den Haag: Van Goor Zonen, 1968. (FHL# 949.2/E2tl)

Genealogy

More than any other Europeans, the Dutch have actively traced their genealogy and published the results. This interest is reflected in the number of records available, the number of indexes to those records, the existence of a government-supported "Central Bureau for Genealogy," and numerous published family histories--over 300 listed under **Netherlands/Genealogy**. Since the locality section of the FHLC lists family histories only by author, it is easiest to access these histories by using the Surname section of the FHLC as explained in Chapter 10 , "Tools, Resources, and Previous Research."

In addition to published books, Dutch genealogical periodicals also discuss many families (see *Periodicals* below) as do some U.S. genealogical periodicals and manuscript collections. Fortunately, an excellent, fairly comprehensive reference work indexes the major surnames in these compilations:

Beresteyn, E. A. van. *Genealogisch Repertorium.* Den Haag: Centraal Bureau voor Genealogie, 1972. (FHL# 949.2/-D25b/1972)

History

The FHLC has few local histories dealing with a specific town, and those are often short picture books with only a general sketch of the area's history and little attention to individuals. Histories are available for most provinces, but again they include very little information on individuals.

However, by far the largest history collection in the FHLC is general histories of the Netherlands. While they are not specific about small localities, they do help give an understanding of the historical forces that affected ancestors. Virtually all of this collection is in Dutch.

Motley, John Lothrop. *History of the United Netherlands: From the Death of William the Silent to the Twelve Years' Truce-1609.* 4 vols. New York: Harper & Brothers, 1870. (FHL# 949.2 H2mo)

_____. *The Rise of the Dutch Republic.* 2 vols. London: Swan Sonnenschein & Co., 1899. (FHL# 949.2/H2m)

Language and Languages

The Dutch language is not difficult for a researcher to work with. It is very similar to German and Danish and shares many roots with English cognates. Most of the civil and church records are clearly formatted and use similar words. Dictionaries are also available in the library.

Cassell's English-Dutch, Dutch-English Dictionary, New York: Macmillan, 1982. (FHL# 439.31321/ca272)

Maps

Kuyper, J. *Gemeente-atlas van Nederland: naar officieele bronnen bewerkt.* 11 vols. Leeuwarden: Hugo Suringan, c.1955. (FHL# 949.2/E3k or microfilm 1181567)

Military Records

The library has a very good collection (over 1,600 reels) of Dutch military records covering enlisted men, draftees, and officers. Service records are arranged by the unit in which the soldier served and cover about 1795 to the 1920s. Unfortunately, few indexes are available to determine the unit in which an ancestor served.

These records are filed under **Netherlands/General** in the FHLC.

Nobility

Vorstermann Van Oyen, A. A. *Dictionnaire nobiliaire.* La Haye: C. Van Doorn, 1886. (FHL# 949.2/D22vo)

Notarial Records

Dutch notarial records can contain almost any legal document and typically include wills and codicils, marriage contracts, deeds, guardianship, and apprenticeship papers. Generally, they are cataloged by the locality where the notary lived, which generally corresponds to a municipality.

Indexes were required by law in 1803 but are rare before then. However, some records include tables of contents.

Some notarial records date to the mid-1500s; most of those before 1811 are microfilmed. Part of the collection extends to 1842; but after that date, they are not available to the public. Like court records, they can be difficult to use but may carry a prominent family back to a date earlier than the local church records or solve a problem in identifying an ancestor and his or her family.

Periodicals

Dutch genealogists in the Netherlands have produced over a dozen regularly published periodicals dealing exclusively with genealogy. Many of them publish local family lineages which can be of great benefit to the researcher. The library has an excellent collection of these references, most of them indexed in *Genealogisch Repertorium* (see *Genealogy* above). Two of the major periodicals still being published are:

Gens Nostra, periodical of the Netherlands Genealogical Society, Amsterdam, 1946-date. (FHL# 949.2/D25g)

De Nederlandsche Leeuw, periodical of the Genealogical-Heraldic Society of the Netherlands, 1883-date. (FHL# 949.2B2ned)

Population Registers

Beginning in 1811, some provinces and localities kept a population register. Formats vary, but typically, registers were ledger-style books listing each household and information on each family such as birth, marriage, and death dates, religion, occupation, removals, etc. After 1850, these registers were kept nationally. In the 1930s, the format was changed to a card which is kept for each family.

When an individual or family moves to another locality within the Netherlands, that town receives copies of the cards. Many of the early registers have been microfilmed to 1910 and sometimes later, but recent cards are protected by privacy laws.

Population registers generally are cataloged under the name of the specific municipality. These records supplant the pre-1850 censuses and are useful in tracking family groups, moves, and emigrations.

Bibliography

For further information on research in the Netherlands see:

Franklin, Charles M. *Dutch Genealogical Research*. Indianapolis, Ind.: Ye Olde Genealogie Shoppe, 1982. (FHL# 949.2/D27cf)

Nederhand, Erica Hartman. *Ancestral Research in the Netherlands: Textbook for an Advanced Study in Dutch Records and Methods of Genealogical Research*. 2 vols. Salt Lake City: Genealogical Society of Utah, 1966. (FHL# 949.2/D27ne or microfilm 845093)

The Family History Library has produced several helpful research aids. Most of the papers in Series C deal with Dutch records and usage, often in great depth. The series is cataloged collectively under FHL# 929.1/G286gs/Ser. C but have been microfiched separately. Here is a listing by the number within Series C, the title, and the microfiche number:

3."Major Genealogical Record Sources in the Netherlands." 6000039

5."Guide to Genealogical Sources in the Netherlands–Zeeland." 6000041

6."Guide to Genealogical Sources in the Netherlands–Gronningen." 6000042

7."Guide to Genealogical Sources in the Netherlands–Friesland." 6000043

8."Guide to Genealogical Sources in the Netherlands–Overijssel. 6000044

9."Guide to Genealogical Sources in the Netherlands–Gelderland." 6000045

10."Guide to Genealogical Sources in the Netherlands–North Holland." 6000046

11."Guide to Genealogical Sources in the Netherlands–Utrecht." 6000047

12."Guide to Genealogical Sources in the Netherlands–Limburg." 6000048

13."Guide to Genealogical Sources in the Netherlands–North Brabant." 6000049

14."Guide to Genealogical Sources in the Netherlands–South Holland." 6000050

15."Guide to Genealogical Sources in the Netherlands–Drenthe." 6000051

20."Church Records of the Netherlands–Remonstrant Church." 6000052

21."Church Records of the Netherlands–Mennonites." 6000053

22."Church Records of the Netherlands–Dutch Reformed." 6000054

23."Church Records of the Netherlands–Walloon or French Reformed." 6000055

24."Church Records of the Netherlands–Evangelical Lutheran and Restored Evangelical Lutheran." 6000056

25."Church and Civil Records of Amsterdam, the Netherlands, before 1811." 6000355-6000356

26."Church Records of the Netherlands–Roman Catholic." 6000058

28."The Origins of Names and Their Effect on Genealogical Research in the Netherlands." 6000059

32."Historical Background Affecting Genealogical Research in the Netherlands." 6000060

BELGIUM

Historical Background

800	Charlemagne unites the Frankish kingdom.
1477	Austrian Hapsburgs obtain control of Belgium.
1506	Spanish Hapsburgs obtain control of Belgium.
1598	Belgium achieves independence.
1621	Belgium returns to the control of Spain.
1713	Spain gives Belgium to Austria.
1797	Napoleon conquers Belgium.
1815	Belgium and the Netherlands united at Napoleon's defeat.

1831 Belgium declares independence from the Netherlands.

1898 Flemish recognized as official language, with French.

1919 Treaty of Versailles grants controls of Eupen and Malmedy to Belgium.

Settlement and Migration

Belgium was conquered by the Franks in the 400s and has seen little immigration since then, although many wars and changes of possession have encouraged some emigration. Persecution of the Protestants in the 1500s and 1600s caused additional emigration, often to Germany and the Netherlands. During the nineteenth century, some Belgians joined the general economic migration from Europe to the United States.

Belgium Library Collection

The Family History Library has an excellent and growing collection of records for Belgium. Most important are its civil registration and church records which presently cover almost every locality in the country.

The library also has a host of additional records and other research tools which make Belgian research relatively easy. Many of these records, particularly church records, civil registration, notarial records, and population registers, are so similar to the same records discussed under France and/or the Netherlands that they will not be discussed here.

Belgium is divided into nine provinces which form the subdivisions used in describing the records available for Belgium. Most of the collection consists of local records cataloged by the specific town, parish, or civil registration district to which the records apply, within the province to which the locality belongs.

There are no major primary collections cataloged nationwide (like the U.S. censuses), except for a set of military records. Many of the remaining sources listed in the general Belgium section are finding aids and other research tools.

Archives and Libraries

The National (or Royal) Archives in Brussels also serves as the archive for the province of Brabant. Each of the other eight provinces has provincial archives for local church and civil records.

In addition, the provinces of Luxembourg, Liege, Hainant, Namur, Oost, and West Vlanderen have additional archives which serve specific areas of the province. The library has an excellent collection of guides and inventories to most of these archives. The FHLC also has inventories for many family archives in Belgium.

Church Records

The Roman Catholic Church has always been the dominant church in Belgium. Even today, over 90 percent of the population consider themselves Catholic. Church records before 1795 are stored in provincial archives and indexed parish by parish, which makes research much quicker.

The library has microfilmed almost all pre-1795 parish registers, plus some to later dates. They appear in the catalog under the name of the parish which is usually the same as the town (commune). Catholic records are in Latin. Protestant records, where they exist, are in French or Flemish. This excellent repertory lists which records are available from which parishes for which years:

Douxchamps, Herve. *Repertorium der oude parochieregisters in Belgie*. Brussel: Herve Douxchamps, 1985. (FHL# 949.3/-K22c)

Civil Registration

The library has microfilmed civil registration records from most towns from 1795 to the 1870s. Decennial indexes generally begin by 1802. In some provinces, such as Antwerpen, the indexes have been filmed together and are listed under the province. However, they are still arranged town by town.

Court Records

Court records are generally deposited at provincial archives. The Family History Library has microfilms of those from some provinces, usually cataloged by town. They may include probate, guardianship, civil, and criminal suits, land entries, and other records.

Emigration and Immigration

Very few emigration sources are available for Belgium in the Family History Library. However, the Antwerp Municipal Archives have passports, emigration registers, hotel registers (for persons awaiting departure), and other records that have not been microfilmed. A small set of Antwerp departure lists covers 1854-55 (FHL# 392910-392912). These lists are indexed in:

Hall, Charles. *The Antwerp Emigration Index*. Logan, Utah: Everton Publishers, c.1980. (FHL# 949.321/A1/W22h)

Many Belgians also left through French or Dutch ports, but these records are not in the library either. U.S. arrival lists may be helpful in documenting an immigrant. See the FHLC heading **U.S./Emigration-Immigration** for more information.

Gazetteers

De Seyn, Eug. *Geschied- en Aardrijkskundig Woordenboek der Belgische Gemeenten*. 2d rev. ed. 2 vols. Turnhout: Uitgaven Brepols, n.d. (FHL# 949.3/E5sa)

Genealogy

The library has over fifty Belgian family histories as well as inventories to numerous family archives. In addition, many briefer genealogies are published in local periodicals. These and many other sources of published genealogies are cataloged or indexed in a repertory:

Leenaerts, Remy J. *Algem*een genealogish - repertorium voor de Zuidlijke Nederlanden. 8 vols. Handzame: Familia et Patria, 1969-date. (FHL# 949.3/A3L, microfiche [vol. 1-5] 6000821)

History

Belgian histories typically do not include much information about specific persons other than the ruling class. The library has very few local histories and only a small collection of general histories. Almost all are written in Flemish or French. One of the best is:

Meeus, Adrien de. *Histoire de Belgique.* Paris: Librairie Plon, 1928. (FHL# 949.3/H2m)

Language and Languages

Belgium is a bilingual country. French is spoken in the southern or Walloon provinces while Flemish, a Dutch dialect, is spoken in the northern areas. Brabant and Brussels are truly bilingual with both languages being used there. Generally, the records will be written in the language common to the area with the exception of the Latin church records. For a Flemish dictionary see:

Clerck, Walter de. *Zuid Nederlands Woordenboek.* 's-Gravenhage, Netherlands: Martinus Nijhoff, 1981. (FHL# 439.313/C594n)

Maps

The library has a few maps of Belgium to help you locate your ancestral town. Also, the gazetteer listed above contains detailed provincial maps.

Europe Road Map 1:200000: Belgium and Luxembourg. Washington, D.C.: Army Map Service, 1942. (FHL# 949.3/E7e or microfiche 6000801)

Military Records

The Family History Library has not specifically collected Belgium military records but some deposited in various archives were included in the microfilming. Many of these records are conscription lists for specific towns or provinces; they are cataloged by jurisdiction in the FHLC. One large collection (108 reels) records enlistment rolls of officers and some regimental rolls for the entire country, arranged by regiment, from 1830 to 1898. A partial index is available: see microfilms 714259, 717448-717449, 717462, and 717493.

Nobility

The FHLC lists about twenty-five books dealing with the history and genealogy of noble Belgian families. For further sources, consult **Belgium/Heraldry** and **Belgium/[Province]/Nobility.** See also Chapter 28, "Medieval Families."

Coomans de Brachene, Oscar. *Tables ascendantes ou quartiers généalogique des families de la Noblesse Belge.* 2 vols. Ninove: Imprimere Anneessens, 1947. (FHL# 949.3/D2c or microfiche 6053501)

Notarial Records

Notarial records rank third in quantity behind church records and civil registration in the Belgian collection. Generally, they are cataloged according to the town where the notary resided. If his territory covered all or part of a province, the records are listed under that province.

Periodicals

The library has copies of most of the Belgian genealogical periodicals. Two major ones are:

Vlaamse Stam: tijdschrift voor familiegeschiedenis. Buizingen: Vlaamse Vereniging voor Familiekunde, 1965+. (FHL# 949.3/B2v)

Les Cahiers Leopoldiens 2d ser. Brussels, n.p., 1961+. (FHL# 949.3/B2C)

Population Registers

Population registers in Belgium resemble those in the Netherlands. Some begin as early as 1796, but most date from about 1847. The library has many of these, but not all. They are cataloged according to the town where they were kept.

Bibliography

Martens-Melengreau, Julienne. *Manuel du Généalogiste: conseils et renseignements.* Brussels: S.C.G.D., 1980. (FHL# 949.3/D27m)

Nederhand, Erica Hartman. *Ancestral Research in Belgium.* Salt Lake City, Utah: n.pub, 1973. (FHL# 949.3/D27n)

LUXEMBOURG

Historical Background

963	City of Luxembourg founded.
1308	Count Henry IV becomes king of Germany.
1354	Emperor Charles IV makes Luxembourg a duchy.
1445	Luxembourg incorporated into Duchy of Burgundy.
1482	Hapsburgs obtain Luxembourg.
1555	Spanish domination begins.
1684	Luxembourg captured by France.
1697	Returned to Spain.
1713	Granted to Austrian Hapsburgs.

1795	Becomes part of French Republic under Napoleon.
1815	Congress of Vienna makes Luxembourg a Grand Duchy under rule of the Netherlands.
1839	Separated from Belgium, semi-independent, but ruled by the Netherlands.
1890	Full independence under new royal house, Duke Adolphus of Nassau-Weilburg.

Settlement and Migration

Modern Luxembourgers are descended from the Franks who invaded the area in the 400s, and the Treveri tribe which settled there even earlier. Since then, the duchy has seen little immigration. The eastern part of Luxembourg is closely tied to Germany in culture and language, while the western portion is tied to France and Belgium, which retained a large portion of Luxembourg's territory when it broke from the Netherlands in 1831. Emigration has been minor, chiefly to the larger cities of Europe and to America.

Luxembourg Library Collection

The Family History Library has a fairly comprehensive collection of primary records for the Grand Duchy of Luxembourg, much of it consists of church and civil registration records for its 130 towns (communes). The rest of the collection is quite small, consisting mostly of reference books and other genealogical tools. The church and civil records are very similar to those in France and the Netherlands and will not be detailed here.

The library's catalog for Luxembourg uses its thirteen cantons as subdivisions under which town records are listed. The gazetteer listed below will help identify in which canton a particular town is found. The FHLC also includes a cross-reference at the beginning of the Luxembourg locality microfiche which lists alphabetically each town for which the library has records and the canton under which the records are cataloged.

Archives and Libraries

Ruppert, P. *Les Archives du Gouvernment du Grand-Duché de Luxembourg: inventaires sommaires.* Luxembourg: La Cour Victor Bück, 1910. (FHL# 949.35/A5is or microfilm 1045438)

Biography and Genealogy

Biographie nationale du pays de Luxembourg depuis ses origines jusqu'à nos corrigée. 2d ed., rev. and corrected. Luxembourg: Imprimerie de la cour Victor Bück, 1957. (FHL# 920.04935/B52b)

Church Records

Luxembourg is almost exclusively Roman Catholic. Parish records generally begin in the early- to mid-1600s. The library has microfilm copies of most parish registers to about 1800.

Civil Registration

Civil registration of births, marriages, and deaths began in 1797. The library has copies of these records to 1880 for most towns. Decennial indexes generally begin in 1803.

Gazetteers

Luxembourg Gazetteer. Salt Lake City: Genealogical Society of Utah, 1964. (FHL# 949.35/E5L or microfilm 1184064)

Includes a listing of smaller villages and hamlets and to which town and canton they belong.

History

The library has very few histories of Luxembourg, none of them comprehensive. Rather, each focuses on a specific period. The best historical treatment of Luxembourg is generally found in books on Belgian or Dutch history or in works dealing with the Low Countries. Encyclopedias, especially *Encyclopedia Britannica* (15th edition), are good sources for a historical overview.

Maps

See the reference under Belgium for the best source.

Nobility

Schleich de Bossé, Jean Robert. *La noblesse an Grand-Duché de Luxembourg.* 2d ed., 2 vols. Luxembourg: Éditions du Centre, 1957, 1959. (FHL# 949.35/D5s or microfiche 6000663)

Records by Jurisdiction

France

Departments	Archives & Libraries	Bibliography	Biography	Cemeteries	Census	Church Directories	Church History	Church Records	Civil Registration	Court Records	Description & Travel	Dictionaries	Directories	Emigration/Immigration	Gazetteers	Genealogy	Heraldry	Historical Geography	History	Land & Property	Language	Maps	Military Records	Minorities	Names, Geographical	Names, Personal	Naturalization	Nobility	Notarial Records	Periodicals	Population	Probate Records	Public Records	Social Life	Societies	Taxation
France	•	•	•	•	•	•	•	•	•	•	•	•	•	•	•	•	•	•	•	•	•	•	•	•	•	•		•	•	•	•	•		•	•	•
Ain	•		•				•	•	•						•	•	•		•			•						•								
Aisne	•						•	•	•						•				•	•		•														
Allier	•		•												•	•			•	•		•														
Alpes Maritimes*	•				•			•	•	•						•			•	•		•		•				•	•							
Ardeche*	•						•	•	•					•	•	•	•		•	•		•			•			•				•				
Ardennes*	•							•	•						•	•			•			•								•						
Ariege	•						•		•					•		•				•		•	•					•	•	•						
Aube	•							•	•						•				•	•		•	•					•	•							
Aude*	•		•				•	•	•						•	•			•			•								•						
Aveyron	•						•	•	•							•						•													•	
Bas-Rhin*	•		•		•	•	•	•	•				•	•	•	•	•		•	•		•	•	•		•			•	•			•			•
Basses-Alpes	•		•						•							•						•						•								
Basses-Pyrenees	•						•	•							•	•	•		•	•		•						•				•				
Belfort*	•				•		•	•	•				•	•	•				•			•		•					•	•					•	•
Bouches-du-Rhone	•		•					•	•				•		•	•			•			•	•				•									
Calvados*	•							•	•		•				•	•	•					•				•								•		•
Cantal	•		•					•	•				•		•	•						•						•								
Charente	•							•	•						•	•						•						•	•							
Charente-Maritime	•		•					•	•					•	•	•			•	•		•						•						•		
Cher	•							•	•	•					•	•	•		•			•						•								
Correze	•		•						•						•	•			•	•		•						•	•							
Corse	•								•						•		•		•	•																
Cote D'Or*	•							•	•	•					•	•				•		•	•						•			•				
Cotes-du-Nord	•		•			•			•										•	•		•														
Creuse	•							•	•	•					•	•			•	•		•														
Deux-Sevres	•						•		•					•	•	•			•			•		•	•											
Dordogne	•							•	•						•	•	•		•	•		•	•		•			•								
Doubs	•							•	•							•				•		•				•	•		•	•						
Drome*	•		•					•	•				•		•	•			•	•		•				•										
Eure*	•								•						•	•	•		•	•		•					•		•	•				•	•	•
Eure-et-Loire	•		•					•	•	•					•				•			•														
Finistere	•		•						•										•			•														
Gard*	•							•	•	•					•	•	•		•	•		•														•
Gers	•						•		•					•					•	•		•														
Gironde	•							•	•						•	•			•			•	•		•							•				
Haut-Rhin*	•		•	•	•	•		•	•					•	•	•	•		•	•		•														•
Haute-Garonne	•						•		•	•				•	•	•			•	•		•														
Haute-Loire	•						•	•								•			•			•						•								
Haute-Marne*	•							•	•	•	•								•			•														
Haute-Saone*	•				•			•	•	•				•		•				•		•				•		•								
Haute-Savoie*	•		•		•		•	•	•						•	•			•	•		•	•					•								•
Haute-Vienne	•		•						•						•	•			•			•						•								
Hautes-Alpes	•		•						•						•	•	•		•	•		•			•											
Hautes-Pyrenees							•							•					•	•		•														
Herault*	•						•	•	•							•	•		•			•														
Ille-de-Vilaine	•		•					•	•		•					•	•		•			•														
Indre	•		•				•	•	•						•	•	•		•	•		•						•								
Indre-et-Loire*	•		•				•	•	•						•	•			•	•		•														

Records by Jurisdiction

France (cont.)

Departments	Archives & Libraries	Bibliography	Biography	Cemeteries	Census	Church Directories	Church History	Church Records	Civil Registration	Court Records	Description & Travel	Dictionaries	Directories	Emigration/Immigration	Gazetteers	Genealogy	Heraldry	Historical Geography	History	Land & Property	Language	Maps	Military Records	Minorities	Names, Geographical	Names, Personal	Naturalization	Nobility	Notarial Records	Periodicals	Population	Probate Records	Public Records	Social Life	Societies	Taxation
Isere	•						•	•	•						•	•			•			•						•								
Jura	•							•	•							•			•			•				•		•								
Landes	•						•	•	•										•	•		•														
Loire-et-Cher*	•		•					•	•		•				•	•			•	•		•														
Loire	•						•	•							•	•	•		•			•						•				•				
Loire-Atlantique	•		•				•	•	•	•	•					•	•		•	•		•														
Loiret	•		•					•							•				•			•														
Lot	•								•					•		•	•		•			•														
Lot-et-Garonne*	•							•	•													•						•	•				•			
Lozere	•															•	•		•			•							•							
Maine-et-Loire	•		•					•	•						•	•		•	•	•		•						•	•							
Manche	•								•							•	•		•			•				•		•						•		
Marne	•							•	•						•				•			•							•							
Mayenne	•		•						•							•			•			•		•				•								
Meurthe-et-Moselle*	•		•					•	•	•	•				•	•						•		•				•	•				•			
Meuse*	•		•					•	•		•											•						•								
Morbihan	•		•						•							•			•			•														
Moselle*	•		•					•	•	•	•				•	•				•		•						•	•							
Nievre*	•							•	•					•	•	•				•		•						•	•							
Nord*	•							•	•							•	•		•			•			•					•						
Oise*	•					•		•	•						•				•	•		•														
Orne	•							•	•							•	•		•	•		•				•		•		•				•		
Pas-de-Calais	•							•	•	•					•	•	•		•			•				•										•
Puy-de-Dome			•						•						•	•						•			•			•								
Pyrenees-Atlantiques	•																		•					•						•				•		
Pyrenees-Orientales	•		•													•			•			•												•		
Rhone*	•						•	•	•						•	•	•		•			•						•	•							
Saone-et-Loire	•								•						•	•						•				•			•							
Sarthe	•							•	•	•					•	•	•		•			•			•			•	•							
Savoie*	•		•		•			•	•					•	•	•	•		•	•		•	•		•	•		•							•	
Seine*	•							•	•						•				•	•		•														•
Seine-et-Marne*	•						•	•	•						•				•			•			•											
Seine-et-Oise*	•	•			•			•	•						•				•	•		•		•				•	•							
Seine-Maritime*	•							•	•	•	•				•	•	•					•	•		•	•		•						•		•
Somme	•							•	•						•	•	•		•	•		•						•	•							
Tarn	•													•		•			•			•														
Tarn-et-Garonne	•							•						•		•	•		•			•														
Var	•		•						•						•	•						•						•								
Vaucluse	•		•					•	•	•					•	•						•						•								
Vendee	•						•	•	•							•	•		•	•		•						•								
Vienne	•						•	•	•	•					•	•				•		•														
Vosges*	•		•					•	•		•				•	•			•			•						•	•							
Yonne	•							•	•						•	•			•			•							•							

* Indicates that Departmental Archives have been microfilmed; hence, church and civil records are available for most towns.

Records by Jurisdiction **France** Regions / Old Provinces	Archives & Libraries	Bibliography	Biography	Cemeteries	Census	Church Directories	Church History	Church Records	Civil Registration	Court Records	Description & Travel	Dictionaries	Directories	Emigration/Immigration	Gazetteers	Genealogy	Heraldry	Historical Geography	History	Land & Property	Language	Maps	Military Records	Minorities	Names, Geographical	Names, Personal	Naturalization	Nobility	Notarial Records	Periodicals	Population	Probate Records	Public Records	Social Life	Societies	Taxation
Alsace			•		•	•	•							•	•	•	•		•	•		•		•			•	•	•	•						•
Anjou																•		•				•						•								
Artois																•																				•
Auvergne			•													•	•		•									•								
Basse Normandie																																		•		
Bearn																	•		•																	
Berry																•	•											•								
Bourbonnais			•													•	•			•																
Bourgogne										•						•		•	•	•								•								
Bretagne	•		•				•		•		•					•	•		•							•		•								
Champagne									•							•			•									•								
Dauphine	•		•				•	•	•					•			•		•									•								
Franche-Comte			•				•		•							•	•							•				•								
Gascogne							•									•	•		•									•								
Ile-de-France															•				•									•								•
Languedoc							•				•					•	•		•							•		•								
Limousin			•												•	•			•																	
Lorraine			•		•	•	•		•		•			•	•	•	•		•			•		•				•	•				•			
Lyonnais							•										•					•						•			•					
Maconnais																•	•																			
Maine																			•									•								
Marche															•	•			•																	
Normandie	•		•						•		•					•	•		•							•		•						•		
Orleanais			•				•									•																				
Paris	•		•												•																					
Pays-Basque															•				•																	
Picardie															•	•	•		•									•		•					•	
Poitou							•								•	•	•		•									•		•						•
Provence			•				•								•	•		•			•							•		•		•				
Roussillon			•												•	•		•																•		
Saintonge																•																				
Touraine																		•																		
Vivaris																	•	•																		•

Records by Jurisdiction — Netherlands

Provinces	Archives & Libraries	Bibliography	Biography	Cemeteries	Census	Church Directories	Church History	Church Records	Civil Registration	Court Records	Description & Travel	Dictionaries	Directories	Emigration/Immigration	Gazetteers	Genealogy	Heraldry	Historical Geography	History	Land & Property	Language	Maps	Military Records	Minorities	Names, Geographical	Names, Personal	Naturalization	Nobility	Notarial Records	Periodicals	Population	Probate Records	Public Records	Social Life	Societies	Taxation
Netherlands	•	•	•	•	•		•	•	•	•	•	•		•	•	•	•		•	•	•	•	•	•	•	•		•	•	•			•	•		•
Drente	•	•	•	•	•		•	•	•	•	•	•				•			•	•	•		•			•		•	•					•		•
Friesland	•		•	•			•	•	•	•						•	•		•		•		•			•		•	•				•			•
Gelderland	•	•	•					•	•	•				•		•	•		•	•					•			•	•	•			•			•
Groningen	•			•			•	•	•	•						•	•		•	•			•	•		•		•	•				•			•
Limburg	•		•	•				•	•							•	•		•			•						•	•	•						
Noord Brabant	•			•			•	•	•							•			•	•						•			•				•			
Noord Holland	•			•				•	•	•						•			•	•					•			•	•							
Overijssel	•	•		•			•	•	•	•						•	•		•	•				•	•			•	•							•
Utrecht	•			•			•	•	•	•						•			•	•						•			•	•			•			
Zeeland	•						•	•	•					•		•	•		•				•			•			•	•			•			•
Zuid Holland	•			•				•	•	•						•			•	•		•						•	•	•						•

Records by Jurisdiction — Belgium

Provinces	Archives & Libraries	Bibliography	Biography	Cemeteries	Census	Church Directories	Church History	Church Records	Civil Registration	Court Records	Description & Travel	Dictionaries	Directories	Emigration/Immigration	Gazetteers	Genealogy	Heraldry	Historical Geography	History	Land & Property	Language	Maps	Military Records	Minorities	Names, Geographical	Names, Personal	Naturalization	Nobility	Notarial Records	Periodicals	Population	Probate Records	Public Records	Social Life	Societies	Taxation
Belgium	•	•	•				•	•		•	•	•		•	•	•	•		•	•	•	•	•	•	•	•	•	•	•	•		•			•	•
Antwerpen	•							•	•	•						•												•	•	•	•	•	•			•
Brabant	•							•	•	•						•	•			•		•				•	•		•	•	•					
Hainaut	•		•	•				•	•							•	•		•	•		•						•	•		•		•			•
Liege	•							•	•	•				•		•			•	•							•	•	•		•					
Limburg	•		•	•				•	•							•	•						•					•			•					
Luxembourg	•							•	•						•	•			•									•								
Namur	•						•	•	•							•			•									•	•							
Oost-Vlaanderen	•			•				•	•	•	•					•	•		•				•					•	•		•					
West-Vlaanderen	•	•		•	•		•	•	•							•	•					•	•						•				•			

Records by Jurisdiction — Luxembourg

Counties	Archives & Libraries	Bibliography	Biography	Cemeteries	Census	Church Directories	Church History	Church Records	Civil Registration	Court Records	Description & Travel	Dictionaries	Directories	Emigration/Immigration	Gazetteers	Genealogy	Heraldry	Historical Geography	History	Land & Property	Language	Maps	Military Records	Minorities	Names, Geographical	Names, Personal	Naturalization	Nobility	Notarial Records	Periodicals	Population	Probate Records	Public Records	Social Life	Societies	Taxation
Luxembourg	•	•	•				•	•	•		•				•	•	•		•	•	•	•			•			•		•			•	•		
Capellen								•	•																											
Clervaux								•	•																											
Diekirch								•	•																											
Echternach								•	•																											
Esch-sur-Alzette								•	•																											
Grevenmacher								•	•																											
Luxembourg-Campagne								•	•																											
Luxembourg-Ville								•	•																											
Mersch								•	•																											
Redagne								•	•																											
Remich								•	•																											
Vlanden								•	•																											
Wiltz								•	•																											

Chapter 23

South America

Harold D. Ethington

The South American collection is composed of two basic parts. The first is the 360 shelf feet of manuscripts, books, and other printed materials. The second is the collection of microfilmed records that now totals an estimated 150,000 reels of film measuring 100 feet each. While the value of the books and other shelf materials is considerable, it is the microfilmed copies of millions of original entry source documents that gives this collection its uniqueness and research potential.

The films are almost always tied to a specific country, but the same cannot be said of the published part of the collection. Almost all of the Latin American Europeans came from two relatively small countries – Spain and Portugal. This stock, when mixed with the native Americans, produced a people with a commonality of heritage, although widely distributed over a large geographical area.

For this reason, a great number of published volumes deal with subjects that surpass the boundaries of a particular country. A young American girl, of what she thinks is Mexican extraction, finds that her family name of Ojeda is actually a Chilean family, and ultimately from Andalucia, Spain. Spanish Conquistadors moved and established alliances with local women freely over vast distances in the New World. Native Americans identified with their kinfolk and clans, recognizing natural boundaries, rather than lines on a map.

For two centuries, all of Spain's territory in South America, except Venezuela, was included in a single unit called the viceroyalty of Peru. But, because administration of so vast an area proved difficult, other viceroyalties were created in the eighteenth century. Then, the viceroyalty of New Granada comprised the northern part of the continent and the viceroyalty of Rio de la Plata the central and southern part.

The Spanish colonies were ruled from Spain by the Council of the Indies, set up at Seville in 1524. In the colonies, the viceroy exercised supreme power and often dominated the audiencia, the advisory council and supreme court of the viceroyalty. The important unit of social and economic life was the encomienda, one or more Indian villages governed by a Spanish proprietor (encomendero), who required serfs labor of the Indians, but was responsible for their education and religious instruction. The encomienda was abolished late in the eighteenth century, but the great estates of today are a survival of the system.

Colonial commerce, traffic, and immigration were controlled from Spain by the Casa de Contratacion (House of Trade) until 1790. Trade was rigidly regulated for the benefit of the mother country, and non-Spanish immigrants were excluded.

South America Library Collection

Archives and Libraries

The Family History Library has a number of volumes dealing with contents of South American archives and libraries, most of which deal with a specific subject, such as papers of past governors or politicians. The following are representative of what is included in the collection:

Gomez-Cañedo, Lino. *Los Archivos de la Historia de América.* 2 vols. México, D.F.: Instituto Panamericano de Geografía e Historia, Comisión de Historia, 1961. (FHL# 980/A3gl)

Hill, Roscoe R. *Los Archivos Nacionales de la América Latina.* (The National Archives of Latin America) La Habana: Archivo Nacional de Cuba, 1948. (FHL# 980/J5h)

Includes history, description of the collection, and a listing of the publications of each archive.

Torres-Lanzas, Pedro. *Catálogo de Legajos del Archivo General de Indias.* (Catalog of Legal Documents in the General Archive of Indias.) Sevilla: Tip. Zarzuela, 1921. (FHL# 980/A1, no. 15)

Catalog of account documents dealing with Spanish America housed in the Archivo General de Indias.

Woodbridge, Henry C. and Dan Newberry, eds. *Basic List of Latin American Materials in Spanish, Portuguese and French.* Amherst, Mass.: Salalm, 1975. (FHL# 980/A3b)

See FHLC heading **South America/Archives and Libraries** for a complete list of holdings on this subject.

Biography

The library has biographies or biographical reference materials dealing with a variety of subjects, most of which are narrow in scope. The following are representative of the collection (see FHLC heading **South America/Biography** for a complete list of holdings and call numbers):

Lewin, Boleslao. *Mártires y Conquistadores Judiós en la América Hispana.* Buenos Aires: Editorial Candelabro, 1954. (FHL# 980/D3l)

Boyd-Bowran, Peter. *Indice Geobiográfico de Cuarenta Mil Pobladores Españoles de América in el Siglo XVI.* Bogotá: Instituto Caro y Cuervo, c.1964. (FHL# 9980/W2b)

Index of 40,000 Spanish settlers to the Americas in the sixteenth century.

Dantin Cereceda, Juan. *Exploradores y Conquistadores de Indias.* (Explorers and Conquerors of the Americas) Madrid: Consejo Superior de Investigaciones Científicas, 1966. (FHL# 980/E3e or microfilm 0896837)

Transcriptions of documents describing the geography and native people of the Americas.

The library also has the handwritten journal of Mormon missionaries Fenton L. Williams, Jr., and John Harris Crosby, describing their 1950 trip through South America collecting genealogical data (FHL# 980/D2w).

History

Thirty-two different histories are in the library's collection including H. H. Bancroft's works and a delightfully new approach to the subject:

Herring, Hubert. *A History of Latin America.* (New York: Alfred A. Knopf, 1982). (FHL# 980/H2h)

Also noteworthy is:

Pastells, R. P. Pablo. *Historia de la Compañia de Jesús en la Provincia del Paraguay.* 8 vols. Madrid, Spain: Libreria General de Victoriano Suárez, 1972. (FHL# 980/K2s)

Names, Personal

In almost 20,000 pages, authors Alberto and Arturo Garcia Carraffa have documented some 18,000 Spanish-American surnames, giving place of origin, illustrious descendants, coats of arms, and other family information on names from Aanda to Urriza.

Carraffa, Alberto García y Arturo García Carraffa. *Diccionario Heráldica y Genealógico de Apelidos Españoles y Americanos.* 86 vols. Madrid, Spain: Nueva Imprenta Radio, S.A., 1952. (FHL# 980/D24g) Library has 86 vols, through the letter "U."

The library also has several other volumes dealing with the complexity of Spanish personal names. See FHLC heading **South America/Names-Personal** for titles and call numbers.

Native Races

Steward, Julian H. *Handbook of South American Indians.* 7 vols. New York: Cooper Square Publishers, 1963. (FHL# 980/F3h)

The library also has ten other works on this subject: See FHLC heading **South America/Native Races** for titles and call numbers.

ARGENTINA

Historical Background

516	Juan Diaz de Solís is the first European to discover the Rio de la Plata and claims the area for Spain.
1526-32	Sebastian Cabot sails up the Rio de la Plata and founds a brief settlement established on the lower Parana called Ft. Sancti Spiritus.
1534	Royal and Supreme Council establishes Spanish dominion over the area.
1535	Expedition of Don Pedro de Mendoza begins permanent colonization of La Plata (area of today's Argentina).
1536	Mendoza founds the settlement of Nuestra Señora Santa Maria del Buen Aire (Our Lady Saint Mary of the Fair Wind). Querendi Indians occupy the area.
1537	Fort is established at Asuncion to which the Spanish political headquarters is transfered. Domingo de Irala is elected governor.
1541	The settlement at Buen Aire is abandoned.
1542-44	Alvar de Vaca brings more colonists from Brazil, but he is denied his rightful governorship by Irala.
1542	Area of current-day Argentina is under the juridiction of the Viceroyalty of Peru established by Spain to govern colonial territory in South America.
1553-96	Communities of Santiago del Estero, Tucuman, Cordoba, Salta, La Rioja, Jujuy, Mendoza, San Juan, and San Luis are established by Spaniards who formerly settled in Peru and Chile.
1573	Juan de Garay and colonists from Asunción found Sante Fe.
1580	Garay arrives in the area formerly called Buen Aire and refounds the settlement,

renaming it Ciudad de la Santísima Trinidad y Puerto de Santa María de Buenos Aires.

1620 The Province of Buenos Aires, consisting of the city and the northern half of present-day Argentina, is removed from Asuncion's jurisdiction.

1714 Royal and Supreme Council is shorn of power.

1721 Economic progress is enhanced by political measures.

1764 French occupy the Falkland Islands.

1776 Viceroyalty of La Plata is established, including most of present-day Bolivia, Paraguay, Uraguay, and Argentina, with Buenos Aires as the capital; the area is no longer under Peruvian viceroyalty.

1806-07 British occupy Buenos Aires and then Montevideo, stimulating nationalism and insurrection in the Rio de la Plata. The British are soon ousted.

1810 Direct Spanish authority is terminated as a junta of the provinces of the Rio de la Plata is established in the name of Ferdinand VII of Spain during the threat of Napoleon.

1813-16 Viceroyalty is divided into provinces; authority is placed in a director; congress convenes at Tucumán.

1816 Congress declares the independence of the United Provinces of the Rio de la Plata with Buenos Aires its capital.

1820s Independence leaves the question of federal or unitary government; many wish to annex Paraguay and Uraguay into the new nation. First English immigrate to Argentina.

1825 War with Brazil begins over possession of Uruguay.

1828 Uraguay gains independence as a result of the war with Brazil.

1829 Period of anarchy in the provinces is ended by the governorship of Juan Manuel de Rosas. Argentina becomes a presidential republic and Buenos Aires develops into a capital district.

1835 Argentine Confederation is governed with absolute authority by Rosas.

1852-59 Federal constitution and presidency is instituted by Justo de Urquiza after overthrowing Rosas.

1856 Rosario is made the chief port city.

1860 The state is reconstituted.

1862 Period of stablity is begun when Buenos Aires becomes supreme over the remainder of the nation and the capital is kept here for five years.

1863 Welsh, sponsored by the Welsh Emigration Society, first arrive in Argentina; colonies are organized in Patagonia.

1865-70 War ensues with Paraguay.

1868-80 Two successful administrations improve immigration, education, and commerce and open the southern frontiers through subjugation of the Indians.

1869 First census is taken, indicating a population of over 1,700,000.

1871 British Consul reports that 10,533 British subjects are residing in Buenos Aires.

1873 Lincolnshire, England, artisans who had previously settled in Asunción, Paraguay, migrate to Argentina.

1874-80 European immigration is encouraged by the Argentine government by facilitating the purchase of government land.

1880 The provinces are consolidated into the Argentine Republic. City of Buenos Aires is restructured as a federal district for the capital, while its province becomes equal to the others in the federation.

1880s Irish Catholics settle in Argentina.

1884 Anti-semitic leader, Dr. Forster, leads immigrants to Argentina.

1890s Jews are brought to Argentina from Russia by the Judeo-German philanthropist Baron Maurice de Hirsch, settling in Sana Fe and Entre Ríos.

1890-1904 Economic rehabilitation is undertaken and hostile boundary disputes with Chile and Brazil are settled.

Settlement and Migration

The modern-day territory of Argentina was populated only after the other Spanish colonies had been well established. Santiago del Estero was founded in 1553, San Juan and Mendoza in 1562, Tucumán in 1565, Córdoba in 1573, Santa Fe in 1573, Buenos Aires in 1580, Salta in 1582, Corrientes and Parana in 1588, La Rioja in 1591, and San Luis in 1596. The inhabitants of these cities and their surrounding areas were the total population of Argentina until independence in 1810. In 1617, Argentina had four provinces: Buenos Aires, Santa Fe, Corrientes, and Concepción.

In 1776, the Viceroyship of Río de la Plata was created, encompassing modern day Argentina, Paraguay, Bolivia, and Uruguay. In 1810, Argentina proclaimed its independence from Spain, and in 1811, 1825, and 1828, Paraguay, Bolivia, and Uruguay also separated themselves from the Viceroyship of Lima.

Modern-day Argentina is divided into a federal district, twenty-two provinces, and the federal territory of Tierra del Fuego. The federal district is divided into ten jurisdictions, each of which sends copies of all vital records to the central office. The index to these records is organized first alphabetically, second, according to gender, and third according to class of record. The library does not have this index.

The provinces are divided into departments, and these in turn are divided into *municipalidades.* Each *municipio* (singular form of municipalidades) has a civil registration, one or more public notaries, civil and criminal courts, and a municipal governor who administers the sale of lands, etc. The greater Buenos Aires area is divided into nineteen *partidos* or districts. Parish registers have, for the most part, been well preserved and have been filmed by the Family History Library. The oldest began in Cordoba, in the first half of the seventeenth century.

The oldest civil registrations began, also in Cordova, 3 January 1881, although it was not instituted by law until 10 August 1886. By about 1889, civil registration had been established in all the country with the exception of Chaco (1906).

The notarial records of the country are found in various places. For 1584-1883, those of the federal district are found in the General Archive of the Nation. Those of the provinces are found in the provincial archives with the records of courts, judiciaries, histories, etc.

The censuses of 1869 and 1895 have been filmed by the Family History Library. There are many other censuses and tax rolls in Argentina, the majority of which are found in the provincial archives. These records are inventoried in Church of Jesus Christ of Latter-day Saints publication *Fuentes Principales de Registros Genealógicos en Argentina* (Salt Lake City: Genealogy Library, 1977) which is available at the International Reference Desk.

Argentina Library Collection

Archives and Libraries

The library has guides to a number of Argentina's archives and libraries, including:

Fernández-Olguín, Eduardo. *Los Archivos de la Ciudad de Corrientes.* (The Archives of the City of Corrientes) Buenos Aires: Imprenta y Casa Editora Coni, 1921. (FHL# 982/A1 no. 12)

Indice des Archivo del Gobierno de Buenos Aires, Correspondiente al Año de 1810. (Index to the Holdings of the Archive of Gobierno of Buenos Aires for the Year 1810) Buenos Aires: Imprenta de La Tribuna, 1869. (FHL# 982/A3i or microfilm 0496677, item 2)

Includes a partial list of the collection.

See FHLC heading **Argentina/Archives and Libraries** for a complete list of holdings and call numbers for this subject.

Biography

The library has a significant collection of biographical works for Argentina. Those with a nation-wide scope include:

Diccionario Biográfico, Provincia de Buenos Aires. (Biographical Dictionary, Province of Buenos Aires.) Buenos Aires: Signos Editorial Argentino, 1954. (FHL# 982.12/-D36d or microfilm 1162469)

Gori, Gaston. *Familias Fundadoras de la Colonia Esperanza.* Santa Fe, Argentina: Libreria y Editorial Colmegna, 1974. See FHLC for call numbers.

Lafuente-Machain, Richardo de. *Conquistadores del Río de la Plata.* Buenos Aires: Tallares Graficos de Sebastian Amorrortu, 1937. (FHL# 982/D3lm)

Udaondo, Enrique. *Diccionario Biográfico Argentino.* (Biographical Dictionary of Argentina) Austin, Tex.: Goligtly-Payne-Coon, 1957. Microfilm of original publication: Buenos Aires: Editorial Coni, 1938. (FHL# microfilm 0038829)

See FHLC heading **Argentina/Biography, Argentina/Genealogy,** and **Argentina/Family History** for call numbers and additional titles.

Census Records

Census records filmed to date by the library are generally indexed in the Family History Library Catalog (FHLC) by province. However, 159 reels for the 1895 census of Buenos Aires have been cataloged under **Argentina/Census.** See that heading for call numbers.

Encyclopedias and Dictionaries

The library has both the *Gran Enciplopedia Argentina,* 9 vols. (1953) (FHL# 982/A5g) and the *Diccionario Historico Argentina,* 6 vols., 1953. (FHL# 982/H26d).

Gazetteers

Office of Geography, Department of the Interior. *Argentina: Official Standard Names Approved by the U.S. Board on Geographic Names.* Washington, D.C.: Department of the Interior, 1968. (FHL# 982/E5u)

Genealogy, Sources

La Sociedad Genealógica de la Iglesia de Jesucristo de los Ultimos días. *Fuentes Principales de Registros Genealógicos en Argentina.* Salt Lake City, Utah: The Church of Jesus Christ of Latter-day Saints, 1977. (FHL# 929.1/-G286gs/Ser. H/no.7)

One of a series of pamphlets on record sources worldwide, this publication, written in Spanish and not translated, is a guide to using genealogical sources in Argentina and at the Family History Library.

History

The Family History Library has more than fifty histories for Argentina, including:

Santillan, Diego Abad de. *Historia Argentina.* 3 vols. Buenos Aires: Tipográfica Editora Argentina, 1965. (FHL# 982/H2a)

Almost 2,000 pages of text, paintings, maps, and photographs. Cover pre-colonial to modern times.

See FHLC heading **Argentina/History** for a complete list of holdings and call numbers for this subject. Local history titles are cataloged under **Argentina/[Province]/[City]/History.**

Historical and Genealogical Periodicals

The library has publications of various historical institutions, but only a few dealing with genealogy. See FHLC heading **Argentina/History-Periodicals** and **Argentina/Genealogy-Periodicals** for titles and call numbers.

Minorities

The library has at least one book on each of these minorities: Irish, Italian, German, Spanish, Polish, Welsh, Jewish (five books), Catalan, and Portuguese. See FHLC heading **Argentina/Minorities** for titles and call numbers.

Maps

The library has eleven different maps or map sets of Argentina. The most comprehensive is:

(Argentine) Instituto Geográfico Militar. *Carta Topográfico de Argentina (scale 1:500,000)*. Buenos Aires: El Instituto, 1939-75. 69 maps. (FHL# 982/E7ag)

Names, Personal

Calvo, Carlos. *Origen de Familias en la República de Argentina*. 5 reels. Salt Lake City: Genealogy Society of Utah, 1975. (FHL# microfilm 11023913-1102917)

Gives the Old World place of origin and current general area of residence for approximately 6,000 surnames in alphabetical order. Original is a typewritten card index.

Granillo, Arturo. *El Nombre de la Mujer Casada* (The Name of the Married Woman). Cordoba, Argentina: Universidad Nacional de Córdoba, 1953. (FHL# 982/P3g) Discusses surnames of married women.

Vital Records

The library has filmed both church records and civil registration for births, marriages, deaths, confirmations, etc. throughout the country, but filming is not complete for all provinces. Civil records date from the late 1800s while church records are found (variously) from the early 1600s to the present. Here is a by-province list with the number of reels (9,756, total) containing vital records and census information: Buenos Aires, 4,237; Capital Federal, 71; Catamarca, 234; Chaco, 17; Chubut, 5; Cordoba, 1,403; Corrientes, 228; Entre Ríos, 321; Formosa, 1; Jujuy, 119; Loja, 4; Malvinas, 0; Mendoza, 253; Misiones, 51; Neuquén, 18; La Pampa, 50; Patagonia, 0; Río Negro, 28; La Rioja, 111; Salta, 323; San Juan, 198; San Luis, 32; Santa Cruz, 4; Santa Fe, 1,320; Santiago, 253; Tierra Del Fuego, 3; and Tucumán, 472.

BOLIVIA

Historical Background

600-1100	Rise and fall of the great Tiahuanaco empire extending over the Peruvian coast with its center in the altiplano region.
1400s	Area is dominated by 12 nations of Aymara-speaking Indians, subjugated by the Quechuan-speaking Indians who dominate the Incan empire and many of which immigrated into the area of the Aymaras. These two languages are spoken by the majority of Bolivians today.
1500s	Area becomes well-populated by the Spaniards after the conquest of Latin America because of its mines and other rich resources.
1538	Hernando Pizarro conquers the Indians of Bolivia.
1550-70	Cities of Chuquisaca, Potosí, and La Paz are established.
1559	Upper Peruvian government is founded as the *audiencia* of Charcas with Chuquisaca as the capital, originally subject to the Viceroyalty of Peru.
1661-1824	Indians in Bolivia periodically rebel against Spanish authority.
1776	Ending subservience to the Viceroyalty of Peru, most of present-day Bolivia, Paraguay, Uruguay, and Argentina are united in the Viceroyalty of La Plata, of which Buenos Aires is the capital.
1781	Indians beseige the city of La Paz for nine months.
1809	Wars of Independence in South America are stimulated by revolts at Chuquisaca and La Paz, which are suppressed by the Spanish forces.
1824	Spanish forces are defeated at Ayachuco in Peru.
1825	A congress convening at Chuquisaca declares Charcas independent and renames the region the Republic of Bolívar (Bolivia).
1826-28	Bolivar and Sucre organize the fledgling state of Bolivia. Peru recognizes Bolivia's independence and Bolivia claims the territory on the coast from Cape Sama to the Loa River.
1835-39	Confederation unites Bolivia and Peru, but the union is dissolved by opposing Argentina and Chile.
1841-57	Economic development and government reforms are instituted by various administrations.
1866	Treaty results in the ceding by Bolivia to Chile of the territory between the Salado

	River and and the Pacific, parallel to the Andes. Brazil also claims a large area on the Paraguay and Madeira Rivers.
1874	Boundary between Bolivia and Chile is fixed at 24th parallel.
1884	Chile takes control of the Atacama Desert, Bolivia's only coastal region and access to the sea, at the Treaty of Valparaiso which ends the War of the Pacific.
1888-92	Railway provides Bolivia with an access to the coast.
1889	Boundary disputes with Argentina are ended by treaty.
1899	Discovery of tin begins vast mining operations.
1903	Acre district is ceded to Brazil after its Brazilian inhabitants declared it and independent state. Brazil in turn provides Bolivia with an outlet to the sea around the cataracts of the Madeira.
1904-09	Public worship other than Roman Catholicism is permitted among other governmental reforms.
1904	Treaty between Chile and Bolivia formally ends the War of the Pacific, with Chile maintaining control of the Bolivian littoral (the coastal Atacama Desert) and plans for a railway to be built by Chile for Bolivia begun. Bolivia recongnizes Chilean control of the area between 23rd and 24th parallel.
1920	In the long-standing dispute over the areas of Tacna and Arica, Bolivia claims that neither Chile nor Peru is entitled to those provinces, yet no resolution is made.
1921-30	Presidencies of Bautista Saavedra and Hernando Siles.
1929	Bolivia permanently loses Atacama, but retains use of the Chilean-built railway.

Settlement and Migration

The city of Charchas, also known as Rancheria de la Plata, Chuquisaca, and Sucre, was founded in 1539. By 1545, Potosi had been established. It would become the largest city in the New World before 1600, with a population of approximately 120,000. In 1559, the Audencia of Charcas was formed, the colonial judicial/administrative body. In South America, only Lima was more important. The boundaries of Charcas reached from Collao (Ayaviri and Asillo) in the north (including the provinces of Sayabamba, Carabaya Moxos, and Chunchos) to Chaco, including the jurisdictions of Tucuman, Juries, and Diaguitas, ultimately fading somewhere in the indefinite regions of the Pampa. In 1617, the Rio de la Plata government was organized, taking jurisdiction over what is modern-day Argentina and the surrounding areas.

The diocese of La Plata was established in 1552 and included all the territory of Charcas. The first division came in 1563 when the bishopric of Santiago de Chile was formed, followed in 1570 by Tucuman. In 1605, the diocese of Nuestra Señora de la Paz was headquartered in Chuquiabo. Its territory, taken from the Diocese of La Plata, included La Paz, Collao, the districts of Chucuita and Paucarcolla, and the major part of Oruro and Cochabamba. La Paz was subordinate to Lima. At this same time, the diocese of San Lorenzo de la Barrance was growing. It was also known as Mizque, (later Santa Cruz), and included the territories of Moxos, Chiquitos, La Barranca, Mizque, Los Yungas de Pocona, and El Valle de Cliza.

After the establishment of La Paz and Santa Cruz, the bishopric of La Plata was elevated to archdiocese (1609). Until 1825, it had as subordinates the diocese of La Paz, Santa Cruz, Paraguay, Tucuman, and Buenos Aires.

Bolivia's original territory covered a vast area, including a long stretch of coastal ports. In 1884, it lost the provinces of Antofagasta and Atacama to Chile and part of Gran Chaco and the Arce district to Brazil in 1899. The country is divided into nine departments *(departamentos)* and eighty-seven provinces, each divided into *secciones* and *municipios.*

Bolivia Library Collection

The Family History Library's Bolivian collection is small in comparison to others and consists mainly of printed materials. A general overview of the principal features of the collection is offered here.

Biography

Among the several biographical titles, the following cover a broad spectrum of Bolivia's people:

Costa de la Torre, Arturo. *Hombres Célebres de Bolivia.* La Paz, Bolivia: Imprenta y Libreria Renovacion, 1970. (FHL# 984/D3c)

Biographies of Juan Ondarza and Abdon Senen founder of Antofagasta, with historical notes about the Bolivian Pacific coast.

Montenegro R., Edmundo. *Diccionario Biográfico de Personalidades en Bolivia.* (Biographical Dictionary of Personalities of Bolivia) La Paz: Edumndo Montenegro R., 1968. (FHL# 984/D3m or microfilm 0908253, item 4)

Census Records

The quality and availability of Bolivian census materials varies greatly with the time period and the area covered. For a complete discussion of these records, see La Sociedad Genealogica. *Fuentes Principales de Registros Genealógicas en Bolivia.* (Salt Lake City: La Sociedad Genealógica, 1977). No call number. Available for purchase at the International Reference Copy Center of the main library for a nominal amount.

Church Directories

Guía Eclesiástica, Bolivia, 1977. La Paz: n.pub., 1977. (FHL# 984/K24g/1977)

Gazetteers

Ayala Z., Alfredo. *División Política y Administrativa de la República de Bolivia El Año 1973.* La Paz: Editorial Don Bosco, 1973. (FHL# 984/A1/no.3)

Particularly useful for following name changes over the years for cities and departments.

Blanco, Federico. *Diccionario Geográfico-Departamento de Cochabamba.* La Paz: Taller Tipo-Litográfica, 1901. (FHL# 984.23/E24b)

Includes short historical notes. Uses the proximity method of location. The library has a similar volume for the department of Chuquisaca-Sociedad Geografica Sucre. *Diccionario Geográfico del Departamento de Chuquisaca.* (Sucre, Bolivia: Imprento Bolivar, 1903). (FHL# 984.24/E5s).

Genealogy, Sources

La Sociedad Genealógica. *Fuentes Principales de Registros Genealógicas en Bolivia.* Salt Lake City: La Sociedad Genealogicas, 1977. (FHL# 929.1/G286gs/Ser. H/no.15)

Explains how Bolivian records have been created and assembled, describes the contents of the various source documents, specifies location, and discusses their usefulness to the researcher.

History

Among the library's fifteen volumes of general Bolivian history is this excellent guide to history and customs:

Weil, Thomas E. *Area Handbook for Bolivia.* Washington, D.C.: American University, 1973. (FHL# 984/H6a)

For histories of departments, *cantones,* and some towns, see **/History** under each designation. One history containing a list of the original (1571) inhabitants is:

Macedonio Urquidi, José. *El Origen de La Noble Villa de Oropesa (Cochabamba).* Cochabamba, Bolivia: La Municipalidad de Cochabamba, 1949. (FHL# 984.2301/H2m)

Maps

The library has military maps on a scale of 1:50,000 for the departments of Cochabamba, La Paz, Potosí, Santa Cruz, Sucre, and Oruro. See **Bolivia/Maps**.

Vital Records

The library has not yet filmed civil records but has filmed most of the extensive church records. Most records begin in the 1500s and extend to the 1970s and 1980s. The following is a breakdown of the 2,603 reels available: Choquisaca, 140; Cochabamba, 671; Jujuy, 8; Oruro, 223; Pando, 0; La Paz, 828; Potosi, 478; Santa Cruz, 165; and Tarija, 90.

BRAZIL

Historical Background

1500	Pedro Alvarez Cabral discovers Brazil.
1500-21	Several royal expeditions and trading posts are established through private enterprise from Portuguese in the area claimed in South America.
1521-30	John III of Portugal begins systematic colonization of the Brazilian area. The coasts of present-day Brazil are patrolled to protect Portugal's interests.
1530-32	São Vicente is founded and early industries are developed by a colonizing expedition led by Martim Alfonso de Sousa.
1540	King of Portugal divides area into *capitanias* with *donatorios* acting as hereditary feudal lords.
c.1540	Convicts from Portugal are shipped to the colony.
1549	Thome de Souza becomes the first governor-general of Portuguese America and founds São Salvador (Bahia). Colonization continues. Jesuit priests begin taking part in colonization and converting the natives to Roman Catholicism.
1551	Government is given supreme authority over religious activities and appointments in America, while the Bishopric of Bahia, under the Archbishopric of Lisbon, is created.
1555	French protestants led by Nicolas Durand de Villegagnon settle on the Bay of the Rio de Janeiro.
1567	French are ousted from Rio de Janeiro and the settlement is reestablished under the Brazilian governor, Mem de Sá.
1581-1640	During the union of Spain and Portugal, Brazil is attacked by Spain's enemies.
1612-21	A town is established by France on the island of Maranhão in northern Brazil, but the Portuguese force its surrender and found Belem on the mainland. The State of Maranhao is created and remains independent of Brazil.
1624-45	The Dutch endeavor colonization of the area under Portuguese claim and maintain, under the Dutch West India Company, control of an area from the Sao Francisco River to Maranhão. The Portuguese later overthrow Dutch rule in the region.
1630	Dutch take Pernambuco and control the city.

1645 Spanish Jesuits are subjected to slave-raiding parties which promote Portuguese rule in the north, while Portuguese Jesuits establish missions in the south, coming into conflict with the Paulistas.

1661 Peace is attained between the Portuguese and Dutch.

1680 Colonia is established by the Portuguese in order to gain possession of the left bank of the Rio de la Plata (Banda Oriental), but the territory frequently changes hands between Portugal and Spain.

1897 Slaves far out number their white masters in the Palmares Republic.

1700s Planters from the coast and Portuguese from Europe rush into the newly discovered coal regions.

1708 The Paulistas are conquered by the Portuguese in the War of the Emboabas.

1709-48 Various captaincies of São Paulo (1709), Minas Gerais (1720), Matto Grosso (1744), and Goyáz (1748) are established with captain-generals subject directly to the Portuguese sovereign.

1710 Rio de Janeiro is sacked and occupied by the French because of the alliance between England and Portugal during the War of Spanish Succession.

1710-11 The native Brazilians of Olinda cede the seat of government to Recife after losing the War of the Mascates.

1720 Paulistas are forced by Portugal to cede Minas Gerais.

1750-80 No Line of Demarcation has been surveyed, so Portuguese expansion proceeds without bounds. Spain recognizes Portugal's claim to the basins of the Amazon and Paraná. Further vast claims are later established.

1750-77 Government is unified with the capital at Rio de Janeiro and Maranhão being incorporated into Brazil. Brazilians take government posts. The Jesuits are expelled.

1807-08 Prince John sets up a regency for Portugal and Brazil, moving to and placing his capital at Rio de Janeiro.

1808 France invades Brazil.

1808-16 Industry, communications, agriculture, the royal press, the Bank of Brazil and other areas are developed during John's reign. Brazil becomes part of the United Kingdom of Portugal, Brazil, and Algarves.

1816-21 The areas of Montevideo and Artigas are annexed to Brazil and the Cisplatine Province, although projects to annex other parts of the Rio de la Plata are halted.

1817 Courts are transfered to Brazil, but expenditures and discrimination against the Brazilians causes a revolution that failed in Pernambuco.

1820 The regency is overthrown in Portugal and the king forced to return to Portugal and accept a new constitution.

1821-22 The Cortes of Portugal resubjugates Brazil and replaces the commercial monopoly there. These actions arouse hostile resent in the Brazilians.

1822 Dom Pedro is declared Pedro I of Brazil, terminating Portuguese rule, and secures the province of Sao Paulo.

1828 The Banda Oriental (Uruguay) becomes independent of Portugal. The Cisplatine Province is also lost to Argentina.

1831-40 Anarchy develops while a regency is in place, until Pedro II succeeds in 1840.

1850-70 Great progress takes place in all aspects of Brazilian life: agriculture, commerce, industry, transportation.

1850 Estimated population: 8,000,000 including 2,500,000 slaves. Law passes which ends the slave trade.

1865 The Empire of Brazil and Argentina sign an alliance against Paraguay; 6,000 slaves belonging to the Crown gain freedom by volunteering to fight against Paraguay.

1870 Republican party formed and republicanism grows popular.

1871 All negro children born after this date are free; all slaves belonging to the nation or employed by the Crown and those abandoned by their masters or for whom title of inheritance was doubtful are emancipated.

1872 Estimated population: over 10,000,000 including 1,500,000 slaves.

1884 Slaves are freed in the province of Ceará.

1888 Complete emancipation is ordered without recompense to owners of slaves. Many slaves move to Uraguay.

1889 Emperor is deposed and republic is proclaimed. Industry and agriculture are improved, but government is plagued by illiteracy, political inexperience, and tendencies toward militarism.

1891 New constitution and president set up called the United States of Brazil.

1895-1906 Various boundary disputes with Argentina (1895 to gain the Acre region), France (1900), Bolivia (1903), England (1904), and Holland (1906), are settled peacefully.

1920-35 Period of extensive immigration to Brazil, especially of Spaniards and Italians. Population reaches over 47,500,000.

Settlement and Migration

Brazilians combine Portuguese, African, and Indian stocks, and Brazilian culture reflects the influences of Iberia, Africa, and Europe, while its political philosophy has been influenced by Western Europe and North America.

Brazil was formally claimed for Portugal by Pedro Alvares Cabral in 1500. In 1530 the Portuguese crown financed a colonizing expedition under Martim Alfonso de Sousa that settled São Vincente in 1532. Shortly thereafter, the Portuguese monarch, Dom Joao III, divided the Brazilian coastline into fifteen hereditary, virtually feudal captaincies *(capitanias)* assigned to individuals *(donatórios)* who would assume the financial burdens of settlement in exchange for broad governing powers and profitmaking possibilities. The captaincies were demarcated only by latitude and extended indefinitely into the interior. Only two, those at Sao Vicente and Pernambuco, were notably successful.

Brazil is the only country in South America which was still a monarchy until the nineteenth century. Independence from Portugal, gained without violence, was proclaimed in 1822. The people instituted an empire, rather than a republic as did neighboring countries.

Brazil's empire lasted sixty-seven years (1822-89). The story of independent Brazil falls into six chapters: Emperor Pedro I (1822-31); the regency (1831-40); Pedro II (1840-89); the first republic (1889-1930); the dictatorship of Getúlio Vargas (1930-45); and the second republic (1945-). History credits the cohesive power of the crown with holding Brazil together rather than seeing provinces splinter into separate nations as did Gran Colombia, Peru, and the provinces of La Plata.

The principal political subdivisions of Brazil are one federal district, twenty-two states, and four territories. The states range in size from the enormous Amazonas, with 13 percent of the national territory, to tiny Guanabara, with less than 1 percent.

The states are subdivided into *municípios,* which are roughly the equivalent of counties. They are established according to population and taxable income and have increased from 1,574 in 1940, to 3,720 in 1963, and reportedly to over 4,000 in 1969. In 1968, there were thirty-eight in Sao Paulo alone. Like the states, *municípios* vary greatly in size. In the Amazon wilderness there are several larger than Portugal.

Brazil Library Collection

Archives and Libraries

The Family History Library has inventories or catalogs of a serveral Brazilian archives or libraries, including:

Guia dos Arquivos de Instituicoés Religiosas e Beneficentes. (Guide to the Archives of Religious and Charitable Institutions) Rio de Janiero: Arquivo Nacional, 1975. (FHL# 981/A1 no. 1)

Moya, Salvador de. *Catálogo de Autores Genealógicos.* São Paulo: Departamento de Cultura, 1937. (FHL# 981/A1 no. 15)

Bibliography of Brazilian and Portuguese authors who have written works of a genealogical nature.

See FHLC heading Brazil/Archives and Libraries for a complete list of titles and call numbers.

Biography and Genealogy

The Family History Library has an extensive list of titles dealing with history and genealogy. The majority of the history titles are national in scope and the genealogy holdings address a specific family or surname. See FHLC heading **Brazil/History** and **Brazil/Genealogy** for a list of complete holdings and call numbers.

Church History, Church Records

The library has seventy-seven reels of trial documents for New Christians (Marranos) taken prisoner for religious infractions in Brazil between 1610 and 1700. They were sent to Portugal to face trial by the Inquisition. Trial documents include genealogical information to prove their descent.

Consult the FHLC under **Brazil/Church History** for call numbers.

Colonization

Cidade Rio de Janeiro. *Hospediaria de Imigrantes. Registros de Imigrantes.* Salt Lake City: Filmed by the Sociedad Genealógica de Utah, 1981. 72 microfilm reels. Microfilm of original records of the City of Rio de Janiero. See FHLC heading **Brazil/Colonization** for call numbers.

Cidade São Paulo. *Hospedaria de Imigrantes. Matrículas de Imigrates.* Salt Lake City: Sociedad Genealógica de Utah, 1981. 55 microfilm reels. Microfilm of original records of the City of São Paulo. See FHLC heading **Brazil/-Colonization** for call numbers.

Other noteworthy titles under this heading include:

Rio de Janeiro (cidade), Hospedaria e Imigrantes. *Registros de Imigrantes.* Salt Lake City: Genealogical Society of Utah, 1981. 130 microfilm reels. See FHLC heading **Brazil/-Colonization** for call numbers.

Records of immigrants entering or leaving Rio de Janeiro, also entering or leaving the hostelry in Rio de Janeiro (1808-1922). Many lists of passengers and ships.

São Paulo, Hospedaria de Imigrantes. *Matrículas de Imigrantes.* Salt Lake City: Genealogical Society of Utah, 1981. 58 microfilm reels. For call numbers, consult the FHLC under **Brazil/Colonization**.

Emigration and Immigration

The library has many noteworthy titles about this subject including:

Bahia (Estado), Brasil, Archivo Público. *Títulos de Residência a Estrangeiros.* Salt Lake City: Filmed by the Genealogical Society of Utah, 1983. 5 microfilm reels. (FHL# microfilm 1366174-1366178)

Microfilm of original manuscripts at the Public Archives in the State of Bahia. Contains records of immigrants to Brazil who entered at the port of Salvador, Bahia between 1839 and 1854.

Bas-Rhin Archives Departmentales. *Emigration pour d'Amérique et des Autres Pays.* Salt Lake City: Filmed by the Genealogical Society of Utah, 1973. 4 microfilm reels. (FHL# microfilm 1070233-1070236)

Microfilm of original records at the Archives Departmentales at Strasbourg, France. Includes emigration documents of French citizens immigrating to the United States and other countries between 1803 and 1869.

Igreja Catolica, Bom Jesus do Calvário (Rio de Janeiro). *Registros Paroquiais, 1828-1837.* Salt Lake City: Filmed by the Genealogical Society of Utah, 1978. (FHL# microfilm 1252871, item 14)

Microfilm of original manuscripts at the Arquivo da Cúria Metropolitâna do Rio de Janeiro. Includes registers of baptisms and marriages of foreigners in Rio de Janeiro performed at the parish church of Good Jesus of Mount Calvary.

Koeniglisches Landeskommisariat, Kusel [Bayern]. *Auswanderungen, 1815-1850.* Salt Lake City: Filmed by the Genealogical Society of Utah, 1965. 7 microfilm reels. (FHL# microfilm 0500174-0500180)

Microfilmed from original minuscripts at the Landratsamt Kusel. Includes immigrations to Poland, Brazil, the United States, and internal migrations.

Registro de Estrangeiros. 3 vols. Rio de Janeiro: Ministério da Justiça e Negocios Interiores, Arquivo Nacional, 1961-1964. (FHL# 981/W2b or microfilm 1090236)

Register of foreigners entering at Rio de Janeiro.

Rio de Janeiro (cidade), Hospedaria de Imigrantes. *Registros de Imigrantes.* Salt Lake City: Filmed by the Genealogical Society of Utah, 1981. 72 microfilm reels. (FHL# microfilm 1285633-1285705)

Microfilm of original manuscripts at the National Archives at Rio de Janeiro. Includes records of immigrants entering and leaving the port of Rio de Janeiro between 1808 and 1869. Contains some ship passenger lists.

Gazetteers

Directoria General dos Correios. *Guia Postal.* 2 vols. Rio de Janeiro, Brazil: Typ. da Directoria General dos Correios, 1930. (FHL# 981/E8d)

Postal guide and very comprehensive. Twenty maps show even foot trails and horse paths.

See also:

Office of Geography, Dept. of the Interior. *Brazil, Official Standard Names Approved by the Board on Geographic Names.* Washington, D.C.: Department of the Interior, 1963. (FHL# 981/E5u)

Guardianship and Ward records

Arquivo Nacional. *Tutelas e Curatelas.* Rio de Janeiro, Brazil: El Arquivo, 1965. (FHL# 981/P2t)

Lists 1,600 guardianships granted in the early part of the nineteenth century along with names of parents and all children plus location of the case file.

History

The library has fifty histories of Brazil. Noteworthy are:

Pombo, Rocha. *Historia do Brasil.* 5 vols. Rio de Janeiro, Brazil: W. M. Jackson, Inc., 1953. (FHL# 981/H2p) In Portuguese.

Weil, Thomas E. *Area Handbook for Brazil.* Washington, D.C.: U.S. Government Printing Office, 1971. (FHL# 981/H6a)

Excellent overview in English of Brazil's peoples, lands, history, and institutions.

Historical/Genealogical Periodicals or Series

The library's collection includes seven periodicals dealing with Brazilian history and genealogy in addition to these:

Revista do Instituto de Estudios Genealógicos. 7 vols. São Paulo: Instituto de Estudos Genealogicos, 1937-43. (FHL# 981/B2r)

Revista Genealógica Brasileira. 9 vols. São Paulo: Instituto Genealogica Brasileiro, 1940-48. (FHL# 981/B2b or microfilm 0962536-0973040)

Maps

Drawn to a scale of 1:500,000, this set of sixty-eight maps covering the entire country is the most detailed and comprehensive in the library's collection:

Ol Conselho Nacional de Geografia. *Carta do Brasil.* Rio de Janeiro, Brazil: El Conselho, 1945-67. (FHL# 981/E7b)

The library also has several large atlases and map sets or books for Brazil.

Minorities

At the conclusion of the United States Civil War, about 20,000 Southerners moved to Brazil, where they established several colonies in the state of Sao Paulo. See:

Harter, Eugene C. *The Lost Colony of the Confederacy.* Jackson: University Press of Mississippi, 1986. (FHL# 981/F2h) Indexes 350 surnames.

Oliveira, Betty Antunes de. *Tombstone Records of the Campo Cemetery.* Brasilia: Gráfica do Senado Federal, 1978. (FHL# 981.61/S2/V3a)

Includes tombstone inscriptions of North Americans buried at Campo Cenetery.

Other groups treated in the sixty-two books cataloged under minorities are Jews, Poles, Japanese, Italians, Germans, French, Dutch, and Ukrainians.

Paleography

The Genealogical Department of the Church of Jesus Christ of Latter-day Saints. *Basic Portuguese Paleography.* Salt Lake City: Genealogical Society of Utah, 1978. (FHL# 929.1/G286gs/H20)

Discusses handwriting styles, unfamiliar and Latin terms, abbreviations, names and naming customs, occupations, titles, surnames, and Portuguese grammar.

Vital Records

The library has filmed vital records throughout Brazil. Civil registration is incomplete (major metropolitan areas only) and census records are absent, but church records are relatively complete. These records occupy more than 18,000 reels and represent millions of original source documents from the early 1600s through the early 1900s.

These records are cataloged in the FHLC by **Brazil/[State]/[Municipio]/Church Records** and **Brazil/[State]/[Municipio]/Civil Registration.**

CHILE

Historical Background

c.1520	Ferdinand Magellan is the first European to visit Chile.
1536	Spanish conquest of the western coast of South America begins; 70 years are taken to subdue the native peoples. Diego de Almagro marches from Peru to take possession of Chile.
1540-43	Pedro de Valdivía leads in the conquest of Chile for Spain.
1541	Valdivia establishes Santiago.
1536-1800	Colonial period of history. Demographically, the population becomes homogeneously mestizo (mixed native and European blood) very early. Socioeconomically, there are only two classes: the Spanish bureaucrats, the landlords, and the merchants who form the rich upper crust in one group; and the laborers on the other hand who compose the majority of the population.
1800-1900	Later immigration of Europeans does not effect the population significantly and are plagued by disease.
1810-12	A junta is established to rule Chile in the name of Ferdinand VII of Spain while he is occupied with the advances of Napoleon.
1814	Peru defeats Chile and captures Santiago. Royal government is reestablished.
1817	Jose de San Martin occupies Santiago with his army and Bernardo O'Higgins is named supreme director.
1818	The independence of Chile is proclaimed and a highly-centralized government is developed under O'Higgins.
1824	O'Higgins opens up new lands and gives them to his country's landless peasants.
1826	Federalism is adopted under the executive administration of Ramon Freire.
1829-30	Civil war occurrs between the Conservative and Liberal parties, from which the Conservatives emerge victorious to begin a long rule with a powerful presidency in Chile. Roman Catholicism remains the official religion.
1833	Constitution is accepted; right to vote is given to those men above 25 years of age who can read and write, thus perpetuating the landed gentry's leadership role.
1839	Chilean war breaks up Confederation of Peru and Bolivia.
1841-51	Under the administration of Bulnes, Chile extends power over the area of the Straits of Magellan. A Liberal Party reforms in opposition of conservative oligarchy.
1879-83	Chile emerges as the dominant power in South America after the War of the Pacific.
1883	Peru cedes the province of Tarapaca to Chile and Chile is to occupy Tacna and Arica for a period of ten years, at which time a plebiscite is to be held.
1884	By treaty, Chile maintains possession of The Bolivian littoral, including the Atacama desert and its mines. Church and state remain unseparated.
1891	Civil war institutes the principals of parliamentary government.
1891-96	Under the direction of the Congressional Party, the president gives a large decree of self-government to the local institutions.
1901	Boundary disputes with Argentina are narrowly negotiated without war. The Liberal Party becomes the dominant faction in Chile.
1907	By this time, the population has become 3,000,000.
1920s	Extensive social, political, and religious reforms are instituted by the Liberal Alliance Party. Chile remains neutral in World War I.

Settlement and Migration

Chile was under the jurisdiction of the Viceroyalty of Peru from 1510 to 1810. Remote, yielding little mineral treasure, and with few tractable Indian slaves, Chile was a second-class colony. In the early 1800s, its total population was little more than a half million, including some 100,000 unassimilated Indians in the south, about 150,000 Creoles (citizens of pure Spanish bloodlines who were born in South America), 20,000 *peninsulares* (Spanish citizens born in Spain), 250,000 mestizos, 4,000 blacks, and a few British, French, Italians, Germans, and others. A few powerful families, among whom Basques were conspicuous, owned the major share of the good land.

In September 1810, a junta was appointed which professed loyalty to the monarch, King Ferdinand VII of Spain, but which decreed free trade, dissolved the royal *audiencia*, and entered into relations with the junta in Buenos Aires.

From 1811 to 1814, the Chilean patriots quarreled among themselves. A royalist plot to restore colonial rule was countered by José Miguel Carrera, a hothead aristocrat of twenty-six who seized dictatorial power, refused to accept edicts from Spain, set up a printing press, founded a secondary school called the National Institute, opened a few primary schools, organized a public library, and adopted a national flag, all while continuing to profess allegiance to Ferdinand.

His despotic course incited the first families of Santiago to revolt under the leadership of Bernardo O'Higgins between 1811 and 1814. Spanish forces marched on Santiago and, in October, 1814, routed the troops of both Carrera and O'Higgins, forcing these rivals into Argentina.

Restored Spanish power, 1814-17, was exercised so ruthlessly that the patriots were able to organize another uprising under Jose de San Martin and O'Higgins. In February 1817, after an incredible march over the Andes, San Martin and O'Higgins with five thousand men defeated the Spanish troops at Chacabuco. Chile declared its independence a year later on 12 February 1818, confirmed two months later by a decisive victory at Maipu. In 1987, the Chileans numbered 12,042,000. A homogeneous people, they are chiefly a blend of Spanish and Araucanian. A few old families boast pure Spanish blood. There are more than 50,000 survivors of the Araucanians but they play little part in Chilean life. The colonial period never saw more than a few thousand black slaves; their descendants have long since been assimilated. During the nineteenth and twentieth centuries, immigration from Europe was steady but scant, bringing in altogether scarcely more than a 100,000 English, Germans, Irish, French, Italians, and Yugoslavs. Most of them are fully assimilated and retain few ethnic ties. Prominent Chilean families bear such names as Edwards, Cos, Korner, Braun, Swinburne, Balfour, Schnacke, Frei, and Muller. The one conspicuous exception to assimilation is the a colony south of Valdivia, established by Germans around 1900 and now, in the third generation, numbering between 30,000 and 40,000. They farm, conduct businesses, and retain their German language and customs.

Chile Library Collection

Archives and Libraries

The library has a compendium of genealogical, biographical, and historical items in the National Archive of Chile in Santiago (see FHL# 983/A3p) and the catalog for the Archivo de la Real Audiencia de Santiago (Archive of the royal Audience of Santiago). (FHL# microfilm 1410452, items 5-6).

Biography, Genealogy, Family History

The library has these biographies and histories, as well a many others pertaining to individuals or groups and a plethora of Chilean history titles:

Fuentes, Jordi. *Diccionario Histórico de Chile.* 2d ed. Santiago: Editorial del Pacifico, 1965. (FHL#983/H26f)

Figueroa, Virgilio. *Diccionario Histórico, Biográfico y Bibliográfico de Chile.* 5 vols. Nedeln, Lichtenstein: Kraus Reprint, 1974. (FHL#983/D36fd)

Roa y Ursua, Luis de. *El Reyno de Chile.* Valladolid, Spain: Talleres Tipográficos "Cuesta," 1945. (FHL# 983/D3r)

Discusses more than 4,000 individuals, 1535-1810.

Census Records

The library has eight reels of census and tax roll information dating from 1777 cataloged under **Chile/Census** or **Chile/[Province]/Census.**

Court Records

The library has four reels of judicial records from the colonial period (1609-1828) cataloged under **Chile/Colonization/ Court Records.** (FHL# microfilm 1410451-1410452, 1398481-1398482)

Gazetteers

The library has gazetteers for Chile compiled in 1867, 1899, and 1888. Each briefly comments on local history and defines locations in relation to major landmarks. The most complete listing of Chilean place names is:

Office of Geography, Department of Interior. *Chile: Official Standard Names.* Washington, D.C.: Department of the Interior, 1967. (FHL# 983/E5u)

Gives locations by latitude and longitude.

Genealogy, Sources

Genealogy Society of the Church of Jesus Christ of Latter-day Saints. *Fuentes Principales de Registros Genealógicas en Chile.* (Principal Sources of Genealogical Records in Chile). Salt Lake City: Genealogical Society of Utah, 1977. (FHL# 929.1/G286/gs/Ser. H/no.4)

Genealogical/Historical Periodicals or Series

The library has these two periodicals or series dealing with genealogy and history:

Boletín de la Academia Chilena de la Historia, Santiago de Chile. Santiago: Imprenta Universitaria, 1933-date. Library has 82 vols. (FHL# 983/B2b or microfilm 0844997-0845000, 0873803-0873810)

La Sociedad Chilena de Historia y Geografía. *Revista Chilena de Historia y Geografía.* 138 vols. Santiago: Imprenta Universitaria, 1911-date. See FHLC heading **Chile/History-Periodicals** for call numbers.

History

Encina, Francisco A. *Historia de Chile*. 20 vols. 1938, rpt. ed., Santiago, Chile: Editorial Nascimiento, 1955. (FHL# 983/H2cm) Includes a three-volume summary.

The library also has twenty-five books on the general history of Chile and at least thirteen on the history of the Catholic Church in the country. See FHLC headings **Chile/History, Chile/Genealogy/** and **Chile/Church History**.

Maps

Grau, Pedro Cunill. *Atlas Histórico de Chile.* Santiago de Chile: Sociedad Teuto-Chilena, 1961. (FHL# 983/E7cg)

Approximately thirty maps provide an orientation to the influence of geography on Chile's history.

For contemporary maps, consult the FHLC under **Chile/Maps**.

Minorities

The Swiss, Jews, Chilenos in California (USA), Germans in Chile, Poles, Vascos (Basque), and Montañeses (highland) minorities are each the subject of at least one book.

Vital Records

The library has filmed church and civil vital records extensively throughout the Chile. Here is a by-province list with the number of reels (9,742, total) of vital records filmed: Aconcagua, 414; Antofagast , 142; Arauco , 127; Atacama, 271; Bio Bio, 202; Cautin, 122; Chiloé, 283; Colchagua, 326; Concepción, 403; Coquimbo, 464; Linares, 148; Llanquihue, 97; Magallanes, 54; Malleco, 102; Maule, 284; Nuble, 970; O'Higgin, 432; Osorno, 90; Santiago, 2,808; Talca, 700; Tarapa, 320; Valdivia, 126; and Valparaíso, 857.

COLOMBIA

Historical Background

1499	Alonso de Ojeda reaches the north coast of Columbia.
1509	Ojeda and Diego de Nicuesa recieve royal grants and promote settlement.
1525	First permanent settlement in what is to become New Granada is made at Santa Marta by Rodrigo de Bastidas.
1533	Cartagena is founded by Pedro de Heredia, directed by royal authority.
1535-38	Gonzalo Jiménez de Quesada leads an expedition up the Magdalena river and at the plateau of Bogota founds Sante Fe de Bogota, the future capital.
1549	The Audiencia of New Granada is founded, including Cartagena, Popayán, and Santa Fe (the seat of government).
1739	The Viceroyalty of New Granada is established to incorporate Panama, Venezuala, and Quito.
1781	Widespread revolt occurs in opposition to attempts to increase royal revenues. The revolts were calmed by the viceroy.
1808	Junta is set up in the name of Ferdinand VII in Quito, deposing the president, but royal authorities later overthrow this insurgency. The viceroyalty also establishes a junta with the viceroy at its head, but the viceroy is deposed and provicial juntas are instituted.
1811-13	Cartagena and Cundinamarca declare independence separately. The Act of Federation of the United Provinces of New Granada is composed, but largely unaccepted. In 1813, Bolivar becomes dictator of Caracas under authority of the cabildo in Bogotá.
1814	Cartagena and Cundimarca are brought back under control of the central government of New Granada.
1815	Pablo Morillo arrives from Spain with 10,000 troops and brings royal authority back to virtually all of New Granada.
1818-19	Simon Bolivar marches into Colombia and defeats the Spanish at Boyacá. He takes control and becomes president of the area of the lower basin of the Orinoco, headquartered ar Angostura. The Congress thereof, after the defeat of the royal troops by Bolivar, proclaims that New Granada, Venezuela, and Quito constitute Great Colombia, the latter two provinces of which are liberated and incorporated from royal authority in the 1820s.
1820	Ecuador joins the Colombian confederates.

1829-31 Separatism dissolves the union and the Republic of New Granada becomes a separate state with a centralized constitution. The borders of the Republic of New Granada correpond to those of present-day Columbia. Sectional rivalry, opposing political factions, and the Church hinder the new state.

1837 Civil wars begin as disunity leads to violence.

1843 A new centralized government is adopted.

1846 A treaty with the United States of America grants New Granada sovereignty over the Isthmus of Panama.

1849-53 Rivers are opened for foreign trade. A new constitution is adopted. The Church loses governmental power. Slavery is abolished.

1855 Panama is given federal status and the path is cleared for other provinces who wish such status.

1858 Certain provinces accept federal government with considerable autonomy and the central, yet weak, government becomes known as the Granadan Confederation.

1860 Cauca and other states become independent of Granada.

1861-63 After civil war, the seven sovereign states are proclaimed in union as the United States of Colombia.

1867-80 Characterized by weak administrations.

1886 A newly accepted constitution restores a centralized government, in which the papacy is given significant power and Roman Catholicism is declared the state religion.

1900-03 Civil war is prolonged, with the eventual ascendency of the Conservatives.

1903 Panama becomes independent of Colombia, but the latter refuses to recognize such independence for over a decade.

1907 Colombia cedes to Brazil territory around the mouth of the Caqueta River and the headwaters of the Rio Negro.

1922 Colombia gains land disputed with Venezuala by the award of the Swiss Federal Council. Boundary disputes are also settled with Peru.

Settlement and Migration

Colombia was named in honor of Christopher Columbus, although the first European in the area was Alonzo de Ojeda, in 1499. Colonization began almost at once, and with the founding of Bogatá in 1538, this region, under the name of New Granada, became the center of Spanish rule in the New World. Most major cities were founded prior to 1600.

The Audiencia de Santa Fe de Bogotá was established in 1550 with jurisdiction over the governors of Santa María, Cartagena, Antioquia, Popayán, Riohacha, Tunja, Bogatá, and the plains of Casanare and San Martin.

In 1564, the Spanish crown formed the New Kingdom of Granada de Tierra Firme with jurisdiction over the modern-day countries of Panama and Colombia (excluding Popayán). In 1717, the Viceroyship of Nueva Granada was organized. The area was divided into fourteen administrative districts, each of which was subdivided into provinces and later *municipalidades* (municipalities). These divisions covered the modern-day territories of Panama, Ecuador, Colombia, and Venezuela.

The viceroyship Nueva Granada continued until 1723 when it ceased to function. It was reestablished in 1740 and functioned until Panama and Ecuador declared their independence in 1822. Colombia commemorates 20 July 1810 as its independence day.

Between 1810 and 1819, Colombian patriots fought Spain in a prolonged war of independence. On 17 December 1819, the revolutionaries established the Republic of Greater Colombia (Panama, Venezuela, Colombia and Ecuador). In 1830, Panama and Colombia declared themselves to be the Republic of New Granada. Renamed the Republic of Colombia in 1886, Panama seceeded from it in 1903.

Colombia is divided into sixteen departments, four *intendencias,* and four *comisarias.*

Colombia Library Collection

Biography

The library has a large collection of books pertaining to Colombian biography. See FHLC heading **Colombia/Biography** for a complete list with call numbers.

Acosta de Samper, Soledad. *Biografiás de Hombres Ilustres.* Bogotá, Colombia: n.pub., c.1882. (FHL# 986.1/D3a)

Biographies of more than 300 discoverers and conquerors of Colombia. One chapter about dogs used in subduing the native population, even giving their names, genealogies, and biographies.

Census Records

The library has two reels of census records covering the period 1777-84. Consult the FHLC under **Colombia/Census** for call numbers.

Church Directories

Iglesia Católica. *Parroquias de Colombia Según Jurisdicciones: Directorio.* Bogotá: Iglesia Católica, 1974. (FHL# 986.1/K22s) The parishes of Colombia by jurisdiction.

Church Records

The library has professions of faith (loyalty to the Catholic Church) by Colombians required by the Spanish Inquisition, 1612-1799, on fifteen reels. Consult the

FHLC under **Colombia/Church Records**. No index is indicated.

Colonization

The library has nine reels under this heading containing an inventory of documents related to newly discovered lands and an index. They contain names of soldiers, magistrates, and judges; wills; deeds; ships' passenger lists and manifests; and other materials.

Gazetteers

Office of Geography, Department of the Interior. *Colombia, Official Standard Names.* Washington, D.C.: Department of the Interior, 1964. (FHL# 986.1/E5u)

Lists all place names in the country, giving location by latitude and longitude.

Esquerra O., Joaquín. *Diccionario Geográfico de los Estados Unidos de Colombia.* Bogota: J. B. Gaitan, 1876. (FHL# 986.1/E5e)

Brief description and histories for locations in 1876.

Genealogy, Sources

Genealogy Department of the Church of Jesus Christ of Latter-day Saints. *Fuentes Principales de Registros Genealógicos en Colombia.* Salt Lake City: Church of Jesus Christ of Latter-day Saints, 1977. (FHL# 929.1/G286gs)

History

An extensive source of historical, biographical, and genealogical information is the following periodical:

Academia Colombiana de Historia. *Boletín de Historia y Antiquedades.* Bogotá: Editorial Kelly, 1964. (FHL# 986.1/B2b) The library has vols. 51-65 (March 1964-June 1978)

_____. *Historia Extensa de Colombia.* 25 vols. Bogota: The Academy, 1974. (FHL# 986.1/H2ac)

The library has only Volume 8 (Nueva Granada), Volume 13 (Historia Eclesiástica), Volume 17 (Historia Diplomática), and Volume 24 (Las Ciencias en Colombia).

Friede, Juan. *Documentos Ineditos Para La Historia de Colombia.* 10 vols. Bogotá: Academia Colombiana de Historia, 1955. (FHL# 986.1/H2e)

Documents held in the Archivo General de Indias de Sevilla, unedited, for 1509-50, indexed by individual. Often contain testimony (depositions) of common people called as witnesses.

The library also has thirty-five other histories. For histories of states or departments, consult the FHLC under **Colombia/[State or Department]/History.**

Maps

Ministerio de Hacienda. *Mapa Vial de Colombia.* N.p.: Instituto Geográfico "Agustín Codazzi," 1973. (FHL# 986.1/E7m)

Contains most place names for Colombia on a scale of 1:1,500,000.

Ministerio de Hacienda. *Mapa División de Vicarias Arciprestazgos y Parroquias de la Ciudad de Bogotá.* N.p.: Instituto Geografico "Agustín Codazzi," 1971. (FHL# 946.141/B1/E7b)

Map of Bogota at a scale of 1:25,000.

Vital Records

The library has filmed neither civil registrations nor parish records. Its holdings consist of two reels listing members, births, marriages, and deaths for the First Baptist Church in San Andres and Providencia, 1852-1959. See FHLC heading **Colombia/Vital Records** for call numbers.

ECUADOR

Historical Background

1000-1487	Area is in the Kingdom of Quitu, ruled by the Shyris, the sovereigns of the Cara Indians.
1487	Territory is united with the Inca Empire.
1525	Francisco Pizarro and others discover the village of Tumbes on the Peruvian coast.
1526	Bartolome Ruiz is the first European to visit the Ecuadorian shores; he arrives at the Esmeraldas, and with others, ventures on to Atacamas.
1529	Francisco Pizarro is appointed captain-general with rights of discovery and conquest in Ecuador and Peru.
1531	Pizarro returns to Tumbes and marches south to the banks of the Piura River where he establishes a settlement called San Miguel in present-day Peru.
1534-51	Sebastian de Belalcázar, lieutenant of Pizarro, conquers the region of Quito (later known as Ecuador) and founds the city of San Francisco de Quito.
1540	Amazon River is discovered by Spaniards; the region of Ecuador becomes part of the Viceroyalty of Peru.
1500s	Colony exists of large estates worked by the Indian peoples, in the central area of Ecuador. Coast of Ecuador is not utilized extensively during colonial period, although some shipbuilding is done. Eastern slopes are dominated by Indians, the only white settlers being missionaries. Galápagos Islands are little more than a hideout for pirates.

1563 The *audiencia* of Quito is established.
1571 Spanish invade Ecuador.
1587 Severe earthquake ruins settlements.
1592 Quito citizens revolt against royal taxes.
1600-1800 Quito remains the political and cultural center of the area of Ecuador, although Guayaquil gradually takes over as the economic center of the area.
1645 Series of major earthquakes destroy many communities.
1717 Administrative authority over the region is transferred to the Viceroyalty of Santa Fe de Bogota.
1722 Governmental authority is returned to Peru.
1739 Bogota becomes administrative headquarters for Ecuador again.
1765 Citizens in Quito rebel against their rulers.
1770 Indians protest and revolt against oppresion.
1776 Quito becomes a part of the Viceroyalty of New Granada.
1790 Indians again rebel over oppressive treatment.
1808 The president of Quito is driven from office and a junta imposed, but royalist forces suppress the uprising.
1819 The Congress of Angostura declares Great Columbia to consist of New Granada, Quito, and Venezuala, with Bolivar as dictator.
1822 Quito is liberated by Antonio José de Sucre from Spain in the battle of Pinchincha and unites with Great Columbia; Simon Bolivar and José de San Martín meet Spanish at Guayaquil.
1830 The Republic of Ecuador is created with Juan Flores as president. Roman Catholicism is proclaimed the exclusive religion.
1831 Border disputes arise with Peru.
1834 Civil war ends with compromise between the two political factions in Ecuador, the Conservatives led by Flores, and the Liberals led by Rocafuerte.
1835 A new constitution forms a republican government.
1845-60 Period of instability and revolt within Ecuador.
1856 Boundary between Ecuador and New Granada is fixed.
1861-75 Gabriel García Morena rules with absolute authority. Administrative, financial, and military reforms are instituted. Only Catholics are allowed to vote during his tenure.
1862 Concordat with the Church occurs, giving them extensive power within Ecuador. By 1869, Ecuador is virtually a theocracy.
1875-95 Period of conflict between Liberals and Conservatives.
1881 Anti-Catholic and anti-feudal reforms are instituted under new leadership by Eloy Alfaro and Leonidas Plaza.
1895-1916 Liberal movements restrict power of the Church and bring a period of reform to Ecuador.
1904 Ecuador respects claims by Brazil of territory between the Caqueta and Amazon rivers. Border disputes with Peru are not resolved.
1906 Ecuador accepts its twelfth constitution.
1934 Ecuador enters the League of Nations.
1935-37 Dictatorship of Paez.

Settlement and Migration

When the Spanish conquistadors reached South America, Ecuador's advanced agricultural Indians had only recently been absorbed into the Inca empire. After Francisco Pizarro gained control of Peru, he sent Sebastian de Belalcazar northward in 1533. Ecuador's area became part of the Spanish Viceroyalty of Peru and remained under Spanish rule until freed by revolutionary troops in 1822. It first joined with Colombia and Venezuela in the republic of Greater Colombia, under the presidency of Simón Bolivar. In 1941, Peru invaded Ecuador and took possession of part of its eastern province. Since then, Ecuador's boundaries have not changed.

Ecuador's parish registers date from the first colonial years. Most notarial records have been preserved in historical archives, and judicial and notarial libraries throughout the country. Deeds are in the Municipal Archive in Quito, the National Archives of History in Quito, and the National Archives of History in Bogota. Tax lists date from early colonial times, and the first national census was taken in 1780.

Civil registration of vital statistics commenced in 1901, and has, in addition to the registration of births, marriages, and deaths, the registration of acknowledgement of children, legitimations, and adoptions.

Ecuador Library Collection

Archives and Libraries

A helpful pamphlet (ten pages) explains how best to extract genealogical information from the two principal archives in Ecuador: The National Archive of History in Quito, and the Historical Archive of Guayas in Guayaquil .

Freile-Granizo, Juan de. *Breve Guía de Fuentes Genealógicas En Dos Archivos Ecuatorianos.* N.p.: n.pub., 1972. (FHL# 986.6/A1/no.3)

See also his more complete inventory and explanation of the Archivo Nacional de Historia in *Guía del Archivo*

Nacional de Historia. n.p.: n. pub, 1973. (FHL# 986.6/-A3f)

Biography

The library has an extensive collection of Ecuadorian biographics. See FHLC heading **Ecuador/Biography** for a complete list of titles and call numbers in addition to:

Borrero Crespo, Maximiliano. *Orígenes Cuencanos.* 2 vols. Cuena-Ecuador: Talleres Graficos de la Universidad de Cuenca, 1960. (FHL# 986.623/C1/D2b)

400 families of Cuenca listed alphabetically; for most he gives both ancestry and descendants.

Marchant, B. Perez. *Diccionario Biográfico del Ecuador.* (Biogaphical dictionary of Ecuador.) Quito, Ecuador: Escuela de Artes Y Oficios, 1928. (FHL# 986.6/D3d or microfilm 1162425, item 6)

Gazetteers

Office of Geography, Department of the Interior. *Names Approved by the U.S. Board on Geographical Names.* Washington, D.C.: Department of the Interior, 1957. (FHL# 986.6/E5u)

Genealogical and Historical Periodicals

The library has a collection of five periodicals relating to the genealogy and history of Ecuador, see FHLC headings **Ecuador/History-Periodicals** and **Ecuador/-Genealogy-Periodicals** for titles and call numbers.

Genealogy, Sources

Genealogical Department of the Church of Jesus Christ of Latter-day Saints. *Fuentes Principales de Registros Genealógicos en Ecuador.* Salt Lake City: Church of Jesus Christ of Latter-day Saints, 1977. (FHL# 929.1/G286gs/-Ser. H/no.13)

History

The library has fourteen books or microfilms on Ecuador's history. An excellent introduction in English to the history and culture of the country is:

Erickson, Edwin E., et al. *Area Handbook for Ecuador.* Washington, D.C.: U.S. Government, 1966. (FHL# 986.6/H6a)

For local histories, consult the FHLC under **Ecuador/[Department]/History.**

Maps

Ecuador Instituto Geográfico Militar. *Mapa de Ecuador, Escala 1:100,000 (Set of 28 maps).* Quito, Ecuador: El Instituto, 1968-74. (FHL# 986.6/E3ei) Located on the atlas stand.

Vital Records

Civil registration has been required in Ecuador since 1901. However, the library has only church records of births, baptisms, marriages, and deaths and only for some provinces:

PROVINCE	CITY	YEARS
Azuay	Ona	1726-1923
Azuay	Paccha	1701-1959
Azuay	Palmas	1889-1971
Azuay	Pan	1809-1980
Azuay	Paute	1701-1945
Azuay	Pucara	1789-1927
Azuay	Quingeo	1835-1980
Azuay	San Bartolome	1738-1966
Azuay	San Christobal	1837-1973
Azuay	San Christobal	1916-52
Azuay	San Fernando	1837-1968
Azuay	San Juan	1835-1937
Azuay	Santa Ana	1908-36
Azuay	Santa Isabel	1823-1969
Azuay	Sayausi	1908-49
Azuay	Sidcay	1663-1972
Azuay	Sigsig	1818-1980
Azuay	Sigsig	1748-1957
Azuay	Sinincay	1853-1950
Azuay	Turi	1853-1944
Azuay	Valle	1802-1960
Choquisaca	Muyupampa	1897-1930
Esmeraldas	Concepcion	1832-1929
Esmeraldas	Esmeraldas	1832-1929
Esmeraldas	Rio Verde	1872-1929
Guayas	Guayaquil	1862-1928
Guayas	Guayaquil	1725-1977
Loja	Alamor	1852-1932
Loja	Amaluza	1787-1926
Loja	Carimanga	1720-1921
Loja	Catacocha	1780-1954
Loja	Celica	1782-1924
Loja	Chaquarpampa	1817-1923
Loja	Chuquiribamba	1695-1927
Loja	Gonzanama	1675-1926
Loja	Guachanama	1606-1945
Loja	Loja	1668-1926
Loja	Loja	1688-1928
Loja	Loja, El Valle	1720-1925
Loja	Malacatos	1704-1932
Loja	Manu	1853-1932
Loja	Nambucola	1883-1934
Loja	Olmedo	1917-42
Loja	Quilanga	1869-1940
Loja	San Lucas	1877-1930
Loja	San Pedro	1790-1936
Loja	Sanaguro	1818-1943
Loja	Urdaneta	1868-1930
Loja	Vilcabamba	1704-1932
Loja	Vilcabamba	1852-1937
Loja	Zapotillo	1892-1910
Loja	Zozoranga	1770-1942
Manabi	Bahia de Caraque	1846-1927
Manabi	Bellavista	1882-1923
Manabi	Calceta	1880-1940
Manabi	Canoa	1846-1927
Manabi	Canuto	1866-1931
Manabi	Chone	1818-1926
Manabi	Jipijapa	1882-1923
Manabi	Pedro Pablo Gomez	1882-1923
Manabi	Santa Ana	1852-1922
Manabi	Tosagua	1863-1928

FRENCH GUIANA

Historical Background

1500	Vincente Yanez Pinzon, an associate of Christopher Columbus, explores the coast of Guiana.
1500s	Explorers frequent the area in search of El Dorado, the "City of Gold."

1604	A French nobleman chooses the site for Cayenne.
1618	The French begin making settlement in the Guianas.
1637	The town of Cayenne is established by merchants from Rouen, in France. This first settlement attempt fails.
1664	Dutch inhabit Cayenne, but are evicted by the French.
1667	Guiana settlement is sacked by the English.
1676	Guiana settlement is invaded by the Dutch.
1700	Portuguese accept the Amazon River as the southeastern boundary of the French settlement.
1713	Under the Treay of Utrecht, the boundary is moved 50 miles north.
1713-62	Series of governors rules French Guiana.
1762	Jesuits are expelled from Guiana and 10,000 Amerinds are dispersed.
1763-65	Kourou expedition, composed of many European immigrants, ends in the death of many settlers.
1794-1805	Political deportees resulting from the French Revolution are sent from France to Guiana.
1802	Although slavery has been formally abolished, slave labor is still common.
1809	Colony is seized by the Portuguese.
1817	French reclaim colony.
1827-46	Thriving colony of freed slaves is established at Mana.
1848	Slavery is finally abolished to the ruin of most plantations. Guianans gain full French citizenship.
1848-55	Immigrant groups are brought to alleviate disaster resulting from emancipation; only the Asian Indians are effective.
1852	Saint-Laurent-du-Maroni is established, the first convict settlement. Penal colonies continue for over 90 years.
1855	Gold is discovered in French Guiana and agriculture is downplayed.
1946	Territory becomes a French *departement.*

The region of Guiana in northwest South America includes Guyana (formerly British Guiana), French Guiana, and Suriname (the Dutch portion of Guiana).

Settlement and Migration

French Guiana, with a territory of 34,750 square miles, has 82,700 inhabitants (1985 estimate). In 1613 the Dutch attempted colonization of the area, but passed the area to Portugal in the 1620s. It went back to the Dutch in 1666. The French gained control through a settlement with the Dutch in 1676, involving disputed land both in South America and Europe.

In 1852, the French government established a penal colony on three tiny islands; after their release, many convicts were stranded because they lacked the means to return to Europe Their descendants formed much of the white population. The penal colonies were abolished 1946-53.

Other settlers include blacks and Indo-Chinese. Most of them are mine, plantation, or road laborers. About 3,000 South American Indians live in the jungles. Cayenne, on the island of Cayenne, is the capital and main seaport. Only a few thousand acres of the country are under cultivation.

To develop further the resources of the interior, France in 1930 set it up as a separate colony, hoping to encourage development and further settlement, but the effort produced only marginal results. In 1946, French Guiana became an Overseas Department in the French Union.

French Guiana Library Collection

[Note: French Guiana is listed in the FHLC as Guiana.]

Census Records

Hebert, Donald J. *Acadians in Exile.* Cecilia, La.: Hebert Publications, 1980. (FHL# 971.6/D2h)

1765 census of Sinnamary, Cayenne, listing the names, ages, country of origin, and physical condition of 138 Acadians, a large French ethnic group from Acadia, France. Arranged both alphabetically and in the original order (pp. 583-97).

Vital Records

Marielle Campeau, *Checklist of Parish Registers.* (Ottawa, Canada: Public Archives of Canada, 1975). (FHL# 971/A3cm) indicates that copies of parish records for three French Guianan parishes are available from the Public Archives of Canada in Ottawa, though they are not available at the Family History Library: Cayenne (St. Sauveur de Cayenne) – births, deaths, marriages (1764-92); Kourou – births, deaths (1763-64, 1768, 1770); and Sinnamary (St. Joseph de Sinnamary) – births, deaths, marriages (1764-67, 1771-67, 1784-92).

The library has two reels of civil registration records for the city of Oiapoque. These films contain information on births, marriages, and deaths, 1738-1870 and are cataloged under **Guiana/Cayenne/Oyapock/Civil Registration**.

GUYANA (formerly British Guiana)

Historical Background

1498	Christopher Columbus sights the coast of Guiana.
1500-1600	Futile attempts are made at colonization by the Dutch, English and French.
1600-1800	The Dutch are the leading colonists of the Guianas, although the English and French colonize also.
1616	The Dutch and English together begin settling the Guianas; by this date, Dutch settlements exist on the Courantyne, Essequibo, and Cayenne rivers.
1621	Dutch West India Company and the slave trade are established.
1651	British colony established on the Surinam River.
1660	Imported slaves constitute a large portion of the population.
1667	British lose present-day Surinam to the Dutch.
1674	Cayenne is established as French territory.
1732	Berbice estuary is settled. Fort is established on Fort Island.
1738-72	Development of the Demerara region begins.
1780-1815	Settlements change hands frequently in the wars between the colonizing countries.
1780-96	Longchamps (Georgetown) is founded.
1796-1814	Longchamps rests in the possession of the British.
1807	Slave trade is abolished.
1814	British purchase Demerara, Berbice, and Essequibo.
1831	Berbice, Demerara, and Essequibo are united as British Guiana.
1834	Emancipation occurrs.
1860	Settlement begins on the Rapunni savanna.
1879	Gold is discovered in the Guianas.
1889	North Western District is organized.
1891	Constitutional structure of government is simplified by the British.
1928	Crown-colony system is introduced.
1953	New constitution is accepted.

The region of Guiana in northeastern South America includes Guyana (formerly British Guiana), Surinam (the Dutch portion of Guiana), and French Guiana.

The area now known as Guyana, formerly British Guiana, was first partially settled by the Dutch in the early 1600s. After years of boundary disputes and conflicting claims, it was ceded to Great Britain in 1814 and named British Guiana. On 26 May 1966, British Guiana became an independent member of the Commonwealth under the name of Guyana.

Guyana Library Collection

History

The dispatches of Guyana settler Storm Van's Gravesande over a period of thirty-four years (1738-72) if reprinted in full would fill twenty-one volumes of 300 pages each. These dispatches, written with conscientious care and laborious detail, reveal the daily patterns of early Guiana colonial life. Now edited, and produced by the Hakluyt Society, they are fascinating reading for the student of British Guianan history:

Van's Gravesande, Storm. *The Rise of British Guiana.* C. A. Harris and J. A. J. de Villiers, eds. Wiesbaden, West Germany: The Hakluyt Society, 1967. (FHL# 988.1/H2s)

For a broad overview of Guyana history, see:

U.S. Government, Department of the Interior. *Area Handbook for Guyana.* Washington D.C.: Government Printing, 1971. (FHL# 988.1/H6a)

Native Races

At the request of the Reverend Ernest Hawkins, Reverend W. H. Brett set forth in 1851 his experiences and observations of the native races of what was then simply Guiana. The result is a fascinating first-hand glimpse into a world virtually unaffected by 200 years of marginal contact with the European nations:

Brett, W. H. *The Indian Tribes of Guiana.* New York: Robert Carter and Brothers, 1852. (FHL# 988.1/F3b)

Vital Records

The library has no copies of vital records, civil or church, for British Guyana. However, due to the boundary changes in the area over the years, you should check all three current-day Guyana nations as well as Venezuela and Brazil for such records.

PARAGUAY

Historical Background

1525-28	First known Europeans visit the area, Alejo García and Sebastian Cabot.
1537	Area is claimed for Spain and the first permanent settlement is founded at Asuncion in 1537.
1588	Jesuits arrive in Paraguay to establish missions.
1600-1700	Region is chiefly noted for autonomous communities of Indians converted to Christianity, which are run by Jesuit missionaries.

1607 First American Provincia Jesuitica is founded.

1610 Mission of San Ignacio is established by the Jesuits.

1644 People revolt against the Jesuits' control of property.

1717 Another revolt ends in defeat for the people who agree to honor the orders of the Spanish government.

1721-35 Jose de Antequera is appointed to resolve a conflict between the *cabildo* of Asuncion and the governor of Paraguay and is chosen governor by the support of the cabildo. He leads a popular rebellion against Spanish authority, but this insurrection is eventually suppressed totally.

1767 Over 30 working missions exist in the Parana-Uraguay basin, but the king of Spain banishes Jesuit priests and seizes their property.

1776 Most of present-day Bolivia, Paraguay, Uraguay, and Argentina are united to from the Viceroy of Rio de la Plata, with Buenos Aires as its capital.

1811 The Paraguayans overthrow the royal governor and establish a revolutionary junta at Asuncion after the forces of Buenos Aires are defeated. Paraguay becomes the first state in the Spanish New World to assert and maintain its independence from Spain.

1814-17 San Martín establishes himself at Mendoza and prepares to carry out plans for a campaign to liberate Chile and attack Peru.

1816-40 Jose Gaspar Rodríguez de Francia becomes Perpetual Dictator of Peru and under his authoritarian government also becomes head of the Paraguayan Church. The docile Guarani people have little defense. Francia isolates the Parguayan country, promotes nationalism, and decreases the influence of the upper classes and the Church.

1840 A period of anarchy threatens Paraguay after the death of Francia.

1844-62 Paraguayan independence is reaffirmed and the presidency continued, though it is largely dictorial in nature. Paraguayan territorial claims are settled with Argentina, Brazil, the United States, and Great Britain. Population is over 1,000,000.

1865-70 War is brought about with Brazil, Argentina, and Uruguay over territorial claims. Paraguay is virtually annihalated and the population drastically reduced. Paraguay loses 55,000 square miles of land but constitutional government is restored.

1874 Eight hundred artisans from Lincolnshire, England, settle near Asunción; after a year or more, most move to Argentina.

1878 Paraguay gains land from Argentina by decision of the President of the United States.

1872-1912 Political instability occurs after the Paraguayan War and the Radical Party controls activities.

1893 Two hundred and fifty immigrants from Sydney, Australia, are sponsored by the New Australian Co-operative Settlement Association; they first settle at Villarica, Paraguay.

1894 A second group, this one from Adelaide, Sydney, follows to Paraguay.

1912-16 The presidency of Edward Schaerer brings about an era of progress and political stability. Paraguay remains neutral during World War I.

1932-35 After war with Chile, Paraguay gains the greater part of the Chaco territory.

1936 A military revolt occurs and Rafael Franco declares Paraguay a totalitarian state.

1937 A constitutional presidency is resumed in Paraguay.

Settlement and Migration

Portuguese Alejo García crossed the region now known as Paraguay about 1524. In 1526, Sebastain Cabot claimed the land for Spain; and from 1536 to 1776, the Paraguayn capital of Asuncion was the administrative center of Today's Argentina, Uruguay, Paraguay, and parts of Bolivia. The Jesuits, who dominated the country from 1610 to 1767, introduced European plants and animals and taught the Indians farming methods.

When Paraguay threw off Spain's rule in 1811, it came under the control of a series of dictators. The first, Jose Gaspar Rodriguez de Francia (1814-40), almost completely barred foreign trade. A later ruler, Francisco Solano Lopez, led the country into a war with Argentina, Brazil, and Uruguay which lasted five years and cost Paraguay 300,000 men. It lost the Chaco area to Bolivia in the Chaco War of the 1930s, which was also costly in lives and money.

The people of Paraguay are chiefly of mixed blood. They are descendants of the Spanish settlers and Guarani Indian tribes. There are only a few pure-blooded Indians today, most of them living in the Chaco. Still fewer people are of pure Spanish blood. Paraguay encourages immigrants but is too remote to attract them in numbers. Colonies of Mennonites from Canada, Russia, Poland, Germany, and the United States have settled in the Chaco. Guarani is spoken more widely than Spanish.

Politically, Paraguay is divided into sixteen departments and the capital. Ecclesiastically, Paraguay is divided into several archdioceses.

Parish records are generally in poor condition, and

many have disappeared altogether. There are very few records from the colonial period.

Civil registration was mandated 26 September 1880 but did not begin to function until 1898 and 1899. The Direccion General del Registro Civil in the capital is divided into ten sections and annexes under the direction of the Director General. In the rest of the country, justices of the peace (Jueces de Paz) are responsible to create and care for these records. A branch of the national archives in Asuncion has a copy of each record. Indexes are available.

The records of the capital are in alphabetical order by surname. The other records are indexed first by location, then alphabetically by surname. There are many records of illegitimate children, legitimations, recognizements, and adoptions in the civil registers of Paraguay.

Paraguay Library Collection

Archives and Libraries

The library has only one small volume describing part of the contents of the Archivo de la Asuncion del Paraguay. (FHL# 989.2/A1/no.1).

Biography/Genealogy

The library has biographical and genealogical works or references for Paraguay. See FHLC heading **Paraguay/History** and **Paraguay/Genealogy** for a complete list of titles and call numbers.

Gazetteers

Office of Geography, Department of the Interior. *Paraguay: Official Standard Names Approved by the U.S. Board on Geographic Names.* Washington, D.C.: U.S. Government, 1957. (FHL# 989.2/E5u)

Genealogy, Sources

The most comprehensive study available of genealogical records in Paraguay is:

Genealogical Department of the Church of Jesus Christ of Latter-day Saints. *Fuentes Principales de Registros Genealogicos en Paraguay.* Salt Lake City: The Church of Jesus Christ of Latter-day Saints, 1977. (FHL# 929.1/G286/gs/Ser. H/no.16)

History

The library has some twenty books or manuscripts on the history of Paraguay. All are in Spanish, and most were written in the twentieth century. Consult the FHLC under **Paraguay/History** or **Paraguay/[Province]/History.** Some of these volumes deal with specific provinces or cities.

Maps

This small historical atlas is useful in determining the political jurisdiction of different parts of the country at different time periods:

Martinez, Marcelino Machuca. *Mapas Históricos del Paraguay Gigante.* Asuncion, Paraguay: n.pub., c.1950. (FHL# 989.2/E7m)

da Ponte, Alberto. *Mapa de la República del Paraguay.* N.p.: El Instituto Geografico Militar, 1971. (FHL# 989.2/E7po) Scale of 1:2,000,000.

U.S. Army Map Service. *Paraguay City Maps 1:12,500.* Washington, D.C.: U.S. Army Map Service, [c.1960s]. (FHL# 989.2142/A1/E7a) Shows major buildings, cemeteries, and city streets.

Minorities

An exceptionally well prepared history on the Mennonite Colony of Fernheim, 1930-80 is:

Dverksen, Hans, and Jacob Harder. *Fernheim, 1930-1980.* Filadelfia, Paraguay: Administracion de la Colonia Fernheim, 1980. (FHL# 989.224/H2d)

Other minorities discussed in separate works are the Poles and the Italians.

Names, Personal

The importance and meaning of native names in Paraguayan society is in:

Cadogan, Leon. *Mil Apellidos Guaraníes* (One Thousand Guarani Surnames). Asuncion, Paraguay: Editorial Toledo, 1960. (FHL# 989.2/A1/no.3)

Vital Records

Civil registration dates from 1898-99, but the library does not yet have these records. However, church records dating from the eighteenth century have been filmed and are available. Here is a by-province list of a total of 571 films: Amambry, 25; Asunción, 128; Boqueron, 11; Caaguazu, 47; Cental, 74; Chaco, 0; Concepcion, 57; Cordiller, 48; Guaira, 47; Itapua, 3; Misiones, 17; Neembucu, 18; Paraguarí, 72; Presidente Hayes, 1; and San Pedro, 23.

PERU

Historical Background

1524-28 Francisco Pizarro begins the conquest of Peru and learns of the extant advanced Inca culture. His first two expeditions reach the San Juan Rier and the Gulf of Guyaquil and Tubez.

1529 The Spanish Crown gives Francisco Pizarro the right of discovery and conquest in the province of Peru.

1531 With Gonzalo and Hernando, Pizarro strengthens the Tumbez settlement and founds San Miguel.

1532 Pizarro captures and kills the Incan monarch, Atahualpa, at their meeting and paralyzes the Incan government.

1533-35 Pizzaro takes control of Cuzco, the Incan capital, secures Quito, and founds Lima.

1535-45 The Spaniards extended their territory to the area around Lake Titicaca and found Chuqisaca. The mines of Potosi are opened. Cali and Popayan are also established. Expansion of territory continues: Almagro advances to the Maule River; the Spaniards expand into Chile; Valdivia founds Santiago.

1537-41 Civil war ensues between the Spanish, as a result of which both Almagro and Pizarro are assassinated and the royal governor Vaca de Castro comes into power.

1542 The Viceroyalty of Peru is established.

1550-51 Royal authority is administrated by the *audiencia* of Lima.

1551 First university in South America is founded at Lima and called San Marcos.

1557-61 The town of Mendoza is founded as conquest extends into Cuyo from the Straits of Magellan.

1569-81 Francisco Alvarez de Toledo rules as viceroy and proves a magnificent magistrate in organizing the colonies.

1570 Inquisition is established in Peru.

1650 Cuzco is nearly destroyed by a series of earthquakes.

1600-1800 Peru lies under the Spanish crown. Unlike many other American states, Peru remains loyal to Spain because of its aristocracy, the large number of Spaniards in the area, and the concentration of Spanish presence in Lima. Outsiders eventually force Peru into independence.

1809-13 Political insurgencies and establishments of juntas in Chuquisaca, La Paz, Cuzco, Quito, and Santiago are suppressed by royal authority.

1821 José de San Martín of Chile, who has entered Peru in 1820 to take Lima and depose the viceroy, proclaims the independence of Peru, assuming authority as protector.

1823 Bolívar is proclaimed dictator.

1824 Spain is expelled from Peru when its troops are defeated by Bolivar at the battle of Ayacucho. Sucre invades Charcas and convenes the new congress.

1825 The congress designates the new state the Republic of Bolívar.

1825-27 Bolivar aids the Peruvian government in its start, and Bolivia becomes a separate state.

1829 Peru takes Guayaquil but is defeated at Tarqui by Sucre.

1835-39 Short-lived Peruvian-Bolivian Federation exists until Chile declares war.

1842-62 Civil war ensues, after which Ramon Castilla is dictator for over fifteen years, instituting administrative, religious, and social reforms.

1864 Spain, never having recognized Peruvian independence, seizes the Chincha Islands.

1865-86 War is declared against Spain, but ended by treaties.

1872 Manuel Pardo becomes the first civilian President of Peru.

1879-84 Chile emerges victorious from the War of the Pacific and gains Tarapace, Tacna, Arica, Lima, and the Atcama desert. Peru cedes the former three in a treaty.

1890s The question of Tacna and Arica, after a plebiscite promised by Chile does not materialize, is not solved.

1899-1903 Boundary disputes with Ecuador and Brazil develop.

1908-12 Diplomatic relations with Chile are severed. Peru acknowledges Brazilian rule over part of Arce. A boundary treaty is undertaken with Brazil.

Settlement and Migration

In 1524, Francisco Pizarro first explored Peru for Spain. Returning in 1531 with a small army, he conquered the Inca empire and killed Atahualpa, the Inca chief.

Peru remained under Spanish domination for almost 300 years. During the independence movements of the early nineteenth century, Peru remained loyal to the Spanish crown. Peruvian independence was a virtual byproduct of the successes of other Spanish colonies in their wars of independence. Following the Argentine liberator San Martin's capture of Lima in 1821, independence was proclaimed.

In 1836 General Andres Santa Cruz united Peru with Bolivia to create the Peru-Bolivia confederation, which broke up in 1839 after a military defeat from Chile. Disorders followed until a stable government was set up in 1844. In 1879, Peru was defeated in a war with Chile and lost Tarapaca, Tacna, and Arica. A 1929 agreement left Arica with Chile and gave Peru back Tacna plus protectorate rights in Arica.

Modern Peru is divided into twenty-four departments, 141 provinces, and 1,321 municipalities. About half the people are Indians. The others are whites or mestizos (mixed white and Indian blood).

Peru Library Collection

Archives and Libraries

The library has guides, indexes, or catalog copies for these archives or libraries. (See FHLC heading **Peru/Archives and Libraries** for descriptions and call numbers: Catalogo Del Archivo General de la Nacion,Catalogo Del Archivo Historico Militar del Peru, and La Seccion Republicana del Archivo Historico de Hacienda.)

Biography

The library has numerous biographical works or references for Peru, including:

Garbin, Raul. *Diccionario Biográfico del Perú.* Lima: Escuelas Americans, 1944. (FHL# 985/D3d)

Martin, Luis. *Daughters of the Conquistadores: Women of the Viceroyalty of Peru.* Alubquerque: University of New Mexico Press, 1983. (FHL# 985/H2ml)

Mendiburu, Manuel de. *Diccionario Histórico-Biográfico del Perú.* 11 vols. Lima: Enrique Palacios, 1931-38. (FHL# 985/D3m or microfilm 1162472-1162473)

Census Records

Peru has taken a general census in 1535, 1569, 1791, 1836, 1850, 1862, 1876, 1940, 1961, and 1972. Those for 1876, 1940, 1961, and 1972 have been published but are held by the National Office of Statistics and Census and are not available to the public.

The library has a few census records cataloged under **Peru/Census.**

Encyclopedias and Dictionaries

Tauro, Alberto. *Diccionario Enciclopédico del Perú.* 3 vols. n.p., Argentina: Editorial Juan Mejia Baca, 1966.

The book is cataloged with the call number 030.85/T194d; however, the volumes are marked correctly 985/A5de and are shelved with the Peruvian collection. Explains archaic words and terms peculiar to Peru. Contains many biographies of famous Peruvians, both living and dead.

Noteworthy also is the eleven-volume set of the *Diccionario Histórico-Biográfico del Perú,* with updates through 1938. (FHL# 985/D3m).

Gazetteers

The library has several gazetteers dealing with Peru as a whole, as well as some that deal with certain departments. Most comprehensive but lacking historical or etymological notes is:

Division of Geography, Department of the Interior. *Official Standard Names Approved by the U.S. Board on Geographic Names.* Washington, D.C.: Central Intelligence Agency, 1955. (FHL# 985/E5p)

Genealogy

Persons and families under suspicion of religious heresy by the Catholic Church's Inquisition between 1600 and 1800 were required to submit genealogies to prove that they were not descended from heretics. One book below explains the inquisition in detail and discusses the gathered information on Peruvians, is:

Lohmann Villena, Guillermo. *Informaciones Genealógicas de Peruanos Seguidas Ante el Santo Oficio.* N.p.: n.pub., 1957. (FHL# 985/D2l)

See also a collection of fourteen reels identified as follows for 1575-1746:

Archivo Historico Nacional. *Procesos de Fe, Lima* (Proceedings of Faith, Lima). Madrid: Centro Nacional de Microfilm, 1977. (FHL# microfilm 1224016-1224029)

Genealogical/Historical Periodicals or Series

The library has a sizeable collection of genealogical and historical periodicals that are useful to researchers. See FHLC heading **Peru/History-Periodicals** and **Peru/Genealogy-Periodicals** for a complete list of titles and call numbers.

Genealogy, Sources

Genealogical Department of the Church of Jesus Christ of Latter-day Saints. *Fuentes Principales de Registros Genealógicos en Perú.* (Principal Sources of Genealogical Records in Peru). Salt Lake City: Church of Jesus Christ of Latter-day Saints, 1977. (FHL# 929.1/G286gs/Ser. H/no.14)

History

Garcilaso de la Vega, born in Cuzco in 1539 to a Spanish noble father and an Indian mother who was a second cousin of the last two Incan rulers, wrote a general history of Peru in 1612. It is one of first hand experiences among Incan and Spanish family members, and reflects an intimate knowledge of the people and their ways. Translated now into English, this is one of the most important works available today on the ancient culture of Peru.

de la Vega, Garcilaso. *Royal Commentaries of The Incas.* Harold V. Livermore, trans. 2 vols. Austin: University of Texas Press, 1966. (FHL# 985/H29)

Martin, Luis. *Daughters of the Conquistadores: Women of the Viceroyalty of Peru.* Albuquerque: University of New Mexico Press, 1983. (FHL# 985/H2ml)

A sociological analysis of colonial attitudes towards daughters, wives, concubines, mothers, the unmarried, the divorced, and the unconventional. Includes many names and family relationships. Indexed.

The library has more than sixty-two listings under **Peru/History** or **Peru/[Department** and/or **City]/History.**

Maps

Instituto Geográfico Nacional de Perú. *Mapos Físicos y Políticos de los Departamentos de Peruú* (Physical and Political Maps of the Departments of Peru). Lima: Instituto Geográfica National de Perú, 1973-84. (Map case FHL# 985/E7pi) 16 maps, very detailed.

Minorities

The library has books on Chinese, Indian, Yugoslav, Japanese, Jewish, and Polish minorities in Peru cataloged under **Peru/Minorities**.

Native Races

Riveros, Edmundo Rey. *El Censo y Los Aborígenes Selvícolas de Nuestra Amazonia* (The Census and the Jungle Aborigines of Our Amazonia). Lima: Revista Militar, 1957. (FHL# 985/A1/no.17)

An analysis of tribal names, locations, and estimated populations, especially useful in relating a tribal name to a specific geographic location and governmental jurisdiction.

Some twenty additional volumes are cataloged under **Peru/Native Races.**

Notarial Records

Notarial records include references to almost every aspect of daily living, and consequently the names of persons and families involved. The name of the notary is especially useful in locating records relating to a particular area and time period.

The Archive. *Indice de Notarios de Lima y Callao Cuyos Protocolos se Hallan en el Archivo Nacional del Perú* (Index of Notaries of Lima and Callao Whose Registries Are Found in the National Archive of Peru). Lima: Gil-Lama, 1928. (FHL# 985/A1/no.2)

The library has twenty reels of notarial records for 1538-1893 (many years and areas not included) cataloged under **Peru/Notarial Records**.

Vital Records

Civil registration was established by law in 1852, but runs generally from 1886 to the present. The library has not yet filmed these records. However, it has filmed church records from earliest colonial times. Here is a by-department list of 2,180 microfilms: Amazonas, 52; Ancash, 182; Arequipa, 194; Azuay, 10; Cajamarca, 301; Callao, 40; Cuzco, 1; Ica, 102; Huánuco, 3; Junín, 75; Lambayeque, 109; Libertad, 14; Lima, 880; Madre de Dios, 52; Puno, 138; San Martín, 2; and Tacna, 25.

SURINAME (formerly Dutch Guiana)

Historical Background

pre-1500	Inhabitants consist of Surinen (previously driven away), Carib, Arawak, and Warrow Indians.
1499	Alonso de Ojeda, serving Italian navigator Amerigo Vespucci, lands on the northeast coast of South America, called Guiana by the Indians.
1593	The Spanish officially take possession of the Guianan coast, but place no settlements.
1593-1651	Dutch, British, and French expeditions visit the area.
1616	British and Dutch simultaneously establish settlements in the Guianas; British control the region of Suriname.
1651	Francis Willoughby, an Englishman, founds the first successful settlement in Suriname, welcoming settlers from other South American and West indian colonies.
1665	Over 500 plantations exist in the region of present-day Suriname. Jewish migrants to the Suriname settlement, coming from a Dutch colony on the Berbice estuary, erect the first synagogue in the Western Hemisphere.
1667-1816	Period of economic decline and political turmoil occurs in Suriname, including slave rebellions. Surinam changes hands frequently between England, France, and the Netherlands.
1670	Large percentage of the population of Suriname consists of imported Negro slaves.
1816	Dutch gain permanent control of Suriname under the Treaty of Paris.
1863	Slavery is abolished and Surinam begins to import workers from China, Java, and India.
1900	90% of all agricultural products are being grown on plantations.
1900-40	Plantation dominance gradually decreases.
1940-54	Dutch divert resources from the East Indies to invest in Suriname.
1950	Suriname gains some autonomy.
1954	Suriname becomes a self-governing region of the Kingdom of the Netherlands.

Settlement and Migration

The region of Guiana in northestern South America consists of Guyana (formerly British Guiana), Suriname (the Dutch portion of Guiana), and French Guiana.

The Dutch first appeared on the rivers of Guiana as traders in 1598 and established a fort in 1613 on the Corantijn River. In 1621, the Dutch goverment granted the Dutch West India Company a charter which brought the proprietorship of all Dutch establishments on the Guiana coast into that company's hands. By 1665, the Dutch had made settlements on the rivers Berbice, Pomeroon, and Essequibo.

English interest in Guiana dates from 1596, when Walter Raleigh published his *Discoveries of the Large, Rich and Beautiful Empire of Guiana,* in which he described his experiences on that coast the year before. Attempts at settlement proved unsuccessful; and by 1665, the only one English settlement on the Suriname River flourished.

The British ceded its claims to Dutch Guiana in 1667 in return for New Amsterdam (New York). About 54,300 square miles in area, Suriname has 395,000 inhabitants (1985 estimate). About one third live in Paramaribo, the capital. Most are mine and plantation workers, chiefly Hindus, Japanese, Chinese, and blacks. In the interior are 40,000 "bush negroes," descendants of escaped slaves. There are about 4,000 whites. United States troops occupied the country during World War II to protect its bauxite deposits.

Guiana Library Collection

Archives and Libraries

Meilink-Roelofsz, M[arie] A[ntoinette] P[etronella]. *Een Archiefreis in West-Indie: De Caribbean Archives Conference in Jamaica.* N.p.: n.pub., 1966. (FHL# 972.986/A5mr)

Contains a discussion of public archives and private Dutch archives in Suriname. In Dutch.

History

Goslinga, Cornelis C. *The Dutch in the Caribbean and on the Wild Coast 1580-1680.* Gainsville: University of Florida Press, 1971. (FHL# 972.9/H2g)

Contains the most complete Suriname history.

This study of the boundaries of Dutch Guiana is helpful in determining which country might hold historical records for a given period:

Sluiter, Engel. *Dutch Guiana: A Problem in Boundaries.* rpt. from *The Hispanic American Historical Review,* 13, no. 1, (Feb. 1933) N.p.: n.pub., n.d. (FHL# 988.3/H2s)

Minorities

The library has small volumes dealing with both Portuguese Jews and Indonesian emigration and colonization in Suriname cataloged under **Suriname/Emigration/Colonization.**

Vital Records

The library has these vital records: Lutheran Church–baptisms, marriages, 1742-1828; Dutch Reformed–baptisms, marriages, 1687-1828; Catholic Church–baptisms, marriages, 1742-1830; Civil registration–divorces, marriages, 1795-1831; German Jews–births, deaths, 1773-1838; Portuguese Jews–births, deaths, 1742-1828; Christian Brotherhood–baptisms, deaths, 1779-1828; and civil registration–burials, 1723-1827.

Uruguay

Historical Background

pre-1600	Area is inhabited by the Charruas Indian tribes.
1600s	European cattle ranches in the area are the only Western inhabitation.
1680	Portuguese found a settlement at Colonia del Sacramento on and in order to gain control of the left bank of the Río de la Plata, the region called the Banda Oriental, which later became Uruguay.
1680-1722	The area of the Banda Oriental changes hands frequently between the Spanish and Portuguese.
1723	Spain begins effective sovereignty in the region with the establishment of Montevideo.
1750	Spain gains control of Colonia.
1776	Uruguay forms part of the Viceroyalty of Rio de la Plata.
1808	Prince John of Portugal tries to annex the Banda Oriental to Brazil.
1811-14	Forces of Buenos Aires and revolutionary Uruguans led by Jose Artigas end Spanish control in the Banda Oriental (which is also claimed by both Portugal and the provinces of the Rio de la Plata).
1816-21	Brazil takes control of the Banda Oriental from Artigas and incorporates it as the Cisplatine Province in 1821.
1828	To end a war between Brazil and Argentina over the Banda Oriental, the area becomes the sovereign nation of the Banda Oriental del Uruguay.
1836-43	Period of unrest develops between two political factions headed by Oribe and Rivera.
1843-51	Oribe begins an eight-year seige of Montevideo and blockade of the Rio de la Plata.
1851	The opposing Colorado faction is restored to power by treaty. Brazil annexes the Misiones territory from Uruguay.
1863-65	Internal disorder continues between the Blancos and Colorados factions, while

	Brazil occupies many Uruguayan border towns.
1865	Flores, the Colorado president, assumes the government. Uruguay enters the Paraguayan War.
1872-1907	Colorados remain in power despite conflict. Public education and other advances are developed.
1919	New constitution lessens the presidential powers, creates a national council of administration, and disestablishes the Roman Catholic Church.
1933	Gabriel Terra establishes a temporary dictatorship.
1934	National presidency of Uruguay is resumed.

Settlement and Migration

The territory known today as La República Oriental del Uruguay (The Eastern Republic of Uruguay), was discovered by Don Juan Diaz de Solis in 1516 while he was exploring the coast of South America for the Spanish crown. Solis, and part of his crew, upon coming ashore, were killed by the Charraus Indians. In 1624, the Spanish established a small colony on the Rio Negro. Nevertheless, Jesuit missionaries provided the major colonization efforts for the next century.

The Spanish crown established a government in the city of Montevideo in 1749. Later, with the establishment in 1776 of the Viceroyalty of Rio de la Plata in Buenos Aires, the territory came under the jurisdiction of the viceroy seated there. In 1828, Uruguay declared its independence. A hero of the revolution, General Fructuoso Rivera, was elected first president in 1830.

The Catholic Church is the dominant religion, but Uruguay practices freedom of worship and the country has many protestant sects, Jewish synagogues, and oriental religions. Most church records with the exception of Catholic records are too recent to be helpful to the genealogist.

In 1919, the country was divided into two dioceses (Salta and Melo), and the Archdiocese of Montevideo. In 1961 there were nine dioceses (Canelones, Florida, Maldonado, Melo, Mercedes, Minas, Salto, San Jose de Mayo, and Tacuarembo), and the Archdiocese of Montivideo. Sixty-five extant Catholic parishes were established prior to 1900. Each has records in good condition.

Civil registration began to function in 1879 in the departments with copies going to the Direccion General del Registro Civil in Montevideo. This archive has an index by year, department, judicial section, and surname, that runs from 1879 to 1920. Since 1920, the index is kept by year, department, and surname.

The Archivo General de la Nación in Montevideo has notarial records, census records, tax rolls, military registrations, property records, deeds, and civil and criminal records, dating from colonial times.

Uruguay Library Collection

Archives and Libraries

The library has inventories, registers, copies of the card catalog, or other materials describing the contents of the following archives or libraries:

Archivo General de la Nacion. *Catalogo de Libros del ex "Archivo General Administrativo.* Montevideo: n. pub., 1965. (FHL#989.5/A5uc)

Catalog of books of the former General Administrative Archive.

Archivo General de la Nación. *Inventario de los Fondos Documentales de Archivo General de la Nacion.* Montevidea: n. pub., 1965. (FHL# 989.5/A5a or microfilm 0897479, item 3)

Inventory of documents in the National Archive of Uruguay.

_____. *Catálogo Descriptivo, VII: Coleccion de Manuscritos.* Montevideo: A. Montverde, 1953. (FHL# 989.5/A5m or microfilm 0896736, item 2)

Descriptive catalog of manuscripts in the National Historical Museum of Uruguay.

Musso, Luis Alberto. *Archivos del Uruguay.* Montevideo: n. pub., 1974. See FHLC for call numbers.

Biography

The library has a number of Uruguayan biographical works for titles and call numbers see FHLC heading Uruguay/Biography.

De-María, Isidoro. *Rasgos Biográficos de Hombres Notables de la República Oriental del Uruguay.* Montevideo: Claudio Garcia, 1939. (FHL# 989.5/D3d or microfilm 0496912, item 2-5)

Biographical sketches of notable men of Uruguay, including some from Argentina.

Fernandez Saldana, José María. *Diccionario Uruguayo de Biografiás, 1810-1940.* Montevideo: Editorial Amerindia, 1945. (FHL# 989.5/D3fd)

Census Records

Censuses after 1802 contain a great deal of family information. These records are in the office of the Direccion General de Estadissticas y Censos (General Director of Statistics and Census) in Montevideo and the library has no copies.

Genealogy

A German emigrant in 1936, Juan Alejandro Apolant, made himself an expert on Uruguayan history and genealogy: "The Inhabitants of Montevideo in its First Forty Years: Relationships, Ancestors, Cognations [blood relationships], and Descendants." The book is fully indexed, and both the strengths and weaknesses of genealogical evidences are addressed:

Apolant, Juan Alejandro. *Genesis de la Familia Uruguaya.*

Montevideo: Imprenta Vinaak, 1975. (FHL# 989.5/-D2pa)

Genealogy, Sources

Genealogical Department of the Church of Jesus Christ of Latter-day Saints. *Fuentes Principales de Registros Genealogicos en Uruguay.* Salt Lake City: Church of Jesus Christ of Latter-day Saints, 1974. (FHL# 929.1/G28gs/Ser. H/no.6)

History

The library has over thirty histories cataloged, some for individual departments or cities. Among the historical or genealogical periodicals in the collection are the *Revista del Instituto de Estudios Genealógicos del Uruguay.* (FHL# 989.5/D25).

Gazetteers

Ministerio de Economía y Finanzas. *Indice Toponímico de los Lugares Poblados.* Montevideo: El Ministerio, 1972. (FHL# 989.5/E2u)

Araujo, Orestes. *Diccionario Geográfico del Uruguay.* Montevideo: Imprenta Artistica, 1900. (FHL# 989.5/E5a)

Office of Geography, Department of the Interior. *Uruguay, Official Standard Names.* Washington, D.C.: U.S. Department of the Interior, 1956. (FHL# 989.5/E5u)

Maps

Uruguay, Servicio Geográfico Militar. *República Oriental del Uruguay: Carta Geográfica.* N.p.: El Servicio, [c.1970s]. (FHL# 989.5/E7m) Scale of 1:500,000.

Minorities

The library has books dealing with the following minorities: Basques, Germans in La Plata, Swiss, Italians, the Waldenses, Europeans, Poles, Mennonites, and Gallegans (from Galicia, Spain).

Vital Records

Civil registration of births, deaths, and marriages, etc. date from the middle of the nineteenth century. These records are kept in departmental capitals with copies in the Direccions General del Registro Civil in Montevideo. [compare above; not spelled the same] The library has no civil records but has the following parish records. Here is a department and city list: Colonia-Carmelo, Colonia, Colonia Valdense, Nueva Helvecia, Nueva Palmira, and Rosario; Durazno-Durazno, Farruco, San Borja, Santa Rosa, and Sarandi del Yi; Flores-Trinidad; Florida-Florida; Salto-Salto; San Jose-Libertad and San Jose de Mayo; and Soriano-Dolores, Mercedes, and Villa Soriano.

VENEZUELA

Historical Background

1535-39	Nikolaus Federmann, a German, attempts to conquer and settle Venezuela.
1528	4,000 Negroes are imported to work on Venezuelan grants.
1538	Gonzalo Jimenez de Quesada is thc first to arrive in Venezuela.
1550	Quesada receives appointment from Spain and returns to Bogota as its Marshal.
1555	Valencia is founded.
1567	Caracas is established.
1610	Peter Claver reaches Cartagena.
1616	Dutch and English form the first permanent settlement in the neighboring Guianas.
1767	Spain expels all Jesuit priests from its territories.
1806	Francisco de Miranda's attempt to liberate Venezuela fails.
1808	Revolutionary movement which eventually leads to independence begins in Caracas.
1810	War of independence begins in Venezuela.
1811	Independence is proclaimed by Venezuela; a republic is established.
1812	Severe earthquake occurs in Venezuela.
1814	Bolivar loses several battles in the wars for independence from Spain.
1815	The republic fails.
1817	In Venezuela, Bolivar's army gathers manpower as cavalry units, who have previously fought for Spain, are added; English and Irish veterans of the Napoleonic Wars are also enlisted.
1818	Bolivar re-establishes the republic; he is named president and commander-in-chief.
1819	Bolivar iş named President and Commander-in-Chief of Venezuela; Bolivar defeats a Spanish army at Boyaca, Colombia.
1821	Only one major Spanish army remains in Venezuela, and it is crushed by Simon Bolivar's troops; the region is proclaimed as a single state called Great Colombia; Congress at Cucuta declares children of slaves are free at birth.
1822	Great Colombia's southern borders remain uncertain.
1830	Great Colombia is dissolved; Venezuelan constitution provides for a centralized government and abolishes the supporting taxes for the Catholic Church,

	making it dependent upon the government.
1853	New Constitution is anti-clerical.
1857	Pro-church faction takes power.
1870	Downgrading of the Catholic Church continues; Protestant missionaries are encouraged; civil marriage is established, freedom of religion is confirmed, and education is taken from the control of the church and given to the state.

Settlement and Migration

In 1814-15, particularly, a great number of Venezuelans emigrated to the Virgin Islands, especially to Santo Tomas.

The great majority of Venezuelans are mixed Spanish and native American (mestizos). The pure whites number only about 10 percent, and the blacks and Indians total twenty percent. Until the late 1930s nearly three-fourths of the people could not read nor write.

Venezuelan parish registers have not been well maintained over the years. The Archive of the Archdeaconry of Caracas has much of what has survived, and the Family History Library has it cataloged (FHL# 987/A1 no.1). Many regional parish registers from the Marida area have been gathered in the Diocesan Archive of the Catholic Church in the city of Mérida. That archive is located in the Mérida Seminary building. Civil registration for the country began in 1873 and became effective several years thereafter. The first national censuses were taken in 1873, 1881, and 1920.

Venezuela Library Collection

Archives and Libraries

Occupying almost ten feet of shelf space, the *Boletin del Archivo Nacional* (Bulletin of the National Archives of Venezuela) is an important genealogical and historical information. The publication runs from September 1826 through December 1981 and contains most issues of this periodical.

Archivo General de la Nación-Venezuela. *Boletín del Archivo General de la Nación*. Caracas: The Archive, 1926-81. (FHL# 987/B2V)

Biography

The library has a number of biographical works on Venezuela cataloged under Venezuela/Biography and **Venezuela/[State]/Biography.**

Census Records

The library has no census records but has tax records for 1756-98. Consult the FHLC under **Venezuela/Census.**

Lombardi, John V. *People and Places in Colonial Venezuela.* Don Mills, Ontario: Fitzhenry and Whiteside, Ltd., c.1976. (FHL# 987/X4L)

Detailed demographic study of colonial parishes but gives few names.

Church Directories

Catholic Church. *Anuario de la Iglesia Católica en Venezuela.* Caracas: Centro de Investigaciones Sociales y Socio-Religiosas, 1969. (FHL# 987/K22c)

Contains names and addresses of Catholic Church officials. See also 1975 edition. (FHL# 987/K24c)

Colonization

The library has nine reels inventorying business documents related to the newly discovered lands. Records include information on soldiers, magistrates, judges, wills, deeds, ships' passenger lists and manifests, and other materials. The works are indexed and cataloged under **Venezuela/Colonization-Inventories, Registers, Catalogs.**

Gazetteers

Office of Geography, Department of the Interior. *Venezuela, Official Standard Names Approved by the U.S. Board on Geographic Names.* Washington, D.C.: Central Intelligence Agency, 1961. (FHL# 987/E5u)

Very detailed; locates sites by latitude and longitude.

Genealogy, Sources

Genealogical Department of the Church of Jesus Christ of Latter-day Saints. *Fuentes Principales de Registros Genealógicos en Venezuela.* Salt Lake City: Church of Jesus Christ of Latter-day Saints, 1976. (FHL# 929.1/G28gs/Ser. H/no.11)

History

In 1771-84, Bishop Mariano Marti conducted an extensive tour of the Diocese of Caracas, including much information on individuals and their family relationships in his eight-volume journal.

Gomez Cañedo, Lino, ed. *Obispo Mariano Martí: Documentos Relativos a su Visita Pastoral de la Diócesis de Caracas.* 8 vols. Caracas: Fuentes para la Historia Colonial de Venezuela, 1969. (FHL# 987.7/K2m) In Spanish.

The library has approximately twenty other specialized histories (military, religious, clerical, revolutionary, etc.), plus histories on each state and federal district.

Maps

Ministerio de Obras Públicas. *Mapa Físico y Político de la República de Venezuela.* Caracas: Ministerio de Obras Públicas, 1955. (FHL# 987/E7vm) Scale of 1:1,000,000; six maps.

Minorities

Emmanuel, Isaac S. *The Jews of Coro, Venezuela.* Cincinnati Ohio: Hebrew Unia College-Jewish Institute of Religion, 1973. (FHL# 987/A1/no.2) Covers 1828-1970. Gives vital records of individuals involved. In English.

A discussion of approximately 3,500 Basque immigrants to Venezuela in the eighteenth century is:

Amezaga Aresti, Vicenti de. *El Elemento Vasco en el Siglo XVIII Venezolano.* Caracas: Tipografica Vargas, 1966. (FHL# 987/F2a) In Spanish.

For discussions of German colonies in Venezuela, see **Venezuela/Emigration and Immigration.**

Politics, Government/Handbooks, Manuals, etc.

Central Intelligence Agency. *Area Handbook for Venezuela.* Washington, D.C.: U.S. Government Printing Office, 1971. (FHL# 987/H6a)

In English. An excellent introduction to the land, peoples, and institutions.

Vital Records

The library has no vital records. Civil registration of births, marriages, and deaths began in 1873 and are available within the various jurisdictions. See FHLC heading **Venezuela/[Province]/Civil Registration.**

The library has three volumes of vital statistics dealing with Caracas (1577-1616) (FHL# 987.7/C1/K29l), Sucre (Petare 1822-25) (FHL# 987.52/P1/N2c), and Zulia (Maracaibo 1723-75) (FHL# 987.23/M1/A3nr).

Chapter 24

Central America and Mexico

Harold D. Ethington

CENTRAL AMERICA

History and Settlement

Central America consists of seven nations lying between Mexico on the north and Colombia on the south: Belize, Costa Rica, El Salvador, Guatemala, Honduras, Nicaragua, and Panama.

Chief among the native populations of the area before the arrival of Europeans were the Maya Indians, who flourished from about A.D. 250 to 900 with their skillfully engineered cities, pyramids, temples, and canals. They also had a complex solar calendar and a system of hieroglyphic writing.

In 1501, Rodrigo de Bastidas and Juan de la Cosa of Spain explored the Central American coast. In 1502 on his fourth voyage, Columbus sailed down the coast from Honduras to Panama. By 1525, the Spanish conquest was complete and much of the native population was killed or enslaved.

In 1570, the Spanish established an administrative center called an *audiencia* in Guatemala with jurisdiction over all of Central America except Panama. It was a subdivision of the Viceroyalty of New Spain, which governed most of the Spanish colonies in North America from its headquarters in Mexico City.

In 1808, Napoleon I of France occupied Spain and forced the Spanish king into exile. Taking advantage of these European distractions, the Audiencia of Guatemala declared its independence on 14 September 1821, removing all of Central America from Spanish control except for Panama, which broke away the same year and became a province of the newly independent nation of Colombia.

From January 1822 to March 1823, Costa Rica, El Salvador, Guatemala, Honduras, and Nicaragua were legally part of Mexico. In 1823, these states formed the United Provinces of Central America and completed a strong states'-rights constitution in November 1824. Attempts at unity ultimately failed, however, and the final Federal Congress on 30 May 1838 declared the states free to constitute themselves as they might deem best.

Prior to 1821, Mexico and Central America had been governed under the Viceroyalty of New Spain (Nueva España) which included all of Mexico, Central America, and North America from the Pacific Ocean to the Mississippi river. This huge territory, one of five viceroyalties in the New World, was subdivided into smaller administrative units, chiefly *presidencias* and *captaincies-general.* Both captains general and presidents were direct appointees of the king, both reported to the king and received orders directly from him, often paying no more than lip service to the viceroy.

The most immediate level of Spanish rule were the offices of *corregidores* (governors) and *alcaldes mayores.* These local officials exercised great control over the lives of their subjects and were replaced in 1790 by a system of "intendentes." Resentment at this governmental change was one of the major factors which eventually led to the 1821 Declaration of Independence by the Mexican and Central American states.

Central American Library Collection

Archives and Libraries

Perhaps the most important archive for Central American research is the Archivo General de Centroamérica in Guatemala City, Guatemala. This archive has gathered materials from throughout Central America from the colonial era (prior to 1821) and has allowed the Family History Library to film most, if not all, of the documents relating to genealogical research – more than 3,600 reels. For a meticulous index, see:

Weathers, Shirley A. *Bibliographic Guide to the Guatemalan Collection*. Salt Lake City, Utah: University of Utah Press, 1981. (FHL# 972.81/A3w)

Discussed further in *Archives and Libraries* in the section on Guatemala below.

Gropp, Arthur E. *Guide to the Libraries and Archives in Central America and the West Indies, Panama, Bermuda, and British Guiana*. New Orleans: Middle America Research Institute, 1941. (FHL# 972.8/A2g; note, however, that the call number on the book itself is 972.8/A3g)

Hill, Roscoe R. *Los Archivos Nacionales de la América Latina.* La Habana, Cuba: Archivo Nacional de Cuba, 1948. (FHL# 980/ J5h)

Emigration and Immigration

Boyd-Bowman, Peter. *Indice Geobiográfico de Cuarenta Mil Pobladores Españoles de América en el Siglo XVII*. Mexico: Academia Mexicana de Genealogía y Heráldica, A.C., 1968. (FHL# 980/W2b)

In Spanish. Contains names and places of origin for some 40,000 settlers during the colonial period. The names are indexed several different ways.

Genealogy and Heraldry

The library has seven different guides to record sources and research that include information on Latin America in particular. Consult the Family History Library Catalog (FHLC) under **Central America/-Genealogy/Heraldry**.

History

The library has twenty-seven volumes cataloged under **Central America/History**, including treatments of native Americans, Jews, ancient history, commercial history, and colonial history. Three works of special note are:

Bancroft, Hubert Howe. *History of the Pacific States of North America.* 3 vols. San Francisco, Calif: A. L. Bancroft, 1882-87. (FHL# 972.8/H2b)

_____. *Native Races.* 2 vols. San Francisco, Calif: A. L. Bancroft, 1882-87. (FHL# 980/F36)

These five volumes contain fascinating details; footnotes are especially useful in understanding historical events.

Herring, Hubert. *A History of Latin America from the Beginning to the Present*. New York: Alfred A. Knopf, 1962. (FHL# 980/H2h)

Lengthy (843 pages) and refreshingly insightful. Excellent annotated reading list.

MacLeod, Murdo J. *Spanish Central America: A Socioeconomic History, 1520-1720*. Berkeley, Calif.: University of California Press, 1973. (FHL# 972.8/H2ma)

A detailed (554 pages) look at the social and economic history of Central America.

Maps

The library has ten entries cataloged under **Central America/Maps**. Among the most useful are:

United States. Army Map Service. *Central America, Scale 1:250,000*. 11 fiche. Washington D.C,: U.S. Army Map Service, 1929-30. (FHL# microfiche 6030549)

Covers Central America, Mexico, and Panama; includes the smallest settlements and street details for the larger cities. Cemeteries noted on the city maps. Microfiche format makes use difficult.

Monteiro, Palmyra V. M. *A Catalogue of Latin America Flat Maps, 1926-1964.* Austin, Tex.: Institute of Latin America/ University of Texas at Austin, c.1967. (FHL# 980/A3m)

A bibliographic guide to maps held by the Library of Congress, the US Army Map Service, and others.

Minorities

Liebman, Seymour B. *Los Judíos en México y América Central: Fe, Llamas, Inquisicion.* Mexico D.F.: Siglo Veintiuno Editores, c.1973. (FHL# 972/F2Li)

An excellent history of Jews in Central America.

Names, Personal

Gorden, Raymond L. *Spanish Personal Names.* Yellow Spring, Ohio: Antioch College, 1968. (FHL# 980/D4g)

Excellent guide to the difficulties of alphabetizing Spanish names.

United States Bureau of the Census. *Tentative 1980 Census Spanish Surname List (unedited)*. Washington D.C.: The Bureau, [c.1970s]. (FHL# 980/D4u)

Provides examples of Spanish surnames in proper alphabetical order.

Native Races

The library has twelve titles cataloged under **Central America/Native Races**. The most important is:

Wauchope, Robert, ed. *Handbook of Middle American Indians.* 16 vols. Austin: University of Texas Press, 1962-76. (FHL# 972.8/F3h)

Notarial Records

Archivo General de Centroamérica. Notarial Records, 1508-1898. 877 reels. Indexed on 101 reels. See **Central America/Notarial Records** for call numbers.

As George Ryskamp noted in *Tracing Your Hispanic Heritage* (Riverside, Calif.: Hispanic Family History Research, 1984):

> Notary records cover the full breadth and depth of life: wills, adoptions, emancipations, sales of rural and urban land, construction of buildings, proof of purity of blood, nobility records, transfers of titles, dowries, rescue of captives, sale of slaves, marriage contracts, sale

of cloth, sale of horses, printing of books, commissioning of famous works of art, apprenticeship papers, proofs of origin for emigrants, and contracts with teachers. . . . For those whose ancestors had sufficient social or financial status to use notarial services, these records will provide the greatest amount of human interest and daily life information about their ancestors.

BELIZE

History and Settlement

Located on the eastern coast of Central America and bounded by Guatemala and Mexico, Belize (known as British Honduras before 1964) is the second smallest of the seven Central American nations. With its British background, its small population (155,000), and its unique blend of Anglo-Saxon, black Hispanic, and native American races, it presents special problems for the genealogical researcher.

Founded by accident in 1638 by a group of shipwrecked British seamen near the mouth of the Belize River, the settlement was known as Belize, Belice, or the Honduran Bay Settlement. A British enclave surrounded by hostile Spanish neighbors, it struggled for 200 years before gaining recognition and protection as a British colony and is still part of the Commonwealth system administered by Great Britain.

The library has no microfilms of Belize's civil records or inventories of its holdings. It has thirteen volumes of reference books and short histories written between 1944 and 1976, which will identify agencies and groups for direct correspondence. Among the most useful are:

Caribbean Council of Churches. *Handbook of Churches in the Caribbean.* Bridgetown, Barbados: Christian Action for Development in the Caribbean, 1973. (FHL# 972.9/K24c)

Lists ministers' names, telephone numbers, denominations, and church addresses for Caribbean nations including Belize (also listed as British Honduras in different sections of the directory).

Gregg, A. R. *British Honduras.* London: Her Majesty's Stationery Office, c.1968. (FHL# 972.82/E6g) Indexed.

Setzekorn, William David. *Formerly British Honduras: A Profile of the New Nation of Belize.* Athens, Ohio; University Press, 1981. (FHL# 972.82/H6sw) Indexed.

Winzerling, E. O. *The Beginning of British Honduras, 1506-1765.* New York: North River Press, 1946. (FHL# 972.82/H2w)

In the late 1950s, a Mennonite colony settled in the Blue Creek, Shipyard, and Spanish Lookout areas. See:

Sawatzky, Harry Leanard. *They Sought a Country: Mennonite Colonization in Mexico, with an Appendix on Mennonite Colonization in British Honduras.* Berkeley: University of California Press, 1971. (FHL# 972/F2s)

Redekop, Calvin Wall. *The Old Colony Mennonites: Dilemmas of Ethnic Minority Life.* Baltimore, Md: Johns Hopkins Press, c.1969. (FHL# 972/F2r)

United States Board on Geographic Names. *British Honduras: Official Standard Names Approved by the U.S. Board on Geographic Names.* Washington, D.C.: U.S. Office of Geography, 1956. (FHL# 972.82/E5u)

Twenty-five pages. Locates over 2,000 place names and identifies the geography of each.

Until the Genealogical Society initiates a filming project in Belize, the most productive research route may be corresponding directly with the agencies concerned.

COSTA RICA

History and Settlement

Costa Rica was discovered in September 1502 by Christopher Columbus on his fourth voyage to the "Indies." Since few Indians survived the following years of Spanish dominion, its small native work force did not attract the same type of colonization as elsewhere in Latin America, and the area was mostly settled by Europeans who did not intermarry with Indians to the same extent as those in other areas of Latin America.

During the colonial period, the majority of the people lived in Alajuela, Cartago, Heredia, and San José. Aside from frequent small skirmishes among these four cities to establish a governing capital, the country was largely free from the continual conflicts that tormented the other Central American states.

During the colonial period, Costa Rica was a province of the Capitan General of Guatemala under the Viceroy of New Spain. After the governing body of Guatemala declared its independence in 1821, Costa Rica, along with El Salvador, Guatemala, Honduras, and Nicaragua, were legally part of Mexico. In 1823, these countries formed the United Provinces of Central America, which Costa Rica joined on 2 November 1824. The federation dissolved in 1848, and Costa Rica declared its independence.

Today, Costa Rica is divided into provinces *(provincias)*, regions *(cantones)*, districts *(distritos)*, and wards *(barrios)* or villages *(caseríos)*. The ecclesiastical divisions are the Archdiocese of San Jose, the dioceses of San Isidro, El General, Alajuela, and Tilaran, and the Vicarage of Limon.

Costa Rica Library Collection

Biography

In addition to one 1945 edition of *Who's Who in Latin America* and histories of the Peralta, Rodríguez, and Quirós families, the library has an excellent 631-page work on the people of Cartago:

Gamboa, Jesus Mata. *Monografía de Cartago.* Cartago, Costa Rica: El Heraldo, 1930. (FHL# 972.862/A5m)

Church Directories, History

Iglesia Católica. *Estado del Clero de la Provincia de Costa Rica.* San Jose, Costa Rica: Metropolitana, 1966. (FHL# 972.86/K24e)

Emigration and Immigration

Leopold, Werner F. *Der Deutsche in Costa Rica.* Hamburg: Verlag Hanseatischer Merkur, 1966. (FHLC# 972.86/-F2L)

Identifies some German immigrants by name.

Gazetteers

United States Board on Geographic Names. *Costa Rica: Official Standard Names Approved by the U.S. Board on Geographic Names.* Washington, D.C.: U.S. Office of Geography, 1956. (FHL# 972.86/E5u)

Genealogy

Martínez, Victor Sanabria. *Genealogías de Cartago Hasta 1850.* 40 vols. Photocopy of typescript. San Jose, Costa Rica: n.pub., 1957. (FHL# 972.86/D2s)

The forty-year effort of the Archbishop of San Jose. Deals with Cartago, San Jose, Heredia, and Alajuela. Includes births, deaths, marriages, and many other genealogical events up to about 1850. Fully indexed in the last volume. Not cataloged in the FHLC.

The Costa Rican Academy of Genealogical Science has published twenty-eight volumes on the colonial period and contemporary families, 1953-81:

La Academia Costarricense de Ciencias Genealógicas. *Revista de la Academia Costarricense De Ciencias Genealógicas.* San Jose, Costa Rica: n.pub., 1953-1981. 28 vols. (FHL# 972.86/B2ac)

History

The library's collection includes nine historical works. The most complete, though dated, is:

Calvo, Joaquín Bernardo. *República De Costa Rica. Apuntamientos Geográficos, Estadísticos, e Históricos.* San José, Costa Rica: Nacional, 1866. (FHL# 972.86/H2c)

The library has short works on Guanacaste and Heredia.

Maps

The following map gives a detailed view of the country from both a scale of 1:500,000 (whole country) and a scale of 1:250,000 (area from Turrialba on the east to Ramon on the west):

Instituto Geográfico de Costa Rica. *Mapa Físico Político.* San José, Costa Rica: Instituto Geográfico de Costa Rica, 1971. (FHL# 972.86/E7g)

Migration

Consejo Interamericano Económico y Social. *Migraciones Internas en Costa Rica.* Washington, D.C.: Union Pan-Americana, 1956. (FHL# 972.86/W21c)

Notarial Records

See discussion in the section on *Central America, General,* above.

Social Life and Customs

Blutstein, Howard I. *Area Handbook for Costa Rica.* Washington D.C.: n.pub., 1970. (FHL# 972.86/H6a)

Vital Records (Civil and Church)

The library has filmed both civil and church vital records. The list below gives the areas covered and the earliest and latest dates of records; coverage may not be complete within the dates. Most items include births, marriages, deaths, confirmations and baptisms; most are indexed.

AREA		YEARS
Alajuela	civil	1888-1947
Alajuela	Alajuela, Pilar	1790-1965
Alajuela	Alajuela, Catedral	1805-1840
Alajuela	Atenas	1846-1932
Alajuela	Grecia	1847-1980
Alajuela	Naranjo	1865-1940
Alajuela	Orotina	1902-1933
Alajuela	Palmares	1866-1951
Alajuela	Sabanilla	1897-1931
Alajuela	San Antonio de Belén	1862-1949
Alajuela	San Mateo	1877-1945
Alajuela	San Pedro	1861-1963
Alajuela	San Ramón	1848-1967
Alajuela	Sarchi Norte	1887-1964
Cartago	civil	1888-1931
Cartago	Cartago, El Carmen	1595-1942
Cartago	Cartago, Tobosi	1738-1930
Cartago	Cot	1738-1930
Cartago	Juan Vinas	1870-1934
Cartago	Orosi	1765-1900
Cartago	Pacayas	1905-1908
Cartago	Paraiso, Rescate	1824-1951
Cartago	Paraiso, Ujarras	1728-1841
Cartago	Quircot	1738-1930
Cartago	San Rafael	1861-1947
Cartago	Tejar	1914-1947
Cartago	Tobosi	1738-1930
Cartago	Tres Rios	1756-1970
Cartago	Turrialba	1897-1962
Costa Rica	civil	1888-1947
Guanacaste	civil	1888-1933
Guanacaste	Bagaces	1821-1955
Guanacaste	Canas	1866-1936
Guanacaste	Filadelfia	1894-1933
Guanacaste	Guanacaste	1790-1826
Guanacaste	Liberia	1818-1942
Guanacaste	Nicoya	1783-1933
Guanacaste	Santa Cruz	1825-1941
Heredia	civil	1888 1931
Heredia	Barba	1713-1952
Heredia	Heredia, Concepción	1720-1936
Heredia	Heredia, San Pablo	1897-1949
Heredia	Heredia, San Rafael	1886-1974
Heredia	Santa Barbara	1852-1934
Heredia	Santo Domingo	1853-1953
Limón	civil	1888-1931
Limón	Guapiles	1908-1941
Limón	Limón	1891-1935
Limón	Talamanca	1881-1960
Puntarenas	civil	1888-1934
Puntarenas	Esparta	1706-1934
Puntarenas	Puntarenas	1850-1935
San José	civil	1888-1931
San José	Acosta San Ignacio	1899-1935
San José	Alajuelita	1845-1940
San José	Asserri	1782-1942

San José	Curridabat	1812-1946
San José	Desamparados	1825-1931
San José	Escazo	1799-1935
San José	Guadalupe	1852-1936
San José	Piedras Negras	1908-1932
San José	San Isidro Coronado	1871-1932
San José	San José El Carmen	1738-1970
San José	San José Mercedes	1882-1935
San José	San José Dolores	1909-1935
San José	San José Soledad	1909-1933
San José	San Juan	1837-1969
San José	San Pablo	1898-1980
San José	San Pedro	1861-1944
San José	San Vincente	1851-1936
San José	Santa Ana	1880-1952
San José	Santiago	1800-1934
San José	Villa Colón	1767-1963

EL SALVADOR

History and Settlement

Nahua Indians reached the El Salvador area as early as 3000 B.C. to be followed by other peoples. Ruins of the huge Maya pyramids, built between A.D. 100 and 1000 still stand in western El Salvador. The Pipil Indians were those dominant in the area when the Spanish conquest occurred in 1524-25. With fewer mineral resources, it attracted fewer settlers than other Central American countries. They were mostly farmers.

In 1821, El Salvador broke away from Spanish domination with the other Central American colonies and joined with all but Panama to form the United Provinces of Central America in 1823. When the federation dissolved in 1838, El Salvador formally withdrew, declaring its independence in 1841.

El Salvador contains fourteen departments, each governed by a governor under the Ministerio de Gobernacion. The departments are comprised of 260 *municipios* formed from fifty-seven cities *(ciudades)*, sixty-nine villages *(villas)*, and 134 settlement *(pueblos)*. *Municipios* and the churches maintain records. Unfortunately, the records of the government were destroyed by a fire in the National Palace in 1889; and even more have been destroyed due to earthquakes, humidity, insects, and political unrest.

The General Archives in Guatemala are very important to the El Salvador researcher. They contain millions of historical facts, including prime genealogical information.

El Salvador Library Collection

Archives and Libraries

The following volume describes books or documents microfilmed by a unit of the El Salvador UNESCO mission 1955-59 (250,000 pages or individual documents):

Colom, Francisco Sevillano. *Lista de Materias Microfilmados (El Salvador)*. San Salvador, El Salvador: UNESCO, 1958. (FHL# 972.84/A3i/1958).

Biography

Ministerio de Educación. *Biográfias de Vicentinos Ilustres*. San Salvador, El Salvador: Ministerio de Educación, 1962. (FHL # 972.8426/S1/D3s)

Contains short biographies of some thirty prominent citizens of San Vicente.

Census Records

Census records for El Salvador are available for 1746-55 and 1802-03. 3 reels. Cataloged in the FHLC under **El Salvador/Census.**

Church Records

Catholic Church records of confirmations, baptisms, marriages, and deaths 1743-1947, are available in one collection of 274 reels divided into two parts. The first part is for the Palacio Arzobispal in San Salvador, while the second part is for all other parishes. Check the FHLC under **El Salvador/Church Records** for call numbers.

Iglesia Católica. *Palacio Arzobispal (San Salvador). Registros Parroquiales, 1743-1947*. Salt Lake City: Sociedad Genealógica de Utah, 1978-79.

Various individual parish records have been filmed and are cataloged in the FHLC under **El Salvador/-[Department]/[City]/Church**.

Genealogy

A complete survey of genealogical sources for the country of El Salvador is:

Genealogical Society of the Church of Jesus Christ of Latter-day Saints. *Fuentes Principalesude Registros Genealógicas en El Salvador*. Salt Lake City: Genealogical Society of Utah, 1975. (FHL# 929.1/G286gs/Ser. H/no.8)

Gazetteers

Jiménez, Br. Thomas Fidias. *Toponimia Arcaica de El Salvador*. San Salvador, El Salvador: Tipografía La Unión, Dutriz Hnos., 1936. (FHL# 972.84/E2j)

Classified by department. Gives Spanish translations and explanations of original Indian place names.

Ministerio de Economía. *Diccionario Geográfico de la República de El Salvador*. San Salvador, El Salvador: Ministerio de Economía, 1945. (FHL# 972.84/E5c)

Ministerio de Obras Públicas. *Diccionario Geográfico de El Salvador*. 5 vols. San Salvador, El Salvador: Instituto Geográfico Nacional de El Salvador, 1970. (FHL# 972.84/E5s/vols.1-5)

You must know which department a particular city is in before you can use this work.

United States Board on Geographic Names. *El Salvador, Official Standard Names Approved by the U.S. Board on Geographic Names*. Washington, D.C.. U.S. Office of Geography, 1956. (FHL# 972.84/E5u)

History

Of the two official government histories written in the early 1900s the following is more complete and useful:

Barberena, Santiago I. *Historia de El Salvador: Epoca Antigua y de la Conquista*. San Salvador, El Salvador: Ministerio de Educacion, 1914. (FHL# 972.84/H26)

An excellent introduction to the culture of El Salvador is:

Blutstein, Howard I. *Area Handbook for El Salvador.* Washington, D.C.: U.S. Government, 1971. (FHL# 972.84/-H6a)

Maps

El Salvador Ministerio de Obras Públicas. *Mapas Departmentales del País.* San Salvador, El Salvador: Ministerio de Obras Públicas, 1964-70. (FHL# 972.84/E7es)

Scale: 1:100,000; one map per each of the fourteen departments.

Notarial Records

See discussion in the section on *Central America, General,* above.

Vital Records

Vital records from civil registration and church records have been filmed throughout El Salvador, including some property records dating from the early 1500s. See also *Church Records* above. For call numbers, consult the FHLC under **El Salvador/[Department]/ Church Records Or Civil Registration.** Listed below are the numbers of reels per department: Ahuachapán, 105; Cabañas, 50; Chalatenango, 408; Chiloe [*sic*], 5; Cuscatlán, 215; La Libertad, 252; La Paz, 71; La Unión, 38; Morazán, 44; San Miguel, 109; San Salvador, 469; San Vicente, 17; Santa Ana, 130; Sonsonate, 113; and Usulután, 124.

GUATEMALA

History and Settlement

The earliest well-known Indian society at Las Charcas in the highlands, dates from the 1000s B.C. The Maya Indian civilization, with its beautiful palaces, pyramids, and temples of limestone, flourished between A.D. 300 and 900, centered in Guatemala. Their civilization had dwindled and most of the Maya were living in the highlands by the time the Spanish arrived from Mexico in 1523 and subdued the area.

In 1570, Spain established the *audiencia* of Guatemala, a high court of judges and administrators and the chief source of legal authority in most of Central America. The capital was moved from Santiago at Tecpan to Ciudad Vieja in 1527, to Antigua in 1543, and to Guatemala City in 1773.

On 15 September 1821, Guatemala declared its independence with the other Central America states, became part of the Mexican empire, and then broke away in 1823 to form the United Provinces of Central America, which dissolved in 1838. Guatemala declared its own independence in 1847.

Forty-three percent of the people are Indian, 1 percent European, and the rest mostly Latinos, a mixture of Caucasian and Indian. Some blacks live around Barrios and Livingston with some Indian-black "mulattoes" inhabiting the Pacific littoral and lowland. Under Spanish law, intermarriage with blacks was illegal. Most blacks in Guatemala are descendants of those brought in from Jamaica to work on the plantations.

The Indians are divided into about twenty different language groups, the six foremost being Maya, Quiché, Mam, Pocomam, Chol, and Carib. They have largely retained their native religions in addition to Catholicism.

Indian records are virtually nonexistent. The Spaniards burned what they found during the conquest in hopes of hastening conversions. Some royal Indian pedigrees have survived, but most are based on legends. Some Indian records are reportedly in the Vatican Archive.

Guatemala Library Collection

Archives and Libraries

The Archivo General de Centroamérica (General Archives of Central America) in Guatemala City is a valuable repository of impressive amounts of civil, government, and judicial documentation of colonial Guatemala, as well as some major document groups for the nineteenth and early twentieth centuries. The Genealogical Society of Utah has filmed over 3,600 reels of documents, including most, if not all, of the following types: probate cases, marriage information, legal processes, census and tribute records, notary records, and land records. They are cataloged in:

Weathers, Shirley A. *Bibliographic Guide to the Guatemalan Collection.* Salt Lake City: University of Utah Press, 1981. (FHL# 972.81/A3w)

Indexed by document type, location by modern name, time period, and reel numbers. Explanations of entries included. An indispensable research guide.

Census Records

See the FHLC under **Guatemala/[Department]/Census.**

Gazetteers

United States Board on Geographic Names. *Guatemala Official Standard Names Approved by the United States Board on Geographic Names.* Washington, D.C.: U.S. Office of Geography, 1965. (FHL# 972.81/E5u)

Instituto Geografía Nacional. *Suplemento del Diccionario Geográfica de Guatemala 1961-1964.* Guatemala City: Instituto Geografico Nacional de Guatemala, 1968. (FHL# 972.81/E5g/Supp. vols. 1-2)

Genealogy

An excellent source for detailed information on selected Guatemalan individuals and families is:

Academia Guatemalteca de Estudios Genealógicos, Heráldicos, e Históricos. *Revista de la Academia Guatemalteca de Estudios Genealógicos, Heráldicos e Históricos (vols 1-6).* Guatemala City: Tipografía Nacional de Guatemala, 1967-72. (FHL# 972.81/B2r/1-6)

A complete survey of genealogical sources for Guatemala is contained in:

The Genealogical Society of the Church of Jesus Christ of Latter-day Saints. *Major Genealogical Record Sources in Guatemala.* Salt Lake City: Church of Jesus Christ of Latter-day Saints, 1970. (FHL# 929.1/G286gs/Ser. H/no. 1.)

History

The library has various histories of the departments of Guatemala. Check the FHLC under **Guatemala/[Department]/History.** One rather complete departmental history is:

Villacorta C., and J. Antonio. *Monografía del Departamento de Guatemala.* Guatemala City: Tipografía Nacional, 1926. (FHL# 972.8152/H2v)

For an excellent introduction to the history and culture of Guatemala, see:

Dombroinski, John. *Area Handbook for Guatemala.* Washington, D.C.: U.S. Government, 1968. (FHL# 972.81/H6a)

Maps

Most detailed of the several maps in the library collection is:

U.S. Army Corps of Engineers. *Map of Guatemala, scale 1:250,000.* Washington, D.C.: Dirección General de Cartografía, 1959. (FHL# 972.81/E7u)

Notarial Records

See discussion in the section on *Central America, General,* above.

Vital Records

The library has filmed vital records created by both church and state throughout the country. They generally date from about 1820 for civil records. Records before that date are indexed under holdings of the Archivo General de Centroamerica. (See *Archives and Libraries* above.) For call numbers, check the FHLC under **Guatemala/[Department/Church Records.** Census, tax, and an assortment of other church and state records are included in the collection. See also **Guatemala/-[Department]/Census** and **Tax** headings. Below is a list of the departments of Guatemala and the number of reels available on each: Alta Verapaz, 360; Baja Verapaz, 299; Chimaltenango, 446; Chiquimula, 339; El Quiché, 62; Esquintla, 241; Guatemala, 1459; Huehuetenango, 429; Izabal, 45; Jalapa, 788; Petén, 35; Progreso, 144 Quezaltenango, 876; Quiché, 256; Retalhuleu, 160; Sacatepéquez, 517; San Marcos, 390; Santa Rosa, 268; Sololá, 341; Suchitepéquez, 329; Totonicapán, 199; and Zacapa, 202.

HONDURAS

History and Settlement

Honduras means "depths" in Spanish, probably a reference to the deep waters off the northern coast. Honduras is the second largest country in area among the Central American republics.

An important Maya center flourished at Copan until the 800s, but the city was already in ruins when Christopher Columbus landed at Cape Honduras on his fourth voyage in 1502 and claimed the land for Spain.

In 1539, Honduras, together with the other Central American states except for Panama, came under the *audencia* of Guatemala and remained part of that administrative division for the remainder of the colonial period. In 1570, silver discovered in the highlands produced a great influx of fortune seekers and a rapid increase in the population of Tegucigalpa. The coastal zone at the side of the Caribbean Sea became a favored refuge of pirates who attacked the colonial ports and preyed upon Spanish treasure-ships. Toward the end of the eighteenth century, this region with its hardwood forests attracted the English, who controlled the Mosquito Coast from the San Juan River in Nicaragua to Belize, as well as the Bay Islands. The Spanish resented, but were unable to repel, the intrusion.

On 15 September 1821, Honduras declared its independence from Spain with the other Central America states, became part of the Mexican empire, and then broke away in 1823 to form the United Provinces of Central America, which dissolved in 1838.

Honduras's present local jurisdictions consist of eighteen departments with 281 municipal entities. Six percent of the population is Indian, 91 percent is Spanish-Indian, and 3 percent is Caucasian, blacks, Asians, etc. About 89 percent of the people profess Catholicism, with twenty Protestant churches comprising the remaining 11 percent.

The Catholic Church established the bishopric of the province of Honduras as the auxiliary of the Archbishop of Mexico in 1527 but with no designated seat. The Pope later fixed the seat in the port of Trujillo, making it auxillary to Guatemala; and it received its first bishop in 1539. In 1559, Fray Jeronimo de Corella moved the episcopal seat to Comayagua, then the capital. In 1916, the seat was moved to Tegucigalpa, where an archdiocese was established with authority over the diocese of Santa Rosa de Copan and the Vicariato Apostolico de San Pedro Sula. In 1949 the Prelate Nullis of Olancho was formed from the archdiocese of Tegucigalpa. In 1963, Pope John XXIII re-established the old Diocese of Comayagua, and ultimately the Vicariato Apostolico de San Pedro Sula was elevated to diocese status on 27 July 1963.

Each division of the central government, each department, each municipality, and the church has archives. Only the National Archive has records dating as far back as the fifteenth century.

Honduras Library Collection

Archives and Libraries

Descriptions of the microfilmed contents of the National Archives of Honduras are:

Colom, Francisco Sevillano. *Lista de Materiales Microfilmados (of the National Archives of Honduras)*. 2 vols. Tegucigalpa, Honduras: UNESCO, 1958. (FHL# 972.83/A3i/1958)

Instituto Pan Americano de Geografía e Historia. *Honduras, Guía de los Documentos.* Mexico: UNESCO, 1967. (FHL# 972.83/A3i)

Biography

Morazán, Don Francisco. *Memorias del Benemérito General Don Francisco Morazán (1840)*. Tegucigalpa, Honduras: Rouge Hermanos y Comp., 1870. (FHL# 972.83/-A1/nos.1-9)

Morazan was president of the Central American Union for the few years it existed.

Colonization

The library has filmed military records, ship passenger lists, judicial decrees, wills, and other documents about Honduras in the Archivo General de Indias, in Seville, Spain.

Archivo General de Indias. *Sección de Contratación Inventorias.* 9 reels. Madrid: División General de Archivos y Bibliotecas, 1971. Consult the FHLC for call numbers.

Gazetteers

The most comprehensive is:

United States Board on Geographic Names. *Honduras: Official Standard Names Approved by the US Board on Geographic Names.* Washington, D.C.: U.S. Office of Geography 1956. (FHL# 910/UN3g/no.27)

For several short works listing the original native names of locations, check the FHLC under **Honduras/[Department]/Gazetteers**

Genealogy

The most comprehensive and useful guide to genealogical sources in Honduras is:

The Genealogical Society of the Church of Jesus Christ of Latter-day Saints. *Fuentes Principales de Registros Genealógicos en Honduras.* Salt Lake City, Utah: The Church of Jesus Christ of Latter-day Saints, 1975. (FHL# 929.1/G286gs/Ser. H/no.8) In Spanish.

History

The library has nine books dealing with the history of Honduras. Chamberlain is the most comprehensive; Valladares is typical of department histories written during the early 1900s. Consult the FHLC under **Honduras/[Department]/History.**

Chamberlain, Robert S. *The Conquest and Colonization of Honduras.* New York: Octagon Books Inc., 1966. (FHL# 972.83/H2ch)

Valladares R., and Juan B. Valladares. *La Virgen de Suyapa.* Tegucigalpa, Honduras: Talleres Tipo-Lito, 1946. (FHL# 972.8332/S1/K2v)

Land and Property

The library has three reels of property records (1570-1820) relating to Honduras during the colonial period.

Guatemala Capitania General Real Audiencia. *Tierras y Propiedades, 1570-1820.* Salt Lake City: Sociedad Genealógica de Utah, 1970. (FHL# microfilm 0744758-0744760).

Maps

The smallest scale map of Honduras in the library's collection is:

Paz, Jesús Aguilar. *Mapa General de la República de Honduras, escala 1:500,000.* Brasil: Servicio Grafico de I.B.G.E., c.1954. (FHL# 972.83/E7h)

Notarial Records

See discussion in the section on *Central America, General,* above.

Probate Records, Public Records, Church Records, Civil Registration, and Vital Statistics

Prior to 1820, all government records were created under the Captania General of Guatemala. Those records remain largely in Guatemala in the National Archives. Among those filmed by the Family History Library are wills (*Testamentos*, 1633-1819), 28 reels, cataloged under **Honduras/Probate Records.**

Other vital records for Honduras, both civil registration and church records from the colonial period to the present, are cataloged in the FHLC under **Honduras/[Department]/ Church Records** or **Civil Registration.** The library currently holds the following number of reels for each department:

Atlándida, 23; Choluteca, 44; Colón, 15; Comayagua, 55; Copán, 93; Cortés, 59; El Paraiso, 168; Francisco Morazán, 352; Intibuca, 84; Islas de la Bahía, 7; Lempira, 236; La Paz, 43; Ocotepeque, 43; Olancho, 2; Santa Barbara, 126; Valle, 27; and Yoro, 20.

MEXICO

History and Settlement

Mexico was inhabited from prehistoric times by nomadic tribes, who probably arrived as early as 10,000 B.C. Between 6500 and 1500 B.C., Indians in the Puebla region discovered how to grow corn and became farmers. Between 1200 and about 100 B.C., the Olmec civilization flourished, including beautiful carved stone statues, a counting system, and a calendar. Its Classic Period, characterized by huge pyramids, came between A.D. 250 and 900, paralleling the climax of the Maya civilization and the Zapotecs in the south. The fierce Toltec Indians established their empire during the 900s, with its capital at Tula, north of present-day Mexico City. The last and greatest Indian empire was that of the Aztec, which flourished from the mid-fourteenth century until the Spanish conquest, 1519-21.

King Charles I of Spain granted huge estates to the *conquistadores,* established a Council of the Indies to make laws for the Spanish-American colonies in 1524, and created the first *audencia* in 1527, headed by a viceroy.

The Mexican war of independence, timed to take advantage of Spain's war with France, began on 15 September 1810. Independence was declared in 1813 but was not finally won until 1821. Mexico became a republic with a federalist constitution in 1824. A border dispute with the United States turned into war (1846-48). French troops occupied Mexico City in 1863 and installed Maximilian, brother of the Austrian emperor and then an ally of Napoleon's, as emperor. Mexican nationalists reclaimed the government in 1867.

Mexico is a federal republic, divided into twenty-nine states, two territories, and one federal district.

Mexico Library Collection

The library's large collection of Mexican materials can be divided into two major categories: (1) seventy-two shelf feet of manuscripts and printed materials, and (2) more than 131,000 microfilm reels.

The printed materials are easier to use than the microfilms cataloged before 1968. With the exception of the parish and civil vital records, many of these microfilms suffer from inefficient cataloging methods (spot checking rather than reading in full) and inaccurate translations of the titles carried by the original work. A few documents ("fugitive" materials) were missed in cataloging and lie between indexed portions of film. More recent work has been done accurately. Haigh's study of the collection in 1978 concluded that, with the exception of 3,600 reels filmed in 1973, most of the films have been accurately and completely identified.

For information on the scope of this collection and guides in using it, see:

Cottler, Susan M., Roger M. Haigh, and Shirley A. Weathers, eds. *Preliminary Survey of the Mexican Collection.* Salt Lake City: University of Utah Press, 1978. (FHL# 972/A3cs; 1979 Supplement FHL# 972/A3h)

Haigh, Roger M., and David J. Robinson. *Research Inventory of the Mexican Collection of Colonial Parish Registers.* Salt Lake City: University of Utah Press, 1980. (FHL# 972/A3rr)

Identifies the content of each reel with film number. Organized geographically by states, then *municipio.* Maps included of each *municipio* locating each parish.

Note that where the *Preliminary Survey* gives only the beginning and ending years with the total number of films (1616-1960, 462 rolls), both the *Research Inventory* and the FHLC list years and type of documents for each reel. Also, note that the *Research Inventory* has indexed the rolls down to the parish level ("El Sagrario"), while the FHLC has stopped at the *municipio* level (Aguascalientes, Aguascalientes).

Both the *Preliminary Survey* and the *Research Inventory* have extensive introductions that provide an excellent background for understanding the nature of the Mexican Collection – its accumulation, its composition, its deficiencies, and most of all, its tremendous potential.

Biography

The library has a large collection of biographies on the following people and groups, including:

Bravo Ugarte, José. *Diócesis y Obispos de la Iglesia Mexicana, 1519-1965.* [Dioceses and Bishops of the Mexican Church 1519-1965.] Mexico: Editorial Jos, 1965. (FHLC# 972/k216)

Other books cataloged under **Mexico/Church History** include Mormon settlements in northern Mexico, Baptists, Presbyterians, the Spanish Inquisition, Jesuits, and Franciscans.

Church Records

Procesos del Santo Oficio de México, 1522-1820. Salt Lake City: Genealogical Society of Utah, 1952-1954. 322 reels. Filmed from original records. See Mexico/Church Records for call numbers.

About half of these reels, "Genealógico de los Procesados," consist of genealogies to show that an accused person was unrelated to anyone convicted of a heresy.

Gazetteers

United States Board on Geographic Names. *Mexico, Official Standard Names Approved by the U.S. Board on Geographic Names.* Washington, D.C.: U.S. Office of Geography, 1956. (FHL# 972/E5u or microfilm 873799)

Locates all place names in Mexico by longitude and latitude.

For other gazetteers, check the FHLC under **Mexico/-Gazetteers.**

Genealogy

The library has several different genealogical or historical periodicals, including:

Memorias de La Academia Mexicana de Genealogía y Heráldica. 1745-1968. Annual. Mexico City: Mexican Academy of Genealogy and Heraldry. (FHL# 972/B2a)

Boletín del Archivo General de La Nación. 1930-1959. Quarterly. Mexico City: Mexican Academy of Genealogy and Heraldry. (FHL# 972/B2bo)

Spanish American Genealogical Helper. 1971-80. Annual. Torrence, Calif: The Augustan Society. (FHL# 929.18/-Au45s)

Aparicio y Aparicio, Edgar Juan. *Genealogical Research in Mexico and Central America.* Salt Lake City: Genealogical Society of the Church of Jesus Christ of Latter-day Saints, 1969. (FHL# 929.1/W893/F15b)

The Genealogical Society of the Church of Jesus Christ of Latter-day Saints. *Fuentes Principales de Registros Genealógicos en México.* Salt Lake City: Church of Jesus Christ of Latter-day Saints, [c.1960s]. (FHL# 929.1/G286gs/Ser. H/no.2)

History

In 1600, Don Fernando de Alva Ixtlilxóchitl (born 1575 in Teotihuacán and governor of Texcoco in 1618) began writing the history of the Texcoco people he lived among. An educated man for his day, Ixtlilxochitl worked with other native Americans who entrusted to him their oral and written history. Although his two surviving volumes have not yet been translated into English, they are a highly valuable primary source about the Spanish conquerors and the history of the conquered:

Alva Ixtlilxochitl, Fernando de. *Obras Históricas de don Fernando de Alva Ixtltlxóchitl.* 2 vols. México: Alfredo Chavero, 1952. (FHL# 972/H2i)

Highly detailed, informative, and interesting, Hubert Howe Bancroft's six volumes on the history of Mexico are still one of the best researched works available:

Bancroft, Hubert Howe. *History of Mexico.* 6 vols. San Francisco, Calif.: History Company, Publishers, 1883-88. (FHL# 972/H2b)

See also Bancroft works that deal with Northern Mexico and Texas in the U.S./Canadian book area (FHL# 979/B4b/vols. 15-16)

The library also has a large collection on the history of the Inquisition in Mexico. Consult the FHLC under **Mexico/History/Inquisition.**

Unique problems of foreigners in New Spain in the 1700s developed because Spanish kings felt foriegners were a threat to imperial, religious, and mercantile security. They were considered undesirables and not allowed to immigrate to Spanish America between 1501 and 1760. The history of immigrants to Mexico is discussed in this work, which also includes a list of names:

Nunn, Charles F. *Foreign Immigrants in Early Bourbon Mexico: 1700-1760.* Cambridge, England: Cambridge University Press, 1979. (FHL# 972/H2n)

In its large history collection on Mexico, the library also has at least one history for each state. Consult the FHLC under **Mexico/[State]/History.**

Maps

The library has many maps or map sets, virtually spanning its history from pre-colonial days to the present. An excellent set of forty-seven maps, scale 1:500,000, used effectively with a current gazetteer is:

Comision Intersecretarial Coordinadora Del Levantamiento de la República Mexicana. *Estados Unido de México.* La Comisión: México, 1957. (FHL# Map Case 972/E7eu/1-7)

Not cataloged in FHLC.

Newspapers, Bibliography

Charnu, Steven M. *Latin American Newspapers in the United States Libraries.* Austin: University of Texas Press, 1968. (FHL# 980/A3L)

Vital Records

The library has microfilmed vital records from throughout Mexico. Church records normally contain baptisms, marriages, confirmations, and burials. State records contain information on births, marriages, and deaths. Interspersed among these records are other documents: illegitimate baptisms, confirmation records, baptismal records by caste, marriage records by caste, death records by caste, wills, church records, membership lists (cofradías), marriage banns, divorces, cordilleras, criminal cases, miscellaneous documents, secret baptisms, secret marriages, guardianship records, and adoptions

For a complete guide to the inclusion and location of these other types of records, see discussion on Haigh under the introduction to *Mexico Library Collection* above.

The most important part of the research collection is the more than 112,000 reels taken in 1,115 parishes and hundreds of governmental repositories. For call numbers, consult the FHLC under **Mexico/Vital Records** or FHL# 972/A3r.

NICARAGUA

History and Settlement

Like its other Central American neighbors, Nicaragua dates its independence from Spain from 15 September

1821. Since then, this small country has seen a continual procession of foreign powers, adventurers, bankers, dictators, and even the U.S. Marines.

For a concise history of Nicaragua with attention to details of interest to genealogical researchers, see:

The Genealogical Society of the Church of Jesus Christ of Latter-day Saints. *Fuentes Principales de Registros Genealógicas en Nicaragua.* Salt Lake City: Genealogical Society of Utah, n.d., pp. 2-4. (FHL# 929.1/G286GS/Ser. H/no.10) Spanish.

Nicaragua Library Collection

Filming of records for Nicaragua has not been completed. For records generated before about 1820, see the General Archives for Central America in Guatemala City.

Biography

In addition to a 1945 *Who's Who* of Latin America, the library has histories of the Arellano and Bernard families. Consult the FHLC under **Nicaragua/Biography**.

Census

The library has two reels of tax lists, 1662-1703, and 1794-95.

Church Directories, Church History

Of the three books cataloged under this heading, the most helpful is:

Catholic Church. *Anuario Eclesiástico de Nicaragua. (The Catholic Directory of Nicaraguan Ecclestiastical Divisions.)* Leon, Nicaragua: Editorial Hospicio, 1967. (FHL# 972.85/K24a)

Civil Registration, Court Records

The library has one reel on marriages (1754), four reels of court judgements (1795-1806), and two of wills (1603-1749, 1635, 1651, and 1772). For call numbers, consult the FHLC under **Nicaragua/Court Records**.

Gazetteers

United States Board on Geographic Names. *Nicaragua: Official Standard Names Approved by the U.S. Board on Geographic Names*. Washington, D.C.: U.S. Office of Geography, 1956. (FHL# 972.85/E5u)

Genealogy

The library has seven reels of "Informacion Personal" (usually taxes) for 1541-1813 under this heading in the FHLC.

For a survey of genealogical sources available for Nicaragua, see:

The Genealogical Society of the Church of Jesus Christ of Latter-day Saints. *Fuentes Principales de Registros Genealógicos en Nicaragua*. Salt Lake City: Church of Jesus Christ of Latter-day Saints, n.d. (FHL# 929.1/G286gs)

Nicaraguan records created prior to 1820 are generally found in the National Archives of Central America in Guatemala City, Guatemala. See discussion under *Archives and Libraries,* Central America, General.

History

The library has at least one history for each of the ten departments. Consult the FHLC under **Nicaragua/-[Department]/History.** Such histories usually contain a great deal of local detail. For national histories, see:

Academia de Geografía e Historia de Nicaragua. *Revista de la Academia de Geografía e História de Nicaragua.* Managua, Nicaragua: La Academia, 1936-68. (FHL# 972.85/H25r)

Molina, Argüello Carlos. *Misiones Nicaragüenses en Archivos Europeos.* México: Instituto Pan Americano de Geografía e Historia, Comisión de Historia, 1957. (FHL# 972.85/H2m)

Contains abstracts of official correspondence with Spain during the colonial period.

Notarial Records

See discussion under *Central America, General,* above.

Pensions

Pensions vested during 1659, 1691, 1695, and 1792 (all under the Capitanía General of Guatemala) have been recorded and filmed on one reel (FHL# microfilm 0745814, item 2), cataloged under **Nicaragua/Pensions.**

Probate Records

Probates generated during 1603-1749 and 1772 are microfilmed on two reels (FHL# 0745811-0745812), cataloged under **Nicaragua/ Probate Records**.

Taxation

The library has six reels of tax lists for 1624-1819 (FHL# 0744398-0744402, 0746865).

Land and Property

The library has nine reels of land and property records for 1579-1893 on nine reels cataloged under **Nicaragua/-Leon/Land and Property.**

Panama

History and Settlement

Panama was discovered by Rodrigo de Bastidas in 1501. In 1502 Christopher Columbus, during his fourth voyage, touched the shores of the area. In 1509 the conquistadors, under Vasco Nuñez de Balboa, established a colony at Santa Maria la Antigua del Darien and Balboa soon became governor. His successor established Panama City in 1519.

Until 1535, Panama was under the jursidiction of Santo Domingo. From 1535 to 1538, it was subject to the Viceroyship of Peru, self-governing between 1538 and 1543, subject to the Viceroyship and boundaries of Guatemala until 1563, when it became a separate Viceroyship of Panama. In 1717 it again came under the Viceroyship of Peru, was self-governing from 1722 to 1739, came under the jurisdiction of Santa Fe de Bogota from 1739 to 1751, then the Viceroyship of Neuva Granada.

With the declaration of independence from Spain in 1821, Panama elected to be a province of Colombia. In 1903, it became an independent nation.

Panama is divided into the provinces *(provincias)* of Bocas del Toro, Chiriqui, Veraguas, Herrera, Los Santos, Coclé, Colón, Panama, San Blas, and Darien. The provinces are divided into municipalities *(municipalidades)*.

The Catholic Church established the Diocese of Panama in 1513 as an auxiliary of the Archbishopric of Lima. In 1553, it became part of the newly established Archbishopric of Santa Fe de Bogotá. In 1926, it became an archbishopric. Today the country is divided into the following ecclesiastical jurisdictions: The Archdiocese of Panama, the dioceses of David, Santiago de Veraguas, the Prelacy Nullius de Bocas del Toro, and the Apostolic Vicarship of Darien.

Panama Library Collection

Biography

Susto, Juan Antonio. *Panameños de la Epoca Colonial en el Archivo General de Indias de Sevilla.* Domingo: n.pub., 1930. (FHL# 986.2/D3a)

Church Directories, Church History

The library has several church histories and directories. The most genealogically valuable is:

Church of Jesus Christ of Latter-day Saints. *Mexican Mission, Annual Genealogical Reports of the Canal Zone, 1947-1951.* Salt Lake City: Church of Jesus Christ of Latter-day Saints, 1953. (FHL# microfilm 0038824)

Colonization, Inventories, Registers, Catalogs

The library has nine reels of business documents with an index of individuals involved in dealings between Panama and Spain during the colonial period. (FHL# 1223681-1223689) Consult the FHLC under **Panama/-Colonization/Inventories/Registers/Catalogs.**

Gazetteers

The library has six different volumes on travel, description, and place names. The most detailed is:

United States Board of Geographic Names. *Panama and the Canal Zone: Official Standard Names Approved by the U.S. Board of Geographic Names.* Washington D.C.: U.S. Office of Geography, 1969. (FHL# 972.87/E5u)

Genealogy

For a full description of genealogical sources in Panama, see:

The Genealogical Society of the Church of Jesus Christ of Latter-day Saints. *Fuentes Principales de Registros Genealógicos en Panama.* Salt Lake City: Church of Jesus Christ of Latter-day Saints, n.d. (FHL# 929.1/G286gs/Ser. H/no.5)

History

The library has eighteen Panamanian histories, including:

Pereira Jiménez, Bonifacio. *Historia de Panamá: Texto para uso de los colegios oficiales y particulares de la Republica.* Panama: n.pub., 1969. (FHL# 986.2/H2p)

Maps

The library has several different series of maps. The most detailed is a twelve-map series:

Panamá Ministerio de Obras Públicas. *Mapa general de la República de Panamá, escala 1:250,000.* Panama Instituto de Geográfico Nacional: Panamá: n.pub., 1966. (FHL# 972.87/F7t; note, on the maps, the call number is 972.87/E7t)

Torres Lanzas, Pedro. *Relación Descriptiva de los Mapas, Planos, etc. de las Antiguas Audiencias de Panamá, Santa Fe, y Quito Existentes en el Archivo General de Indias.* Madrid: Tip. de la Revista de Arch. Bibl. y Museos., 1904. (FHL# 980/A3tL)

A bibliography of maps and plans housed in the Archive General de Indias in Madrid, Spain, dealing with the old *audiencias* of Panama, Santa Fe de Bogotá, and Quito.

Military Records

The library has three reels of Spanish military records held in Simancas, Spain, on military service in Columbia, Ecuador, and Panama from 1787 to 1800. Consult the FHLC under **Panama/Military Records.**

Social Life and Customs

Written for Americans, this book is an excellent introduction to the social life and customs of Panama:

Weil, Thomas E. et al. *Area Handbook for Panama.* Washington, D.C.: U.S. Government Printing Office, 1972. (FHL# 986.2/H6a)

The library has four other books dealing with this subject.

Church Records

Catholic Church records containing genealogical data have been filmed throughout the country. The area, record type, and time periods are listed below. The years are inclusive, but coverage may not be complete within those years. Some items are indexed. See the FHLC under **Panama/Church Records.**

Chapter 25

South Pacific: Australia, New Zealand,and the South Pacific Islands

Gordon L. Remington

AUSTRALIA

Historical Background

1642	Dutch explorer Abel Tasman visits various parts of Australia.
1769-77	Voyages of Captain James Cook bring Australia to English attention.
1788	First settlement at Sidney Cove. New South Wales established as penal colony.
1803-04	First settlement in Tasmania.
1824	First settlement in Queensland, at Moreton Bay.
1825	Tasmania established as a separate colony called Van Diemen's Land.
1826	First permanent settlement in Western Australia at Swan River.
1829	Swan River Colony established, basis for the state of Western Australia.
1834	First permanent settlements in Victoria.
1842	South Australia becomes a separate colony.
1849	Convicts sent to Western Australia.
1851	Victoria established as a separate colony; gold rushes in New South Wales and Victoria attract many immigrants.
1856	Name of Van Diemen's Land changed to Tasmania.
1868	Last transportation of convicts to Australia.
1869	Darwin founded, later capital of the Northern Territory.
1901	Commonwealth of Australia proclaimed; New South Wales, Queensland, South Australia, Tasmania, Victoria, and Western Australia become the six states of Australia. Australia becomes a Dominion in the British Empire.
1911	Australian Capital Territory established.
1912	Northern Territory transferred from South Australia to the federal government.
1931	Australia joins British Commonwealth of Nations.

Settlement and Migration

After the loss of Britain's American colonies in 1783, there was no place to send convicts who would previously have been transported out of England. The need for a penal colony ultimately forced the British government to experiment in the South Pacific. In 1788, eleven ships carrying about 1,350 people arrived at what is now Sydney and established the colony of New South Wales. In 1792, the first free settlers arrived in New South Wales.

Settlement of Australia continued by both free and convict immigrants. Free immigrants came either by their own means or with government assistance. Convicts could earn remission of their sentences, but they could never return to England. Many immigrants came as part of the penal establishment, as soldiers or officials.

The convict immigrants were almost entirely from the British Isles. Most were convicted of what, by modern standards, would be minor crimes. After the Irish Revolution of 1798, many Irish political prisoners were also transported to Australia.

The free settlers, too, were largely from Britain and Ireland; but other countries were eventually represented, in particular, Germany. Many Chinese and other Asians have also settled in Australia. Australia's immigration policies have varied over the years. After World War II, Australia opened its doors to many European refugees. In recent years, immigrating to Australia has become more difficult.

Because each state operated as an independent colony prior to 1901, government organizations and record keeping differ slightly from one state to another. The units of local government in each state and the Northern Territory are: New South Wales – cities, municipalities, and shires; Northern Territory – cities and municipalities; Queensland – cities, towns, and shires; South Australia – cities, corporate towns, and district council areas; Tasmania – cities and municipalities; Victoria – cities, towns, and boroughs; and Western Australia – cities, towns, and shires.

As of 1984, Australia had almost 900 local government entities with various powers. The Family History Library Catalog (FHLC) is organized by state and then by the name of the local government entity in which or by which the record was created. Many of the records of genealogical value (with the exception of cemetery, church, and newspaper records) are cataloged at the state level. To locate a particular town or borough in its proper state, consult:

Division of National Mapping, Department of Minerals and Energy. *Australia 1:250,000 Map Series Gazetteer.* Canberra: Australian Government Publishing Service, 1975. (FHL# 994/E5am)

Norfolk Island, technically a self-ruling territory, is included in the FHLC for Australia.

It should be noted that every state except Western Australia was at one time under the jurisdiction of New South Wales. Records relating to individuals who settled in Australia prior to the establishment of the colony in which the settlement was eventually included may be found in New South Wales.

Australia Library Collection

The extent and variety of records from Australia available at the Family History Library defies a listing of every single type of record. This discussion of records available will concentrate on major record groups and give examples from each state, where applicable. For an excellent discussion of the types of records available for each state, consult:

Hall, Nick Vine. *Tracing Your Family History in Australia: A Guide to Sources.* Adelaide: Rigby Publishers, 1985. (FHL# 994/D23v)

This work surpasses Niel T. Hansen's *Guide to Genealogical Sources: Australia and New Zealand* (Prahran, Australia: Hall's Book Store Printery, 1962) in currency, comprehensiveness, and readability. Use Vine Hall to determine what types of records exist for each state, then consult the FHLC to see if that particular record is available at the library.

Certain Australian records are restricted by the Family History Library. Sometimes, but not always, they will bear the notation: "The information in these records shall not be used so as to cause pain or embarrassment to any living person." These records are restricted because they either deal directly with convict records or with records which may indicate convict status. They are located in Special Collections and may be searched after you sign an agreement not use the records "so as to cause pain or embarrassment to any living person." The agreement form is available in Special Collections. These records are not avilable through the branch library system.

This restriction, in force at the time the Family History Library acquired the records, has since been abolished in Australia. It may be only a matter of time before the restriction at the Family History Library is also lifted.

Archives and Libraries

Each Australian state maintains its own archives, and a number of research libraries have genealogically valuable material. The Family History Library has the following guides to archives and libraries in its collection:

Australia (General)

Ives, Alan. *Archives in Australia.* 7 vols. Canberra: Pearce Press Processed Publications, 1978. (FHL# 994/J53i)

Principal Manuscript Collections in the National Library of Australia. Canberra: National Library of Australia, 1973. (FHL# 994/A1/no.29)

New South Wales

New South Wales, Archives Authority. *Concise Guide to the State Archives of New South Wales.* Sydney: The Authority 1969. (FHL# Q/994.4/A35/g/no.13)

See also quarterly supplement.

Queensland

Queensland State Archives. *Provenance Catalogue.* 2 reels. Salt Lake City: Genealogical Society of Utah, 1981. (FHL# microfilm 1239122-1239123)

South Australia

Price, A. Grenfell. *Libraries in South Australia: A Report of an Inquiry Commissioned by the South Australian Government into the System of Management of Libraries Maintained or Assisted by the State.* Adelaide: Libraries Board of South Australia, 1969. (FHL# 994.23/J5p)

Tasmania

Tasmania State Archives. *General Index, 1803-1940.* 4 reels. Salt Lake City: Genealogical Society of Utah, 1975. (FHL# microfilm 0918580-0918583)

Victoria

Brown, Frances, Dom Meadley, and Marjorie Morgan, eds. *Family and Local History Sources in Victoria.* Blackburn: Custodians of Records, 1983. (FHL# 994.5/D23f)

Biography

Biographical material can be found in printed and manuscript form on the national, state, and local level in the library's collection. Some examples of biographical materials are:

Mennell, Philip. *The Dictionary of Australasian Biography: Comprising Notices of Eminent Colonists from the Inauguration of Responsible Government down to the Present Time 1855-1892.* 1892; microreproduction, Salt Lake City: Genealogical Society of Utah, 1982. (FHL# microfilm 0284858)

Pike, Douglas, Bede Nairn, and Geoffrey Serle, eds. *Australian Dictionary of Biography.* 9 vols. Carlton, Victoria/London: Melbourne University Press/Cambridge University Press, 1966-work in progress. (FHL# 994/D36a)

Serle, Percival. *Dictionary of Australian Biography.* 2 vols. 1949; microreproduction, 2 reels, Salt Lake City: Genealogical Society of Utah, 1959. (FHL# microfilm 0209242-0209243)

Some examples of manuscript biographical material are:

Biographical Index (South Australia). 2 reels. Salt Lake City: Genealogical Society of Utah, 1963. (FHL# microfilm 041860-041861)

Biography Index (Victoria). 28 reels. Salt Lake City: Genealogical Society of Utah, 1984. (FHL# microfilm 1363965-1363981, 1364013-1364024)

Erickson, Rica, comp. *Western Australia Biographical Card Collection of Persons Resident in the State Prior to 1915.* 9 reels. Salt Lake City: Genealogical Society of Utah, 1982. (FHL# microfilm 1363635-1363639, 1363642-1363643, 1363651-1363652)

Cemeteries

The Family History Library has a large collection of cemetery records (monumental inscriptions) for Australia. Check the FHLC under **Australia/Cemeteries, Australia/[State]/Cemeteries**, and **Australia/-[State]/[City or Borough]/Cemeteries.**

Census

A regular census has been taken in Australia since the 1840s, but most of the schedules have been destroyed as a matter of public policy. A few surviving schedules are available at the Family History Library. This register of what is available, including microfilm call numbers, has been prepared by the library staff:

Church of Jesus Christ of Latter-day Saints Genealogical Department. *Index to the Australian Census Records in the British Collection of the Family History Library, Salt Lake City, Utah.* Salt Lake City: Genealogical Society of Utah, 1985. (FHL# 994/X22c)

Here is a list of what is available by state and year:

New South Wales

1806 (FHL# microfilm 0587930)

1828 (FHL# microfilm 0942055-0942056, 0917871-0917872, index on 0930427-0930430)

Both are restricted, but the 1828 census has been published in Malcolm R. Sainty and Keith A. Johnson, eds. *Census of New South Wales, November 1828* (Sydney: Library of Australian History, 1980). (FHL# Q/994.4/X2c).

1841 (FHL# microfilm 0288560-0288561 or 091873)

1891 see FHLC or the census register; 36 microfilm reels not in numerical sequence

Northern Territory

1881, 1891, 1901 (FHL# microfilm 0416828)

Queensland

none available.

South Australia

1841 (FHL# microfilm 0304789)

Tasmania

1837 (FHL# microfilm 0284640)

1842 (FHL# microfilm 0284641-0284649)

1843 (FHL# microfilm 0284650-0284655)

1848 (FHL# microfilm 0284656-0284667)

1851 (FHL# 0284668-0284671)

An index to the above censuses (except 1837) can be found on FHL# microfilm 0416842-0416843.

Victoria

1836, 1838 (FHL# microfilm 0209172)

1836 (FHL# microfilm 0918991)

1838 (FHL# microfilm 0918991)

1841 (FHL# microfilm 0917874)

Western Australia

1832 (FHL# 994.1/X2b)

1837 (FHL# 994.1/X2c or microfilm 0973232 or 1363694, published) (FHL# microfilm 0284826, manuscript)

Church Records

The Family History Library has many church records, both film copies of originals and abstracts, from Australia. Most Church of England records from major cities are available. It should be noted that some of the earlier church records identify convict origins and so are restricted. Check the FHLC under **Australia/[State]/-[City or Borough]/Church Records.**

Civil Registration

The Family History Library has Australian Civil Registration Indexes for all six states. The time period covered is from the start (variable for each state) civil registration to 1896/1906, depending on the state. The information given on birth, marriage, and death records varies from state to state. For information on the nature of civil registration in each state, consult:

Hall, Nick Vine. *Tracing Your Family History in Australia: A Guide to Sources.* Adelaide: Rigby Publishers, 1985. (FHL# 994/D23v)

The reference staff at the Family History Library has prepared a register of civil registration indexes:

Church of Jesus Christ of Latter-day Saints, Genealogical Department. *Guide to the Australian Civil Registration Indexes Available in the LDS Family History Library.* Salt Lake City: Genealogical Society of Utah, c.1986. (FHL# 994/V22g)

Here is a brief state-by-state synopsis of the civil registration indexes:

New South Wales

Index to Baptisms, pre-1856

Index to Marriages, pre-1856

Index to Burials, pre-1856

Index to Births, 1856-99

Index to Marriages, 1856-99

Index to Deaths, 1856-99

Queensland

Country Death Index, 1856-94

Brisbane Death Index, 1856-94

Queensland Death Index, 1895-99

Brisbane Marriage Index, 1856-93

Country Marriage Index, 1856-93

Queensland Marriage Index, 1894-99

South Australia

Birth Index, 1842-1906

Marriage Index, 1842-1906

Death Index, 1842-1905

Tasmania

The library has both indexes and records to 1899. Consult the FHLC for specific years and call numbers.

Victoria

Index to Early Church Records, 1838-53 (baptisms, marriages, burials)

Index to Births, 1853-95

Index to Deaths, 1853-95

Index to Marriages, 1853-95

Western Australia

Index to Births, 1840-95

Index to Marriages, 1841-96

Index to Deaths, 1841-96

Indexes are sometimes subdivided into sections covering different periods of time, and hundreds of microfiche are often involved. The FHLC will give specific references.

Correctional Institutions

Under this heading fall all records of convicts transported to Australia between 1788 and 1868. Records exist only for the states of New South Wales, Queensland, Tasmania, and Western Australia, as South Australia and Victoria were not founded as penal colonies.

The records include convict pardons, remissions of sentences, tickets to leave, correspondence concerning convicts, etc. Because these records are not easily accessible through the library or its branches, consult Vine Hall's description of what is available for each state and compare those listings with the FHLC.

These records are quite important; but due to the current restrictions, a detailed summary will not be presented here.

Directories

Directories or almanacs are available for major cities and also for whole states. Due to the lack of census records, directories are an important tool for locating a person in place and time. Consult the FHLC under **Australia/[State]/[City or Borough]/Directories.**

Emigration and Immigration

These records are one of the most important groups in Australian genealogical research. The passenger arrival lists will often contain detailed information about the immigrant, including exact place of origin.

The Family History Library has a variety of records associated with shipping and passenger arrivals. These indexes to passenger lists are available:

Queensland

Card Index to Immigrants Arriving in Queensland: 1848-1912. 55 reels. Salt Lake City: Genealogical Society of Utah, 1981. reels. (FHL# microfilm 1238963-1239122, 1363525-1363526)

South Australia

Index to Inwards Passenger Lists, 1846-1887 Published in New South Wales Newspapers. 8 reels. Salt Lake City: Genealogical Society of Utah, 1963. (FHL# microfilm 0416862-0416869)

Tasmania

Alphabetical List of Convicts Arriving in Tasmania, 1804-1853. 8 reels. Salt Lake City: Genealogical Society of Utah, 1975. (FHL# microfilm 0918587-0918591, 0830273, 0952486-0952487)

Western Australia

Card Index to Passengers Arriving in Western Australia, 1829-1890. 4 reels. Salt Lake City: Genealogical Society of Utah, 1961. (FHL# microfilm 0284818-0284821)

Where an index is not available, you must know the ship on which your ancestor arrived. Many records will indicate this information. Once you know the name of the ship, you can search shipping registers to find the exact arrival date, and then search the passenger lists. Many of the records essential for this process are available at the Family History Library.

History and Genealogy

There is a great deal of historical and compiled genealogical material for Australia available at the Family History Library. Check the FHLC under **Australia/-[State]/[City** or **Borough]/History** or **/Genealogy**, and also **/[State]/History** or **/Genealogy**, and **Australia/-History** or **Genealogy.**

Land and Property

The granting of land to ex-convicts and to free settlers played an important role in the development of Australia. The Crown had a virtual monopoly on land grants, and the easy terms on which land could be acquired was an inducement for settlement and expansion.

The Family History Library has a few land records for each state, but the collection is by no means comprehensive. Check **Australia/[State]/Land and Property** to see if land records are available. A useful work for the early period is:

Johnson, Keith A., and Malcolm R. Sainty. *Land Grants 1788-1809, New South Wales, Norfolk Island, Van Diemen's Land.* North Sydney: Genealogical Publications of Australia, 1974. (FHL# Q/994/R2j)

Maps and Gazetteers

The Family History Library has a variety of maps and gazetteers. Check the FHLC for the locality and state of interest; also check on the national level for maps of Australia in general.

Military Records

The Family History Library has few original military records from Australia on microfilm, but there are a number of printed works concerning Australian soldiers in native wars, the Boer War, and World Wars I and II.

Native Races

Unlike the New Zealand Collection, the Family History Library's Australia Collection has few sources relating to the Aborigines. See the FHLC under **Australia/Native Races** for the few printed works available.

Naturalization

Naturalization was not a requirement in Australia for non-British immigrants, but it did grant certain rights to the individual who went through the process, particularly in regard to land ownership. The following naturalization records are available at the Family History Library:

New South Wales

Naturalization Papers and Index, 1849-1904

Queensland

Indexes to Naturalization, 1858-1902

Oaths of Allegiance, 1858-1904

South Australia

Certificates of Naturalization and Index, 1858-1903

Tasmania

Miscellaneous Papers, 1836-80

Victoria

Certificates of Naturalization and Index, 1858-1903

Western Australia

Naturalization Register, 1841-1903

Naturalization Certificates, 1871-1903

Check the FHLC for specific call numbers and years.

Newspapers and Obituaries

The Family History Library has some original newspapers on microfilm, but most records under this heading are compiled abstracts of vital information from newspapers. Check the FHLC under **Australia/-[State]/[City** or **Borough]/** to see what is available.

Periodicals

There are a number of genealogical and historical periodicals available for each state. An important periodical for Australia in general is:

Descent: The Official Journal of the Society of Australian Genealogists. Surry Hills, Australia: The Society, 1961-to date. (FHL# 994/B2au)

Probate Records

The Family History Library has probate records for five of the six states. The Supreme Court or Probate Court in each state is responsible for probating or administering an estate. Probate records available at the Family History Library are:

New South Wales

New South Wales Probate Office. *Lexicographical Index of the Estates of Deceased Persons in New South Wales 1800-1901.* 2 reels. Salt Lake City: Genealogical Society of Utah, 1963. (FHL# microfilm 0388342-0388343).

New South Wales Probate Office. *Registers of Copy of Wills in New South Wales 1800-1931.* 68 reels. Salt Lake City: Genealogical Society of Utah, 1963. (FHL# microfilm 0388344-0388411)

New South Wales Supreme Court. *Probate Papers 1790-1814.*

Salt Lake City: Genealogical Society of Utah, 1963. (FHL# microfilm 0388294)

Queensland

Queensland Supreme Court (Brisbane: Southern District). *Ecclesiastical Files, 1857-1922.* 208 reels. Salt Lake City: Genealogical Society of Utah, 1976-77. (See FHLC; call numbers not consecutive.)

Queensland Supreme Court (Rockhampton: Central District).

Ecclesiastical Files, 1896-1944. 21 reels. Salt Lake City: Genealogical Society of Utah, 1975. (FHL# microfilm 0919169-0919189)

Queensland Supreme Court (Townsville: Northern District).

Ecclesiastical Files, 1875-1906. 14 reels. Salt Lake City: Genealogical Society of Utah, 1976. (FHL# microfilm 0919035-0919047, 0919190)

South Australia

None available.

Tasmania

Tasmania Supreme Court. *Register of the Granting of Letters of Administration, 1868-1896.* Salt Lake City: Genealogical Society of Utah, 1975. (FHL# microfilm 0952988)

Tasmania Supreme Court, *Registers of the Granting of Probate, 1868-1904.* Salt Lake City: Genealogical Society of Utah, 1975. (FHL# microfilm 0952354)

Victoria

Victoria Probate Office. *Index to Probate Applications 1853-1959.* 26 reels. Salt Lake City: Genealogical Society of Utah, 1959. (FHL# microfilm 0209288-0209313)

Victoria Probate Office. *Register of Wills 1841-1900.* 37 reels. Salt Lake City: Genealogical Society of Utah, 1962. (FHL# microfilm 0388474-0388510)

Western Australia

Western Australia Supreme Court. *Probate Records 1832-1940.* 50 reels. Salt Lake City: Genealogical Society of Utah, 1975. (See FHLC; call numbers not consecutive.)

Public Records

The heading **/Public Records** can cover many different types of government-generated records. The library has many records about the day-to-day business of the penal colonies, although some are restricted.

Other headings under which similar records are cataloged include **/Court Records, /Officials and Employees,** and **/Politics and Government.**

Voting Registers

Electoral rolls, like directories, are an important census substitute. The Family History Library has Australia's complete 1960 electoral roll (124 volumes), plus these electoral rolls for the following states and time periods in the nineteenth century (check the FHLC for call numbers):

New South Wales 1869-91, 1842-1900

Queensland 1862-1905

Victoria 1856-86 (sporadic)

Western Australia 1870-1900

NEW ZEALAND

Historical Background

1300s	Maoris arrive in New Zealand.
1642	Dutch explorer Abel Tasman is first European known to visit New Zealand.
1770s	Captain James Cook circumnavigates New Zealand.
1792-1841	Sporadic settlement by sealers, whalers, escaped convicts from Australia. New Zealand technically under the jurisdiction of New South Wales.
1814	First English missionaries arrive.
1840	Great Britain takes formal possession of New Zealand; Treaty of Waitangi guarantees rights of Maoris. First organized settlements established.
1841	New Zealand becomes a British colony separate from Australia; administered by the New Zealand Company.
1848	Beginning of non-compulsory civil registration of births and deaths.
1852	New Zealand granted self-government.
1852-76	Struggle between central government and powerful provincial governments.
1850	Beginning of compulsory civil registration of births, marriages, and deaths.
1860-71	Maori Wars.
1864	Capital transferred from Auckland to Wellington.
1865	Native Lands Act establishes Maori Land Courts.
1876	Reorganization of government; provinces become less powerful.
1907	New Zealand granted Dominion status in the British Empire.
1931	New Zealand joins British Commonwealth of Nations.

Settlement and Organization

Maoris arrived in New Zealand from other South Pacific Islands in the fourteenth century and settled the

North Island. By 1642, their settlements had spread to the South Island as well, but the major Maori concentration remained on the North Island.

Sporadic settlement by Europeans, mostly sealers and whalers, commenced in 1792. English missionaries arrived in 1814, but it was not until the British government took formal possession of New Zealand in 1840 that organized settlements were established. A colony of Nonconformists settled at New Plymouth in 1840, and colonies of Scots Presbyterians and Episcopalians settled on the South Island under the auspices of the New Zealand Company.

Most settlers came from the British Isles; but in the twentieth century, immigrants from other European, Asian, and American countries have also arrived.

Provinces based on the original colonies were the most effective form of government until 1876, but they were highly autonomous, giving only nominal deference to the central government. When the central government was strengthened in 1876, the provinces were stripped of most of their powers but remained organizational entities. Provinces are further subdivided into counties, cities, and boroughs, all independent of one another. Additional jurisdictions include districts for public administration of land registration, water supply, education, etc., which do not conform to the province/-county system.

The names of New Zealand's provinces are: Auckland, Canterbury, Hawke's Bay, Marlborough, Nelson, Otago, Southland, Taranaki, Wellington, and Westland.

The FHLC divides New Zealand according to its ten provinces. Records created by or in the various administrative units are then listed in the province in which that administrative unit is located. For example, to access cemetery records for the borough of One Tree Hill, you must know the province in which it is located. These books are helpful:

Wards, Ian, ed. *New Zealand Atlas.* Wellington: A. R. Shearer, Government Printer, 1976. (FHL# 993.1/E6w)

Wise's New Zealand Guide. Dunedin, NZ: H. Wise & Co., Ltd., 1969. (FHL# 993.1/E6g)

If these volumes are not available in your branch libraries, you can determine the provinces in which counties, boroughs, and cities are located by consulting the following list. The other administrative districts must still be located through one of the above references. In addition, some of these counties, cities, and boroughs may now be obsolete, having been combined with others. Nevertheless, if a record was created under its jurisdiction at one time, it may still be listed under that name in the FHLC.

The FHLC also includes the headings **/North Island** and **/South Island** for the two main land masses of New Zealand. General records (collections of cemetery records, for instance) are listed under these headings. The Chatham Islands, technically a county in Canterbury Province, also have a separate listing in the FHLC. Following is a list of the location of counties, cities, and boroughs by Province:

County	**Province**
Akaroa	Canterbury
Akitio	Wellington
Amuri	Canterbury
Ashburton	Canterbury
Ashley	Canterbury
Atwater	Marlborough
Bay of Islands	Auckland
Bruce	Nelson
Buller	Otago
Chatham Islands	Canterbury
Cheviot	Canterbury
Clifton	Taranaki
Clutha	Otago
Cook	Auckland
Coromandel	Auckland
Dannevirke	Hawke's Bay
Egmont	Taranaki
Eketahuna	Wellington
Ellesmere	Canterbury
Eltham	Taranaki
Eyre	Canterbury
Featherston	Wellington
Fiord	Southland
Franklin	Auckland
Golden Bay	Nelson
Great Barrier Islands	Auckland
Grey	Westland
Hauraki Plains	Auckland
Hawere	Auckland
Hawke's Bay	Hawke's Bay
Heathcote	Canterbury
Hobson	Auckland
Hokianga	Auckland
Horowhenua	Wellington
Hurunui	Canterbury
Hutt	Wellington
Inangahua	Nelson
Inglewood	Taranaki
Kaikoura	Marlborough
Kairanga	Wellington
Kiwitea	Wellington
Lake	Otago
Mackenzie	Canterbury
Malvern	Canterbury
Manawatu	Wellington
Mangonui	Auckland
Maniototo	Otago
Mantikau	Auckland
Marlborough	Marlborough
Masterton	Wellington
Matamata	Auckland
Mount Herbert	Canterbury
Ohinemuri	Auckland
Opotiki	Auckland
Oroua	Wellington
Otamatea	Auckland
Otorohanga	Auckland
Oxford	Canterbury
Pahiatua	Wellington
Paparua	Canterbury
Patea	Taranaki
Piako	Auckland
Pohangina	Wellington
Raglan	Auckland
Rangiora	Canterbury
Rangitikei	Wellington
Rodney	Auckland
Rotorua	Auckland
Silverpeaks	Otago
Southland	Southland
Stewart Island	Southland
Stratford	Taranaki
Strathallan	Canterbury

Taieri	Otago
Taranaki	Taranaki
Taumarunui	Auckland
Taupo	Auckland
Tauranga	Auckland
Thames	Auckland
Taupeka	Otago
Vincent	Otago
Waiapu	Auckland
Waiheke Island	Auckland
Waihemo	Otaho
Waikato	Auckland
Waikohu	Auckland
Waikouaiti	Otago
Waimari	Canterbury
Waimarino	Wellington
Waimate	Canterbury
Waimate West	Taranaki
Waimea	Nelson
Waipa	Auckland
Waipara	Canterbury
Waipawa	Hawke's Bay
Waipukurau	Hawke's Bay
Wairarapa South	Wellington
Wairewa	Canterbury
Wairoa	Auckland
Waitaki	Otago
Waitemata	Auckland
Waitomo	Auckland
Waitotara	Wellington
Wallace	Southland
Wanganui	Wellington
Westland	Westland
Whakatane	Auckland
Whangarei	Auckland
Whangaroa	Auckland
Woodville	Hawke's Bay

City	Province
Auckland	Auckland
Birkenhead	Auckland
Christchurch	Canterbury
Dunedin	Otago
East Coast Bays	Auckland
Gisborne	Auckland
Hamilton	Auckland
Hastings	Hawke's Bay
Invercargill	Southland
Lower Hutt	Wellington
Manukau	Auckland
Mount Albert	Auckland
Napier	Hawke's Bay
Nelson	Nelson
New Plymouth	Taranaki
Palmerston N.	Wellington
Papakua	Auckland
Papatoetoe	Auckland
Porirura	Wellington
Takapuna	Auckland
Tauranga	Auckland
Timaru	Canterbury
Upper Hutt	Wellington
Waitemata	Auckland
Wanganui	Wellington
Wellington	Wellington
Whangarei	Auckland

Borough	Province
Alexandria	Otago
Arrowtown	Otago
Ashburton	Canterbury
Balclutha	Otago
Blenheim	Marlborough
Bluff	Southland
Cambridge	Auckland
Carterton	Wellington
Cromwell	Otago
Dannevirke	Hawke's Bay
Dargaville	Auckland
Devonport	Auckland
Eastbourne	Wellington
Eketahuna	Wellington
Ellerslie	Auckland
Eltham	Taranaki
Featherston	Wellington
Feilding	Wellington
Foxton	Wellington
Geraldine	Canterbury
Glen Eden	Auckland
Gore	Southland
Green Island	Otago
Greymouth	Westland
Greytown	Wellington
Havelock North	Hawke's Bay
Hawera	Taranaki
Helensville	Auckland
Henderson	Auckland
Hokitika	Westland
Howick	Auckland
Huntly	Auckland
Inglewood	Taranaki
Kaiapoi	Canterbury
Kaikohe	Auckland
Kaitaia	Auckland
Kaitangata	Otago
Kapiti	Wellington
Kawerau	Auckland
Lawrence	Otago
Levin	Wellington
Lyttleton	Canterbury
Martinborough	Wellington
Marton	Wellington
Masterton	Wellington
Matamata	Auckland
Mataura	Southland
Milton	Otago
Morrisville	Auckland
Mosgiel	Otago
Mount Eden	Auckland
Mount Maunganui	Auckland
Mount Roskill	Auckland
Mount Wellington	Auckland
Murupara	Auckland
Naseby	Otago
New Lynn	Auckland
Newmarket	Auckland
Ngaruawahia	Auckland
Northcote	Auckland
Oamuru	Otago
Ohakune	Wellington
Onehunga	Auckland
One Tree Hill	Auckland
Otahuhu	Auckland
Otaki	Wellington
Paeroa	Auckland
Pahiatua	Wellington
Patea	Taranaki
Petone	Wellington
Picton	Marlborough
Port Columbus	Otago
Pokekohe	Auckland

Putaruru	Auckland
Queenstown	Otago
Raetihi	Wellington
Rangiora	Canterbury
Riccarton	Canterbury
Richmond	Nelson
Riverton	Southland
Roxburgh	Otago
Runanga	Westland
St. Kilda	Otago
Stratford	Taranaki
Taihape	Wellington
Tapanui	Otago
Taumarunui	Auckland
Taupo	Auckland
Tawa	Wellington
Te Aroha	Auckland
Te Awamatu	Auckland
Te Kuiti	Auckland
Temuka	Canterbury
Te Puke	Auckland
Thames	Auckland
Tokora	Auckland
Taukau	Auckland
Waihi	Auckland
Waimate	Canterbury
Waipawa	Hawke's Bay
Waipukurau	Hawke's Bay
Wairoa	Hawke's Bay
Waitara	Taranaki
Waiuku	Auckland
Westport	Nelson
Winton	Southland
Woodville	Hawke's Bay

New Zealand Library Collection

Most of the Family History Library's New Zealand collection consists of two groups of records: Maori Land Court records and cemetery records. One reason for these emphases is the government restrictions placed on public records; another is LDS missionary activities among the Maori population.

In many cases, separate records are kept for Maoris – not because of racial prejudice but because Maori customs of land tenure, inheritance, and marriage differ significantly from European customs.

In the descriptions that follow, specialized records will receive more attention. For more conventional records, you will simply be referred to the FHLC.

Archives and Libraries

The National Archives of New Zealand in Wellington is the repository for most records of historical value created by government entities. The Family History Library has several inventories of the various types of records located at the National Archives. For an introduction to research at the archives, see:

A Guide for Genealogical Searching at National Archives. Wellington: National Archives, 1984. (FHL# 993.1/A3gf)

Of New Zealand's other libraries, two of the most useful to genealogists are the Alexander Turnbull Library in Wellington and the Hocken Library in Dunedin. The Family History Library has a few catalogs and inventories for these libraries, including the periodical *The Turnbull Library Records* (1967-to date), published by the Friends of the Turnbull Library. For a useful overview of archives and libraries in New Zealand, see:

Hansen, Niel T. *Guide to Genealogical Sources: Australia and New Zealand.* Prahran, Australia: Hall's Book Store Printery, Ltd., 1962. (FHL# 994/D27h)

Somewhat dated but a good summary of the records available for New Zealand and how to find them. Neglects Maori records; somewhat stilted writing style.

Biography

Biographical material can be found for a few of New Zealand's provinces at the Family History Library. See other headings under **New Zealand/Genealogy.** Examples of printed and manuscript biographical material are:

The Cyclopedia of New Zealand: Industrial, Descriptive, Historical, Biographical, Facts, Figures, Illustrations. 6 vols. bound in 7. Wellington: Cyclopedia Company, 1897. (FHL# 993.1/D3c or microfilm 0287489-0287493)

Contains many thumbnail sketches of locally prominent people in the late nineteenth century. Each volume represents a different province.

Hinton, Mrs. N., comp. *Hawke's Bay Biographical Index: 1860-1982.* 8 reels. Salt Lake City: Genealogical Society of Utah, 1983. (FHL# microfilm 1363717-1363724)

Represents material taken from a variety of sources, including cemeteries, newspapers, and shipping lists.

Cemeteries

Cemetery records, known in New Zealand as monumental inscriptions, are available for almost every locality in addition to compilations of records on the county, province, and island level. Check the FHLC under **New Zealand/[Province]/[Locality]/Cemeteries.**

Church Records

As with cemetery records, check the FHLC under **New Zealand/[Province]/[Locality]/Church Records.** Original records and abstracts of church records are available, but on a more limited scale than cemetery records.

Civil Registration/Vital Records

The Family History Library does not have any official vital records for New Zealand. Records cataloged under these headings are mostly printed abstracts, with some overlap with church and cemetery records.

Court Records

Maori Land Court records are cataloged under **New Zealand/[Province]/Native Races.** Other court records are mostly printed copies of the originals.

Directories

Some general directories for New Zealand are available. Also see **New Zealand/[Province]/[Locality]/Almanacs or /Directories.**

Emigration and Immigration

The Family History Library has a wealth of material on immigrants to New Zealand in the nineteenth century. A basic overview is:

Spoonley, P., K. A. Carwell-Cooke, and A. D. Trlin. *Immigrants and Immigration: A New Zealand Bibliography.* N.Z.: Department of Sociology, Massey University, 1982. (FHL# 993.1/W23s)

For the period when the New Zealand Company governed New Zealand, see:

Emigration Lists, 1839-1850. 2 reels. Salt Lake City: Genealogical Society of Utah, 1961. (FHL# microfilm 0287437-0287438)

New Zealand Company Embarkation Register, 1839-1850. Salt Lake City: Genealogical Society of Utah, 1961. (FHL# microfilm 0287503)

(New Zealand Company) Embarkation Register: Indexing Cards of the Alexander Turnbull Library. 3 reels. Salt Lake City: Genealogical Society of Utah, 1961. (FHL# microfilm 0287421-0287423)

For immigration records after 1852, check the FHLC under **New Zealand/Emigration and Immigration**; also see the same heading under **[Province]/[Port].** Some examples are:

New Zealand, Department of Immigration. *Emigration to Canterbury: Lyttelton Shipping Lists, 1853-1885.* 3 reels. Salt Lake City: Genealogical Society of Utah, 1973. (FHL# microfilm 1066501-1066503)

_____. *Passenger Lists from British Isles to New Zealand, 1871-1888.* 25 reels. Salt Lake City: Genealogical Society of Utah, 1961. (FHL# microfilm 0287439-0287463)

Passenger Lists from Foreign Ports to Canterbury 1855-1871. 5 reels. Salt Lake City: Genealogical Society of Utah, 1961. (FHL# microfilm 0287464-0287468)

Genealogy

The Family History Library has a number of compiled collections of genealogically relevant material for both Europeans and Maoris. See **New Zealand/[Province]/Genealogy/Maori Land Court Records.** See also **New Zealand/[Province]/Native Races** and **New Zealand/[Province]/[Locality]/Genealogy.**

History

Histories and historical material are available for most provinces. A good general history of New Zealand is:

Oliver, W. H., and B. R. Williams. *The Oxford History of New Zealand.* Wellington: Oxford University Press, 1981. (FHL# 993.1/H2oh)

Land and Property

The Family History Library does not have any of the original records relating to land transactions of Europeans. A few abstracts and printed works may be found under **New Zealand/Land and Property.** For Maori Land Court records, see **New Zealand/[Province]/Native Races.**

Maps

A number of maps and atlases are available. See the FHLC under **New Zealand/[Province]/[Locality]/-Maps.**

Military Records

The Family History Library has mostly printed works relating to New Zealand soldiers in the Maori Wars, the Boer War, and World Wars I and II. Among the original records under this heading are:

British Half Pay Civil Pension List, 1865-1887. Salt Lake City: Genealogical Society of Utah, 1961. (FHL# microfilm 0287477)

British Military and Civil Pension Registers, 1865-1891. 3 reels. Salt Lake City: Genealogical Society of Utah, 1961. (FHL# microfilm 0287474-0287476)

Imperial Pensions Index Book 1845-1887. Salt Lake City: Genealogical Society of Utah, 1961. (FHL# microfilm 0287477)

Native Races

A wealth of material on the history and culture of the Maoris is available at the Family History Library under **/Native Races, /Folklore, /Social Life and Customs, /Language, /Genealogy,** and **/Court Records.**

Perhaps the most important original records relating to the Maoris are the **New Zealand/[Province]/Maori Land Court Records.** Under the Treaty of Waitangi in 1840, the Maoris retained possession of their land and the right to sell it to European settlers. Unfortunately, land ownership was not clearly defined by European terms, and many disputes over ownership arose because one tribe of Maoris sold land claimed by another. In addition, the already warlike Maoris began conquering each other's land to sell it to Europeans. The tensions resulting from conflicting land claims were a contributing cause to the Maori Wars of 1860-71.

Recognizing that settlement of land disputes would help to keep the country at peace, the government passed the Native Lands Act in 1865, which established courts in which various Maoris could present their claims to a particular piece of land. The court considered all land ownership changes after 1840 as invalid.

Land ownership was often based on inheritance, and the Maoris would recite long pedigrees from the original Maori settler to establish proof of ownership. Some of these pedigrees, based on oral tradition, extend back to the fourteenth century.

The land court districts did not conform to the provincial or county systems. Courts were held at different places each year in each district, so the same piece of land could be disputed in different courts at different times. The reference staff at the Family History Library has prepared a guide to the Maori Land Court records, also available on microfilm at branch libraries:

Church of Jesus Christ of Latter-day Saints, Genealogical Society. *Register of New Zealand Maori Land Court Minute Books 1865-1961.* Salt Lake City: Genealogical Society of Utah, 1964. (FHL# 993.1/A6m or microfilm 0599501)

This register uses a Family History Library cataloging number which is now obsolete and must be converted to to the current catalog number before a film can be ordered through the branch library.

The land court records are in both English and Maori. A useful, if somewhat technical study of the Maori Land Court system is:

Smith, Norman. *Maori Land Law.* Wellington: A. H. and A.W. Reed, 1960. (FHL# 993.1/R2s)

The library also has compiled Maori genealogies (often based on land court records) and taped oral genealogies.

Newspapers and Obituaries

The Family History Library has a few original newspapers on microfilm, but most records under these headings are printed abstracts. To see what papers are available for a given locality and time period, consult the work below, then check the FHLC:

Harvey, D. R. *Union List of New Zealand Newspapers before 1940 Preserved in Libraries, Newspaper Offices, Local Authority Offices and Museums in New Zealand.* Wellington: National Library of New Zealand, 1985. (FHL# 993.1/B33h)

Periodicals

See, for example:

The New Zealand Genealogist. Auckland: The New Zealand Society of Genealogists, 1970-to date. (FHL# 993.1/B2na)

The New Zealand Journal of History. Auckland: University of Auckland, 1967-to date. (FHL# 993.1/B2new)

Probate Records

All probate records of Europeans fall under the jurisdiction of the Supreme Court of New Zealand, which has Registries in the following cities and boroughs: Auckland, Blenheim, Christchurch, Dunedin, Gisborne, Greymouth, Hamilton, Invercargill, Masterton, Napier, New Plymouth, Palmerston North, Timaru, Wanganui, Wellington, Westport, and Whangarei.

The Family History Library has probate records for the following Registries and years; they are listed by province below:

Auckland

Auckland, 1842-1900 (FHL# 0799727-0799742, 0774563-0774580)

Gisborne, 1879-1900 (FHL# 0794271-0794272)

Canterbury

Christchurch, 1855-1900 (FHL# 0797828-0797846)

Timaru, 1898-1900 (FHL# 0797089)

Hawke's Bay

Napier, 1862-1900 (FHL# 0794636-0794651)

Marlborough

Blenheim, 1875-1908 (FHL# 0797547-0797550)

Nelson

Westport, 1856-1906 (FHL# 0793361-0793374)

Otago

Dunedin, 1851-1907 (FHL# 0797847-0797855, 0798412-0798429, 0796471-0796486)

Southland

Invercargill, 1863-1904 (FHL# 0794998-0795000, 0797106-0797119)

Wellington

Wellington, 1842-1900 (FHL# 0794526-0794561, 0794652-0794670)

Westland

Greymouth, 1868-1901 (FHL# 0797070-0797072)

These records are cataloged in the FHLC, under **New Zealand/[Province]/[City or Borough]/Probate Records.** Because the jurisdiction of the probate Registry offices did not conform to province boundaries, you should also check neighboring provinces. Indexes or registers are available for all of the probate Registries listed above except Gisborne. A useful, if technical explanation of the probate system is:

Grace, G. J. *Dobbie's Probate and Administration Practice.* Wellington: Butterworths, 1966. (FHL# 993.1/S2y)

Maori estates are probated or administered under the Maori Land Court.

Public Records

A variety of records can be found cataloged under **New Zealand/Public Records, /Officials and Employees,** and **/Politics and Government** and the same headings at the provincial level as well. Some of these records consist of official correspondence or relate to the day-to-day running of the government.

Voting Registers

Although all of New Zealand's censuses from the nineteenth century to the present have been destroyed as a matter of public policy, electoral rolls survive and are available at the Family History Library. While the electoral rolls do not give as much detail as the census, they will at least locate a person in place and time and give name, address, and occupation.

Electoral rolls are available from 1865 to 1957. The reference staff at the Family History Library has prepared a register of the available rolls; it is on microfilm and circulates to branch libraries:

Church of Jesus Christ of Latter-day Saints, Genealogical Society. *New Zealand Electoral Rolls Register.* Salt Lake City: Genealogical Society of Utah, 1966. (FHL# 993.1/X3n or microfilm 0599501)

This register uses a cataloguing number which is now obsolete and must be converted to the current system before a film can be ordered through the branch center library.

Besides the electoral rolls kept at the national level, some electoral rolls can be found at the provincial level for both the period prior to 1865 when national registration began; after 1865, provincial records usually duplicate the records kept at the national level. Check the FHLC under **New Zealand/[Province]/Voting Registers.**

SOUTH PACIFIC ISLANDS

The Family History Library's collections for the island nations and dependencies in the South Pacific vary widely. All of the islands have been under the control of a foreign colonial power at one time, and many still are. Thus, their record-keeping systems have been influenced by the colonial power. This list of South Pacific islands summarizes the foreign powers which have controlled or presently control them:

American Samoa	U.S. since 1899
Caroline Islands	Germany 1885-1919, Japan 1919-47, U.S. since 1947
Christmas Islands	Great Britain to 1958, Australia since 1958
Cocos (Keeling)	Australia since 1984
Cook Islands	New Zealand to 1965, self government since 1965
Easter Island	Chile
Fiji	Great Britain to 1970, independent since 1970
French Polynesia	Overseas Territory of France
Guam	Spain 1521-1898, U.S. since 1898
Kiribati (Gilbert)	Great Britain to 1979, independent since 1979
Loyalty Islands	Dependency of New Caledonia (French)
Mariana Islands	Spain 1521-1899, Germany 1899-1919, Japan 1919-47, U.S. since 1947
Nauru	Germany 1886-1918, Australia (Trust) 1918-68, independent since 1968
New Caledonia	Overseas Territory of France.
Niue	New Zealand
Papua-New Guinea	South: Great Britain 1884-1905, North: Germany 1884-1918, Australia (Trust) 1905/1918-75, independent since 1975
Pitcairn Island	Great Britain (Bounty mutineers settled here 1790)
Solomon Islands	Great Britain 1890s-1978, independent since 1978
Tokelau	New Zealand
Tonga	Great Britain 1900-70, independent since 1970
Tuvalu (Ellice)	Great Britain 1900-78, independent since 1978
Vanuatu (New Hebrides)	Anglo-French 1906-80, independent since 1980
Wallis and Futuna	Overseas Territory of France
Western Samoa	Germany 1899-1911, New Zealand (Trust) 1919-62, independent since 1962

In addition to the nations and dependencies on this list, the FHLC also catalogs some general sources under the headings **Melanesia, Micronesia, Oceania,** and **Polynesia**, regional geographical terms for large groups of islands.

Because of LDS missionary efforts, every island or island group has some sources in the Family History Library. Many of the Fiji and Papua-New Guinea civil registration records, patterned after the British and Australian systems, have been microfilmed. Oral genealogies have been taped or written down for many islands, particularly Tonga and Samoa. A wealth of material, much of it on local culture, is cataloged under **[Nation]/Native Races/Ethnology, /Folklore,** and **/Social Life and Customs.**

A typical South Pacific source is:

Cole, William A., and Elwin W. Jensen, comps. *The Cole-Jensen Collection: Oral Genealogies and Genealogical Information Collected from the Polynesian Peoples and from the Pacific Islands.* 9 reels. Salt Lake City: Genealogical Society of Utah, 1984. (FHL# microfilm 1358001-1358009)

Records by Jurisdiction **Australia** States	Archives & Libraries	Bibliography	Biography	Business Records	Cemetery	Census	Church History	Civil Registration	Correctional	Court	Description & Travel	Directories	Emigration/Immigration	Gazetteers	Genealogy	History	Land & Property	Language	Maps	Migration	Military	Native Races	Naturalization	Newspapers	Obituaries	Occupations	Periodicals	Probate	Public Records	Schools	Social Life	Taxation	Vital Records	Voting Registers
Australia General	•	•	•	•	•	•	•	•	•	•	•	•	•	•	•	•	•		•	•	•	•	•	•	•	•	•	•	•	•	•	•	•	•
Capital Territory	•				•										•	•			•								•							
New South Wales	•		•	•	•	•	•	•	•	•	•	•	•	•	•	•	•		•			•	•	•		•		•	•	•	•		•	•
Northern Territory					•	•				•						•			•												•			
Queensland	•			•	•			•	•		•	•	•	•	•	•	•		•			•	•	•	•	•		•	•	•		•	•	•
South Australia	•		•	•	•	•	•			•	•	•	•		•	•	•		•				•	•	•			•	•	•	•	•	•	
Tasmania	•		•	•	•	•	•	•	•	•		•	•	•	•	•	•		•			•	•	•		•	•	•	•			•	•	•
Victoria	•	•	•	•	•	•	•					•	•	•	•	•	•		•				•		•	•	•	•	•	•		•	•	•
Western Australia	•	•	•		•	•	•		•			•	•	•	•	•	•		•				•			•		•	•			•	•	•
Norfolk Island					•						•		•			•	•		•									•	•					

Records by Jurisdiction **New Zealand** Islands	Archives & Libraries	Bibliography	Biography	Business	Cemeteries	Census	Church History	Church Records	Civil Registration	Court Records	Description & Travel	Directories	Emigration/Immigration	Folklore	Gazetteers	Genealogy	History	Land & Property	Language	Maps	Military History	Military Records	Native Races	Newspapers	Obituaries	Pensions	Periodicals	Probate Records	Schools	Social Life	Taxation	Vital Records	Voting Registers
New Zealand	•	•	•	•	•	•	•	•	•	•	•	•	•	•	•	•	•	•	•	•	•	•	•	•	•	•	•	•	•	•	•	•	•
North Island																•	•	•		•			•									•	
Auckland	•	•	•		•		•	•	•	•	•	•	•	•	•	•	•	•		•			•	•			•	•	•	•		•	•
Hawke's Bay					•			•	•	•		•	•			•	•	•					•	•				•		•			•
Taranaki					•			•					•			•	•	•				•	•					•	•			•	•
Wellington	•				•				•		•		•				•			•	•	•	•	•	•			•	•	•			•
South Island			•		•			•								•	•	•		•												•	
Canterbury			•		•			•			•	•	•			•	•	•		•								•	•	•		•	•
Marlborough					•					•			•			•	•											•					
Nelson				•	•					•	•		•			•	•			•			•	•				•	•			•	•
Otago			•	•	•		•					•	•				•	•		•								•					•
Southland			•				•			•							•											•	•				
Westland			•							•							•															•	
Chatham Islands																		•												•		•	

Records by Jurisdiction

South Pacific Islands

Islands	Biography	Census	Church Records	Description & Travel	Directories	Emigration & Immigration	Gazetteers	Genealogy	History	Land & Property	Maps	Native Races	Newspapers	Public Records	Vital Records
American Samoa			•		•		•	•	•			•			•
Caroline Islands							•	•	•	•					
Christmas Islands							•								
Cocos Islands							•				•				
Cook Islands			•	•			•	•	•	•	•	•			
Easter Islands				•				•	•			•			
Fiji			•	•	•	•	•	•	•	•	•	•		•	•
French Polynesia			•	•				•	•	•	•	•	•	•	•
Guam									•			•	•		
Kiribati							•	•	•			•			
Loyalty Islands									•						
Mariana Islands							•			•		•			
Marshall Islands							•								
Melanesia Islands			•	•				•	•		•	•			
Micronesia			•	•			•	•	•	•	•			•	
Nauru				•			•								
New Caledonia	•			•		•						•			
Niue		•							•		•	•			
Oceania			•	•		•	•	•	•	•	•	•			
Papua-New Guinea	•	•	•	•	•	•	•	•	•	•	•	•	•	•	•
Pitcairn Island			•	•			•		•						•
Polynesia			•	•		•	•	•	•	•	•	•			
Solomon Island						•	•	•	•			•			
Tokelau				•			•		•			•			
Tonga			•	•	•		•	•	•	•	•	•			
Tuvalu				•				•	•			•			•
Vanuatu			•		•	•	•	•	•	•					•
Wallist Futuna								•				•			
Western Samoa			•		•			•	•			•			•

Chapter 26

The Caribbean Islands

Johni Cerny

BERMUDA

The Bermuda Islands are named after a Spanish sea captain named Juan Bermudez who discovered them in 1515. The English named them the Somers Islands in honor of British Admiral Sir George Somers who put into Bermuda in 1609 en route to Virginia when his ship, the *Sea Venture,* was damaged in a hurricane while carrying settlers to Virginia.

Somers built two small vessels on the island and stocked them with pigeons, turtles, live pigs, and dried fish. He landed his passengers and provisions at Jamestown, Virginia, in 1610.

The history of the Bermuda Islands is linked closely with that of the United States. Once the Virginia Company in England heard glowing reports about the island, it amended its charter to include the islands, renaming them Virginiola. The first group of settlers sent to colonize the islands left England in 1612.

Three years later the new colony at Virginiola was sold to the "Governor and Company of the City of London for the Plantacion of the Somer [*sic*] Islands." Daniel Tucker, a Virginia colonist, served as the governor of the new colony.

Once the transition was accomplished, the colony was surveyed and divided into eight tribes (parishes or counties). Each tribe was laid out in plots for leasing to settlers who were required to buy supplies from and sell their produce to the new company.

After the land was divided, the new company discovered that there was less land than they had planned on, and Order No. 212 in the Laws of the Bermuda Company dated 1622 provided for maintaining a large piece of land in Virginia which was made over to the Bermuda Company by the Virginia Company. The land, in Chesterfield County, Virginia, is still known as the Bermuda Hundred.

Self-government in the islands began 1 August 1620 when the second British colonial legislature met in the parish church of St. Georges, Bermuda, under an ordinance of the Bermuda Company.

Bermuda Colony land was leased and later granted to early settlers. Grievances against the Bermuda Company were heard by the crown between 1670 and 27 November 1684 when the company's charter was revoked.

Attempts to create an agricultural economy in Bermuda failed, but ship building became a valuable industry there. Salt ponds for evaporating salt from sea water by the heat of the sun produced salt for trade with England and other European countries. In Newfoundland and Nova Scotia, the Bermudians exchanged salt for salt fish to be traded in the West Indies for sugar and rum which were then bartered for barrels of salt beef and pork in the American colonies or for clothing and hardware in England.

Though sympathetic to the principles of the American protest at the onset of the revolution, the islands remained loyal to the crown. When Britain prohibited trade with the American colonies, Bermuda was hard pressed because its people lived on provisions from the American colonies. Some Bermudians chose to transfer large amounts of gun powder to the colonies in exchange for trade allowances at American ports.

Shipping played an important role in Bermuda's history, especially in relationship to the United States and its wars. The islands served as a second center for Civil War blockade runners. Cotton selling for four cents in the south was bringing sixty cents a pound in England.

Eventually, shipping lost its place at the forefront of the islands' economy and Bermudians were forced to turn to agriculture during the nineteenth century and then to tourism during the twentieth century.

Bermuda Library Collection

Bermuda records and publications are cataloged and shelved in the Latin America book and film area of the Family History Library.

Archives and Libraries

Rowe, Helen. *A Guide to the Records of Bermuda.* Hamilton: Bermuda Archives, 1980. (FHL# 972.8/A2g)

Church History

Smith, T. Watson. *History of the Methodist Church Within the Territories Embraced in the Late Conference of Eastern British America.* 1877; rpt. ed., Salt Lake City: Genealogical Society of Utah, 1971. (FHL# microfilm 0856140)

Church Records

Church of England. Parish Church of St. Euestatius (Netherlands Antilles). *Parish Register Transcripts, 1773-1778, Including St. George Marriages.* N.p.: n.pub., n.d. (FHL# 972.977/A1/no.1 or microfiche 6030542)

Nester, Ruth A. *Records of Bermuda: St. Ann Church, Southampton Parish: Burials, 1858-1958 and Christenings, 1912-1930, St. Mark Church: Burials, 1845-1907.* Spokane, Wash.: The author, 1959. (FHL# 972.99/V2r)

_____. *Register of Baptisms, Marriages, and Burials, St. George's Parish, 1755-1802, and Old Devonshire Church.* Typescript, n.d. (FHL# 972.99/V2reg)

Gazetteers

United States Board on Geographic Names. *British West Indies and Bermuda: Official Standard Names Approved by the U.S. Board on Geographic Names.* Washington, D.C.: U.S. Office of Geography, 1955. (FHL# 972.9/E5us or microfilm 0873794)

Genealogy

Mercer, Julia E. *Bermuda Settlers of the 17th Century: Genealogical Notes from Bermuda.* Baltimore, Md.: Genealogical Publishing Company, 1982. (FHL# 972.99/D2mj)

History

Kennedy, Jean de Chantal. *Biography of a Colonial Town: Hamilton, Bermuda, 1790-1897.* Hamilton, Bermuda: Bermuda Book Stores, 1963. (FHL# 972.99/D3k)

Lefroy, John Henry, Sir. *Memorials of the Discovery and Early Settlement of the Bermudas or Somers Islands, 1515-1685.* 2 vols. London: Longmans, Green, 1877-79. (FHL# 972.99/H2l)

Murray, Hugh. *An Historical and Descriptive Account of British America: Comprehending Canada Upper and Lower, Nova Scotia, New Brunswick, Newfoundland, Prince Edward Island, the Bermudas, and the Fur Countries.* 3 vols. Edinburgh: Oliver and Boyd, 1839. (FHL# 971/H2mu or microfilm 0982219, items 1-3)

Smith, John. *The General Historie of Virgina, New England and the Summer Isles.* 2 vols. New York: Macmillan, 1907. (FHL# 970/H2s)

Wilkinson, Henry C. *Bermuda in the Old Empire War: 1684-1784: A History of the Island from the Dissolution of the Somers Island Company until the End of the American Revolutionary War.* London: Oxford University, 1973. (FHL# 972.99/H2wi or microfilm 1102984, item 1)

Maps

Wells, Edward. *A New Map of the Most Considerable Plantations of the English in America.* London: T. W., 1738. (FHL# 970/E7w) Photocopy of original map.

Periodicals

The Bermuda Historical Quarterly. Hamilton: The Quarterly, Vols. 1-38, 1944-82. (FHL# 929.99/B3b)

BARBADOS

Barbados, claimed by English sailors in 1624 in the name of King James I, was the third West Indian Island to be settled by English colonists during the first half of the seventeenth century. (Bermuda was established in 1612 and St. Kitts in 1623.) King James granted the island to James Ley, who became first Earl of Marlborough. Ley sponsored a colonizing venture by Sir William Courteen which resulted in the settlement of Hole Town in 1627.

According to English businessmen, Barbados was perfect for growing sugarcane except for the lack of a sizeable labor force. They resolved the labor problem by importing slaves, as they did on the other islands. They divided the island into large estates and then populated each estate with an adequate slave labor force.

By 1640 Barbados had a population of 30,000, of which less than one percent were slaves. However, by 1645, nearly twenty percent of the population was slaves, and the white population had increased by only a few hundred. In 1685, over 45,000 slaves lived on the island.

The white population began to decrease after 1685 and stood at 12,000 in 1700. Many white families went to Virginia where they established plantations, which also used slave labor. Other white families returned to England or immigrated to South America and Australia.

Barbados Library Collection

Barbados records and publications are cataloged and shelved in the Latin America book and film area of the Family History Library.

Bibliography

Chandler, M. J. *A Guide to Records in Barbados.* Oxford, England: Blackwell, 1965. (FHL# 972.981/A3ch)

Handler, Jerome S. *A Guide to Source Materials for the Study of Barbados History.* Carbondale: Southern Illinois University Press, 1971. (FHL# 972.981/H23h)

Census Records

Barbados census records in the library collection are a hodge-podge of enumerations taken from a number of printed sources, including:

Kent, David L. *Barbados and America.* Arlington, Va.: C. M. Kent, 19[illegible]. (FHL# 972.981/[illegible]) Principally a transcription of documents in the Public Records Office, London, which includes census returns for 1680 and 1715.

Governor of Barbados. *The Dispatches of Governor, Sir Jonathan Atkins, Relating to the Population of the Island of Barbados,* A.D. 1679-1680. Salt Lake City: Genealogical Society of Utah, 1979. (FHL# microfilm 1162149, item 9) Contains the names of landowners, with the number of acres owned, number of white servants and black slaves owned by each.

Brandow, James C., ed. *Omitted Chapters from Hotten's Original Lists of Persons of Quality and Others Who Went from Great Britain to the American Plantations, 1600-1700.* Baltimore, Md.: Genealogical Publishing Co., 1982. (FHL# 972.981/X2oc) Supplement to John Camden Hotten's 1880 publication.

Hotten, John Camden. *The Original Lists of Persons of Quality and Others Who Went from Great Britain to the American Plantations, 1600-1700.* New York: n.p., 1880, rpt. Baltimore, Md.: Genealogical Publishing Company, 1968. (FHL# 973/W2h, 1968) Supplement includes census returns, parish registers, and militia rolls from the Barbados census of 1679 and 1680.

Governor of Barbados. *A Census of the Island of Barbados, West Indies [1715].* Salt Lake City: Genealogical Society of Utah, 1979. (FHL# microfilm 1162149, item 2-1162150) Originals in the Department of Archives, Blackrock, Barbados. The 1715 census was taken by church wardens of the parishes under the direction of Governor Robert Lowther.

Church Records

Barbados Registration Office. *Parochial Registers, 1849-1900.* 106 reels. Salt Lake City: Genealogical Society of Utah, 1978. See Family History Library Catalog (FHLC) under **Barbados/Church Records** for film numbers. Filmed from transcripts in the Department of Archives, Blackrock, Barbados. Series B consists of copies of Anglican parochial registers, 1849-85. After 1885, it consists of registers of all denominations. Registers list baptisms, marriages, and burials.

Barbados Registration Office. *Parochial Registers, 1660-1887.* Salt Lake City: Genealogical Society of Utah, 1978. (FHL# microfilm 1159600-1159603) Microfilm of civil transcripts of church records at the Department of Archives, Blackrock, Barbados. Civil transcripts of baptisms, marriages, and burials recorded by Wesleyan, Catholic, Moravian, Jewish, and other non-Anglican congregations. Includes indexes.

Sanders, Joanne McRee, ed. *Barbados Records, Baptisms 1643-1800.* Baltimore, Md.: Genealogical Publishing Co., 1984. (FHL# 972.981/K29s)

———. *Barbados Records, Marriages 1643-1800.* Houston, Tex.: Sanders Historical Publications, 1982. (FHL# 972.981/K29sj)

Gazetteers

United States Board on Geographic Names. *British West Indies and Bermuda: Official Standard Names Approved by the U.S. Board on Geographic Names.* Washington, D.C.: U.S. Office of Geography, 1955. (FHL# 972.9/E5us)

Genealogy

Brandow, James C. *Genealogies of Barbados Families, 1650-1652.* Georgetown, British Guiana: Argosy Press, 1877. (FHL# 972.981/D29g)

History

The library has ten histories of Barbados. See **Barbados/History** for others not cited below.

Schomburgh, Robert Herman. *The History of Barbados.* 1848; rpt. ed., New York: A. M. Kelley, 1971. (FHL# 972.981/H2s)

Maps

Wells, Edward. *A New Map of the Most Considerable Plantations of the English in America.* London: T. W., 1738. Photocopy of original map. (FHL# 970/E7w)

See FHLC under **Barbados/Maps** for additional holdings.

Probate Records

Sanders, Joanne McRee, ed. *Barbados Records, Wills and Administrations.* 3 vols. Houston, Tex.: Sanders Historical Publications, 1979-81. Volume 1, 1639-80, Volume 2, 1681-1700, Volume 3, 1701-25. (FHL# 972.981/P2s)

BAHAMAS

Today the Bahamas consist of an archipelago of nearly 700 islands and 2,000 cays (islets) scattered over 760 miles of the Atlantic Ocean southeast of the United States. According to tradition, Christopher Columbus discovered San Salvador (Watling Island) in 1492, but Spain made no use of the Bahamas except to enslave and deport the Arawak inhabitants.

In 1647, the Eleutherian Adventurers' Company arrived and colonized the islands for England. The first group of settlers included only a few people from England and others from the Bermudas. They settled among pirate crews who planned Caribbean shipping raids from the islands.

King Charles II of England granted the Bahamas to six of the lords proprietors of Carolina in 1670; however, the governors they appointed were unable to control the pirates and settlements were unsuccessful. Ten years later, in 1680, the Spanish began a series of attacks upon New Providence. They combined forces with the French in 1703 and nearly conquered the English settlement in the Bahamas.

The English crown took control of the islands in 1729 and made them peaceful and law-abiding settlements. England surrendered the Bahamas to Spain in 1782 during the American Revolution, but the Treaty of Versailles returned the islands to Britain in 1783 in exchange for eastern Florida. Nearly 3,000 American loyalists who had fled to Florida during the war immigrated to the Bahamas with their slaves.

The Bahamas played an important role in the blockade-running trade during the American Civil War. Shipments from England to Confederate ports went through the Bahamas, enabling the islands to prosper. The same arrangement brought additional prosperity during Prohibition (1920-33) when rum-runners established their headquarters in the Bahamas.

England continued to rule the Bahamas until 10 July 1973 when Prince Charles, representing Queen Elizabeth II, ended 300 years of colonial rule. The Bahamas became the Commonwealth's thirty-third independent member.

Bahamas Library Collection

Bahamanian records and publications are cataloged and shelved in the Latin America book and film area of the Family History Library.

Archives and Libraries

Saunders, D. Gail, and E. A. Carson. *Guide to the Records of the Bahamas.* Nassau: Government Printing Department, Commonweah of the Bahamas, 1983. (FHL# 972.96/A5s)

Business Records and Commerce

Saunders, D. Gail, and E. A. Carson. *Trading and Other Company Records, 1861-1953, of the Bahama Islands.* New Providence, Nassau: Dakota Southern Microfilm Service, Inc. 1956. (FHL# microfilm 223455-223462) Microfilmed from original holograph.

Colonization

Riley, Sandra. *Homeward Bound.* Miami: Island Research, 1983. (FHL# 972.96/H2rs) A history of the Bahama Islands to 1850.

Court Records

Bahamas Registrar General. *Indentures (New Series), 1954-1960.* 173 reels. New Providence, Nassau: Dakota Southern Microfilm Service, Inc., 1956-60. (FHL# 223485-223657) See FHLC under **Bahamas/Court Records** for date and volume number on each film reel.

_____. *Dowers, 1791-1917.* New Providence, Nassau: Dakota Southern Microfilm Service, Inc., 1956. (FHL# microfilm 223463-223466) Microfilmed from original manuscripts in the Bahama Islands.

_____. *Mortgages, Bonds, Bills of Sale, Deeds of Gift, Power of Attorney, 1764-1882.* New Providence, Nassau: Dakota Southern Microfilm Service, Inc., 1955-56. (FHL# 223445-223454) Microfilmed from original manuscripts in the Bahama Islands.

_____. *Chancery Records, 1800-1859.* New Providence, Nassau: Dakota Southern Microfilm Service, Inc., 1956. (FHL# microfilm 223467-223468)

Emigration and Immigration

Bethel, A. Talbot. *The Early Settlers of the Bahama Islands.* Norfolk: Rounce and Wortley, n.d. (FHL# 972.96/H2e) Includes a brief account of the American Revolution and historical facts taken from the Bahamas archives.

History

Riley, Sandra. *Homeward Bound.* Miami: Island Research, 1983. (FHL# 972.96/H2rs) A history of the Bahama Islands to 1850.

Land and Property

Bahamas Registrar General. *Deeds, 1788-1955.* 298 reels. New Providence, Nassau: Dakota Southern Microfilm Service, Inc., 1956. (FHL# microfilm 223157-223444) See **Bahamas/Land and Property** for year and volumes included in each reel.

_____. *Deeds of Conveyance, Mortgages, Leases, Bonds, Bills of Sale, Assignments, Power of Attorney, 1860-1956.* New Providence, Nassau: Dakota Southern Microfilm Service, Inc., 1956. (FHL# microfilm 223474-223484)

_____. *Leases, 1846-1860.* New Providence, Nassau: Dakota Microfilm Service, Inc., 1956. Microfilmed from original manuscripts in the Bahama Islands. (FHL# microfilm 223474)

_____. *Mortgages, Bonds, Bills of Sale, Deeds of Gift, Power of Attorney, 1764-1882.* New Providence, Nassau: Dakota Southern Microfilm Service, Inc., 1955-56. (FHL# microfilm 223445-223545)

Probate Records

Bahamas Registrar General. *Indentures (New Series), 1954-1960.* New Providence, Nassau: Dakota Southern Microfilm Service, Inc., 1956-60. (FHL# microfilm 223485-223498) Includes wills.

Vital Records

Bahamas Registrar General. *Birth, Marriage, and Death Registers, 1850-1960.* New Providence, Nassau: Dakota Southern Microfilm Service, Inc., 1959-60. (FHL# microfilm 222931-223062) Microfilmed from original records of the Bahama Islands.

PUERTO RICO

Christopher Columbus discovered Puerto Rico when he landed on the island's west coast 19 November 1493. Columbus named the island San Juan Bautista (St. John the Baptist), and its capital city was established at Puerto Rico (Rich Port). The capital was renamed San Juan after 1521 and the island became Puerto Rico.

Spanish colonization of the island began in 1508, when Juan Ponce de Leon, a member of Columbus's crew and discoverer of Florida, took possession of the island and conquered the 30,000 Taino Indians living there with a force of fifty men. Before the end of the sixteenth century, few Indians lived on the coastal plains; but large numbers thrived in the mountains where they ultimately intermarried with the Spanish and were assimilated into the larger society.

Sugarcane came to Puerto Rico from Hispaniola in 1515; and three years later, African slaves were imported to supplement the Indian labor force. Puerto Rican colonists also grew smaller quantities of cotton, ginger, cacao, and indigo. Tobacco was introduced as a commercial crop around 1615 and coffee a century later.

Puerto Rico was attacked by the British in 1595 and again in 1598 when George Clifford, third Earl of Cumberland, captured San Juan for a few months. The island remained peaceful until 1625 when the Dutch tried unsuccessfully to take it but managed only to burn San Juan. The English tried to capture the island in 1797 but also failed.

The first Puerto Rican census in 1765 lists a population of 45,000 - 5,000 of them slaves. The Spanish ruled Puerto Rico much as it did Mexico and restricted foreign trade until 1804. The first newspaper on the island, *La Gaceta*, was founded in 1807.

Latin Americans were plagued by revolution after revolution during the early 1800s, and people began to escape unrest there by migrating to Puerto Rico. By 1832, the island boasted 330,000 inhabitants.

Puerto Rico achieved provincial status in 1869, after several minor attempts at revolution between 1835 and 1868. Slavery was abolished in 1873, and Puerto Rico became an autonomous government in 1897, a few months before the Spanish-American War began 21 April 1898. At the war's end, the island was ceded to the United States under the terms of the Treaty of Paris signed 10 December 1898. Between 1899 and 1940, the island's population rose from 953,000 to 1,869,000.

Puerto Rico Library Collection

Puerto Rican records and publications are cataloged and shelved in the Latin America book and film area of the Family History Library.

Archives and Libraries

Gomez-Canedo, Lino. *Los Archivos Historicos de Puerto Rico* (The Historical Archives of Puerto Rico). San Juan de Puerto Rico: Archivo General de Puerto Rico, 1964. (FHL# 972.95/A3gc)

Biography

The library's Puerto Rico collection includes several biographical titles. See **Puerto Rico/Biography** for a complete list. This heading includes no English works.

Rosa-Nieves, Cesareo, and Esther M. Melon. *Puertorican Biographies.* Sharon, Conn.: Troutman Press, c.1970. (FHL# 920.0795/R71b)

Census Records

United States Bureau of the Census. *Report on the Census of Puerto Rico, 1899.* Washington, D.C.: Government Printing Office, 1900. (FHL# 972.95/X2p/1899)

Emigration and Immigration

Cifre de Loubriel, Estela. *La Immigracion a Puerto Rico durante el Siglo XIX* (Immigration to Puerto Rico During the Nineteenth Century). San Juan de Puerto Rico: Instituto de Cultura Puertoriqueno, 1964. (FHL# 972.95/W2ci or microfilm 924457, item 1)

Galinez Suarez, Jesus. *Puerto Rico en Nueva York* (Puerto Ricans in New York). Buenos Aires, Argentina: Editorial Tiempo Contempraneo, 1968. (FHL# 974.71/F2g)

Gazetteers

Arana-Soto, S. *Diccionario Geografico de Puerto Rico* (Geographical Dictionary of Puerto Rico). San Jose: n.pub., 1978. (FHL# 972.95/E26a)

Genealogy

The three titles cataloged under this heading deal with specific families. See **Puerto Rico/Genealogy.**

History

Alegria, Ricardo E. *Discovery, Conquest, and Colonization of Puerto Rico, 1493-1599.* San Juan de Puerto Rico: Coleccion de Estudios Puertoriquenos, 1971. (FHL# 972.95/W7a) In English.

Gomez, Juan Gualberto, and Antonio Sendras Burin. *Bosquejo de la Historia de Puerto Rico, 1493-1891* (Outline of the History of Puerto Rico, 1493-1891). N.p.: n.pub., c.1900. (FHL# 972.95/H2g)

Van Milleldyk, Rudolph Adams. *The History of Puerto Rico from the Spanish Discovery to the American Occupation.* New York: Arno Press, 1975. (FHL# 972.95/H2v)

See FHLC under **Puerto Rico/History** for complete list of titles on this subject.

Naturalization and Citizenship

Cifre de Loubriel, Estela. *Catalogo de Extranjeros Residentes en Puerto Rico en el Siglo XIX* (Catalog of Resident Foreigners in Puerto Rico in the Nineteenth Century). Rio Piedras, P.R.: Ediciones de la Universidad de Puerto Rico, 1962. (FHL# 972.95/W2c)

Slavery and Bondage

Secretaria del Gobierno Superior Civil de Puerto Rico. *Registro Central de Esclavos, 1872* (Slave Schedules of Puerto Rico, 1872). Washington, D.C.: National Archives and Records Services, 1969. (FHL# microfilm 475649-475656)

DOMINICAN REPUBLIC

When Christopher Columbus landed at Hispaniola in 1492 during his maiden voyage, the Caribs, a nomadic tribe with South American origins after whom the Caribbean Sea is named, and the peaceful Tainos Indians inhabited the island.

Columbus left a few sailors to establish a settlement on the north coast, but the Indians killed them. Upon his return, Columbus established another colony farther south, Santo Domingo, where gold was reported.

Hispaniola, as the Dominican Republic was known then, was the first fully Spanish settlement in the New World. It is the site of the oldest cathedral, monastery, university, and hospital in the Americas. The Spanish established class and caste orders and developed a slave-based economy that exploited the native populations.

Hispaniola flourished while it met Spain's demand for gold and silver, but eventually it was eclipsed by the more spectacular colonies in Mexico and Peru. By 1550, the island was virtually abandoned.

Three centuries later, the French claimed the western third of the island and a new slave-based economy developed through the production of sugar cane in an area that would later become the independent nation of Haiti.

Spain ceded the eastern two-thirds of Hispaniola to France in 1795 as a result of the French Revolutionary War. Encouraged by the French Revolution, slaves revolted against the existing inhumane conditions on the island. They overthrew French rule and also the remaining Spanish contingency in the east. Their freedom was short-lived, since the British intervened in 1809 and reunited the colony with Spain.

In 1821, the Dominican Republic declared its independence and formed a republic consisting of the eastern two-thirds of the island.

A few weeks later, Haitians took over the entire island. Jean Pierre Boyer governed as president and, though viewed as cruel and barbarous, freed the slaves. The island's history is a succession of Haitian and Dominican Republic dictators. The United States assumed control of the Dominican Republic, 1916-24. Since then, it has come under the rule of several dictators, including Vasquez and Trujillio.

Dominican Republic Library Collection

Dominican Republic records and publications are cataloged and shelved in the Latin America book and film area of the Family History Library.

Biography

Garcia, Jose Gabriel. *Rasgos Biograficos de Dominicano Celebres* (Biographical Sketches of Famous Dominicans). Santo Domingo, R.D.: Editor de Caribe, D. por A. 1971. (FHL# 972.93/D3g)

Martinez, Rufino. *Biografico Historico Dominicano 1821-1930* (Dominican Biographical History, 1821-1930). Santo Domingo, R.D.: Universidad Autonoma de Santo Domingo, 1971. (FHL# 972.93/D3m)

Church Records

The library has a large collection of Dominican Republic church records; however, they are cataloged under a town, district, or city heading. For example: If the Guerra Catholic Church records are the subject of interest, see the FHLC under **Dominican Republic/Distrito Nacional, Guerra** for a list of the records included in the collection.

Civil Registration

The library has a large collection of Dominican Republic civil registration records; however, they are cataloged under a town, district, or city heading. For example: If the La Vega civil registration records are the subject of interest, see the FHLC under **Dominican Republic/La Vega, La Vega/Civil Registration** for a complete list of the records included in the collection.

Gazetteers

Gentil, Robert. *Grande Geographie de L'ile d' Haiti* (Geography of the Island of Haiti). Paris: Imprimerie Goupy, G. Maurin, Successeur, 1896. (FHL# 972.94/E6g) In French.

Genealogy

Larrazabal Blanco, Carlos. *Familias Dominicanas* (Dominican Families). 54 vols. Santo Domingo: Academia Dominicana de La Historia, 1967-80. (FHL# 972.93/D2L)

Rodriguez Demorizi, Emilio. *Familias Hispanoamericanas* (Spanish American Families). Ciudad Trujillo, R.D.: Editora Montalvo, 1959. (FHL# 972.93/D3r)

History

The library has a substantial number of titles dealing with Dominican Republic history. See **Dominican Republic/History** for a complete list of that subject's titles.

Maps

Among a significant number of Dominican Republic maps, is G. DeLisle's *Carte de L'Isle de Saint Dominique*

(Paris: DeLisle, 1725) (FHL# 972.93/E7d). See FHLC under **Dominican Republic/Maps** for a complete list of maps on file.

Vital Records

See *Civil Registration*.

Records by Jurisdiction **Puerto Rico** Municipalities and Towns	Biography	Census	Church Records	Genealogy	History	Occupations	Slavery	Civil Registration
Arecibo								
Manati				•				
Utuado		•					•	•
Bayamon								
Naranjito			•					
Guayama								
Aguas Buenas			•					
Aibonito			•					
Arroyo			•		•			
Barranquita			•					
Caguas			•		•			
Cayey			•					
Comerio			•					
Guayama			•					
Maunabo			•					
Patillas			•					
Salinas			•					
Humacao								
Ceiba			•					
Fajardo			•					
Gurabo			•					
Humacao			•					
Juncos			•					
Las Piedras			•					
Luquillo			•					
Naguabo			•					
San Lorenzo			•					
Yabucoa			•					
Mayaguez	•							
Cabo Rojo	•				•	•		
Guanica			•					
Guayanilla			•					
Mayaguez					•			
San German					•			
Yauco			•					
Ponce								
Coamo			•					
Jayuya			•					
Juana Diaz			•					
Penuelas			•					
Playa de Ponce			•					
Ponce			•					
Santa Isabel			•					
Rio Piedras								•
San Juan					•			

Records by Jurisdiction **Dominican Republic** Provinces and Municipalities	Church Records	Civil Registration	Land & Property	Maps	Notarial Records
Azua					
Azua	•	•			
Baoruco					
Baoruco	•				
Neiba		•			
Barahona					
Barahona	•	•			
Cabral		•			
Enriquillo		•			
Dajabon					
Dajabon		•			
Distrito Nacional					
Guerra	•	•			
Jaina	•				
Los Alcarrizos	•	•			
Los Minas	•				
Ozama Arriba	•				
Santo Domingo	•	•			
Villa Mella	•	•			
Duarte					
Castillo	•	•			
Pimentel	•	•			
San Francisco de Macoris	•	•			
Villa Riva	•	•			
El Seibo					
Duverge	•				
El Seibo	•	•			
Hato Mayor Del Rey	•	•			
Miches		•			
Sabana De La Mar	•	•			
Espaillat					
Moca	•	•			
San Jose De Las Matas	•				
Independencia					
Duverge	•	•			
La Altagracia					
Bonao	•	•			
Salvaleon De Higoey	•	•			
La Estrelleta					
Banica	•	•			
Elias Pina	•	•			
La Romana					
La Romana		•			
La Vega					
Jarabacoa	•	•			
La Vega	•	•			
Maria Trinidad Sanchez					
Cabrera	•	•			
Matanzas	•	•			

Records by Jurisdiction **Dominican Republic (cont.)** Provinces and Municipalities	Church Records	Civil Registration	Land & Property	Maps	Notarial Records
Nagua		•			
Moncion					
Moncion		•			
Monticristi					
Monticristi	•	•			
Peravia					
Bani	•	•			
Neiba	•				
San Jose De Ocoa	•	•			
Puerto Plata					
Altamira	•	•			
Imbert	•	•			
Luperon		•			
Puerto Plata	•	•			
Salcedo					
Salcedo	•	•			
Samana					
Sabana De La Mer	•				
Samana	•				
Sanchez	•	•			
San Cristobal					
Monte Plata	•	•			
San Cristobal	•	•			
San Juan Bautista					
De Bayaguana	•	•			
Yamasa	•	•			
San Juan					
El Cercado	•	•			
Las Matas De Farfan	•	•			
San Juan	•				
San Pedro De Macoris					
La Romana	•				
Los Llanos	•	•			
San Pedro De Macoris	•	•			
Sanchez Ramirez					
Cevicos	•	•			
Cotui	•	•			
Santiago					
Pera	•	•			
San Jose De Las Matas	•	•			
Santiago De Los Caballeros	•	•			
Santo Tomas De Janico	•	•			
Santiago Rodriguez					
Sabaneta		•			
Santo Domingo					
Santo Domingo				•	
Tellillo					
Bayaguana					•
Valverde					

Records by Jurisdiction **Dominican Republic (cont.)** Provinces and Municipalities	Church Records	Civil Registration	Land & Property	Maps	Notarial Records
Esperanza		•			
Valverde		•			

Chapter 27

Africa

Johni Cerny

The Family History Library's cataloged African collection consists primarily of South African records; however, a substantial number of records from other African nations have been microfilmed but are not yet cataloged. Here is a list of uncataloged microfilmed records available upon request at the Family History Library at the International Reference Desk.

Senegal: church and civil records.

The Gambia: oral genealogies, miscellaneous church and civil records.

Zimbabwe: colonial civil and church records, excluding Dutch Reformed Church records.

Namibia: court and estate records.

St. Helena: British East Indies Company records from the 1700s, British colonial records, no church records.

Mauritius: church records and civil registration from the early 1700s.

SOUTH AFRICA

Settlement and Migration

The Dutch East India Company established a colony at Cape Town, South Africa, around 1652 as a stop-off point for its ships going to and from India. Farmers and artisans were needed to provide food and services to keep the colony going and the company granted them land to encourage them to stay.

The Dutch had South Africa to themselves, as far as European competitors were concerned, until 600 French Huguenots arrived in 1688. While their religious beliefs and practices were their primary reasons for leaving Europe, they quickly assimilated into the Dutch population.

The Dutch Reformed Church was the official church of the East India Company and the only religion practiced in South Africa until 1780 when German immigrants established a Lutheran Church at Cape Town.

Dutch King William V of Orange escaped the Netherlands to take refuge in England when French armies conquered his country in 1795. The British crown assumed control of Cape Town from 1795 to 1802. The French took over the colony, 1803-06, but the British regained control in 1806 and the tide of British migration began. Nearly 76,000 Englishmen arrived between 1806 and 1875. Another wave of migration between 1904 and 1946 brought another 85,000 English immigrants to the colony.

South African Library Collection

Almanacs

Smith, H. H. *African Court Calendar for 1801.* 1801; rpt. ed., Cape Town: South African Library, c.1970. (FHL# 968.7/B4s/no. 1)

Archives and Libraries

Pama, Cornelis, ed. *The South African Library: Its History, Collections, and Librarians, 1818-1968.* Cape Town: A. A. Balkema, 1968. Text in English and Afrikaans. (FHL# 968/A5p)

See the Family History Library Catalog (FHLC) under **South Africa/Archives and Libraries** for a long list of titles on this subject.

Bibliography

Muller, C. F. J., F. A. Van Jaarveld, and Theo Van Wijk, eds. *A Select Bibliography of South African History.* Pretoria: University of South Africa, 1966. (FHL# 968/A3ms)

Musiker, Reuben. *Guide to South African Reference Books.* 4th ed. rev. Cape Town: A. A. Balkema, c.1965. (FHL# 968/A3m)

Saunders, Christopher. *Historical Dictionary of South Africa.* Metuchen, N.J.: Scarecrow, 1983. (FHL# 968/H26s)

See the FHLC under **South Africa/Bibliography** for additional titles.

Biography

De Krock, J. W., ed. *Dictionary of South African Biography.* Cape Town: Nasionale Boekhandel Bpk., 1968. (FHL# 968/D3ds)

Philip, Peter. *British Residents at the Cape, 1795-1819.* Cape Town: David Philip, 1981. (FHL# 968/D3pp) Biographical records of 4,800 pioneers.

Rosenthal, Eric. *Southern African Dictionary of National Biography.* London: Frederick Warne and Co. Ltd., 1966. (FHL# 968/D3r)

Church Directories

Almanak van die Nederduitsch Hervormde Kerk van Afrika (Directories of the Dutch Reformed Church of Africa). Krugersdorp: N. H. W. Pers, 1909. (FHL# 968/K24a)

See the FHLC under **South Africa/Church Directories** for additional titles.

Church History

The library has several books on this topic, including:

Brown, William Eric. *The Catholic Church in South Africa.* Wheathampstead, England: Anthony Clarke Books, c.1960. (FHL# 968/K2b)

Franken, Johan Lambertus Machiel. *Die Hugenote aan die Kaap* (Huguenots in South Africa). Pretoria: Die Staatsdrukker, 1978. (FHL# 968/B4a/yr.41)

Wigman, A. Theodore. *The History of the English Church and People in South Africa.* 1895; rpt. ed., New York: Negro University Press, 1969. (FHL# 968/K21w)

Civil Registration

South Africa Office of the Registrar of Births, Marriages, and Deaths. *Natal Marriage Registers, 1845-1899.* 44 reels. Salt Lake City: Genealogical Society of Utah, 1982. Microfilm of originals at the Central Archives Depot, Pretoria. See the FHLC under **South Africa/Civil Registration** for film numbers.

______. *Cape Province Marriage Registers, 1696-1899.* 327 reels. Salt Lake City: Genealogical Society of Utah, 1982. Microfilm of originals at the Central Archives Depot, Pretoria. Text in Afrikaans and English. See the FHLC under **South Africa/Civil Registration** for film numbers.

______. *Orange Free State Marriage Registers, 1848-1899.* 45 reels. Salt Lake City: Genealogical Society of Utah, 1982. Microfilm of originals at the Central Archives Depot, Pretoria. Text in Afrikaans and English. See the FHLC under **South Africa/Civil Registration** for film numbers. Certificates arranged by district and then chronologically.

______. *Transvaal Marriage Registers, 1861-1899.* 44 reels. Salt Lake City: Genealogical Society of Utah, 1982. Microfilm of originals at the Central Archives Depot, Pretoria. Text in Afrikaans and English. Certificates are arranged by district for groups of years before 1889. See the FHLC for call numbers.

Colonization Indexes

Wiid, Edith. *Genealogical Card Indexes for South Africa.* Salt Lake City: Genealogical Society of Utah, n.d. (FHL# microfilm 1367170-1367175) Indexes at the Mowbray Chapel, Capetown, South Africa.

Directories

See the FHLC under **South Africa/Directories** for a complete listing of holdings.

Emigration and Immigration

The library has an extensive collection of South African emigration and immigration titles. See **South Africa/Emigration and Immigration** for a complete list.

Gazetteers

Nienaber, P. J. *Suid-Afrikaanse Pleknaamwoordeboek* (Dictionary of South African Place Names). Kaapstad: Tafelberg-Uitgewers, 1971. (FHL# 968/E2n)

Genealogy

Grobbelaar, Pieter W. *Families, Familiename en Familiewapens.* (Families, Family Names and Family Coats of Arms) Kaapstad: Tafelberg Uitgevers, c.1975. (FHL# 968/B2f)

Kannemeyer, A. J. *Hugenote-Familieboek* (Huguenot Family Book). Kaapstad: Unie-Volkspers, 1940. (FHL# 968/D2k) Alphabetical list of Huguenot families from France.

Pama, Cornelis. *Die Groot Afrikaanse Familienaamboek* (Heads of Families and Family Names for the Afrikaaners of South Africa). Kaapstad: Human and Rosseau, 1983. (FHL# 968/D2pc)

Redelinghuys, J. H. *Die Afrikaner-Familienaamboek.* (The Afrikaner Family Name Book) Kaapstad: Publisitas, c.1954. (FHL# 968/D2r) Alphabetical list of South African surnames and early genealogies.

See the FHLC under **South Africa/Genealogy** for additional books on this topic.

Genealogy Handbooks, Manuals, Etc.

Lombard, R. T. J. *Handbook for Genealogical Research in South Africa.* Pretoria: Human Sciences Research Council, 1977. (FHL# 968/D25lr)

See the FHLC under **/Genealogy/Handbooks, Manuals, etc.** for additional books on this topic.

History

The library has an enormous collection of South African histories cataloged under **South Africa/History.**

Language and Languages

Boshoff, S. P. E. *Radiopraatjies oor Afrikaans* (Radio Chats on Afrikaans). Johannesburg: Voortrekkerpers Beperk, 1960. (FHL# 968/A8b) Articles on the origin, development, and characteristics of the Afrikaans language.

Maps

The library has a large collection of South African maps. See the FHLC under **South Africa/Maps** for additional books on this topic.

Military Records

South African military records in the library collection focus on the Boer War. See **South Africa/Military Records** for a complete list of holdings in addition to:

South Africa Government Archives (Pretoria). *Archives of the Officer Charged with Gathering Information Concerning Deaths Among the Republican Fighting Forces and the Civilian Population, (RS), 1899-1902.* Salt Lake City: Genealogical Society of Utah, 1982. (FHL# microfilm 1295350-1295351) Microfilm of originals at the Transvaal Archives Depot, Pretoria.

After the Boer War, inquiries concerning deaths during the war were forwarded to P. L. A. Goldman in 1906 to make a survey of casualties among the Republican fighting forces and the civilian population. Registers include deaths of burghers on commando raids and names of persons in concentration camps.

Minorities

Minorities in South Africa include the African population, Cornish immigrants, Jews, French Huguenots, Germans, and Scandinavians. See the FHLC under **South Africa/Minorities** for a complete list of holdings.

Names

Rosenthal, Eric. *South African Surnames.* Cape Town: H. Timmins, c.1965. (FHL# 968/D4r)

Periodicals

Johannesburg Public Library, comp. *Index to South African Periodicals, 1960-1969.* Pretoria: The State Library, n.d. (FHL# microfilm 6340193-6340410)

_____. *Index to South African Periodicals, 1970-1974.* Pretoria: The State Library, 1978. (FHL# microfilm 6340042-6340191)

See the FHLC under **South Africa** for other subjects in the library collection.

Records by Jurisdiction **South Africa** Provinces and Towns	Almanacs	Archives & Libraries	Biography	Business	Census	Church History	Church Records	Civil Registration	Colonization	Court Records	Directories	Emigration/Immigration	Genealogy	Guardianship	Heraldry	History	Land & Property	Maps	Military Records	Minorities	Native Races	Naturalization	Orphans/Orphanages	Probate Records	Schools	Taxation	Voting Registers
Cape Province	•	•	•	•	•	•	•	•	•	•	•	•	•	•	•	•	•	•	•	•	•	•	•	•			
Albany District								•	•							•											
Albert District								•																			
Aliwal North District								•																			
Barkly West District								•																•			
Beaconsfield District								•																			
Beaufort West Dist.								•																			
Bedford District								•																			
Caledon District								•																			
Cape District								•																			
Cape Town		•			•	•	•	•				•	•			•											
Colesburg District								•																			
Cradock District								•								•											
Douglas District								•																			
East London										•																	
Encobo District								•																			
Fort Beaufort District								•																			
George District								•																			
Graff Reinet District								•				•															
Grahamstown.	•					•									•												
Herbert District													•														
Hopefield District								•																			
Kat River																•											
Kimberley District								•																•			
King Wm's Town Dist.													•								•						
Kurman													•														
Lady Frere District								•																•			
Laingsburg District								•																			
Lovedale																•											
Malmesbury							•																				
Malmesburey District								•																			
Paarl							•																				
Peddie																•											
Port Elizabeth						•																					
Postmasburg													•														
Queentown																•											
Robbeneiland							•																				
Salem																•											
Somerset							•																				
Southwell																•											
Stellenbosch							•						•														
Stellenbosch District								•																			
Swellendam District								•																			
Tarkastad District								•																			
Taung Dist.													•														
Transkei District								•																			
Tulbaugh District					•			•																			
Uitenhage District								•																			
Upington District								•																			

Records by Jurisdiction **South Africa (cont.)** Provinces and Towns	Almanacs	Archives & Libraries	Biography	Business	Census	Church History	Church Records	Civil Registration	Colonization	Court Records	Directories	Emigration/Immigration	Genealogy	Guardianship	Heraldry	History	Land & Property	Maps	Military Records	Minorities	Native Races	Naturalization	Orphans/Orphanages	Probate Records	Schools	Taxation	Voting Registers
Vryburg													•								•						
Walvis Bay							•																				
Worcester District								•																			
Natal		•	•		•			•	•	•		•	•			•			•					•			
Durban							•																				
Pietermaritzburg							•																		•		
Weenen							•																				
Zululand							•			•														•			
Orange Free State		•						•								•			•					•			
Blomfontein							•																				
Smithfield							•																				
Transvaal		•				•	•	•		•	•		•			•			•		•	•		•	•	•	•
Barberton District								•																•			
Bloemhof								•									•							•			
Hamanskraal													•								•						
Heidelberg							•																				
Johannesburg		•									•					•		•	•								
Johannesburg District								•																•			
Klerksdorp								•														•		•			
Leydsdorp													•								•						
Litchenberg District								•																•			
Marico District																								•			
Middleburg District								•																			
Potchefstroom Dist.								•																			
Pretoria		•					•				•							•									
Sekhukhuneland													•								•						
Sibasa District													•														
Soweto						•																					
Tzaneen													•								•						
Wakkerstroom Dist.							•																	•			
Waterberg District								•														•		•			

Chapter 28

Medieval Families Identification Unit

Paul C. Reed

Complexities in documenting the genealogy of royalty led the Genealogical Department of the Church of Jesus Christ of Latter-day Saints to create a special unit, the Royalty Identification Unit, to deal with such research. Since its creation, its responsibility has been expanded to include all individuals born before 1500; and in 1986, its name was changed to the Medieval Families Identification Unit. The unit is not limited to a geographical area such as Virginia or Norway, but rather deals with noble genealogies of any period and all individuals born before 1500.

The Medieval Families Identification Unit primarily extracts and compiles royal, noble, and medieval genealogies; and its present area of concentration is Continental Europe. All noble oriental genealogies are sent to the Nihon Keizu Kyokai (Japan Genealogical Library) in Tokyo. It also audits and reviews all temple ordinance submissions for persons born before 1500.

This unit consists of two divisions: (1) a small core staff that researches, documents, and evaluates material pertinent to its assigned area, and (2) a large number of volunteers who extract all of the genealogically important material from single sources. The information thus prepared is compiled on family group sheets and eventually entered into the Personal Ancestral File (PAF).

All of the family groups sheets thus prepared are housed in the Medieval Families Identification Unit with past submissions from patrons of the Family History Library and the old Royalty Identification Unit. The vast majority of these tens of thousands of family groups sheets, however, do not meet current genealogical standards of accuracy. Eventually, all of the contents will be upgraded and entered into the PAF system.

Researchers in the Medieval Families Identification Unit systematically extract and evaluate all available information on one house or dynasty before beginning on another. In this way, an accurate record can be kept of completed material. The list below shows the Euroepan houses already completed or those (marked with an asterisk) currently being extracted:

Althann*
Alvensleben
Andrassy
Anhalt
Ansbach
Arkel
Asperen
Attems
Auersperg
Austria (royalty of)
Babenberg*
Baden
Banffy
Barclay*
Barcsay
Batory
Bathory
Batthyany
Bavaria
Baynham*
Bayreuth
Beichlingan
Bentheim
Berclay*
Berka
Berkeley
Bethlen
Biberstein
Birkenfeld
Blamont
Blankenburg
Bohemia (royalty of)
Borsselen
Boskovice
Bourbon
Bourchier*
Braganza*
Brandenburg
Braose*
Breunner
Bronchorst

Oldenburg
Oppersdorf
Orlamunde
Ortenburg
Palatine
Palffy
Pallant
Pechy
Perenyi
Pernstein
Pirkstejn*
Plantagenet
Plesse
Pluh*
Poland (royalty of)
Pomerania
Poniatowski
Portugal* (royalty of)
Poyntz
Promnitz*
Prussia (royalty of)
Puckler
Querfurt
Radziwill
Rakoczi
Rantzau*
Regenstein
Revay
Reuss*
Rhedey
Rietberg
Rozmberk
Rugen
Russia (royalty of)*
Russia (grand duchy of)*
Saint John*
Salm
Saltykov*
Sapieha
Saxe-Altenburg
Saxe-Coburg

Brunswick
Budovec
Bulmer
Calvert*
Castell*
Cimburk
Criechingen
Csaky
Culemburg
Dassel
Denmark (royalty of)
Dessewffy
Deitrichstein
Dolgorukij
Dosa (Dozsa)
East Friesland
East Pomerania
Egmond
England (royalty of)
Eotvos*
Eppenstein
Erbach
Esterhazy*
Festetics
Fitz Harding*
Fitz William*
Forgach*
France (royalty of)
Frangepan
Furstenberg
Galizcia*
Gleichen
Greece (royalty of)
Grey*
Hackenborn
Hallermund
Hanau
Hanover
Hapsburg
Harant
Hastings*
Hatzfeld*
Henneberg
Hesse
Heukelom
Heydeck
Hohenzollern
Holland (royalty of)
Holstein
Holy Roman Empire, 1452-1526
Honstein
Hornes
Hoya
Hradec
Hungary (royalty of)
Hungerford*
Huszar
Illyeshazy
Isenburg
Jagietto
Karolyi
Katzenelnbogen
Khevenhuller
Kinsky
Kostka
Kounice
Krajir
Kranichfield
Krasinski
Kravar
Krinecky
Kunstat
Landsteijn
Leiningen
Leszczynski
Leuchtenberg
Lichtemberk
Saxe-Eisenach
Saxe-Eisenburg
Saxe-Gotha
Saxe-Hildburghausen
Saze-Jena
Saxe-Meinigen
Saxe-Romild
Saxe-Saalfield
Saxe-Weimar
Saxony-Merseberg
Saxony-Weissenfeld
Saxony-Zeitz
Sayn
Schalksberg
Shaumburg-Lippe
Schenkoedra-Tautenberg
Schenk von Landsbergg
Schenk von Tautenberg
Schladen
Schleswig-Holstein
Schlik
Schonborn
Schwarzburg
Schwarzenberg
Scotland* (royalty of)
Scrope*
Sedlacek
Seinsheim
Selberk
Selms
Shaun
Silesia (royalty of)
Simmern
Sobieski
Solms
Spain (royalty of)
Spanheim
Spee
Spencer-Churchill
Spiegelberg
Sponheim
Stanley
Starhemberg
Stein
Sternberk
Stewart* (1265-1659)
Steyr
Stolberg
Stuart*
Sulzbach
Svihovsky
Sweden (royalty of)
Sydenham*
Szapolyay
Szechenyi
Szilahyi
Teixeira*
Teleky
Thuringia
Thurzo
Tokoly
Tonna
Torning
Tracy*
Trauttmansdorff
Trcka
Troppau (royalty of)
Valdsteijn
Valkenburg
Valkenstein
Vartemberk
Vasa*
Veldenz
Verney
Volmestein
Waldeck
Waldenberg
Lichtenberg
Limburg
Lindsay*
Lippe
Lobkovice
Lonyay
Lowenstein
Lumley*
Luxembourg*
Mattesdon*
Mecklenburg
Meissen
Metternich*
Michalovice
Mors
Munsterberg
Nadasoly
Nassau
Neuberg
Nevill/Neville
Oettingen
Wartenberg
Waldock
Wends
Werberg
Werle
Wernigerode
Wertheim
Westerburg
Wied
Windischgraetz
Wolfenbuttel
Wolfstein
Wunstorf
Wurttemberg
Zamoyski
Zerotin
Ziegenhain
Zollern
Zrinyi
Zweibrucken

The thousands of other family group records held in the Medieval Families Identification Unit, most submitted when research standards were less exacting, deal mainly with British royal houses. Many ancestors common to millions of American have already had their temple ordinances completed through the submission of these records, but the genealogical information they are based upon tends to contain a high proportion of error and is of little use to the contemporary medievalist. They were usually combined from secondary sources that do not cite their sources or provide primary documentation.

Patrons should be particularly wary of three publications that have been extremely popular in the past but have been shown to contain many errors and inaccuracies:

Wurts, John S. *Magna Charta*. 8 vols. New York: Brookfield Publishing Co., 1942-c.1958. (FHL# 942/D2wj)

Call, Michel L. *Royal Ancestors of Some L.D.S. Families*. Orem, Utah: by the author, 1975. Supplements A-E (FHL# 929.7/C13r)

Virkus, Frederick Adams. *The Compendium of American Genealogy*. 7 vols. 1925-42. rpt. ed., Baltimore: Genealogical Publishing Company, 1968. See the FHLC for call numbers.

Because these sources are themselves riddled with errors, so are the family group records based on them. Material submitted for either temple ordinance work or the PAF must use as many primary sources or as many well-documented secondary sources as possible. Examples of reliable secondary sources are cited in the Selected Bibliography.

Official policy does not allow patrons to submit royal names for temple ordinance work. Before submitting the names of any nobility or gentry, patrons should first check the medieval Temple Index Bureau (TIB), (FHL# 884548-884577 and 1263086-1263088). For a description of these films see Laureen R. Jaussi and Gloria D. Chaston, comps., *Register of Genealogical Society Call Numbers, Volume I: A Companion to Fundamentals of Genealogical Research* (Provo, Utah: The Genealogy

Tree, n.d.), pp. 3-9. Several copies of this book are at the LDS register table (FHL# 979.225/Sl/A3j).

Patrons should also search the Family Group Record Archives, as well as the International Genealogical Index. If the ancestors are not located in any of these sources, well-documented family group records may be submitted to the Medieval Families Identification Unit.

Jurisdiction List

The Jurisdiction list and index were created by the Medieval Families Identification Unit to help patrons locate noble European ancestry; it is kept at the International Reference Desk.

The Jurisdiction List has two sections. The first is an index which lists alphabetically the names and titles of ruling houses. Most names listed refer first to the geographical area over which the house ruled but may also be the name of a particular dynasty. The geographical or dynastic name is followed by a source number. These numbers pertain to sources which include genealogical information on that house or the ruling dynasty of that geographical region.

Each source in the Jurisdiction List has been assigned a unique number. For instance, *21* refers to George Edward Cokayne, *The Complete Peerage.* (See bibliography for complete citation.)

The second part of the Jurisdiction List is a list of the 855 sources in order of their unique source numbers. Most of the classic reference works of the past (Isenberg, Stokvis, Anselm (Anselme de Saint Marie), are included. The reference works themselves, of course, usually contain their own detailed indexes. However, the Jurisdiction List can give the patron a good working knowledge from which to continue research.

A copy of the Jurisdiction List–two black binders sometimes called the "Royalty Binders"–is kept at the reference desk of the International Reference Area. Some of the sources on the Jurisdiction List are no longer in the Family History Library Catalogue (FHLC). If you have difficulty finding something, have a record attendant trace it on the computer.

Select Bibliography

Virtually no source is free from error. Therefore, a good research rule when dealing with nobility or gentry is to check every available source. Local, county, and regional histories are indispensable. They usually summarize the descent of local rulers, often citing charters, deeds, and other documents. To locate histories, search the FHLC for the geographical area of interest under the heading **History**. For example, if you are interested in the Halifax family of Yorkshire, look under these subheadings: **England/Yorkshire/History**; or under **England/Yorkshire/Halifax/History**.

Publications of local historical, archaeological, and antiquarian societies can also be helpful. Check the subheadings **Periodicals** and **Societies** under the geographical area you are searching. They frequently contain articles detailing early families and transcribe otherwise unavailable or unknown local records.

Foremost among modern genealogical periodicals is *The Genealogist*, edited by Niel D. Thompson, F.A.S.G., F.S.G., and published in New York by the Association for the Promotion of Scholarship in Genealogy, Ltd., 1980-date (FHL# 929.105/G286n). This publication is noted for the detailed and accurate articles which it contains. Many of these articles deal with medieval or noble genealogies.

Below is an annotated bibliography of sources dealing with European nobility. These general sources should be used in addition to the sources specific to a single country or region. Also search the FHLC under **Europe/Nobility**, and **Europe/Genealogy**.

General Reference

Schwennicke, Detlev. *Europäischen Stammtafeln.* Marburg, West Germany: J. A. Stargartd, 1978-present. (FHL# Q/940/D5es New Series)

This monumental effort supersedes the past work of Wilhelm Karl, Prinz von Isenburg, *Stammtafeln zur geschichte der Europäischen Staaten* (Marburg, West Germany: J. A. Stargardt, 1953). (FHL# 940/D22f). It covers, or will eventually cover, all the major noble houses of Europe, in addition to many minor dynasties. The Family History Library has eight volumes: (1) Kings, kaisers, and archdukes of Germany and the Holy Roman Empire; (2) The other houses of Europe (including the Netherlands, Belgium, France, Spain, Portugal, Great Britain, Scandinavia, Italy, the Slavic houses, and the Byzantine imperial families); (3) Illegitimate children and branches without noble status; (4) Standesherrliche Häuser I.; (5) Not yet published; (6) Alten Lotharingien I; (7) Alten Lotharingien II.; (8) West, Middle, and Northern European families; (9) Middle Rhine, Upper Rhine, and Burgundy.

Stokvis, A. M. H. J. *Manuel d'Histoire de Généalogie et de Chronologie de Tous les Etats du Globe.* 3 vols. 1888-93; rpt. ed., Leiden: B. M. Israël, 1966. (FHL# vol. 1, microfilm 1059451, item 1; vol. 2, microfilm 1059451, item 2; vol. 3, microfilm 1059452, in two parts)

Stovkis includes extensive chronological tables and genealogical tables of African, American, Arabic, Indian, and Oriental rulers as well as the usual European/British houses. He usually highlights only the direct male lines, omitting wives and other children unless they are the heirs/heiresses or heads of other dynasties. Even though this book is more accurate than many others, it must still be used with caution.

Pryce, Frederich R. *A Guide to European Genealogies Exclusive of the British Isles.* Tyler's Green, High Wycombe, U.K.: University Microfilms, Ltd., 1965. (FHL# 940/D22p)

Paget, Gerald. "Genealogies of the European Families from Charlemagne to the Present." Typescript, 1957. (FHL# microfilm 170050-170062)

This twelve-volume typescript covers many of the minor dynasties missed by Stokvis, Isenburg, and

Schwennicke, such as the minor branches of the de Baux family. Paget cites the source from which each genealogy is taken, but his work is only as accurate as those sources. He cites histories, genealogies, etc., rather than primary sources like court records.

Hübner, Johann. *Genealogische Tabellen, nebst denen darzu gehörigen genealogischen Fragen: zur Erläuterung der politischen Historie.* Leipzig, Germany: Johan Friedrich Glieditschens seel. Sohn., 1737-44. (FHL# microfilm 001247, item 3-001249)

These volumes must be used with caution. The German and Dutch tables are the most accurate, the Spanish tables the least accurate.

Country-by-Country Sources

Albania (see also under Byzantine Empire)

Sturdza, Mihail-Dimitri. *Dictionnaire Historique et Généalogique des Grandes Familles de Grèce, d'Albanie et de Constantinople.* Paris: by the author, 1983. (FHL# 949.5/D5s)

This volume covers a large portion of the nobility of Greece, Albania, and Turkey, as well as the rulers of the Byzantine Empire. He relies on the works of Rüdt-Collenberg, among others.

Arabic/Islamic Dynasties

Wüstenfeld, Ferdinand. *Register zu den Genealogische Tabellen der Arabischen Stämme und Familien, mit Historischen und geographischen Bemerkungen*. Gottengen: Dieterichschen Buchhandlung, 1852. (FHL# Q/953/D2wx, with charts in a separate volume.)

This series of tables covers a wide array of traditional Arabic genealogies, frequently including wives and daughters. It is divided into two sections: (1) "Ismâ'ilite" covering charts A-Z, and (2) Yemen Arabs covering charts 1-23. A transliteration table for Arabic/German conversion is on p. xiii.

De Zambaur, Eduard. *Manuel de Généalogie et de Chronologie pour l'Histoire de l'Islam*. Osnabrück, West Germany: Biblioverlag, 1976. (FHL# Q/929.1/Z14m, or microfilm 441499)

Lane-Poole, Stanley. *The Mohammedan Dynasties: Chronological and Genealogical Tables with Historical Introductions.* New York: Frederick Ungar Publishing Co., 1965. (FHL# 956/D51)

This famous work covers many of the smaller dynasties in Spain and Africa as well as the caliphal houses.

Austria (see also under Holy Roman Empire)

Rouille, Marcel [Michel] Dugast. *Les Maisons Souveraines de l'Autriche: Babenberg, Habsbourg (Habsbourg-d'Espagne), Habsbourg-Lorraine (Lorraine)*. Paris: by the author, 1967. (FHL# 929.7/D878ma)

Belgium (see also under France)

Prior to 1830, the region now known as Belgium was comprised of the counties of Brabant, Flanders, and Hainau, with other minor divisions. Researchers should also check these regional listings in the FHLC under **/Periodicals, /History,** and **/Nobility.** See also regional publications like *Tablettes du Hainaut: Généalogie-Histoire-Héraldique* (FHL# 949.341/D2t) and *Tablettes Généalogique, Historique, Héraldiques de Flandres* (FHL# 949.31/D2t).

Annuaire de la Noblesse de Belgique. Brussels: A. van Dalen, 1847-89. (FHL# 949.3/D22a). This work continued to be published after 1890 under the title *La Noblesse Belge.* Brussels: Imprimerie Veuve Monnom, 1890-1929. (FHL# 949.3/D22a).

Le Parchemin: Bulletin de l'Office Généalogique et Héraldique de Belgique. Bruxelles: Office Généalogique et Héraldique de Belgique, 1936-December 1985. Bi-monthly-.(FHL# 949.3/D25p)

Bulgaria

Romanoff, Prince Dimitri. *The Order, Medals and History of the Kingdom of Bulgaria.* [Denmark]: Balkan Heritage, 1982. (FHL# 949.77/D6r)

This volume deals mainly with Bulgarian royalty since the 1700s and includes genealogical tables of the royal house of Bulgaria and the house of Battenberg. For earlier royalty, search the FHLC under **Bulgaria/History**.

Byzantine Empire

The Byzantine Empire succeeded the Eastern Roman Empire and covered Greece, Turkey, parts of the southern Balkans, many of the crusading states of the Middle East, and other sections of Asia Minor. The last remnant of this empire was conquered by the Ottoman Turks in 1461.

Sturdza, Mihail-Dimitri. *Dictionnaire Historique et Généalogique des Grandes Familles de Grèce, d'Albanie et de Constantinople.* Paris: by the author, 1983. (FHL# 949.5/D5s)

This volume covers a large portion of the nobility of Greece, Albania, and Turkey, as well as the rulers of the Byzantine Empire. He relies on the works of Rüdt-Collenberg, among others.

Rüdt-Collenberg, Count W. H. *The Rupenides, Hethumides and Lusignans: The Structure of the Armeno-Cilician Dynasties.* Paris: Imprimerie A. Pignie, 1963. (FHL# 956.6/D2r)

This work details the dynasties created by European crusaders who conquered lands in the Middle East, founded dynasties, and interrmarried with local as well as European dynastics. It also details the local Turkish, Armenian, Mongolian, and other ruling families of the Middle East. Charts include their marriages with many of the ruling families of Europe. Other valuable works on the nobility of this region by the same author can be located in the FHLC, **Author/Title** section.

Czechoslovakia (see also under Slavic)

Sedlácek, August. *Hrady, zámky a tvrz e království ceského.* 5

vols. Prague: Nákladem Knihtiskárny Frantiskasimácka, 1882-1927. (FHL# Q/943.7/D22s)

Wegener, Wilhelm. *Die Premysliden.* Published as part of *Genealogische Tafeln zur Mitteleuropaischen Geschichte.* Gottingen, Germany: Heinz Reise Verlag, 1962-69. (FHL# 940/D22w)

Denmark (see under Scandinavia)

England (see under Great Britain)

Finland (see under Scandinavia)

France

Arnaud, Etienne. *Répertoire de Généalogies Francaises Imprimées.* 3 vols. Nancy, France: Berger-Levrault, 1978. (FHL# 944/D23a)

Very useful to researchers dealing with a given surname. De Saint Marie, Anselme. *Histoire généalogique et chronologique de la maison royale de France . . .* 9 vols. 1726; rpt. ed., (New York and London: Johnson Reprint Corporation, 1967). (FHL# 944/D5a or microfilm 532231-532239). See also the revision, FHL# 661978-661979, which includes a comprehensive index.

This book, one of the most extensive works in the Family History Library on French royal/noble houses, begins with French rulers of the fifth century and traces most of the major houses to the 1700s, including such bordering suzerains as the counts of Flanders, dukes of Burgundy, and counts of Lorraine.

Affonso, Domingos se Araujo, et al. *Le Sang de Louis XIV.* 2 vols. Braga, Portugal: n.p., 1961-62. (FHL# Q/929.244/-L929a)

This work is a genealogical listing of descendants of Louis XIV, king of France and Navarre (1638-1715).

Sirjean, Gaston. *Encyclopedie généalogique de maisons souveraines du monde.* Paris: n.p., 1959. (FHL# 940/D25s)

The Family History Library has two volumes of this multi-volumed work; they deal with French royalty and nobility.

Garnier, Ed[uard]. *Tableaux généalogique des souverains de la France et de ses grands feudataires.* 2 vols. Paris: Librarie A. Frank, 1863. (FHL# 944/D22g)

These pedigrees rely on material housed in the French archives, some of it faulty. However, they are still helpful.

de La Chesnaye-Desbois, Francois Alexandre Aubert. *Dictionnaire de la Noblesse, contenant les généalogies, l'histoire et la chronologie des familles nobles de la France.* 19 vols. Paris: Schlessinger Freres, 1863-77. (FHL# microfilm 661873-661882)

This source concentrates on French nobility and gentry rather than royalty.

Greece (see under Byzantine Empire)

Germany (see under Holy Roman Empire)

Great Britain

The Family History Library possesses more sources on British nobility and medieval ancestry than on any other area. Here are some of the more useful:

General Aids

Cheney, C. R., ed. *The Handbook of Dates for Students of English History.* London: Offices of the Royal Historical Society, 1955. (FHL# Ref/942/C4rg/no.4)

Many medieval British records are dated according to the reigns of monarchs, feast days, and saints' days. This volume explains the Julian (Old Style) Calendar, the Gregorian (New Style) Calendar, lists the regnal years of the British sovereigns and popes, saints' days, festivals, legal chronology, and the Easter tables.

Fryde, E. B., et al., eds. *Handbook of British Chronology.* London: Offices of the Royal Historical Society, 1986. (FHL# Ref/942/C4rg/no.2).

This book details the chronology of the Anglo-Saxon rulers of England; the rulers of England, Wales, Scotland, and the Isle of Man; the English, Irish, and Scottish officers of state, the archibishops and bishops; dukes, marquesses, and earls; the English and British Parliaments; and the provincial and national councils of the Church in England.

Lists and Indexes

The List and Index Society has published extensive lists, indexes, and calendars of English civil, governmental, and legal records held in the Public Records office. Even though most of these records are not available at the Family History Library, the society's publications will help you find primary records held in other repositories. See:

List and Index Society. London: Swift, 1965-present. (FHL# Q/942/B4pro)

List and Index Society. New York: Kraus Reprint Corp., 1966-present. (FHL# Q/942/B4Pre)

Peerage, Baronetage, and Knighthood

Cokayne, George Edward. *The Complete Peerage of England[,] Scotland[,] Ireland[,] Great Britain[,] and the United Kingdom[,] Extant, Extinct, or Dormant.* 12 vols. London: St. Catherine Press, Ltd., 1910-59. Rev. by the Hon. Vicary Gibbs. (FHL# Brit Ref/942/D22cok; or vols. 1 and 2: 973308; vols. 3 and 4: 978309; vol. 5: 973310; vols. 6 and 7: 973311; vol. 8: 973312; vol. 9: 973313; vol. 10: 973314; vols. 11 and 12, part 1: 973316; and vol. 12, part 2: 073316, item 2 and 973371, item 1)

This work should be the first consulted when an ancestor is known as a peer of the British realm. However, it does not usually detail the younger children or daughters of a peer unless they become involved in the inheritance of the title.

Brydges, Sir Egerton. *Collins's Peerage of England: Genealogical, Biographical, and Historical.* London: T. Bensley, 1812. (FHL# 942/D22be or microfilm 824368-824372, item 1)

Though not as accurate as *The Complete Peerage,* Brydges provides more detail on the younger children of peers.

G.E.C. [Cokayne, George Edward.] *The Complete Baronetage, 1611-1880.* 5 vols. Exeter, Great Britain: W. Pollard, 1900-06. (FHL# 942/D22cg; or vols. 1 and 3: 547502 and vols. 2, 4, 5: 962204)

This work is similar to *The Complete Peerage* and is the most accurate of works on baronetage. The Family History Library also has Burke's *Peerage and Baronetage* for 1828, 1829, 1840, 1845, 1847, 1852, 1854, 1865, 1876, 1878, 1879, 1880, 1883, 1884, 1887 (K-Z only for this year), 1892, 1894, 1895, 1904, 1915, 1926, 1934 (Volume 3 only for this year), 1938, 1949, and 1980. See FHLC for complete listing of call numbers. These and other works by Burke such as *Commoners, Landed Gentry,* and *Extinct Peerage* should be used with caution, since many of the earlier pedigrees contain errors. They are helpful as supplemental sources, however. The library also has the works of Debrett, Dod, Foster, Jacob, Kimber, Lodge, Paget, Ridgway, Stockdale, and Whitaker on peerage and baronetages.

Pine, L[eslie] G[ilbert]. *The New Extinct Peerage, 1884-1871; containing extinct, abeyant, dormant, and suspended peerage with genealogies and arms.* London: Heraldry Today, c.1972. (FHL# 942/D22pn)

This work continues Burke's *Extinct Peerage* down to about 1970.

______. *The Story of the Peerage.* Edinburgh: N. Blackwood, 1956. (FHL# 942/D22pee)

This book supplies a useful introduction to the development of British peerage.

Shaw, William A. *The Knights of England: A complete record from the earliest time to the present day of the knights of all orders of chivalry in England, Scotland, and Ireland and of knights bachelors.* 2 vols. London: Central Chancery of the Orders of Knighthood, 1906. (FHL# microfilm 990305, items 1 and 2; and microfilm 990286, items 2 and 3)

Nocolas, Sir Nicholas Harris. *History of the Orders of Knighthood of the British Empire. . .* 4 vols. London: William Pichering for John Hunter, 1982. (FHL# Q/942/D22n)

England

Three indispensable bibliographical indexes will aid the researcher in locating British family histories, county and local histories, periodicals, and other sources. They are organized by surname. Most of the sources cited can be located in the FHLC, either under **Author/Title** or **Locality**. These bibliographies, however, do not cover Irish, Scottish, or Welsh families in the same depth as British families.

Marshall, George W. *The Genealogist's Guide.* Baltimore: Genealogical Publishing Company, 1980. (FHL# 929.142/M356g or microfilm 496451, item 2)

Whitmore, J. B. *A Genealogical Guide.* London: Walford Brothers, 1953. (FHL# 929.142/M356g supp.) An edition was also printed by the Harleian Society, (FHL# 942/B4h, vols. 99, 101, 102, 104; or 162,084, item 3, and 162085, items 1, 2, 4)

Barrow, Geoffrey B. *The Genealogist's Guide: An Index to Printed British Pedigrees and Family Histories 1950-1975; Being a Supplement to G. W. Marshall's* Genealogist's Guide *and J. B. Whitmore's* Genealogical Guide. London: Research Publishing, 1977. (FHL# 929.142/M356g, 1950-75 or microfiche 6026284.

The Family History Library also holds some English court and manorial records. Such records as Calendar of Close Rolls, Calendar of Patent Rolls (1216-1578), *Curia Regis* Rolls, Calendar of Assize Records, Calendar of Inquisitions Miscellaneous, Feudal Aids, Calendar of Fine Rolls, the *Testa de Nevill,* the Red Book of the Exchequer, etc., can be located in the FHLC under **England/Court Records** and **England/Land Records.** Publications of countywide records may be located by looking under the same subdivisions under each county name.

Jacob, Lance, comp. *Printed Visitation Pedigrees of England.* Salt Lake City: Genealogical Society, 1981. (FHL# Brit Ref/942/D23j)

Sixteenth- and seventeenth-century monarchs periodically sent out heralds to verify that those using coats of arms had valid rights to them. These heralds recorded pedigrees showing the descent of the individual from an ancestor with the right and also described the immediate family of the informant. These pedigrees are known as "visitations." The Genealogical Society compiled this index since, though most visitation pedigrees are indexed in Marshall, Whitmore, and Barrow, the documents themselves are not always easy to locate. This index is organized by county or region and includes the year(s) of the visitation, bibliographical information, and the call number. It also lists visitations not held by the library. See publications of the Harleian Society (FHL# 942/B4h).

Smith, Frank, et al. "An Inventory of Genealogical Sources in the British Collection of the Family History Library." Typescript. 49 binders. Salt Lake City: Genealogical Society, 1986. (Kept at the British Reference Desk.)

This compilation, created by volunteers from the British collection's books and microfilms, is more detailed than the FHLC. At the beginning of each binder is a subject list of the information contained within it. Subjects are arranged in two sections, the first topically, the second chronologically. All subjects are broken down into 100-year periods before 1500. After 1500, the groupings are by fifty-year period. Among medieval subjects covered in this inventory are assize rolls, 1248-1482; cartularies, 1100s-1800s; chancery proceedings, 1386-1875; chantry records, 1100s-1800s; charter rolls, 1199-1517; churchwardens' accounts, 1200-present; close rolls, 1205-1903; Court of Requests, 1485-1642; Court of Star Chamber, late 1400s-1656; *Curia Regis* rolls, 1194-1241; deeds, 1200-present; the Domesday Book, 1086-87; Eyre rolls, 1201-1482; Feet of Fines, 1182-1834; hundred rolls, 1216-1307; *Inquisitions Ad Quod Damnum,* 1216-1485; Inquisitions Post Mortem,

1216-1649; letters patent, 1200-1844; manor court rolls, 1200-1900; patent rolls, 1202-1958; pipe rolls, 1156-1832; plea rolls, 1218-1875; quarter sessions, 1350-present; recognizances, 1205-1903; subsidy rolls, 1154-1700s; and tithe records, 1200-1834.

The inventory also lists all pedigrees of three consecutive generations or more not found in Marshall, Whitmore, or Barrow, expands their indexes, covers England and Wales as general areas, and provides separate entries on each county in England and Wales.

Ireland

In addition to the sources cited below, the researcher should search the FHLC under **Ireland/Nobility, Ireland/Genealogy** and under the name of the family of interest in the FHLC Surname Index. The Family History Library recently microfilmed many valuable Irish records, discussed in Chapter 16.

Archdall, Mervyne, ed. *The Peerage of Ireland, or A genealogical history of the present nobility of that kingdom. . .* Dublin: J. Moore, 1789. (FHL# 941.5/D22lo; or vols. 1-2: microfilm 908431; vols. 3-5: microfilm 908432; vols. 6-7: microfilm 908433)

This volume, a revision of John Lodge, *The Peerage of Ireland,* 2 vols. (London: n.pub., 1754) is one of the better published but lacks the reliability of Cockayne's *The Complete Peerage*, which contains the most accurate versions of such confused ancestries as the Geraldines, Fitz Geralds, etc. Archdall makes a useful companion to *The Complete Peerage,* however, since it details younger children.

Hogan, James. *The Irish Law of Kingship, with Special Reference to Ailech and Cenel Eoghain.* Dublin: Hodges Figgis and Co., 1932. (FHL# 941.5/D5h)

This work is a detailed treatise on laws concerning early Irish kingship and includes charts of the royal house of Dal Riada (early Scotland). Reprinted from *Proceedings of the Royal Irish Academy* 40 (March 1932), Section C, no. 3 (complete issue). See also *The Journal of the Royal Historical and Archaeological Association of Ireland,* 1859-present, originally the *Kinlkenny Archaeological Society*, c.1851-53. At some point, the sponsoring society became the Royal Society of Antiquaries of Ireland. The journal has published many articles on the early Irish houses, including charts constructed from traditions and myths of the descent of Irish rulers from Adam.

O'Hart, John. *The Irish and Anglo-Irish Landed Gentry.* Shannon: Irish University Press, 1969. (FHL# 941.5/D220h)

This work is particularly helpful for its coverage of the Cromwellian period when many Anglo-Norman families settled in Ireland, plus later Irish gentry. Not recommended is his *Irish Pedigrees; or, The Origin and Stem of the Irish Nation,* 5th ed. (Baltimore: Genealogical Publishing Co., 1976). (FHL# 941.5/D2oha/1976). It is basically a list of pedigrees without documentation and is quite inaccurate when dealing with Anglo-Norman lines. To be avoided for the same reasons is William P. Durning/Ulliam O'Duirnin, *If You're a Wee Bit Irish: A Chart of Old Irish Families Collected from Folk Tradition* (La Mesa, California: The Irish Family Names Society, 1978). (FHL# 941.5/D2od).

Burke, Sir Bernard. *Burke's Genealogical and Heraldic History of the Landed Gentry of Ireland.* London: Burke's Peerage Ltd., 1958. (FHL# 941.5/D22bu/1958)

_____. *Burke's Irish Family Records.* London: Burke's Peerage, Ltd., 1976. (FHL# 941.5/D22bur/1976)

This book is the successor to *Burke's Genealogical and Heraldic History of the Landed Gentry of Ireland.*

Curtis, Edmund, ed. *Calendar of Ormond Deeds (1172-1603).* 6 vols. Dublin: The Stationary Office, 1932-43. (FHL# 941.5/R2orm)

This work provides valuable land and court records. Researchers should search the FHLC under **Ireland/Court Records** and **Ireland/Land Records.**

Hennessy, William M., ed. *Annals of Ulster. Otherwise, Annals of Senat; A Chronicle of Irish Affairs from* A.D. 431 to A.D. 1540. 4 vols. Vol. 1 edited by Hennessy. Vols. 2, 3, 4, edited by B. MacCarthey. Dublin: Alexander Thom and Co., 1887-1901. (FHL# 941.6/H2hul)

This work is a compilation of family histories and chronicles. For similar works, search the FHLC under **Ireland/History** and the same heading for counties or towns of interest.

Scotland

Stuart, Margaret. *Scottish Family History: A Guide to Works of Reference on the History and Genealogy of Scottish Families.* Edinburgh; Oliver and Boyd, 1930. (FHL# Ref/941/A3s or microfiche 6026373)

Ferguson, Joan P. S., comp. *Scottish Family Histories Held in Scottish Libraries.* Edinburgh: Scottish Central Library, 1960. (FHL# Ref/ 941/D23f. An eleven-leaf typescript supplement by the author, n.d., is on microfilm: 1239087, item 6)

Stuart's and Ferguson's works are similar to *The Genealogist's Guide* and should be used together when researching early Scottish families.

Paul, Sir James Balfour. *The Scots Peerage.* 12 vols. Edinburgh: David Douglas, 1904-14. (FHL# 941/D22p)

This source lists Scottish peers and their families. It is footnoted and well indexed.

Douglas, Robert. *The Peerage of Scotland: containing the historical and genealogical account of the nobility of that kingdom. . .* Edinburgh: n.p., 1764. (FHL# microfilm 252997) 2nd rev. ed. Edinburgh: A. Constable, 1813. (FHL# Q/941/D22d)

Douglas's work is good for an eighteenth-century compilation but repeats some early traditions (such as identifying MacDuff as Earl of Fife) that are no longer accepted by scholars.

Crawfurd, George. *The Peerage of Scotland: containing a historical and genealogical account of the nobility of that kingdom. . .* Edinburgh: by the author, 1716. (FHL# microfilm 994026, item 6)

Crawfurd's work is the predecessor of Douglas's *Peerage* and should be used with caution.

Anderson, Marjorie O. *Kings and Kingship in Early Scotland.*

Totowa, New Jersey: Rowman and Littlefield, 1973. (FHL# 941/D22p)

This source is an outstanding study on the vague and controversial topic of early Scottish and Pict rulers.

It is important to study Scottish history in conjunction with early ruling genealogies. Historical works are listed in the FHLC under **Scotland/History**. The Family History Library's holdings of sasines and other valuable court and land records are discussed in Chapter 17.

Wales

An "Inventory of Genealogical Sources in the Welsh Collection," similar to that described for England, arranges genealogically important information held by the Family History Library under subject headings. This inventory is in the same format as its corresponding English collection discussed above.

Bartrum, Peter C. *Welsh Genealogies,* A.D. 300-1400. [Wales]: University of Wales Press, c.1980. (FHL# microfiche 6025561)

These twenty-five microfiche contain most the traditional medieval Welsh pedigrees. An extensive index identifies the source each individual was located in. A general preface explains the format, the contents of the pedigrees, and the index.

Bartrum, Peter C. *Welsh Genealogies,* A.D. 1400-1500. 18 vols. Aberystwyth, Wales: National Library of Wales, 1983. (FHL# 942.9/D2bw)

This work continues the previous compilation and has a similar format of pedigrees and a detailed index. However, the preface to the first volume, not repeated here, should be read to understand fully the contents. Both works are based on the traditional pedigrees of the Welsh bards and other sources such as Lewys Dwynn, *Heraldic Visitations of Wales,* 2 vols. (Llandovery: William Rees, 1856) (FHL# 942.9/D23d) and many of the publications and periodicals of Welsh genealogical, historical, and archaeological societies. Although Bartrum does not cite original records, such as ancient deeds, he has avoided many errors and clarified a number of common discrepencies frequently found in other recitations. Anglo-Saxon Marcher families are also charted in the pedigrees.

Holy Roman Empire

After the break-up of Charlemagne's empire, the German states eventually united (c.1000s) in a federation called the Holy Roman Empire or the German Empire which lasted until 1806. It also included, at times, the Netherlands, Burgundy, and Italy. Works on Germanic *adel* (nobility) therefore contain noble families within the boundaries of the old empire. Many works deal with German rulers, houses, and dynasties. Search the FHLC by region, political subdivision, or city under **Nobility** and **Genealogy**. Also use Schwennicke (listed in this bibliography under General Reference).

Wollmershäuser, Friedrich R. "German Noble Descent: A Realistic View." Paper presented to the National Genealogical Conference, Utah Genealogical Society Association, August 1985, Salt Lake City. Copy located at the Medieval Families Identification Unit.

This paper briefly lists many sources for research on German noble families as well as the difficulties entailed in actually proving family traditions of descent from nobility.

Behling, Dorothy L. "Nobly Speaking." [A series of articles.] *German Genealogical Digest* 1985-date. (FHL# 943/B2g)

These articles explain for a beginning researcher how to use the extensive sources related to Germanic nobility available at the Family History Library.

Von Hefner, Otto Titan. *Stammbuch des blühenden und ausgestorbenen Adels in Deutschland*. 4 vols. bound in 2. Regensburg: Georg Joseph Manz, 1860-66. (FHL# 943/D22h or microfilm 491136)

This source lists all noble houses, both extinct and extant, up to its publication, in alphabetical order. It lists family members, describes the family's residence, and defines its suzerainty.

Bibliotheca Familiarium Nobilium: Repertorium gedruckter Familien-Geschichten und Familien-Nachrichten. Ein handbuch für sämmler, genealogische Forscher und Bibliothekare. 2 vols. Neustrelitz: Gundlachs Antiquariat, 1897. (FHL# 940/D23g or microfilm 496454; 1883 ed. on microfilm 492935)

Kneschke, Ernst Heinrich. *Neues allegemeines deutsches Adels-Lexicon* . . . Leipzig: Friedrich Voigt, 1959-70. (FHL# 943/D22kn or microfilm 496835-496838)

The Gotha Books

Justus Perthes published his first compilation of Germanic nobility in Gotha in 1764, thus giving this series, all of them published by his family, its common name. The series continues to 1942 and forms the basic sources from which a German noble ancestry is commonly built. The Gotha Books were published in several series, enumerated below. See **Author/Title** for microfilm numbers; they were not filmed in a continuous sequence and have many different numbers. However, all are indexed in a major work:

Von Fritzch, Thomas Freiherr. *Die Gothaischen taschenbucher, Hofkalender und Almanach.* Limburg/Lahn: C. A. Starke, 1968), vol. 2, pp. 185-349. (FHL# 943/B4da)

This index gives the history of the Gotha series, describes each volume, defines terminology, and gives the history of the publishing house. The families are arranged in alphabetical order.

1. *Gothaischer Hofkalender zum Nutzen und Vergnügen eingericht[et].* 181 vols. Gotha: Perthes, 1765-1942. (FHL#943/D5ad [vols 1-169, 179-81]); 79 reels)

This series lists the families of German princes (kings, grand dukes, margraves, etc.) The title varies from year to year. Von Fritzch's index designates this series by H.

2. *Gothaisches genealogisches Taschenbuch der gräflichen Häuser.* 115 vols. Gotha: Perthes, 1825-1942. (FHL# 943/D2ge; 80 reels)

Von Fritzch's index designates this series by G and *G.

3. *Gothaisches genealogisches Taschenbuch der frieherrlichen*

Häuser. 92 vols. Gotha: Perthes, 1848-1942. (FHL# 943/D2gd; also 79 reels)

Von Fritzch's index designates this series by F and *F.

4. *Gothaisches genealogisches taschenbuch der uradeligen Häuser*. 41 vols. Gotha: Perthes, 1900-42. (FHL# 943/D2gc; also 33 reels)

This series lists lesser nobles who inherited their titles. Von Fritzch's index designates this series by *A.

5. *Gothaisches genealogisches taschenbuch der briefadeligen Häuser*. 34 vols. Gotha: Perthes, 1907-42. (FHL# 943/D2gb; also 29 reels.

This series lists houses created by the ennobling of commoners. Von Fritzch's index designates this series by A.

In *Die Gothaischen taschenbücher*, pp. 350-415, Von Fritzch also indexes the following series:

1. *Genealogisches taschenbuch der Ritter- und Adelsgeschlechter*. 19 vols. 9 vols. published Brunn: Buschak & Irrgang, 1870-84; 10 vols. published Brunn: Irrgang, 1885-94. (FHL# 943/D2gf)

Von Fritzch's index designates this series by T.

2. Von Dachenhausen, Alexander Freiherr. *Genealogisches Taschenbuch des Uradels*. 2 vols. Brunn: Friedrich Irrgang, 1891, 1893. (FHL#943/D22gt or microfilm 824310)

Von Fritzch's index designates this series by S.

3. *Handbuch des Preuss ischen Adels*. 2 vols. Berlin: Ernst Siegfried Mitter und Sohn, 1982. (FHL# 943.1/D22h or microfilm 823863)

Von Fritzch's index designates this series by P.

4. *Jahrbuch des deutschen Adels*. 3 vols. Berlin: W. T. Bruer, 1896-99. (FHL# 943/B5j or microfilm 824303-824305)

Von Fritzch's index designates this series by J.

5. *Genealogisches taschenbuch der Adeligen Häuser Osterreichs*. 5 vols. Wien: Otto Maass, 1905-13. (FHL# 943.6/B5g)

Von Fritzch's index designates this series by O.

6. *Wiener genealogisches Taschenbuch*. 8 vols. Schriftl: Hans von Stratowa, 1926-37. (FHL# 943.6/B5w)

Von Fritzch's index designates this series by W.

Von Ehrenkrook, Hans Friedrich, ed. *Genealogisches Handbuch des Adels*. Limburg an der Lahn: C. A. Starke, 1951-present. The editor since 1965 is Walter von Hueck. This publication appears in five series: (1) *Fürstliche Häuser*, (2) *Gräfliche Häuser*, (3) *Frieherrlichen Häuser*, (4) *Adelige Häuser*, and (5) *Adelslexikon*, complete through letter I. (FHL# 943/D2ga)

An index to volumes 1-41 appears in *Stammfolgen-Verzeichnisse für das genealogische Handbuch des Adels und das deutsche Geschlechterbuch*. Limburg an der Lahn: C. A. Starke, 1969. (FHL# 943/D5h).

Huberty, Michel et al. *L'Allemagne dynastique: Les quinze familles qui ont fait l'Empire*. 4 vols. Le Perreux-sur-Marne, France: Alain Giraud, 1979-present. (FHL# 943/D5h)

Work in progress. Among the fifteen families to be documented are: Volume 1: Hesse-Reuss-Saxe; Volume 2: Anhalt-Lippe-Würtemberg; Volume 3: Bunswick-Nassau-Schwarzbourg; and Volume 4: Wittelsbach.

The Euler Collection

Dr. Friederich Euler amassed an immense collection (350 reels of microfilm) of material pertaining primarily to notable or "leading" German individuals between the tenth and twentieth centuries. Also known as *Fuehrende Persoenlichkeiten*, it contains information not available anywhere else in the library. Euler did not always cite sources, and many cannot be reconstructed. This collection is cataloged in the **Author/Title** FHLC. The material is arranged alphabetically by surname, but patrons should search under all possible spelling variants of each surname, paying particular attention to such prefixes as *von*. Binder 17, kept at the International (European) Register Table, contains a detailed list of the surnames on each film.

Hungary

Kempelen, Béla, ed. *Magyar Nemes Családok I. Kötet*. 11 vols. Budapest: Grill Károly Könyvkiadóvállalata, 1911-32. (FHL# 943.9/D5k or microfilm 973233-973238, item 1)

This series is an alphabetical listing of noble families of Hungary.

Turul, A Magyar Heraldikai és Genealogiai Társaság. 64 vols. Budapest: Kiadja A Magyar Heraldikai és Genealogiai Társaság, 1883-1950. (FHL# 943.9/B2t)

Nagy, Iván. *Magyarország családai czimerekkel és nemzedékrendi táblákkal*. 13 vols. Pest: Friebeisz Istvan, 1857-65. (FHL# 943.9/D5n or microfilm 973241-973244, and 1045308-1045309)

Wertner, Mór. *Az Arpádok csaleadi törtenete*. Nagybecskerek, Hungary: Pleitz Fer Pal, 1892. (FHL# microfilm 865450)

This source is a genealogy of the house of Arpad from the ninth to the fourteenth century.

Von Barcsay-Amant, Zoltán. *Adeliges Jarhbuch*. 63 vols. Luzern, Switzerland: n.pub., n.d. (FHL# 942.9/D55aj)

This series, a yearbook of Hungarian nobility, was known as *Nemesi évkönyv*, 1923-35. (Budapest: May Nyomda Részvnytársaság, 1923-35). During 1936-43, it was again called *Adeliges Jahrbuch* and continued publication through 1985.

Ireland (see under Great Britain)

Italy

Spreti, Vittorio. *Enciclopedia storico-nobilaire italianna*. 8 vols. Milan: Ed. Enciclopedia Storico-nobiliare Italiana, 1928-35. (FHL# 945/D56s)

Dizionario Biografico Degli Italiani. 30 volumes to date. Roma: Enciclopedia Italiana, 1960-present. (FHL# 945/D3db)

This remarkably detailed biographical dictionary contains articles on notable Italians followed by extensive bibliographies. The first thirty volumes cover Aa-Crispolto.

Litta, Pompeo. *Famigie Celebri Italiane*. 12 vols. Milan: Paolo Emilio Giusti, 1819-71. (FHL# microfilm 761764-761769)

Revista del Collegio Araldico. Roma: Collegio Araldico, c.1903-present. (FHL# 945/B2r)

Published annually. Also called *Revista Araldica.*

Lithuania (see under Slavic)

Luxembourg (see also under France)

Schleich de Bossé, Jean Robert. *La Noblesse au Grand-Duché de Luxembourg.* 2 vols. Luxembourg: Editions du Centre, 1957, 1979. (FHL# 949.35/D5s or microfiche 6000773)

The Netherlands (see also France and Holy Roman Empire)

Other sources may be found under **Netherlands/Nobility** and **Netherlands/Periodicals.**

De Nederland's Adelsboek: Histirisch Gedeeslte. 77 vols. by 1986. 'S-Gravenhage: W. P. van Stockum & Zoon, 1925-present. (FHL# 949.2/D55na)

Dek, A. W. E. *Genealogie van het Vorstenhuis Nassau.* Zaltbommel Europese Bibliotheck, 1970. (FHL# 929.2492/N187d)

Norway (see under Scandinavia)

Poland (see under Slavic)

Portugal

De Sousa, Antonio Caetano. *Historia Genealogica de casa real Portuguesa* 12 vols. 1735; rpt. ed., Coimbra: Atlântida, 1946-55. (FHL# 946.9/D2s)

Gayo, Felgueiras. *Nobiliario de Familias de Portugal.* 33 vols. Braga, [Portugal]: Oficinas Graficas da Pax, 1938-42. (FHL# 946.9/D2g)

De Dornellas, Affonso. *Historia e Genealogia.* 14 vols. bound in 7. Lisbon: Livraria Ferin, 1913. (FHL# 946.9/H2d)

Romania

Lecca, Octav-George. *Familiile Boerestf Române: Istoric si genealogie.* Bucharest: n.p., 1899. (FHL# microfilm 441412)

Russian Empire (see under Slavic)

Scandinavia

In Viking days before the tenth century, Scandinavia was a loose configuration of petty kingdoms grouped around trading centers. They eventually developed into nation-states, but their political history continued to overlap: at one time Denmark ruled Norway, and Sweden ruled both Norway and Finland. Consequently, works on Scandinavian nobility frequently cross today's national boundaries.

Køngsfeldt, J. P. F. *Genealogisk-historiske tabeller over de Nordiske rigers kongeslaegter: Anden omarbeidede udgave.* Copenhagen: Den Danske Historiske Forening, 1865. (FHL# microfilm 1124504, item 3)

Kønigsfeldt covers the ruling families of Denmark, Norway, and Sweden. Although sources and comments are heavily footnoted, much of the early material is based on Norse sagas and cannot be authenticated.

Denmark

Danmarks Adels Aarbog. Copenhagen: P. G. Philipsens Boghandel, 1884-1965. (FHL# 948.9/D55d or microfilm 1124534-1124545)

Brenner, S. Otto. *Nachkommen Gorms des Alten (König von Dänemark).* Copenhagen: Personalhistorik Institut, 1964. (FHL# 929.2489/G68b or microfilm 897500, item 1)

This source traces the descendants of King Gorm of Denmark (c.939) through the sixteenth generation.

Finland

Aminoff, Torsten G. *Finlands ridderskaps och adelskalender.* Helsingfors: Frenckellska Tryckeri Ahtiebolagets Förlag, 1858-1980. (FHL# 948.97/D25f)

Norway

Lande, Harald. *Norges Konger og Dronninger i Tusen År.* Oslo: J. W. Cappelens Förlag, 1945. (FHL# Q/948.1/D51)

Sweden

Swartz, Erick C:son. *Genealogia Gothica.* 2 vols. Stockholm: n.p., 1930, 1937. (FHL# 948.5/D2s or microfilm 1124504, item 1-2)

This work details the Swedish royal family from 639 to 1936.

Wrangel, F. U., and Otto Bergström. *Svenska Adelns Ättartavlor.* 2 vols. Stockholm: Norstedt, 1897, 1900. (FHL# 948.5/D5w or microfilm 1124532)

Scotland (see under Great Britain)

Slavic

The Slavic peoples dominated eastern Europe from the time of the Roman Empire. The western Slavs became the Poles, Czechs, Slovaks, and Moravians; the southern Slavs the Serbs, Croats, and Slovenes. The eastern Slavs spread throughout western Russia and are closely related to the Lithuanians. Because historical boundaries differ from contemporary ones, studies of Slavic nobility frequently cross political boundaries.

Manteuffla, Tadeusza, ed. *Nauki Pomocnicze Historri.* Warsaw: Panstwowe Wyda Wnictwo Naukowe, 1959. (FHL# microfilm 232852)

This source covers many Slavic and Germanic noble houses. However, the tables do not always agree with German *adel* books, and the names are reproduced in Slavic form. Thus, it is is easy to be confused about the identity of an individual when comparing the two sources.

Wegener, Wilhelm. *Genealogische Tafeln zur Mitteleuropaischen Geschichte.* 1 vol. Gottingen: Heinz Reise Verlag, 1962-69. (FHL# 940/D22w)

This source covers many royal and noble Slavic houses.

Lithuania

The grand duchy of Lithuania covered most of present-day Lithuania and the Ukraine. In 1386, it united with Poland. Works relating to both contemporary nations must be searched when tracing a noble family from either Poland or Lithuania.

Wolffa, Jozef. *Ród Gediminä: dodatki i poprawki.* Krakow: Anczycai Spółki, 1886. (FHL# microfilm 865179, item 1)

Poland

Dworzaczek, Wlodzimierz. *Genealogia.* 2 vols. Warsaw: Panstwowe Wydawnictwo Naukowe, 1959. (FHL# microfilm 1181597, item 1, and 232852)

This guide to research techniques for Polish nobility includes extensive bibliographies of source material. Most of this work is written in Polish.

Balzer, Oswald. *Genealogia Piastów.* Krakow: Akademia umieje tnosci, 1895. (FHL# microfilm 865445)

This work details families of the Piastów dynasty of Poland, tenth to sixteenth centuries.

Wutke, Konrad. *Stamm- und Übersichtstafeln der Schlesischen Piasten: aus Grund von H. Grotefends Stammtafeln der Schlesischen Fürsten bis zum Jahre 1740.* Breslau: Königliche-Universitäts-und- verlagsbuchhandlund, 1910. (FHL# Q/940/D22gs)

Boniecki, Adam, and Arthur Reiski, eds. *Herbarz Polski: wiadomosci historyczno-genealogiczne o rodach szlacheckich.* 16 vols. Warsaw: Mikrofilmowato Arch Gebethner i Wolff, 1899-1912. (FHL# vols. 1-4, Aa-Dowiakowsky: microfilm 127686; vols. 5-8, Dowiattowie-Jelonek, microfilm 127687; vols. 9-13, Jelowacy-Laspoccy, microfilm 127688; vols. 14-15 Lasoccy-Lopuscy, microfilm 127689; vols. 15-16, Liwscy-Uzupelnienia do czesci I, microfilm 865218)

This work is a comprehensive source on the genealogy and heraldry of Polish nobility. Books on Polish heraldry ("herbarz Polski") are very helpful in establishing connections between Polish nobles of the same surname. For other books on this subject see the FHLC under **Poland/Nobility**, and **Poland/Genealogy.**

Russian Empire

De Baumgarten, N. "Généalogies des branches régnantes des Rurikides du XIIIe siècle au XVIEe siècle." *Orientalia Christiana* 35, no. 94 (1934): whole issue. (FHL# 947/D22ba)

This publication was issued by the Pontificum Institutum Orientalium Studiorum in Rome.

_____. "Généalogies et mariages occidentaux des Rurikides russes du Xe au XIIIe siècle." *Orientalia Christiana* 9, no. 35 (1927): whole issue. (FHL# 929.247/R882b)

Durasov, V. *Rodoslovnaya kniga Vserossijskago Dvoryanstva.* Grad Sv. Petra [St. Petersburg]: n.p., 1906. (FHL# microfilm 127799)

This source gives the lineages of Russian nobility.

Ikonnokov, Nicolas. *"La Noblesse de Russie."* Typescript. 1951-56. First series: 27 vols.; second series: 3 vols.; supplements 1-2. (FHL# 947/D22ba)

After the Russian Revolution of 1912, many Russian nobles fled to France, where some of the best recent works on Russian nobility have been produced. A detailed revision of Ikonnokov's series is D. Schakhovskovy, ed., *Societe et Noblesse Russe* (Rennes: Universite de Haute Bretegne, 1978). (FHL# 947/D5s). The Family History Library has only Volume 1, A-Apl. For yearbooks on Russian nobility, usually in Russian, check the FHLC under **Russian Empire/Nobility.**

Spain

De Bethencourt, Francisco Fernandez. *Historia Genealógica y Heráldica de la Monarquía Española: Casa Real y Grandes de Espana.* 9 vols. Madrid: Establecimiento Tipográphico de Enrique Teodoro, 1889-1912. (FHL# Q/946/D22b)

Garcia Carraffa, Alberto and Arthuro. *Diccionario Heráldico y Genealógico de Appellidos Españoles y Americanos.* 86 vols. Madrid: Nueva Impenta Radio, 1952-63. (FHL# 980/D24g or microfilm 035111, item 3-035122)

These volumes deal extensively with noble families in Spain and in its former American colonies. They are listed in alphabetical order with a bibliography following each family entry. The Family History Library has volumes A-Ur. The author died before completing his project.

Hildalguia: La Revista de Genealógia, nobleza y armas. 34 vols. to May 1986. Madrid: n.p., 1953-present. (FHL# 946/B2n)

This series focuses on Spanish nobility. *Hildalguia* is not always accurate, but its articles supply information not available from other sources in the Family History Library.

Garcia Cubero, Benito Municio Cristobal Luis. *Bibliografia heráldico-nobiliaria de la Biblioteca nacional de Madrid.* Madrid: Ediciones Hidalguia, Instituto Luis de Salazar y Castro, 1958. (FHL# 946/A3mc)

Sweden (see under Scandinavia)

Switzerland (see also under France and Holy Roman Empire)

Genealogisches handbuch zur Schwiezer Geschichte. 3 vols. Zürich: Schulthess, 1900-43. (FHL# 949.4/D22s or microfilm 491156)

This source describes the history and descendants of noble Swiss families from 1142 to 1911.

Von Gauen, J. P. Zwicky. *Schweizorisches Geschlechterbuch.* 12 vols. Basel: Kommission Sverlag von C. F. Lendorff, 1905-65. (FHL# 949.4/D2z)

This source lists Swiss nobility from 1223 to 1965.

Union of Soviet Socialist Republics (see under Slavic, Russian Empire)

Wales (see under Great Britain)

Contributors

William L. Arbuckle was born in 1930 in central Ohio. He graduated from Ohio University and did graduate work at the University of Utah and Arizona State University. He served as a lieutenant in the United States Air Force. In 1963 Mr. Arbuckle began a career in genealogy by tracing his own ancestry. The Genealogy Department of the LDS Church in Salt Lake City has accredited him in Scotland and British Canada. He has worked as a full-time professional genealogist since 1973.

Mr. Arbuckle has lectured at the Family History Library in Salt Lake City and at the annual conference held jointly by Brigham Young University, the Utah Genealogical Society, and many local and state societies.

Johni Cerny is a native of Kansas City, Missouri, and holds a degree in Social Work and Genealogical Research from Brigham Young University. She is president and founder of Lineages, Inc., the nation's largest genealogical research firm, and has been tracing people's ancestry for nearly twenty-five years – first as a hobbyist and later as a professional genealogist after a brief career as a captain in the U.S. Army Ordnance Corps. She is a specialist in tracing black slave, Colonial Virginian, and immigrant ancestry and has taught classes on southern states research at Brigham Young Univeristy. She has also given lectures about proving family traditions, immigration and naturalization, and tracing black slave ancestry in the American South, and she has given various courses dealing with aspects of genealogy in the marketplace and as a business. She is engaged in tracing the origins and ancestry of those associated with the Second Germanna Colony in Virginia and is conducting research into Elvis Presley's ancestry for future publication.

Ms. Cerny is a trustee and immediate past-treasurer of the Association of Professional Genealogists and is a delegate from that organization to the Genealogical Coordinating Committee and the Federation of Genealogical Societies. As member of the National Genealogical Society, she wrote "From Maria to Bill Cosby: A Case Study in Tracing Black Slave Ancestry" for the *National Genealogical Society Quarterly*, (March, 1987) and has lectured at NGS national conferences. She is a member of the New England Historic and Genealogical Society, a member and past-president of the Professional Chapter, Utah Genealogical Association, American Society of Indexers, and a number of other organizations. She received the Grahame T. Smallwood Award of Merit for service to the Association of Professional Genealogists (1985) and the Federation of Genealogical Societies Award of Merit for *The Source: A Guidebook of American Genealogy*.

Her publications include the award-winning book *The Source: A Guidebook of American Genealogy* (1984) with Arlene Eakle, now in its fifth printing; *Ancestry's Guide to Research: Case Studies in American Genealogy* (1985) with Arlene Eakle now in its fourth printing; *A Guide to German Parish Registers, Vols. 1-3* (1988). Works in progress include *Printed Sources: A Guide to Secondary Sources in American Genealogy* with Wendy Elliott; *Before Germanna: The Origins and Ancestry of Those Associated with the Second Germanna Colony of Virginia* with Gary J. Zimmerman; *The Ancestry of American Immigrants from Wuerttemberg,* 20 vols., an untitled book about Elvis Presley's ancestry, and a number of journal articles.

Richard W. Dougherty, who holds a Ph.D. in history from the University of Wisconsin-Madison, has been a professional genealogist since 1979. A Fulbright Scholar at the University of Bonn, Germany, his area of research specialization is tracing immigrant ancestors from Germany and central Europe. Accredited by the Family History Library in German research, he is also a member of the Concordia Historical Institute and the National Genealogical Society as well as the Association of Professional Genealogists. He served as president of the Professional Chapter of the Utah Genealogical Association and is currently serving on the Executive Board of the UGA. He is the author of the chapters on family and home sources and American church records in *The Source: A Guidebook of American Genealogy.*

Wendy L. Elliott, a native of California and graduate of California State University at Fullerton (B.S. in history), is executive vice-president and research director of Lineages, Inc., in Salt Lake City. After fifteen years as a hobbyist, she has been a professional genealogist for the past ten years and a certified genealogist since 1980, specializing in southern, midwestern, and Colonial Virginia research, along with black American ancestry and migration.

Ms. Elliott is the past-president of the California State Genealogical Alliance; Nantucket Chapter, Colonial Dames of the Seventeenth Century; and Belle Boyd Chapter, Daughters of the Confederacy. She served as secretary for the National Society, Descendants of Early Quakers and for the Southwest Oral History Association. She is a member of over twenty genealogical and historical societies and ten heritage societies. She co-founded the Yorba Linda (California) Genealogical Society. She is a member of the Association of Professional Genealogists and the National Genealogical Society.

A nationally known lecturer, she has taught genealogical research courses at California State University, Fullerton, and Brigham Young University in Provo, Utah.

Many of her genealogical research articles can be found in national publications and she has authored a series of research guides including *U.S. Migration Patterns, Research in Quaker Records,* and *Using Land Records to Solve Research Problems.* She wrote *From Boyt to Boyette: The Descendants of Thomas Boyet.* Works in progress include *Printed Sources: A Guide to Secondary Sources in American Genealogy* with Johni Cerny.

Harold D. Ethington, a 1971 graduate of Brigham Young University, holds a degree in business management. He has served as an officer and director of Lineages, Inc., since its founding in 1983. He has been involved in genealogical research for twenty-six years and is a specialist in locating and using unindexed source documents on the local level. As president of the Ethington Family Organization, he traveled and spoke widely to various groups about the preservation of family histories, the presentation of family history on film and micro-media, and the use and function of family organizations. His publications include *Five Hundred Ethington Family Groups Sheets, 1773-1978 to the Seventh Generation* (1978); *One Thousand Historical References to Ethington and Related Family Names, 1700-1850* (1979); and the short subject film *They Too are Real People* (1978).

Marlene M. Marino, a professional genealogist, lecturer, and instructor, is vice-president of the Professional Chapter, Utah Genealogical Association. She has worked for the Genealogical Department of the Church of Jesus-Christ of Latter-day Saints in negotiating microfilming contracts, as a microfilmer in the Midwest, and as an acquisition specialist in Salt Lake City. Ms. Marino is serving an eighteen month assignment as a part-time volunteer reference consultant at the United States and Canada Reference desk.

As a member of the National Genealogical Society, she served as the hospitality chairman of the 1985 National Conference. She specializes in southern, midwestern, and Pacific northwest research, with emphasis on early Tennessee and Colonial Virginia.

Kory L. Meyerink was born in Greenwich, Connecticut, to a Dutch immigrant father and a mother whose roots go generations into New England and New York. His eighteen year hobby of genealogy became his profession eight years ago. A graduate of Brigham Young University, he also resided in Germany for two years, becoming fluent in that language. Conversant with German and Dutch records, he specializes in northern and eastern United States research and in finding the hometowns of German, Dutch, and other European immigrants.

Accredited in German as well as midwestern, eastern and New England research in the United States, he is currently a trustee of the Association of Professional Genealogists. He is also the state registrar for the Utah Society, Sons of the American Revolution, a society of which he has served in a number of capacities. He has worked for the LDS Family History Library as a reference consultant on a part-time basis and contributed two chapters to *The Source: A Guidebook of American Genealogy.* Among his other activities he is presently pursuing a Masters of Library Science.

Glade I. Nelson, a native of Maeser, Utah, has been actively involved in genealogy for over thirty years. He is an accredited genealogist and an officer in several family organizations. Employed by the Genealogical Department of the Church of Jesus Christ of Latter-day Saints since 1978, Mr. Nelson has been the manager of the Records Extraction Program and manager of the Worldwide Family History Centers Support Section. He also serves as the Family History Department coordinator for Latin America.

Mr. Nelson is the immediate past-president of the Association of Professional Genealogists, having served as president from 1984 to 1986. He is a delegate to the Federation of Genealogical Societies, representing the Genealogical Society of Utah. He is also a member of the National Genealogical Society, the New England Historic and Genealogical Society, and the Society of Australian Genealogists.

His publications include several genealogical articles in *The American Genealogist, The Virginia Genealogist,* and the *Genealogical Journal.* He has researched extensively in New England, New York, England, Scotland and France. His major projects include researching the Challis/Chellis family of New England and documenting the ancestry and descendants of the Plantagenet Kings of England.

Paul C. Reed is a professional genealogist from Salt Lake City. He specializes in medieval English and Colonial Virginia research. Mr. Reed belongs to several genealogical societies, is past-president of the Salt Lake Chapter, Sons of the American Revolution, and presently serves as second vice-president of the Utah State Society of the Sons of the American Revolution. An author of several articles, he is working on two books dealing with research in medieval English records and tracing the noble ancestry of southern colonial immigrants.

Gordon L. Remington is a professional genealogist residing in Salt Lake City, Utah.

Sheri E. Slaughter holds a Bachelor's degree in Child Development from the University of Utah, and has an arts and commercial background. Her nineteen years as a genealogist was inspired by stories of her father's Mormon Battalion trek told to her by her grandmother. Of English, German and Swedish ancestry, she is of the fourth generation of her family in Utah.

Clifford L. Stott, a native of Massachusetts, is a professional genealogist specializing in New England research. He studied at Brigham Young University and is accredited by the Family History Library. Mr. Stott has been involved in New England research for fifteen years and is also a recognized authority on Utah territorial history. He authored *Search for Sanctuary: Brigham Young and the White Mountain Expedition* (1984).

Gary J. Zimmerman, Accredited Genealogist, began researching his own family at age twelve. At twenty-one, he was the youngest person to become accredited by the Genealogical Department. Since then, he has made a name for himself with three volumes of *German Immigrants*. Future publications will include transcriptions of passenger lists from New Orleans and Hamburg.

Appendix A

100 Genealogical Reference Works On Microfiche

This list describes 100 reference works frequently used by Family History Library patrons, available on approximately 1,200 microfiche and prepared especially for branch center libraries in the United States and Canada.

The list is arranged by country and by state within the United States. The author, title, and original publication information is presented for each entry, followed by the microfiche call number.

Canada

Crossby, Peter Alfred, ed. *Lovell's Gazetteer of British North America.* Montreal: John Lovell & Son, 1881. (FHL# microfiche 6010015-6010020)

A gazetteer of place names in Canada. Includes topographical and statistical descriptions of the cities, towns, and counties in existence in 1881.

De Marce, Virginia Easley. "Canadian Participants in the American Revolution, an Index." Typescript, 1980. (FHL# microfiche 6046783)

A valuable register of Canadians (mainly from Ontario) who participated in the American Revolutionary War. Shows the soldier's name, where he was stationed, rank, time period, family information, age, and service record in the British Army or militia.

Lovell's Canadian Dominian Directory for 1871. 9 vols. Montreal: John Lovell, 1871. (FHL# microfiche 6046766)

A directory of persons residing in Canada listed in city and township directories. The names and occupations of heads of households are listed. Every household in the town may not be represented, especially in the rural areas. The directory can be used to determine a possible residence in the 1871 census. Vol. 1 includes an index of towns and historical sketches. Vols. 2-4 include towns in Ontario. Vols. 5-7 include towns in Quebec. Vol. 8 includes towns in Nova Scotia, New Brunswick, and Newfoundland. Vol. 9 includes Prince Edward Island and miscellaneous data.

"Recensements du Quebec." 7 vols. (FHL# microfiche 6046792)

A collection of census records for several major cities in Quebec, Canada. Vol. 1 includes 1666 census of Quebec City; lists names, ages, occupations; not indexed. Vol. 2 includes 1667 census of Quebec city; indexed. Vol. 3 includes 1760-62 censuses of Trois Rivieres; not indexed. Vol. 4 includes 1744 census of Quebec city; not indexed. Vol. 5 includes 1671-1711 censuses of Terreneuve and Plaisance; not indexed; 1731 census of Montreal; indexed. Vol. 6 includes 1765 census of Montreal and Trois Rivieres; 1762 census of Quebec City; not indexed. Vol. 7 includes 1792, 1795, 1798, 1805 censuses of Quebec Parish; indexed.

Reed, William D. *The Loyalists in Ontario; the Sons and Daughters of the American Loyalists of Upper Canada.* Lambertville, N.J.: Hunterdon House, 1973. (FHL# microfiche 6046758)

A valuable collection of names and genealogical data concerning British loyalists of the American Revolutionary War in the United States and Canada. Also includes those who married loyalists 1750-1850.

Denmark

The Church of Jesus Christ of Latter-day Saints, Genealogical Dept. *Danish-Norwegian Paleography.* Research papers, series D, no. 16. Salt Lake City, 1976. (FHL# microfiche 6030017)

Basic instruction in reading and interpreting Danish and Norwegian handwritten documents. Includes examples.

The Church of Jesus Christ of Latter-day Saints, Genealogical Dept. *Major Genealogical Record Sources in Denmark.* Research papers, series D, no. 5. Salt Lake City, 1974. (FHL# microfiche 6030005)

Basic guide to genealogical research in Denmark. Includes descriptions of sources available for research.

Danmark. Udgivet af Generaldirekotratet for Post og Telegrafvaesenet. *Post- og Telegraf Adressebog for Kongeriget Danmark, 1960.* Copenhagen, 1960. (FHL# microfiche 6030021-6030026)

A postal guide and gazetteer of place names in Denmark. Shows parishes, towns, and political jurisdictions.

England and Wales

Bartholomew, John. *The Survey Gazetteer of the British Isles.* 9th ed. Edinburgh: Bartholomew, 1952. (FHL# microfiche 6020337-6020344)

A gazetteer of place names throughout the British Isles. It is an excellent tool for locating smaller places, although it does not give great detail on each place.

Lewis, Samuel. *A Topographical Dictionary of England.* 4 vols. London: S. Lewis & Co., 1831. (FHL# microfiche 6340019-6340034)

An excellent gazetteer for determining the ecclesiastical jurisdictions of places in England so that parish registers, probate records, and marriage licenses can be found more easily. It also gives good historical background on each parish and a description of schools, churches, and other institutions in the area.

Lewis, Samuel. *A Topographical Dictionary of Wales.* 2 vols. London: S. Lewis, 1833. (FHL# microfiche 6026723)

An excellent gazetteer for determing the ecclesiastical jurisdictions of places in Wales so that parish registers, probate records, and marriage licenses may be found more easily. It also gives good historical background on each parish and a description of schools, churches, and other institutions in the area.

Richards, Melville. *Welsh Administrative and Territorial Units: Medieval and Modern.* Cardiff: University of Wales, 1969. (FHL# microfiche 6026396)

An excellent finding tool for locating a parish or smaller locality in North and South Wales. It lists the parish in which a small town or village is located.

Wilson, John Marius. *The Imperial Gazetteer of England and Wales.* Edinburgh: A. Fullarton, 1870. (FHL# microfiche 6020308-6020336)

An excellent gazetteer of place names throughout England and Wales. It shows jurisdictional, institutional, and political information for each of the towns, villages, and counties in England and Wales. It also indicates if a particular place is a parish or not, and the civil registration district to which the parish belongs. The Family History Library Catalog uses the spellings and jurisdictions in this gazetteer as a standard for its listings.

Street Index, 1841 Census [England and Wales]. 3 vols. Typescript. (FHL# microfiche 6026393)

Index of 1841 street names for the cities of Liverpool, Leeds, Southampton, and parts of Greater London. It is excellent for narrowing down census searches in these large cities.

Census of 1851 Street Addresses, England and Wales. 19 vols. Typescript. (FHL# microfiche 6054458-6054472)

Index of 1851 street names for all major cities throughout England and Wales and most of Greater London. It is excellent for narrowing down census searches in these cities.

Street Index, 1861 Census [England and Wales]. 8 vols. Typescript. (FHL# microfiche 6026702)

Index of 1861 street names for most major cities throughout England and Wales, although it is missing some major cities such as parts of Greater London. It is excellent for narrowing down census searches in these cities.

1871 Street Index [England and Wales]. 16 vols. Typescript. (FHL# microfiche 6054442-6054457)

Complete index of 1871 street names in all major cities throughout England and Wales. It is excellent for narrowing down census searches in the large cities.

Street Index, 1881 Census, England and Wales. 27 vols. Typescript. (FHL# microfiche 6026715)

Complete index of 1881 street names in all major cities throughout England and Wales. It is excellent for narrowing down census searches in the large cities.

France

France, Secrétariat d'Etat aux Posteset Télécommunications. *Code Postal.* Paris: Imprimerie Nationale, 1979. (FHL# microfiche 6000824)

A postal guide and gazetteer of place names in France. Shows department jurisdictions for cities and towns.

Germany

Eger, Wolfgang. *Die protestantischen Kirchenbücher der Pfalz.* Veröffentlichungen des Vereins für Pfälzische Kirchengeschichte, vol. 8. Zweibrücken: Prot. Landeskirchenrats de Pfalz, 1960. (FHL# microfiche 6000835)

A descriptive guide to the parishes and available Protestant parish registers for the Palatine area of Germany. Shows parishes, towns, and an inventory of the church records.

Endler, Carl August and Albrecht, Edm. *Mecklenburgs familiengeschichtlichen Quellen.* Hamburg: Richard Hermes, 1936. (FHL# microfiche 6000834)

A descriptive guide to the parishes and available parish registers of the Mecklenburg area of Germany. Shows parishes, towns, and an inventory of the church records.

Jensen, Larry O. *A Genealogical Handbook of German Research.* Pleasant Grove, Ut: L. Jensen, 1978. (FHL# microfiche 6000366-6000368)

A basic guide to genealogical research in Germany. Includes descriptions and examples of the records, handwriting samples, and research strategies.

Die Kirchenbücher in Baden. Inventare der nichtstaatlichen Archive in Baden-Württemberg, pt. 4. Karlsruhe: G. Braun, 1975. (FHL# microfiche 6000833)

A descriptive guide to the parishes and available parish registers of the Baden area of Germany. Shows parishes, towns, and an inventory of the church records.

Müller, Friedrich. *Müllers grosses Deutsches Ortsbuch.* 12th ed. Kaemmerer, M. *Müllers Verzeichnis der jenseits der Oder-Neisse gelegenen, unter fremder Verwaltung stehenden Ortschaften.* Wuppertal-Barmen: Post-und Ortsbuchverlag, 1958. (FHL# microfiche 6000340-6000354)

A gazetteer of place names for modern Germany. Includes both East and West Germany. Shows towns, counties, districts, and other jurisdictions, and the local civil registration offices in Germany. Also includes an index of German places now located in Poland and the Soviet Union.

Stumpp, Karl. *The Emigration from Germany to Russia in the Years 1763-1862.* Tübingen: K. Stumpp, 1972. (FHL# microfiche 6000829)

A documentary showing the origins and history of many German families who moved to Russia.

Uetrecht, E., ed. *Meyers Orts- und Verkehrslexikon des Deutschen Reiches.* 2 vols. Leipzig: Bibliographisches Institut, 1912-13. (FHL# microfiche 6000001-6000029)

An excellent gazetteer of place names for the German Empire of 1871-1918. Shows parishes, civil registry offices, court and political jurisdictions. The Family History Library Catalog uses the spellings and jurisdictions in this gazetteer for its listings.

Ireland

Ireland. Registrar General. *Alphabetical Index to the Townlands and Towns of Ireland.* Dublin: Alexander Thom, 1877. (FHL# microfiche 6020345-6020353)

An excellent tool for finding a particular townland or town in Ireland. Shows civil parishes, cities, and the county in which a townland is found. This helps to locate church and other records. Information given is based on the 1871 census of Ireland.

The Parliamentary Gazetteer of Ireland. 10 parts. Dublin: A. Fullarton, 1844. (FHL# microfiche 6020358-6020382)

An excellent gazetteer of place names for Ireland. Shows the civil parish, the barony, and the county for each place. Also gives background information and a description of major industries, institutions, schools, and churches in the area.

LDS

Jenson, Andrew. *Encyclopedic History of the Church of Jesus Christ of Latter-day Saints.* Salt Lake City: Deseret News Pub. Co., 1941. (FHL# microfiche 6053258)

A guide to the early wards, branches, districts, missions, and stakes of the church. Shows organization dates and changes in church jurisdictions prior to 1941, and some data on early local and general church leaders.

"Index to Andrew Jenson's *Encyclopedic History of the Church of Jesus Christ of Latter-day Saints.*" Typescript, 1975. (FHL# microfiche 6051304)

A comprehensive alphabetical index to Jenson's *Encyclopedic History of the Church.*

Norway

The Church of Jesus Christ of Latter-day Saints, Genealogical Dept. *Danish-Norwegian Paleography.* Research papers, series D, no. 16. Salt Lake City, 1976. (FHL# microfiche 6030017)

Basic instruction in reading and interpreting Danish and Norwegian handwritten documents. Includes examples.

Helsing, Klaus, and Lundh, Ragnar. *Norsk Stedfortegnelse: Postadressbog for Norge.* 2 vols. Kristiania [Oslo]: Poststyrelsen, 1901. (FHL# microfiche 6030038-6030049)

A postal guide and gazetteer of place names in Norway. Shows towns, parishes, clerical districts, and county jurisdictions.

Smith, Frank, and Thomsen, Finn A. *Genealogical Guidebook and Atlas of Norway.* Logan, Ut.: Everton, 1974. (FHL# microfiche 6030098)

A basic guide to genealogical research in Norway. Includes descriptions of the sources, examples, and maps.

Poland

Jodlowska, J., ed. *Spis Miejscowosci Polskiej Rzeczypospolitej Ludowej.* Warsaw: Wydawnictwa Komunikacji i Lacznosci, 1967. (FHL# microfiche 6000369-6000383)

A gazetteer of place names for modern Poland. Shows towns, districts, and province jurisdictions, and local civil registration offices.

Scotland

Groome, Francis H. *Ordnance Gazetteer of Scotland.* 3 vols. in 6. Edinburgh: Thomas C. Jack, Grange Pub. Works, 1883-86. (FHL# microfiche 6020391-6020411)

An excellent gazetteer of place names for Scotland. Shows the parish in which a particular place is found, historical background information, and a description of major industries, institutions, schools, and churches in the area.

Wilson, John. *The Gazetteer of Scotland.* Edinburgh: W. & A. K. Johnston, 1882. (FHL# microfiche 6026374)

A good listing of most Scottish place names. It gives a good historical background on the places listed, and some data on institutions and churches in the area.

Spain

Diccionario Geográfico Postal de España. Madrid: Avizau y Compania, 1880. (FHL# microfiche 6053502)

A postal guide and gazetteer of place names for Spain. Shows cities, towns, parishes, municipalities, and province jurisdictions.

Sweden

Johansson, Carl Erik. *Cradled in Sweden: A Practical Guide to Genealogical Research in Swedish Records.* Logan: Everton, 1972. (FHL# microfiche 6030093-6030095)

A basic guide to genealogical research in Sweden. Includes descriptions of sources, examples, and research strategies.

Sverige. Postverket televerket och Statens Järnvägar. *Svensk Ortförtechning: Till Bruk för Trafikverken och Deras Kunder.* Stockholm, 1960. (FHL# microfiche 6030028-6030037)

A postal guide and gazetteer of place names in Sweden. Shows towns, parishes, and county jurisdictions.

Switzerland

Les Noms de Famille Suisses, Familiennamenbuch der Schweiz, I Nomi Di Famiglia Svizzeri. Zürich: Polygraphischer Verlag, 1940. (FHL# microfiche 6053507)

A guide to locating family surnames in Switzerland. Shows town of origin for each Swiss family surname.

United States

A Century of Population Growth From the First Census of the United States to the Twelfth, 1790-1900. 1909. Reprint. Baltimore: Genealogical Pub. Co., 1969. (FHL# microfiche 6010073-6010076)

A detailed description of changes in the population of the United States documented through each of the federal censuses from 1790 to 1900. Shows trends of immigration, natural growth, racial characteristics, national origin, religion, etc. Includes an analysis of common surnames and spelling variations shown in the census records and other useful information.

Colange, Leo de. *The National Gazetteer: A Geographical Dictionary of the United States.* 2 vols. 1884. Reprint. Ann Arbor, Mich.: University Microfilms, 1972. (FHL# microfiche 6046725)

A gazetteer of place names in the United States. Shows towns, townships, counties, states, and other jurisdictional and geographical features important for research. Particularly useful for identifying place names in the 1880 census.

Daughters of the American Revolution. *The Rolls of Honor (Ancestor's Index) in the Lineage Books of the National Society of the Daughters of the American Revolution.* 4 vols. 1916-39. Reprint (4 vols. in 2). Baltimore: Genealogical Pub. Co., 1972. (FHL# microfiche 6051292)

An index of the persons who lived at the time of the American Revolutionary War, or participated in it, and who are ancestors of those descendants who have documented their lineage with the Daughters of the American Revolution (DAR). This index leads to 160 volumes of lineage books which provide summaries of each member's ancestry.

Hayward, John. *A Gazetteer of the United States of America.* Hartford, Conn.: Case, Tiffany, 1853. (FHL# microfiche 6046770)

A gazetteer of place names in the United States. Shows towns, townships, and other geographical features useful in locating genealogical records in the United States at an early period. Particularly useful with the 1850 census.

Kirkham, E. Kay. *A Genealogical and Historical Atlas of America.* Logan, Ut.: Everton, 1976. (FHL# microfiche 6010066-6010069)

A set of useful maps and gazetteer of place names for the United States and Canada. Includes historical changes in the development of the United States.

McMullin, Phillip, ed. *Grassroots of America: A Computerized Index to the American State Papers, Land Grants and Claims (1789-1837).* Salt Lake City: Gendex, 1972. (FHL# microfiche 6051323)

A valuable index to the land grants and other records published in the American State Papers. Shows the name of the grantees and the volume and page number. States emphasized in the index are Alabama, Arkansas, Florida, Georgia, Illinois, Indiana, Iowa, Louisiana, Michigan, Minnesota, Mississippi, Missouri, and Wisconsin.

Savage, James. *A Genealogical Dictionary of the First Settlers of New England.* 4 vols. 1860-62. Reprint. Baltimore: Genealogical Pub. Co., 1981. (FHL# microfiche 6019972)

A valuable collection of genealogical data on early immigrants to the United States. Includes data on places of origin in England and elsewhere. Shows three generations of those who came before 1692.

The Pension Roll of 1835. 4 vols. Baltimore: Genealogical Pub. Co., 1968. (FHL# microfiche 6046995)

A report of those receiving or applying for pensions in the United States as a result of service in the Revolutionary War, the War of 1812, or other military service. Lists those who were alive in 1835, or died shortly before that date. Arranged alphabetically within states and counties.

U.S. National Historical Publications and Records Commission. *Directory of Archives and Manuscripts Repositories in the United States.* Washington, D.C.: National Archives and Records Service, 1978. (FHL# microfiche 6010080-6010089)

A valuable list of records repositories and archives in the United States. Shows addresses, jurisdictions, and a brief description of holdings.

United States Official Postal Guide, 1905. Washington, D.C.: GPO, 1905. (FHL# microfiche 6051281)

A postal guide and gazetteer of place names in the United States. Particularly useful with the 1900 census.

California

Bancroft, Hubert Howe. *California Pioneer Register and Index, 1542-1848, Including Inhabitants of California 1769-1800 and List of Pioneers: extracted from The History of California by Hubert Howe Bancroft.* Baltimore: Regional Pub. Co., 1964. (FHL# microfiche 6051337)

An extensive list of early California pioneers. Includes biographical and genealogical information.

Connecticut

Connecticut. Adjutant General's Office. *Record of Service of Connecticut Men in the...*I. *War of the Revolution*. II. *War of 1812.* III. *Mexican War.* Hartford, Conn.: Case, Lockwood, and Brainard, 1889. (FHL# microfiche 6046698)

Vol. I includes lists of regiment members for the Revolutionary War, pensioners, and brief regimental histories. Vol. II includes lists of regular army servicemen who fought in the War of 1812. Shows name, rank, place, and length of service. Vol. III includes lists of Regular Army Servicemen for the Mexican War. Shows name, rank, date mustered, and where served.

Georgia

Maddox, Joseph T., and Carter, Mary. *37,000 Early Georgia Marriages*. Georgia, 1975. (FHL# microfiche 6046751)

Lists of marriages from early Georgia county records as transcribed in genealogical periodicals. Arranged alphabetically within 29 counties by the name of the groom from the early 1700s to 1800s.

Maddox, Joseph T., and Carter, Mary. *40,000 Early Georgia Marriages*. Georgia, 1975. (FHL# microfiche 6051217)

Additional lists of marriages from early Georgia county records. Includes twenty additional counties.

Illinois

Beck, Louis Caleb. *A Gazetteer of the States of Illinois and Missouri.* 1823. Reprint. New York: Arno Press, 1975. (FHL# microfiche 6010063)

A gazetteer of place names in Illinois and Missouri published at a very early date. Includes historical, topographical, and statistical data on the towns, villages, and counties of these states.

Irons, Victoria, and Brennan, Patricia C. *Descriptive Inventory of the Archives of the State of Illinois.* Springfield: Illinois State Archives, 1978. (FHL# microfiche 6046721)

A checklist and description of the holdings and arrangement of records at the Illinois State Archives.

U.S. Congress. House. *War of 1812 Bounty Lands in Illinois.* 26th Congress, 1st sess., House Document 262. Reprint. Thomson, Ill.: Heritage House, 1977. (FHL# microfiche 6051272)

An index of veterans of the War of 1812 who filed bounty land warrant applications in the Illinois military land tract. Shows name, rank, unit, and location of the land.

U.S. Illinois Historical Records Survey. *Guide to Public Vital Statistics Records in Illinois.* 1941. Reprint. Thomson, Ill.: Heritage House, 1976. (FHL# microfiche 6051164)

A checklist of existing state and local public records of births, marriages, divorces, and deaths in Illinois. Includes a history of record keeping in the state, and abstracts of the laws affecting it.

Indiana

The Indiana Gazetteer. Indianapolis: E. Chamberlain, 1849. (FHL# microfiche 6051129)

A gazetteer of place names in Indiana published at an early date. Includes historical, topographical, and statistical data on the towns, villages, and counties of Indiana.

Iowa

Idaho State Historical Society Genealogical Library. "Index to Iowa Soldiers." 7 vols. Typescript, 1979. (FHL# microfiche 6051153)

An index to the names of soldiers of the Civil War listed in the *Roster and Record of Iowa Soldiers in the War of the Rebellion.* (6 vols. on 5 microfilm reels: 987646-987650).

Iowa Postal History Society. *Alphabetical Listing of Iowa Post Offices, 1833-1970.* Iowa Postal History Society, 1970. (FHL# microfiche 6051285)

A list of all post offices established in the state of Iowa. Includes those that have been discontinued.

Kentucky

Jillson, Willard Rouse. *Old Kentucky Entries and Deeds: A complete Index to All of the Earliest Land Entries, Military Warrants, Deeds and Wills of the Commonwealth of Kentucky.* 1926. Reprint. Baltimore: Genealogical Pub. Co., 1969. (FHL# microfiche 6051260)

An index to early land records of Kentucky. Shows location of the land and the names of the individuals involved in the grant or transfer.

Sutherland, James Franklin. *Some Original Land Grant Surveys Along Green River in Lincoln and Casey Counties, 1781-1836.* N.p., 1975. (FHL# microfiche 6051189)

An index and register of land grants for early Kentucky counties. Includes names of grantees and location of the land as well as information concerning research techniques.

Taylor, Philip Fall. *A Calendar of the Warrants for Land in Kentucky, Granted for Service in the French and Indian War.* Baltimore: Genealogical Pub. Co., 1967. (FHL# microfiche 6019959)

An index and register of early land grants in Kentucky. Shows names of grantees and location of the land.

Maine

Noyes, Sybil; Libby, Charles Thornton; and Davis, Walter Goodwin. *Genealogical Dictionary of Maine and New Hampshire.* 2 vols. Portland, Me.: Southworth-Anthoensen Press, 1928-39. (FHL# microfiche 6046621)

Genealogical and biographical information concerning early families residing in Maine and New Hampshire. Arranged alphabetically.

Maryland

Cotton, Jane Baldwin, comp. *Maryland Calendar of Wills.* 8 vols. Baltimore: Kohn & Pollock, 1906-28. (FHL# microfiche 6046924)

Abstracts and index of all names mentioned in colonial wills of Maryland, 1635-1743.

Massachusetts

Massachusetts. Commissioner of Public Records. *Report of the Custody and Condition of the Public Records of Parishes, Towns, and Counties of Massachusetts.* Boston: Wright & Potter Printing Co., 1889. (FHL# microfiche 6046869)

A descriptive inventory of Massachusetts public records. Shows types of records kept, the years covered, the location of the records, physical condition, and whether they are indexed.

Nason, Elias. *A Gazetteer of the State of Massachusetts.* Boston: B. B. Russell, 1874. (FHL# microfiche 6046886)

A gazetteer of place names for the state of Massachusetts. Includes topographical, statistical, and historical descriptions of the cities, towns, villages, and counties in the state.

Pope, Charles Henry. *The Pioneers of Massachusetts.* 1900. Reprint. Baltimore: Genealogical Pub. Co., 1965. (FHL# microfiche 6046669)

A list of early pioneers and settlers of Massachusetts, with genealogical and biographical information from colonial town and church records.

Michigan

Blois, John T. *Gazetteer of the State of Michigan.* Detroit: Sydney L. Rood, 1839. (FHL# microfiche 6051130)

A gazetteer of place names for the state of Michigan published at an early date. Includes topographical, statistical, and historical descriptions of the cities, towns, and counties in the state.

Missouri

Beck, Louis Caleb. *A Gazetteer of the States of Illinois and Missouri.* 1823. Reprint. New York: Arno Press, 1975. (FHL# microfiche 6010063)

Ellsberry, Elizabeth Prather, comp. *Bible Records of Missouri.* 8 vols. Chillicothe, Mo.: E. P. Ellsberry, 1963. (FHL# microfiche 6051119)

An extensive collection of abstracted Bible records for the state of Missouri. Includes records of births, marriages, deaths, etc., recorded in private Bibles and journals.

New Hampshire

Hayward, John. *A Gazetteer of New Hampshire.* Boston: John P. Jewett, 1849. (FHL# microfiche 6019968)

A gazetteer of place names in the state of New Hampshire. Includes descriptions of the towns, districts, counties, and physical features as they existed at the time.

Noyes, Sybil; Libby, Charles Thornton; and Davis, Walter Goodwin. *Genealogical Dictionary of Maine and New Hampshire.* 2 vols. Portland, Me.: Southworth-Anthoensen Press, 1928-1939. (FHL# microfiche 6046621)

Genealogical and biographical information concerning early families residing in New Hampshire and Maine. Arranged alphabetically.

New Jersey

Gordon, James F. *A Gazetteer of the State of New Jersey.* Trenton: D. Fenton, 1834. (FHL# microfiche 6046927)

A gazetteer of place names for the state of New Jersey published at an early date. Includes descriptions of the cities, towns, and counties of the state as they existed at the time.

New York

Bailey, Rosalie Fellows. *Guide to Genealogical and Biographical Sources for New York City, Manhattan, 1783-1890.* New York: R. Bailey, 1954. (FHL# microfiche 6051128)

A list of sources of genealogical and biographical information in old New York City for the years 1783-1890. Shows type of information and where it is available.

Fernow, Berthold, comp. & ed. *Calendar of Wills on File and Recorded in the Offices of the Clerk of the Court of Appeals, of the County Clerk at Albany, and of the Secretary of State, 1626-1836.* New York: Colonial Dames of the State of New York, 1896. (FHL# microfiche 6046668)

Abstracts and index of wills recorded at Albany for the state of New York and for the county of Albany. Includes the names of the testators and heirs and other valuable genealogical information.

New York County. Surrogate's Court. *Abstracts of Wills on File in the Surrogate's Office, City of New York, 1665-1801.* 17 vols. New York Historical Society Collections, vols. 25-41. New York: New York Historical Society, 1892-1913. (FHL# microfiche 6046928)

Abstracts and index of original wills filed in New York City prior to 1801. Includes names of testators and heirs, and other genealogically valuable data.

French, John Homer. *Gazetteer of the State of New York.* 8th ed. Syracuse, N.Y.: R. P. Smith, 1860. (FHL# microfiche 6046699)

A gazetteer of place names in the state of New York. Includes topographical, statistical, and historical descriptions of the cities, towns, villages, and counties of the state as they existed at the time, as well as many prominent state and community leaders.

Place, Frank, II, comp. *Index of Personal Names in J. H. French's Gazetteer of the State of New York.* Cortland, N.Y.: Cortland County Historical Society, 1962. (FHL# microfiche 6051206)

An index of personal names appearing in French's gazetteer.

U.S. New York Historical Records Survey. *Guide to Public Vital Statistical Records in New York State (Including New York City).* 3 vols. Albany, 1942. (FHL# microfiche 6046676)

A descriptive inventory and register of birth, marriage, and death records for the state of New York. Shows types of records that exist for various time periods, and the location and custody of the records.

North Carolina

Daughters of the American Revolution, North Carolina. *Roster of the Soldiers from North Carolina in the American Revolution.* N.p.: North Carolina DAR, 1932. (FHL# microfiche 6046553)

A list of soldiers, officers and enlisted men who served in the Continental Army from the state of North Carolina. Includes military land warrants, pensioners, and heirs of those who died in service.

Grimes, John Bryan. *Abstracts of North Carolina Wills, 1690-1760.* 1912. Reprint. Baltimore: Genealogical Pub. Co., 1967. (FHL# microfiche 6046876)

Abstracts and index of all early North Carolina wills. These were filed in the Office of the Secretary of State. Shows names of testators, heirs, and other genealogical data.

Grimes, John Bryan. *North Carolina Wills and Inventories.* Raleigh: Edwards & Broughton, 1912. (FHL# microfiche 6051125)

Abstracts and index of wills and inventories on file at the office of the North Carolina Secretary of State for the years 1733-73. Shows names of testators, heirs, and other genealogical data.

Olds, Fred A. *An Abstract of North Carolina Wills from About 1760 to About 1800.* 1925. Reprint. Baltimore: Genealogical Pub. Co., 1965. (FHL# microfiche 6019970)

Abstracts of wills for all North Carolina counties from 1760 to 1800. Arranged alphabetically for each county. Shows names of testators, heirs and other genealogical data.

Ohio

Bell, Carol Willsey. *Ohio Wills and Estates to 1850: An Index.* Columbus: C. W. Bell, 1981. (FHL# microfiche 60512[illegible])

An index of wills and inventories filed in Ohio county courthouses prior to 1850. Shows name of testator, and the date and county where filed.

Ohio State Library. *County by County in Ohio Genealogy.* Columbus, 1978. (FHL# microfiche 6046719)

A descriptive list of genealogical materials available at the State Library in Columbus, Ohio.

Pennsylvania

Daly, John, and Weinberg, Allen. *Genealogy of Philadelphia County Subdivisions.* 2nd ed. Philadelphia: Department of Records, 1966. (FHL# microfiche 6046613)

Historical maps, chronology, and description of the political subdivisions and city wards in Philadelphia. Shows creation dates and jurisdictions of the various divisions throughout their existence.

Gordon, Thomas F. *A Gazetteer of the State of Pennsylvania.* Philadelphia: T. Belknap, 1832. (FHL# microfiche 6053251)

A gazetteer of place names for the state of Pennsylvania. Includes topographical, statistical, and historical descriptions of the cities, towns, villages, and counties in existence at the time.

South Carolina

Charleston Free Library. *Index to Wills of Charleston County, South Carolina, 1671-1868.* 1950. Reprint. Baltimore: Genealogical Pub. Co., 1974. (FHL# microfiche 6051308)

A name index to all of the wills filed in Charleston County prior to 1868. This court covered the entire state and colony for the early years. Shows the name of the testator and location of the estate.

Houston, Martha Lou, comp. *Indexes to the County Wills of South Carolina.* 1939. Reprint. Baltimore: Genealogical Pub. Co., 1964. (FHL# microfiche 6046877)

Name indexes to the wills filed in the county probate courts in South Carolina for the years 1766-1864. Includes all counties organized before 1853 except Charleston county. Arranged alphabetically within each county.

Tennessee

U.S. Tennessee Historical Records Survey. *Guide to Public Vital Statistics in Tennessee.* Nashville, 1941. (FHL# microfiche 6046959)

A descriptive inventory and register of birth, marriage, and death records for the state of Tennessee. Includes a history of the types of records and information on how they are available.

U.S. Tennessee War Services Section. *Guide to Church Vital Statistics in Tennessee.* Nashville, 1942. (FHL# microfiche 6051201)

A descriptive inventory and register of church records in the state of Tennessee. Includes a synopsis of record keeping in major churches and information on where records are available.

Texas

Kinney, John M., comp. *Index to Applications for Texas Confederate Pensions.* Revised ed. Revised by Peggy Oakley. Austin, Tex.: Texas State Library, Archives Division, 1977. (FHL# microfiche 6019976)

An index of names of Confederate Civil War veterans who applied for pensions from the state of Texas. Includes accepted and rejected applications. The actual files are available on 700 reels of microfilm of Confederate pensioners.

White, Gifford. *1830 Citizens of Texas.* Austin, Tex.: Eakin Press, 1983. (FHL# microfiche 6051297)

A census list of persons residing in Texas prior to 1830; taken from various tax lists, land records, and other sources.

Utah

Esshom, Frank. *Pioneers and Prominent Men of Utah.* 1913. Reprint. Salt Lake City: Western Epics, 1966. (FHL# microfiche 6053257)

A biographical encyclopedia of early Utah residents. Includes photographs, portraits, and genealogical data.

"Registry of Names of Persons Residing in the Various Wards as to Bishop's Reports, Salt Lake City, Dec. 28, 1852." Typescript. (FHL# microfiche 6051208)

A list of early residents of Utah based on reports of members made by The Church of Jesus Christ of Latter-day Saints in 1852. Shows names and places of residence at the time.

Virginia

Gannett, Henry. *A Gazetteer of Virginia.* Washington, D.C.: GPO, 1904. (FHL# microfiche 6019559)

A gazetteer of place names in the state of Virginia. Includes topographical, statistical, and historical descriptions of the cities, towns, and counties of the state in existence at the time.

Stewart, Robert Armistead. *Index to Printed Virginia Genealogies.* 1930. Reprint. Baltimore: Genealogical Pub. Co., 1965. (FHL# microfiche 6019375)

An index of names appearing in early published genealogies of Virginia families.

Swem, Earl Gregg. *Virginia Historical Index.* 2 vols. Roanoke, Va.: Stone Printing, 1934-36. (FHL# microfiche 6046961)

An index of names appearing in several important works including the *Virginia Historical Register, Tyler's Quarterly Historical and Genealogical Magazine,* the

Virginia Magazine of History and Biography, the *William and Mary Quarterly,* the *Calendar of Virginia State Papers, Henning's Statutes at Large,* the *Norfolk County, Virginia Antiquary,* etc. Many of these works are available in the Family History Library on microfilm, or at local libraries.

U.S. Virginia Historical Records Survey. *Inventory of the Church Archives of Virginia; Dover Baptist Association.* Richmond, 1939. (FHL# microfiche 6046547)

An index and register of Baptist church records in Virginia. Includes historical sketches and records of individual churches.

Wisconsin

Hunt, John Warren. *Wisconsin Gazetteer.* Madison: B. Brown, 1853. (FHL# microfiche 6051150)

A gazetteer of place names for the state of Wisconsin. Includes topographical, statistical, and historical descriptions of cities, towns, and counties in existence at the time.

U.S. Wisconsin Historical Records Survey. *Directory of Churches and Religious Organizations in Wisconsin.* Madison, Wis., 1941. (FHL# microfiche 6051165)

A descriptive list of religious denominations and organizations in Wisconsin. Shows organization dates, locations, and other useful data.

Index

This index includes the authors and titles of bibliographic works cited as well as subjects. *A, An,* and *The* have been dropped at the beginnings of titles, but added at the end when their omission would make the title unclear. Short titles with ellipses have been used for some works. Record collections known by an individual's name are cited by surname: Hale, Charles R., Collection. No individual counties, subdivisions of countries, or cities appear as individual entries, due to the geographical organization of the book. The exception is a country or kingdom that no longer exists, such as Bohemia. Excluded are groups or agencies as authors, names of wars, and titles that refer so specifically to a particular record type in a particular locale that the reader would most probably look for it only by area–i.e., church records, published directories, census records, maps, tax records, military records, cemetery inscriptions, land records, and tax records. Due to restrictions of space, the majority of book titles listed are in English. Diacritical marks and accents have been omitted. All named individuals who are authors, editors, compilers, etc., are indexed.

A

B

C

D

E

F

G

H

I

J

K

L

M

N

O

P

T

U

Y

Z

NEW HANOVER COUNTY PUBLIC LIBRARY
8175